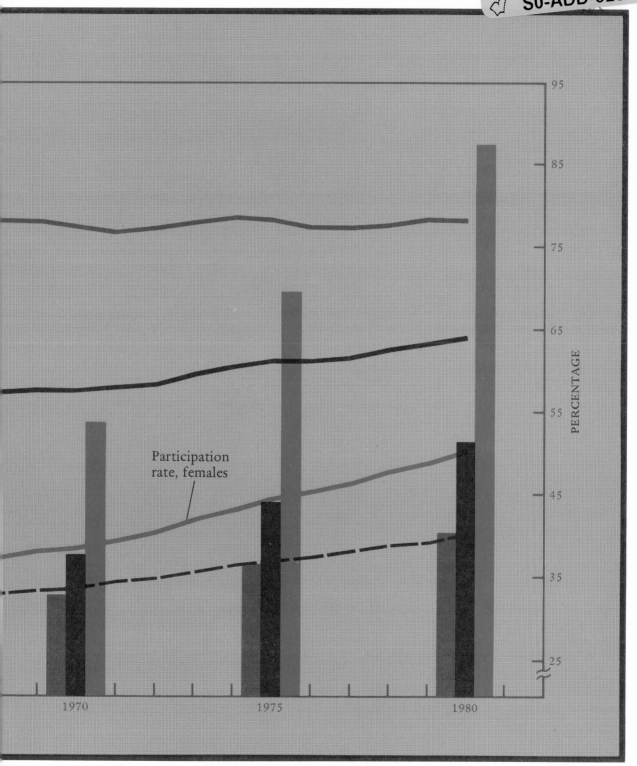

Participation
rate, females

Economics

Economics

FOURTH EDITION

Richard G. Lipsey
Queen's University

Douglas D. Purvis
Queen's University

Gordon R. Sparks
Queen's University

Peter O. Steiner
The University of Michigan

HARPER & ROW, PUBLISHERS, New York
Cambridge, Philadelphia, San Francisco,
London, Mexico City, São Paulo, Sydney

1817

SPONSORING EDITOR: John Greenman
DEVELOPMENT EDITOR: Mary Lou Mosher
PROJECT EDITOR: Nora Helfgott
DESIGNER: Emily Harste
DESIGN SUPERVISION: Helen Iranyi
SENIOR PRODUCTION MANAGER: Kewal K. Sharma
COMPOSITOR: Ruttle, Shaw & Wetherill, Inc.
PRINTER AND BINDER: Kingsport Press
ART STUDIO: Danmark and Michaels Inc. and Fine Line
  Illustrations Inc.
COVER PHOTO: Ed Cooper, Shostal

ECONOMICS, Fourth Edition

Library of Congress Cataloging in Publication Data
Main entry under title:

Economics.

  Rev. ed. of: Economics / Richard G. Lipsey, Gordon R. Sparks, Peter O. Steiner. 3rd ed. c1979.
  Includes index.
  1. Economics. I. Lipsey, Richard G., 1928–
II. Lipsey, Richard G., 1928–   Economics.
HB171.5.E334 1982   330   81–20100
ISBN 0–06–044075–9   AACR 2

Brief Contents

PART ONE
The Nature of Economics   **1**

  1 The Economic Problem, 2
  2 Economics as a Social Science, 20
  3 The Role of Statistical Analysis, 32
  4 An Overview of the Economy, 46

MICROECONOMICS

PART TWO
A General View of the Price System   **65**

  5 Demand, Supply, and Price, 66
  6 Elasticity of Demand and Supply, 86
  7 Supply and Demand in Action I:
     Price Controls and Agricultural Problems, 98
  8 Supply and Demand in Action II:
     International Trade and Exchange Rates, 128

PART THREE
Demand   **151**

  9 Household Consumption Behavior, 152
 10 Demand Theory in Action, 176

PART FOUR
Production and Cost   **191**

 11 The Firm, Production, and Cost, 192
 12 Production and Cost in the Short Run, 207
 13 Production, Substitution, and
     Productivity Increases: Cost in the Long
     and Very Long Run, 220

PART FIVE
Markets and Pricing   **247**

 14 Pricing in Competitive Markets, 248
 15 Pricing in Monopoly Markets, 271

16 Industrial Organization and Theories of
    Imperfect Competition, 289
17 Price Theory in Action, 309
18 Monopoly Versus Competition, 324
19 Who Runs the Firm and for What Ends? 343

PART SIX
Factor Pricing and the Distribution of Income 361
20 The Distribution of National Income, 362
21 Labor Markets and the Determination
    of Wages, 385
22 Interest and the Return on Capital, 412
23 Poverty, Inequality, and Mobility, 431

PART SEVEN
The Market Economy: Problems and Policies 449
24 Microeconomic Policy I: Benefits and
    Costs of Government Intervention in the
    Market Economy, 450
25 Microeconomic Policy II: Public Finance and
    Public Expenditure, 477

PART EIGHT
Resource Allocation in an Open Economy 503
26 International Trade and Protection, 504
27 Energy Policy: A Case Study, 534

MACROECONOMICS

PART NINE
National Income and Fiscal Policy 559
28 Aggregate Demand and Aggregate Supply, 560

29 The Concepts of National Product and
    National Income, 578
30 What Determines National Income? 595
31 Changes in National Income, 610
32 Cycles and Fluctuations in
    National Income, 626
33 National Income, International Trade, and
    the Balance of Payments, 650
34 Fiscal Policy, 673

PART TEN
Money, Banking, and Monetary Policy 701
35 The Nature and Importance of Money, 702
36 International Monetary Systems, 728
37 The Banking System and
    the Supply of Money, 749
38 The Macroeconomic Role of Money and the
    Theory of Monetary Policy, 768

PART ELEVEN
Macroeconomic Policy 799
39 The Nature of Unemployment and Inflation, 800
40 Macroeconomic Policy and the
    Balance of Payments, 836
41 Macroeconomic Experience, 855
42 Current Issues in Macroeconomic Policy, 878

PART TWELVE
Economic Growth and Comparative Systems 907
43 Growth in Developed Economies, 908
44 Growth and the Less-developed
    Countries, 928

Detailed Contents

Preface, xix

PART ONE
The Nature of Economics   1

1
THE ECONOMIC PROBLEM   2
Economic Problems of the Eighties, 3
  Unemployment and Inflation, 3
  Energy, 3
  Productivity and Growth, 4
  Growth and Pollution, 5
  Poverty and Wealth, 5
  The Role of Government, 6
What Is Economics? 6
  Resources and Commodities, 6
  Scarcity, 7
  Choice, 7
  A Classification of Economic Problems, 9
  Economics: A Working Definition, 12
Economic Analysis and Economic Policy, 12
  The Pervasiveness of Policy Decisions, 12
  The Roles of the Economist in Economic Policy, 12
  Economic and Political Objectives, 17

2
ECONOMICS AS A SOCIAL SCIENCE   20
  The Distinction Between Positive and Normative, 20
  The Scientific Approach, 22
  Is Human Behavior Predictable? 23
  The Nature of Scientific Theories, 24
  What Is a Theory and How Is It Tested? 25
  Economics as a Developing Science, 29

3
THE ROLE OF STATISTICAL ANALYSIS 32
Index Numbers, 32
Index Numbers of Prices, 33
Index Numbers of Physical Outputs, 35
The Accuracy and Significance of Index Numbers, 36
Measurement and Testing of Economic Relations, 36
Techniques for Testing Theories, 37
The Statistical Testing of Economic Theories:
An Example, 38
Evaluating the Evidence, 42

4
AN OVERVIEW OF THE ECONOMY   46
The Evolution of Market Economies, 46
Surplus, Specialization, and Trade, 47
Factor Services and Division of Labor, 47
Scarcity and the Allocation of Resources, 48
The Decision Makers, 48
Households, 48
Firms, 50
Central Authorities, 50
Other Decision Makers, 51
Markets and Economies, 51
Markets, 51
Economies, 51
Sectors of an Economy, 52
How Individual Markets Work:
An Overview of Microeconomics, 53
The Circular Flow:
From Microeconomics to Macroeconomics, 55
An Overview of Macroeconomics, 55
Micro- and Macroeconomics Compared, 57
Alternative Economic Systems, 57
Differences Between Economies, 58
Whose Values? 60
Incentive Systems, 61
Ends and Means, 61
Comparative Systems: A Final Word, 62

PART TWO
A General View of the Price System   65

5
DEMAND, SUPPLY, AND PRICE   66
The Basic Theory of Demand, 66
The Nature of Quantity Demanded, 67

What Determines Quantity Demanded? 68
Demand and Price, 68
The Demand Schedule and the Demand Curve, 69
The Basic Theory of Supply, 73
The Nature of Quantity Supplied, 74
What Determines Quantity Supplied? 74
Supply and Price, 74
The Supply Schedule and the Supply Curve, 75
The Determination of Price by Demand and Supply, 78
The "Laws" of Supply and Demand, 80
The Theory of Price in an Inflationary World, 82

6
ELASTICITY OF DEMAND AND SUPPLY 86
Demand Elasticity, 86
Price Elasticity: A Measure of the Responsiveness of
Quantity Demanded to Price Changes, 88
Other Demand Elasticities, 92
Supply Elasticity, 94

7
SUPPLY AND DEMAND IN ACTION I: PRICE CONTROLS AND AGRICULTURAL PROBLEMS   98
The Theory of Price Controls, 99
Quantity Exchanged at Non-equilibrium Prices, 99
Effective Ceiling Prices, 100
Allocating a Commodity in Short Supply, 100
The Experience with Ceiling Prices, 102
Rent Controls, 102
The Theory of Ceiling Prices Applied
to Rent Controls, 103
Special Aspects of the Housing Market, 103
Supply Response to Changes in Rents, 106
The Demand for Rental Housing, 107
When Rent Controls Work: Short-term Shortages, 107
When Rent Controls: Fail: Long-term Shortages, 108
What Are the Alternatives? 110
The Problems of Agriculture, 110
Long-term Trends, 111
Short-term Fluctuations, 112
Agricultural Stabilization and Support Plans, 114
Problems with Agricultural Stabilization
and Support Plans, 117
Agricultural Policy in Canada, 118
Has the Farm Problem Disappeared? 121
Four General Lessons About Resource Allocation, 123
Costs May Be Shifted, But They Cannot Be
Avoided, 123
Free-market Prices and Profits Encourage
Economical Use of Resources, 123

Controls Inhibit the Allocative Mechanism, 124
Controls Require Alternative
Allocative Mechanisms, 124

8
**SUPPLY AND DEMAND IN ACTION II:
INTERNATIONAL TRADE AND EXCHANGE
RATES**   128
The Nature of International Trade, 128
The Expansion of the Consumption Possibility
Set Through Trade, 129
The Determination of Imports and Exports:
A Simple Example, 131
The Nature of Exchange Rates, 133
The Effects of Changes in the Exchange Rate, 135
The Determination of Exchange Rates, 136
Equilibrium Exchange Rates in a
Competitive Market, 138
Changes in Exchange Rates, 140
Domestic Inflation and the Exchange Rate, 141
Foreign Inflation and the Exchange Rate, 142
Central Bank Management of Exchange Rates, 142
Fixed Versus Floating Exchange Rates, 147
The Canadian Dollar Exchange Rate, 147

PART THREE
Demand   151

9
**HOUSEHOLD CONSUMPTION
BEHAVIOR**   152
The Relation Between Market and Household
Demand Curves, 153
The Marginal Utility Theory of Household Behavior, 153
Marginal and Total Utility, 153
Maximizing Utility, 156
Applying the Distinction Between Marginal and
Total Utility, 159
Household Choice: An Alternative Analysis, 165
The Budget Line, 165
Indifference Curve Analysis, 168

10
DEMAND THEORY IN ACTION   176
Measurement of Demand, 177
Modern Measures of Demand, 177
Problems of Measurement, 179

Criticisms of Demand Theory, 181
Does Demand Theory Make Unreasonable
Assumptions About Rational Household Decision
Making? 181
Is Demand Theory Only an Elaborate Way of Saying
That Anything Can Happen? 182

PART FOUR
Production and Cost   191

11
THE FIRM, PRODUCTION, AND COST   192
The Organization of Production, 193
Proprietorships, Partnerships, and Corporations, 193
The Rise of the Modern Corporation, 195
The Firm in Economic Theory, 195
Cost and Profit to the Firm, 197
The Meaning and Measurement of Cost, 197
The Measurement of Opportunity Cost
by the Firm, 199
Profits: Their Meaning and Significance, 203

12
**PRODUCTION AND COST IN THE
SHORT RUN**   207
Real Choices Open to the Firm, 208
Time Horizons for Decision Making, 208
Connecting the Runs: The Production Function, 210
Short-run Choices, 210
Total, Average, and Marginal Products, 210
The Shape of the Marginal and
Average Product Curves, 212
Short-run Variations in Cost, 214

13
**PRODUCTION, SUBSTITUTION, AND
PRODUCTIVITY INCREASES: COST IN
THE LONG AND VERY LONG RUN**   220
The Long Run: No Fixed Factors, 220
Conditions for Cost Minimization, 221
The Principle of Substitution, 222
Cost Curves in the Long Run, 223
The Relation Between Long-run and
Short-run Costs, 225

Shifts in Cost Curves, 226
Isoquants: An Alternative Analysis of the Firm's
   Input Decisions, 227
The Very Long Run: Progress and Productivity, 232
The Nature and Significance of Productivity, 232
Major Sources of Increasing Productivity, 234
Invention, 235
Incentives and Disincentives for Innovation, 240
How Much Productivity Growth Do We Want? 242

PART FIVE
Markets and Pricing   247

14
PRICING IN COMPETITIVE MARKETS   248
Firm Behavior and Market Structure, 248
The Significance of Market Structure, 249
Behavioral Rules for the Profit-maximizing Firm, 250
The Elements of the Theory of Perfect Competition, 251
The Assumptions of Perfect Competition, 251
Demand and Revenue Curves for the Perfectly
   Competitive Firm, 253
Short-run Equilibrium: Firm and Industry, 254
Equilibrium Output of a Firm in Perfect Competition,
   254
Short-run Supply Curves, 255
The Determination of Short-run Equilibrium Price,
   256
Short-run Profitability of the Firm, 257
Long-run Equilibrium, 257
The Effect of Entry and Exit, 257
The Level of Cost at Equilibrium, 259
The Long-run Response of a Perfectly Competitive
   Industry to a Change in Technology, 259
Industries That Are Declining Due to a Steady
   Decrease in Demand, 261
The Appeal of Perfect Competition, 264
The Noneconomic Appeal of Competition, 264
The Economic Appeal of Perfect Competition:
   Efficiency, 264
Some Words of Warning About the Efficiency of
   Perfect Competition, 267

15
PRICING IN MONOPOLY MARKETS   271
A Monopolist Selling at a Single Price, 271
The Monopolist's Revenue Curves, 272
Profit Maximization in a Monopolized Market, 274

Equilibrium of the Firm and Industry, 275
The Inefficiency of Monopoly, 276
The Nature and Extent of Monopoly Power, 278
Measuring Monopoly Power, 279
Price Discrimination, 280
Why Price Discrimination Pays, 281
When Is Price Discrimination Possible? 281
A Formal Analysis of Price Discrimination, 284
The Positive Effects of Price Discrimination, 285
The Normative Aspects of Price Discrimination, 286
Price Discrimination: Systematic and Unsystematic,
   286

16
INDUSTRIAL ORGANIZATION AND
THEORIES OF IMPERFECT
COMPETITION   289
Structure of the Canadian Economy, 290
Two Groupings of Canadian Industries, 290
Patterns of Concentration in Manufacturing, 291
Intermediate Market Forms, 292
**Competition Among the Few: The Theory of
Oligopoly, 296**
Administered Prices Under Oligopoly, 297
Theoretical Approaches to Oligopolistic Behavior, 297
Empirically Based Approaches to Oligopolistic
   Behavior, 298
Barriers to Entry, 300
Price Inflexibility: Is There a Kinked Demand
   Curve? 305
Oligopoly and Resource Allocation, 306

17
PRICE THEORY IN ACTION   309
**Problems in Attempts to Monopolize Perfectly
Competitive Industries, 309**
Cheating: The Instability of Producers' Associations,
   310
Partial Participation: Milk Withholding in Wisconsin,
   311
Control of Entry: The Price of Haircuts, 312
Substitutes: The Decline and Fall of a Patent
   Monopoly, 314
OPEC and the Price of Gasoline, 315
Before OPEC: Energy Binge, 315
OPEC's Embargo, 316
OPEC: Supply Limitation as a Long-run Strategy, 319
The Situation in 1980, 320
Kinds of Energy Policy, 320
The Debate About Strategy, 321

18
MONOPOLY VERSUS COMPETITION   324

Comparisons Between Monopoly and Competition, 325
The Effect of Changes in Cost on Price and Quantity Produced, 325
The Monopolization of a Competitive Industry with No Change in Costs, 326
The Effect of Market Structure on Cost, 326
The Incentive to Innovate, 328
Public Policy Toward Monopoly: Combines Laws, 330
The Nature of Competition Policy, 331
Canadian Competition Policy, 332
Public Policy Toward Monopoly: Public Utility Regulation, 334
Natural Monopoly, 334
The Theory of Natural Monopoly Regulation, 336
Problems of Implementing the Theory, 336
Evaluating Public Utility Regulation, 338

19
WHO RUNS THE FIRM AND FOR WHAT ENDS?   343

Do Firms Manipulate the Market? 344
The Hypothesis That Firms Control the Market, 344
The Evidence for the Hypothesis, 345
Doubts About the Hypothesis, 346
Who Controls the Modern Firm?: Alternative Maximizing Theories, 348
The Hypothesis of Minority Control, 349
The Hypothesis of Intercorporate Control Groups, 349
The Hypothesis of the Separation of Ownership from Control, 350
Do Firms Maximize Anything?: Nonmaximizing Theories of the Firm, 352
Nonmaximization Due to Ignorance, 352
Nonmaximization by Choice, 353
Evolutionary Theories, 356
The Significance of Nonmaximizing Theories, 357
A Final Word: The Importance of Profits, 357

PART SIX
Factor Pricing and the Distribution of Income   361

20
THE DISTRIBUTION OF NATIONAL INCOME   362

Problems of Distribution, 362
The Theory of Distribution, 364

The Demand for Factors, 365
The Downward Slope of the Demand Curve, 365
What Determines the Elasticity of Factor Demands? 366
The Marginal Productivity Theory of Distribution, 367
Important Misconceptions About Marginal Productivity Theory, 368
The Supply of Factors, 369
The Total Supply of Factors, 369
The Supply of Factors to Particular Uses, 373
The Price of Factors in Competitive Markets, 376
Factor Price Differentials, 377
Transfer Earnings and Economic Rent, 378
Policy Implications of the Distinction Between Rents and Transfer Earnings, 380
What Question Does the Theory Answer? 381

21
LABOR MARKETS AND THE DETERMINATION OF WAGES   385

Theoretical Models of Wage Determination, 386
A Union in a Competitive Labor Market, 386
A Monopsonistic Labor Market Without a Union, 387
A Union in a Monopsonistic Market, 388
Labor Market Institutions, 389
The Evolution of the Modern Union, 393
Requirements of a Successful Union, 394
The Historical Development of Unions in North America, 395
Methods and Objectives of the Modern Union, 397
Restricting Supply to Increase Wages, 398
Competing Goals, 400
Minimum Wages and Employment, 401
Effective Minimum Wages in a Competitive Labor Market, 401
Effective Minimum Wages in a Monopsonistic Labor Market, 404
Discrimination in Labor Markets, 404
A Model of the Effects of Discrimination, 405
Female-Male Differentials in Labor Markets, 407
Who Loses from Discrimination? 409

22
INTEREST AND THE RETURN ON CAPITAL   412

The Productivity or Efficiency of Capital, 413
The Rate of Return on Capital, 413
The Value of an Asset, 417
A Theory of Interest Rate Determination, 418
The Demand for Additional Capital by a Firm, 418
The Economy as a Whole, 419
Further Determinants of the Market Rate of Interest, 420
A Complication: Many Rates of Interest, 422

Sources of Funds for Investment, 423
  Financing the Modern Corporation, 423
  Stocks and Stockholders, 423
  Bonds and Bondholders, 424
  Loans from Financial Institutions, 424
  Reinvested Profits, 424
  Securities Markets (Stock Markets), 425

23
POVERTY, INEQUALITY, AND MOBILITY 431

The Distribution of Income Between Rich and Poor: The Problem of Poverty, 431
  The Concept of Poverty, 432
  Who Are the Poor? 433
  Why Are There Poor? 433
  "Waging War" on Poverty, 434
  The Nature of Current Programs, 436
The Relevance of Distribution Theory, 437
  Do Market Conditions Determine Factor Earnings? 438
  Do Factors Move in Response to Changes in Earnings? 441

PART SEVEN
The Market Economy: Problems and Policies 449

24
MICROECONOMIC POLICY I: BENEFITS AND COSTS OF GOVERNMENT INTERVENTION IN THE MARKET ECONOMY 450

Market Success, 451
  The Interdependent Economy, 451
  How Markets Coordinate, 451
  What Do Markets Do Well? 452
  Qualifications About Market Success, 454
Market Failure, 455
  Externalities as a Source of Inefficiency, 455
  Market Imperfections and Impediments as a Source of Inefficiency, 458
  The Neglect of Nonmarket Goals as a Source of Market Failure, 459
Responding to Market Failure, 460
  The Tools of Microeconomic Policy, 460

  Government Attempts to Correct Market Failure: Benefits and Costs, 463
Government Failure and the Theory of Government Intervention, 466
  Causes of Government Failure, 466
  The Reality of Government Failure, 467
  The Theory of Government Intervention to Correct Market Failure, 468
  Government Intervention in Canada Today, 470

25
MICROECONOMIC POLICY II: PUBLIC FINANCE AND PUBLIC EXPENDITURE 477

Taxation as a Tool of Micro Policy, 478
  Taxes and the Distribution of Income, 478
  Can Progressivity Be Increased? 481
  How Much Progressivity Is Desirable? 484
  Tax Structure and the Allocation of Resources, 484
  Tax Incidence, 485
Public Expenditure as a Tool of Micro Policy, 487
  Public Expenditures and Redistribution of Income, 490
  Intergovernmental Transfers as a Form of Redistribution, 490
  Government Expenditure and Resource Allocation, 494
Evaluating the Role of Government, 498
  Do Benefits of Government Programs Exceed Costs? 498
  The Balance Between Private and Public Sectors, 499
  What Is the Role of Government Today? 500

PART EIGHT
Resource Allocation in an Open Economy 503

26
INTERNATIONAL TRADE AND PROTECTION 504

The Gains from International Trade, 505
  Interpersonal, Interregional, and International Trade, 505
  Sources of the Gains from Trade, 505
  Additional Sources of the Gains from Trade: Learning by Doing and Economies of Scale, 509
  Terms of Trade, 510

The Debate About Protectionism, 512
  Methods of Protectionism, 512
  Free Trade Versus Protectionism, 514
  Trade and Protectionism, 516
Canadian Trade Policy, 521
  The Foreign Ownership Issue, 527

27
ENERGY POLICY: A CASE STUDY   534
  Domestic Patterns of Energy Production and
    Consumption, 535
  International Developments, 537
  Canadian Energy Prices in the 1970s, 537
The Two-price System, 540
**The Debate About Establishing Parity with
  World Prices, 542**
  A Fallacious Argument for Not Moving to Parity, 542
  The Argument for Parity, 543
  Arguments Against Parity, 547
**Current Issues in Energy Policy: The National
  Energy Program, 553**

PART NINE
National Income and
Fiscal Policy   559

28
AGGREGATE DEMAND AND
AGGREGATE SUPPLY   560
What Is Macroeconomics? 560
  Micro and Macro Compared, 560
  Some Major Macroeconomic Issues, 561
  Key Macro Variables: Definition and Behavior, 561
Aggregate Demand and Aggregate Supply, 567
  The Shapes of the Aggregate Curves, 567
  Shifts in the Aggregate Curves, 569
  Aggregate Demand and Supply in Action, 569
  The Shapes of the Aggregate Curves Explained, 571
  The Game Plan, 575

29
THE CONCEPTS OF NATIONAL PRODUCT
AND NATIONAL INCOME   578
National Income Accounting, 578
  The Output-expenditure Approach to
    National Income, 579

  The Factor Payments (Factor Income) Approach, 584
  Related Measures of National Income, 587
Interpreting National Income Measures, 587
  Money Values and Real Values, 588
  Total Output and Per Capita Output, 589
  Omissions from Measured National Income, 590
  Which Measure Is Best? 592

30
WHAT DETERMINES NATIONAL
INCOME?   595
Desired Expenditure, 595
  Desired Consumption Expenditure, 597
  Other Categories of Desired Expenditure, 602
  The Aggregate Desired Expenditure Function, 602
Determining Equilibrium National Income, 604
  Desired Expenditure Equals National Income
    in Equilibrium, 604
  A Graphical Illustration of Equilibrium, 605
**The Relation Between Aggregate Demand and
  Aggregate Expenditure, 606**

31
CHANGES IN NATIONAL INCOME   610
Why National Income Changes, 610
  Movements Along Curves Versus Shifts of Curves, 610
  Shifts in the Desired Expenditure Function, 612
**The Multiplier: A Measure of the Magnitude of
  Changes in Income, 616**
  Definition of the Multiplier, 617
  The Multiplier: An Intuitive Statement, 617
  The Multiplier: A Graphical Analysis, 617
  The Size of the Multiplier, 618
  How Large Is the Multiplier in Canada? 619
Inflationary and Deflationary Gaps, 621
  Using the Concepts of the "Gaps," 623

32
CYCLES AND FLUCTUATIONS IN
NATIONAL INCOME   626
  The Historical Record, 626
  Is There a Principal Cause of Cycles? 629
Shifts in Consumption, 630
  Shifts in the Relationship Between Consumption
    and Disposable Income, 630
  Shifts in the Relationship Between Disposable
    Income and National Income, 631
Shifts in Exports, 632

Investment and Its Determinants, 632
Why Does Investment Change? 634
Investment in Inventories, 635
Investment in Residential Construction, 637
Business Fixed Investment, 637
The Accelerator Theory of Investment, 640
Government and Cyclical Fluctuations, 642
Government Expenditures on Goods and Services, 642
Government Transfer Payments, 642
Elements of a Theory of Fluctuations, 642
The Terminology of Business Fluctuations, 643
Cumulative Movements and Turning Points, 644
The Variety of Cyclical Fluctuations, 646
Fluctuations: A Consensus View? 647

33
NATIONAL INCOME, INTERNATIONAL TRADE, AND THE BALANCE OF PAYMENTS   650
The Historical Record, 651
National Income and the Balance of Trade, 652
International Transmission of Business Cycles: The Export Multiplier, 652
The Net Export Function, 652
Net Exports and Domestic Absorption, 658
Net Exports and Aggregate Demand, 662
Canada's Balance of International Payments, 663
The Nature of Balance-of-Payments Accounts, 663
Major Categories in the Balance-of-Payments Accounts, 665
The Relation Among Current, Capital, and Official Accounts, 667
Balance-of-Payments Deficits and Surpluses, 668
Canada's Balance-of-Payments Experience, 669

34
FISCAL POLICY   673
The Theory of Fiscal Policy, 674
The Budget Balance, 674
Fiscal Policy When Private Expenditure Functions Do Not Shift, 675
Fiscal Policy When Private Expenditure Functions Are Shifting, 677
Tools of Fiscal Policy, 678
Automatic Tools of Fiscal Policy: Built-in Stabilizers, 678
Discretionary Fiscal Policy, 682

Fiscal Policy in Action, 685
Judging the Stance of Fiscal Policy, 686
The Great Depression and World War II, 686
The Postwar Period, 688
Proposals Concerning the Budget Balance, 692
The National Debt, 694

PART TEN
Money, Banking, and Monetary Policy   701

35
THE NATURE AND IMPORTANCE OF MONEY   702
The Nature of Money, 702
What Is Money? 702
Do We Need Money? 704
The Origins and Growth of Metallic Money, 705
The Evolution of Paper Money, 706
Deposit Money, 710
Near Money and Money Substitutes, 711
Changing Concepts of What Is Money, 712
The Importance of Money, 712
The "Real" and Money Parts of the Economy, 712
The Experience of Price Level Changes, 713
Why Inflations Matter, 715
The Classical Quantity Theory, 720
The Transactions Demand for Money, 720
Assumptions of the Quantity Theory, 721
Money, Prices, and Output in the Classical Quantity Theory, 723

36
INTERNATIONAL MONETARY SYSTEMS   728
Before World War II, 729
The Gold Standard in Theory, 729
Actual Experience of the Gold Standard, 730
The 1930s: Experimentation with Fluctuating Rates, 731
The Rise and Fall of the Bretton Woods System, 1944–1972, 732
The International Monetary Fund, 733
Problems of an Adjustable Peg System, 733
Collapse of the Bretton Woods System, 736

The Present System: Its Nature and Its Problems, 739
A Dirty Float, 739
Survival of the IMF in a World of Floating
Exchange Rates, 740
Current Problems, 740
The Challenge for the 1980s, 745
An International Reserve Currency, 745
The Management of Exchange Rates, 745
The Need for Cooperation, 746

37
THE BANKING SYSTEM AND THE
SUPPLY OF MONEY   749

The Chartered Banks, 750
Banks as Profit-seeking Institutions, 752
The Creation and Destruction of Money, 753
A Monopoly Bank, a Single New Deposit, 754
Many Banks, a Single New Deposit, 756
Many Banks, Many Deposits, 758
Excess Reserves and Currency Drains, 759
Central Banks, 760
Basic Functions of a Central Bank, 760
Control of the Money Supply, 762
Open Market Operations, 762
Other Central Bank Policies, 765

38
THE MACROECONOMIC ROLE OF
MONEY AND THE THEORY OF
MONETARY POLICY   768

The Demand for and the Supply of Money, 768
Kinds of Assets, 768
What Determines the Supply of Money? 770
What Determines the Demand for Money? 770
The Determination of Monetary Equilibrium:
The Transmission Mechanism, 774
From Monetary Disequilibrium to Changes in the
Rate of Interest, 774
From Changes in the Rate of Interest to Shifts in
Aggregate Expenditure, 776
The Transmission Mechanism Summarized, 776
The Theory of Monetary Policy, 776
Policy-induced Monetary Disequilibrium, 777
The Strength of Monetary Policy, 778
Changes in the Price Level, 779
The Shape of the Aggregate Demand Curve, 779
Equilibrium National Income and the Price Level, 782

The Price Level and the Monetary Adjustment
Mechanism, 782
Frustration of the Monetary Adjustment
Mechanism, 785
A Few Implications, 786
Instruments and Objectives of Monetary Policy, 786
Controlling National Income Through Monetary
Policy, 788
Targets of Monetary Policy: Money Supply Versus
Interest Rates, 789
The Shift from Interest Rates to the Money Supply
as the Primary Target Variable, 791
Monetary Policy: Some Interim Conclusions, 796

PART ELEVEN
Macroeconomic Policy   799

39
THE NATURE OF UNEMPLOYMENT
AND INFLATION   800

Unemployment, 801
Why Policymakers Are Concerned, 801
Causes of Unemployment, 802
Measured and Nonmeasured Unemployment, 804
Tools for the Control of Unemployment, 804
Experience of Unemployment, 805
Inflation, 808
The Definition of Inflation, 808
Why Policymakers Are Concerned, 808
Classification of the Causes of Inflation, 809
Demand-pull Theories of Inflation, 812
Supply-side Theories of Inflation, 812
Demand-Supply Theories of Inflation, 814
The Control of Inflation: Validated and
Unvalidated Inflation, 817
Experience of Inflation, 818
A Link Between Inflation and Unemployment, 820
The Intermediate Section of the Aggregate Supply
Curve, 821
Validated Demand Inflation: An Unemployment-
Inflation Trade-off? 824
Validated Demand Inflation and Accelerating
Inflation, 825
The Phelps-Friedman Theory: Accelerating Inflation
and an Unstable Phillips Curve, 825
Implications of the Phelps-Friedman Theory, 829

40
MACROECONOMIC POLICY AND THE BALANCE OF PAYMENTS 836
Macroeconomic Policy and the Current Account, 836
The Current Account and Domestic Policy Objectives, 837
Expenditure-changing and Expenditure-switching Policies, 840
Macroeconomic Policy and the Capital Account, 841
An Alternative Concept of External Balance, 843
Macroeconomic Policy Under Fixed Exchange Rates, 844
Macroeconomic Policy Under Flexible Exchange Rates, 845
Fiscal Policy Under Flexible Rates, 846
Monetary Policy Under Flexible Rates, 846
Canadian Experience with Flexible Exchange Rates, 847

41
MACROECONOMIC EXPERIENCE 855
The 1930s: Depression Economics, 855
The 1940s: Full Employment and Inflation, 856
The 1950s: The Goal of Full Employment Without Inflation, 857
The 1960s: Inflation-Unemployment Trade-offs and More Demand Inflation, 859
The 1970s: Inflation, Stagflation, and the "Failure of Conventional Wisdom," 861
The Control of Aggregate Demand and the Control of Inflation, 876

42
CURRENT ISSUES IN MACROECONOMIC POLICY 878
Control of Inflation in the 1980s, 879
Causes of Inflation, 879
An Appropriate Target Rate of Inflation, 880
Possible Cures for Inflation, 881
Controversies over Stabilization Policy, 887
Causes of Cyclical Fluctuations, 888
Control of Cyclical Fluctuations: Monetary Versus Fiscal Policy, 890
The Micro Foundations of Monetarism and Neo-Keynesianism, 894
One Monetarist Microeconomic Model, 895
The Neo-Keynesian Micro Foundations, 897
Differences in the Two Models, 899
How Much Unemployment at Full Employment? 902
The Composition of Macro Variables, 903

PART TWELVE
Economic Growth and Comparative Systems 907

43
GROWTH IN DEVELOPED ECONOMIES 908
The Nature of Economic Growth, 908
The Definition of Economic Growth, 909
The Cumulative Nature of Growth, 910
Benefits of Growth, 911
Costs of Growth, 913
Growth as a Goal of Policy: Do the Benefits Justify the Costs? 916
Theories of Economic Growth, 917
Growth in a World Without Learning, 917
Growth with Learning, 918
A Contemporary View of Growth, 919
Are There Limits to Growth? 923

44
GROWTH AND THE LESS-DEVELOPED COUNTRIES 928
The Uneven Pattern of Development, 928
Barriers to Economic Development, 931
Population Growth, 931
Natural Resources, 932
Inefficiency in the Use of Resources, 933
Inadequate Human Resources, 934
Institutional and Cultural Barriers, 934
The Challenge to Development Policy, 935
Some Basic Choices, 937
How Much Government Control? 937
What Sorts of Education? 939
What Population Policy? 939
How to Acquire Capital? 940
Alternative Development Strategies, 943
Agricultural Development, 944
Specialization in a Few Commodities, 946
Import Substitution Industrialization, 946
Industrialization for Export, 947
Commodity Price Stabilization Agreements, 948
A New International Economic Order (NIEO)? 949
Some Controversial Unresolved Issues, 951

APPENDIXES

Appendix to Chapter 2
MORE ON FUNCTIONAL RELATIONS A-2
Functional Relations: The General Expression of Relations Among Variables, A-2

Functional Forms: Precise Relations Among
Variables, A-3
Error Terms in Economic Hypotheses, A-3

Appendix to Chapter 3
GRAPHING ECONOMIC MAGNITUDES   A-5

Graphing Economic Observations, A-5
Graphing Functions, A-8

Appendix to Chapter 6
ELASTICITY: A FORMAL ANALYSIS   A-11

Point Elasticity According to the Approximate
Definition, A-11
Point Elasticity According to the Precise Definition, A-14

Appendix to Chapter 7
ELEMENTS OF DYNAMICS   A-16

Lags in Adjustment of Supply, A-17
The Relevance of Statics and Dynamics in
Evaluating the Price System, A-20

Appendix to Chapter 9
**THE DERIVATION OF THE DEMAND
CURVE FROM INDIFFERENCE CURVES**   A-21

Derivation of Demand Curves, A-21
The Slope of the Demand Curve, A-22

Appendix to Chapter 11
**BALANCE SHEETS, INCOME
STATEMENTS, AND COSTS OF
PRODUCTION: TWO VIEWS**   A-25

An Example, A-25
An Accountant's Balance Sheet and Income
Statement, A-26
An Economist's Balance Sheet and Income
Statement, A-28

Appendix to Chapter 14
**MORE ON LONG-RUN COMPETITIVE
EQUILIBRIUM**   A-30

Long-run Equilibrium Implies Minimum Attainable
Costs, A-30

Long-run Responses to Changes in Demand, A-31
The Long-run Industry Supply Curve, A-32
The Existence of Long-run Competitive Equilibrium, A-35

Appendix to Chapter 20
**THE DERIVATION OF THE DEMAND FOR
FACTORS**   A-37

Appendix to Chapter 34
**THE PERMANENT-INCOME HYPOTHESIS
AND THE LIFE-CYCLE HYPOTHESIS**   A-39

Variables, A-39
Assumptions, A-41
Implications, A-41
Conclusion, A-43

Appendix to Chapter 38
**MONEY IN THE NATIONAL INCOME
MODEL**   A-44

The Interest Rate and Aggregate Expenditure:
The *IS* Curve, A-44
Liquidity Preference and National Income:
The *LM* Curve, A-45
Macroeconomic Equilibrium Determination of
National Income and the Interest Rate, A-46
The Price Level and Aggregate Demand, A-47

Appendix to Chapter 42
**MORE ON MONETARY VERSUS FISCAL
POLICY**   A-49

The Relative Effectiveness of Monetary and Fiscal
Policy, A-49
The Monetary Mechanism and Aggregate Demand, A-51

Mathematical Notes   M-1
Glossary
Index

Preface

Our basic motivation in writing *Economics* remains to provide a book that reflects the enormous changes in economics over the last 40 years. Economics is always changing, but in the years since World War II there has been a change of such importance that we do ourselves and our students a great disservice if we neglect it. During this period economics has moved very rapidly toward becoming a genuine science. We apply the term *science* neither to praise nor to castigate economics, but to describe its movement toward the characteristic that distinguishes any science: the systematic confrontation of theory with observation.

The quotation from Lord William Beveridge on page xxix of this book is our text — in the preacher's sense of that word. Beveridge was scolding the profession in 1937, but things since then have clearly changed for the better. Today we all agree that economics is not a stage on which we parade our pet theories and ask to have them admired solely for their elegance or their conclusions, nor is it a container in which we collect quantities of unrelated institutional and statistical material about the economy. Economists are making a serious attempt to push back the frontiers of ignorance about the economic environment in order both to understand it and to control it. As we repeatedly discover, new problems and new phenomena challenge our existing knowledge. Economists must therefore continually be concerned with the relations among theory, institutions, and facts and must regard every theory as subject to empirical challenge.

A second major theme of this book concerns

the relations between economic theory and economic policy. An appreciation of these relations is not new to economics. Indeed, many nineteenth-century economists expressed the modern view that although economic theory can show us some of the consequences of our actions, it can never show us what we ought to do. What is new today is the realization of how little can be said about policy on the basis of the purely qualitative theories, and the resulting successful application of the quantitative revolution of the last 40 years to matters of policy. Four decades of systematic observations have provided us with a much better idea of how things are related to one another quantitatively, and this knowledge has greatly increased the economist's power to say sensible and relevant things about public policy. This is not to deny that there are still great areas where economists' knowledge is painfully sparse, as the current debates about how to cope with the twin problems of unemployment and inflation, and on the relative efficacy of monetary and fiscal policy, remind us.

The third major feature of the book relates to the way we view modern students. We have tried in several different ways to be as honest with them as is possible within the confines of an introductory textbook. No subject worth studying is always easy, and we have not glossed over hard points just because they are hard. We have tried to follow Einstein's advice: make things as simple as possible, but not simpler. We do not approve of slipping particularly hard bits of analysis past students without letting them see what is happening and what has been assumed, nor do we approve of teaching them things they will have to unlearn if they go on in economics (a practice sometimes justified on the grounds that it is important to get to the big issues quickly).

Every student who continues in economics soon learns that, although economics has many triumphs to its credit, there are areas where present knowledge is woefully inadequate. It is sometimes argued that in an elementary course such inadequacies should be played down or altogether suppressed so that beginning students will not lose faith in their subject. We reject this view. Both the students' education and our subject depend upon careful criticism. We have devoted some space to examining both sensible and foolish criticisms of economic theories. In doing this, we hope to give students some inkling of how it is possible to criticize effectively, and hence to improve, the existing body of economic theory.

Effective criticism of existing ideas is the springboard to progress in science, and we believe that an introduction to economics should also introduce students to methods for testing, criticizing, and evaluating the present state of the subject. We do not accept the notion that if you suggest the possibility of criticism to students, they will make hasty and confused criticisms. Students will always make criticisms and evaluations of their courses, and their criticisms are much more likely to be informed and relevant if they are given both practice and instruction in how to go about challenging in an effective, constructive manner what they have been taught rather than reverting to mere dogmatic assertion of error or irrelevance.

MAJOR REVISIONS IN THIS EDITION

This revision is the most comprehensive we have undertaken since the appearance of the first edition. Users of previous editions will want to check the details of the new table of contents carefully. The most basic change is the revision of the core of macroeconomic theory and policy, as described in detail below. But other major changes have been made throughout the book, including the addition of more than 40 new boxes dealing with a wide range of applied issues. We believe our treatment is now more up-to-date, more relevant to contemporary Canadian issues, and easier for students. Only time—and your letters—will tell us if we are right.

Changes in International Trade and Finance

We have reorganized and rewritten much of this material, not only to take into account several major developments but also to further develop the theme introduced in the third edition of integrating the international material into the rest of the text. We have also considerably expanded the coverage of policy issues that arise in an open economy such as Canada, including a completely new chapter on energy policy (Chapter 27) and an extended treatment of national income and the balance of payments in one unified chapter (Chapter 33).

Chapter 8, "International Trade and Exchange Rates," has been completely rewritten so that the material is treated as a basic application of the tools of supply and demand. The basic approach has been changed so that the focus is on the modern analysis of the "small open economy" which acts as a price-taker in world markets. Attention is directed to the roles of domestic supply and demand in determining the *volume* of exports and imports. This analysis is simpler and more closely related to earlier chapters than the "Keynesian-elasticities" approach used previously.

Chapter 27 in the third edition, "Canada's Trade Policy and Tariff Policy," has been dropped; the material on the balance of payments is now in the new Chapter 33, and the material on tariff policy is included with that on the gains from trade in Chapter 26, "International Trade and Protection." This chapter also contains new material reflecting the rising importance of nontariff barriers to trade, which threaten a reversal of the long-term trend away from economic protectionism. The reorganized Chapter 26 is combined with the new Chapter 27 (dealing with energy policy in Canada) to form a new section on "Resource Allocation in an Open Economy" (Part Eight).

Chapter 36, "International Monetary Systems," has been updated and now immediately follows Chapter 35, "The Nature and Importance of Money," allowing a more unified treatment of the role of money in exchange and a parallel development of the classical quantity theory of money and the operation of the international gold standard.

Chapter 40, "Macroeconomic Policy and the Balance of Payments," has been revised extensively to draw on the new material presented in Chapter 33 and to emphasize the problems of stabilization policy in an open economy operating under flexible exchange rates.

Chapter 43, "Comparative Economic Systems," has been dropped. The basic theoretical issues are now covered in Chapter 4 while the country-specific discussions are incorporated into Chapters 19 and 43.

Changes in Microeconomics

In addition to the revised Chapter 8, supply and demand in action has been extended in Chapter 7 to add a fuller discussion of rent control and a summary section on general lessons about resource allocation.

In this revision we have expanded the discussion of just when and how markets prove to be efficient and inefficient. This affects Chapters 14, 15, 18, and 24. We have also added a parallel discussion of government success and government failure—see especially the final half of Chapter 24, which also now includes the discussion of social cost.

Among the new applications of economics to current microeconomic problems is an extended discussion of OPEC and the price of gasoline (Chapter 17) and several boxes dealing with Canadian policy issues.

To make room for these and other additions, some of the third edition coverage of long-run equilibrium has been placed in an appendix, where it remains available to those who wish to assign it but can be readily omitted.

Changes in Basic Macroeconomics

Parts Eight, Nine, and Ten of the third edition (Parts Nine, Ten, and Eleven of this edition) have been totally rewritten to let aggregate demand and aggregate supply curves bear much of the weight of the analysis. This has a number of substantial advantages for teaching economics in the 1980s. First, the price level can be allowed to vary from the outset. Our experience is that contemporary students become increasingly restive with a treatment that holds the price level constant while most of national income theory is being covered. Second, it is much easier to deal with supply shocks and to explain stagflation. Third, the treatment of the definition and determination of national income can be greatly simplified. The present Chapter 29 is very much simpler than its third edition counterpart, Chapter 28. Gone are the four increasingly complex economies (spendthrift, frugal, governed, and open) with which we formerly built the analysis. Gone too is the withdrawals-injections explanation of equilibrium. (These concepts, in the Swedish process-analysis tradition, have much to commend them, but many students find them harder than the more static approach embodied in aggregate demand and supply diagrams.) One important pedagogical payoff to our current approach is the overview of recent economic events that can be provided at the very outset in Chapter 28 and in detail in Chapter 41.

No approach is without its own difficulties. The major difficulty with aggregate demand-supply lies in the instability of the aggregate supply curve. Although the economy can move up and down a given aggregate demand curve in response to shifts in aggregate supply, the reverse is not true. The aggregate supply curve will itself shift in response to some aggregate demand curve shifts, owing partly to the downward rigidity of prices. The complications inherent in this instability of the aggregate supply curve can often be sidetracked, where they are unimportant, by using a kinked aggregate supply curve (that suppresses the intermediate gradually rising portion) and this we do where we can. A second difficulty is that the downward slope of the aggregate demand curve cannot be fully explained until after money is introduced. The full explanation does not come, therefore, until Chapter 38.

The shift to an aggregate demand-aggregate supply approach pervades Part Nine ("National Income and Fiscal Policy"), Part Ten ("Money, Banking, and Monetary Policy"), and Part Eleven ("Macroeconomic Policy").

In addition to this major change in approach, a number of other significant changes have been made in these parts. The chapter on fiscal policy has been heavily revised to eliminate policy debates from previous decades in favor of such current debates as "Can and should the budget be balanced?" and "How can the stance of fiscal policy be judged?" "The Macroeconomic Role of Money and the Theory of Monetary Policy" (Chapter 38) has been completely rewritten. The explanation of the demand for money now is rooted in the analysis of Tobin rather than Keynes. The chapter includes the full explanation of the shape of the aggregate demand curve as well as an explanation of why continuous inflations require monetary validation. Chapter 39 provides an expanded discussion of employment, inflation, and the possible relation between the two as well as the rather difficult analysis of the Phelps-Friedman theory of expectational inflation and stagflation.

Many students have read or heard that economists cannot understand the inflation-unemployment experience of the last decade. They will be pleasantly surprised in reading the wholly new Chapter 41, "Macroeconomic Experience," to learn that economics can yield a good explanation of the decade-by-decade experience of the economy over the last half century.

The discussion of current policy issues in macroeconomics has been updated and expanded. Among the topics receiving expanded attention are wage and price controls, monetary gradualism, rational expectations, and the so-called natural rate of unemployment.

TEACHING AIDS

Tag lines and captions for figures and tables. The boldface tag line below the figure or table indicates succinctly the central conclusion intended by the illustration; the lightface caption provides information needed to reach that conclusion. Titles, tag lines, and captions are, with the figure or table, a self-contained set, and many students find them a useful device for reviewing a chapter.

Boxes. The material in colored "boxes" contains examples or materials that are relevant extensions of the text narrative but need not be read in sequence.

End-of-chapter material. Each chapter contains a summary, a list of topics for review, and a set of discussion questions. The questions are particularly useful for class discussion or for "quiz sections." They are answered in the *Instructor's Manual.*

Mathematical notes. Mathematical notes to the body of the text are collected in a self-contained section at the end of the book. Since mathematical notation and derivation is not required to understand the principles of economics, but is helpful in more advanced work, this seems to us to be a sensible arrangement. It provides clues to the uses of mathematics for the increasing numbers of students who come to beginning economics with some background in math, without encumbering the text with notes that may appear formidable to those who find mathematics arcane or frightening. Students with a mathematical background have many times told us they find the notes helpful.

Glossary. The glossary covers widely used definitions of economic terms. Because some users treat micro- and macroeconomics in that order, and others in reverse order, words in the glossary are printed in boldface type when they are first mentioned in *either half* of the text.

Endpapers. Inside the front cover is a figure, new to this edition, that represents Canadian labor market developments by sex, 1953–1980. Inside the back cover is a list of the most commonly used abbreviations in the text as well as a set of useful data about the Canadian economy.

Supplements

Our book is accompanied by a workbook, *Study Guide and Problems,* prepared by Professors Douglas A. L. Auld and E. Kenneth Grant. It is designed to be used either in the classroom or by the students working on their own.

An *Instructor's Manual,* prepared by us, and a *Test Bank* prepared under our supervision are available to instructors adopting the book.

USING THE BOOK

This textbook reflects to some extent the way its authors would teach their own courses. Needs of students differ; some want to have material that goes beyond the average class level, but others have gaps in their backgrounds. To accommodate the former, we have included more material than we would assign to every student. Also, because there are many different kinds of first-year economics courses in colleges and universities, we have included more material than normally would be included in any single course. Requests and suggestions from users of previous editions have prompted us to include some additional alternative material.

Although teachers can best design their own courses, it may be helpful if we indicate certain views of our own as to how this book *might* be adapted to different courses.

Sequence

Because the choice of order between macro and micro is partly a personal one, it cannot be decided solely by objective criteria. We believe that in the 1970s there are good reasons for preferring the micro–macro order. Whereas in the immediate post-World War II years, the major emphasis was on the development of both the theory and the policy implications of Keynesian economics, the thrust over the last ten years has been to examine the micro underpinnings of macro functions and to erect macroeconomics on a firmer base of micro behavioral relations. Changes have occurred not only in economic theory but in the problems that excite students. Although macroeconomic problems such as inflation and unemployment are still of great concern, many of the problems that students find most challenging today—poverty, pollution, and managing wage and price controls—are microeconomic in character. The micro–macro order, moreover, reflects the historical evolution of the subject. A century of classical and neoclassical development of microeconomics preceded the Keynesian development of macroeconomics.

For those who prefer the macro–micro order and who wish to reverse the order of our book, we have attempted to make reversibility virtually painless. The overview chapter that ends Part One has been built up to provide an improved base on which to build either the microeconomics of Part Two or the macroeconomics of Part Nine. Where some microeconomic concepts were required—as in the macro investment chapter—we have added brief sections to make the treatment self-contained, while providing review material for those who have been through the microeconomic section.

One-Term Courses

Thorough coverage of the bulk of the book supposes a two-term course in economics. A number of first courses in economics are only one term (or equivalent) in length and our book can be easily adapted to such courses. Suggestions for use of this book for such courses are given on pages xxv–xxvi. We recognize that for any one-term course a choice must be made among emphases. Most one-term survey courses necessarily give some coverage to theory and to policy, to micro- and macroeconomics, but the relative weights vary. Instructors will wish to choose the topics to be included or excluded and to vary the order to suit their own preferences.

ACKNOWLEDGMENTS

The starting point for this book was *Economics,* Sixth Edition, by Richard G. Lipsey and Peter O. Steiner. It would be impossible to acknowledge here all the teachers, colleagues, and students who contributed to that book. Hundreds of users have written to us with specific suggested improvements, and much of the credit for the fact that the book does become more and more teachable belongs to them. We can no longer list them individually but we thank them all most sincerely.

Charles Burton provided absolutely first-rate research assistance. We also express thanks to Michael Abbott, John Helliwell, Frank Lewis, Nancy Olewiler, and Brian Scarfe for detailed comments and suggestions for revision of particular chapters. A few individuals provided reviews of the third edition that were most helpful in preparing the present edition. These are Delbert C. Ogden, University of Calgary (who also revised the Test Bank); Bruce W. Wilkinson, University of Alberta; and Gerald E. Clarke, Carleton University. Douglas Auld and Kenneth Grant, who prepared the study guide, have contributed to this edition as well.

Special thanks is due to Patricia Casey-Purvis, Ellen McKay, and especially Marlene Rego for careful and efficient handling of the manuscript at all stages.

This edition introduces a new member to our team of authors, Professor Douglas D. Purvis of Queen's University. He would like to dedicate this edition to Jaime and Joshua, who have been dedicated to him for so long.

Richard G. Lipsey
Douglas D. Purvis
Gordon R. Sparks
Peter O. Steiner

Suggested Outline for a One-Term Course[1]

Basic core chapters for courses covering both micro and macro

INTRODUCTION

1 The Economic Problem
2 Economics as a Social Science
4 An Overview of the Economy

MICROECONOMICS

5 Demand, Supply, and Price
6 Elasticity of Demand and Supply
11 The Firm, Production, and Cost
12 Production and Cost in the Short Run
13 Production, Substitution, and Productivity Increases: Cost in the Long and Very Long Run
14 Pricing in Competitive Markets
15 Pricing in Monopoly Markets
24 Microeconomic Policy I: Benefits and Costs of Government Intervention in the Market Economy

MACROECONOMICS

28 Aggregate Demand and Aggregate Supply
29 The Concepts of National Product and National Income
30 What Determines National Income?
31 Changes in National Income
34 Fiscal Policy
35 The Nature and Importance of Money
37 The Banking System and the Supply of Money
39 The Nature of Unemployment and Inflation (to page 820)

[1] A one-term course can cover about 20 to 22 full chapters. The core consists of about 18 chapters. Selections from other chapters, as listed on page xxvi or according to the instructor's own preferences, can produce courses with various emphases.

Chapters that can be added to give different emphases to different courses[2]

MICROECONOMICS

* 7 Supply and Demand in Action I: Price Controls and Agricultural Problems
  8 Supply and Demand in Action II: International Trade and Exchange Rates
 17 Price Theory in Action
*18 Monopoly Versus Competition
 20 The Distribution of National Income
*21 Labor Markets and the Determination of Wages
*23 Poverty, Inequality, and Mobility
*25 Microeconomic Policy II: Public Finance and Public Expenditure
*26 International Trade and Protection
*27 Energy Policy: A Case Study

MACROECONOMICS

 38 The Macroeconomic Role of Money and the Theory of Monetary Policy
*40 Macroeconomic Policy and the Balance of Payments
*41 Macroeconomic Experience
 42 Current Issues in Macroeconomic Policy
 43 Growth in Developed Economies
*44 Growth and the Less-developed Countries

[2] Chapters shown with an * are particularly appropriate for courses with a heavy policy orientation. Chapters not listed here or in the core seem to us to be of lower priority in a one-term course, but they are not necessarily too difficult.

To the Student

A good course in economics will give you some real insight into how an economy functions and into some of the policy issues that are currently the subject of serious debate. Like all rewarding subjects, economics will not be mastered without effort. A book on economics must be worked at. It cannot be read like a novel.

Each student must develop an individual technique for studying, but the following suggestions may prove helpful. It is usually a good idea to read a chapter quickly in order to get the general run of the argument. At this first reading you may want to skip the "boxes" of text material and any footnotes. Then, after reading the topics for review and the discussion questions, reread the chapter more slowly, making sure that you understand each step of the argument. With respect to the figures and tables, be sure you understand how the conclusions stated in the brief tag lines below each table or figure have been reached. You should be prepared to spend time on difficult sections; occasionally, you may spend an hour on only a few pages. Paper and a pencil are indispensable equipment in your reading. It is best to follow a difficult argument by building your own diagram while the argument unfolds rather than by relying on the finished diagram as it appears in the book. It is often helpful to invent numerical examples to illustrate general propositions. The end-of-chapter questions require you to apply what you have studied. We advise you to outline answers to some of the questions. In short, you must seek to understand economics, not to memorize it.

After you have read each part in detail, reread

it quickly from beginning to end. It is often difficult to understand why certain things are done when they are viewed as isolated points, but when you reread a whole part, much that did not seem relevant or entirely comprehensible will fall into place in the analysis.

We call your attention to the glossary at the end of the book. Any time you run into a concept that seems vaguely familiar but is not clear to you, check the glossary. The chances are that it will be there, and its definition will remind you of what you once understood. If you are still in doubt, check the index entry to find where the concept is discussed more fully. Incidentally, the glossary, along with the captions under figures and tables and the end-of-chapter summaries,

may prove very helpful when reviewing for examinations.

The bracketed colored numbers in the text itself refer to a series of over 50 mathematical notes that are found starting on page M-1. For those of you who like mathematics or prefer mathematical argument to verbal or geometric exposition, these may prove useful. Others may ignore them.

We hope that you will find the book rewarding and stimulating. Students who used earlier editions made some of the most helpful suggestions for revision, and we hope you will carry on the tradition. If you are moved to write to us, please do.

Einstein started from facts—the Morley-Michelson measurements of light, the movements of the planet Mercury, the unexplained aberrancies of the moon from its predicted place. Einstein went back to facts or told others where they should go to confirm or to reject his theory—by observation of stellar positions during a total eclipse. . . .

. . . It is not necessary, of course, for the verification of a new theory to be done personally by its propounder. Theoretical reasoning from facts is as essential a part of economic science as of other sciences, and in a wise division of labour there is room, in economics, as elsewhere, for the theoretician pure and simple, for one who leaves the technical business of verification to those who have acquired a special technique of observation. No one demanded of Einstein that he should visit the South Seas in person, and look through a telescope; but he told others what he expected them to see, if they looked, and he was prepared to stand or fall by the result. It is the duty of the propounder of every new theory, if he has not himself the equipment for observation, to indicate where verification of his theory is to be sought in facts—what may be expected to happen or to have happened if his theory is true, what will not happen if it is false.

[Now consider by way of contrast the behaviour of the participants in a current controversy in economics.] . . . None of them takes the point that the truth or falsehood of . . . [a] theory cannot be established except by appeal to facts; none of them tests it by facts himself. The distinguishing mark of economic science, as illustrated by this debate, is that it is a science in which verification of generalisations by reference to facts is neglected as irrelevant.

. . . I do not see how . . . [members of the public who survey the controversy] can avoid the conclusion that economics is not a science concerned with phenomena, but a survival of medieval logic, and that economists are persons who earn their livings by taking in one another's definitions for mangling. . . .

I know that in speaking thus I make enemies. I challenge a tradition of a hundred years of political economy, in which facts have been treated, not as controls of theory, but as illustrations. I shall be told that in the Social Sciences verification can never be clean enough to be decisive. I may be told that, in these sciences, observation has been tried and has failed, has led to shapeless accumulations of facts which themselves lead nowhere. I do not believe for a moment that this charge of barrenness of past enquiries can be sustained; to make it is to ignore many achievements of the past and to decry much solid work that is being done at this School and elsewhere. But if the charge of barrenness of realistic economics in the past were justified completely, that would not be a reason for giving up observation and verification. It would only be a reason for making our observations more exact and more numerous. If, in the Social Sciences, we cannot yet run or fly, we ought to be content to walk, or to creep on all fours as infants. . . . For economic and political theorising not based on facts and not controlled by facts assuredly does lead nowhere. . . .

There can be no science of society till the facts about society are available. Till 130 years ago we had no census, no knowledge even of the numbers and growth of the people; till 15 years ago we had no comprehensive records about unemployment even in this country, and other countries are still where we were a generation or more ago; social statistics of every kind—about trade, wages, consumption—are everywhere in their infancy. . . .

From Copernicus to Newton is 150 years. Today, 150 years from the *Wealth of Nations*, we have not found, and should not expect to find, the Newton of economics. If we have traveled as far as Tycho Brahe we may be content. Tycho was both a theorist and an observer. As a theorist, he believed to his last day in the year 1601 that the planets went round the sun and that the sun and the stars went round the earth as the fixed centre of the universe. As an observer, he made with infinite patience and integrity thousands of records of the stars and planets; upon these records Kepler, in due course, based his laws and brought the truth to light. If we will take Tycho Brahe for our example, we may find encouragement also. It matters little how wrong we are with our theories, if we are honest and careful with our observations.

Extracts from Lord William Beveridge's farewell address as Director of the London School of Economics, June 24, 1937. Published in *POLITICA*, September, 1937.

Economics

Part One

The Nature
of Economics

The Economic Problem

Many of the world's most compelling problems are economic. The dominant problem of the 1930s was the massive unemployment of workers and resources known as the Great Depression. The wartime economy of the 1940s solved that problem but created new ones, especially the question of how quickly to reallocate scarce resources between military and civilian needs. By the 1950s inflation was appearing as a major problem in many countries. It is still with us. Much attention in the 1960s was devoted to trying to understand and to combat a slowdown in the pace of economic growth. The central problems of the 1970s were the rising cost of energy — oil prices increased tenfold over the decade — and the emergence of the disturbing combination of high unemployment *and* high rates of unemployment. Problems change from decade to decade, yet there are always problems.

Of course, not all of the world's serious problems are primarily economic. Political, biological, social, cultural, and philosophic issues often predominate. But no matter how "noneconomic" a particular problem may seem, it will almost always have a significant economic dimension.

The crises that lead to wars often have economic roots. Nations fight for oil and rice and land to live on, although the rhetoric of their leaders evokes God and Glory and the Fatherland. Arabs and Israelis fight for a homeland, to be sure, but also for pastures and farms and water and transportation routes.

A population explosion threatens to overrun the globe as a result of humanity's spectacular ability to reduce mortality rates much faster than birth rates. The current rate of world population growth is 2.2 persons a second, or about 70 million per year. The causes are mainly biological, medical, and cultural, but the economic consequences are steady pressures against the available supplies of natural resources and agricultural land. Unless the human race can find ways to increase its food supply as fast as its numbers, increasing millions face starvation.

Race is not primarily an economic phenomenon, but the problem of racial discrimination has important economic effects on individuals and on the economy. It means untapped human talent. It means a waste of social resources. It means children growing up undernourished, undereducated, unqualified for good jobs, and hostile to an alien world.

Economic Problems of the Eighties

UNEMPLOYMENT AND INFLATION

Virtually every minister of finance in recent history has included in his budget speeches a statement establishing full employment and stable prices as twin goals of economic policy. Reasonable as that may sound as a goal of policy, the fact is that we have seldom had both full employment and completely stable prices at the same time, and as the eighties began we had neither. At the start of the decade, unemployment stood at almost 8 percent of the labor force and prices were rising at an annual rate of 10 percent.

How did the unprecedented persistence of both "too high" unemployment and "too high" inflation arise, and how may it be avoided? Are zero unemployment and zero inflation reasonable *long-run* goals? What is an acceptable level of unemployment? Can we be sure we will never again experience the trauma of the 1930s, when up to a quarter of all those who sought work were unable to find it?

What is an acceptable amount of inflation? Will not any inflation ultimately get out of hand and wipe out the value of money and savings? Why do prices in some countries rise 30 percent or 40 percent a year while in others they rise at a rate of 5 or 6 percent? Why did inflation accelerate dramatically over most of the world in the early 1970s? Why did consumer prices in Canada rise by only 30 percent between 1960 and 1970 but by more than 90 percent between 1970 and 1980? Can a country control inflation? Why do we sometimes have both high unemployment and high inflation?

These questions concern the stability of the economy and the causes and consequences of depression and inflation. They also concern the ability of people, individually or through governments, to control and change their economic environment.

ENERGY

Energy is vital to an industrial economy — energy to drive its factories, to fuel its cars, to heat and light its homes and offices, and to do a myriad of other tasks. Over the last 200 years, North American output has grown, and with it has grown North America's demand for the earth's limited fossil fuels.

Throughout most of our history the increase in energy consumption caused no serious problems because new supplies were discovered as rapidly as old ones were exhausted. In 1970, world consumption of crude oil amounted to 17.5 billion barrels but proven world reserves were thirty-five times this amount. Canada's ratio of reserves to production stood at about twenty to one. However, since then there has been a dramatic turn of events with increasing demand for energy not being matched by a corresponding increase in the rate of discovery of new reserves. By the end of 1973, Canada's reserves-to-production ratio had fallen to thirteen to one. At this point in time, the world was rudely awakened to the new energy realities by the formation of the OPEC cartel, which restricted supplies of Middle Eastern oil and boosted the price from around $3 per barrel to more than $10. The price of oil has continued to rise; early in 1981 it was about $41 a barrel.

Do these trends portend an inevitable exhaustion of our energy resources and thus a limit to the future growth of both our population and our standard of living, or are they a temporary and transitory phenomenon? A great debate has developed concerning the appropriate response to the skyrocketing price of energy. Some have argued that if the government does not force us to make major changes now in how we use fuel, we will face disaster before the end of the century. Others, less alarmed, have argued that the price rises now occurring will lead to an automatic correction of the problem by decreasing the amount of energy we consume and at the same time making it profitable to discover or develop new sources of energy. They believe that the problems are transitory, that they will exist only for the next ten or twenty years and then be solved. Which group is closer to the truth?

Canada and the United States, with one-twentieth of the world's population, use one-third of the world's energy. To what extent are the *world's* supplies of oil and gas (e.g., in Alberta, in the USSR, in Saudi Arabia, and under the oceans) adequate to the world's demands for energy? If they are adequate, is the shortage currently experienced by many Western industrialized nations only a problem in trade, transportation, or foreign policy? To what extent can nuclear or solar energy render coal and oil and gas as unnecessary as oil and gas rendered whale oil?

In terms of energy supplies, Canada is one of the world's more fortunate countries. To what extent should we restrict exports of oil and natural gas so as to preserve scarce supplies for our own use? How should Canada respond to the dramatic increase in the world price of oil? Should we insulate domestic consumers from world prices by holding down the price of our own oil within Canada? Many argue that the answer to this last question is no because holding down the price encourages wasteful use of a scarce resource and only postpones the inevitable adjustment to higher prices that we will have

to make when our low-cost reserves are exhausted. Canada has very large potential supplies of oil in the Athabasca tar sands, but they can be extracted only at a much higher cost than that of extracting conventional oil.

These questions concern our ability to discover and bring to market the basic resources we need, our ability to make more resources available by trade with other countries, our ability to find new substitutes for depleted resources, and our ability to adapt to scarcities by changing our techniques of production. The questions also concern the roles of the free price system and of government intervention in the workings of our market economy.

PRODUCTIVITY AND GROWTH

Canadians pride themselves on having one of the highest standards of living in the world and a rate of growth in the output of goods and services per person that resulted in a doubling of the standard of living every generation. This happened most recently between 1947 and 1972. During the 1970s the annual rate of growth in the economy averaged 4.2 percent, significantly less than the 5.2 percent average of the 1960s. And while the 1960s saw one of the longest periods of *sustained* growth in the nation's history, growth in the 1970s was sporadic. There was a relatively severe slowdown in 1974–1975 and other, more minor periods of low growth.

Output per person continued to increase throughout the seventies at about its postwar average. However, growth in output per person *employed*, often called productivity, slowed dramatically during the seventies. While productivity grew at an average annual rate of 2.7 percent between 1947 and 1973, during the last half of the seventies it averaged less than 1 percent annually. Since productivity growth accounts for much of the growth in total output produced in the economy, this slowdown is a matter of major significance.

Why did output per person in the economy

continue to grow at its historic rate while output per person employed slowed? The proportion of the population employed, called the participation rate, grew rapidly in the 1970s. This was the result of entry into the labor force of the large youth population of the "baby boom" generation, of an ever-increasing proportion of women in the labor force, and of a large influx of new immigrants, most of whom entered the labor force. This growth in participation cannot go on forever, and unless productivity once again begins to grow rapidly, we can look forward to a slowing of the rate of growth of output per person in the country. A slowing of the growth rate from 3.5 percent annually to 1 percent annually may not seem very significant until we realize that at the former rate output per capita doubles in about twenty years (about a generation) while at the latter rate it takes almost *seventy* years for output per capita to double!

Canada has not suffered in isolation. Growth in output in the United States between 1970 and 1975 dropped to half that of the 1947–1970 period, and from 1975 to 1980 it dropped to a third. The downturn suffered in the United States in 1974–1975 was much more severe than that experienced in Canada. The United States, Germany, France, Italy, and Japan have all experienced lower productivity growth since 1973 than during the prior ten-year period.

What caused this loss of momentum in the economy? Some of it was due to the changing composition of output; in particular, the rapid growth of employment in the petroleum industry was largely associated with increased exploration activity, not increased current production of oil and gas. But the statistics also show a decreasing share of the nation's output going into new machines, equipment, and factories as well as a falloff in the rate of invention and innovation. But what *causes* these things? Is it the unstable and uncertain state of today's economy? Is it the burden of high taxes on people and businesses? Is it the heavy drain imposed on the economy by government regulating business in more and more ways in order to provide cleaner, safer working conditions, bigger unemployment benefits, and more generous pensions and medical care?

Can we find ways to reverse the slowdown in our nation's growth? Will it require more government involvement with the market—or less?

GROWTH AND POLLUTION

Do we *want* another century of rapid growth and industrialization? Without the automobile, the airplane, and electricity, ours would be a different and less comfortable world. But because of them air pollution has become a major problem. Without steel and cement and factories and tractors, the industrial development of the past century would have been impossible; with them, the volume of wastes discharged into water and air has grown to alarming proportions. Insecticides have increased agricultural production manyfold and virtually eliminated malaria and cholera, but they have all but extinguished the peregrine falcon, endangered other species, including *Homo sapiens,* in ways not yet fully known, and biologically destroyed many lakes and streams. Is large-scale pollution the inevitable companion of economic growth? If it is, how much growth do we really want? If it is not, how can we ensure growth with less pollution?

These questions concern the use, and abuse, of society's resources. They are among the basic economic questions, and they involve understanding why markets sometimes fail to work satisfactorily and how to deal with such failures. They also involve understanding why government intervention sometimes works and sometimes fails.

POVERTY AND WEALTH

A third of the world's population suffers from malnutrition. According to the Economic Council of Canada, about one Canadian in five lives in poverty. Poverty is a major problem in Canada despite the fact that the average Canadian is richer than ever before and the material standard of living in this country is close to the highest yet experienced anywhere. How can this be? Who are the poor, and what makes them so? Will poverty take care of itself as we continue to grow richer? Can poverty ever be eliminated in Canada? In the world? Why does the average standard of living rise rapidly in some countries, slowly in others, and not at all in still others? Is equality of income a desirable or attainable national goal?

These questions involve two basic economic issues: what determines the level of income and what determines the distribution of that income.

Medical science has greatly improved what can be done for victims of accident or disease. But costs have risen to the point where a major operation or illness is far beyond the capacity of an average family to afford out of its earnings or savings. In Canada and many other advanced economies the majority of these costs are paid by the government. The United States is currently debating whether it too should consider similar legislation. Should the government provide medical and hospital care to all who need it, as a matter of giving every man, woman, and child an equal right to life and health?

THE ROLE OF GOVERNMENT

What things should the government do, and what things should it leave to private decision makers? Do we, as John Kenneth Galbraith charges, allocate too little to government expenditure on such valuable things as health and education, while growing sated with privately produced goods such as big cars and electric can openers? Do we instead, as Milton Friedman charges, have the government do badly many things private groups could do well? Or do we do both?

Is there an economic limit to government spending or to the national debt? What is the debt, and how does it arise? Why do economists insist that if one Canadian gets more dollar bills he or she will be richer, but if all Canadians simultaneously get more dollar bills they will not in aggregate be richer?

Government involvement in the economy affects the working of what is already a complex economic system. How the economy operates and how differently it would operate with different institutions are current and compelling concerns of economists.

What Is Economics?

We have listed a few issues that are important today and on which economic analysis is supposed to shed light. One way to define the scope of economics is to say that it is the social science that deals with such problems. Fifty years ago such all-embracing definitions were popular. Perhaps the best known was Alfred Marshall's: "Economics is a study of mankind in the ordinary business of life." Because economic problems have certain common features, one may, by looking at them, arrive at a more penetrating definition.

The problems of economics arise out of the use of scarce resources to satisfy unlimited human wants. Scarcity is inevitable and is central to economic problems.

What are society's resources? Why is scarcity inevitable? What are the consequences of scarcity?

RESOURCES AND COMMODITIES

A society's resources consist of the free gifts of nature, such as land, forests, and minerals; human resources, both mental and physical; and all sorts of man-made aids to further production, such as tools, machinery, and buildings. Economists call such resources **factors of production**[1] because they are used to *produce* those things that people desire. The things produced are called **commodities.** Commodities may be divided

---

[1] The definitions of the terms in **boldface** type are gathered together in the glossary at the end of the book.

into goods and services. **Goods** are tangible (e.g., cars or shoes), and **services** are intangible (e.g., haircuts or education). Notice the implication of positive value contained in the terms "goods" and "services." (Compare the terms "bads" and "disservices.")

Goods and services are the means by which people seek to satisfy some of their wants. The act of making goods and services is called **production,** and the act of using them to satisfy wants is called **consumption.** For most people in most societies goods are not regarded as desirable in themselves; few people want to pile them up endlessly in warehouses, never to be consumed. They are valued because people want the services they provide. An automobile, for example, helps to satisfy its owner's desires for transportation, mobility, and possibly status.

SCARCITY

For all practical purposes, human wants may be regarded as limitless. An occasional individual may "have everything," but human capacity to generate new wants as fast as old ones are satisfied is well known to psychologists. For the overwhelming preponderance of the world's 4 billion human beings, *scarcity* is real and ever present. In relation to the desires of individuals (for more and better food, clothing, housing, schooling, vacations, entertainment, etc.), the existing supply of resources is woefully inadequate; there are enough to produce only a small fraction of the goods and services that people desire.

Is not Canada rich enough that scarcity is nearly banished? After all, we have been characterized as an affluent society. Whatever affluence may mean, it does not end the problem of scarcity. Most households that earn $50,000 a year (a princely amount by worldwide standards) have no trouble spending it on things that seem useful to them. Yet it would take many times the present output of the Canadian economy to produce enough to allow all Canadian households to consume that amount.

CHOICE

Because resources are scarce, all societies face the problem of deciding what to produce and how to divide it among their members. Societies differ in who makes the choices and how they are made, but the need to choose is common to all.

Just as scarcity implies the need for choice, so choice implies the existence of cost.

Opportunity Cost

A decision to have more of one thing requires a decision to have less of something else. It is this fact that makes the first decision costly. We offer first a trivial example and then one that vitally affects all of us; both examples involve precisely the same fundamental principles.

Consider the choice that must be made by a small boy who has 10¢ to spend and who is determined to spend it all on candy. For him there are only two kinds of candy in the world: gumdrops, which sell for 1¢ each, and chocolates, which sell for 2¢. The boy would like to buy 10 gumdrops and 10 chocolates, but he knows (or will soon discover) that this is not possible. (In technical language, it is not an *attainable combination* given his scarce resources.) There are, however, several attainable combinations that he might buy: 8 gumdrops and 1 chocolate, 4 gumdrops and 3 chocolates, 2 gumdrops and 1 chocolate, and so on. Some of these combinations leave him with money unspent, and he is not interested in them. Only six combinations (as shown in Figure 1-1) are both attainable and use all his money.

After careful thought, the boy has almost decided to buy 6 gumdrops and 2 chocolates, but at the last moment he decides that he simply must have 3 chocolates. What will it cost him to get this extra chocolate? One answer to this question is 2 gumdrops. In order to get the extra chocolate he must sacrifice 2 gumdrops, as is seen in Figure 1-1. Economists say that the opportunity cost of the third chocolate is what he must sacrifice in order to get it, which in this case is 2 gumdrops.

FIGURE 1–1

A Choice Between Gumdrops and Chocolates

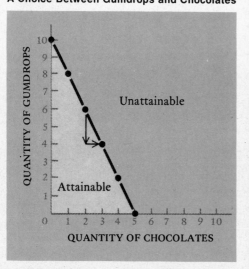

A limited amount of money forces a choice among alternatives. Six combinations of gumdrops and chocolates are attainable and use all of the boy's money. The downward-sloping line provides a boundary between attainable and unattainable combinations. The arrows show that the opportunity cost of 1 more chocolate is 2 gumdrops. In this example, the opportunity cost is constant and therefore the boundary is a straight line.

Another answer is that the cost of the third chocolate is 2¢, but given the boy's budget and his intentions, this answer is less revealing than the first one. Where the real choice is between more of this and more of that, the cost of "this" is fruitfully looked at as what you must sacrifice of "that." The idea of **opportunity cost** is one of the central insights of economics.

Every time one is forced by scarcity to make a choice, one is incurring opportunity costs. These costs are measured in terms of forgone alternatives.

Production Possibilities

Although the previous example concerned a minor consumption decision, the essential nature of the decision is the same whatever the choice being considered.

Exactly the same problems arise, for example, in the important social choice between military and nonmilitary goods—between swords and plowshares. In recent years about 2 percent of the Canadian gross national product was spent for national defence. The government of Canada made a choice as to the relative amounts of the production of goods for civilian consumption and the production of armaments. Such a choice is similar in form to the one facing the boy deciding what candies to buy with his dime. It is not possible to produce an unlimited quantity of both military and civilian goods. If we have full employment of resources and we wish to produce more arms, then we must produce less of all other goods, thereby reducing the quantity of goods available to satisfy civilian wants. The opportunity cost of more military goods is forgone civilian goods, and somehow a choice must be made.

The choice is illustrated in Figure 1-2. Because resources are limited, some combinations—those that would require more than the total available supply of resources for their production—cannot be obtained. The downward-sloping curve on the graph divides the combinations that can be obtained from those that cannot be obtained. Points to the right of this curve cannot be obtained because there are not enough resources; points to the left of the curve can be obtained without using all of the available resources; and points on the curve can just be obtained if all the available resources are used. The curve is called the **production possibility boundary.** It slopes downward because, when all resources are being used, to get more of one kind of goods, some of the other kind must be sacrificed.

A downward-sloping production possibility boundary illustrates three concepts: scarcity, choice, and opportunity cost.[2] Scarcity is implied

[2] The importance of scarcity, choice, and opportunity cost has led many to define economics as the problem of allocating scarce resources between alternative and competing ends. The issues emphasized by this definition are very important, but, as will be seen in the next section, there are other, equally important issues in economics that the definition does not stress.

by the unattainable combinations above the boundary; choice, by the need to choose among the attainable points; opportunity cost, by the downward slope of the boundary.

The production possibility boundary in Figure 1-2 is drawn *concave* downward, which means that more and more civilian goods must be given up to achieve equal successive increases in military goods. This shape implies that the opportunity cost grows larger and larger as we increase

the amount of arms produced. (Drawn as a straight line, as in Figure 1-1, the curve implies that the opportunity cost of each good stays constant, no matter how much of it is produced.) As we shall see, there are reasons to believe that the rising opportunity cost case applies to many important choices.

A CLASSIFICATION OF ECONOMIC PROBLEMS

Modern economies involve thousands of complex production and consumption activities. While the complexity is important, many basic decisions that must be made are not very different from those made in a primitive economy in which people work with few tools and barter with their neighbors. Nor do capitalist, socialist, and communist economies differ in their need to solve the same basic problems, though they do differ, of course, in how they solve the problems. Most problems studied by economists fall within six areas.

1. What Goods and Services Are Being Produced and in What Quantities?

This question concerns the allocation of scarce resources among alternative uses, called **resource allocation.** Any economy must have some mechanism for making decisions on the problem of resource allocation.

How are choices made between points such as *a* and *b* in Figure 1-2? In free-market economies, most decisions about the allocation of resources are made through the price system. In other systems, more of the decisions are made by central planners. Economists are interested in the consequences of different kinds of decision making on resource allocation.

2. By What Methods Are Goods and Services Produced?

Generally, there is more than one technically possible way in which a commodity can be made. Agricultural commodities, for example, can be

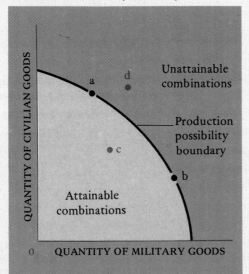

FIGURE 1–2
A Production Possibility Boundary

QUANTITY OF CIVILIAN GOODS

Unattainable combinations

a   d

Production possibility boundary

c

b

Attainable combinations

0   QUANTITY OF MILITARY GOODS

The downward-sloping boundary shows the combinations that are just attainable when all of the society's resources are efficiently employed. The quantity of military goods produced is measured along the horizontal axis, the quantity of civilian goods along the vertical axis. Thus any point on the diagram indicates some amount of each kind of good produced. The production possibility boundary separates the attainable combinations of goods such as *a, b,* and *c* and unattainable combinations such as *d.* It slopes downward because resources are scarce: more of one good can be produced only if resources are freed by producing less of the other good. Points *a* and *b* represent efficient combinations that use all of society's resources. Point *c* represents either inefficient use of resources or failure to use all the available resources.

produced by taking a small quantity of land and applying to it large quantities of fertilizer, labor, and machinery or by using a large quantity of land and applying only small quantities of fertilizer, labor, and machinery. Either method can be used to produce the same quantity of some crop.

Which alternative method should be adopted? A common criterion is the avoidance of inefficient methods. Any scheme of production that uses all of society's resources but produces inefficiently leads to an output combination that falls *inside* the production possibility boundary (at a point such as *c* in Figure 1-2). It would be possible to get more of either (or both) goods by using more efficient methods of production. Because resources are scarce, efficient methods of production are desirable. Economists are interested in distinguishing between efficient and inefficient methods, in determining how the choice of efficient methods can be assured, and in learning why inefficient methods are sometimes chosen.

3. What Quantities of Goods and Services Are Being Consumed and by Whom?

The production possibility boundary indicates the alternative combinations of goods that an economy can produce, but the combination of goods that it consumes need not be the same. *International trade* allows the bundle of goods consumed to differ from the bundle of goods produced. More of one good can be consumed than is produced, the difference being made up by imports of the good from foreign countries. Similarly, if more is produced than is consumed, the excess can be exported. Thus, while point *d* in Figure 1-2 is not an attainable combination of goods in terms of domestic production, it might be attainable as a consumption point. For example, point *d* would represent a consumption point if production were at point *b* and the economy were to export military goods (thereby reducing the level of domestic utilization of military goods below the level of domestic production) and import civilian goods (thereby raising the level of domestic consumption of civilian goods above the level of domestic production).

The production of goods and services generates income whether the goods are consumed domestically or sold abroad. Economists are interested in what determines how a nation's total income is distributed among such groups as landowners, laborers, and capitalists or among other groups such as farmers, union members, and the poor. They are interested also in the consequences of government intervention designed to change the distribution of income by using devices such as progressive income taxes, minimum wage laws, and programs of social insurance.

These first three questions fall within **microeconomics,** which concerns the allocation of resources and the distribution of income as they are affected by the workings of the price system and by some government policies.

4. Are the Country's Resources Being Fully Utilized, or Are Some Lying Idle and Thus Going to Waste?

It may seem strange that this question needs to be asked at all. Surely, if resources are so scarce that there are not enough of them to produce all urgently required goods, then available resources will not be left idle. Yet one of the most disturbing characteristics of free-market economies is that such waste sometimes occurs. Unemployed workers would like to have jobs, the factories in which they could work are available, the managers and owners would like to be able to operate their factories, raw materials are available in abundance, and the goods that could be produced by these resources are needed by individuals in the community. But for some reason nothing happens.

Massive unemployment occurred in the Great Depression of the 1930s. Although that disastrous experience—20 percent unemployment—has not been repeated, the problem is still with us in significant though lesser degree. In 1978, for example, unemployment reached 8.5 percent. Unemployment forces the economy *inside* its production possibility boundary, at a point such as *c* in Figure 1-2.

Unemployment of resources is thus similar to an inefficient use of them (discussed above under question 2) in that both lead to production inside the full-employment production possibility boundary. They are not the same problem, however, and the remedies are very different.

5. Is the Purchasing Power of Money and Savings Constant, or Is It Being Eroded Because of Inflation?

The world's economies have often experienced periods of prolonged and rapid changes in price levels. Over the long swing of history, price levels have sometimes risen and sometimes fallen. In recent decades, however, the course of prices has almost always been upward. The seventies saw a period of accelerating inflation in Canada and in most of the world.

Inflation reduces the purchasing power of money and savings. It is closely related to the amount of money in the economy. Money is the invention of human beings, not of nature, and the amount in existence can be controlled by them. Economists ask many questions about the causes and consequences of changes in the quantity of money and the effects of such changes on the price level. They also ask about other causes of inflation.

6. Is the Economy's Capacity to Produce Goods Growing or Remaining the Same over Time?

Productive capacity grows rapidly in some countries and slowly in others, and in some countries it actually declines. Generally the most rapid growth in productive capacity has occurred in those countries that already have relatively high standards of living. As a result, living standards diverge more and more between the "have" and the "have not" countries. Growth in productive

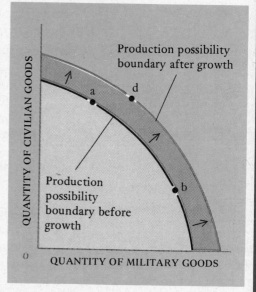

FIGURE 1–3

The Effect of Economic Growth on the Production Possibility Boundary

Economic growth shifts the boundary outward and makes it possible to have more of all commodities. Before growth in productive capacity, points *a* and *b* were on the production possibility boundary and point *d* was an unattainable combination. After growth, point *d* and many other previously unattainable combinations are attainable, as shown by the dark shaded band.

capacity can be represented in a production possibility diagram as a pushing outward of the boundary, as shown in Figure 1-3. If the economy's capacity to produce goods and services is growing, combinations that are unattainable today will become attainable tomorrow. Clearly, in an economy in which not nearly enough can be produced to satisfy all wants, growth will be important because growth makes it possible to have more of all goods. But growth is not free. What are the ways in which growth occurs and what are its costs?

Questions 4 to 6 fall within **macroeconomics,** the study of the determination of economic aggregates such as total output, total employment, the price level, and the rate of economic growth.

ECONOMICS: A WORKING DEFINITION

The six-way classification just discussed does not embrace all the things that interest economists. Additional topics such as the problems of international borrowing or comparative economic systems might be included in one or more of those categories, or they might be treated separately. Similarly, the theory of economic policy might be regarded as affecting all of the problem areas mentioned, or it might be treated separately.

Our purpose in listing these problem areas is to outline the scope of economics more fully than can be done with short definitions. Economics today is regarded much more broadly that it was even half a century ago. Earlier definitions stressed the alternative and competing uses of resources. Such definitions focused on choices between alternative points on a stationary production possibility boundary. Important additional economic problems concern failure to achieve the boundary (problems of inefficiency or underemployment of resources) and the outward movement of the boundary over time (problems of growth and development).

Economics, broadly defined, concerns:

1. **The ways in which a society uses its resources and distributes the fruits of production to individuals and groups in the society.**
2. **The ways in which production and distribution change over time.**
3. **The efficiencies of economic systems.**

Economic Analysis and Economic Policy

Economics helps in understanding and predicting some aspects of human behavior. People, by nature curious about their environment, want to predict this behavior in order that they may control their environment and adapt it to their needs.

THE PERVASIVENESS OF POLICY DECISIONS

Governments derive their authority to form and carry out policy from their police power—indeed, the words "policy" and "police" come from the Greek word for state, *politeia*.

Some governments lean toward a policy of laissez faire, or noninterference; others toward a policy of attempting strict control over every facet of the economy.

All governments have economic policies. Even the decision not to act but to let nature take its course is a policy decision.

Whether to rely on marketplace decision making or to replace it is as much a policy decision as is a government's decision to tax cigarettes.

Every year thousands of economic policy decisions are made by municipal, provincial, and federal governments. Most of them are never seriously debated. Nor is every facet of existing policy debated anew each year; indeed, many policy decisions now in force (such as giving unions the right to organize) were made decades ago. Only a few policy issues attract attention and become the subject of earnest and heated argument in a particular year.

THE ROLES OF THE ECONOMIST IN ECONOMIC POLICY

Any policy action has two aspects: the goals (or ends) that the decision makers are attempting to achieve and the means by which the desired ends are to be achieved. The governments in Canada simultaneously pursue many broad policy goals such as efficient use of resources, growth, justice, national security, and economic stability. Economists do not establish goals, but they are often involved in helping to resolve conflicts among competing goals, in forging the links between goals and the means available to achieve them, and in evaluating policy proposals.

Defining Conflicts of Policy

Governments have many goals. A particular policy that serves one goal may hinder another and have no effect on yet a third. Unemployment compensation, for example, may promote justice by protecting unemployed families from debilitating hardships; at the same time it may hinder the quickness with which labor moves from labor-surplus to labor-scarce occupations, thereby decreasing efficient uses of resources. Moreover, it will have no effect one way or the other on air pollution.

Economics has a large role to play in defining goal conflicts by identifying the effects, indirect as well as direct, of a proposed policy. Raising the minimum wage may seem extremely desirable to people who believe that the lowest-paid workers are not getting enough income to live at a decent standard of living. But if that policy results in some workers being laid off and becoming unemployed, the benefits to those who get higher wages must be balanced by the costs of the extra unemployment.

Proposing Policies

It is frequently the role of the economist to suggest policies. Given a statement of objectives, economic analysis can be used to invent or publicize proposed policies that will achieve the objectives. Economists in and out of government have had a major impact on policy. The Council of Economic Advisers has played a particularly active role in policy decisions in the United States. In this country the Economic Council of Canada has contributed to policy formation through its Annual Reviews, published each year since 1964. Among academic economists who have influenced policy in Canada, the most outstanding figure has been the late W. A. Mackintosh, whose influence spanned a period of fifty years. A frequent vehicle for extragovernmental

influence on policy is the Royal Commission. The report of the Carter Commission, a recent notable example, is well known within and outside Canada as a classic statement of the equity aspects of taxation.

Forming and Evaluating Policies

Economists must frequently determine whether a particular policy proposal—which may or may not have originated with them—is the best way to meet a particular problem. While each issue has its own special characteristics, there are also common concerns. Five main questions need to be asked in every case: (1) What are the policy goals? (2) Do the proposed means achieve those goals? (3) What costs are directly imposed? (4) Do the proposed means have adverse side effects? (5) Are there better alternative means?

Consider an example. A team of economists is asked to evaluate a proposal that the federal government institute rationing of gasoline by issuing coupons to every registered automobile owner. Each dated coupon permits the holder to purchase a specific number of gallons of gasoline during a specific week. How might the economists go about evaluating this proposal?

The economists would start by asking what goals gasoline rationing is meant to achieve. They might find that its purpose is, first, to limit total purchases of gasoline to a specific number of gallons per week and, second, to do so in a way that shares the reduction in gasoline supply equitably among all drivers.

Given these goals, the economists would next ask how well the proposal meets them. If the authorities can effectively enforce the rule that gasoline not be sold without coupons, the quantity of coupons will assure that no more than that number of gallons will be sold. This amount will be an upper limit, not the actual quantity, because it takes *both* money and coupons to get gasoline. Some users will not want to buy their full allotment of gasoline; others will want to buy more than they are allowed.

The number of coupons issued that will actu-

Disagreement among Economists*

If you listen to a discussion among economists on "As It Happens" or "Sunday Morning" or if you read about their debates in the daily press or weekly magazines, you will find economists constantly disagreeing among themselves. Indeed, it used to be said in the United Kingdom that, if you asked 10 economists for their opinion on any matter, you would get 11 answers — 1 from each of any 9 economists and 2 from Keynes.† Indeed, one very widespread reason for rejecting economists' advice is that they never completely agree on any issue. Why do economists constantly disagree, and what should we make of this fact?

One reason for disagreement may be the public's demand for disagreement. Let us assume that all economists were in fact agreed on some proposition, for example, that unions are not a major cause of inflation. This view would be unpalatable to some. Those who are hostile to unions, for instance, would like to blame inflation on them and would be looking for an intellectual champion. Fame and fortune would await the economist who espoused this cause, and a champion would soon be found.

This phenomenon has been called "Yas's Law": demand for dissent creates its own supply of dissent.‡ The operation of the law was evident in the United States, for example, in 1962–1964, when the U.S. Congress was debating a tax cut proposed by the President. The vast majority of U.S. economists supported the tax cut as being a necessary stimulus to sagging economic activity at the time. A relatively little-known economist named Charles Killingsworth was, however, catapulted to nationwide fame as one of the few economists who would argue on public platforms against the cut.§

Yas's Law precludes unanimity among economists on any issue over which the public or policymakers are split. This forces anyone wanting to know the weight of professional opinion to form a judgment on the proportion of the profession who support some proposition. In the case of the U.S. tax cut, there was an overwhelming and obvious majority; when there is more dissent, however, an assessment of the balance of professional opinion can be difficult because there are neither relevant opinion polls nor other objective ways of testing it.

This discussion brings up a second reason for apparent professional disagreement, media

---

*Box adapted from R. G. Lipsey, "Economists, Policy Makers and Economic Policy," in *Economic Policy Advising in Canada, Essays in Honour of John Deutsch*, D. Smith (ed.), C. D. Howe Institute, Montreal, 1981.
†J. M. Keynes was Britain's most famous economist. As the founder of macroeconomic theory his influence persists to this day. We will hear much more about him in the second half of this book.

‡ Yas is Say spelt backward after J. B. Say, a nineteenth-century French economist who said that there could never be too much production in the economy because supply creates its own demand.
§ Killingsworth was, of course, sincere, but if sincere dissentors had been unavailable, the potential for fame and fortune would have brought an opportunistic dissentor to the fore.

---

ally be used may be hard to predict. It will certainly be less than the total number issued if there is no legal way to transfer surplus coupons from those who would not use them to those who want extra coupons. While the coupons are not transferable, there may nevertheless be an illegal trade in the coupons unless the government takes severe measures to prevent it.

The economists may well conclude that the proposal can achieve its first objective, to control the quantity of gasoline actually sold. Examining the second objective, however, they may find that issuing coupons to *owners* does not achieve equal treatment of *drivers*. Some persons own

coverage. Anyone interested in professional opinion needs to assess the weight of the opinion on either side of any issue. When the media cover an issue, they naturally wish to give both sides of it. Normally, the public will hear one or two economists for each side of a debate, regardless of whether the profession is divided right down the middle or is nearly, but not quite, united. For example, the public will not know that in one case a reporter could have chosen from dozens of economists to present each side while in a second case the reporter had to spend three days trying to locate someone willing to take one side because nearly all economists contacted were willing to take the other. There are issues over which as much as 80 to 90 percent of the profession are on one side. However, the media, in their desire to show both sides of the case, present the public with the appearance of a profession equally split over all matters. It is indeed unfortunate that some method of weighing professional opinion cannot be devised.

A third reason for disagreement is that economists are not equally well informed on any given policy problem. The explosion of knowledge during recent decades has forced a high degree of specialization onto those economists who wish to stay near the frontiers of their subject. Thus, for example, one economist, when asked about Canada's inflation rate or its currency's exchange rate, could give an answer that was at least based on a knowl-edge of the relevant facts, theories, and controversies. When asked about energy policy, however, he might have to base his answer on somewhat general considerations. The scope of current knowledge is such that every economist, no matter what his expertise, will be ignorant of basic facts and theoretical controversies of some aspects of the discipline.

The diversity of opinion on a particular subject is often greater among the entire body of economists than among those economists who are specialists in the subject. This is particularly so because a consensus reached by specialist researchers often takes some years to filter through to nonspecialists. Nevertheless, a reporter thinks nothing of phoning a local undergraduate economics lecturer for a view on some technical issue with regard to energy policy; and if a second reporter reaches an expert on, say, inflation, that economist may give a view on the energy policy issue with the apparent firmness and authority of a genuine expert.

Thus anyone seeking to discredit economists' advice by showing that they disagree over every issue will have no trouble supporting his or her case. But those who wish to know if there is a majority view or even a strong consensus will find one on a surprising number of issues. Of course, there are also genuine disagreements among economists on many issues—especially concerning recent and incompletely understood events, and controversies at the frontiers of current research.

two or more cars; others own no car and depend on borrowed or rented cars. Moreover, some persons must drive long distances to and from work, while others need not. The rationing plan tends to impose equal mileage, not equal sacrifice of mileage, on coupon receivers. Thus it imposes a greater sacrifice on people who need to drive above average distances and a lesser sacrifice on people who drive below average distances. The same allotment of gallons per week may seem generous to a retired couple living in Prince Edward Island and ridiculously small to a ranching couple in British Columbia.

On the basis of this much analysis, the economists are likely to report that the plan does not meet its second objective. They will urge rejection or modification of the proposal. They will also point out that a revised allocation plan, based on demonstrated needs plus a small free-driving allowance, would correct the deficiency. Yet there are many other difficulties. Let us suppose that a number of modifications in the plan have been made and that the economists have concluded it will fulfill its basic purposes.

The economists will now ask how costly the plan would be to put into effect and enforce. They would estimate the direct costs of printing and distributing the coupons, of developing and running an allocation system, of establishing a means to hear the inevitable appeals from outraged citizens, of policing the use of coupons, and of enforcing the nontransferability of coupons. The total estimated costs would be reported to the policymakers. If the costs seemed too large relative to the benefits, the entire plan might be dropped right there. But suppose the costs, although large, seem to be small enough to be offset by the benefits of the gasoline rationing scheme.

Next the economists might search for ways in which this policy serves or conflicts with other goals. Does it serve the public interest by encouraging production of more efficient cars? Does it work against the public interest by encouraging crime in the form of the counterfeiting or theft of ration coupons or the bribing of officials who allocate coupons? Does it fail to prevent some people from using gasoline frivolously while it forces others to curtail vital activities? There are a host of similar questions to be asked.

Ideally, the existence and importance of each side effect must be estimated. When a policy action helps to achieve one goal but hinders the attainment of others, it is necessary to establish trade-offs among them. Usually there will be some rate at which people will be willing to trade a loss in one direction for a gain in another. Let us suppose that if this were the end of the matter,

the economists and policymakers would conclude that, all things considered, the gasoline rationing plan is better than nothing and deserves further study.

The final step for the economists is to consider whether modifications of the plan, or alternatives to it, will achieve the goals equally well but at lower cost or less sacrifice in terms of setbacks to other policy objectives. They may well consider, for example, whether allowing the coupons to be sold will lead to fairer, more efficient gasoline usage, less crime, and smaller enforcement costs. Another proposal they may consider is to discourage gas consumption by a 50¢ per gallon gasoline tax, combined with a series of money grants to poorer people who must drive as part of their work.

This final step is very important. It compares a particular feasible proposal, not only against "do nothing," but against other feasible proposals.

At any stage of their investigation, the economists may conclude that gasoline rationing is not a very effective means of achieving the policymakers' objectives. (In fact many economists have reached that conclusion.) But suppose that the team of economists concludes that gasoline rationing *does* achieve the desired goals, that the direct costs and undesirable effects in other directions are judged (by the policymakers) to be less important than the desirable effects in achieving the stated policy goals, and that there are no other practicable measures that would better achieve the goals? The team will then conclude that there is a strong case in favor of the proposal.

Do the views—and prejudices—of the investigators have a great deal to do with the outcome of their investigation? A particular group of economists may have strong views on the specific measure it is attempting to assess. If the economists do not like the measure, they are likely to be relentless in identifying costs and searching out possible unwanted effects and somewhat less than thorough in discovering effects that help to achieve the desired goals. It is important though difficult to guard against an unconscious bias of this sort. Fortunately there are likely to be others with different biases. One advantage of publishing evaluations and submitting them to review and discussion is that it provides opportunities for those with different biases to discover arguments and evidence originally overlooked.

ECONOMIC AND POLITICAL OBJECTIVES

Actual policymaking is more complicated than the previous discussion suggests, and a few of the many reasons policy issues get settled in a less systematic fashion deserve mention.

Decisions on interrelated issues of policy are made by many different bodies. Federal and provincial parliaments pass laws, the courts interpret laws, the governments decide which laws to enforce with vigor and which to soft-pedal, the Department of Finance and the Bank of Canada influence monetary factors, and a host of other agencies and semi-autonomous bodies determine actions in respect to different aspects of policy goals. Because of the multiplicity of decision makers, it would be truly amazing if fully consistent behavior resulted. The majority of Canadians believe that there are advantages to this separation of responsibilities, but one of its consequences is that inconsistent decisions will be made.

Furthermore, in a system such as ours, inconsistent decisions may result from political compromises between two or more interested groups, factions, or agencies. Compromises are frequently necessary to reconcile conflicting interests among the provinces or between the federal government and the provinces.

Another problem arises from the fact that legislators in a democracy have their own and their party's reelection as one of their important goals. This means, for example, that any measure that imposes large costs and few benefits obvious to the electorate over the next few years is unlikely to find favor, no matter how large the long-term benefits are. There is a strong bias toward myopia in an elective system. Although much of this bias stems from shortsightedness and selfishness, another part reflects genuine uncertainty about the future. The further into the future the economist calculates, the wider the margin of possible error. It is not surprising that politicians who must worry about the next election often tend to worry less about the long-term effects of their actions. "After all," they may argue, "who can tell what will happen twenty years hence?"

These problems of political decision making are what George Bernard Shaw had in mind when he said that the only strong argument in favor of democracy is that all of its alternatives are even worse.

Summary

1. Economic problems are among the important concerns of every generation. A common feature of such problems is that they concern the use of limited resources to satisfy virtually unlimited human wants.

2. Scarcity is a fundamental problem faced by all economies. Not enough resources are available to produce all the goods and services that people would like to consume. Scarcity makes it necessary to choose. All societies must have a mechanism for deciding what commodities will be produced and in what quantities.

3. The concept of opportunity cost emphasizes the problem of scarcity and choice by measuring the cost of obtaining a unit of one commodity in terms of the number of units of other commodities that could have been obtained instead.

4. Six basic questions faced by all economies are: What goods and services are being produced and in what quantities? By what methods are goods and services produced, and are those methods efficient? What quantities of goods and services are being consumed and by whom? Are the society's resources being fully utilized? What is happening to the purchasing power of money and savings? Is the economy's capacity to produce growing over time or remaining static?

5. Not all economies resolve these questions in the same ways or equally satisfactorily. Economists study how these questions are answered in various societies and the consequences of using one method rather than another to provide answers.

6. Governments, in varying degree, choose to intervene in the functioning of the economy. In so doing, they pursue economic policies.

7. It is necessary to distinguish between certain ends that are being sought and the means by which they will be achieved. Economics does not allow a "scientific" choice between alternative ends: It does not tell which of competing goals should be adopted. Economic analysis can help to determine whether a particular measure contributes to stated goals and at what cost.

8. One of the main reasons particular policies will always be subject to debate and disagreement is that most policies that are effective in bringing us closer to some goals take us further away from others. This leads to policy conflicts, and it is necessary to judge how much of one objective is to be sacrificed in order to get more of another.

Topics for Review

Scarcity and the need for choice
Choice and opportunity cost
Production possibility boundary
Resource allocation
Unemployed resources
Growth in productive capacity
Steps in evaluating economic policies
Conflicts of policies

Discussion Questions

1. What does each of the following quotations tell you about the policy conflicts perceived by the person making the statement and about how he or she has resolved them?

a. President Carter, January 1977: "We've got so many people out of work, and we've got so much unused industrial capacity, that I think if we carefully target employment opportunities around the country, we can decrease unemployment substantially before we start becoming equally concerned about inflation."

b. Russell Baker, commenting on the decision of Nantucket Island residents to approve a Holiday Inn to cater to oil drillers: "Economics compels us all to turn things into slums. Although it will be too bad, it will be absolutely justifiable. An economic necessity. Another step down the ladder to paradise."

c. Time magazine: "Considering our limited energy resources and the growing demand for electricity, the United States really has no choice but to use all of its possible domestic energy sources, including nuclear energy. Despite possible environmental and safety hazards, nuclear power is a necessity."

d. King Khalid of Saudi Arabia: "Increasing oil production in order to lower oil prices would be the most damaging thing that could happen to humanity. Experts say that if oil consumption continues to increase as it has, oil reserves will dry up by the end of this century."

2. "A careful study has shown that students living in apartments receive significantly lower grades than students living in dormitories. The administration has therefore decided to ban apartment living." What do you infer from these statements to be the administration's policy goals? How, apparently, is the administration interpreting the observed events? Could this interpretation of the facts be tested? Can the wisdom of the administration's goals be evaluated?

3. Consider the right to free speech in political campaigns. Suppose that the Flat Earth Society, the Communist party, and the Liberal party all demanded equal time on CBC television in a federal election. What economic questions are involved? Can you see a possible confusion between freedom of speech and free access to scarce resources?

4. What is the major opportunity cost of (a) enrolling in school, (b) taking this course, (c) studying enough to get an A, (d) attending a given lecture?

5. Canada entered World War II with substantial unemployment of resources and moved rapidly to full employment of available resources. Contrast the opportunity costs of fighting the war under these circumstances with the opportunity costs for an economy already at full employment.

6. Evidence accumulates that the use of chemical fertilizers, which increases agricultural production greatly, causes damage to water quality. Show the choice involved between more food and cleaner water in using such fertilizers. Use a production possibility curve with agricultural output on the vertical axis and water quality on the horizontal axis. In what ways does this production possibility curve reflect scarcity, choice, and opportunity cost? How would an improved fertilizer that increased agricultural output without further worsening water quality affect the curve? Suppose a pollution-free fertilizer were developed; would this mean there would no longer be any opportunity cost of using it?

7. What is the difference between scarcity and poverty? If everyone in the world had enough to eat, could we say that food was no longer scarce?

8. Explain why the government cannot avoid making policy decisions on wage and price controls, the size of tariffs, public support of separate schools, and the external value of the Canadian dollar. Was there a policy about wages before any minimum-wage laws were passed?

Economics as a Social Science

2

Economics is generally regarded as a social science. What exactly does it mean to be scientific? Can economics ever hope to be "scientific" in its study of those aspects of human behavior with which it is concerned? The first step in answering these questions is to be able to distinguish between positive and normative statements. The ability to make this distinction has been one of the reasons for the success of science in the last 300 years.

THE DISTINCTION BETWEEN POSITIVE AND NORMATIVE

Positive statements concern what is, was, or will be. **Normative statements** concern what ought to be.

Positive statements, assertions, or theories may be simple or complex, but they are basically about matters of fact.

Disagreements over positive statements are appropriately settled by an appeal to the facts.

Normative statements, because they concern what ought to be, are inextricably bound up with philosophical, cultural, and religious systems. A normative statement is one that makes, or is based on, a value judgment—a judgment about what is good and what is bad.

Disagreements over normative statements cannot be settled merely by an appeal to facts.

The Distinction Illustrated

The statement "It is impossible to break up atoms" is a positive statement that can quite definitely be (and of course has been) refuted by empirical observations, while the statement "Scientists ought not to break up atoms" is a normative statement that involves ethical judgments. The questions "What government policies will reduce unemployment?" and "What policies will prevent inflation?" are positive ones, while the question "Ought we to be more concerned about unemployment than about inflation?" is a normative one. The statement "A government deficit will reduce unemployment and cause an increase in prices" is a very simple hypothesis in positive economics, a hypothesis that can be tested by an appeal to empirical observation, while the statement "Because unemployment ought to matter more than inflation, a government deficit is sound policy" is a normative hypothesis that cannot be settled solely by an appeal to observation.

Having grasped this distinction, be careful not to turn it into an inquiry-stopping, dogmatic rule. From the fact that positive economics does not include normative questions (because its tools are inappropriate to them) it does *not* follow that the student of positive economics must stop her or his inquiry as soon as someone says the word "ought." Consider the statement "It is my value judgment that we *ought to have* rent control because controls are *good*." It is quite in order for a practitioner of positive economics to ask "Why?" It may then be argued that controls have certain consequences and it is these consequences that are judged to be good. But the statements about the consequences of rent control will be positive, testable statements.

Thus the pursuit of what appears to be a normative statement will often turn up positive hypotheses on which the *ought* conclusion depends. For example, there are probably relatively few people who believe that government control of industry is in itself good or bad. Their advocacy or opposition will be based on certain beliefs about relations that can be stated as positive rather than normative hypotheses. For example: "Government control reduces (increases) efficiency, changes (does not change) the distribution of income, leads (does not lead) to an increase of state control in other spheres."

A careful study of this emotive subject would reveal enough positive economic questions to keep a research team of economists occupied for many years.

The Importance of the Distinction

If we think something ought to be done, we can deduce other things that, if we wish to be consistent, ought to be done; but we can deduce nothing about what is done (i.e., is true). Similarly, if we know that two things are true, we can deduce other things that must be true, but we can deduce nothing about what is desirable (i.e., *ought* to be).

The distinction between positive and normative statements is critical because it is logically impossible to deduce normative statements from positive statements and vice versa.

First, consider an example involving both normative and positive statements. Suppose I believe that (1) as a moral principle I ought to be charitable to all human beings. Then if I am told that (2) the inhabitants of China are not Christians but are human beings, it follows that (3) therefore I ought to be charitable toward Chinese. From (1) and (2) a normative rule has been deduced about how I ought to behave in a particular case. However, no positive statement about how I *do* behave can be deduced from (1) and (2).

Now suppose someone else comes along and says, "You ought not to be charitable toward the Chinese because my moral principles dictate that you should be charitable only toward Christians." If an argument arises about whether to be charitable toward the Chinese, this argument will turn on value judgments about how we ought to behave. These are questions on which reasonable people sometimes have to agree to disagree. If both sides insist on holding to their views on charity, even if both are perfectly reasonable, there is no civilized way of forcing either to admit error.

Second, consider an example involving only positive statements. Assume I say that (1) capital punishment is a strong disincentive to murder and that (2) the Chinese abolished capital punishment after the Revolution, so that (3) therefore the number of murders must have risen in China since the Revolution. The two factual statements, (1) and (2), and the deduction that follows from them are all positive statements. Nothing can be deduced about the moral desirability of abolishing capital punishment from statements (1) and (2), even if they are factually correct.

Now suppose you say, "The number of murders has not risen in China since the Revolution; in fact, the number has fallen." If you hold to this view, you must deny one or the other of the first two positive statements. You could deny statement (1) by saying, for example, that capital punishment is actually an incentive to commit murder. You could deny statement (2) by saying, for example, that, although the Chinese pretended to abolish capital punishment as a propaganda move, they in fact retained it after the Revolution. In both cases the disagreement is over factual statements. If enough facts were gathered, and if both parties were reasonable, one party could be forced to admit being wrong.

The distinction between positive and normative allows us to keep our views on how we would like the world to work separate from our views on how the world actually does work. We may be interested in both. It can only obscure the truth, however, if we let our views on what we would like to be bias our investigations of what actually is. It is for this reason that the separation of the positive from the normative is one of the foundation stones of science and that scientific inquiry, as it is normally understood, is usually confined to positive questions.

Positive and Normative Statements in Economics

Economics, like other sciences, is concerned with questions, statements, and hypotheses that could conceivably be shown to be wrong (that is, false) by actual observations of the world. It is not necessary to show them to be either consistent or inconsistent with the facts tomorrow or the next day; it is only necessary to be able to imagine evidence that could show them to be wrong. *Thus an appeal to the facts is an appropriate way in which to deal with them.* Other questions, including normative ones, cannot be settled by a mere appeal to empirical observation. This does not, of course, mean that they are unimportant. Such questions as "Should we subsidize higher education?" and "Should we send food to Iran?" must be decided by means other than a simple appeal to facts. In democratic practice, such questions are usually settled by voting on them.

THE SCIENTIFIC APPROACH

Very roughly, the scientific approach, or the scientific method as it is sometimes called, consists of relating questions to evidence. When presented with a controversial issue, scientists will ask what the evidence is both for and against it. They may then take a stand on the issue, with more or less conviction depending on the weight of the evidence. If there is little or no evidence, scientists will say that at present it is impossible to take a stand. They will then set about searching for relevant evidence. If they find that the issue is framed in terms that make it impossible to gather evidence for or against it, they will then usually try to recast the question so that it can be answered by an appeal to the evidence. This approach to a problem is what sets scientific inquiries off from other inquiries.

In some fields, the scientist, having reframed the question, is able to generate observations that will provide evidence for or against the hypothesis. Experimental sciences such as chemistry and some branches of psychology have an advantage because it is possible for them to produce relevant evidence through controlled laboratory experiments. Other sciences such as astronomy and economics cannot do this. They must wait for natural events to produce observations that may be used as evidence in testing their theories, or they must rely on nonlaboratory experiments that are not fully controlled. An example of the latter is the space probe programs of recent years, which have added greatly to astronomers' knowledge about the universe.

The ease or difficulty with which one can collect evidence does not determine whether a subject is scientific or nonscientific.

How scientific inquiry proceeds and the ease with which it can be pursued do, however, differ substantially between fields in which laboratory experiment is possible and those in which it is not. Some of these differences will be discussed in Chapter 3. Until then we shall consider general problems more or less common to all sciences.

IS HUMAN BEHAVIOR PREDICTABLE?

Natural versus social sciences. Is it possible to conduct a scientific study in the field of human behavior? When considering whether it is possible to make a scientific study of such subjects as the causes of unemployment and the consequences of a large national debt, it is sometimes argued that natural sciences deal with inanimate matter that is subject to natural "laws" while the social sciences deal with human beings who have free will and therefore cannot be made the subject of natural laws.

This view implies that inanimate matter will show stable responses to certain stimuli, but animate matter will not. For example, if you put a match to a dry piece of paper, the paper will burn, whereas if you subject human beings to torture, some will break down and do what you want them to do and others will not. Even more confusing, the same individual may react differently to torture at different times.

Does human behavior show sufficiently stable responses to factors influencing it to be predictable within an acceptable margin of error? This is a positive question that can be settled only by an appeal to evidence and not by *a priori* speculation. (*A priori* may be defined as the use of knowledge that is prior to actual experience.) The question itself might concern either the behavior of groups or that of isolated individuals.

Group versus individual behavior. It is a matter of simple observation that when a group of individuals is considered, they do not behave capriciously but instead display stable responses to various forces that act on them. The warmer the weather, for example, the more people visit the beach and the higher the sales of ice cream and Coca-Cola. It may be hard to say when or why one individual will buy an ice cream cone or a Coke, but a stable response pattern from a large group of individuals can be seen: the higher the temperature, the greater the sales of these two products at the beach.

There are many situations in which group behavior can be predicted accurately without certain knowledge of individual behavior. No social scientist can predict, for example, when an apparently healthy individual is going to die, but death rates for large groups are stable enough to make life insurance a profitable business. This would not be so if group behavior were capricious. Although social scientists cannot predict what particular individuals will be killed in auto accidents in the next holiday weekend, they can come very close to knowing the total number who will die. The more objectively measurable data they have (for example, the state of the weather on the days in question and the change in auto sales over the previous year), the more closely they will be able to predict total deaths.

The well-known fact that pollsters do a good job of predicting elections on the basis of sample surveys provides evidence that human attitudes do not change capriciously. If group behavior were truly capricious, there would be no point in trying to predict anything on the basis of sample surveys. The fact that 80 percent of the voters sampled said they intended to vote for a certain candidate would give no information about the probable outcome of the election. Today's information would commonly be reversed tomorrow.

The difference between predicting individual and group behavior is illustrated by the fact that economists can predict with fair accuracy what households as a group will do when their take-home pay is increased. Some individuals may do surprising and unpredictable things, but the total response of all households to a permanent change in tax rates that leaves more money in their hands is predictable within quite a narrow margin of error. This stability in the response of households' spending to a change in their available income is the basis of economists' ability to predict successfully the outcome of major revisions in the tax laws.

This does not mean that people never change their minds or that future events can be foretold by a casual study of the past. People sometimes think in terms of a simple dichotomy: Either there are historical laws apparent to the casual observer or there is random behavior. They observe a prophet predicting that some change will take place in the future merely because it took place in the past. Upon seeing the prophet make an utterly mistaken prophecy, they conclude that, because the prophet cannot prophesy, human behavior is random and thus unamenable to scientific study. The stability discussed here is a stable response to causal factors (e.g., next time it gets warm, ice cream sales will rise) and not merely inertia (e.g., ice cream sales will go on rising in the future because they have risen in the past).

The "Law" of Large Numbers

Successful predictions about the behavior of large groups are made possible by the statistical "law" of large numbers. Broadly speaking, this law asserts that random movements of many individual items tend to offset one another. This law is based on one of the most beautiful constants of behavior in the whole of science, natural and social, and yet it can be derived from the fact that human beings make errors! The law is based on the *normal curve of error,* which is encountered in elementary statistics.

What is implied by this law? Ask any one person to measure the length of a room and it will be almost impossible to predict in advance what sort of error of measurement he or she will make. Dozens of things will affect the accuracy of the measurement and, furthermore, the person may make one error today and quite a different one tomorrow. But ask a thousand people to measure the length of the same room, and it can be predicted within a very small margin just how this *group* will make its errors. It can be asserted with confidence that more people will make small errors than will make large errors, that the larger the error, the fewer will be the number making it, that roughly the same number of people will overestimate as will underestimate the distance, and that the average error of all individuals will be zero.

If a common cause should act on each member of the group, it is possible to predict the average behavior of the group even though any one member may act in a surprising fashion. If, for example, each of the thousand individuals is given a tape measure that understates "actual" distances, it can be expected that, on the average, the group will underestimate the length of the room. It is, of course, quite possible that one member, who had in the past been consistently undermeasuring distance because of psychological depression, will now overestimate the distance because the state of his health has changed. But some other event may happen to another individual that will turn her from an overmeasurer into an undermeasurer. Individuals may act strangely for inexplicable reasons. But the group's behavior, when the inaccurate tape is substituted for the accurate one, will be predictable precisely because the odd things that one individual does will tend to cancel out the odd things some other individual does.

Irregularities in individual behavior tend to cancel one another out, and the regularities tend to show up in repeated observations.

THE NATURE OF SCIENTIFIC THEORIES

There is abundant evidence of stable response patterns in human behavior. Some regularity between two or more things is observed, and we ask why this should be so. A *theory* attempts to explain why. Once we have a theory it enables us to predict as yet unobserved events. For example, national income theory predicts that an increase in the government's budget deficit will reduce the amount of unemployment. The simple theory of market behavior predicts that, under specified conditions, the introduction of a sales tax will be accompanied by an increase in the price of the commodity concerned and that the price increase will be less than the amount of the tax. It also lets us predict that if there is a partial failure of the potato crop, the total receipts earned by potato farmers will rise!

Theories are used in explaining observed phenomena. A successful theory enables us to predict the consequences of various occurrences.

The Pervasiveness of Theories

Observations concern sequences of events. Any explanation whatsoever of how these events are linked together is a theoretical construction. Theories are what are used to impose order on observations, to explain how what is seen is linked together. Without theories there would be only a shapeless mass of meaningless observations.

The choice is not between theory and observation but between better or worse theories to explain observations.

In a particular case we might see an increase in interest rates followed by a reduction in borrowing by corporations. The practical person may think the link is obvious, and indeed in some sense it may be, but nonetheless it requires a theoretical construction. Before these two events can be linked together, it is necessary to have a theory of what the corporate managers are trying to do and how they try to do it, plus the assumption that the managers know what behavior will achieve their goals.

True in Theory but Not in Practice

Misunderstanding about the place of theories in scientific explanation gives rise to many misconceptions. One of these is illustrated by the phrase "True in theory but not in practice." The next time you hear someone say this (or, indeed, the next time you say it yourself) you should immediately reply, "All right then, tell me what does happen in practice." Usually you will not be told mere facts, but you will be given an alternative theory—a different explanation of the facts. The speaker should have said, "The theory in question provides a poor explanation of the facts" (that is, it is contradicted by some factual observations); "I have a different theory that does a much better job."

WHAT IS A THEORY AND HOW IS IT TESTED?

A theory consists of (1) a set of definitions that clearly define the *variables* to be used, (2) a set of *assumptions* that outline the conditions under which the theory is to apply, (3) one or more *hypotheses* about the relationships of variables, and (4) *predictions* that are deduced from the assumptions of the theory and can be tested against actual empirical observations.

Variables

Theories are concerned with how various things are related to each other. If we know how two things are related, then we know how one of them will change as the other changes. The things that we relate to each other are called variables. A **variable** is some magnitude that can take on different possible values. Variables are the basic elements of theories, and each one needs to be carefully defined.

Price is an example of an important economic variable. The price of a commodity is the amount of money that must be given up to purchase one unit of that commodity. To define a price we must first define the commodity to which it attaches. Such a commodity might be one dozen grade A large eggs. We could then inquire into the price of such eggs sold in, say, supermarkets

Kinds of Variables

Endogenous and Exogenous Variables

Endogenous variables are those that are explained within a theory. **Exogenous variables** are those that influence the endogenous variables but are themselves determined by considerations outside of the theory. Consider the theory that the price of apples in Vancouver on a particular day is a function of several things, one of which was the weather in the Okanogan Valley during the previous apple-growing season. We can safely assume that the state of the weather is not determined by economic conditions. The price of apples in this case is an endogenous variable—something determined within the framework of the theory. The state of the weather in the Okanogan is an exogenous variable; changes in it influence prices because they affect the supply of apples, but the weather is uninfluenced by these prices.

Other words are sometimes used for the same distinction. One frequently used pair is *induced,* for endogenous, and *autonomous,* for exogenous.

Stock and Flow Variables

A distinction between variables that is important in economics is that between stocks and flows. A flow variable has a time dimension; it is so much per unit of time. The quantity of grade A large eggs purchased in Halifax is a flow variable. No useful information is conveyed if we are told that purchases were 2,000 dozen eggs unless we are also told over what period of time these purchases occurred. Two thousand dozen per hour would indicate an active market in eggs, while 2,000 dozen per week would indicate a sluggish market. A stock variable has no time dimension; it is just so much. Thus, if the egg producers' marketing board has 2 million dozen eggs in warehouses around the country, the quantity is a stock. All those eggs are there at one time. The stock variable is just a number, not a rate of flow of so much *per day* or *per month*.

Economic theories use both stock variables and flow variables, and it takes a little practice to keep them straight. The amount of income earned is a flow; there is so much per year or per month or per hour. The amount of a household's expenditure is also a flow—so much spent per week or per month. The amount of money in a bank account or a miser's hoard (earned, perhaps, in the past, but unspent) is a stock—just so many thousands of dollars. What of the interest earned by the miser who puts money into a savings bank? It is a flow. The key test is always whether a time dimension is required to give the variable significant meaning.

in Moose Jaw, Saskatchewan. This would define the variable. The particular values taken on by the variable might be 98¢ on July 1, 1981, $1.02 on July 8, 1981, and 99¢ on July 15, 1981. A series of observations on the values of a variable at different points in time, such as these on egg prices, is called a **time series.**

There are many distinctions between kinds of variables; two of the most important are discussed in the box above.

Assumptions

Assumptions play a vital role in theorizing. Students are often greatly concerned about the justification of assumptions, particularly if they seem unrealistic. Suppose an economic theory starts out: "Assume that there is no government." Surely, says the reader, this assumption is totally unrealistic, and I cannot therefore take seriously anything that comes out of the theory.

But this assumption may merely be the economist's way of saying that, whatever the government does, even whether it exists, *is irrelevant for the purposes of this particular theory.*

Now, put this way, the statement becomes an empirical assertion. The only way to test it is to see if the predictions that follow from the theory do or do not fit the facts that the theory is trying to explain. If they do, then the theorist was correct in the assumption that the government could be ignored for the particular purposes at hand. In this case the criticism that the theory is unrealistic because there really is a government is completely beside the point.

Another important use of an apparently unrealistic assumption may be to outline the set of conditions under which a theory is meant to hold. Consider a theory that assumes the government has a balanced budget. This may mean that the theorist intends that theory to apply only when there is a balanced budget; it may *not* mean that the size of the government's budget surplus or deficit is irrelevant to the theory.[1]

Usually it is not appropriate to criticize the simplifying assumptions of a theory only on the grounds that they are unrealistic. All theory is an abstraction from reality. If it were not, it would merely duplicate the world and would add nothing to the understanding of it. A good theory abstracts in a useful and significant way; a poor theory does not. If we believe that the theorist has assumed away something important for the problem at hand, then we must believe, and try to show, that the conclusions of the theory are contradicted by the facts.

Hypotheses

Relations among variables. The critical step in theorizing is formulating hypotheses. A hypothesis is a statement about how two or more variables relate to each other. For example, it is a basic hypothesis of economics that the quantity produced of any commodity depends, among other things, on its price. Thus the two variables, the price of eggs and the quantity of eggs produced, are related to each other according to an economic hypothesis.

Functional relations. A **function,** or a functional relation, is a formal expression of a relation among variables.

The particular hypothesis that the quantity of eggs produced is related to the price of eggs is an example of a functional relation in economics. In its most general form, it merely says that quantity produced is related to price. More specifically, however, the hypothesis may be that as the price of eggs falls, the quantity produced will also fall. In other words, in this hypothesis price and quantity vary *directly* with each other. In the case of many hypotheses of this kind economists can be even more specific about the nature of the functional relation. On the basis of detailed factual studies, economists often have a pretty good idea of by *how much* quantity produced will change as a result of specified changes in price — that is, about magnitude as well as direction.[2]

Predictions

A scientific prediction is not the same thing as a prophecy.

A scientific prediction is a conditional statement that takes the form: *If* you do this, *then* such and such will follow.

If hydrogen and oxygen are mixed under specified conditions, *then* water will be the result. *If* the government has a large budget deficit, *then* the amount of employment will be increased. It is most important to realize that this prediction is very different from the statement: "I prophesy that in two years' time there will be a large increase in employment because I believe the

---

[1] As the text illustrates, an assumption may mean many different things. When you encounter an assumption in economic theory, ask yourself whether it is being used to convey the idea that (1) the world actually behaves as assumed, (2) the factor under consideration is irrelevant to the theory, (3) the theory only holds when the condition specified in the assumption actually holds, or (4) a convenient fiction is being introduced to simplify some quite complex piece of behavior.

[2] The appendixes for each chapter appear starting on page A-1. The appendix to this chapter (page A-2) gives a more detailed discussion of functional relations.

FIGURE 2–1
The Interaction of Deduction and Measurement in Theorizing

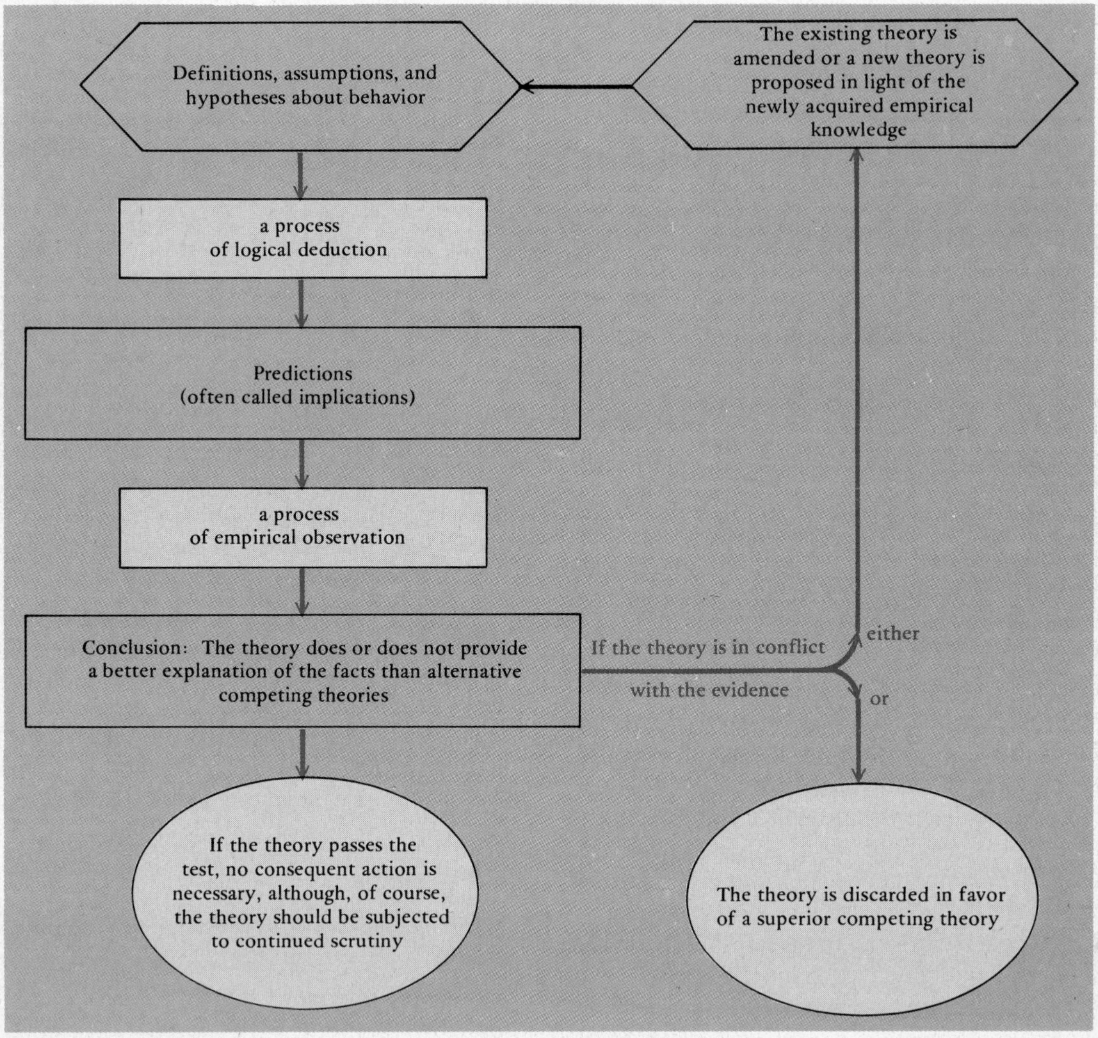

```
┌─────────────────────────┐                  ┌─────────────────────────┐
│ Definitions, assumptions,│◄─────────────────│  The existing theory is │
│ and hypotheses about     │                  │  amended or a new theory│
│ behavior                 │                  │  is proposed in light of│
└─────────────────────────┘                  │  the newly acquired     │
             │                                │  empirical knowledge    │
             ▼                                └─────────────────────────┘
┌─────────────────────────┐
│      a process           │
│  of logical deduction    │
└─────────────────────────┘
             │
             ▼
┌─────────────────────────┐
│      Predictions         │
│ (often called implications)│
└─────────────────────────┘
             │
             ▼
┌─────────────────────────┐
│      a process           │
│  of empirical observation│
└─────────────────────────┘
             │
             ▼
┌──────────────────────────────┐
│ Conclusion: The theory does  │  If the theory is in conflict   either
│ or does not provide a better │
│ explanation of the facts than│  with the evidence               or
│ alternative competing theories│
└──────────────────────────────┘
```

Definitions, assumptions, and hypotheses about behavior

The existing theory is amended or a new theory is proposed in light of the newly acquired empirical knowledge

a process of logical deduction

Predictions (often called implications)

a process of empirical observation

Conclusion: The theory does or does not provide a better explanation of the facts than alternative competing theories

If the theory is in conflict
with the evidence

either
or

If the theory passes the test, no consequent action is necessary, although, of course, the theory should be subjected to continued scrutiny

The theory is discarded in favor of a superior competing theory

Theory and observation are in continuous interaction. Starting (at the top left) with the definitions of terms and the assumptions of a theory, the theorist deduces by logical analysis everything that is implied by the assumptions. These implications are the predictions of the theory. The theory is then tested by confronting its predictions with evidence. If the theory is in conflict with facts, it will usually be amended to make it consistent with those facts (thereby making it a better theory); in extreme cases it will be discarded, to be replaced by a superior alternative. The process then begins again: the new or amended theory is subjected first to logical analysis and then to empirical testing.

government will decide to have a large budget deficit." The government's decision to have a budget deficit or surplus in two years' time will be the outcome of many complex factors, emotions, objective circumstances, chance occurrences, and so on, few of which can be predicted by the economist. If the economist's prophecy about the level of employment turns out to be wrong because in two years' time the government does not have a large deficit, then all that has been learned is that the economist is not a good guesser about the behavior of the government. However, *if* the government does have a large deficit (in two years' time or at any other time) and *then* the amount of employment does not rise, a conditional scientific prediction in economic theory has been contradicted.

Testing Theories

A theory is tested by confronting its predictions with evidence. It is necessary to discover if certain events are followed by the consequences predicted by the theory. For example, is an increase in the government's budget deficit followed by a reduction in unemployment? Testing is never easily accomplished (some of the problems involved are discussed in Chapter 3).

As a generalization, it can be said that theories tend to be abandoned when they are no longer useful. And theories cease to be useful when they cannot predict the consequences of actions in which one is interested better than the next best alternative. When a theory consistently fails to predict better than the available alternatives, it is either modified or replaced. Figure 2-1 summarizes the discussion of theories.

ECONOMICS AS A DEVELOPING SCIENCE

Economics is like other sciences in at least two respects. First, there are many observations of the world for which there are, at the moment, no fully satisfactory theoretical explanations. Second, there are many predictions that no one has yet satisfactorily tested. Serious students of economics must not expect to find a set of answers to all their questions as they progress in their study. Very often they must expect to encounter nothing more than a set of problems that provides an agenda for further research. Even

when they do find answers to problems, they should accept these answers as tentative and ask even of the most time-honored theory, "What observations would be in conflict with this theory?"

Economics is still a young science. On the one hand, economists know a good deal about the behavior of the economy. On the other hand, many problems are almost untouched. Students who decide to specialize in economics may find themselves, only a few years from now, publishing a theory to account for some of the problems mentioned in this book; or they may end up making a set of observations that will refute some venerable theory described in these pages.

A final word of warning: Having counseled a constructive disrespect for the authority of accepted theory, it is necessary to warn against adopting an approach that is too cavalier. No respect attaches to the person who says, "This theory is for the birds, it is *obviously* wrong." This is too cheap. To criticize a theory effectively on empirical grounds, one must demonstrate, by a carefully made set of observations, that some aspect of the theory is contradicted by the facts. This is a task worth attempting, but it is seldom easily accomplished.

Summary

1. It is possible, and fruitful, to distinguish between positive and normative statements. Positive statements concern what is, was, or will be, while normative statements concern what ought to be. Disagreements over positive statements are appropriately settled by an appeal to the facts. Disagreements over normative statements can never be settled by a mere appeal to factual evidence.

2. The success of scientific inquiry depends on separating positive questions about the way the world works from normative questions about how one would like the world to work. The scientific approach involves formulating positive questions precisely enough so that they can be settled by an appeal to evidence and then finding means of gathering or producing the necessary evidence.

3. Some people feel that although natural phenomena can be subject to scientific inquiry and "laws" of behavior, human phenomena cannot. The evidence, however, is otherwise. Social scientists have observed many regular and stable human behavior patterns, and these form the basis for successful predictions of how people will behave under certain conditions.

4. The fact that people sometimes act strangely, even capriciously, does not destroy the possibility of a scientific study of group behavior. Indeed, the odd and inexplicable things that one person does will tend to cancel out the odd and inexplicable things that another person does. Observation of group behavior often discloses fairly stable and predictable responses to things that exert a significant influence on the members of the group.

5. Observations reveal only sequences of events. Theories are designed to give meaning and coherence to these events. Theories thus pervade all attempts to explain events. A theory consists of a set of definitions of the variables to be employed, a set of assumptions giving the conditions under which the theory is meant to apply, and a set of hypotheses about how things behave. Any theory has certain logical implications that must be true if the theory is true.

6. A theory provides predictions of the type *"if* one event occurs, *then* another event will also occur." An important method of testing theories is to confront their predictions with evidence. When theories fail to predict better than the available alternatives, theories tend to be rejected. The progress of any science lies in finding better explanations of events than are now available. Thus, in any developing science, one must expect to discard present theories and replace them with demonstrably superior alternatives. Such a process improves the quality of the explanations.

7. The important concept of a functional relation is discussed in more detail in the appendix to this chapter, which begins on page A-2.

Topics for Review

Positive and normative statements
The law of large numbers and the predictability of human behavior
The roles of variables, assumptions, and predictions in theorizing
Endogenous and exogenous variables
Stock and flow variables
Functional relations
Prediction versus prophecy
The scientific approach

Discussion Questions

1. A baby doesn't "know" of the theory of gravity, yet in walking and eating the child soons learns to use its principles. Distinguish between behavior and prediction of behavior. Does a business executive or a farmer have to understand economic theory to behave in a pattern consistent with economic theory?

2. "If human behavior were completely capricious and unpredictable, life insurance could not be a profitable business." Explain. Can you think of any businesses that do *not* depend on predictable human behavior?

3. Write five statements about inflation. (It does not matter whether the statements are correct, but you should confine yourself to those you think might be correct.) Classify each statement as positive or normative. If your list contains only one type of statement, try to add a sixth statement of the other type. Check the validity of your positive statements as well as you can against the data given in this text (see *Inflation* in the index). If this does not satisfy you about their validity, outline how you would go about completing the test of your statements.

4. Each of the following unrealistic assumptions is sometimes made. See if you can visualize situations in which each of them might be useful.
   a. The earth is a plane.
   b. There are no differences between men and women.
   c. There is no tomorrow.
   d. A bond will pay $100 interest a year forever.

5. "The following theory of wage determination proceeds

on the assumption that labor unions do not exist." Of what use can such a theory be in Canada today?

6. Emotional statements can often be reworded so as to be tested by an appeal to evidence. How might you do that with respect to each of the following assertions?

   a. The Canadian economic system is the best in the world.

   b. The provision of free medical care for more and more people will inevitably end in socialized medicine for all, and socialized medicine will destroy our standards of medical practice by destroying the doctor's incentive to do his or her job well.

   c. The energy crisis is the result of a plot by the oil producers to exploit the public by restricting output to gain profits.

   d. Inflation is ruining the standard of living of the Canadian worker and destroying the integrity of the family.

The Role of Statistical Analysis

3

In this chapter we look at two very different problems in statistics. We study first the important statistical tool of index numbers, which are used throughout economics and occur constantly in this book. You cannot read far in a newspaper or a news magazine without encountering important index numbers such as the Consumer Price Index, measures of productivity growth, and indexes of industrial output. Then we discuss some very general questions concerning the use of theory to measure and test economic relationships.

Index Numbers

Economists frequently seek simple answers to questions such as "How much have prices risen this year?" or "Has the quantity of industrial production increased this year, and, if so, by how much?" There is no perfectly satisfactory answer to the first question because all prices do not move together, nor to the second because one cannot simply add up tons of steel, pieces of furniture, and gallons of gasoline to get a meaningful total. Yet these are not foolish questions. There *are* trends in prices and production, and thus there are real phenomena to describe. It is of no help to someone who asks about price changes over some period to be given a list of 4,682 individual prices and told, "See for yourself, they varied."

Index numbers are statistical measures that are used to give a concise summary answer to the inherently complex questions of the kind just suggested. An **index number** measures the percentage change in some broad average since some base period. As such it points to overall tendencies or general drifts, not to specific single facts. The two most important kinds of index numbers are price indexes and production indexes.

INDEX NUMBERS OF PRICES

A **price index** shows the average percentage change that has occurred in some group of prices over some period of time. The point in time from which the change is measured is called the **base period** (or base year), while the point in time to which the change is measured is called the **given period** (or given year). There are several elements in the definition of index numbers.

First, what group of prices should be used? This depends on the index. The **Consumer Price Index,** known affectionately as the CPI, covers prices of commodities commonly bought by households. Changes in the CPI are meant to measure changes in the typical household's "cost of living." The Wholesale Price Index measures a different group of commodities commonly bought and sold by wholesalers. The "Gross national expenditure implicit price index," or the GNE deflator, as it is sometimes called, is a price index that covers virtually all of the goods and services produced in the economy; it includes not only the prices of consumer goods and services bought by households but the prices of capital goods such as plant and machinery bought by firms.

Second, what kind of average should be used? If all prices were to change in the same proportion, this would not be an important question. A 10 percent rise in each and every price covered means an average rise of 10 percent no matter how much importance we give to each price change when calculating the average. But what if—as is almost always the case—different prices change differently? Now it does matter how much importance we give to each price change.

A rise of 50 percent in the price of caviar is surely much less important to the average consumer than a rise of 40 percent in the price of bread. And this in turn is surely less important than a rise of 30 percent in the cost of housing. Why? The reason is that the typical household spends less on caviar than on bread and less on bread than on housing.

In calculating any price index, statisticians seek to weight each price according to its importance. Let us see how this is done for the CPI. Government statisticians survey periodically a group of households to discover how they spend their incomes. The average bundle of goods bought is calculated, and the quantities in this bundle become the weights attached to the prices. In this way the average price change heavily weights commodities on which consumers spend a lot and lightly weights commodities on which consumers spend only a little. The procedure is illustrated in Table 3-1.

Finally, how is the average change calculated? This is done by comparing the costs of purchasing the typical bundle of commodities in the base period and in the given year. The given year cost is expressed as a percentage of the base period cost, and this figure is the index number of the new period. Thus, for example, a CPI of 110 means that the cost of purchasing the "representative" bundle of goods is 110 percent of what it was in the base period.

A price index number of a given year tells the ratio of the cost of purchasing a bundle of commodities in that year to the cost of purchasing the same bundle in the base year multiplied by 100. [1]

The percentage *change* in the cost of purchasing the bundle is thus the index number minus 100. An index number of 110 indicates a percentage increase in prices of 10 percent over those ruling in the base year.

[1] Notes giving mathematical demonstrations of the concepts presented in the text are designated by colored reference numbers. These notes can be found beginning on page M-1.

TABLE 3–1
The Calculation of a Price Index Covering Three Commodities

Commodity	Quantity in fixed bundle	Base year 1980		Given year 1981	
		Price in 1980	Value in 1980	Price in 1981	Value in 1981
A	500 units	$1.00	$ 500	$2.00	$1,000
B	200 units	5.00	1,000	7.00	1,400
C	50 units	2.00	100	9.60	480
			1,600		2,880

$$\text{Index value } 1980 = \frac{1600}{1600} \times 100 = 100$$

$$\text{Index value } 1981 = \frac{2880}{1600} \times 100 = 180$$

A price index shows the ratio of the costs of purchasing a fixed bundle of goods between two years (multiplied by 100). The cost of purchasing the fixed bundle is calculated at the prices ruling in each year. The index for year 1981 is the cost of purchasing that bundle in 1981 expressed as a percentage of the cost of purchasing the same bundle in the base year (which is 1980 in this example). The price index is thus always 100 in the base year. The index of 180 means that prices have risen on average by 80 percent between the base year and the year in question. This average weights price changes by their *importance* in the average household's budget in the base year.

Some Difficulties

An index number is meant to reflect the broad trend in prices rather than the details. This means that although the information it gives may be extremely valuable, it must be interpreted with care. Here are three of the many reasons why care is required.

First, the weights in the index refer to an average bundle of goods. This average, although "typical" of what is consumed in the nation, will not necessarily be typical of what each household does. The rich, the poor, the young, the old, the single, the married, the urban, and the rural households typically consume bundles that differ from one another. An increase in air fares, for example, will raise the cost of living of a middle-income traveler while leaving that of a poor stay-at-home unaffected. In the example of Table 3-1, the cost of living would have risen by 100 percent, 40 percent, and 380 percent respectively for three different families one of whom consumed only commodity A, one only commodity B, and one only commodity C. The index in the table shows, however, that the cost of living went up by 80 percent for a family that consumed all three goods in the relative quantities indicated.

The more an individual household's consumption pattern diverges from that of the typical pattern used to weight prices in the price index, the less well the price index will reflect the average change in prices relevant to that household.

To assess the importance of this problem, separate indexes are calculated for different subgroups. For example, in the United States since January 1980, there has been both an "all-urban" CPI and a separate index for "urban wage and clerical workers." These indexes differ from one another because the typical consumption pattern of wage and clerical workers differs from that of other urban dwellers. In Canada, various regional price indexes are available.

Second, households usually alter their consumption patterns in response to price changes. A price index that shows changes in the cost of purchasing a fixed bundle of goods does not allow for this. For example, a typical cost of living index for middle-income families at the turn of the century would have given heavy weight to the cost of maids and children's nurses. A doubling of servants' wages in 1900 would have greatly increased the middle-class cost of living. Today it would have little effect, for the rising cost of labor has long since caused middle-income families to cease to employ full-time servants. A household that has dispensed altogether with a commodity whose price is rising rapidly does not have its cost of living rise as fast as a household that continues to consume that commodity in an undiminished quantity.

A fixed-weight price index tends to overstate cost of living changes because it does not allow for changes in consumption patterns that shift expenditure away from commodities whose prices rise most and toward those whose prices rise least.

Third, as time goes by, new commodities enter the typical consumption bundle and old ones leave. A cost of living index in 1890 would have had a large item for horse-drawn carriages but no allowance at all for automobiles and gasoline.

A fixed-weight index makes no allowance for the rise of new products nor for the declining importance of old ones in the typical household's consumption bundle.

The longer the period of time that passes, the less some fixed consumption bundle will be typical of current consumption patterns. For this reason Statistics Canada, the government body responsible for the CPI, makes a new survey of household expenditure patterns about once every ten years and revises the weights. The base period is then usually changed to conform to the year in which the new set of commodity weights was calculated. At the beginning of the 1980s the CPI stood at 197 (base 1971). This meant that the cost of purchasing the bundle of goods bought by a typical household in 1971 had risen 97 percent in the intervening nine years. (Nine years is a long time for a fixed-weight price index to be used, and soon Statistics Canada will be estimating a new set of weights preparatory to shifting the base year of the CPI to some year in the early 1980s.)

INDEX NUMBERS OF PHYSICAL OUTPUTS

There are many output indexes, and the Index of Real Domestic Product in Manufacturing is one of the leading economic indicators. This index stood at 134.1 in January 1979 but had fallen to 128.2 in June 1980. In each case, 1971 was the base period (for which the index was 100). This means that whatever the index measured was 34.1 percent higher in January 1979 than in the base period, but fell 5.9 points (approximately 5 percent) in the next 17 months. To the extent that the index is meaningful it measures both the growth of the Canadian economy in the period 1971–1980 and a recession between early 1979 and mid 1980. But what exactly does the index measure?

Like the price indexes discussed above, it is an average of the changes in thousands of individual items. It is not hard to measure the change in production of tons of steel from month to month or year to year, nor that of tires or television sets. It is somewhat harder to measure the quantity of printing, of furniture, and of aircraft because the unit of output is less well defined; but these too can be approximated.

The compilers of the Index of Real Domestic Product in Manufacturing first compute indexes of the change in quantity of output for individual industries and then combine them into an overall index by using the value of output in each industry as a weighting device. Table 3-2 illustrates in simplified form the kind of computation for a two-industry world. The final computation says the index has increased by 29.2 percent between 1980 and 1981. This is the weighted average of the 25 percent increase in production of industry A and the 50 percent increase in industry B. Nothing tangible increased by 29.2 percent. Yet this average reflects the fact that both industries expanded output and that industry A was in the aggregate five times as important as industry B. The procedure used in Table 3-2 can be extended to include thousands of commodities, and this leads to an overall index

TABLE 3–2

The Calculation of a Quantity Index

	Output		Quantity relative	Value of output (billions of dollars)	
	1980 (Q_0)	1981 (Q_1)	Q_1/Q_0	V_0	$\frac{Q_1}{Q_0} \times V_0$
Industry A	40,000 tons	50,000 tons	1.25	$10	$12.5
Industry B	200,000 yards	300,000 yards	1.50	2	3.0
Total				$12	$15.5
Index value (1980 = 100)				100	129.2

This quantity index weights quantity changes by the relative importance of the quantities in the base year. The increase in quantity in each industry is shown in the "quantity relative" column, Q_1Q_0. Industry A is more important than industry B, as is shown by V_0, the values of outputs in the base year (here 1980). Thus industry A gets greater weight in computing the price index. The total value of output in 1980 was $12 billion. The last column shows the increase in value of output caused by the increase in quantity, assuming that prices and relative importance of the two commodities did not change. This computed value is $15.5 billion for 1981. The index for 1981 is

$$\frac{15.5}{12.0} \times 100 = 129.2$$

of physical production. Compilers of index numbers of physical output face many practical problems—which products to include, how to adjust for changes in quality of product, and which values to use as weights.

THE ACCURACY AND SIGNIFICANCE OF INDEX NUMBERS

Index numbers of either price or output are by their very nature crude approximations. Given the changing nature of goods and products over time (a 1967 car is different from a 1981 car) and the changing relative importance of different commodities (the declining role of food in consumers' total budgets and the rising role of services), any fixed bundle of commodities becomes out of date very quickly. But if an important trend of prices or production is under way, there is need to measure it approximately.

It would be foolish to make very much of the fact that the Consumer Price Index rose from 180.8 to 181.3 (1971 = 100) between November and December 1978, for an index number is the average of many changes. Some prices rose and others fell; some rose a lot, others very little, and so on. When the net change is so small, it may not mean very much by itself. This result, however, taken in conjunction with similar monthly increases throughout that year and the next, revealed a strong inflationary trend.

Index numbers are useful, then, as general indicators. Yet people often become mesmerized by them and treat them as though they had an accuracy that their compilers do not claim for them. Being aware of their limitations should not lead one to neglect index numbers for the useful information they do show: average changes over time.

Measurement and Testing of Economic Relations

It is one thing for economists to theorize that two variables are related to each other; it is quite another for them to be able to say *how* these variables are related. Economists might generalize on the basis of a casual observation that when households receive more income, they are likely to buy more of most commodities. But precisely how much will the consumption of a particular commodity rise as household incomes rise? Are there exceptions to the rule that the purchase of a commodity rises as income rises? For estimating precise magnitudes and for testing general rules or hypotheses, common sense, intuition, and casual observation do not take us very far. More systematic statistical analysis is required.

Statistical analysis is used to test the hypothesis that two things are related and, when they are, to estimate the numerical values of the function that describes the relation.

In practice, the same data can be used simultaneously to test whether a relationship exists and, when it does exist, to provide a measure of it.

TECHNIQUES FOR TESTING THEORIES

The techniques used to test theories differ considerably between those disciplines that can use laboratory methods and those that cannot.

Laboratory Sciences

In some sciences all the observations required for testing theories can be obtained from controlled experiments made under laboratory conditions. In these experiments all the factors that are thought to affect the outcome of the process being studied are held constant. These factors are then varied one by one and the influence of each variation observed.

Suppose chemists have a theory predicting that the rate at which a substance burns is a function of (1) the rate at which oxygen is made available during the process of combustion and (2) the chemical properties of the substance. To test this theory that may take many identical pieces of a substance and burn them, varying the amount of available oxygen in each case. This procedure will show how combustion varies with the quantity of oxygen supplied. They may then take a number of substances with different chemical compositions and burn them, using identical amounts of oxygen in each case. This procedure will show how combustion varies with chemical composition.

Being able to conduct such experiments, scientists are never forced to use data in which both chemical composition and the quantity of oxygen vary at once. Laboratory conditions serve to hold other factors constant and to produce data for situations in which factors can be varied one at a time.

Nonlaboratory Sciences

In many sciences factors cannot be isolated individually in laboratory experiments. In these sciences observations can be used to establish relationships and to test theories, even though they show what happens when several causes operate at the same time.

Consider the hypothesis that the health of an adult depends on that adult's diet as a child. Clearly, hundreds of factors affect the health of adults: heredity, conditions of childhood other than nutrition, and various aspects of adult environment. There is no acceptable way to examine this hypothesis as a controlled experiment, for scientists cannot subject a group of children to varying diets and then ensure that all other influences are the same as each person grows into an adult.

Are we then to conclude that the hypothesis cannot be tested because other factors cannot be held constant? No, because to do so would be to deny many advances in medicine, biology, and other life sciences made during the last 100 years. Testing is more difficult where laboratory methods cannot be used, but not only is it possible, it is frequently done.

In a situation in which many influences vary at once, data must be used carefully. If only two men are studied and it is found that the one with the better nutritional standards during youth has the poorer adult health record, this finding would not disprove the hypothesis that a good diet contributes to better health. It might well be that some other factor has exerted an overwhelming influence. The less healthy man may have lived most of his adult life in a disease-ridden area, while the healthier man may have lived in a relatively healthy place. A single exception does not disprove the hypothesis that two variables are related as long as we admit that other variables can also influence the outcome. But if thousands of people are studied with respect to childhood diet and adult health record, individual irregularities may be expected to cancel out and an underlying regularity to show up.

Contrast this strategy of basing decisions on a large number of observations with the practice in much ordinary conversation of acting as though a single contrary case disproved a theory. Notice how often one person advances a possible relation (e.g., between legal education and some facet of character) and someone else "refutes" this theory by citing a single counterexample (e.g., "Ralph Nader went to law school and did not turn out like that").

THE STATISTICAL TESTING OF ECONOMIC THEORIES: AN EXAMPLE

Economics is a nonlaboratory science. It is rarely possible to conduct controlled experiments with the economy. However, millions of *uncontrolled experiments* are going on every day. Households are deciding what to purchase in the face of changing prices and incomes; firms are deciding what to produce and how to produce it; and government is intervening with taxes, subsidies, and controls.

Because all these acts can be observed and recorded, a mass of data is produced continually by the economy. Most items in which economists are interested, such as the volume of unemployment, the level of prices, and the distribution of income, are influenced by a large number of factors, all of which vary simultaneously. If economists are to test their theories about relations in the economy, they must use statistical techniques designed for situations in which other things could not be held constant.

Consider testing the hypothesis that the quantity of beef purchased by low-income and middle-income North American households increases as their incomes increase. To begin with, observations should be made of household income and beef purchases. It is impossible to list all the households involved, so a small number

(called a **sample**) must be observed on the assumption that they are typical of the entire group.

The Sample

We start by observing a sample of three households. The data listed on Table 3-3 may lead us to wonder whether the hypothesis is wrong, but before we jump to that conclusion we note that "by chance" the three households selected may not be typical of all the households in the country. Expenditure on food, for example, is influenced by factors other than income. Possibly these other factors just happen to be the dominant forces in the three cases.

Increasing the number of households in the sample may reduce the chances of consistently picking untypical households. Suppose the next sample checked is larger: it consists of 100 households selected from among friends and acquaintances. A statistician points out, however, that the new group is a *biased* sample, for it contains households from only a limited geographical area, probably with only a limited occupational range, and possibly with incomes very similar to one another. (Since the way in which purchases of beef vary as income varies is of special interest, this last point is likely to have serious consequences.) As a result of these limitations, it is unlikely that this sample of households will be representative of all low-income and middle-income households in the group in which we are interested.

TABLE 3-3
Three Observations on Beef Purchases and Income

Household	House-hold income	Beef purchases, pounds per week
1	$9,000	5.10
2	11,000	5.05
3	13,000	4.93

These three observations suggest that beef purchases go down as income rises, but a sample of three is too small to be reliable.

The statistician suggests that a random sample of households be taken. A **random sample** is one chosen according to a rigidly defined set of conditions that guarantees, among other things, that every household in which we are interested has an equal chance of being selected. Choosing the sample in a random fashion has two important consequences.

First, it becomes more unlikely that the sample will be unrepresentative of all households. Second, and more important, it allows us to calculate just how likely it is that the sample is unrepresentative in any given aspect by any stated amount. This second result is important because it allows us to make statements about the probability that the behavior of all households will differ by any quantitative amount from that of households in the sample. The reason this can be done is that the sample was chosen by chance and chance events are predictable.

That chance events are predictable may sound paradoxical. But if you pick a card from a deck of ordinary playing cards, how likely is it that you will pick a heart? an ace? an ace of hearts? You play a game in which you pick a card and win if it is a heart and lose if it is anything else; a friend offers you $5 if you win against $1 if you lose. Who will make money if the game is played a large number of times? The same game is played again, but now you get $3 if you win and pay $1 if you lose. Who will make money over a large number of draws? If you know the answers to these questions (we will bet that most of you do), you must believe that chance events are in some sense predictable.

Suppose that a random sample of 4,827 households has been chosen. (How representative the sample is of all relevant households can be checked by comparing some characteristic of the households in it with a result that is known to hold for all households, e.g., how many have two cars or incomes over $8,000?) Once the sample is chosen and checked for representativeness, the information required from it is collected. In this case, the information desired is the income of each household and its weekly purchases of beef.

FIGURE 3–1
A Scatter Diagram Relating Beef Purchases to Income

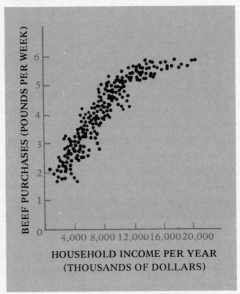

The scatter pattern shows a clear tendency for beef consumption to rise with income. Household income is measured along the horizontal axis and purchases of beef along the vertical axis. Each dot represents the beef purchases of one household. The dots fall within a narrow, rising band, suggesting the existence of a systematic relationship. (There are 4,827 observations in the original sample, but only a sample of these is shown in the figure because a scatter diagram with 4,827 points would be unintelligible.)

Analysis of the Data

There are several ways in which the data may be used to evaluate the hypothesis. One is the **scatter diagram.**[2] Figure 3-1 is a scatter diagram that relates household income to purchases of beef. The pattern of the dots suggests that there is a strong tendency for purchases of beef to be

[2] The appendix to this chapter, which begins on page A-5, outlines the elements of graphs and the graphical analysis of economic data and of functional relations between economic variables. If you find graphical analysis baffling, you might read this appendix now.

higher, the higher is household income. It thus supports the hypothesis.

There is some scattering of the dots because the relationship is "not perfect"; in other words, there is some variation in food purchases that cannot be associated with variations in household income. These "unexplained variations" in beef purchases occur for two main reasons. First, factors other than income influence beef purchases, and some of these other factors will undoubtedly have varied between the households in the sample. Second, there will inevitably be some errors in measurement. For example, a household might incorrectly report its beef purchases.

Another way to examine the hypothesis that beef purchases vary directly with income is with a cross-classification table. Table 3-4 cross-classifies households by their income and their average beef purchases. At the loss of considerable detail, the table makes clear the general

TABLE 3–4
Income Class and Average Beef Purchases

Annual household income	Average weekly beef purchases in pounds	Number of households
$0– 1,999	2.13	532
2,000– 3,999	2.82	647
4,000– 5,999	3.70	692
6,000– 7,999	4.25	867
8,000– 9,999	4.86	865
10,000–11,999	5.16	513
12,000–13,999	5.20	371
14,000–15,999	5.30	159
16,000–17,999	5.52	121
18,000–19,999	5.90	60

Average beef purchases rise steadily as income rises. This sample of 4,827 U.S. households has been cross-classified according to income and average beef purchases. Thus, in the first row, the 532 households with incomes below $2,000 per year are grouped together and their average beef purchases calculated. In the second row, all households with incomes between $2,000 and $3,999 have been grouped together. This method reduces a mass of 4,827 pairs of observations to a mere 10.

tendency for beef purchases to rise as income rises.

While both the scatter diagram and the cross-classification table reflect the general relationship between beef purchases and household income, neither concisely characterizes the specific relationship. **Regression analysis,** a widely used technique, provides quantitative measures of what the relationship is and how closely it holds. Regression analysis may be used if certain conditions are fulfilled.[3] A **regression equation** represents the best estimate of the *average* relationship between household income and beef purchases. Such an equation for our example will describe the tendency for higher household income to be associated with higher consumption of beef.[4]

A measure of how closely the relationship holds can be obtained by calculating the percentage of the variance in household expenditure on beef that can be accounted for by variations in household income.[5] This measure is called the **coefficient of determination** (r^2). It indicates, specifically in this case, the proportion of the variance in beef purchases that can be "explained" by associating it with variations in household incomes.

A "significance test" can be applied to determine the odds that the relation discovered in the sample does not exist for the whole population but has arisen by chance because the households selected happen not to be representative of the households in which we were interested. It turns out, in this example, that there is less than one chance in 1 million that the rising pattern of dots

[3] The detailed discussion of techniques and conditions is left to courses in statistics and econometrics.

[4] The equation of a straight line fitted to the data shown in Figure 3-1 is $B = 2.35 + 0.24Y$, where B is purchases of beef in pounds and Y is income in thousands of dollars per year. The equation shows that for every increase of $1,000 in household income, beef consumption tends to increase by about a quarter of a pound per week. The straight line is only an approximation to the true relation, which the scatter diagram suggests has a slight curvature.

[5] *Variance* is a precise statistical measure of the amount of variability (dispersion) in a set of data.

shown in Figure 3-1 would have been observed if there were no increasing relation between income and beef purchases for U.S. households. Since this chance is very small, we believe the hypothesis that these two variables—beef purchases and household income—are in fact positively related. Statistically the relationship is said to be "significant."

Extending the Analysis

The scatter diagram shows that *all* the variation in households' purchases of beef cannot be accounted for by observed variations in household income. If it could, all the dots would lie on a line. Since they do not, some other factors must influence food expenditure. What could make one household with an income of $12,000 buy 20 percent more beef than another household with the same income?

One possible reason is that households in different parts of the country may have been faced with different prices of beef. (There will be other reasons, such as family size and religion, but price is an important second reason.) Assume that the survey also collected data on the prices of various cuts of beef in each city or town from

which a household in the sample bought its meat. These data were then used to calculate the average price of beef facing each household.

There are now *three* observations for each of the 4,827 households: annual income, weekly purchases of beef, and average price of beef facing it. How should these data be handled? Unfortunately, the scatter diagram technique is not available because the relation between three data cannot easily be shown on a two-dimensional graph.

Instead the data may once again be grouped. This time there are two variables that are thought to influence beef consumption, and the data have to be cross-classified in a more complicated manner, as shown in Table 3-5. (To prevent the table from becoming too large, households have been lumped into income groups of $4,000. This is only a matter of convenience; the classification can be made as detailed as required.)

The device of cross-classification shown in Table 3-5 demonstrates clearly the way in which we hold one variable constant while allowing another to vary. Reading across any row, income is held constant within a specified range and price is being varied; reading down any column, price is held constant within a specified range and income is being varied.

TABLE 3–5
Average Weekly Beef Purchases (in Pounds) Cross-Classified by Income and Price

Annual household income	Average price of beef per pound			
	$1.60–1.99	$2.00–2.39	$2.40–2.79	$2.80–3.19
$0– 3,999	2.65	2.59	2.51	2.43
4,000– 7,999	4.14	4.05	3.94	3.88
8,000–11,999	5.11	5.00	4.97	4.84
12,000–15,999	5.35	5.29	5.19	5.07
16,000–19,999	5.79	5.77	5.60	5.53

Beef purchases vary directly with income and inversely with price. Each row in the table shows the effect of price on the purchases of beef for a given level of income. For example, reading across the second row, households with incomes between $4,000 and $7,999 bought an average of 4.14 pounds of beef when the price was between $1.60 and $1.99, 4.05 pounds when the price was between $2.00 and $2.39, and so on. The declining numbers across each row suggest that beef purchases decline as prices rise, for particular income groups. Each column of the table shows the effect of income on purchases of beef for a given price of beef.

To estimate a numerical relation between household income, average price, and beef purchases, **multiple regression analysis** may be used.[6] It allows estimation of both the separate and joint effects on beef purchases of variations in the price of beef and variations in household income by fitting to the data an equation that "best" describes them. It also permits measurement of the proportion of the total variation in beef purchases that can be explained by associating it with variations both in income and in price. Finally, it permits use of significance tests to determine how likely it is that the relations found in the sample are the result of chance rather than an underlying relationship for all households. Chance enters because, by bad luck, an unrepresentative sample of households might have been chosen.

EVALUATING THE EVIDENCE

Statistical techniques can help to measure the nature and strength of economic relationships and show how probable it is that a certain result has occurred by chance. What they cannot do is prove that a hypothesis is either true or false. Nor can they tell us when the hypothesis should be accepted or rejected.

Can a Hypothesis Be Proven True or False?

Most hypotheses in economics are universal hypotheses. They say that whenever certain specified conditions are fulfilled, cause X will always produce effect Y. Such universal hypotheses cannot be proven correct with 100 percent certainty. No matter how many observations are collected that agree with the hypothesis, there is always

some chance that a long series of untypical observations has been made or that there have been systematic errors of observation. After all, the mass of well-documented evidence accumulated several centuries ago on the existence of the power of witches is no longer accepted, even though it fully satisfied most contemporary observers. The existence of observational errors — even on a vast scale — has been shown to be possible, although (one fervently hopes) it is not very frequent. Observations that disagree with the theory may begin to accumulate, and after some time a theory that looked nearly certain may begin to look rather shaky.

By the same token a universal hypothesis can never be proven false with 100 percent certainty. Even when current observations consistently conflict with the theory, there are the same possibilities of the selection of a large number of untypical cases or systematic errors of observation. For instance, evidence was once gathered "disproving" the hypothesis that high income taxes tend to discourage work. More recent research suggests that economists may have been wrong to reject the theory that high taxes tend to discourage work. As a result of measurement errors and bad experimental design, the conflicting evidence may not have been as decisive as was once thought.

There is no absolute certainty in any knowledge. No doubt some of the things we now think true will eventually turn out to be false, and some of the things we currently think false will eventually turn out to be true. Yet while we can never be certain, we can assess the balance of evidence.

Some hypotheses are so unlikely to be true, given current evidence, that for all practical purposes we may regard them as false. Other hypotheses are so unlikely to be false, given current evidence, that for all practical purposes we may regard them as true.

This kind of practical decision must always be regarded as tentative. Every once in a while we will discover that we have to change our mind:

---

[6] Where three or more variables are involved, "multiple" rather than "simple" regression is used. The symbol R^2 (instead of r^2) is used for the coefficient of determination in a multiple regression analysis.

something that looked right will begin to look doubtful, or something that looked wrong will begin to look possible.

The Decision to Reject or Accept

In general, a hypothesis can never be proved or refuted conclusively, no matter how many observations are made. Nonetheless, since decisions have to be made, it is necessary to accept some hypotheses (to act as if they were proven) and to reject some hypotheses (to act as if they were refuted). Just as a jury can make two kinds of errors (finding an innocent person guilty or letting a guilty person go free) so can statistical decision makers make two kinds of errors. They can reject hypotheses that are true, and they can accept hypotheses that are false. Luckily, like a jury, they can also make correct decisions—and indeed they expect to do so most of the time.

Although the possibility of error cannot be eliminated in statistics, it can be controlled.

The method of control is to decide in advance how large a risk to take of rejecting a hypothesis if it is in fact correct.[7] Conventionally in statistics this risk is often set at 5 percent or 1 percent. When the 5 percent cutoff point is used, we will reject the hypothesis if the results that appear to contradict it could have happened by chance no more than one time in 20. Using the 1 percent decision rule gives the hypothesis a greater measure of reasonable doubt. A hypothesis is rejected only if the results that appear to contradict it could have happened by chance no more than one time in 100.

When action must be taken, some rule of thumb is necessary. But it is important to understand, first, that no one can ever be *certain* about being right in rejecting any hypothesis and, second, that there is nothing magical about arbitrary

cutoff points. Some cutoff point must be used whenever decisions have to be made.

Finally, recall that the rejection of a hypothesis is seldom the end of inquiry. Decisions can be reversed should new evidence come to light. Often the result of a statistical test of a theory is to suggest a new hypothesis that "fits the facts" better than the old one. Indeed, in some cases just looking at a scatter diagram or making a regression analysis uncovers apparent relations that no one anticipated and leads economists to formulate a new hypothesis.

Summary

1. Index numbers are summary measures that give the average percentage change in a set of related items between a "base" year and another "given" year.

2. The Consumer Price Index (CPI) measures the percentage change in the cost of purchasing a typical bundle of commodities since the base year. It is thus a measure of the average change in prices in which each price is "weighted" by the importance of that commodity in the typical consumption bundle.

3. Some problems with index numbers are: (1) the weights on which they are based are broad averages that do not reflect each individual's expenditure pattern, (2) the fixed weights make no allowance for changes in consumption patterns that occur in response to price changes, and (3) the fixed weights cannot allow for important new products, the decline of old ones, and changes in the quality of commodities that continue to be bought. For these and other reasons the weights are revised periodically.

4. Quantity indexes measure average changes in quantities of commodities where each quantity is weighted by its value in the base year.

5. Index numbers measure broad trends, and therefore not too much importance should be given to small changes. However, they provide very valuable information—provided it is under-

---

[7] Return to the jury analogy: Our notion of a person being innocent unless the jury is persuaded of guilt "beyond a reasonable doubt" rests on our wishing to take only a small risk of rejecting the hypothesis of innocence if the person being tried is in fact innocent.

stood that they are only meant to reflect major changes.

6. Theories are tested by checking their predictions against actual evidence. In some sciences, these tests can be conducted under laboratory conditions where only one thing changes at a time. In other sciences, testing must be done using the data produced by the world of ordinary events, where many factors are changing all at once. Modern statistical analysis is designed to test hypotheses where many variables are changing at once.

7. Sample data are often used in testing economic hypotheses. If the sample is random, the probability of the measured characteristics of the sample being misleading (because of the unlucky choice of a nonrepresentative sample) can be calculated.

8. Scatter diagrams are relatively simple devices for exploring the presence of systematic relationships between two variables. Regression analysis permits more specific measures of the relationship: what it is, how closely it holds, and whether or not it is "significant."

9. Hypotheses involving several variables require more sophisticated statistical techniques such as use of complex cross-classification tables and multiple regression analysis, each of which attempts to identify the separate and joint effects of several variables on one another.

10. While statistical tests allow us to assess the probability that what we observe is consistent with a particular hypothesis, they never allow determination of the truth or falsity of a hypothesis beyond any doubt. Because it is often necessary to act as though certain hypotheses are true and others false, decision rules may be required. Two frequently used cutoff points are 5 percent and 1 percent.

11. Methods of graphing economic observations and functional relations are further discussed in the appendix to this chapter, which begins on page A-5.

Topics for Review

Price indexes and quantity indexes
Base years and given years
Quantity weights in price indexes
Value weights in quantity indexes
Problems with fixed-weight indexes calculated over long time periods
The twofold role of statistical analysis: measurement and testing
Cross-classification tables
The difference between proving a hypothesis true and accepting the hypothesis
The difference between proving a hypothesis false and rejecting the hypothesis

Discussion Questions

1. According to a senior vice-president of Mellon Bank: "When it comes to forecasting the economy, the stock market has as good a record—if not better—than most economists." Can this hypothesis be tested? If so, how? If not, why not?
2. In the seventies the cost of automobile insurance rose sharply. The American Automobile Association said its increase was due not (as some charged) to the passage by many states of no-fault insurance laws but to the inflation in the costs of parts used in repairing cars. How might the AAA's hypothesis be tested?
3. "The simplest way to see that capital punishment is a strong deterrent to murder is to ask yourself whether you might be more inclined to commit murder if you knew in advance that you ran no risk of ending in the electric chair, the gas chamber, or on the gallows." Comment on the methodology of social investigation implied in this statement. What alternative approach would you suggest?
4. There are hundreds of eyewitnesses to the existence of flying saucers and other UFOs. There are films and eyewitness accounts of Nessie, the Loch Ness monster. Are you persuaded of their existence? If not, what would it take to persuade you? If so, what would it take to make you change your mind?
5. What is the role of the law of large numbers in making economic statements testable? Does not the fact that it depends on errors mean that any science that relies on it will be inviting errors?
6. A classic example of biased sampling was the attempt made by the *Literary Digest* in 1936 to predict the result of the U.S. presidential election. The magazine fore-

cast a substantial Republican victory, and its subsequent demise has been attributed to this error. (Franklin D. Roosevelt won every state but Maine and Vermont from Republican Alfred Landon, and the political platitude "As Maine goes, so goes the nation" was reworded to "As Maine goes, so goes Vermont.") The *Literary Digest* poll was based on a random sample of names in telephone directories. Can you spot a potential flaw in this sample? Remember that this happened in 1936. Would the same bias have existed if the survey had been made in 1976? By 1948 the selection of the sample was much more sophisticated, but the Roper polls predicted Dewey over Truman by such a substantial margin that polling was discontinued after September 30. Truman, of course, won the election. What was the nature of the sampling error this time?

7. Look up in the *Bank of Canada Review* the behavior of the major categories of the CPI over the last two years. Compare the rise in the costs of living of someone who spent most of his income on food and someone who spent her income in proportion to the overall CPI weights. What commodity groups would have heavy weights in the budget of a person whose cost of living had risen much less than the average? In the budget of a person whose cost of living had risen much more than the average?

An Overview of the Economy

4

The Evolution of Market Economies

The great seventeenth century British political philosopher Thomas Hobbes described life in a state of nature as "nasty, brutish and short." Modern study of the several surviving food-gathering societies suggests that Hobbes' ideas were wide of the mark. In fact societies in the pre-agricultural stage are characterized by a

relative simplicity of the material culture (only 94 items exist among Kung bushmen); the lack of accumulation of individual wealth [and mobility]. . . . Subsistence requirements are satisfied by only a modest effort—perhaps two or three days work a week by each adult; they do not have to struggle over food resources; the attitudes toward ownership are flexible and their living groups open. Such features set hunters and gatherers apart from more technologically developed societies whose very survival depends upon their ability to maintain order and to control property.[1]

Most of the characteristic problems of economics do not arise in these primitive societies. Indeed the economic problem as we know it today has been with us a mere eight or ten thousand years, or relatively little more than an instant of the millions of years in which humanoid creatures have been on earth. It began with the original agricultural revolution, when human beings first found it possible to stay in one place and survive. Gradually abandoning their nomadic life of hunting and food gathering, people settled down to tend crops that they had learned

[1] *The Times Atlas of World History* (Maplewood, N.J.: Hammond, 1979), page 39.

to plant and animals that they had learned to domesticate. All societies since that time have faced the problem of choice under conditions of scarcity.

SURPLUS, SPECIALIZATION, AND TRADE

Along with permanent settlement, the agricultural revolution brought surplus production: farmers could produce substantially more than they needed to survive. The agricultural surplus allowed the creation of new occupations and thus new economic and social classes such as artisans, soldiers, priests, and government officials. Freed from having to grow their own food, these new classes turned their talents to performing specialized services and producing goods other than food. They also produced more than they themselves needed, so they traded the excess to obtain whatever they required.

Economists called this allocation of different jobs to different people **specialization of labor.** Specialization has proven extraordinarily efficient compared to universal self-sufficiency for at least two reasons. First, individual talents and abilities differ, and specialization allows each person to do the job he or she can do relatively best, while leaving everything else to be done by others. People not only do their own thing; they do their own best thing. Second, a person who concentrates on one activity becomes better at it than could a jack-of-all trades.

The exchange of goods and services in early societies commonly took place by simple mutual agreement among neighbors. In the course of time, however, trading became centered in particular gathering places called markets. Today we use the term **market economy** to refer to a society in which people specialize in productive activities and meet most of their material wants through exchanges voluntarily agreed upon by the contracting parties.

Specialization must be accompanied by trade. People who produce only one thing must trade most of it to obtain all the other things they require.

The earliest market economies depended on **barter,** the trading of goods directly for other goods. But barter can be a very costly process in terms of time spent searching out satisfactory exchanges. *Money* evolved to make trade easier. It eliminates the inconvenience of barter by allowing the two sides of the barter transaction to be separated. If a farmer has wheat and wants a hammer, he does not have to search for an individual who has a hammer and wants wheat. He merely has to find someone who wants wheat. The farmer takes money in exchange, then finds another person who wishes to trade a hammer and swaps the money for the hammer.

By eliminating the need for barter, money greatly facilitates trade and specialization.

FACTOR SERVICES AND DIVISION OF LABOR

Market transactions in early economies mainly involved goods and services for consumption. Producers specialized in making a commodity and then traded it for the other products they needed. The labor services required to make the product would usually be provided by the makers themselves, by apprentices learning to be craftsmen, or by slaves. Over the last several hundred years many technical advances in methods of production have made it efficient to organize agriculture and industry on a very large scale. These technical developments have made use of what is called the **division of labor.** This term refers to specialization within the production process of a particular commodity. The labor involved is divided into a series of repetitive tasks, and each individual does a single task that may be just one of hundreds of tasks necessary to produce the commodity. Today it is possible for an individual to work on a production line without knowing what commodity emerges at the end of that line!

To gain the advantages of the division of labor it became necessary to organize production in large and expensive factories. With this development workers lost their status as craftsmen (or peasants) and became members of the working class, wholly dependent on their ability to sell their labor to factory (or farm) owners and lacking a plot of land to fall back on for subsistence in times of need. The day of small craftsmen who made and sold their own goods was over. Today's typical workers do not earn their incomes by selling commodities they personally have produced; rather they sell their labor services to firms and receive money wages in return. They have increasingly become cogs in a machine that they do not fully understand or control.

SCARCITY AND THE ALLOCATION OF RESOURCES

The term **allocation of resources** refers to the way in which the available factors of production are distributed among the various uses to which they might be put. All economies that have existed since the original agricultural revolution have been faced with the problem of scarcity. There are not enough resources to produce all of the goods and services that could be consumed. It is therefore necessary to allocate the available resources among their various possible uses and in so doing to choose what to produce and what not to produce. In a market economy, millions of consumers decide what commodities to buy and in what quantities; a vast number of firms produce these commodities and buy the factor services that are needed to make them; and millions of factor owners decide to whom they will sell these services. These individual decisions collectively determine the economy's allocation of resources.

In a market economy, the allocation of resources is the outcome of countless independent decisions made by consumers and producers, all acting through the medium of markets.

Our main objective in this chapter is to provide an overview of this market mechanism.

The Decision Makers

Economics is about the behavior of people. Much that we observe in the world, and that

economists assume in their theories, can be traced back to decisions made by individuals. There are millions of individuals in most economies. To make a systematic study of their behavior more manageable, we categorize them into three important groups: households, firms, and central authorities. These groups are economic theory's cast of characters, and the stage on which their play is enacted is the market.

HOUSEHOLDS

A **household** is defined as all the people who live under one roof and who make, or are subject to others making for them, joint financial decisions. Economic theory gives households a number of attributes.

First, it assumes that each household makes consistent decisions, as though it were composed of a single individual. Thus economists ignore many interesting problems of how the household reaches its decisions. Intrafamily conflicts and the moral and legal problems concerning parental control over minors are dealt with by other social sciences.[2] These problems are avoided in economics by the assumption that the household is the basic decision-making atom of consumption behavior.

Second, we assume that each household is consistently attempting to achieve some goal when it makes choices. In demand theory we assume that the goal of the household is the maximization of its *satisfaction* or *well-being* or *utility,* as the concept is variously called. The household tries to do this within the limitations of its available resources.

Third, we assume that households are the principal owners of factors of production. They sell the services of these factors to firms and receive their incomes in return.

Is it correct to assume that factors of production are principally owned by households? It is

---

[2] In academic work, as elsewhere, a division of labor is useful. However, it is important to remember that when economists speak of *the* consumer or *the* individual, they are in fact referring to the group of individuals composing the household. Thus, for example, the commonly heard phrase *consumer sovereignty* really means *household sovereignty.*

The Division of Labor

Adam Smith began his famous treatise on *The Wealth of Nations* with a long study of the division of labor. Among other things, he had this to say.

The greatest improvements in the productive powers of labour . . . have been the effects of the division of labour.

To take an example . . . the trade of the pinmaker; a workman not educated to this business (which the division of labour has rendered a distinct trade), nor acquainted with the use of the machinery employed in it could scarce, perhaps, with his utmost industry, make one pin in a day, and certainly could not make twenty. But in the way in which this business is now carried on . . . it is divided into a number of branches. . . . One man draws out the wire, another straightens it, a third cuts it, a fourth points it, a fifth grinds it at the top for receiving the head; to make the head requires two or three distinct operations; to put it on, is a peculiar business, to whiten the pins is another; it is even a trade by itself to put them into the paper; and the important business of making a pin is, in this manner, divided into about eighteen distinct operations, which, in some manufactories, are all performed by distinct hands, though in others the same man will sometimes perform two or three of them.

Smith observes that even in smallish factories, where the division of labor is exploited only in part, output is as high as 4,800 pins per person per day!

Later Smith discusses the general importance of the division of labor and the forces that limit its application.

Each animal is still obliged to support and defend itself, separately and independently, and derives no sort of advantage from that variety of talents with which nature has distinguished its fellows. Among men, on the contrary, the most dissimilar geniuses are of use to one another; the different produces of their respective talents, by the general disposition to truck, barter, and exchange, being brought, as it were, into a common stock, where every man may purchase whatever part of the produce of other men's talents he has occasion for.

As it is the power of exchanging that gives occasion to the division of labour, so the extent of this division must always be limited by the extent of that power, or, in other words, by the extent of the market. When the market is very small, no person can have any encouragement to dedicate himself entirely to one employment for want [i.e., lack] of the power to exchange all that surplus part of the produce of his own labour, which is over and above his own consumption, for such parts of the produce of other men's labour as he has occasion for.

Smith notes that there is no point in specializing to produce a large quantity of pins, or anything else, unless there are enough persons making other commodities to provide a market for all the pins that are produced. Thus the larger the market, the greater the scope for the division of labor and the higher the resulting opportunities for efficient production.

obvious that labor is "owned" by those individuals who sell their labor and receive wages and salaries in return. Most capital equipment is owned by firms; but firms are in turn owned by households. Corporations, for example, are owned by the households that hold those companies' stocks. These households provide firms with the money needed to carry on business, and they receive the firms' profits as their income.

Land is owned by households and firms—which are in turn owned by households. A household may use its land itself, or it may make the land available to some other user in return for rent, which becomes the household's income.[3]

Again, we assume that in making these deci-

[3] The main group that owns capital and land without itself being a household, or being owned by a household, is the government.

sions on how much to sell and to whom to sell it, each household seeks to maximize its utility.

FIRMS

A **firm** is defined as the unit that employs factors of production to produce commodities that it sells to other firms, to households, or to the central authorities (defined below). For obvious reasons a firm is often called a *producer*. Economic theory gives firms several attributes.

First, economists assume that each firm makes consistent decisions, as though it were composed of a single individual. Thus economic theory ignores the internal problems of who reaches particular decisions and how they are reached. In doing this, economists assume that the firm's internal organization is irrelevant to its decisions. This allows them to treat the firm as the atom of behavior on the production or supply side of commodity markets, just as the household is treated as the atom of behavior on the consumption or demand side.

Second, economists assume that most firms make their decisions with a single goal in mind: to make as much profit as possible.[4] This goal of *profit maximization* is analogous to the household's goal of utility maximization. There is a difference, however; although household satisfaction cannot be directly measured, a firm's profits can be. (The assumption of profit maximization has come under serious criticism, and currently there are several competing theories of the motivation of firms. Alternative theories of firm behavior are treated later in the micro part of this book. Meanwhile, we can go far using the simple assumption of profit maximization.)

Third, economists assume that firms in their role as producers are the principal users of the services of factors of production. In markets where factor services are bought and sold, the roles of firms and households are thus reversed from what they are in commodity markets: in factor markets firms do the buying and households do the selling.

CENTRAL AUTHORITIES

The **central authorities,** often called "the government," are defined to be public agencies, government bodies, and other organizations belonging to or under the direct control of governments. Municipal and provincial governments, as well as the federal government, are included. In Canada the term "central authorities" includes federal Parliament, the provincial legislature, the Bank of Canada, the city council, commissions and regulatory bodies, the police force, and all other government bodies that exercise control over the behavior of firms and households. It is not important to draw up a comprehensive list of all central authorities, but one should have in mind a general idea of the organizations that have legal and political power to exert control over individual decision makers and over markets.

It is *not* a basic assumption of economics that the central authorities always act in a consistent fashion or as though they were a single individual. Some important reasons for this may be mentioned here. First, the mayor of Vancouver, a member of the Legislative Assembly of Manitoba, and a member of Parliament from Quebec represent different constituencies, and therefore they may express different and conflicting views and objectives.

Second, individual public servants, whether elected or appointed, have personal objectives (such as staying in office, achieving higher office, power, prestige, and personal aggrandizement) as well as public service objectives. Although the balance of importance given to the two types of objectives will vary among persons and among types of office, both will almost always have some importance. It would be a rare member of Parliament, for example, who would vote against a measure that slightly reduced the "public

---

[4] There is a second class of firms: nonprofit organizations such as hospitals and private universities. They employ factors of production to produce a commodity that they sell on the market. But they are in business as a public service, not to make profits.

good" if this vote almost guaranteed his defeat at the next election. ("After all," he could reason, "if I am defeated, I won't be around to vote against *really* bad measures.")

For these and other reasons, conflict between different central bodies is the subject of much of the theory about the control of the economy.

OTHER DECISION MAKERS

Although in basic economic theory we can get away with three sets of decision makers, it is worth noting that there are others. Probably the most important are charities such as the Canadian Cancer Society and funding organizations such as the Donner Foundation. These bodies are responsible for allocating some of the economy's resources. They ensure, for example, that resources are channeled to medical and academic research. In most cases, however, these organizations do not directly produce goods.

Markets and Economies

We have seen that firms, households, and central authorities are the main actors in the economic drama. Their action takes place in individual markets.

MARKETS

The word "market" originally designated a place where goods were traded. The St. Lawrence Market in Toronto is a world-famous modern example of markets in the everyday sense, and most cities have produce markets where fresh produce is brought early in the morning and promptly sold. Much early economic theory attempted to explain price behavior in just such markets. Why, for example, can you sometimes obtain tremendous bargains at the end of the day and at other times get what you want only at prices that appear exorbitant in relation to prices quoted only a few hours before?

As theories of market behavior were developed, they were extended to cover commodities such as wheat. Wheat produced anywhere in the world can be purchased almost anywhere else in the world, and the price of a given grade of wheat tends to be nearly uniform the world over. When we talk about the wheat market, the concept of a market has been extended well beyond the idea of a single place to which the producer, the storekeeper, and the homemaker go to sell and to buy.

For present purposes, a **market** is satisfactorily defined as an area over which buyers and sellers negotiate the exchange of a well-defined commodity. Economists distinguish two broad types of markets: **product markets,** in which firms sell their output of goods and services, and **factor markets,** in which households sell the services of the factors of production they control.

ECONOMIES

An **economy** is rather loosely defined as a set of interrelated production and consumption activities. It may refer to this activity in a region of one country (*the economy of Newfoundland*); it may refer to this activity in a country (*the Canadian economy*); or it may refer to this activity in a group of countries (*the economy of Western Europe*). In any economy the allocation of resources is determined by the production, sales, and purchase decisions made by firms, households, and central authorities.

A **free-market economy** is an economy in which the decisions of individual households and firms (as distinct from the central authorities) exert the major influence over the allocation of resources.[5]

The opposite of a free-market economy is a **command economy,** in which the major decisions

---

[5] Free-market economies are sometimes called capitalist economies; in fact, the term "capitalist" is often used as a synonym for "free market." In Marxist literature "capitalist" refers to the private ownership of the factor of production, capital. But it is possible to be capitalist in Marx's sense of the word and yet have overwhelming public intervention into markets. Thus "capitalist" (private ownership of capital) does not mean the same as "free (uncontrolled) market." For most purposes of modern economics, it is who controls the markets rather than who owns the capital that is the important matter.

about the allocation of resources are made by the central authorities and in which firms and households produce and consume only as they are ordered.

The terms *free market* and *command economy* are used to describe tendencies that are apparent, even though no real economies rely solely either on free markets or on commands. Thus in practice all economies are **mixed economies** in the sense that some decisions are made by firms and households and some by central authorities.

SECTORS OF AN ECONOMY

Parts of an economy are usually referred to as **sectors** of that economy. For example, the agricultural sector is the part of the economy that produces agricultural commodities.

Market and Nonmarket Sectors

Producers make commodities. Consumers use them. There are two basic ways in which commodities may pass from one group to the other: they may be sold by producers and bought by consumers through markets; or they may be given away.

When commodities are bought and sold, producers must cover their costs with the revenue they obtain from selling the product. We call this production *marketed production,* and we refer to this part of the country's activity as belonging to the **market sector.**

When the product is given away, the costs of production must be covered from some source other than sales revenue. We call this production *nonmarketed production,* and we refer to this part of the country's activity as belonging to the **nonmarket sector.** In the case of private charities, the money required to pay for factor services may be raised from the public by voluntary contributions. In the case of production by governments—which accounts for the bulk of nonmarketed production—the money is provided from government revenue, which in turn comes mainly from taxes.

Whenever a government enterprise *sells* its output, its production is in the market sector. But much state output is in the nonmarket sector by the very nature of the product provided. For example, one could hardly expect the criminal to pay the judge for providing the service of criminal justice. Other products are in the nonmarket sector because governments have decided that there are advantages to removing them from the market sector. This is the case, for example, with most of Canadian education. Public policy places it in the nonmarket sector even though much of it could be provided by the market sector.

All of a country's national product can be assigned to either the market sector or the nonmarket sector of the economy.[6]

The Public and Private Sectors

The productive activity of a country is often divided in a different way than between market and nonmarket sectors. In this alternative division, the **private sector** refers to all production that is in private hands and the **public sector** refers to all production that is in public hands. The distinction between the two sectors depends on the legal distinction of ownership. In the private sector, the organization that does the producing is owned by households or other firms; in the public sector, it is owned by the state. The public sector includes all production of goods and services by central authorities plus all production by nationalized industries that is sold to consumers through ordinary markets.

The distinction between market and nonmarket sectors is economic: it depends on whether or not the costs of producing commodities are recovered by selling them to their users. The distinction between the private and the public sectors is legal: it depends on whether the producing organizations are privately or publicly owned.

---

[6] The assignment is obvious when the product is sold for a price that covers its full costs or is given at a zero price. But what of products that are sold for a price that does not cover full costs? In these cases production falls partly into one sector and partly into the other. If, for example, 10 percent of costs is covered by small charges made to users and 90 percent by the government, then the production is 10 percent in the market sector and 90 percent in the nonmarket sector.

HOW INDIVIDUAL MARKETS WORK: AN OVERVIEW OF MICROECONOMICS

Early economists observed the market economy with wonder. They saw that most commodities were made by a large number of independent producers and yet in approximately the quantities that people wanted to purchase them. Natural disasters aside, there were neither vast surpluses nor severe shortages of products. They also saw that in spite of the ever-changing requirements in terms of geographical, industrial, and occupational patterns, most laborers were able to sell their services to employers most of the time.

How does the market produce this order in the absence of conscious coordination by the central authorities? It is one thing to have the same good produced year in and year out when people's wants and incomes do not change; it is quite another thing to have production adjusting continually to changing wants, incomes, and techniques of production. Yet this *relatively* smooth adjustment is accomplished by the market—albeit with occasional, and sometimes serious, interruptions.

The great discovery of eighteenth century economists was that the price system is a social control mechanism.

Adam Smith, in his classic *The Wealth of Nations,* published in 1776, spoke of the price system as "the invisible hand." It allows decision making to be decentralized under the control of millions of individual producers and consumers but nonetheless to be coordinated. Two examples may help to illustrate how this coordination occurs.

A Change in Demand

For the first example, assume that households wish to purchase more of some commodity than previously. To see the market's reaction to such a change, imagine a situation in which farmers find it equally profitable to produce either of two crops, carrots or brussels sprouts, and so are willing to produce some of both commodities, thereby satisfying the demands of households who wish to consume both. Now imagine that consumers develop a greatly increased desire for brussels sprouts and a diminished desire for carrots. This change might have occurred because of the discovery of hitherto unsuspected nutritive or curative powers of brussels sprouts, or it might have been the result of a successful advertising campaign on the part of the association of brussels sprout producers: "Eat brussels sprouts; they're grown *above* ground." Whatever the reason, there has been a major shift toward sprouts and away from carrots.

What will be the effects of this shift? When consumers buy more brussels sprouts and fewer carrots, a shortage of brussels sprouts and a glut of carrots develop. In order to unload their surplus stocks of carrots, merchants reduce the price of carrots—in the belief that it is better to sell them at a reduced price than not to sell them at all. Sellers of brussels sprouts, however, find that they are unable to satisfy all their customers' demands for that product. Sprouts have become a scarce commodity, so the merchants charge more for them. As the price rises, fewer people are willing and able to purchase sprouts. Thus making them more expensive limits the demand for them to the available supply.

Farmers see a rise in the price of brussels sprouts and a fall in the price of carrots. Brussels sprout production has become more profitable than in the past: the costs of producing sprouts remain unchanged at the same time that their market price has risen. Similarly, carrot production will be less profitable than in the past because costs are unchanged but the price has fallen. Attracted by high profits in brussels sprouts and deterred by low profits or potential losses in carrots, farmers expand the production of sprouts and curtail the production of carrots. Thus the change in consumers' tastes, working through the price system, causes a reallocation of resources—land and labor—out of carrot production and into brussels sprout production.

As the production of carrots declines, the glut

of carrots on the market diminishes and their price begins to rise. On the other hand, the expansion in brussels sprout production reduces the shortage and the price begins to fall. These price movements will continue until it no longer pays farmers to contract carrot production and to expand brussels sprout production. When the dust settles, the price of sprouts is higher than it was originally but lower than it was when the shortage sent the price soaring before output could be adjusted; and the price of carrots is lower than it was originally but higher than when the initial glut sent the price tumbling before output could be adjusted.

The reaction of the market to a change in demand leads to a transfer of resources. Carrot producers reduce their production; they will therefore be laying off workers and generally demanding fewer factors of production. Brussels sprout producers expand production; they will therefore be hiring workers and generally increasing their demand for factors of production.

Labor can probably switch from carrot to sprout production without much difficulty. Certain types of land, however, may be better suited for growing one crop rather than the other. When farmers increase their sprout production, their demands for those factors especially suited to sprout production also increase—and this creates a shortage of these resources and a consequent rise in their prices. Meanwhile, with carrot production falling, the demand for land and other factors of production especially suited to carrot growing is reduced. A surplus results, and the prices of these factors are forced down.

Thus factors particularly suited to sprout production will earn more and will obtain a higher share of total national income than before. Factors particularly suited to carrot production, however, will earn less and will obtain a smaller share of the total national income than before.

Changes of this kind will be studied more fully later; the important thing to notice now is how a change in demand initiated by a change in consumers' tastes causes a reallocation of resources in the direction required to cater to the new set of tastes.

A Change in Supply

For a second example, consider a change originating with producers. Begin as before by imagining a situation in which farmers find it equally profitable to produce either sprouts or carrots and in which consumers are willing to buy, at prevailing market prices, the quantities of these two commodities that are being produced. Now imagine that, at existing prices, farmers become more willing to produce sprouts than in the past and less willing to produce carrots. This shift might be caused, for example, by a change in the costs of producing the two goods—a rise in carrot costs and a fall in sprout costs that would raise the profitability of sprout production and lower that of carrot production.

What will happen now? For a short time, nothing at all; the existing supply of sprouts and carrots on the market is the result of decisions made by farmers at some time in the past. But farmers now begin to plant fewer carrots and more sprouts, and soon the quantities on the market begin to change. The quantity of sprouts available for sale rises, and the quantity of carrots falls. A shortage of carrots and a glut of sprouts results. The price of carrots consequently rises, and the price of sprouts falls. This provides the incentive for two types of adjustments. First, households will buy fewer carrots and more sprouts. Second, farmers will move back into carrot production and out of sprout production.

This example began with a situation in which there was a shortage of carrots that caused the price of carrots to rise. The rise in the price of carrots removed the shortage in two ways: it reduced the quantity of carrots demanded and it increased the quantity offered for sale (in response to the rise in the profitability of carrot production). Remember that there was also a surplus of brussels sprouts that caused the price to fall. The fall in price removed the surplus in two ways: it encouraged the consumers to buy more of this commodity and it reduced the quantity of sprouts produced and offered for sale (in response to a fall in the profitability of sprout production).

These examples illustrate a general point:

The price system is a mechanism that coordinates individual, decentralized decisions.

The existence of such a control mechanism is beyond dispute. How well it works in comparision with alternative coordinating systems has been in serious dispute for over a hundred years. It remains today a major unsettled social question.

The Circular Flow: From Microeconomics to Macroeconomics

Figure 4-1 illustrates the two sets of markets, factor markets and product markets, through which the decisions of firms and households are coordinated. Consider households first. The members of households want commodities to keep them fed, clothed, housed, entertained, healthy, and secure; they also want them to educate, edify, beautify, stupefy, and otherwise amuse themselves. Households have, in varying amounts, resources with which to attempt to satisfy these wants. But not all their wants can be satisfied with the resources available. Households are forced, therefore, to make choices as to what goods and services to buy in product markets that offer them myriad ways to spend their incomes.

The signals to which households respond are product-market prices; for each given set of prices, households make a set of choices. In so doing they also, in the aggregate, affect those prices. The prices also serve as signals to firms of what goods *they* may profitably provide. Given technology and the cost of factors, firms must choose among the products they might produce and sell, among the ways of producing them, and among the various quantities (and qualities) they can supply. By so doing, the firms too affect prices.

Firms must buy factors of production. The quantities demanded depend on the firms' production decisions, which in turn depend on consumers' demands. The demands for factors will in turn affect the prices of labor, managerial skill,

raw materials, buildings, machinery, use of capital, land, and all other factors. The households who are owners of factors (or who possess the skills that can provide the factor services) respond to factor prices and make *their* choices about where to offer their services. These choices determine factor supplies and affect factor prices. Payments by firms to factor owners provide the owners of the factors with incomes. The recipients of these incomes are households whose members want commodities to keep them fed, clothed, housed, entertained. We have now come full circle!

The action of the drama involves firms and households inextricably bound up with each other. Payments flow from households to firms and back to households again.

AN OVERVIEW OF MACROECONOMICS

The idea of payments and incomes flowing in a closed circuit, suggested in Figure 4-1, is basic to macroeconomics. The figure shows flows in two directions. The counterclockwise flows are those of factor services from households to firms and of commodities from firms to households. These are called **real flows.** The clockwise flows are those of money from firms to households (to pay for factor services bought by firms) and from households to firms (to pay for the commodities bought by households). These are called **money flows.** The money spent to purchase factor services becomes income to the households who sell the factor services, and the money spent by households to buy the goods produced by firms becomes the income of the firms. If households spent *all* the income they received on buying goods and services produced by firms, and if firms distributed *all* the income they received to households either by purchasing factor services or by distributing profits to their owners, then the circular flow would be very simple indeed. Everything that households received would be passed on to firms, and everything that firms received would be passed on to households. The circular flow would be a completely closed system.

FIGURE 4-1

The Circular Flows of Goods and Services and Money Payments Between Firms and Households

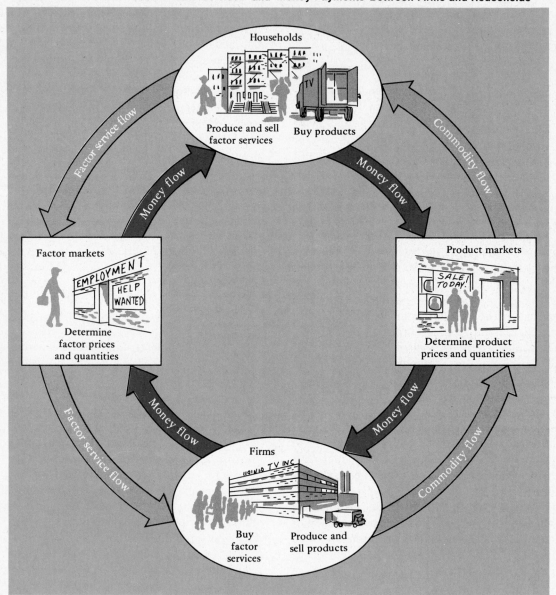

The interaction of firms and households in factor and product markets generates both real and money flows. Factor services are sold through factor markets. The real flow is of factor services from households to firms and the money flow is of income from firms to households. Goods and services for consumption are sold through product markets. The real flow is of goods and services from firms to households and the money flow is of payments from households to firms.

However, there are two main reasons why the circular flow is not a completely closed system. First, neither households nor firms spend all of the income they receive on purchasing goods and services from the other. Households, for ex-ample, have to pay income taxes, and some of their after-tax-income is saved. Some of the money that households do spend on purchasing goods and services goes to governments rather than firms because of sales taxes; only what is left becomes the receipts of firms. Furthermore, not all of the income received by firms is paid out to factors; some is paid to governments in the form of business taxes, and some is saved by the firms.

The second reason why the circular flow of income is not a completely closed system is that firms receive income that does not arise from the spending of households, and households receive income that does not arise from the spending of firms. When governments spend money on goods and services that are produced by firms, for example, this creates income for the firms that does not arise directly out of the expenditure of private households. When governments hire the services of civil servants, mine inspectors, road builders, and other workers, they create income for households that does not arise directly out of the spending of firms. Similarly, if some firms purchase machines and equipment (say, out of funds borrowed from banks), this creates income for the other firms that manufacture the equipment (and for the households that supply the required factor services); but such income does not arise directly out of household spending.

There is a basic element of circularity in the economy because much income received by households is passed on to firms and much income received by firms is passed on to households. But there are also incomes received by one group and not passed on to the other and incomes received by one group that do not arise out of the spending of the other.

It should be intuitively clear from this discussion that the size of the total incomes received by households and firms depends not only on their total purchases from one another but also on what they receive from other sources of spending. Macroeconomics studies the determinants of all these flows of spending. Why are they the size they are, and why do they change? These are important questions since the flows themselves determine the total output produced, the total income earned, and the total amount of employment available.

MICRO- AND MACROECONOMICS COMPARED

Microeconomics deals with the determination of prices and quantities in individual markets and with the relations among these markets. Microeconomics thus looks at the details of the market economy. In contrast, macroeconomics suppresses much detail and paints the economy with a very broad brush. Macroeconomics deals with such aggregates as the total flow of payments from households to firms and the total flow of factor income from firms to households.

Microeconomics and macroeconomics look at different aspects of the circular flow of income. Both deal with important questions concerning the functioning of the economy. Whichever is studied first, it is important to remember that they are complementary, not competing, theories and that both are needed for a full understanding of the functioning of a modern economy.

Alternative Economic Systems

Economics is concerned with the basic questions, What is produced? How is it produced? How is the product distributed? In this book, these and related questions will be examined in the context of a market economy in which private firms and households interact in markets with some assistance and interference from the government. This kind of economy fits the pattern of Canada, the United States, Britain, western Europe, and other areas of the world that together are inhabited by less than a quarter of the world's population. We study this kind of economy for several reasons. First, this is the kind of economy *we* live in. Second, it is the economic environment in which the serious study of economics was born and has grown.

Today, however, more than a billion people, a third of the world's population, live in the Soviet Union and China, countries that explicitly reject our kind of economic system. At least another third of the world's population live in countries whose economies have not yet developed to the point where the model of either the free-market or the managed economy fits them closely; many are "uncommitted" economically as well as politically.

Can the same theories and measurements be applied to economies quite different from the free-market economy? So far as economics describes the ways in which people respond to incentives and mobilize scarce means to given ends, the same economic principles are applicable under a variety of different institutional, political and social arrangements.

All economies face scarcity, and all must decide how to allocate scarce goods; all may face problems of inflation, unemployment, balance-of-payments deficits, and unsatisfactory rates of growth.

So far as economic analysis concerns these topics, it can contribute valuable insights even where familiar institutions are modified or absent. Furthermore, the study of different economic systems may provide clues to the strengths and weaknesses of different forms of economic organization.

DIFFERENCES BETWEEN ECONOMIES

It is common to speak of the economic systems of "capitalism," "socialism," and "communism" as if they were the only three paths to basic economic decisions. But this is at best a simplification and at worst a confusion. There are dozens of economic systems in existence today, not three. Just as there are many differences among Canada, the United States, the United Kingdom, Germany, Sweden, Japan, France, Greece, and Brazil, so are there differences among the institutions of the Soviet Union, China, Poland, Bulgaria, Cuba, Czechoslovakia, and Yugoslavia. Countries are dissimilar in many respects: in who owns resources, in who makes decisions, in the role of governmental planning, in the nature of the incentives offered to people, and in the way that the economy performs.

Which dissimilarities are important? Differences of opinion about the answer to this question may lead to important disparities in evaluation. Canadians may view their economy as being the reason for their high standard of living and see in their well-stocked stores proof of the superiority of free enterprise capitalism. Russians may look at their economy and see, in its rapid and purposeful growth and the absence of urban unemployment, proof of its superiority to the North American economy. Sweden's slum-free public housing, nationalized medicine, and high productivity in privately owned industry may lead Swedes to regard their "mixed" economy as very satisfying.

Ownership of Resources

Who owns a nation's farms and factories, its coal mines and forests? Who owns its railways and airways. Who owns its streams and golf courses? Who owns its houses and hotels?

The answers to these questions differ in different countries. One characteristic of the system called capitalism is that the basic raw materials, the productive assets of the society, and the final goods are predominantly privately owned by individuals singly or in groups. By this standard, Canada is predominantly a capitalistic economy, although many of its resources are in fact held in public rather than private hands. It is possible to conceive of a society with full and complete private ownership of resources, but none has ever existed, and we suspect that if it did the citizens would soon get together and buy back from private owners lands to create public parks and buildings to house government offices and the nation's army. In Canada, public ownership extends beyond the usual basic services such as schools, the post office, and local transport systems to include most electric power supplies, health insurance, the Canadian Broadcasting Corporation, Canadian National Railways, and Air Canada. Crown corporations (publicly owned business enterprises) also operate in areas such as mining and chemicals, but the pattern of ownership remains predominantly private.

FIGURE 4–2
Estimated Differences in Ownership Patterns for Selected Countries

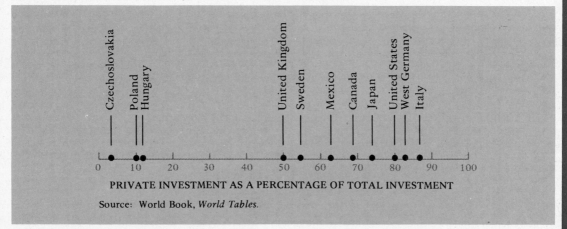

PRIVATE INVESTMENT AS A PERCENTAGE OF TOTAL INVESTMENT

Source: World Book, *World Tables.*

Actual economies never rely solely on private or solely on public investment. These estimates are based on the percentage of gross fixed investment accounted for by the private sector. Such investment provides additions to the stock of productive capital. Private capital investment plays a role even in Communist countries; public capital is a significant part of investment in all countries.

In contrast, socialism envisions a society in which the ownership of productive assets is public. Communism theoretically is opposed to any form of private property. Today there are no completely communistic or socialistic societies. In the Soviet Union, virtually all factories are state-owned and an attempt has been made to collectivize all farms, but though the Soviets officially designate their economy as socialistic, there are three sectors of that economy—agriculture, retail trade, and housing—where some private ownership exists. If the USSR is not a pure socialist economy, it is sufficiently near the public ownership end of the spectrum to distinguish it from Canada and the United States near the private ownership end.

Other countries fall between them on the spectrum. Great Britain has six times in this century elected Labor governments that have been officially committed to socialism to the point of nationalizing key industries: railroads, steel, coal, gas, electricity, atomic power, postal services, telephones, telegraphs, airlines, and some trucking. Although many key industries are publicly owned, the bulk of industries that produce goods and services for household comsumption and capital goods for firms are privately owned and controlled. Ownership patterns are genuinely variable rather than of an either/or variety. Figure 4-2 shows the division of fixed investment between public and private sectors in 11 countries.

With respect to the ownership of resources—and virtually every other dimension of an economy—three basic points are worth remembering.

1. **Every real economy is "mixed" rather than pure.**
2. **Among countries the mixture differs in ways that are appreciable and significant.**
3. **Over time, the mixture changes.**

The Decision Process (Coordinating Principles)

A distinction is sometimes made between two kinds of systems: a *market system,* in which decisions are made impersonally and in a decentralized way by the interaction of individuals in markets, and a *command system,* in which centralized decision makers decide what is to be

TABLE 4-1
Comparative Economic Systems: Ownership and Decision Patterns

Decision pattern	Ownership pattern	
	Predominantly private	Predominantly public
Predominantly decentralized with use of market	United States	Yugoslavia
Predominantly centralized with use of command principle	Nazi Germany	USSR

Each of these combinations of private and public ownership and centralized and decentralized control has occurred in practice. This table is a simplification that highlights differences among economic systems. Ownership and decision patterns are *variables;* it would be an interesting exercise to use a grid that gives several, rather than just two, gradations for each variable and then attempt to place current and past economies in the appropriate cells.

done and issue appropriate commands to achieve the desired results.

Again, no country offers an example of either system working along, but it is true that some economies—those of Canada, the United States, France, and Yugoslavia, for example—rely much more heavily on market decisions than do the economies of East Germany, the Soviet Union, and Cuba. Yet even in Canada the command principle has some sway: minimum wages, quotas on some agricultural outputs, and wartime priorities are obvious examples. More subtle examples concern public expenditures and taxes that in effect transfer command of some resources from private individuals to public officials.

In the planned economies of the Soviet bloc, where plans and targets, quotas and directives are important aspects of the decision-making system, there is substantial command at work. But markets are used too. At the retail level, for example, people can spend their incomes with substantial discretion on a wide variety of goods.

Table 4-1, though it suppresses many subtle distinctions, focuses on important tendencies in certain twentieth century economies by a simple classification according to ownership and decision patterns. The table suggests at once that communist countries such as the USSR and Yugoslavia differ significantly from each other as well as from Canada.

Much economic behavior depends more on the decision pattern than on the ownership pattern. Thus in the United Kingdom, while a large number of key industries are publicly owned, their control is vested in semi-autonomous boards over which Parliament exerts very little control. By and large, the boards try to make their enterprises profitable, and to the extent that they succeed, their behavior will be similar to that of profit-seeking privately owned firms. In predicting their market behavior, economic theorists need not concern themselves with the legal distinction between public and private ownership any more than they need concern themselves with the distinction between corporations and partnerships.

In contrast, firms in Hitler's Germany were under a high degree of state control, even though technically they were privately owned. An attempt to predict their behavior using the profit-maximizing model would not have been successful because the central decision makers guiding their actions were concerned with goals quite different from profit maximization.

WHOSE VALUES?

In the market and command systems different groups make the relevant decisions. It follows that different people's judgments will determine those decisions.

In a capitalistic market economy, dollars "vote." The demands of consumers for goods exert a major influence on the nature of the goods produced. Traditionally this is called consumer sovereignty, but it should be noted both that the rich consumer has more say than the poor one and that firms have a great deal of control over what is and is not produced. In an unfettered market economy, the initial distribution of income and wealth influences the nature of economic decisions because it determines who has the dollars that exercise the effective demands. Mixed economies often use public policies to modify the decisions that would emerge from the uses of private purchasing power, but they are best regarded as supplementing rather than challenging the principle of consumer and producer sovereignty.

Early Marxists attacked the notion of a market-oriented value system. One of the great slogans of the utopian Marxists was "From each according to his ability, to each according to his need." Such a slogan does not solve the allocational problem: in a world in which desires for goods and services exceed the capacity to produce them, someone has to judge who needs what and then take steps to provide it.

In general, in command systems some group must decide what is to be produced and who is to get it. Because no one has yet devised a scheme by which everyone would automatically give according to his or her ability and in which everyone's needs would be clear to all, decisions have to be made. Whoever makes the decisions might do so on the basis of majority preferences, with each person having one vote, regardless of his or her share of the income. (Cooperatives operate on this principle, each *member* having one vote; the contrast with a corporation, where each *share* has one vote, is marked.) Alternatively, each decision maker might decide on the basis of his or her own preferences (autocracy) or those of a particular group. Or the decision maker might decide on the basis of what he or she thinks is "good for the people."

Different systems are likely to reflect the values of different groups. Planned systems reflect the values of the central authorities somewhat more strongly than do market systems.

INCENTIVE SYSTEMS

Psychologists know that people (and most other living creatures) respond to reward and punishment. Incentives may be of two main kinds—the carrot or the stick—and of almost infinite varieties. Direct monetary rewards, in the form of wages or profits or bribes, are well understood. Indirect monetary rewards, such as special housing, vacations, or subsidized education, are not always as readily identified, but they can be effective. Nonmonetary "carrots" include praise, medals, certificates, and applause. Fines, prison terms, and other penalties are used to punish aberrant behavior in all societies; in some societies coercion and fear provide even stronger motivation.

Capitalistic market economies place major reliance on monetary incentives. Monetary incentives to the individual in a socialistic society are not very different from those in a capitalistic economy. Differential earnings for different occupations are used in socialist economies, and piece rates are common. Gifts and bonuses of housing, cars, and other sought-after goods or privileges are used and valued. Large accumulations of assets are not permitted, but the importance of this is in dispute. There are no millionaires in the Soviet Union, but the desire for power is perhaps as important as the desire for wealth in both capitalistic and socialistic societies.

The big difference in incentive systems lies in whether those responsible for production respond to what it is *profitable* to produce or whether they respond to what they are directed to produce. In the first case, profits can provide their own reward in terms of bonuses, salaries, dividends, and perhaps the funds to permit growth and the accumulation of power. In the second case, it is necessary to provide incentives to managers and workers to achieve the assigned quotas.

ENDS AND MEANS

Many, perhaps most people in Western societies value the *means* of the free market and democratic processes even more highly than they value the *ends* of high and rising living standards. Most North Americans distrust the agglomeration of central power and the loss of democratic institutions that accompany communism or any other form of centrally administered command economy. Many believe that there is no need to choose between means and ends because they feel that the free market and democracy produce better results than do alternative systems in terms of both means and ends.

How many Canadians would decide to go over to the Soviet system, even if it could be *proved* that the Soviet system was certain to produce a higher growth rate than the free-market system? In the 1930s it was believed that fascist dictatorships were more efficient than democracies. Mussolini, it was said, "made the Italian trains run on time." It is debatable that the belief was correct, but most people accepted it. Yet few Canadians advocated that Canada become a fascist dictatorship.

In many less-developed countries, ordinary people often put more importance on the ends, higher living standards, than on the means of achieving them. They may regard a change of means per se as unimportant. The choice between a centralized and a decentralized economy may seem to be simply one of which group will exploit them—government officials or powerful monopoly interests. If a highly planned communistic economy offers them a good chance of a 4 percent growth rate, while a democratically oriented market society offers 2 percent, they may well choose the planned society. To warn them that in so choosing they may throw away their freedom is likely to evoke the reply, What has freedom meant to us in the past but the freedom to be hungry and exploited?

COMPARATIVE SYSTEMS: A FINAL WORD

Perhaps the most important empirical observation about different economies is that a wide variety of economic systems seem able to coexist and are successful.

No economic system seems to do everything better than any major competing system; indeed, each has its strengths and weaknesses relative to alternative systems. To talk of "better" and "worse" in this context may itself be misleading: different economic systems imply different choices between current and future consumption, between individual or collective choices, between degrees of freedom or coercion, between stability and growth.

The economic institutions of a society reflect in part its values, but they also reflect habits and traditions, experiments and inertia. These institutions change with time in given countries and vary at a given time among countries. In the variety of experience economists hope to find many clues as to which instruments best achieve which ends.

In the contemporary experience, it looks as if the command principle makes the management of certain macro policies much easier than it is in a market system, but it also appears that it is less well suited than the market to handling micro allocations. While a command system can achieve great sacrifices in the short run, the growth evidence suggests no simple conclusion, for many countries with very different economic systems have achieved rapid growth. It is clear that markets are less personal than bureaucrats, and this makes them more acceptable to many people because they are less arbitrary and less subject to autocratic abuse.

Summary

1. This chapter provides an overview of the workings of the market economy. All modern economies are based on specialization and division of labor, which necessitate the exchange of goods and services. Exchange takes place in markets and is facilitated by the use of money. Much of economics is devoted to a study of how free markets work to coordinate millions of individual, decentralized decisions.

2. In economic theory, three kinds of decision makers—households, firms, and central authori-

ties—interact in markets. It is assumed that households seek to maximize their satisfaction (to the best of their ability) and that firms seek to maximize their profits, but that central authorities may have multiple objectives.

3. A market is defined, for the present, as an area over which buyers and sellers negotiate the exchange of a well-defined commodity. A free-market economy is one in which the allocation of resources is determined by the production, sales, and purchase decisions made by firms and households acting in response to such market signals as prices and profits.

4. Subdivisions of an economy are called sectors. Two common divisions of an economy are into market and nonmarket sectors, and into public and private sectors. These divisions cut across each other; the first is based on the economic distinction of how costs are covered, and the second is based on a legal distinction of ownership.

5. The price system provides a set of signals that reflects changes in demand and supply and to which producers and consumers can react individually but in a nonetheless coordinated manner.

6. The interactions between households and firms through markets are illustrated in a circular-flow diagram that traces both goods and money flows between households and firms. The real flows of goods and services from households to firms and from firms to households play a major role in generating the circular flow of income. This is the key concept of macroeconomics.

7. Not all income received by households is spent for the output of firms, and some income received by firms is not paid out to households. Also some payments to firms do not result from the spending of households, and some payments to households do not result from the spending of firms. The flows of expenditure in the economy determine total output, total income, and total employment.

8. Macroeconomics is largely concerned with what determines the size of the expenditure flows in the economy as a whole. Microeconomics is concerned with behavior in individual markets and the interrelations among markets. Microeconomics and macroeconomics are complementary parts of economic theory. They study different aspects of a single economic system, and both are needed for an understanding of the whole.

9. Actual economies can differ from one another in a great variety of ways, and such capsule characterizations as "capitalism," "socialism," and "communism" represent simplifications of complex matters.

10. Among the important dimensions in which economies can differ from one another are (a) the pattern of ownership of goods and resources; (b) the nature of the decision process used, with a particularly important distinction concerning "command" versus "market" decision mechanisms; (c) whose values control the economy and how these values are articulated; (d) the nature of the incentive systems used; and (e) the relative concern about ends and means.

Topics for Review

Specialization and the division of labor
Economic decision makers
Markets and market economies
The private sector and the public sector
Market and nonmarket sectors
The price system as a social control mechanism
Linkages between firms and households
The circular flow of income
Real flows and money flows
The relation between microeconomics and macroeconomics
Alternative economic systems

Discussion Questions

1. Suggest some examples of specialization and division of labor among people you know.
2. There is a greater variety of specialists and specialty stores in large cities than in small cities having the

same average income of the population. Explain this in economic terms.

3. Define the household of which you are a member. Consider your household's income last year. What proportion of it came from the sale of factor services to firms? Identify the other sources of income. Approximately what proportion of the expenditures by your household became income for firms?

4. "It is not from the benevolence of the butcher, the brewer, or the baker that we expect our dinner, but from their regard to their self-interest. We address ourselves, not to their humanity, but to their self-love, and never talk to them of our necessities, but of their advantages." Do you agree with this quotation from *The Wealth of Nations?* How are "their self-love" and "our dinner" related to the price system? What are assumed to be the motives of firms and of households?

5. Trace the effect of a sharp change in consumer demand away from cigarettes and toward chewing gum as a result of continuing reports linking smoking with lung cancer and heart disease. Can producers of cigarettes do anything to prevent their loss of profits?

6. Make a list of decision makers in the Canadian econ-omy today that do not fit into the categories of firm, household, and central authority. Are you sure that the concept of a firm will not stretch sufficiently to cover some of the items on your list?

7. Consider a major baby boom such as occurred following World War II. Trace out some significant microeconomic and macroeconomic effects of such a boom. Is there a clear line between them in every case?

8. Can you visualize one $20 bill being used in transactions that create $200 of income in one month? If so, how? If not, why not? Can you visualize it not being used in any transactions that create income in one month? If so, how? If not, why not? Do your answers imply that money and income are not related to one another?

9. "What the world of economics needs is an end to ideology and *isms.* If there is a best system of economic organization, it will prove its superiority in its superior ability to solve economic problems." Do you agree with this statement? Would you expect that if the world survives for another 100 years, a single form of economic system would be found superior to all others? Why or why not?

Part Two

A General View of the Price System

Demand, Supply, and Price

5

Some people believe that economics begins and ends with the "law" of supply and demand. It is, of course, too much to hope for "economics in one lesson." (An unkind critic of a book with that title remarked that the author needed a second lesson.) The so-called laws of supply and demand are an important beginning in the attempt to answer vital questions about the workings of a market system.

A first step is to understand what determines the demands for commodities and the supplies of them. Then we can see how supply and demand operate together to determine price and how the price system as a whole allows the economy to reallocate resources in response to changes in demand and in supply. Supply and demand prove to be helpful concepts in discussing both the price system's successes and its failures. They also can be used to discuss the consequences of particular forms of government intervention such as price controls, minimum-wage laws, and sales taxes.

The Basic Theory of Demand

Canadian consumers spent about $150 billion on goods and services in 1979. What was it spent on, and why? Table 5-1 shows the composition of this expenditure and how it has changed in 25 years. Economists ask many questions about the pattern of consumer expenditure: Why is it what it is at any moment of time? Why does it change in the way it does? Why did the fraction of total consumer expenditure for food decline from more than one-fourth in 1930 to less than one-sixth today? Why did Canadian consumers allocate about 6 percent of their total expenditure to automobile transportation in 1930 and over 10 percent in the 1960s? (In the period 1942–1945 they spent less than 4 percent on automobile transportation and purchases of new cars fell almost to zero. Why?) Why do Canadians now heat their homes with electricity, oil, and natural gas whereas twenty years ago they used coal? Why do people who build houses in Norway and western North America rarely use brick while it is commonly used in Great Britain and eastern North America? Why have the maid and the washerwoman been increasingly replaced by the vacuum cleaner and the washing machine?

THE NATURE OF QUANTITY DEMANDED

The total amount of a commodity that all households wish to purchase is called the **quantity demanded** of that commodity.[1] It is important to notice three things about this concept. First, quantity demanded is a *desired* quantity. It is how much households are willing to purchase, given the price of the commodity, other prices, their incomes, tastes, and so on. This may be a different amount than households actually succeed in purchasing. If sufficient quantities are not available, the amount households wish to purchase may exceed the amount they actually do purchase. To distinguish these two concepts, the term *quantity demanded* is used to refer to desired purchases, and phrases such as **quantity actually bought,** or **quantity exchanged** are used to refer to actual purchases.

Second, *desired* does not refer to idle dreams or future possibilities but to effective demands — that is, to the amounts people are willing to *buy* given the price they must pay for the commodity.

---

[1] In this chapter we concentrate on the demand of *all* households for commodities. Of course, what all households do is only the sum of what each individual household does, and in Part Three we shall study the behavior of individual households in greater detail.

TABLE 5–1
Composition of Personal Consumption Expenditures, 1951 and 1976-1979 (Percentages)

	1951	1976-1979
Durable goods	11.9	15.1
Automobile and parts	6.5	7.9
Furniture and household equipment	3.9	4.9
Other	1.5	2.3
Semidurable goods	16.9	12.6
Clothing and footwear	10.5	7.2
Other	6.4	5.4
Nondurable goods	39.7	30.9
Food	22.9	15.1
Electricity, gas, and other fuels	3.8	3.7
Gasoline, oil, and grease	2.3	5.7
Other	10.7	6.7
Services	31.5	41.4
Housing and household services	12.5	14.0
Health services	3.1	2.9
Other	15.9	24.5

Source: Statistics Canada, 13–531, 13–20; Department of Finance, *Economic Review.*

The declining relative importance of food and clothing and the rising importance of gasoline and oil and services of all kinds stand out.

For persons intending to spend $100 this year on a commodity whose price is $20, the quantity demanded is 5 units even though they would prefer to consume much more if only they did not have to pay for it.

Third, quantity demanded refers to a continuous *flow* of purchases. It must therefore be expressed as so much per period of time: 1 million oranges *per day,* 7 million *per week,* or 365 million *per year.* If you were told, for example, that the quantity of new television sets demanded (at current prices) in Canada was 100,000, this would mean nothing until you were also told the period of time involved. One hundred thousand television sets demanded *per day* would be an enormous rate of demand; 500,000 *per year* would be a very small rate. (The important distinction between stocks and flows was discussed in the box on page 26.)

WHAT DETERMINES QUANTITY DEMANDED?

How much of some commodity will all households be willing to buy per month? This amount will be influenced by a number of variables. The following are the most important. [2]

1. The commodity's own price.
2. The prices of related commodities.
3. Average household income.
4. Tastes.
5. The distribution of income among households.
6. The size of the population.

This list of variables that influence the quantity of a commodity demanded is even longer than it looks, for *many* prices are covered under the second point. We can neither develop a simple theory nor understand the separate influence of each variable if we start by trying to consider what happens when everything changes at once.

Fortunately, there is an easier way: We can consider the influence of the variables one at a time. To do this, we hold all but one of them constant. Then we let that one selected variable vary and study how it affects quantity demanded. We can do the same for each of the other variables in turn, and in this way we can come to understand the importance of each.[2] Once this is done, we can aggregate the separate influences of two or more variables to discover what would happen if several things changed at the same time—as they often do in practice.

Holding all other influencing variables constant is often described by the words "other things being equal" or by the equivalent Latin phrase, *ceteris paribus*. When economists speak of the influence of the price of wheat on the quan-

tity of wheat demanded *ceteris paribus*, they refer to what a change in the price of wheat would do to the quantity demanded if all other factors that influence the demand for wheat did not change.

DEMAND AND PRICE

We are interested in developing a theory of how commodities get priced. Thus we are necessarily interested in the influence on quantity demanded of each commodity's own price. We begin by holding all other influences constant and asking: How do we expect the quantity of a commodity demanded to vary as its own price varies?

A basic economic hypothesis is that the lower the price of a commodity, the larger the quantity that will be demanded, other things being equal.

Why might this be so? Commodities are used to satisfy desires and needs, and there is almost always more than one commodity that will satisfy any given desire or need. Such commodities compete with one another for the purchasers' attention. Hunger may be satisfied by meat or vegetables, a desire for green vegetables by broccoli or spinach. The need to keep warm at night may be satisfied by several woollen blankets or one electric blanket, or for that matter by a sheet and a lot of oil burned in the furnace. The desire for a vacation may be satisfied by a trip to the lake or to the mountains, the need to get there by different airlines, a bus, a car, even a train. And so it goes: Name any general desire or need, and there will be at least two and often dozens of different commodities that will satisfy it. Even something so basic as the body's need for fluid may be satisfied by drinking water, tea, coffee, Coke, 7-Up, lemonade, beer, and so on.

We can now see what happens if we hold income, tastes, population, and the prices of all other commodities constant and vary only the price of one commodity. As that price goes up, the commodity becomes an increasingly expensive way to satisfy a want. Some households will stop buying it altogether; others will buy smaller amounts; still others will continue to buy the same quantity. Because many households will

---

[2] A relation in which many variables—in this case average income, population, tastes, and many prices—influence a single variable—in this case quantity demanded—is called a *multivariate* relation. The technique of studying the effect of each of the influencing variables one at a time, while holding the other variables constant, is common in science and mathematics. Indeed it is such a common procedure that there is a mathematical concept, the partial derivative, explicitly designed to accomplish this task.

switch wholly or partially to other commodities to satisfy the same want, it follows that less will be bought of any commodity whose price has risen. As meat becomes more expensive, for example, households may switch to some extent to meat substitutes; they may also forgo meat at some meals and eat less meat at others. As carrots get increasingly expensive, people may switch to brussels sprouts or broccoli to satisfy their desire for vegetables.

Alternatively, a fall in a commodity's price makes it a cheaper method of satisfying a want. Purchasers as a whole will buy more of it. Consequently they will buy less of similar commodities whose prices have not fallen and which as a result have become expensive *relative to* the commodity in question. As pocket calculators have fallen in price over the last 10 or 15 years, more and more of them have been purchased. When a bumper tomato harvest drives prices down, shoppers switch to tomatoes and cut their purchases of many other vegetables that now look relatively more expensive.

THE DEMAND SCHEDULE AND THE DEMAND CURVE

How can the relationship between quantity demanded and price be portrayed? One method is to use a **demand schedule.** This is a numerical tabulation showing the quantity that is demanded at selected prices.

Table 5-2 is a hypothetical demand schedule for carrots. It lists the quantity of carrots that would be demanded at various prices on the assumption that average household income is fixed at $20,000 (and that tastes and all other prices do not change.) The table gives the quantities demanded for six selected prices, but actually there is a separate quantity that would be demanded at each possible price from one cent to several hundreds of dollars.

A second method of showing the relation between quantity demanded and price is to draw a graph. The six price-quantity combinations shown in Table 5-2 are plotted on the graph shown in Figure 5-1, which has price on the vertical axis

TABLE 5–2
A Demand Schedule for Carrots

	Price per ton p	Quantity demanded when average household income is $20,000 per year (thousands of tons per months) D
U	$ 20	110.0
V	40	90.0
W	60	77.5
X	80	67.5
Y	100	62.5
Z	120	60.0

The table shows the quantity of carrots that would be demanded at various prices, *ceteris paribus.* Row W indicates that if the price of carrots were $60 per ton, consumers would desire to purchase 77,500 tons of carrots per month, given the values of other variables that may affect quantity demanded (such as average household income).

FIGURE 5–1
A Demand Curve for Carrots

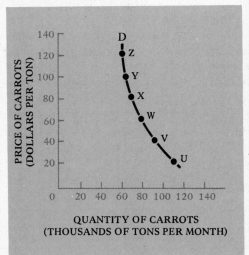

This demand curve relates quantity demanded to the price of carrots; its downward slope indicates that quantity demanded increases as price falls. There are six points corresponding to the price-quantity combinations shown in Table 5-2. Each row in the table defines a point on the demand curve. The smooth curve drawn through all of the points and labeled *D* is the demand curve.

and quantity on the horizontal axis. The smooth curve drawn through these points is called a **demand curve.** It shows the quantity of carrots that purchasers would like to buy at each price. The curve slopes downward to the right; this indicates that the quantity demanded increases as the price falls.

A single point on the demand curve indicates a single price-quantity combination. Notice that while any point on the demand curve represents a specific quantity demanded, the demand curve as a whole shows more.

The whole demand curve represents the complete relation between quantity demanded and price, other things being equal.

When economists speak of the conditions of demand in a particular market as being given or known, they are referring not just to the particular quantity being demanded at the moment (i.e., not just to a particular point on the demand curve) but to the entire demand curve—to the complete functional relation whereby desired purchases are related to all the possible alternative prices of the commodity.

Thus the term **demand** refers to the entire relation between price and quantity (as shown, for example, by the schedule in Table 5-2 or the curve in Figure 5-1). In contrast, a single point on a demand schedule or curve is the *quantity demanded* at that point (for example, at point W in Figure 5-1, 77,500 tons of carrots a month are demanded at a price of $60 a ton).

Shifts in the Demand Curve

The demand schedule is drawn up, and the demand curve plotted, on the assumption of *ceteris paribus.* But what if other things change, as surely they must? What, for example, if households find themselves with more income? If households spend their extra income, they will buy additional quantities of commodities *even though prices have not changed.*

But if households increase their purchases of any one commodity whose price has not changed, the purchases cannot be represented on

the original demand curve. When they are represented on a new demand curve, the new curve must be to the right of the old curve. Thus the rise in household income has shifted the demand curve to the right. This illustrates the operation of an important general rule.

A demand curve is drawn on the assumption that everything except the commodity's own price is held constant. A change in any of the variables previously held constant will shift the demand curve to a new position.

A demand curve can shift in many ways; two of them are particularly important. If more is bought at *each* price, the demand curve shifts right so that each price corresponds to a higher quantity than it did before. If less is bought at *each* price, the demand curve shifts left so that each price corresponds to a lower quantity than it did before.

The influence of changes in variables other

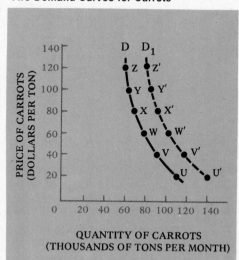

FIGURE 5-2
Two Demand Curves for Carrots

QUANTITY OF CARROTS
(THOUSANDS OF TONS PER MONTH)

The rightward shift in the demand curve from *D* to *D₁* indicates an increase in the quantity demanded at each price. The lettered points correspond to those in Table 5-3. A rightward shift in the demand curve indicates an increase in demand in the sense that more is demanded at each price and that a higher price would be paid for each quantity.

TABLE 5–3
Two Alternative Demand Schedules for Carrots

Price per ton p	Quantity demanded when average household income is $20,000 per year (thousands of tons per month) D		Quantity demanded when average income is $24,000 per year (thousands of tons per months) D_1	
$20	110.0	(U)	140.0	(U')
40	90.0	(V)	116.0	(V')
60	77.5	(W)	100.8	(W')
80	67.5	(X)	87.5	(X')
100	62.5	(Y)	81.3	(Y')
120	60.0	(Z)	78.0	(Z')

An increase in average income increases the quantity demanded at each price. When average income rises from $20,000 to $24,000 per year, quantity demanded at a price of $60 per ton rises from 77,500 tons per month to 100,800 tons per month. A similar rise occurs at every other price.

Thus the demand schedule relating columns p and D is replaced by one relating columns p and D_1. The graphical representations of these two functions are labeled D and D_1 in Figure 5–2.

than price may now be studied by determining how changes in each variable shift the demand curve. Any change will shift the demand curve to the right if it increases the amount people wish to buy, other things remaining equal, and to the left if it decreases the amount households wish to buy, other things remaining equal.

Average household income. If the income of the average household increases, households can be expected to purchase more of most commodities even though commodity prices remain the same. Considering all households, we expect that no matter what price we pick, more of any commodity will be demanded than was previously demanded at the same price. This shift is illustrated in Table 5-3 and Figure 5-2.

A rise in average household income shifts the demand curve for most commodities to the right. This indicates that more will be demanded at each possible price.

Other prices. We saw that the downward slope of a commodity's demand curve occurs because the lower its price, the cheaper the commodity is, relative to other commodities that can satisfy the same needs or desires. Those other commodities are called **substitutes.** Another way to accomplish the same change in relative cheapness is for the price of the substitute commodity to rise. For

example, carrots can be made cheap relative to cabbage either by lowering the price of carrots or by raising the price of cabbage. Either change will tend to increase the amount of carrots households are prepared to buy.

A rise in the price of a substitute for a commodity shifts the demand curve for the commodity to the right. More will be purchased at each price.

For example, a rise in the price of a substitute for carrots could shift the demand curve for carrots from D to D_1 in Figure 5-2.

Another class of commodities is called **complements.** These are commodities that tend to be used jointly with each other. Cars and gasoline are complements; so are golf clubs and golf balls, electric stoves and electricity, an airplane trip to Banff and lift tickets on the mountain. Since complements tend to be consumed together, a fall in the price of either will increase the demand for both.

A fall in the price of a complementary commodity will shift a commodity's demand curve to the right. More will be purchased at each price.

For example, a fall in the price of airplane trips to Banff will lead to a rise in the demand for lift tickets at Banff even though their price is unchanged.

Tastes. Tastes have a large effect on people's desired purchases. A change in tastes may be long lasting, such as the shift from fountain pens to ball-point pens or from slide rules to pocket calculators. Or it may be a short-lived fad such as the craze for hula hoops or pet rocks. In either case a change in tastes in favor of a commodity shifts the demand curve to the right. More will be bought at each price.

Distribution of income. If a constant total of income is redistributed among the population, demands may change. If, for example, the government increases the deductions for children on the income tax and compensates by raising basic tax rates, income will be transferred from childless persons to heads of large families. The type of commodity more heavily bought by the childless will decline in demand, while that bought by those with large families will increase in demand.

A change in the distribution of income will shift to the right the demand curves for commodities bought most by those gaining income. On the other hand, it will shift to the left the demand curves for commodities bought most by people losing income.

Population. Population growth does not by itself create new demand. The additional people must have purchasing power before demand is changed. Extra people of working age, however, usually means extra output, and if they produce, they will earn income. When this happens, the demand for all the commodities purchased by the new income earners will rise. Thus it is usually (although not always) true that:

A rise in population will shift the demand curves for commodities to the right, indicating that more will be bought at each price.

These shifts are summarized in Figure 5-3 and its caption.

Movements Along the Demand Curve Versus Shifts of the Whole Curve

Suppose you read in today's newspaper that the rising price of housing has caused a declining

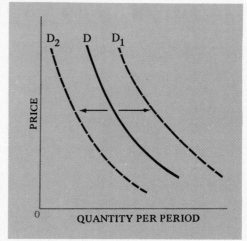

FIGURE 5–3
Shifts in the Demand Curve

A shift in the demand curve from *D* to *D₁* indicates an increase in demand; a shift from *D* to *D₂* indicates a decrease in demand. An increase in demand means more is demanded at each price. Such a rightward shift can be caused by a rise in income, a rise in the price of a substitute, a fall in the price of a complement, a change in tastes in favor of the commodity, an increase in population, and a redistribution of income toward groups who favor the commodity.

A decrease in demand means less is demanded at each price. Such a leftward shift can be caused by a fall in income, a fall in the price of a substitute, a rise in the price of a complement, a change in tastes against the commodity, a decrease in population, and a redistribution of income away from groups who favor the commodity.

demand as people have found ways of economizing on their use of housing. Then tomorrow you read that the rising price of housing has been caused by a rising demand for housing. The two statements appear to contradict each other. The first associates a rising price with a declining demand, the second associates a rising price with a rising demand. How can both statements be true? The answer is that they refer to different things. The first describes a movement along a demand curve in response to a change in price;

the second describes a shift in the whole demand curve. Using the words "rising demand" or "declining demand" in each case can only cause confusion.

Consider first the statement that less is being bought because it has become more expensive. This refers to a movement along a given demand curve, to a change between two specific quantities being bought, one before the price rose and one afterward. Any one point on a demand curve represents a specific amount being bought at a specified price. It represents, therefore, a particular quantity demanded. A movement along a demand curve is referred to as a change in the quantity demanded. [3]

A movement down a demand curve is called an increase (or a rise) in the quantity demanded; a movement up the demand curve is called a decrease (or a fall) in the quantity demanded.

Now consider the shift in demand. We have seen that *demand* refers to the whole demand curve. Economists reserve the term **change in demand** to describe a shift in the whole curve — that is, a change in the amount that will be bought at *every* price.

An *increase in the demand* means that the whole demand curve has shifted to the right; a *fall in demand* means that the whole demand curve has shifted to the left.

To illustrate this terminology, look again at Table 5-3. When average income is $20,000, an increase in price from $60 to $80 decreases the *quantity demanded* from 77.5 to 67.5 thousand tons a month. An increase in average income from $20,000 to $24,000 increases *demand* from D to D_1.

The Basic Theory of Supply

The Canadian economy produced goods and services worth $260 billion in 1979. A broad classification of *what* was produced is given in Table 5-4. Economists have as many questions to ask about production and its changing composition

as they do about consumption. The percentage distributions in Table 5-4 illustrate some of the basic changes in composition of output. Even more dramatic changes are visible in more detailed data.

For example, through the 1960s and early 1970s the chemical, petroleum, and electrical products industries all grew in relative importance. In the mid seventies, export-oriented industries such as forest products, primary metals, and transportation equipment all suffered declines. And at the end of the decade investment-oriented industries such as machinery, electrical products, and metal fabricating were growing rapidly.

Economists want to know why. Why did the aluminum industry grow faster than the steel industry? Why, even within a single industry, did some firms prosper and grow, others hold their

TABLE 5–4

Domestic Product by Industry of Origin, Selected Years (Percentage Distribution)

Industry group[a]	1961	1971	1979
	Percentage distribution		
Agriculture, forestry, fishing, and trapping	6.6	4.6	3.8
Mining, quarrying, and oil wells	4.7	4.1	3.4
Manufacturing	26.8	24.6	23.7
Construction	6.3	7.6	6.7
Transportation, storage, and communication	10.8	9.8	11.0
Utilities	3.0	2.9	3.5
Wholesale and retail trade	13.8	12.5	13.0
Finance, insurance, and real estate	13.0	12.8	14.1
Other Services	15.0	21.1	20.8
Total	100.0	100.0	100.0

Source: Statistics Canada, 11–003, 13–201.
[a] Excluding government and government enterprises.

Since 1961 agriculture, mining, and manufacturing have all declined in relative importance, while utilities, finance, and services have gained. Construction, transportation, and trade show considerable fluctuation with no evident trend.

own, and still others decline and fail? Why and how do firms and industries come into being? All these questions and many others are aspects of a single question: *What determines the quantities of commodities that firms will produce and offer for sale?*

Full discussion of these questions of supply will come later (in Part Five). For now it is enough (1) to develop the basic relation between the price of a commodity and the quantity that will be produced and offered for sale by firms and (2) to understand what forces lead to shifts in this relationship.

Much of what needs to be said about supply parallels what we have said about demand.

THE NATURE OF QUANTITY SUPPLIED

The amount of a commodity that firms wish to sell is the **quantity supplied** of that commodity. This is the amount that firms are willing to offer for sale; it is not necessarily the amount they succeed in selling. The term **quantity actually sold** or **quantity exchanged** indicates what they actually succeed in selling. Quantity supplied is a flow: it is so much per unit of time, per day, per week, or per year.

Notice that while we use different terms (quantity demanded and quantity supplied) to distinguish desired purchases from desired sales, we use the same term, *quantity exchanged,* to describe actual purchases and actual sales. This reflects an important fact of life: although households may desire to purchase an amount that differs from what sellers desire to sell, they cannot succeed in buying what someone else does not sell. A purchase and a sale are merely two sides of the same transaction. Looked at from the buyer's side, there is a purchase; looked at from the seller's side, there is a sale.

Since desired purchases do not have to equal desired sales, different terms are needed to describe the two separate amounts. But because the quantity actually purchased must be the same amount as the quantity actually sold, both can be described by a single term, quantity exchanged.

WHAT DETERMINES QUANTITY SUPPLIED?

How much of a commodity will firms be willing to produce and offer for sale? The amount will be influenced by a number of variables. The following are the most important: [4]

1. The commodity's own price.
2. The prices of other commodities.
3. The costs of factors of production.
4. The goals of the firm.
5. The state of technology.

The situation is the same here as it is on the demand side. The list of influencing variables is long, and we will not get far if we try to discover what happens when they all change at the same time. So again we use the very convenient *ceteris paribus* technique to study the influence of the variables one at a time.

SUPPLY AND PRICE

Since we want to develop a theory of how commodities get priced, we are necessarily interested in the influence on quantity supplied of a commodity's own price. We start by holding all other influences constant and asking: How do we expect the quantity of a commodity supplied to vary with its own price?

A basic economic hypothesis is that for many commodities the higher their price, the larger the quantity that will be supplied, other things being equal.

Why might this be so? It is because the profits that can be earned from producing a commodity are almost certain to increase if the price of that commodity rises while the costs of factors used to produce it remain unchanged. Furthermore, if the prices of other commodities remain unchanged, the profits that can be earned by producing them will be unchanged, and as a result there will be a rise in *relative* profitability of producing the commodity whose price has risen. This will make firms, which are in business to earn profits, wish to produce more of the commodity whose price has risen and less of other commodities.

Notice, however, the qualifying word "many" in the hypothesis stated above. "Many" is used because, as we shall see in Part Five, there are exceptions to this rule. Although the rule states the usual case, a rise in price (*ceteris paribus*) is not always necessary to call forth an increase in quantity in the case of all commodities.

THE SUPPLY SCHEDULE AND THE SUPPLY CURVE

The general relationship just discussed can be illustrated by a supply schedule that shows the quantities that producers would wish to sell at alternative prices of the commodity. A **supply schedule** is analogous to a demand schedule: the former shows what producers would be willing to sell, while the latter shows what households would be willing to buy at alternative prices of the commodity. Table 5-5 presents a hypothetical supply schedule for carrots.

A **supply curve,** the graphic representation of the supply schedule, is illustrated in Figure 5-4. Once again, while each point on the supply curve represents a specific price-quantity combination, the whole curve shows more.

The whole supply curve represents the complete relation between quantity supplied and price, other things being equal.

TABLE 5-5
A Supply Schedule for Carrots

	Price per ton *p*	Quantity supplied (thousands of tons per month) *S*
u	$ 20	5.0
v	40	46.0
w	60	77.5
x	80	100.0
y	100	115.0
z	120	122.5

The table shows the quantities that producers wish to sell at various prices, *certeris paribus.* For example, row y indicates that if the price were $100 per ton, producers would wish to sell 115,000 tons of carrots per month.

When economists speak of the conditions of supply as being given or known, they refer not just to the particular quantity being supplied at the moment (that is, not to just a particular point on the supply curve) but to the entire supply curve, to the complete functional relation by which desired sales are related to all possible alternative prices of the commodity.

Supply refers to the entire relation between supply and price. A single point on the supply schedule or curve refers to the *quantity supplied* at that price.

Shifts in the Supply Curve

A shift in the supply curve means that at each price a different quantity will be supplied than previously. An increase in the quantity supplied at each price is shown in Table 5-6 and graphed

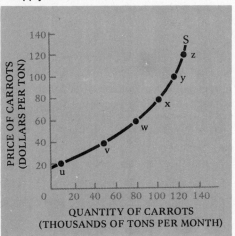

FIGURE 5–4
A Supply Curve for Carrots

This supply curve relates quantity supplied to the price of carrots; its upward slope indicates that quantity supplied increases as price increases. There are six points corresponding to the price-quantity combinations shown in Table 5-5. Each row in the table defines a point on the supply curve. The smooth curve drawn through all of the points and labeled *S* is the supply curve.

TABLE 5–6
Two Alternative Supply Schedules for Carrots

Price per ton p	Quantity supplied before cost-saving innovation (thousands of tons per month) S		Quantity supplied after the innovation (thousands of tons per month) S_1	
$ 20	5.0	u'	28.0	u'
40	46.0	v'	76.0	v'
60	77.5	w'	102.0	w'
80	100.0	x'	120.0	x'
100	115.0	y'	132.0	y'
120	122.5	z'	140.0	z'

A cost-saving innovation increases the quantity supplied at each price. As a result of the cost-saving innovation, quantity supplied at $100 per ton rises from 115,000 to 132,000 tons per month. A similar rise occurs at every price. Thus the supply schedule relating p and S is replaced by one relating p and S_1.

in Figure 5-5. This change appears as a rightward shift in the supply curve. In contrast, a decrease in the quantity supplied at each price would appear as a leftward shift. A shift in the supply curve must be the result of a change in one of the factors that influence the quantity supplied other than the commodity's own price. The major possible causes of such shifts are summarized in the caption of Figure 5-6 and are considered briefly below.

For supply, as for demand, there is an important general rule.

A change in any of the variables (other than the commodity's own price) that affect the amount of a commodity that firms are willing to produce and offer for sale will shift the whole supply curve for that commodity.

Other prices. Commodities may be substitutes or complements in production as well as in consumption. Land that grows wheat can also grow corn, or it can be used to raise hogs. Suppose the price of corn falls and as a result corn is less profitable to produce. Some farmers will shift from corn to wheat production. Thus a fall in the price of corn may shift the supply curve of wheat to the right, indicating that at each price of wheat more will be supplied than before.

Since commodities are alternative outputs for producers, a fall in the price of one commodity may shift the supply curve of another to the right.

Prices of factors of production. The price paid for a factor of production is a cost to a firm that

FIGURE 5–5
Two Supply Curves for Carrots

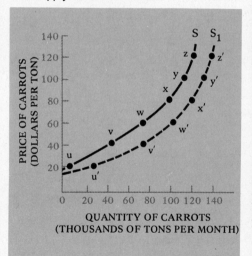

The rightward shift in the supply curve from S to S_1 indicates an increase in the quantity supplied at each price. The lettered points correspond to those in Table 5-6. A rightward shift in the supply curve indicates an increase in supply in the sense that more carrots are supplied at each price.

FIGURE 5-6
Shifts in the Supply Curve

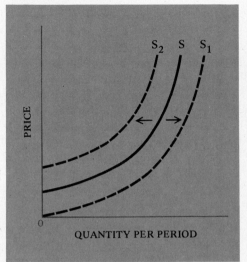

A shift in the supply curve from S to S_1 indicates an increase in supply; a shift from S to S_2 indicates a decrease in supply. An increase in supply means more is supplied at each price. Such a rightward shift can be caused by some kinds of changes in producers' goals, improvements in technology, decreases in the prices of other commodities, and decreases in the prices of factors of production that are important in producing the commodity.

A decrease in supply means less is supplied at each price. Such a leftward shift can be caused by some kinds of changes in producers' goals, increases in the prices of other commodities, and increases in the prices of factors of production that are important in producing the commodity.

uses it. A change in factor prices changes the quantity that producers will be willing to offer for sale because it changes costs and hence profits. Just as profits are increased by an *increase* in the commodity's price, factor costs remaining constant, so are they increased by a fall in factor prices, the price of the commodity remaining constant. A rise in factor prices reduces the profitability of a commodity at any given price of that commodity. The initial profitability can be restored only if the price of the commodity rises.

A rise in the costs of factors of production shifts to the left the supply curve of a commodity that uses that factor, indicating that less will be supplied at any given price.

The goals of the firm. In elementary economic theory, the firm is assumed to have the single goal of profit maximization. Firms might, however, have other goals either in addition to or as substitutes for profit maximization. If the firm worries about risk, it will pursue safer lines of activity even though they promise lower probable profits. If the firm values size, it may produce and sell more than the profit-maximizing quantities. If it worries about its image in society, it may forsake highly profitable activities (such as the production of napalm) when there is major public disapproval. However, as long as the firm prefers more profits to less, it will respond to changes in the profitabilities of alternative lines of action, and supply curves will slope upward.

A change in the importance that firms give to other goals will shift the supply curve one way or the other, indicating a changed willingness to supply the quantity at any given price and hence a changed level of profitability.

Technology. At any time, what is produced and how it is produced depends on what is known. Over time knowledge changes; so do the quantities of individual commodities supplied. The enormous increase in production per worker that has been going on in industrial societies for about 200 years is largely due to improved methods of production. Yet the Industrial Revolution is more than a historical event; it is a present reality. Discoveries in chemistry have led to lower costs of production of well-established products, such as paints, and to a large variety of new products made of plastics and synthetic fibers. The invention of transistors and silicon chips has revolutionized production in television, high-fidelity equipment, computers, and guidance-control systems.

Any technological change that decreases production costs will increase the profits that can be earned at any given price of the commodity.

Since increased profitability tends to lead to increased production, this change will shift the supply curve to the right, indicating an increased willingness to produce the commodity and offer it for sale at each possible price.

Movements Along the Supply Curve Versus Shifts of the Whole Curve

As with demand, it is important to distinguish movements along supply curves from shifts of the whole curve. The term **change in supply** is reserved for a shift of the whole supply curve. This means a change in the quantity supplied at each price of the commodity. A movement along the supply curve indicates a *change in the quantity supplied* in response to a change in the price of the commodity. Thus an *increase in supply* means that the whole supply curve has shifted to the right; an *increase in the quantity supplied* means a movement upward to the right along a given supply curve.

The Determination of Price by Demand and Supply

So far demand and supply have been considered separately. The next question is: How do the two forces interact to determine price in a competi-

tive market? The theory that answers this question is called **price theory.** (In developing this theory we shall continue, until the final section of this chapter, with the simplifying assumption that all forces that might influence demand or supply, other than the commodity's own price, are held constant.)

Table 5-7 brings together the demand and supply schedules from Tables 5-2 and 5-5. The quantities of carrots demanded and supplied at each price may now be compared (see column 4 of Table 5-7).

There is only one price, $60 a ton, at which the quantity of carrots demanded equals the quantity supplied. At prices of less than $60 a ton there is a shortage of carrots because the quantity demanded exceeds the quantity supplied. This is often called a situation of **excess demand** or, what is the same thing, one of deficient supply. At prices greater than $60 a ton there is a surplus of carrots because the quantity supplied exceeds the quantity demanded. This is called a situation of **excess supply** or one of deficient demand.

In order to discuss the determination of market price, suppose first that the price is $100 a ton. At this price, 115,000 tons would be offered for sale but only 62,500 tons would be demanded. There would be excess supply of 52,500 tons a month. We assume that sellers will then cut their prices in order to get rid of this

TABLE 5-7
Demand and Supply Schedules for Carrots and Equilibrium Price

(1) Price per ton p	(2) Quantity demanded (thousands of tons per month) D	(3) Quantity supplied (thousands of tons per month) S	(4) Excess demand (+) Excess supply (−) (thousands of tons per month) $D - S$
$ 20	110.0	5.0	+105.0
40	90.0	46.0	+ 44.0
60	77.5	77.5	0.0
80	67.5	100.0	− 32.5
100	62.5	115.0	− 52.5
120	60.0	122.5	− 62.5

Equilibrium occurs where quantity demanded equals quantity supplied—where there is neither excess demand nor supply. These schedules are those of Tables 5-2 and 5-5. The equilibrium price is $60. For lower prices there is excess demand; for higher prices there is excess supply.

surplus and that purchasers, observing the stock of unsold carrots, will offer less for what they are prepared to buy.

The tendency for buyers to offer, and sellers to ask for, lower prices when there is excess supply implies a downward pressure on price.

Next consider the price of $20 a ton. At this price, there is excess demand. The 5,000 tons produced each month are snapped up very quickly, and 105,000 tons of desired purchases cannot be made. Rivalry between would-be purchasers may lead to their offering more than the prevailing price in order to outbid other purchasers. Also, perceiving that they could have sold their available supplies many times

over, sellers may begin to ask a higher price for the quantities that they do have to sell.

The tendency for buyers to offer, and sellers to ask for, higher prices when there is excess demand implies an upward pressure on price.

Finally, consider a price of $60. At this price, producers wish to sell 77,500 tons a month and purchasers wish to buy that quantity. There is neither a shortage nor a surplus of carrots. There are no unsatisfied buyers to bid the price up, nor are there unsatisfied sellers to force the price down. Once the price of $60 has been reached, therefore, there will be no tendency for it to change.

An equilibrium implies a state of rest, or bal-

Supply and Demand: What Really Happens

"The theory of supply and demand is neat enough," said the skeptic, "but tell me what really happens."

"What really happens," said the economist, "is that first, demand curves slope downward; second, supply curves slope upward; third, prices rise in response to excess demand; and fourth, prices fall in response to excess supply."

"But that's theory," insists the skeptic. "What about reality?"

"That is reality as well," said the economist.

"Show me," said the skeptic.

The economist produced the following passages from recent newspaper articles.

Increased demand for macadamia nuts causes price to rise above competing nuts. Major producer now plans to double the size of its orchards during the next five years.

* * *

The ghost town of de Lamar, Idaho, is a mute witness to the recent unprofitability of silver min-

ing. But now silver is stirring again. Prices rose between 1970 and 1979 from $1.30 an ounce to about $50.00, making it economical to begin mining again. De Lamar is now coming back in production at a rate that is expected soon to make it the third largest silver producer in the U.S.

* * *

The average price of cocoa beans has dropped about 50 cents a pound since last November because of increases in supplies.

* * *

The effects of [the first year of] the deregulation of U.S. airlines have been spectacular: cuts in air fares of up to 70 percent in some cases, record passenger jam-ups at the airports, and a spectacular increase in the average load factor [the proportion of occupied seats on the average commercial flight]. (In the second year of airline deregulation airline prices have risen substantially as airlines passed on the rising cost of aviation fuel.)

The skeptic's response is not recorded, but you will have no trouble telling which clippings illustrate which of the economist's four statements about "what really happens."

ance, between opposing forces. The **equilibrium price** is the one toward which the actual market price will tend. It will persist once established, unless it is disturbed by some change in market conditions.

The price at which the quantity demanded equals the quantity supplied is called the equilibrium price.

Any other price is called a **disequilibrium price**: quantity demanded does not equal quantity supplied, and price will be changing. A market that exhibits excess demand or excess supply is said to be in a state of **disequilibrium.**

When the market is in equilibrium, quantity demanded equals quantity supplied. Anything that must be true if equilibrium is to be obtained is called an **equilibrium condition.** In the competitive market, the equality of quantity demanded and quantity supplied is an equilibrium condition. **[5]**

This same story is told in graphic terms in Figure 5-7. The price of $60 is the equilibrium price because there is neither excess supply nor excess demand. All other prices are disequilibrium prices, and if they occur, the market will not be in a state of rest. At prices below the equilibrium, there will be shortages and rising prices; at prices above the equilibrium, there will be surpluses and falling prices.

The quantities demanded and supplied at any price can be read off the two curves, while the magnitude of the shortage or surplus is shown by the horizontal distance between the curves at each price. The figure makes it clear that the equilibrium price occurs where the demand and supply curves intersect. Below that price there will be a shortage and hence an upward pressure on the existing price. Above it there will be a surplus and hence a downward pressure on price. These pressures are represented by the vertical arrows in the figure.

THE "LAWS" OF SUPPLY AND DEMAND

Changes in any of the variables other than price that influence quantity demanded or supplied will

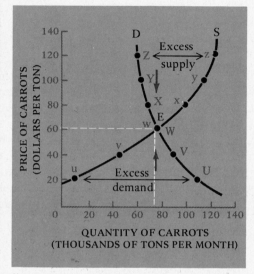

FIGURE 5-7

The Determination of the Equilibrium Price of Carrots

The equilibrium price corresponds to the point where demand and supply curves intersect. Point *E* indicates the equilibrium. At a price of $60, quantity demanded equals quantity supplied. At prices above the equilibrium, there is excess supply and downward pressure on price. At prices below equilibrium, there is excess demand and upward pressure on price.

cause a shift in either the supply curve or the demand curve (or both). There are four possible shifts: (1) a rise in demand (a rightward shift in the demand curve); (2) a fall in demand (a leftward shift in the demand curve); (3) a rise in supply (a rightward shift in the supply curve); and (4) a fall in supply (a leftward shift in the supply curve).

To analyze the effects of any of these shifts we use the method known as **comparative statics.** We start from a position of equilibrium and then introduce the change to be studied. The new equilibrium position is determined and compared with the original one. The differences between the two positions of equilibrium must be due to the changes in the data that were introduced—for everything else has been held constant. The term is *comparative statics* because the method of an-

FIGURE 5-8
The "Laws" of Supply and Demand

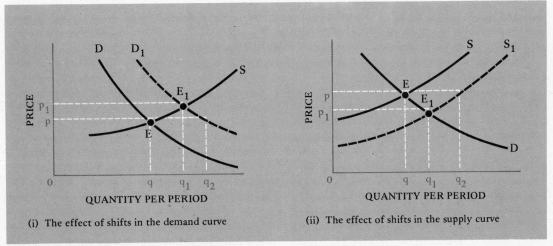

(i) The effect of shifts in the demand curve

(ii) The effect of shifts in the supply curve

The effects on equilibrium price and quantity of shifts in either demand or supply are called the laws of supply and demand.

A rise in demand. In (i) if demand rises from D to D_1, excess demand of q-q_2 develops at price p. Price and quantity both rise to their new equilibrium values at p_1 and q_1.

A fall in demand. In (i) if demand falls from D_1 to D, an excess supply develops at p_1. Price and quantity both fall to their new equilibrium values at p and q.

A rise in supply. In (ii) if supply rises from S to S_1, excess supply of q-q_2 develops at p. Price falls and quantity rises to their new equilibrium values at p_1 and q_1.

A fall in supply. In (ii) if supply falls from S_1 to S, an excess demand develops at p_1. Price rises and quantity falls to their new equilibrium values at p and q.

alysis is to compare two positions of static equilibrium.

Figure 5-8 shows the effects of these four shifts, which are the four so-called laws of supply and demand.[3]

1. **A rise in demand causes an increase in both the equilibrium price and the equilibrium quantity exchanged.**
2. **A fall in demand causes a decrease in both the equilibrium price and the equilibrium quantity exchanged.**
3. **A rise in supply causes a decrease in the equilibrium price and an increase in the equilibrium quantity exchanged.**
4. **A fall in supply causes an increase in the equi-**

librium price and a decrease in the equilibrium quantity exchanged.

In this chapter we have studied many forces that can cause demand or supply curves to shift. These were summarized in Figures 5-3 and 5-6. By combining this analysis with the four "laws" of supply and demand, we can take many real-world events that cause demand or supply curves to shift and link them to resulting changes in market prices and quantities. To take one example, a large rise in the price of beef will lead to an increase in both the price and the quantity exchanged of both chicken and pork (because a rise in the price of one commodity causes a rightward shift in the demand curves for its substitutes).

The theory of the determination of price by demand and supply is beautiful in its simplicity yet, as we shall see, powerful in its wide range of applications.

[3] The detailed argument in each case follows that of pages 78–80 and Figure 5-7 as to what happens when supply does not equal demand. Be sure you understand the market *behavior* that gives rise to each of the four "laws" summarized here.

Laws, Predictions, Hypotheses

In what sense can the four propositions developed for supply and demand be called laws? They are not like acts passed by Parliament, interpreted by courts, and enforced by the police; they cannot be repealed if people do not like their effects. Nor are they like the laws of Moses, revealed to man by the voice of God. Are they "natural laws" similar to Newton's law of gravity? It was clearly this last sense that classical economists had in mind when they labeled them as laws, and it was Newton's laws that they had in mind as analogies.

The term *law* is used in science to describe a theory that has stood up to substantial testing. A law of this kind is not something that has been proven to be true for all times and all circumstances, nor is it regarded as immutable. As observations accumulate, laws may often be modified or the range of phenomena to which they apply may be restricted or redefined. Einstein's theory of relativity, for one example, forced such amendments and restrictions on Newton's laws.

The "laws" of supply and demand have stood up well to many empirical tests, but no one believes that they explain all market behavior. Indeed the range of markets over which they seem to meet the test of providing accurate predictions is now much smaller than it was 80 years ago. It is possible—though most economists would think it unlikely—that at some future time they would no longer apply to any real markets. They are thus laws in the sense that they predict certain kinds of behavior in certain situations and the predicted behavior occurs sufficiently often to lead people to continue to have confidence in the predictions of the theory. They are not laws—any more than are the laws of natural science—that are beyond being challenged by present or future observations that may cast their predictions in doubt. Nor is it a heresy to question their applicability to any particular situation.

Laws, then, are hypotheses that have led to predictions that seem to account for observed behavior. They are theories that seem—in some circumstances at least—to have survived attempts to refute them and have proven useful. It is possible, in economics as in natural sciences, to be impressed both with the "laws" we do have and with their limitations: to be impressed, that is, both with the power of what we know and with the magnitude of what we have yet to understand.

THE THEORY OF PRICE IN AN INFLATIONARY WORLD

Up to now we have developed the theory of the prices of individual commodities under the assumption that all other prices remained constant. Does this mean that the theory is inapplicable to an inflationary world when virtually all prices are rising? Fortunately the answer is no.

The key lies in what are called relative prices. We have mentioned several times that what mattered for demand and supply was the price of the commodity in question relative to the prices of other commodities. A **relative price** measures the price of the specific commodity relative to other prices.

In an inflationary world we are often interested in the price of a given commodity as it relates to the average price of all other commodities. If, during a period when the general price level rose by 40 percent, the price of oranges rose by 60 percent, then the price of oranges rose relative to the price level as a whole. Oranges became *relatively* expensive. However, if oranges had risen in price by only 30 percent when the general price level rose by 40 percent, then the relative price of oranges would have fallen. Although the money price of oranges rose substantially, oranges became *relatively* cheap.

In Lewis Carroll's famous story *Through the Looking Glass,* Alice finds a country where you have to run in order to stay still. So it is with inflation. A commodity's price must rise as fast as the general level of prices just to keep its relative price constant.

It has been convenient in this chapter to analyze a change in a particular price in the context of a constant price level. The analysis is easily extended to an inflationary period by remembering that any force that raises the price of one commodity when other prices remain constant will, given general inflation, raise the price of that commodity faster than the price level is rising. For example, a change in tastes in favor of carrots that would raise their price by 20 percent when other prices were constant, would raise their price by 32 percent if at the same time the general price level goes up by 10 percent.[4] In each case the price of carrots rises 20 percent *relative to the average of all prices.*

In price theory, whenever we talk of a change in the price of one commodity we mean a change relative to all other prices.

If the price level is constant, this change requires only that the money price of the commodity in question should rise. If the price level is itself rising, this change requires that the money price of the commodity in question should rise faster than the price level.

Summary

1. The amount of a commodity that households wish to purchase is called the quantity demanded. It is a flow expressed as so much per period of time. This quantity is determined by the commodity's own price, the prices of related commodities, average household income, tastes, the

distribution of income among households, and the size of the population.

2. Quantity demanded is assumed to increase as the price of the commodity falls, *ceteris paribus.* The relationship between quantity demanded and price is represented graphically by a demand curve that shows how much will be demanded at each market price. A movement along a demand curve indicates a change in the quantity demanded in response to a change in the price of the commodity.

3. The demand curve shifts to the right (an increase in demand) if average income rises, if the price of a substitute rises, if the price of a complement falls, if population rises, or if there is a change in tastes in favor of the product. The opposite changes shift the demand curve to the left (a decrease in demand). A shift of a demand curve represents a change in the quantity demanded at each price and is referred to as a change in demand.

4. The amount of a commodity that firms wish to sell is called the quantity supplied. It is a flow expressed as so much per period of time. This quantity depends on the commodity's own price, the prices of other commodities, the costs of factors of production, the goals of the firm, and the state of technology.

5. Quantity supplied is assumed to increase as the price of the commodity increases, *ceteris paribus.* A movement along a supply curve indicates a change in the quantity supplied in response to a change in price.

6. The supply curve shifts to the right (an increase in supply) if the prices of other commodities fall, if the costs of producing the commodity fall, or if, for any reason, producers become more willing to produce the commodity. The opposite changes shift the supply curve to the left (a decrease in supply). A shift in the supply curve indicates a change in the quantity supplied at each price and is referred to as a change in supply.

7. The equilibrium price is the one at which the

----

[4] In the first case the price level is 100 and an index of carrot prices rises from 100 to 120 ($100 \times 1.2 = 120$). In the second case the index of the price level becomes 110 and the index of carrot prices must rise to 132 ($110 \times 1.2 = 132$).

quantity demanded equals the quantity supplied. At any price below the equilibrium there will be excess demand, while at any price above the equilibrium there will be excess supply. Graphically, equilibrium occurs where demand and supply curves intersect.

8. Price is assumed to rise when there is a shortage and to fall when there is a surplus. Thus the actual market price will be pushed toward the equilibrium price, and when it is reached, there will be neither shortage nor surplus and price will not change until either the supply curve or the demand curve shifts.

9. Using the method of comparative statics, the effects of a shift in either demand or supply can be determined. A rise in demand raises both equilibrium price and quantity; a fall in demand lowers both. A rise in supply raises equilibrium quantity but lowers equilibrium price; a fall in supply lowers equilibrium quantity but raises equilibrium price. Those are the so-called laws of supply and demand.

10. Price theory is most simply explained against a backdrop of a constant price level. Price changes discussed in the theory are changes *relative to* the average level of all prices. In an inflationary period, a rise in the relative price of one commodity means that its price rises more than does the price level; a fall in its relative price means that its price rises by less than does the price level.

Topics for Review

Quantity demanded and quantity exchanged
Demand schedules and demand curves
Quantity supplied and quantity exchanged
Supply schedules and supply curves
Movements along a curve and shifts in the curve
Changes in quantity demanded and changes in demand
Changes in quantity supplied and changes in supply
Equilibrium, equilibrium price, and disequilibrium
The determination of equilibrium
Comparative static analysis
The "laws" of supply and demand
Relative price

Discussion Questions

1. What shifts in demand or supply curves would produce the following results? (Assume that only one of the two curves has shifted.)
   a. The price of pocket calculators has fallen over the last few years and the quantity exchanged has risen greatly.
   b. As the Canadian standard of living rose over the past three decades, both the prices and the consumption of prime cuts of beef rose steadily.
   c. During the recession of 1974-1975 the prices *and* quantities exchanged of lead, copper, and tin fell substantially.
   d. Because federal safety and antipollution regulations have led to large increases in the cost of producing automobiles, it has been suggested that if strong regulations continue, the prices of cars will rise and the sales of cars will fall.
2. Explain each of the following in terms of changes in supply and demand.
   a. DuPont increased the price of synthetic fibers, although it acknowledged demand was weak.
   b. Some of the first $10 Canadian Olympic coins were imperfectly stamped. Dealers and collectors are paying as much as $500 for these flawed pieces.
   c. "Master Charge has replaced sugar-daddy," a Beverly Hills furrier said, explaining the rise in sales of mink coats.
   d. The Edsel was a lemon when produced in 1958-1960 but is now a best seller among cars of its vintage.
   e. When a frost hit the Florida citrus industry, a spokesperson for the Israel citrus marketing board said Mediterranean producers would receive better prices for their crops everywhere in the world.
3. Suppose that tape recorder producers find that they are selling more tape recorders at the same price than they did two years ago. Is this a shift of the demand curve or a movement along the curve? Suggest at least four reasons why this rise in sales at an unchanged price might occur.
4. What would be the effect on the equilibrium price and quantity of marijuana if its sale were legalized? What would be the effect on the equilibrium prices of gold and paper if all the world's banks sold their gold supplies and replaced them with paper certificates that were officially accepted as reserves?
5. The relative price of a color television set has dropped drastically over time. Would you explain this falling

price in terms of demand or supply changes? What factors are likely to have caused the demand or supply shifts that did occur?

6. Classify the effect of each of the following as: (a) a decrease in the demand for fish, (b) a decrease in the quantity of fish demanded, or (c) other. Illustrate each diagrammatically.

a. The government of Iceland bars fishermen of other nations from its waters.

b. People buy less fish because of a rise in fish prices.

c. The Roman Catholic Church relaxes its ban on eating meat on Fridays.

d. The price of beef falls and as a result households buy more beef and less fish.

e. In the interests of training marine personnel for national defense, the government decides to subsidize the fishing industry.

f. It is discovered that eating fish is better for one's health than eating meat.

7. "The effect of price changes often eludes analysis. For example, two of the food groups that have shown absolute decreases in consumption per capita—flour and potatoes—have also shown decreases in price relative to the prices of all goods. Consumption of meat per capita has been rising in the face of an increase in relative prices." Do the changes elude your analysis? How would you reword this statement to make clear what you think did happen?

Elasticity of Demand and Supply

When flood damage led to major destruction of the North American onion crop, onion prices rose generally. In one city they rose 42 percent in one week. Not surprisingly consumption fell. Very often it is not enough to know merely whether quantity rises or falls in response to a change in price; it is also important to know by how much. In this case, the press reported that the effect was to cause many consumers to stop using onions altogether and to substitute onion salt, sauerkraut, cabbage, and other products. Other consumers still bought onions but in reduced quantities. Overall consumption was down sharply. Were aggregate dollar sales of onions (price *times* quantity) higher or lower? The data above do not tell, but this is the sort of information that may matter a good deal. A government concerned with the effect of a partial crop failure on farm income will not be satisfied with being told that food prices will rise and quantities consumed will fall; it will need to know by approximately how much they will rise and fall if it is to assess the effects on farmers.

Demand Elasticity

Suppose there is a fall in the supply of a farm crop. The two parts of Figure 6-1 show the same leftward shift in the supply curve. Because the demand curves are different, the effects on equilibrium price and quantity are different. In the first case, the quantity demanded varies greatly with price. A small rise in price restores equilibrium by removing the excess demand. In the sec-

FIGURE 6-1

The Effect of the Shape of the Demand Curve

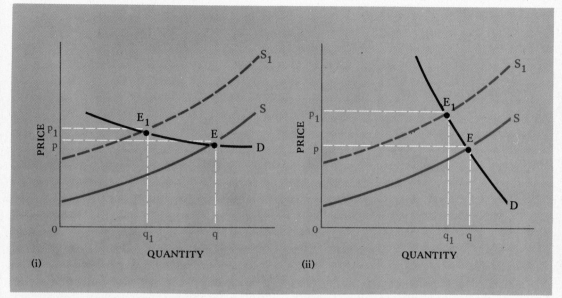

The flatter the demand curve, the less is the change in price and the greater is the change in quantity. Both parts of the figure show the same leftward shift in the supply curve. In each part, initial equilibrium is at price *p* and output *q* and the new equilibrium is at *p*₁ and *q*₁. In (i) the effect of the shift in supply from *S* to *S*₁ is a slight rise in the price and a large decrease in quantity. In (ii) the effect of the identical shift in the supply curve from *S* to *S*₁ is a large increase in the price and a relatively small decrease in quantity.

ond case, the quantity demanded is very insensitive to price changes and equilibrium is restored only when a large price rise has called forth the extra quantity necessary to satisfy the almost unchanged quantity demanded.

The difference may have great policy significance. Consider what would happen if the government persuaded farmers to produce more of a certain crop. (It might, for example, pay a subsidy to farmers for growing this crop.) If the government is successful, then at every possible price of the product there will be an increase in the quantity that farmers would be willing to produce. Thus the whole supply curve of the product would shift to the right. This may be visualized in both parts of Figure 6-1 by assuming that the supply curve shifts from S_1 to S.

Figure 6-1(i) illustrates a case in which the quantity that consumers demand is very sensi-

tive to price changes. The extra production brings down price, but because the quantity demanded is very responsive, only a small change in price is necessary in order to restore equilibrium. The effect of the government's policy, therefore, is to achieve a large increase in the production and sales of this commodity and only a small decrease in price.

Figure 6-1(ii) shows a case in which the quantity demanded is quite unresponsive to price changes. As before, the increase in supply at the original price causes a surplus that brings the price down. But this time the quantity demanded by consumers does not increase very much in response to the fall in price. Thus the price continues to drop until, discouraged by lower and lower prices, farmers reduce the quantity supplied very nearly to the level attained before they received the increased incentive to produce. The effect of the government's policy is to bring about a large fall in the price and only a small increase in the quantity produced and sold.

In comparing the cases diagrammed in Figure 6-1, it can be seen that the government's policy has exactly the same effectiveness as far as farmers' willingness to supply the commodity is concerned (the supply curve shifts are identical). But the effects on the equilibrium price and quantity are very different because of the different degrees to which the quantity demanded by consumers responds to price changes. If the purpose of the policy is to increase the quantity of this commodity produced and consumed, then the policy will be a great success when the demand curve is similar to the one shown in Figure 6-1(i), but it will be a failure when the demand curve is similar to the one shown in Figure 6-1(ii). If, however, the main purpose of the policy is to achieve a large reduction in the price of the commodity, the policy will be a failure when demand is as shown in (i) but it will be a great success when demand is as shown in (ii).

A shift in supply can have very different effects, depending on the shape of the demand curve.

PRICE ELASTICITY: A MEASURE OF THE RESPONSIVENESS OF QUANTITY DEMANDED TO PRICE CHANGES

When considering the responsiveness of the quantity demanded to changes in price, we may wish to make statements such as "The demand for carrots was more responsive to price changes ten years ago than it is today" or "The demand for meat responds more to price changes than does the demand for green vegetables." In order to make such comparisons, a measure of the degree to which quantity demanded responds to changes in price is required.

In the previous examples it was possible to make comparisons between the two demand curves in Figure 6-1 on the basis of their geometrical steepness, because the curves were both drawn on the same scale. Thus, for any given price change, the quantity changes more on the flatter curve than it does on the steeper one. However, it can be very misleading to inspect a *single* curve and to conclude from its general appearance something about the degree of responsiveness of quantity demanded to price changes. You can make a curve appear as steep or as flat as you like by changing the scales. For example, a curve that looks steep when the horizontal scale is 1 inch = 100 units will look much flatter when 1 inch = 1 unit if the same vertical scale is used in each case.

Instead of gaining a vague general impression from the shape of demand curves, one could note the actual change in quantity demanded in response to a certain price change. But it would still be impossible to compare degrees of responsiveness for different commodities.

Assume that we have the information shown in Table 6-1. Should we conclude that the demand for radios is not so responsive to price changes as the demand for beef? After all, price cuts of 20¢ cause quite a large increase in the quantity of beef demanded but only a small increase in radios.

There are two problems here. First, a reduction in price of 20¢ will be a large price cut for a low-priced commodity and an insignificant price cut for a high-priced commodity. The price reductions listed in Table 6-1 represent very different fractions of the total prices. Actually it is more revealing to know the percentage change in the prices of the various commodities. Second,

TABLE 6–1
Price Reductions and Corresponding Increases in Quantity Demanded

Commodity	Reduction in price	Increase in quantity demanded
Beef	$.20 per pound	7,500 pounds
Men's shirts	.20 per shirt	5,000 shirts
Radios	.20 per radio	100 radios

TABLE 6-2
Price and Quantity Information Underlying Data of Table 6-1

Commodity	Unit	Original price	New price	Average price	Original quantity	New quantity	Average quantity
Beef	per pound	$ 1.70	$ 1.50	$ 1.60	116,250	123,750	120,000
Men's shirts	per shirt	8.10	7.90	8.00	197,500	202,500	200,000
Radios	per radio	40.10	39.90	40.00	9,950	10,050	10,000

These data provide the appropriate context of the data given in Table 6-1. The table relates the $.20 per unit price reduction of each commodity to the actual prices and quantities demanded.

by an analogous argument, knowing the quantity by which demand changes is not very revealing unless the level of demand is also known. An increase of 7,500 tons is quite a significant reaction of demand if the quantity formerly bought was 15,000 tons, but it is only a drop in the bucket if the quantity formerly demanded was 10 million tons.

Table 6-2 shows the original and new levels of price and quantity. Changes in price and quantity expressed as percentages of the average prices and quantities are shown in the first two columns of Table 6-3.[1] **Elasticity of demand,** the measure of responsiveness of quantity demanded to price changes, is defined as [6]

percentage change in quantity demanded
percentage change in price

When it is necessary to distinguish this measure of elasticity from other related concepts, it is sometimes called "price elasticity of demand," since the variable causing the change in quantity demanded is the commodity's own price.

[1] The use of averages is designed to avoid the ambiguity caused by the fact that, for example, the $.20 change in the price of beefsteak is a different percentage (11.8) of the original price, $1.70, than it is (13.3) of the new price, $1.50. We want the elasticity of demand between any two points (*A* and *B*) to be independent of whether we move from *A* to *B* or from *B* to *A*; as a result, using either "original" prices and quantities or "new" prices and quantities would be less satisfactory than using averages. In this illustration, $.20 is unambiguously 12.5 percent of $1.60 and applies to a price increase from $1.50 to $1.70, as well as to the decrease discussed in the text.

Interpreting Numerical Values of Elasticity of Demand

Because demand curves slope downward an *increase* in price is associated with a *decrease* in quantity demanded and vice versa. Since the percentage changes in price and quantity have opposite signs, demand elasticity is a negative number. We shall follow the usual practice of ignoring the negative sign and speak of the measure as a positive number, as we have done in Table 6-3. Thus, the more responsive the quantity demanded (radios relative to beef in the example), the greater the elasticity of demand and the higher the measure (2.0 compared to 0.5).

The numerical value of elasticity can vary from zero to infinity. Elasticity is zero if there is

TABLE 6-3
The Calculation of Demand Elasticities

Commodity	(1) Percentage decrease in price	(2) Percentage increase in quantity	(3) Elasticity of demand (2) ÷ (1)
Beef	12.5	6.25	0.5
Men's shirts	2.5	2.5	1.0
Radios	0.5	1.0	2.0

Elasticity is the percentage change in quantity divided by the percentage change in price. The percentage changes are based on average prices and quantities shown in Table 6-2. For example, the $.20 per pound decrease in the price of beef is 12.5 percent of $1.60. A $.20 change in the price of radios is only 0.5 percent of the average price per radio of $40.

FIGURE 6–2
Elasticity Along a Straight-Line Demand Curve

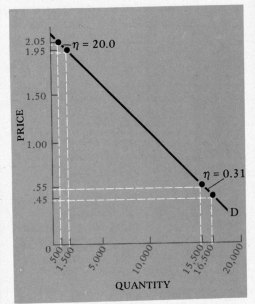

Moving down a straight-line demand curve, elasticity falls continuously. On this straight line, reduction in price of 10¢ always leads to the same increase (1,000 units) in quantity. Near the upper end of the curve, however, where price is $2 and quantity is 1,000 units, a reduction in price of 10¢ (from $2.05 to $1.95) is only a 5 percent reduction, but the 1,000-unit increase in quantity is a 100 percent increase. Elasticity, which is often symbolized by the Greek letter eta (η), is 20. At the price of 50¢ and quantity of 16,000 units, a price reduction of 10¢ (from 55¢ to 45¢) leads to the same 1,000-unit increase in demand. A 20 percent price decrease combines with a 6.25 percent quantity increase to give an elasticity of 0.31.

no change at all in quantity demanded when price changes, that is, when quantity demanded does not respond to a price change. The larger the elasticity, the larger is the percentage change in quantity for a given percentage change in price. As long as the elasticity of demand has a value of less than one, however, the percentage change in quantity is less than the percentage change in price. When elasticity is equal to one, then the

two percentage changes are equal to each other. When the percentage change in quantity exceeds the percentage change in price, the value for the elasticity of demand is greater than one.

When the percentage change in quantity is less than the percentage change in price (elasticity less than one), the demand is said to be **inelastic.** When the percentage change in quantity is greater than the percentage change in price (elasticity greater than one), the demand is said to be **elastic.** This terminology is important, and you should become familiar with it.

A demand curve need not—and usually does not—have the same elasticity over every part of the curve. Figure 6-2 shows that a downward-sloping, straight-line demand curve does not have a constant elasticity. The only two cases in which a straight line has constant elasticity are when it is vertical and when it is horizontal. Figure 6-3 illustrates three special demand curves with constant elasticities.

Elasticity of Demand and Changes in Total Expenditure and Total Revenue

Money spent in purchasing a commodity is received by the sellers of the commodity. The total amount spent by purchasers is thus the gross revenue of the sellers. How does total expenditure made by purchasers of a commodity or total gross revenue received by sellers of a commodity (the same thing) react when the price of a product is changed? The simplest example will show that total revenue may rise or fall in response to a decrease in price. Suppose 100 units of a commodity are being sold at a unit price of $1. The price is then cut to 90¢. If the quantity sold rises to 110, the total revenue of the sellers falls from $100 to $99; but if quantity sold rises to 120, total revenue rises from $100 to $108.

Generally what happens to total revenue depends on the price elasticity of demand. If this is less than unity (that is, less than one), the percentage change in price will exceed the percentage change in quantity. The price change will then dominate so that total revenue will change in the same direction as the price changes. If,

FIGURE 6-3
Three Demand Curves

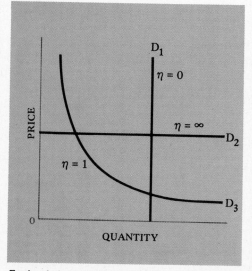

Each of these demand curves has constant elasticity. D_1 has *zero elasticity:* the quantity demanded does not change at all when price changes. D_2 has *infinite elasticity:* there exists a small price increase that decreases quantity demanded from an indefinitely large amount to zero. D_3 has *unit elasticity:* a given percentage increase in price brings an equal percentage decrease in quantity at all points on the curve.

however, elasticity exceeds unity, the percentage change in quantity will exceed the percentage change in price. The quantity change will then dominate so that total revenue will change in the same direction as quantity changes (that is, in the opposite direction to the change in price).

Notice what happened to total revenue when price fell in the example of radios, shirts, and beef. (The calculations are shown in Table 6-4.) In the case of beef, the demand is inelastic and a cut in price lowered the revenue of sellers; in the case of radios, the demand is elastic and a cut in price raised the revenue earned by sellers. The borderline case is men's shirts; here the demand elasticity is unity and the cut in price leaves total revenue unchanged.

These examples illustrate more general relationships:

1. **If demand is elastic, a fall in price increases total expenditure and a rise in price reduces it.**
2. **If demand is inelastic, a fall in price reduces total expenditure and a rise in price increases it.**
3. **If elasticity of demand is unity, a rise or a fall in price leaves total expenditure unaffected.** [7]

Consider two real examples. When a bumper potato crop in North America sent prices down 50 percent, quantity sold increased only 15 percent and potato farmers found their revenues falling sharply. Demand was clearly inelastic. When in the 1970s Salt Lake County's Utah Transit Authority cut its bus fares from 25 cents to 15 cents for the average journey, the volume of passenger traffic increased from 4.4 million to 14 million journeys within two years and revenues rose sharply. Demand was clearly elastic.

TABLE 6-4
The Changes in Total Revenue (Total Expenditure) for the Example of Table 6-2

Commodity	Price × quantity (original prices and quantities)	Price × quantity (new prices and quantities)	Change in revenue (expenditure)	Elasticity of demand from Table 6-3
Beef	$ 197,625	$ 185,625	−$12,000	0.5
Men's shirts	1,599,750	1,599,750	0	1.0
Radios	398,995	400,995	+ 2,000	2.0

Whether revenue increases or decreases in response to a price cut depends on whether demand is elastic or inelastic. The $197,625 figure is the product of the original price of beef ($1.70) and the original quantity (116,250 pounds). The $185,625 is the product of the new price ($1.50) and quantity (123,750), and so on.

What Determines Elasticity of Demand?

A great deal of work has been put into the measurement of demand elasticity, and in Chapter 10 we summarize some actual measurements. One of the most important determinants of elasticity is undoubtedly the degree of availability of close substitutes. Some commodities, such as margarine, cabbage, pork, and Fords, have quite close substitutes—butter, other green vegetables, beef, and similar makes of cars. A change in the price of these commodities, *the prices of the substitutes remaining constant,* can be expected to cause much substitution—a fall in price leading consumers to buy more of the commodity in question and a rise in price leading consumers to buy more of the substitute. Other commodities, such as salt, housing, and all vegetables as a group, have few if any satisfactory substitutes, and a rise in their price can be expected to cause a smaller fall in quantity demanded than would be the case if close substitutes were available.

To a great extent, elasticity depends on how widely or narrowly a commodity is defined.

Food and shelter are necessities in the sense that life cannot go on without some minimum quantity of them. It is a fact that food as a whole has an inelastic demand over a large price range. It does not follow, however, that any one food, such as white bread or cornflakes, is a necessity in the same sense. There is every reason to believe that the quantity demanded for any one food can and will fall greatly as a result of a rise in its price.

OTHER DEMAND ELASTICITIES

The purpose of measuring demand elasticity is to discover the degree to which the quantity demanded responds to a change in one of the factors that influence it. So far the response of the quantity of a commodity demanded to changes in the commodity's own price has been considered. It is also important to know how demand responds to changes in incomes and the prices of other goods.

Income Elasticity of Demand

The responsiveness of demand to changes in income is termed **income elasticity of demand,** and it is defined as

percentage change in quantity demanded
percentage change in income

For most goods, increases in income lead to increases in demand and income elasticity will be positive. These are called **normal goods.** Goods for which consumption decreases in response to a rise in income have negative income elasticities and are called **inferior goods.**

The income elasticity of normal goods may be less than unity (inelastic) or greater than unity (elastic), depending on whether (say) a 10 percent increase in income leads to less than or more than a 10 percent increase in the quantity demanded. Not surprisingly, different commodities have different income elasticities (as the studies examined in Chapter 10 show). Goods that consumers at a given level of income regard as necessities tend to have lower income elasticities than do luxuries, for the obvious reason that as incomes rise it becomes possible for households to devote a smaller proportion of their income to meeting basic needs and a larger proportion to buying things they have always wanted but could not afford.

The reaction of demand to changes in income is extremely important. In most Western economies we know that economic growth has caused the level of income to double every 20 to 30 years over a sustained period of at least a century. This rise in income is shared to some extent by most of the households in the country. As they find their incomes increasing, they increase their demands for most commodities. But the demands for some commodities such as food and basic clothing will not increase very much as incomes rise while the demands for other commodities increase rapidly as incomes rise. In developing countries such as Ireland and Mexico the

Terminology of Elasticity

TERMINOLOGY	NUMERICAL MEASURE OF ELASTICITY	VERBAL DESCRIPTION
A. Price elasticity of demand [supply]		
Perfectly or completely inelastic	Zero	Quantity demanded [supplied] does not change as price changes
Inelastic	Greater than zero, but less than one	Quantity demanded [supplied] changes by a smaller percentage than does price
Unit elasticity	One	Quantity demanded [supplied] changes by exactly the same percentage as does price
Elastic	Greater than one, but less than infinity	Quantity demanded [supplied] changes by a larger percentage than does price
Perfectly, completely, or infinitely elastic	Infinity	Purchasers [sellers] are prepared to buy [sell] all they can at some price and none at all at an even slightly higher [lower] price
B. Income elasticity of demand		
Inferior good	Negative	Quantity demanded decreases as income increases
Normal good	Positive	Quantity demanded increases as income increases:
Income inelastic	Greater than zero, less than one	less than in proportion to income increase
Income elastic	Greater than one	more than in proportion to income increase
C. Cross elasticity of demand		
Substitute	Positive	Price increase of a substitute leads to an increase in quantity demanded of this good (and less of the substitute)
Complement	Negative	Price increase of a complement leads to a decrease in quantity demanded of this good (and less of the complement)

demand for durable goods is increasing most rapidly as household incomes rise, while in North America it is the demand for services that is rising most rapidly. The uneven impact of the growth of income on the demands for different commodities has very important effects on the economy and groups in it, and these will be studied at several different points in this book.

The income elasticity of a particular good is expected to be different at widely different income levels. Consider how a family's diet may change as its income level rises. When incomes are very low, households may eat virtually no meat and consume lots of starchy foods such as bread and potatoes; at higher levels, they may eat the cheaper cuts of meat and more green vegetables along with their bread and potatoes; at yet higher levels they are likely to eat more (and more expensive) meat, to substitute frozen for canned vegetables, and to eat a greater variety of foods. In this sequence the income elasticity of hamburger may be high at low levels of income but decrease as income rises and steak replaces hamburger. Different commodities will show different patterns. Potatoes are likely to exhibit low income elasticity while steak proves to be income-elastic over a wide range of income.[2] Figure 6-4 shows one particular pattern of income elasticity varying with income.[3]

[2] It is common to use the terms *income-elastic* and *income-inelastic* to refer to income elasticities of greater or less than unity. See the box on page 93.

[3] The curve in Figure 6-4, like the demand curve studied in Chapter 5, shows the relation of quantity demanded to *one* variable, *ceteris paribus*. This time the variable is income instead of price. (An increase in price of the commodity, incomes remaining constant, would shift downward the curve shown in Figure 6-4).

In this chart, in contrast to the ordinary demand curve, quantity demanded is on the vertical axis. This follows the usual practice of putting the to-be-explained variable (called the dependent variable) on the vertical axis and the explanatory variable (called the independent variable) on the horizontal axis. It is the ordinary demand curve that has the axes "backwards." This practice dates to Alfred Marshall's *Principles of Economics* (1890), the classic that is one of the foundation stones of modern price theory. [8] For better or worse, Marshall's scheme is now used by everybody—although mathematicians never fail to wonder at this further example of the odd ways of economists.

Cross Elasticity

The responsiveness of demand to changes in the prices of other commodities is called **cross elasticity of demand.** It is defined as

$$\frac{\text{percentage change in quantity demanded of one good, } X}{\text{percentage change in price of another good, } Y}$$

Cross elasticity can vary from minus infinity to plus infinity. Complementary commodities will have negative cross elasticities. Cars and gasoline, for example, are complements. A large rise in the price of gasoline will lead (as it has in North America) to a decline in the demand for cars as some people decide to do without a car and others decide not to buy a second (or a third) car. Substitute commodities have positive cross elasticities. Cars and public transport are substitutes. A large rise in the price of cars (relative to public transport) would lead to a rise in the demand for public transport as some people shifted from cars to public transport.

Measures of cross elasticity sometimes prove helpful in defining whether producers of similar products are in competition with each other. Glass bottles and tin cans have a high cross elasticity of demand. The producer of bottles is thus in competition with the producer of cans. If the bottle company raises its price, it will lose substantial sales to the can producer. Men's shoes and women's shoes have a low cross elasticity. Thus a producer of men's shoes is not in close competition with a producer of women's shoes. If the former raises its price, it will not lose many sales to the latter.

Supply Elasticity

The concept of elasticity relates to supply as well as to demand. Just as elasticity of demand measures the response of quantity demanded to changes in any of the forces that influence it, so elasticity of supply measures the response of quantity supplied to changes in any of the forces that influence it. We will focus on the commodity's own price as a factor influencing supply.

FIGURE 6–4
An Income-Consumption Curve Relating Quantity Demanded to Level of Income

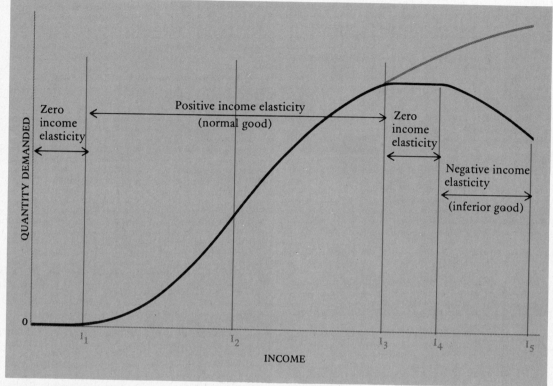

Different shapes of the curve relating quantity demanded to income correspond to different ranges of income elasticity. The product whose income-consumption curve is shown by the heavy curve is a normal good for incomes up to I_3 and an inferior good above I_4. Whenever the curve is horizontal (from 0 to I_1 and from I_3 to I_4) income elasticity is zero. Between I_1 and I_2 quantity demanded is rising proportionally more rapidly than income (income elasticity greater than plus unity); between I_2 and I_3 quantity demanded is rising but less than proportionally (income elasticity greater than zero, less than unity). Different commodities will have different patterns: For example, if the income-consumption curve for some commodity was the heavy curve to I_3 and the screened curve thereafter, that commodity would not be an inferior good at any level of income.

Elasticity of supply measures the responsiveness of the quantity supplied to a change in the commodity's own price. It is defined as

$$\frac{\text{percentage change in quantity supplied}}{\text{percentage change in price}}$$

The supply curves considered in this chapter all have positive slopes: an increase in price causes an increase in quantity sold. Such supply curves all have positive elasticities.

There are important special cases. If the supply curve is vertical—the quantity supplied does not change as price changes—elasticity of supply is zero. This would be the case, for example, if suppliers produced a given quantity and dumped it on the market for whatever it would bring. A horizontal supply curve has an infinitely high elasticity of supply: A small drop in price would reduce the quantity producers are willing to supply from an indefinitely large amount to zero. Between these two extremes elasticity of supply will vary with the shape of the supply curve.[4]

What Determines Elasticity of Supply?

Supply elasticities are very important for many problems in economics. The brevity of this discussion reflects two main facts. First, much of the treatment of demand elasticity carries over to the case of supply and does not need repeating. Second, there will be more about the determinants of supply elasticity in Part Four.

In the meantime it should be noted that supply elasticity depends to a great extent on how costs behave as output is varied. If costs of production rise rapidly as output rises, then the stimulus to expand production in response to a price rise will quickly be choked off by increases in costs. In this case supply will tend to be rather inelastic. If, however, costs rise only slowly as production increases, a rise in price that raises profits will call forth a large increase in quantity supplied before the rise in costs puts a halt to the expansion in output. In this case supply will tend to be rather elastic.

Summary

1. Elasticity of demand (also called *price elasticity*) is a measure of the extent to which the quantity demanded of a commodity responds to a change in its price. We define it as the percentage change in quantity divided by the percentage change in price that brought it about. Elasticity is here defined to be a positive number that varies from zero to infinity.

2. When the numerical measure of elasticity is less than one, demand is *inelastic*. This means that the percentage change in quantity is less than the percentage change in price that brought it about. When the numerical measure exceeds

unity, demand is *elastic*. This means that the percentage change in quantity is greater than the percentage change in price that brought it about.

3. Elasticity and total revenue of sellers are related in this way: If elasticity is less than unity, a fall in price lowers total revenue; if elasticity is greater than unity, a fall in price raises total revenue; and if elasticity is unity, total revenue does not change as price changes.

4. The main determinant of the price elasticity of demand is the availability of substitutes for the commodity. The more and better the substitutes, the higher the elasticity.

5. Income elasticity is the percentage change in quantity demanded divided by the percentage change in income that brought it about. The income elasticity of demand for a commodity may well change as income varies. For example, a commodity that has a high income elasticity at a low income (because increases in income bring it within reach of the typical household) may have a low or negative income elasticity at higher incomes (because with further rises in incomes it can be replaced by a superior substitute).

6. Cross elasticity is the percentage change in quantity demanded divided by the percentage change in the price of some other commodity that brought it about.

7. Elasticity of supply is an important concept in economics. It measures the ratio of the percentage change in the quantity supplied of a commodity to the percentage change in its price. It is the analogue on the supply side to the elasticity of demand.

8. An appendix to this chapter, for students with some mathematical background, extends the analysis.

Topics for Review

Elasticity of demand
Significance of elastic and inelastic demands
The relation between demand elasticity and total expenditure

---

[4] Steepness, which relates to absolute rather than percentage changes, is *not* always a reliable guide. As is proven in the appendix to this chapter, any upward-sloping straight line through the origin has an elasticity of $+1.0$ over its entire range.

Income elasticity of demand
Normal goods and inferior goods
Cross elasticity of demand
Elasticity of supply

Discussion Questions

1. What, if anything, does the following newspaper quotation tell you about the elasticity of demand for public transportation? "Ridership always went up when bus fares came down, but the increased patronage never was enough to prevent a decrease in overall revenue."

2. What would you predict about the relative price elasticity of demand of (a) food, (b) meat, (c) beef, (d) chuck roast, (e) Loblaw chuck roast? What would you predict about their relative income elasticities?

3. The price of gasoline has risen substantially over the last decade.
   a. How would you have expected demand to respond the first year or two after the price increases began?
   b. How would you expect demand to have responded after a decade of price rises?

4. If the elasticity of demand for railway passenger travel is unity in the neighborhood of present prices and the railways are losing money on their passenger traffic, how (if at all) can they make their passenger service profitable?

5. Consider the demand for margarine expressed in this quotation: "We always buy Fleischmann's now—I don't even have butter in the house. In the beginning it was the price, now I don't even consider that. We're very cholesterol conscious in our family." Interpret this in terms of elasticity of demand for butter and for margarine.

6. What elasticity measure or measures would be useful in answering the following questions?
   a. Will cheaper transport into the central city help keep downtown shopping centers profitable?
   b. Will raising the bulk-rate postage rate increase or decrease the postal deficit?
   c. Are producers of toothpaste and mouthwash in competition with each other?
   d. Would an increase in gas field prices solve the natural gas shortage within a decade?
   e. Would raising Canadian oil prices to the world price level help to reduce Canadian oil imports by a significant amount?
   f. In the mid 1970s there was considerable new planting of cocoa trees. Why, when the additional output began to come on the market in 1979, did the price of cocoa fall drastically even though the increase in supply was as yet very modest?

Supply and Demand in Action I: Price Controls and Agricultural Problems

7

The laws of supply and demand and the concepts of elasticity of demand and supply have immediate application to many real-world problems. Consider, for example, recent developments in the world market for wheat. During the period 1972–1974 the available supply was reduced by crop failures, particularly in the Soviet Union, and drought conditions in a broad band of countries across Africa, Asia, and Australia. As a result, the price of wheat rose to a level more than double that which had prevailed over the previous ten years. Then there was a dramatic reversal in the 1976–1977 crop year, when Canada and several other producers harvested record crops and the price plummeted.

These facts suggest why even the simple theory of demand and supply is so useful. The fluctuations in the supply of a perishable product had just the effects that microeconomics predicts for products with inelastic demands.

In this chapter and the next we apply the basic concepts of elasticity of demand and supply and the method of comparative statics. The method, it will be recalled, is to start from a position of equilibrium—say, in the market for soybeans—and introduce the change to be studied—for example, a shift to the left of the supply curve. Then we determine the new equilibrium position and compare it with the original one. The differences between the two positions of equilibrium (higher price, lower quantities actually exchanged) can be attributed to the change introduced, for that is the only change that has been allowed to occur.

Predictions can be made not only about the movements of prices and quantities in response to changes. In this chapter we also analyze what the basic model predicts about the market response to controls placed on prices charged or quantities exchanged. In the following chapter we focus on international aspects of supply and demand where domestic prices must equal those prevailing in foreign markets.

The Theory of Price Controls

It is common in wartime, and increasingly frequent in peacetime, for governments to fix maximum prices at which some goods and services may be sold. The government of Canada attempted to control inflation during the period 1975–1978 by establishing the Anti-Inflation Board, which set maximum permissible increases in wages and prices. In a number of provinces this was accompanied by controls on the prices at which apartments could be rented, and in most cases the controls are still in place even though the Anti-Inflation Board has been disbanded.

In a free market, price tends to move toward its equilibrium value, where the quantities demanded and supplied are equal. Government price controls are designed to cause the market price to differ from its equilibrium value. In so doing they cause quantity demanded to differ from quantity supplied at the controlled price. This in turn leads to further consequences.

QUANTITY EXCHANGED AT NON-EQUILIBRIUM PRICES

In competitive markets, price tends to change whenever quantity supplied does not equal quantity demanded. Thus price will move toward its equilibrium value, where there are neither unsatisfied suppliers nor unsatisfied demanders. However, price controls create the possibility that price may be held indefinitely at a disequilibrium value. When this happens, what determines the quantity actually traded on the market? A moment's thought will show that any voluntary market transaction requires both a willing buyer and a willing seller. This means that if quantity demanded is less than quantity sup-

plied, the former will determine the amount actually exchanged and the rest of the quantity supplied will remain in the hands of the unsuccessful sellers. On the other hand, if quantity demanded exceeds quantity supplied, the latter will determine the amount actually traded and the rest of the quantity demanded will represent desired purchases of unsuccessful buyers.

At any disequilibrium price, quantity exchanged is determined by the *lesser* of quantity demanded or quantity supplied.

This is shown graphically in Figure 7-1. Quantity exchanged at any price is determined by the curve *on the left* at that price—that is, the demand curve above, and the supply curve below, the equilibrium price.

FIGURE 7-1
The Determination of Quantity Exchanged in Disequilibrium

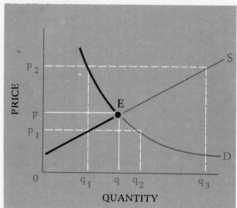

In disequilibrium, quantity exchanged is determined by the *lesser* of quantity demanded or quantity supplied. At p the market is in equilibrium with quantity demanded equal to quantity supplied at q. For prices below p, such as p_1, the quantity exchanged will be determined by the supply curve. For example, the quantity q_1 will be exchanged at the disequilibrium price p_1 in spite of the excess demand of q_1q_2. For prices above p, such as p_2, the quantity exchanged will be given by the demand curve. For example, the quantity exchanged will be only q_1 at the price p_2 in spite of the excess supply of q_1q_3. Thus the heavy black line shows the whole set of actual quantities exchanged, at different prices.

Although frequently referred to as fixed or "frozen" prices, most price controls specify the highest permissible price, often called the **ceiling price,** that producers may legally charge. Sometimes controls state that certain goods and services cannot be sold *below* some minimum price, known as a **price floor.** The principal examples of a price floor in Canada today are agricultural price-support programs, discussed later in this chapter, and minimum wage laws, discussed in Chapter 21.

EFFECTIVE CEILING PRICES

If the ceiling price is set at or above the equilibrium price, it will have no effect because equilib-

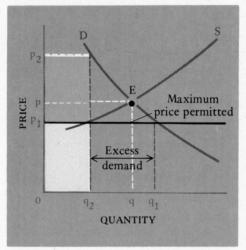

FIGURE 7-2
A Price Ceiling and Black Market Pricing

A ceiling price below the equilibrium price causes excess demand and invites a black market. Equilibrium price is at *p*. If a price ceiling is set at p_1, the quantity demanded will rise to q_1 and the quantity supplied will fall to q_2. Quantity actually exchanged will be q_2. Although excess demand is q_2q_1, price may not legally rise to restore equilibrium. If all the available supply of q_2 were sold on a black market, price to consumers would rise to p_2, with black marketeers earning receipts shown by the shaded areas. The dark shaded area is the profit of those who buy at the ceiling price and sell at the black market price.

rium will still be attainable and will not be inconsistent with the ceiling price required by law. If, however, the ceiling price is set below equilibrium, it is binding.[1] This means that the free-market price must be reduced. The forced reduction will cause a fall in the quantity supplied, an increase in the quantity demanded, and a shortage of the commodity (see Figure 7-2). A first prediction of the effect of price control in a competitive market is:

Binding ceiling prices lead to excess demand for the commodity, and the quantity exchanged will fall below its equilibrium amount.

In inflationary situations, price controls often take the form of "freezing" prices at current free-market levels. At the moment of imposition the price control is not effective, but as inflation occurs the free-market price would rise, and thus the controlled price becomes an effective ceiling price.

ALLOCATING A COMMODITY IN SHORT SUPPLY

What happens to the excess demand that is always produced by binding price ceilings? The free-market way of eliminating excess demand is to allow price to rise so as to allocate the available supply among would-be purchasers. Since this does not happen, some other method of allocation must be adopted. Experience shows that certain alternatives are likely.

If stores sell their available supplies on a first-come, first-served basis, people will rush to those stores that are said to have stocks of any commodity in short supply. In Europe during World II, the word—even the rumor—that a shop was selling supplies of a scarce commodity could cause a local stampede. Buyers often spent hours in line, waiting to get into the shop, and supplies were usually exhausted long before all were served. Standing in lines is a way of life in many command economies today.

---

[1] Binding price controls are sometimes said to be "effective"; this is a very special meaning of the word effective.

A different system will develop if storekeepers individually decide who will get the scarce commodities. Goods may be kept "under the counter" and sold only to regular customers. This happened in the United States in 1978, during periods of gasoline shortages, as some gas station operators sold only to their regular customers. When sellers decide to whom they will (and will not) sell scarce supplies, allocation is by **sellers' preferences.**

If the government dislikes the distribution that results from sellers' preferences, it can do at least two things.

First, it can pass laws requiring suppliers to sell on a first-come, first-served basis. To the extent that such "nondiscrimination" legislation is effective, it leads to allocation according to willingness to stand in line. These laws are not easily enforceable, however, and there is little doubt that some available supplies are sold to favored customers according to sellers' preferences.

Second, a more drastic measure, the government can ration the commodity. To do so, it prints only enough coupons to match the available supplies and then distributes the coupons to purchasers, who will need both money and ration coupons to buy the commodity. The coupons may be distributed equally among the population or on the basis of age, family status, occupation, or any other criterion.

Rationing substitutes the central authorities' preferences for the seller's preferences in allocating a price-controlled commodity.

Coupon rationing appeals to many people because other schemes, such as first-come, first-served or allocation by sellers' preferences, may appear arbitrary or capricious—and thus unfair.

Black Markets

Ceiling prices, with or without rationing, usually give rise to black markets. A **black market** is one in which goods are sold (illegally) at prices above the legal maximum price. For most products there are many retailers, and although it may be easy to police the producers, it is often impossible to control effectively the price at which retailers sell to the general public.

Suppose the government can control producers but not retailers. Production remains unchanged because the producers would continue to receive the uncontrolled price for their product. At the retail level, however, the opportunity for a black market arises because purchasers are willing to pay more than the ceiling price for the limited amounts of the commodity that are available. The theory of supply and demand leads to this prediction:

The potential for a black market always exists when binding price ceilings are imposed because it will pay someone to buy at the controlled price and sell at the black market price.

Figure 7-2 illustrates the limiting case in which all the available supply is sold on a black market. The development of such a market depends on there being a few people willing to risk heavy penalties by running a black market supply organization and a reasonably large number of persons prepared to purchase goods illegally on such a market. This case is extreme because there are honest people in every society and because governments ordinarily have considerable power to enforce their price laws. Usually some, not all, of a price-controlled commodity is sold at a black market price. (It is a revealing comment on human nature that there are few known cases in which binding price ceilings were not accompanied by the growth of a black market.)

Does the existence of a black market mean that the goals sought by imposing a price ceiling have been thwarted? This question can be answered only when we know what the government hopes to achieve with its ceiling price. Governments may be interested mainly in (1) restricting production (in order perhaps to release resources for war production), (2) keeping prices down, or (3) satisfying notions of equity in the consumption of a commodity that is temporarily unusually scarce. Ceiling prices with a black market achieve the first but not the second and third objectives. The second objective is frustrated to the extent that goods find their way onto the black market. If equity is the goal, an effective price ceiling on manufacturers plus an extensive black market at the retail level will produce the worst possible results. There will be less to go around than if there were no controls, and the available quantities will tend to go to those with the most money and the least social conscience.

THE EXPERIENCE WITH CEILING PRICES

There is evidence to confirm all these predictions about ceiling prices. Practically all belligerent countries in World War I and World War II put ceilings on prices of certain key items made exceptionally scarce by wartime requirements. These ceilings were always followed first by shortages, second by either the introduction of rationing or the growth of some alternative method of allocation such as sellers' preferences, and third by the rise of a black market. Price ceilings were more effective in limiting consumption than in controlling prices, although they did restrain price increases because the patriotic response of many people to wartime controls led them to do without rather than to patronize the black market.

A more comprehensive kind of ceiling price control is sometimes attempted in peacetime, in an effort to curb inflation. A freeze is put on virtually all prices. But if there is general excess demand, this kind of policy is sure to fail unless something is done to attack the causes of the excess of demand over supply. Price freezes sometimes work for a while, but eventually the backlog of purchasing power bursts out somewhere, and black markets follow. Pressure builds up on the government to remove the controls. Only after prices rise do supplies increase. This happened in the United States after the Nixon administration imposed a price freeze in 1971, it happened to some extent in Canada after the AIB was disbanded, and it has happened throughout the world whenever general ceiling prices have been imposed.[2]

Rent Controls

A widespread growing use of ceiling prices in North America today relates to the rental of houses and apartments for private occupancy. Rent controls have been used in many places the world over, and the consequences have almost always been the same: the creation of a severe housing shortage, private allocation systems, and a black market. For example, in order to make up the difference between the controlled rent and the free-market rent, the landlord may charge the new tenant a grossly inflated sum for a few shabby sticks of furniture. Alternatively, landlords may ration in accordance with their own preferences for tenants and discriminate against families with young children or on some other basis.

As we have noted, the use of rent controls is increasing in Canada. Controls have existed in New York City since World War II; more recently they have been introduced or seriously advocated in many other American cities. In Sweden and Britain, where rent control on unfurnished apartments has existed for decades, housing shortages are endemic except in neighborhoods where population is declining. Whole areas of London are full of abandoned, rotting houses that would have lasted for centuries but which, at controlled rentals, did not even pay the owner the cost of upkeep. When British controls were extended to furnished apartments in 1973, the supply of such accommodations dried up, at least until loopholes were found in the law. When rent controls were initiated in Rome in 1978, a housing shortage developed virtually overnight. This kind of rent control-induced shortage led University of Chicago Professors George Stigler

---

[2] A detailed discussion of the Canadian experience after the Anti-Inflation Board was disbanded appears on pages 867–873.

and Milton Friedman to point to the conflict between "ceilings" and "roofs."

Rent controls are spreading in North America, yet many advocates of such controls seem to have little appreciation of their consequences. Economic theory makes a number of predictions that are useful in understanding the current experience with rent controls and in predicting the consequences. In what follows, we consider the implications of rent controls that are applied uniformly to all rental accommodations; qualifications that arise when rent controls are less comprehensive are outlined at the end of this section.

THE THEORY OF CEILING PRICES APPLIED TO RENT CONTROLS

Rent controls are just a special case of ceiling prices. Controls are usually imposed to freeze rents at their current level at a time when equilibrium rents are rising either because demand is shifting rightward (due to forces such as rising population and income) or because supply is shifting leftward (due to forces such as rising costs). The result is that soon rents are being held below the free-market equilibrium level and excess demand appears. Figure 7-2 can be applied to rent controls. The following predictions about rent controls are simply applications to housing of results that apply to any commodity subject to binding ceiling prices.

1. There will be a housing shortage in the sense that quantity demanded will exceed quantity supplied.
2. The actual quantity of accommodation will be less than if free-market rents had been charged.
3. The shortage will lead to alternative allocation schemes. Landlords may allocate by sellers' preferences, or the government may intervene. In the housing market, government intervention usually takes the form of security-of-tenure laws, which protect the ten-

ant from eviction and thus give existing tenants priority over potential new tenants.
4. Black markets will appear. Landlords may require large lump-sum entrance fees from new tenants. In general, the larger the housing shortage, the bigger the sum required. In the absence of security-of-tenure laws, landlords may force tenants out when their leases expire, and they may even try to evict them in order to extract a large entrance fee from new tenants.

SPECIAL ASPECTS OF THE HOUSING MARKET

Housing has unusual attributes that make the analysis of rent controls somewhat special. The most important is the nature of the commodity itself. So far in this book we have mainly considered markets for commodities that are consumed soon after they are purchased. But housing is an example of a **durable good,** a good that yields its services only gradually over an extended period of time. Once built, an apartment lasts for decades or even centuries, yielding its valuable services continuously over that time. Thus the supply of rental accommodation depends on the *stock* of rental housing available, and in any year it is composed mainly of buildings built in prior years. The stock is added to by conversions of housing from other uses and construction of new buildings, and it is diminished by conversions to other uses and demolition or abandonment of existing buildings whose economic life is over. The stock usually changes slowly from year to year.

These considerations mean we can draw more than one supply curve for rental accommodation, depending on how much time is allowed for reactions to occur to any given level of rents. We shall distinguish just two such curves. The *long-run supply curve* relates rents to the quantity of rental accommodation that will be supplied after sufficient time has passed for all adjustments to be made. The *short-run supply curve* relates rents to quantity supplied when only a short time — say, a few months — is allowed for adjustments

Rent Control in Paris*

A dollar a month will pay a wage earner's rent in Paris.† Such cheapness is amazing. Rent is reckoned as equal in cost to transport to and from work. To put it another way, a month's rent for a large family of six costs as much as eleven packets of cigarettes. Parisians spend on entertainment every month far more than they pay for three months' rent.

Even in a very modest budget such an expenditure absorbs but a small part of income. On average, rent makes up 1.4 percent of a wage earner's expenditures. Such low rents are not a privilege confined to wage earners. Rent seldom rises above 4 percent of any income; frequently it is less than 1 percent.

This may seem a very desirable state of affairs. It has its drawbacks. While you pay no more than these quite ridiculous prices if you are lucky enough to be in possession of a flat, if you are searching for lodgings you cannot find them at any price. *There are no vacant lodgings,* nor is anyone going to vacate lodgings which cost so little, nor can the owners

*This account is excerpted from a longer paper, "No Vacancies," first published in the United States in 1948 and reprinted in F. A. Hayek et al., *Rent Control—A Popular Paradox* (Vancouver B.C.: Fraser Institute, 1976) pp. 105–112. The author, Bertrand de Jouvenal, is a noted French journalist. The general situation described here still exists today.

† All prices are in terms of 1946 dollars. To think of them in 1982 terms, multiply by four.

expel anyone. Deaths are the only opportunity.

Young couples must live with in-laws, watching out for deaths. Tottering old people out to sun themselves will be shadowed back to their flat by an eager young wife who will strike a bargain with the *concierge,* so as to be first warned when the demise occurs. Other apartment chasers have an understanding with the undertakers.

There are two ways of obtaining an apartment which death has made available. Legally, you may obtain from a public authority a requisition order: you will usually find that the same order for the same apartment has been given to other candidates. The illegal method is the surest: deal with the heir, and with his complicity immediately carry in some pieces of your furniture. As soon as you are in, you are king of the castle.

Buying one's way into an apartment will cost anything from $500 to $1,500 per room. At such prices wage earners may as well give up hope of setting up house; they will have to stay with their families.

There are some 84,000 buildings for habitation in Paris: 23,000 were built before 1850; 48,000 before 1880; 75,000 were built before World War I.

Sixteen thousand buildings are in such a state of disrepair that there is nothing that can

to be made in response to a change in rents. We shall assume that in the short run very few new conversions and very little new construction can occur.

The Long-run Supply Curve

Among the many suppliers of rental accommodation are large investment companies and individuals with modest savings invested in one or two small apartments. There is a large potential source of supply, for it is relatively easy to build a new apartment or to convert an existing house and offer its units for rent. If the expected return from investing in new apartments rises significantly above the return on comparable other investments, there will be a flow of investment funds into the building of new apartments. How-be done but pull them down. Nor are the remainder altogether satisfactory. To go into sordid details, 82 percent of Parisians have no bath or shower, more than half must go out of their lodgings to find a lavatory, and a fifth do not even have running water. Little more than one in six of existing buildings is pronounced in good condition by the public inspectors. Lack of repair is ruining even these.

Owners can hardly be blamed. They are not in a financial position to keep up their buildings, let alone improve them. To take an example, here is a lady who owns three buildings containing 34 apartments, all inhabited by middle-class families. Her net loss from the apartments, after taxes and repairs, is $80 a year. Not only must her son put her up and take care of her, but he must also pay out the $80. She cannot sell; there are no buyers.

When the owner tries to cut down the repairs, he runs great risks. One postponed repairs on his roofs, and rain filtering into an apartment spoiled a couple of armchairs. He was sued for damages and condemned to pay a sum amounting to three years of the tenant's paltry rent.

The miserable condition of owners is easily explained. While rents since 1914 have multiplied 6.8 times, taxes have grown 13.2 times and the cost of repairs has increased from 120 to 150 times the 1914 price!

A "right" has developed, the "right" to dig in. The French now have struck roots in their rented lodgings. One cannot allow the owner to dispossess tenants, because in that case he might so easily make an agreement secretly with a new tenant: rent control implied necessarily the denial of the owner's right to evict. The tenant's right to retain possession has been confirmed and the rent is raised slightly from time to time.

If a builder were now to put up flats similar to those in existence, these new apartments would have to be let for prices representing ten times present rent ceilings, in order to reward the costs of construction and the capital invested. As long as the rents of existing buildings are held down artificially far below costs, it will be psychologically impossible to find customers at prices ten times higher, and hence construction will not be undertaken.

Such is the differential between the legal and the economic price of lodgings that even the most fervent advocates of freedom are scared at the prospect of a return to it. They feel that if the right to dismiss tenants and the right to bargain and contract with them were restored, evictions could not be executed, the whole nation of tenants sitting down to nullify the decision. The thing, they say, has now gone too far; the price of rent is too far removed from the cost.

ever, if the return from apartments falls significantly below that obtainable on comparable investments, funds will go elsewhere. The construction of new apartments will fall off and possibly stop altogether. Old apartments will not be replaced as they wear out, so the quantity available will fall drastically. Therefore the long-run supply curve of apartments is highly *elastic*.

The Short-run Supply Curve

Now consider the supply response over a few months. What if rents rise? Even though it immediately becomes profitable to invest in new apartments, it may well take years for land to be obtained, plans drawn up, and construction completed. Thus a long time may pass between the decision to create more apartments and the occupancy by tenants of the new apartments built in response to market signals. Of course some existing housing can be more quickly converted to rental uses, but in many cases even this is likely to take more than a few months.

What if rents fall? New construction will fall off, and this will surely decrease the supply at some time in the future. It will, however, pay the owners of existing apartments with no attractive alternative use of their rental units to rent them for whatever they will earn, providing that the rentals at least cover current out-of-pocket costs such as taxes and heating. Some rental housing can be abandoned or converted to other uses, but, again, this will not usually happen very quickly.

Thus the short-run supply curve that relates rentals to the quantity supplied tends to be quite *inelastic* at the level of the quantity currently supplied. The longer the time horizon, the less inelastic it will be. For the very short run, however, it is likely to be almost completely inelastic.

SUPPLY RESPONSE TO CHANGES IN RENTS

If rents rise, what will the supply response be? In the short run, the quantity will remain more or less the same because the short-run supply curve is inelastic. For a while existing landlords will make **windfall profits,** profits that bear no relation to current or historical costs. Yet these profits are the spur to the long-run allocation of resources. New construction will begin, and after a year or two new rental units will begin to come onto the market. The quantity will continue to expand until a new point on the long-run supply curve has been attained.

If rents decrease, the quantity supplied will also remain more or less unchanged because of the inelastic short-run supply curve. But the profitability of supplying rental accommodations will fall, and new construction will be curtailed as a result. How long will it be before the current stock of old housing shrinks to its new point on the long-run supply curve?

Because houses are durable, they will not quickly disappear. But owners of rental properties can speed the shrinkage in various ways. Some apartments can be withdrawn from the rental market and sold to owner-occupiers more or less on an "as is" basis. Others can be converted into cooperatives or condominiums. Other apartments occupy land with valuable alternative uses. If rents fall far enough, it will pay to demolish those apartments and use the land for something else, but it requires a substantial and long-lasting fall in rents before demolition costs are worth incurring.

Many existing apartment buildings and other rental accommodations have no real alternative uses and will continue to serve as apartments until they are abandoned as useless. Yet the useful life of an apartment depends on how well it is maintained. In general, the less spent on maintenance and repairs, the shorter the structure's effective life. The lower the rents, the less will it pay landlords to spend on upkeep, and thus the faster will the apartment "wear out."

If rental revenues fall below the minimum costs of operation (which include taxes and heating), the owner may simply abandon the apartment. Although this may sound extreme, it has happened repeatedly in North America and Europe. When it happens, a stock of housing that might have lasted decades or even centuries is dissipated within a few years.

The special features of the housing market lead to an important additional prediction about rent controls.

Because the long-run supply curve of rental housing is highly elastic, rent controls that hold rents below their free-market levels for an extended period will inevitably lead to a large reduction in the quantity of rental housing available.

This prediction is illustrated in Figure 7-3. The speed with which the reduction occurs will depend on the extent to which controlled rents depart from their free-market levels: the greater the discrepancy, the faster the rental housing stock will shrink.

FIGURE 7-3
Effects of Rent Control in the Short and Long Run

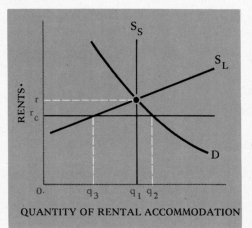

QUANTITY OF RENTAL ACCOMMODATION

Rent controls cause housing shortages that worsen as time passes. The controlled rent, r_c, is below the equilibrium rent, r. The short-run supply of housing is the inelastic curve S_s. Thus quantity supplied remains at q_1 in the short run, and the housing shortage is q_2q_1. Over time the quantity supplied shrinks as shown by the long-run supply curve S_L. In long-run equilibrium there are only q_3 units of rental accommodation, far fewer than when controls were instituted. Since the long-run supply is quite elastic, the housing shortage of q_3q_2 that occurs after supply has fully adjusted ends up being much larger than the initial shortage of q_2q_1.

THE DEMAND FOR RENTAL HOUSING

There are many reasons to expect the demand for apartments and other forms of rental housing to be quite elastic. As the price of rental accommodation in an area rises, each of the following will occur.

1. Some people will stop renting and buy instead.
2. Some will move to where rental housing is cheaper.
3. Some will economize on the amount of housing they consume by renting smaller, cheaper accommodations (or renting out a room or two in their present accommodations).

4. Some will double up and others will not "undouble" (for example, young adults will not move out of parental homes as quickly as they might otherwise do).

Such occurrences contribute to a substantial elasticity of the demand for rental housing: Increases in rents will sharply decrease the quantity demanded.

The effect of rent controls is to prevent such increases in rents from occurring. Thus, even while the supply of rental housing is shrinking for the reasons discussed above, the signal to economize on rental accommodation is *not* given through rising rentals. The housing shortage grows as the stock of rental accommodation shrinks while nothing decreases the demand for it. This too is illustrated in Figure 7-3.

WHEN RENT CONTROLS WORK: SHORT-TERM SHORTAGES

Pressure for rent controls seems to arise in response to rapidly rising rents for housing. The case for controlling rising rentals is strongest when the shortages causing the increasing rents are temporary.

Suppose there is a temporary influx of population into an area. Perhaps a pipe-line or a power complex is being built, and many workers are required for the construction even though few will remain behind to run the automated equipment. When the construction workers flood in, market rents will rise. New construction of apartments will not occur, however, because investors recognize the rise in demand and rentals as temporary. In this case, rent control may stop existing owners from gaining windfall profits, with few harmful supply effects since a long-run supply response is not expected in any case. After the boom is over, demand will fall and free-market rents will return to the controlled level (their original level). Controls may then be removed with little further effect. This is illustrated in Figure 7-4.

FIGURE 7-4
Rent Controls in Response to Increasing Demand

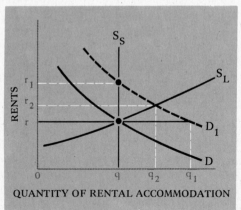

QUANTITY OF RENTAL ACCOMMODATION

Rent controls prevent a temporary skyrocketing of rents when demand rises, but they also prevent the long-term supply adjustment to demand increases.

Temporary demand fluctuations. The short-run supply curve S_S applies. In the free market a temporary rise in demand from D to D_1 and then back to D will change rents from r to r_1 and then back to r. Rent control would hold rents at r throughout; it would create a housing shortage due to excess demand of qq_1 as long as demand was D_1, but it would not affect the quantity of housing available.

Permanent changes in demand. The long-run supply curve S_L applies. A permanent rise in demand from D to D_1 will cause free-market rents to rise from r to r_1 and then to fall to r_2 as the quantity of accommodation supplied grows from q to q_2. Controlling the rent at r, in order to prevent windfall profits, produces a permanent housing shortage of qq_1.

Even in cases where rent controls have no long-run adverse effect, there will be some disadvantages. At controlled rents there will be a severe housing shortage but no incentive to existing tenants to economize on housing and no incentive for potential suppliers to improvise by finding ways of providing extra short-run accommodation. If rents rise on the free market, existing tenants will economize and some tenants and owners will find it profitable to rent out rooms. Even though the supply of permanent apart-

ments does not change, the supply of casual temporary accommodation (mobile homes, for example) will increase. Such reactions are induced by the signal of rising rents but inhibited by controls.

WHEN RENT CONTROLS FAIL: LONG-TERM SHORTAGES

Long-run Increases in Demand

What if the rise in demand for rental accommodation is not temporary, and the ability to expand supply is not limited arbitrarily by government decree? Increases in rentals give the signal that apartments are very profitable investments. A consequent building boom will lead to increases in the quantity supplied, and it will continue as long as large profits can be earned.

If rent controls are imposed in the face of such long-term increases in demand, they will prevent short-run windfalls, but they will also prevent the needed long-run construction boom from occurring. Thus controls will convert a temporary shortage into a permanent one. This too is illustrated in Figure 7-4.

Inflation in Housing Costs

A second situation in which rent controls fail comes about when they are introduced to protect tenants from rent increases in an inflationary world. Inflation raises both the costs of construction of new housing and the costs of operating and maintaining existing housing. As we saw in Chapter 5, a rise in costs shifts the supply curve upward and to the left.

Fixed rent controls in an economy that is experiencing a steady inflation will produce a housing shortage that grows over time. If inflation is combined with growth in demand, the growth in the housing shortage becomes very large (see Figure 7-5).

The Clamor for Rent Control

In the face of the predicted and observed consequences, why does rent control persist and even grow? The answer is largely that the primary victims of rent control do not identify themselves as such, while the primary beneficiaries do.

Whatever the overall effects of rent control, existing tenants who can stay in their present locations will benefit from it. Existing tenants know that rent controls hold down the cost of housing. (The only risk to them comes if landlords allow their apartment buildings to deteriorate.) And existing tenants constitute an important political constituency for rent controls.

Many renting families live on incomes that are small, fixed, and being eroded steadily by inflation. Renters include a disproportionate fraction of the aged, the unemployed, welfare recipients, and members of minority groups. They also include many students. A high percentage of these groups are paying at least half their money incomes to a landlord (who seems never to be in view except to collect the rent), and these groups are truly being squeezed by the rising costs of everything. (Of course not all existing renters are poor, nor landlords rich.)

If the beneficiaries of rent control are existing tenants, who are the victims? The housing shortage hurts those who will want rental housing that will not be there in the future. The elderly couple who fight to keep rent control on the apartment they occupy are behaving wholly in their own best interest. But they are making life more difficult for the next generation of aged couples, many of whom will not find housing of the same quality if rent controls are kept. The welfare family protected today will have a hard time finding housing if it moves when the opportunity for a job arises or when its present apartment house is abandoned. Minority groups generally will find that their members are hurt in the long run by the steadily shrinking quantity and quality of available rental housing.

Why do so many people favor rent controls when control-induced shortages will make it more difficult for them to find a suitable apartment? The answer, when it is not an ideological dislike of landlords, seems to be that they do not recognize the link between the lower rents they will pay—if they are lucky enough to find a rent controlled apartment where they want it—and the *decreased chance* of finding such an apartment. If they knew that rent control was the reason they had to wait so long and search so hard to find accommodation, they might prefer to pay the free-market rent. But they do not know this—and once "in," they will be protected by rent controls.

Thus the call for rent control comes both from existing tenants, who gain at the expense of those who do not have secured leases in rental housing, and from potential tenants, who underestimate the adverse effects on *them* of the rent control-induced housing shortage. In contrast, the *articulate* opposition is the much smaller (and less sympathetic) group of landlords. The silent victims, who are the future unsuccessful searchers for rental units, may never realize the causal link between rent controls and the housing shortage from which they suffer.

That many individuals are either selfish or myopic in calling for rent control is understandable. That their leaders and public representatives do not appreciate and weigh the long-term consequences is less comprehensible except in very political terms. Worldwide experience as well as economic theory demonstrates that rent controls create shortages, that shortages do not benefit the population as a whole, that the real costs of providing housing do not diminish when controls are imposed, and that when the private market does not provide housing, either tenants will bear the cost by doubling up or doing without or public taxes will have to be raised to provide public housing. Perhaps the politicians are myopic too, judging next month's election (and hence today's constituency) to be more important than the adverse, long-run future effects.

FIGURE 7-5
An Ever-growing Housing Shortage

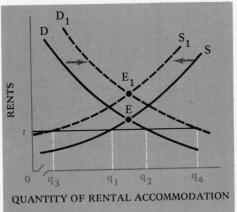

QUANTITY OF RENTAL ACCOMMODATION

In a growing, inflation-prone economy, rent controls will cause the housing shortage to worsen year by year. In a growing economy the demand curve is continually shifting rightward as more people with higher real incomes demand more housing. In an inflationary economy the supply curve is continually shifting leftward because construction, maintenance, and operating costs are rising. Such shifts when combined with rent controls cause the housing shortage to grow over time. For example, when the curves are D and S, rent control at r is accompanied by a housing shortage of q_1q_2. When the curves have shifted to D_1 and S_1, however, the same controlled rent causes an overall housing shortage of q_3q_4.

WHAT ARE THE ALTERNATIVES?

Advocates of continuing rent controls often say that construction costs are now too high to erect buildings that offer apartments at rents that middle-class people can afford. What are the alternatives? One possibility is to let rents rise on the free market sufficiently to cover costs. If "middle-class people" (and others) really decide they cannot afford these apartments and will not rent them, then the building of apartments will cease. It is more likely, however, in light of past consumer behavior, that agonizing choices will be made to spend a higher proportion of total income on housing and/or to economize on housing.

A second possibility is to control rents below the cost of new building, with the inevitable consequence of a shortage of rental housing that grows as the stock of rental accommodation wears out and is not replaced. A further alternative is for government to step in with public housing and fill the gap between total demand and private supply. Subsidized public housing will then be financed at the taxpayer's expense (since the high costs of housing must be paid by someone).

The costs of providing additional housing cannot be voted out of existence; they can only be transferred from one set of persons to another.

In Canada, some modifications to rent control programs have been introduced to deal with some of the issues raised in this chapter. For example, in Vancouver controls do not apply to apartments renting for more than a stated limit, and in Ontario they do not apply to new buildings. Although both policies still involve the transfer of costs and benefits from one group to another and both still lead to some of the problems with rent controls outlined before, they both attempt to avoid the costs associated with the induced reduction of supply associated with a comprehensive rent control policy.

Some European countries, notably Great Britain and Sweden, have been through the whole process of imposing rent controls to protect tenants and ending up with excess demand and an increasingly expensive program of subsidized public housing. In the face of other public needs, they are trying to give more scope to private markets for housing, but policies of rent controls are always politically popular. Only time will tell how far North America is to travel the same path. Economics cannot tell society which hard choice to make, but it can show what the choices are. The greatest danger is that the long-run costs will be neglected in making the choice.

The Problems of Agriculture

Finding satisfactory solutions to their "farm problem" has been one of the major challenges to policymakers in most nations in the non-Communist world. Farm incomes appear to be typically lower and less stable than those in other industries and occupations. The Canadian farm population of about two million constitutes 10 percent of the total population and provides 7 percent of the total labor force but earns less than 5 percent of national income. A variety of techniques of government intervention have been tried, including price supports, crop insurance, transportation and storage subsidies, and the operation of marketing boards, but the problems remain.

The farm problem is interesting because of the importance of farmers in Canadian life. It is also important because the key features of it — sharply fluctuating prices that are outside the producer's control, inelastic demand curves, and a low income elasticity of demand in a society that is exhibiting steady growth — are found singly and in various combinations in many of the economy's markets, farm and nonfarm alike.

LONG-TERM TRENDS

Paradoxically, it has been steady growth over time in the productive capacity and wealth of the North American economy that has caused many long-term problems for agriculture. Pressure has come from both the demand and the supply sides of agricultural markets.

Demand. Workers can produce more per worker than they previously did. In this century output per worker in Canada has increased at an average annual rate of almost 2 percent. Such increases in production lead to increases in the income of the population. How do households wish to consume their extra income? The relevant measure is income elasticity of demand, which measures the effect of increases in income on the demands for various goods. Income elasticities vary considerably among goods. At the levels of income existing in Canada and other advanced industrial nations, most foodstuffs have low income elasticities because most people are already well fed. When these people get extra income, they tend to spend much of it on con-

sumers' durables, entertainment, and travel. Thus, as incomes grow, the demand for agricultural goods tends to increase relatively slowly (if population remains relatively stable).

If productivity is expanding uniformly among industries, the demands for goods with low income elasticities will be expanding more slowly than output. In such industries excess supplies will develop, prices and profits will be depressed, and resources will be induced to move elsewhere. Exactly the reverse will happen for industries producing goods with high income elasticities. Demands will expand faster than supplies, prices and profits will tend to rise, and resources will move into the industries producing these goods.

Supply. The need to transfer resources out of agricultural industries is even greater than would be required by their low income elasticities. The reason is that growth in agricultural productivity has been well *above* the average for the economy. Encouraged by government-financed research, by subsidies, and by a government-assured demand for farm output at a stable price, agricultural productivity has increased enormously in this century. Since 1947, for example, Canadian farm output per agricultural worker has grown at the rate of about 5 percent per year, nearly twice the rate of growth of total output per worker.

These productivity increases tend to shift the supply curves of agricultural goods to the right, indicating a greatly increased ability and willingness to produce at each price. If resources had not been reallocated out of farming, there would have been enormous increases in output, which could hardly have been sold within Canada or exported at any price.

Reallocations of resources in a free-market economy are expected to take place under the incentives of low prices, low wages, and depressed incomes in the declining sector, and high prices, wages, and incomes in the expanding sector. But incentives of this kind prove painful — indeed pain is the spur — to those who live and work on farms, especially when resources move slowly in response to depressed incomes. It is one thing for the farmer's son or daughter to move to the city; it may be quite another for the farmer and the farmer's parents, who are set in their ways. Because farmers are people—and voters—governments tend to respond to their cries for help in overcoming the depressed conditions in agriculture that free markets often produce.

Notice that the same problem exists for any industry where growth in demand is low while productivity growth is high. It is quite possible that in the future a similarly gradual but continuing decline will affect durable consumer goods industries such as automobiles and refrigerators.

SHORT-TERM FLUCTUATIONS

Short-term volatility of prices is typical of many agricultural markets. Why do such fluctuations occur?

Farm crops are subject to variations in output because of many factors completely beyond farmers' control. Some variation is simply a matter of season, but pests, floods, and lack of rain can drastically reduce farm output, and exceptionally favorable conditions can cause production greatly to exceed expectations. By now you should not be surprised to hear that such unplanned fluctuations in output cause fluctuations in farm prices. Not only does price theory predict this obvious consequence, it also predicts other, less obvious ones that help us to understand some of the farmer's problems.

The basic behavior is illustrated in Figure 7-6. Because demand curves slope downward, variations in farm output placed on the market cause price fluctuations in the opposite direction to crop sizes. A bumper crop sends prices down, a small crop sends them up. The price change will be larger, the less elastic the demand curve.

Because agricultural products tend to have inelastic demands, fluctuations in prices tend to be large in response to unplanned changes in production.

What are the effects on the receipts of farmers? If the commodity in question has an elasticity of demand greater than unity, increases in the quantity supplied will raise farmers' receipts and decreases will lower farmers' receipts. If the demand is inelastic, farmers' receipts will rise when price rises and fall when price falls.

If demands are inelastic, good harvests will bring reductions in total farm receipts and bad harvests will bring increases.

Because most farm products have inelastic demands, farm receipts tend to vary inversely with crop size. When nature is bountiful and produces a bumper crop, farmers' receipts dwindle; when nature is moderately unkind and output falls unexpectedly, their receipts rise. The interests of the farmer and the consumer are exactly opposed in such cases. This conflict was dramatically illustrated in 1972 and 1973 when worldwide grain failures sent grain prices skyrocketing and farm incomes up—and triggered the largest rise in consumer food prices in 25 years. In 1976 fair weather and bumper crops brought relief in the supermarkets but led to lower incomes to farmers.

Cyclical Fluctuations in Prices and Incomes

As the tide of national and international prosperity ebbs and flows, demand curves for all commodities rise and fall. The effects on prices and outputs depend on the elasticity of *supply*.[3] Industrial products typically have rather elastic supply curves, so shifts in demand cause fairly large changes in outputs but only small changes in prices. Agricultural commodities as a whole often have rather inelastic supplies because acreage and labor devoted to agricultural uses is

---

[3] The appendix to this chapter pursues the theory that a further source of short-run fluctuations lies in the possibility that cycles are introduced by supply *lags* in response to changes in demand. The appendix provides an excursion into what is called *dynamic analysis*; the example is that of the famous hog cycle.

FIGURE 7-6
The Effect on Price of Unplanned Variations in Output Depends on Elasticity of Demand

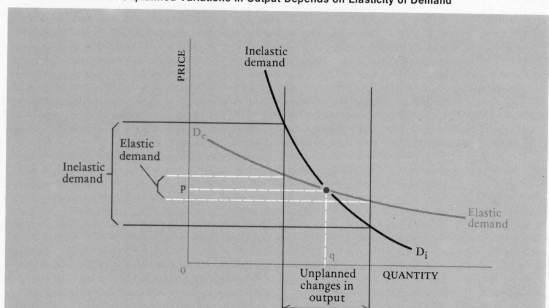

An unplanned fluctuation in output of a given size leads to a much sharper fluctuation in price if the demand curve is inelastic than if it is elastic. Suppose the expected price is p and the planned output q. The two curves D_i and D_e are *alternative* demand curves. If actual production always equaled planned production, the equilibrium price and quantity would be p and q with either demand curve. Unplanned variations in output, however, cause quantity to fluctuate year by year between q_1 (a bad harvest) and q_2 (a good harvest). When demand is inelastic (shown by the heavy curve), prices will show large fluctuations. When demand is elastic (shown by the screened curve), price fluctuations will be much smaller.

not quickly transferred to nonagricultural uses when demand falls and then returned to agriculture quickly when demand rises.

Given an inelastic supply curve for agricultural products as a whole, farm prices, farm receipts, and farm income will be very sensitive to demand shifts, as Figure 7-7(i) illustrates. A sharp drop in demand (a leftward shift of the demand curve) will cause hardship among those whose income depends on farm crops.

However, in comparing the position of agriculture with that of industry, it is incomes received —not prices—that matter. Figure 7-7(ii) deals with the effects of a shift in demand where output

rather than price is decreased sharply. It shows that a very elastic supply can be as much a curse as a very inelastic one in the face of a decrease in demand! The loss in receipts in Figure 7-7(ii) is primarily due to a decline in quantity sold rather than a decline in price, but that does not make it less painful.[4]

---

[4] Farm income is not simply farm profits, for the wages paid to farm labor are also incomes attributable to farming. Similarly, the incomes earned in industry include the wages and salaries of workers as well as the profits of business people. When output drops greatly, as in Figure 7-7(ii), many business people will lay off workers, and so on. This reduces incomes earned from industrial production.

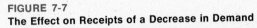

FIGURE 7-7
The Effect on Receipts of a Decrease in Demand

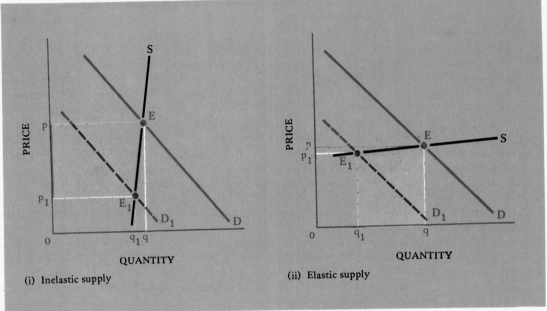

(i) Inelastic supply

(ii) Elastic supply

Either an inelastic or an elastic supply curve can lead to a sharp decrease in receipts, but the effect on prices is very different in the two cases. In each part of the diagram, when demand decreases from D to D_1, price and quantity decrease to p_1 and q_1 and total receipts decline by the shaded area. In (i) the cause is mainly the sharp decrease in price. Output and em- ployment remain high, but the drastic fall in price will reduce or eliminate profits and put downward pressure on wages. In (ii) the cause is primarily the sharp decrease in quantity. Employment and total profits earned fall drastically, though wage rates and profit margins on what is produced may remain close to their former level.

In addition to changes in domestic demand, the Canadian agricultural sector has to contend with cycles in economic conditions in other countries because about 20 to 25 percent of farm production is exported. (The wide fluctuations in exports of wheat are shown below in Figure 7-12.)

AGRICULTURAL STABILIZATION AND SUPPORT PLANS

Governments throughout the world intervene in agricultural markets in attempts to deal with the problems just studied. They try to stabilize agricultural prices and incomes in the face of short- term and uncontrollable fluctuations in supply and cyclical fluctuations in demand. They also seek to support agricultural prices and incomes at levels sufficient to guarantee farmers what is regarded as reasonable or decent living standards. In so doing they often weaken the incentive for resources to leave farming, and thus, if there is a long-run problem, make it worse.

Because income stabilization and price stabilization are not the same, there has been confusion about what is intended in schemes designed to achieve "orderly agricultural marketing." We shall consider several schemes.

Suppose the supply curve in each case refers to planned (or average) production per year, but actual production fluctuates around that level. In a free market, as we have seen, this causes both prices and farmers' receipts to fluctuate widely from year to year.

The Ever-Normal Granary

One method of preventing fluctuations in prices and gross receipts is for individual farmers to form a producers' association that tries to stabilize — to keep "ever normal" — the supply *actually coming onto the market,* in spite of variations in production. It does this by storing a crop, say grain, in years of above average production and selling out of its storage elevators in years of below average production.

Since one farmer's production is an insignificant part of total production, there is no point in an individual farmer's holding some production off the market in an effort to prevent a fall in price in a year of bumper crops. But if all farmers get together and agree to vary the supply coming onto the market, then, collectively, they can have a major effect on price. The appropriate policy is illustrated in Figure 7-8.

Since revenues accrue to the producers when the goods are actually sold on the market, total revenues can be stabilized by keeping sales constant at the equilibrium output even though production varies. This can be accomplished by adding to or subtracting from inventories the excesses or shortages of production.

The fully successful ever-normal granary stabilizes both prices and revenues of producers.

The costs of this plan are those of providing storage and of organizing and administering the program. A potential danger is that the producers' association will sell on average less than is produced (in order to get higher prices) and will find itself with ever-increasing stockpiles of the crop.

The first significant attempts by Canadian farmers to control market supply occurred in the 1920s when western wheat producers formed wheat pools in each of the prairie provinces. Their marketing functions were later taken over by the federal government through the establishment of the Canadian Wheat Board.

Government Price Supports at the Equilibrium Price

Because there are many difficulties in organizing and administering private stabilization schemes such as the ever-normal granary, why cannot the government do the same thing and do it more efficiently?

Suppose the government, instead of the producers' association, enters the market, buying in the market and adding to its own stocks when there is a surplus and selling in the market —

FIGURE 7-8
Stabilizing Sales Despite Variable Production: The Ever-normal Granary

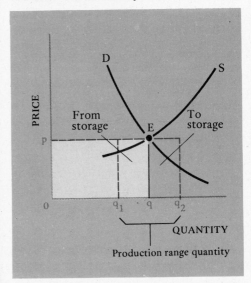

The ever-normal granary scheme sells the equilibrium quantity each year even though actual production varies. The planned supply curve is S; p and q are the equilibrium price and quantity. Actual production varies between q_1 and q_2. When production is q_2 the producers' association sells q and stores qq_2. When production is q_1 it still sells q, supplementing the current production by selling q_1q from its stored crops. Producers' revenue is stabilized at $p \cdot q$ (the shaded area) every year.

FIGURE 7-9
Government Price Supports at the Equilibrium Price

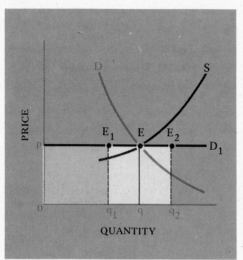

QUANTITY

Government price supports at the equilibrium price stabilize prices and do not accumulate surpluses but cause revenues to vary directly with production. Actual production varies around the equilibrium level of q. When production is q_2 the government buys qq_2 and stores it. When production is q_1 the government sells q_1q from storage. The quantity sold to the public is always q, and this stabilizes price at p. The government policy converts the demand curve to D_1. If q is average production, there is no trend toward accumulation of storage crops.

Farmers' revenue varies from pq_1 (the darker shaded area) when production is q_1, to pq_2 (the entire shaded area) when production is q_2.

thereby reducing its stocks—when there is a shortage. If it had enough grain elevators and warehouses, and if its support price were set at a realistic level, the government could stabilize prices indefinitely. But, as Figure 7-9 illustrates, it would not succeed in stabilizing farmers' revenues and incomes, for farmers would find their revenues high with a bumper crop and low with a poor crop.

Government price supports at the equilibrium price would not stabilize revenues. They would however reverse the pattern of revenue fluctua- tion of a crop with inelastic demand and a fluctuating supply.

In effect, the government policy imposes a demand curve that is perfectly elastic at the support price. This stabilizes price, but it does not stabilize receipts to producers.

Government Stabilization of Farmers' Revenues by Open Market Purchases and Sales

Obviously there must be a government buying and selling policy that will stabilize farmers' receipts. What are its characteristics? As has been seen, too much price stability causes receipts to vary directly with production and too little price stability causes receipts to vary inversely with production. It appears that the government should aim at some intermediate degree of price stability. If the government allows prices to vary in inverse proportion to variations in production, then receipts will be stabilized. A 10 percent rise in production should be met by a 10 percent fall in price, and a 10 percent fall in production by a 10 percent rise in price.

To stabilize farmers' receipts, the government must make the demand curve facing the farmers one of unit elasticity. It must buy in periods of high output and sell in periods of low output, but only enough to let prices change in inverse proportion to farmers' output.

Government Price Supports Above the Free-market Equilibrium Level

To avoid long-term problems, the government policy just described should allow prices to fluctuate around the free-market level. In practice, however, stabilization plans involving price supports usually set prices above the average free-market equilibrium level. Partly this is due to the fact that stabilization is not the only goal, and there is a desire to assure farmers a standard of living comparable with that of city dwellers. This involves attempting to *raise* farm incomes in addition to stabilizing them.

Here too the government buys in periods of high output and sells in periods of low output, but on average it buys much more than it sells. This is illustrated in Figure 7-10.

Stabilization of prices above the free-market equilibrium level is an example of establishing a price floor below which the commodity cannot be sold. Whenever price is maintained above the free-market level, the quantity that suppliers wish to sell will exceed the quantity demanded. Either an unsold surplus will exist or someone — in this case, the government — must step in and buy the excess production. In the average year there is a surplus, and this results in a situation in which over time the stabilizing authority buys more than it sells, so unsold surpluses accumulate. The cost to the taxpayers includes any part of the outlay not ultimately recovered by sale of the crop, plus costs of storage, handling, and administration.

PROBLEMS WITH AGRICULTURAL STABILIZATION AND SUPPORT PLANS

A first difficulty of plans that seek to raise farm income by raising prices above free-market levels is the tendency to accumulate surpluses. Eventually, if agricultural surpluses persist, the stored crops will have to be destroyed, dumped on the market for what they will bring, or otherwise disposed of at a fraction of their cost. If the crops are thrown on the market and allowed to depress the price, then the original purposes for which the crops were purchased — price stabilization and raising of farm incomes — are defeated. If the crops are destroyed or allowed to rot, the efforts of a large quantity of the country's scarce factors of production (the land, labor, and capital that went into producing the stored goods) will have been completely wasted.

Destroying crops is a vexing moral problem when millions are starving, but if the stored crops are not to depress the price, they must be kept off the market. Giving crops away to those who would not otherwise buy them is sometimes attempted but is hard to achieve. Selling grain at

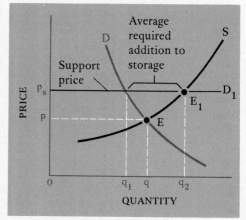

FIGURE 7-10
Price Supports Above the Equilibrium Price

The support price becomes a price floor, and the government must purchase the excess supply at that price. Average annual demand and supply are D and S. The free-market equilibrium is at E. If the government will buy any quantity at p_s, the demand curve becomes the black curve D_1 and equilibrium shifts to E_1. The average addition to storage is the quantity q_1q_2. The government purchases add to farmers' receipts and to government expenditures.

cut-rate prices for conversion to gasohol has recently been proposed.

Any of these "solutions" will mean that the agricultural support program will show a deficit, for goods will have been purchased that cannot be sold except at a large loss. This deficit means that taxpayers generally will be paying farmers for producing goods that no one in the nation is willing to purchase at prices that come near to covering costs.

When support schemes begin to produce ever-larger surpluses, the next step is often to try to limit each farmer's production. Quotas may be assigned to individual farmers and penalties imposed for exceeding the quotas. Or bonuses may be paid for leaving the land idle and for plowing crops under. Such measures waste resources because the desired output could be produced with fewer resources and the remaining resources used to produce other goods. All they

Of Rotten Eggs and Curdled Milk

EGGS ROT IN A HUNGRY WORLD*

The federal Canadian Egg Marketing Agency was established for the basic purpose of ensuring that farmers made a profit on their eggs. Eggs rating the subsidized price to producers were supposed to be produced under provincial quotas, many of which have been exceeded. Smaller producers were not under the quota.

The result has been more eggs than consumers could consume, especially at the high price ensured by CEMA's guaranteed price to the farmers. Eggs bought at 67 cents a dozen have been stored to be sold for processing by drying or freezing at 26 cents. But there are too many eggs even for the processors. The freshest eggs for processing (subsidized by Canadians) go to processors in the United States.

Canadian producers are therefore being stuck by CEMA with the older eggs, of which 10 to 30 per cent are rotten. Some are so old and so bad that they are being condemned by Department of Agriculture inspectors in storage warehouses.

As the Consumer Association of Canada has complained to Prime Minister Pierre Trudeau, this is wasteful and CEMA is "a mismanaged monopoly." Yet federal Agriculture Minister Eugene Whelan has said that he will ask his Cabinet colleagues to pay $5 million to $6 million to relieve part of the $10 million debt into which CEMA has fallen.

CEMA has stimulated over-production, pushed egg prices in Canada so high that many Canadians have had to cut their consumption, provided bargain fresh and processed eggs to U.S. customers at the cost of the Canadian taxpayers who can't afford them themselves, and let uncounted thousands of eggs rot.

CURDLED MILK†

More to be censured than pitied, federal Agriculture Minister Eugene Whelan has done it again. His ludicrous attempts to bottle up

---

*Adapted from an editorial in the Toronto *Globe and Mail,* August 1, 1974.

† Adapted from an editorial in the *Edmonton Journal,* April 22, 1976.

---

dispense with is the visible symbol of trouble, the accumulating surpluses.

A second difficulty arises because the long-term need to reallocate resources out of agriculture (a result of the low income elasticity of demand) will conflict with plans designed to stabilize farm incomes at a high level. A program that succeeds in giving the rural sector a high level of income will partially frustrate the market mechanism for inducing excess resources to move out of agriculture. Indeed it may make matters worse. If the artificially profitable and stable market provides a stimulus for research and development that greatly increases productivity in the farm sector, it will shift the supply curve to the right, creating a further excess of quantity supplied over quantity demanded at the stabilized price.

AGRICULTURAL POLICY IN CANADA

Marketing Boards and the Use of Quotas

The primary method by which agricultural stabilization is attempted in Canada is through the

overproduction of the Canadian dairy industry have gone sour. By supporting the price of skim milk powder at 68 cents a pound this year (a four-cent increase) Mr. Whelan has succeeded in alienating farmers, maddening consumers and upsetting cabinet colleagues.

All this has come about because Mr. Whelan got his thinking crossed up. He decided that farmers were entitled to a bigger share of the country's wealth and boosted the base milk price from $9.41 per hundred-weight to $11.02. These increases were in no way related to production costs but rather were a case of giving farmers "what was their due."

It hadn't occurred to the minister what the dairymen's response would be. They overproduced to the point of creating huge surpluses of powdered milk, mountains of it that cost money to store and more money to ship. There's a surplus of the stuff all over the producing world and on the international market its price has fallen to 20 cents per pound, delivered. This is the powdered milk that Canadians must buy at 68 cents wholesale. Incredible, isn't it?

Mr. Whelan's sorry attempts to extricate himself from the quicksands of this un-manageable surplus have led him to fine, in effect, dairymen who continue to overproduce and to cut their deliverty quotas by 15 percent.

That's how Eugene Whelan is "helping" the dairymen. On top of this, the dairymen will suffer from reduced domestic consumption, the result of higher shelf prices in the market place.

It hasn't occurred to Mr. Whelan that this country would be better off if he subsidized Canadian consumers rather than his export program. That he could, at the price of admitting his mistakes, cut the powdered milk price still further and sell his surplus to domestic livestock producers as protein supplement. He refused to do this last year, and Canadian feed makers paid 38 cents a pound for powdered milk while it was sold to feed makers abroad at six cents.

Canadian consumers have every right to be asking why they are subsidizing milk powder for countries that don't want it. With the aroma of 28 million rotten eggs still hanging about, they are being stuck with costs related to the storage and sale of 300 million pounds of powdered milk.

operation of marketing boards. Sales through them account for about one-half of all farm cash receipts. Most marketing boards were established under provincial legislation, but their ability to control markets has been constrained by lack of cooperation among them. To alleviate this problem, the federal government has attempted to coordinate provincial activities through the Agricultural Products Marketing Act of 1972. One of the first boards to be established under this act was the Canadian Egg Marketing Agency, which soon became a classic case of price supports leading to accumulation of surpluses — in this case, rotting eggs. The Canadian Dairy Commission has created similar conditions in the market for skim milk powder (see box).

Typically the method used to stave off surplus production is to establish quotas that limit the output of each individual producer. To the extent that the total quota allocation is less than the free-market equilibrium quantity, the marketing board can maintain the price above the equilibrium level without generating surpluses and provide holders of quotas with profits in excess of those they would earn in a free market (see Fig-

FIGURE 7–11
Price Support Through the Use of Quotas

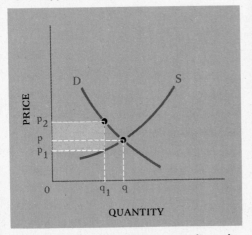

A quota below the equilibrium quantity maintains the price above the equilibrium level without generating surpluses. If a total quota of q_1 is enforced, the price will rise to p_2. Since the supply curve indicates that in a free market producers would be willing to supply q_1 at a lower price p_1, the effect is to provide holders of quotas with additional profit represented by the shaded area.

ure 7-11). If the right to produce conferred by a quota is transferable either by itself or jointly with the farm to which it is attached, it will have a market price. For example, it has been estimated that the right to produce broiler chickens in Ontario commands a price in the neighborhood of $5 per bird. A farmer wishing to enter the industry at what is said to be a minimum efficient family farm level (50,000 birds) would have to pay something like $250,000 for the right to produce, over and above the cost of buildings, equipment, and land.

The high value placed on quotas is an indicator of the success of marketing boards in raising the incomes of farmers. On the other hand it suggests that consumers are providing a very substantial subsidy. On the basis of data on quota values, Professors Grubel and Schwindt have estimated that the operation of the British Columbia Milk Board in 1975 cost consumers in

that province about $12 million per year or about $48 on the average for a family of four.[5]

Besides being costly to consumers, it is not clear that quotas distribute income in favor of the farmers most in need. In particular, new producers who wish to enter the industry must purchase quotas from existing holders, so the benefit of the extra profits accrues entirely to those who received the initial allocation and thereby reaped a windfall gain.

The Marketing of Wheat

The origins of government involvement in the marketing of Canadian wheat can be traced back to the early 1900s, when disparities in bargaining power emerged between western farmers and grain buyers. The growers' associations protested that unfair practices and control of country prices were carried out by the companies controlling the elevators to which the farmers delivered their grain. The government's response was limited; except for the World War I period, government intervention before 1930 was confined to regulation of marketing procedures such as grading, inspection, and provision of railway facilities, and provincial government participation in and subsidization of cooperative elevator companies.

Heavy involvement by the government of Canada in the marketing of wheat arose out of the disruptions of the Great Depression. Pressures to establish a national marketing board had built up during the 1920s, when the growers' vulnerability to the vagaries of the international wheat situation became the dominant concern, the proportion of output exported having grown to more than 70 percent. Under the Canadian Wheat Board Act of 1935, the procedure was established by which the federal cabinet sets annually a minimum initial price at which wheat will be purchased by the board. After the wheat delivered to the board has been sold, the pro-

[5] H. W. Grubel and R. W. Schwindt, *The Real Cost of the B.C. Milk Board* (Vancouver, B.C.: Fraser Institute, 1977).

ceeds in excess of initial payments are distributed to the producers. When sales yield less than the initial payments, the loss is absorbed by the federal treasury. During the first eight years of its existence, the Wheat Board operated alongside the open market so that deliveries to the board fluctuated according to the relationship between its price and the market price. Compulsory marketing through the Wheat Board was instituted in 1943 and has been maintained to the present time.

The recent wheat situation. Ideally, the role of the Canadian Wheat Board should be to bargain effectively in the international market and to dampen fluctuations in the incomes of producers by accumulating stocks in years of high yield and/or weak demand and running down stocks in the opposite circumstances. Judged by the statistics for recent years, the board has not been very successful (see Figure 7-12).

During the 1960s it had to contend with fluctuations in yield per acre from a low of 17.9 bushels in 1959–1960 to a high of 27.9 bushels in 1966–1967. Export demand varied between a low of 277 million bushels and a high of 585 million bushels, with large contracts with the USSR and China accounting for a substantial portion of the strong demand experienced in the mid 1960s. The carryover of wheat in storage was clearly substantially above the level necessary to provide a buffer stock. This resulted in a substantial burden on the federal government, which is committed to paying part of the cost of storage.

In an attempt to reduce the level of accumulated stocks, the government resorted at the end of the 1960s to a wheat acreage reduction scheme under which compensation payments were made to farmers who reduced their acreage below 1969 levels. As can be seen from Figure 7-12, a substantial reduction in seeded acreage and production was induced, but ironically this was accomplished just as world markets were about to make a dramatic about-face. Exports returned to the high levels experienced

in the mid sixties (again much of the increase was accounted for by sales to the USSR), and by the end of 1972–1973 stocks had fallen to the lowest level since 1952.

Carryover stocks remained low until the 1976–1977 crop year, when the prairie crop reached a record level of 840 million bushels. At the same time production increased in the United States and the Soviet Union, and the international market was once again flooded with wheat. Predictably, prices sagged, falling below $3 a bushel, compared with the peak level of $6 reached in late 1974. This depressed market was costly to Canadian taxpayers because the federal government is committed to maintaining farm incomes. (Under the Western Grain Stabilization Plan, established in 1975, participating farmers are guaranteed that their net cash receipts will not fall below the average of the preceding five years.)

Over the four crop years ending in mid 1980, exports recovered steadily if not sensationally. Despite bumper crops of more than 700 million bushels in both 1977–1978 and 1978–1979 (due to record yields both years of over 28 bushels per acre), stocks were historically low in August 1980. However, the world grain market was disrupted by the U.S. embargo on exports to the Soviet Union following the latter's incursion into Afghanistan, and the repercussions of this will be felt, particularly in carryover stocks, for years to come.

HAS THE FARM PROBLEM DISAPPEARED?

Until five or ten years ago most economists would have agreed that despite substantial government intervention — or perhaps because of it — the agricultural sector was still a major trouble spot in the economy and farm policy an expensive but predictable failure.

Yet few would have urged the government to cease its intervention altogether. For to leave to the price mechanism the task of reallocating resources out of farming would mean facing the

FIGURE 7–12
Canadian Wheat Production

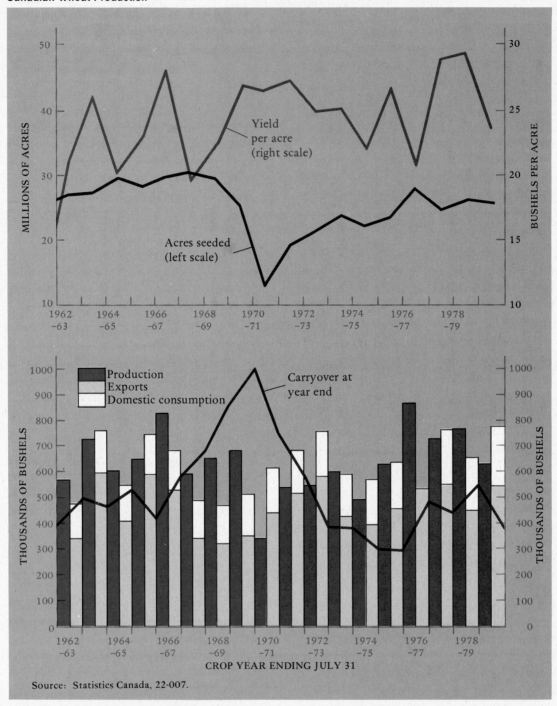

Source: Statistics Canada, 22-007.

Variations in output and demand lead to fluctuations in carryover stocks of wheat. The top panel illustrates the behavior of acres seeded to wheat and yield per acre. These are the determinants of annual variations in the total wheat crop, and translate into the colored bars in the bottom panel, which indicate yearly pro-duction. The white and gray bars in the bottom panel indicate domestic consumption and exports of wheat, respectively. The difference between production and total consumption equals the change in carryover stocks as indicated by the black line in the bottom panel.

prospect of a more or less permanently depressed sector of the community. It is doubtful that any Canadian political party would be willing to accept the social and political consequences of leaving this sector to fend for itself.

Recent unexpected events have raised the possibility that our past policy has not been so disastrous after all and that by good luck if not by good judgment our accumulated surpluses have found an important use. Growing world population, growing world income, and some massive crop failures around the world have created the spectre of a worldwide food shortage and of hunger and starvation.

Whether or not these developments portend the end of the "farm problem" and the beginning of a long-awaited era of farm prosperity is not yet clear. There is no doubt that the *need* for food and other agricultural products throughout the world is high and rising because of the population explosion. But will this need be translated into *demand,* in the sense of willingness to purchase at the prices required to bring forth supply? Will Canadian agriculture, with its high wages and high expectations for farmers' incomes (based as they are on our standards of income), be able to compete successfully in world markets? (Canadian households are finding Canadian food prices "out of sight," and those prices will look even higher in New Delhi.) If the answers to these questions are yes, all may be well; if no, the farm problem may soon be severe again. It is as yet too early to tell.

Four General Lessons About Resource Allocation

We have examined several examples of government intervention in markets that might have been left unregulated. Public debate about the desirability of more or less intervention is lively today, both with respect to deregulation in areas of existing regulation and with respect to imposing wage and price controls to cope with the ever-rising prices in our inflationary economy.

Our discussion suggests four widely applicable lessons.

1. COSTS MAY BE SHIFTED, BUT THEY CANNOT BE AVOIDED

Production, whether in response to free-market signals or to government controls, uses resources; thus it involves costs to members of society. If it takes 5 percent of the nation's resources to provide housing to some stated average standard, then those resources will not be available to produce other commodities. For society there is no such thing as free housing. The average standard of living depends on the amounts of resources available to the economy and the efficiency with which these resources are used. *It follows that costs are real* and are incurred no matter who provides the goods. Rent controls, housing subsidies, or public provision of housing can change the share of the costs of housing paid by particular individuals or groups — lowering the share for some, raising the share for others — but they cannot make the costs go away.

Different ways of *allocating* the costs may also affect the total amount of resources used, and thus the amount of costs incurred. Controls that keep prices and profits of some commodity below free-market levels will lead to increased quantities demanded and decreased quantities supplied. Unless government steps in to provide additional supplies, fewer resources will be allocated to producing the commodity. If government chooses to supply all the demand at the controlled prices, more resources will be allocated to it, which means fewer resources will be devoted to other kinds of goods and services. The opportunity cost of more housing is less of something else.

2. FREE-MARKET PRICES AND PROFITS ENCOURAGE ECONOMICAL USE OF RESOURCES

Prices and profits in a market economy provide signals to both demanders and suppliers. Prices that are high and rising (relative to other prices) provide an incentive to purchasers to economize on the commodity. They may choose to satisfy the want in question with substitutes whose prices have not risen so much (because they are less costly to provide) or to satisfy less of that want by shifting expenditure to the satisfaction of other wants. There is substantial scope for such economizing reactions even for commodities as "necessary" as housing: *some* housing is necessary, but a particular quantity is not.

On the supply side, rising prices tend to produce rising profits. High profits attract further resources into production. Short-term windfall profits that bear no relation to current costs repeatedly occur in market economies; they cause resources to move into those industries with profits until profits fall to levels that can be earned elsewhere in the economy.

Falling prices and falling profits provide the opposite motivations. Purchasers are inclined to buy more; sellers are inclined to produce less and to move resources out of the industry and into more profitable undertakings.

The pattern we have described may be summarized:

Free-market prices and profits are signals to producers and consumers. Changing relative prices and profits signal a need for change to which consumers and producers respond.

3. CONTROLS INHIBIT THE ALLOCATIVE MECHANISM

Some controls prevent prices from rising (in response, say, to an increase in demand). If the price is held down, the signal is never given to consumers to economize on a commodity that is in short supply. On the supply side, when prices and profits are prevented from rising (on the grounds, for example, that no more than a "fair" return should be earned at all times), the profit signals that would attract new resources into the industry are never given. The shortage continues, and the movements of demand and supply that would resolve it are not set in motion.

In the opposite case, where there is excess supply, an appropriate response would be some increase in quantity purchased and some decrease in production accompanied by a shift of resources to production of other, more valued commodities. Falling prices and profits would motivate such shifts. When prices are prevented from falling in the face of temporary surpluses (on the grounds, for example, that producers of an essential product must have a fair return guaranteed to them), the signals that would increase purchases or push resources out of an industry are never given.

The results tend to be the same no matter what the motives for intervention. For rent controls and other maximum prices, public policy rests on the view that consumers need protection from producers. Landlords who provide rental accommodations are left to bear any windfall losses themselves yet are prevented from earning windfall gains. In agriculture, however, public policy since the 1930s had often taken the opposite view: to protect farmers at the expense of consumers or taxpayers.

The underlying reasons for these views are complex. One may start with stereotypes of rich landlords, poor tenants, struggling family farmers, and beleaguered taxpayers. Yet even superficial analysis shows that these are only stereotypes, that there are lots of struggling landlords, rich tenants, and corporate farms.

4. CONTROLS REQUIRE ALTERNATIVE ALLOCATIVE MECHANISMS

If the price system with its profit incentives is not used to allocate resources, alternative methods will necessarily appear. Temporary fluctuations in demand and supply will give rise to severe shortages and surpluses. During times of shortages, allocation will be by sellers' preferences unless the state imposes rationing. During periods of surplus, there will be unsold supplies or illegal price cutting unless the state buys and stores the surpluses. Long-run changes in demand and costs will not induce resource reallocations through private decisions. As a result, the state will be put under strong, long-run pressure to step in. It will have to force or order resources out of industries where prices are held too high—as it has tried to do in agriculture. It will also have to force or order resources into industries where prices are held too low—as it can do, for example, by providing public housing.

Whenever a specific alternative scheme of allocation is imposed, it is costly in a number of additional ways. First, the allocation itself usually requires the use of resources for administering and enforcing the rules. Second, the use of the state's power takes the mixed economy one step further away from the free enterprise economy and toward a command economy. Third, the freedom of some individuals to act in what they consider their own best interest is limited. Sometimes the benefits of the policies will justify the costs, sometimes they will not. Justified or not, the costs are always present and are often large.

Summary

1. The elementary theory of supply, demand, and price provides powerful tools for analyzing and understanding some real-world problems and policies. The chapter illustrates this with respect to price controls and agricultural policies.

2. Price ceilings are binding ("effective") whenever they hold price below the free-market equilibrium price. Binding ceiling prices cause shortages to appear, lead to allocation by sellers' or government's preferences, and provide a strong incentive for black marketeers to buy at the controlled price and sell at the higher free-market price.

3. Rent controls are a persistent and spreading form of price ceiling. The major effect of rent control is a shortage of rental accommodation that grows worse because of a slow but inexorable decline in the quantity of rental housing.

4. Rent controls can be an effective response to temporary situations in which there is a ban on

building or a transitory increase in demand. They will almost surely fail when they are introduced as a response to a long-run increase in demand or to inflation in the costs of providing rental housing.

5. Agricultural commodities are subject to wide fluctuations in market prices, and these often lead to fluctuations of producers' incomes. This is because of year-to-year unplanned fluctuations in supplies combined with inelastic demands, and because of cyclical fluctuations in demands combined with inelastic supplies. Where demand is inelastic, large crops tend to be associated with low total receipts and small crops with high total receipts.

6. Fluctuations in farmers' gross receipts can be reduced by a producers' association that stores crops unsold when output is high and sells from inventories when output is low, or by appropriate government purchases and sales in the open market.

7. Price stabilization schemes historically tend to involve stabilization above average free-market equilibrium levels. The result is a buildup of surpluses. To avoid these surpluses, marketing boards in Canada have established quotas that limit the output of individual producers.

8. The long-term problems of agriculture arise from a high rate of productivity growth on the supply side and a low income elasticity on the demand side. This means that, unless many resources are being transferred out of agriculture, quantity supplied will increase faster than quantity demanded year after year. If existing prices are maintained, and if farmers are guaranteed a market for all of their output at these prices, the yearly farm surplus will tend to increase.

9. All wheat produced in Canada is marketed through the Canadian Wheat Board. Wide fluctuations in yields and export demand have hampered its efforts to stabilize the incomes of growers. Carryover stocks grew rapidly during the 1960s but were reduced to historically low levels the mid1970s as a result of an upturn in world demand. In the late 1970s, record yields and bumper crops led to some increase in carryover stocks, but growth in exports was also rapid so that at the end of the decade stocks were still historically low.

10. The early 1970s witnessed a worldwide food shortage and a boom in agriculture. Whether this promises an end to long-term farm problems depends on whether our farm products will remain competitive in world markets at prices that the world's growing population will pay. The late 1970s experienced both bumper crops domestically and buoyant world demand.

11. Four general lessons about resource allocation are: (1) costs may be shifted, but they cannot be avoided, (2) free-market prices and profits encourage economical use of resources, (3) controls inhibit the allocative mechanism, and (4) controls require alternative allocative mechanisms.

Topics for Review

Comparative statics
Ceiling prices and price floors
Black markets
Allocative function of windfall profits
The effect of controls on allocation
Alternative allocative mechanisms
Price supports at and above the level of free-market equilibrium
Price stabilization versus income stabilization
Income elasticity and long-term resource reallocation

Discussion Questions

1. "When a controlled item is vital to everyone, it is easier to start controlling the price than to stop controlling it. Such controls are popular with consumers, regardless of their uneconomic consequences. In this respect oil price controls resemble rent controls." Explain why it may be uneconomic to have such controls, why they may be popular, and why, if they are popular, the government might nevertheless choose to decontrol prices.

2. "Since the demand for these exceeds the supply, applications should be made well in advance." This is from a university catalog's description of married students' quarters. Comment on the allocative system being used by the university authorities.

3. Medical and hospital care in Britain is provided free to individuals by the National Health Service, with the costs paid by taxation. Some British doctors complain that patients want "too much" medical care; patients complain that they have to wait "too long" in doctors' offices for the care they get and months or years for needed operations. Use the theory of supply and demand to discuss these complaints. Would you expect a private (pay) medical market to grow up alongside the National Health Service? Would you expect the government to welcome or discourage such a second service?

4. Predict the consequences of extending the legal minimum wage to the services of children, including those for mowing lawns and babysitting.

5. Consider a law school that has 1,000 qualified applicants for 200 places in the first-year class. It is debating a number of alternative admission criteria: (a) a lottery, (b) date of initial application, (c) grades, (d) recommendations from alumni, (e) place of residence of applicant. An economist on the faculty determines that if the tuition level were doubled, the excess demand would disappear. Argue for (or against) using the tuition rate to replace each of the other suggested criteria.

6. The demand for housing (rented or owned) is downward sloping. List some of the reasons why a rise in the price of all forms of housing (due to, say, a rise in construction costs) would lead to a reduction in the quantity of housing demanded. Do some of the reasons apply particularly to rental housing? To owner-occupied housing?

7. It is sometimes asserted that the rising costs of construction are putting housing out of the reach of ordinary citizens. Determine who bears the cost when rentals are kept down by (a) rent controls, (b) a subsidy to tenants equal to some fraction of their rent payments, and (c) low-cost public housing.

8. In England rents are set by public bodies that are instructed to fix fair rents without regard for local conditions of demand and supply. What might this mean? Analyze some of the effects of this policy on the workings of local housing markets.

9. After the 1980 provincial election in Ontario, in which the Progressive Conservatives won a majority, there

was considerable speculation that rent controls would be abandoned. Gordon Walker, the minister responsible for housing policy, announced that while some relaxation of controls might be considered for rural areas with high vacancy rates, controls would remain in places where they are needed, such as metropolitan Toronto with its low vacancy rate. What is meant by the phrase "where they are needed"? Analyze the effects of this type of selective rent control policy.

10. In 1974 the Kenya Meat Commission (KMC) decided it was undemocratic to allow meat prices to be out of the reach of the ordinary citizen. It decided to freeze meat prices. Six months later, in a press interview, the managing commissioner of the KMC made each of the following statements.

   a. "The price of almost everything in Kenya has gone up, but we have not increased the price of meat. The price of meat in this country is still the lowest in the world."

   b. "Cattle are scarce in the country, but I do not know why."

   c. "People are eating too much beef, and unless they diversify their eating habits and eat other foodstuffs the shortage of beef will continue."

   Do the facts allegedly make sense, given KMC's policy?

11. Use a supply and demand diagram to illustrate the cost to the taxpayers of a deficiency payment scheme under which the government pays producers the difference between the market price and a fixed guaranteed price.

12. What would be the effects of a university policy that dictated equal pay to every university teacher of given age whatever his or her ability and field of study?

13. It has been said that the success of agriculture has benefited everyone but the farmer. In the light of what you have learned in this chapter, explain the background of this statement.

14. "If a farmer borrows money to buy a mechanical picker that replaces 100 hand pickers, this may make his operations more profitable in an average year while simultaneously leaving him more vulnerable to even minor cyclical downturns." Explain.

Supply and Demand in Action II: International Trade and Exchange Rates

8

We have seen that goods and services are traded among the households and firms of a single nation. They are also traded among units located in different nations. **International trade** refers to all exchanges of goods and services that take place across national boundaries.

In Chapter 4 we found that efficiency gains arise from specialization and that specialization must be accompanied by trade. This applies as much to international situations as it does to internal, or *intra*national, situations. The present chapter uses the basic tools of supply and demand to study the markets for goods that enter into international trade, called **exports** and **imports**, and the complications that arise because different countries use different currencies. (A later chapter takes up in more detail the fundamental question of what determines the gains that are derived from trade between nations and then examines the pros and cons of interfering with the flow of international trade.)

The Nature of International Trade

International trade comes about when nations take advantage of the efficiency gains that arise from specialization. International trade is important because it allows the bundle of goods that a country consumes to differ from the bundle of goods that it produces. More generally, international trade allows the set of goods available for consumption, called the **consumption possibility set,** to differ from the bundle of goods actually produced and from the set of goods that could be produced, as determined by the production possibility boundary. A country that engages in international trade may effectively transform one kind of good, say agricultural products, into another, say manufactured products, by exporting agricultural products to other countries and importing manufactured goods. In order to export agricultural products, the country must produce more agricultural products than it consumes. Conversely, imports of manufactured goods allow domestic consumption of such goods to exceed domestic production.

An economy that engages in international trade is called an **open economy;** one that does not is called a **closed economy.** In this chapter we examine a simple case, that of the small open economy. A **small open economy** exerts no influence on the world prices of traded goods. Its exports and imports are small in relation to the total volume of world trade, and therefore changes in the quantities that it exports and imports do not influence the prices established in world markets. For many countries and commodities, this is a reasonable assumption.

THE EXPANSION OF THE CONSUMPTION POSSIBILITY SET THROUGH TRADE

In **autarky,** a situation in which there is no international trade, an economy consumes those goods, and only those goods, that it produces. By allowing the goods consumed by a nation to differ from the goods produced, international trade actually *expands* the consumption possibility set.

This expansion has two distinct stages. One occurs for a *given* production point on the production possibility curve. The other arises out of the possibility of choosing a different production point in the presence of international trade than would be chosen in autarky.

Expansion in Consumption Opportunities with Given Production

The first stage is straightforward. Given its production choice, in autarky the economy must consume the same quantities of those goods

it chooses to produce. When trade is possible, a wide variety of consumption combinations is possible, *including the no-trade option.* For our small open economy, the ratio at which goods can be exchanged in international markets, called the **terms of trade,** is a constant.[1] When production, say of agricultural goods, exceeds desired consumption, the surplus goods may be exchanged at a fixed ratio for manufactured goods. When production of agricultural goods is less than desired consumption, more can be obtained in exchange for manufactured goods. A wider range of combinations of final consumption of agricultural and manufactured goods is available even when production is unchanged. This is illustrated in Figure 8-1 (i) and (ii).

Expansion in Consumption Opportunities with Variable Production

Of course production may change. The second expansion of the consumption possibility set is a further consequence of the fact that international trade allows the separation of production decisions from consumption decisions. Without the possibility of international trade, an economy's choice of which bundle of goods it will produce must be related to its decision as to which bundle of goods it will consume. With the possibility of trade, the choice of a production bundle can be altered to reflect the relative value placed on goods by international markets.

Suppose a country is producing less manufactured goods than it wishes to consume. In the absence of trade, production would adjust to satisfy domestic desires and there would be an increase in the quantity of manufactured goods produced. With trade, the extra manufactured goods can be imported, adjustment in production need not respond to the domestic excess demand, and indeed the quantity of manufactured goods produced may in fact *decrease.* The decrease in production of manufactured goods re-

---

[1] The terms of trade indicate the number of units of the export good required to pay for one unit of the import good. The role of the terms of trade in influencing the gains from trade is discussed in Chapter 26.

FIGURE 8–1
The Effects of International Trade on the Consumption Possibility Set

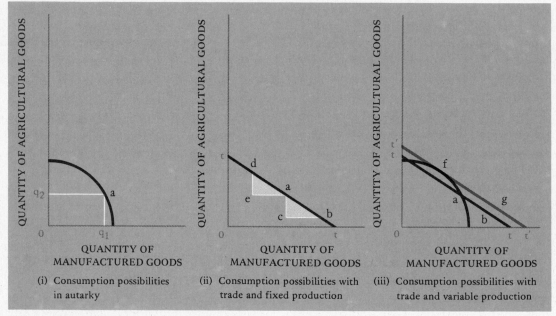

(i) Consumption possibilities
in autarky

(ii) Consumption possibilities with
trade and fixed production

(iii) Consumption possibilities with
trade and variable production

International trade creates gains in the form of increased consumption opportunities that arise from (1) the possibility of consuming a bundle of goods different from what is produced and (2) the possibility of specializing in production. In (i) production is at point a; with no international trade consumption is also at point a. In (ii) production remains fixed at point a but now the possibility of international trade means that consumption need not be at point a. Agricultural goods can be exchanged for manufactured goods in the ratio indicated by the line tt, thereby enlarging the consumption possibility set to the line tt. For example, if consumption were at b, ac units of agricultural goods could be exported and cb units of manufactured goods imported. Alternatively, if consumption were at d, ed units of agricultural goods could be imported and ea units of manufactured goods exported.

In (iii) the consumption possibility set is shifted to the line $t't'$ by changing production from a to f and thereby increasing the country's degree of specialization in agricultural goods. For any point on the original consumption possibility set, tt, there is a point on the new set, $t't'$, which allows more consumption of each good. Compare, for example, points b and g. Notice also that, except at the zero trade point f, the new consumption possibility set lies everywhere above the production possibility curve.

leases resources that can then be used to increase the production of agricultural products. Consumption opportunities are improved if the economy obtains more manufactured goods for consumption by producing and exporting agricultural goods than by increasing output of manufactured goods and reducing that of agricultural goods. This is illustrated in Figure 8-1 (ii) and (iii).

Summary of Sources of Expansion of Consumption Possibilities Through International Trade

We have just seen that international trade leads to an expansion of the set of goods that could be consumed in the economy by (1) permitting the possibility of consuming goods different from those produced and (2) permitting a change in the pattern of production. These effects can be summarized:

For a country with a *given* production possibility curve, international trade expands the consumption possibility set beyond that which prevails in autarky. In an open economy, the consumption of some goods (imports) exceeds domestic production and the production of other goods (exports) exceeds domestic consumption. The expansion of consumption opportunities arises directly from the opportunity to trade and indirectly from the opportunity to specialize in production.

In Figure 8-1 the movement from (i) to (ii) corresponds to the direct gain and the movement from (ii) to (iii) corresponds to the indirect gain. In Figure 8-1 we consider only situations of **balanced trade** — where the value of goods imported is exactly matched by the value of goods exported. (In Chapter 33, we consider situations of unbalanced trade, wherein the difference between the value of exports and imports gives rise to a transfer of a financial claim on one economy to the other.)

Stage two of the increase in consumption opportunities arises from appropriate specialization in production. In our example, the economy expands its opportunities by increasing the production of agricultural goods and decreasing the production of manufactured goods. Economists often refer to this as exploiting the country's **comparative advantage.** The benefits that arise in moving from the autarky or no-trade position at point *a* in Figure 8-1 (i) to the trading position in Figure 8-1 (iii) are called the **gains from trade.** These topics are taken up in more detail in Chapter 26; here we focus on the markets for imports and exports.

THE DETERMINATION OF IMPORTS AND EXPORTS: A SIMPLE EXAMPLE

Suppose the economy in our example is an exporter of agricultural goods. In order for trade to be balanced, the economy must be importing some other good — in our example, manufactured goods. This is illustrated in Figure 8-2. At the

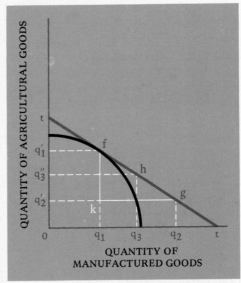

FIGURE 8–2
An Example of Agricultural Exports Balanced by Manufactured Imports

Exports of agricultural products are balanced by imports of manufactured goods as the economy trades along the consumption possibility set given by *tt*. Production is at point *f*, allowing q_1 of manufactured goods and q_1' of agricultural goods to be produced. Consumption is at point *g*, where q_2 of manufactured goods and q_2' of agricultural goods are consumed. Exports of agricultural goods are $q_1' - q_2'$ (=*fk*). Imports of manufactured goods are $q_2 - q_1$ (=*kg*). At the terms of trade given by *tt*, *fk* and *kg* have equal values. A shift in demand from manufactured goods toward agricultural goods moves the consumption point from *g* to *h*; imports of manufactured goods fall to $(q_3 - q_1)$ and exports of agricultural goods fall to $(q_1' - q_3')$.

prevailing terms of trade, exports of agricultural goods, *fk*, are equal in value to imports of manufactured goods, *kg*.

Exports. Domestic supply and demand curves for a typical exported agricultural good, say wheat, are shown in Figure 8-3. In the example, equilibrium occurs at a price different from that at which domestic supply and demand are equal.

Assuming a small open economy (that the world price is given) amounts to assuming that foreign demand for the export good is perfectly elastic at the world price. The world price will be quoted in terms of the foreign currency; the Canadian price must equal that world price adjusted for the exchange rate. The **exchange rate** is the ratio at which the domestic currency can be exchanged for the foreign currency. For the moment we will treat the exchange rate as given; later we will consider the effects of a change in the exchange rate and then examine the forces that work to determine the exchange rate.

In Figure 8-3 the world price adjusted for the exchange rate is such that domestic supply exceeds domestic demand. This is consistent with equilibrium because the excess supply is exported. For a traded commodity such as wheat, domestic demand and supply do not determine the domestic price. A world price is determined in world markets by world demand and world supply; the domestic price must be equal to this world price adjusted for the exchange rate between domestic and foreign currencies. Instead, domestic supply and demand determine the *quantity* to be traded. The determination of the quantity of wheat to be exported is shown in Figure 8-3.

Note that for the exported goods in Figure 8-3, the world price exceeds the price that would have prevailed in the absence of trade, p_a. The latter is often referred to as the **autarky price.** It is the higher external valuation which makes it in the country's interest to export the good. (This point is developed further in Chapter 26.) The higher world price also induces the economy to specialize in producing more of the export good than it would in autarky.

Imports. The market for a typical imported good, say British steel, is in an analogous situation, as depicted in Figure 8-4. Because the world price is below the domestic autarky price, there is an excess of domestic demand over domestic supply. The excess demand is satisfied by imports.

Determination of Price and Quantity in Markets for Traded Goods

In Chapter 5 we learned that demand and supply interact to determine the price and quantity exchanged in a particular market. That analysis has to be modified when the market in question is the domestic market for a good that is traded internationally.

For an open economy, equilibrium in a particular market is consistent with domestic demand for that product being different from domestic supply. If at the world price domestic demand exceeds supply, the good will be imported; if domestic supply exceeds demand, the good will be exported.

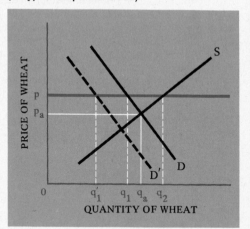

FIGURE 8–3
The Domestic Supply and Demand for Wheat (a Typical Exported Good)

Exports are determined by the domestic excess supply of a tradeable good at the world price. *D* and *S* are the domestic demand and supply schedules. In autarky, at price p_a quantity q_a will be produced and consumed domestically. If the world price of wheat, *p*, exceeds the autarky price, p_a, the country will export wheat. At the world price *p*, quantity supplied will be q_2, domestic consumption will be q_1, and $q_2 - q_1$ will be exported. A fall in domestic demand to *D'* increases the quantity exported to $q_2 - q_1'$.

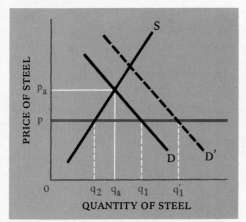

FIGURE 8-4
The Domestic Supply and Demand for Steel (a Typical Imported Good)

Imports are determined by the excess domestic demand for a tradeable good at the world price. *D* and *S* are the domestic demand and supply schedules. In autarky, at price p_a quantity q_a will be produced and consumed domestically. If the world price of steel, *p*, is less than the autarky price, p_a, the country will import steel. At the world price *p*, quantity supplied will be q_2, domestic consumption will be q_1, and $q_1 - q_2$ will be imported. A rise in domestic demand to *D'* increases the quantity imported to $q_1' - q_2$.

Effects of Changes in Domestic Supply and Demand

Suppose that domestic residents experience a change in taste. At the same prices and values of other variables that influence quantity demanded, people decide to consume less wheat and more steel. This decision is illustrated in Figure 8-3 where the demand for wheat shifts to the left and in Figure 8-4 where the demand for steel shifts to the right. At the prevailing world prices, the shifts lead to an increase in the quantity of wheat exported and an increase in the quantity of steel imported. If these shifts were common to all agricultural and manufactured products, they might show up in Figure 8-2 as a movement of the consumption point from *g* to *h*.

Since the economy we are studying is assumed to be very small relative to the rest of the world, these changes do not have a noticeable effect on world prices. The result of the shifts in demand is a change in the *quantities* of imports and exports. The assumption that world prices are constant means that in effect the domestic economy can buy or sell any quantities it wants on world markets. The world demand for wheat is presumed to be infinitely elastic, so the increase in the quantity of wheat that the country *desires* to export in Figure 8-4 is also the *actual* increase in wheat exports.

The effects of a change in domestic supply can also be studied. For example, an increase in domestic wages would increase the cost of producing both wheat and steel, and it would reduce the quantity that would be supplied domestically at each price. The reader can verify that this would lead to an increase in the quantity of British steel imported and a decrease in the quantity of wheat exported.

For a small open economy with a given exchange rate, changes in domestic supply and demand lead to changes in quantities imported and exported rather than to changes in domestic prices.

In our terminology, a large country is one that would exert some influence on world prices so that *both* quantities and prices would change in response to shifts in domestic demands and supplies. These complications we ignore for the present; however, the qualification that the exchange rate remain unchanged is an important one, and we turn now to a closer look at the exchange rate.

The Nature of Exchange Rates

One of the major differences between international trade and interregional trade (trade within one country) is that while different regions of the same country use the same money, different nations do not. The currency of one country is generally acceptable within the bounds of that country, but usually it will not be accepted by households and firms in another country.

When Canadian producers sell their products, they require payment in Canadian dollars, for they must meet wage bills, pay for raw materials, and reinvest or distribute their profits. When the goods are sold in Canada, there is no problem; the purchasers will pay dollars for them. However, when a Canadian producer sells goods to an Indian importer, either the Indian must exchange rupees for dollars to pay for the goods or the Canadian producer must accept rupees. The producer will accept rupees if they can be exchanged for the required dollars. The same holds true for producers in all countries; they must eventually receive payment for the goods they sell in terms of the currency of their own country.

In general, trade between nations can occur only if it is possible to exchange the currency of one nation for that of another.

Foreign exchange refers to the actual foreign currency, or various claims on it such as cheques and promises to pay, that are traded for each other. The exchange rate is the price at which purchases and sales of foreign currency or claims on it take place; it is the amount of one currency that must be paid in order to obtain one unit of another currency. For example, in 1980 the exchange rate between British currency (called "pounds sterling" and indicated by the symbol £) and Canadian dollars was approximately £1 = \$2.75. Thus one pound exchanged for two dollars and seventy-five cents, and one dollar exchanged for approximately £0.36.

What is the mechanism for exchanging currencies? International payments that require the exchange of one national currency for another can be made in a bewildering variety of ways, but in essence they involve the exchange of currencies between people who have one currency and require another.

Suppose that a Canadian auto dealer wishes to purchase a British sports car to sell in Canada. The British manufacturer will require payment in sterling. If the car is priced at £4,000, the Canadian importer can go to a local bank and purchase a "draft" for £4,000 to send to the British dealer. The exchange rate determines the price charged for the draft, so if the rate is \$2.75 = £1, the Canadian dealer would pay \$11,000 (plus a small commission). The effect of this transaction on the banks in the two countries is shown in Table 8-1.

Suppose now that in the same period of time a British wholesaler wishes to purchase 20 Canadian refrigerators to sell in Britain. If the refrigerators are price at \$550 each, the Canadian seller will require a total payment of \$11,000. To make

TABLE 8-1
Changes in the Balance Sheets of Two Banks as a Result of International Trade

U.K. bank			Canadian bank		
Assets	Liabilities		Assets	Liabilities	
No change	(1) Deposits of car exporter	+£4,000	No change	(1) Deposits of car importer	−\$11,000
	(2) Deposits of refrigerator importer	−£4,000		(2) Deposits of refrigerator exporter	+\$11,000
	Net change	0		Net change	0

International transactions involve a transfer of deposit liabilities among banks. The table records two separate international transactions at an exchange rate of £1 × \$2.75: (1) a Canadian purchase of a British car for £4,000 (= \$11,000), and (2) a British purchase of Canadian refrigerators for \$11,000 (= £4,000). The Canadian's import of a car reduces deposit liabilities to Canadian citizens and increases deposit liabilities to British citizens. The Britisher's import of refrigerators does the opposite. When a series of transactions are equal in value, there is only a transfer of deposit liabilities among individuals within a country. The Canadian refrigerator manufacturer received (in effect) the dollars the Canadian car purchaser gave up to get a British-made car.

this payment, the British importer goes to the bank, gives the bank £4,000, and receives a draft for $11,000. When the Canadian seller deposits this draft, the Canadian bank acquires a claim against a British bank; the effect of this transaction is also shown in Table 8-1.

The two transactions cancel each other out. There is no net change in international liabilities, and no money need pass between British and Canadian banks to effect the transactions. Each bank merely increases the deposit of one domestic customer and lowers the deposit of another. Indeed, as long as the flow of payments between the two countries is equal (Canadians pay as much to British residents as British residents pay to Canadians), all payments can be managed as in the previous examples, and there will be no need for a net payment from British banks to Canadian banks.

When the flow of payments is not the same in both directions, the difference is referred to as the **balance of trade.** When exports exceed imports, a country has a **trade surplus;** when imports exceed exports, it has a **trade deficit.** Later we consider the problems that arise when trade is not in balance.

THE EFFECTS OF CHANGES IN THE EXCHANGE RATE

So far we have treated the exchange rate as though it remained constant. In fact the exchange rate has fluctuated a great deal in the past. We want eventually to address the question of what determines the exchange rate and to explain the fluctuations observed in Figure 8-10. But first we need to identify the main effects of a change in the exchange rate.

A change in the market-determined value of the exchange rate is called an **appreciation** when the value of the currency in question rises and a **depreciation** when the value of the currency falls. For example, if the exchange rate between pounds sterling and Canadian dollars changes from £1 = $2.50 to £1 = $2.75, the value of the Canadian dollar will have depreciated by 10 percent relative to the pound.[2] A sale of $10.00 on the foreign exchange market would now yield only £3.64, whereas before the depreciation it would have yielded £4.00. A sale of £10.00 on the foreign exchange market would now yield $27.50, whereas before the change it would have yielded only $25.00.

To see the effects of changes in the exchange rate, let us return to our example of a country that is exporting wheat and importing steel. As before, we assume that the country is small enough that it does not influence the world prices of these commodities. A 10 percent depreciation of the country's currency would mean that the domestic currency prices of the two goods must rise by 10 percent. Since the sale of a unit of wheat still yields the same amount of foreign exchange, it now yields 10 percent more in terms of domestic currency. Domestic purchasers too will have to pay the higher price, for if the domestic price did not rise, producers would prefer to sell only in the export market. Similarly, the purchase of steel still requires the same amount of foreign currency, but 10 percent more of the domestic currency must be paid to obtain the required amount of foreign currency. Thus the domestic currency price of imported steel also rises by 10 percent.

These effects are illustrated in Figures 8-5 and 8-6. In the market for wheat, the increase in the domestic price causes the quantity supplied to rise and the quantity demanded domestically to fall. As a result, the quantity exported, which is equal to the excess of the quantity supplied over the quantity demanded domestically, *rises.* For the imported good, the domestic price rise also causes quantity supplied to increase and quantity demanded to fall. Since the initial situation, shown in Figure 8-6, was one where domestic

[2] When the exchange rate is expressed in this way, as the price of a unit of foreign exchange, a depreciation occurs when the exchange rate rises. When the exchange rate is expressed as the amount of foreign currency that is equivalent in value to one dollar, a depreciation is associated with a fall in the exchange rate. When the price of one pound sterling rises from $2.50 to $2.75, the pound sterling equivalent of one dollar falls from £0.40 to £0.36.

supply exceeded domestic demand, this response reduces that excess. As a result the quantity imported *decreases*.

For a small country, a depreciation of the domestic currency causes the domestic prices of traded goods to rise, thereby increasing the quantity supplied and reducing the quantity demanded domestically. Therefore the volume of exports increases while the volume of imports falls.

Similarly, an *appreciation* of the domestic currency *lowers* the domestic prices of traded goods. This leads to a reduction in the quantity supplied and an increase in the quantity demanded domestically for both; the quantity of steel imports now rises while the quantity of wheat exports falls.

FIGURE 8–5

The Effects of an Increase in the Domestic Currency Price of an Exported Good (Wheat)

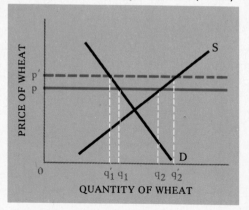

An increase in the domestic currency price of export goods leads to an increase in the volume of exports. Exports of wheat are determined by the domestic excess supply of the tradeable good at the domestic price. (The domestic price is the world price adjusted by the exchange rate.) D and S are the domestic demand and supply schedules. If the world price expressed in domestic currency is p, quantity q_2 will be produced, of which q_1 will be consumed domestically and $q_2 - q_1$ will be exported. A depreciation of the domestic currency or an increase in the world price causes the domestic currency price to rise to p'. As a result, domestic consumption falls to q_1', quantity supplied rises to q_2', and exports rise to $q_2' - q_1'$.

FIGURE 8–6

The Effects of an Increase in the Domestic Currency Price of an Imported Good (Steel)

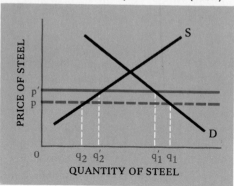

An increase in the domestic currency price of import goods leads to a decrease in the volume of imports. Imports of steel are determined by the domestic excess demand for steel at the domestic price. (The domestic price is the world price adjusted by the exchange rate.) D and S are the domestic demand and supply schedules. If the world price expressed in domestic currency is p, quantity q_1 will be consumed, of which q_2 will be produced domestically and $q_1 - q_2$ will be imported. A depreciation of the domestic currency or an increase in the world price causes the domestic currency price to rise to p'. As a result, quantity supplied rises to q_2', domestic consumption falls to q_1', and imports fall to $q_1' - q_2'$.

THE DETERMINATION OF EXCHANGE RATES

The theory that we develop here applies to all exchange rates, but for convenience we shall continue to deal with the example of trade between Canada and Britain and with the determination of the rate of exchange between their two currencies, dollars and pounds sterling.

Because one currency is traded for another on the foreign exchange market, it follows that to desire (demand) dollars implies a willingness to offer (supply) pounds, while an offer (supply) of dollars implies a desire (demand) for pounds.

If at an exchange rate of £1 = $2.75 British importers demand $5.50, they must be offering

£2; if Canadian importers offer $5.50, they must be demanding £2. For this reason, the theory can deal either with the demand for and the supply of dollars, or with the demand for and the supply of pounds sterling; both need not be considered. We shall conduct the argument in terms of the supply, demand, and price of dollars (quoted in pounds).

The Demand for Dollars

Demand for dollars in the foreign exchange market arises to finance purchases by foreigners from Canadians. In addition to the purchase of exports studied before, there are purchases of assets previously owned or newly issued by Canadians (and Canadian governments). Such purchases are called **capital flows.** They play an important role in exchange markets, and we shall study them in detail later in the book; for the present we continue to focus on international trade in goods and services.

Consider again our representative traded goods, wheat exports and steel imports. What are the implications of transactions in these goods for the foreign exchange market? We found that a depreciation of the dollar led to an increase in the quantity of wheat exports. Since the pound sterling price of wheat is constant, the supply of pounds on the foreign exchange market has increased. But a dollar is now worth less in terms of pounds, so more dollars are now demanded on the foreign exchange market.

Figure 8-7 plots the price of dollars (measured in pounds) on the vertical axis and the quantity of dollars on the horizontal axis. Moving down the vertical scale, the dollar becomes cheaper (it is worth fewer pounds); its value is depreciating on the foreign exchange market. Moving up the scale, the dollar becomes more expensive; it is appreciating on the market.

What is the shape of the demand curve for dollars? As we have just seen, if the dollar depreciates, the British will buy more Canadian wheat and will require more dollars for this purpose. The quantity of dollars demanded will rise. In the opposite case, if the dollar appreciates, the

British will buy less Canadian goods and will thus demand fewer Canadian dollars.

The demand curve for dollars on the foreign exchange market is downward-sloping when plotted against the sterling price of dollars.

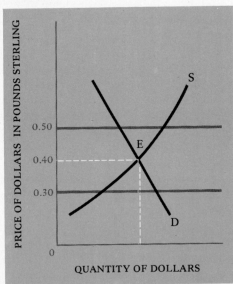

FIGURE 8–7
An Exchange Rate Determined on a Competitive Market

PRICE OF DOLLARS IN POUNDS STERLING

QUANTITY OF DOLLARS

The equilibrium exchange rate equates the demand and supply on the foreign exchange market. The curve S is the supply of dollars to the foreign exchange market. It is upward-sloping because an increase in the value of the Canadian dollar leads to lower domestic import prices and hence more imports; more dollars are supplied in exchange for foreign exchange with which to purchase the imports. The curve D is the demand for dollars on the foreign exchange market. It slopes downward to the right because an increase in the value of the Canadian dollar leads to lower domestic prices of export goods; less goods are exported, so fewer dollars are demanded on the foreign exchange market. The quantity of dollars demanded is equal to the quantity supplied at a price of £0.40 per dollar (or £1 = $2.50). If the exchange rate is too low, say $1 = £0.30, there is excess demand for dollars and the exchange rate is bid up. If the exchange rate is too high, say $1 = £0.50, there is excess supply of dollars and the exchange rate is bid down.

The Supply of Dollars

Because of the symmetrical nature of foreign exchange markets, the sources of the supply of dollars to the foreign exchange market are merely the opposite side of the demand for pounds. Who wants to sell dollars for foreign exchange? Canadians seeking to purchase foreign goods and services (and assets) will require foreign exchange to make those transactions, and hence they will wish to supply dollars in exchange for foreign currencies.

When the dollar depreciates, the Canadian price of British imports rises. Canadians will buy less of the now more expensive British goods. Whether or not they spend fewer dollars buying them will depend on how elastic the domestic supply and demand are. If the percentage reduction in imports exceeds the percentage increase in prices, money expenditures on imports—and hence the supply of dollars on the foreign exchange market—will fall.[3] The amount of dollars being offered in exchange for pounds sterling in order to pay for imports thus falls.

When the dollar appreciates in value, British exports to Canada become cheaper, more will be sold, and more dollars will be spent on them. Thus more dollars will be offered in exchange for pounds in order to obtain the foreign exchange needed to pay for the extra imports. This is illustrated by the supply curve in Figure 8-7.

The supply curve of dollars on the foreign exchange market is upward-sloping when plotted against the sterling price of dollars.

EQUILIBRIUM EXCHANGE RATES IN A COMPETITIVE MARKET

Consider an exchange rate that is set on a free market. Like any perfectly competitive price, this rate fluctuates freely according to the conditions of demand and supply. (While we continue to focus on the determination of the equilibrium exchange rate between the dollar and the pound, you should be aware of the fact that there exist exchange rates for many pairs of currencies. See the discussion in the box.)

Assume that the current price of dollars is so low (say, £0.30 in Figure 8.7) that the quantity of dollars demanded exceeds the quantity supplied. This reflects the fact that at that exchange rate, desired payments to Canada by holders of sterling exceed desired payments to Britain by holders of dollars. This situation is one in which *desired payments* are not in balance. Dollars will be in scarce supply; some people who require dollars to make payments to Canada will be unable to obtain them, and the price of dollars will be bid up. The value of the dollar vis-à-vis the pound will appreciate, or the value of the pound vis-à-vis the dollar will depreciate, which is the same thing.

As the sterling price of dollars rises, the dollar price of Canadian export goods falls. Hence the quantity of exports falls, as does the quantity of Canadian dollars demanded on the foreign exchange market. This is a movement along the demand curve *D* in Figure 8-7. However, the appreciation of the dollar also leads to a fall in the dollar price of imports into Canada. Hence a larger quantity will be sold and, on the assumption that the response of imports is elastic, the quantity of Canadian dollars supplied will rise. This is a movement along the supply curve *S* in Figure 8-7.

Thus a rise in the price of the dollar reduces the quantity demanded and increases the quantity supplied. Where the two curves intersect, quantity demanded equals quantity supplied, and the exchange rate is in equilibrium.

What happens if the price of dollars is too high? The quantity of dollars demanded will be less than the quantity of dollars supplied. With the dollar in excess supply, some people who wish to convert dollars into pounds will be unable to do so. The price of dollars will fall, fewer dollars will be supplied, more will be demanded, and an equilibrium will be reestablished.

---

[3] This is the case of an elastic import demand, probably the most relevant case empirically and certainly the easiest to consider. If import demand is inelastic, the supply curve for dollars may be upward sloping; this raises potential problems that are of some interest but too complex to be pursued in a first-year textbook.

Multilateral Exchange Rates

Because Canada trades with many countries, there are exchange rates between the Canadian dollar and many other currencies. In February 1981 the Canadian dollar was worth approximately 0.83 U.S. dollars, 0.36 British pounds, 1.82 German marks, and 172 Japanese yen.

Equilibrium in the market for Canadian dollars does not require that the demand for Canadian dollars by residents of any one country be equal to the supply of Canadian dollars being offered in exchange for that particular country's currency. Equilibrium is established when the total demand for Canadian dollars is equal to the supply of Canadian dollars being offered in exchange for all foreign currencies. In other words, equilibrium does not require that Canada's trade be in balance with each individual country but, rather, that our total exports and imports be in balance.

At the same time, equilibrium can exist in the market for all currencies simultaneously only when there are no opportunities for profitable **arbitrage**. Arbitrage operations consist in buying currencies in markets where they are cheap and selling them where they are dear so as to make a profit on the transaction.

Exchange rates are generally specified in terms of the U.S. dollar. Once the rates between the U.S. dollar and two other currencies are determined, there is only one rate between the other two currencies that will *not* allow buyers and sellers of foreign exchange to engage in profitable arbitrage.

Consider an example. Suppose that on a particular day the U.S. dollar is worth £0.60 and 800 lire. Given the two rates, the only rate between lire and sterling that rules out profitable arbitrage operations is £0.60 = 800 lire, which is the equivalent of £1 = 1,333 lire. The table gives an example in which the exchange rate between the pound and the lira is out of line with the other two. Such "disorderly cross-rates" will be quickly eliminated in a free market. Arbitragers will buy lire with dollars and sell lire against pounds. If rates are free to vary, this will tend to bid the rates toward a consistent level where it is no longer possible to make profits by arbitrage. If rates are fixed by central authorities, such disorderly cross-rates could not long be sustained, but while they were, they would provide a gift to everyone who was informed enough to take advantage of them.

One unit of this currency	Exchanges for the stated number of units of this currency		
	U.S. Dollar	Lira	Pound
U.S. Dollar	1	800	0.60
Lira	0.00125	1	0.000909
Pound	1.67	1,100	1

Disorderly cross-rates mean that a profit can be made merely by buying and selling currencies at existing rates in different markets. In this example, a trader can start with $2 and purchase 1,600 lire. He or she can then use the lire to purchase £1.45, which can be exchanged for $2.42. The profit is $0.42 on an investment of $2, or 21 percent. Because the transactions can be effected quickly and with large amounts of money, very large profits can be earned. Because this is possible, however, such rates will not long persist.

A competitive foreign exchange market is like other competitive markets in that the forces of demand and supply tend to lead to an equilibrium price at which quantity demanded equals quantity supplied.

CHANGES IN EXCHANGE RATES

What causes exchange rates to vary? The simplest answer to this question is changes in demand or supply in the foreign exchange market. Anything that shifts the demand curve for dollars to the right or the supply curve for dollars to the left increases the equilibrium exchange rate and thus leads to an appreciation of the dollar. Anything that shifts the demand curve for dollars to the left or the supply curve for dollars to the right decreases the equilibrium exchange rate and leads to a depreciation of the dollar. This is nothing more than a restatement of the laws of supply and demand, applied now to the market for foreign currencies.

But what causes the shifts in demand and supply that lead to changes in exchange rates? There are many causes, some of them transitory and some persistent. Several are related to trade flows.

A Change in Tastes

Earlier we considered the effects on exports of wheat and imports of steel of a change in Canadian preferences away from wheat and in favor of steel. These effects were illustrated in Figures 8-3 and 8-4. At each exchange rate the increased volume of exports leads to an increased demand for Canadian dollars in the foreign exchange market: in Figure 8-8 the demand for dollars in the foreign exchange market shifts to the right. At the same time, the reduced volume of imports (shown in Figure 8-4) reduces at each exchange rate the supply of dollars on the foreign exchange market: in Figure 8-8 the supply of dollars shifts to the left. The extra demand for dollars in combination with the reduced supply of dollars raises the equilibrium price of dollars. Thus an increased preference on the part of Canadian con-

FIGURE 8–8

The Effects of Shifts in the Demand and Supply of Dollars in the Foreign Exchange Market

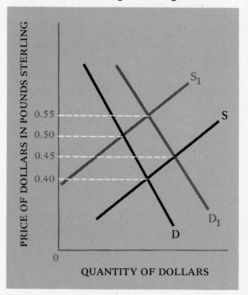

An increase in the demand for dollars or a decrease in the supply of dollars causes the dollar to appreciate in terms of pounds; a decrease in demand or an increase in supply causes the dollar to depreciate in terms of pounds. A shift in preference from imported goods to exported goods causes D to rise to D_1 and S to shift to S_1; the exchange rate rises from £0.40 to £0.55. An increase in costs in the export industry causes the demand for dollars to shift from D_1 to D, causing the exchange rate to fall from £0.55 to £0.50. An increase in costs in the import industry shifts S_1 to S, causing the exchange rate to fall from £0.50 to £0.40. Domestic inflation causes S_1 to shift to S and D_1 to shift to D; the exchange rate falls from £0.55 to £0.40. Foreign inflation causes S to shift to S_1 and D to shift to D_1; the exchange rate rises from £0.40 to £0.55.

sumers for exported goods at the expense of imported goods will lead to an appreciation in the value of the dollar (a depreciation in the value of the pound).

The effect of an increase in preference for the imported good is left to the reader to determine as an exercise.

Increases in the Costs of Domestic Production

A rise in the supply price of domestic exports. Suppose that there is an increase in the cost of growing wheat, measured in terms of the domestic currency. At any domestic price of wheat, less wheat will be supplied; that is, the supply curve of wheat shifts up and to the left. In turn, at any given exchange rate, the quantity of wheat exports will fall and hence the demand for dollars on the foreign exchange market will also fall. The demand for dollars shifts left, say from D_1 to D in Figure 8-8, leading to a fall in the price of Canadian dollars in terms of pounds sterling. The increase in Canadian costs of production in the export sector leads to a depreciation of the dollar and an appreciation of the pound.

A rise in the domestic cost of producing imported goods. Suppose instead that domestic costs rose in the manufacturing sector. (Because manufactured goods are imported in our example, we can call this the import-competing sector.) An increase in domestic costs causes the supply curve to shift left, thereby reducing the quantity supplied at any given domestic price. In turn, the quantity of imports at any given exchange rate will rise, causing the supply of dollars to the foreign exchange market to increase, say from S_1 to S in Figure 8-8. Again the increase in domestic costs of production, this time in the import-competing sector, leads to a depreciation of the Canadian dollar.

The Connection Between the Import and Export Markets

The determination of the exchange rate in the foreign exchange market creates an important relationship between the markets for traded goods. As we have seen, the supply of dollars to the foreign exchange market arises from the need for foreign exchange with which to purchase imports, and the demand for dollars on the foreign exchange market arises from the sale of foreign exchange earned by sales of exports. Hence the interaction of supply and demand in the foreign exchange market involves an interaction between markets for exports and markets for imports. This can be seen by further analysis of the effects of domestic cost increases.

Consider first the effects on the import-competing (manufactured goods) sector of an increase in costs in the export (agricultural goods) sector. As we have seen, this leads to a leftward shift in the demand for dollars on the foreign exchange market and a depreciation of the Canadian dollar. In terms of the manufactured goods sector, this means an increase in the Canadian dollar price of manufactured goods and hence a decrease in the quantity of imports. This leads to a decrease in dollars supplied to the foreign exchange market, reflecting (in Figure 8-8) the movement along the supply curve that occurs when equilibrium is reestablished in the foreign exchange market after the shift in the demand curve from D_1 to D.

The effects of an increase in costs in the import-competing sector are similar. The supply of dollars now shifts to the right. The depreciation leads to an increase in the dollar price of agricultural goods and an increase in the quantity of dollars demanded on the foreign exchange market. This reflects a movement along the demand curve in response to the shift in the supply curve from S_1 to S.

Having seen how a particular change in one traded goods market leads to changes in prices and quantities in other traded goods markets, we turn now to an example of a *common* disturbance introduced into the markets for both exports and imports.

DOMESTIC INFLATION AND THE EXCHANGE RATE

Suppose that the Canadian economy is experiencing inflationary pressures in the sense that domestic wages and money incomes are rising. In this event domestic supply and demand curves in all goods markets will be shifting upward. For those goods, such as non-traded services, for which the domestic price is determined by domestic supply and demand, prices will therefore be rising. But for traded goods, for which the price is determined in world markets, the dollar prices will be constant and thus the *relative* prices of traded goods will be falling. As a result quantity demanded would be increasing and quantity supplied would be decreasing. Could this situation continue?

Since foreign prices are not changing, in order for domestic prices of traded goods to be constant, the exchange rate must also be constant. But the upward drift in the domestic demand and supply for exported agricultural goods will lead to a decrease in the quantity exported, as Figure 8-3 shows. This will reduce the quantity of dollars demanded on the foreign exchange market. Similarly, the upward drift of the domestic demand and supply for imported manufactured goods will, as Figure 8-4 shows, cause the quantity of imports to increase. This will increase the supply of dollars to the foreign exchange market.

In terms of the foreign exchange market, the increased imports of manufactured goods induced by the domestic inflation leads to a shift downward and to the right of the supply of dollars. Similarly, the reduced exports of manufactured goods leads to a shift downward and to the left of the demand for dollars. Hence domestic inflation leads to a depreciation of the Canadian dollar and an increase in the dollar prices of traded goods. These price increases then tend to roughly parallel the increases in wages and non-traded goods prices; if domestic inflation were 10 percent and the induced depreciation were also 10 percent, there would be no change in relative prices. The increases in traded goods prices also offset the initial effects of the upward shifts in the demand and supply curves for traded goods on the quantities of imports and exports so that these quantities would not then be much affected by the domestic inflation.

Domestic inflation, other things being equal, will lead to a depreciation of the Canadian dollar.

The price advantage for foreign-manufactured imported goods and the price disadvantage for domestically produced export goods caused by the inflation is, at least to some degree, offset by the lower value of the Canadian dollar.

FOREIGN INFLATION AND THE EXCHANGE RATE

At a given exchange rate, foreign inflation causes the domestic prices of traded goods to rise. As we saw in Figures 8-5 and 8-6, this leads to an increase in the volume of exports, a decrease in the volume of imports, and consequently a trade account surplus. Can this situation persist?

In terms of the foreign exchange market, the trade surplus caused by the foreign inflation is reflected in an excess demand for dollars. This is illustrated in Figure 8-8 where the initial equilibrium exchange rate is £0.40. The increase in exports causes the demand for dollars to shift from D to D_1, and the decrease in imports causes supply to shift from S to S_1. As a result the value of the Canadian dollar appreciates. The appreciation lowers the domestic price of traded goods and thus offsets the initial inflationary pressure arising from the foreign inflation. This important result is one desirable property of market-determined exchange rates.

Market-determined exchange rates, other things being equal, will insulate the domestic economy from foreign inflation. Foreign inflation will lead to an appreciation of the domestic currency, thereby offsetting the inflationary pressure on the domestic prices of traded goods.

This issue is pursued further in the box on pages 144–145.

CENTRAL BANK MANAGEMENT OF EXCHANGE RATES

So far we have considered exchange rates that are left completely free to be determined by the market forces of demand and supply. Such rates are called free, or **flexible**, or **floating exchange rates**. In practice, however, exchange rates are seldom left entirely free from influence by the central authorities.

Fixed Exchange Rates

From the end of World War II until the early 1970s, the rates of exchange between most currencies were set, or pegged, within very narrow limits by each country's own central bank. Such rates are commonly called *pegged* or **fixed exchange rates.** When rates are fixed, fluctuations in the demand for and supply of dollars vis-à-vis other currencies are not allowed to affect the actual exchange rate. But of course they will create situations of disequilibrium in which there is excess demand or supply in the foreign exchange market.

While the government can fix the exchange rate of its currency, it cannot usually prevent shifts from developing in the demand for and supply of its currency. The government must then take steps to eliminate the excess demand or the excess supply, or it must be prepared to change the exchange rate from one fixed level to another. A change in the rate at which a currency is fixed by its government is called a **revaluation** when the currency is increased in value and a **devaluation** when the currency is reduced in value.

Managing Fixed Exchange Rates

How can a government manage a fixed exchange rate in order to avoid the need for devaluation or revaluation? In our simple example, where only Canada and Britain trade with each other, there are *two* currencies but only *one* exchange rate between them. Thus the governments of Canada and Britain cannot make independent decisions on fixing the exchange rate between their two currencies. In practice, countries with a fixed exchange rate generally maintain the external value of their currency in terms of the U.S. dollar and allow arbitrage to determine rates vis-à-vis other currencies, as explained in the box on page 139. Therefore we need to consider the ex-

change rate between the Canadian dollar and the U.S. dollar.[4]

Having chosen a fixed exchange rate against the U.S. dollar, the Canadian authorities then manage matters so that the selected rate can actually be maintained. They must be prepared to offset imbalances in demand and supply by government sales or purchases of forein exchange. In the face of short-term fluctuations in market demand and supply, the central authorities can maintain a fixed exchange rate by entering the market and buying and selling as required to stabilize the price.

As long as the central authorities attempt to maintain an exchange rate *that equates demand and supply on average,* the policy can be successful. Sometimes the authorities will be buying, and at other times they will be selling, but their reserves will fluctuate around a constant average level.

However, if there is a permanent shift in one of the curves that causes the pegged rate to differ substantially from the long-term equilibrium rate, it will be very difficult to maintain the fixed rate. For example, if there is a major inflation in Canada and prices remain stable in the United States, the equilibrium value of the Canadian dollar will fall. In a free market the Canadian dollar would depreciate and the U.S. dollar appreciate, but this is a managed market, not a free market. If the Bank of Canada persists in trying to maintain the original rate, it will have to meet the excess demand for U.S. dollars by selling its reserves of U.S. dollars. It can continue this policy only as long as it has reserves that it is willing to spend to maintain the artificially high price of Canadian dollars. The Bank cannot do this indef-

---

[4] When there are *n* countries, having *n* independent currencies, there is room for only *n* − 1 independent decisions on the price of foreign exchange. In practice, what happens is that each country other than the United States sets the price of its currency in terms of U.S. dollars and intervenes in its own foreign exchange market to maintain the fixed price. Any country can change the price of its currency vis-à-vis all others by changing the rate at which its currency is convertible into U.S. dollars. In this sense the U.S. dollar is the international unit of account.

Foreign Inflation: Imported or Insulated?

Two distinct circumstances can lead to an appreciation of the Canadian dollar. One is a change in the price at which the Bank of Canada intervenes in the foreign exchange market, the other is a change in the foreign prices of traded goods in the absence of Bank of Canada intervention. The two circumstances have very different implications for the "competitiveness" of domestic industry. Many critics of Bank of Canada policy in the 1970s argue that the Bank has failed to recognize the distinction between the two cases. Let us examine this contention.

At given foreign currency prices of traded goods, an increase in the foreign exchange value of the Canadian dollar as maintained by the Bank of Canada will lead to a reduction in the foreign demand for exports (because the Canadian price of goods abroad rises in terms of the foreign currency) and an increase in the Canadian demand for imported goods (because the Canadian price of foreign imports falls). Output or employment in both the export sector (agriculture) and the import-competing sector (manufacturing) will fall. This case is one in which appreciation of the Canadian dollar is harmful to the international competitive position of Canadian industry because it raises domestic costs and prices relative to those of foreign-based industry.

At given values of the exchange rate and domestic prices, an increase in foreign currency prices of traded goods leads to an increase in foreign demand for Canadian exports and a reduction in Canadian demand for imports from abroad. The first increases the demand for Canadian dollars on the foreign exchange market; the second leads to a reduction in the supply of Canadian dollars on that market. As a result the value of Canadian dollars in terms of foreign currency is bid up. This appreciation offsets the inflationary effects of the foreign price rise; the domestic prices of both export and import-competing goods is unaltered, as is the domestic output of

both goods. In this sense, the flexible exchange rate is said to insulate the domestic economy from foreign inflation. This case is one in which appreciation of the Canadian dollar is *not* harmful to the international competitive position of Canadian industry; the appreciation is a response to foreign disturbances and is instrumental to the process that restores domestic costs and prices to their initial position relative to those of foreign industries.

It is often true that appreciation of the Canadian dollar is detrimental to domestic industry. This is the analysis of the first case above, the case of constant foreign prices. However, when the appreciation is a *result* of increases in foreign prices, as in the second case above, then the increase in the value of the Canadian dollar is simply a part of the adjustment process and will not hurt the competitive position of either the export industry in world markets or the import-competing industry in domestic markets. Nevertheless, in the face of foreign inflation, increases in the value of the Canadian dollar are often opposed, and that opposition is sometimes strong enough to influence domestic policy.

What happens when foreign prices increase and the exchange rate is not allowed to appreciate in the manner outlined above? The answer is simple; the Canadian currency price of traded goods must also rise. In the end Canadian prices must equal foreign prices adjusted for the exchange rate. If the exchange rate does not change, Canadian prices must change. This is known as "imported inflation."

The full mechanism by which this occurs will be spelled out in a later chapter; for now we see that there are two options in the face of foreign inflation. One is to let the Canadian dollar appreciate and hence insulate Canadian prices from the effects of the foreign prices. If the cause of the appreciation is truly foreign inflation, then the appreciation will not be harmful to the competitiveness of the domestic industries. The second option is to maintain the exchange rate fixed by the operations of the Bank of Canada and to allow foreign inflation to translate itself into domestic inflation. The apparent benefits to Canadian industry of avoiding appreciation and taking this second option are in fact an illusion; domestic inflation will ensue, and it will bring about the increase of domestic relative to foreign prices and costs.

Many economists argue that precisely such a mistake was made in Canada in 1974–1975. At that time OPEC price increases caused enormous increases in inflation in our major trading partners, in particular the United States. Canada then was basically self-sufficient in oil and hence was not adversely affected by the oil shock. At the same time, the Bank of Canada resisted the upward pressure on the value of the Canadian dollar resulting from the American inflation. The decrease in the relative price of Canadian goods led to an increase in exports and a decrease in imports, causing an excess demand for Canadian dollars on the foreign exchange market. The Bank of Canada met this excess demand by selling Canadian dollars, thereby stabilizing the exchange rate. Although Canada was on a *de jure* floating exchange rate at that time, the exchange rate did not in fact perform its "insulation" function because it was not allowed to float *de facto*. By fixing the exchange rate, the

Bank of Canada allowed the rapid takeoff into double-digit inflation in the rest of the world to result in a similar inflation in Canada.

This policy error is not unique to the Canadian experience; it is similar to what has happened in other high-inflation countries such as Israel and Sweden. Attempts to protect the domestic export sector from the supposed ravages of appreciation end in a situation of imported inflation. But in fact the *real* position of the domestic export sector is ultimately the same. Either the exchange rate appreciates, allowing domestic money wages and prices to remain constant, or the exchange rate is held constant and domestic inflation occurs. In the latter event, the inflation bids up domestic wages, causing the domestic price of the export good to rise. The competitiveness of the export sector remains the same as under the flexible exchange rate option because in both cases the foreign currency prices of our export goods rise.

Similar arguments were being made when the United States inflation rate took off to 16 and 17 percent in early 1979; there was pressure on the Bank of Canada to intervene to prevent the Canadian dollar from appreciating. Fortunately, the high American inflation did not last very long, and the problem disappeared . . . for the time being. But what would have happened if the U.S. inflation had persisted? Have we learned, or will we repeat past mistakes?

initely because sooner or later its reserves will be exhausted. (The opposite case of stable prices in Canada and inflation in the United States is discussed in the box.)

The management of a fixed rate is illustrated in Figure 8-9. When the rate is not near the free-market equilibrium rate, controls of various sorts may be introduced to attempt to shift the demand curve for foreign exchange so that it intersects

the supply curve at a rate close to the controlled rate. This is usually done by restricting imports of goods and services or by restricting the export of capital.

If the authorities cannot shift demand and supply in order to keep the equilibrium rate approximately as high as the fixed rate, they will have no alternative but to devalue the domestic currency when they run out of reserves.

FIGURE 8–9
A Fixed Exchange Rate

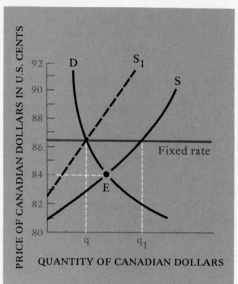

When an exchange rate is fixed at other than the equilibrium rate, there will be either persistent excess demand or persistent excess supply. The demand and supply curves of Canadian dollars in the absence of government controls are D and S; equilibrium is at E with a price of 84 U.S. cents per dollar. (The U.S. dollar is worth $1.19 Canadian.) The government then fixes the exchange rate at 86.5 U.S. cents per dollar, thereby overvaluing the Canadian dollar. There is now an excess of dollars supplied over dollars demanded of qq_1. To maintain the fixed rate without losing reserves, it is necessary to shift either the demand curve or the supply curve (or both) so that the two intersect at, or very near, the fixed rate. For example, controls on foreign spending by Canadians that shifted the supply curve to S_1 would make the fixed rate a viable one. If the curves are not shifted, the fixed rate will have to be supported by reducing Bank of Canada reserves of U.S. dollars by qq_1 per period.

Managed Flexible Rates

In the present-day system, exchange rates are not stabilized at an announced par value. Nevertheless governments, working through their central banks, intervene from time to time to influ-

ence the exchange rate and prevent sharp or sudden changes in it. What tools does the government have for this task?

For one, the government can attempt to influence the long-term equilibrium exchange rate by various forms of payments or trade restrictions. Suppose there is an excess supply of one currency and thus downward pressure on the exchange rate. If domestic holders of the currency are forbidden to buy all the foreign currency they wish, this will decrease the supply. Sometimes countries restrict the use of their domestic currency by requiring licences for the purchase of foreign exchange. This is called "blocking" the currency. If imports are restricted, there will be less need to sell the home currency to acquire foreign exchange.

Another method for bringing the market into line with the current exchange rate is to manipulate the short-term interest rate in order to induce short-term capital to enter or leave the country. If the Canadian government wishes to increase the demand for Canadian dollars, it can raise interest rates above world market levels. This will cause some foreign investors to shift their excess cash out of pounds and marks and into dollars for the purpose of buying government bonds or other dollar financial assets. For as long as the inflow persists, the demand for Canadian dollars on the foreign exchange market will be high, so the value of the dollar will be held higher than it otherwise would be. But as soon as interest rates fall, a reverse flow will occur and put downward pressure on the dollar.

A third form of intervention is for the central bank to attempt to iron out short-term and medium-term fluctuations in the exchange rate through open market purchases and sales of foreign exchange. If the Bank of Canada enters the foreign exchange market to sell Canadian dollars and buy foreign exchange, this will cause the dollar to depreciate. If it does the opposite, buying Canadian dollars and selling foreign exchange, this will cause the Canadian dollar to appreciate. The exchange rate can be stabilized against short-run fluctuations in this way, and it can even be held above its equilibrium value for as long as the Bank wishes to invest its reserves of foreign exchange.

FIXED VERSUS FLOATING EXCHANGE RATES

The main difference between managed flexible rates and managed fixed rates is that with the former the government is not committed to defending a publicly announced rate; it can resist changes it thinks are transitory and yield to changes it believes are the result of long-term forces. Until the 1970s most governments maintained fixed exchange rates.

Throughout the 1950s and 1960s a long debate raged among economists and bankers about the relative merits of fixed versus floating exchange rates. The whole argument (with a few major exceptions) was more notable for the passions involved than for the objectivity used in assessing empirical evidence. The supporters of fixed rates held that the stability of such rates is conducive to trade and that free-market rates might fluctuate so erratically as to disturb the free flow of international trade and to impair long-run industrial planning based on a reasonable assessment of a country's ability to sell goods abroad.

In the event, exchange rates were freed in the early 1970s. None of the predicted drastic consequences ensued. Exchange rates have fluctuated, but in the main their movements have followed long-run trends due to such factors as relative international rates of inflation. Short-term fluctuations have occurred, but they do not seem to have been of sufficient magnitude to upset seriously the rising flows of worldwide international trade.

THE CANADIAN DOLLAR EXCHANGE RATE

Over the past half century the external value of the Canadian dollar has fluctuated between a low of 82.7 U.S. cents in December 1931 and a maximum value just over 105 U.S. cents during the late 1950s (see Figure 8-10). Both fixed-rate and floating-rate regimes were in force at different times during this period. Between 1926 and 1929 a fixed rate was maintained by Canada, as well as by most other countries, by maintaining convertibility into gold at a fixed price (see pages 729–730). A floating rate was adopted early in 1929 and maintained through the unsettled periods of the Great Depression until the outbreak of World War II, when a fixed par value of 90.9 U.S. cents was established.

During the war the higher rate of price increase experienced in the United States led to upward pressure on the equilibrium exchange rate, and an accumulation of foreign exchange reserves was required to maintain the existing fixed rate. Consequently the par value was raised to 100 U.S. cents in 1946, but losses of reserves were experienced at this level, and the wartime par value was reestablished in 1949 when the pound sterling was depreciated. In 1950 the Canadian dollar came under strong upward pressures and the decision was made to allow it to float. Under the influence of free-market forces, the Canadian dollar soon rose above parity with the U.S. dollar and remained there until 1961.

The upward pressure on the Canadian dollar eased in 1960, and a rapid downward movement was precipitated in 1961 by statements by the minister of finance that the government wished to see a lower exchange rate and was prepared to intervene in the market if necessary. Downward pressure soon built up as holders of Canadian dollars rushed to exchange them for U.S. dollars in anticipation of a falling rate, and the government found itself selling rather than buying U.S. dollars. In order to eliminate the great market uncertainties that it had itself created, the government decided to return to a fixed rate. A par value of 92.5 U.S. cents was established May 2, 1962, and the government committed itself to intervening in the market to keep the rate within 1 percent on either side of the par value.[5]

[5] This commitment put Canada in the same position as other countries that maintained fixed exchange rates under the rules of the International Monetary Fund (see Chapter 36).

Exchange Rates and National Pride

It is interesting, sociologically and psychologically, that the value of exchange rates often becomes an important symbol of national pride. To understand some of the actions of governments, one must understand that great symbolic value is often attached to the price of a country's currency in the foreign market. During the 1950s, for example, the fact that the Canadian dollar was worth more than the U.S. dollar was a source of great satisfaction to many Canadians. The fall in the value of the Canadian dollar in 1977–1978 was equally a source of great concern to many Canadians.

The economist does not seek to explain this phenomenon, but he or she may wonder at it. No doubt there are circumstances when a rise in the value of a country's currency should be taken as a good sign. There are other circumstances in which such a change is symptomatic of undesirable domestic conditions. For example, a major depression in Canada could easily lead to a rise in the external value of our currency because a fall in income leads to a decline in the demand for imports. The presence of a depression is hardly a cause for national congratulation.

Alternatively, a large flow of foreign investment leading to increased foreign control of Canadian industry would cause an appreciation of the exchange rate. It is an odd fact that many Canadians are proud when the Canadian dollar rises above the American dollar on the foreign exchange market and simultaneously gravely concerned about the inflow of foreign capital that is the direct cause of the high rate!

Exchange rates can appreciate or depreciate for many different reasons, and to take the price of one's currency per se as a symbol of national pride is to commit oneself in advance to being proud of a great variety of different events.

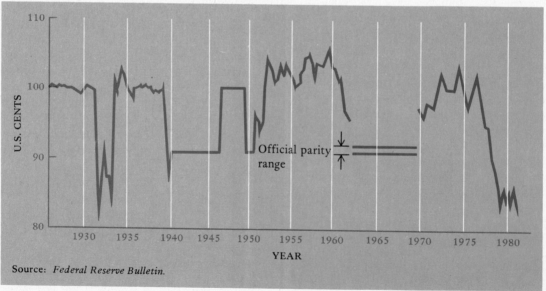

FIGURE 8–10
The Exchange Rate of the Canadian Dollar in U.S. Funds

Source: *Federal Reserve Bulletin.*

The Canadian dollar has fluctuated between 82.7 and just over 105 U.S. cents. The exchange rate has been fluctuating in response to market forces since mid 1970. This was also the case during the 1930s and the 1950s.

With the Canadian dollar depreciated, the competitive position of Canadian exports improved and imports became more expensive; as a result the trade balance moved into a surplus position. In 1970 a record merchandise trade surplus of close to $3 billion led to strong upward pressure on the Canadian dollar. During the first five months of 1970, maintenance of the fixed exchange rate entailed an accumulation of foreign exchange reserves of about $850 million, an increase of 25 percent over the volume held at the end of 1969. The government finally gave up the fight and, beginning June 1, Canada was back on a floating exchange rate. By early 1972 a premium over the U.S. dollar had also been reestablished, and the rate rose to almost 104 U.S. cents in 1974.

Since then there have been wide fluctuations. By the end of 1977 the rate had fallen below 90 U.S. cents for the first time since the early 1930s, and it has stayed well below 90 U.S. cents, often falling below 85 U.S. cents and occasionally below 83 U.S. cents. In later chapters we return to a broader discussion of the exchange rate and the role of international capital flows.

Summary

1. International trade allows the quantities of particular goods consumed to differ from the quantities produced. This leads to an expansion of the consumption possibility set.

2. If the domestic supply of a good exceeds the demand at prevailing world prices, the good will be exported. If domestic demand exceeds supply, the good will be imported.

3. International trade can occur only if it is possible to exchange the currency of one country for that of another. The exchange rate between two currencies is the amount of one currency that must be paid in order to obtain one unit of the other currency.

4. Exchange rates in a free market are determined by supply and demand. The supply of Canadian dollars (the demand for foreign exchange) arises from Canadian imports, and the demand for domestic currency (the supply of foreign exchange) arises from Canadian exports.

5. A depreciation of the Canadian dollar raises the domestic price of Canadian exports and increases the quantity of dollars demanded; at the same time it raises the dollar price of imports from abroad and thus lowers the quantity of dollars supplied to buy foreign exchange to be used to purchase foreign goods. Thus the demand curve for dollars is downward-sloping and the supply curve of dollars is upward-sloping when the quantities demanded and supplied are plotted against the price of dollars measured in terms of a foreign currency.

6. The Canadian dollar will tend to appreciate on the foreign exchange market if (among other things) there is a change in tastes in favor of Canadian export goods, a fall in the supply price of Canadian goods, or a foreign inflation. The dollar will tend to depreciate if there is a domestic inflation.

7. Where more than two currencies are involved, there will be an exchange rate between each pair of currencies. Arbitrage is the buying and selling of foreign exchange with a view to making a profit by buying where a given currency is cheap and selling where it is dear. The possibility of such arbitrage operations ensures that disorderly cross-rates among several currencies cannot long persist.

8. From the end of World War II to the early 1970s most countries maintained fixed exchange rates. Fixed rates pose two main problems: (a) If there are long-term shifts in demand and supply in the foreign exchange market, the fixed rate must be changed periodically to accommodate such shifts or controls must be used to prevent the disequilibrium in demand and supply from occurring. (b) Short-term fluctuations must be ironed out by the central authorities' sales and purchases of foreign exchange; these sales and purchases require that a reserve of gold and foreign exchange be held. The world is now on a system where many exchange rates are left to be determined by the forces of demand and supply on a relatively free market.

9. Canada has adopted both fixed and floating exchange rates at different times over the past 50 years. During the 1950s the exchange rate of the Canadian dollar fluctuated according to market forces and rose to a premium over the U.S. dollar. A fixed rate of 92.5 U.S. cents was established in 1962 and abandoned in 1970.

Topics for Review

The determination of quantities of imports and exports
Foreign exchange and exchange rates
The determination of the equilibrium exchange rate
Fixed versus flexible exchange rates
Appreciation, depreciation, revaluation, and devaluation
Imported inflation

Discussion Questions

1. In Figure 8-1 (iii), what is the opportunity cost, in terms of agricultural goods, of consuming an additional unit of manufactured goods at point a if the additional manufactured goods are obtained (i) through domestic production and (ii) through trade?

2. Recast Figure 8-7 as the demand and supply for pounds sterling in terms of the dollar price of pounds sterling. What is the equilibrium price? How does the equilibrium quantity of pounds sterling exchanged compare to the equilibrium quantity of dollars in Figure 8-7? How could the shifts in the S and D curves of Figure 8-8 be shown in your diagram?

3. What would the effect be on the supply and/or demand for Canadian dollars on the foreign exchange market of the following events? Indicate, using a diagram, the effect on the equilibrium exchange rate.
   a. Rising labor costs in Canadian manufacturing lead to a worsening ability to compete in world markets.
   b. The quantity of coffee imports is reduced, but the value of imported coffee increases because of price increases.
   c. A major U.S. newspaper switches from a U.S. newsprint producer to a cheaper Canadian source of paper.
   d. Japanese cars make further inroads into the Canadian market.

4. "In order to maintain a fixed exchange rate, Canada must maintain a rate of growth of the general price level in Canada equal to the average rate of growth of prices in the rest of the world; under flexible rates this is not necessary." Explain.

5. Can speculation occur in foreign exchange markets when exchange rates are fixed? When they are free to fluctuate? Under what circumstances will speculation help to stabilize fluctuations in exchange rates?

6. Suppose that in the foreign exchange market £1 = $2.00. 1 French franc=$0.20, and £1=12 French francs. How could an arbitrager make a profit? Assuming flexibility in exchange rates, how would such arbitrage eliminate this profit possibility? What would happen if exchange rates were fixed at these levels?

7. In recent years money wages have risen substantially faster in Canada than in the United States. Many Canadians have expressed the fear that their rapidly rising costs will price them out of U.S. markets. Did this fear make sense when the Canadian exchange rate was fixed relative to the American dollar? Does it make sense today when exchange rates are free to vary on the open market?

Part Three

Demand

Household Consumption Behavior

9

Early economists, struggling with the problem of what determines the relative prices of commodities, encountered what they came to call the **paradox of value:** necessary commodities such as water have prices that are low compared to the prices of luxury commodities such as diamonds. Water is necessary to our existence, these economists of some 200 years ago argued, while diamonds are frivolous and could disappear from the face of the earth tomorrow without causing any real upset. Does it not seem odd, then, that water is so cheap and diamonds are so expensive? It took a long time for economists to resolve this apparent paradox, so it is not surprising that even today the confusion persists in many quarters and clouds some current policy discussions.

We have already met one answer: It is supply and demand, not "necessity" or "luxury," that determine price in any competitive market. The equilibrium price that equates supply and demand is relatively low for water and relatively high for diamonds. But why is the demand for a necessity not enough to assure that its price will be high? After all, water is essential to life itself.

To address this more fundamental question we must go behind the market demand curve, which is the aggregate of all households' desired purchases at each possible price, and consider the behavior and motivation of individual households. This involves looking first at the relation between the market demand curve and the demand curves of individual households, then at individual behavior.

THE RELATION BETWEEN MARKET AND HOUSEHOLD DEMAND CURVES

Market demand curves tell how much is demanded by all purchasers. For example, in Figure 5-1 (see page 69) the market demand for carrots was 90,000 tons when the price was $40 per ton. This 90,000 tons is the sum of the quantities demanded by millions of different households. It may be made up of 4 pounds for the Mc-Daniels, 7 pounds for the Belangers, 1.5 pounds for the Wilsons, and so on. The demand curve for carrots also tells us that when the price rises to $60, aggregate quantity demanded falls to 77,500 tons per month. This quantity too can be traced back to individual households. The McDaniels might buy only 3 pounds, the Belangers 6.5 pounds, and the Wilsons perhaps none at all. Notice that we have now described two points, not only on the market demand curve but on the demand curves of each of these households.

Aggregate behavior is merely the sum of the behavior of individual households. The market demand is the horizontal sum of the demand curves of the individual households.

It is the *horizontal* sum because we wish to add quantities demanded at a given price, and quantities are measured in the horizontal direction on a conventional demand curve graph. This process is illustrated in Figure 9-1.

The Marginal Utility Theory of Household Behavior

MARGINAL AND TOTAL UTILITY

The satisfaction someone receives from consuming commodities is called his or her **utility.** The total utility obtained from consuming some commodity can be distinguished from the marginal utility of consuming one unit more or one unit less of it.

FIGURE 9–1

The Relation Between Household and Market Demand Curves

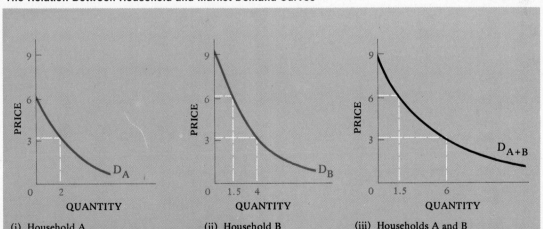

(i) Household A

(ii) Household B

(iii) Households A and B

An aggregate demand curve is the horizontal sum of the individual demand curves of all households in the market. The figure illustrates aggregation over only two households. At a price of $3, household A pur-chases 2 units and household B purchases 4 units; thus together they purchase 6 units. No matter how many households are involved the process is the same.

Total utility refers to the total satisfaction from consuming some commodity. **Marginal utility** refers to the change in satisfaction resulting from consuming a little more or a little less of the commodity. Thus, for example, the total utility of consuming ten units of any commodity is the total satisfaction that those ten units provide. The marginal utility of the tenth unit consumed is the satisfaction added by the consumption of that unit — or, in other words, the difference in total utility between consuming nine units and consuming ten units.[1]

The significance of this distinction can be seen by considering two questions: (1) If you had to give up consuming one of the following commodities completely, which would you choose: water or the movies? (2) If you had to choose between one of the following, which would you pick: increasing your water consumption by 35 gallons a month (the amount required for an average bath) or attending one more movie a month?

In (1) you are comparing the value you place on your total consumption of water with the value you place on all your attendances at the movies. You are comparing the *total utility* of your water consumption with the *total utility* of your movie attendances. There is little doubt that everyone would answer (1) in the same way, revealing that the total utility derived from consuming water exceeds the total utility derived from attending the movies.

In (2) you are comparing the value you place on a small addition to your water consumption with the value you place on a small addition to your movie attendances. You are comparing your *marginal utility* of water with your *marginal utility* of movies. The response to choice (2) is far less predictable than the response to choice (1).

Some might select the extra movie; others

might decide they have seen all the movies they can stand (marginal utility of another visit to the movies, *zero*) and would select the extra water. Furthermore, their choice would depend on whether it was made at a time when water was plentiful, so that they had more or less all the water they wanted (marginal utility of a little more water, *low*), or when water was scarce, so that they might put quite a high value on obtaining a little more water (marginal utility of a little more water, *high*).

Choices of type (1) are encountered much less commonly than are choices of type (2). If our income rises a little, we have to decide to have some more of one thing or another. When we find that we are overspending, or when our income falls, we have to decide what to cut down on, to have a little less of this or a little less of that.

Real choices are rarely conditioned by total utilities; it is marginal utilities that are relevant to choices concerning a little more or a little less.

The Hypothesis of Diminishing Marginal Utility

The basic hypothesis of utility theory, sometimes called the law of diminishing marginal utility, is:

The utility that any household derives from successive units of a particular commodity will diminish as total consumption of the commodity increases, the consumption of all other commodities being held constant.

Consider further the case of water. Some minimum quantity is essential to sustain life, and a person would, if necessary, give up all his or her income to obtain that quantity of water. Thus the marginal utility of that much water is extremely high. More than this bare minimum will be drunk, but the marginal utility of successive glasses of water drunk over a period will decline steadily.

Evidence for this hypothesis will be considered later, but you can convince yourself that it is at least reasonable by asking yourself a few questions. How much money would induce you to cut

---

[1] Here and elsewhere in elementary economics it is common to use interchangeably two concepts that mathematicians distinguish between. Technically, *incremental* utility is measured over a discrete interval, such as from nine to ten, while marginal utility is a rate of change measured over an infinitesimal interval. But common usage applies the word *marginal* when the last unit is involved, even if a one-unit change is not infinitesimal. [9]

your consumption of water by one glass per week? The answer is, very little. How much would induce you to cut it by a second glass? By a third glass? To only one glass consumed per week? The answer to the last question is, quite a bit. The fewer glasses you are consuming already, the higher the marginal utility of one more or one less glass of water.

But water has many uses other than for drinking. A fairly high marginal utility will be attached to some minimum quantity for bathing, but much more than this minimum will only be used for more frequent baths and for having a water level in the tub higher than is absolutely necessary. The last weekly gallon used for bathing is likely to have quite a low marginal utility. Again, some small quantity of water is necessary for tooth brushing, but many people leave the water running while they brush. They can hardly pretend that the water going down the drain between wetting and rinsing the brush has a high utility. When all the extravagant uses of water by the modern consumer are considered, it is certain that the marginal utility of the last, say, 30 percent of all units consumed is very low, even though the total utility of *all* the units consumed is extremely high.

Utility Schedules and Graphs

Assuming that utility can be measured, it is possible to illustrate the hypothesis. The schedule in Table 9-1 is hypothetical. It merely illustrates the assumptions that have been made about utility. The table shows that total utility rises as the number of movies attended each month rises. Everything else being equal, the household gets more satisfaction, the more movies it consumes each month—at least over the range shown in the table. But the marginal utility of each additional movie per month is less than that of the previous one (even though each movie adds something to the household's satisfaction). The marginal utility schedule declines as quantity consumed rises. The same data are shown graphically in the two parts of Figure 9-2. [10]

TABLE 9-1
Total and Marginal Utility Schedules

Number of movies attended (per month)	Total utility	Marginal utility
0	0	
		30
1	30	
		20
2	50	
		15
3	65	
		10
4	75	
		8
5	83	
		6
6	89	
		4
7	93	
		3
8	96	
		2
9	98	
		1
10	99	

Total utility rises but marginal utility declines as the consumption of this household increases. The marginal utility of 20, shown as the second entry in the last column, arises because total utility increased from 30 to 50—a difference of 20—with attendance at the second movie. Technically this is ''incremental utility'' over the interval from 1 to 2 units. To indicate that the marginal utility is associated with the change from one rate of movie attendances to another, the figures are recorded between the rows. When plotting marginal utility on a graph, it is plotted at the midpoint of the interval over which it is computed.

Can marginal utility reach zero? With many commodities there is some maximum consumption after which additional units give no additional utility. If the individual were forced to consume more, the additional units would actually reduce his or her total utility.

Cigarettes are an obvious example. There is a maximum number of cigarettes that most people would smoke per day, even if they did not have to worry about cost. For nonsmokers that number is zero. Few smokers would want to go to the point of chain-smoking from the second they awoke until the moment they fell asleep. Long before consumption reached this point, additional cigarettes smoked would cease to add to utility and would begin to subtract from it; that is, additional cigarettes would have a negative

FIGURE 9–2
Total and Marginal Utility Curves

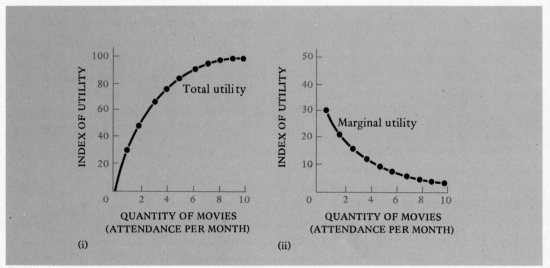

The total utility curve rises but the marginal utility curve falls as the quantity consumed rises. The dots reflect the points listed in Table 9-1; smooth curves have been drawn through them.

marginal utility or, as it is sometimes called, a marginal *disutility*. The same is true of many other commodities such as food, alcoholic beverages, and most recreation. (Although a few fanatics might be happy to play golf from sunup to sunset seven days a week for the rest of their lives, most people would not.)

MAXIMIZING UTILITY

A basic assumption of the economic theory of household behavior is that households consistently follow a particular rule.

The members of a household are assumed to maximize their total utility.

This is one way of saying that the members of households try to make themselves as well off as they possibly can in the circumstances in which they find themselves. Sometimes this assumption is taken to mean that households are narrowly selfish and have no charitable motives. Not so; if,

for example, the household derives utility from giving its money away to others, this can be incorporated into the analysis. The marginal utility it gets from a dollar given away can be compared with the marginal utility it gets from a dollar spent on itself.

The Equilibrium of a Household

How can a household adjust its expenditure so as to maximize the total utility of its members? Should it go to the point at which the marginal utility of each commodity is the same, that is, the point at which it would value equally the last unit of each commodity consumed? This would make sense only if each commodity had the same price per unit. But if a household must spend $3 to buy an additional unit of one commodity and only $1 for a unit of another, the first commodity would represent a poor use of its money if the marginal utility of each were equal: It would be spending $3 to get satisfaction that it could have acquired for only $1.

The household maximizing its utility will allocate its expenditure among commodities so that the utility of the last dollar spent on each is equal.

Imagine that the household is in a position in which the utility of the last dollar spent on carrots yields three times the utility of the last dollar spent on brussels sprouts. In this case total utility can be increased by switching a dollar of expenditure from sprouts to carrots and gaining the difference between the utilities of a dollar spent on each.

The utility-maximizing household will continue to switch its expenditure from sprouts to carrots as long as a dollar spent on carrots yields more utility than a dollar spent on sprouts. But this switching reduces the quantity of sprouts consumed and, given the law of diminishing marginal utility, raises the marginal utility of sprouts; at the same time, it increases the quantity of carrots consumed and thereby lowers the marginal utility of carrots. Eventually the marginal utilities will have changed enough so that the utility of a dollar spent on carrots is just equal to the utility of a dollar spent on sprouts.

At this point there is nothing to be gained by a further switch of expenditure from sprouts to carrots. If the household persisted in reallocating its expenditure, it would further reduce the marginal utility of carrots (by consuming more of them) and raise the marginal utility of sprouts (by consuming less of them). Total utility would then be lower because the utility of a dollar spent on sprouts would now exceed the utility of a dollar spent on carrots.

Let us now leave carrots and sprouts and deal with commodities in general. Denote the marginal utility of the last unit of X by MU_x and its price by p_x. Let MU_y and p_y refer to a second commodity. The marginal utility per dollar of X will be MU_x/p_x. For example, if the last unit adds 30 units to utility and costs \$2, then its marginal utility per dollar is $30/2 = 15$.

The condition required for a household to maximize its utility is, for any pair of commodities,

$$\frac{MU_x}{p_x} = \frac{MU_y}{p_y} \qquad [1]$$

This says that the household will allocate its expenditure so that the utility gained from the last dollar spent on each commodity is equal.

This is the fundamental equation of the utility theory of demand. Each household demands each good (for example, movie attendance) up to the point at which the marginal utility per dollar spent on it is the same as the marginal utility of a dollar spent on another good (for example, water). When this condition is met, the household cannot shift a dollar of expenditure from one commodity to another and increase its utility.

An Alternative Interpretation of Household Equilibrium

It is possible to rearrange the terms in equation [1] to gain an additional insight into household behavior.

$$\frac{MU_x}{MU_y} = \frac{p_x}{p_y} \qquad [2]$$

The right-hand side of this equation is given to the household by the market; it states the *relative* price of the two goods. It is determined by the market and is outside the control of the individual household, which reacts to these market prices but is powerless to change them. The left-hand side concerns the ability of the goods to add to the household's satisfaction; it is within the control of the household. In determining the quantities of different goods it buys, the household determines also their marginal utilities. (If you have difficulty seeing why, look again at Figure 9-2(ii).)

If the two sides of equation [2] are not equal, the household can increase its total satisfaction by rearranging its purchases. Assume, for example, that the price of a unit of X is twice the price of a unit of Y, $(p_x/p_y = 2)$, while the marginal utility of a unit of X is three times that of a unit of Y, $(MU_x/MU_y = 3)$. It will now pay the household to buy more X and less Y. If, for example, it reduces its purchases of Y by two units, it will free enough purchasing power to buy a unit of X. Since one new unit of X bought yields 1.5 times the satisfaction of two units of Y forgone, this switch is worth making. What about a further switch of X for Y? As the household buys more X and less Y, the marginal utility of X will fall and the marginal utility of Y will rise. The household will go on rearranging its purchases — reducing Y consumption and increasing X consumption — until, in this example, the marginal utility of X is only twice that of Y. At this point there is no further room to increase total satisfaction by rearranging purchases between the two commodities.

Now consider what the household is doing. It is faced with a set of prices that it cannot change. The household responds to these prices, and maximizes its satisfaction, by adjusting the things it can change — the quantities of the various goods it purchases — until equation [2] is satisfied for all pairs of commodities.

This sort of equation — one side representing the choices the outside world gives decision makers and the other side representing the effect of those choices on their welfare — recurs in economics again and again. It reflects the equilibrium position reached when decision makers have made the best adjustment they can to the external forces that limit their choices.

When all households are fully adjusted to a given set of market prices, each and every household will have identical ratios of its marginal utilities for each pair of goods. This is because each household faces the same set of market prices. Of course a rich household may consume more of each commodity than will a poor household. The rich and the poor households (and every other household) will, however, adjust their *relative* purchases of each commodity so that the relative marginal utilities are the same for each household. Thus, if the price of X is twice the price of Y, each household will purchase X and Y to the point at which the household's marginal utility of X is twice its marginal utility of Y.

The Derivation of the Household's Demand Curve[2]

To derive the household's demand curve for a commodity, it is only necessary to ask what happens when there is a change in the price of that commodity. To do this for candy, take equation [2] and let X stand for candy and Y for all other commodities. Assume that candy involves such a small proportion of the consumer's total expenditure that the marginal utilities of all other goods are unaffected when the household spends a little more or a little less on candy. If total expenditure on candy rises from \$1 a month to \$2 in response to a 10 percent fall in the price of candy, this represents a large increase in candy consumption, and the marginal utility of candy must fall. But the extra dollar spent on candy may mean only 1¢ less spent on each of a hundred different commodities, and this reduction in the consumption of each of them is so small that it will have a negligible effect on their marginal utilities.

What will happen if, with all other prices constant, the price of candy rises? The household that started from a position of equilibrium will now find itself in a position in which[3]

$$\frac{MU \text{ of candy}}{MU \text{ of } Y} < \frac{\text{price of candy}}{\text{price of } Y} \qquad [3]$$

To restore equilibrium, it must buy less candy, thereby raising its marginal utility until once again equation [2] is satisfied (where X is candy). The common sense of this is that the marginal utility of candy *per dollar* falls when its price rises. The household began with the utility of the last dollar spent on candy equal to the utility of the last dollar spent on all other goods, but the rise in candy prices changes this. The household buys less candy (and more of other goods) until the marginal utility of candy rises enough to make the utility of a dollar spent on candy the

[2] This section, which derives from utility theory the prediction that demand curves slope downward, may be omitted without loss of continuity.

[3] The inequality sign (<) always points to the smaller of two magnitudes. When the price of candy rises, the right-hand side of equation [2] increases. Until the household adjusts its consumption patterns, the left-hand side will stay the same. Thus equation [2] is replaced by inequality [3].

same as it was originally. Thus, if candy prices have doubled, the quantity purchased must be reduced until the marginal utility of candy has doubled.

This analysis leads to the basic prediction of demand theory.

A rise in the price of a commodity (with income and the prices of all other commodities held constant) will lead to a decrease in the quantity of the commodity demanded by each household.

If this prediction is valid for each household, it is also true for all households taken together. Thus the theory predicts a downward-sloping market demand curve.

APPLYING THE DISTINCTION BETWEEN MARGINAL AND TOTAL UTILITY

The Paradox of Value Revisited

We saw at the beginning of this chapter that early economists found it paradoxical that the market often valued necessary commodities such as water much lower than it valued such luxuries as diamonds. To state the "paradox" they distinguished a commodity's *value in use* (its total utility) and its *value in exchange* (its total market value, that is, price *times* quantity).[4] It seemed reasonable to them that commodities with high use values should have high market values. A precise statement of what they expected is: For any two commodities, the ratio of their values in exchange should conform to the ratio of their values in use. In the case of water and diamonds this led to the *incorrect* prediction that

$$\frac{p \times q \text{ of diamonds}}{p \times q \text{ of water}} = \frac{\text{total utility of diamonds}}{\text{total utility of water}} \quad [4]$$

The paradox of value was resolved when later economists discovered that equation [4] was inconsistent with the assumption that households

[4] The total utilities of two commodities cannot be simply related to their relative market *prices*, since the latter can be made anything we want by choosing the units appropriately. For example, one barrel of diamonds is expensive relative to one barrel of water, but a one-carat diamond is cheap relative to one reservoir full of water.

are utility maximizers. The reason is that utility-maximizing behavior relates *marginal* utilities to prices (as shown in equation [2]), not total utilities to total values purchased (as hypothesized in equation [4]).

Thus, for example, the fact that air is free means that people will use it until its marginal utility is zero. However, its zero value in exchange does not preclude its having a high value in use (total utility). To understand the case of water and diamonds, remember that water is cheap because there is enough of it that people consume it to the point at which its *marginal* utility is very low; they are not prepared to pay a high price to obtain a little more of it. Diamonds are expensive because they are scarce (the owners of diamond mines keep diamonds scarce by limiting output), and those who buy them have to stop at a point where marginal utility is still high; they are prepared to pay a high price for an additional diamond.

Elasticity of Demand, Necessities and Luxuries

Closely related to the paradox of value is the idea of relating elasticities to total utilities. It is possible to define necessities and luxuries in terms of total utilities. Certain commodities, called luxuries, have low total utilities; they can be dispensed with altogether if circumstances require. Other commodities, called necessities, are essential to life; they have high total utilities because certain minimum quantities of them are essential indeed.

So far so good. Error often creeps in, however, when people try to use commonsense knowledge about luxuries and necessities to predict demand elasticities and to dispense with the need for measurement. They argue that since luxuries can easily be given up, they will have highly elastic demands because when their prices rise, households can stop purchasing them. On the other hand, necessities have almost completely inelastic demands because when prices rise, households have no choice but to continue to buy them.

If it worked, this approach would save us time; we would have to determine only whether a particular commodity was a necessity or a luxury to be able to predict its elasticity of demand. But

elasticity of demand depends on marginal utilities, not total utilities.

Demand theory leads to the prediction that when the price of a commodity—say, eggs—rises, the household will reduce its purchase of eggs enough to increase their *marginal* utility to the point where the marginal utility per dollar spent on eggs is the same as for other commodities whose prices did not rise. But will the reduction in quantity required to raise the marginal utility be a little or a lot? This depends on the shape of the marginal utility curve in the range that is relevant. If the marginal utility curve is flat, a large change in quantity is required and demand will be elastic. If the curve is steep, a small change will suffice and demand will be inelastic. Figure 9-3 considers several possibilities in response to a doubling in the price of eggs. It leads to these important conclusions:

The response of quantity demanded to a change in price (i.e., the elasticity of demand) depends on the marginal utility over the relevant range and has no necessary relation to the total utility of the good.

"Just" Prices

The emotional reaction to goods is often a response to their total utilities rather than to their marginal utilities. We often hear an argument such as this: Water is a necessity of life of critical importance to rich and poor; it is wrong, therefore, to make people pay for so necessary a commodity.

Such views often produce curious results. If, for example, water is provided free instead of at a modest cost, the extra consumption that will occur will be for many uses that yield a relatively low utility (such as letting the water run while brushing teeth). The relevant question when deciding between a zero price and a modest price for water is not "Is water so necessary that we do not want to deprive anyone of *all* of it?" but rather "Are the marginal uses of water such that we do not want to discourage anyone from using water for these purposes?" Clearly, the two questions can be given different answers.

FIGURE 9–3
The Relation of Elasticity of Demand to Utility

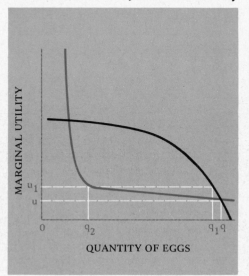

Elasticity of demand is determined by marginal utilities in the relevant range, not total utilities. The household originally consumes q dozen eggs per month, and the last egg consumed has a marginal utility of u. The price of eggs now doubles. To achieve a new equilibrium the household must cut its egg consumption until the marginal utility of eggs doubles, rising from u to u_1. If the black line is the household marginal utility curve, consumption only falls to q_1 and the household will have a very inelastic demand curve for eggs. If, however, the colored line is the household's marginal utility curve, consumption falls to q_2 and the household will have a very elastic demand curve. While the shape of the marginal utility curve in the relevant range is thus important, its shape outside of this range is irrelevant. To see this, let the colored curve have two alternative shapes in the range above u_1. The dark curve indicates a much higher total utility of the first units consumed than does the light curve, yet these alternative shapes have no influence on the household's behavior when it seeks to raise the marginal utility of eggs from u to u_1.

What Do Attitude Surveys Measure?

Consider a type of survey that is popular both in the daily newspapers and in sociology and political science. These surveys take the form of asking such questions as:

Do you like the Progressive Conservatives more than the New Democrats?

In deciding to live in area A rather than B, what factors influenced your choice? List the following in order of importance: neighbors, schools, closeness to swimming area, price and quality of housing available, play areas for children, general amenities.

In choosing a university, what factors were important to you? List in order of importance: environment, academic excellence, residential facilities, parents' opinion, school opinion, athletic facilities, tuition.

You should be able to add other examples to this list (which was drawn from real cases). *All of the above survey questions, and most of those you will be able to add, attempt to measure total rather than marginal utilities.* There is of course nothing illegal or immoral about this. People are free to measure anything that interests them, and in some cases knowledge of total utilities may be of practical value. But in many cases actual behavior will be determined by marginal utilities, and anyone who attempts to predict such behavior from a (correct) knowledge of total utilities will be hopelessly in error.

Where the behavior being predicted involves an either-or decision, such as a vote for the PC or the NDP candidate, the total utility that is attached to each choice will indeed be what matters because the voters are choosing one or the other. But where the decision is marginal, between a little more and a little less, total utility is not what will determine behavior.

A recent newspaper poll in a large midwestern city showed that two-thirds of the city's voters rated its excellent school system as one of its important assets. Yet in a subsequent election the voters turned down a school bond issue. Is this irrational behavior, as the newspaper editorials charged? Does it show a biased sample in the poll? It demonstrates neither. The poll measured the people's assessment of the total utility derived from the school system, while the bond issue vote depended on the people's assessment of the marginal utility of a little more money spent on the school system. There is nothing contradictory in anyone's feeling that the total utility of the city's fine school system is very large but that the city has other needs that have a higher marginal utility than further money spent on school construction.

A recent survey showed—paradoxically, it claimed—that many parents are getting more pleasure from their families just at the time that they are electing to have smaller families. There is nothing paradoxical about a shift in tastes that increases the marginal utility of the first two or three children and reduces the marginal utility of each further child. Nor is there any paradox in a parent's getting a high total utility from the total time spent with the children but assigning a low marginal utility to the prospect of spending a little additional time with them each evening.

Evidence about the consumption of water at various prices suggests that the marginal utility curve for water is shaped like the curve in Figure 9–4. The difference between providing water free and charging a modest price for it may mean a great deal in the quantity of water consumed. The additional water is costly to provide, and its provision requires scarce resources that could have been used to produce other things. If the utility of the commodities forgone is higher than the utility of the extra water consumed, then people are worse off as a result of receiving water free. A charge for water would release resources from water production to produce goods that yield a higher utility. Of course some minimum quantity of water could be provided free to every household, but the effects of this would be very different from those of making water generally free.

FIGURE 9–4
A Hypothetical Marginal Utility Curve for Water

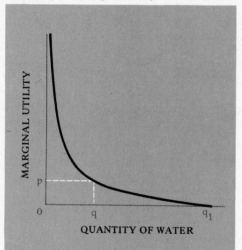

The imposition of a modest price may greatly reduce the quantity of water consumed without causing a large total sacrifice in the utility derived from water consumption. If water is priced at p, consumers will consume q units per month. Lowering the price to zero would increase the consumption to q_1. Much of the water that a household would consume at a zero price has a very low marginal utility.

Similar considerations apply to food, medical services, and a host of other commodities that are necessities of life but that have numerous extravagant uses which yield low utility and which will only be indulged if the commodity is very cheap or free.

Free Goods and Scarce Goods

A **free good** is one for which no price needs to be paid. Since a household's total utility can always be increased by consuming more of any good having a positive marginal utility, it follows that free goods will be consumed up to the point where their marginal utilities are zero.

Free goods may arise naturally or through government policy. When a good is naturally free, the amount supplied by nature is so plentiful that every household can consume it to the point of zero marginal utility without exhausting the available supply. When a good that is not naturally free is provided free to consumers by government policy, households will once again consume it to the point of zero marginal utility even though the last unit is costly to produce.

A **scarce good** is one that commands a positive price. It follows that scarce goods will have positive marginal utilities. Most goods are scarce. Not enough can be produced to satisfy demand at a zero price.

The meaning of the scarcity principle first discussed in Chapter 1 may now be reinterpreted. If all goods had zero prices, the total amounts that people would want to consume would greatly exceed the amounts that could be produced by all of the economy's resources. Thus goods are scarce in relation to households' potential demands, and resources are scarce in relation to households' desires for the goods they can produce.

Consumers' Surplus

Assume that you would be willing to pay as much as $100 a month for the amount of a commodity you consume rather than do without it.

Further, assume that you actually buy the commodity for $60 instead of $100. What a bargain! You have paid $40 less than the top figure you were willing to pay. Yet this sort of bargain is not rare; it occurs every day in any economy where prices do the rationing. Indeed it is so common that the $40 "saved" in this example has a name: *consumers' surplus*. A precise definition will come later; in the meantime, let us see how this surplus arises.

Consumers' surplus is a direct consequence of diminishing marginal utility. To illustrate the connection, suppose we have collected the information shown in Table 9-2 on the basis of an interview with Mrs. Schwartz. Our first question is, If you were getting no milk at all, how much would you be willing to pay for one glass per week? With no hesitation, she replies, $3. We then ask, If you had already consumed that one glass, how much would you pay for a second glass per week? After a bit of thought she answers, $1.50. Adding one glass per week with each question, we discover that she would be willing to pay $1 to get a third glass per week and 80¢, 60¢, 50¢, 40¢, 30¢, 25¢, and 20¢ for successive glasses from the fourth to the tenth glasses per week. The information shows that she puts progressively lower valuations on each additional glass of milk, and this illustrates the general concept of diminishing marginal utility.

But Mrs. Schwartz does not have to pay a different price for each glass of milk she consumes each week. Instead she finds that she can buy all the milk she wants at the prevailing market price. Suppose the price is 30¢. She will buy eight glasses per week (one each weekday and two on Sunday) because she values the eighth glass just at the market price while valuing all earlier glasses at higher amounts. Because she values the first glass at $3 but gets it for 30¢, she makes a "profit" of $2.70 on that glass. Between her $1.50 valuation of the second glass and what she has to pay for it she clears a "profit" of $1.20. She clears 70¢ on the third glass, and so on. These "profit" amounts are called her consumers' surpluses on each glass. They are shown in column 3 of the table; the total surplus is $5.70 per week.[5]

While other consumers would put different numerical values into Table 9-2, diminishing marginal utility implies that the figures in column 2 would be declining for each consumer. Since a consumer will go on buying further units until the value he or she places on the last unit equals the market price, it follows that there will be a consumers' surplus on every unit consumed except the last one.

TABLE 9–2
Consumers' Surplus on Milk Consumption by One Consumer

(1) Glasses of milk consumed per week	(2) Amount the consumer would pay to get this glass	(3) Consumers' surplus if milk costs 30¢ per glass
First	$3.00	$2.70
Second	1.50	1.20
Third	1.00	0.70
Fourth	0.80	0.50
Fifth	0.60	0.30
Sixth	0.50	0.20
Seventh	0.40	0.10
Eighth	0.30	0.00
Ninth	0.25	——
Tenth	0.20	——

Consumers' surplus on each unit consumed is the difference between the market price and the maximum price the consumer would pay to obtain that unit. The table shows the value that a single consumer, Mrs. Schwartz, puts on successive glasses of milk consumed each week. Because marginal utility declines, she would pay successively lower amounts for each additional unit consumed. As long as she would be willing to pay more than the market price for any unit, she will buy that unit and obtain a consumers' surplus on it. The marginal unit is the one valued just at the market price and on which no consumers' surplus is earned.

[5] Instead of summing her consumers' surplus on each glass, we could arrive at the same total in a different way. First, add up the valuation she places on each of the eight glasses. This total value is $8.10. Then determine what she actually paid: 8 × .30 = $2.40. Subtract $2.40 from $8.10, and the consumers' surplus is $5.70.

FIGURE 9-5
Consumers' Surplus for an Individual

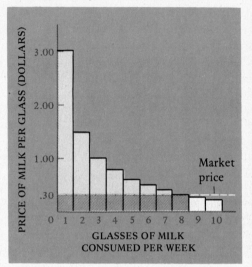

Consumers' surplus is the sum of the extra valuations placed on each unit over and above the market price paid for each. This figure is based on the data in Table 9-2. Mrs. Schwartz will pay the dark shaded area for the eight glasses of milk she will consume per week when the market price is 30¢ a glass. The total value she places on these eight glasses is the entire shaded area. Hence her consumers' surplus is the light shaded area.

FIGURE 9-6
Consumers' Surplus for the Market

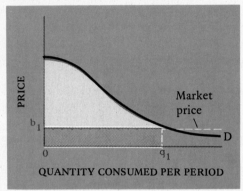

Total consumers' surplus is the area under the demand curve and above the price line. The demand curve shows the amount consumers would pay for each unit of the commodity if they had to buy their units one at a time. The area under the demand curve shows the total valuation consumers place on all units consumed. For example, the total value that consumers place on q_1 units is the entire shaded area under the demand curve up to q_1. At a market price of p_1 the amount paid for q_1 units is the dark shaded area. Hence consumers' surplus is the light shaded area.

In general, **consumers' surplus** is the difference between the total value consumers place on all the units consumed of some commodity and the payment they must make to purchase the same amount of that commodity. The total value placed by each consumer on the total consumption of some commodity can be estimated in at least two ways: The valuation that the consumer places on each successive unit may be summed; or the consumer may be asked how much he or she would pay to consume the amount in question if the alternative were to have none of the commodity.[6]

The data in columns 1 and 2 of Table 9-2 give Mrs. Schwartz's demand curve for milk. It is her demand curve because she will go on buying glasses of milk as long as she values each glass at least as much as the market price she must pay for it. When the market price is $3 per glass, she will buy only one glass; when it is $1.50, she will buy two glasses—and so on. The total valuation is the area below her demand curve, and consumers' surplus is that part of the area that lies above the price line. This is shown in Figure 9-5. Figure 9-6 shows that the same relation holds for the smooth market demand curve that indicates the total amount all consumers would buy at each price.

---

[6] This is only an approximation, but it is good enough for our purposes. More advanced theory shows that the calculations presented here ignore an "income effect." As a result they slightly overestimate consumers' surplus. Although it is sometimes necessary to correct for this bias, no amount of re-

finement upsets the general result that we establish here: When consumers can buy all units they require at a single market price, they pay much less for the quantity consumed than they would be willing to pay if faced with the choice between that amount and nothing.

Household Choice: An Alternative Analysis

The marginal utility approach to household behavior came first historically, and it is still valued because of the great insights that the concept of marginal utility opened up. With the publication in 1939 of Sir John R. Hicks' classic *Value and Capital,* an alternative approach often called indifference curve analysis became popular in English-language economics.[7] This is not a competing theory but a slightly different way of looking at choices by households. Its major innovation was to dispense with the notion of a *measurable* concept of utility that is required by marginal utility theory.

THE BUDGET LINE

Consider a household faced with the choice between only two goods, food (F) and clothing (C). (Such choices between two goods reveal everything necessary for elementary theory.) Assume that the household has a certain money income, say $120 a week, and that the prices for food and clothing are fixed—at the outset at $4 a unit for food and $2 a unit for clothing. The household does not save; its only choice is in deciding how much of its $120 to spend on food and how much to spend on clothing.

The household's problem is illustrated by the line *ab* in Figure 9-7, which shows the combina-

---

[7] Hicks, whose career has been spent mainly at Oxford, was the first British recipient of the Nobel prize in economics, for the contributions to economics that he made in *Value and Capital* and elsewhere. He did not invent indifference curve analysis; he took over, popularized, and extended the use of a concept developed by the great Italian economist Vilfredo Pareto in the first decade of this century. As is so often true in science, it is not the discoverer or the inventor, but the one who makes the timely and insightful application, who has the major impact. Thus it was Hicks, not Pareto, who led to the almost universal use of indifference analysis by economists in the 1940s and 1950s. Pareto in his time was following "hints" given in 1896 by the American economist Irving Fisher and in a slim volume published in 1886 by the Italian engineer Giovanni Antonelli. Such is the history of ideas.

FIGURE 9–7
Budget Lines

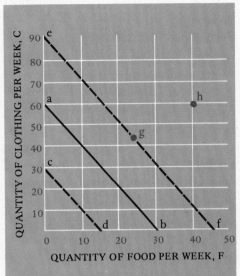

The budget line shows the quantities of goods available to a household given its money income and the prices of the goods it buys. Any point indicates a combination (or *bundle*) of so much food and so much clothing. Point *h,* for example, indicates 60 units of clothing and 40 units of food per week. With an income of $120 a week and prices of $4 for food and $2 clothing, the household's budget line is *ab.* This line shows all the combinations of F and C available to a household spending that income at those prices.

An increase in money income from $120 to $180, with money prices of F and C constant, shifts the budget line outward, parallel to itself, to *ef.* A decrease in money income to $60 shifts the budget line to *cd.*

---

tions of food and clothing available to it. The household could spend all its income on clothing and obtain 60C and no F per week. Or it could decide to have 1F each week, at a cost of $4, and only 58$C$. It could also go to the other extreme and purchase only food, buying 30F and no C.

When all the points indicating combinations that are available to the household if it spends all its income are joined, the result is called the household's **budget line.** (It is also sometimes called an "isocost" line since all points on the line represent bundles of goods with the same total cost of purchase.)

Among the important properties of the budget line are the following. (You should check enough examples against Figure 9-7 to satisfy yourself that they are true.)

1. Points on the budget line represent bundles of commodities that exactly use up the household's income. (Try, for example, the point 20C and 20F.)
2. Points between the budget line and the origin represent bundles of commodities that use up less than the household's income. (Try, for example, the point 20C and 10F.)
3. Points above the budget line represent combinations of commodities costing more to purchase than the household's present income. (Try, for example, the point 30C and 40F.)

The budget line shows all combinations of commodities that are available to the household given its money income and the prices of the goods that it purchases, if it spends all its income on them.

Changes in Money Income

What happens to the budget line when money income changes? If the household's money income is halved from $120 to $60 per week, prices being unchanged, then the amount of goods it can buy will also be halved. If it spends all its income on clothing, it will now get 30C and no F (point c in Figure 9-7); if it spends all its income on food, it will get 15F and no C (point d). All possible combinations now open to the household appear on budget line cd, which is closer to the origin than the original budget line.

If the household's income rises to $180, it will be able to buy more of both commodities than it could previously. The budget line shifts outward. If the household buys only clothing, it can have 90C; if it buys only food, it can have 45F; if it divides its income equally between the two goods, it can have 45C and 22.5F.

Variations in the household's money income, with prices constant, shift the budget line parallel to itself.

Proportional Changes in Prices of Both Goods

Changing both prices in the same proportion shifts the budget line parallel to itself in the same manner that a money income change shifted it. Doubling both prices with money income constant halves the amount of goods that can be purchased and thus has exactly the same effect on the household's budget line as halving money income with money prices constant. In both cases the household's original budget line is shifted inward.

It is now apparent that it is possible to have exactly offsetting changes in prices and money incomes. A change in money income and a *proportional* change of the same amount in all money prices leaves the position of the budget line—and hence the real choices available to the household—unchanged.

The **indexing** of money values is an arrangement that automatically increases them as the average level of all prices rises during an inflation. For example, when money wages are indexed, they are increased in proportion to increases in the price level. The purpose of indexing is to accomplish the offsetting changes analyzed in the preceding paragraph. Prices rise, shifting inward the budget line for a constant money income. Indexing then raises incomes in proportion to the price rise. This shifts the budget line back to its original position and leaves the purchasing power of wages unaffected by the inflation.

Changes in Relative Prices

Absolute price or *money price* or merely *price* of a commodity means the amount of money that must be spent to acquire 1 unit of the commodity. A **relative price** is the ratio of two absolute prices. The statement "the price of F is $2" refers to an absolute price; "the price of F is twice the price of C" refers to a relative price.

A change in a relative price can be accomplished either by changing both of the money

FIGURE 9–8

The Effect on the Budget Line of Changes in the Price of Food

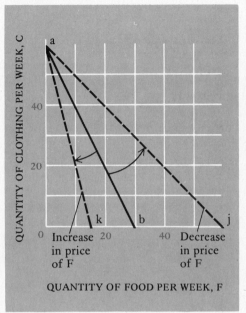

A change in the price of one commodity changes relative prices and thus changes the slope of the budget line. The original budget line *ab* arose from a money income of $120, with units of *C* priced at $2 and units of *F* at $4. A fall in the price of *F* to $2 doubles the quantity of *F* obtainable for any given quantity of *C* purchased and pivots the budget line outward to *aj*. A rise in the price of *F* to $8 reduces the quantity of *F* obtainable and pivots the budget line inward to *ak*.

prices in different proportions or by holding one price constant and changing the other. It is useful for our purposes to do the latter. The effects of such a change are shown in Figure 9-8. The basic conclusion that emerges is this:

A change in relative prices — such as occurs when one price changes while the other price remains constant — changes the slope of the budget line.

The economic significance of the slope of the budget line for food and clothing (which we have just seen to be related to the relative prices of the two commodities) is that it reflects the opportunity cost of food in terms of clothing. To increase food consumption with expenditure constant, one must move along the budget line, consuming less clothing. Suppose the price of food (p_F) is $2 and the price of clothing (p_C) is $1. With income fixed, it is necessary to forgo the purchase of 2 units of clothing to acquire 1 unit extra of food. The opportunity cost of food in terms of clothing is thus 2 units of clothing. But it can also be stated as p_F/p_C, which is the relative price. Notice that this relative price ($p_F = 2p_C$) is consistent with an infinite number of absolute prices. If $p_F = \$40$ and $p_C = \$20$, it still takes the sacrifice of 2 units of clothing to acquire 1 unit of food. This shows that it is relative, not absolute, prices that determine opportunity cost. The general conclusion is that the opportunity cost of *F* in terms of *C* is measured by the slope of the budget line or (the equivalent) by the relative price ratio. [11]

The Basic Conclusions Restated

It may be helpful to restate the earlier conclusions in terms of absolute and relative prices. (You should reread what has gone before if you cannot prove them yourself.)

1. A change in money income, with absolute prices constant, shifts the budget line parallel to itself — inward toward the origin when income falls and outward away from the origin when income rises.
2. An equal proportional change in all absolute prices leaves relative prices unchanged. Multiplying all money prices by the same constant, with money income constant, has exactly the same effect on the budget line as dividing money income by the same constant with money prices constant.
3. An equal percentage change in all absolute prices and money income leaves the budget line exactly where it was before the changes occurred.
4. A change in relative prices causes the budget line to change its slope.

Real and Money Income

A household's **money income** is its income measured in money units, so many dollars and cents per month or per year. A household's **real income** is the purchasing power of its money income, that is, the quantity of goods and services that can be purchased with its money income.

If money prices remain constant, any change in money income will cause a corresponding change in real income. If the household's money income rises by 10 percent (say from $10,000 to $11,000), the household can if it wishes buy 10 percent more of all commodities—its real income has also risen by 10 percent.

If prices change, however, real and money incomes will not change in the same proportion—indeed, they can easily change in opposite directions. Consider a situation in which all money prices rise by 10 percent. If money income falls, or rises by any amount less than 10 percent, real income falls. If money income also rises by 10 percent, real income will be unchanged. Only if money income rises by more than 10 percent will real income also rise.

Changes in real income are shown graphically by shifts in the budget line. When the budget line in Figure 9-7 shifts outward, away from the origin, real income rises. When the line shifts inward, toward the origin, real income falls.

If we are interested in the household's potential standard of living, we are interested in its ability to purchase goods and services; this is appropriately measured by real income, not by money income.

INDIFFERENCE CURVE ANALYSIS[8]

What the household does is determined by both what it can do and what it would like to do. The budget line shows what the household *can do,* the choices that it can make given its money in-

come and the prices of the commodities that it buys. What the household *wants to do* is determined by its tastes.

An Indifference Curve

Take an imaginary household and give it some quantity of each of the two goods, say 18 units of clothing and 10 units of food. (A consumption pattern for a household that contains quantities of two or more distinct goods is called a *bundle* or a *combination* of goods.) Now offer the household an alternative bundle of goods, say 13 units of clothing and 15 units of food. This alternative has 5 fewer units of clothing and 5 more units of food than the first one. Whether the household prefers this bundle depends on the relative valuation that it places on 5 more units of food and 5 fewer units of clothing. If it values the extra food more than the forgone clothing, it will prefer the new bundle to the original one. If it values the food less than the clothing, it will prefer the original bundle.

There is a third alternative: If the household values the extra food the same as it values the forgone clothing, it would gain equal satisfaction from the two alternative bundles of food and clothing. In this case the household is said to be indifferent between the two bundles.

Assume that after much trial and error a number of bundles have been identified, each of which gives equal satisfaction. These are shown in Table 9-3.

There will of course be combinations of the two commodities other than those enumerated in the table that will give the same level of satisfaction to the household. All of these combinations are shown in Figure 9-9 by the smooth curve that passes through the points plotted from the table. This curve is an indifference curve. In general, an **indifference curve** shows all combinations of goods that yield the same satisfaction to the household. A household is *indifferent* between the combinations indicated by any two points on one indifference curve.

Any points above and to the right of the curve

show combinations of food and clothing that the household would prefer to combinations indicated by points on the curve. Consider, for example, the combination of 20 food and 18 clothing, which is represented by point g in the figure. Although it might not be obvious that this bundle must be preferred to bundle a (which has more clothing but less food), it is obvious that it will be preferred to bundle c, because there is both less clothing and less food represented at c than at g. Inspection of the graph shows that *any* point

TABLE 9–3
Alternative Bundles Giving a Household Equal Satisfaction

Bundle	Clothing	Food
a	30	5
b	18	10
c	13	15
d	10	20
e	8	25
f	7	30

These bundles all lie on a single indifference curve. Since all of these bundles of food and clothing give equal satisfaction, the household is "indifferent" among them.

FIGURE 9–9
An Indifference Curve

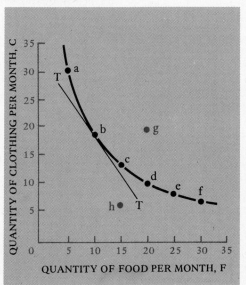

An indifference curve shows combinations of food and clothing that yield equal satisfaction and among which the household is indifferent. Points a to f are plotted from Table 9-3. The smooth curve through them is an indifference curve; each combination on it gives equal satisfaction to the household. Point g above the line is a preferred combination to any point on the line; point h below the line is an inferior combination to any point on the line. The slope of the line T-T gives the marginal rate of substitution at point b. Moving down the curve from b to f the slope flattens. This shows that the more food and the less clothing the household has, the less willing it will be to sacrifice further clothing to get more food.

above the curve will be obviously superior to *some* points on the curve in the sense that it will contain both more food and more clothing than those points on the curve. But since all points on the curve are equal in the household's eyes, the point above the curve must be superior to *all* points on the curve. By a similar argument, points below and to the left of the curve represent bundles of goods that are inferior to bundles represented by points on the curve.

The Marginal Rate of Substitution

How much clothing would the household be prepared to give up to get one more unit of food? The answer to this question measures what is called the marginal rate of substitution of clothing for food. The **marginal rate of substitution (MRS)** is the amount of one commodity a consumer would be prepared to give up to get one more unit of another commodity. The first basic assumption of indifference theory is that the algebraic value of the MRS is always negative. This means that to gain a positive change in its consumption of one commodity, the household is prepared to incur a negative change in its consumption of a second.

Graphically the negative marginal rate of substitution is shown by the downward slope of all indifference curves. (See for example the curve in Figure 9-9.)

The Hypothesis of Diminishing Marginal Rate of Substitution

The second basic assumption of indifference theory is that the marginal rate of substitution between any two commodities depends on the amounts of the commodities currently being consumed by the household. Consider a case where the household has a lot of clothing and only a little food: Common sense suggests that the household might be willing to give up quite a bit of its plentiful clothing in order to get one unit more of very scarce food. Now consider a case where the household has only a little clothing and quite a lot of food: Common sense suggests that the household would be willing to give up only a small amount of its scarce clothing in order to get one more unit of already plentiful food.

This example illustrates the hypothesis of the **diminishing marginal rate of substitution.** In terms of our clothing-food example, the hypothesis states that the less clothing and the more food the household has already, the smaller will be the amount of clothing it will be willing to give up to get one further unit of food.

The hypothesis says that the marginal rate of substitution changes systematically as the amounts of two commodities presently consumed vary. Take any two commodities, *A* and *B*. The more *A* and the less *B* the household currently has, the less *B* will it be willing to give up to get a further unit of *A*. The graphical expression of this hypothesis is that the slope of any indifference curve becomes flatter as the household moves downward to the right along the curve. [12] In Figure 9-9 a movement downward to the right means less clothing and more food is being consumed. The decreasing steepness of the curve means that less and less clothing will be sacrificed to get one further unit of food.

The hypothesis is illustrated in Table 9-4, which is based on the example of food and clothing in Table 9-3. The last column of the table shows the rate at which the household is prepared to sacrifice units of clothing per unit of food obtained. At first the household will sacri-

TABLE 9–4
The Marginal Rate of Substitution Between Clothing and Food

Movement	(1) Change in clothing	(2) Change in food	(3) Marginal rate of substitution (1) ÷ (2)
From *a* to *b*	−12	5	−2.4
From *b* to *c*	− 5	5	−1.0
From *c* to *d*	− 3	5	− .6
From *d* to *e*	− 2	5	− .4
From *e* to *f*	− 1	5	− .2

The marginal rate of substitution of clothing for food declines as the quantity of clothing in the bundle declines and the quantity of food increases. This table is based on Table 9–3. When the household moves from *a* to *b*, it gives up 12 units of clothing and gains 5 units of food; it remains at the same level of overall satisfaction. The household at point *a* was prepared to sacrifice 12 clothing for 5 food (i.e., $^{12}/_5 = 2.4$ units of clothing per unit of food obtained). When the household moves from *b* to *c*, it sacrifices 5 clothing for 5 food (a rate of substitution of 1 unit of clothing for each unit of food).

fice 2.4 units of clothing to get 1 unit more of food, but as its consumption of clothing diminishes and that of food increases, the household becomes less and less willing to sacrifice further clothing for more food.[9]

The Indifference Map

So far we have constructed only a single indifference curve. However, there must be a similar curve through other points in Figure 9-9. Starting at any point, such as *g*, there will be other combi-

---

[9] Movements between widely separated points on the indifference curve have been examined. In terms of a very small movement from any of the points on the curve, the rate at which the household will give up clothing to get food is shown by the slope of the tangent to the curve at that point. The slope of the line *T* which is a tangent to the curve at point *b* in Figure 9-9 may thus be thought of as the slope of the curve at that precise point. It tells us the rate at which the household will sacrifice clothing per unit of food obtained when it is currently consuming 18 clothing and 10 food (the coordinates of point *b*).

nations that will yield equal satisfaction to the household and, if the points indicating all of these combinations are connected, they will form another indifference curve. This exercise can be repeated as many times as we wish, and as many indifference curves as we wish can be generated. The farther any indifference curve is from the origin, the higher will be the level of satisfaction given by any of the combinations of goods indicated by points on the curve.

A set of indifference curves is called an **indifference map,** an example of which is shown in Figure 9-10. It specifies the household's tastes by showing its rate of substitution between the two commodities for every level of current consumption of these commodities. When economists say that a household's tastes are *given,* they do not mean that the household's current

consumption pattern is given; rather, they mean that the household's entire indifference map is given.

The Equilibrium of the Household

Indifference maps describe the preferences of households. Budget lines describe the possibilities open to the household. To predict what households will actually do, both sets of information must be put together. This is done in Figure 9-11. The household's budget line is shown in the figure by the straight line, while its tastes are shown by its indifference map (a few of whose curves are shown in the figure). Any point on the budget line is attainable. But which point will actually be chosen by the household that is interested in maximizing its satisfactions?

Since the household wishes to maximize its satisfactions, it wishes to reach its highest attainable indifference curve. Inspection of the figure shows that if the household purchases any bundle on its budget line where an indifference curve cuts the budget line, a higher indifference curve can be reached. Only when the bundle purchased is one where an indifference curve is tangent to the budget line is it impossible for the household to alter its purchases and reach a higher curve.

The household's satisfaction is maximized at the point at which an indifference curve is tangent to its budget line.

At such a tangency position, the slope of the indifference curve (the marginal rate of substitution of the goods in the household's preferences) is the same as the slope of the budget line (the relative prices of the goods in the market). The common sense of this result is that if the household values goods at a different rate than the market does, there is room for profitable exchange. The household can give up some of the good it values relatively less than the market and take in return some more of the good it values relatively higher than the market does. When the household is prepared to swap goods at the same rate as they can be traded on the market, there is

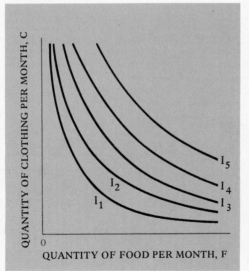

FIGURE 9–10
An Indifference Map

An indifference map consists of a set of indifference curves. All points on a particular curve indicate alternative combinations of food and clothing that give the household equal satisfaction. The further the curve from the origin, the higher the level of satisfaction it represents. Thus I_5 is a higher indifference curve than I_4 and represents a higher level of satisfaction.

FIGURE 9–11
The Equilibrium of a Household

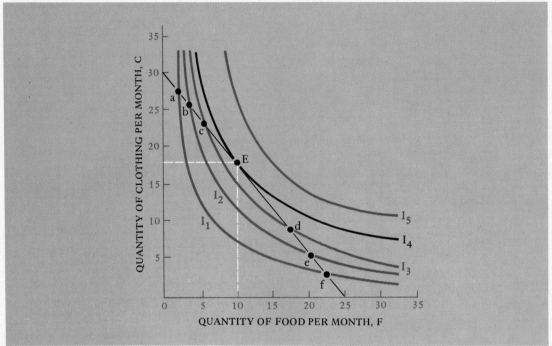

Equilibrium occurs at *E* where an indifference curve is tangent to the budget line. The household has an income of $750 a month and faces prices of $25 a unit for clothing and $30 a unit for food. A combination of *C* and *F* indicated by point *a* is attainable, but by moving along the budget line higher indifference curves can be reached. The same is true at *b* and *c*. At *E*, how-ever, where an indifference curve is tangent to the budget line, it is impossible to reach a higher curve by moving along the budget line. If the household did alter its consumption bundle by moving from *E* to *c* or *d*, for example, it would move to lower indifference curves and thus to lower levels of satisfaction.

no further opportunity for it to raise its satisfaction by substituting one commodity for the other.

The household is presented with market information (prices) that it cannot itself change. It adjusts to these prices by choosing a bundle of goods such that, at the margin, its own subjective evaluation of the goods conforms with the evaluations given by market prices.

The Reaction of the Household to a Change in Income

We have seen that a change in income leads to parallel shifts of the budget line — inward toward the origin when income falls and outward away from the origin when income rises. For each level of income there will be an equilibrium position at which an indifference curve is tangent to the relevant budget line. Each such equilibrium position means that the household is doing as well as it possibly can for that level of income. If we move the budget line through all possible levels of income, and if we join up all the points of equilibrium, we will trace out what is called an **income-consumption line,** an example of which is shown in Figure 9-12. This lines shows how consumption bundles change as income changes, with relative prices held constant.

FIGURE 9–12
The Income-Consumption Line

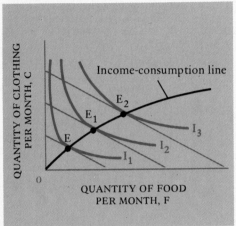

The income-consumption line shows how the household's purchases react to a change in income with relative prices held constant. Increases in income shift the budget line out parallel to itself, moving the equilibrium from E to E_1 to E_2. By joining up all the points of equilibrium, an income-consumption line is traced out.

FIGURE 9–13
The Price-Consumption Line

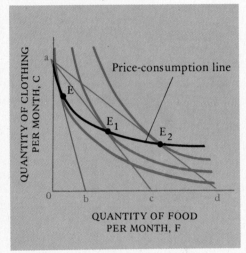

The price-consumption line shows how the household's purchases react to a change in one price with money income and other prices held constant. Decreases in the price of food (with money income and the price of clothing constant) pivot the budget line from ab to ac to ad. The equilibrium position moves from E to E_1 to E_2. By joining up all the points of equilibrium, a price-consumption line is traced out.

The Reaction of a Household to a Change in Price

We already know that a change in the relative price of the two goods changes the slope of the budget line. If the price of food is varied continuously, there will be an equilibrium position for each price. Connecting these traces out a **price-consumption line,** as in Figure 9-13. Notice that as the relative price of food and clothing changes, the relative quantities of food and clothing purchased also change. In particular, as the price of food falls the household buys more food.[10]

We are now very close to deriving a demand curve for food. Figure 9-13 shows how the quantity of food consumed varies as the price of food varies. This gives us the information needed to

plot a demand curve. All we need to do is to transfer this information to a new diagram with the price of food on one axis and the quantity of food consumed on the other.[11]

Summary

1. Marginal utility theory distinguishes between the total utility gained from the consumption of all units of some commodity and the marginal utility resulting from the consumption of one more unit of the commodity. The basic assumption about a household's tastes made in utility theory is that the utility the household derives from the consumption of successive units of a

---

[10] There is a rarely encountered but theoretically possible exception to this rule, a Giffen good, that is described in the appendix to this chapter.

[11] The derivation of demand curves from indifference curves is further explored in the appendix to this chapter.

commodity per period of time will diminish as the consumption of that commodity increases.

2. The household maximizes its utility and thus reaches equilibrium when the utility derived from the last dollar spent on each commodity is equal. Another way of putting this is that the marginal utilities derived from the last unit of each commodity consumed will be proportional to their prices.

3. It is vital to distinguish between total and marginal utilities because most choices are related to marginal utilities and cannot be predicted from a knowledge of total utilities. The paradox of value involved a confusion between total and marginal utilities. Whether goods are "necessities" or "luxuries," while perhaps determining the total utilities they produce, tells nothing about marginal utilities. But it is marginal utilities that are required for defining elasticity and understanding market behavior.

4. Indifference curves and indifference theory provide an alternative way of studying household consumption behavior. The basic constructs of indifference curve analysis are the budget line and the indifference map.

5. Consumers' surplus arises when a household can purchase every unit of a commodity at a price equal to the value that it places on the last unit purchased. Diminishing marginal utility implies that the household places a higher value on all other units purchased and hence that all but the last unit purchased will yield a consumers' surplus.

6. While the budget line describes what the household *can* purchase, indifference curves describe the household's tastes and, therefore, refer to what it would *like* to do. A single indifference curve joins combinations of commodities that give the household equal satisfaction and among which it is therefore indifferent.

7. The basic hypothesis about tastes is that of diminishing marginal rate of substitution. This hypothesis states that the less of one good and the more of another that the household has, the less willing it will be to give up some of the first good to get a further unit of the second.

8. The household maximizes its satisfactions, given its budget line, at the point at which an indifference curve is tangent to its budget line.

9. The income-consumption line shows how quantity consumed changes as income changes. The price-consumption line shows how quantity consumed changes as relative prices change. When prices change, the household will consume relatively more of the commodity whose relative price falls and relatively less of the commodity whose relative price rises.

10. The appendix to this chapter carries further the derivation of downward-sloping demand curves using indifference theory. It also considers the theoretical possibility that a demand curve could slope upward.

Topics for Review

Market demand and individual household demand curves
The hypothesis of diminishing marginal utility
Conditions for maximizing utility
The interpretation of $MU_x/MU_y = p_x/p_y$
The paradox of value
Consumers' surplus
The budget line
Real income and money income
Indifference curves and indifference maps
The marginal rate of substitution
The tangency of the budget line and an indifference curve
The price-consumption and income-consumption lines

Discussion Questions

1. Why is market demand the *horizontal* sum of individual demand curves? Is the vertical sum different? What would a vertical sum of individual demand curves show? Can you imagine any use of vertical summation of demand curves?
2. Which of the choices implied below involve a consideration of marginal utilities and which total utilities?
   a. Seventeen-year-olds should be given the vote.

b. A diet calls for precisely 1,200 calories per day.

c. My doctor says I must give up smoking and drinking or else accept an increased chance of heart attack.

d. In 1976 Armand Hammer decided to buy the Rembrandt painting *Juno* for a record $3.25 million and called it the "crown jewel of my collection."

e. I enjoyed my golf game today, but I was so tired that I decided to stop at the 17th hole.

f. A general with limited reserves wonders whether to reinforce her left flank or her right flank or to distribute the reserves thinly between the two.

3. Are the transactions described in the following quotations consistent with the utility of the commodity? Interpret "worthless" and "priceless" as used here.

a. "Bob Koppang has made a business of selling jars of shredded U.S. currency. The money is worthless, and yet he's sold 53,000 jars already and has orders for 40,000 more—at $5.00 a jar. Each jar contains about $10,000 in shredded bills."

b. "Leonardo da Vinci's priceless painting *Genevra de' Benci* was sold to the National Gallery of Art for $5 million."

4. The *New York Times* called it the great liver crisis. Chopped liver is a delicacy on the table, particularly the kosher table, but in the late 1970s it was a glut on the market. Prices had sunk to a 20-year low as supplies had risen to an all-time high because of a very high cattle slaughter. What do the following quotations from the *Times'* story tell you about the marginal and total utility of liver?

a. "Grade A-1 liver is being used for cats and dogs instead of people. It's unheard of, it's a waste," says the manager of Kosher King Meat Products. "Even Israel is drowning in chopped liver."

b. "They're falling all over their feet to sell to me," said the president of Mrs. Weinberg's Kosher Chopped Liver Co., which uses 3,500 pounds of liver daily. "I've been offered prices so low I can't believe them."

c. "The nature of people being what they are, even though they like a good bargain, they're not going to eat something that doesn't agree with their taste."

5. Suppose that a person has 24 hours in the day and can work at a wage of $3 per hour for as many hours as he wants. Ignoring taxes and his possible need for sleep, draw the budget line between leisure and money income. How does the budget line change if the wage rate rises to $4 per hour? Show that this person will not necessarily work longer just because his wage has risen.

6. A person has 20 hours a week that he wishes to allocate between reading history and playing hockey. He can read one chapter (carefully) every two hours and complete one hockey game every 30 minutes.

a. Given a 20-hour time budget, graph his budget line.

b. What is the price of a hockey game in terms of chapters?

c. What is the price of a chapter in terms of hockey games?

d. Suppose that because of general fatigue as the term progresses the time required to do both activities doubles. Draw a new budget line.

7. Is a household relatively better off if its money income is decreased by 10 percent or if the prices of all the goods it buys are increased by 10 percent? Does it matter in answering this question whether the household spends all its income?

8. Some people do not care about the difference between two similar products. To see what effect this would have on their behavior, draw a typical indifference curve of a woman who values white and whole wheat bread identically. Show her consumption equilibrium position when the price of white bread is held constant at $1 a loaf while that of whole wheat changes from 80¢ to $1 to $1.20. How does this behavior differ from that of a household that likes both kinds of bread but values them differently?

9. Between 1977 and 1978 per capita after-tax money income in Canada rose by 10.1 percent while the CPI rose by 8.9 percent. What happened to real disposable income per capita?

Demand Theory in Action

10

Students of economics, along with many critics of the subject, often find demand theory excessively abstract. How can so unrealistic a theory, they ask, have any application to the real world?

Yet applied economists use the results of demand theory, abstract or not, in their everyday work. Indeed much of what economists do to earn a living involves demand measurements. Economists are asked by electric power commissions to draw up long-term investment plans based on the projected future demand for electric power. The National Parks Branch calls on economists to review its system for setting its price of admission to its parks. Whether—and to what extent—raising tolls will help ease the deficits of the Metropolitan Toronto transit system and the St. Lawrence Seaway are questions that cannot be answered correctly without a knowledge of price elasticity of demand. When the FAO (the United Nations Food and Agricultural Organization) or a marketing board wants to make agricultural demand projections by crops and areas, it needs to know income elasticities of demand. Many industries need to know the cross elasticities of demand for their products with oil and gas in order to estimate the effects on them of the sharply rising prices of oil and gas.

To deal effectively with many substantive issues, knowledge of relevant demand conditions is essential. Fortunately a great deal of the demand information that the economist requires is available. In this chapter we look at some of the empirical knowledge that has been collected over the last few decades.

Even where information is not already available, it is often possible to obtain it without great cost or difficulty. The appropriate methods have been carefully worked out. Solutions to two of the most troubling measurement problems are discussed at the end of the first part of the chapter.

Critics of demand theory do not quarrel with the *need* for demand information, or even with the usefulness of applied economics, but they have often suggested that the theory is only an elaborate way of saying that anything can happen. Others have suggested that it is based on totally unrealistic assumptions about how households actually behave. Thoughtful students are often worried by such doubts. In the second part of this chapter we consider such criticisms and show that they do not point to fatal flaws in demand theory.

Measurement of Demand

MODERN MEASURES OF DEMAND

Many statistical problems associated with demand measurement were solved earlier in this century. Since that time large quantities of data on demand elasticities have been accumulated. The value of these data to the applied economist is the ultimate proof of the usefulness of demand theory.

Price Elasticities

Table 10-1 shows a few estimated price elasticities of demand, covering agricultural and non-agricultural commodities. Much pioneering work on demand measurement concerned the price elasticity of demand of agricultural products. This attention was due in part to the large price variations (caused by fluctuating crop yields and competitive market conditions) in those commodities; such price variations provided the empirical evidence needed to measure demand elasticities. It was due also to concern about the level of farm incomes and the relation of farmers' welfare to fluctuating crops. Professors Henry Schultz in the United States and Richard Stone in the United Kingdom were prominent in these efforts. Many agricultural research centers extended this work and even today produce estimates of price elasticities of foodstuffs. These data mostly confirm the general belief in low price elasticities for individual crops and for food products as a whole.

TABLE 10-1
Estimated Price Elasticities of Demand (Selected Commodities)[a]

Inelastic demand (less than unity)	
Apples (Canada)	0.1
Sugar	0.3
Public transportation	0.4
All foods	0.4
Gasoline	0.6
All clothing	0.6
Butter (Canada)	0.8
Consumer durables	0.8
Demand of approximately unit elasticity[b]	
Beef	
Beer	
Marijuana	
Elastic demand (greater than unity)	
Furniture	1.2
Electricity	1.3
Domestic lamb and mutton (UK)	1.5
Automobiles	2.1
Millinery	3.0

[a] For the United States except where noted.
[b] Greater than 0.9 and less than 1.1.

The wide range of price elasticities is illustrated by these selected measures. These elasticities, from various studies, are representative of literally hundreds of existing estimates. Explanations of some of the differences are discussed in the text.

The policy payoff of this knowledge in terms of understanding the farm problem was enormous; it represents an early triumph of empirical work in economics. (See the discussion in Chapter 7.)

Although agricultural commodities often have inelastic demands, notice in Table 10-1 that some commodities, such as beef in the United States and domestically produced lamb and mutton in the United Kingdom, have been found to be elastic. The reason for this is that they have close substitutes.

For example, British households can choose between locally produced lamb and mutton and imported lamb and mutton (which typically has a somewhat lower quality and price than the domestic product). Similarly, American households can and do choose between beef, pork, and chicken on the basis of price. The broader the category of related products, the lower the observed price elasticity of demand.

Although the importance of the agricultural problem led early investigators to concentrate on the demand for foodstuffs, modern studies have expanded to include virtually the whole range of commodities on which the household spends its income.

How then can we explain the relatively low (0.8) price elasticity for durables shown in Table 10-1? Again, the answer lies partly in the broadness of the category. Demand for individual categories of durable goods tends to be elastic; for example, the demand for furniture is shown in Table 10-1 to be elastic. But for durables as a group, demand is also inelastic because by their very nature replacement of durables can be postponed with greater ease than can purchases of nondurables such as foodstuffs.

Because most specific manufactured goods have close substitutes, studies show they tend to have price-elastic demand. Millinery, for example, has been estimated to have an elasticity of 3.0. In contrast, "all clothing" tends to be inelastic.

The accumulated data on price elasticity confirm this generalization:

Any one of a group of close substitutes will tend to have an elastic demand, even though the demand for the group as a whole may be inelastic.

Income Elasticities

Table 10-2 provides a sample of the data on income elasticities. Because the demand over time for particular basic commodities is so greatly affected by income elasticities, the FAO has estimated income elasticities for dozens of products, country by country.

TABLE 10-2

Estimated Income Elasticities of Demand (Selected Commodities)[a]

Inferior goods (negative income elasticities)	
Milk	−0.3
Starchy roots	−0.2
Inelastic normal goods (0.0 to 1.0)	
Coffee (U.S.)	0.0
Wine (France)	0.1
Vegetables	0.2
All food (U.S.)	0.2
Poultry	0.3
Beef and Veal	0.4
Housing (U.S.)	0.6
Cigarettes (U.S.)	0.8
Elastic normal goods (greater than 1.0)	
Gasoline (U.S.)	1.1
Cream (U.K.)	1.7
Wine	1.8
Consumer durables (U.K.)	1.8
Poultry (Ceylon)	2.0
Restaurant meals (U.K.)	2.4

[a] For Canada except where noted.

Income elasticities vary widely across commodities and sometimes across countries. The basic source of food estimates by country is the FAO, but many individual studies have been made. Explanations of some of the differences are discussed in the text.

These data tend to show that the more basic or staple a commodity, the lower is its income elasticity: food as a whole has an income elasticity of 0.2, durables of 1.8. In Canada, milk and such starchy roots as potatoes are inferior goods; their quantity consumed falls as income rises.

Does the distinction between luxuries and necessities explain differences in income elasticities? The table suggests that it does. The case of meals eaten away from home is one example; such meals are almost always more expensive, calorie for calorie, than meals prepared at home. It would thus be expected that at lower ranges of income restaurant meals would be regarded as an expensive luxury, but the demand for them would expand substantially as households became richer. This is in fact what happens.

Does this mean that the market demand for the foodstuffs that appear on restaurant menus will also have high income elasticities? Generally the answer is no; when a household eats out rather than preparing meals at home, the main change is not in what is eaten but in who prepares it. The additional expenditure on "food" goes mainly to pay the wages of cooks and waiters and to yield a return on the restaurateur's capital. Thus, when a household expands its expenditure on restaurant food by 2.4 percent in response to a 1 percent rise in its income, most of the extra expenditure on "food" goes to workers in the service industry; little, if any, finds its way into the pockets of farmers. Here is a striking example of the general tendency for households to spend a higher proportion of their incomes on services as their incomes rise.

Empirical studies tend to confirm that, as income rises, household expenditures follow broadly similar paths in different countries. Summarizing recent studies, Robert Ferber wrote that they "tend to bear out earlier findings on income elasticity yielding low elasticities for food and housing, elasticities close to unity for clothing and education, and higher elasticities for various types of recreation, personal care, home operation and other services."

The accumulated data on income elasticity confirm this generalization:

The more basic an item in the consumption pattern of households, the lower its income elasticity.

Cross Elasticities of Demand

Many of the most interesting studies of cross elasticity have been made to determine whether specific products are substitutes as part of antitrust inquiries (see Chapter 18, page 334). Whether cellophane and Saran Wrap, or aluminum cable and copper cable, are or are not substitutes may determine questions of monopoly under the law. As we have seen, the positive or negative sign and the size of cross elasticities sheds light on whether or not goods are substitutes.

Other Variables

Modern studies show that demand is influenced by many socioeconomic factors — family size, age, geographical location, type of employment, wealth, and income expectations — not included in traditional demand theory. Although significant, the total contribution of all these factors to changes in demand is small. Typically, less than 30 percent of the variations in demand are accounted for by these "novel" factors, with a much higher proportion governed by the traditional variables of prices and current incomes.

PROBLEMS OF MEASUREMENT

The knowledge of demand elasticities that we have just surveyed could not be developed until econometricians overcame major problems in measuring demand relationships. One particular aspect of such measurement is troubling to many students: Since in a market economy all kinds of things are happening at once, how can they be sorted into neat theoretical categories? When market demand changes over time, invariably the influences that affect demand will all be changing. What, for example, is to be made of the observation that the quantity of butter consumed per capita rose by 10 percent over a period in which average household income rose by 5 percent, the price of butter fell by 3 percent, and the price of margarine rose by 4 percent?

A first set of questions concerns how much of the change is due to income elasticity of demand, how much to price elasticity, and how much to the cross elasticity between butter and margarine. If there is only one observation, the question cannot be answered. If, however, there is a large number of observations showing, say, quantity demanded, income, price of butter, and price of margarine every month for four or five years, it is possible, as we saw in Chapter 3, to discover the separate influence of each of the variables. The most frequently used technique for estimating the separate effect of each variable on demand is called multiple regression analysis,

The Identification Problem

The three-part diagram below illustrates the so-called identification problem. If, as in (i), the demand curve stays put while the supply curve moves up and down — perhaps because of crop variations in some agricultural commodity — then market observations in prices and quantities (shown by the black dots) trace out the demand curve. If, as in (ii), the supply curve stays put while the demand curve moves about — owing perhaps to changes in the number of consumers or their incomes — then market observations trace out the supply curve.

So far so good. But what if both curves shift randomly back and forth between the four positions shown in (iii)? In such a situation a series of market observations will be obtained that will not trace out either the demand or the supply curves that generated them. A few such points are shown in the panel. Points E_1, E_2, E_3, and E_4 — market observations of quantities and prices at different times — do not *identify* either the demand curve or the supply curve.

The identification problem is surmountable. The key to identifying the demand and supply curves separately is to bring in other variables than price and then to relate demand to one (or more) of them and supply to *some other* variables. For example, supply of the commodity might be related not only to the price of the commodity but also to its costs of production; demand might be related not only to the price of the commodity but also to consumers' incomes. Provided that both of these other factors, cost of production and income, vary sufficiently, it is possible to determine the relation between quantity supplied and price as well as the relation between quantity demanded and price.

Neglect of the identification problem can cause serious errors in interpreting economic data. Consider this analysis: "Last year the price of scotch whisky rose by 10 percent and scotch imports hardly fell at all, so we know that the market for scotch must have a low elasticity of demand." Has the analysis really identified the demand curve? It may have if the rise in price reflects a shift of the supply curve. But if the rise in price was due mainly to a rise in demand for scotch, the analysis may actually have discovered that the short-run supply curve of scotch is very inelastic (because scotch takes several years to manufacture). The general rule to keep in mind is that, unless there is additional information that provides clues to how much each curve shifted, nothing can be told about the shape of either the demand or the supply curve from price and quantity data alone.

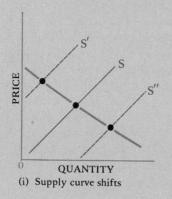

(i) Supply curve shifts

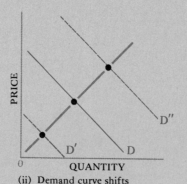

(ii) Demand curve shifts

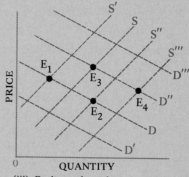

(iii) Both supply and demand curves shift

which can be used directly to estimate each of the elasticities mentioned.

A second set of questions concerns using data on quantity actually *consumed* to estimate quantity *demanded*. The problem arises because both demand shifts and supply shifts can change the quantity actually consumed, and thus the shape of the demand curve may not be definitively established from data on prices and quantities alone. This **identification problem,** too, can yield to statistical solution, as suggested in the box.

Criticisms of Demand Theory

Some critics dismiss demand theory, saying that it is based on the ridiculous assumption that all households make decisions using careful marginal calculations about the effects of minor adjustments in expenditure patterns. They argue that this assumption might describe the behavior of a few record-keeping middle-class groups but not that of most households.

Other critics maintain that demand theory has little real content. According to them, the theory is a complex theoretical apparatus that offers little more than the proposition that most demand curves slope downward most of the time. If this is all we get from the elaborate theory, then demand theory really is a lot of sound and fury signifying (almost) nothing. What about these criticisms?

DOES DEMAND THEORY MAKE UNREASONABLE ASSUMPTIONS ABOUT RATIONAL HOUSEHOLD DECISION MAKING?

In developing the theory of household behavior in Chapter 9, we deduced that if households wished to maximize their utility or satisfaction, they would vary their consumption patterns so that relative marginal utilities would be exactly proportional to relative market prices (marginal utility theory) or marginal rates of substitution would be exactly equal to relative market prices (indifference theory). It is tempting to dismiss these theories out of hand with the objection that it is unrealistic to pretend that households always act with the mechanical consistency that such theories apparently assume. After all, most of us know people who occasionally buy strawberries in spite of, or even because of, a rise in their price, or who spend a week's pay on a binge or a frivolous purchase.

To see what to make of such conflicting observations, it is helpful to distinguish three possible uses of demand theory. The first use is to study the aggregate behavior of all households—as illustrated, for example, by the market demand curve for a product. The second use is to make statements about an individual household's probable actions. The third use is to make statements about what each household will certainly do.

Now consider an automobile firm that is wondering about the effect on its sales of a price increase. Clearly the first use of demand theory is what interests the automobile firm. It does not care what every last household will do, nor, really, does it care what *you* will do; it wants to know whether in the aggregate, and by how much, its sales will decrease if it raises prices.

This aggregate use of demand theory is the most common one in economics. The analysis of Chapters 7 and 8, you will recall, depended on having knowledge of the shapes of relevant market demand curves. It did not, however, require that we know the behavior of each individual household. The second use of demand theory, though much less common than the first, is occasionally important; it is sometimes desirable to be able to say what a single household (or a group of households) will probably do. The third use is by far the least important, for it is rarely necessary, possible, or even interesting to try to state categorically what each household will always do.

The criticisms cited at the beginning of this section apply only to the third use of demand theory. The observations referred to earlier refute only the prediction that *all* households *always* behave as assumed by the theory. In order to predict the existence of a relatively stable downward-sloping market demand curve (the first use), or to predict what an individual household will probably do (the second use), we do not require that *all* households behave as is assumed by the theory all of the time. Consider two illustrations.

First, some households may always behave in a manner not assumed by the theory. Households whose members are mental defectives or have serious emotional disturbances are obvious possibilities. The inconsistent or erratic behavior of such households will not cause market demand curves to depart from their downward slope, provided these households account for a minority of total purchasers of any product. Their erratic behavior will be swamped by the normal behavior of the majority of households.

Second, an occasional irrationality or inconsistency on the part of every household will not upset the downward slope of the market demand curve so long as these isolated inconsistencies do not occur at the same time in all households. As long as such inconsistencies are unrelated across households, occurring now in one and now in another, their effect will be offset by the normal behavior of the majority of households.[1]

The downward slope of the demand curve requires only that at any moment of time most households are behaving as assumed by the theory. This is compatible with inconsistent behavior on the part of some households all of the time and on the part of all households some of the time.

IS DEMAND THEORY ONLY AN ELABORATE WAY OF SAYING THAT ANYTHING CAN HAPPEN?

Demand theory predicts that the quantity of a good demanded varies with its own price, the prices of other goods, income, and tastes. Critics argue that because quantity demanded may rise,

fall, or stay unchanged as any one of these influencing factors changes, the theory is merely an elaborate way of saying anything can happen.

While it is true that anything can happen, this does not mean that every possible outcome is equally likely. Because theory and empirical work tell us when one outcome is more likely than another, the theory is useful.

To discuss this issue it is necessary to consider the relation between quantity demanded and each of the variables that influence it. We shall ask in each case whether the theory offers interesting or useful predictions about the behavior of demand and then whether there is evidence confirming these predictions.

Quantity Demanded and the Commodity's Own Price

Early demand theory predicted that all demand curves must always slope downward. This prediction was known for a long time as the law of demand: The price of a product and the quantity demanded vary inversely with each other. Criticisms of the law of demand have taken various forms, focusing on the Giffen good, the conspicuous consumption good, and (by far the most important) the good whose demand is perfectly inelastic.

The Giffen good. Great interest was attached to an apparent refutation of the law of demand by the Victorian economist Sir Robert Giffen. Giffen is supposed to have observed that during the nineteenth century a rise in the price of imported wheat led to an increase in the price of bread, but that the consumption of bread by the British working class increased. If this observation is correct (i.e., if Giffen really made it—which now appears to be in doubt—and if his measurements were correct), it would refute the prediction that *all* demand curves *always* slope downward. It would not be inconsistent with the theory because this is precisely the sort of exception envisaged by modern theory and mentioned in the

---

[1] See the discussion in Chapter 2, pages 23–24.

appendix to Chapter 9. This kind of exception is, in any case, extraordinarily limited in theory and is all but unknown in actuality.[2]

Conspicuous consumption goods. Thorstein Veblen in *The Theory of the Leisure Class* (1899) suggested that some commodities were consumed not for their intrinsic qualities but because they carried a snob appeal. The more expensive such a commodity became, the *greater* might be its ability to confer status on its purchaser.

This is, of course, possible. Elizabeth Taylor and Joe Namath may buy diamonds, not because they particularly like diamonds per se but because they wish to show off their wealth in an ostentatious but socially acceptable way. They are assumed to value diamonds precisely because they are expensive; thus a fall in price might lead them to stop buying diamonds and to switch to a more satisfactory object of conspicuous consumption. People of this sort will have upward-sloping *individual* demand curves for diamonds. They may also behave in the same way with respect to luxury cars; they may buy them *because* they are expensive.

However, no one has ever observed statistically an upward-sloping *market* demand curve for commodities such as diamonds or luxury cars. The reason for this, notwithstanding the snob appeal of certain goods, is easy to discover. Consideration of the countless lower-income consumers who would be glad to buy diamonds or Cadillacs if only they were sufficiently inexpensive suggests that upward-sloping demand curves for a few individual wealthy households

are much more likely than is an upward-sloping market demand curve for the same commodity. Recall the discussion (page 182) about the ability of the theory of the downward-sloping demand curve to accommodate odd behavior on the part of a small group of households. In this case the "odd" group is the group of the rich rather than that of the mentally defective or the emotionally disturbed.

Perfectly inelastic demand curves. Even if demand curves do not slope *upward to the right* as the previous cases have suggested, the substantial insight provided by the law of demand would be diminished if there were many important commodities for which changes in price had virtually no effect on quantity demanded.

It is surprising how often the assumption of a vertical demand curve is implicit. A common response of urban bus or subway systems to financial difficulties is to propose a percentage fare increase equal to the percentage their deficit is of their revenues. It was once widely argued that the demand for gasoline was virtually perfectly inelastic—on the ground that people who had paid thousands of dollars for cars would never balk at a few pennies extra for gas. The events of recent years have proven how wrong that argument was: Higher gas prices have led to smaller cars, to more car pools, to more economical driving speeds, and to less pleasure driving.

As we have seen, a mass of accumulated evidence suggests that most demand curves do in fact slope downward to an appreciable degree.

For practical purposes, the hypothesis of the downward-sloping demand curve can be regarded as conforming with the evidence.

Most firms have an intuitive idea of the elasticities they face, although they seldom use the economist's language in referring to them. There is also evidence that even sophisticated business executives may underestimate price elasticities and thus overprice their commodities. For example, the transatlantic airlines bitterly resisted the efforts of English entrepreneur Sir Freddie

[2] The commodity must be a good with a large negative income effect (an inferior good) *and* play so large a part in most households' budgets that an increase in its price leads to a large decrease in households' real incomes. An example might be bread in a very poor economy where it is the diet staple. Suppose, in such an economy, that the price of bread rises sharply. This may be expected to lead to larger expenditures on bread, which will further impoverish many households to the point where they are forced to substitute bread (even though it is more expensive) for other more luxurious forms of nourishment.

Product Quality, Consumer Information, and the "Market for Lemons"

The theory of demand predicts that utility-maximizing consumers will demand goods up to the point where the marginal utility per dollar spent is equal for all goods consumed. One criticism often levied against that theory is that this condition places unreasonable demands on consumers' ability to ascertain the quality of alternative goods available in order to determine their various marginal utilities. After all, in this modern commercial age new products are continuously being introduced into the market. Some turn out to be highly desirable; others turn out to be a waste of money. It is often very hard for consumers to determine, at least initially, the quality of these new goods before making a decision about purchasing them. The term *rip-off* probably gets used more regarding purchases of new goods than regarding established, well-known products.

Indeed, ignorance concerning new products does pose serious problems for consumers. And poor consumer information about the quality of new products appears to present opportunities for quick profits to be earned by supplying low-quality, new products. Does this also render our theory of consumer demand useless?

One possible reaction to a lack of information about product quality is for consumers to judge the quality of a product by its price. How often have you made a purchase when you knew little about the product, and done exactly this? When buying a first set of skis or a new cartridge for your stereo, for example, did you just assume that the more expensive ones were better? Do you necessarily choose the cheaper of two brands of wine, neither of which you know anything about?

What happens to demand theory when consumers act this way? The theory predicts that a reduction in price will lead to an increase in demand. But if a decrease in price leads consumers to reduce their perception of the quality of the product, then there will not necessarily be an increase in demand. This is illustrated in the figure. Suppose D_0 is the original demand curve; its position depends upon consumers' perception of quality. The negative slope of D_0 reflects the usual increase in quantity demanded associated with a fall in price; although perception of product quality is constant along D_0, diminishing marginal utility still leads to a negative relationship between price and quantity. Suppose now that the initial price is p_0; then q_0 will be the quantity demanded. What would happen if p_0 were to be reduced to p_1?

The basic theory predicts quantity demanded will increase along D_0 from q_0 to q_1. But if the reduction in price leads consumers

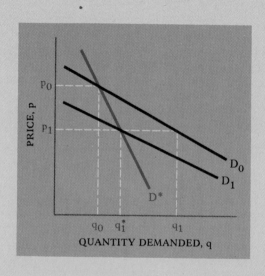

to reduce their view of the quality of the product, the demand curve shifts down from D_0 to D_1. Since consumers' perception of the quality of the product has fallen, the marginal utility they anticipate from consumption of any particular quantity of the good is also lower. At each price, less would now be bought. As a result the fall in price from p_1 to p_0, increases the quantity demanded by much less than the original demand curve D_0 suggested it would; in the figure quantity demanded falls only to q_1^*. In fact, if the shift in demand due to changed perception of quality were large enough, quantity demanded need not rise at all. The actual demand curve in the absence of good information about product quality, D^*, may therefore be much less elastic than if consumers were informed. The inelasticity of the demand curve means of course that there is less incentive for producers to lower price.

Inadequate information about product quality may well lead to this price inelasticity of demand. But it is surely a transitory phenomenon. After continued exposure in the market, first-hand knowledge of a product's quality will place consumers on their "true" demand curve. Low-quality products will have small demand, and high-quality products will be desired in larger numbers. A product's reputation for quality will hinge on more reliable information than just its price; brand names are one attempt to get consumers to associate high standards of quality with particular products.

It is clear that the problem of judging quality is much greater for newly consumed goods than for regularly purchased ones. It can be profitable for a producer to bring a new product of inferior quality into the market and make a large profit before information about his product's quality spreads. Hence a valuable service is often provided by consumers'

protection legislation such as "truth-in-packaging" and "truth-in-advertising" as well as by private, consumer-information-oriented organizations.

While this issue is of primary concern for newly marketed products, it also has application to consumer durables where resale markets exist for used items. University of California Professor George Akerlof has argued that in such markets it makes sense for consumers to estimate quality by price. For example, any particular vintage of automobiles may include a certain proportion of "lemons." Purchasers of new cars of a certain vintage take a chance on their car turning out to be a lemon. Those who are unlucky and get a lemon are more likely to resell their car then those who are lucky and get a quality car. Hence in the used car market there will be a disproportionately large number of lemons for sale. Thus, buyers of used cars are right to be suspicious of why the car is for sale while salespeople are quick to invent reasons ("It was owned by a little old lady who only drove it on Sundays"). Because it is very difficult for a buyer to identify a lemon before buying it, he or she will be prepared to buy a used car only at a price low enough to offset the increased probability that it is a lemon. This, Akerlof maintains, explains why one-year old cars typically sell for a discount much larger than can be explained by the physical depreciation that occurs in one year.

Consumers certainly do not have perfect information, and this in turn clearly hinders the straightforward application of the laws of supply and demand. But this is not necessarily an indictment of the theory of demand. With appropriate extensions, the theory of demand is, as we have seen, a useful tool for studying the problems caused by incomplete information.

Laker to introduce his cut-price "skytrain" between London and New York. When the service was finally introduced in the mid 1970s, the other carriers slashed prices on standby tickets in self-defense. And they were surprised at the overwhelming increase in demand as the low fares attracted a new type of traveler. Demand rose and the number of empty seats fell. Soon it was clear that the lower fares were increasing revenues and profits.[3] Cases in which companies have raised prices and been surprised at the resulting drop in sales have also been documented.

Quantity Demanded and Household Income

Demand theories give no single prediction about how quantity demanded changes as income changes. They say that a rise in income may cause the quantity demanded to rise, to fall, or to remain unchanged. This states only that anything can happen; hence it makes no useful prediction about what could be expected to happen to demand when income changes. But "anything can happen" does not mean that the theory is empty; various kinds of empirical observations help to make it meaningful.

The approximate income elasticity of demand often tends to be identifiable from the technical data about commodities. An inferior good is typically the cheaper and less satisfactory of a number of commodities, all of which satisfy more or less the same need. Consider transport. When people are very poor, they walk. At a slightly higher level of income, they can acquire a bicycle; cycling was the dominant form of transport for industrial workers in Europe as recently as the 1950s. At higher levels of income, motorized bicycles, motor scooters, and motorcycles can be substituted for bicycles; Italy was once overrun with motor scooters, and enormous numbers of

them are still used by workers in Portugal. Finally, a level of income is reached, as it was in the more advanced industrial countries of Western Europe during the 1950s and 1960s, at which ordinary workers feel they can get rid of their two-wheeled conveyances and buy an automobile. For each of these modes of transportation there is a range of income over which the income elasticity of demand is high, and then a higher range over which the income elasticity falls and eventually becomes negative.

Another important set of empirical observations shows clearly that income elasticities change only gradually over time. Over the last 40 years, many service industries have encountered income elasticities that are well in excess of unity and rising over time. These elasticities are not expected to drop suddenly to very low levels, and thus it is possible to predict that, unless service industries achieve rates of productivity growth very much higher than the national average, there will be a continuing pressure coming from the price system for more resources to move into the service industries. The fact that income elasticities are known not to change rapidly or capriciously permits predictions about the near future on the basis of present knowledge.

A third set of observations reveals that with respect to broad categories of consumption expenditure, households in any one Western country behave in a fashion roughly similar to those in other Western countries. (Indeed, it is not even clear that the qualification *Western* is necessary if income levels are approximately the same.) At low income levels, food tends to have a fairly high income elasticity of demand, but as the level of income rises, the income elasticity of demand for food tends to fall well below unity, so that only a small amount of any additional income gets spent on food. This phenomenon has been observed in every growing country that has approached the levels of income currently enjoyed by North America and Western Europe. Thus it can be predicted that as long as productivity growth continues in agriculture, the long-run drift from the land will continue in Western

---

[3] Although air fares have since risen as a result of rising fuel costs, the standby fares introduced to compete with Laker's low skytrain fares remain *relatively* cheap ways of crossing the Atlantic.

countries, and that when other countries of the world succeed in achieving sustained rates of growth, they will encounter within a predictable time period the problem of a declining agricultural sector.

Similarly, a significant phenomenon of the past two decades in North America and the most highly developed countries of Western Europe is that the income elasticity of demand for consumer durables has been declining, while that for many services has been rising. Other countries can look forward to similar pressures on the pattern of resource allocation within a generation.

The real incomes of most Western countries are doubling every 30 years or so. Thus, over such a period of time, changes in income exert a major influence on changes in demand.

A knowledge of what income elasticities are and are likely to be is one of the most potent tools at the economist's command for predicting the future needs of the economy in many different aspects.

Quantity Demanded and the Prices of Other Commodities

The theory of demand predicts that the quantity demanded of one commodity may be affected by the changing prices of other commodities: It will tend to increase as the price of a complementary good declines (because they are used jointly), and it will tend to decrease as the price of a substitute good declines (because its users shift to the now relatively cheaper substitute). Of course there are also many pairs of commodities which are sufficiently unrelated that the price of one has no appreciable effect on the quantity demanded of the other. These three reactions—quantity demanded rising, falling, or remaining unchanged—cover all conceivable possibilities. The basic theory does not rule out any possibility, so by itself it is of no more use in predicting the reactions to changes in the prices of other goods than it is in predicting reactions to changes in income.

Just as with income, however, this is not the end of the story. It is often possible to tell from the technical nature of the goods alone which will be substitutes and which complements. Although the demand for factors of production will not be considered fully until Part Six, it is worth noting here just how often technical data tell where to expect complementarity and where substitutability. Steel plates, electric welders, and welder operators are complementary, so it can be predicted that a fall in the price of any one will lead to an increase in the demand for all three. Cranes and crane operators, steam shovels and trucks, trains and rails, roads and signs, any piece of equipment and its human operator—all are examples of pairs of goods that are complements for each other. For each set of complementary goods, it can be expected that a fall in the price of one good will lead to a rise in demand for the others.

A similar list of inputs that are substitutes might include such items as wood, bricks, and concrete in construction; manure and artificial fertilizers; a roomful of statistical clerks with desk calculators and a small electronic digital computer. With these pairs of substitute goods, it can be expected that a fall in the price of one of them will lead to a fall in the demand for the other.

There are also consumers' goods for which complementarity or substitutability can be predicted in advance. Complementarity exists, for example, between razors, razor blades, and shaving cream; golf clubs and golf balls; grass seed and lawn mowers; electric stoves and electricity; houses and mortgages; wedding rings and the services of obstetricians, marriage guidance counselors, and divorce court judges. The list of substitute goods might include such obvious examples as cabbage and spinach, beef and pork, private cars and public transport, gas stoves and electric stoves, and vacations in the Maritimes and on the Italian Riviera. It could be extended indefinitely. If the technical data tell which goods are substitutes and which are complements, then the effect of a change in the price of one good on the demand for the other can be predicted.

Quantity Demanded and Tastes

Changes in demand that are due to changes in taste cannot be identified because taste changes cannot be measured. This usually causes trouble when the relation between demand and other factors is considered. Whenever something happens that does not agree with theory, it is always possible that a change in tastes accounted for what was seen. Say, for example, incomes and other prices were known to be constant, while the price of some commodity rose and, at the same time, more was bought. This could mean an upward-sloping demand curve or a shift in the demand curve caused by a change in tastes.

If there are only two observations, it will be impossible to distinguish between the two possibilities because there is no independent way of telling whether tastes changed. But if there are many such observations, it is possible to get some idea of where the balance of probabilities lies between the two situations. Assume, for example, that we have 26 observations on prices and quantities of some commodity whose price has changed once a week over a six-month period. Assume further that *after removing the effects estimated to be due to changes in income,*[4] price and quantity changed in the same direction each week. Now it will be hard to avoid the conclusion that the evidence conflicts with the hypothesis of a downward-sloping demand curve.

Of course, this conflict can be explained away by saying that tastes must have changed in favor of this commodity each time that its price rose and against the commodity each time that its price fell. This "alibi" can be used with effect to explain away a single conflicting observation, but it would be uncomfortable to use the same alibi 26 times in six months—"uncomfortable" because the situation is extremely improbable. [13] Instead one would suspect a fault in the hypoth-

esis that quantity demanded and price vary inversely with each other in the case of this commodity.

This is now a problem in statistical testing. Economists will not usually abandon a theory as a result of only one conflicting observation, but they are prepared to abandon it as soon as the accumulating evidence makes it seem very unlikely that the theory is correct. Thus, statistically, the theory is testable.

Summary

1. Knowledge of demand elasticities is of major importance in applied economics. Modern work on the measurement of demand has provided a great deal of evidence on the size of the reaction of quantity demanded to prices, incomes, and other socioeconomic data.

2. The price elasticity of a commodity group tends to be higher the more narrowly it is defined and the more adequate are its substitutes. Any one of a group of close substitutes will tend to have an elastic demand even though the group as a whole has a highly inelastic demand.

3. Income elasticity tends to be lower the more basic, or staple, is the commodity. Thus luxuries tend to have higher income elasticities than necessities. The patterns of measured income elasticity are remarkably similar across countries.

4. Economists concerned with the measurement of demand have faced and surmounted a number of serious technical problems. Regression analysis has proved useful in dealing with situations where many things vary at once.

5. Demand theory does not, as some critics assert, assume that all households act with perfect rationality all of the time. The predictions of demand theory about the market demand function require only that at any one time most of the households in the market are behaving as assumed by the theory.

---

[4] This can be done through multiple regression analysis or other sophisticated statistical techniques. (See Chapter 3.)

6. The fact that anything can happen in modern demand theory does not mean the theory is useless, for economists can specify the conditions under which different outcomes are to be expected. The so-called law of demand leads to the prediction that the market demand curve for a commodity will slope downward and to the right except in very special circumstances. Possible exceptions to the general prediction of demand have been suggested but have received no empirical support. A great accumulation of empirical evidence supports the law of demand.

7. While demand theory makes no single prediction about the effect of a change in income on quantity demanded, useful predictions can be made about the relationship because (a) it is often possible to identify approximate income elasticities from technical data; (b) income elasticities change gradually rather than erratically from year to year; (c) income elasticities tend to be similar at similar levels of income in different countries, so that knowledge of what happened at a certain level of income in country A helps to predict what will happen when country B reaches that same level of income.

8. While demand theory makes no single prediction about the effect on the quantity demanded of a change in the price of another commodity, the theory is nevertheless useful because it is often possible to tell from technical data alone whether goods are complements or substitutes.

9. Changes in tastes are an ever-present possible alibi to explain away any observations that appear to conflict with the theory. If prices are cut and less is sold, one can always say that the price cut just happened to be accompanied by a change in tastes away from the commodity. However, when there is a large number of observations of changing prices and quantities, it is possible to calculate the probability that taste changes account for what was seen. If, to save a hypothesis, highly improbable circumstances are needed, it is preferable to reject the hypothesis.

Topics for Review

The role of statistical measurement of demand

The difference between price and income elasticities and what such elasticities show

The difference between an inferior good and a Giffen good

The difference between a luxury and a conspicuous consumption good

The difference between inelastic and perfectly inelastic demand curves

Discussion Questions

1. When no-frills houses came on the market, they were regarded as a response to high prices. But they have captured more of the market than expected. Some builders estimate they may ultimately constitute 80 percent of all houses sold. Suggest alternative explanations of this unexpected success. A leading builder says, "It's just like people driving smaller cars and drinking beer instead of Scotch." Is it also like students wearing long hair instead of short, or today's parents having fewer children than their parents did? Which of these things represent changes in taste and which represent responses to changes in prices or incomes? If you don't know, what economic data would be useful in answering the question?

2. "A survey shows that most people prefer butter to margarine." What exactly might this mean? Supposing it to be true, can you account for the facts that many people buy some of both butter and margarine each month and that in total more pounds of margarine are sold than pounds of butter?

3. In the early empirical studies of demand theory, agricultural products were studied extensively. Can you think of a reason why these early studies were able to identify many demand curves without great difficulty?

4. A reliable newspaper reports that synthetic motor oil is gaining in sales despite its high price relative to natural oil. What can account for a synthetic oil's selling at $3.95 a quart when the best conventional oils were readily available at about $1.00?

5. Predict the effect on the demand for owner-occupied housing of (a) a rise in mortgage interest rates, (b) a decline in the price of rental housing. If over the period in which both (a) and (b) occurred the quantity of new housing sold increased, what would you conclude about the theory of demand? What would happen to the demand for owner-occupied

housing if federal tax laws were revised to allow a deduction for mortgage interest payments?

6. It has been observed recently that obesity is a more frequent medical problem for the relatively poor than for the middle-income classes. Can you use the theory of demand to shed light on this observation?

7. At an auction in New Orleans a buyer paid $14,200 for a 1806 bottle of Chateau Lafite-Rothschild. Wine authorities say it may not even be drinkable. But the bottle may be the last of its kind, and the buyer said he wanted it for his collection. Does this behavior suggest an upward-sloping demand curve for luxuries? If the wine is undrinkable, will the price paid for the bottle prove to have been unwisely high?

8. Suggest commodities that you think might have the following patterns of elasticity of demand.
   a. High income elasticity, high price elasticity
   b. High income elasticity, low price elasticity
   c. Low income elasticity, low price elasticity
   d. Low income elasticity, high price elasticity

9. Look at Table 10-1. Can you suggest why gasoline is inelastic but electricity is elastic? Why is furniture more elastic than all consumer goods taken together?

10. Look at Table 10-2. Can you suggest why gasoline is more income elastic than cigarettes or housing? Or why coffee is less income elastic than beef?

Part Four

**Production
and Cost**

The Firm, Production, and Cost

11

Ask almost anyone you know to name ten North American business firms. The odds are overwhelming that their lists will include some of these firms: General Motors Corporation, U.S. Steel, General Electric, American Telephone & Telegraph, Dow Chemical, Standard Oil, Du Pont, Canadian Pacific, United Airlines, the Prudential Insurance Company, and the National Broadcasting Company. Drive around Gananoque, Ontario, and note at random ten firms that come into view. They will probably include an A & P supermarket, Harding's Drug Store, a Shell service station, Donevan's Hardware, the Modern Café, and the Bank of Montreal. Drive through Manitoba or Saskatchewan and look around you: Every farm is a business firm as well as a home.

Firms develop and survive because they are efficient institutions for organizing resources to produce goods and services and for organizing their sale and distribution. While General Motors, the Modern Café, and the Manitoba farm are all *firms*, what do they have in common? It is not hard to count ways in which they are different. But there may also be insight to be gained in treating them all under a single heading. This is what economic theory does. Economists usually assume that the firm's behavior can be understood in terms of a common motivation. Whether the firm is Ma and Pa's Bar and Grill or the Ford Motor Company and whether a particular decision is made by the board of directors, the third vice-president in charge of advertising, or the owner-manager is regarded as irrelevant to predicting what decisions are made.

Before studying how the firm is treated in economic theory, we shall examine more closely the firm in North America today, to see from what we are abstracting. Criticisms that the theory neglects differences among firms will be considered in Chapter 19.

The Organization of Production

PROPRIETORSHIPS, PARTNERSHIPS, AND CORPORATIONS

There are three major forms of business organization: the single proprietorship, the partnership, and the corporation. In the **single proprietorship,** a single owner makes all decisions and is personally responsible for everything done by the business. In the **partnership,** there are two or more joint owners. Either may make binding decisions, and each partner is personally responsible for everything done by the business. In the **corporation,** the firm legally has an entity of its own. The owners (the stockholders) are not each personally responsible for everything that is done by the business. Owners elect a board of directors who hire managers to run the firm under the board's supervision.

In most sectors of the Canadian economy the corporation is the dominant form of organization. In 1966, 63 percent of the establishments in the manufacturing industries were those of incorporated companies. Moreover, the average size of corporate establishments was much larger; their share of employees was 92 percent and their share of the value of shipments was 95 percent. Only in agriculture and in services (e.g., medicine, law, barbering, accounting) is the corporation relatively unimportant, and even here its share of the business is steadily rising.

The Proprietorship and the Partnership: Advantages and Disadvantages

The major advantage of the single proprietorship is that the owner can readily maintain full control over the firm. The owner is the Boss. The disadvantages are, first, that the size of the firm is limited by the capital the owner can personally raise and, second, that the owner is personally responsible in law for all debts of the firm.

The ordinary (or general) partnership overcomes to some extent the first disadvantage of the proprietorship but not the second. Ten partners may be able to finance a much bigger enterprise than could one owner, but they are still subject to unlimited liability. Each partner is fully liable for all the debts of the firm. This liability is independent of the amount of money a particular partner may have invested in the firm. If a tenth partner makes $1,000 available (or $100, or nothing, for that matter) when joining a firm that subsequently goes bankrupt with debts of $100,000, this individual, and each of the other nine partners, is fully liable for the $100,000. If none of the other partners has salable personal assets, while the tenth partner has a house, a car, furniture, and some investments, he or she may lose all personal possessions so that the debts of the partnership can be cleared.

Obviously, people with substantial personal assets will be unwilling to enter a partnership unless they have complete trust in the other partners and a full knowledge of all the obligations of the firm. This need for trust is compounded because each partner usually has full power to sign contracts that bind the firm in its ordinary lines of business. One partner's fortune is at the mercy of every other partner's judgment. As a direct consequence of this authority and of the fact of unlimited liability, it is difficult to raise money through a partnership from persons who wish to invest but not be active in the business. Investors may be willing to put up $1,000 but unwilling to jeopardize their entire fortune; if, however, a person joins a partnership in order to do the former, he or she may also do the latter.

A further disadvantage of an ordinary partnership is that any time a partner dies or resigns the partnership agreement must be redrawn. This may make it difficult to have as a partner someone who is not genuinely interested and involved in the business but who wants to invest in it. For such a partner may decide at any time to liquidate his or her interest and so dissolve the partnership.

The **limited partnership** is designed to avoid some of these difficulties. General partners continue to have unlimited authority and unlimited liability, but there will also be limited partners. The limited partner's liability is restricted to the amount that he or she has invested in the firm. Such partners do not participate in the management of the firm or engage in agreements on behalf of the partnership. In effect, the limited partnership permits some division of the functions of decision making, provision of capital, and risk taking.

In most respects, this division of responsibility is more effectively achieved through the corporation. But there are certain professions in which general partnership is traditional. These include law, medicine, and (until very recently) brokerage. Partnerships survive in these fields partly because each depends heavily on a relationship of trust with its clients, and the partners' unlimited liability for one another's actions is thought to enchance public confidence in the firm.

The Corporation: Advantages and Disadvantages

The corporation is regarded in law as an entity separate from the individuals who own it. It can enter into contracts, it can sue and be sued, it can own property, it can contract debts, and it can generally incur obligations that are the legal obligations of the corporation *but not of its owners.* This means that the corporation can enter into contracts in its own right and that its liability to adhere to such contracts can be enforced only by suing the corporation, not by suing the owners. The right to be sued may not seem to be an advantage, but it is, because it makes it possible for others to enter into enforceable contracts with the corporation.

Although some corporations are very small or are owned by just a few stockholders who also manage the business, the most important type of corporation is one that sells shares to the general public. The company raises the funds it needs for the business by the sale of stock, and the shareholders become the company's owners. They are entitled to share in corporate profits. Profits, when paid out, are called **dividends. Undistributed profits** also belong to the owners, but they are usually reinvested in the firm's operations. If the corporation is liquidated, shareholders split up any assets that remain after all debts are paid.

Diffuse ownership of corporate shares usually means that the owners cannot all be managers. Stockholders, who are entitled to one vote for each share they own, elect a board of directors. The board defines general policy and hires senior managers who are supposed to translate this general policy into detailed decisions.

Should the company go bankrupt, the personal liability of any one shareholder is limited to whatever money that shareholder has actually invested in the firm. This is called **limited liability.**

From a shareholder's viewpoint, the most important aspect of the corporation is limited liability.

The corporation's advantage is that it can raise capital from a large number of individuals, each of whom shares in the firm's profits but has no liability for corporate action beyond risking the loss of the amount invested. Thus investors know their exact maximum risk and may simply collect dividends without needing to know anything about the policy or operation of the firm that they own collectively. Because shares are easily transferred from one person to another, a corporation has a continuity of life unaffected by frequent changes in the identity of its owners.

From the individual owner's point of view, there are disadvantages in investing in a corporation. First, the owner may have little to say about the management of the firm. For example, if those who hold a majority of the shares decide that the corporation should not pay dividends, an individual investor cannot compel the payment of "his" share of the earnings. Second, the income of the corporation is taxed twice. The corporation is taxed on its income at a rate of nearly 50 percent before dividends are paid. Dividends are paid out of the after-tax income. Then individual stockholders are also taxed on any dividends paid to them. This "double taxation" of corporate income is only partially offset by the dividend tax credit provisions of the Canadian income tax, and some view it as clearly unfair and discriminatory. Others see it as the price to be paid for the advantage of incorporation. Judging from the continuing importance of the corporation in North America, despite corporate income taxes of about 50 percent, the price has not been prohibitive.

THE RISE OF THE MODERN CORPORATION

The corporate form of organization is employed today wherever large enterprises are found. The principal reason is that is has decisive advantages over any other form in raising the vast sums of capital required for major enterprises. Historically, wherever and whenever large accumulations of capital in a single firm were required, the limited liability company developed. The corporate form has spread even to the service industries and agriculture, as firms in these industries grew to the point where they needed a lot of capital to function effectively.

Although historians have found roots of the corporation in Roman law and in the medieval guild system, the direct predecessor of the modern corporation was the English chartered company of the sixteenth century. The Muscovy Company, granted a charter in 1555, the East India Company, first chartered in 1600, and the Hudson's Bay Company, chartered in 1609 and still going strong in Canada 370 years later, are famous early examples of joint-stock ventures with limited liability. These companies were granted charters by the Crown so that English merchants could trade with particular regions. The special needs for many investors to finance a ship that would not return with its cargo for years —if it returned at all—made this *exceptional* form of organization seem desirable.

In the next three centuries, the trading company's critical attributes (e.g., large capital requirements and need to diversify risk) were seen to exist in other fields, and charters were granted in the fields of insurance, turnpikes and canals, and banking, as well as foreign trade. The Industrial Revolution, which made the large firm efficient, extended the needs for large amounts of capital committed over long periods of time to many more fields, and during the nineteenth century the demand for a general rather than a special privilege of incorporation became strong. General laws permitting incorporation with limited liability, *as a matter of right rather than special grant of privilege,* became common in England and in North America during the late nineteenth century.

Today incorporation is relatively routine, although it is subject to a variety of provincial laws. Moderate fees are charged for the privilege of incorporation, and a company can choose to incorporate either federally or under the regulations of one of the provinces.

THE FIRM IN ECONOMIC THEORY

General Motors and Alice's Restaurant certainly make decisions in different ways. Indeed, within a single large corporation not all decisions are made by the same people or in the same way. Nor are all decisions equally important. To take an example, someone at General Motors decided to introduce a new model car in 1975. Someone else decided to call it the Chevette. Someone else decided how and where to produce it. Someone else decided its price. Someone else decided how to promote its sales. The common aspect of these decisions is that all were in pursuit of the same goal—the manufacture and sale of successful automobiles and other products to earn profits for the owners of General Motors.

Economic theory assumes that the same principles underlie each decision made within a firm and that the decision is uninfluenced by who makes it. Thus the firm can be regarded as a decision-making unit with objectives and a unit that makes decisions designed to achieve those objectives.

Motivation: Profit Maximization

It is assumed that the firm makes decisions in such a way that its profits will be as large as possible. In technical language, it is assumed that the firm *maximizes its profits*. The concept of profits requires careful definition, which will be given later in this chapter. For now we may treat it in the everyday sense of the difference between the value of the firm's sales and the costs to the firm of producing what is sold.

The assumption of profit maximization provides a principle by which a firm's decisions can be predicted.

Economists predict the firm's behavior in regard to the choices open to it by studying the effect that making each of the choices would have on the firm's profits. They then predict that from these alternatives the firm will select the one that produces the largest profits.

At this point you may well ask if it is sensible to build an elaborate theory on such a simple assumption about the motives of business people. Of course some business people are inspired by motives other than an overwhelming desire to make as much money as possible. Cases in which they use their positions to seek political influence or pursue charitable objectives are not difficult to document.

This theory does not say, however, that profit is the *only* factor that influences business people. It says only that profits are so important that a theory that assumes profit maximization to be the business firm's sole motive will produce predictions that are substantially correct. It follows that to point out that business people are *sometimes* motivated by considerations other than profits does not refute the theory. It is always possible that the profit-maximizing assumption could be substantially wrong. If so, the way to demonstrate this is to show that the predictions following from the theory are inconsistent with the facts.

Why is this assumption made? First, it is necessary to make *some* assumption about what motivates decision makers if the theory is to predict how they will act. Second, a great many of the predictions of theories based on this assumption have been confirmed by observation. Third, there is no general agreement that an alternative assumption has yet been shown to yield substantially better results. However, the assumption has been criticized, and alternatives have been suggested (see Chapter 19).

Factors of Production

The firm is in business to make profits. It does this by producing and selling one or more commodities. Production is roughly like a sausage machine. Certain elements, such as raw materials and the services of capital and labor, are fed in at one end, and a product emerges at the other. The materials and factor services used in the production process are called **inputs,** and the products that emerge are called **outputs.** One way of looking at the process is to regard the inputs as being combined to produce the output. Another equally useful way is to regard the inputs as being used up, or sacrificed, in order to gain the output.

Each distinct input into the production process can be regarded as a factor of production. Literally hundreds of inputs enter into the output of a specific good. Among the inputs entering into automobile production are, to name only a few, sheet steel, rubber, spark plugs, electricity, machinists, cost accountants, fork-lift operators, managers, and painters. These inputs can be grouped into four broad classes: (1) those that are inputs to the automobile manufacturer but outputs to some other manufacturer, such as spark plugs, electricity, and sheet steel; (2) those that are provided directly by nature, such as land; (3) those that are provided directly by households, such as labor; and (4) those that are provided by the machines used for manufacturing automobiles.

The first class of inputs is made up of goods produced by other firms. These products appear as inputs only because the stages of production are broken up between different firms so that, at any one stage, a firm is using as inputs goods produced by other firms. If these products are traced back to the firms that provided them, it will be found that they were produced with the same four types of inputs.

Eventually, however, if these products are traced back to their sources, all production can be accounted for by the services of only three kinds of inputs, which are often called the basic factors of production. All the gifts of nature, such as land and raw materials, the economist calls **land.** All physical and mental efforts provided by people are called **labor** services. All machines and other production equipment are grouped in a category called **capital,** defined as man-made aids to further production.

Extensive use of capital—the services of machines and other capital goods—is one distinguishing feature of modern as opposed to primitive production. Instead of making consumer goods directly with only the aid of simple natural tools, productive effort goes into the manufacture of tools, machines, and other goods that are desired not in themselves but as aids to making further goods. The use of capital goods renders the production processes *roundabout.* Instead of making what is wanted directly, a roundabout process first makes tools that will subsequently be used to make what is finally wanted.

Economic Efficiency

Firms must decide not only what and how much to produce but by what method goods will be produced. In general, there is more than one way to produce a given product. Indeed, if this were not the case, there would be no need for firms to face the decision of *how* to produce. It is possible to produce agricultural commodities by farming a small quantity of land, combining a great deal of labor and capital with each acre of land, as is done in Belgium; it is also possible to produce the same commodities by farming a great deal of land, using only a small amount of labor and capital per acre of land, as is done in Australia.

What does it mean to ask which process is best? One meaning of "best" is that, if the output is the same, the best process is the one that uses the fewest inputs or, in other words, the one that is technically most efficient. **Technological efficiency** measures use of inputs in physical terms; **economic efficiency** measures use in terms of costs.

The economically most efficient method is the one that *costs* the least. Economic efficiency depends on factor prices *and* on technological efficiency.

Cost and Profit to the Firm

THE MEANING AND MEASUREMENT OF COST

Economic efficiency has been defined in terms of cost. But what is cost? **Cost,** to the producing firm, is the *value* of the factors of production used in producing its output.

Notice the use of the word "value" in the definition. A given output produced by a given technique, say 6,000 cars produced each week by American Motors with its present production methods, will have a given set of inputs associated with it—so many working hours of various

Technological Versus Economic Efficiency: An Example

Suppose, given the state of technology, there are only four known ways to produce 100 widgits per month:

	Quantity of inputs received	
	Capital	Labor
Method A	6	200
Method B	10	250
Method C	10	150
Method D	40	50

Method B is technologically inefficient because it uses more of both inputs than does method A. It thus wastes 4 units of capital and 50 units of labor. Among the other three methods, method A uses the least capital, but it is the most labor-using.* Method D conserves labor but uses much more capital. Method C is intermediate between them. (If you are tempted to consider method D tech-

nologically most efficient because it uses only 90 units of all resources, think again.)

Methods A, C, and D are all technologically efficient because no one of them uses more of both resources than either of the others.

Which one is the least costly—that is, is economically efficient? We cannot tell without knowing the costs of capital and of labor. Economic efficiency depends on factor prices. Consider the three cases shown in the table below. As we move from Case I to II to III, a unit of labor becomes increasingly expensive *relative to* a unit of capital.

Method A is economically efficient when labor is cheap relative to capital. Method C becomes efficient when labor gets somewhat more expensive relative to capital. Finally, when labor gets very expensive relative to capital, method D, which uses least labor per unit of capital, becomes economically efficient.

To test your understanding, answer these questions:

1. Can a technologically *inefficient* method ever be economically efficient?
2. Is there a set of factor prices for which *both* method C and method D will be economically efficient?

* This is yet a third concept of efficiency, "engineering efficiency," in which least use of a particular factor is involved. When engineers speak of the efficiency of an engine, they may mean how much of the fuel it turns into power. Similarly, a maker of labor-saving machines might consider method D the most efficient because it uses the least amount of labor.

	Factor prices per unit		Total cost of factors		
	Capital	Labor	Method A	Method C	Method D
Case I	$50	$3	$ 900	$950	$2,150
Case II	20	5	1,120	950	1,050
Case III	15	5	1,090	900	850

types of laborers, supervisors, managers, and technicians, so many tons of steel, glass, and aluminum, so much electric light and other services, and so many hours of the time of various machines. To know the cost of this diverse set of factor inputs, the value of each in money terms must be calculated. The sum of these separate costs is the total cost to American Motors of producing 6,000 cars per week. "Costing" may be very easy or very difficult.

Purpose in Assigning Costs

Economists' interest in costs is a direct consequence of the notion that factor services are scarce and, as a result, valuable. Thus, in using them up to produce outputs, the firm uses things that have value. From the point of view of a profit-maximizing firm, the profit from production consists of the difference between the value of the outputs and the value of the inputs. Knowing costs, then, is a precondition to knowing profits, and knowing profits is necessary to understanding behavior. An economist might discuss this behavior for several reasons: (1) to *describe* the actual behavior of a firm, (2) to *predict* how the firm's behavior will respond to specified changes in the conditions it faces, (3) to *help* the firm make the best decisions it can in achieving its goals, and (4) to *evaluate* how well firms use scarce resources.

The same measure of cost need not be correct for all of these purposes. For example, if the firm happens to be misinformed about the value of some resource, it will behave according to that misinformation. In describing or predicting the firm's behavior, economists should use the information the firm actually uses, even if the economist knows it is incorrect. But in helping the firm to achieve its goals, economists should substitute the correct information.

Economists use a well-established definition of costs in solving problems of the kind cited in items 3 and 4 of the above list. If business people use the same definition and have the same information, the economist's definition will be appro-priate for problems of types 1 and 2 as well. This will be assumed for the moment.

Opportunity Cost

Although the details of economic costing vary, they are governed by a common principle that is sometimes called user cost but is more commonly called **opportunity cost.**

The cost of using something in a particular venture is the benefit forgone (or opportunity lost) by not using it in its best alternative use.

An old Chinese merchants' proverb says: "Where there is no gain, the loss is obvious." The economic sense of this proverb is that the merchant who shows no gain has wasted time — time that could have been used in some other venture. The merchant has neglected the opportunity cost of his time.

What is given up *is* the cost of the indicated action. One of the problems in evaluating costs is that different people (or groups) may see or care about different alternatives. Jones sees the alternative to watching television on a Saturday afternoon as playing golf; his wife regards the alternative as a family outing. For the present, analysis will be limited to cost as seen by the firm. In Chapter 24 other points of view will be considered.

THE MEASUREMENT OF OPPORTUNITY COST BY THE FIRM

In principle, measuring opportunity cost is easy. The firm must assign to each factor of production it has used a monetary value equal to what it has sacrificed in order to use the factor. Applying this principle to specific cases, however, reveals some tough problems.

Purchased and Hired Factors

Assigning costs is a straightforward process when factors purchased in one period are used up in the same period and where the price the

Opportunity Cost More Generally

Opportunity cost plays a vital role in the economic analysis, but it is a fundamental principle that applies to a wide range of situations. It is one of the great insights of economics. Consider some examples:

■ George Bernard Shaw, on reaching his 90th birthday, was asked how he liked being 90. He is reputed to have said, "It's fine, when you consider the alternative."

■ Llewelyn Formed likes to watch the evening news on both CBC and CTV. If he finally settles on CTV, what is the opportunity cost of this decision?

■ M. C. Pigg, a 31-year-old bachelor, is thinking about marrying at last. But, although he thinks Miss Piggy is a lovely girl, he figures that if he marries her, he will give up the chance of wedded bliss with another girl he may meet next year. So he decides to wait a while. What additional information do you require to determine the opportunity cost of the decision?

■ Serge Ginn, M.D., complains that now that he is earning large fees he can no longer afford to take the time for a vacation trip to Europe. In what way does it make sense to say that the opportunity cost of his vacation depends on his fees?

■ Ms. Anne Thrope doesn't like bankers, so she keeps her life's savings of $10,000 hidden in her mattress. What does it cost her per year to dislike bankers? One answer might be that it is the loss of interest she would have earned if she had placed her money in savings account at 5 percent ($500 per year) plus the added cost of the extra fire and theft insurance she carries on her house and belongings. This is the right answer if she regards the savings account as her best alternative. (She could dislike bankers and still earn money on her savings by investing in government bonds, real estate, or stocks. But perhaps Ms. Thorpe dislikes governments, risk, and businessmen, too.)

■ Hard-Luck Harry loses $100 a week in a dice game. He knows the game is crooked but plays anyway because, as he says, "it's the only game in town." A reform mayor is elected and shuts down all gambling establishments. What is the opportunity cost to Harry?

firm pays is set on a competitive market by the forces of supply and demand. Many raw material and intermediate-product purchases fall into this category. From the point of view of the firm purchasing in a competitive market, if it pays $25 per ton for coal delivered to its factory, it has sacrificed its claims to whatever else $25 can buy, and thus the purchase price is a reasonable measure of the opportunity cost to it of using one ton of coal.

For hired factors of production, where the rental price is the full price, the situation is identical. Borrowed money is paid for by payment of **interest**. An **interest rate** is the money price paid to use $1 for one year. Interest payments measure the opportunity cost of borrowed funds. Most labor services are hired, but typically the cost is more than the wages paid because employers usually must contribute to social insurance, to pension funds, to unemployment and disability insurance, and to other fringe benefits. The cost of these benefits must be added to the direct wage in determining the opportunity cost of labor services used.

Imputed Costs

The cost must also be assessed for factors of production that the firm uses but neither purchases nor hires for current use. Since no payment is made to anyone outside the firm, these costs are not so obvious. They are called **imputed costs.** If the most profitable lines of production are to be discovered, the opportunity cost of these factors should be reckoned at values that reflect what the firm might earn from the factors if it shifted them to their next best use. Some important imputed costs arise because of the use of owners' money, the depreciation of capital equipment, the need to compensate risk taking, and the need to value any special advantages (such as franchises or patents) that the firm may possess.

The cost of money. Consider a firm that uses $100,000 of its own money that it could instead have loaned out at interest at a rate of 10 percent per year.

Thus $10,000 (at least) should be deducted from the firm's revenue as the cost of funds used in production. If, to continue the example, the firm makes only $6,000 over all other costs, then one should say not that the firm made a profit of $6,000 by producing but that it lost $4,000. For if it had closed down completely and merely loaned out its money to someone else, it could have earned $10,000.

The cost of money may be higher than this if the best alternative use of the money could yield more than the market interest rate. Many firms cannot obtain nearly as much money as they would wish by borrowing. If a firm is rationed in the amount of funds if can borrow, it will place a high value on the funds that it does have. In these circumstances, the firm must look at the other ventures it might have undertaken in order to assign opportunity cost because its inability to raise all the capital it wants means that it will be unable to do all the things it wants. Many business firms operate with "cut-off rates of return" that approximate the opportunity cost of money

to the firm. They are chosen to approximate the return on projects that the firm cannot undertake because it lacks sufficient funds.[1]

Depreciation. The costs of using assets owned by the firm, such as buildings, equipment, and machinery, consist of the cost of the money tied up in them and a charge, called **depreciation,** for the loss in value of the asset because of its use in production. Depreciation includes both the loss in value due to physical wear and tear and that due to obsolescence. The economic cost of using an asset for a year is the loss in value of the asset during the year.

Accountants use several conventional methods of depreciation based on the price originally paid for the asset. One of the most common is *straight-line depreciation,* in which the same amount of historical cost is deducted in every year of useful life of the asset. While historical costs are often useful approximations, they may in some cases differ seriously from the depreciation required by the opportunity cost principle. Consider two examples of the possible error involved.

Example 1. A woman buys a $6,000 automobile that she intends to use for six years. She may think that, using straight-line depreciation, this will cost her $1,000 per year. But if after one year the value of her car on the used-car market is $4,000, it has cost her $2,000 to use the car during the first year. Why should she charge herself $2,000 depreciation during the first year? After all, *she* does not intend to sell the car for six years. The answer is that one of the purchaser's alternatives was to buy a one-year-old car and operate it for five years. Indeed,

---

[1] Empirical studies of certain manufacturing industries suggest that the opportunity cost of money is substantially higher than the rate of interest on bonds and long-term loans. An accurate figure may well be as high as 35 percent. The fact that it is so high helps explain why many firms are anxious to retain a major portion of their profits and why many stockholders (who do not have similar personal investment opportunities) are willing to have corporations pay dividends that are substantially less than earnings and reinvest the remainder to earn their internal rate of return.

that is the very position she is in after the first year. Whether she likes it or not, she has paid $2,000 for the use of the car during the first year of its life. If the market had valued her car at $5,500 after one year (instead of $4,000), the depreciation would have been only $500.

Example 2. In the previous example an active used-asset market was considered. At the other extreme, consider an asset that has no alternative use. This is sometimes described as the case of "sunk" costs. Assume that a firm has a set of machines it purchased some time ago for $100,000. These machines should last ten years, and the firm's accountant calculates the depreciation costs of these machines by the straight-line method at $10,000 per year. Assume also that the machines can be used to make one product and nothing else. Since they are installed in the firm's plant, they cannot be leased to any other firm, and their scrap value is negligible. In other words, the machines have no value, except to this firm in its current operation. Assume that if the machines are used to produce this product, the cost of all other factors utilized will amount to $25,000, while the goods produced can be sold for $29,000.

Now, if the accountant's depreciation "costs" of running the machines are added in, the total cost of operation comes to $35,000; with revenues at $29,000, this makes an annual loss of $6,000 per year. It appears that the goods should not be made!

The fallacy in this argument lies in adding in a charge based on the historical cost of the machines as one of the costs of current operation. The machines have no alternative uses whatsoever. Clearly their opportunity cost is zero. The total costs of producing this line of goods is thus only $25,000 per year (assuming all other costs have been correctly assessed), and the line of production shows an annual profit of $4,000, not a loss of $6,000.

To see why the second calculation leads to the correct decision, notice that if the firm decides this line of production is unprofitable and does not continue it, it will have no money to pay out and no revenue received on this account. If the firm takes the economist's advice and pursues the line of production, it will pay out $25,000 and receive $29,000, thus making it $4,000 per year richer than if it had not done so. Clearly, production is worth undertaking. The amount the firm happened to have paid out for the machines in the past has no bearing whatever on deciding the correct use of the machines once they are installed on the premises.

Bygones are bygones; they should have no influence on deciding what is currently the most profitable thing to do.

The "bygones are bygones" principle extends well beyond economics and is often ignored in poker, in war, and perhaps in love. Because you have invested heavily in a poker hand, a battle, or a courtship does not mean you should stick with it if the prospects of winning become very small. At every moment of decision, you should be concerned with how benefits from this time forward compare with current and future costs.

Risk taking. One difficult problem in imputing costs concerns the evaluation of the service of risk taking. Business enterprise is often a risky affair. The risk is borne by the owners of the firm who, if the enterprise fails, may lose the money they have invested in the firm. The owners will not take these risks unless they receive a remuneration in return. They expect a return that exceeds what they could have obtained by investing their money in a virtually riskless manner, say, by buying a government bond.

In the sense in which the term is used here, risk taking is a factor of production and thus has a cost. It is a service that must be provided if the firm is to carry on production, and it must be paid for by the firm. If a firm does not yield a return sufficient to compensate for the risks involved, the firm will not be able to persuade people to contribute money to it in return for a part ownership in the firm.

Investors demand a higher return on a risky venture than on a sure one because, in addition to having their capital used, they take the chance of never getting it back. In order to earn the required return on their total investments—the successful and the unsuccessful—investors require a greater return on the successful investments.

Suppose, in investing $100,000 in a class of risky ventures, a businesswoman expects that most of the ventures will be successful but some will fail. In fact she expects about $10,000 worth to be a total loss. (She does not know which specific projects will be the losers, of course.) Suppose further that she requires a 20 percent return on her total investment. In order to earn $20,000 profit and recover the $10,000 expected loss, she needs to earn $30,000 profit on the $90,000 of successful investment. This is a rate of return of $33\frac{1}{3}$ percent. She charges 20 percent for the use of the capital, $13\frac{1}{3}$ percent for the risk she takes.

Special advantages. Suppose a firm owns a valuable patent or a highly desirable location, or produces a popular brand-name product such as Coca-Cola, Chevrolet, or Labatt's 50. Each of these involves an opportunity cost to the firm in production (even if it was acquired free) because if the firm does not choose to *use* the special advantage itself, it could sell or lease it to others. Typically, the value of these advantages will differ from their historical cost.

PROFITS: THEIR MEANING AND SIGNIFICANCE

Profits, although often defined loosely in everyday usage, may be given a series of more precise definitions. **Economic profits** on goods sold are defined as the difference between revenues received from the sale and the opportunity cost of the resources used to make them. (If costs are greater than revenues, such "negative profits" are called *losses*.)

This definition includes in costs (and thus excludes from profits) the imputed returns to capital and to risk taking. This use of the words

TABLE 11–1
The Calculation of Economic Profits: An Example

Gross revenue from sales	$1,000
Less: direct costs of goods sold (materials, labor, electricity, etc.)	650
"Gross profits" (or "contributions to overhead")	350
Less: indirect costs (depreciation, overhead, management salaries, etc.)	140
"Net profits" before income taxes	210
Less: imputed charges for own capital used and for risk taking } = "normal profits"	100
Economic profits before income taxes	110
Less: income taxes payable	100
Economic profits after income taxes	$ 10

The main difference between "economic profits" and the usual everyday definition of profits is the subtraction of imputed charges for use of capital owned by the firm and for risk taking. Income tax is levied on whatever definition of profits the taxing authorities choose, usually closely related to "net profits."

"profit" and "loss" gives specialized definitions to words that are in everyday use. They are therefore a potential source of confusion to the student who runs into other uses of the same words. Table 11-1 may help clarify the definition.

Some economists, while following substantially the same definitions, label as **normal profits** the imputed returns to capital and risk taking just necessary to prevent the owners from withdrawing from the industry. These normal profits are, of course, what has been defined as the opportunity costs of risk taking and capital. Whatever they are called, they are costs that have to be covered if the firm is to stay in operation in the long run.

Other Definitions of Profits

Business firms define profits as the excess of revenues over the costs with which accountants provide them. We will explore in the appendix to this chapter some of the differences between accountants' and economists' views of business transactions. Some of these differences affect the meaning of profits. Accountants do not include as costs charges for risk taking and use of owners' own capital, and thus these items are recorded by businesses as part of their profits. When a businessman says he *needs* profits of such and such an amount in order to stay in business, he is making sense within his definition, for his "profits" must be large enough to pay for those factors of production that he uses but that the accounting profession does not include as costs.

The economist would express the same notion by saying that the business needs to cover *all* its costs, including those not accepted by accounting conventions. If the firm is covering all its costs (in the sense that we have defined costs), then it could not do better by using its resources in any other line of activity than the one currently being followed. Indeed, it would probably do worse in most other lines of activity.

A situation in which revenues equal costs (economic profits of zero) is a satisfactory one— because all factors, hidden as well as visible, are being rewarded at least as well as in their *best* alternative uses.

With zero profits then, in the economist's sense of that concept, you can do no better, although you might do worse. To reverse the Chinese proverb cited earlier, "Where there is no loss compared to the best alternative use of every factor, the gain is obvious."

The income tax authorities have yet another definition of profits, which is implicit in the thousands of rules as to what may and may not be included as a deduction from revenue in arriving at taxable income. In some cases, the taxing authorities allow more for cost than the accountant recommends; in other cases, they allow less.

It is important to be clear about different meanings of the term "profits," not only to avoid fruitless semantic arguments, but because a theory that predicts that certain behavior is a function of profits defined in one way will not

necessarily predict behavior accurately, given some other definition. For example, if economists predict that new firms will seek to enter an industry whenever profits are earned, this prediction will frequently be wrong if the accountants' definition is used to determine profits. The definition of profits as an excess over all opportunity costs is for many purposes the most useful, but in order to apply it to business behavior or to tax policy, appropriate adjustments must be made. And in order to apply accounting or tax data to particular theories, the data must be rectified.

Profits and Resource Allocation

When resources are valued by the opportunity cost principle, their costs show how much these resources would earn if used in their best alternative uses. If there is an industry in which all firms' revenues exceed opportunity costs, all the firms in that industry will be earning profits. Thus the owners of factors of production will want to move resources into this industry because the earnings potentially available to them are greater there than in alternative uses of the resources. If in some other industry firms are incurring losses, some or all of this industry's resources are more highly valued in other uses, and owners of the resources will want to move them to those other uses.

Economic profits and losses play a crucial signaling role in the workings of a free-market system.

Profits in an industry are the signal that resources can profitably be moved into the industry. Losses are the signal that the resources can profitably be moved elsewhere. Only if there are zero economic profits is there no incentive for resources to move into or out of an industry.

Summary

1. The firm is the economic unit that produces and sells commodities. The economist's definition of the firm abstracts from real-life differences in size and form of organization of firms.

2. The single proprietorship, the partnership, and the corporation are the major forms of business organization in Canada today. The corporation is by far the most common business wherever large-scale production is required. The corporation is recognized as a legal entity; its owners, or shareholders, have a liability that is limited to the amount of money they have actually invested in the organization. Corporate ownership is readily transferred by sale of shares in organized securities markets.

3. Economic theory assumes that the same principles underlie each decision made within the firm and that the actual decision is uninfluenced by who makes it. The key behavioral assumption is that the firm seeks to maximize its profit.

4. Production consists of transforming inputs (or factors of production) into outputs (or goods and services). It is often convenient to divide factors of production into categories. One common classification is land, labor, and capital. Land includes all primary products, labor means all human services, and capital denotes all man-made aids to further production. An outstanding feature of modern production is the use of capital goods and roundabout methods of production.

5. Because there is more than one way to engage in production, the firm must decide *how* to produce. Efficiency is a measure of the relative amount of input necessary to produce a given output. Technological efficiency evaluates units of input in physical terms. Economic efficiency evaluates them in terms of costs.

6. The opportunity cost of using a resource is the value of that resource in its best alternative use. If the opportunity cost of using a resource in one way is less than or equal to the gain from using the resource in this way, there is no superior way of using it.

7. Measuring opportunity cost to the firm requires some difficult imputations in cases involving resources not purchased or hired for current use. Among these imputed costs are those for use of owners' money, depreciation, risk taking, and any special advantages that the firm may possess.

8. A firm maximizing profits, defined as the difference between revenue and opportunity cost, is making the best allocation of the resources under its control, according to the firm's evaluation of its alternatives.

9. Profits and losses provide important signals concerning the reallocation of resources. Profits earned in an industry provide a signal that more resources can profitably move into the industry. Losses show that some resources have more profitable uses elsewhere and serve as a signal for them to move out of that industry.

10. The appendix to this chapter introduces balance sheets and profit and loss statements and uses them to discuss some of the differences between the concepts of profits used by accountants and economists.

Topics for Review

The firm in theory and in the Canadian economy
The role of profit maximization
Single proprietorship, partnership, and corporation
Advantages of the corporation
Factors of production
Economic efficiency
Opportunity costs
Economic and other definitions of profits
Profits and resource allocation

Discussion Questions

1. Many modern firms go through stages of being in turn a single proprietorship, a partnership, and a corporation. Can you suggest why such an evolution might be sensible? If you were to start a business, which form would you choose? Why?

2. Can the economic theory of the firm be of any help in analyzing the productive decisions of such nonprofit organizations as governments, churches, and universities? What, if any, role does the notion of opportunity cost play for them?

3. In *The Engineers and the Price System* Thorstein Veblen argued that businessmen who made decisions about financing, pricing, and the like were largely superfluous to the operation of a business. In his view, knowledge of the technology would be sufficient to ensure efficient operation of firms. Discuss Veblen's contention.

4. "There is no such thing as a free lunch." Can anything be costless? Gas stations have traditionally provided free services, including windshield cleaning, air pumps for tire inflation, and road maps. Now many sell road maps and have discontinued free services. Indeed, self-service stations are becoming increasingly popular with motorists who like the lower gas prices of those stations. Under what conditions will profit-maximizing behavior lead to the coexistence of full-service and self-service gas stations? What would determine the proportions in which each occurred?

5. What is the opportunity cost of:
   a. a politician being fined $10,000 and sent to prison for one year
   b. lending $500 to a friend
   c. not permitting a $116 million electric power dam to be built because it would destroy the snail darter, a rare 3-inch-long fish found only in that particular river
   d. towing icebergs to Saudi Arabia to provide drinking water at the cost of 50¢ per cubic meter

6. Is straight-line depreciation an appropriate method of assessing the annual cost to the typical household of using a passenger automobile? Some firms that use trucks allocate the cost on a per-mile basis. Why might this method be more nearly appropriate for trucks than for automobiles owned by households?

7. Having bought a used car from Smiling Sam for $900, you drive it two days and it stops. You now find that it requires an extra $500 before it will run. Assuming that the car is not worth $1,400 fixed, should you make the repairs?

8. "The higher the opportunity cost, the poorer the investment." Do you agree with this statement? If you do not, how could you formulate the maxim so that you did agree?

9. Which concept of profits is implied in the following quotations:
   a. "Profits are necessary if firms are to stay in business."
   b. "Profits are signals for firms to expand production and investment."
   c. "Increased depreciation lowers profits and thus benefits the company's owners."

Production and Cost in the Short Run

12

The Canadian automobile industry in 1979 consisted of four firms who together produced and sold 1.2 million new motor vehicles. However, their individual shares of the market were not anything like equal. General Motors sold 53 percent. Ford sold 28 percent, Chrysler sold 17 percent, and American Motors sold 2 percent. The prices charged for comparable models were approximately the same, but the profits *per automobile* made and sold were very different for the companies not only in 1979 but on the average over many years. General Motors has consistently shown the highest profit per unit: Ford has been next most profitable, while Chrysler and American Motors each earned much lower profits per car than the other two. In 1979 Chrysler's losses in its combined North American operations of about $1 billion threatened the ability of that company to continue in business and led to massive loan guarantees of $1.5 billion from the U.S. government to the parent company and $200 million from the Canadian federal government to Chrysler Canada. Ford, too, lost money on its North American operations, but foreign operations kept it in the black overall.

One reason for the differences in profitability lies in the *cost* of making and selling a car, which tends to be lower the more cars are produced. Over the past 40 years several once-profitable smaller producers, among them Packard, Crosley, Studebaker, and Kaiser-Frazer, were unable to increase their volume and found that costs had become greater than revenues. They left the industry after suffering heavy losses. This experience illustrates one aspect of the theory of cost of production: cost of production per unit may be very different for different levels of output.

A different aspect of the theory of costs relates to factor prices. When rising chicken feed prices reached the point where it cost more to feed chickens as they grew than they sold for when fully grown, chicken farmers shut down temporarily. Similarly, when meat packers were squeezed between the legal maximum price at which they could sell and the rising cost of the livestock they bought, some of them suspended production.

In order to understand firms' behavior, we need to know what determines their costs of production and how those costs vary as output varies. The principle of opportunity cost shows how to put a money value on the factor services that are used up in the process of production. These money values for all the factor services used to produce a certain output are added up to get the total cost of producing that output. But how are these costs related to output?

Real Choices Open to the Firm

Consider a firm producing a single product in a number of different plants. If its rate of sales has fallen off, should production be reduced correspondingly? Or should production be held at the old rate and the unsold amounts stored up against an anticipated future rise in sales? If production is to be reduced, should a single plant be closed or should all plants be operated fewer hours per week? If demand increases sharply and unexpectedly, how can more production be squeezed out of the existing facilities?

All these matters concern how best to use *existing* plant and equipment. They also involve time periods too short to build new plants or to install more equipment. The decisions made will be implemented quickly: A plant can be shut down on a week's notice, overtime can be increased tomorrow, and new production workers can be added as soon as they can be hired and trained.

More weighty decisions must be made when managers do long-range planning. Should the firm adopt a highly automated process that will greatly reduce its wage bill, even though it must borrow large sums of money to buy the equipment? Or should it continue to build new plants that use the same techniques it is now using? Should it build new plants in an area where labor is plentiful, but that is distant from its sources of raw materials? These matters concern what a firm should do when it is changing or replacing its plant and equipment. Such decisions may take a long time to put into effect.

In the above examples, managers make decisions from known possibilities. Large firms also have research and development staffs whose job it is to discover new methods of production. But the firm must decide how much money to devote to this function and in what areas the payoff for new development will be largest. If, for example, a shortage of a particular labor skill or raw material is anticipated, the research staff can be told to try to find ways to economize on that input or even eliminate it from the production process.

TIME HORIZONS FOR DECISION MAKING

In order to reduce to manageable proportions the decisions firms are constantly making, economists organize the decisions into three theoretical groups: (1) How best to employ existing plant and equipment (the "short run"). (2) What new plant and equipment and production processes to select, given the framework of known technical possibilities (the "long run"). (3) What to do about encouraging the invention of new techniques (the "very long run"). In using these periods economists abstract from the more complicated nature of real decisions and focus on the key factors that restrict the range of choice in each set of decisions.

The Short Run

Short-run decisions are those made when the quantity of some inputs cannot be varied. The firm cannot get more of the **fixed factors** than it has on hand, and it is committed to make any money payments that are associated with these fixed factors.[1] Factors that can be varied in the short run are called **variable factors.**

In the short run, what matters is that at least one significant factor is fixed. The factor is fixed in the sense that while the firm may or may not use all that it has, it cannot get more for the duration of the short run. The fixed factor is usually an element of capital (such as plant and equipment), but it might be land, the services of management, or even the supply of skilled labor.

The short run does not correspond to a definite number of months or years. In some industries it may extend over many years; in others it may be only a matter of months or even weeks. Furthermore, it may last a different period of time in an expanding phase of an industry than in a contracting one.

In the electric power industry, for example, it takes three or more years to acquire and install a steam-turbine generator. An unforeseen increase in demand will involve a long period during which the extra demand must be met as best it can with the existing capital equipment. Once installed, this equipment has a very long life, and a decrease in demand leaves the firm committed, possibly for decades, to all the costs of this equipment that do not vary with output.

In contrast, a machine shop can acquire new equipment or sell existing equipment in a very few weeks, so the short run is correspondingly short. An increase in demand will have to be met with the existing stock of capital for only a brief time, after which it will be possible to adjust the stock of equipment to the level made desirable by the higher demand.

The Long Run

Long-run decisions are those made when the inputs of all factors of production may be varied but the basic technology of production is unchanged. Again, the long run does not correspond to a specific period of time.

The special importance of the long run in production theory is that it corresponds to the situation facing the firm when it is planning to go into business, to expand the scale of its operations, to branch out into new products or new areas, or to modernize, replace, or reorganize its method of production.

The firm's *planning decisions* characteristically are made with fixed technical possibilities but with freedom to choose from a variety of production processes that will use factor inputs in different proportions.

The Very Long Run

Unlike the short and the long run, the **very long run** concerns the opportunities arising from changing technology. A central characteristic of modern industrial society has been the continuously changing technology that leads to new and improved products and new and improved production methods. Some of these technological advances arise from within the firm as part of its own research and development efforts. For example, much of the innovation in cameras and films has been due to the efforts of the Kodak and Polaroid companies. Or firms may merely adopt technological changes made by other firms. For example, the transistor and the electronic chip have revolutionized dozens of industries that had nothing to do with developing them in the first place. In either case, decisions are required on the part of the firm as to how much to spend in its efforts to change the firm's technology either by developing new techniques or adapting techniques developed by others.

[1] Sometimes it is physically impossible to increase the quantity of a fixed factor in a short time. For instance, there is no way to build a hydroelectric dam or a nuclear power plant in a few months. Other times it might be physically possible, but prohibitively expensive, to increase the quantity. For example, a suit-manufacturing firm could conceivably rent a building, buy and install new sewing machines, and hire a trained labor force in a few days if money were no consideration. Economists regard prohibitive cost along with physical impossibility as a source of fixed factors.

CONNECTING THE RUNS: THE PRODUCTION FUNCTION

Although it is convenient to treat production decisions in several stages—or in separate compartments—they are thoroughly interrelated. The plant built today (a long-run decision) affects tomorrow's short-run decisions. Similarly, an alternative to coping with a plant of inadequate size by running overtime shifts (a short-run expedient) is constructing a new wing (a long-run decision) or an entirely new plant (another long-run decision) or searching for a new technique of production (a very-long-run decision).

The various "runs" are simply different aspects of the same basic problem: getting output from inputs efficiently. They differ in terms of what the firm is able to change.

The relation between factor services used as inputs into the production process and the quantity of output obtained is called the **production function.** A simplified production function in which there are only two factors of production, labor and capital, will be considered here, but the conclusions apply equally when there are many factors. The variation of output and cost under the assumption that one of the two factors is fixed is examined in this chapter. (Capital is taken to be the fixed factor and labor the variable one.) The long-run situation in which both factors can be varied is covered in the next chapter.

Short-run Choices

TOTAL, AVERAGE, AND MARGINAL PRODUCTS

Assume that a firm starts with a fixed amount of capital (say, 4 units) and contemplates applying various amounts of labor to it. Table 12-1 shows three different ways of looking at how output varies with the quantity of the variable factor. As a first step, some terms need to be defined.

1. **Total product** (*TP*) means the total amount produced during a given period of time by all the

TABLE 12-1

The Variation of Output with Capital Fixed and Labor Variable

(1) Quantity of labor (L)	(2) Total product (TP)	(3) Average product (AP)	(4) Marginal product (MP)
0	0	—	
1	15	15.0	15
2	34	17.0	19
3	48	16.0	14
4	60	15.0	12
5	62	12.4	2

The relation of output to changes in the quantity of labor can be looked at in three different ways. Capital is assumed to be fixed at 4 units. As the quantity of labor increases, the rate of output (the total product) increases. Average product increases at first and then declines. The same is true of marginal product.

Marginal product is shown between the lines because it refers to the *change* in output from one level of labor input to another. When graphing the schedule, *MPs* of this kind should be plotted at the midpoint of the interval. Thus, graphically, the marginal product of 12 would be plotted to correspond to quantity of labor of 3.5.

factors of production employed. If the inputs of all but one factor are held constant, total product will change as more or less of the variable factor is used. This variation is shown in columns 1 and 2 of Table 12-1, which gives a total product schedule. Figure 12-1(i) shows such a schedule graphically. (The shape of the curve will be discussed shortly.)

2. **Average product** (*AP*) is merely the total product per unit of the variable factor, labor. The number of units of labor will be denoted by *L*.

$$AP = \frac{TP}{L}$$

It is shown in column 3 of Table 12-1. Notice that as more of the variable factor is used, average product first rises and then falls. The level of output (34 units in the example) where average product reaches a maximum is called the **point of diminishing average productivity.**

3. **Marginal product** (*MP*), sometimes called

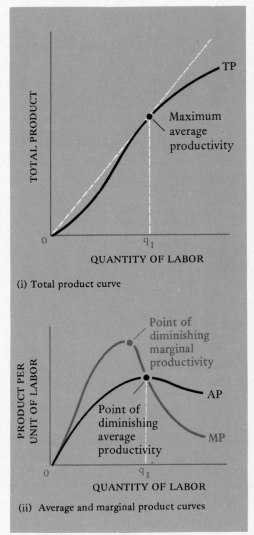

FIGURE 12–1
Total, Average, and Marginal Product Curves

(i) Total product curve

(ii) Average and marginal product curves

TP, AP, and *MP* **curves often have the shapes shown here.** (i) The total product curve shows total product steadily rising, first at an increasing rate, then at a decreasing rate. This leads both average and marginal product curves in (ii) to rise at first and then decline. The point of maximum average product (also called the point of diminishing average productivity) is q_1. At this point $MP = AP$.

incremental product, is the change in total product resulting from the use of 1 unit more of the variable factor.[2] **[14]**

$$MP = \frac{\Delta TP}{\Delta L}$$

Computed values of marginal product are shown in column 4 of Table 12-1. The figures in this column are placed between the other lines of the table to stress that the concept refers to the *change* in output caused by the *change* in quantity of the variable factor. For example, the increase in labor from 3 to 4 units ($\Delta L = 1$) raises output by 12 from 48 to 60 ($\Delta TP = 12$). Thus the *MP* equals 12, and it is recorded between 3 and 4 units of labor. Note that the *MP* in the example rises and then falls. The level of output where marginal product reaches a maximum is called the **point of diminishing marginal productivity.**

Figure 12-1(ii) plots average product and marginal product curves. Although three different schedules are shown in Table 12-1 and three different curves are shown in Figure 12-1, they are all aspects of the same single relationship that is described by the production function. As we vary the quantity of labor, with capital fixed, output changes. Sometimes it is interesting to look at the total increase in output, sometimes at the average increase, and sometimes at the marginal increase.

Finally, bear in mind that the schedules of Table 12-1 and the curves of Figure 12-1 all assume a specified quantity of the fixed factor. If the quantity of capital had been, say, 6 or 10 instead of the 4 units that were assumed, there would be a different set of total product, average product, and marginal product curves. The reason for this is that if any specified amount of labor has more capital to work with, it can produce more output—that is, its total product will be greater.

---

[2] The Greek delta (Δ) is a standard symbol meaning "the change in." Thus ΔL is read "a change in the quantity of labor." For the definition of marginal product we want a 1-unit change in labor, that is, $\Delta L = 1$.

Diminishing Returns

The phenomenon of eventually diminishing returns when more of a variable factor is applied to one or more fixed factors is illustrated by the following examples. In each case you should be able to identify the variable factor and the fixed factor or factors, as well as the "product" that is subject to diminishing returns.

■ When Southern California Edison was required by the State of California to modify its Mojave power plant to reduce the amount of fly ash emitted into the atmosphere, it discovered that a series of filters applied to the smokestacks could do the job. A single filter eliminated half the discharge. Five filters in series reduced the fly ash discharge to the three percent allowed by law. When a state senator proposed a new standard that would permit no more than one percent fly ash emission, the company brought in experts who testified that such a requirement (if it could be met) would require at least 15 filters per stack and would triple the cost.

■ Experimenters with chemical fertilizers at the Rothampsted Experimental Station, an agricultural research institute in Hertfordshire, England, in 1921 applied different amounts of a particular fertilizer to ten apparently identical quarter-acre plots of land. For one such test, using identical seed grain, the results were:

Plot	Fertilizer dose	Yield index*
1	15	104.2
2	30	110.4
3	45	118.0
4	60	125.3
5	75	130.2
6	90	132.4
7	105	131.9
8	120	132.3
9	135	132.5
10	150	132.8

*Yield without fertilizer = 100

You may find it useful to compute the average and marginal product of fertilizer and identify the (approximate) points of diminishing average and marginal productivity.

■ Idaho's Salmon River, a noted sport fishing river, has become the center of a thriving, well-promoted tourist trade. As the fishing pressure in the Salmon River has increased, the total number of fish caught has steadily increased; but the number of fish per person

THE SHAPE OF THE MARGINAL AND AVERAGE PRODUCT CURVES

The Law (Hypothesis) of Diminishing Returns

The variations in output that result from applying more or less of a variable factor to a given quantity of a fixed factor are the subject of a famous economic hypothesis. Usually it is called the **law of diminishing returns.**

The hypothesis states that if increasing amounts of a variable factor are applied to a given amount of a fixed factor, eventually a situation will be reached in which each additional unit of the variable factor adds less to total product than did the previous unit.

The common sense of diminishing marginal product is that the fixed factor limits the amount of additional output that can be realized by adding more of the variable factor. The hypothesis of diminishing returns predicts only that sooner or later the *MP* curve will decline. It is conceivable that marginal returns might diminish from

fishing has decreased, and the average hours fished for each fish caught has increased. The average weight of the fish caught has remained the same.

■ Gallup, Roper, and all other pollsters, as well as all students of statistics, know that you can use a sample to estimate characteristics of a very large population. Even a relatively small sample can provide a useful estimate—at a tiny fraction of the cost of a complete enumeration of the population. However, sample estimates are subject to *sampling error*. If, for example, 38 percent of a sample approves of a certain policy, the percentage of the population that approves of it is likely to be close to 38 percent, but it might well be anywhere from 36 to 40 percent. The theory of statistics shows that the size of the expected sampling error can always be reduced by increasing the sample size. The 4 percent interval (in the example above) could be cut in half—to 2 percent—by *quadrupling* the sample size. That is, if the original sample had been 400, a new sample of 1,600 would halve the expected error. To reduce the interval to 1 percent, the new sample would have to be quadrupled again—to 6,400. In other words, there are diminishing marginal returns to sample size.

■ During World War II decisions had to be made repeatedly concerning how many bombs to drop on a particular military target. Given the scarcity of bombs and bombers, an overbombing of one site would have an opportunity cost: it would leave other targets untouched. Consider the bombing of a German steel mill. The first bomb, even if it were a direct hit, could not knock out the factory; thus, if the goal was to stop steel production, the amount of effective damage would be expected to increase with further bombs. Eventually, when the operation of the steel plant had been crippled, additional bombs, while adding to the problems of resuming production, would surely have less marginal effect than earlier ones because much of their force would only redistribute the rubble from earlier hits.

■ An oldtime Texas rancher interviewed in a television documentary, *The New Dust Bowl?*, denied vehemently that there was a serious water problem in his state. "The water's there, just like it's always been," he said. "Get yourself a rig and start drilling. Either you'll hit oil, in which case you'll forget about water, or you'll find water. I've been doing it for 30 years. Used to hit water at 12 to 18 feet; now it's more like 70 to 80 feet, but it's there just the same."

the outset, so that the first unit of labor contributes most to total production and each successive unit contributes less than the previous unit. (This is the case in what is known as the Cobb-Douglas production function.) It is also possible for the marginal product to rise at first and decline later.[3] The reason is clear when seen in the context of the organization of production.

Consider the use of a variable number of workers in a manufacturing operation. If there is only one worker, that worker must do all the tasks, shifting from one to another and becoming competent in each. As a second, third, and subsequent workers are added it is often possible to break the tasks into a large number of separate jobs, with each laborer specializing in one job and becoming expert at it. This process is called the *division of labor*. If additional workers permit more and more efficient divisions of labor, marginal product will be rising. This may go on for some time, but (according to the hypothesis

[3] Thus what is called the law of diminishing marginal returns might more accurately be described as the law of eventually diminishing returns.

of diminishing returns) the scope for such economies must eventually disappear and sooner or later the marginal products of additional workers must decline. When this happens each additional worker will increase total output by less than the previous worker increased it. This sort of case is the one illustrated in Figure 12-1, where marginal product rises at first and then declines. Eventually marginal product may reach zero and even decline. It is not hard to see why, when you consider the extreme case where there are so many workers in a limited space that additional workers simply get in the way.

The hypothesis is usually described in terms of diminishing marginal returns, but it can equally well be stated in terms of diminishing average returns. The law of diminishing *average* returns states that if increasing quantities of a variable factor are applied to a given quantity of fixed factors, the average product of the variable factor will eventually decrease. [15]

The Significance of the Law of Diminishing Returns

There is a great deal of empirical confirmation of both diminishing marginal and diminishing average returns. (Some examples are reflected in the box.) One might, however, wish that it were not so. The consequence of diminishing returns is easily seen in a single example. If the hypothesis were not true, there would be no reason to fear that the world population explosion will bring with it a food crisis. If the marginal product of additional workers applied to a fixed quantity of land were constant, then world food production could be expanded in proportion to the population merely by keeping a constant fraction of the population on farms. But with fixed techniques, the hypothesis of diminishing returns predicts an inexorable decline in the marginal product of each additional laborer because an expanding population has a fixed world supply of agricultural land. Thus, unless there is a continual improvement in the techniques of production, continuous population growth will bring with it,

according to the hypothesis of diminishing returns, declining average living standards and eventually widespread famine.

This was the gloomy prediction of the early nineteenth century English economist Thomas Malthus. No wonder economics was popularly known at the time as the dismal science!

The Relation Between Marginal and Average Curves

Notice that in Figure 12-1(ii) the *MP* curve cuts the *AP* curve at the latter's maximum point. Although the relation between marginal and average curves is a mathematical one and not a matter of economics, it is important to understand how these curves are related [16]

The average product curve slopes upward as long as the marginal product curve is above it; it makes no difference whether the marginal curve is itself sloping upward or downward. The common sense of this relation is that if an additional worker is to raise the average product of all workers, his or her output must be greater than the average output of all other workers. It is immaterial whether the new worker's contribution to output is greater or less than the contribution of the worker hired immediately before; all that matters is that his or her contribution to output exceeds the average output of *all* workers hired previously. (The relation between marginal and average measures is further illustrated in the box about Ted Williams.)

SHORT-RUN VARIATIONS IN COST

We now shift our attention from the firm's production function to its costs. We consider firms that are not in a position to influence the prices of the factors of production they employ. These firms must pay the going market price for all factors.[4] Given the prices paid for factors and the

---

[4] The important problems that arise when the firm is in a position to influence the prices it pays for its factors of production are considered in Chapter 21.

The Batting Average of Ted Williams: Marginal and Lifetime

The relationship between "marginal" and "average" concepts is very general. An illuminating example comes from the *Baseball Encyclopedia*. The table gives the batting average (number of hits — output — divided by official times at bat — input) of Ted Williams over his illustrious career with the Boston Red Sox. For each year, column 2 gives his batting average for his whole major-league career before that year. It is his lifetime average on opening day. Column 3 gives his average during the current, or "marginal," year.

Whenever his current year average is above the lifetime-to-date average, the latter rises. See, for example, 1941, 1948, and 1957. Whenever his current year is below the lifetime, the latter falls. See, for example, 1946, 1950, and 1959. This is true whether the marginal itself is rising or falling. For example, both 1950 and 1951 were below average years for Williams and lowered his average, even though 1951 was better than the previous year had been (marginal rising) and 1950 was worse than the previous year had been (marginal falling). *If the average is to fall, all*

that matters is that the marginal is below the average.

Year	(1) Games played	(2) Lifetime batting average on opening day	(3) Batting average during year
1939	149	.000	.327
1940	144	.327	.344
1941	143	.335	.406
1942	150	.359	.356
1943–45*	0	.358	—
1946	150	.358	.342
1947	156	.355	.343
1948	137	.353	.369
1949	155	.355	.343
1950	89	.354	.317
1951	148	.351	.318
1952–53*	43	.348	.406
1954	117	.350	.345
1955	98	.349	.356
1956	136	.350	.345
1957	132	.349	.388
1958	129	.352	.328
1959	103	.351	.254
1960	113	.346	.316
Lifetime	2292	.344	

*Military service

physical returns summarized by the product curves, the costs of different levels of output can be calculated.

Cost Concepts Defined

The following brief definitions of several cost concepts are closely related to the product concepts just introduced.

1. **Total cost** (*TC*) means the total cost of producing any given level of output. Total cost is divided into two parts, total fixed costs (*TFC*) and total variable costs (*TVC*). **Fixed costs** are those that do not vary with output; they will be

the same if output is 1 unit or 1 million units. These costs are also often referred to as "overhead costs" or "unavoidable costs." All costs that vary directly with output, rising as more is produced and falling as less is produced, are called **variable costs**. In the example of Table 12-1, since labor was the variable factor of production, the wage bill would be a variable cost. Variable costs are often referred to as "direct costs" or "avoidable costs."

2. **Average total cost** (*ATC*), also called **average cost** (*AC*), is the total cost of producing any given output divided by the number of units produced, or the cost per unit. *ATC* may be

TABLE 12–2
The Variation of Costs with Capital Fixed and Labor Variable

Labor (L)	Output (q)	Total cost ($)			Average cost ($ per unit)			Marginal cost (MC)
		Fixed (TFC)	Variable (TVC)	Total (TC)	Fixed (AFC)	Variable (AVC)	Total (ATC)	
0	0	100	0	100	—	—	—	
1	15	100	10	110	6.67	0.67	7.33	0.67
2	34	100	20	120	2.94	0.59	3.53	0.53
3	48	100	30	130	2.08	0.62	2.71	0.71
4	60	100	40	140	1.67	0.67	2.33	0.83
5	62	100	50	150	1.61	0.81	2.42	5.00

The relation of cost to level of output can be looked at in several different ways. These cost curves are computed from the product curves of Table 12–1, given the price of capital of $25 per unit and the price of labor of $10 per unit. Notice that the average curves are cost per unit of output. Thus, for example, the *ATC* of $3.53 arises because 34 units of output cost a total of $120. The marginal cost of $.71

shown in the next line is the increase in total cost of $10 associated with hiring one more laborer *divided by* the increase in output of 14 caused by employing one more laborer (output rises from 34 to 48).

For graphical purposes, marginal costs should be plotted midway in the interval over which they are computed. The *MC* of $0.71 would be plotted at output 41.

divided into **average fixed costs** (*AFC*) and **average variable costs** (*AVC*) in the same way that total costs were divided.

Although average *variable* costs may rise or fall as production is increased (depending on whether output rises more rapidly or more slowly than total variable costs), it is clear that average fixed costs decline continuously as output increases. A doubling of output always leads to a halving of fixed costs per unit of output. This is a process popularly known as "spreading one's overhead."

3. **Marginal cost** (*MC*), sometimes called **incremental cost,** is the increase in total cost resulting from raising the rate of production by 1 unit. Because fixed costs do not vary with output, marginal fixed costs are always zero. Therefore marginal costs are necessarily marginal variable costs, and a change in fixed costs will leave marginal costs unaffected. For example, the marginal cost of producing a few more potatoes by farming a given amount of land more intensively is the same, whatever the rent paid for the fixed amount of land. [17]

These three measures of cost are simply different ways of looking at a single phenomenon. They are mathematically interrelated.

Short-run Cost Curves

Take the production relationships in Table 12-1. Assume that the price of labor is $10 per unit and the price of capital is $25 per unit. The cost schedules computed for these values are shown in Table 12-2.[5]

Figure 12-2 plots cost curves that are similar in shape to those arising from the data in Table 12-2. Notice that the marginal cost curve cuts the *ATC* and *AVC* curves at their lowest points. This is another example of the relation (discussed above) between a marginal and an average curve. The *ATC* curve, for example, slopes downward as long as the marginal cost curve is below it; it makes no difference whether the marginal cost curve is itself sloping upward or downward.

In Figure 12-2 the average variable cost curve reaches a minimum and then rises. With fixed factor prices, when average product per worker is a maximum, average variable cost is a minimum. [18] The common sense of this proposition is that each additional worker adds the same

[5] If you do not see where any of the numbers come from, review Table 12-1 and the definitions of cost just given.

amount to cost but a different amount to output, and when output per worker is rising, the cost per unit of output must be falling – and vice versa.

The hypothesis of eventually diminishing average productivity implies eventually increasing average variable costs.

Short-run *ATC* curves are often drawn U-shaped. This reflects the assumptions that (1) average productivity is increasing when output is low but (2) at some level of output average productivity begins to fall fast enough to cause average variable costs to increase faster than average fixed costs fall. When this happens, *ATC* increases.

The Definition of Capacity

The output that corresponds to the minimum short-run average total cost is often called by economists and business people the **capacity** of the firm. Capacity, in this sense, is not an upper limit on what can be produced. Instead it is the largest output that can be produced without encountering rising average costs per unit. In the example of Figure 12-2(ii) capacity output is q_c units, but higher outputs can be achieved, provided the firm is willing to accept the higher per-unit costs that accompany output "above capacity." A firm producing with **excess capacity** is producing at an output smaller than the point of minimum average total cost.

FIGURE 12–2
Total, Average, and Marginal Cost Curves

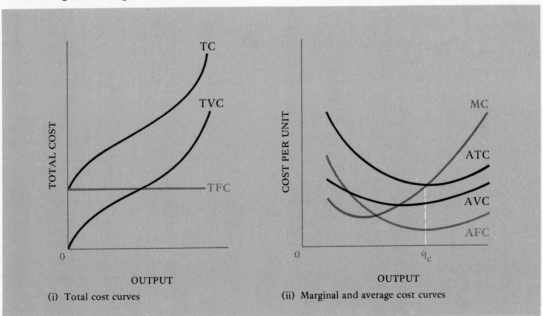

(i) Total cost curves

(ii) Marginal and average cost curves

TC, AC, and *MC* curves often have the shapes shown here. (i) Total fixed cost does not vary with output. Total variable cost and the total of all costs *(TC = TVC + TFC)* rise with output, first at a decreasing rate, then at an increasing rate. The total cost curves in (i) give rise to the average and marginal curves in (ii). *AFC* declines as output increases. *AVC* and *ATC* fall and then rise as output increases. *MC* does the same and intersects *ATC* and *AVC* at their minimum points. Capacity output is q_c, the minimum point on the *ATC* curve.

The technical definition gives the word "capacity" a meaning different from that in everyday speech, but the concept proves useful, and in any case it is widely used in economic and business discussions.

A Family of Short-run Cost Curves

A short-run cost curve shows how costs vary with output for a given quantity of the fixed factor—say a given size of plant.

There is a different short-run cost curve for each given quantity of the fixed factor.

A small plant for manufacturing nuts and bolts will have its own short-run cost curve. A medium-size plant and a very large plant will each have its own short-run cost curve. If a firm expands and replaces its small plant with a medium-size plant, it will move from one short-run cost curve to another. This change from one plant size to another is a long-run change. How short-run cost curves of plants of different size are related to each other is studied in the next chapter.

Summary

1. The firm's production decisions can be classified into three groups: (a) how best to employ existing plant and equipment (the short run); (b) what new plant and equipment and production processes to select, given the framework of known technical possibilities (the long run); and (c) what to do about encouraging, or merely adapting to, the invention of new techniques (the very long run).

2. The short run involves decisions in which one or more factors of production are fixed. The long run involves decisions in which all factors are variable, but in which technology is unchanged. In the very long run, technology can change.

3. The production function describes the ways in which different inputs may be combined to produce different quantities of output. Short-run and long-run situations can be interpreted as implying different kinds of constraints on the production function. In the short run, the firm is constrained to use no more than a given quantity of some fixed factor; in the long run, it is constrained only by the available techniques of production.

4. The theory of short-run cost behavior depends on the productivity of variable factors when applied to fixed factors. The concepts of total, average, and marginal product represent alternative ways of looking at the relation between output and the quantity of the variable factor of production.

5. The hypothesis, or "law," of eventually diminishing returns asserts that if increasing quantities of a variable factor are applied to a given quantity of fixed factors, the marginal product and the average product of the variable factor will eventually decrease. This hypothesis leads directly to implications of rising marginal and average costs.

6. Given physical productivity schedules and the costs per unit of factors, it is a simple matter of arithmetic to develop the whole family of short-run cost curves.

7. Short-run average total cost curves are drawn as U-shaped to reflect the expectation that average productivity increases for small outputs but eventually declines sufficiently rapidly to offset advantages of spreading overheads. The output corresponding to the minimum point of a short-run average total cost curve is called the plant's capacity.

8. There is a whole family of short-run cost curves, one for each quantity of the fixed factor.

Topics for Review

Short run, long run, and very long run
Marginal and average productivity
The hypothesis of diminishing returns
The relation between marginal and average curves
The relation between productivity and cost

Marginal cost and average cost
Capacity and excess capacity

Discussion Questions

1. Is the short run the same number of months for increasing output as for decreasing it? Must the short run in industry A be the same length for all firms in the industry? Under what circumstances might the short run actually involve a longer time span than even the very long run?
2. How would the following factors increase or reduce the relative importance of short-run decisions for management?
   a. a guaranteed annual employment contract of at least 48 40-hour weeks of work for all employees
   b. a major economic depression during which there is substantial unemployment of labor and in which equipment is being used at well below capacity levels of production
   c. a speeding up of delivery dates for new easy-to-install equipment
3. Indicate whether each of the following conforms to the hypothesis of diminishing returns; and, if so, whether it refers to marginal or average returns, or both.
   a. "The bigger they are, the harder they fall."
   b. As more and more of the population receive smallpox vaccinations, the reductions in the smallpox disease rate for each additional 100,000 vaccinations become smaller.

c. For the seventh year in a row, the average depth of drilling required to hit oil increased.
   d. Five workers produce twice as much today as ten workers did 40 years ago.
4. Consider the education of a human being as a process of production. Regard years of schooling as one variable factor of production. What are the other factors? What factors are fixed? At what point would you expect diminishing productivity to set in? For an Einstein would it set in during his lifetime?
5. Suppose that each of the following news items is correct. Discuss each in terms of its effects on the level of average total cost.
   a. The Ontario Ministry of Education reports that the increasing level of education of our youth has led both to higher productivity and to increases in the general level of wages.
   b. During the winter of 1977 many factories in the United States were forced by fuel shortages to reduce production and to operate at levels of production far below capacity.
   c. For the third year in a row, the Post Office's production exceeded its capacity.
   d. NASA reports that the space program has led to development of electronic devices that have brought innovations to many industries.
6. "Because overhead costs are fixed, increasing production lowers costs. Thus small business is sure to be inefficient. This is a dilemma of modern society which values both smallness *and* efficiency." Discuss.

Production, Substitution, and Productivity Increases: Cost in the Long and Very Long Run

13

While an analysis of the short-run behavior of the firm is important to an understanding of how markets work to allocate resources, it neglects the major sources that have led to high and rising standards of living for much of the world's population. In this chapter we turn to the firm's long-run behavior, when it is free to vary all factors of production. Should the firm adopt a technique that uses a great deal of capital and only a small amount of labor? Or should it adopt a technique that uses less capital and more labor? What implications will these decisions have for the firm's costs?

In the second part of the chapter we examine the improvements in techniques and productivity that so dramatically increased output and incomes in North America for more than 100 years but more recently have shown signs of a slowdown. The causes of the rapid growth and the present slowdown are subject to some debate; we shall discuss briefly what is known about them.

The Long Run: No Fixed Factors

The long run is a situation in which all factors can be varied. When this is the case, there are alternative ways of achieving the same total output, and it is necessary to choose among them. The long run is concerned with firms' planning how to design their plant and equipment for maximum profits.

The hypothesis of profit maximization provides a simple rule for doing this: Any firm that is trying to maximize its profits should select the method that produces its output at the lowest possible cost. This implication of the hypothesis of profit maximization is called the implication of **cost minimization.**

From the alternatives open to it, the firm chooses the least costly ways of achieving any specific output.

If there is a stable, required output rate, and if the costs of factors are known, that is all there is to it. In other words, the firm selects the economically efficient way of producing any level of output.

These long-run planning decisions are important because today's variable factors are tomorrow's fixed factors. A firm deciding on a new plant and the machinery to go into it will choose among many alternatives. But once installed, the new equipment is fixed for a long time. If the firm errs now, its survival may be threatened; if it estimates shrewdly and its rivals do not, it may reward both its owners and its foresighted managers with large profits and bonuses.

These decisions are among the most difficult and important the firm makes. They are difficult because the firm must anticipate what methods of production will be efficient not only today but in the years ahead, when costs of labor and raw materials may have changed. The decisions are difficult, too, because the firm must estimate how much output it will want to be producing. Is the industry of which it is a member growing or declining? Is it going to increase or decrease its share of the market? Will new products emerge to render its buggy whips less useful than an extrapolation of past sales suggests?

CONDITIONS FOR COST MINIMIZATION

What should the firm do to make its costs as low as possible? The firm does not have the least costly method of production if it is possible to substitute one factor for another so as to keep its output constant while reducing its total cost.

This idea can be stated more formally: The firm should substitute one factor (for example, capital) for another factor (for example, labor) as long as the marginal product of the one factor *per dollar expended on it* is greater than the marginal product of the other factor *per dollar expended on it*. The firm cannot have minimized its costs as long as these two magnitudes are unequal. Using K to represent capital, L labor, and p the price of a unit of the factor, the necessary condition of cost minimization may be stated:

$$\frac{MP_K}{p_K} = \frac{MP_L}{p_L} \qquad [1]$$

This equation is analogous to the condition for the utility-maximizing household, given on page 157, in which the household equated the marginal utility per dollar of two goods.[1]

To see why this equation needs to be satisfied if costs of production are really minimized, suppose that the left-hand side of [1] is equal to 10, showing that the last dollar spent on capital produced 10 units of output, while the right-hand side is equal to 4, showing that the last dollar spent on labor added only 4 units to output. In such a case, the firm, by using $2.50 less of labor, would reduce output by 10 units. But it could regain that lost output by spending $1 more on capital.[2] Making such a substitution of capital for labor would leave output unchanged and reduce cost by $1.50. Thus the original position was not the cost-minimizing one. Whenever the two sides of [1] are not equal, there are factor substitutions that will reduce costs.

By rearranging the terms in [1] we can look at the cost-minimizing condition a bit differently.

$$\frac{MP_K}{MP_L} = \frac{p_K}{p_L} \qquad [2]$$

The ratio of the marginal products on the left-

---

[1] In the section which begins on page 227, the condition is given a graphic analysis similar to that given household behavior in the second half of Chapter 9.

[2] The argument in the previous two sentences assumes that the marginal products do not change when expenditure is changed by a few dollars.

hand side compares the contribution to output of the last unit of capital and the last unit of labor. If the ratio is 4, this means 1 unit more of capital will add four times as much to output as one unit more of labor. The right-hand side shows how the cost of 1 unit more of capital compares to the cost of 1 unit more of labor. If it is also 4, it does not pay the firm to substitute capital for labor or vice versa. But suppose the right-hand side is 2. Capital, although twice as expensive, is four times as productive. It will pay the firm to switch to a method of production that uses more capital and less labor. If, however, the right-hand side is 6 (or *any* number more than 4), it will pay to substitute labor for capital.

This formulation shows how the firm can adjust the elements over which it has control (the quantities of factors used, and thus the marginal products of the factors) to the prices or opportunity costs of the factors given to it by the market. A precisely analogous adjustment process is involved when households adjust their consumption of goods to the market prices of those goods (see page 173).

THE PRINCIPLE OF SUBSTITUTION

Suppose that a firm is producing where the cost-minimizing conditions shown in [1] or [2] are met but that the cost of labor increases while the cost of capital remains unchanged. As we have just seen, the least-cost method of producing any output will now use less labor and more capital than was required to produce the same output before the factor prices changed. The prediction called the **principle of substitution** follows from the assumption that firms try to minimize their costs.

Methods of production will change if the relative prices of factors change. Relatively more of the cheaper factor will be used and relatively less of the more expensive one.

This prediction plays a central role in the way the market system allocates resources because it relates to the way the individual firm will respond to changes in relative factor prices. Such changes in relative factor prices are caused by the changing relative scarcity of factors to the economy as a whole. The individual firm is thus motivated to use less of factors that have become scarcer to the economy.[3]

The Significance of the Principle of Substitution to the Economy as a Whole

The relative prices of factors of production will tend to reflect their relative scarcities. One country has a great deal of land and a small population. Here the price of land will be low while, because labor is in short supply, the wage rate will be high. Producers of agricultural goods will tend to make lavish use of the cheap land while economizing on expensive labor; thus a production process will be adopted that utilizes a low ratio of labor to land.

A second country is small in area and has a large population. Here the demand for land will be high relative to its supply, and land will be relatively expensive while labor will be relatively cheap. Firms producing agricultural goods will tend to economize on land by using a great deal of labor per unit of land; thus a productive process will be adopted that uses a high ratio of labor to land.

Similar decisions will be made with respect to the relative scarcity of any factor. If capital is scarce relative to other factors, it will be expensive; firms following their own self-interest will use it sparingly. If capital is plentiful relative to other factors, it will be cheap and firms will adopt production processes that make lavish use of capital.

Thus relative factor prices will reflect the relative scarcities (in relation to demand) of different factors of production: abundant factors will have prices that are low relative to the prices of factors that are scarce. Firms seeking their own

[3] A numerical example of the principle of substitution is shown on page 198. As labor became relatively more expensive, moving from Case I to Case III, the firm shifted from method A, using much labor, to method D, using less labor.

private profit will be led to use large amounts of the factors that are plentiful in the country and to economize on factors that are scarce.

Once again we see that the price system is an automatic control system. No single firm needs to be aware of national factor surpluses and scarcities. Prices determined in the competitive market tend to reflect them, and individual firms that never look beyond their own private profit are nonetheless led to economize on factors that are scarce to the nation as a whole. Thus the price system leads profit-maximizing firms to take account of the nation's relative factor scarcities when deciding which of the possible methods of production to adopt.

This discussion suggests why methods of producing the same commodity differ among countries. In Canada, where labor is highly skilled and very expensive, a steel company may use elaborate machinery to economize on labor. In China, where labor is abundant and capital scarce, a much less mechanized method of production is appropriate. The Western engineer who believes that the Chinese lag behind Westerners because they are using methods long dismissed in the West as inefficient may be missing the truth about economic efficiency in use of resources. The frequent suggestion that to aid underdeveloped countries we only have to export Western "know-how" is incomplete.

COST CURVES IN THE LONG RUN

There is a best (least-cost) method of producing each level of output when all factors are free to be varied. In general this method will not be the same for different levels of output. If factor prices are given, a minimum cost can be found for each possible level of output and, if this minimum achievable cost is expressed as an amount per unit of output, we can obtain the long-run average cost of producing each level of output. When this information is plotted on a graph, the result is called a **long-run average cost curve** (*LRAC*). Figure 13-1 shows such a curve.

This long-run average cost curve is determined by the technology of the industry (which is assumed to be fixed) and by the prices of the factors of production. It is a "boundary" in the sense that points below the curve are unattainable, points on the curve are attainable if sufficient time elapses for all factors to be adjusted, and points above the curve are also attainable. Indeed, points above the *LRAC* curve may represent the best that can be done in the short run when all factors are not freely variable.

The *LRAC* curve divides the cost levels that are attainable with known technology and given factor prices from those that are unattainable.

The Shape of the Long-run Average Cost Curve

The long-run average cost curve shown in Figure 13-1 falls at first and then rises. This curve is often described as U-shaped, although "saucer-shaped" might be more descriptive.

Decreasing costs. Over the range of output from zero to q_m the firm has falling long-run average costs. An expansion of output results in a reduction of costs per unit of output once enough time has elapsed to allow adjustments in the techniques of production. Since the prices of factors are assumed to be constant, the reason for the decline in costs per unit must be that output increases faster than inputs as the scale of the firm's production expands. Over this range of output the firm is often said to enjoy long-run **increasing returns.**[4] Increasing returns may arise as a result of increased opportunities for specialization of tasks made possible by the division of labor even with no substitution of one factor of production for another. Or they may arise because of factor substitution. Even the most casual observation of the differences in production

---

[4] Economists shift back and forth between speaking in physical terms (i.e., increasing *returns* to production) and cost terms (i.e., decreasing *costs* of production). Thus the same firm may be spoken of as having decreasing costs or enjoying increasing returns.

FIGURE 13–1
A Long-run Average Cost Curve

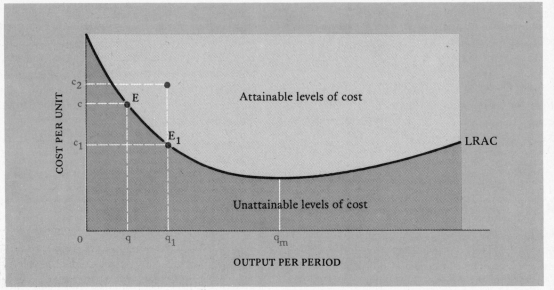

The long-run average cost curve provides a boundary between attainable and unattainable levels of cost. If the firm wishes to produce output q, the lowest attainable cost level is c per unit. Thus point E is on the *LRAC* curve. E_1 represents the least-cost method of producing q_1. Suppose a firm is producing at E and desires to increase output to q_1. In the short run it will not be able to vary all factors, and thus costs above c_1, say c_2, must be accepted. In the long run a plant optimal for output q_1 can be built and cost of c_1 can be attained. Output q_m is that at which the firm attains its lowest possible per unit cost of production for the given technology and factor prices.

technique used in large-size and small-size plants shows the differences in factor proportions. These differences arise because large, specialized equipment is useful only when the volume of output that the firm can sell justifies its employment.

For example, assembly line techniques, body-stamping machinery, and multiple-boring engine-block machines in automobile production are economically efficient only when individual operations are repeated thousands of times. Using elaborate harvesting equipment (which combines many individual tasks that would otherwise be done by hand and by tractor) provides the least-cost method of production on a big farm but not on a few acres.

Typically, as the level of planned output increases, capital is substituted for labor and complex machines for simpler machines. Automation is a contemporary example. Electronic devices can handle huge volumes of operations very quickly, but unless the level of production requires very large numbers of operations, it does not make sense to use automation.

Increasing costs. Over the range of outputs greater than q_m the firm encounters rising costs. An expansion in production, even after sufficient time has elapsed for all adjustments to be made, will be accompanied by a rise in average costs per unit of output. If costs per unit of input are constant, this rise in costs must be the result of an expansion in output less than in proportion to the expansion in inputs. Such a firm is said to suffer long-run **decreasing returns.**[5] Decreasing returns imply that the firm suffers some diseconomy of scale. As its scale of operations increases, diseconomies—of management or otherwise—are encountered that increase its per unit costs of production.

Lowest LRAC. At output q_m in Figure 13-1 the firm has reached its lowest possible long-run costs per unit of output. While every point on the *LRAC* is efficient in the sense that *that output* is not attainable at a lower cost per unit (given current technology and factor prices), the output q_m is efficient in a second sense: no other output can be produced at so low a cost. Under certain conditions, called those of perfect competition, each firm in equilibrium will produce at the minimum point on its *LRAC*. (See Chapter 14 and its appendix for a full discussion of this proposition.)

Constant returns. In Figure 13-1 the firm's long-run average costs fall to output q_m and rise thereafter. Another possibility should be noted: The firm's *LRAC* might have a flat portion over a range of output around q_m. With such a flat portion, the firm would be encountering constant costs over the relevant range of output. This would mean that the firm's average costs per unit of output were not changing as its output changed. Since factor prices are assumed to be fixed, this must mean that the firm's output is increasing exactly as fast as its inputs are increasing. Such a firm is said to be encountering **constant returns.**

THE RELATION BETWEEN LONG-RUN AND SHORT-RUN COSTS

The various short-run cost curves mentioned at the conclusion of Chapter 12 and the long-run

curve studied in this chapter are all derived from the same production function. Each assumes given prices for all factor inputs. In the long run, all factors can be varied; in the short run, some must remain fixed. The long-run average cost curve (*LRAC*) shows the lowest cost of producing any output when all factors are variable. The short-run average cost curve (*SRAC*) shows the lowest cost of producing any output when one or more factors is not free to vary.

The short-run cost curve cannot fall below the long-run curve because the *LRAC* curve represents the *lowest* attainable costs for every output. It might be the same curve if precisely the same size plant were the best for any level of output. But that is not likely. The usual situation is that as the level of output is increased, a larger plant makes it possible to lower unit costs. Thus a larger plant is required to achieve the lowest attainable costs. This is shown in Figure 13-2.

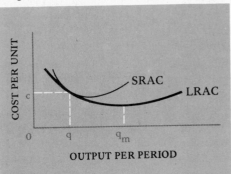

FIGURE 13-2
Long-run and Short-run Average Cost Curves

The short-run average cost curve is tangent to the long-run curve at the output for which the quantity of the fixed factors is optimal. If output is varied around *q* units with plant and equipment fixed at the optimal level for producing *q*, costs will follow the short-run cost curve. While *SRAC* and *LRAC* are at the same level for output *q*, since the fixed plant is optimal for that level, for all other outputs there is too little or too much of the fixed factor and *SRAC* lies above *LRAC*. If some output other than *q* is to be sustained, costs can be reduced to the level of the long-run curve when sufficient time has elapsed to adjust all factor inputs.

---

[5] Long-run decreasing returns differ from the short-run diminishing returns that we encountered earlier. In the short run at least one factor is fixed and the law of diminishing returns ensures that returns to the variable factor will eventually diminish. In the long run all factors are variable and it is possible that physically diminishing returns would never be encountered—at least as long as it was genuinely possible to increase inputs of all factors.

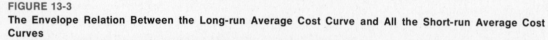

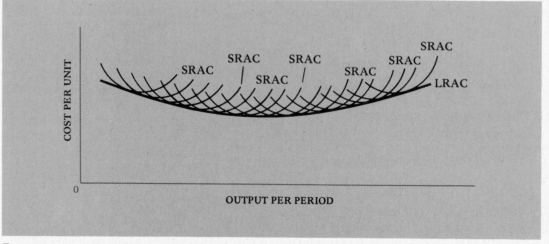

FIGURE 13-3
The Envelope Relation Between the Long-run Average Cost Curve and All the Short-run Average Cost Curves

To every point on the long-run cost curve there is an associated short-run curve tangent at that point. Each short-run curve shows how costs vary if output varies, with the fixed factor held constant at the level that is optimal for the output at the point of tangency.

We saw at the end of Chapter 12 that a *SRAC* curve such as that in Figure 13-2 is one of many such curves. Each curve shows how costs vary as output is varied from a base output, holding some factors fixed at the quantities most appropriate to the base output (see Figure 13-3). The long-run curve is sometimes called an **envelope curve** because it encloses the whole family of short-run curves. Each short-run cost curve is tangent to (touches) the long-run curve at the level of output for which the quantity of the fixed factor is optimal and lies above it for all other levels of output.

SHIFTS IN COST CURVES

The cost curves derived so far show how cost varies with output, given constant factor prices and fixed technology. Changes in either technological knowledge or factor prices will cause the entire family of short-run and long-run cost curves to shift. Loss of existing technological knowledge is rare, so technological change normally works in only one direction, to shift cost curves downward. Improved ways of making existing commodities will mean that lower cost methods of production become available. Technological change is discussed later in this chapter.

Factor price changes can exert an influence in either direction. If a firm has to pay more for any factor that is uses, the cost of producing each level of output will rise; if the firm has to pay less, costs will fall.

A rise in factor prices shifts the family of short-run and long-run cost curves upward. A fall in factor prices or a technological advance shifts the entire family of cost curves downward.

Although factor prices usually change gradually, they sometimes rise suddenly and drastically. This was the case in the seventies. One reason was the sharp general inflation that beset the Canadian economy; a second reason was the sudden and dramatic increase in energy prices that was triggered by the rise in the price of oil following the formation of OPEC.

World oil prices quadrupled within a year and

had increased tenfold by the end of the decade; while Canadian oil prices did not keep pace, they nevertheless rose substantially. (See the discussion in Chapter 27.) The effect of this was to shift upward the cost curves of all users. The size of the shift varied from product to product, depending on how important particular inputs were to total production. Oil price increases had some effects on almost all industries, and they had a major effect on such industries as synthetic rubber, plastics, and airlines.

ISOQUANTS: AN ALTERNATIVE ANALYSIS OF THE FIRM'S INPUT DECISIONS[6]

The production function gives the relation between the factor inputs that the firm uses and the output that it obtains. In the long run the firm can choose among many different combinations of

TABLE 13-1
Alternative Methods of Producing 6 Units of Output: Points on an Isoquant

Method	K	L	ΔK	ΔL	Rate of substitution ΔK/ΔL
a	18	2			
b	12	3	−6	1	−6.0
c	9	4	−3	1	−3.0
d	6	6	−3	2	−1.5
e	4	9	−2	3	−0.67
f	3	12	−1	3	−0.33
g	2	18	−1	6	−0.17

An isoquadrant describes the firm's alternative methods for producing a given output. The table lists some of the methods indicated by a production function as being available to produce 6 units of output. The first combination uses a great deal of capital (*K*) and very little labor (*L*). Moving down the table, labor is substituted for capital in such a way as to keep output constant. Finally, at the bottom, most of the capital has been replaced by labor. The rate of substitution between the two factors is calculated in the last three columns of the table. Note that as we move down the table, the absolute value of the rate of substitution declines.

[6] The material in this section can be omitted without loss of continuity.

inputs that will yield it the same output. The production function and the choices open to the firm can be given a graphical representation using the concept of an isoquant.

A Single Isoquant

Table 13-1 gives a hypothetical illustration of those combinations of two inputs (labor and capital) that will each serve to produce a given quantity of output. The data from Table 13-1 are plotted in Figure 13-4. A smooth curve is drawn through the points to indicate that there are addi-

FIGURE 13-4
An Isoquant for Output of Six Units*

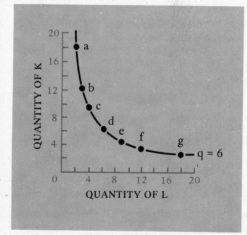

Isoquants are downward-sloping and convex. The downward slope reflects the requirement of technological efficiency. A method that uses more of one factor must use less of the other factor if it is to be technologically efficient. The convex shape of the isoquant reflects a diminishing marginal rate of substitution. Starting from point *a*, which uses relatively little labor and much capital, and moving to point *b*, 1 additional unit of labor can substitute for 6 units of capital (while holding production constant). But from *b* to *c*, 1 unit of labor substitutes for only 3 units of capital. The geometrical expression of this is that moving along the isoquant to the right, the slope of the isoquant becomes flatter.

* The lettered points are plotted from the data in Table 13-1.

tional ways, not listed in the table, of producing 6 units.

This curve is called an **isoquant.** It shows the whole set of technologically efficient possibilities for producing a given level of output – 6 units in this example.[7] It is analogous both to the contour line on a map that shows all points of equal altitude and to an indifference curve that shows all combinations of commodities that yield an equal utility.

As we move from one point on an isoquant to another we are *substituting one factor for another* while holding output constant. If we move from point *b* to point *c*, we are substituting 1 unit of labor for 3 units of capital. The **marginal rate of substitution** measures the rate at which one factor is substituted for another with output held constant. Graphically the marginal rate of substitution is measured by the slope of the isoquant at a particular point. Table 13-1 shows the calculation of some rates of substitution between various points of the isoquant. [19]

The marginal rate of substitution is related to the marginal products of the factors of production. To see how, consider an example. Assume that at the present level of inputs of labor and capital the marginal product of a unit of labor is 2 units of output while the marginal product of capital is 1 unit of output. If the firm reduces its use of capital and increases its use of labor to keep output constant, it needs to add only one-half unit of labor for one unit of capital given up. If, at another point on the isoquant with more labor and less capital, the marginal products are 2 for capital and 1 for labor, then the firm will have to add two units of labor for every unit of capital it gives up. The general proposition is:

The marginal rate of substitution is equal to the ratios of the marginal products of the two factors of production.

Isoquants satisfy two important conditions:

they are downward-sloping and they are convex viewed from the origin.[8] What is the economic meaning of each of these conditions?

The downward slope indicates that each factor input has a positive marginal product. If the input of one factor is reduced and that of the other is held constant, output will be reduced. Thus, if one input is decreased, production can only be held constant if the other factor input is increased. The marginal rate of substitution has a negative value: Increases in one factor must be balanced by decreases in the other factor if output is to be held constant.

To understand convexity, consider what happens as the firm moves along the isoquant of Figure 13-4 downward and to the right. Labor is being added and capital reduced so as to keep output constant. If labor is added in increments of exactly one unit, how much capital may be dispensed with each time? The key to the answer is that both factors are assumed to be subject to the law of diminishing returns. Thus the gain in output associated with each additional unit of labor added is *diminishing* while the loss of output associated with each additional unit of capital forgone is *increasing*. It therefore takes ever-smaller reductions in capital to compensate for equal increases in labor. This implies that the isoquant is convex viewed from the origin.

An Isoquant Map

The isoquant of Figure 13-4 referred to 6 units of output. There is another isoquant for 7 units, another for 7,000 units, and a different one for every rate of output. Each isoquant refers to a specific output and connects alternative combinations of factors that are technologically efficient methods of achieving that output. If we plot a representative set of these isoquants on a single graph, we obtain an **isoquant map** like that in Figure 13-5. The higher the level of output

---

[7] This is an example of graphing a three-variable function in two dimensions. See page 169 for another illustration.

[8] The same two basic conditions are satisfied by the indifference curves of consumer theory.

FIGURE 13-5
An Isoquant Map

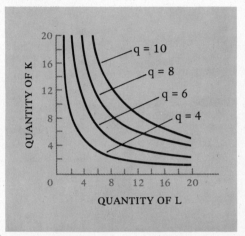

An isoquant map shows a set of isoquants, one for each level of output. The figure shows four isoquants drawn from the production function and corresponding to 4, 6, 8, and 10 units of production.

firm. The higher the level of expenditure, the farther the isocost line is from the origin.

In Figure 13-7 the isoquant and isocost maps are brought together. The economically most efficient method of production must be a point on an isoquant that just touches (i.e., is tangent to) an isocost line. If the isoquant cuts the isocost line, it is possible to move along the isoquant and reach a lower level of cost. Only at a point of tangency is a movement in either direction along the isoquant a movement to a higher cost level. The lowest attainable cost of producing 6 units is $24. This cost level can be achieved only by operating at *A,* the point where the $24 isocost line is tangent to the 6-unit isoquant. The lowest average cost of producing 6 units is thus $24/6/ = $4 per unit of output.

The least-cost position is given graphically by the tangency point between the isoquant and the isocost lines.

along a particular isoquant, the further away from the origin it will be.

Isoquants and the Conditions for Cost Minimization

Finding the efficient way of producing any output requires finding the least-cost factor combination. To find this combination when both factors are variable, factor prices need to be known. Suppose, to continue the example, that capital is priced at $4 per unit and labor at $1. In Chapter 9 a budget line was used to show the alternative combinations of goods a household could buy; here an **isocost line** is used to show alternative combinations of factors a firm can buy for a given outlay. Four different isocost lines appear in Figure 13-6. The slope of each reflects *relative* factor prices, just as the slope of the budget line in Chapter 9 represented relative product prices. For given factor prices a series of parallel isocost lines will reflect the alternative levels of expenditure on factor purchases that are open to the

FIGURE 13-6
Isocost Lines

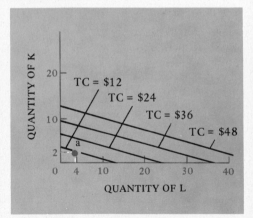

Each isocost line shows alternative factor combinations that can be purchased for a given outlay. The graph shows the four isocost lines that result when labor costs $1 a unit and capital $4 a unit and expenditure is held constant at $12, $24, $36, and $48 respectively. The line labeled *TC* = $12 represents all combinations of the two factors that the firm could buy for $12. Point *a* represents 2 units of *K* and 4 units of *L*.

FIGURE 13-7
The Determination of the Least-cost Method of Output

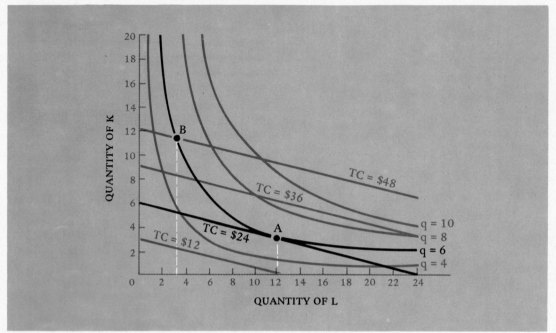

Least-cost methods are represented by points of tangency, such as **A**, between isoquant and isocost lines. The isoquant map of Figure 13-5 and the isocost map of Figure 13-6 are brought together. Consider point *A*. It is on the 6-unit isoquant and the $24 isocost line. Thus it is possible to achieve the output *q* = 6 for a total cost of $24. There are other ways to achieve this output, for example at point *B*, where *TC* = $48. Moving along the isoquant from point *A* in either direction increases cost. Similarly, moving along the isocost line from point *A* in either direction lowers output. Thus either move would raise cost per unit.

Notice that point *A* in Figure 13-7 indicates not only the lowest level of cost for 6 units of output but also the highest level of output for $24 of cost.[9]

The slope of the isocost line is given by the ratio of the prices of the two factors of production. The slope of the isoquant is given by the ratio of their marginal products. When the firm reaches its least-cost position, it has equated the price ratio (which is given to it by the market prices) with the ratio of the marginal products (which it can adjust by varying the proportions in which it hires the factors). In symbols,

$$\frac{MP_K}{MP_L} = \frac{p_K}{p_L}$$

This is equation [2] on page 221. We have now derived this result by use of the isoquant analysis of the firm's decisions. **[20]**

Isoquants and the Principle of Substitution

Suppose that with technology unchanged—that is, with the isoquant map fixed—the price of one factor changes. Suppose that with the price of capital unchanged at $4 per unit, the price of labor rises from $1 to $4 per unit. Originally, the efficient factor combination of producing 6 units

[9] Thus we find the same solution if we set out *either* to minimize the cost of producing 6 units of output *or* to maximize the output that can be obtained for $24. One problem is said to be the "dual" of the other.

was 12 units of labor and 3 units of capital. It cost $24. To produce that same output in the same way would now cost $60 at the new factor prices. Figure 13-8 shows why that is not efficient: The slope of the isocost line has changed, which makes it efficient to substitute the now relatively cheaper capital for the relatively more expensive labor.

This illustrates the principle of substitution:

Changes in relative factor prices will cause a partial replacement of factors that have become relatively more expensive by factors that have become relatively cheaper.

Of course, substitution of capital for labor cannot fully offset the effects of a rise in cost of labor, as Figure 13-8(i) shows. Consider the output attainable for $24. In the figure there are two isocost lines representing $24 of outlay—at the old and new price of labor. The new isocost line

for $24 lies everywhere inside the old one (except where no labor is used). The isocost line must therefore be tangent to a lower isoquant. This means that if production is to be held constant, higher costs must be accepted—but because of substitution it is not necessary to accept costs as high as would accompany an unchanged factor proportion. In the example 6 units can be produced for $48 rather than the $60 that would have been required if no change in factor proportions had been made.

This leads to the predictions that:

A rise in the price of one factor with all other factor prices constant will (1) shift upward the cost curve of commodities that use that factor and (2) lead to a substitution of factors that are now relatively cheaper for the factor whose price has risen.

Both predictions were stated earlier in this

FIGURE 13-8

The Effects of a Change in Factor Prices on Costs and Factor Proportions

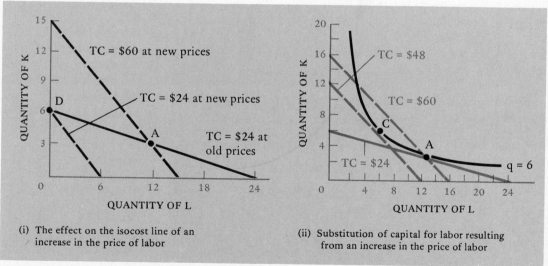

(i) The effect on the isocost line of an increase in the price of labor

(ii) Substitution of capital for labor resulting from an increase in the price of labor

An increase in the price of labor pivots the isocost line inward and thus increases the cost of producing any output. It also changes the slope of the isocost line and thus changes the least-cost method of producing. (i) The rise in price of L from $1 to $4 a unit (price of K constant at $4) pivots the TC line inward. Any output previously produced for $24 will cost more at the new prices if it used any amount of labor. The new cost of producing A rises from $24 to $60. (ii) The steeper isocost line is tangent to the isoquant at C, not A. Costs at C are higher than they were before the price increase but not as high as if the factor substitution had not occurred.

chapter; now they have been derived formally using the isoquant technique.

The Very Long Run: Progress and Productivity

Three sets of changes in the very long run tend to dominate the production function. All are related to technology, broadly defined. The first is the change in the techniques available for producing existing products. Over an average person's lifetime, these changes often can be dramatic. Seventy years ago roads and railways were built by gangs of workers using buckets, spades, and draft horses; today bulldozers, steam shovels, giant trucks, and other specialized equipment have completely banished the workhorse from construction sites and to a great extent have displaced the worker with his shovel. Indeed, the pace of general mechanization has been so fast that within the space of one lifetime, humanity's more than 4,000-year partnership with the horse in war and peace all but came to an end. About the same amount of coal is produced today as 50 years ago, but the number of coal miners is less than one-tenth of what is was then.

Second is the change in new goods and services that become available. Television, polio vaccine, nylon clothing, and many other consumer products of today did not exist two generations ago. Other products are so changed that their nominal connection with the "same" commodity produced in the past is meaningless. A 1981 Ford automobile is very different from a 1931 Ford. Modern jets such as the jumbo 747, the new 787, and the supersonic Concorde are each revolutionary compared with the DC-3, which itself barely resembled the *Spirit of St. Louis.* In their first year of operation, 100 Boeing 747s logged passenger miles that would have required a fleet of 23,000 DC-3s.

Third, improvements in such things as health and education improve the quality of labor services. Today's managers and workers are in better health and are better clothed and better housed than their counterparts in their grandparents' generation. On the average they are better educated. Even unskilled workers today tend to be literate and competent in arithmetic, and their managers are apt to be trained in modern scientific methods of business control.

These kinds of technological change have been vital features of the so-called developed (or industrialized) countries. Recently there has been evidence of a slowdown in the rate of technological change. To understand either the historical growth or the recent slowdown, it is necessary to understand the forces that affect technological change. Is it influenced significantly by the decisions of firms? Is it encouraged or discouraged significantly by government policies and external events? Answers to these questions are vital to an understanding of the long-run story of production and cost.

THE NATURE AND SIGNIFICANCE OF PRODUCTIVITY

In discussing these issues, it is not helpful simply to discuss the cost of a well-defined unit of a well-defined product. Measuring output and cost in a world of changing products is hard and involves a serious index number problem.[10] Economists utilize the notion of **productivity,** defined as a measure of output per unit of resource input, instead of simply the cost of a unit of output. This does not resolve the difficulties of measuring output, but it shifts the attention to society's ability to get more and better output out of the basic resources of the economy. One widely used measure of productivity is output per worker.[11] Labor is taken as representative of the economy's basic resources because we are a society of people and we value our leisure. There is enough year-to-year stability in the nature of products produced that rates of increase in productivity year by year provide measures of progress caused by technical change.

[10] See page 32 for a discussion of index numbers.
[11] It is the measure we shall use. Other possible measures include output per hour of labor and output per person.

FIGURE 13-9
Productivity Growth in Canada, Selected Periods, 1947–1980

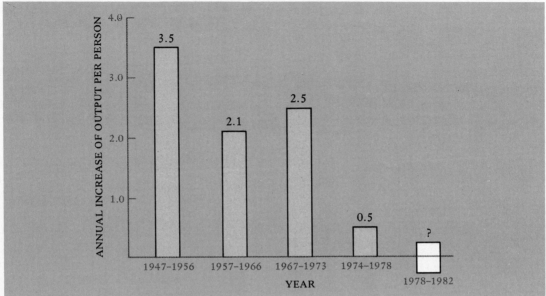

The historical rate of growth of productivity of almost 3 percent per year has declined sharply since 1973. Each bar shows the average annual increase in output per employed person over the period indicated. Until 1973 such productivity increases were usually be-tween 2 and 3.5 percent. They fell to .5 percent over the period 1974–1978, and provisional estimates suggest that productivity actually fell during 1979 and early 1980.

Productivity increases are a potent force for increasing living standards. In Canada there is no doubt that over the last 100, 50, or even 20 years, the material standard of living of the typical family has increased enormously. Indeed, our great-grandparents would have regarded today's standard of living in most industrialized countries as unattainable (if not incomprehensible).

Figure 13-9 shows the average increases in productivity in Canada over the recent past. The apparently modest rate of increase of output per worker of 2 percent per year leads to a doubling of output per worker every 35 years. Productivity in North America increased at more than this rate over the past 100 years. On average, since World War II productivity growth in Canada has been nearly 3 percent per year, a rate that doubles output per worker every 23 years.

In other countries the rate of growth has been higher. In Germany productivity increased at 5 percent per year, doubling output every 14 years, and in Japan it has increased at more than 9 percent per year—a rate that doubles output per worker approximately every 8 years! In many countries productivity growth at a stable rate came to be taken for granted, to be expected. Productivity growth was not something to be worried about but to be counted on.

When productivity growth in Canada dropped sharply after 1973, it caused surprise and some alarm. During 1978 productivity did not increase appreciably, and that did nothing to alleviate fears that the days of substantial automatic increases in productivity were past.

Why do we care about productivity growth? If there is less productivity growth with the same level of employment, the rate of increase of real output declines. Combined with declining employment, it may actually contribute to declining output per person. Decreases in rates of productivity growth can also add to inflationary pressures. In recent decades Canadians have come to expect to receive the gains in productivity in the form of wage and profit increases. If productivity increases at 4 percent per year, factor prices can increase 4 percent per year on average without leading to price increases. But the same factor price increases become inflationary once productivity growth falls below that level.

MAJOR SOURCES OF INCREASING PRODUCTIVITY

The decline in the historical rate of productivity growth has led to a good deal of research into the causes of productivity changes.

Productivity is defined as output per hour worked. Thus anything that increases output while keeping hours worked the same, or that decreases the hours required to attain the same output, increases productivity. Several major historical sources of productivity increase have been identified.

Energy Substitution

One principal means has been the increasing reliance on inanimate energy for production. Energy to plow fields, to turn machines, to move goods, to provide heat, and to transform natural resources is a major determinant of the productive power of an economy. In 1900 more than half of all energy requirements was supplied by human beings, horses, mules, and oxen. By 1980 animal and human power provided less than 10 percent of all energy; it has been increasingly replaced by such inanimate sources of power as coal, oil, gas, and water power. Total energy from these fuels increased by much more than did population over the first seven decades of this century. This reflected the development of new methods for substituting relatively cheap energy for relatively expensive labor.

This source of the historical trend toward ever-increasing energy substitution cannot be expected to continue as energy becomes relatively scarce and therefore relatively more expensive. Just as falling energy costs led to rapidly rising productivity, rising energy costs may be expected to slow the productivity increase. Much of the future of energy substitution will depend on the effectiveness of policies designed to discover new and cheaper sources of fuel.

Substitution of Capital for Labor

A major means of increasing productivity has been the substitution of machinery and equipment for labor. In manufacturing, transportation, communications, and mining, the process of substitution of capital for labor is so obvious that we need only mention it. It has been large also in agriculture and in some services. This substitution can be measured by changes in the amount of capital per worker, which has steadily increased over the last 100 years and has been accompanied by increasing productivity.

Three motives for this substitution can be identified. The first is the rising price of labor relative to capital goods. The second is the development of new, improved (i.e., more productive) machines to replace older ones. The third is the opportunity provided by population growth, and by growth in demand, to utilize more capital to take advantage of economies of the larger scale that growth fosters.

As industrialization proceeds, the opportunities for the substitution of capital for labor naturally decline somewhat simply because there is less and less labor left to substitute for. At the extreme, once a process is fully automated, no further substitution is possible.

Improved Characteristics of Labor

While an "hour of work" is a readily measurable unit of human labor effort and is thus a convenient yardstick for measuring productivity, the things a human being can do in one hour vary greatly. One individual's contribution to the level of output in a single hour will depend on his or her health, education, and training. Over the last 100 years the level of these things in the population (and therefore in the work force) has steadily increased and has led to continuing increases in the productivity of labor. Because of their beneficial effects on production, expenditures on health, education, and training are sometimes spoken of as investments in human capital.

The effective use of an individual's labor skills requires that they be available in the right place at the right time. A skilled mechanic may be needed in Kamloops, but if he or she is trapped by education, ill health, or poverty in Oshawa, neither the individual nor the national product will benefit. Education and health are now known to increase the adaptability and mobility of labor between jobs, occupations, and places—and thus to contribute indirectly as well as directly to rising productivity.

Other Sources of Productivity Increase

While the three sources just described have all been major contributors to productivity increases in virtually every industrializing society, there are dozens of other, individually smaller yet cumulatively large sources of increasing productivity. Let us name two.

One is the increase in the quality of many nonlabor inputs into production. For example, the kind and quality of metals has changed: steel replaces iron and aluminum substitutes for steel in a process of change that makes a statistical category such as "primary metals" seem unsatisfactory and obsolete. Even for a given category, such as "steel," today's product is lighter, stronger, and more flexible than the product manufactured only 15 years ago.

Another secondary source of productivity increases may be described as managerial. Better organization of production will in itself account for increases in productivity. New ideas raise efficiency when they are applied to new products or new processes. Imagination can design a more efficient assembly line with no change in the quantity, quality, or proportions of factors.

INVENTION

Invention is the discovery of something new, such as a new production technique or a new product. **Innovation** is the introduction of an invention into use. Invention is a necessary precondition to innovation.

Invention is cumulative; a useful invention is used, a useless one is discarded. Except where whole societies disappear, knowledge is seldom lost, and the state of technical knowledge improves or stays the same. For this reason, the cumulative impact of many small inventions may be fully as large as or larger than that of the occasional dramatic invention such as the steam engine, the cotton gin, or the sewing machine. Indeed, none of these famous inventions burst into full bloom as a result of a single act of creative inspiration; each depended on the contributions of prior inventors. The backlog of past inventions constitutes society's technical knowledge, and in turn it conditions innovation.

To understand innovation and productivity increases, then, we must first understand what creates the pool of inventions from which innovation will occur. While there are many motives that spur invention, there is no longer any doubt that major changes in the store of technical knowledge are the result of expenditures on research and development (R&D) by private firms, by the government, and by scholars and scientists in universities and other nonprofit and nongovernmental research institutions.

Money can buy invention. In the United States in 1980, about $50 billion was devoted to R&D expenditures, of which roughly 40 percent was expended by the federal government, 40 percent in private industry, and the rest in universities and other places. Among the corporate research centers are such giants as AT&T's Bell Labs (with 17,000 employees) and the research centers of IBM and General Electric in New York and Texas Instruments in Texas.

Foreign Investment and the Level of R&D Expenditure in Canada

Canada ranks lower than most other industrial nations in the proportion of GNP it spends on research and development, and one reason often cited for this is the extensive foreign ownership of Canadian industry. What are the evidence and the theory regarding the influence of foreign investment on R&D expenditure?

The evidence suggests that R&D expenditure is low for *all* companies in the Canadian economy, both foreign and domestically owned. A commonly heard argument is that "small" Canadian markets allow only low-volume production in Canada and that the small scale cannot support the high cost of R&D. Is there a relationship between these factors and foreign ownership? Does foreign ownership imply a further reduction in R&D expenditure relative to the already below-average R&D expenditure of Canadian-owned firms?

Economic theory does not suggest a definite relationship between foreign ownership and R&D expenditure. On the one hand, foreign-owned subsidiaries may do less R&D than domestic firms because there are economies-of-scale in research that cause parent companies to keep their research at home. On the other hand, foreign-owned subsidiaries might do *more* research than Canadian-owned firms because as multinationals they can afford R&D that small Canadian firms cannot. True, subsidiaries do less research than their parents; but the question remains, do foreign subsidiaries do less research than Canadian companies?

Professor A. E. Safarian of the University of Toronto, in the first significant research on the topic in the mid 1960s, could find no relationship between foreign ownership and R&D in Canada. More recent work under Professor Richard Caves of Harvard University has found a *positive* relationship between foreign ownership and R&D. However, the direction of causality in this relationship is not clear. Firms in industries that by nature involve high R&D expenditure are more likely to engage in foreign investment than are firms in low

In Canada, R&D expenditure represents only about half as large a proportion of GNP as it does in other industrialized countries; moreover, this proportion fell from about 1.3 in 1967 to about 0.9 in 1977. The federal government accounts for only about 11 percent of R&D expenditure in Canada. One reason why both government and total R&D expenditure is so low is the relatively small role played by the military in Canada. A more controversial issue is whether the substantial foreign ownership of Canadian industry leads to low R&D expenditure; this and related policy problems are taken up in the boxes.

In January 1981 the federal government announced a program to encourage R&D expenditure in Canada, with the announced objective of total R&D expenditure reaching 1.5 percent of GNP by 1985. The program calls for growth in federal government research spending of 17 percent a year over the five-year period. In 1979 government spending was just under $1 billion (compared with the $20 billion spent by the U.S. government); under the program it would grow to $2.5 billion by 1985.

R&D by businesses is sometimes very applied (to develop a new carburetor, for example), but company-financed basic research has led to

R&D industries. This is because the expansion of the scale of production and sales allows a payoff from the large but intangible R&D assets. In other words, the larger the scale, the lower the cost of fixed R&D expenditure *per unit of output*. Controlling for this effect by adjusting R&D expenditure in Canadian industries by that in their U.S. counterpart tends to restore the standard view that there is a negative relationship between foreign ownership and expenditure on R&D.

Studies of particular industries show that the effects might go either way. A strong positive effect of foreign ownership on R&D has been found in the machinery industry, and especially in the aircraft industry, while in chemicals and electrical equipment the influence is apparently negative.

The late Harry Johnson, a famous Canadian economist who taught at the University of Chicago and the London School of Economics, was fond of emphasizing that through parent-subsidiary technology transfer, Canada gets the benefits of foreign R&D very cheaply. Others believe that importing the results of R&D is undesirable *per se* because it replaces R&D expenditure in Canada. However, the fact that R&D is imported does not eliminate its *benefits*. Canada's access to new technology is not accurately measured by domestic R&D expenditure because subsidiaries have ready access to new technology developed in the parent companies. This frees Canadian resources for direct participation in production and other activities while allowing Canadian technology to keep pace rapidly and perhaps cheaply with new developments in the rest of the world.

Sometimes parent-subsidiary transfers are the best way of acquiring foreign technology, sometimes not. One problem that remains is the evaluation of the real price paid for R&D transferred to Canada via parent-subsidiary ties. How do we measure the gains from R&D? How do we know to whom the benefits accrue? The broader issue of whether Canada needs a policy to foster R&D is taken up in the accompanying box.

major breakthroughs. The transistor and the silicon chip, for example, are revolutionizing data processing, communications, and many other fields. In Canada federal government R&D expenditures led to the development of the highly successful Candu reactor. The results of federal government research efforts in the United States were most visible in the crash programs that led to the atomic bomb in World War II and the exploration of space in the 1960s. Out of those efforts have come a host of products and processes that have proven useful in the production of goods and services for consumption and have led to productivity increases. Solar energy is a potential area of expanded federal research. Scientific and medical R&D efforts in the universities and in hospitals, often financed by private foundations or public appeals for funds, have transformed the world we live in.

Some critics of programs to encourage more R&D expenditures have argued that the important kinds of invention, the kinds that really affect productivity, would occur with or without such expenditures. Much of what is called R&D, they say, is merely cosmetic—designed to sell the "new improved" brand of soap, cereal, or clothing—rather than material change. A great deal of evidence now contradicts this view and

Should Canada Adopt Policies to Promote R&D Expenditure?

The consensus view is that Canada as a nation spends a below average amount on R&D. Is government action to promote R&D expenditure called for?

To begin with, we might look a little more closely at the evidence that Canadian expenditure on R&D is low. In *The Weakest Link: A Technological Perspective on Canadian Industrial Underdevelopment,* published in 1978, the Science Council of Canada claims that "Canada's R&D performance is about the worst of the western world!" Does this claim stand in the face of facts?

The question is highly controversial, for measurement problems in assessing R&D performance are severe. In a critique of the Science Council, Professor Kristian Palda of Queen's University argues that current estimates of Canadian R&D expenditure are in fact serious underestimates. He writes:

The leading edge of innovative industrial activity is widely found in small enterprises launched by engineers or scientists. These entrepreneurs . . . are designated as executive rather than research personnel and their fairly high salaries are not carried on the R&D line of their corporate financial statements. In Canada, due to the heavy representation of the small-scale manufacturing firm this undoubtedly leads to a substantial underestimate of industrial R&D effort and personnel. The exclusion of pilot plant investment in what is clearly a major development effort by Syncrude contributes also . . . to a Canadian underestimate.

In addition, "high technology" itself is difficult to define; in some circumstances it could mean "capital intensive," in others it could mean "value added per employee," in still others it could mean "skill level requirements per employee." The blanket application of any one definition leads to absurd results. Professor Palda notes that if, for example, high technology were defined as an industry where expenditures on research make a large contribution to the productivity of that industry, then agriculture would be the most technology-intensive industry in North America. Yet the Science Council does not even consider agriculture in its dismal overview of Canada's technological development.

Thus there is reason for being skeptical of blanket statements about the state of R&D expenditure in Canada.

There is the related question, given the presence of foreign-owned subsidiaries in the Canadian economy, of whether the percentage of R&D expenditure within Canada is a relevant measure of technical performance. One study conducted by the federal Ministry of State for Science and Technology estimated that in one year in the mid1970s the cost of "invisible" R&D performed for Canadian subsidiaries by their parent firms was $688 million, compared to the cost of actual R&D performed in Canada by foreign-controlled subsidiaries of $282 million. Canada may or may not be backward in its research *performance,* but that it suffers in terms of *access* to R&D results seems implausible.

shows that productivity growth is to a significant degree a response to expenditures on R&D. Those countries (particularly Germany and Japan) that have stepped up their R&D expenditures have experienced much higher levels of productivity growth than have countries (Canada, the United States, and the United Kingdom) that have let such expenditures lag. Similarly, in-

Some groups have lobbied actively for policies to encourage R&D expenditure in Canada. But R&D expenditure alone does not guarantee improved economic performance, and the policy proposals emerging from these sources have met with much criticism from economists. Doubts have been raised not only about the claim that Canada needs more R&D but also about the ability of public sector intervention to stimulate more R&D.

What particular strategies or policies are involved? One often quoted strategy is to "pick winners" and subsidize them. This approach raises two questions: Is the political will strong enough to let the losers sink and is the political intellect strong enough to identify the potential winners? Another proposal is to subsidize R&D directly. But it is possible that if governments actively promoted R&D, the private sector would reduce its R&D expenditure correspondingly. And because R&D requires a large sales volume to make it work, giving R&D subsidies to firms that do not have a sufficient market may well be a waste of money. Technological improvements are of no advantage when they do not contribute to a marketable product; hence access to a large market is necessary.

A related proposal is to screen the import of foreign technology into Canada. Presumably this would stimulate R&D expenditure by keeping foreign technology out. Some would prefer to try to direct the import of technology into Canadian firms rather than to foreign subsidiaries. This would tend to reduce the role of foreign ownership in the Canadian economy, but it would result in a slower transmission of new technology and a higher price for what is transmitted.

Common to all these proposals is the advocacy of increased government involvement to promote "high technology" industries. But what are the costs of such intervention? Foreign experience tells us that the costs could be enormous. In examining the French experience with nuclear energy, aerospace computers, and electronics, Professor Palda shows that technology was ultimately imported from abroad only after expensive domestic programs had failed to be technically or economically successful. On the basis of France's experience, Canada would be well advised to assess carefully the prospective costs and benefits of the ambitious program suggested by the Science Council in *The Weakest Link*.

Most economists remain rather skeptical about the need for and the effectiveness of R&D policies. In an Ontario Economic Council study in 1977, Professor Donald McFetteridge of Carleton University argued that researchers have yet to produce any statistical evidence that the rate of return to industrial and R&D development in Canada is positive —let alone so high that it should be favored over alternative uses of our scarce investment money.

dustries that are major R&D spenders (chemicals, electrical equipment, air transport) have maintained productivity growth much better than others that engage in very little R&D (steel, leather, construction). Of course some sectors that do little R&D, such as coal mining and farming, may buy their equipment from industries that do a great deal, and thus they achieve gains in productivity. Such an industry is buying R&D in the price it pays for its equipment.

INCENTIVES AND DISINCENTIVES FOR INNOVATION

Innovation requires both the availability of technical knowledge and its introduction into use. New methods, machines, materials, and products are introduced not "because they are there" but because (and when) it appears *profitable* to introduce them. Productivity growth may decline because the profit incentives to innovate are weak or nonexistent. Profit incentives in turn are affected by many aspects of the economic climate. Many contemporary scholars see changes in the latter as the main reason for the lagging productivity growth of the Canadian economy.

The Growth Rate of the Economy

The opportunities for the profitable introduction of innovations are much greater in a growing economy than in a stagnant one. New machines and new methods are more easily introduced when new needs arise because the extra demand must be met by additional machines rather than by the continued use of existing but less advanced machines that may still have productive life. The durability of existing equipment slows innovation in an industry that is not growing. An electric power commission faced with an increase in demand will introduce the latest kind of steam turbine generator and use it alongside older vintages of turbine generators until they wear out. A power commission that is not growing will postpone its modernization, perhaps for decades. A growing industry often has profitable opportunities for investment in additional machines as well as machines geared to larger scale of output. It may also have incentives to introduce new products. Every time it seeks new investment it is likely to look at the latest, most modern technology available. The introduction of that technology leads to productivity increases.

A growing economy can also adapt more easily to the changing skills requirements of its labor force. It is often as hard to retrain existing workers as it is to retool existing machines; it is relatively easy to educate and train new entrants into the labor force with the new skills they will need. Moreover, the presence of job and promotion opportunities in new occupations where there is no long seniority problem to overcome tends to motivate young people preparing for entry into the labor force to acquire the requisite skills.

One of the sources of the slowdown of productivity growth in Canada in the 1970s was the slowdown in the rate of growth of output of the economy. That slowdown was in good part a deliberate response by government, which sought to restrain the inflationary pressures of the 1970s by reducing total demand. As a result fewer industries and companies were expanding and less investment was taking place. When investment is not rapid, the capital stock is neither growing nor improving very rapidly.

When investment fell during the 1970s, not only did productivity growth slow on that account, but the number of new job opportunities also fell, and this had a secondary dampening effect on productivity.

Stagnation in growth of output leads to less investment, less innovation, fewer jobs, and fewer incentives to acquire special skills. Thus it tends to retard productivity increases.

The Level of Capacity Utilization

There are several reasons why an economy with substantial economic slack (in capacity utilization or in labor utilization) may find its productivity growth slowing. One of the most important is that in such a period new investment is likely to fall sharply as expansion is postponed. Firms with excess capacity not only delay expansion, they postpone replacing existing equipment as it wears out. Since new investment is a main source of introducing innovations, the postponement of investment is directly harmful to productivity growth.

Second, bottlenecks in production are infrequent when there is general slack in the economy. Bottlenecks trigger both the substitution of one input for another and the invention of substitutes for scarce items. With excess capacity, firms' activities are likely to shift to attempts to increase demand rather than to reduce costs.

The failure of the Canadian economy to achieve anything like full utilization of its capacity during the period 1975–1980 added a cyclical damper to productivity growth that accentuated the effects of the slowdown in economic growth.

Shifts in Demand and the Composition of Output

Industries, and sectors of the economy, differ greatly from one another in what is called their technological base, that is, in their opportunities for increasing productivity. It is much harder for social workers to increase their output (cases handled per year) than it is for airline pilots to increase their output (passenger miles flown per year). This has nothing to do with the skill or the dedication of the social worker and the pilot; it concerns the nature of their tasks and the tools at their disposal. The bigger, faster plane that increases the pilot's productivity has no counterpart for the social worker.

The overall productivity level of the economy is the weighted average of the level of productivity of its sectors. If production shifts from high productivity sectors to low productivity sectors, aggregate productivity falls even though the level of productivity in each individual sector remains unchanged. The same is true of growth in productivity. Suppose, for example, there are only two sectors. In "manufacturing" productivity grows at 5 percent per year; in "services" productivity grows by 1 percent per year. If each sector produces one-half of total output, total productivity growth will be 3 percent per year. But if services becomes 75 percent of the total

and manufacturing 25 percent, the aggregate productivity increase will fall to 2 percent.[12]

In the early stages of industrial development, factors of production tend to be shifting from sectors where productivity is both low and only slowly increasing (such as subsistence agriculture) to sectors where it is higher and more rapidly growing. This leads to sharp rises in productivity levels and rates of productivity growth. As economies become more fully industrialized, one kind of slowdown is that the opportunities for shifting resources out of low productivity sectors decrease: the smaller the sectors become, the less possible is further shrinkage.

A second kind of shift also occurs because the nature of goods and services that the population wants may change. Many commodities with high income elasticities of demand have relatively low productivity and a low technical base. This is true, for example, of services designed to provide amenities of various kinds, including civic services such as garbage collection, parks, police protection, and libraries. Demands for medical and hospital care increase relative to demands for copper, manufactured goods, and transportation. Similarly, such things as clean air and safer consumer products may be desired even though they add to the costs of the goods produced.

There is little doubt that some of the decrease in productivity growth in Canada in the 1970s reflected these kinds of shifts in the demands for various goods. One major shift was the rapid growth in employment in the oil- and natural gas-related industries. Measured productivity in these industries has recently been very low. Between 1967 and 1973 the growth of productivity in the petroleum and natural gas extraction industry averaged 7 percent per year. Then, between 1974 and 1978, oil and natural gas output per person employed *declined* at an average rate

---

[12] In the first case productivity growth is $\frac{1}{2} \times 5 + \frac{1}{2} \times 1 = 3$ percent. In the second case productivity growth is $\frac{1}{4} \times 5 + \frac{3}{4} \times 1 = 2$ percent.

of about 10 percent. Output in this sector fell in response to policy initiatives aimed at conserving oil and gas resources for domestic needs, and in response to other factors. However, employment increased steadily in these industries as exploration and development activity quickened and as more labor-intensive synthetic oil facilities were expanded. Productivity developments in the oil- and natural gas-related industries and in pipelines are responsible for a significant portion (the Department of Finance has estimated it to be about 25 percent) of the reduction in the rate of growth of overall productivity over the five years 1974–1978. Yet these developments do not help to explain the further decline in labor productivity in the economy as a whole in 1979, for output in those sectors rose very rapidly in 1979.

The Institutional Climate

The profits from innovation depend largely on such things as the tax laws and regulatory requirements. If innovators are allowed to reap large gains from successful innovations, they will be more likely to take the risks of innovation. Innovation can be encouraged by investment credits, patent laws, low tax rates, government subsidies, and government-assisted R&D. It can be discouraged by regulatory burdens involving environmental impact statements, safety regulation, and the hassles and delays involved in meeting government requirements. Many regulatory commissions restrict what firms can do and limit entry into fields in which an innovative firm might see profit opportunities.

A different aspect of the institutional climate is the ability and desire of the members of a relatively rich country to protect individuals and firms from the harsh forces of economic competition. The rigors of the marketplace may compel improving productivity because it is essential to survival; protecting people may remove the incentives. Foreign competition that threatens domestic firms may spur them to adopt more efficient techniques; restrictions on that competition may remove the need and the incen-

tive for such innovations. Similarly, the protection of unemployed labor by various welfare schemes, while ameliorating the distress of workers, decreases their geographic and occupational mobility.

Many believe that the institutional climate in Canada has become increasingly hostile to private innovation in recent decades and that high taxes, government regulation, and economic protection have all added to the forces that inhibit innovation and growth.

HOW MUCH PRODUCTIVITY GROWTH DO WE WANT?

Decreases in cost levels that are possible by choosing among known techniques and among alternative levels of output are limited in scope. We can never do better than a 100 percent utilization of what is currently known. Yet improvements by invention are potentially limitless. For this reason, the long-term struggle to get more from the world's limited resources is critically linked to discovery.

Economics used to be known as the dismal science because some of its predictions were dismal. The classical economists' basic prediction about the long run was that world population would continue to expand and the pressure of more and more persons on the world's limited resources would cause a decline in output per person. Human history would be one of more and more people living less and less well, with the surplus of persons that could not be supported at all dying off in plague, famine, and pestilence. This prediction has been dramatically correct in some of the countries now called underdeveloped. It has, however, been wrong for the industrial countries for several reasons. First, because of voluntary restriction on population growth, the population did not expand as rapidly as was foreseen by economists writing before the wide availability of birth control techniques. Second, pure knowledge and its applied techniques have expanded so rapidly during the last 150 years that our ability to squeeze more out of limited resources has expanded faster than the population has expanded.

Even in the industrial nations the race between consumption and production is a close one, and if the rate at which the frontiers of knowledge are being expanded should again fall below the rate of population increase, economics may once again become a dismal science.

Undesired Restraints

Some of the sources of decreasing rates of productivity growth are plainly undesired. These include a sluggish economy and the failure of firms and households to fully adapt to higher energy prices.

Government policies (considered in full in the macroeconomic section of this book) are designed to avoid economic slack and to stimulate innovation. Similarly, energy policies may reduce the impact of the oil price increases.

Quite apart from government actions, the market mechanism, if allowed to work. will tend to lessen the force of these inhibitions to growth in productivity. Consider, for example, the slowdown in growth of productivity due to increases in oil prices. One may expect the higher price of oil and the products that use it to have several effects that mitigate the energy shortage. One effect is to stimulate the search for new methods of finding oil. A second is to lead people to economize on oil consumption by discovering oil-saving techniques. A third is to encourage the development of new sources of fuel that will substitute for oil. The most publicized alternatives are nuclear and solar energy. But inventors also consider what others regard as fanciful. Two companies in the United States have already signed agreements to provide 1.2 billion cubic feet of "bio-gas" made from cow manure. Its proponents claim that it is in every way as good as natural gas and that it could supply up to 15 percent of total American energy requirements if all the available cow manure were utilized.

It is worth noticing that these adaptations *will result from* the price rise. There are those who urge the government to hold down the price of oil during this period of shortage for political reasons or to save households and firms from the hardships that a rising price of oil imposes on them. But such a policy, if it occurs, will inhibit the long-run process that promises to free us from such a heavy dependence on foreign oil.

Desired Restraints on Productivity?

Others aspects of the slowdown in productivity growth may not be remedied—not because we do not understand them, but because they are the by-products of desired changes. The shift to production of commodities with high income elasticities but low productivity levels is the most obvious example. The population evidently does not want more goods if it means less police protection, or more food at the cost of less recreation even though such shifts would increase productivity growth.

Growth in productivity has often been accompanied by increased pollution and more industrial accidents. Whether cleaner air and more safety are demanded by the public or are instead part of the bureaucratic burden imposed on an unwilling populace is a matter of debate. To many in the business community, big government is guilty of slowing productivity growth by its policies. To others, such efforts are desirable. They argue that a cleaner environment, safer working conditions and products, and better health are also forms of output—output that people have indicated they prefer to faster cars and more lethal pesticides.

"Progress," as measured by productivity growth, is thus no longer an unquestioned overriding goal of society. Progress has come to mean growth, and growth has long meant industrialization. Applied to the economy as a whole, industrialization and its accompanying changes in productivity clearly have vastly increased our material well-being and permitted more and more people to escape the ravages of hunger and the relentless struggle to subsist.

But nothing is without its cost, and in the case

of growth this is increasingly being recognized. The gasoline engine, the steel mill, the jet airplane, DDT, plastics, and the skyscraper with its hundreds of thousands of electric lights are the artifacts of our progress over the last century. Have they lowered the quality of life, while raising the standard of living?

Just as humankind can benefit (at some stage in its development) from more production of luxuries and less of basic necessities, so too may it benefit from more amenities and lower productivity growth. To the extent that it can, a slower rate of productivity growth may reflect a better life, not a worsening one.

Summary

1. There are no fixed factors in the long run. The profit-maximizing firm chooses, from the alternatives open to it, the least costly way of achieving any specific output. A long-run cost curve represents the boundary between attainable and unattainable levels of cost for the given technology.

2. The principle of substitution says that efficient production will substitute cheaper factors for more expensive ones. If the relative prices of factors change, relatively more of cheaper factors and relatively less of more expensive ones will be used.

3. The shape of the long-run cost curve depends on the relationship of inputs to outputs as the whole scale of a firm's operations changes. Increasing, constant, and decreasing returns lead to decreasing, constant, and increasing long-run average costs.

4. The relation between long-run and short-run cost curves is shown in Figures 13-2 and 13-3. Every "long-run" cost corresponds to *some* quantity of each factor and is thus on some short-run cost curve. The short-run cost curve shows how costs vary when that particular quantity of a fixed factor is used to produce outputs greater than or less than those for which it is optimal.

5. Cost curves shift upward or downward in response to changes in the prices of factors or the introduction of changed technology. Increases in factor prices shift the cost curves upward. Decreases in factor prices or technological advances that make it possible to produce the same amount of output with lower quantities of all inputs shift cost curves downward.

6. An isoquant is a "contour line" that shows all of the combinations of factors that can be used to produce a given amount of output. The slope of the isoquant is the marginal rate of substitution between the two factors of production, and it is equal to the ratio of their marginal products.

7. An isoquant is downward-sloping because both factors have positive marginal products. If one is diminished, the other must be increased if output is to be held constant. The isoquant is convex viewed from the origin because both factors have diminishing marginal productivity as a result of which equal reductions in one factor (rising marginal productivity) must be compensated for by larger and larger increases in the other factor (falling marginal productivity).

8. An isoquant map is a series of isoquants, each one of which gives the combinations of two factors that will produce a given level of output.

9. The firm will be minimizing its costs of producing a given level of output if it produces where an isoquant is tangent to an isocost line. This implies that the ratio of the marginal products of the factors is equal to the ratio of their prices.

10. A change in factor prices will lead all firms to substitute the factor whose relative price falls for the factor whose relative price rises. Thus the cheaper any one factor is relative to other factors, the larger is the quantity of that factor firms will desire to use.

11. Over extended periods, the most important influence on costs of production and the standard of living has been the increases in output made possible by new technology and reflected in increasing productivity. The relatively modest rate of productivity increase of 3 percent per year leads to a doubling of output per worker every 23 years.

12. Major sources of productivity growth in industrializing countries have been the increased use of inanimate energy, the substitution of capital for labor, improved health, the education and training of labor, improved materials, and better organization of production.

13. Behind improvements in productivity lie invention and innovation. Invention—the discovery of new methods—occurs in many ways, but research and development expenditures play a major role. Changes in the level and type of R&D can be traced in an economy's productivity record.

14. Innovation requires invention and also profitable opportunities for the introduction of available knowledge. The economic climate (its growth and its level of capacity utilization), the instutional climate, and the differences in technological possibilities in sectors where demand is growing and declining all affect the opportunities for innovation.

15. The slowdown in productivity growth in Canada during the 1970s, with its consequent reduction in the average growth rate of living standards, was due to a combination of circumstances: lower growth in national output, economic slack, increased regulatory burdens, and a shift in demand from high productivity to lower productivity activities.

16. Not all of the slowdown in measured productivity growth represents a worsening of the quality of life. Material progress leads both to more goods and services per person and to opportunities for better living. Yet progress of this kind is not an unmixed blessing; pollution of the environment accompanies growth, and an increased number of injuries and accidents occur. Whether the current level of government regulation of health and safety has gone too far is an issue highly debated today.

Topics for Review

The implication of cost minimization
The interpretation of $MP_k / MP_L = p_K/p_L$
The principle of substitution
Increasing, decreasing, and constant returns
The envelope curve
A single isoquant and an isoquant map
The marginal rate of substitution
The tangency of an isoquant and an isocost line at the least-cost position
Substitution along an isoquant as a result of a change in relative factor prices
The distinction between production and productivity
The level of productivity and the rate of growth of productivity
Sources of increasing productivity
Invention and innovation
Research and development (R&D)
Determinants of innovation

Discussion Questions

1. Why does the profit-maximizing firm choose the least costly way of producing any given output? Might a nonprofit-maximizing organization such as a university or a church or a government intentionally choose a method of production other than the least costly one? Might an ordinary business corporation do so intentionally?

2. In Dacca, Bangladesh, where gasoline costs $3 a gallon and labor is typically paid less than 20¢ an hour, Abdul Khan pedals a bicycle-ricksha (pedicab) for his living. It's exhausting work that is coming under increasing attack by those who feel it is an inhumane practice. "We really want to get rid of them and move to motorized taxis, but I'm afraid it will take a long, long time," says the Bangladesh information officer. Ricksha drivers earn $2 a day, which is more than a skilled worker gets in Dacca. Explain the use of pedicabs in Dacca but not in New York or Tokyo. Comment on the information officer's statement.

3. Use the principle of substitution to predict the effect of each of the following:

   a. During the 1960s salaries of professors rose much more rapidly than those of teaching assistants. During the 1970s salaries of teaching assistants rose more than those of professors.

   b. The cost of land in big cities increases more than the cost of high-rise construction.

   c. Gold leaf is produced by pounding gold with a hammer. The thinner it is, the more valuable. The price of gold is set on a world market, but the price of labor varies among countries. Gold leaf is thinner in some countries than in others.

   d. OPEC keeps oil prices increasing faster than prices of most other raw materials.

4. The long-run average cost curve can be thought of as consisting of points from each of a number of short-run average cost curves. Explain in what sense any point on the long-run curve is also on some short-run curve. What is the meaning of a move from one point on a long-run cost curve to another point on the same curve? Contrast this with a movement along a short-run curve.

5. The director of federal energy programs urged the American people to make necessary "long-run adjustments to the energy shortage by reducing energy input per unit of output." How exactly might this be done? Is this use of "long-run" the economists' use of that concept?

6. Israel, a small country, imports the "insides" of its automobiles but manufactures the bodies. If this makes economic sense, what does it tell us about cost conditions of automobile manufacture?

7. In each of the following situations, what is the shape of each isoquant, and how will the factor combination for a particular output be affected by changes in the relative prices of the factors?

   a. The two factors of production are perfect substitutes (that is, either can substitute for all of the other; for example, soybean oil and peanut oil in making shortening).

   b. The two factors of production are perfect complements (that is, they must be used in fixed proportions; for example, taxis and taxi tires).

8. Name five important modern products that were not available when you were in elementary school. Make a list of major products that you think have increased their sales at least tenfold in the last 30 years. Consider to what extent the growth in each series may reflect product or process innovation.

9. By 1980 thousands of firms had switched from an eight-hour day, five-day week, to a four-day week, with each day ten hours long. Output per week appears to have increased significantly. Is this an increase in productivity? Is it an innovation? Would you predict that this success will lead to a general substitution of the four-day week for the five-day week wherever the latter is now standard?

10. What do you believe to have been the primary spur for each of the following inventions and innovations: color television, the cotton gin, nuclear power, penicillin, the assembly line, radar, the smashing of the atom, the nuclear bomb, the Frisbee, synthetic rubber, polio vaccine, the airplane, motion pictures, and the wheel? Are any of these attributable to more than one source?

11. Each of the following is a means of increasing productivity. Discuss which groups within the society might oppose each one.

    a. A labor-saving invention that permits all goods to be manufactured with less labor than before.

    b. A rapidly increasing growth of population in the economy.

    c. Removal of all government production safety rules.

    d. A reduction in corporate income taxes.

    e. Discovery of a new, cheap substitute for oil.

Part Five

Markets
and Pricing

Pricing in Competitive Markets

14

Is Goodyear in competition with Goodrich? Does Eaton's compete with Simpsons? Is the farmer from Brandon, Manitoba, in competition with a wheat farmer from Biggar, Saskatchewan? In the ordinary meaning of the noun "competition" and the verb "compete," the answers to the first two of these questions are plainly yes, and the answer to the third question is probably no.

Goodyear and Goodrich both advertise extensively to persuade tire buyers to buy *their* product. Goodrich has even been known to confuse the issue: "See that blimp up there? It's theirs, not ours. If you want Goodrich tires you'll just have to remember Goodrich." Everyone knows that Eaton's and Simpsons watch each other like hawks and that swarms of comparison shoppers check their respective prices and qualities every day. But there is nothing that the Manitoba farmer can do that will affect the sales or the profits of the Saskatchewan farmer.

Firm Behavior and Market Structure

To sort out the questions of who is competing with whom and in what sense do they compete, it is necessary to distinguish between the behavior of individual firms and the type of market in which the firms operate. Economists use the term *market structure* to refer to the latter concept. The concept of competitive behavior is quite distinct from the concept of competitive market structure. The degree of *competitive behavior* refers to the degree to which individual firms actively compete with one another. The degree of *competitiveness of the market structure* refers to the extent to which individual firms have power over that market—power to influence the price or other terms on which their product is sold. In everyday use "competition" usually refers only to competitive behavior; economists, however, are interested both in the behavior of individual firms and in market structures.

Goodrich and Goodyear certainly engage in competitive (i.e., rivalrous) behavior. It is also true that both individually and together they have some power over the market. Either firm could raise its prices and still continue to sell tires; each has the power to decide—within limits set by buyers' tastes and the prices of competing tires—what price consumers will pay for its own product.

The Manitoba and the Saskatchewan wheat farmers do not engage in active competitive behavior with each other. They operate, however, in a market over which they have no power. Neither has significant power to change the market price for its wheat by altering its behavior.

At one extreme of competitive market structures, economists use a theory in which no single firm has any market power. There are so many firms that each must accept the price set by the forces of market demand and supply. In this theory of the perfectly competitive market structure there is no need for individual firms to behave competitively with respect to one another since none has any power over the market. One firm's ability to sell its product is uninfluenced by the behavior of any other firm. The apparent paradox that interfirm competition does not occur in perfectly competitive markets is resolved when we recognize the distinction between interfirm competitive *behavior* and the competitive *structure* of the market in which the firm operates.

The theory of the perfectly competitive market

structure applies directly to a number of real-world markets. It also provides a benchmark for comparison with other market structures in which there are so few firms that each has some significant market power.

THE SIGNIFICANCE OF MARKET STRUCTURE

Although market demand curves and cost curves of individual firms are the basic elements of the theory of product pricing, they are not in themselves sufficient to provide a theory of price. Hypotheses are needed that tell how these elements interact and finally come together in the market. At the outset we need to define two basic concepts, the market and the industry.

From the point of view of a household, the **market** consists of those firms from which it can buy a well-defined product; from the point of view of a firm, the market consists of those buyers to whom it can sell a well-defined product. A group of firms that sells a well-defined product, or closely related set of products, is said to constitute an **industry.** The market demand curve is the demand curve for an industry's product. An industry may sell in many different markets.

Consider a firm that produces a specific product for sale in a particular market and competes for customers with other firms in the same industry. If a profit-maximizing firm knows precisely the demand curve it faces, it knows the price it could charge for each rate of sales and thus knows its potential revenues. If it also knows its costs, the firm can readily discover the profits that would be associated with any rate of output and can choose the rate that maximizes its profits. But what if the firm knows its costs and only the *market* demand curve for its product? It does not know what its own sales would be. In other words, the firm does not know its *own* demand curve. In order to determine what fraction of the total market demand will be met by other sellers, it needs to know how other firms will respond to its change in price. If it reduces its price by 10 percent, will other sellers leave their prices unchanged or will they also reduce them? If they reduce their prices, will they do so by less than 10 percent, by exactly 10 percent, or by more than 10 percent? Obviously, each possible outcome will have a different effect on the firm's sales and thus on its revenues and profits.

The answers to questions about the relation of a firm's demand curve to the market demand curve depend on such variables as the number of sellers in the market and the similarity of their products. These are aspects of **market structure,** which is defined as the characteristics of market organization that are likely to affect a firm's behavior and performance.

For example, if there are only two large firms in an industry, each may be expected to meet most price cuts that the other makes; but if there are 5,000 small firms, a price cut by one may go unmatched. If two firms are producing identical products, they may be expected to behave differently with respect to each other than if they were producing similar but not identical products.

 The central hypothesis of industrial organization economics is that firm behavior will be affected by market structure.

There are many other aspects of market structure that may affect firm behavior, such as the ease of entering the industry, the nature and size of the purchasers of the firm's products, and the firm's ability to influence demand by advertising. To reduce these aspects to manageable proportions, economists have focused on a few theoretical market structures that they believe represent a high proportion of the cases actually encountered in market societies. In this chapter and the next two, we shall look at four market structures: perfect competition, monopoly, monopolistic competition, and oligopoly.

Before considering any of these market structures, it is useful to deal with the rules of behavior common to all firms that seek to maximize their profits.

BEHAVIORAL RULES FOR THE PROFIT-MAXIMIZING FIRM[1]

A firm should produce only if it will do better than it could by not producing. The firm always has the option of producing nothing. If it produces nothing, it will have an operating loss equal to its fixed costs. If it decides to produce, it will add the variable cost of production to its fixed costs and the receipts from the sale of its products to its revenue. If revenue exceeds variable cost, it will pay the firm to produce; if revenue is less than variable cost, the firm will actually lose less by not producing than by producing. This leads to the first rule for profit maximizing:

Rule 1. A firm should not produce at all if the average revenue from its product does not equal or exceed its average variable costs. [21]

If a firm decides that, according to rule 1, production is worth undertaking, it must decide how much to produce. Common sense dictates that on a unit-by-unit basis, if any unit of production adds more to revenue than it does to cost, that unit will increase profits; if it adds more to cost than to revenue, it will decrease profits. If the firm is in a position where a further unit of production will increase profits, it should expand output; if it is in a position where the last unit of production decreased profits, it should contract output. The notion of the change in cost brought about by an additional unit is, of course, marginal cost (MC). A parallel concept, **marginal revenue** (MR), may be defined as the change in total revenue resulting from the sale of one additional unit.

A second rule may now be stated formally:

Rule 2. Assuming that it pays the firm to produce at all, it will be profitable for the firm to expand output whenever marginal revenue is greater than marginal cost; expansion should thus continue until marginal revenue equals marginal cost. [22]

---

[1] Formal proofs of the propositions discussed in the text are given in the Mathematical Notes.

These two rules can be restated as three necessary conditions for a firm to be maximizing its profits. It must be producing an output where (a) price is at least as great as average variable cost, (b) marginal revenue equals marginal cost, and (c) the marginal cost curve cuts the marginal revenue curve from below.[2] **[23]**

These rules apply to all profit-maximizing firms whatever the market structure in which they operate. The rules refer to the firm's costs and its revenues. Before we can apply the rules we need to consider particular market structures in order to provide links between the demand curve for an industry's product and the demand curves—and thus the revenue curves—facing individual firms.

The Elements of the Theory of Perfect Competition

THE ASSUMPTIONS OF PERFECT COMPETITION

The theory of **perfect competition** is built on two critical assumptions, one about the behavior of the individual firm and one about the nature of the industry in which it operates.

The *firm* is assumed to be a **price taker;** that is, the firm is assumed to act as though it can alter its rate of production and sales within any feasible range without such action having a significant effect on the price of the product it sells. Thus the firm must passively accept whatever price happens to be ruling on the market.

The *industry* is characterized by **freedom of entry and exit;** that is, any new firm is free to set up production if it so wishes, and any existing firm is free to cease production and leave the industry. Existing firms cannot bar the entry of new firms, and there are no legal prohibitions on entry or exit.

The ultimate test of the theory based on these assumptions will be the usefulness of its predictions, but because students are often bothered by the first assumption, it is worth examining whether it is in any way reasonable. To see what is involved in the assumption of price taking, contrast the demands for the products of an automobile manufacturer and a wheat farmer.

An automobile manufacturer. General Motors is aware that it has market power. If it substantially increases its prices, sales will fall off; if it lowers prices substantially, it will sell more of its products. If GM decides on a large increase in production that is not a response to a known or anticipated rise in demand, it will have to reduce prices in order to sell the extra output. The automobile manufacturing firm is *not* a price taker. The quantity that it is able to sell will depend on the price it charges, but it does not have to accept passively whatever price is set by the market. In other words, the firm manufacturing automobiles is faced with a downward-sloping demand curve for its product. It may select any price-quantity combination consistent with that demand curve.

A wheat farmer. In contrast, an individual firm producing wheat is just one of a very large number of firms all growing the same product; one firm's contribution to the total production of wheat will be a tiny drop in an extremely large bucket. Ordinarily the firm will assume that it has no effect on price and will think of its own demand curve as being horizontal. Of course the firm can have *some* effect on price, but a straightforward calculation will show that the effect is small enough that the firm can justifiably neglect it.

The market elasticity of demand for wheat is approximately 0.25. This means that if the quantity of wheat supplied in the world increased by 1

---

[2] The third condition is designed to distinguish between profit-maximizing and profit-minimizing positions. Consider a situation in which *MC* cuts *MR* from above: For outputs to the left of the intersection marginal cost exceeds marginal revenue, which indicates that these units reduce profits and thus that profits could be increased by *reducing* output. For outputs to the right of the intersection marginal revenue exceeds marginal cost, which indicates that these units increase profits and thus that profits could be increased by *increasing* output. The intersection must thus represent minimum profits.

TABLE 14-1

The Calculation of a Firm's Elasticity of Demand (η_F) from Market Elasticity of Demand (η_M)

Given

$\eta_M = 0.25$

World output $= 200$ million tons

Firm's output increases from 40,000 to 60,000 tons, a 40% increase over the average quantity of 50,000 tons

Step 1. Find the percentage change in world price

$$\eta_M = -\frac{\text{percentage change in world output}}{\text{percentage change in world price}}$$

$$\text{Percentage change in world price} = -\frac{\text{percentage change in world output}}{\eta_M}$$

$$= -\frac{\frac{1}{100} \text{ of } 1\%}{0.25}$$

$$= -\frac{4}{100} \text{ of } 1\%$$

Step 2. Compute the firm's elasticity of demand:

$$\eta_F = -\frac{\text{percentage change in firm's output}}{\text{percentage change in world price}}$$

$$= -\frac{+40\%}{-\frac{4}{100} \text{ of } 1\%} = +1000$$

Because even a large change in output to the firm is a minute change in world wheat production, the effect on world price is very small. Thus the firm's elasticity of demand is high. This table relies on the concept of elasticity of demand developed in Chapter 6. Step 1 shows that a 40 percent increase in the firm's output leads to only a tiny decrease in the world's price. Thus, as step 2 shows, the firm's elasticity of demand is very high: 1000.

The arithmetic is not important, but understanding why the wheat farm will be a price taker in these circumstances is vital.

percent, the price would have to fall by 4 percent to induce the world's wheat buyers to purchase the whole crop. Even huge farms produce a very small fraction of the total crop. In a recent year an extremely large Canadian wheat farm produced about 50,000 tons, only about 1/4,000 of the world production of 200 million tons. Suppose a large wheat farm increased its production by 20,000 tons, say from 40,000 to 60,000 tons. This would be a big percentage increase in its own production but an increase of only 1/100 of 1 percent in world production. Table 14-1 shows that this increase would lead to a decrease in the world price of 4/100 of 1 percent (4¢ in $100) and give the firm an elasticity of demand of 1,000! This is a very high elasticity of demand; the farm would have to increase its output 1,000 percent to bring about a 1 percent decrease in the price of wheat. Because the farm's output cannot be varied this much, it is not surprising that the firm regards the price of wheat to be unaffected by any change in output that it could conceivably make.

It is only a slight simplification to say that the firm is unable to influence the world price of wheat and that it is able to sell all that it can produce at the going world price. In other words, the firm is faced with a perfectly elastic demand curve for its product—it is a price taker.

The difference between firms producing wheat and firms producing automobiles is one of degree of market power. The wheat firm, as an insignificant part of the whole market, has no power to influence the world price of wheat. But the automobile firm does have power to influence the price of automobiles because its own production represents a significant part of the total supply of automobiles.

DEMAND AND REVENUE CURVES FOR THE PERFECTLY COMPETITIVE FIRM

Students sometimes confuse the individual firm's demand curve under perfect competition with the market demand curve for the product. The market demand curve is downward-sloping for the reasons we discussed in Part Three. A consequence, as we saw, is that a rightward shift of the supply curve will lead to a fall in market price, other things being equal.

The demand curve facing a single firm in perfect competition is infinitely elastic because variations in its production *over the range that we need to consider for all practical purposes* will have such a small effect on price that the effect can safely be assumed to be zero. Of course, if the single firm increased its production by a vast amount, a thousandfold say, this would cause a significant increase in supply and the firm would be unable to sell all it produced at the going price. The perfectly elastic demand curve does not mean that the firm could actually sell an infinite amount at the going price; rather, that the variations in production *that it will normally be practicable for the firm to make* will leave price virtually unaffected. This is shown in Figure 14-1.

Total, Average, and Marginal Revenue Costs

The notions of total, average, and marginal revenue are the demand counterparts of the notions of total, average, and marginal cost that we considered in Chapter 12. We focus now on the receipts to a seller from the sale of a product.

Total revenue (TR) is the total amount received by the seller. If q units are sold at p dollars each, $TR = p \cdot q$. (The dot between p and

FIGURE 14-1
Three Demand Curves of Differing Elasticity

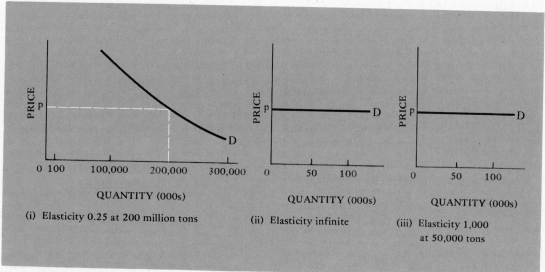

(i) Elasticity 0.25 at 200 million tons

(ii) Elasticity infinite

(iii) Elasticity 1,000 at 50,000 tons

For practical purposes, the demand curves in (ii) and (iii) are indistinguishable from each other. The firm's demand curve in (iii) appears horizontal because of the change in the quantity scale compared to (i). If the quantity scale in (i) were stretched to 1,000 times its present size, that demand curve, too, would appear horizontal.

TABLE 14-2
Revenue Concepts for a Price-taking Firm

Price p	Quantity q	$TR = p \times q$	$AR = TR/q$	$MR = \Delta TR/\Delta q$
$3.00	10	$30.00	$3.00	
3.00	11	33.00	3.00	$3.00
3.00	12	36.00	3.00	3.00
3.00	13	39.00	3.00	3.00

When price is fixed, $AR = MR = p$. Marginal revenue is shown between the lines because it represents the change in total revenue (e.g., from $33 to $36) in response to a change in quantity (from 11 to 12 units),

$$MR = \frac{36-33}{12-11} = \$3 \text{ per unit.}$$

q is a "times" sign, frequently used instead of $p \times q$, to avoid confusion with variables labeled x.)

Average revenue (AR) is the amount of revenue *per unit* sold. This is the price of the product.

Marginal revenue (MR), sometimes called incremental revenue, has already been defined. It is the change in total revenue resulting from the sale of an additional unit of the commodity. [24]

Calculations of these revenue concepts for a price-taking firm are illustrated in Table 14-2. The table shows that as long as the firm's output does not affect the price of the product it sells, both average and marginal revenue will be equal to price at all levels of output. Thus, graphically (as in Figure 14-2), average revenue and marginal revenue are both horizontal lines at the level of market price. Since the firm can sell any quantity it wishes at this price, the same horizontal line is also the *firm's* demand curve.

ar = mr

If the market price is unaffected by variations in the firm's output, then the firm's demand curve, the average revenue curve, and the marginal revenue curve coincide in the same horizontal line.

Total revenue, of course, does vary with output; since price is constant, it follows that total revenue rises in direct proportion to output.

FIGURE 14-2
Revenue Curves for a Price-taking Firm

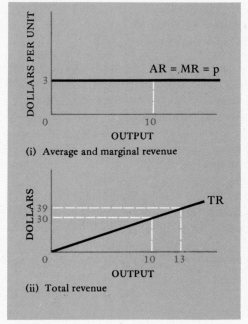

(i) Average and marginal revenue

(ii) Total revenue

This is a graphic representation of the revenue concepts of Table 14-2. Because price does not change, neither marginal nor average revenue varies with output. When price is constant, total revenue is a rising straight line from the origin.

Short-run Equilibrium: Firm and Industry

EQUILIBRIUM OUTPUT OF A FIRM IN PERFECT COMPETITION

The firm in perfect competition is a price taker and can adjust to varying market conditions only by changing the quantity it produces. In the short run it has fixed factors, and the only way to vary its output is by using more or less of those factors that it can vary. Thus the firm's short-run cost curves are relevant to its output decision.

We saw earlier that any profit-maximizing firm will seek to produce at a level of output where marginal cost equals marginal revenue. In the immediately preceding section we saw that a perfectly competitive firm's demand and marginal revenue curves coincide in the same horizontal line whose height represents the price of the product. Thus price equals marginal revenue. It follows immediately that a perfectly competitive firm will equate its marginal cost of production to the market price of its product (as long as price exceeds average variable cost).

The market determines the highest price at which the firm can sell its product. The firm picks the quantity of output that maximizes its profits. This is the output for which $p = MC$. When the firm is maximizing profits, it has no incentive to change its output. Therefore, unless prices or costs change, the firm will continue producing this output because it is doing as well as it can do, given the situation. The firm is said to be in **short-run equilibrium**, which is illustrated in Figure 14-3.

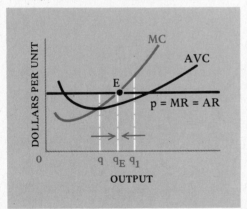

FIGURE 14-3
The Equilibrium of a Competitive Firm

The firm chooses the output for which p = MC above the level of AVC. When $p = MC$ as at q_E, the firm would decrease its profits if it either increased or decreased its output. At any point left of q_E, say q, price is greater than the marginal cost, and it pays to increase output (as indicated by the left-hand arrow). At any point to the right of q_E, say q_1, price is less than the marginal cost, and it pays to reduce output (as indicated by the right-hand arrow). The equilibrium output for the firm is q_E.

The perfectly competitive firm is a mere quantity adjuster. It pursues its goal of profit maximization by increasing or decreasing quantity until it equates its short-run marginal cost with the prevailing price of its product—a price that is given to it by the market.

The market price to which the perfectly competitive firm responds is itself set by the forces of demand and supply. The individual firm, by adjusting quantity produced to whatever price is ruling on the market, helps to determine market supply. The link between the behavior of the firm and the behavior of the competitive market is provided by the market supply curve.

SHORT-RUN SUPPLY CURVES

The supply curve shows the relation between the quantity supplied and price. For any given price we need to ask what quantity will be supplied. This question may be answered by supposing that a price is specified and then determining how much each firm will choose to supply. Then a different price is supposed and quantity supplied again determined—and so on, until all possible prices have been considered.

The Supply Curve of One Firm

Figure 14-4(i) shows a firm's marginal cost curve with four alternative demand curves. The firm's marginal cost curve gives the marginal cost corresponding to each level of output. A supply curve is needed that gives the quantity the firm will supply at every price. For prices below AVC, the firm will supply zero units (rule 1). For prices above AVC, the firm will equate price and marginal cost (rule 2 modified by the proposition that $MR = p$ in perfect competition). From this it follows that:

In perfect competition the firm's supply curve has the identical shape as the firm's marginal cost curve above AVC.

FIGURE 14-4
Deriving the Supply Curve for a Price-taking Firm

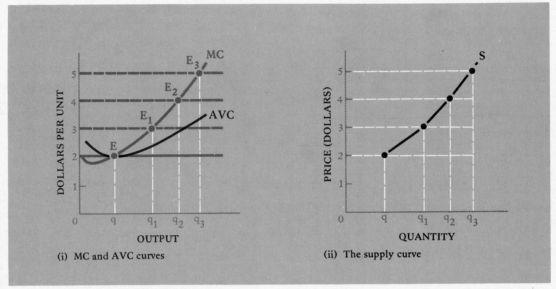

(i) MC and AVC curves (ii) The supply curve

For a price-taking firm, the supply curve has the same shape as its *MC* curve above the level of *AVC*. As prices rise from $2 to $3 to $4 to $5, the firm wishes to increase its production from *q* to q_1 to q_2 to q_3. For prices below $2, output would be zero because the firm is better off if it shuts down. The point *E*, where price equals *AVC*, is called the shutdown point. The firm's supply curve is shown in (ii).

The Supply Curve of an Industry

Figure 14-5 illustrates the derivation of an industry supply curve for an example of only two firms. The general result is that:

> **In perfect competition the industry supply curve is the horizontal sum of the marginal cost curves (above the level of average variable cost) of all firms in the industry.**

The reason for this is that each firm's marginal cost curve tells us how much that firm will supply at any given market price, and the industry supply curve is the sum of what each firm will supply at each market price.

This supply curve, based on the short-run marginal cost curves of the firms in the industry, is the industry's **short-run supply curve.**

THE DETERMINATION OF SHORT-RUN EQUILIBRIUM PRICE

The short-run supply curve and the demand curve for the industry's product together determine the market price. (This happens in the manner analyzed in Chapter 5.) Although no one firm can influence market price significantly, the collective actions of all firms in the industry (as shown by the industry supply curve) and the collective actions of households (as shown by the industry's demand curve) together determine market price at the point where the demand and supply curves intersect.

At the equilibrium market price each firm is producing and selling a quantity for which its marginal cost equals the market price. No firm is motivated to change its output in the short run. Since total quantity demanded equals total quan-

FIGURE 14-5
The Derivation of an Industry Supply Curve

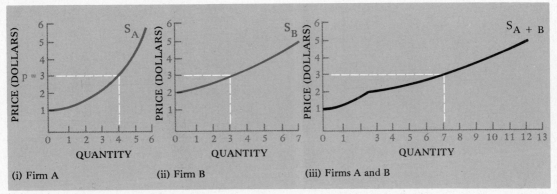

(i) Firm A (ii) Firm B (iii) Firms A and B

The industry supply curve is the horizontal sum of the supply curves of each of the firms in the industry. At a price of $3 firm A would supply 4 units and firm B would supply 3 units. Together, as shown in (iii), they would supply 7 units. If there are hundreds of firms, the process is the same: Each firm's supply curve (which is derived in the manner shown in Figure 14-4) shows what the firm will produce at any given price p. The industry supply curve relates the price to the sum of the quantities produced by each firm. In this example, because firm B does not enter the market at prices below $2, the supply curve S_{A+B} is identical with S_A up to price $2 and is the sum of $S_A + S_B$ above $2.

tity supplied, there is no reason for market price to change in the short run; the market and all the firms in the industry are in short-run equilibrium.

SHORT-RUN PROFITABILITY OF THE FIRM

Although we know that when the industry is in short-run equilibrium, the competitive firm is maximizing its profits, we do not know *how large* these profits are. It is one thing to know that a firm is doing as well as it can in particular circumstances; it is another to know how well it is doing.

Figure 14-6 shows three possible positions for a firm in short-run equilibrium. In all cases, the firm is maximizing its profits by producing where $p = MC$, but in (i) the firm is making losses, in (ii) it is just covering all costs, and in (iii) it is making profits in excess of all costs. In (i) it might be better to say that the firm is minimizing its losses rather than maximizing its profits, but both state-

ments mean the same thing. The firm is doing as well as it can, given its costs and prices.

Long-run Equilibrium

While Figure 14-6 shows three possible short-run equilibrium positions for the profit-maximizing firm in perfect competition, not all of them are possible equilibrium positions in the long run.

THE EFFECT OF ENTRY AND EXIT

The key to long-run equilibrium under perfect competition is entry and exit. We have seen that when firms are in *short-run* equilibrium, they may be making profits or losses or just breaking even. Since costs include the opportunity cost of capital, firms that are just breaking even are doing as well as they could if they invested their capital elsewhere. Thus there will be no incentive for existing firms to leave the industry; neither will there be an incentive for new firms to

FIGURE 14-6
Alternative Short-run Equilibrium Positions of a Competitive Firm

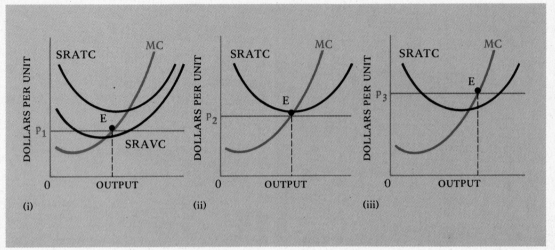

(i)   (ii)   (iii)

When it is in short-run equilibrium, a competitive firm may be suffering losses, breaking even, or making profits. The diagrams show a firm with given costs faced with three alternative prices p_1, p_2, and p_3. In each part of the diagram E is the point at which $MC = MR =$ price. Since in all three cases price exceeds AVC the firm is in short-run equilibrium.

In (i) price is p_1 and the firm is suffering losses because price is below average total cost. Since price exceeds average variable cost, it pays the firm to keep producing, but it does *not* pay it to replace its capital equipment as the capital wears out.

In (ii) price is p_2 and the firm is just covering its total costs. It does pay the firm to replace its capital as it wears out since it is covering the full opportunity cost of its capital.

In (iii) price is p_3 and the firm is earning profits in excess of all its costs.

enter the industry, for capital can earn the same return elsewhere in the economy. If, however, existing firms are earning profits over all costs, including the opportunity cost of capital, new capital will enter the industry to share in these profits. If existing firms are making losses, capital will leave the industry because a better return can be obtained elsewhere in the economy. Let us consider the process in a little more detail.

If all firms in the competitive industry are in the position of the firm in Figure 14-6(iii), new firms will enter the industry, attracted by the profits being earned by existing firms. Suppose that in response to high profits for 100 existing firms, 20 new firms enter. The market supply curve that formerly added up the outputs of 100 firms now must add up the outputs of 120 firms. At any price, more will be supplied because there are more suppliers.

This shift in the short-run supply curve, with an unchanged market demand curve, means that the previous equilibrium price will no longer prevail. The shift in supply will cause the equilibrium price to fall, and both new and old firms will have to adjust their output to this new price. This is illustrated in Figure 14-7. New firms will continue to enter and price will continue to fall until all firms in the industry are just covering their total costs. Firms will then be in the position of the firm in Figure 14-6(ii), which is called a *zero-profit equilibrium*.

Profits in a competitive industry are a signal for the entry of new capital; the industry will expand, forcing price down until the profits fall to zero.

If the firms in the industry are in the position of the firm in Figure 14-6(i), they are suffering losses. They are covering their variable costs, but the return on their capital is less than the opportunity cost of this capital; the firms are not covering their total costs. This is a signal for the exit of firms. As plant and equipment are discarded they will not be replaced. As a result, the industry's short-run supply curve shifts left and market price rises. Firms will continue to exit and price will continue to rise until the remaining firms can cover their total costs—that is, until they are all in the zero-profit equilibrium illustrated in Figure 14-6(ii). Exit then ceases.

Losses in a competitive industry are a signal for the exit of capital; the industry will contract, driving price up until the remaining firms are covering their total costs.

In all of this we see profits serving their function of allocating resources among the industries of the economy.

FIGURE 14-7
The Effect of New Entrants on the Supply Curve

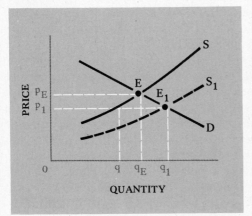

New entrants shift the supply curve to the right and lower the equilibrium price. Initial equilibrium is at E. If the supply curve shifts to S_1 by virtue of entry, the equilibrium price must fall to p_1 while output rises to q_1. At this price before entry, only q would have been produced. The extra output is supplied by the new productive capacity.

THE LEVEL OF COST AT EQUILIBRIUM

An industry is nothing more than a collection of firms; for an industry to be in long-run equilibrium each firm must be in long-run equilibrium. It follows that when a perfectly competitive industry is in long-run equilibrium, all firms in the industry will be selling at a price equal to minimum average total cost—that is, they must be in zero-profit equilibrium, as in Figure 14-6(ii). This result plays an important role in the appeal that perfect competition has had to economists, as we shall see. (Further discussion of the level of cost in long-run equilibrium will be found in the appendix to this chapter.)

Let us now apply this theory to two commonly observed situations.

THE LONG-RUN RESPONSE OF A PERFECTLY COMPETITIVE INDUSTRY TO A CHANGE IN TECHNOLOGY

Consider an industry in long-run equilibrium. Since the industry is in equilibrium, each firm must be in zero-profit equilibrium. Now assume that some technological development lowers the cost curves of newly built plants. Since price is just equal to the average total cost for the old plants, new plants will now be able to earn profits, and more of them will now be built. But this expansion in capacity shifts the short-run supply curve to the right and drives price down. The expansion in capacity and the fall in price will continue until price is equal to the *ATC* of the *new* plants. At this price old plants will not be covering their long-run costs. As long as price exceeds their average variable cost, however, such plants will continue in production. As the outmoded plants wear out they will gradually disappear. Eventually a new long-run equilibrium will be established in which all plants use the new technology.

What happens in a competitive industry in which technological change occurs not as a single isolated event but more or less continuously?

FIGURE 14-8
Plants of Different Vintages in an Industry with Continuing Technical Progress

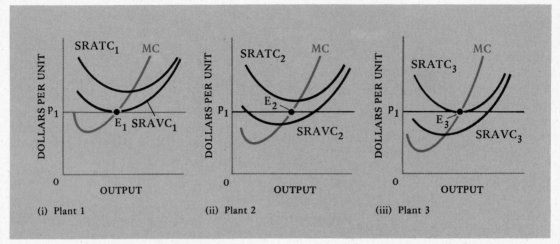

(i) Plant 1   (ii) Plant 2   (iii) Plant 3

Entry of progressively lower-cost firms forces price down, but older plants with higher costs remain in the industry as long as price covers average variable cost. Plant 3 is the newest plant with the lowest costs. Price will be determined by the average total costs of plants of this type since entry will continue as long as the owners of the newest plants expect to earn profits from them. Plant 1 is the oldest plant in operation; it is just covering its *AVC*, and if the price falls any further it will be closed down. Plant 2 is a plant of intermediate age. It is covering its variable costs and earning some return on its capital. The return will shrink over time as entry of new plants with lower and lower costs drives price lower and lower.

Plants built in any one year will tend to have lower costs than plants built in any previous year. This is a common occurrence in the real world; it is illustrated in Figure 14-8. Such industries have a number of interesting characteristics.

One is that plants of different ages and different levels of efficiency will exist side by side. This characteristic is dramatically illustrated by the variety of vintages of steam turbine generators found in any long-established electric power commission. Critics who observe the continued use of older, less efficient plants and urge that "something be done to eliminate these wasteful practices" miss the point of economic efficiency. If the plant is already there, the plant can be profitably operated as long as it can do anything more than cover its variable costs. As long as a plant can produce goods that are valued by consumers at an amount above the value of the resources currently used up for their production (variable costs), the value of society's total output is increased by using that plant to produce goods.

A second characteristic of such an industry is that price will be governed by *the minimum ATC of the most efficient plants*. Entry will continue until plants of the latest vintage are just expected to earn normal profits over their lifetimes. The benefits of the new technology are passed on to consumers because all units of the commodity, whether produced by new or old plants, are sold at a price that is related solely to the *ATC* of the new plants. Owners of older plants find their returns over variable costs falling steadily as more and more efficient plants drive the price of the product down.

A third characteristic is that old plants will be discarded (or "mothballed") when the price falls below their *AVC*. This may occur well before the plants are physically worn out. In industries with continuous technical progress, capital is usually discarded because it is economically obsolete, not because it has physically worn out. This illustrates the economic meaning of obsolete:

Old capital is obsolete when its average variable cost exceeds the average total cost of new capital.

INDUSTRIES THAT ARE DECLINING DUE TO A STEADY DECREASE IN DEMAND

What happens when a competitive industry in long-run equilibrium begins to suffer losses due to a permanent and continuing decrease in the demand for its products? As demand declines, price falls and firms that were previously covering *ATC* are not now able to do so. They find themselves in the position shown in Figure 14-8(ii). Firms earn losses instead of breaking even, and the signal for exit of capital is given. But exit takes time. The economically correct response to a steadily declining demand is not to replace old equipment but to continue to operate with existing equipment as long as the firm can cover its variable costs of production.

Gradually equipment will break down and not be repaired or replaced. The capacity of the industry will shrink, slowly at first. If demand keeps declining, capacity must keep shrinking.

Declining industries typically present a sorry sight to the observer. Revenues are below long-run total costs, and as a result new equipment is not brought in to replace old equipment as it wears out. The average age of equipment in use thus rises steadily. The untrained observer seeing the industry's very real plight is likely to blame it on the antiquated equipment in use.

The antiquated equipment in a declining industry is the effect rather than the cause of the industry's decline.

It would not usually make sense for firms to modernize in the face of steadily falling demand even when new, improved equipment is available. To do so would increase the industry's capacity and its output, thereby making its overall plight still worse. Price would fall even more rapidly, adding further to the losses of existing firms.

A striking example of the confusion of cause and effect in a declining industry occurred during the debate over the nationalization of the coal industry in Great Britain in the period between the two world wars.

The view that public control was needed to save an industry from the dead hand of third-rate, unenterprising private owners was commonly held about the British coal industry and was undoubtedly a factor leading to its nationalization in 1946. This view was held by the commission which reported in 1926 on the state of the coal industry: "It would be possible to say without exaggeration of the miners' leaders that they were the stupidest men in England, if we had not had frequent occasion to meet the owners."

The late Sir Roy Harrod, a leading British economist from the 1920s to the 1960s, shocked many by taking the opposite view, arguing that the rundown state of the coal industry in South Wales and Yorkshire represented the correct response of the owners to the signals of the market.

Economic efficiency does not consist in always introducing the most up-to-date equipment that an engineer can think of but rather in the correct adaptation of the amount of new capital sunk to the earning capacity of the old asset. In not introducing new equipment, the managements may have been wise, not only from the point of view of their own interest, but from that of national interest, which requires the most profitable application of available capital . . . it is right that as much should be extracted from the inferior mines as can be done by old-fashioned methods [i.e., with equipment already installed], and that they should gradually go out of action.[3]

The general point that Professor Harrod makes is extremely important. It is in the public and the private interest that what appear to be antiquated methods be employed in declining industries. Capital resources are scarce; to install new plant and equipment in a genuinely declining

---

[3] Roy Harrod, *The British Economy* (New York: McGraw-Hill, 1963), page 54.

Government Support of Threatened Firms

Troubled industrial giants pose serious concerns for policymakers. Whether it be the Chrysler Corporation, Massey Ferguson, or a large textile firm, the threatened bankruptcy of such a company often calls forth a government policy to support that company. The British government has a long history of supporting troubled industrial giants, and although such support is less far-reaching and more recent in Canada than in Britain, our policy could easily move piecemeal in the British direction. In the United States the Reagan administration has overcome its dedication to market forces by protecting the domestic auto industry, first by continuing support to Chrysler and then by negotiating with Japan a voluntary reduction in Japanese car sales to the United States.

FIRMS THAT CAN COVER VARIABLE COSTS

What is often forgotten is that real capital equipment does not crumble away just because a firm goes bankrupt. As long as the real capital can cover its variable costs of operation, someone will find its operation profitable.

A company may get into financial difficulties for many reasons. It may have been mismanaged, or the demand for its product may have declined. It may be able to cover its variable costs but unable to meet its debt obligations. Its creditors—both its suppliers and those who have lent it money by buying its bonds—may then foreclose, driving the firm into bankruptcy. Whether the result of mismanagement or a decline in demand, the essential problem is that the firm has too much (real) capital and hence cannot earn an adequate return on it. There is not enough to pay dividends on the equity capital or interest on the debt capital.

If the firm goes bankrupt for either reason, its shareholders—and possibly also its creditors—will suffer the initial losses. The firm, however, will be reorganized. Its capital will continue to operate, and it will continue to employ workers. Some cutbacks and firings may be involved in making the firm once again viable. But the capital is still there. As long as it can earn anything above its variable costs, the firm's creditors can operate it and regain some of what the firm owes to them.

When the government steps in to save a trouble firm from bankruptcy, it is common for policymakers to say they are doing this to save x thousand jobs, where x thousand is the total employment of the company. This is almost never correct. If variable costs can be covered and some additional return earned, it will always pay someone to operate the firm; no one's interests will be served by merely scrapping the capital. The government is saving the investments of the owners and creditors of the firm, not the jobs of the work force.

FIRMS THAT CANNOT COVER VARIABLE COSTS

Sometimes firms do go out of business because the industry in which they are located is declining and there is not enough room for all the existing firms. In this case the firms will find that they are no longer able to cover even their variable costs of production. They will then go out of business, and all their employees will lose their present jobs.

This process is as old as history and as fundamental as economic growth. As growth proceeds, the pattern of demands and costs shifts; some industries decline and others expand. So we can always expect to find declining industries, and in them firms that are closing their doors and creating unemployment. However, we can also expect to find expanding industries, and in them growing firms that are seeking to expand their employment.

When the government steps in and supports the declining industries, the consequences can be serious. The nation's scarce resources are wasted when they are used to produce goods that consumers value less than the cost of the variable inputs that make up those goods. When the government then adds additional capital to the industries, it is capital that not only cannot contribute as much to the value of output as could capital in other industries, it is capital that can earn no positive return at all. The amount that consumers are willing to pay to purchase the output contributed by the extra capital does not even cover the variable costs of production.

To prop up declining industries is to reduce the growth rate by preventing the factors of production—labor and capital—from moving to sectors that are growing. Sooner or later such support becomes impossible; as demand continues to fall, the subsidy required to support the declining industry increases until, as more firms and more industries become involved, the subsidy load becomes unbearable. *To attempt to freeze a particular industrial pattern in a changing world is to impose heavy and growing costs on the economy and in the end to attempt an impossible task.*

REGIONAL POLICY

The third major reason for supporting industries that are unable to stand on their own relates to regional policy. Industries in the Maritimes, and some other parts of the country, are sometimes subsidized because policymakers believe that living standards in these areas would otherwise be too low. In effect this represents a transfer of income in the form of a subsidy from wealthier areas to poorer areas. While the payment of subsidies from the better off to the less well off may appeal to many of us in the interests of justice, the subsidizing of inefficient industries nevertheless represents an inefficient way to effect the income transfer.

The payment of direct transfers where the recipients may then spend the money as they wish might be a more efficient method of effecting such transfers. However, this is often less liked by many because it creates a direct gift rather than a chance to be employed (even though the employment is not efficient from the nation's point of view).

Canadian regional policies raise complicated issues with respect to equity and justice. Consider the magnitude of the problem. It is quite possible for a well-to-do- major part of the country to subsidize a less well-to-do smaller part of the country (small in terms of population and resources) as, for example, when the rest of Canada subsidizes industries in the Maritimes. Whether or not this is efficient, the policy is certainly possible and will not "break the bank." But if a major part of the country's industry, such as the industrial sector of Quebec and Ontario, were to be subsidized in the same way, the burden would quickly become intolerable. While 90 percent of the people can heavily subsidize 10 percent of the people, the reverse is not possible. If the center of the industrial part of the country were to be propped up by large subsidies, who would pay the subsidies? Therefore, although we could continue to subsidize inefficient industries in small parts of the country indefinitely, the development of a tendency to subsidize a major part of the industrial structure in the center of the country must be viewed with some alarm. The British experience shows that this can become extremely costly and in the end succeeds not in saving the industries but only in delaying their demise—at large national costs. And when the government finally withdraws its support, the decline is much more abrupt and hence more difficult to adjust to than it would have been had the industry been allowed to decline gradually under the market force of steadily declining demand.

People interested in Canada's continued economic growth must hope, then, that the government of Canada will continue to understand the process of growth and to understand that the decay of certain industries and the collapse of certain firms is an inevitable part of growth. The government, we hope, will also understand that the appropriate response is to provide welfare and retraining schemes that cushion the blow of change, moderating the effects on the incomes of those who lose their jobs and making it easier for them to retrain and transfer to expanding sectors of the economy. Appropriate intervention intended to increase mobility and reduce the social and personal costs of mobility is a viable long-run policy. To try to freeze the existing structure by shoring up the inevitably declining industry is not.

industry is to use the nation's scarce resources of new capital where they will not lead to the largest possible increases in the value of output.

The Appeal of Perfect Competition

The theory of perfect competition shows that profit-maximizing price-taking firms, responding to prices set by the impersonal forces of supply and demand, will be motivated to provide all commodities for which total revenues are equal to or greater than total costs. They will be motivated to produce every unit for which price is greater than marginal cost, and they will thus expand production up to the point where price equals marginal cost. The entry and exit of firms will, in long-run equilibrium, push prices to the level of minimum average total costs—that is, to the lowest level attainable for the given technology and factor prices.

Consider an economy in which every industry operates as a perfectly competitive industry. For the nineteenth century liberal economists, such a world was more than a theoretical model, it was a most attractive ideal. One of them, Bascom, glowingly characterized such an economic system as "more provocative of virtue than virtue herself." The appeal of a competitive economy has both noneconomic and economic aspects.

THE NONECONOMIC APPEAL OF COMPETITION

In a perfectly competitive economy there are many firms and many households. Each is a price taker, responding as it sees fit, freely and without coercion, to signals sent to it by the market. For one who believes in the freedom of individuals to make decisions, and who distrusts all power groups, the perfectly competitive model is almost too good to be true. No single firm and no single consumer has any power over the market. Individual consumers and producers are passive quantity adjusters who respond to market signals.

Yet the impersonal force of the market produces an appropriate response to all changes. If tastes change, for example, prices will change, and the allocation of resources will change in the appropriate direction. Throughout the entire process, no one will have any power over anyone else. Dozens of firms will react to the same price changes, and if one firm refuses to react, there will be countless other profit-maximizing firms eager to make the appropriate changes.

Because the market mechanism works, it is not necessary for the government to intervene. Market reactions, not public policies, will eliminate shortages or surpluses. There is no need for government regulatory agencies or bureaucrats to make arbitrary decisions about who may produce what, or how to produce it, or how much it is permissible to charge for the product. If there are no government officials to make such decisions, there will be no one to bribe to make one decision rather than another.

In the impersonal decision-making world of perfect competition, neither private firms nor public officials wield economic power. The market mechanism, like an invisible hand, determines the allocation of resources among competing uses.

THE ECONOMIC APPEAL OF PERFECT COMPETITION: EFFICIENCY

Resources are scarce relative to the wants of society's members, so it is desirable not to waste the resources we have. The most obvious way to waste resources is not to use them at all. When labor is unemployed and factories lie idle (as occurs in serious depressions), their potential current output is lost. If these resources could be reemployed, total output would be increased and hence everyone could be made better off.

But full employment of resources by itself is not enough to prevent the waste of resources. Even when resources are being fully used, they may be used inefficiently.

Let us look at three possible sources of inefficiency in resource use.

1. If firms do not use the least costly method of producing their chosen outputs, they will waste resources. By adopting the least costly method they would free resources to be used to make other commodities. In a firm that achieves its monthly production of 30,000 pairs of shoes at a resource cost of $400,000 when it could be done at a cost of only $350,000, resources are being used inefficiently. If the lower cost method were used, $50,000 worth of other commodities could be produced each month by transferring the resources saved to their best alternative use.

2. If some firms are too large and others too small, each will not be producing at the lowest point on its long-run average cost curve. Thus any given level of the industry's production will use more resources than is necessary.

3. If too much of one product and too little of another is produced, resources are also being used inefficiently. To take an extreme example, say that so many shoes were produced that their *marginal* utility was zero while the marginal utility of coats remained high at the current level of output. Since no one places any value on the last pair of shoes produced, while everyone places a high value on an additional coat, no one will be made worse off by reducing the output of shoes, yet someone will be made better off by using the resources to increase the production of coats.

These examples suggest that we must refine our ideas of the waste of resources beyond the simple notion of ensuring that all resources are used. Economists define rather precisely what is meant by efficiency and inefficiency in resource use.

Resources are said to be used *inefficiently* when it would be *possible* by using them differently to make at least one household better off without making any household worse off. Conversely, resources are said to be used *efficiently* when it is *impossible* by using them differently to make any one household better off without making at least one other household worse off.

Inefficiency implies that we can help someone without hurting someone else. Efficiency implies that we cannot. When resources are already being used efficiently, we can only make one household better off at the cost of making another household worse off.

Efficiency in the use of resources is often called **Pareto-efficiency** or **Pareto-optimality** in honor of the great Italian economist Vilfredo Pareto (1848–1923), who pioneered the study of efficiency.

So much for the meaning of efficiency; now how do we achieve it? The three sources of inefficiency numbered above suggest important conditions that must be fulfilled if economic efficiency is to be attained.

Productive Efficiency

The first condition of economic efficiency is that whatever output the *firm* selects must be produced at the lowest possible cost of producing that level of output. Otherwise more resources will be used for this output than are necessary. This condition will be fulfilled by any profit-maximizing firm. A firm is obviously not maximizing its profits when it produces its desired output at a higher cost than is necessary.

The second condition is that the costs of producing the *industry* output should be as low as possible. This condition is fulfilled under perfect competition. We saw on page 258 that when a perfectly competitive industry is in long-run equilibrium, every firm is producing at the minimum point on its long-run average total cost curve.

These two conditions concern what is called **productive efficiency.** The first guarantees that firms produce on, rather than above, their long-run average total cost curves. The second guarantees that firms produce at the point of *lowest* long-run average total cost. Together they ensure that each product is produced as cheaply as possible.

Allocative Efficiency

The third condition concerns the appropriate mix of products. Resources are not being used efficiently when they are being used to produce products that no one wants. **Allocative efficiency** refers to the allocation of resources among the economy's various industries; it obtains when it is impossible to change that allocation in such a way as to make someone better off without making someone else worse off.

What is the right mix? How many shoes and how many coats should be produced for allocative efficiency? The answer is that (under certain conditions that we shall specify later) the allocation of resources to any one commodity is efficient when its price is equal to its marginal cost of production, that is, $p = MC$.

This rather subtle condition has been one of the most influential ideas in the whole of economics. To understand it, we need to remind ourselves of two points established earlier: first, the price of any commodity indicates the value that each household places on the last unit of the commodity that it consumes (per period); second, marginal cost indicates the value that the resources used to produce the marginal unit of output would have in their best alternative uses.

The first proposition follows directly from marginal utility theory (see page 163). A household will go on increasing its rate of consumption of a commodity until the *marginal* valuation that it puts on the commodity is equal to its price. The household gets a consumers' surplus on all but the marginal unit because it values them more than the price it has to pay. On the marginal unit, however, it only "breaks even" because the valuation placed on it is just equal to its price.

The second proposition follows from the nature of opportunity cost (see page 199). The marginal cost of producing some commodity is the opportunity cost of the resources used. Opportunity cost means the value of the resources in their best alternative uses.

To see how these propositions fit together, assume that shoes sell for $30 a pair but have a marginal production cost of $40. If one less pair of shoes were produced, the value that households place on the pair of shoes not produced would be $30. But by the meaning of opportunity cost, the resources that would have been used to produce that pair of shoes could instead produce other goods (say a coat) valued at $40. If society can give up something its members value at $30 and get in return something its members value at $40, the original allocation of resources is inefficient. Someone can be made better off, and no one need be worse off. This is easy to see when the same household gives up the shoes and gets the coat. But it follows even when different households are involved, for the gaining household can compensate the losing household and still come out ahead.

Assume next that shoe production is cut back until the price of a pair of shoes rises from $30 to $35 while its marginal cost falls from $40 to $35. The efficiency condition is now fulfilled in shoe production because $p = MC = \$35$. Now if one less pair of shoes were produced, $35 worth of shoes would be sacrificed while at most $35 worth of other commodities could be produced with the freed resources. In this situation the allocation of resources to shoe production is efficient because it is not possible to change it and make someone better off without making someone else worse off. If one household were to sacrifice the pair of shoes, it would give up goods worth $35 and would then have to get all of the new production of the alternative commodity produced just to break even. It cannot gain without making another household worse off. The same argument can be repeated for every commodity, and it leads to this conclusion:

The allocation of resources among commodities is efficient when for each commodity price equals marginal cost.

Allocative efficiency is thus satisfied when $p = MC$ in all industries. For every industry in perfect competition, $p = MC$ in equilibrium. Thus:

Universal perfect competition fulfills the condition for allocative efficiency by ensuring that price equals marginal cost in every industry.

A Graphic Interpretation of Allocative Efficiency

Consider a competitive industry where forces of demand and supply establish a competitive price. Because the industry supply curve represents the sum of the marginal cost curves of the firms in the industry, the market clearing price is one at which $p = MC$. In the figure, such a price is shown as p^*, and the corresponding output is q^*. For every unit produced up to this output, the value consumers would be willing to pay (as shown by the demand curve) is greater than the opportunity cost of the resources used to produce it (as shown by the $S = MC$ curve).

The shaded areas represent the excess of consumer variation over opportunity cost. It is customary to divide the total shaded area into two parts: that above the price line (dark shade) is called *consumers' surplus* (encountered in Chapter 9); that below the price line (light shade) is an analogous quality called *producers' surplus* — because producers would have been willing to provide each unit at its marginal cost but are actually paid p^* (which is greater than marginal cost for all but the last unit). The two shaded areas together represent the *sum* of consumers' surplus and producers' surplus.

Allocative efficiency is achieved when the sum of the surpluses is maximized. This occurs at the output q^*, where $p = MC$. For any output less than q^*, such as q_1, a slight increase in output toward q^* would lead to an addition to both consumers' and producers' surplus. This is because at the level of output q_1, consumers' valuation of the commodity, p_1, exceeds the opportunity cost of producing it, c_1. For any output greater than q^*, such as q_2, this is not the case. For every unit beyond q^* the demand curve (what consumers would pay) is below the supply curve (what producers must be paid). Extra units beyond q^* would subtract from both producers' and consumers' surpluses.

Thus producers' plus consumers' surplus is maximized *only* at output q^*. If some invisible authority were to instruct producers to "maximize the sum of producers' and consumers' surplus," producers would produce every unit up to q^*. The perfectly competitive market price, p^*, provides exactly that signal!

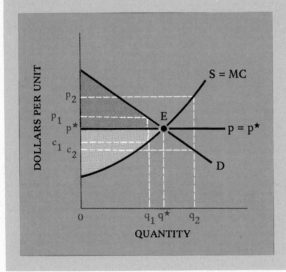

SOME WORDS OF WARNING ABOUT THE EFFICIENCY OF PERFECT COMPETITION

An economy that consisted of perfectly competitive industries would in equilibrium achieve allocative efficiency. Further, if the costs for each such industry were the lowest costs attainable, the economy would also achieve productive efficiency in the production of every commodity. This is because the forces of competition push equilibrium price to the level where $p = MC = ATC$.

Before jumping to the conclusion that perfect competition is the best of all possible worlds and that government policy ought to do everything possible to achieve it, we must consider certain qualifications. Four will be mentioned here, to be developed in later chapters.

Costs may be higher under perfect competition than under alternative market structures. In a competitive industry, production occurs at the lowest level of cost attainable by the competitive firm. But, as we shall see, it is possible that the existence of unexploited economies of large-scale production can render an industry made up of competitive firms less productively efficient than (say) a monopoly. It is also possible that firms in a perfectly competitive industry may not innovate as rapidly as firms in another industry structure, and thus the cost of producing the competitive output will not be as low as it might be.

These matters are discussed more fully in Chapters 15, 16, and 18.

Perfect competition may not pertain simultaneously everywhere in the economy. Our argument about allocative efficiency rested on $p = MC$ everywhere in the economy. But there may be some industries where price does not and cannot equal marginal cost. (The reasons will be explored in Chapter 18.) In such a world there is no general presumption of what the effect will be of prices equaling marginal costs *somewhere* in the economy. Thus, if price does not equal marginal cost in industry A, the fact that $p = MC$ in industry B may not lead to allocative efficiency.

This proposition illustrates what is known as the "theory of the second best": We may know how to identify the best of all possible worlds (from the limited point of view of the optimum we are discussing), but we may have a harder task when attempting to rank order two situations in the very imperfect world in which we live.

Private costs may be poor measures of society's costs. Producing a good up to the point at which the price just equals the *firm's* marginal cost is efficient from society's point of view only if the firm's private costs reflect the opportunity costs to society of using the resources elsewhere. As we shall see in Chapter 24, this is often not the case because of what are called externalities. For example, if the competitive firm uses resources it does not pay for (such as the clean air around its factories), it may produce too much output and too much pollution to be efficient. It does so because *its* own marginal costs fail to include the value that members of society place on some of the resources (clean air) it uses up.

Efficiency is not the only goal. A competitive economy distributes output as well as produces it. A freely functioning competitive economy might produce a distribution of income consisting of one millionaire and 999 paupers. Such an economy can be just as efficient, even more efficient, than an economy with 1,000 persons of roughly equal income. Before one can speak of a competitive economy as being "virtuous," one must consider goals other than efficiency. This matter is discussed further in Chapter 24.

Summary

1. Competitive behavior is concerned with how individual firms compete against each other; competitive market structure is concerned with the degree of power that individual firms have to influence such market variables as the price of the product. Under perfect competition individual firms are powerless to influence market price. Therefore they do not have any incentive to indulge in competitive behavior against their fellow producers in the same industry.

2. A profit-maximizing firm will produce at an output where (a) price is at least as great as average variable cost, (b) marginal cost equals marginal revenue, and (c) the marginal cost curve cuts the marginal revenue curve from below.

3. The two critical assumptions of the theory of perfect competition are that firms are price

takers and that the industry displays freedom of entry and exit. A firm that is a price taker will adjust to different market conditions by varying its output.

4. The perfectly competitive firm's short-run supply curve is the same shape as its MC curve above AVC. The perfectly competitive industry's short-run supply curve is the horizontal sum of its firms' supply curves (i.e., the horizontal sum of the firms' marginal cost curves).

5. When perfectly competitive firms are in short-run equilibrium, they must, if they are producing at all, be covering their variable costs. But they may be making losses (price less than average total cost), making profits (price greater than average total cost), or just covering all costs (price equal to average total cost).

6. In the long run, profits or losses will lead to the entry or exit of capital from the industry. Entry of new firms or exit of existing firms will push a competitive industry to a long-run zero-profit equilibrium and move production to the level of minimum average total cost. Long-run equilibrium is discussed at greater length in the appendix to this chapter.

7. The long-run response of a growing, perfectly competitive industry to steadily changing technology is the gradual replacement of less efficient plants and machines by more efficient ones. Older machines will be utilized as long as price exceeds AVC; then they will be discarded and replaced by newer, more modern ones.

8. The long-run response of a declining industry will be to continue to satisfy the remaining demand from its existing machinery as long as price exceeds AVC. Despite the appearance of being antiquated, this is the correct response in the face of steadily falling demand.

9. The great appeal of the theory of perfect competition as a means of organizing production has both noneconomic and economic elements. The noneconomic appeal lies in the decentralized decision making of myriad firms and households. No individual exercises power over the market.

At the same time, it is not necessary for the government to intervene to determine resource allocation and prices; thus there is no need for government agencies to exercise arbitrary or bureaucratic power.

10. The economic appeal of a world of perfect competition arises from the fact that, under certain conditions, it exhibits both productive and allocative efficiency. Productive efficiency is achieved because the same forces that lead to long-run equilibrium lead to production at the lowest attainable cost. Allocative efficiency is achieved because in competitive equilibrium, price equals marginal cost for every product. If this condition is met in all industries, there will be no shift of resources that can increase the satisfaction of any household without decreasing it for some other household. Other terms for allocative efficiency are *Pareto-optimality* and *Pareto-efficiency*.

11. The efficiency of perfect competition should be understood yet interpreted with caution. Four qualifications to its being "ideal" are: (a) costs may be higher under perfect competition than under alternative market structures; (b) perfect competition may not pertain simultaneously everywhere in the economy; (c) private costs may be poor measures of society's costs; (d) efficiency is not the only goal of the members of society. Because of the first three, competitive equilibrium in a particular industry may not even be efficient. Because of the fourth, even an efficient competitive equilibrium may be regarded as less than ideal in its results.

Topics for Review

Competitive behavior and competitive market structure
Behavioral rules for the profit-maximizing firm
Price taking and a horizontal demand curve
Average revenue, marginal revenue, and price under perfect competition
The relation of the industry supply curve to firms' marginal cost curves
Short-run and long-run equilibrium of firms and industries

Productive and allocative efficiency

Pareto-optimality (and Pareto-efficiency)

Discussion Questions

1. Consider the suppliers of the following commodities. What are the elements of market structure that you might want to invoke to account for differences in their market behavior? Could any of them be characterized as perfectly competitive industries?

   a. television broadcasting

   b. automobiles

   c. sand and gravel

   d. medical services

   e. mortgage loans

   f. retail fruits and vegetables

   g. soybeans

2. Which of the following observed facts about an industry are inconsistent with its being a perfectly competitive industry?

   a. Different firms use different methods of production.

   b. There is extensive advertising of the industry's product by a trade association.

   c. Individual firms devote 5 percent of sales receipts to advertising their own product brand.

   d. There are 24 firms in the industry.

   e. The largest firm in the industry makes 40 percent of the sales and the next largest firm sells 20 percent, but the products are identical and there are 61 other firms.

   f. All firms made large profits in 1980.

3. In which of the following sectors of the Canadian economy might you expect to find competitive behavior? In which might you expect to find industries that were classified as operating under perfectly competitive market structures?

   a. manufacturing

   b. agriculture

   c. transportation and public utilities

   d. wholesale and retail trade

   e. criminal activity

4. In the 1930s the U.S. coal industry was characterized by easy entry and price taking. Because of large fixed costs in mine shafts and fixed equipment, however, exit was slow. With declining demand, many firms were barely covering their variable costs but not their total costs. As a result of a series of mine accidents, the federal government began to enforce mine safety standards, which forced most firms to invest in new capital if they were to remain in production. What predictions would competitive theory make about market behavior and the quantity of coal produced? Would coal miners approve or disapprove of the new enforcement program?

5. Suppose entry into an industry is not artificially restricted but takes time because of the need to build plants, acquire know-how, and establish a marketing organization. Can such an industry be characterized as perfectly competitive? Does ease of entry imply ease of exit, and vice versa?

6. What, if anything, do each of the following tell you about ease of entry or exit in an industry?

   a. Profits have been very high for two decades.

   b. No new firms have entered the industry for 20 years.

   c. The average age of the firms in a 40-year-old industry is less than seven years.

   d. Most existing firms are using obsolete equipment alongside newer, more modern equipment.

   e. Profits are low or negative; many firms are still producing, but from steadily aging equipment.

7. In the 1970s grain prices in North America rose substantially relative to other agricultural products. Explain how each of the following may have contributed to this result; then consider how a perfectly competitive grain industry might be expected to react in the long run.

   a. Crop failures caused by unusually bad weather around the world in several years.

   b. Rising demand for beef and chickens because of rising population and rising per capita income.

   c. Great scarcities in fishmeal, a substitute for grain in animal diets, because of a mysterious decline in the anchovy harvest off Peru.

   d. Increased Soviet purchases of grain on the world market.

Pricing in Monopoly Markets

15

Is Bell Canada a monopoly? How about IBM, International Nickel, and the National Hockey League? Just as the word "competition" has both an everyday meaning and a more specialized technical one, so too does the word "monopoly." Monopoly, as economists use the concept, is a market structure that leads to certain predicted kinds of market behavior.

The word "monopoly" comes from the Greek words *monos polein*, which mean "alone to sell." It is convenient for now to think of **monopoly** as the situation in which the output of an entire industry is controlled by a single seller. This seller will be called the monopolist. Later in this chapter we will define monopoly in a less restrictive way.

A Monopolist Selling at a Single Price

Consider first an industry producing a single product in which a monopolist sets a price and supplies the entire quantity that buyers wish to purchase at that price. In contrast to the competitive firm, the monopolist is a price setter, not a price taker. The monopolistic firm faces a downward-sloping demand curve and can pick any price-quantity combination on the demand curve. The monopolist is sometimes said to be able to *administer* its price. This means that it, unlike the perfect competitor, can and usually does select its own price.

THE MONOPOLIST'S REVENUE CURVES

Because the monopolistic firm is assumed to be the only producer of a particular product, its demand curve is identical with the demand curve for that product. The market demand curve, which shows the aggregate quantity that buyers will purchase at every price, also shows the quantity that the monopolist will be able to sell at any price it sets. Given the market demand curve, the monopolist's average revenue and marginal revenue curves can be readily deduced.

When the seller charges a single price for all

TABLE 15-1

The Relation of Average Revenue and Marginal Revenue: A Numerical Illustration

Price $P = AR$	Quantity q	$TR = p \times q$	$MR = \Delta TR / \Delta q$
$9.10	9	$81.90	
9.00	10	90.00	$8.10
8.90	11	97.90	7.90

Marginal revenue is less than price because price must be lowered to sell an extra unit. A monopolist can choose either the price or the quantity to be sold. But choosing one determines the other. In this example, to increase sales from 10 to 11 units, it is necessary to reduce the price on all units sold from $9 to $8.90. The extra unit sold brings in $8.90, but the firm sacrifices 10¢ on each of the 10 units that it could have sold at $9 had it not wanted to increase sales. The net addition to revenue is the $8.90 minus 10¢ times 10 units, or $1, making $7.90 altogether. Thus the marginal revenue resulting from the increase in sales by 1 unit is $7.90, which is less than the price at which the units are sold.

Marginal revenue is shown displaced by half a line to emphasize that it represents the effect on revenue of the *change* in output.

FIGURE 15-1

The Effect on Revenue of an Increase in Quantity Sold

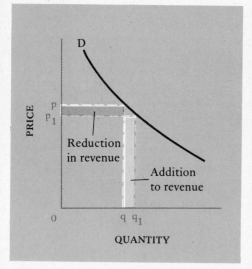

For a downward-sloping demand curve, marginal revenue is less than price. A reduction of price from p to p_1 increases sales by 1 unit from q to q_1 units. The revenue from the extra unit sold (i.e., its price) is shown as the lighter shaded area. But to sell this unit, it is necessary to reduce the price on each of the q units previously sold. This loss in revenue is shown as the darker shaded area. Marginal revenue of the extra unit is equal to the *difference* between the two areas.

units sold, average revenue per unit is identical with price. Thus the market demand curve is also the average revenue curve for the monopolist. But marginal revenue is less than price because the monopolist has to lower the price that it charges on *all* units in order to sell an *extra* unit. (Figure 15-1). **[25]** This is an important difference from the case of perfect competition; it is explored numerically in Table 15-1 and graphically in Figure 15-1.

Figure 15-2 illustrates the average and marginal revenue curves for a monopolist, based on a downward-sloping straight-line demand curve.[1]

---

[1] It is helpful (for sketching revenue curves, etc.) to remember that if the demand curve is a downward-sloping straight line, the *MR* curve also slopes downward and is twice as steep. Its price intercept (where $q = 0$) is the same as that of the demand curve, and it cuts the quantity axis (where $p = 0$) at just half the output that the demand curve does. **[26]**

FIGURE 15-2

Demand, Average Revenue, and Marginal Revenue Curves for a Monopolist

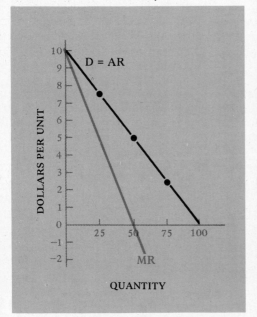

For the monopolist, *MR* does not equal price. The demand curve is the *AR* curve; the *MR* curve is below and steeper than the *AR* curve because the demand curve slopes downward.

Marginal Revenue, Total Revenue, and Elasticity of Demand

A demand curve represents a single relationship between quantity and price, but there are many different ways of looking at this relationship.

Figure 15-3 shows how total revenue and elasticity of demand (η) are related to *AR* and *MR*. Consider first that part of the demand curve where elasticity is greater than one. This means that total revenue rises as quantity increases, and hence the total revenue curve is upward-sloping. Because total revenue is increasing as quantity is increasing, marginal revenue must be positive. Next consider the point at which elasticity of demand is exactly unity. Here total revenue remains constant as quantity sold increases. This

implies that marginal revenue is zero. Consider finally the part of the demand curve where elasticity is less than one. This means that total revenue falls as quantity increases, and hence the total revenue curve is now downward-sloping. This implies that marginal revenue is negative.

FIGURE 15-3

The Relation of Total, Average, and Marginal Revenue to Elasticity of Demand

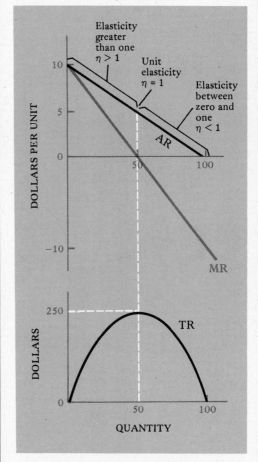

When *TR* is rising, *MR* is greater than zero and elasticity is greater than unity. In this example, for outputs from 0 to 50, marginal revenue is positive, elasticity is greater than unity, and total revenue is rising. For outputs from 50 to 100, marginal revenue is negative, elasticity is less than unity, and total revenue is falling.

Marginal revenue thus goes from positive to negative as the demand curve goes from elastic to inelastic, or (what is the same thing) as the total revenue curve stops rising, reaches its maximum, and begins to fall. (The relation between elasticity and total revenue was examined in Chapter 6.)

This relationship has an immediate and important implication. Since marginal cost is greater than zero, the profit-maximizing monopoly (which produces where MR equals MC) will produce where MR is positive, that is, where demand is elastic.

A profit-maximizing monopolist will never push its sales of a commodity into the range over which the commodity's demand curve becomes inelastic.

The common sense of this is that if demand is inelastic, marginal revenue is negative. Thus the monopolist can both increase revenue and reduce cost by reducing its sales.

PROFIT MAXIMIZATION IN A MONOPOLIZED MARKET

To describe the profit-maximizing position of a monopolist, we need only bring together information about the monopolist's revenues and its costs and apply the rules developed in Chapter 14.

The monopolist produces an output such that marginal revenue equals marginal cost. The price corresponding to that output is given by its demand curve.

This profit-maximizing position is shown in each part of Figure 15-4.

Note for future reference one respect in which this monopolistic equilibrium differs from that of a firm in perfect competition. While a competitive firm produces at an output where $p = MC$, the monopolistic firm produces at an output where p is greater than MC. Later we shall return to discuss some implications of this.

FIGURE 15-4
The Profit-maximizing Position of a Monopolist

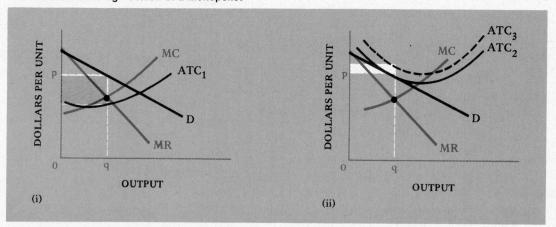

(i)

(ii)

Profit-maximizing output is _q_, where _MR_ = _MC_; price is above _MC_. The rules for profit maximization require $MR = MC$ and $p > AVC$. (AVC is not shown in the diagram, but it would be below ATC.) This happens at output q. Whether or not there are profits depends on the position of the ATC curve. In (i) where average total cost is ATC_1, there are profits, as shown by the shaded area. In (ii) where average total cost is ATC_2, profits are zero. If average total costs rose to ATC_3, the monopolist would suffer losses, as shown by the white area in (ii).

The Profits of a Monopolist

The fact that a profit-maximizing monopolist produces at an output where $MR = MC$ says nothing about how large profits will be — or even whether there will be monopoly profits. Profits may exist, as shown in Figure 15-4(i), and indeed they may persist for a long time because entry of new firms does not push price down to the level of average total cost.

But, as Figure 15-4(ii) shows, the profit-maximizing monopolist may be suffering losses too. Nothing guarantees that a monopolist will make profits. If the ATC curve is shifted upward from the level in Figure 15-4(i) while all other curves are left unchanged, profits will shrink as the curve moves up. When the ATC curve gets so high that it just touches the demand curve, as ATC_2 does in Figure 15-4(ii), the monopolist does better at that output than at other levels of output, but it has zero profits.

A Monopolist's Supply Curve?

In describing the monopolist's profit-maximizing behavior, we did not introduce the concept of a supply curve, as we did in the discussion of perfect competition. A supply curve relates the quantity supplied to the price offered. In perfect competition, the industry short-run supply curve is known as soon as the marginal cost curves of the individual firms are known. This is because the profit-maximizing firms equate marginal cost to price. Given marginal costs, it is possible to know how much will be produced at each price.

In monopoly a unique relation between market price and quantity supplied does not exist.

Like all profit-maximizing firms, a monopolistic firm equates marginal cost to marginal revenue; but, unlike firms in perfect competition, for the monopolist marginal revenue does not equal price. Because the monopolist does *not* equate marginal cost to price, it is possible for different demand conditions to give rise to the same output but to differing prices.[2]

EQUILIBRIUM OF THE FIRM AND INDUSTRY

When a monopolist is the only producer in an industry, there is no need for separate theories of the firm and the industry, as is necessary with perfect competition. The monopolist *is* the industry. Thus the profit-maximizing position of the firm shown in Figure 15-4 is the short-run equilibrium of the industry.

In a monopolized industry, as in a perfectly competitive one, profits provide an incentive for new firms to enter. If such entry occurs, the equilibrium position will change and the firm will no longer be a monopolist. **Barriers to entry** are impediments to the entry of new firms into an industry.

If monopoly is to persist in the long run, there must be barriers to the entry of other firms into an industry.

Barriers may come about in many ways. Patent laws, for instance, may create and perpetuate monopolies by conferring on the patent holder the sole right to produce a particular commodity. A firm may be granted a charter or a franchise that prohibits competition by law. Monopolies may also arise because of economies of scale. The established firm that is able to produce at a lower cost than any new, small competitor may well retain a monopoly through a cost advantage.

A monopoly may also be perpetuated by force or by threat. Potential competitors can be intimidated by threats ranging from sabotage to a price war in which the established monopoly has sufficient financial resources to ensure victory.

---

[2] In order to know the amount produced at any given price, it is necessary to know something about the shape and position of the marginal revenue curve in addition to knowing the marginal cost curve. This means that there is not a supply curve independent of the demand curve for the monopolist's product.

It is the barriers to entry in one form or another that allow a monopolist to earn profits that persist in the long run. In perfect competition, an equilibrium in which firms earn profits can occur in the short run but cannot last longer than it takes for entry to force prices down to the level of average total cost. Because there may well be no entry, the short-run profitable equilibrium of a monopolist can continue indefinitely.

THE INEFFICIENCY OF MONOPOLY

In Chapter 14 we saw that (subject to certain qualifications) perfect competition produces efficient results. By leading firms to produce at levels of output at which $p = MC$ and $p = ATC$, it satisfies conditions of both productive and allocative efficiency.

Productive Efficiency or Inefficiency

We cannot make a specific prediction about productive efficiency under monopoly, except to say that (unlike the situation in perfect competition) there is no necessary force to push production to the level where cost of production is a minimum. The output of a monopolized industry will in general be different from that of a competitive industry. While a monopolist will choose to produce its profit-maximizing output at the lowest cost *for that output*, there is no assurance that its chosen output will be the least-cost output. It may be, or it may not be. Figure 15-5 illustrates two possible cases. In Figure 15-5(i) production is at the level of minimum *ATC*; in Figure 15-5(ii) it is not.

Why might a monopolist that wishes to maximize profits not choose the output with the

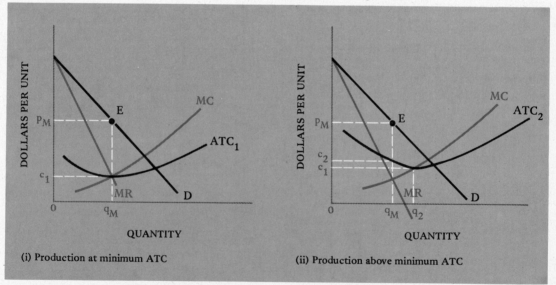

FIGURE 15-5

Monopolistic Equilibrium With or Without Production at Minimum Average Total Cost

(i) Production at minimum ATC

(ii) Production above minimum ATC

The equilibrium output, where *MR* = *MC*, may occur but need not occur at minimum *ATC*. The D, MR, and MC curves are identical in the two parts of the diagram. Equilibrium price and output are p_M and q_M in each case. The diagrams differ in the position of average total cost. In (i) minimum *ATC* occurs at the equilibrium output. In (ii) actual average total cost of c_2 is greater than minimum attainable average total cost of c_1, which would require output q_2. Nothing in the theory of monopoly forces equilibrium to occur at minimum average total cost.

lowest per unit cost of production? The answer is that when choosing a level of output, the monopolist affects *both* the level of cost and the price it will receive for that output. A competitive firm, a price *taker,* can always increase profits in the short run by producing at lower average total costs. A monopolist, a price *setter,* faces a downward-sloping demand curve and may profitably accept higher average total costs if price is high enough to offset the increased unit costs. In the example of Figure 15-5(ii), at the output where *ATC* is a minimum, marginal revenue is less than marginal cost. Thus a profit-maximizing monopolist that found itself at that output would choose to decrease output, thereby increasing profits despite increased average total costs.

A monopolistic firm may or may not operate at the output that achieves minimum attainable average total costs.

Allocative Inefficiency (Price Greater than *MC*)

The fact that the monopolist produces where price is greater than marginal cost violates the conditions for allocative efficiency (discussed on page 266). When price equals marginal cost, consumers pay for the last unit purchased an amount just equal to the opportunity cost of producing that unit. But at a monopoly price and output, price is greater than marginal cost. Thus consumers pay for the last unit an amount that exceeds the opportunity cost of producing it. This is illustrated in Figure 15-6. Consumers would be prepared to buy additional units for an amount greater than the cost of producing these units. Recall that opportunity cost is the market value consumers would receive if the resources were used in their best alternative use. Some consumers could be made better off, and none worse off, by shifting extra resources into production of this commodity. In other words, allocative efficiency could be improved by increasing production of the product.

The monopoly output is not allocatively efficient; equivalently, it is not Pareto-optimal.

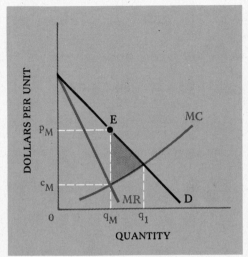

FIGURE 15-6
The Allocative Inefficiency of Monopoly

Because monopolistic equilibrium occurs where price is greater than marginal cost, it is not allocatively efficient. A monopolist chooses price p_M and output q_M. At that output, consumers put a value of p_M on the last unit produced, but the resources used to produce that last unit have a lower value, c_M, in their best alternative uses. Every unit between q_M and q_1 would cost less to produce than the value consumers place on it. Output q_M is thus allocatively inefficient. The shaded area is sometimes described as the deadweight loss due to the allocative inefficiency of monopoly.

The Inefficiency of Monopoly: A Warning

Just as the conclusion that perfect competition is efficient was subject to some words of warning (see page 267), so too are the conclusions about the inefficiency of monopoly. The detailed comparison of monopoly and competition we defer to Chapter 18, but a preview is in order. Much of the case against monopoly depends on the monopoly's having the same costs as a competitive industry. This assumption has been called into question in the very long run. Specifically, if monopolists engage in more innovation than would firms in a competitive industry, the cost curves of the industry may shift downward enough to offset any short-run inefficiency. (The

The Allocative Inefficiency of Monopoly: A Graphic Interpretation

In the box on page 267, we gave a graphic interpretation of allocative efficiency. That analysis can be extended here, with reference to the figure below.

Allocative efficiency occurs at the output q_c where $p = MC$. The monopolist restricts output so that price, p_M, is greater than marginal cost. It does so to increase profits: the monopolist gains (at the expense of consumers) by raising price and restricting output. *But the monopolist's gain is smaller than consumers' losses.* This can be seen in the diagram. First

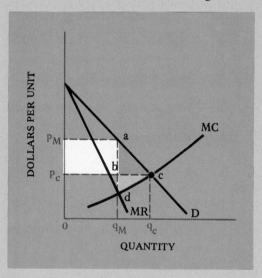

consider the effect on the producer of raising the price from p_c to p_M, noting that as a result output sold falls from q_c to q_M. On the first q_M units there is a big increase in the producer's profits, shown by the white rectangle $P_c P_M ab$. To be sure, the producer loses some profits on the reduction in sales from q_M to q_c; these lost profits are shown by the light shaded area bcd. The net gain to the producer is the white rectangle *minus* the light shaded triangle. Now consider consumers. Their loss of consumers' surplus is the white rectangle *plus* the dark shaded triangle abc.

The white rectangle is a pure redistribution from consumers to the monopolist. It reflects extra payments on the first q_M units. Such a redistribution does not affect allocative efficiency. But the two shaded areas are losses to one group that are not gains to the other group. They are a deadweight loss and are a measure of the allocative inefficiency of monopoly.

The monopolist, by restricting output and raising price above the competitive level, gains a larger share of a smaller "pie." The deadweight loss arises because of the decrease in the size of the pie caused by not producing units that consumers value above the opportunity cost of production.

important question of the influence of market structure on innovation is discussed in Chapter 18.)

The Nature and Extent of Monopoly Power

The *theory* of monopoly just developed assumes that the monopolist has no expectation of competition.

It is difficult to imagine a firm without *any*

competition. A firm may have a complete monopoly on a particular product at a given moment, but every product has some present or potential substitute for the services it provides. Some products have fairly close substitutes, and even a single seller producing such a product will have close rivals. Other products may have no existing close substitute, but new products may be developed that will compete with it. For these reasons it is useful to recognize monopoly power as a variable that can be relatively slight or nearly complete, rather than as an attribute which either does or does not exist.

Monopoly power exists to the extent that a firm is insulated from loss of customers to other sellers.

How is the extent of monopoly power to be defined? The mere fact that a firm's demand curve slopes downward means that if the firm raises its price, it will lose some sales. But there may be limits on the firm's power over price other than the slope of the market demand curve. Any producer facing a downward-sloping demand curve could choose the price-quantity combination (where $MR = MC$) that appears to maximize its profits. *But this price might not turn out to be the long-run profit-maximizing price* because the choice of a particular price-quantity combination may itself lead to changes in the behavior of other firms that in turn *shift* the original firm's demand curve. If, for example, a firm raises its price and (as an indirect result) its demand curve shifts to the left, its sales and profits will be less than the firm would have expected on the basis of the original demand curve.

Consider an example. The Coca-Cola Company is the sole producer of Cola-Cola and faces a downward-sloping demand curve. But the Coca-Cola Company is not a complete monopolist. To see why, suppose that the demand curve for Coke shows that if the price is cut by 20 percent *and* if all other soft drink suppliers keep their prices at their present levels, sales of Coke will increase by 50 percent. This would almost surely result in an increase in the company's profits. Since the Coca-Cola Company is unquestionably free to cut price by 20 percent, why does it not do so? The answer is that if it did, other soft drink prices would not remain unchanged—and the company knows this. The very action of reducing prices would almost surely cause sellers of other soft drinks to reduce *their* prices. If they did so, Coca-Cola's sales would not increase as much as its *ceteris paribus* demand curve predicts. Sales would not increase by 50 percent; instead they might increase by (say) only 10 percent. In such an event the company's profits would decrease rather than increase. Thus the Coca-Cola Company, while it has a monopoly of Coca-Cola sales, does not have a monopoly of soft drink sales, although it may well have some market power.

The larger the *shifts* in a demand curve that are induced by a firm's changing its price, the less is that firm's monopoly power. Such shifts have two main sources. The first (as in the Coca-Cola example) is the price reactions of existing producers of substitute products. The second is the entry of new firms that succeed in capturing part of the sales that the monopolist included in "its" demand curve. Such shifts in the demand curve, from either cause, limit the market power of the firm and reduce its profits.

Since no firm is perfectly insulated from all competition for all time, total monopoly power does not exist. Monopoly power is a variable.

It matters a good deal that monopoly power is measured in terms of "more" or "less" rather than "you have it" or "you don't." One consequence is that a monopoly over a single product does not necessarily confer a high degree of monopoly power. A single producer of a product with many close substitutes (e.g., Coke) may have less monopoly power than either of two firms that produce a product with few close substitutes (e.g., soap). A second consequence is that it is not necessarily true that effective monopoly power increases as the number of firms in an industry decreases. For example, less monopoly power may be exercised in an industry where the only two or three firms compete vigorously than in an industry where eight or ten firms cooperate with each other. Such firms could agree among themselves to set a common price and/or to share the market and act in exactly the same way as if they were a single-firm monopoly. Such behavior is known as **collusion.**

MEASURING MONOPOLY POWER

In order to use the theory of monopoly, we must be able to define monopolistic markets. Furthermore, it is a matter of public policy that uncontrolled monopoly power is undesirable. Government agencies, such as the Competition Board, which enforce these policies, must know where monopoly power exists if they are to control or eliminate it.

Measuring monopoly power is not easy. Ideally, outputs and profits of firms in any industry should be compared with what prices, outputs, and profits would be if all firms were under unified (monopoly) control and were fully insulated from entry. But this hypothetical comparison does not lend itself to measurement.

Concentration Ratios

In practice, two alternative measures are widely used. The first of these is the **concentration ratio,** which shows the fraction of total market sales controlled by the largest group of sellers. Common types of concentration ratios cite the share of total market sales made by the largest four or eight firms. How well concentration ratios measure effective monopoly power is a matter of substantial debate among economists.

A first problem is to define the market with reasonable accuracy. For one example, concentration ratios in national cement sales are low, but they understate the market power of cement companies because heavy transportation costs divide the cement *industry* into a series of regional *markets,* in each of which there are relatively few firms. (We shall discuss problems of market definition further in Chapter 18.)

A second problem is the interpretation of concentration ratios. Are they adequate proxies for the intensity of competition? Clearly, market share is one measure of the *potential* power to control supply and set price. The inclusion in concentration ratios of the market shares of several firms rests on the possibility that large firms will, in one way or another, adopt a common price-output policy that is no different from the policy they would adopt if they were in fact under unified management.

Such common behavior may occur with or without an actual agreement to collude. Lawyers speak of **conscious parallel action** and economists of **tacit collusion** to refer to noncollusive parallel *tual* exercise of monopoly power only if overt or tacit collusion occurs.

High concentration ratios may be necessary for the exercise of monopoly power, but they are not sufficient. They tend to show the potential for monopoly power but not necessarily the actuality.

Profits as a Measure of Monopoly Power

Many economists, following the lead of Professor Joe S. Bain, use profit rates as a measure of monopoly power. By "high" profits, the economist means returns sufficiently in excess of all opportunity costs that potential new entrants desire to enter the industry. Persistently high profits, so goes the logic, are indirect evidence that neither rivalry among sellers nor entry of new firms prevents existing firms from pricing as if they were monopolists.

Using profits in this way requires care because, as we have seen (page 203), profits as reported in firms' income statements are not pure profits over opportunity cost. In particular, allowance must be made for differences in risk and in required payments for the use of owners' capital.

While neither concentration ratios nor profit rates are ideal measures of the degree of market power that a firm, or group of firms, actually exercises, both are of value and are widely used. In fact, concentration ratios and high profit rates are themselves correlated. Because of this, alternative classifications of markets and industries, according to their monopoly power measured in these two ways, do not differ much from one another. In spite of the difficult problems of measuring monopoly power, the theory of monopoly is widely used by economists and policymakers.

Price Discrimination

Raw milk is often sold at one price when it is to go into fluid milk, but at a lower price when it is to be used to make ice cream or cheese. Lawyers often charge for their services according to the incomes of their clients. Movie theaters may have lower admission prices for children than for adults. Railways charge different rates per ton mile for different products. Air Canada charges a wide variety of prices for a flight from Vancouver to Toronto, depending on how far in advance the seat is purchased. Electric power commissions sell electricity more cheaply for industrial than for home use. Universities in Ontario charge foreign graduate students higher tuition. Japanese steel companies sell steel more cheaply in Canada than in Japan.

Such price differences could never persist under perfect competition. Yet many of these examples have existed for decades. Persistent price differences clearly require the exercise of some monopoly power because the seller is exerting influence over the price at which its product is sold. Why should a firm want to sell some units of output at a price well below the price it gets for other units? Why, in other words, does it practice price discrimination?

Price discrimination occurs when a producer sells a specific commodity to different buyers at two or more different prices, for reasons not associated with differences in cost. Not all price differences represent price discrimination. Quantity discounts, differences between wholesale and retail prices, and prices that vary with the time of day or the season of the year are not generally considered price discrimination because the same physical product sold at a different time or place or in different quantities may have different costs. If an electric power commission has unused capacity at certain times of day, it may be cheaper to provide service at those hours than at peak demand hours. When price differences reflect cost differences, they are nondiscriminatory. However, when price differences rest merely on different buyers' valuations of the same product, they are discriminatory. It does not cost a movie theater operator less to fill a seat with a child than an adult, but it may pay to let the children in at a discriminatory low price if few of them would attend at the full adult fare.

WHY PRICE DISCRIMINATION PAYS

Persistent price discrimination comes about either because different buyers may be willing to pay different amounts for the same commodity or because one buyer may be willing to pay different amounts for different units of the same commodity.

Consider differences among buyers. Think of the demand curve for a market containing individual buyers, each of whom has indicated the price he or she is prepared to pay for a single unit. Suppose a single price is charged. For each unit sold, buyers were willing to pay *at least* the price indicated. If the seller can make every buyer pay the maximum he or she is willing to pay, the seller can increase its profits by capturing the amounts in excess of the single price that buyers were willing to pay. In other words, the firm can capture the buyer's consumers' surplus.

WHEN IS PRICE DISCRIMINATION POSSIBLE?

However much the local butcher might like to charge the banker's wife twice as much for hamburger as he charges the taxi driver, he cannot succeed in doing so. Madame Banker can always shop for meat in the supermarket, where her husband's occupation is not known. Even if the butcher and the supermarket agreed to charge her twice as much, she could hire the taxi driver to shop for her. The surgeon, however, may succeed in discriminating (if all reputable surgeons will do the same) because it will not do the banker's wife much good to hire the taxi driver to have her operations for her.

To succeed in price discrimination, a seller must be able to control what is offered to a particular buyer and must be able to prevent the resale of the commodity from one buyer to another.

The first of the two conditions—control over supply—is the feature that makes price discrimination an aspect of the theory of monopoly.

International Price Discrimination: Dumping and the Rationale for Antidumping Policy

Monopolists can and will discriminate when it is possible for them to "separate" markets. This can occur, for example, where markets are divided by political boundaries. Restrictions on international trade can prevent the resale activities that would otherwise make it impossible for a monopolist to price discriminate. A straightforward application of Figure 15-7 shows that a domestic firm which is a competitor in its export market but which has monopoly power in the home market (due, say, to restrictions on imports) will charge a higher price at home than abroad. In that situation the firm produces where marginal cost equals the international price and then sells in the domestic market the quantity for which marginal revenue equals marginal cost.

When a firm sells abroad at lower prices than it charges domestically, it is said to be *dumping*.* Dumping has occurred recently, for example, with exports of Japanese steel into North American markets. Not surprisingly, the North American steel industry has requested help from the respective federal governments. To understand the issues, we need to understand a bit more about dumping.

Motives for dumping. Japanese producers dump steel in North America because it is profitable for them to do so. There are several reasons why it might pay them to sell more cheaply here than at home.

1. It may be a sensible long-term strategy because of economies of scale in production and the fact that the Japanese home market is permanently too small to support an industry of efficient size. In such circumstances, to have an efficient industry requires an export market, but to achieve that market, a low-price policy may be

required. Dumping in this case, by making it possible to produce output at the lowest possible cost per unit, benefits both domestic and foreign customers.

2. It may be a sensible middle-term strategy to provide a market for efficiently produced steel for a period—say, five or ten years—until Japanese markets are able to absorb the entire output of Japanese production.

3. It may be a sensible cyclical strategy to provide a market for output in periods when Japanese demand is low, thereby utilizing the capacity required to meet maximum Japanese demands in periods of boom and expansion. Sales in the export market simply permit Japanese production to continue on an even level over the cycle.

4. It may be a predatory strategy designed to destroy the foreign industry. After foreign plants have shut down, prices can be raised to exploit the foreigner's new dependence on imports.

Effects on the buying country. Suppose Canada is the "beneficiary" of dumped Japanese steel, that is, steel sold at less than the Japanese domestic price and (let us suppose) below the average cost of production in Canada. If such sales continue, they will either eliminate the Canadian industry or force it to become competitive by becoming more efficient. However unfair this may sound to Canadian steel makers, it will benefit Canadian steel buyers for as long as they are able to buy cheaper steel.

No matter what the Japanese producers' motives, the Canadian steel industry and the United Steelworkers of America will want the government to stop this, for it threatens their profits and their jobs.

Suppose the government chooses to look beyond the political pressures of the moment and to do what is best for the national interest.

*Occasionally dumping is defined as selling abroad at a price below marginal cost, but we shall use the conventional definition given in the text.

Here it matters which of the four motivations explains the dumping. If the Japanese are prepared to supply cheap steel on a permanent basis, it would surely benefit Canadians to buy Japanese steel and use Canadian resources to produce something in which we have a comparative advantage. This is the case for doing nothing to protect the domestic steel industry.

However, if cheap Japanese steel would destroy the Canadian industry without replacing the need for it—that is, for any of the last three listed reasons—then sufficient protection to preserve a viable industry may be required. This is the valid case for protectionism.*

The problem for policy is to diagnose what is happening and to adopt rules that will preserve needed industries without depriving Canadian buyers of cheaper sources of supply. Currently there is controversy about what is really happening in the case of Japanese steel. Advocates of protection for the North American steel industry maintain that dumping is occurring because of short-run predatory behavior of the Japanese steel industry; many economists believe that no protection is warranted because the situation appears to them to be simply a reflection of long-run efficient operation of the Japanese industry.

Antidumping Provisions

Under the Anti-Dumping Act of 1968, Canadian producers who believe that competing foreign goods are being dumped in Canada may complain to the deputy minister of National Revenue. If, on the basis of an initial inquiry, the deputy minister finds that dumping which may cause material injury is occurring, he will impose a provisional duty and refer the

case to the Anti-Dumping Tribunal (ADT). The ADT conducts a more thorough investigation and makes a final recommendation to the minister. If material injury is found to be present (or anticipated), dumping duties will be levied. From 1969 to 1977 there were 57 inquiries, and material injury was found in 18 cases.

The United States has announced *trigger prices* that are usually equal to the domestic prices in the exporting country. If a foreign producer were to sell in the United States below a trigger price, antidumping proceedings would be initiated. Canada has no explicit trigger price system, but there is little doubt that there are implicit, unannounced price floors that inhibit dumping by foreign producers.

Two features of the trigger price system make it highly protectionist. First, the setting of trigger prices above the marginal costs of an industry subject to decreasing costs assures that much price discrimination that may be mutually beneficial to foreign producers and domestic buyers will be challenged. Second, the trigger prices become in effect minimum prices that no foreign producer dare undercut. Thus the provisions inhibit foreign competition and serve as nontariff barriers to trade, both where dumping is beneficial to domestic interests and where it is not.

A particularly bizarre feature of the trigger price rule is that when a foreign country is caught dumping, it is "penalized" by being forced to raise its prices. This taxes domestic consumers and transfers the income to the supposed villains, the foreigners. If protection were desired, a more sensible response would be to tax the foreign goods, thereby raising the domestic price and the desired protection but transferring the proceeds from the increased price to the domestic government rather than to the foreign producers.

* The fact that three of the four motives listed lead to the protectionist position does not mean that they are three times as likely to apply as the other motive.

The second of the two conditions—ability to prevent resale—tends to be associated with the character of the product or the ability to classify buyers into identifiable groups. Services are less easily resold than goods; goods that require installation by the manufacturer (e.g., heavy equipment) are less easily resold than are movable goods such as household appliances. An interesting example of nonresalability occurs in the case of plate glass. Small pieces sell much more cheaply per square foot than bigger pieces, but the person who needs glass for a $6' \times 10'$ picture window cannot use four pieces of $3' \times 5'$ glass.

Transportation costs, tariff barriers, and import quotas separate classes of buyers geographically and may make discrimination possible. One aspect of international price discrimination is discussed in the box starting on page 282.

The examples just discussed relate directly to discrimination among classes of buyers. Discrimination among units of output follows similar rules. The tenth unit purchased by a given buyer in a given month can be sold at a different price than the fifth unit only if the seller can keep track of who buys what. This can be done by the seller of electricity through meter readings or by the magazine publisher, who can distinguish between renewals and new subscriptions. The operator of a car wash and the manufacturer of aspirin find it more difficult, although by such devices as coupons and "one-cent" sales, they too can determine which unit is being purchased.

It is, of course, not enough to be able to separate buyers or units into separate classes. For price discrimination to be profitable, the different groups must have different degrees of willingness to pay. The hypothesis of diminishing marginal utility (see page 154) would lead to the prediction that different valuations are placed by an individual on different units, and differences in income and tastes would lead to the prediction that different subgroups will have different elasticities of demand for a given commodity. Thus the potential for profitable price discrimination is often present. [27]

A FORMAL ANALYSIS OF PRICE DISCRIMINATION

Consider a monopolist that sells a single product in two distinct markets, A and B. Customers in one market cannot buy in the other, either directly or by having a customer in the other market resell the product to them; the two markets are completely insulated from each other. The demand and marginal revenue curves are shown in parts (i) and (ii) of Figure 15-7.

Since the monopolist can price discriminate, there is no need to equate prices in the two markets. How then will the monopolist behave in each market? The simplest way to discover what should be done is to imagine the monopolist deciding how best to allocate *any* given output, q^*, between the two markets. Because output is fixed (arbitrarily at q^*), there is nothing the monopolist can do about costs. The best thing to do therefore is to maximize the revenue that is received by selling q^* in the two markets. *To do this the monopolist will allocate sales between the markets until the marginal revenues of the last unit sold in each are the same.*

Consider what would happen if this strategy were not followed. If the marginal revenue of the last unit sold in market A exceeded the marginal revenue of the last unit sold in market B, the monopolist would keep the overall output constant at q^* but reallocate a unit of sales from market B to market A, thereby gaining a net addition in revenue equal to the difference between the marginal revenues in the two markets. Thus it will always pay a monopolist to reallocate a given total quantity between markets as long as marginal revenues are not equal in the two markets.

How can we determine the profit-maximizing output and prices? If we assume that marginal cost varies with output as shown in part (iii) of Figure 15-7, we cannot just put the *MC* curve onto the diagram for each market, for the marginal cost of producing another unit for sale in market A will depend on how much is being produced for sale in market B, and vice versa. To determine

FIGURE 15-7
A Discriminating Monopolist

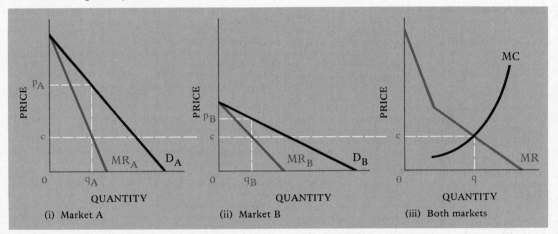

(i) Market A	(ii) Market B	(iii) Both markets

A monopolist that can discriminate between markets will allocate output between them so that marginal revenues in each will be equal. Total output will be such that marginal cost equals *overall* marginal revenue. The solid black lines in (i) and (ii) depict the individual market demand curves; the colored lines indicate the respective marginal revenue curves. For each common marginal revenue, total quantity can be found by adding the quantities in each market; this yields the overall marginal revenue curve in (iii).

Profit-maximizing total output is at *q* in (iii), where *MR* and *MC* intersect. Because marginal revenue is *c* in each market, market outputs are q_A and q_B respectively. Although marginal revenue is equal in the two markets, the prices P_A and P_B (read off the demand curves) are not.

what overall production should be, we need to know *overall* marginal revenue. To find this we merely sum the separate quantities in each market that correspond to each particular marginal revenue. This follows from the fact that at any value of total production, sales will be allocated so as to equate marginal revenues in the two markets. If, for example, the tenth unit sold in market A and the fifteenth unit sold in market B each have a marginal revenue of $1 in their separate markets, then the marginal revenue of $1 corresponds to overall sales of 25 units (divided into 10 units in A and 15 in B). This is shown in Figure 15-7.

THE POSITIVE EFFECTS OF PRICE DISCRIMINATION

The positive consequences of price discrimination are summarized in two propositions.

1. **For any given level of output, the most profitable system of discriminatory prices will provide higher total revenue to the firm (and thus also higher average revenue) than the profit maximizing single price.**

To see that this is reasonable, remember that a monopolist with the power to discriminate *could* produce exactly the same quantity as a single-price monopolist and charge everyone the same price. Therefore it need never get *less* revenue, and it can do better if it can raise the price on even one unit sold.

2. **Output under monopolistic discrimination will generally be larger than under single-price monopoly.**

To see that this is reasonable, remember that a single-price monopolist stops selling at an output where price is greater than *MC*. Suppose the monopolist is able to sell additional units without reducing the price on all earlier units. Since price is greater than *MC* on some units not yet sold, it will be profitable to lower the price a bit and sell additional units. It follows that when a firm can price its product unit by unit, it will pay it to produce more than if it were limited to a single price.

THE NORMATIVE ASPECTS OF PRICE DISCRIMINATION

The predicted combination of higher average revenue and higher output does not in itself have any *normative* significance. It will typically lead to a different distribution of income and a different level of output than when the seller is limited to a single price. The ability of the discriminating monopolist to capture some of the consumers' surplus will seem undesirable to consumers but not to the monopolist. How outsiders view the transfer may depend on who gains and who loses.

If discrimination leads a firm to produce a larger output, it will *decrease* the allocative inefficiency or monopoly noted on page 278. The common sense of this is that a monopolistic firm which must charge a single price produces less than the perfectly competitive industry because it is aware that by producing and selling more it drives down the price against itself. Price discrimination allows it to avoid this disincentive. To the extent that the firm can sell its output in separate blocks, it can sell another block without spoiling the market for the block already being sold. In the case of *perfect* price discrimination, where every unit of output is sold at a different price, the profit-maximizing firm will produce every unit for which the price charged can be greater than or equal to its marginal cost. It will, therefore, produce the same output as the firm in perfect competition.

Under perfect price discrimination as well as under perfect competition, the price of the last unit sold will equal marginal cost. As a result, allocative inefficiency is avoided.

Economists can specify the different effects of different kinds of pricing behavior. Having specified the differences, people can debate their desirability. Economic analysis can describe the consequences of price discrimination, but it cannot finally evaluate them.

This remark may not satisfy the student who is aware that price discrimination has a bad reputation among economists and lawyers. The very word "discrimination" has odious connotations. Laws make certain kinds of price discrimination illegal. But was discrimination by airlines in giving students lower standby fares really bad? Whether an individual judges price discrimination as "evil" depends on the details of the case as well as on personal value judgments.

PRICE DISCRIMINATION: SYSTEMATIC AND UNSYSTEMATIC

The discussion so far has been concerned with systematic and persistent price discrimination. Systematic price discrimination most often consists of classifying buyers according to their age, location, industry, income, or the use they intend to make of the product, and then charging different prices for the different "classes" of buyers. It may also take other forms, such as charging more for the first unit bought than for subsequent units, or vice versa.

Another sort of price discrimination is common. Any firm that occasionally gives a favorite customer a few cents off, or shaves its price to land a new account, is also engaged in price discrimination. If these practices are used irregularly, they are called unsystematic discrimination. Such discrimination is not really part of the price structure, and we have ignored it here. This does not mean that it is unimportant; on the contrary, unsystematic price discrimination plays a major role in the dynamic process by which prices change in response to changed conditions of supply and demand.

The causes and consequences of systematic as opposed to unsystematic price discrimination are very different.

The law, however, is generally unable to distinguish between the two kinds of price discrimination and so hits at both. Legislation, motivated solely by a desire to attack systematic discrimination, may have unforeseen and possibly undesired effects on unsystematic discrimination. Because unsystematic price discrimination is important for the working of competition, prohibiting it may aid the maintenance of monopoly power.

Summary

1. Our analysis of monopoly begins with two simplifying assumptions: first, that an entire industry is supplied by a single seller, called a monopolist; second, that the monopolist sets a single price and supplies the entire quantity that buyers wish to purchase at that price.

2. Under these circumstances, the monopolist's own demand curve is identical with the market demand curve for the product. The market demand curve is the monopolist's average revenue curve. The marginal revenue resulting from the sale of another unit by a monopolist will always be less than the price obtained for that unit.

3. When the monopolist is maximizing profits (i.e., producing where $MR = MC$), marginal revenue will be positive, and thus elasticity of demand will be greater than unity. The amount of profits that a monopolist earns is not predicted by the theory. The amount may be large, small, zero, or negative in the short run, depending on the relation of demand and cost.

4. The presence of profits in a monopolized industry provides the same incentive to entry as it does in perfect competition. Therefore, for monopoly profits to persist in the long run, there must be effective barriers to entry. Such barriers include patent laws, charters or franchises, economies of scale, and coercive tactics.

5. Monopolists producing where $MR = MC$ and with price greater than MC do not achieve the efficiencies associated with perfect competition.

There is no assurance in equilibrium that the output produced is that for which ATC is a minimum. Also, the conditions of allocative efficiency are not met. In restricting output the monopolist does not produce the output that maximizes the sum of consumers' and producers' surplus.

6. There is no such thing as a complete monopoly. Monopoly power is limited by the presence of existing substitute products, by the development of new products, and by the possibility of entry of new firms.

7. Monopoly power exists to the extent that a firm is insulated from loss of customers to other sellers. The degree of monopoly power may best be thought of as a quantitative variable. Two widely used measures of the degree of monopoly power are concentration ratios and the comparison of profits in one industry with those earned in other industries of similar risk and invested capital.

8. Price discrimination occurs when different units of the same commodity are sold for different prices, for reasons not associated with differences in costs. Different buyers may be charged different prices, or the same buyer may be charged different prices on different units of the commodity purchased.

9. The conditions under which a seller can succeed in charging discriminatory prices are, first, that it can control the supply of the product offered to particular buyers and, second, that it can prevent the resale of the commodity from one buyer to another.

10. Commodities that are highly susceptible to price discrimination include services, equipment requiring installation by the manufacturer, and commodities whose buyers can be isolated geographically by transport costs or international trade barriers.

11. Two predictions about price discrimination are (a) for any given level of output, the best system of discriminatory prices will provide higher total revenue to the firm than the best single price, and (b) output will usually be larger than under a single-price monopoly.

12. The consequences of price discrimination can differ from case to case. Price discrimination affects the distribution of income, the quantities produced, and the allocation of resources. Any individual is almost certain to evaluate individual cases differently, whatever his or her personal set of values. Further, there are important differences in the effects of systematic and unsystematic price discrimination.

Topics for Review

The relationship of price and MR for a monopolist
The relationships among MR, TR, and elasticity
Allocative inefficiency of monopoly
Measures of monopoly power
Price discrimination
Conditions that make price discrimination both possible
    and profitable

Discussion Questions

1. Imagine a monopoly firm with fixed costs but no variable or marginal costs—for example, a firm owning a spring of water that produces indefinitely, once certain pipes are installed, in an area where no other source of water is available. What would be the firm's profit-maximizing price? What elasticity of demand would you expect at that price? Would this seem to be an appropriate pricing policy if the water monopoly were municipally owned? Suppose now that entry becomes easy because of the discovery of many additional springs. What price behavior would you expect to occur? What price equilibrium would be predicted?

2. Suppose that only one professor teaches economics at your school. Would you say this professor is a monopolist who can exact any "price" from students in the form of readings assigned, tests given, and material covered? Suppose that two additional professors are hired; has whatever monopoly power that existed been decreased?

3. Each of the following has some "monopoly power": Xerox Corporation, Pepsi-Cola Company, Gulf Oil, OPEC, the Post Office, Bell Canada. In each case, what do you think is the basis of the monopoly power? How might you decide which of the organizations listed has the greatest degree of monopoly power?

4. Which of these industries—licorice candy, copper wire, outboard motors, coal, local newspapers—would you most like to monopolize? Why? Does your answer depend on several factors or just one or two? Which would you as a consumer least like to have monopolized by someone else? If your answers are different in the two cases, explain why.

5. A movie exhibitor, Aristotle Murphy, owns movie theaters in two Nova Scotia towns of roughly the same size, 50 miles apart. In Monopolia he owns the only chain of theaters; in Competitia there is no theater chain, and he is but one of a number of independent operators. Would you expect movie prices to be higher in Monopolia than in Competitia in the short run? In the long run? If differences occurred in prices, would Mr. Murphy be discriminating in price?

6. Airline rates to Europe are higher in summer than in winter. Canadian railways charge lower fares during the week than on weekends. Electric power commissions charge consumers lower rates, the more electricity they use. Are these all examples of price discrimination? What additional information would you like to have before answering?

7. Discuss how each of the following represents price discrimination. In your view, which are the most socially harmful?
    a. standby fares on airlines that are a fraction of the full fare
    b. standby fares, as above, available only to bona fide students under 22 years of age
    c. first class fares that are 50 percent greater than tourist fares, recognizing that two first class seats use the space of three tourist seats
    d. negotiated discounts from list price, where sales personnel are authorized to bargain hard and get as much in each transaction as the traffic will bear
    e. higher tuition for foreign students at provincial universities
    f. higher tuition for law students than for history students
    g. rental of heavy-duty equipment, with charges based on hours of usage per month, rather than sale of the equipment outright

Industrial Organization and Theories of Imperfect Competition

16

Texaco, Shell, and Mobil are three of the "major" oil companies. They are not, singly or collectively, monopolists nor are they firms in perfect competition. Yet they are typical of many real firms in our economy. Similar comments apply to Molson's and Labatt's. Do the two basic theories of pricing behavior we have studied — perfect competition and monopoly — have any relevance to their behavior?

The essential features of perfect competition are that each firm sells a product sufficiently similar to those sold by its numerous competitors that no one firm has any power to influence price (firms are price takers) and that the industry exhibits freedom of entry and exit. The essential features of monopoly are blockaded entry and a demand curve that is substantially the same for the firm and for the industry. Do the theories of perfect competition and monopoly provide a sufficient basis for predictions about price and market behavior in the real economy? Fifty years ago most economists would have said yes; today most would say no, although the matter is still in dispute.

This chapter looks first at some statistics to see how well the assumptions about monopoly and competition *describe* the Canadian economy. This is not the whole of the matter, for it is the method of science to abstract from the full complexity of reality, and it might well be that descriptively unrealistic models were analytically adequate to make predictions that were confirmed by observations. If this were true, one would be able to predict the behavior of all

Canadian industries by classifying each as competitive or monopolistic *for purposes of predicting responses.* Many economists believe that although the models of monopoly and perfect competition are clearly useful, there is a need for other models as well. This chapter suggests some of them.

Structure of the Canadian Economy

Our first task is to analyze how well the models of perfect competition and monopoly describe Canadian firms and industries.

TWO GROUPINGS OF CANADIAN INDUSTRIES

It is relatively easy to divide much of Canadian industry into two broad groups, those with a large number of relatively small firms and those with a few relatively large firms. If these two groups are described by the two market forms we have studied so far, then it must be perfect competition for the first and monopoly for the second.

Sectors with Many Small Firms

Between 40 and 50 percent of the economy's national product is produced by industries made up of a large number of small firms. This includes most agricultural production, most services (travel agents, lawyers, plumbers, television technicians, etc.), most retail trade (stores, gas stations, etc.), most wholesale trade, most construction, and industries whose major business is exchange (real estate agents, stockbrokers, etc.).

The competitive model, with the addition of government intervention where necessary, does quite well in describing many of these industries. This is obviously so where the business of the industry is exchange rather than production. Foreign exchange markets and stock exchanges are notable examples. Agriculture also fits fairly well in most ways; the individual farmer is clearly a price taker, entry into farming is easy, and exit is possible though not in fact very rapid. Many basic raw materials such as iron ore, tin, and copper are sold on world markets where prices fluctuate continually in response to changes in demand and supply.

Some other industries, however, do not seem to be described by the perfectly competitive model even though they contain many firms. In the retail trades and services, for example, most firms have some influence over prices. The local grocery, supermarket, discount house, and department store not only consider weekend specials and periodic sales important to business success, they spend a good deal of money advertising them. In wholesaling, the sales representative is regarded as a key figure — which would not be true if the firm could sell all it wished at a given market price. Moreover, each store in these industries has a unique location that may give it some local monopoly power over nearby customers.

The first group of industries therefore contains some that are clearly described by the model of perfect competition and many others that are not.

Sectors with a Few Large Firms

About an equal percentage of the national product is produced by industries dominated by a few large firms. Included are most manufacturing industries, which together constitute the largest sector of the Canadian economy.

A casual look at the manufacturing sector can be misleading if one does not distinguish between products and firms. In some manufacturing industries there are many differentiated products produced by only a few firms. In soaps and detergents, for example, a vast variety of products is produced by a mere two firms, Lever Brothers and Procter & Gamble. Similar circumstances exist in chemicals, breakfast foods, cigarettes, and numerous other industries where many more or less competing products are in each case produced by a very few firms. Clearly these industries are not perfectly competitive. Yet neither do they appear to be monopolies, for the few firms typically compete energetically against each other.

Cases of single-firm monopolies outside the regulated industries are few. They include the Eddy Match Company, which was virtually the sole producer of wooden matches in Canada between 1927 and 1940, and Canada Cement Limited, which produced nearly all the output of cement until the 1950s. At the time of the Royal Commission on Price Spreads (1935), Canadian Industries Limited produced all ammunition and explosives, the Consolidated Mining and Smelting Company produced over 90 percent of lead and over 70 percent of zinc, and 70 percent of the nickel used in Canada was refined by the International Nickel Company.

Many of the large companies no longer hold such dominant positions in their respective markets. Imperial Oil Company refined approximately 80 percent of all gasoline sold in Canada in 1921, but the company's percentage of total output had fallen to 55 percent by 1932 and to 38 percent in 1968. In the mid 1930s approximately 70 percent of tobacco output was accounted for by the Imperial Tobacco Company; by 1968 the company's sales represented only 42 percent of industry output.

The most striking cases of monopoly in today's economy are in transportation and public utilities. All railway rates in Canada are regulated by the Railway Transport Committee of the Canadian Transport Commission. Telephone rates of the two federally chartered companies, Bell Canada and British Columbia Telephone, are also subject to the regulation of the Canadian Transport Commission, and the rates of companies operating in the Atlantic and Prairie provinces fall under provincial regulation. Even here, however, the monopoly sometimes exists only because of government regulation. For example, if a legal monopoly were not enforced by the government, postal and parcel delivery services would be fiercely competitive. In other cases a monopoly that seems quite unassailable will not persist over the decades. Technological breakthroughs have already been made that will make voice communication a competitive in-

dustry in the foreseeable future. The days of the monopoly of the telephone company are clearly numbered.

Monopoly and perfect competition do not *describe* **much of the Canadian economy. Many industries with numerous firms depart from some of the conditions of perfect competition; most industries with no more than a few firms depart from the conditions of monopoly.**

PATTERNS OF CONCENTRATION IN MANUFACTURING

Table 16-1 shows four-firm concentration ratios in selected Canadian manufacturing industries. Many of these industries approximate neither pure competition nor single-firm monopoly.

TABLE 16-1
Concentration Ratios in Selected Manufacturing Industries, 1974

Industry	Four-firm concentration ratio (percent)
Breweries	94.8[a, b]
Cane and beef sugar procedures	92.0
Aluminum rolling, casting, etc.	91.3
Motor vehicles	90.1
Cement	83.1
Distilleries	82.6
Iron and steel mills	76.8
Petroleum refining	67.8
Agricultural implements	67.4[a]
Radio and television sets	59.1
Sporting goods	51.8
Soft drinks	50.4
Motor vehicle parts	46.2
Dairy products	37.3
Bakeries	37.0
Pulp and paper mills	34.0
Pharmaceuticals and medicines	25.6
Shoes	24.3
Men's clothing	12.7
Women's clothing	7.5

Source: Statistics Canada, 31-402.
[a] Figure given is for 1968; figure for 1974 is secret.
[b] Six-firm concentration ratio is 100.0.

Concentration varies greatly among manufacturing industries. The concentration ratios show the share of the industry's shipments accounted for by the four largest firms.

The concentration ratios alone provide limited information about the state of competitive rivalry, though they have long been used as an index of monopoly power. There is often intense rivalry in such concentrated industries as distilling, brewing, cigarette producing, and automobile manufacturing. Moreover, concentration ratios computed on a national basis neglect the regional nature of many markets. The cement industry would not appear to be a monopoly, since four firms account for 70 percent of industry output. It has been estimated, however, that 90 percent of cement is shipped less than 60 miles; therefore there may be substantial regional monopoly power within the industry. In other industries the concentration ratios may overstate the degree of monopoly power. The fact that four firms account for 84 percent of aluminum rolling and casting may be misleading because aluminum competes with many other metals that are substitutes in a number of uses. Similarly, the high concentration in automobiles overstates the degree of monopoly power in that industry, for it does not take into account the effect of import competition from the Volkswagens, Datsuns, and Toyotas that are now so familiar on Canadian streets.

Canada and the United States. It is of some interest to compare the concentration in manufacturing industries in Canada with that in the United States. In some respects the Canadian economy differs materially from the U.S. economy. The population in Canada is slightly more than 10 percent of the U.S. population, while GNP is slightly less than 10 percent of the U.S. level. Foreign trade is of greater importance in the Canadian economy than in the American. However, similarities in standard of living, consumption patterns, and education in the two countries have resulted in some similarity in industrial structure.

Yet it is apparent that the Canadian manufacturing sector is more concentrated than the American. A study published by the Department of Consumer and Corporate Affairs in 1971 yielded 116 industries or groups of industries for which meaningful comparisons between the United States and Canada could be made. The date obtained, given in Table 16-2, indicate the relatively higher concentration in Canadian manufacturing. Recent studies indicate that this basic relationship has continued to hold.

INTERMEDIATE MARKET FORMS

The need for intermediate categories to describe the Canadian economy is suggested by Table 16-3, which shows that in just over one-half of the industries in the sample the four largest firms account for more than 50 percent of industry output. It is clear that it would be inaccurate to describe the Canadian economy as competitive. Yet in over 75 percent of the industries, the four largest firms control less than 75 percent of industry output. It is also clear that it would be inaccurate to describe the Canadain economy as monopolistic.

The inability of the theories of monopoly and perfect competition to describe the modern economy made economists of 50 years ago uncomfortable. And uncomfortable economists theorize. Some of the resulting theories were appealing in part because they were descriptively realistic. This appeal was expressed by Professor R. L. Bishop when he said that with these alternative theories, economists were at last able to explain "why we are a race of eager sellers and coy buyers, with purchasing agents getting the Christmas presents from the salesmen rather than the other way around."

Monopolistic Competition

Dissatisfaction with the polar cases of perfect competition and monopoly led in the 1930s to the development of a new theory of a market structure called monopolistic competition. The theory was developed in two classic books, one by the American economist Edward Chamberlin, the other by the British economist Joan Robinson.

This is the famous **excess capacity theorem** of monopolistic competition.

Productive efficiency is not achieved under monopolistic competition because firms do not produce at their lowest attainable cost.

This prediction, over which a seemingly endless controversy raged for decades, is illustrated graphically in Figure 16-1(ii).

The modern conclusion, however, is that when a choice must be made on how many products to produce, "productive efficiency" is no longer desirable. Let us see why this is so. People have different tastes; some prefer one differentiated product and some another. Each brand of breakfast food, for example, has its sincere devotees. This creates a trade-off between producing more products to better satisfy diverse tastes and producing any given set of products at the lowest possible cost. The larger the number of differentiated products in existence, the further to the left of the least-cost level of output the production of each product will be, but the more it will be possible to satisfy diverse tastes. Under these conditions, consumers' satisfactions are not maximized by increasing production of each product until each is produced at its least-cost point. Instead the number of differentiated products must be increased until the gain from adding one more equals the loss from having to produce each existing product at a higher cost (because less of each is produced). For this reason, among others, the charge that monopolistic competition would lead to a waste of resources is no longer accepted as necessarily, or even probably, true.

Monopolistic competition after 40 years. Monopolistic competition produced a revolution in economists' attitudes. However, there was a long debate over what it actually predicted and how empirically relevant the theory was. Today the debate has subsided somewhat, with the realization that—at least in manufacturing—product differentiation occurs mainly where a small group rather than a large group of firms compete with each other.

Although there are many industries in which a large number of slightly differentiated products compete for the buyers' attention, in most such cases the industries have only a few firms, each of which sells a large number of products. Consider the soap and detergent industry. Among the well-known brands currently on sale in Canada are Cheer, Dash, Dawn, Gain, Oxydol, Tide, Dreft, Ivory Snow, Ivory Liquid, Joy, Cascade, Camay, Lava, Safeguard, Zest, Mr. Clean, Top Job, Spic and Span, Comet, and Cinch. Surely this is impressive differentiation, and the fact that most of the names are familiar to most Canadians shows that they are advertised effectively.

At first glance, the above list of products might appear to provide a perfect example of monopolistic competition. But *every one* of the products named above is manufactured by a single company, Procter & Gamble, which, with Lever Brothers, dominates sales of soaps, cleansers, and detergents in Canada. Clearly such industries are not the large-group case envisaged by the framers of the theory of monopolistic competition.

Thus it is the small-group case of "differentiated oligopoly" rather than the large-group case of monopolistic competition that seems relevant today.[1] Indeed, in the last half of the 1970s there was a great outburst of theorizing about all aspects of product differentiation. Significantly, the theory that studies market structures where a small number of firms compete to sell a large number of differentiated products has taken the name *monopolistic competition.* The term now

---

[1] At first sight retailing may appear to be closer to the conditions of monopolistic competition than is manufacturing. Certainly every city has a very large number of retailers selling any one commodity. The problem is that they are differentiated from each other mainly by their geographical location, each firm having only a few competing close neighbors. Thus a model of interlocking oligopolies (a market form to be discussed in the next section), with every firm in close competition with only a few neighbors, seems to be a better model for retailing than the large-group monopolistic competition model, in which every firm competes directly with a large number of other firms. But this too is subject to current controversy.

refers to any industry in which more than one firm sells differentiated products.

This modern theory is the direct descendant of the earlier theories of monopolistic competition. The focus remains on product differentiation and on industrial structures thought to describe the nature of the modern economy. The new theory is consistent with the famous propositions of Chamberlin and Robinson that it pays firms to differentiate their products, to advertise heavily, and to engage in other forms of nonprice competition. These are characteristics to be found in the world but not in perfect competition. Most of the modern theory of product differentiation relates to industries with a small number of firms. This is the theory of oligopoly, to which we now turn our attention.[2]

Oligopoly

Manufacturing industries are often characterized by small groups of firms rather than large groups.[3] **Oligopoly** is a market structure in which there are relatively few firms that have enough market power that they may not be regarded as price takers (as in perfect competition) but are subject to enough rivalry that they cannot consider the market demand curve as their own. In most of these cases entry is neither perfectly easy nor wholly blockaded. In many industries, a small number of firms—between three and a dozen—tend to dominate the industry, and newcomers find it hard to establish themselves.

While the automobile industry in Canada and the United States is a somewhat extreme example of this, its experience is revealing. Today three large firms and one much smaller firm constitute the industry. No one has successfully entered the industry in the more than 50 years since the Dodge brothers split with Ford and started making their own cars. Henry Kaiser attempted to enter in 1946. His Kaiser-Frazer came on the market, but despite the postwar boom in car sales the company suffered staggering losses and quietly withdrew in 1953. Recently foreign automobile firms have been setting up plants in the United States. These are not new entrants into the world's automobile industry, however, but merely new plants being set up by old established firms.

What makes the automobile industry unusual is the absence of a "competitive fringe." The situation in the cigarette industry is similar. In contrast, there are 49 firms in the flour and breakfast cereal industry, but the 29 smallest firms together account for only 12 percent of value of output. In the United States there are 136 tire and tube manufacturing companies, of which the 100 smallest supply in aggregate less than 2 percent of the market. Oligopoly is not inconsistent with a large number of small sellers when the "big few" dominate the decision making in the industry.

Competition Among the Few: The Theory of Oligopoly

One of the most striking contrasts between perfectly competitive and oligopolistic markets concerns the behavior of prices. In perfect competition prices change daily, even hourly, in response to changes in demand and supply. Oligopolistic prices change less frequently. Manufacturers of radios, automobiles, television sets, and men's suits do not change their prices with anything like the frequency that prices change in markets for basic materials or stocks and bonds. If you price a man's suit or a lady's skirt today in your local store, chances are that the price will be the same when you return to the store tomorrow. Of course prices do change, but in oligopolistic in-

---

[2] Chamberlin considered the small-group case, but in the historical development of the subject it was his large-group case that was treated as important. The essence of monopolistic competition as understood by Chamberlin, and by the economics profession at the time, was the large group case.

[3] Oligopolies may be present even in nationally unconcentrated industries. A national concentration ratio is relevant where there is one national market. But if transport costs mean that the country is split up into numerous regional markets, each one may contain a small number of oligopolistic firms.

dustries prices usually change by relatively large amounts at discrete intervals in time. Book publishers and appliance manufacturers, for example, typically announce list prices for their products and change them infrequently. These prices do not change in response to every small fluctuation in demand and costs, although they do change in response to large or persistent changes.[4]

ADMINISTERED PRICES UNDER OLIGOPOLY

A major difference between perfectly competitive and oligopolistic firms is that the former are price takers while the latter are price setters. A wheat farmer must accept the market price of wheat, but a producer of television sets must *decide* what price to charge for its product. We say that the oligopolistic firm administers its price. An **administered price** is a price that is set by conscious decision of the seller rather than by the impersonal forces of demand and supply.

In determining price an oligopolist has to consider demand, costs, and the prices of competing products.

When all of these influencing factors have been taken into account, the oligopolist must still decide what price to put on its product. Having decided on an administered price, the oligopolistic firm must accept the consequences: its sales will be determined by the demand curve for its product. An increase or decrease in demand is signaled to the firm by a rise or a fall in its sales at the administered price. In contrast, in perfect competition a change in demand is signaled to the firm by a change in its market price.

[4] There tends to be more short-run price competition in the retailing of goods produced by oligopolists than among the oligopolists themselves. For example, the average discount that automobile retailers are prepared to negotiate with their customers may fluctuate continually with market prices even though the prices they pay to the manufacturer may remain stable from month to month.

THEORETICAL APPROACHES TO OLIGOPOLISTIC BEHAVIOR

Homogeneous Products

A pathbreaking attack on the oligopoly problem occurred as long ago as 1838, the work of the French economist A. A. Cournot. He dealt with the special case of an industry containing only two firms, called a **duopoly**. The two firms sold an identical product. He had each choose its profit-maximizing output on the assumption that the other firm would hold its own output constant. He then showed that if each firm in turn adjusted to the last move made by its competitor (on the assumption that the competitor would make no further move), a stable equilibrium would be reached in which the market was divided between the two firms in a definite way. Each firm would charge the same price as the other, and that price would be higher than the perfectly competitive price but lower than the price a monopolist would charge. This finding established oligopoly as a truly intermediate case between perfect competition and monopoly.

Firms in the situation analyzed by Cournot will raise price and lower output when costs rise, and they will usually raise price and raise output when demand increases. Thus changes in price and quantity are in the same direction as under perfect competition, though the magnitude of the changes will be different.

The equilibrium Cournot analyzed has survived in modern theorizing. It is now called a Nash or a Cournot-Nash equilibrium. It is the equilibrium that results when each firm makes its decisions on the assumption that all other firms' behavior will be unchanged.

Nash equilibria can be determined for many oligopolistic situations. Their properties can be compared with the equilibria that would result from perfect competition and from monopoly (usually, higher prices and lower output than under competition; lower prices and higher output than under monopoly). The price-quantity differences can also be studied when equilibrium changes under the impact of shifts in input costs or demand for the industry's output.

Unfortunately the Cournot-Nash assumption, that each firm takes its rival's behavior as given, seems inapplicable to many small-group situations. The Ford Motor Company knows (or quickly learns) that if it slashes the prices of some of its cars, GM, Chrysler, and American Motors will react by adjusting their prices on comparable cars. Similar considerations apply when General Mills considers changing the advertising for one of its breakfast cereals or Lever Brothers the prices of its soaps.

Thus not only must an oligopolistic firm be concerned with how *buyers* of its products will react to changes it makes, it must anticipate how each of a few identified rival *sellers* will react. The firm's policy must depend on how it *thinks* its competitors will react to its moves, and the outcome of the firm's policy will depend on how they do in fact react. Here there is no simple, unique set of rules for the equilibrium either of the firm or of the small group of firms that constitutes the industry. Neither is there a set of simple predictions about how the firms will react, either individually or collectively, to various changes in taxes, costs, and demand. Much depends on the policy that the firm pursues, on the policies that its competitors pursue, on how each reacts to the other's changes, and on how each thinks the other will react.

Economists have sometimes tackled this problem of interactions by assuming that each firm makes its decisions subject to what are called *conjectural variations*. A firm making, say, a price decision conjectures what variations its choice would induce its rivals to make in their prices. The Cournot-Nash equilibrium is the special case where conjectural variations are zero. Firm A sets its price on the conjecture that its rivals will not vary their prices in response to firm A's decision, and its rivals do the same.

Of course a wide range of conjectural variations is possible. For example, firm A might assume that whatever price it sets, its rivals will set the same price. Equilibrium can be shown to exist for many conjectural variations, and the properties of these equilibria (price, quantity, etc.) can be compared with the equilibria that would result if the industry were either perfectly competitive or fully monopolized.

The problem with the conjectural variations approach is that it is difficult to state conjectural variations that are anything other than mechanical rules. Such rules ignore subtle considerations of strategy such as bluff and counterbluff that may be relevant in real situations of small-group competition. More important perhaps, they neglect the learning and adaptation that characterize most real industries.

Differentiated Products

Cournot's analysis dealt with oligopolists selling homogeneous products. Another set of oligopoly problems arises when firms sell differentiated products. For example, one brand of cigarettes sold by the Imperial Tobacco Company differs not only from all other brands sold by that company but from all brands sold by competing companies. With differentiated products, each product is distinct from every other product.

One of the puzzles of such oligopolies is why each firm sells a number of similar products that compete actively with many other products sold by the *same* company. One part of the answer may lie in consumers' tastes; another part may lie in the desire to make more difficult the entry of new firms into the industry. We shall study this question later in this chapter.

EMPIRICALLY BASED APPROACHES TO OLIGOPOLISTIC BEHAVIOR

Because the oligopoly problem is so complex, some economists have sought to build a theory from observations of the behavior of oligopolistic firms. These economists believe that we need to begin with detailed knowledge of the actual behavior of such firms. The knowledge is then used to narrow the range of theoretically possible cases by selecting those that actually occur.

In this section we shall (1) describe one major empirically based hypothesis about oligopoly behavior, (2) describe briefly a number of subsidiary hypotheses concerning forces that pull in opposite directions, and (3) discuss at greater length one or two hypotheses that seem to shed some light on real oligopolistic behavior.

The Hypothesis of Qualified Joint Profit Maximization

While explicit collusion is illegal in Canada, why cannot a small group of firms that recognize their interdependence simply act in a common manner? Such tacit collusion has been called "quasi-agreement" by Professor William Fellner. If all firms behave as though they were branches of a single firm, they can achieve the ends of a monopolist by adopting price and output policies that will maximize their *collective* (joint) *profits*. Every firm is interested, however, in *its own* profits, not the industry's profits, and it may pay one firm to depart from the joint profit-maximizing position if, by so doing, it can increase its share of the profits.

The hypothesis of qualified joint profit maximization thus rests on the notion that a firm in an oligopolistic industry is responsive to *two* sets of influences.

Any oligopolistic firm wants to cooperate with its rivals to maximize their joint profits; it also wants to receive as large a share of the profits as possible.

Consider the conflicting pressures on an oligopolistic firm when it chooses its price. First, if firms in a group recognize that they are *interdependent* and face a downward-sloping demand curve, they will recognize that their joint profits depend on the price that each of them charges. This pulls each firm to cooperate with its rivals in charging the same price that a single firm would charge if it monopolized the industry.

Second, despite this pull an aggressive seller may hope to gain more than its rivals by being the first to cut price below the monopoly level.

But if it does this, other firms may follow and the total profits earned in the industry will fall as prices are pushed below their joint profit-maximizing level. A firm that initiates such a price-cutting strategy must balance what it expects to gain by securing a larger *share* of the profits against what it expects to lose because there will be a smaller total of profits to go around.

The hypothesis of qualified joint profit maximization is that the relative strength of the two tendencies (toward and away from joint profit maximization) varies from industry to industry in a systematic way that may be associated with observable characteristics of firms, markets, and products. Let us consider some examples.

Some Specific Hypotheses About Oligopolistic Behavior

1. *The tendency toward joint maximization is greater for small numbers of sellers than for larger numbers.* Here the argument concerns both ability and motivation. When there are few firms, they will know that there is no chance that any one of them can gain sales without inducing retaliation by its rivals. At the same time, a smaller number of firms can tacitly coordinate their policies with less difficulty than a larger number.

2. *The tendency toward joint maximization is greater for producers of very similar products than for producers of sharply differentiated products.* The argument here is that the more nearly identical the products of sellers, the closer will be the direct rivalry for customers and the less the ability of one firm to gain a decisive advantage over its rivals. Thus, other things being equal, such sellers will prefer joint efforts to achieve a larger pie to individual attempts to take customers away from each other.

3. *The tendency toward joint maximization is greater in a growing than in a contracting industry.* The argument here is that when demand is growing, firms can utilize their capacity fully without resorting to attempts to "steal" their rivals' customers. In contrast, when firms have

excess capacity, they are tempted to give discounts or secret price concessions in order to pick up customers. Eventually their rivals will retaliate, and large price cuts may become general.

4. *Tacit price fixing to maximize joint profits will cause nonprice competition that will take the industry away from its joint maximizing position.* The argument here is that when firms seek to suppress their basic rivalry by agreeing, tacitly or explicitly, not to engage in price competition, rivalry will break out in other forms. Firms then seek to maintain or increase their market shares through excessive advertising, quality changes, the establishment of new products, bonuses, giveaways, and a host of other schemes for gaining at the expense of their rivals while leaving the list prices of products unchanged.

5. *The tendency toward joint profit maximizing is greater, the greater are the barriers to entry of new firms.* The high profits of existing firms will attract new entrants, who will drive down price and reduce profits. Less of this will occur, the greater are the barriers to entry. Thus the greater the entry barriers, the closer the profits of existing firms can be to their joint maximizing level. Such barriers to entry may be natural or created by the firm.

BARRIERS TO ENTRY

Suppose firms in an oligopolistic industry succeed in raising prices above long-run average total costs so that economic profits are earned. Why do these profits not cause further firms to enter the industry? Why does entry not continue until the extra output forces price down to the level where only the opportunity cost of capital is being earned (i.e., economic profits are zero)?

The answer lies in *barriers to entry,* which are anything that puts new firms that wish to enter an industry at a significant competitive disadvantage relative to existing firms in the industry. Barriers are of three sorts: natural barriers, barriers created by the firms already in the industry, and barriers created by government policy. We discuss the first two in this chapter.

Natural Barriers

Natural barriers to entry may result from an interaction between market size—as shown by the market demand curve—and economies of scale—as shown by the firm's long-run average total cost curve (*LRATC*).

One type of natural barrier depends on the shape of the *LRATC* curve and in particular on what is called **minimum efficient scale** (*MES*). This term refers to the smallest size firm that can reap all the available economies of large scale.

Suppose the technology of an industry is such that the typical firm's *MES* is 10,000 units a week at an *ATC* of $10 per unit and that at a price of $10 the total quantity demanded is 30,000 units per week. Clearly there is room for no more than three plants of efficient size—and hence three firms at most will serve this market. The industry will naturally tend to be oligopolistic.

Now say that demand expands to 35,000 units at a price of $10. There is still not room for a fourth plant operating at *MES,* but the existing firms can raise their prices above $10 a unit and earn a profit above total costs.

Natural barriers to entry occur when the output at which *MES* is achieved is large relative to total demand. Under these circumstances a small number of existing firms may earn profits without inducing a further firm to enter the market.

A second type of natural cost barrier occurs when there are **absolute cost advantages.** This means that existing firms have average cost curves that are significantly lower over their entire range than those of potential new entrants. Among possible sources of such an advantage are control of crucial patents or resources, knowledge that comes only from "learning by doing" in the industry, and established credit ratings that permit advantageous purchasing and borrowing. Each of these may be regarded as only a temporary disadvantage of new firms, which, given time, might develop their own know-how, patents, and satisfactory credit ratings.

This kind of barrier, however, makes it possible for existing firms to charge a price such that although existing firms earn profits, new entrants may face losses for some time after entry. This price is known as a **limit price.** The early losses, which persist until the new firms' *ATC*s fall to the level of the going price, can make entry seem sufficiently unprofitable—in spite of the expectation of later profits—to prevent entry.

Firm-created Barriers to Entry

If natural entry barriers do not exist, oligopolistic firms can earn long-run economic profits only if they can create barriers that prevent their profits from attracting new entrants into the industry.

Predatory pricing. One way of doing this is to create a situation that threatens a new entrant with losses in spite of the fact that existing firms are earning profits. For example, prices may be cut to or below cost whenever entry occurs, then raised after the new entrant has given up.

There is much controversy concerning predatory pricing. Some economists argue that pricing policies that appear to be predatory can be explained by other motives and that existing firms only hurt themselves when they engage in such practices instead of reaching an accommodation with new entrants. Others argue that predatory pricing seems to have been observed and that it is in the long-run interests of existing firms to punish new entrants even when it is costly to do so in the short run.

Whatever the outcome of this debate among economists, the courts have taken the position that predatory pricing does occur. A number of firms have been convicted of using it in restraint of trade.

Preemptive expansion in an expanding market. Say the market is growing (demand curve shifting outward) to an extent that there will be room for each of three existing firms to open one more plant operating at *MES* every four years beginning in 1980. If the firms were not worried about entry, each would build a new plant in 1980, 1984, 1988, and so on. But faced with this strategy, a new firm could build a plant in 1983, 1987, and so on—and thus be in possession of a market when the new plant became profitable a year later. The investment in fixed capital represents a commitment to the market. The first three plants that get in will have preempted the new part of the market, and it will not pay anyone else to build yet another plant because four new plants would all lose money.

In order to prevent this from happening, existing firms will be tempted to build their new plants long before the demand expands enough for them to be operated at a profit. Once the plant is built it will not pay a new firm to build a further plant, and the existing firms will remain in possession of the market when demand expands sufficiently to allow the new plant to cover its costs. Existing firms may well be in a much stronger position to expand in anticipation of future demand than potential new firms. This type of entry-preventing strategy—building new capacity to serve an expanding market before it is needed—has been alleged to occur in several oligopoly and monopoly situations.

Advertising. Suppose there are few scale economies so that a new firm can reach minimum costs at an output that is low relative to total industry output. Thus there are only weak barriers to entry. (This may well be the case, for example, in the cigarette and soap industries.) Existing firms can create entry barriers by imposing fixed costs on new entrants. These fixed costs raise the *MES* of all firms, including new entrants.

Advertising is one such policy. Where there is much effective brand-image advertising, a new firm will have to spend a great deal on advertising its product in order to bring it to the public's attention. If the firm's sales are small, advertising costs *per unit sold* will be very large. Only when sales are large, so that the advertising costs can be spread over a large number of units, will costs per unit be brought down to a level low enough that they will not confer a significant competitive disadvantage on the new firm.

MES, Industry Rationalization, and the Eastman-Stykolt Hypothesis

Declining costs can lead to a minimum scale at which production is efficient. For many industries this *MES* exceeds the total domestic market for the product. Importing the commodity from larger foreign countries would then be cheaper than producing it domestically, and competitive forces would lead to the elimination of the domestic industry.

Professors Harry Eastman and Stephen Stykolt of the University of Toronto and other economists have argued that many Canadian industries are in this situation and that without tariffs and other forms of protection from foreign competition the domestic industries might disappear. The protection so afforded allows domestic production in these industries to be profitable even at a scale well below the industry's *MES*.

In the view of many economists, by propping up such industries and hence preventing resources from moving to more productive uses, this policy has resulted in a costly and inefficient industrial structure. Such protection has also, it is contended, led to the extensive foreign ownership of Canadian industry, for many of the protected industries are dominated by foreign-owned multinational corporations that build branch plants in Canada as a way of circumventing the trade barriers that make it unprofitable to export to Canada directly.

What would happen if the barriers to trade were removed? Would these corporations then serve the Canadian market more efficiently from their lower-cost U.S. plants? To answer this question, we must examine further the sources of the economies of scale.

In many industries scale economies arise from the ability to sustain long production runs. With a small market, there is then a trade-off between efficient scale and product diversity. For example, the Canadian pulp and paper industry, if it were to produce solely for the domestic market, would operate inefficiently because of the costs of having to change production runs frequently in order to produce paper of different weights, grades, colors, and widths. One possible response to moving to freer trade would be for the domestic industry to specialize in only a few particular products lines, thereby lengthening production runs and reaping the economies of scale. However, most domestic production would then be exported; product diversity in domestic consumption would have to be provided by imports.

Figure 16-2 illustrates how heavy advertising can shift the cost curves of a firm with a low *MES* to make it one with a high *MES*. In essence, what happens is that a scale advantage of advertising is added to a low *MES* of production with the result that the overall *MES* is raised. Thus a new entrant who must both produce and advertise finds itself at a substantial cost disadvantage relative to its established rivals.

A firm with no natural entry barriers may be able to create them by use of nonprice competition. Advertising of course does things other than create barriers to entry. Among them, it may perform the useful function of informing buyers about their alternatives, thereby making markets work more smoothly. Indeed, a new firm may find that advertising is essential, even when existing firms do not advertise at all, simply to call attention to its entry into an industry where it is unknown.

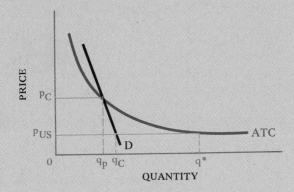

demand curves *for a particular product line.* *MES* is reached at an output level of q^*, far in excess of the domestic demand q_C at the price corresponding to *ATC* for the efficient scale of output. Protection of the domestic industry allows the Canadian price p_C to exceed the foreign price p_{US} and leads to output and consumption of q_p. Free trade causes prices to fall to p_{US}, domestic demand rises to q_C, and domestic output rises to the efficient level, q^*. The difference between domestic production and consumption, q^*q_C, is exported. For other product lines, the removal of protection barriers also causes prices to fall and domestic demand to grow, but the demand is satisfied by imports. Hence the advantages of efficiency in production and diversity in consumption are realized.

This specialization in narrow product lines and the resultant *intraindustry* trade is often called *rationalization* of the domestic industry.* Such a process provides the domestic economy with the twin benefits of efficient scale in production and diversity in consumption. This is illustrated in the figure.

The figure shows the *ATC* and domestic

Such rationalization is possible through explicit international agreement. Is it possible without such agreement? One example of such an angreement is the Automotive Products Trade Act (the "Auto Pact") passed in Canada in 1965. An assessment of the Auto Pact and a discussion of the contrasting case of industries where rationalization occurs without explicit agreement appear in the twin boxes on pages 522–523 and 524–525.

---

*Intraindustry trade occurs when a country simultaneously exports and imports goods produced in the same industry. For example, Canada engages in intraindustry trade in automobiles.

Brand proliferation. Many products have several characteristics, each of which can be varied over a wide range. Thus there is room for a large number of similar products, each with a somewhat different mix of characteristics. Consider the many different kinds of breakfast cereals or cars. The multiplicity of brands is in part a response to consumers' tastes. If you doubt this, try to persuade a sports car addict to switch to a standard four-door sedan, or try to get a lover of

Granola to switch to Sugar Puffs, or try to make all the members of one family eat the same cereal every day of the week.

Product proliferation can also serve as a barrier to entry. Because there are some economies of scale in producing every differentiated product, an infinite variety cannot be provided. Even though a small group of consumers could be found who would prefer each of 10,000 different breakfast cereals, their demands would

FIGURE 16-2
Advertising Cost as a Barrier to Entry

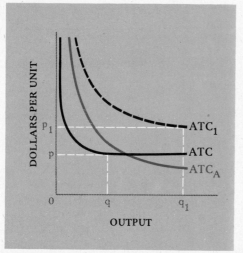

Large advertising costs can increase the *MES* of production and thereby increase entry barriers. The *ATC* curve shows that the *MES* without advertising is at *q*. The curve *ATC*_A shows that advertising cost per unit falls as output rises. Advertising increases total cost to *ATC*_1 and raises *MES* to *q*_1. Advertising has given a scale advantage to large sellers and has thus created a barrier to entry.

not be large enough to cover the costs of production. Thus there is room in the market for perhaps only 50 or 60 brands rather than a few thousand. By producing many kinds of cars, cereals, or soaps and adding new ones whenever demand either increases or shifts toward a different mix of characteristics, existing firms can make it more difficult for new firms selling a differentiated product to enter the industry.

Having many differentiated products confers other advantages on existing firms. If the product is one in which consumers switch brands frequently, then increasing the number of brands sold by existing firms will reduce the expected sales of a new entrant. Say that an industry contains three large firms, each selling one brand of cigarettes, and say that 30 percent of all smokers choose brands in a random fashion each year. If a new firm enters the industry, it can expect to

pick up 25 percent of these smokers (it has one brand out of a total of four available brands). This would give it 7.5 percent (25 percent of 30 percent) of the total market the first year merely as a result of picking up its share of the random switchers, and it would keep increasing its share year by year thereafter.[5] If, however, the existing three firms had five brands each, there would be fifteen brands already available and a new small firm selling one new brand could expect to pick up only one-sixteenth of the brand switchers, giving it less than 2 percent of the total market the first year, and its gains in subsequent years would also be less.

Applications of the Theory of Entry Barriers

The hypothesis that nonprice competition can create barriers to entry helps to clarify two apparently paradoxical aspects of everyday industrial life: the fact that one firm may sell many different brands of the same product, and the fact that each firm spends considerable sums on advertising, competing against its own products as well as those of rival firms. The soap and cigarette industries provide classic examples of this behavior; both industries contain only a few firms that sell a large number of differentiated products.

Part of the reason surely lies in differences among consumers' tastes. Yet another part of the reason may lie in the creation of entry barriers. Here the explanation is that technological barriers to entry are weak in these industries: a small plant can produce at an average total cost just about as low as that of a large plant.

Product differentiation and brand-image advertising can be used to create substantial barriers to entry where natural barriers are weak.

To the extent that these practices raise entry barriers, they allow existing firms to move in the direction of joint profit maximization without fear

[5] Because it is smaller than its rivals, it will lose fewer customers to them by random switching than it will gain from them.

of a flood of new entrants attracted by the high profits.

PRICE INFLEXIBILITY: IS THERE A KINKED DEMAND CURVE?

It has frequently been observed that administered prices change less frequently than do prices determined in competitive markets. One way of putting this is to say that administered prices show some inflexibility in the face of short-term fluctuations in demand and costs.

A sufficient explanation may be found in two forces. The first is the relatively flat short-run average cost curves frequently found for manufacturing firms, which mean that costs per unit remain roughly constant as output varies in response to short-term or cyclical variations in demand. The second is the extra costs of changing administered prices. They include the costs of printing new list prices for the many products of a typical multiproduct firm, the costs of notifying all customers, the accounting difficulty of keeping track of frequently changing prices, and the loss of customer and retailer loyalty due to the uncertainty caused by frequent changes in prices.

A different kind of explanation that still has some adherents was offered many years ago by Paul Sweezy. His explanation was based on a novel demand curve for the oligopolist firm. This demand curve is based on different conjectural variations for price increases and price decreases. Each oligopolist conjectured that its rivals will match any price decreases it makes but will not follow it in any price increases. If the firm raises its price and no one follows, it will lose market share and its sales will fall off rapidly; its demand curve will be very flat. If the firm lowers its price and everyone follows, it will not gain market share and its sales will expand only in proportion to the expansion in the industry's sales. The demand curve for price cuts will thus be steeper than the demand curve for price increases.

These conjectural variations give rise to the kinked demand curve hypothesis, which is explained in Figure 16-3. This kink in the demand curve causes a discontinuity in the marginal revenue curve. [28]

With the kinked demand curve there is an interval in which the firm's profit-maximizing price will be unchanged despite changing economic conditions.

Whether or not the kink is an important element in the theory of oligopoly pricing is still debated; for many economists the evidence seems to relegate the kink to the role of an interesting but infrequent special case. In any event, the kink does not offer a general theory of oligopoly price; it predicts a tendency for a price, once set, to be maintained, but it says nothing about what price is set initially.

FIGURE 16-3
The Kinked Demand Curve

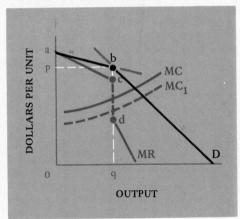

With a kinked demand curve prices tend to be inflexible despite changes in cost. At the market price p, the firm sells q. It believes that if it lowers price, everyone else will follow suit, and its sales will increase along the demand curve bD. But the firm believes that if it raises price, no one else will follow, and its sales will follow the demand curve ba. The black curve abD is the firm's perception of its own demand curve. The corresponding marginal revenue curve is the *discontinuous* curve $acdMR$. A shift in marginal cost from MC to MC_1 changes neither the price nor the output that maximizes profits.

OLIGOPOLY AND RESOURCE ALLOCATION

Behavior of oligopolistic industries is much more complex than behavior under perfect competition or under monopoly. If oligopolists made simplistic Cournot-Nash assumptions, behavior would be relatively easy to predict. As it is, interactions are obvious and oligopolistic firms must—and plainly do—take account of them. The equilibrium reached will then depend on each firm's conjectural variations. No one pattern dominates. However, there can be little doubt that oligopoly is genuinely different from either perfect competition or monopoly.

Firms in oligopolistic markets (as well as monopolies) administer their prices. The market signaling system works slightly differently when prices are determined by the market than when they are administered. Changes in the market conditions for both inputs and outputs are signaled to the perfectly competitive firm by changes in the *prices* of its inputs and its outputs. Changes in the market conditions for inputs are signaled to the oligopolist by changes in the prices of its inputs. Changes in the market conditions for the oligopolist's product are signaled, however, by a change in sales at the administered price.

The oligopolist that administers its price gets a signal when the demand for its product changes, the signal taking the form of a variation in its sales. The perfectly competitive firm receives a signal of the same change in demand through a change in the market price that it faces.

Rises in costs of inputs will shift cost curves upward, and oligopolistic firms will be led—if the shift is not reversed—to raise price and lower output. Rises in demand will cause the sales of oligopolistic firms to rise. Firms will then respond by increasing output, thereby increasing the quantities of society's resources that are allocated to producing that commodity.

The market system reallocates resources in response to changes in demand and costs in roughly the same way under oligopoly as it does under perfect competition.

Although the market system allocates resources under oligopoly in a manner that is qualitatively similar to what happens under perfect competition, the actual allocation is not likely to be the same. Generally, oligopolistic industries will earn profits and will charge prices that exceed marginal cost (because the firms face downward-sloping demand curves and will equate marginal cost to marginal revenue, not to price). In this respect oligopoly is similar to monopoly.

There is a wide range of oligopolistic behavior. Some oligopolies succeed in coming close to the sort of joint profit maximization that would characterize monopoly. Others compete so intensely among themselves that they approximate competitive prices and outputs. The allocative consequences vary accordingly.

In some respects, oligopolistic industries differ from either perfect competition or monopoly: they may exhibit more price rigidity, more advertising, and more product differentiation. There may also be some tendency for more nonprice competition than consumers want.

Oligopoly is an important market structure in today's economy because there are many industries where the *MES* is simply too large to support a perfectly competitive market. Oligopoly will not, in general, achieve the optimal allocative efficiency of perfect competition. Rivalrous oligopoly, however, may produce more satisfactory results than monopoly. The defense of oligopoly as a market form is that it may be the best of the available alternatives where the *MES* is large. The challenge to public policy is to keep oligopolists competing. Public policies with this objective are discussed in Chapter 18.

Summary

1. A review of the structure of the Canadian economy shows that while there are both large-firm and small-firm sectors, most of the industries involved do not conform descriptively to the models of either perfect competition or monopoly.

2. Monopolistic competition is a market structure in which firms sell a differentiated product. Large-group monopolistic competition does not seem to apply to a significant number of industries in today's world.

3. Differentiated products abound, but generally they are produced in industries that contain a small number of firms each one of which sells many such products. This is small-group oligopoly.

4. The basic characteristics of oligopoly are that the firms in an industry recognize that they are interdependent and that anything that one firm does will probably lead to a reaction by rival sellers.

5. Oligopolists must administer their prices. Their prices are not changed with the frequency that prices change in perfect competition.

6. There is no simple set of predictions about the outcome of oligopolistic situations. Everything depends on the strategies adopted by the various rivals. Therefore, instead of a single theory, there are many possible patterns of behavior to understand, explain, and predict. A very general hypothesis of qualified joint profit maximization says that firms that recognize that they are rivals will be motivated by two sets of opposing forces, one set moving them toward joint profit maximization and the other moving them away from it.

7. In order to suggest the way in which observable variables such as size and number of sellers, nature of the product, and conditions of demand may influence the two sets of opposing forces, five specific hypotheses are suggested. The list is illustrative of a much larger list that might be provided.

8. Oligopolies persist because of barriers to entry, which may be natural or created. Natural barriers include large minimum efficient scales

and absolute cost advantages. Firm-created barriers may include predatory pricing, preemptive expansion in a growing market, advertising, and brand proliferation.

9. One possible explanation of price rigidity under oligopoly is the kinked demand curve.

10. Under oligopoly the price system works to reallocate resources in response to changes in demand and costs in qualitatively the same way as it does under perfect competition. Oligopoly may not be as efficient as perfect competition, but it is responsive to major changes in economic conditions.

Topics for Review

Concentration ratios
Product differentiation
The excess capacity theorem
Administered prices
Barriers to entry
Minimum efficient scale
Absolute cost advantages

Discussion Questions

1. Is the consumer benefited by lower prices, by higher quality, by more product variety, by advertising? If trade-offs are necessary (more of one means less of another), how would you evaluate their relative importance with respect to the following products?
   a. vitamin pills
   b. beer
   c. cement
   d. bath soap
   e. women's dresses
   f. television programs
   g. prescription drugs
2. White sidewall tires cost about $1 per tire more to manufacture than black sidewall tires, and they lower somewhat the durability of tires. At the retail level the extra cost of a white sidewall tire is at least $5 per tire. Yet 70 percent of all passenger car tires manufactured in North America in 1980 were the white sidewalls. What, if anything, do these facts tell you about the market structure of the manufacture, distribution,

or marketing of automobile tires? If white sidewalls are found to be somewhat more likely to suffer blow-outs, should their use be prohibited by law?

3. It is sometimes said that there are more drugstores and gasoline stations than are needed. In what sense might that be correct? Does the consumer gain anything from this plethora of retail outlets? How would you determine the optimal number of movie theaters or gasoline stations in a city of 100,000 people?

4. Are any of the following industries monopolistically competitive? Explain your answer.
   a. textbook publishing (fact: there are over 50 elementary economics textbooks in use somewhere in North America this year)
   b. university education
   c. cigarette manufacture
   d. restaurant operation
   e. automobile retailing

5. It has been estimated that if automobile companies did not change models for 10 years, the cost of production would be reduced by approximately 30 percent. In view of this fact, why are there annual model changes? Which, if any, of the reasons you have suggested depend on the industry's being oligopolistic? Should frequent model changes be forbidden by law?

6. Compare and contrast the effects on the automobile and the wheat industries of each of the following.
   a. The effect of a large rise in demand on quantity sold.
   b. The effect of a large rise in costs on price.
   c. The effect on price of a temporary cut in supplies coming to market due to a three-month rail strike.

d. The effect on price and quantity sold of a rush of cheap foreign imports.
e. The effects of a large rise in the price of one of the industry's important imports.
In the light of your answers discuss general ways in which oligopolistic industries fulfill the same general functions as do perfectly competitive industries.

7. It is illegal in Canada for competitors to fix prices by agreement, yet conspiracies have been discovered and punished. Why should firms take the risk of collusion when it is perfectly legal for each to simply charge the price that maximizes the joint profits of the group? What factors might you hypothesize that would make collusion more (or less) likely?

8. Consider the effect on competition of each of the following.
   a. banning cigarette advertising
   b. limiting the number of taxicab licences in a city
   c. requiring all automobile manufacturers to produce a 90 percent pollution-free car by 1984

9. Many people in advertising have thought that economists, with their emphasis on efficiency in the allocation of resources, have not been duly appreciative of the role of advertising in influencing consumer preferences. What roles does economic analysis give to advertising? Which are regarded as improving resource allocation and which as worsening it?

10. Does the kinked demand curve rest on a state of mind of buyers, of sellers, or on actual market conditions? Would such a state of mind, or such conditions, be more likely in a period of great excess capacity or a period of shortages? Could cost changes ever cause prices to change under the kinked demand theory?

Price Theory in Action

17

Price theory helps us to understand and to make predictions about things that are reported in the newspapers every day: the effect of a grain shortage on the price of chicken feed, for example, and the increased use of car pools when the price of gasoline rose. In this chapter we apply price theory to real-world situations. In the first section the theories of monopoly and perfect competition are used to study how producers in competitive industries often try, through collective action, to obtain monopolistic profits but fail to do so perfectly. In the final section we examine the impact of a successful cartel, OPEC, on an economy that had come to take cheap and abundant energy for granted.

Problems in Attempts to Monopolize Perfectly Competitive Industries

Sellers of goods and services often seek collective action to raise what they consider excessively low prices. Cocoa producers in west Africa, wheat producers in the United States and Canada, the Organization of Petroleum Exporting Countries (OPEC), coffee growers in Brazil, taxi drivers in many cities, and labor unions throughout the world have all sought to obtain, through collective action, some of the benefits of departing from perfectly competitive situations. Basically they have sought to form organizations to regulate the output and sales of the goods or services they supply.

The motive behind this drive for monopoly power is easy to understand. The equilibrium position of a perfectly competitive industry is one in which a restriction of output and a consequent increase in price will always increase the profits of all producers. This is particularly obvious when (as is so often the case with agricultural goods) the demand for the product is inelastic at the equilibrium price; then marginal revenue is negative. Because marginal cost is positive, since it surely costs something to produce every extra unit, a reduction in output will not only raise the total revenues of producers, it will also reduce total costs.

It is equally true that the industry's profits can always be increased, even if demand is elastic at the competitive equilibrium price. At such an equilibrium, each firm is producing where marginal cost equals price. Because the market demand curve slopes downward, the industry's marginal revenue is less than price—and thus less than marginal cost. Therefore, in competitive equilibrium, the last unit sold necessarily contributes more to the industry's costs than to its revenue.

In a perfectly competitive industry, profits will increase if the producers enter into an effective agreement to restrict output.

The big "if" is the ability to form and maintain an *effective* agreement. A **cartel** is an organization of producers designed to eliminate competition among its members, usually by restricting output. OPEC is the best known and most effective cartel of modern times. (We examine some aspects of its workings in the final section of this chapter.) Its success comes about because (a) it has been able to prevent cheating, (b) it has been supported by most oil producers, (c) entry into large-scale oil exportation is difficult, and (d) there are relatively few adequate substitutes for oil in the short run. Why each of these features of OPEC is important to its success is illustrated in the following case studies.

CHEATING: THE INSTABILITY OF PRODUCERS' ASSOCIATIONS

A **producers' association** is a joint selling organization for a group of producers. Such an association often acts as a cartel and attempts to reduce the output of a commodity by getting each producing firm to agree to restrict its output. While there is an incentive under perfect competition for all producers to enter into such an agreement, there is also an incentive for each producer to violate it.

To see how this would happen, consider a producers' association that raises prices by cutting production. Suppose that every firm except one restricts its output. That one firm will be doubly well off in that it can sell its original output at the new, higher price received by all other firms that have restricted their production. But the same would be true for *each* firm.

An association organized mainly to restrict output is subject to competing pressures, illustrated in Figure 17-1. Each of the firms is better off if the association is formed and is effective; but each firm is even better off if every other firm plays ball while only it does not. Yet if everyone cheats (or stays out of the association), everyone will be worse off.

Producers' associations will tend to be unstable because of the incentives for individual producers to violate the quotas.

The history of schemes to raise farm incomes by limiting crops bears ample testimony to the accuracy of this prediction. Crop restriction agreements often break down, and prices fall, as individuals exceed their quotas. The great bitterness and occasional violence that is sometimes exhibited by members of crop restriction plans against nonmembers and members who cheat is readily understandable. So far the OPEC coun-

FIGURE 17-1
The Dilemma of Producers' Associations

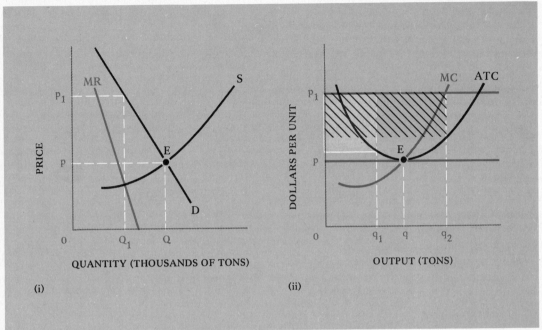

All producers benefit when they restrict output; any one producer will benefit even more if others reduce output but it does not. Market conditions are represented in (i), conditions for an individual producer in (ii). (Note the change of scale.) Before the association is formed, the market is in competitive equilibrium at price p and output Q, and the individual producer is producing output q and just covering costs. An association is formed and reduces industry output to Q_1 by persuading each producer to produce only q_1. This output, where supply equals marginal revenue, maximizes joint profits with price p_1. The individual producer earns profits shown by the shaded area.

Once price is raised to p_1, however, the individual producer would like to increase output to q_2 and thus earn the profits shown in the diagonally striped area. But if all producers try to increase their outputs, price will fall back toward p.

tries have resisted the temptation to cheat, perhaps because of their political unity.

PARTIAL PARTICIPATION: MILK WITHHOLDING IN WISCONSIN

We have seen the need to police the activities of members of any output-restricting scheme. Another well-documented case shows the problems that occur when the producers' association covers substantially less than the total number of producers in the industry.

In the late 1960s there were 72,000 dairy farmers in Wisconsin, of whom about 4,300 were members of a militant group known as the National Farmers Organization. The NFO members controlled about 6 percent of the milk produced in the state. Angry about low milk prices and recognizing the inelasticity of the market demand curve, the NFO in 1967 proposed to withhold milk from the market. By dumping it in rivers, fields, and roads, they hoped to dramatize the plight of the dairy farmer and raise the price of milk by 20 percent. The elasticity of demand for milk is approximately 0.5; to achieve a 20 percent price increase would require a reduction in quantity sold of about 10 percent.

The NFO urged all farmers, whether members or not, to join them, but only members withheld supplies, and they withheld *all* their milk. During a three-week period, member farmers removed about 40 million pounds of milk (enough for 18 million quarts), or about 6 percent of the total usually supplied during the three-week period. Even if this withholding action had had the full effect predicted by the theory, given the 6 percent withheld and the elasticity of demand of 0.5, it would have raised prices by 12 percent and *benefited the farmers who were continuing to produce,* not those who were dumping their milk. The participants lost approximately $1.7 million, or an average of $400 each, in the action. The action failed because the total response was too small and too unevenly shared. Any increase in price would have persisted only as long as reduction in flow continued. Withholding milk for a week or three weeks and then resuming full production would at most drive prices up only until supply increased and brought them down.

A monopoly would seek to decrease the supply as a long-term policy. For a producers' association to achieve the same results would require a long-term withholding, and this could benefit the withholders only if a great majority of producers shared both in the withholding and in the production of what was sent to market. When the NFO failed to enlist the general support of milk producers, its attempts to raise the incomes of its members was doomed to fail.

Whether the NFO was foolish is another matter. If its purpose was to raise the income of its members by direct market action, it clearly (and predictably) failed. If, however, the primary purpose was to achieve a political solution, it may be that the dramatic and expensive action demonstrated the intensity of the members' feelings of grievance. Yet many of the NFO members believed they would succeed because of the laws of supply and demand. Even a neophyte economist could have told them otherwise.

CONTROL OF ENTRY: THE PRICE OF HAIRCUTS

Including all the producers in the industry and being able to police their actions is not enough for the success of a profit-increasing scheme. It is also necessary to prevent new producers, attracted by the monopoly profits resulting from output restriction, from entering the industry.

An example concerns the efforts of men's barbers in a particular city to avoid the rigors of competition. Assume that there are many barber shops and freedom of entry into barbering: anyone who qualifies can set up as a barber. Assume that the going price for haircuts is $5 and that at this price all barbers believe their income is too low. The barbers hold a meeting and decide to form a trade association. They agree on the following points: First, all barbers in the city must join the association and abide by its rules; second, any new barbers who meet certain professional qualifications will be required to join the association before they are allowed to practice their trade; third, the association will recommend a price for haircuts that no barber shall undercut.

The barbers intend to raise the price of haircuts in order to raise their incomes. You are called in as a consulting economist to advise them as to the probable success of their plan. What do you predict?

The first thing you need to know is whether the organization is strong enough to enforce its minimum price on members and to prevent barbers from operating outside the organization. If it is not this strong, you will predict that their plan will not succeed in raising the price above the market level. But suppose you are persuaded that the organization does have the requisite strength to enforce a price rise to, say, $7. What are your predictions about the consequences?

You now need to distinguish between the short-run and the long-run effects of an increase in the price of haircuts. In the short run the number of barbers is fixed. Thus, in the short run, the answer is simple enough: It all depends on the elasticity of the demand for haircuts.

If the demand elasticity is less than 1, total expenditure on haircuts will rise and so will the incomes of barbers; if demand elasticity exceeds 1, the barbers' revenues will fall. Thus you need some empirical knowledge about the elasticity of demand for haircuts. You will probably have to try to gain some idea of demand elasticity by studying the effects of changes in haircut prices either at other times or in other places.

When you propose making such a study, one of the leaders of the organization (who has taken a course in economics) tells you not to waste your time, haircuts are a necessity, and therefore their demand is almost perfectly inelastic. You reject this argument for two reasons. You realize, first, that the time between haircuts is by no means fixed. An increase in the average period between haircuts from four weeks to six weeks would represent a 33 percent fall in quantity demanded. If such a change were occasioned by, say, a 25 percent rise in price, the elasticity of demand over this range would be 1.33. You realize also that people can have their hair cut elsewhere than in a barbershop. The sale of hair clippers for home use keeps rising in North America as a direct response to sharp rises in the relative price of haircuts.

Let us suppose, however, that on the basis of the best available evidence you estimate the elasticity of demand over the relevant price range to be 0.45. You then predict that barbers will be successful in raising incomes in the short run. A 40 percent rise in price will be met by an 18 percent fall in business, so the total revenue of the typical barber will rise by about 15 percent.[1] In predicting the consequences, you will also want to estimate the length of the short run for this industry.

Now what about the long run? If barbers were just covering costs before the price change, they will now be earning profits. Barbering will become an attractive trade relative to others requiring equal skill and training, and there will be a flow of barbers into the industry. As the number of barbers rises, the same amount of business must be shared among more and more barbers, so the typical barber will find business—and thus profits—decreasing. Profits may also be squeezed from another direction. With fewer customers coming their way, barbers may compete against one another for the limited number of customers. The association does not allow them to compete through price cuts, but they can compete in service. They may spruce up their shops, offer their customers expensive magazines to read, and so forth. This kind of competition will raise operating costs.

These changes will continue until barbers are just covering their opportunity costs, at which time the attraction for new entrants will subside. The industry will settle down in a new long-run equilibrium in which individual barbers make incomes only as large as they did before the price rise. There will be more barbers than there were in the original situation, but each barber will be working for a smaller fraction of the day and will be idle for a larger fraction (the industry will have excess capacity). Barbers may prefer this situation; they will have more leisure. Customers may or may not prefer it: They will have shorter waits even at peak periods, and they will get to read a wide choice of magazines, but they will pay more for haircuts.

But you were hired to report to the barbers with respect to the effect on their incomes, not their leisure. The report that you finally present will say: "You will succeed in the short run (because you face a demand curve that is inelastic), but your plan is bound to be self-defeating in the long run unless you are able to prevent the entry of new barbers."

The important lesson to be learned is this:

Unless producers can control entry, they cannot succeed in keeping earnings above the competitive level in the long run.

---

[1] Suppose the quantity of haircuts originally was 1,000. At $5 this produced revenue of $5,000. A rise in price to $7 and a fall in quantity to 820 creates revenue of $5,740, a 14.8 percent increase. More generally, let p and q be the price and quantity before the price increase. Total revenue after the increase is $TR = (1.40p)(.82q) = 1.148pq$.

If price competition is ruled out, profits will be driven down by the entry of new firms and the resulting creation of excess capacity. Producers' associations that are successful in keeping earnings up are those that are successful in restricting entry.

SUBSTITUTES: THE DECLINE AND FALL OF A PATENT MONOPOLY

The case of the barbers suggests that monopoly profits cannot be maintained unless there are effective barriers to entry. Even if prices are not brought down by new entrants (because of effective group control over price), excess capacity will continue to develop until each firm's profits are reduced to zero. How easy is it to raise barriers to entry to protect monopoly profits? One might think that a patent that confers a legal monopoly to produce a product would be sufficient, but restriction is not that simple.

Profits are a challenge to those who want their share of them; they are the carrot of the free enterprise system, and no producer is immune to potential competition from those who would compete for his or her share of the consumer's dollar. Consider the case of ball-point pens.

In 1945, Milton Reynolds acquired a patent on a new type of pen that wrote with a ball bearing rather then a conventional nib. He formed the Reynolds International Pen Company, capitalized at $26,000, and began production on October 6, 1945.

The Reynolds pen was introduced with a good deal of fanfare by Gimbels, a New York City department store which guaranteed that the pen would write for two years without refilling. The price was set at $12.50 (the maximum price allowed by the wartime Office of Price Administration). Gimbels sold 10,000 pens on October 29, 1945, the first day they were on sale. In the early stages of production, the cost of production was estimated to be around 80¢ per pen.

The Reynolds International Pen Company quickly expanded production. By early 1946 it employed more than 800 people in its factory and was producing 30,000 pens per day. By March 1946 it had $3 million in the bank.

Macy's, Gimbels' traditional rival, introduced an imported ball-point pen from South America. Its price was $19.98 (production costs unknown).

The heavy sales quickly elicited a response from other pen manufacturers. Eversharp introduced its first model in April, priced at $15. In July 1946 *Fortune* magazine reported that Sheaffer was planning to put out a pen at $15, and Eversharp announced its plan to produce a "retractable" model priced at $25. Reynolds introduced a new model but kept the price at $12.50. Costs were estimated at 60¢ per pen.

The first signs of trouble emerged. The Ball Point Pen Company of Hollywood (disregarding a patent-infringement suit) put a $9.95 model on the market, and a manufacturer named David Kahn announced plans to introduce a pen selling for less than $3. *Fortune* reported fears of an impending price war in view of the growing number of manufacturers and the low cost of production. In October, Reynolds introduced a new model, priced at $3.85, that cost about 30¢ to produce.

By Christmas 1946 approximately 100 manufacturers were in production, some of them selling pens for as little as $2.98. By February 1947 Gimbels was selling a ball-point pen made by the Continental Pen Company for 98¢. Reynolds introduced a new model priced to sell at $1.69, but Gimbels sold it for 88¢ in a price war with Macy's. Reynolds felt betrayed by Gimbels. Reynolds introduced a new model listed at 98¢. By this time, ball-point pens had become economy rather than luxury items but were still highly profitable.

In mid 1948 ball-point pens were selling for as little as 39¢ and costing about 10¢ to produce. In 1951 prices of 25¢ were common. Ever since then the market has been saturated with a wide variety of models and prices, ranging from 19¢ up. Their manufacture is only ordinarily profitable. Ball-point pens were no passing fad, as everyone knows; their introduction has fundamentally changed the writing implement industry.

The ball-point pen example has interested observers in many fields. Lawyers have been concerned about the ease with which patent rights were circumvented. Psychologists have noted the enormous appeal of a new product even at prices that seemed very high. Advertising people have regarded it as a classic case of clever promotion.

From the point of view of economic theory, it illustrates several things:

1. A firm that innovates, taking the risks of introducing a new product, may gain a temporary monopoly. In the short run such a monopoly can charge prices not remotely equal to costs and earn enormous profits.
2. Entry of new firms (even in the face of obstacles) will often occur in response to high profits.
3. Entry will, in time, drive prices down to a level more nearly equal to the costs of production and distribution.
4. The lag between an original monopoly and its subsequent erosion by entry may nevertheless be long enough that the profits to the innovator, as well as to some of the imitators, may be very large.[2]

The case of the ball-point pen is not an isolated one; it is typical of what happens when a successful innovation brings a new product onto the market. A more recent example is the pocket calculator that has ousted the slide rule as the applied scientist's constant companion. It is so easy to operate that it is carried and used regularly by many who would never have used a slide rule. When first introduced in the early 1970s, pocket calculators were relatively expensive, often costing over $100. They were also relatively crude in their capabilities. Nonetheless they proved popular; sales and profits rose, and firms rushed to enter the lucrative new field. Competition led simultaneously to product improvement and price reduction. Today calculators that perform basic calculations can be bought for about $10, and sophisticated scientific

and programmable pocket calculators can be bought for under $50.

OPEC and the Price of Gasoline

In 1973, in the aftermath of the Arab-Israeli war, members of OPEC placed an embargo on exports of Mideast oil. When that embargo was lifted, OPEC established and maintained a fourfold increase in the price of oil; since then there have been a number of increases, including a further doubling in 1979. Details of Canadian developments and policies in response to these events are presented in Chapter 27. In the present chapter we consider some of the broader developments and reactions in the U.S. and Canadian economies, focusing in particular on the automobile industry and its response to the skyrocketing price of gasoline.

In 1980 gasoline was approximately four times as expensive as it had been a decade earlier. The number of gasoline stations had fallen, and gasoline price wars, a not uncommon event in the 1960s, were almost unheard of. The share of imported cars in the North American market had risen from about 5 percent to 22 percent. Sales of cars of North American manufacture had fallen from 11 million to 9 million per year, even though big discounts were being offered in the winter of 1980, and North American cars had become smaller and more fuel efficient than the gas guzzlers of a decade earlier. All but one of the North American auto companies were having a hard time; Chrysler was on the edge of bankruptcy, and Ford was reporting large losses. These factors can be understood largely in terms of the theories of supply and demand, competition and monopoly, with some government intervention thrown in. What happened?

BEFORE OPEC: ENERGY BINGE

During the half century before 1973, North Americans increased their consumption of energy at an annual rate of about 5 percent—enough to double consumption every 14 years.

[2] It is estimated that Reynolds earned profits as high as $500,000 *in a single month*—about 20 times its original investment.

FIGURE 17-2
Gasoline Prices in an Era of Unlimited Supply

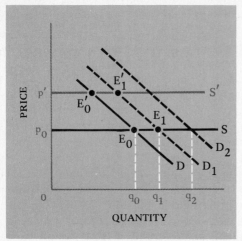

With a horizontal long-run supply curve, demand can increase year by year with no increase in price. S is a long-run supply curve that is perfectly elastic at price p_0. Suppose S applies to the United States in the early 1970s. The various demand curves refer to different years; each year the demand curve shifts rightward as gasoline consumption increases. There is no gasoline shortage on the horizon. The U.S. equilibrium in year 0 is E_0, and it is expected to shift to E_1 in year 1, with larger consumption but no increase in price above p_0.

The screened supply curve S' is also perfectly elastic—at a higher price, p'. Suppose it reflects the supply in European countries that have levied a high tax on gasoline. For the same set of demand curves, equilibrium consumption is much lower in European countries than in America, yet there too it increases year by year, with no increase in price, as shown by E_0' and E_1'.

That energy came increasingly from oil and gas, the use of which soared. Much of this surge resulted from the growing use of the mass-produced automobile. Automobiles became the symbol of the North American dream. As North American households became richer they tended to buy larger numbers of ever faster, bigger, and more lavishly equipped cars—to say nothing of trailers, vans, and recreational vehicles. Year by year the demand for gasoline to power these internal combustion engines rose. Yet the price of

gasoline remained low, so low that throughout this period the cost of fuel remained a trivial part of the cost of owning and operating a car.

This epoch of ever-increasing demand at a constant price is analyzed in Figure 17-2. The long-run supply curve seemed to be almost perfectly elastic at a low price. For every barrel of oil produced, another was discovered. Although everyone knew this could not go on forever, a rising supply price was far in the future. Indeed, the enormous quantities of oil being discovered and produced in the Middle East so threatened the profitability of the domestic oil industries that North American governments took steps to protect domestic companies from the imports of cheap foreign oil. The U.S. government imposed quotas that limited imports of foreign oil. In Canada the "Ottawa Valley Line" was established in 1961 to provide a protected market in the west for Canadian oil. Various tax incentives were also provided in both Canada and the United States to encourage domestic exploration and production.

The fact that the demand curve shifted rightward year after year was not a cause for alarm; indeed, the reverse was true: Energy fueled the increasing productivity that led to ever-rising material standards of living. North America rode on cheap and plentiful oil.

North Americans traveling abroad were amused by the small, cramped cars they saw and rented, and they were appalled by the high cost of gasoline. The high prices abroad were due to very high taxes on gasoline, and the higher prices led to lower gasoline consumption. Europeans drove smaller cars, waited until they reached a higher level of income before buying a car (or buying a second car), and relied more on bicycles and public transportation. The European situation is also shown in Figure 17-2.

OPEC'S EMBARGO

Although not all North America's oil came from abroad, a virtually horizontal supply curve of the sort shown in Figure 17-2 was due to the willingness of oil exporters in the Middle East to supply as much oil as North America and European countries wanted at a fixed price. What would happen if and when the oil exporters changed their mind?

The world found out in 1973 with the onset of the OPEC oil embargo. The "Ottawa Valley line" and associated policies had been so successful that Canada was a net oil exporter in 1973. The withdrawal of OPEC oil from world markets generated general shortages and led to an increase in the world price of oil. For Canada this increased the opportunity cost of oil exports (see Chapter 27) but did not create shortages of the dimension experienced by oil-importing countries that suddenly had to rely on much more limited non-OPEC sources. They discovered that supply from these sources was not perfectly elastic. The change in shape of the supply curve for oil-importing countries due to OPEC is illustrated in Figure 17-3.

The theory of supply and demand leads to two clear predictions: a sharp rise in gasoline prices due to the upward shift of the supply curve, and a significant reduction in consumption as households adjusted to the new price level. These predictions rest on two assumptions: first, that consumers would reduce consumption rapidly in response to any price increase that occurred; second, that price was free to rise in response to the embargo-induced scarcity. Neither assumption was correct in 1974. For reasons discussed below, consumer response to increased energy costs occurs only over time, and governments in both Canada and the United States intervened to restrict the price increases that actually occurred. The experience of the United States, a net oil importer, provides an interesting case study of shortages created by preventing prices from adjusting.

Gasoline Price Controls in the United States

It happened that at the time of the OPEC embargo the United States government was setting maximum prices for gasoline. General price and wage controls had been imposed by the Nixon

FIGURE 17-3
The Effect of the OPEC Embargo

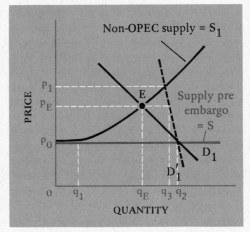

A change in gasoline supply, government price control, and short-run demand inelasticity all contribute to a large shortage of gasoline. Before the embargo, supply was S and demand D_1. The oil embargo shifts the supply curve to S_1. A new long-run equilibrium would occur at E, with price rising to p_E and consumption falling to q_E. Government maximum price controls prevented such a price rise. If price is held at p_0, excess demand of $q_1 q_2$ will appear.

Even if the government allows price to rise immediately to p_E, a shortage of $q_E q_3$ will occur because the short-run demand curve D_1' is much less elastic than the long-run curve D_1. A short-run price of p_1 would clear the market, but such a high price is not permitted by government, which does not want to allow windfall profits. Yet unless price rises to p_1 there will be excess demand in the short run and the need for some other means of allocation of gasoline.

administration in 1971. Most items had been decontrolled by the time of the embargo, but not gasoline. The result was predictable: a sudden, sharp gas shortage at the controlled prices. Lines developed, and stations ran out of gas and closed down. Rumors that the Amityville Shell station had gas on a summer Friday afternoon led to a colossal traffic jam as thousands of drivers tried to get there to fill their tanks before supplies ran out.

When price does not allocate limited supplies, there is always a need for alternative allocation schemes. Many gas stations would sell only to regular customers. Others sold only a few gallons at a time, thereby increasing the customer's time spent in line. Others exacted hidden prices by selling gas in large quantities only to those who bought tires, batteries, or windshield wipers (at very favorable prices). Travelers spent endless hours searching for gas or sitting in lines. The government was urged to allocate gasoline on a fair and equitable basis, both to dealers and, by issuing ration coupons, to consumers.

While the government did not adopt gasoline rationing, it took some steps. It permitted some price rises, and it attempted to allocate gasoline to the hardest hit areas. It imposed lower speed limits, and it exhorted people to form car pools. Some state governments imposed rationing through odd-even day sales and by closing stations on Sundays. These expedients helped reduce waiting lines. But even after prices had been allowed to rise to what approximated new equilibrium levels, the shortages continued. Why?

Price Increases and Demand Adjustments

In response to a sharp rise in the price of gasoline, households and firms would be expected to consume less of it, as the demand curve shows. Yet price rises had less effect on consumption than suggested by a downward-sloping demand curve such as D_1 in Figure 17-3. The reason is that it takes time to achieve adjustments in quantity demanded in response to a rise in price.

For example, if they had expected gasoline to cost $1.50 a gallon, the suburban Smith family would not have built their life style around two cars that gave only 12 and 15 miles to the gallon. They might not have moved to a location where a 20-mile commute to work and the ferrying of children to school, lessons, doctor's appointments, and parties were required daily. And they certainly would not have bought a fancy recreational vehicle for family vacations. But having done all those things, the Smiths were stuck and had to make the best of it. They began to use their cars more sparingly, but it would have been

silly to leave them in the garage and take taxis. (The *variable* cost of using the family car was less than the *total* cost of a taxi ride.) They tried to sell the RV, but the few people who answered their ad in the local paper were willing to pay only a small fraction of the price the Smiths thought was fair.

Up to now we have not needed to distinguish between short-run and long-run adjustments to changes in price. But for a commodity such as gasoline that is consumed along with other, durable goods, *time* is a key element in the adjustment process. It is necessary to recognize short-run as well as long-run demand curves.

The longer the period of time for adjustment, the greater will be the possibilities for substituting for commodities whose relative price is rising. Thus, in general, the longer the period of time, the more elastic the demand curve will be.

In the very short run, the only way to use less gasoline is to drive less. Over a longer time, people have many options. They can change the kind of car they drive. They can move closer to work and make other changes in their life-style.

Such adjustments began to occur very quickly. Producers and distributors of small, fuel-saving cars, such as American Motors and Volkswagen, found demand for their products rising; other automobile manufacturers found large cars not selling. The latter stoped production and laid off workers while they strained to shift production into their relatively few plants suitable for producing small cars. Used-car dealers found that their big cars would not sell but their small cars were being snapped up at existing prices—so they changed the structure of their prices.

The full adjustment to smaller, more efficient cars had not been accomplished by the end of the decade, but more of it occurs every year. The adjustment is made more difficult to the extent that the demand for energy continues to grow as part of the long-term trend.

We can capture the spirit of the adjustment problem by using only two demand curves, a relatively elastic long-run demand curve and a relatively inelastic short-run curve. See Figure 17-3.

In economic terms, the short-run demand curve for gasoline was much less elastic than the long-run curve. As shown in the figure, such an inelastic demand curve would lead to shortages in the short run even if price jumped at once to the new long-run equilibrium price, p_E. Not only would the Smiths have to pay the new and outrageous higher price, they could not even then be sure of getting gas at that price!

There is of course *some* price at which demand can be equated with supply even in the short run. But neither the government nor the gasoline station operators were willing to let price rise to that level. The more inelastic the demand curve, the greater the windfall profits will be if price rises are used to eliminate excess demand. The government decided not to allow "profiteering" as a result of the unfortunate OPEC-induced gas shortage. Prices would be allowed to rise, but only by a "reasonable amount" based on cost. The government kept maximum prices on gasoline well below those that would have cleared the market. Private operators were reluctant to charge even as much as the government allowed. Ernie Weaver at the local filling station did not want to sell gas for which he had paid 70¢ a gallon for $1.20 or more a gallon. He believed that if he did, his customers would never forgive him for gouging them. Yet even at 85¢ a gallon they complained and asked bitterly whether he was planning to retire soon to Florida.

OPEC: SUPPLY LIMITATION AS A LONG-RUN STRATEGY

The oil embargo created a shortage of oil in the United States, but it did not lead to profits for the oil-producing countries. There were no sales by OPEC, and hence there were no revenues. But the experience showed the oil exporters how dependent North Americans (and others) were on their product, and how willing they were to pay more for gasoline.[3] What Ernie Weaver

[3] By 1976 Canada had again become a net oil importer and was once again dependent on imported oil supplies. See Chapter 27.

would not do, Sheik Yamani, the oil minister of Saudi Arabia, would do: restrict output, raise price, and earn huge profits.

Oil exporters in Saudi Arabia, Kuwait, and Iran could increase profits by restricting output and raising price, just as others can who cartelize a previously competitive industry. The sons of the sheiks had attended the Harvard Business School and learned all about monopolies and cartels. After the embargo, the oil-producing countries did not return to unlimited supply but instead adopted a regime of carefully controlled supply. Producing a limited supply, combined with the ever-rising demand for oil, will keep prices high. See Figure 17-4. By taking into ac-

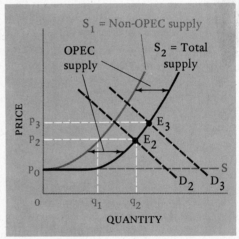

FIGURE 17-4
OPEC as a Cartel

Given a sharply rising non-OPEC supply curve of oil, the members of OPEC can determine equilibrium prices by choosing their contribution to total supply. The curve S_1 represents the non-OPEC supply of the product. If OPEC were prepared to supply unlimited quantities at p_0, the supply curve would be S and the situation shown in Figure 17-2 would be restored. But by fixing its production, OPEC can determine the new total (OPEC + non-OPEC) supply curve S_2. OPEC can, for given demand curves and non-OPEC supplies, pick a price (such as p_2) and determine what quantity to supply ($q_1 q_2$) to make that the equilibrium price. If demand is increasing, as from D_2 to D_3, the same OPEC supply will lead the price to increase from p_2 to p_3.

count how much non-OPEC oil is produced, the members of OPEC can determine how much they should produce to maximize their own profits.

Once or twice a year OPEC members meet to survey world supply and demand and to set prices. This implies that they also set output quotas for their members, for the high prices can be maintained only if excess production is avoided.

THE SITUATION IN 1980

By 1980 crude oil prices stood at roughly ten times the level of 1970, and the oil producers were among the richest nations in the world. The gasoline shortages of the mid 1970s had largely disappeared in response to a combination of substantial price increases, some allocation of gasoline supplies, some significant demand adjustments, and the introduction of some new, non-OPEC supplies. But the tentative and insecure nature of the balance between demand and supply was illustrated in 1979 by a temporary cutoff of Iranian oil supplies. Neither prices nor allocations adapted quickly enough. Almost overnight, shortages and waiting lines reappeared in the United States. They were followed by another round of major price increases by members of OPEC.

As long as North Americans depend on OPEC oil to meet a significant fraction of their energy needs, OPEC can manipulate its contribution to total world supply so as to serve its own best interests.

KINDS OF ENERGY POLICY

There are several alternative approaches to the kind of energy policy issue posed by the story of gasoline prices. Three of them are: (1) to let the market work, accepting whatever levels of price are necessary to equate supply and demand; (2) to impose price controls on energy and then to ration or otherwise allocate the shortages that will inevitably occur; (3) with or without either of the others, to attempt to *shift* the supply curve rightward (stimulate production) and/or *shift* the demand curve leftward (conserve energy).

Each of these approaches has its supporters. The second is sufficiently similar to rent control (discussed in Chapter 7) to require no further discussion. What of the other two?

Can the Free Market Do the Job?

If all controls on energy prices and production were removed, the price system could equate quantity demanded and quantity supplied. High and rising prices would force consumers to conserve energy and to find relatively cheaper sources for the most expensive kinds of energy. At the same time, high prices would promise high profits to producers who find new supplies of conventional energy or new substitutes for them.

The free-market strategy relies, in the first instance, on *movements along* supply and demand curves. For example, allowing price to rise (in response to a shortage) may eliminate the shortage by decreasing quantity demanded—moving up the demand curve. Yet initial changes may induce *shifts* in the curves. For example, a price rise may lead to windfall profits to producers, which in turn may lead to a new entry that will shift the supply curve rightward.

The fact that the free market can do the job does not necessarily mean it *should* be the chosen strategy. Key questions concern how quickly such results will occur and how much and what sorts of redistribution of income will result. Many critics of the free-market solution believe it may prove highly unfair in its distributive effects. Supporters of the free-market policy recognize such dangers but believe them to be less significant than the dangers inherent in intervention with the market. They also believe that any adverse redistributive effects could be offset by specific measures (such as taxes and subsidies) that are less costly to the economy than any intervention with the free-market price of energy. These issues are discussed in more detail in Chapter 27.

Can Intervention Do the Job?

A more interventionist energy policy means direct government action to shift supply or demand curves relative to what they would otherwise be. On the supply side, for example, the government can give exploration subsidies for oil. As a result, at any given price a larger quantity would be found and produced than before—that is, the supply curve would shift to the right. Other elements of a supply-side policy include providing incentives to hasten research in solar or geothermal energy and subsidizing greater use of the abundant supplies of coal.

On the demand side, people can be motivated to consume less energy by means other than allowing producer's prices to rise—for example, by taxing energy consumption heavily. (For consumers, a 50¢ per gallon tax is like a 50¢ price rise; it moves them up along their demand curves.) Other policies may shift the demand curve leftward. These include rules that compel auto manufacturers to produce more fuel-efficient engines, and subsidies that encourage home insulation, public transporation, and car pooling.

Supporters of interventionist policies believe they will work more fairly than simply letting prices rise. Critics believe that while a wise government might do a better job than the free market, our own government's performance is likely to be much worse.

THE DEBATE ABOUT STRATEGY

The current discussion is in part about which policy to follow and in part about whether there really is a major problem to solve.

The first OPEC price hike in 1973 failed to persuade many people of either the urgency of the problem or its genuineness. Since then most North Americans have come to believe in the problem, yet many think it will go away if only the energy companies would stop gouging the public.

The view that there is no energy problem is plainly wrong as long as the OPEC countries can control oil production. Oil is at present a key to our energy consumption. Just to stabilize the price of oil, given the historical pattern of ever-increasing demand, requires that we increase the supply of oil or oil substitutes *and* reduce the level of demand. If we are unwilling to do those things, we must be prepared to live with steadily rising prices.

Rightward-shifting demand combined with an upward-sloping supply curve inevitably means rising prices or, if prices are held down, ever-increasing shortages.

The way in which the "energy shortage" is resolved involves much more than finding the quickest or fairest way to equate supply and demand. The way in which this is done will also affect the rate of productivity growth, the nature of industrial development, and the quality of life. For one example, if the decision is made not to utilize nuclear energy on the grounds that it involves high safety risks, we will almost surely have higher energy costs and a slower rate of productivity growth than if we do utilize it. If instead we use more high sulfur coal, we will have a dirtier atmosphere. But using nuclear energy, while increasing energy supply, may require safety risks that people find unacceptable, and it may generate widespread protests and demonstrations. Finally, much of the dispute about energy policy concerns the general issue of the effectiveness of government regulation and intervention, which we will discuss in Chapter 24 before turning to a detailed discussion of energy policies in Chapter 27.

Summary

1. Groups supplying goods or services under conditions that approximate those of competitive equilibrium have a strong incentive to organize to restrict output. The reason is that their collective profits will surely increase, since the last units being produced have marginal costs in excess of marginal revenues.

2. To achieve and retain the benefits of monopolization requires more than just agreeing to restrict output. An effective cartel must be able to police and enforce its output quotas because it is in any one producer's interest to cheat. It must also cover most of the output of the industry, control the entry of new producers, and be insulated from too many close substitutes for the product it produces.

3. The NFO's milk-withholding program illustrates the difficulties that face a producers' association that includes only a fraction of the total producers in the industry. The case of the barbers illustrates the importance of entry control. The ball-point pen case illustrates the problem of substitutes.

4. The OPEC cartel has been remarkably successful so far in raising prices and profits. It includes most large oil exporters; it has prevented cheating; entry into oil production is not easy; and adequate substitutes for the amounts of oil OPEC has held off the market are neither easily nor quickly developed.

5. Several aspects of the impact of the rise in the price of gasoline on the Canadian and American economies and on the automobile industry can be traced, using supply and demand analysis. In the era before OPEC, demand for oil products rose steadily in response to low prices and a seemingly highly elastic supply.

6. OPEC changed the supply situation overnight by means of an embargo. In the United States the embargo, combined with government price controls, led to shortages, long lines, and the clamor for government allocation—all predicted by the theory of a price fixed below the equilibrium level.

7. Following the embargo, OPEC has limited the supply of oil through a cartel output restriction strategy that has converted a horizontal supply curve to a steeply rising one. It has managed the price of oil and received enormous monopoly profits from its sale.

8. Even after the price of gasoline was allowed to rise, the short-run inelasticity of demand (due to the durable nature of gasoline-using machines) and the continuing trend for ever more energy consumption kept gasoline scarce and the equilibrium price rising year by year.

9. Possible policy responses to the cartel-imposed supply limitation include (a) accepting whatever free-market price is necessary to equate demand with the new supply, (b) imposing price controls and allocating the inevitably short supplies, (c) attempting to shift the demand curve leftward (conserving energy) and the supply of non-OPEC production rightward (stimulating production). Either the first or the third policy (or a combination of the two) can eventually work to equate demand and supply. The level of price and the distributive consequences of the policies are not the same, and the differences account for a good bit of the sharp current debate about what sort of energy policy to adopt. Other aspects of the debate concern how much loss of productivity growth, pollution, and government intervention North Americans wish to put up with as a consequence of their dependence on OPEC oil.

Topics for Review

The motive for output restriction in a competitive industry
Why cartels may fail to raise profits
Long-run and short-run demand elasticity
Alternative energy policies

Discussion Questions

1. "If producers can sometimes successfully collude and if workers can successfully unite as unions, then consumers can certainly form powerful consumer groups to gain better prices and better products. This is all the easier because there is no law against a consumer boycott." What do you think?

2. Market-sharing and price-fixing agreements (except for agriculture and labor) are violations of the combines laws. Consider the effect of the following on the

ability of firms in the industry to achieve uniform prices:

a. resale price-maintenance laws that allow the manufacturer of a commodity to set minimum prices below which its product may not be sold

b. regulations that set fixed commissions for brokers to charge

c. a trade association that each month publishes the prices charged by each of its members in the previous month.

d. a trade association that publishes "average industry costs of production" every month.

3. Consider the case of barbers. It is common practice for barbers to charge lower prices for children's haircuts than for adults' haircuts. How can you account for this? What does it suggest about the market structure of barbering?

4. Use price theory in discussing the following news stories.

a. The analysis sent out by a leading stock brokerage firm: "Prices of digital watches are following the pattern of pocket calculators—down 25 percent a year. This is just what we expected; it is normal. Expect squeezed profit margins and some bankruptcies."

b. Donald Hollister, inventor of a new long-lasting light bulb that won't burn out for at least 10 years: "Even if this catches on, I expect to do well, but not to make a million dollars. The idea is too simple."

c. "Barbers are providing special inducements to long-haired youths: free beard trims with every haircut."

d. Newspaper report about the growth of a local "gut row": "It's a bit mind boggling to see so many fast-food restaurants in one place. All the national chains are there—Burger King, McDonald's, Shakey's Pizza—and you have your choice of chicken, seafood, barbecue or even native favorites like sau-

sage biscuits. It's great for the family, but nobody's making any money."

5. France is occasionally beset by "artichoke wars." When good weather produces a bumper crop, prices fall sharply and angry farmers from Brittany storm into Paris, even barricading the streets with artichokes in protest. Assuming that not many artichokes are used up in pelting the citizenry of Paris, what would you say to the farmers if called on to advise them? You are expected to be honest with them and to explain both the disadvantages and the advantages of your plan.

6. In 1973 the OPEC cartel agreed to raise petroleum prices. OPEC was to do this by having each member nation raise the tax it charged producers on each barrel. In 1973 the Persian Gulf members of OPEC increased the taxes charged from less than $2 to over $7 a barrel. By 1980 the price of oil was over $20 a barrel. International cartels are notorious for their instability; in what ways is OPEC stronger than a cartel based on agreements among individual firms in different countries?

7. Comment on the following statements about OPEC and the "energy crisis."

a. The Japanese minister of trade and industry, Komoto, responding to an OPEC price increase: "An outrageous act that ignores economic principles and is therefore regrettable."

b. Milton Friedman (in 1976): "OPEC will break up within the next year because it will not be able to withstand the competitive pressure resulting from the vast sources of oil being discovered in many areas."

c. "The only barrier to solving the energy crisis caused by OPEC is the general public's view that there is no real problem."

d. "Nuclear energy, polluting coal, skyrocketing gasoline prices—these are the things that are wrong with North America today."

Monopoly Versus Competition

18

Monopoly has been regarded with suspicion for a very long time. Even today in some quarters it takes a large share of the blame for inflation, for the energy shortage, for discrimination in employment, and for inequalities in income. It is widely believed that modern economic theory has *proved* that monopoly allows the powerful producer to exploit the consumer, while the competitive system always works to the consumer's advantage. In *The Wealth of Nations* (1776), Adam Smith—the founder of classical economics—developed a ringing attack on monopolies and monopolists. Since then most economists have criticized monopoly and advocated freer competition. In Chapters 14 and 15 we saw that perfect competition has appealing features and that it is efficient in ways that monopoly is not.

Is a preference for competition and a distrust of monopoly justified? This chapter carries further the comparison of monopoly and competition in terms of their predicted effects, then looks at the principal policies for dealing with monopoly in Canada. Throughout the discussion, "monopoly" refers to monopoly power, not merely to the case of a single seller. "Competition" refers both to the market structure known as perfect competition and to competitive behavior of firms in a variety of market structures. The context will make it clear which meaning is intended.

Comparisons Between Monopoly and Competition

THE EFFECT OF CHANGES IN COST ON PRICE AND QUANTITY PRODUCED

Cost savings mean fewer resources are used in production than would otherwise be the case. If such cost savings occur, how and to what extent are they passed on to consumers?

Consider the case of an invention that lowers the marginal cost of production. In a perfectly competitive industry, the fact that each firm's marginal cost curve shifts downward means that

the industry supply curve (which is the sum of the marginal cost curves) also shifts downward. As a result of the invention, any given output will be provided at a lower price than before and any given price will call forth a higher output. The cost-saving invention lowers price and raises output. Figure 18-1(i) illustrates this. The effect of an identical change in marginal cost on the price and output of the monopolist is shown in Figure 18-1(ii). The downward-shifting marginal cost curve intersects the marginal revenue curve at a higher level of output than it did previously. Because the demand curve is unchanged, it follows that the price must fall. So the benefit from

FIGURE 18-1
The Effect on Price of a Reduction in Marginal Cost

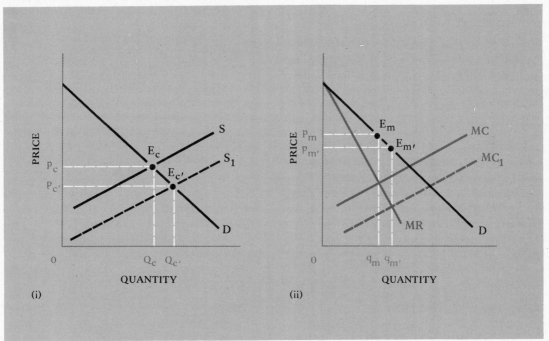

A reduction in marginal cost leads to a greater decrease in price and a greater increase in quantity in a competitive industry than in a monopolized one. The demand curve is the same in both parts of the diagram, and the competitive short-run supply curve (*S*) is the same as the monopolist's marginal cost curve (*MC*). When marginal cost decreases, the curves shift down-

ward to S_1 and MC_1. The new competitive output is where *D* and S_1 cross. The new monopolistic output is where MC_1 and *MR* cross. Because *MR* declines more steeply than *D*, the increase in output (and the consequent decrease in price) is less under monopoly than under competition.

any fall in costs will, to some extent, be passed on to consumers as lower prices in both competition and monopoly.

But while prices will fall in both cases, they will not usually fall to the same degree.

Other things being equal, prices and quantities will change less in monopoly than in competition as a response to a change in marginal costs.

The reason for this is that the monopolist is guided by the marginal revenue curve, which is steeper than the demand curve. The same vertical fall in marginal costs leads to a lesser increase in quantity and thus a lesser fall in price.

THE MONOPOLIZATION OF A COMPETITIVE INDUSTRY WITH NO CHANGE IN COSTS

The classical case against monopoly is to a great extent based on this prediction:

If a perfectly competitive industry should be monopolized, and if the cost curves of all productive units are unaffected by this change, the price will rise and the quantity produced will fall.

Assume that a competitive industry is monopolized as the result of a single firm's buying out all the individual producers and operating each one as an independent plant. Further assume that cost curves are not affected by this change. This means that the marginal costs will be the same to the monopolist as to the competitive industry.

When the industry is monopolized, it becomes profitable to drive price up by restricting output for precisely the same reasons it pays a producers' association to do so (see page 310). As long as neither market demand nor costs change, it will always pay the monopolist that charges a single price to restrict output below, and to raise price above, their perfectly competitive levels (see Figure 18-2).

The consequences of this change in equilibrium price and quantity were presented in Chapters 14 and 15: (1) at competitive but not monopolistic equilibrium, the level of average

FIGURE 18-2
The Monopolization of a Competitive Industry

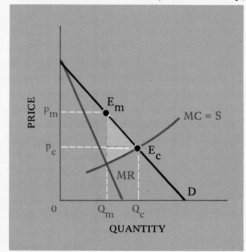

When a competitive industry is monopolized, output falls and price rises and a deadweight loss occurs. The competitive industry's supply curve and the monopolist's marginal cost curve are identical. The industry faces demand curve D. A competitive industry would produce Q_c at price p_c. The monopolist reduces output to Q_m because units between Q_m and Q_c add more to its cost than to its revenue. The shaded area shows that consumers were willing to pay more for each unit of lost output than its marginal cost of production. This deadweight loss of monopolization is a source of allocative inefficiency.

cost is necessarily the lowest attainable, given the technology of the society, and (2) at competitive but not monopolistic equilibrium, $p = MC$, and thus allocative efficiency is achieved.

Under these circumstances, the monopolization of a competitive industry surely introduces allocative inefficiency, and it may lead to productive inefficiency.

THE EFFECT OF MARKET STRUCTURE ON COST

What if costs are not the same for the monopolist as for the competitive industry? Costs may be affected when an industry is monopolized or when a large number of small firms is replaced by a small number of large firms. If any savings occur from combining numerous competing groups into a single integrated operation, the costs of producing any given level of output will be lower than they were previously. If this cost reduction occurs, it will be possible for output to be increased and price to be lowered as a result of the replacement of a perfectly competitive industry by a firm with monopoly power. This may occur in two very different ways.

Advantages of Large Scale

The cost advantage of having one railroad between two points rather than 50 railroads (or one water company in a city, or one telephone system in a country) is obvious. In such situations, it would be inefficient to have a large number of firms each producing a small output at a high cost per unit. If such a situation existed, any firm that grew bigger than its rivals would soon find itself in a position to cut price below its rivals' costs and monopolize the industry. This situation is called **natural monopoly.** It exists where the size of the market allows only one firm of efficient size.

Natural monopoly is just the extreme version of a much more common situation in industrialized countries, in which advantages of scale will make perfect competition wholly unattainable because there is room for only a small number of firms of efficient size.

Today the effective choice is usually not between monopoly and perfect competition but between more or less oligopoly.

Whenever there are long-run advantages of large-scale production, of marketing and distribution, of learning by doing, or of innovation or invention, the minimum efficient size of firms will tend to be large.

When *MES* is large, it is likely that productive efficiency will be improved, rather than worsened, by a shift from competition to a more concentrated market structure.

Lower Levels of Cost of Producing a Given Output

Even if there are no advantages of large-scale *plants,* large *firms* may be able to achieve economies, and thus lower costs, by multiproduct production and associated large-scale distribution, national advertising, and large-scale purchasing. Such economies have been described as **economies of scope** rather than of scale. When such cost reduction occurs, it is possible for output to be increased and price to be lowered as a result of the monopolization of a perfectly competitive industry. The possibility of such a situation is illustrated in Figure 18-3.

Saying that monopoly *may* lead to lower costs does not mean that departures from competition

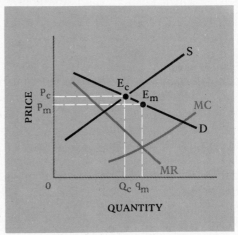

FIGURE 18-3
A Case in Which Monopolization Leads to Lower Prices

If monopolization lowers costs sufficiently, it may lead to greater output and lower price than competition. D and S are the demand and supply curves of a competitive industry that is in equilibrium at E_c with p_c and Q_c. If costs are unaffected by monopolization, S will become the monopolist's marginal cost curve and the monopolist will restrict output and raise price. However, if the monopolization reduces costs to MC, the equilibrium will be at E_m, with p_m less than p_c and q_m greater than Q_c.

must lead to lower costs. A large firm that is protected from competition by an entry barrier may reduce the efficiency of production and so shift marginal and average cost curves upward. In such a case (compared to the competitive industry) monopolization will certainly raise price and lower output.

It is thus possible for changes in market structure to change costs in either direction. The key empirical question is, in what circumstances do large firms in less competitive market structures achieve lower levels of cost than an industry composed of large numbers of small firms? Much of the answer depends on how market structure affects the rate of innovation.[1]

THE INCENTIVE TO INNOVATE

As far as profits are concerned, firms in any market structure have an incentive to innovate in order to find a cost-saving process or a more popular new product. There has been extended debate over which kinds of market structure are most conducive to innovation.

Innovation Under a Monopoly

A monopolist can always increase its profits if it can reduce costs. And because it is able to prevent the entry of new firms into the industry, the additional profits will persist into the long run. Thus, from the standpoint of maximizing profits, the monopolist has both a short-run and a long-run incentive to reduce costs by innovation.

Innovation requires research and development, and that costs money. The monopolistic firm may have an advantage over the competitive firm in that funds for research and development are more readily available to it. In the first place, it may have profits to invest in such ventures even though credit is tight. In the second place, tax laws that permit writing off business expenses may make research and development relatively cheap. Suppose that this year a monopolist expects to make $2 million profit, on which it will have to pay taxes of approximately $1 million. If it spends the $2 million on research and development, it will show no profits for tax purposes this year and the firm will save $1 million in taxes. In effect, it can get $2 million worth of research for only $1 million. Successful research will eventually lead to future profits and will strengthen the firm's position as a monopolist. Of course, in later years it will have to pay taxes on the profits it earns—unless they are again spent on research and development.

Some critics of monopoly concede that innovation occurs but argue that monopolists engage in the wrong kinds of innovation. Monopolists may be expected to give special attention to kinds of innovation that increase or preserve the barriers to entry of potential competitors, as well as undertaking innovations that reduce costs to consumers in the long run.

Innovation Under Competition

The firm in perfect competition has the same profit incentive to innovate as the monopolist, but only in the short run, not in the long run. In the short run, a reduction in costs will allow the firm that was just covering costs to earn profits. In the long run, other firms will be attracted into the industry by these profits. Existing firms will copy the cost-saving innovation, new firms will enter the industry using the new techniques, and the profits of the innovator will eventually disappear.

The effectiveness of profits as an incentive to reduce costs for a firm will depend on the magnitude of the extra profits and the length of time over which they persist.

If it takes only a few months for existing firms and new entrants to copy and install any new invention, then the innovating firm's profits will be above normal for only a short time and the extra profits actually earned may not be sufficient to compensate for the risks and the costs of developing the new innovation. In such cases the

[1] At this time we suggest you read again the discussion of invention and innovation on pages 235–240.

direct incentive to innovate will be absent from a competitive industry. Alternatively, if it takes several years for other firms to copy and install the cost-saving innovation, then the profits earned over these years by the innovating firm might be more than sufficient to compensate for all costs and risks and might yield a handsome profit as well. In this case the incentive to innovate is present in a competitive industry.

The Greater Incentive to Innovate?

Might competition be *more* conductive to innovation than monopoly? Some think so. A monopolist that does not innovate may be missing larger profits, yet it can still have some long-run profits. But, the argument runs, if the competitive firm does not innovate, some of its competitors are likely to do so and it will find itself in a position in which it cannot even keep up with its competitors, thus incurring losses and eventual bankruptcy.

A very different view was that of the distinguished Austrian (and later American) economist Joseph A. Schumpeter. In brief, his argument was that only the incentive of profits leads entrepreneurs to take the great risks involved in innovation, and that monopoly power is much more important than competition in providing the climate under which innovation occurs. The profits of the monopolist provide the incentive for other people to try to get their share. This might involve imitating the monopolist's product (thereby eroding the monopoly market), or it might involve trying to come up with a new product that would better serve the underlying wants that make the monopolist rich. As a result no monopoly will last forever; it will not even last very long if it fails to innovate and to anticipate its future competition. Schumpeter called the process of one monopoly being replaced by another the *process of creative destruction*. In *Capitalism, Socialism and Democracy* (1942) he said:

What we have got to accept is that it has come to be the most powerful engine of that progress and in par-

ticular of the long-run expansion of total output not only in spite of, but to a considerable extent through, this strategy which looks so restrictive when viewed in the individual case and from the individual point of time. In this respect, perfect competition is not only impossible but inferior, and has no title to being set up as a model of ideal efficiency. It is hence a mistake to base the theory of government regulation of industry on the principle that big business should be made to work as the respective industry would work in perfect competition.

Innovation Under Oligopoly

Many students of industrial organization have theorized that intermediate market structures, such as oligopoly, might lead to more innovation than either competitive or monopolistic industries. They argue that the oligopolist is faced by clear and present competition from existing rivals and cannot afford the more relaxed life of the monopolist who might choose not to maximize profits. At the same time, however, the oligopolist expects to keep a good share of the profits it earns because of the barriers to entry and its ability to avoid excessive price competition with existing rivals.

The empirical evidence is broadly consistent with this hypothesis. Professor Jesse Markham of Harvard University recently concluded a survey of empirical findings by saying:

If technological change and innovational activity are, as we generally assume, in some important way a product of organized R&D activities financed and executed by business companies, it is clear that the welfare payoffs that flow from them can to some measurable extent be traced to the doorsteps of large firms operating in oligopolistic markets.

Everyday observation provides some confirmation of this finding. Leading firms that operate in highly concentrated industries, such as Kodak, IBM, du Pont, Bell, Xerox, General Electric, and General Motors, have been highly innovative over many years.[2]

---

[2] The discussion of foreign ownership and R&D expenditure, in the box on page 236, could be usefully reviewed at this point.

While Schumpeter's hypothesis, applied to oligopoly, has substantial credibility, it is also true that the relationship is far from perfect. Some highly oligopolistic American industries, such as steel, appear to have lagged far behind their foreign competitors. Evidently the long, sustained absence of competition led them to become complacent and relatively inefficient. (A Schumpeterian might respond that the result is due to such things as tariff protection and other *governmental* impediments to creative destruction.)

Patents and the Incentive to Innovate

Economists who believe that competitive market structures best serve consumers by assuring them low prices, but who worry about the possible lack of incentives to innovate under competition, believe that other institutions, such as the patent laws, can provide the necessary incentives. Patent laws confer a temporary monopoly on the use of an invention. The intent of patent protection is to lengthen the short-run period during which whoever controls the invention can earn supernormal profits as a reward for inventing it. This is meant to act as a spur to invention and innovation. Whether or not existing patent laws have that effect is subject to substantial debate among economists.

Public Policy Toward Monopoly: Combines Laws

The theory of monopoly leads to three principal predictions. (1) Where monopoly power exists in an industry, it will lead to a restriction on the flow of resources into the industry and thus to the employment of fewer resources than would be used under competitive conditions. (2) Consequently firms with monopoly power will be able to charge higher prices and will be able to earn profits in excess of opportunity costs. (3) Their owners will command a larger share of the national income than they would under conditions

of competition. In short, an economy characterized by firms with monopoly power will lead to a different allocation of resources and a different distribution of income than will an economy composed largely of competitive industries. The belief that competition produced ideal results and monopoly worse results underlies the present-day **combines laws** that prohibit the operation of monopolies, attempts to monopolize, and conspiracies in restraint of trade.

The distributional aspects of monopoly are important. In the industrial sectors of the economy, corporate managers and stockholders are typically of above average income. Thus the higher salaries and higher dividends of corporate monopoly tend to lead to a more unequal distribution of income. On the other hand, monopoly power, when exercised by those who are relatively poor rather than relatively rich, has frequently been supported rather than opposed by the government. For example, the efforts of farmers to increase farm income have been not only condoned but actively promoted by public policies of crop restriction, price supports, and the exemption of marketing boards from combines laws. Labor unions are also exempt from combines laws, and the efforts of unions to achieve some degree of monopoly power over the supply of labor were also supported actively by those public policies that encouraged the growth of unions.

Combines laws attempt to prohibit the acquistiion or exercise of monopoly power by business firms.

The first Canadian policies with respect to anticompetitive practices were proposed in the late nineteenth century, an era when economists believed both that perfect competition produced ideal results and that perfect competition was the feasible alternative to monopoly. The laws that were put in place reflected this attitude; legislation enacted in 1889 made it an offence to combine or agree to lessen competition unduly or restrain trade.

While modern economists are no longer so confident about the feasibility of perfect competition and the evils of monopoly power, competition (and the laws that promote it) is still regarded as playing a key role in the successful working of the market economy. The laws originally adopted in 1889 and 1890 have been changed, but the basic pro-competition stance of those laws still prevails in current legislation.

Noneconomic motives for dealing with the "monopoly problem" also exist. Principal among them is the distrust of power; many people fear the political influence of those with substantial economic power. The hypothesis that big business wields enormous political power and thus threatens the open society is often presented. Such studies may utilize statistics showing the size and share of *total* manufacturing assets held by the nation's largest 200 corporations. This "macroconcentration" does not concern monopoly power in any market; rather, it concerns bigness in the economy.

Compared with the prevalent view in the United States, where the general policy is referred to as an *antitrust policy,* these noneconomic motives have not been so persuasive to Canadian policymakers. In introducing the legislation proposed in 1910, Mackenzie King, then minister of labour, stated during a debate in the House of Commons that "this measure seeks to afford the means of conserving to the public some of the benefits which arise from large organizations of capital. . . ." Throughout the history of Canadian policy, legislation has been directed chiefly at the misuse and abuse of power by large associations and only rarely at combinations per se.

This apparent acceptance of the need for large firms in the business sector has been explained in terms of the *staples theory* of economic growth as developed by the late professors Harold Innis of the University of Toronto and W. A. Mackintosh of Queen's University. Their thesis essentially was that much of Canada's real growth was tied to a succession of export staples such as fur, wheat, lumber, and base metals. The exploitation of these resources required not only large amounts of private capital in a country where capital was scarce, but also substantial "social overhead" capital in the form of an extensive east-west transportation network. In addition, uncertainty was created by the wide price fluctuations to which these products were subject. The result was a reliance on firms with substantial monopoly power and considerable direct government support.

THE NATURE OF COMPETITION POLICY

By and large, economists have regarded monopolistic restrictions on resource flows as being adverse on the grounds that they hinder the efficient use of resources. Because those with monopoly power are usually relatively well off, any redistribution of income toward the monopolist also conflicts with the public's desire for more equality in income distribution. Whenever large firms have acquired sizable shares of the output of major industries, they have usually become objects of public concern, and the clamor for the government to "do something" about monopoly has been loud. Competition policy has been aimed at such firms.

The concern with monopoly power and control of particular product markets, whether by merger or by internal growth of the firm, is only one aspect of competition policy. Also prohibited are restrictive business practices such as some forms of price discrimination, collusive agreements concerning prices to be charged or market shares, and resale price maintenance (control by a manufacturer of the price at which a retailer sells a product). In principle, these activities are prohibited because it is believed that they limit actual or potential competition. In practice, it becomes difficult to determine just when a legal offence has been committed and whether there is in fact a threat to competition from an economic point of view. Ideally the legal judgment should be subservient to the economic analysis, but this is difficult to ensure given the problem of drafting a statute that will cover all future situations and the uncertainty concerning what interpretation the courts will place on its provisions. Most important, economists are frequently not in agreement on the likely consequences of various forms of behavior of firms in oligopolistically or monopolistically competitive markets.

CANADIAN COMPETITION POLICY

Government policy with respect to trusts and industrial combinations in Canada dates from 1888, when a Select Committee of the House of Commons initiated an investigation into alleged combinations in trade. The committee report concluded that combinations detrimental to the public interest existed in several industries, and legislation enacted in 1889 made it an offence to combine or agree to lessen competition unduly or to restrain trade. However, the task of assembling evidence in a combines investigation proved to be beyond the resources of individual injured parties or the ordinary machinery of criminal investigation.

The enactment of the Combines Investigation Act of 1910 was an attempt to remedy this shortcoming. It provided that if a judge concluded that there were reasonable grounds for believing an illegal combine existed, the minister of labour was to appoint a board of three commissioners to carry out a full inquiry and publish a report of its findings. The act did not provide penalties for past actions of a combine, but it did provide fines for continuing practices reported by the board to be detrimental to the public interest.

In framing the 1910 legislation, the Canadian government was influenced by what was regarded as the unhappy experience of the United States with its Sherman Antitrust Act (1890). There was no inclination to emulate the "trustbusting" activities that involved the American antitrust division of the Department of Justice in a large number of prosecutions during the period 1904–1911, when the courts adopted a strict interpretation of the Sherman Antitrust Act.[3] Mackenzie King commented in Parliament:

[3] This period of vigorous prosecution ended with the enunciation by the Supreme Court of the "rule of reason." In forcing Standard Oil Company and American Tobacco Company to divest themselves of a large share of their holdings of other companies, the Court stated that only *unreasonable* combinations in restraint of trade merited conviction under the Sherman Antitrust Act.

I have tried to show that this legislation is not brought in with a view to aiming at the formation of combinations as such, but rather a controlling of their actions, so that they may not unduly embarrass or interfere with the rights of the general public. We have sought to avoid the errors which have exhibited themselves in the legislation of other countries. We have tried to avoid the error which the United States have experienced in going too far in one direciton.[4]

Instead early Canadian legislation relied strongly on the publicity attached to an investigation as a deterrent to restrictive trade practices.

Competition Policy, 1923–1975

The Combines Investigation Act of 1923 formed the basis of competition policy until the end of 1975. Although King, who was then prime minister, retained his faith in the deterrent effect of investigation and publicity, the new law provided punishment for past participation in the formation or operation of a combine. Prosecution could take place even if the combine had ceased its unlawful activities after investigation. To provide greater continuity in the administration of the act, a permanent registrar was empowered to conduct inquiries. In 1935 the legislation was amended to prohibit discriminatory pricing that substantially lessened competition or eliminated a competitor, and in 1951 resale price maintenance was added to the list of proscribed practices.

With these amendments, the legislation prohibited three broad classes of activity: (1) combinations such as price-fixing agreements that unduly lessen competition, (2) mergers or monopolies that may operate to the detriment of the public interest, and (3) unfair trade practices. A large number of cases of unfair trade practices were successfully pursued, but—compared to the U.S. enforcement experience—there was a striking paucity of merger cases. During the sixty years following the first legislation in 1910, only

[4] Debates, House of Commons, Sess. 1909–1910, Vol. IV, p. 6837. See J. A. Ball, *Canadian Anti-trust Legislation* (Baltimore, 1934), chapter 5.

two full-scale cases came before the courts. Both defendants, Canadian Breweries Limited and B. C. Sugar Refining Company, were acquitted by the trial courts and neither decision was appealed. One plea of guilty was entered to a merger charge in 1970, and in 1973 the Crown obtained an order, without a full trial, prohibiting a merger. In 1974, K. C. Irving Limited was convicted, but this judgment was reversed on appeal.

The reason most often cited for the lack of combines enforcement in Canada was the inability of criminal legislation to cope with complex economic issues. Under criminal law, the government must prove beyond a reasonable doubt that the accused has commited the offence. In the United States, most antitrust cases are civil cases in which a lesser standard of proof is required to obtain a conviction. In American merger cases litigated since 1950, for example, when a substantial share of the market has been controlled, the courts have generally found that the merger restricts competition and is therefore illegal.

There is also some doubt whether the penalties imposed for violations in Canada were effective. The most common penalty, the criminal fine, which on only one occasion exceeded $25,000 for a single company, may not have deterred contraventions of the act. Canadian courts have also appeared less willing than American courts to assess economic evidence. Mr. Justice Hope in *R*. v. *Container Materials, Ltd.* (1940) expressed this reluctance with the caveat, "Our Lady of the Common Law is not a professed economist," and Mr. Justice Spence in *R* v. *Howard Smith Paper Mills* (1959) reemphasized the courts' difficulty:

Surely the determination of whether or not an agreement to lessen competition was "undue" by a survey of one industry's profits against profits of industry generally, and a survey of the movement of the prices in that one industry against the movement of prices generally, would put the Court to the essentially non-judicial task of judging between conflicting political theories. It would entail the Court's being required to conjecture — and by a Court it would be nothing more

than mere conjecture, since a Court is not trained to act as an arbitrator of economics — whether better or worse results would have occurred to the public if free and untrammelled competition had been permitted to run its course.

The New Competition Policy

A major review of Canadian legislation was begun in 1966 by the Economic Council of Canada. Its recommendations, published in a report in 1969, together with those of a committee of experts appointed by the Department of Consumer and Corporate Affairs, formed the basis of proposed amendments to the Combines Investigation Act. The amendments were subsequently presented to Parliament in two stages. The Stage II amendments, which proposed the transfer of certain practices from criminal to civil law, recommended the appointment of a Competition Board to replace the courts in the examination of trade practices, and dealt with the issue of mergers and monopolization, had not been passed by the spring of 1981.

The Stage I amendments were proclaimed on January 1, 1976. They included provisions for extending the Combines Investigation Act to service industries, for allowing civil actions to be brought for damages resulting from contraventions of the act, and for strengthening legislation against misleading advertising. However, perhaps the most significant feature of the Stage I amendments is that they give the Restrictive Trade Practices Commission (RTPC) the power to order suppliers to cease certain practices. Previously the RTPC functioned only as an investigative body that could recommend prosecution. The following practices are dealt with:

Refusal to supply. When the business of a complainant is "substantially" affected as a result of a supplier's refusal to sell its product to the complainant, the commission can order the practice to cease. While the force of this provision is to ensure that customers are treated fairly, it also makes some attempt to ensure that unfair demands on suppliers are not made. For example, the act makes clear that a single *brand* does not constitute a separate *product*.

Exclusive dealing. A seller may not require a customer to purchase from it alone, nor may it prohibit the customer from carrying competing products. Yet exclusive dealing is permitted when it is engaged in for a short period of time for the purpose of promoting entry into a new market, or when it occurs between companies that are affiliated in some way.

Market restriction. A seller may not restrict *the way a good is resold* (for example, by requiring certain marketing techniques or granting exclusive territorial dealerships) unless the commission finds that such a practice will facilitate entry into a new market, in which case the practice is permissible for a short period.

Tied sales. A supplier may not require that a buyer of one product buy a second product as a condition of being sold the first.

The sections of the amendments that deal with *misleading advertising* are extensive. Although the commission cannot act directly in such cases, the Department of Consumer and Corporate Affairs has shown itself to be quite willing to prosecute on the advice of the commission. These actions are specifically forbidden:

1. Making a representation to the public in the form of a guarantee, statement, or warranty on the performance, efficacy, or length of life of a product that is not based on adequate or proper tests.
2. Advertising a product at a bargain price when the supplier does not or cannot supply the product in reasonable quantities.
3. Promoting the sale of a product by a contest unless the chances of winning are disclosed *and* the contest is based either on skill or on random selection.
4. Supplying a product at a price higher than the advertised price, except when the advertised price is erroneous and is immediately corrected.

One of the most significant innovations in the proposed and existing amendments to the Com-

bines Investigation Act is the transformation of the Restrictive Trade Practices Commission from a purely investigative body into a board empowered to determine whether the costs of certain types of behavior on the part of individual firms outweighs their benefits. The provisions of the amendments, and the exceptions to them, are by their very nature quite ambiguous. Hence the amendments provide, at best, guidelines for the commission, and the precedents established in individual cases will assume considerable importance.

This theme is important in the determination of public policy toward monopoly. One well-known example is the determination of the optimal Canadian industrial structure. While industries with small firms of uniform size are less able to combine and extract monopoly profits from their domestic customers, they are also less able to exploit economies of scale that would enable them to compete more effectively against large foreign firms. (For a related discussion, see the box on pages 302–303.) Economics can give the policymaker guidance on how to measure the costs and benefits of alternative policies in particular cases. Since the costs may or may not outweigh the benefits of certain actions, it is impossible to give the courts a strict rule as to whether a certain action is "wrong." It is thus appropriate that a specialized tribunal, applying rules set by the government, be employed to pass judgment on whether actions by firms are or are not desirable.

Public Policy Toward Monopoly: Public Utility Regulation

NATURAL MONOPOLY

Natural monopoly arises because of economies of scale (discussed on page 327). Policymakers have not wanted to compel the maintenance of a large number of small, inefficient producers when a single firm would be much more efficient; neither have they wanted to give the natural monopolist the opportunity to restrict output, raise price, and appropriate as profits the gains available by virtue of large-scale production.

The public utility concept grew out of the recognition by economists that when there are major economies of large-scale production, protection of the public interest by competition is impractical if not impossible.

The dilemma of natural monopoly is illustrated in Figure 18-4. To achieve low costs, a single larger producer is necessary, but an unregulated profit-maximizing monopoly would restrict output, raise price, and fail to provide the large volume of output at a low price that the technology makes possible.

One possible response to this dilemma is for government to assume ownership of the single firm and instruct (or delegate to) the managers of the nationalized industry regarding what quantity to produce and what price to charge, in each case being guided by the national interest. Many countries have done precisely that with telephone and railway services, among others. In Canada this solution has been followed, for example, with Canadian National Railways, the CBC, and provincial electric power companies. In other cases, such as telephones, the practice has been to allow private enterprise but to regulate its behavior.

Public utility regulation gives to appropriate public authorities (usually specially constituted regulatory commissions such as the Canadian Transport Commission) control over the price and quantity of service provided by a natural monopoly, with the object of achieving the efficiency of a single seller without the output restriction of the monopolist.

In return for giving a company a franchise or licence to be the sole producer, the public utility regulators deserve the right to regulate its behavior.

Regulation of this kind has been prevalent for almost a century. In Canada, railway rates have been regulated since the passage of the Railway Act of 1888 and public utility regulation has since spread to other forms of transpor-

FIGURE 18-4
The Problem of Natural Monopoly

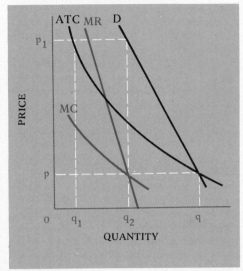

Cost conditions in a situation of natural monopoly are such that a single firm is required to achieve the economies of scale, but a monopolist finds it profitable to restrict output to maximize profits. Because *ATC* declines sharply, efficiency is served by having a single firm. Clearly, one firm producing at q would be more efficient than several firms each producing q_1 at a cost of p_1 per unit. But an unregulated monopoly would restrict output to q_2 and charge price p_1, thereby depriving consumers of the advantages of large-scale production.

tation—airlines, trucking, pipelines—and to the standard utilities—telephone, electricity, water, and gas.

Although regulatory commissions were first created to deal with natural monopoly problems, most regulatory activity is no longer of that kind. Many other commissions have been set up, often referred to as the "alphabet agencies" because of the common use of their initials as shorthand names and the broad spectrum of activities they attempt to regulate. Provincial bodies such as the Ontario Securities Commission (OSC) and the Quebec Securities Commission (QSC) are concerned mainly with consumer protection. The federal National Energy Board (NEB) regulates the interprovincial transmission of oil and natural

FIGURE 18-5
Pricing Strategy for a Regulatory Commission

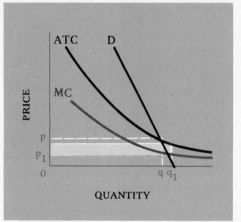

Average cost pricing is the goal of regulatory commissions, which seek the lowest prices possible without losses for natural monopolies. Although perfect competition leads to production where price equals marginal costs, here the price cannot be set at p_1, where demand equals marginal cost, because the firm would necessarily suffer losses (the shaded area). Price p covers all costs (including the opportunity cost of capital). The corresponding output q achieves most of the cost advantages of large-scale output.

gas and must approve exports of electricity, oil, and natural gas. Many activities of the Canadian Radio and Television Commission (CRTC) and the Canadian Transport Commission (CTC) concern the orderly use of airways and skyways — the prevention of chaotic competition. We limit our discussion in this chapter to natural monopoly regulation; some discussion of other regulatory activities will be found in Chapter 24.

THE THEORY OF NATURAL MONOPOLY REGULATION

What price should a regulatory commission permit? It might wish to set price equal to marginal cost (the way it would be in perfect competition), but such a price and quantity would surely lead to losses, for marginal cost is necessarily below average cost when average cost is falling. This is illustrated in Figure 18-5. Some means of continuing subsidization of these losses would be required.

An alternative is to permit the company to charge a price that allows it to cover all its costs and earn a fair return on its investment. In essence, this is the objective of most regulatory commissions with regard to pricing in natural monopoly situations. The theory is extraordinarily simple. The problems of putting the theory into practice are difficult.

PROBLEMS OF IMPLEMENTING THE THEORY

Regulation has aimed at setting prices high enough to permit firms to cover all their costs yet low enough to achieve the large sales required to reap the scale economies that characterize natural monopoly situations. If a regulatory commission knew what the demand curve and the cost curves looked like, it could simply pick the point on the demand curve that corresponded to the lowest price that covered average total costs. But a diagram like that of Figure 18-5 is not usually available. In the absence of reliable demand and cost information, commissions have tended to judge prices according to the level of profits they produce. Generally, having set prices, regulatory agencies permit price increases when profits fall below "fair" levels and require price reductions if profits exceed such levels.

While it is true that if the appropriate price is charged, economic profits will be zero, the reverse is not necessarily true. Profits can be zero because of inefficient operation, misleading accounting, or pricing at the lowest attainable level of average cost. Thus commissions that rely on profits as their guide to pricing must monitor a number of other aspects of the regulated firm's behavior.

The Definition of Costs

If a company is to be allowed to charge a price determined as "cost plus a fair profit" (as the regulators say), and if that price is below the profit-maximizing one, it is clearly in the firm's interest to exaggerate reported costs if it can. One major activity of regulatory commissions has been to define rules of allowable costing, as they affect both permissible rates of depreciation and reasonable expenses and expenditures. Freezing the rate of return removes the profit motive for keeping costs down. But although the firm does not care, the public presumably does, and thus cost supervision is an important activity of public utility regulation. Without it, the regulated industries' managers might have no incentive to be efficient and might simply let costs drift upward.

The Rate Base

Average total cost includes an appropriate rate of return on the capital invested in the business. Suppose it is agreed that a firm should be allowed to earn a rate of return of 8 percent on its capital. The **rate of return** is defined as the ratio of profits to invested capital. What is the value of the capital to which 8 percent is to be applied? The allowable amount is called the **rate base**. There has been no more controversial area than this in public utility regulation. Should the original cost or the reproduction cost of the firm's assets be used? It does not make much difference unless prices are changing, but in the inflationary situation of the last 35 years, reproduction cost is uniformly higher than original costs and thus leads to higher bases, higher permitted profits, and higher rates to users. If the major concern is to generate profits to buy replacement equipment, reproduction cost is appropriate. If the major concern is to generate profits to compensate past capital investments, original cost may be appropriate. Regulatory commissions (and the courts) have vacillated on this issue.

The precise nature of regulatory rules is important because the rules affect the incentives of those regulated. Economists Harvey Averch and Leland Johnson have shown that a regulated utility has a lesser incentive to resist high capital costs than an unregulated one, and that in some circumstances it pays the unregulated utility to buy relatively unproductive equipment. This is true because if profits depend on the rate base, it often pays the firm to increase its rate base. Thus the notion of "necessary and prudent investments" enters into regulatory rules. This tendency for one regulation to lead to a need for yet further regulation has been called the tar-baby effect, after a fictional creature made of tar which overcame an attacker by enmeshing it.

A Fair Return

The permitted rate of return that is implicit in the theory of public utility regulation is the opportunity cost of the owners' capital, with allowances for risk. Regulatory commissions have paid some attention to overall earnings rates in the economy, and the level of permitted earnings has changed slightly over time. But equity and tradition have played a much larger role than considerations of opportunity cost, and regulatory commissions have been slow to adjust permitted rates of return to changing market conditions. For decades permitted rates of return of 6 to 9 percent were employed. But when market interest rates soared to double-digit figures during the late 1970s, the traditional levels were not sufficient to induce new investment. Yet regulatory commissions have been reluctant to permit the large increases in prices that would result from sharp increases in the permitted rate of return.

Risk

Regulated public utilities typically enjoy monopoly positions with respect to what are often essential services. This tends to make them less vulnerable to loss of business than other enterprises that face more direct competition. But they are not free of risk. If a utility is losing money because the demand for its product is declining, and if no adjustment of prices or service can save it, it will eventually discontinue service via bankruptcy or will "sell out" to the public, to be run as a subsidized public enterprise. Investors in many American railways have found this out the hard way.

Even for a utility that stays in business, there is risk. While it is common to speak of the regulatory rate of return as "guaranteed," this is not accurate. In principle, it is a maximum "target" rate of return. Actual earnings may be larger or smaller over the short run because of economic factors and regulatory lags. If actual earnings are larger, the regulatory commission will refuse to grant price increases and may even seek to lower prices and reduce future profits. If actual earnings are lower, the regulatory commission will permit price increases.

It is possible for a utility to earn more than the maximum target rate if it is in an industry where its unregulated profits would be growing. For example, suppose the permitted rate of return is 10 percent and a certain company earns 15 percent in one year. No one confiscates its "excess" return, and it may take the regulatory commission six months or more to reduce rates to the point where earnings are again 10 percent. If this situation tends to recur, the average profit over time will be in excess of 10 percent—possibly well in excess. Of course, in a declining industry or in a rapid inflation the reverse situation can occur, and a firm may find its profits falling short of the permitted rate. Even though its petition to raise prices is approved, the process takes time and the end result is likely to be an average profit rate less than the official permitted rate.

The Curtailment of Service

Because profits are not guaranteed, a regulated utility in a declining industry may have a serious problem. If it is failing to make profits equal to the permitted rate, it may apply for permission to increase its prices, but if its demand is elastic, a rise in rates will lead to a reduction in revenues and may reduce profits. Privately owned urban transit systems and passenger rail lines have proven unprofitable because of secularly declining demand as people shifted to substitutes: private cars and airplanes. Given elastic demand curves, when transport companies raise fares (hoping to increase revenues), they find they only lose more customers to other means of transport.

At this point a bus company, for example, may look to its costs to see how it can avoid losses. Often it finds that some parts of its service (such as routes to outlying neighborhoods) no longer cover the variable costs of providing them, and it proposes to the regulatory authority that this service be dropped. Often the regulators say no. The reason is that they see other considerations in abandoning the bus service (such as increased congestion in the downtown area as even more people use their own cars) that loom large to the regulators but not to the bus company.

The regulators want the regulated company to "cross-subsidize" the less popular routes with profits from the more popular routes.[5] At the same time, they do not want to force the company into bankruptcy. Thus, each time a curtailment of service is proposed, regulators must make the difficult determination of whether the company is merely trying to increase its profits and is shirking its public service responsibility or whether it is truly in trouble.

EVALUATING PUBLIC UTILITY REGULATION

The moral of the public utility experience is that what looks like a simple and straightforward theory of regulating natural monopoly turns out in practice to be highly complex. In large part this is because regulated companies adapt their behavior to the rules that are imposed on them—and thus begins a chain of adaptation and change by regulators and regulated that produces a complex and cumbersome apparatus. Moreover, the need for due process in decisions that affect property rights has made procedures and decisions legalistic and resource-using.

Regulation brings both costs and benefits. Today's great debate is, "Do the benefits justify the costs?" The debate is its most heated with respect to environmental and safety regulatory activities, but it extends to public utility regulation

---

[5] This "cross-subsidization" was dramatically illustrated when the U.S. government deregulated airlines in the late 1970s. Fares on highly profitable transnational flights fell, but those on short commuter flights rose.

as well. The costs of regulation include more than the costs of running regulatory commissions and the costs imposed on the courts by seemingly endless appeals. Regulatory costs are also imposed on businesses that must strive to comply with paperwork.

Professor Richard Posner of the University of Chicago estimated that milk price regulation added about 10 percent to milk prices in the United States. The president's Council of Economic Advisers estimated that regulation accounted for a rise of about one point per year in the cost of living. Murray Weidenbaum of Washington University and Willard Butcher of Chase Manhattan Bank put the cost of regulation even higher: as much as $100 billion per year. Whether these estimates are realistic is debated. And there are, of course, benefits. Ralph Nader and others counter the Weidenbaum "costs" with equally impressive (and equally controversial) dollar estimates of "benefits."

The alleged benefits and costs are difficult—if not impossible—to measure with any precision. Much of the debate is ideological, notwithstanding its expression in terms of dollar estimates of benefits and costs. Is keeping the cost to consumers of electricity artificially low a benefit or a cost? It surely benefits some consumers, yet it just as surely involves some resource misallocation. Are the accidents avoided by industrial safety standards worth the extra expenditures they require? Victims of such accidents may answer differently than those who pay more for the products. These questions are not readily answered on a scientific basis.

Some, including Professor George Stigler of the University of Chicago, believe that the evidence shows that the levels of prices, quantities, and profits are about the same under public utility regulation as they would have been without it; they even go so far as to suggest that unregulated monopoly would have performed better.

The American experience with airline deregulation suggests that it is difficult to evaluate results. Starting in 1978, the Civil Aeronautics Board (CAB) removed regulations on airline rate making and on protecting individual airline routes. The initial responses seemed almost miraculous: tumbling air fares, supersaver discounts, increased air service on popular routes, increased passenger travel, and a boom in the industry. But a year later fares were *up* 25 to 40 percent over the regulated levels, some of the major carriers were having severe financial troubles, service to certain locations had been curtailed, and the euphoria of a year earlier was gone.

Evaluation is difficult here because expenses have increased, especially the price of jet fuel. Has deregulation of the airlines been a success? It will be many years before enough experience exists to permit a definitive evaluation of the benefits and costs of airline deregulation. Without hard evidence, one can find assertions on each side. To the president of United Airlines the answer was that while fares had risen, they had risen much less than would have been the case with regulation—that is, deregulation was a success. To the senior vice-president of American Airlines, deregulation was raising costs and thus prices by encouraging excess capacity on most routes—that is, deregulation was a failure.

Considering regulation generally, there seems in 1981 to be a remarkable consensus that regulation has failed to live up to the expectations held for it. Perhaps the most widely held view is that regulation, even when effective at first, becomes too rigid and unresponsive to change and as a result fails to recognize and to permit such competition as is possible. Given changing technology, yesterday's natural monopoly of a single railway may become but one mode of transportation in a competitive transportation industry. Wire telephone communications are no longer unique, given radio and satellites. Even the Post Office is not the only way to send written messages and parcels from one place to another. Thus the scope of natural monopoly regulation keeps changing. But regulators tend to cling to, and in some cases are legally committed to, rules and assumptions that may no longer fit the world they are regulating.

Changes in regulation in some form or another seem likely to occur over the next decade in response to this growing concensus. Some favor rapid deregulation and reliance on market forces. Others believe that the deficiencies lie in the structure of regulation and that changing the way regulation is carried out will improve matters. Still others think that the failures of regulation require nationalization or new legislation defining a novel approach to what regulators should do.

Which of many proposed directions for regulatory reform will be followed is unclear at this stage. The United States under President Carter saw considerable deregulation activity, and most observers believe that this trend will continue under President Reagan. There is no such trend currently apparent in Canada, though the revisions to the Bank Act passed in 1980 did lift some restrictions with respect to the operations of foreign banks within Canada. However, the present regulatory commissions are not without political support and are generally staunchly defended *by the regulated industries themselves*. For some, this last point is the most telling criticism of all.

Summary

1. Comparison of the models of perfect competition and monopoly reveals that prices will change less in response to cost changes in monopoly than in competition and that if costs, demand, and products are unchanged, the monopolization of a previously competitive industry will lead to a rise in price and a decline in output. In such circumstances, monopoly may lead to both productive and allocative inefficiency.

2. Levels of cost are not independent of market structures. If there are advantages of large scale in production, distribution, marketing, or puchasing, the minimum efficient size of the firm may be too large to be compatible with conditions of perfect competition. In such cases a shift from competition to a more concentrated market structure — oligopoly or monopoly — may lead to lower costs and increased efficiency. Because costs are not independent of market structure, the prima facie case in favor of competition and against concentration of market power is weakened. Most economists believe that substantial competition is compatible with efficient operations of industry and that it is desirable to foster at least that amount of competition.

3. A major issue in the evaluation of different market structures concerns the incentive provided for invention and innovation. Joseph Schumpeter believed that the incentive to innovate was so much greater under monopoly that monopoly was to be preferred to perfect competition. While few modern economists go that far, the empirical evidence suggests that technological change and innovation are to a measurable extent traceable to the efforts of large firms in oligopolistic industries.

4. The implications of the classical view of monopoly and competition led policy in two directions: public utility regulation to deal with natural monopoly and competition policy to deal with others kinds of monopoly.

5. Historically, Canada has not pursued an aggressive competition policy, particularly in comparison with the United States. Early legislation relied strongly on public disclosure rather than penalties as a deterrent to illegal practices. The new Competition Act promises stricter enforcement through the use of civil review procedures rather than criminal prosecution.

6. The philosophy of public utility regulation was to grant a monopoly where necessary to achieve the advantages of large-scale production but to prevent the monopolist from restricting output and raising price. The most common regulatory approach has been to regulate prices. This is done by watching profits: allowing price increases only if necessary to permit the regulated utility to earn a fair return on its capital and requiring price decreases if profits rise above the approved level.

7. Implementation of this straightforward theory encounters difficulties because any set of rules becomes a set of signals that induces patterns of response from those regulated. Thus it has been necessary for regulators to define carefully "proper" costs, how the costs should be measured, the appropriate rate base, what constitute "necessary and prudent" additions to capital equipment, and what constitutes a fair return. They have also been forced to determine when and whether utilities can discontinue providing services to groups in the community from whom (private) revenues do not cover (private) variable costs.

8. The entire regulatory apparatus has come under close scrutiny in recent years. A first step toward deregulation in the United States was the passage in 1978 of the Airline Deregulation Act, which will gradually phase out the existence of the Civil Aeronautics Board, which has controlled both rates and routes. In Canada there has not been a noticeable trend toward deregulation.

9. Regulation is costly, but it may be beneficial. Whether overall public utility regulation has had much effect and, if it has, whether on balance the effect has been beneficial is a matter of lively current debate and research.

Topics for Review

Effects of monopolizing a competitive industry
Competition and allocative efficiency
The effect of market structure on costs
Purposes of competition policy
Natural monopoly
Difficulties of public utility regulation
Deregulation

Discussion Questions

1. "I think there are some people, in and out of government, who get a little confused and associate bigness with badness. Success alone is now evidence enough to warrant intensive scrutiny by the government to determine how the success can be remedied—as if it were some sort of disease. The age of Orwell's doublethink, prophesied for 1984, has come early. For

now, to win is to lose. The real losers are the consumers. They lose the advantages of free competition; new and better products, lower prices and wider choices." Comment on these views of GM Chairman Murphy.

2. "Greater efficiency requires greater size, and greater size means more monopoly. We must recognize that in many sectors of the Canadian economy the quest for efficiency has meant the death of competition." What evidence would you look for to support or challenge this argument?

3. Economists Armen Alchian and Reuben Kessel have advanced the hypothesis that monopolists choose to satisfy more of their nonmonetary aims than do perfect competitors. Consider three aims:
   a. exercising the prejudices of the monopolists against certain racial minorities
   b. enjoying a good life with big expense accounts
   c. promoting their political philosophies by advertising and broadcasting
   What theoretical arguments could support the Alchian-Kessel hypothesis? Would the same arguments apply to oligopolists?

4. Suppose profits are used as a measure of monopoly power in deciding whether to prosecute a combines case. Would such a rule be expected to affect the behavior of firms with high profits? In what ways might changes be socially beneficial and in what ways socially costly?

5. In the early 1960s Carnation, a national firm, was brought to court for selling its products at a lower price in Alberta and British Columbia than in Ontario. It was accused of pursuing this pricing policy for the purpose of driving the regional supplier, which was its only competition in the west, out of business.

6. How would each of the following "facts" affect your view of monopoly?
   a. evidence that most invention was done by educational institutions
   b. evidence that monopolists paid higher wages than competitive firms
   c. evidence that monopolists could afford to, and did, spend more money on quality improvement than did competitive firms
   d. evidence that monopolists tended to have better records in hiring minority groups and handicapped workers

7. Antimonopoly policy might be based on any one of the following: market power (e.g., number of sellers), market conduct (e.g., price fixing), market performance (e.g., high profits). Can you develop arguments

for preferring any one of these bases over the others? Under what circumstances should some aspect of market structure or market conduct be treated as illegal per se—that is, without considering the effect in the particular case?

8. What makes an unregulated business valuable to its owners? In view of your answer, discuss the following remarks. "A regulatory agency affects the value of a regulated business by the level of rates it permits it to charge. But it is already supposed to have ascertained the fair value of the business *before* it sets the rates."

9. "In a competitive market the least-cost production techniques are revealed by entry and exit, while in public utility regulation they are revealed by commission rate hearings. It is easier to fool the commission than the market. Therefore, wherever possible, competition should be permitted." Discuss.

10. It is often asserted that when a regulatory agency such as a public utilities commission is established, it will ultimately become controlled by the people it was intended to regulate. This argument raises the question of who regulates the regulators. Can you identify why this might happen? How might the integrity of regulatory boards be protected?

Who Runs the Firm and for What Ends?

19

Once upon a time most Canadians had great faith in the ability of private firms to produce the goods and services on which the nation's prosperity was founded. Canada had one of the highest living standards in the world, and it seemed to be living proof that North American-style private capitalism not only worked, it worked much better than any known alternative.

Today the public's perception seems to have changed. Private firms no longer enjoy the public's full confidence. Many people question both the morality of business behavior and the ability of business to act as the prime mover of a successful capitalist system. Today many North Americans are in the anomalous position of believing in the free-market private enterprise system in general while harboring deep suspicions about whether our major corporations can or will make it work.

Important questions are involved here. Does the continuing success of the North American economy depend on the initiative of healthy, independent, private firms? Does it depend instead on increased public scrutiny and control of the behavior of these firms? Is the economy's apparent failure to perform as well in the past decade as it did in previous decades due to a failure of private firms? Or is it perhaps due to increasing government interference with their activities?

What light does the theory we have studied so far shed on these important questions? In economic theory firms are users of factors of production and producers of commodities. They face cost and demand curves that are largely determined by forces beyond their control. They seek to maximize their profits by keeping their costs as low as possible and producing to satisfy consumers' demands. They care only about profits, and their decisions are uninfluenced by their internal structure. Thus they contribute to our high living standards by producing, as cheaply as possible, goods that satisfy consumers' demands.

An important body of criticism disputes this standard theory of the firm. It says instead that actual firms have the power to control their market conditions and that they use that power. They manipulate demand by advertising, and they are not under heavy competitive pressure to produce efficiently by holding costs down. Firms, the critics continue, do not even seek to maximize profits. Instead they seek other goals that are determined by their internal structure, and these goals often cause them to behave in ways that are socially undesirable. If true, such criticisms would support the views that firms hinder rather than advance consumer welfare and that they need to be forced by government to act in the social interest.

In past chapters we studied the traditional view that firms serve the interests of consumers. In the present chapter we will study some criticisms of that view. We begin with those that strike at the very core of the standard microeconomic theory.

Do Firms Manipulate the Market?

In conventional theory, demand curves depend decisively on consumers' tastes and incomes and are to a significant degree independent of the actions of firms. Firms are assumed to be in business to make money, which they do by producing and selling the goods and services that consumers want. The successful firm is the one that best satisfies consumers' demands, while the firm that consistently does not do this will eventually fail. The ultimate source of all profits is consumers' desires. (Even monopoly profits depend

on consumers' willingness to buy the product that the monopolist controls.) The need for firms to respond to consumers' desires is an important part of any argument for the free enterprise system. If firms did not so respond, there would be little justification in allowing them to exert major influences on the allocation of the country's resources.

THE HYPOTHESIS THAT FIRMS CONTROL THE MARKET

A very different hypothesis is given its most prominent expression by former Harvard professor John Kenneth Galbraith and consumer advocate Ralph Nader. In this view it is *not* consumers' real wants that create the market signals that in turn provide the profit opportunities that motivate business behavior. Instead, large corporations have great power to create and manipulate demand. Firms must plan and invest for an uncertain future, and the profitability of the enormous investments that they make is threatened by the unpredictability of events. Firms try to make the future less unpredictable by actively manipulating market demand and by co-opting government agencies that are supposed to control their activities.

Manipulation of Demand

The most important source of unpredictable events that may jeopardize corporate investments is unexpected shifts in market demand curves. To guard against the effects of unexpected declines in demand, corporations spend vast amounts on advertising that allows them to sell what they want to produce rather than what consumers want to buy. At the same time, corporations decide not to produce products that consumers would like to buy. This reduces the risks inherent in investing in wholly new and untried products and avoids the possibility that successful new products might spoil the market for an existing product.

According to this hypothesis, we consumers are the victims of the corporations; we are pushed around at their whim, persuaded to buy things we do not really want, and denied products we would like to have. In short we are brainwashed ciphers with artificially created wants, and we have no real autonomy with respect to our own consumption.

Corruption of Public Authorities

A second threat to the long-range plans and investments of corporations comes from uncontrollable and often unpredictable changes in the nature of government interference with the freedom of the corporation. Corporation managers, according to the theory, meet this threat by indirectly subverting public institutions such as universities and regulatory agencies.

Government, instead of regulating business and protecting the public interest, has become the servant of the corporation. It supplies the corporate sector with such essential inputs as educated, trained, healthy, socially secure workers. Government also serves the giant corporation through policies concerning tariffs, import quotas, tax rules, subsidies, and research and development. These policies protect the industrial establishment from competitive pressures and reinforce its dominance and profitability.

Corruption of Our Value System

The managers of modern firms have great power. The corporations they manage earn large profits that can be reinvested to further the achievement of the values of the ruling group, which Galbraith calls the technostructure. The values of this "ruling class" emphasize industrial production, rapid growth, and materialistic aspirations at the expense of the better things of life (such as cultural and aesthetic values) and the quality of the environment.

The New Industrial State

The foregoing is an outline of what Galbraith calls the New Industrial State.[1] If Galbraith's theories of the behavior of modern corporations were substantially correct, we would have to make major revisions in our ideas of how free-market economies work.

According to the concept of the New Industrial State, the largest corporations (1) tend to dominate the economy, (2) largely control market demand rather than being controlled by it, (3) co-opt government processes instead of being constrained by them, and (4) utilize their substantial discretionary power against the interests of society.

THE EVIDENCE FOR THE HYPOTHESIS

Superficially, many facts lend support to Galbraith's hypothesis. The corporate giants are well known to all of us. Leading the *Financial Post's* list of the top 200 Canadian industrial companies is General Motors of Canada with annual sales in excess of $5 billion. Other companies with sales above $2 billion include Imperial Oil, Canadian Pacific, Bell Canada, Massey-Ferguson, Alcan, and International Nickel. If power comes with size, a "few" people—perhaps two or three hundred strategically placed executives of the country's leading corporations—have great power over economic affairs. Moreover, this corporate elite forms in many ways a close-knit group with common values and a (small "c") conservative point of view.[2] They exercise political influence through lobbying, contributions to

---

[1] These views did not originate with the publication in 1967 of Galbraith's book by that title nor with the formation of "Nader's Raiders." Much earlier James Burnham wrote *The Managerial Revolution* and Robert Brady sounded an alarm in *Business as a System of Power*. Thorstein Veblen had predicted the technocratic takeover of society in *The Engineers and the Price System* in 1921, and Karl Marx predicted the subversion of the government bureaucrat by the businessman more than a century ago.

[2] See Peter C. Newman, *The Canadian Establishment*, Vol. 1 (Toronto: McClelland and Stewart, 1975).

political parties, and direct participation in the process of governing.

It is also true, as the hypothesis predicts, that the great corporations, along with many smaller firms, spend vast amounts on advertising. These expenditures are obviously designed to influence consumers' demand, and there is little doubt that if firms such as Lever Brothers, Gulf Oil, Molson's and GM cut their advertising, they would lose sales to their competitors.

Similarly, it is true that much of the pollution of our environment is associated with industries that consist of well-known large firms. If automobiles, steel, oil, industrial chemicals, detergents, and paper are the primary sources of our pollution, surely Ford, Stelco, Dow Chemical, Texaco, Procter & Gamble, and Abitibi Paper are significantly to blame.

DOUBTS ABOUT THE HYPOTHESIS

Sensitivity to Market Pressures

Even the largest, most powerful industries are not immune to market pressures. Ford's Edsel was a classic example of the market's rejecting a product. The penetration of small foreign cars into the North American market forced the automobile industry into first the compact car and then the still cheaper subcompacts. In spite of this, massive losses were suffered by North American automobile manufacturers as consumers turned in very large numbers to foreign cars whose low costs and high gas mileages they preferred even in the face of heavy advertising of North American cars. In similar fashion, changing patterns of demand over time have produced continuous long-term changes in the list of leading companies.

Are these demand shifts explained by the corporate manipulation of consumers' tastes through advertising or by more basic changes? Advertising has two major aspects: it seeks to inform consumers about the available products, and it seeks to influence consumers by altering their demands. The first aspect, informative advertising, plays an important part in the efficient operation of any free-market system; the second aspect is one through which firms seek to control the market rather than be controlled by it.

Clearly, advertising does influence consumers' demand. If GM were to stop advertising, it would surely lose sales to Ford, Chrysler, and foreign imports. But it is hard to believe that the automotive society was conjured up by the advertising industry. When you are persuaded to fly CP Air, your real alternative is hardly a Conestoga wagon, a bicycle, or even a Voyageur-Colonial bus; more likely you are forgoing Air Canada or Pacific Western. Careful promotion can influence the success of one rock group over another, but could it sell the waltz to today's teenager? Advertising—taste making—unquestionably plays a role in shaping demand, but so too do more basic human attitudes, psychological needs, and technological opportunities.

Certainly advertising shifts demands among very similar products. It is hard to believe, however, that the national economy or the average person's system of values would be fundamentally changed if there were available one more or one less make of automobile or television set or brand of shoes. A look at those products that have brought basic changes to the economy— and perhaps to our value systems—suggests that these products succeeded *because consumers wanted them*, not because advertising campaigns brainwashed people into buying them. Consider a few major examples.

The automobile transformed North American society and is in demand everywhere, even in Communist countries where only informative advertising exists. The Hollywood movie had an enormous influence in shaping our world and in changing some of our values; it was—and still is—eagerly attended throughout the world, whether or not it is accompanied by a ballyhoo of advertising. The jet airplane has shrunk the world: It has allowed major league sports to expand beyond those cities in the northeast and midwest that could be reached by an overnight bus or rail journey. It has made the international conference a commonplace, and it has made European, Hawaiian, and Caribbean vacations a reality for many. For better or worse, the birth control pill has revolutionized many aspects of behavior in spite of the fact that it has never been advertised in the mass media. Television has changed the activities of children (and adults) in fundamental ways and has brought viewers a sense of immediacy about distant events that newspapers could never achieve.

The new products that have significantly influenced the allocation of resources and the pattern of society, such as those mentioned above, have succeeded because consumers wanted them; most of those that failed did so because they were not wanted — at least not at prices that would cover their costs of production.

The evidence suggests that the allocation of resources in the economy owes more to the tastes and values of consumers than it does to corporate advertising and related activities.

Who Controls the Government?

Is government subservient to big business? Lobbying is a legal, large-scale activity employed by many groups. Big business has its influence, but so do farmers, labor unions, and small business. Certainly American corporations have sometimes exercised illegal and improper influence on both domestic and foreign governments.

Cases of corrupt behavior have been documented at all levels of government; it does not follow, however, that government is subservient to the corporations and that decision making by the former is *dominated* by the wishes of the latter. In the United States, government contracts bolster the aerospace industry, yet Lockheed's deep financial trouble in the 1970s came in part as a result of government decisions. Tobacco companies have seen government agencies first publicize the hazards of their principal product and then restrict their advertising. Airlines finally lost their decade-long battle to prevent the introduction of the cheap transatlantic air fares pioneered by England's Sir Freddie Laker.

While business often succeeds in attempts to protect its commercial interests through political activity, it does so within limits. Where the truth lies between the extremes of "no influence" and "no limits" is a subject of current research. Yet it does seem safe to say that, first, corporations have a lot of political influence and, second, there are some serious constraints on the ability of corporations to exert political influence over all levels of government.

Neglect of the Public Interest?

One aspect of the Galbraithian critique has found a receptive public: the apparent disregard by large corporations of the adverse effects of productive activities on the environment. The problems of pollution arise from the activities of both small and large corporations and the activities of government units and citizens. Do such polluting activities represent irresponsible behavior by corporations that can be changed by such things as Campaign GM (an effort to make General Motors responsible), or does their correction require direct policy action in the form of rules, regulations, penalties, and tax incentives?

Consumerism is a movement that asserts a conflict between the interests of firms and the public interest. Consumerists hold that the conflict should be removed by pressuring firms to be motivated by the public interest rather than by their stockholders' desires for maximum profits.

Consumerists believe, for example, that GM's directors must be made to recognize that automobiles pollute and cause accidents, and that GM's resources should be invested in the development and installation of safety and antipollution devices. This, they argue, is proper use of GM's funds, even if GM's stockholders do not see it that way and even if automobile purchasers do not want to pay for the extra safety and antipollution devices.

What are the main arguments *for* this view? First, that only the company can know the potentially adverse effects of its actions. Second, that by virtue of holding a corporate charter, the corporation assumes the responsibility to protect the general welfare while pursuing private profits.

What are the main arguments *against* the consumerist view? Managers of companies have neither the knowledge nor the ability to represent the general public interest; they are largely selected, judged, and promoted according to their ability to run a profit-oriented enterprise, and the assumption that they are especially competent to decide broader *public* questions is unjustified. Moral, as distinct from economic, decisions—such as whether or not to make or use nerve gas, to make or use internal combustion engines, to manufacturer or smoke cigarettes, and to manufacture or utilize DDT or aerosol sprays—cannot properly be delegated to corporations or their executives. Some are individual decisions; others require either the expertise or the authority of a public regulatory agency. Whoever makes decisions on behalf of the public must be politically responsible to the public.

Those opposing the consumerist view hold that most required changes in corporate behavior should be accomplished not by exhorting business leaders to behave responsibly, nor by placing consumer representatives on the corporation's board of directors, but by regulations or incentives that force or induce the desired corporate behavior. Let corporations pursue their profits—subject to public laws. For example, legislatures can require that all cars have seat belts or have antipollution valves or meet specific standards of emission levels. Another alternative is to open the way for lawsuits that would either enjoin certain behavior or force corporations to pay for the damages their products cause.

The controversy over policy alternatives is current and important. Much of the credit for the dialogue belongs to Galbraith and Nader. It is essential to recognize that the policy issues at stake—whether and how to change the behavior of corporations—can arise whether corporations are primarily responding to market signals or are impervious to them. If the public does not approve the results of corporate behavior, it will want to control the behavior, whatever the cause, provided the costs—including undesirable side effects—do not exceed the benefits.

Who Controls the Modern Firm?: Alternative Maximizing Theories

Galbraith's is not the only modern criticism of the theory of firm behavior. Most other critics, however, accept (what Galbraith denies) that industries face market demand curves that the firms can influence only slightly. The critics then go on to suggest that firms will behave in ways different from those suggested by profit maximizing. In effect, these theories view firms as maximizers—of something other than profits.

Corporations play a dominant role in much of North American industry, and large corporations have dominant market shares in many industries. But who or what *is* the corporation? In some corporations, a small group or family provided most of the original capital, and the firm grew with little or no sale of equities to the public. Examples are the Ford Motor Company, which until 1956 was wholly owned by the Ford family; the Great Atlantic and Pacific Tea Company, which until recently was controlled by the Hartford family; Molson's Brewery; and the T. Eaton Company. At the other extreme, the giant American Telephone and Telegraph Company is owned by more than 3 million shareholders, no one of whom owns as much as 1 percent of the 700 million outstanding shares.

Between these extremes lie the majority of corporations. The characteristic pattern of corporate ownership is that tens of thousands or hundreds of thousands of shareholders own minute fractions of the total, while dominant groups (often including other corporations) hold from 3 percent to 20 percent of the voting stock.

In major areas of the business world the days of the single proprietor who is both owner and manager of a company are gone forever. Diversification of ownership is a major characteristic of the modern corporation. Does it matter? Traditional profit-maximizing theory answers no. The three hypotheses considered below suggest that the answer is yes.

THE HYPOTHESIS OF MINORITY CONTROL

It is quite possible for the owners of a minority of the stock to control a majority of the shares that are voted and thus to exercise effective control over the decisions of the corporation.

This possibility arises because not all shares are actually voted. Each share of common stock has one vote in a corporation. Shares must be voted at the annual meeting of stockholders, either in person or by assigning a **proxy** to someone attending. Any individual or group controlling 51 percent of the stock clearly controls a majority of the votes. But suppose one group owns 30 percent of the stock, with the remaining 70 percent distributed so widely that few of the dispersed group even bother to vote; in this event, 30 percent may be the overwhelming majority of the shares *actually voted*. In general, a very small fraction (sometimes as little as 5 percent) of the shares actively voted may exercise dominant influence at meetings of stockholders.

The hypothesis of minority control is that a well-organized minority often controls the destiny of the corporation against the wishes of the majority.

Dispersed ownership and minority control are well established in the corporate sector. But the hypothesis requires more than that a minority control the voting shares; it requires that stockholders be able to exert a significant influence on the firm's behavior *and* that the controlling minority have interests and motives different from the holders of the majority of the firm's stock. If all stockholders are mainly interested in having the firm maximize its profits, then it does not matter, as far as market behavior is concerned, which set of stockholders actually influences the firm's policy. There is no accepted evidence to show that controlling groups of stockholders generally seek objectives different from those sought by the holders of the majority of the firm's stock. Of course, disagreements between stockholder groups sometimes arise. A colorful phenomenon in corporation history is the **proxy fight,** in which competing factions of the stockholders (or management) attempt to collect the voting rights of the dispersed and generally disinterested stockholders.

THE HYPOTHESIS OF INTERCORPORATE CONTROL GROUPS

If each member of a small group holds directorships in several companies, the group can control the board of directors of many different companies without being so obvious as to have the identical set of persons on each and every board. By controlling the boards of directors, this group can exert effective and relatively unostentatious control over the companies themselves.

The hypothesis of intercorporate control groups says that otherwise independent companies are subject to common control through interlocking directorates.

The factual basis of this hypothesis is that many individuals are directors of many companies. According to Peter Newman, there are significant interlocking connections among about a quarter of the corporate directors in Canada. In particular he documents the links between the chartered banks and their corporate clients provided by individuals who serve on the boards of both.

For the hypothesis of intercorporate control groups to have implications for behavior requires more than interlocking directorates; it requires that boards of directors be able to control the policies of corporations in ways that would not be approved by managers or by stockholders. Notice that this requirement places the hypothesis in conflict with the previous one, for one cannot hold simultaneously that managers make the effective decisions, ignoring the interests of shareholders and directors, and that directors make the effective decisions, ignoring the interests of managers and shareholders.

There is much evidence about interlocks, but there is no substantial evidence that the common directors exert any significant influence altering the firm's behavior from what it would be if no such interlocking existed. Why, then, do they occur? There may be good reasons, even if such directors do not systematically alter firm behavior. Some individuals are wanted by many corporations for their expertise and the prestige their names convey.

THE HYPOTHESIS OF THE SEPARATION OF OWNERSHIP FROM CONTROL

A different consequence of diversified ownership was suggested in the 1930s by A. A. Berle and Gardiner Means. They hypothesized that, because of diversified ownership and the difficulty of assembling stockholders or gathering proxies, the managers rather than the stockholders or the directors exercise effective control over the corporation.

The hypothesis of the separation of ownership from control is that managerial control occurs and leads to different behavior than would stockholder control.

In the modern corporation the stockholders elect directors, who appoint managers. Directors are supposed to represent stockholders' interests and to determine broad policies that the managers will carry out. In order to conduct the complicated business of running a large firm, a full-time professional management group must be given broad powers of decision. Although managerial decisions can be reviewed from time to time, they cannot be supervised in detail. In fact the links are typically weak enough that top management often does truly control the destiny of the corporation over long periods of time.

As long as directors have confidence in the managerial group, they accept and ratify their proposals, and stockholders elect and reelect directors who are proposed to them. If the managerial group behaves badly, it may later be re-moved and replaced—but this is a disruptive and drastic action, and it is infrequently employed.

Within wide limits, then, effective control of the corporation's activities resides with the managers, who need not even be stockholders. Although the managers are legally employed by the stockholders, they remain largely unaffected by them. Indeed, the management group characteristically asks for, and typically gets, the proxies of a large enough number of stockholders to elect directors who will reappoint it—and thus it perpetuates itself in office.

Professors Berle and Means made a pioneering study of the ownership of the 200 largest non-financial corporations in 1929. They showed that corporations in which no dominant ownership group could be identified as having as much as 10 percent of the stockholdings accounted for 60 percent of the total assets owned by all 200 corporations studied. The percentage of assets thus held is even higher today—above 80 percent. What is the significance of this?

The hypothesis of the separation of ownership from control requires not only that the managers be able to exert effective control over business decisions, but that they wish to act differently from the way the stockholders and directors wish to act. If the managers want to maximize the firm's profits—either because it is in their own interests to do so or because they are legally compelled or voluntarily choose to reflect the stockholders' interest—then it does not matter that they have effective control over decisions.

Only if the managers wish to pursue different goals than those of the owners will the behavior of the firm be different according to whether the managers or the owners exercise effective control.[3] Consider then a theory that takes the separation of ownership and control as its starting point and proceeds on the assumption that managers are motivated by desires other than to maximize the profits of the firm.

[3] The possibility of the separation of ownership and control is one of the contentious points in the debate about the role of foreign ownership of Canadian industry. See the discussion in the box.

How Far Can Corporations Depart from Profit-maximizing Behavior?

Many of the criticisms of modern microeconomic theory assume that firms seek to do things other than maximize their profits. If the present management elects not to maximize its profits, this implies that some other management could make more money by operating the firm. A major restraint on existing managements is the threat of a stockholder revolt or a takeover bid. As we shall see in Chapter 22, the maximum amount one can afford to pay for any asset depends on how much it is expected to earn. If I can make an asset produce more than you, I can rationally outbid you for it.

A management that fails to come close to achieving the profit potential of the assets it controls becomes a natural target for acquisition by a firm that specializes in taking over inefficiently run firms. The management of the acquiring firm makes a **tender offer** (or **takeover bid** as it is sometimes called) to the stockholders of the target firm, offering them what amounts to a premium for their shares, a premium it can pay because it expects to increase the firm's profits. Managers who wish to avoid takeover bids cannot let the profits of their firm slip far from the profit-maximizing level—because their unrealized profits provide the incentives for takeovers.

Some, though by no means all of the so-called conglomerate firms, have specialized in this kind of takeover. In the last decade the example par excellence of this has been International Telephone and Telegraph, which acquired (among other American companies) Avis Car Rental, Continental Baking, Sheraton Hotels, Canteen Food Service, and Hartford Life Insurance. In each case it substantially increased the operating profits of the acquired company after the takeover. One Canadian example is the Power Corporation of Canada, which acquired Canada Steamship Lines, Dominion Glass, Great-West Life Insurance, Imperial Life Insurance, Montreal Trust, and Angus Corporation, among others.

The pressure of the threat of takeovers must be regarded as limiting the discretion of corporate management to pursue goals other than profit maximization.

The Sales Maximization Hypothesis

The theory that firms seek to maximize not their profits but their sales revenue was first advanced by Professor William Baumol of Princeton University. Firms, it is assumed, wish to be as large as possible. Faced with a choice between profits and sales, they would choose to increase sales rather than profits.

This theory begins with the separation of management and ownership. In the giant corporation the managers need to make some minimum level of profits to keep the shareholders satisfied; after that they are free to seek growth unhampered by profit considerations. This is a sensible policy on the part of management, the argument runs, because salary, power, and prestige all vary with the size of a firm as well as with its profits. Generally the manager of a large, normally profitable corporation will earn a salary considerably higher than that earned by the manager of a small but highly profitable corporation.

The sales maximization hypothesis says that managers of firms seek to maximize their sales revenue, subject to a profit constraint.

Sales maximization subject to a profit constraint leads to the prediction that firms will sacrifice some profits by setting price below, and output

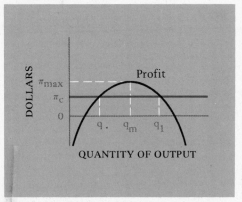

FIGURE 19-1
Output of the Firm Under Satisficing, Profit Maximizing, and Sales Maximizing

The "best" level of output depends on the motivation of the firm. The figure shows the level of profits associated with each level of output. A profit-maximizing firm produces output q_m. A satisficing firm, with a target level of profits of π_c, is willing to produce any output between q. and q_1. A sales-maximizing firm, with a minimum profit constraint of π_c, produces the output q_1. Thus satisficing allows a range of outputs on either side of the profit-maximizing level while sales maximization predicts a higher output than does profit maximizing.

above, their profit-maximizing levels, as illustrated in Figure 19-1.

Do Firms Maximize Anything?: Nonmaximizing Theories of the Firm

Many students of large and complex organizations have been critical of economic theory for regarding modern corporations as "simple profit-maximizing computers." They believe that firms are profit oriented in the sense that, *ceteris paribus,* they prefer more profits to less. They do not believe, however, that firms are profit maximizers.

Maximization has two aspects. A firm is a *local maximizer* if it maximizes profits that can be earned with its present range of commodities and its present markets. A firm is a *global maximizer* if it surveys and chooses from all possible courses of action, which will include new products, new markets, and radically new sales and production techniques. It is fairly easy to gather evidence showing that most firms are not global maximizers; it is more difficult to do the same for local maximization.

NONMAXIMIZATION DUE TO IGNORANCE

A common but misguided line of criticism holds that firms are unable to maximize profits because they cannot equate marginal cost with marginal revenue. This criticism is based on the observation that many accounting practices are not set up to provide managers with marginal information. Indeed, most managers have never even heard of the concepts of marginal cost and marginal revenue. Thus, these critics conclude, firms cannot be maximizing profits because they cannot be using the necessary marginal concepts.

The constructs of the theory of the firm are merely tools employed by economists to predict the consequences of certain behavior patterns. They are not meant to describe how firms reach decisions. Economic theorists use the mathematical concepts of marginal cost and marginal revenue to discover what will happen as long as, by one means or another—by guess, hunch, clairvoyance, luck, or good judgment—firms approximately succeed in maximizing profits. The predictions of the theory are thus independent of the thought processes by which the managers of firms actually reach their decisions.

A famous analogy concerns the determination of how safe it may be for a driver to pass a truck on a two-lane road. The analyst must consider a complex equation relating the automobile's speed, the truck's speed, the car's ability to accelerate, the possibility of an oncoming car (and its speed and distance), weather conditions, and so on. But the driver, unlike the analyst, need not solve a mathematical equation to make his or her decision. Yet if the driver and analyst are competent, both will reach the same decision.

What is at issue, then, is not whether firms calculate and equate marginal magnitudes. The question is whether or not they continually indulge in behavior that tends to choose the most profitable of the available alternatives.

NONMAXIMIZATION BY CHOICE

Alternatives to profit maximization are usually based on observations of actual firms. The observations and the theories all have in common the implication that firms *choose* not to be profit maximizers.

Full-cost Pricing

Most manufacturing firms are price setters: they must quote a price for their products rather than accept a price set on some impersonal competitive market. Profit-maximizing theory requires that these firms change their prices in response to every change in demand and costs that they experience. Yet students of large firms have long alleged that this much price flexibility is not observed. In the short run, prices of manufactured goods do not appear to vary in response to every shift in the firm's demand. Instead they appear to change rather sluggishly.

This short-run behavior is consistent with the hypothesis of **full-cost pricing,** which was originally advanced in the 1930s by Robert Hall, a British economist, and Charles Hitch, an American, following a series of detailed case studies of actual pricing decisions made in and around Oxford, England. Case studies in the intervening decades have continued to reveal the widespread use of full-cost pricing procedures.

The full-cost pricer, instead of equating marginal revenue with marginal cost, sets price equal to average cost at full-capacity output, plus a conventional markup.

The **markup** may be either so much per unit or a percentage of average costs. Price having been set, sales are determined by what can be sold at that price.

The firm changes its prices when its average costs change substantially (as a result of such events as a new union contract or a sharp change in the prices of key raw materials), and it may occasionally change its markup. However, its short-run pricing behavior is rather conventional and is not characterized even by local profit maximization.

Modern supporters of profit-maximizing theory accept the full-cost evidence but argue that it reveals only the administrative procedure by which prices are set from day to day. They hold that management makes frequent changes in markups in an attempt to maximize profits. Thus they believe that, while firms may be full-cost pricers from day to day, they are profit maximizers with respect to their average experience over, say, a year.

Modern critics of profit-maximizing theory accept the evidence that full-cost prices are sometimes changed in the profit-maximizing direction. They hold, however, that the prevalence of conventional full-cost practices shows that prices are typically not at their profit-maximizing level. They also hold that the prevalence of full-cost pricing shows that firms are creatures of custom that make fairly small, profit-oriented changes at fairly infrequent intervals.

Organization Theory

According to profit-maximizing theory, firms constantly scan available alternatives and choose the most profitable ones. A common criticism of this theory is that behavior is influenced seriously by the organizational structure of the firm. **Organization theory** argues that in big firms decisions are made after much discussion by groups and committees and that the structure of the process affects the substance of the decisions.

The central prediction of organization theory is that different decisions will result from different kinds of organizations, even when all else is unchanged.

Labor-Managed Firms

Our analysis of the firm rests on a division between workers and firms. Firms own the capital; make decisions about input combinations, output levels, and prices; and hire workers. Of course, this is not the only possible division. An alternative form of organization is the "worker cooperative" or "collective" whose members both provide labor services to the firm and jointly manage it. Such organizations have often been advocated and formed in various societies; their modern roots lie in the critical reaction to the industrial revolution that began in the eighteenth century. Utopian socialists of that era, including Charles Fourier in France and Robert Owen in England, placed their hopes in autonomous communities organized for the good of all. In his *Parliamentary History of the French Revolution,* published in the mid 1800s, Phillipe Brechez provided the philosophy, theory, and outline for the functioning of "workmen's associations" that embodied worker self-management.

Today various forms of cooperatives or collectives exist in many societies. What happens when workers hire capital, as these situations imply, instead of capitalist entrepreneurs hiring workers, the situation we have analyzed? Some answers can be found by considering the experience in Yugoslavia, where worker-managed firms are prevalent.

In most nonagricultural sectors of the Yugoslav economy, public (state) ownership is retained, but management of the individual enterprises has been turned over to the workers, blue-collar and white-collar alike. They have virtually full authority over all operations, and their pay (above guaranteed minimum wages) is determined by the net income of the enterprise.

A characteristic arrangement might be for the workers in a plant to elect a workers' council, which in turn elects a management board. This board appoints a manager who is responsible to it, but who also has a good deal of discretion. The local political party is consulted in the selection of the manager, and the manager is charged with upholding the state laws as they impinge on the operations of the firm. Any difference from a command system would be mere formality if the managers now received detailed orders from higher up, but they do not. Factors of production and goods are purchased on more or less free markets, and the firm can prosper or suffer. If it prospers, it may reinvest part of its profits (subject only to the restrictions mentioned below), and it may borrow funds from banks and other firms for expansion.

The firm is subject to various taxes on its income, but beyond that its earnings are distributed to the workers. Nominally, workers receive only "profit sharing" and no wages, but the effect of a guaranteed minimum amount to each worker means that profit sharing comes into play only after minimal levels of income have been achieved.

Workers' managements appear to have advantages for the Yugoslavian state. First, an enormous and demanding administrative burden is transferred from central planning to decentralized markets. Second, workers' morale and their productivity seem to have risen in response to their having a real and personal stake in their firm.

Yet economists ask whether such organizations lead to an efficient allocation of society's scarce resources. In the long run, worker-managed (cooperative) firms appear no different from profit-maximizing (entrepreneurial) firms, for labor and capital will enter or exit the industry until their return just matches their opportunity cost elsewhere in the economy. However, in the process of short-run adjustment problems might arise.

In responding to short-run fluctuations in demand, an entrepreneurial firm will adjust so as to equate price to marginal cost. Hence an increase in price will lead to an expansion of output and employment in the short run. A cooperative firm will behave differently in the short run; because wages are not treated as costs, the worker-owners are interested in maximizing the difference between total revenue and nonlabor (fixed) costs *per worker*. With fixed capital, it is in the interest of the worker-owners to have a large work force in order to minimize capital costs per head; with diminishing marginal productivity, it is in their interest to have a small work force in order to maximize the value of output per head. A straightforward application of economic principles suggests that balancing the two opposing forces *at the margin* determines the short-run equilibrium output of the cooperative. An increase in the price of output strengthens the relative force of the second effect, thereby leading to a *decrease* in output and employment.*

Another problem concerns the incentives for capital to enter or leave an industry (a role

*This is true only when the rules of the cooperative permit the dismissal of a worker if it is to the advantage of the remaining workers.

played by profits in Western economies). The Yugoslav solution to the problem is that returns of more than 30 percent in excess of that required to pay the guaranteed minimum wage must be reinvested, while industries that fail to provide at least 70 percent of the wage standard must shut down.

Other problems, familiar from market economies, have also arisen. Once the workers of a firm recognize that their income reflects the firm's revenues, they may be tempted to increase those revenues in any way they can. Indeed, because of the relatively small scale of most Yugoslavian industry, a potentially severe monopoly problem has arisen. Many firms have discovered that they need not be price takers, and (where allowed) they have increased prices and restricted output in textbook profit-maximizing fashion. In a fully market-oriented society, monopoly profits would motivate new firms to enter the industry, and entry would continue until the monopoly profits had been removed. In Yugoslavia there is a more serious problem: Profits accrue to the workers in a firm, but who is motivated to organize the firm in the first place? Sometimes the local community will do so when it has unemployed workers; more often it will wait for some central official to decide that prices are rising too high and that further firms should be encouraged or created.

The 30 percent rule in Yugoslavia is an attempt to deal with this problem, but it works only imperfectly and with a lag. And while it leads to an expansion of capacity in a profitable industry, it does not lead to an increase in the number of firms and thus does not increase competition.

One proposition that follows from this theory is that large and diffuse organizations find it necessary to develop standard operating procedures to help them in making decisions. These decision rules arise as compromises among competing points of view and, once adopted, are changed only reluctantly. An important prediction following from this hypothesis is that the compromises will persist for long periods of time despite changes in conditions affecting the firm. Even if a particular compromise were the profit-maximizing strategy in the first place, it would not remain so when conditions changed. Thus profits will not usually be maximized.

Another prediction is that decision by compromise will lead firms to adopt conservative policies that avoid large risks. Smaller firms not faced with the necessity of compromising competing views will take bigger risks than larger firms.

Organization theorists have suggested an alternative to profit maximization that they call **satisficing**. Satisficing theory was first suggested by Professor Herbert Simon of Carnegie-Mellon University, who in 1978 was awarded the Nobel Prize in economics for his work on firm behavior. Speaking of his theory, he wrote, "We must expect the firm's goals to be not maximizing profits but attaining a certain level or rate of profit, holding a certain share of the market or a certain level of sales."

According to the satisficing hypothesis, firms will strive to achieve certain target levels of profits, but having achieved them, they will not strive to improve their profit position further. This means that the firm could produce any one of a range of outputs that yield at least the target level of profits rather than the unique output that maximizes profits.

EVOLUTIONARY THEORIES

The modern evolutionary theories advanced by such economists as Richard Nelson and Sidney Winter of Yale University build on the earlier theories of full-cost pricing and satisficing. Nelson and Winter argue that firms do not—indeed, could not—behave as profit maximizing predicts. They accept that firms desire profits and even strive for profits; what they deny is that firms maximize globally or even locally.

Evolutionary theorists have gathered much evidence to show that tradition seems to be paramount in planning. The basic effort at the early stages of planning is directed, they argue, toward the problem of performing reasonably well in established markets and maintaining established market shares. They quote evidence to show that suggestions, made by planners in preliminary planning documents, to do something entirely new in some areas, even on a 10-year horizon, are usually weeded out in the reviewing process. They believe that most firms spend very little effort on *planning* to enter entirely new markets, and still less on direct efforts to leave or even reduce their share in long-established markets. These attitudes were illustrated by one firm that, although faced with obviously changing circumstances, reported, "We have been producing on the basis of these raw materials for more than 50 years with success, and we have made it a policy to continue to do so."

Concepts of Evolutionary Theory

The evolutionary theory of the firm draws many analogies with the biological theory of evolution. Here are two of the most important.

The genes. In biological theory, behavior patterns are transmitted over time by genes. Rules of behavior fulfill the same function in the evolutionary theory of the firm. In Sidney Winter's words:

That a great deal of firm decision behavior is routinized . . . is a "stylized fact" about the realities of firm decision process. Routinized . . . decision procedures . . . cover decision situations from pricing practices in retail stores to such "strategic" decisions as advertising or R and D effort, or the question of whether or not to invest abroad.

Winter talks of firms "remembering by doing" according to repetitive routines. He adds that government policymakers tend to have unrealistic expectations about firms' flexibility and responsiveness to changes in market incentives. These expectations arise from the maximizing model, whose fatal flaw, Winter alleges, is to underestimate the importance and difficulty "of the task of merely continuing the routine performance, i.e., of preventing undesired deviations."

The mutations. In the theory of biological evolution, mutations are the vehicle of change. In the evolutionary theory of the firm this role is played by innovations. Some innovations are similar to those discussed in Chapter 13, the introduction of new products and new production techniques. However, a further important class of innovations in evolutionary theory is the introduction of new rules of behavior. Sometimes innovations are thrust on the firm; at other times the firm consciously plans for and creates innovations.

According to maximizing theory, innovations are the result of incentives—the "carrot" of new profit opportunities. In evolutionary theory, the firm is much more of a satisficer, and it usually innovates only under the incentive of the "stick" either of unacceptably low profits or some form of external prodding. Firms change routines when they get into trouble, not when they see a chance to improve an already satisfactory performance. For example, in the growing markets of the 1960s many firms continued all sorts of wasteful practices that they shed fairly easily when their profits were threatened in the more difficult 1970s.

THE SIGNIFICANCE OF NONMAXIMIZING THEORIES

An impressive array of evidence can be gathered in apparent support of various nonmaximizing theories. What would be the implications if they were accepted as being better theories of the behavior of the economy than profit maximization?

If nonmaximizing theories are correct, the economic system does not perform with the delicate precision that follows from profit maximization. But the system described by evolutionary theory *does* function. Firms sell more when demand goes up and less when it goes down. They also alter their prices and their input mixes when hit with the "stick" of sufficiently large changes in relative input prices.

Evolutionary theory does not upset the broad case for the price system: that it produces a coordinated response from decentralized decision makers to changes in tastes and costs.

But *profit-oriented* nonmaximizing firms will also exhibit a great deal of inertia. They will not respond quickly and precisely to small changes in market signals from either the private sector or government policy. Neither are they likely to make radical changes in their behavior even when the profit incentives to do so are large.

Nonmaximizing models imply sensitivity of the price system to large but not to small changes in signals caused by changes in demand, costs, or public policy.

A Final Word: The Importance of Profits

Economics is a continually developing subject; its theories are under constant scrutiny and even attack. Some of the major debates concerning the profit-maximizing theory of the firm have been reviewed in this chapter. On the one hand, the Galbraithian view that firms create their own market conditions seems difficult to maintain in the face of the evidence. On the other hand, it seems unlikely that simple profit-maximizing theory will be rich enough to capture all aspects of corporate behavior. Thus it may benefit by expansion to include elements of such theories as satisficing, sales maximization, and evolutionary behavior.

Profits, however, are unmistakably a potent force in the life—and death—of firms. The resilience of profit-maximizing theory and its ability to predict how the economy will react to some major changes (such as the recent dramatic increases in energy prices) suggests that firms are at least strongly motivated by the pursuit of profits and that, other things being equal, they prefer more profits to less profits.

If profit-maximizing theory should eventually give way to some more organizationally dominated theory, the new theory will still be a profit-oriented theory. The search for profits and the avoidance of losses is a potent force that drives the economy even when firms do not turn out to be continual profit maximizers.

Summary

1. A sweeping attack on the traditional theory of the behavior of the firm is made by Galbraith, along with Nader and others. He argues that large corporations manipulate markets, tastes, and governments rather than respond to market and governmental pressures. While there is evidence about the undoubted size and influence of large corporations, there is also much evidence of marketing influence on corporate behavior.

2. In recent years, serious concern has developed over whether corporations should represent the interest of their owners and managers or whether they should be responsible to a broader public interest. Consumerists argue for the latter point of view; others prefer to rely on markets and government control to protect the public interest.

3. The widespread ownership of the modern corporation leads to the question, who really controls the modern corporation? Attempts to answer this question have led to alternative theories that firms maximize something other than profits. Three important hypotheses have been advanced.
a. A minority group of stockholders often controls the corporation against the wishes of the majority. The fact of minority control is widely accepted, but there is little evidence to suggest that the minority usually coerce the majority.
b. A small group of people effectively control a large section of the economy through the mechanism of interlocking directorates. This hypothesis is not widely accepted (although interlocking directorships do exist).
c. Because of the widespread ownership of the corporation, stockholders cannot exert effective control over the managers; thus the latter have the real control of the organization and operate it for their advantage rather than that of their stockholders. This hypothesis has some serious, but by no means universal, support.

4. All these hypotheses suggest that firms may seek to maximize something other than profits. One standard alternative is Professor Baumol's hypothesis of sales maximization: firms seek to be as large as possible (judged by sales revenue), subject to the constraint that they achieve a minimum rate of profit.

5. An alternative set of hypotheses denies that firms maximize profits in either the local or the global sense of maximization.
a. The full-cost hypothesis states that firms determine price by adding a customary—and infrequently changed—markup to full costs. This makes their pricing behavior relatively insensitive to short-term fluctuations in demand.
b. Organization theorists also see firms as insensitive to short-term fluctuations in market signals. Their reason lies in the decision-making structure of large organizations, which must

rely on routines and rules of thumb rather than on fresh calculations of profitabilities as each new situation presents itself.

c. Evolutionary theorists build on full-cost and organizational theories. They see the firm as a profit-oriented entity in a world of imperfect information, making small, profit-oriented changes from its present situation but being more resistant to large, "structual" changes. Resources are still reallocated by evolutionary firms as demand and costs shift but usually more in response to the "stick" of threatened losses than the "carrot" of possible extra profits.

6. Under both maximizing and nonmaximizing theories, profits are an important driving force in the economy and changes in demand and costs cause changes in profits, which cause firms to reallocate resources. The speed and precision, but not the general direction of the reallocations, are what is different between maximizing and nonmaximizing theorists.

7. Both satisficing and sales maximization can be stated as genuine alternatives to the theory of short-run profit maximization. The same is possible with long-run profit maximization, but only if the nature of the "long run" is made specific; otherwise, it is simply an alibi or rationalization for every shred of contradictory evidence.

Topics for Review

The New Industrial State
The long-run sensitivity of firms to market pressures
Consumerism
Alternative maximizing theories
Ownership, management, and control of corporate decisions
Sales maximization
Nonmaximizing theories
Full-cost pricing
Satisficing
Evolutionary theories

Discussion Questions

1. In 1976 the automobile manufacturers introduced their 1977 models. GM and American Motors (AMC) put major emphasis on smaller, more economical cars, and Ford and Chrysler stayed with their 1976 model sizes. Read the following news headlines (which appear in chronological order) and then discuss the light they shed on the hypothesis that firms control the market.
   a. "GM's 1977 Line Runs Ahead of the Pack. The big question: Do people want small cars?"
   b. "Ford, Chrysler, beam; AMC in trouble on sales."
   c. "GM's Fuel-Saving Chevette: Right Car at the Wrong Time."
   d. "Price Cuts and Rebates Lift Sales of Small AMC and GM Cars."
   e. "GM Confirms Plans to Drop the Subcompact Vega."
   What do these further events reveal about the same hypothesis? "In 1979 all auto firms sold all the small cars they could produce. But they were left with sizable unsold inventories of large cars, and as a result they are preparing to alter their production mix in favor of small cars."

2. "Because automobile companies were interested only in profits, they would not produce the safer, less polluting, but more expensive cars that the public really wanted. Legislation was necessary, therefore, to force producers to meet consumer needs." Discuss.

3. Assume that each of the following assertions is factually correct. (The first is a matter of current controversy; the rest are unquestioned.) Taken together, what would they tell you about the prediction that big business is increasing its control of the U.S. economy?
   a. The share of total manufacturing assets owned by the 200 largest corporations has been rising steadily for the last 25 years.
   b. The number of new firms begun every year has grown steadily for the last 25 years.
   c. The share of manufacturing in total production has been decreasing for 40 years.
   d. Profits as a percent of national income are no higher now than half a century ago.

4. "The business of the businessman is to run his business so as to make profits. If he does so, he will serve the public interest better than if he tries to decide what is good for society. He is neither elected nor appointed to that task." Discuss.

5. "Our list prices are really set by our accounting depart-

ment: they add a fixed markup to their best estimates of fully accounted cost and send these to the operating divisions. Managers of these divisions may not change those prices without permission of the Board of Directors, which is seldom given. Operating divisions may, however, provide special discounts if necessary to stay competitive.'' Does this testimony by the president of a leading manufacturing company support the full-cost pricing hypothesis?

6. The leading automobile tire manufacturers (Goodyear, Firestone, etc.) sell original equipment (OE) tires to automobile manufacturers at a price below the average total cost of all the tires they make and sell. This happens year after year. Is this consistent with profit-maximizing behavior in the short run? In the long run? If it is not consistent, what does it show? Do OE tires compete with replacement tires?

Part Six

Factor Pricing and the Distribution of Income

The Distribution of National Income

20

PROBLEMS OF DISTRIBUTION

Are the poor getting poorer and the rich richer as Karl Marx thought they would? Are the rich becoming relatively poorer and the poor relatively richer as Alfred Marshall hoped they would? To what extent do such social changes as the increased number of working women or altered public policies on poverty change the distribution of income? Should we reject the view held by Pareto that inequality of income is a social constant determined by forces that are possibly beyond human understanding and probably beyond human influence?

The founders of classical economics, Adam Smith and David Ricardo, were concerned with the distribution of income among what were then the three great social classes: workers, capitalists, and landowners. To deal with this question they defined three factors of production: labor, capital, and land. The return to each of these factors was the income of each of the three classes in society. Smith and Ricardo were interested in what determined the income of each group relative to the total national income, and in how a nation's economic growth affected this income distribution. Their theory predicted that as society progressed landlords would become relatively better off and capitalists would become relatively worse off. Karl Marx provided different answers to the same questions: He concluded that as growth occurred capitalists would become relatively better off and workers relatively worse off (at least until the whole capitalist system collapsed).

TABLE 20-1
Functional Distribution of National Income in Canada, 1979

Type of income	Billions of dollars	Percentage of total
Employee compensation	145.8	71.1
Corporate profits	25.6	12.5
Proprietors' income, including rent	15.0	7.3
Interest	18.6	9.1
Total	205.0	100.0

Source: Statistics Canada, 11–003E.

Total income is classified here according to the nature of the factor service that earned the income. While these data show that employee compensation is about 71 percent of national income, they do not show that workers and their families receive only that fraction of national income. Many households will have income in more than one category listed in the table.

These and similar nineteenth century debates focused on the distribution of total income among the major factors of production, now called the **functional distribution of income.** Table 20-1 shows data for the functional distribution of income in Canada in 1979. Although functional distribution categories (wages, rent, profits) pervade current statistics, much of the attention of non-Marxist economists has shifted to another way of looking at differences in incomes.

Around the beginning of the present century, Pareto studied what is now called the **size distribution of income,** the distribution of income between different households without reference to the social class to which they belonged. He discovered that inequality in income distribution was great in all countries and, more surprising, that the degree of inequality was quite similar from one country to another. Tables 20-2 and 20-3 show that even in Canada in 1979 there were many families with very low incomes and there was much inequality in the distribution of income.

Inequality in the distribution of income is shown graphically in Figure 20-1. This curve of income distribution, called a **Lorenz curve,** shows

TABLE 20-2
Income of Canadian Families, 1979

Income class	Percentage of families
Less than $5,000	4.7
$5,000–6,999	4.7
$7,000–8,999	5.5
$9,000–11,999	7.1
$12,000–14,999	7.4
$15,000–19,999	14.9
$20,000–24,999	16.1
$25,000 or more	39.7

Source: Statistics Canada, 13–206.

Although median family income was about $21,000 in 1979, many families received much less and some a great deal more.

how much of total income is accounted for by given proportions of the nation's families. For example, in 1979 the bottom 20 percent of all Canadian families earned only 5.8 percent of all income earned. The farther the curve bends away from the diagonal straight line, the more unequal is the distribution of income.

There are good reasons why much of the attention of modern economists is devoted to the size distribution rather than the functional distribution of income. After all, some capitalists (such as the owners of small retail stores) are in the

TABLE 20-3
Inequality in Family Income Distribution, 1979

Family income rank	Percentage share of aggregate income
Lowest fifth	5.8
Second fifth	12.9
Middle fifth	18.6
Fourth fifth	24.5
Highest fifth	38.2
	100.0

Source: Statistics Canada, 13–206.

While far from showing overall equality, income distribution is relatively equal for the middle 60 percent of the distribution. If the income distribution were perfectly equal, each fifth of the families would receive 20 percent of aggregate income.

FIGURE 20-1

A Lorenz Curve of Family Income in Canada, 1979

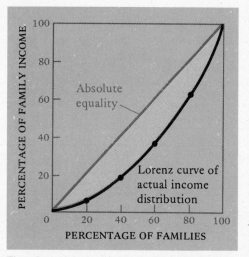

The size of the shaded areas between the Lorenz curve and the diagonal is a measure of the inequality of income distribution. If there were complete income equality, the bottom 20 percent of the income receivers would receive 20 percent of the income, etc., and the Lorenz curve would be the diagonal line. Because the lower 20 percent receive only about 6 percent of the income, the actual curve lies below the diagonal. The lower curve shows actual Canadian data. The extent to which it bends away from the straight line indicates the amount of inequality in the distribution of income.

lower part of the income scale, while some wage earners (such as skilled athletes) are at the upper end of the income scale. Moreover, if someone is poor, it matters little whether that person is a landowner or a worker. Today many who want to decrease inequality focus on influences other than which factor of production is owned by the income earner. Among other influences are race, sex, age, education, occupation, and region of residence.

We shall look closely at the poverty problem in Chapter 23. In order to understand this and other problems concerning the distribution of income, we must first study how the income of house-

holds is determined and what forces cause it to change.

It is tempting to give superficial explanations of differences in income with remarks like, "People are paid what they are worth." But the economist must ask, Worth what to whom? What gives a particular man his value? His wife, his mother-in-law, and his employer may all respond differently. Sometimes people say, "People earn according to their ability." But incomes are distributed in a very much more unequal fashion than any *measured* index of ability, be it IQ, physical strength, or typing skill. In what sense is Tom Watson five times as able a golfer as Curtis Strange? His average score is only 1 percent better, yet he earns five times as much.

If answers couched in terms of worth and ability are easily refuted, so are answers such as, "It's all a matter of luck," or "It's just the system." We want to discover whether the theories of economics provide explanations of the distribution of income that are more satisfactory than the shallow ones mentioned above.

THE THEORY OF DISTRIBUTION

Every element of income has, in a purely arithmetical sense, two components: the quantity of the income-earning service that is provided and the price per unit paid for it. The amount a worker earns in wages depends on the number of hours worked and the hourly wage received. The amount a group of workers (say, union members) earns depends on how many of them there are and how much each earns. The amount of dividends a stockholder receives depends on the number of shares of stock he or she owns and the dividents that each share pays.

Because factor prices are one of two elements that determine factor incomes, a theory of factor prices is essential to a theory of distribution.

The theory of factor prices is just a special case of the theory of price; it depends on the demand for and the supply of factors.

As with the theory of product prices studied in

Chapter 5, the theory of distribution is concerned with *relative* prices. One factor becomes "more expensive" when its price rises relative to that of other factors. In an inflationary world, most prices will be rising, but not at the same rate. So some factors will be becoming relatively more expensive, some relatively cheaper. We shall use the phrase "rise in price" to mean a rise in relative price, and the phrase "fall in price" to mean a fall in relative price. (See pages 82–83 for fuller discussion.)

In this chapter we consider competitive markets. Price theory states that the competitive market price of any commodity or factor is determined by demand and supply. The competitive market determination of the equilibrium price and quantity—and thus the money income—of a factor of production is illustrated in Figure 20-2. Look again at Figure 5-8(i), page 81, to see why this analysis is familiar.

To elaborate on the theory of factor pricing, we need a theory of the demand for factors and a theory of their supply. From them we can derive a theory of the determination of competitive equilibrium prices and quantities. In Chapter 21 we will determine the effect of various departures from competitive conditions such as those brought about by employers' associations and labor unions.

The Demand for Factors

The demand for a factor of production is said to be a **derived demand** because a firm requires labor, raw materials, machines, and other factors of production, not for their own sake, but in order to produce the goods and services that it sells.

The demand for any factor of production depends on the existence of a demand for the goods that it helps to make.

Examples of derived demand are easy to find. The demand for computer programmers and technicians is growing as industry and government use more and more electronic computers.

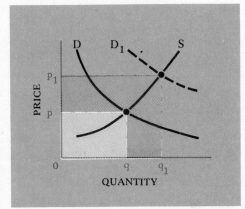

FIGURE 20-2
The Determination of Factor Price and Income in a Competitive Market

Demand and supply for factors determine prices and quantities of factors in competitive factor markets. With demand and supply curve D and S, the price of the factor will be p and the quantity employed q. The total income earned by the factor is the lighter shaded area. A shift in demand from D to D_1 raises equilibrium price and quantity to p_1 and q_1. The income earned by the factor rises by the darker shaded area.

The demand for carpenters and building materials rises or falls with the level of house building. Anything that increases the demand for new housing—population growth, lower interest rates on mortgages, and so on—will increase the demand for the factors required to build houses. Typically, one factor will be used in making many commodities. Steel is used in dozens of industries, as are the services of carpenters.

The total demand for a factor will be the sum of the demands for it in every activity in which it is used.

THE DOWNWARD SLOPE OF THE DEMAND CURVE[1]

The demand curve for a factor of production shows how the quantity demanded of that factor

[1] A more formal derivation of the demand curve for a factor is presented in the appendix to this chapter.

will vary as its price varies, the prices of all other factors remaining constant. Although demand curves for factors generally slope downward, they do so for somewhat different reasons than do demand curves for commodities.

What would happen to quantity demanded if there were a rise in the price of a factor? Because demand is a derived demand, the effect must be traced to the commodities that the factor is used to make. One effect is related to the link between a factor's price and the price of the good or service it helps to produce. Consider for example a rise in the wages of carpenters, which increases the cost of producing houses. The rise in cost shifts the supply curve of houses upward. This leads to a rise in the price of houses and to a decrease in the number of houses sold. If fewer houses can be sold, fewer will be built and lesser quantities of factors will be needed. Thus there will be a decrease in the quantity demanded of the factors used to produce houses.

The second effect relates to substitution among factors: When the price of a factor goes up, relatively cheaper factors will be substituted for the factor whose price has risen. For example, if carpenters' wages rise relative to those of factory workers, some prefabricated door and window frames made by factory workers will be used in place of on-the-job carpenters. This is simply the principle of substitution in operation.

Demand curves for factors slope downward because of (1) the effect of factor price changes on the costs and prices of the commodities the factor makes and (2) the substitution of relatively cheaper for relatively more expensive factors.

WHAT DETERMINES THE ELASTICITY OF FACTOR DEMANDS?

The greater the change in quantity of a factor demanded for a given change in its price, the greater is the elasticity of demand for the factor. Both of the considerations that lead to downward-sloping demand curves play a role in determining elasticity.

The Demand for the Commodities That Use the Factor

Other things being equal, elasticity of demand for a factor will be larger, the more elastic is the demand for the commodity that the factor helps to make. If an increase in the price of the commodity causes a large fall in the quantity demanded (i.e., the demand for the commodity is very elastic), there will be a large decrease in the quantity of the factor now needed. But if the increase in the price of the commodity causes only a small fall in its quantity demanded (i.e., the demand for the commodity is inelastic), there will be only a small decrease in the quantity of the factor now required.

The Importance of the Factor in Total Costs of Production

The elasticity of demand for a factor will be greater, the larger is the fraction of total costs that are payments to the factor. Suppose that wages are 50 percent of the costs of producing a good while raw materials account for 10 percent. A 10 percent rise in the price of labor would raise the cost of producing the commodity by 5 percent (10 percent of 50 percent), but a 10 percent rise in the price of raw materials would raise the cost of the commodity by only 1 percent (10 percent of 10 percent). Thus a 10 percent increase in labor's price would cause a larger increase in the cost of the commodity than a 10 percent rise in the price of raw materials. The larger the increase in cost, the larger the increase in the commodity's price—and hence the larger the decrease in the quantity demanded of the commodity and the factors used to make it.

Substitution of One Factor for Another

Obviously, the greater the substitution of one factor for another in response to changes in relative factor prices, the greater is the elasticity of factor demand. The ease of substitution depends on the substitutes available and technical conditions of production. A contractor in Toronto, Ontario, may normally use Toronto laborers. But should they demand higher wages, the contractor might well be able to bring workers from nearby Mississauga at only the additional cost of daily transportation. It is well known that a bushel of wheat can be produced by combining land either with a lot of labor and a little capital or with a little labor and a lot of capital, and that manufactured goods can be made either by capital-intensive or by labor-intensive techniques. In other cases, short-run substitutions are not simple to make. Recent rises in the price of gasoline have not led quickly to massive substitutions of other fuels.

While it is easy to think of barriers to substitution, they can be exaggerated. Even in the short run it is possible to vary factor proportions in surprising ways. For example, in automobile manufacture and in building construction, glass and steel can be substituted for each other simply by varying the dimensions of the windows. Grain in the form of gasohol can substitute for oil as automobile fuel.

Nor are such direct (if dramatic) short-run substitutions the end of the story. In the long run a factory that has a particular technique embodied in its equipment (and thus cannot easily vary factor proportions in the short run) can be replaced. Plant and equipment are continually being replaced, and more or less capital-intensive methods can be adopted in new plants in response to changes in factor prices. Similarly, engines that use less gasoline per mile (or that use a cheaper fuel) will surely be developed if the price of gasoline remains high.

Determinants of Factor Demand: Summary

The derived nature of the demand for factors, in addition to leading to the prediction of a downward-sloping demand curve, leads to the following predictions about elasticity of demand.

The elasticity of demand for a factor will vary directly with:

1. **the elasticity of demand of the final product it makes**
2. **the proportion of the total cost of production accounted for by the factor**
3. **the ease with which other factors may be substituted for it.**

THE MARGINAL PRODUCTIVITY THEORY OF DISTRIBUTION

Demand for factors is a derived demand. This leads to a proposition that has played an important role in the history of economics.

The conditions for maximizing profits in the short run were discussed in Chapter 14. When one factor is fixed while another is allowed to vary, the profit-maximizing firm increases its output to the level at which the last unit produced adds just as much to costs as to revenue, that is, until marginal cost equals marginal revenue. In other words, the firm will increase production up to the point at which the last unit of the variable factor employed adds just as much to revenue as it does to costs.

All profit-maximizing firms will hire units of the variable factor up to the point at which the marginal cost of the factor equals the marginal revenue produced by the factor.

This implication of profit-maximizing behavior is true of all profit-maximizing firms, whether they are selling under conditions of perfect competition, monopolistic competition, oligopoly, or monopoly. It is merely a logical deduction from two assumptions: (1) that the firm is a profit maximizer and (2) that the firm *buys* its factors in markets in which it is a price taker. (Note that the second assumption says nothing about the firm's behavior in the market in which it *sells* its product.)

Because we use the term "marginal revenue" to denote the change in revenue resulting when the rate of product sales is increased by 1 unit, we shall use another term, **marginal revenue product** (*MRP*), to refer to the change in revenue caused by the sale of the product contributed by *an additional unit of the variable factor.* We may now state more concisely the equilibrium condition stated above:

The marginal cost of the variable factor = The marginal revenue product of that factor [1]

If the firm is unable to influence the price of the variable factor by buying more or less of it (i.e., if the firm is a price taker when *buying* factors), then the marginal cost of the factor is merely its price. The cost, for example, of adding an extra ton of coal is the price that must be paid per ton of coal purchased. In these circumstances, we may state the condition of [1] in this form:

$$w = MRP \qquad [2]$$

where *w* is the price of the factor.

A profit-maximizing firm that is a price taker in factor markets hires a factor up to the point at which its price equals its marginal revenue product.

This is an equilibrium condition for a profit-maximizing firm that does not influence the price of a factor by buying more or less of it. It is sometimes called the **marginal productivity theory of distribution** because it says that, in equilibrium, factors of production will receive a price equal to the value of output that is added by the hiring of an additional (marginal) unit of the factor. This comes about by firms adjusting the quantity of the variable factor they hire at the established market price.

This important yet frequently misunderstood proposition means that, under the circumstances specified, all units of a factor will be paid a price equal to the marginal revenue product of the factor. It applies in long-run equilibrium to all factors because in the long run all factors are variable.

IMPORTANT MISCONCEPTIONS ABOUT MARGINAL PRODUCTIVITY THEORY

In certain quarters "marginal productivity theory" is almost a dirty word, for it seems to say that all factors, including labor, are paid on the same basis and that each unit is paid exactly the value of what it produces. The theory has been criticized on the grounds that it is inhumane and that it implies that the market leads to factor prices that, however low they might be, are "just" because every unit is paid the value of its contribution. Both criticisms rest on misconceptions of what the theory says and implies.

Is Marginal Productivity Theory Inhumane?

Marginal productivity theory does not take into account the differences between human services and other services. Thus the theory is sometimes called inhumane because it treats human labor as it treats a ton of coal or a wagonload of fertilizer. One must be careful to distinguish one's emotional reaction to a procedure that treats human and nonhuman factors alike from one's evaluation of it in terms of economics. Anyone who accepts this criticism must explain carefully why separate theories of the pricing of human and nonhuman factors are needed in order to make predictions about behavior.

The marginal productivity theory is only a theory of the *demand* for a factor. It predicts only what profit-maximizing employers would like to buy. It predicts that desired purchases of a factor depend on the price of the factor, the technical conditions of production, and the demand for the product made by the factor. *Supply* conditions undoubtedly differ between human and nonhuman factors, but these differences are accommodated within the theory of distribution, as we shall see. No evidence has been gathered to indicate that it is necessary to have separate theories of the demand for human and nonhuman factors of production.

Does the Theory Define a Just Distribution of Income?

In a world of perfectly competitive factor markets, the theory predicts that in equilibrium all factors receive payment equal to the values of their marginal products. Some eminent economists in the past spoke as if this led to a just distribution because factors were rewarded according to the value of their own contributions to the national product. "From each according to his ability; to each according to his own contribution" might have been the slogan for this group. One of its most famous exponents was the American economist John Bates Clark (1847–1938). Many critics of the low levels of wages that then prevailed reacted passionately to a theory that was claimed to justify them.

It is not necessary here to enter into normative questions of what constitutes a just distribution of income. It is, however, worth getting the facts straight. According to the marginal productivity theory, each worker does not receive the value of what he or she personally contributes to production. The worker receives instead the value of what one more worker would add to production if that worker were taken on while all other factors were held constant. If one million similar workers are employed, then each of the one million will receive a wage equal to the extra product that would have been contributed by the millionth laborer if he or she had been hired while capital and all other factors remained unchanged. Whether such a distribution of the national product is or is not "just" may be debated. The marginal productivity theory does not, however, contribute to that debate; it does *not* say that each unit of a factor receives as income the value of its own contribution to production. Indeed, where many factors cooperate in production, it is generally impossible to divide total production into the amounts contributed by each unit of each factor of production.

Whether payment according to marginal product is more or less just than payment according to some other criterion has not been generally agreed. However, it is possible both to hold that marginal productivity tends to determine how people get paid and to believe that government policies that change the distribution of income are desirable. Many economists hold both positions.

The Supply of Factors

Some factors, such as exhaustible natural resources, exist in limited quantities. This is true of natural gas and coal, even of sand and gravel. Other factors, such as timber products, beef, machines, and many human services, are renewable. Is it these characteristics or others that make some factors scarce and some plentiful? If we are prepared to pay more for a factor, will we get more of it? What in fact do we need to know to define the supply schedules for factors of production?

Two important economic questions concern the supplies of factors: First, to what extent do economic forces determine the total supply of a factor to the whole economy? Second, to what extent do economic forces determine the supply available to a particular sector of the economy (say, one industry) that wants to purchase only a part of the total supply?

If the total amount of a factor available is too small or too large relative to demand, will such shortages or surpluses correct themselves? If not, what can be done to correct the imbalance? Can a particular firm or industry meet its requirements even when there is an overall shortage of the factor?

THE TOTAL SUPPLY OF FACTORS

It might seem plausible to assume that the total supplies of factors available to the economy are fixed and not subject to economic influences. After all, there is an absolute maximum to the world's land area; there is an upper limit to the number of workers; there is only so much coal, oil, copper, and iron ore in the earth. In none of

What Is a Person Worth?
The Economics of Superstar Salaries

Joe Namath, an aging but flamboyant quarterback with injured knees, was paid $450,000 to play for the New York Jets in 1976, a season in which they won only three of their fourteen games (for the second year in a row). At the end of the dismal season, the Jets owners gladly accepted the resignation of the club's coach but wanted Broadway Joe to play again in 1977 at the same salary. Sportscasters and fans agreed that the team played better and had more chance of winning with their second-string quarterback, who was paid less than one-tenth of Namath's salary. Yet the Jets continued to want to play—and pay—Joe Namath. Was this sound economics?

It was. The principal products the Jets sell are football tickets and television rights to their games. Despite their poor won-lost record, the Jets were in those days a major drawing card not only in New York but throughout the country. Joe Namath was a main reason for this, remembered as the David who in 1969 led the Jets of the scorned American Football League to victory over the mighty National Football League champion Baltimore Colts, quarterbacked by John Unitas. Eight years later thousands of extra fans paid to see the Jets because of Namath. On the road during 1976, the Jets attracted roughly 10,000 more fans per game (in the same stadiums) than did the Buffalo Bills with 1976's reigning superstar, O. J. Simpson. For the season the Jets were estimated to have earned about $240,000 in their share of extra ticket sales for seven games away from home—just because of Namath. At home Namath was credited with attracting more than 10,000 extra fans per game, and this was worth at least another $350,000 in ticket sales to the football club. Add in the additional value in television rights, and Joe was plainly a bargain: his *MRP* was more than his wage. When Namath left the Jets, attendance fell.

When ABC lured Barbara Walters away from NBC with a five-year contract at a million dollars a year, it was economic calculation that was at work, not sympathy for the women's movement. ABC's share of the television news audience had slipped from 23 rating points in 1973 to 19 points in 1976.

Was Barbara worth her million? The critics thought not, but the fact is that if she has raised the rating of ABC by even one point, she will have paid her way. Halfway through her five-year contract, it looks like a financial success for her and for the network.

Before the 1979 baseball season, Pete Rose *at age 37* ("over the hill" for an athlete) signed a four-year contract at $800,000 per year, the highest baseball salary ever paid up to that time. His new employers expected (and have not been disappointed) that the fans who appreciated the acquisition of "Charlie Hustle" would pay to see him play. If they did, it would not matter whether he got 200 hits or batted .300.

Arnold Palmer made golf prizes swell and earnings of professional golfers soar by a magnetic personality that made golf a major spectator sport and brought national television coverage. Nancy Lopez-Melton is now doing the same for women's golf.

Notice that it is not the direct product produced that is responsible for high salaries. It is not yards gained or birdies scored that made Namath and Palmer rich, nor is it interviews conducted or hours on the air that led to Barbara Walters' high salary. It is tickets sold, or advertising sold, that converts the physical feats of these people into marginal revenue product. Will the extraordinary skills of Russian gymnasts or Japanese volleyball players one day make athletes in those sports worth their weight in gold? That will depend on some entrepreneur's ability to generate a market for their product. Whatever happened to Mark Spitz and Eric Heiden?

these cases, however, are we near the upper limits. The *effective* supplies of land, labor, and natural resources are thus not fixed in any meaningful sense. What, then, causes variations in the supply of a factor of production available to the *whole economy?*

The Total Supply of Labor

The total supply of labor means the total number of hours of work that the population is willing to supply. This quantity, which is often called the **supply of effort,** is a function of the size of the population, the proportion of the population willing to work, and the number of hours worked by each individual. These components in turn are affected by many forces.

Population. Populations vary in size and the variations may be influenced to some extent by economic factors. There is some evidence that the birth rate is higher in good times than in bad. Much of the variation in population, however, is explained by sociological and biological reasons rather than economic reasons.

Labor force participation. The number of people in the labor market, the **labor force,** varies considerably in response to economic and social conditions. Generally, a rise in the demand for labor and an accompanying rise in the earnings of labor will lead to an increase in the proportion of the population willing to work. Persistent unemployment may lead unemployed workers to become discouraged about finding a job and to withdraw from the labor force.

Social or legal changes can cause major variations in participation rates. The women's liberation movement, for example, is one cause of the sharply increased labor force participation of females in Canada. The recent report of the Special Senate Committee on Retirement Age Policies, *Retirement Without Tears*, recommended the abolition of mandatory retirement based on age, and recent decisions by the courts and human rights commissions have reinforced the trend toward the elimination of mandatory retirement. This may increase the labor force further if

more of the aged who were previously obliged to retire at 65 decide to stay on the job.

Hours worked. Generally, a rise in real wages such as has occurred in most Western countries over the last two centuries leads people to consume more goods — and to consume more leisure. This means that over time, as wages rise, people are willing to work fewer hours per week, a fact that *ceteris paribus* will lead to a decline in the supply of labor. But incentives such as overtime pay can be used to persuade employees to work more.

Tax rates. Many believe that today's high income taxes tend to reduce the supply of effort by lowering the incentive for people to work. They protest that it is not worth their while to work because of the crushing tax burdens they have to shoulder. Yet such objective evidence as exists suggests that high taxes do not always reduce the supply of effort. To the extent that they do, the aggregate effect may be small. A good deal of research has shown that while some people may work less hard in response to rising taxes, others feel poorer and thus work more to maintain their after-tax incomes. The most recent research suggests at most a small net disincentive up to a level of marginal tax rates of 50 percent, such as exists today in North America.

At tax rates of 75 percent or more, important distortions may occur. In Brtain, where marginal tax rates used to rise to 85 percent at levels of income that would be regarded as moderate in Canada, a "brain drain" occurred in many professional, scientific, and managerial occupations. Low salaries combined with very high tax rates on "extra" earnings to produce dramatic evidence that workers can "vote with their feet" against high taxes on earnings. Such mobility was no doubt made easier by the existence of jobs in other English-speaking countries, principally the United States and Canada.

To reduce the supply of effort is not the only possible response to tax rates regarded as confiscatory. Citizens may vote for politicians who promise to reduce taxes; or they may simply not pay income taxes. Tax avoidance, including outright cheating, may become common and even socially acceptable. The British government estimates that roughly 8 percent of the entire national income arises in cash transactions that avoid taxes because they are never reported. The growth of this "black economy" in Britain is widely believed to have been motivated by the high marginal tax rates. And the desire to avoid taxes may explain the recent rapid growth of bartering in the United States, now estimated to account for $15 to $20 billion of transactions annually.

Inflation, unemployment, and the fear of poverty. Unsettled conditions in the economy and the uncertainties they create tend to increase the supply of effort. People believe they need larger cushions against possible disaster. Rapid inflation during the late 1970s led to some slowing of the previous trend toward voluntary earlier retirement. It is not hard to understand why. While the incomes of the employed tend to rise along with a general inflation, most pensions do not. Inflation at a 10 percent annual rate for 14 years reduces the purchasing power of a pension fixed at $20,000 per year to $5,000. After 21 years its purchasing power would be only $2,500. Those who in a noninflationary world would have been glad to retire at age 60 on $20,000 per year will think twice before doing so if they recognize that they may be reduced to poverty by inflation should they be lucky enough to live to be 80.

This problem would be bad enough, and would in itself lead to deferred retirements, if workers could be sure of what the inflation rate would be during their retirement years. The problem is much worse because the future is in doubt. The inflation rate might average as little as 4 percent a year, or it might reach 20 percent, as it did in Italy and England during the 1970s. At 20 percent per year inflation, purchasing power is halved every 3.5 years. That will reduce the purchasing power of a $20,000 pension to $2,700 after 10 years and a mere $366 after 20 years! Even if the higher inflation rate is not probable,

many will be unwilling to take a voluntary action, such as early retirement, that would prove disastrous if it should happen.

Chronic unemployment poses a similar threat. Many of the employed believe they should earn as much as they can when work is available in order to build up their reserves against the possibility of future layoffs.

These effects will occur whether or not the fears prove to be real. What matters is what people *think* might happen.

Welfare payments, unemployment insurance, etc. Do welfare payments and other aid to the poor make them less willing to take jobs? Some significant disincentives to working have been found, but they do not seem to have a major effect when the financial aids are structured so as to leave those who can work with some incentive to do so. Many of those receiving payments are unable to work. Most who can work find it worthwhile to do so for their sense of participation in society as well as for the extra income. However, for a sizable—and much noticed—number, there is no doubt that welfare has become a substitute for work. And some welfare rules actually discourage work by making welfare recipients turn over as much as two-thirds of any income they might earn.

The Total Supply of Arable Land

If the term "land" is used to refer to the total area of dry land, then the total supply of land in a country will be almost completely fixed. It was nineteenth century practice (following Ricardo) to define land as the *original and inexhaustible powers of the soil.* But dust bowls were a phenomenon unknown to Ricardo, who also did not know that the deserts of North Africa were once fertile plains. Clearly the supply of fertile land is not inexhaustible; considerable care and effort is required to sustain the productive power of land. If the return to land is low, its fertility may be destroyed within a short time. Moreover, scarcity and high prices may make it worthwhile to increase the supply of arable land by irrigation and other forms of reclamation.

The Total Supply of Natural Resources

People worry — usually when it is too late — about exhausting natural resources. Canada's known reserves of oil and natural gas has shrunk from 23.5 times annual consumption in 1965 to 12.6 times annual consumption in 1978. The great iron ore deposits of the Mesabi Range were exhausted in 1965, and America's known supplies of oil and gas had shrunk by 1979 to less than an 11-year supply.[2]

The problem of actual exhaustion of natural resources does not arise as often as one might think. There is frequently a large undiscovered or unexploited quantity of a given resource or of an adequate substitute. The exhaustion of high-grade iron ore reserves in the United States did not end steel production — partly as a result of the discovery of ways to use low-grade iron ores once thought worthless, and partly because new supplies in Labrador and the Caribbean have been developed.

Guessing what will prove to be an effective substitute resource may be difficult. Will solar energy or nuclear fusion one day provide a permanent solution to the energy crisis? A writer in the *Cornell Law Quarterly* in 1930 worried about the upcoming shortage of gasoline. He believed that ordinary alcohol was the answer, and for that reason he urged the repeal of Prohibition! Gasohol may yet prove him to have been a prophet 50 years before his time.

Emerging shortages may lead to their own corrections. As long as oil remains sufficiently valuable, it will pay to find more of it. If the cost of finding oil becomes too high, the supplies that it

is economically feasible to find will decrease — at those prices. Before that event, however, free-market prices would surely rise. A sufficient increase in the price of oil would make it economically worthwhile to process the vast quantities of previously unexploited tar-sands oil. Consumers will feel the scarcity in terms of higher prices, and this will lead them to use less oil; this in turn will decrease the rate of exhaustion of known reserves.

One of the dangers of government regulation is that it may prevent these self-correcting responses. In the United States the Federal Power Commission kept the field price of natural gas artifically low. This encouraged consumption, discouraged exploration, and depleted reserves. Deregulation in 1978 has led to an enormous expansion of known American reserves in a very short time (thereby weakening a potential market for Canadian exports of natural gas).

Ultimately, of course, there is an upper limit, and resources can be totally exhausted; worse, they can be contaminated or otherwise despoiled so as to render them useless long before they have been consumed.

The Total Supply of Capital

Capital is a man-made factor of production, and its supply is in no sense fixed. The supply of capital in a country consists of the stock of existing machines, plant, equipment, and so on. This capital is used up in the course of production, and thus the stock is diminished by the amount that wears out each year. However, the stock of capital is increased each year by the production of new capital goods. Taking the long view and ignoring cyclical fluctuations, there has been a fairly steady tendency in all developed countries for the stock to increase over time.

THE SUPPLY OF FACTORS TO PARTICULAR USES

Plainly it is easier for some users to acquire more of a scarce factor of production than it is for all

[2] It should not be inferred that supplies of oil and gas will be exhausted by 1990. The known supply was reported to be more than 20 years for every year prior to 1972; in other words, each year about as much was discovered as was used. What *is* new in recent years is that discovery has lagged behind production, and thus the number of years of known supply has been shrinking.

users to do so simultaneously. Most factors have many uses; a given piece of land can be used to grow any one of several crops, or it can be subdivided for a housing development. A machinist in Windsor can work in a variety of automobile plants, or in a number of other industries, or even in the physics laboratories at the University of Windsor. A lathe can be used to make many different products and requires no adaptation when it is turned from one use to another.

The total supply must be allocated among all the different uses to which it can possibly be put. If the factor's owners are concerned only with making as much money as they can, they will move their factor to that use at which it earns the most money. Such a movement out of one use and into another would continue until the earnings of each of the units of one kind of factor in all of its various possible uses were the same. Because owners of factors are known to take other things besides money into account—such as risk, convenience, and a good climate—it is not sufficient to consider only monetary incentives; we must consider the sum of monetary and nonmonetary rewards.

The Hypothesis of Equal Net Advantage

The **hypothesis of equal net advantage** says that owners of factors will choose that use of their factors that produces the greatest net advantage to themselves. (Net advantage includes both monetary and nonmonetary rewards.)

This hypothesis plays the same role in the theory of distribution as the assumption that firms seek to maximize profits plays in the theory of production. It leads to the prediction that the units of one kind of factors of production will be allocated among various uses in such a way that their owners receive the same net return in every use.

People often worry about this hypothesis because we do not know how to measure nonmonetary advantages. The hypothesis can be made operational, however, if we assume (as is no doubt often the case) that the differences in nonmone-

tary advantages between two uses of a factor remain relatively constant or change only slowly over time. We can then predict that variations in monetary advantages will widen or narrow the gap and that some resources will flow in response to the change.

A change in the relative rate of pay of a factor between two uses will lead to a shift of some but not all units of that factor to the use whose rate of pay has increased.

This prediction implies a rising supply curve for a factor in any particular use. When the price of a factor rises, more of it will be supplied. Such a supply curve (as all supply curves) can *shift* in response to changes in other variables. One of the variables that can shift the supply curve is a change in the size of nonmonetary benefits.

Factor Mobility

When considering the supply of a factor to a particular use, the most important concept is **factor mobility.** The term is used in the sense of shiftability in use. A factor that shifts easily between uses in response to small changes in incentives is said to be highly mobile. In such a case the factor will be in very elastic supply in any one of its uses because small increases in the price offered will attract a large flow of the factor from other uses. A factor that does not shift easily from one use to another, even in response to large changes in remuneration, is said to be highly immobile. In this case the factor will be in very inelastic supply in any one of its uses because even a large increase in the price offered will attract only a small inflow from other uses.

Mobility of land. Land, which is physically the least mobile of factors, is one of the most mobile in an economic sense. Consider agricultural land. Within a year at most, one crop can be harvested and a totally different crop planted. A farm on the outskirts of a growing city can be sold for subdivision and development on short notice.

Once land is built upon, as urban land usually is, its mobility is much reduced. A site on which a hotel has been built can be converted into an office building site, but it takes a large differential in the value of land use to make it worthwhile because the hotel must be torn down.

Although land is highly mobile between alternative uses, it is completely immobile as far as location is concerned. There is only so much land within a given distance of the center of any city, and no increase in the price paid can induce further land to locate within that distance. This locational immobility has important consequences, including high prices for desirable locations and the tendency to build tall buildings that economize on the use of land where it is very scarce, as in the centers of large cities.

Mobility of capital. Most capital equipment, once constructed, is comparatively unshiftable (immobile) among uses. A great deal of machinery is utterly specific: once built, it must either be used for the purpose for which it was designed or else not used at all. (It is the immobility of much fixed capital equipment that makes the exit of firms from declining industries a slow and difficult process.) Of course many kinds of capital equipment are mobile—a shed may be used for many purposes, and a lathe can be used to make hundreds of products.

Over long periods of time the allocation of a country's capital stock among uses does change substantially. When capital goods wear out, firms might simply replace them with identical goods. But the firm has many other options: It may buy a newly designed machine to produce the same goods, it may buy machines to produce totally different goods, or it may spend its resources in other ways. Such decisions lead to changes in the long-run allocation of a country's stock of capital among various uses.

Labor mobility. Labor is unique as a factor of production in that the supply of the service implies the physical presence of the owner of the source of the service. Absentee landlords can obtain income from land located in remote parts of the world while continuing to live in the place of their choice. Investment can be shifted from iron

mines in northern Minnesota to mines in Labrador while the owners of the capital commute between New York and the French Riviera. But when a worker employed by a firm in Oshawa decides to supply labor service to a firm in Cornwall, the worker must physically travel to Cornwall. This is all quite obvious, but it has an important consequence.

Because of the need for physical presence, nonmonetary considerations are much more important in the allocation of labor than in the allocation of other factors of production.

People may be either satisfied with or frustrated by the kind of work they do, where they do it, those they do it with, and the social status of their occupations. Since these considerations influence their decisions about what they will do with their labor services, they will not move every time they can earn a higher wage.

Nevertheless, according to the hypothesis of equal net advantage, occupational and job movement will occur when there are changes in the wage structure. The mobility that does occur depends on many forces. For example, it is not difficult for a secretary to shift from one company to another or to take a job in Regina instead of in Saskatoon, but it can be difficult for a secretary to become an editor or a fashion model in a short period of time. There are three considerations here: ability, training, and inclination. Lack of any one will stratify some people and make certain kinds of mobility difficult for them.

One important key to labor mobility is time. In the short term it is often difficult for people to change occupations; in the long term it is much easier.

Some barriers may seem insurmountable for a person once his or her training has been completed. It is not easy, and it may be impossible, for a farmer to become a surgeon or for a truck driver to become a professional athlete, even if the relative wage rates change greatly. But the children of farmers, doctors, lawyers, and athletes, when they are deciding how much education or training to obtain, are not nearly as limited in

Labor Mobility and Immobility

Labor mobility—between places, between jobs, between occupations, and even between social classes—has been studied extensively. The studies show, among other things, that:

1. Labor mobility of every kind increases as the time allowed for movement increases.
2. Labor is more mobile between jobs in the same location than between different locations because movement of the family and loss of social contacts are deterrents.
3. Labor is more mobile between jobs in the same occupation than between occupations because of the time required to acquire new skills.
4. Education is more important than family background in determining occupation. While it is still an advantage to have a successful parent (successful in the sense of the parent's having an occupation at the high end of the income scale), it is not nearly as important as it was 50 years ago. What is helpful is having the education that a successful parent helps one acquire.
5. While relative wages do matter, job opportunities are often even more important in

influencing labor movement, both among places and among occupations.

While there are many "man-made" encouragements to labor mobility, such as education, training, and employment agencies, there are also barriers. Many organizations, private and public, adopt policies that affect personnel and impede their mobility as workers. When labor unions negotiate seniority rights for their members, they protect older employees from being laid off but they also make them reluctant to change jobs. When an employer provides employees with a pension plan, the employees may not want to forfeit this fringe benefit by changing jobs.

Unions may also limit entrance into an occupation. Licensing is required in dozens of trades and professions. Barbers, electricians, doctors, and, in some places, even peddlers must have licenses. There is, of course, a perfectly legitimate reason for requiring licences in those cases in which the public must be protected against the incompetent or the quack or the nuisance. Licensing, however, can have the effect of limiting supply. Discrimination based on racial prejudice and other similar attitudes further limit the mobility of labor.

their choices as their parents, who have completed their education and are settled in their occupations.

For this reason the labor force is not static. At one end of the age distribution people enter the labor force from school; at the other end they leave it via retirement or death. The turnover due to these causes is about 3 or 4 percent per year. Over a period of 20 years, a totally different occupational distribution could appear by redirecting new entrants to jobs other than the ones left vacant by workers leaving the labor force, without a single individual ever changing jobs. The role of education in adapting people to available

jobs is very great. In a society in which education is provided to all, it is possible to achieve large increases in the supply of any desired labor skill within a decade or so.

The Price of Factors in Competitive Markets

We have now developed theories of both the demand for and the supply of factors of production. These theories predict a downward-sloping demand curve and an upward-sloping supply curve. This is all that is needed for a theory of factor pricing in competitive markets. If factor prices are free to vary, prices and quantities employed will tend toward the point at which quantity supplied equals quantity demanded. Furthermore, shifts in either the demand for or the supply of factors will have the same effects on prices, quantities, and factor incomes as are predicted by standard price theory.

The theory of factor prices is absolutely general. If one is concerned with labor, one should interpret factor prices to mean wages; if one is thinking about land, factor prices should be interpreted to mean land rents, and so on.

FACTOR PRICE DIFFERENTIALS

Prices of different units of factors such as labor or land vary. Consider the prices of a number of closely related factors such as different kinds of labor. If all these factors were identical and if all benefits were monetary, then all their prices would tend toward the same level. Factors would tend to move from low-priced occupations to high-priced ones. The quantities supplied would diminish in occupations in which prices were low, and the resulting shortage would tend to force prices up; the quantities of factors supplied would increase in occupations in which prices were high, and the resulting surplus would force factor prices down. The movement would continue until there were no further incentives to transfer—that is, until factor prices were equalized. Factor price differentials are commonly seen and may be divided into two distinct types.

Dynamic Differentials

Some factor price differentials reflect a temporary state of disequilibrium. These are self-eliminating and are called **dynamic differentials.** They could equally well be called disequilibrium differentials. They are brought about by circumstances such as the growth of one industry and the decline of another. Such differentials themselves lead to reallocations of factors, and these reallocations will in turn act to eliminate the differentials.

Consider the effect on factor prices of a rise in the demand for air transport and a decline in the demand for railway transport. The theory predicts an increase in the airline industry's (derived) demand for factors and a decrease in the railway industry's demand for factors. Relative factor prices are thus predicted to go up in the airline industry and down in the railway industry. The differential in factor prices will itself foster a net movement of factors from the railway industry to the airline industry, and this movement will cause the dynamic price differentials to lessen and eventually disappear. How long this process takes will depend on how easily factors move from one industry to the other—that is, on the extent of factor mobility.

Equilibrium Differentials

Some factor price differentials may persist in equilibrium without generating forces that eliminate them. These **equilibrium differentials** are related to differences in the factors themselves (e.g., land of different fertilities or labor of different abilities), to differences in the cost of acquiring skills, and to different nonmonetary advantages of different factor employments.

It is usual to pay academic research workers less than they could earn in the world of commerce and industry because there are substantial nonmonetary advantages attached to the former. If labor were paid the same in both employments, many people would try to move out of industry and into academic employment. Excess demand for labor in industry and excess supply in universities would then cause industrial wages to rise relative to academic wages until the movement of labor stopped.

Equilibrium differentials may also be caused by differences in skills. If there is a chronic shortage of skilled workers, the skilled worker will earn more than the unskilled worker. Although there will be some movement from unskilled to skilled jobs, it is not likely to be sufficient to eliminate this differential. People will not acquire scarce skills, even if they are able to do so, unless the differentials in wages remain large enough to pay for the costs and time spent in acquiring them.

It is important to realize that the high pay of the skilled relative to that of the unskilled merely reflects relative demand and supply conditions for the two types of labor. There is nothing in the nature of competitive markets that ensures that skilled workers always get high pay just because they are skilled. When, for example, the demand for expert harness makers declined, they were in excess supply and their wages came down. History is full of examples of highly skilled workers who lost their privileged position when there was a change in the supply of or the demand for their services. Many think it both un-just and incomprehensible that since World War II truck drivers have been earning more money than schoolteachers. Whatever the justice of the matter, it is certainly not incomprehensible; at the same wage there would be excess demand for truck drivers and excess supply of school teachers.

The two kinds of differentials are closely linked to factor mobility and the hypothesis of equal net advantage. Dynamic differentials lead to, and are eroded by, factor movements; equilibrium differentials are explained in part by different nonmonetary benefits and in part by lack of mobility.

Dynamic differentials tend to disappear over time; equilibrium differentials persist indefinitely.

TRANSFER EARNINGS AND ECONOMIC RENT

The amount that a factor must earn in its present use to prevent it from transferring to another use is called its **transfer earnings.** Any excess that it earns over this amount is called its **economic rent.** The distinction is critical in predicting the effects of changes in earnings on the movement of factors.

The concept of economic rent, a surplus over transfer earnings, is analogous to the notion of economic profit as a surplus over opportunity cost.

Origins of the Concept of Economic Rent

The present concept of economic rent arose out of a policy controversy. In the early nineteenth century, when classical economics was in full bloom, there was a controversy about the high price of wheat in England. The high price was causing great hardship because bread was a primary source of food. Some argued that "corn" (then the generic term for all grains) had a high price because landlords were charging very high rents to tenant farmers. In order to meet these land rents, the prices that farmers charged for their corn also had to be raised to a high level. In short, it was argued that the price of corn was high because the rents of agricultural land were high. Those who held this view advocated restricting the power of the landlords and some-how forcing them to behave more reasonably.

Others—including, notably, David Ricardo—held that the situation was exactly the reverse. The price of corn was high, they said, because there was a shortage of corn caused by the Napoleonic wars. Because corn had a high price, it was profitable to produce it and there was keen competition among farmers to obtain land on which to grow corn. This competition in turn forced up the rents of corn land. If the price of corn were to fall so that corn growing became less profitable, then the demand for land would fall and the price paid for the use of land (i.e., its rent) would also fall. Those holding this view advocated removing the tariff so that imported corn could come into the country, thereby increasing the supply and bringing down both the price of corn and that of the land on which it was grown.

Stated formally, the essentials of Ricardo's argument were these: Land was regarded as having only one use, the growing of corn. The supply of land was regarded as unchangeable—that is, in perfectly inelastic supply. Nothing had to be paid to prevent land from transferring to a use other than growing corn because it had no other use. No self-respecting landowner would leave land idle as long as he could obtain some return, no matter how small, by renting it out. Therefore, all the payment to land—that is, rent—was a surplus over and above what was necessary to keep it in its present use. Given the fixed supply of land, the price depended on the demand for land, which was *derived* from the demand for corn. Rent, the term for the payment for the use of land, thus became the term for a surplus payment to a factor over and above what was necessary to keep it in its present use.

The Modern View of Economic Rent

Later two facts were realized. First, land itself often had alternative uses, and from the point of view of any one use, part of the payment made to land would necessarily have to be paid to keep it in its present use. Second, factors of production other than land also often earn a surplus over and above what is necessary to keep them in their present use. Television stars and great athletes, for example, are in short and fairly fixed supply, and their potential earnings in other occupations are probably quite moderate. But because there is a huge demand for their services, as television stars or athletes, they may receive payments greatly in excess of what is needed to keep them from transferring to other occupations.

Thus it appears that all factors of production are pretty much the same; part of the payment made to them is a payment necessary to keep them from transferring to other uses, and part is a surplus over and above what is necessary to keep them in their present use. This surplus is now called economic rent whether the factor is land or labor or a piece of capital equipment.

The Division of Factor Earnings Between Rents and Transfer Earnings

In most cases, the actual earnings of a factor of production will be a composite of transfer earnings and economic rent. It is possible, however, to imagine cases in which all earnings are *either* transfer earnings *or* economic rent. The possibilities are illustrated in Figure 20-3. When the supply curve is perfectly elastic (horizontal), the

FIGURE 20-3

The Division of Factor Payments Between Economic Rent and Transfer Earnings

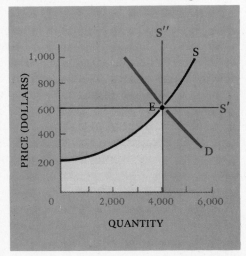

The division of total factor payments between economic rent and transfer earnings depends on the shape of the supply curve. A single demand curve is shown with three different supply curves. In each case the competitive equilibrium price is $600 and 4,000 workers are hired and the total payment to labor ($2,400,000) is represented by the entire shaded area.

(a) When the supply curve rises to the right (the black curve, S) part of the payment is rent, part transfer earnings. The 4,000th worker is just receiving transfer earnings because if the wage falls below $600 a month, he or she will not work. However, other workers would stay in the industry at a lower wage. If a separate bargain were made with each worker so that each was paid only its transfer earnings, the total payment would be the area under the black supply curve, shown as the lighter shaded area. Because the same wage must be paid to everyone, however, the total wage payment is larger, and the extra payment, shown as the darker shaded area, represents economic rent.

(b) When the supply curve is horizontal (the colored line, S') the whole payment is transfer earnings because even a small decrease in price offered would lead all units of the factor to move elsewhere.

(c) When the supply curve is vertical (the colored line, S") the whole payment is rent because a decrease in price would not lead any unit of the factor to move elsewhere.

whole of the price paid is a transfer earning: if the purchasing industry does not pay this price, it will not obtain any quantity of the factor. When the supply curve is perfectly inelastic (vertical), the whole of the payment is an economic rent: even a price barely above zero would not lead suppliers to decrease the quantity supplied. After all, some price is better than none. The price actually paid allocates the fixed supply to those most willing to pay for it.

The more usual situation is that of a gradually rising supply curve. In this case, a rise in the price serves the allocative function of attracting more units of the factor into the employment, but the same rise in the factor's price provides an extra economic rent to all units of the factor already employed. (The owners of these units were willing to supply them at the original price.)

This is quite a general result. If a factor becomes scarce in any or all of its uses, its price will rise. This will serve the allocative function of attracting additional units, but it will also give an economic rent to all units of the factor already in that employment, whose transfer earnings were already being covered.

POLICY IMPLICATIONS OF THE DISTINCTION BETWEEN RENTS AND TRANSFER EARNINGS

Using Wage Increases to Increase the Quantity of a Factor Supplied

If the government of Canada wants more physicists, should it subsidize physicists' salaries? As we have seen, such a policy may well have an effect on supply. It will persuade some students uncertain about whether to become engineers or physicists to become physicists. Whether it is an efficient use of the money will depend on the slope of the supply curve. Clearly, however, raising all physicists' salaries may mean that a great deal of money will have to be spent on extra payments to those who are already physicists. These payments will be economic rents, for existing physicists have demonstrated that they are

prepared to be physicists at their old salaries. If these rents are a large part of the total subsidy, an alternative policy may produce more physicists per dollar. One such alternative is to subsidize scholarships and fellowships for students who will train to become physicists. The National Research Council does precisely this. The effect of such subsidies is to shift the supply curve of physicists to the right.

If the supply curve is quite inelastic, an increase in the quantity supplied may be achieved more easily and at less cost by policies designed to shift the supply curve to the right than by the policy of raising price and moving up the original supply curve. See Figure 20-4.

Urban Land Values and Land Taxes

The high payments made for the services of urban land are largely economic rents. The land is scarce relative to the demand for it, and it commands a price very much above what it could earn in agricultural uses. The payment it receives is thus well in excess of what is necessary to prevent it from transferring from urban uses back to agricultural uses. A society with rising population and rising per capita real income tends also to have steadily rising urban land prices. This fact has created a special interest in taxes on land values.

Suppose there is a tax on the economic rent of land. If the same tax rate is applied to all uses of land, the relative profitability of different uses will be unaffected and a landlord will not be tempted to change the allocation of land among uses. Land will not be forced out of use because land that is very unprofitable will command little rent and so pay little tax. Thus there will be no change in the supply of goods that are produced with the aid of land, and because there is no change in supply, there will be no change in prices.

Furthermore, the tax cannot be passed on to consumers. Farmers will be willing to pay just as much (and no more) as they would have offered previously for the use of land. Agricultural

FIGURE 20-4

Alternative Ways to Increase the Quantity of a Factor Actually Provided

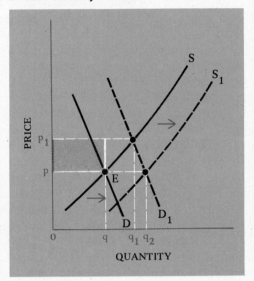

A subsidy that shifts the supply curve may achieve an increase in quantity actually provided without giving economic rents to those previously employed. With demand and supply curves D and S the factor market is in equilibrium at E. An increase in demand to D_1 would bring about an increase in quantity from q to q_1 but only with a sharp rise in factor price from p to p_1. This price rise would give substantial rents to those already employed, as shown by the shaded area. An alternative policy that gives subsidies to new entrants shifts the supply curve to S_1. It provides the additional quantity qq_2 without increasing the payments to units already employed.

prices and rents will be unchanged, and the whole of the tax will be borne by the landlord. The net rents earned by landlords will fall by the full amount of the tax. Therefore a tax on land rents *that are truly economic rents* falls solely on landowners and is not passed on to the users of land or the consumers of the produce of land.

This is the kind of argument that lay behind the popular appeal of the so-called single-tax movement, of which Henry George (1839–1897) was the guiding genius and his book *Progress and Poverty* (1880) the bible. The book was an all-time best-seller among books on economic issues, and George ran for mayor of New York City in 1886 and very nearly won, campaigning as a one-issue candidate. The single-tax movement has only faded in the period since World War II. The chief difficulties with the proposal are that not all land rents are economic rents, not all economic rents are land rents, and the revenues from a land tax would surely not be enough to make it the only tax needed in today's world.

WHAT QUESTIONS DOES THE THEORY ANSWER?

Consider again the questions discussed in the early paragraphs of this chapter. The theory of distribution we have here developed concentrates on the pricing of factors in many of the markets of the economy. We certainly can reject the view that the size distribution of income is beyond understanding, or beyond influence, even if many aspects of what determines incomes remain obscure. We know that when something improves the productivity of a factor, the factor's price will tend to increase. We know that factor mobility and immobility play an important role in the supply of factors to particular uses and thus to the pay of factors in those uses. We know how and why factor price differentials arise. We know that some differentials persist as equilibrium differentials and that others are the signals that lead to their own erosion.

Implicit in this is a large part of the explanation of why some people earn large salaries and incomes and others do not. Thus this theory has a great deal to say about the *size distribution* of income. It is also well understood today that government policies of taxation and expenditure can affect the distribution of income. Income inequality has been diminishing in Canada as a result of systematic attention to problems of poverty, discrimination, and immobility of labor. Although the specific impact of particular programs is often in doubt (and sometimes disappointing), there is no doubt about the government's overall ability to change the distribution of income.

But while the theory answers many questions, it leaves others unanswered. The theory of distribution worked out in this chapter is based on the marginal analysis developed in the last half of the nineteenth century. It emphasizes the determination of both factor and product prices in millions of individual markets. Yet market economies are complex, and it is not easy to go from what happens in one market to what happens in the economy. Consider an example: If the government attempts to increase the income of the poor by giving them amounts of money to be used for rent, how much does this benefit them and how much the landlords from whom they rent? The answer will depend on how much rents go up and how the prices of other items the poor buy are affected.

What does this market-oriented theory of distribution contribute to the broad questions about functional distribution of income considered by Marx and raised before him by Ricardo and Smith? What for example can we say about what determines the share of total income earned by labor? Can we say anything about the distribution of income among labor (wages), capital (interest and profits), and land (rent)? Our theory about individual markets offers few general predictions about the functional distribution of income. It holds that to discover the effect of some change, say a tax or a new union, on the functional distribution between wages, profits, and rent, we would need to be able to discover not only what would happen in each individual market of the economy but also to aggregate to find the overall result.[3] Clearly, we are a long way

from being able to do all this with our present state of knowledge.

It may well be that general predictions about the effects of events, such as the rise of unions, on overall distribution cannot be easily derived. Many economists would argue that economic theory has little to say about great issues raised by the classical economists on the level of labor and capital's overall shares of the total national product. They could also argue that the ability of marginal productivity theory to deal with detailed questions of distribution is nonetheless a remarkable triumph.

One reason that questions concerning the overall functional distribution of income are difficult, and perhaps impossible, to answer is that the broad categories such as "labor" are themselves highly diverse: a theoretical physicist, a baseball superstar, and a bus driver all receive labor income. It makes sense to talk about laws governing distribution into three main factor shares if labor, capital, and land are each relatively homogeneous and each subject to a common set of influences not operating on the other two factors. In fact, however, there may well be as much difference between two different types of labor as between one kind of labor and one kind of machine. Thus there is no more reason to expect that there would be simple laws governing the overall functional distribution of income between land, labor, and capital than to expect that there should be simple laws governing the overall distribution of income between blondes and brunettes or Methodists and Baptists.

Summary

1. The functional distribution of income refers to the shares of total national income going to each of the major factors of production. It focuses on sources of income. The size distribution of income refers to the shares of total national income going to various groups of households. It focuses only on the size of income, not its source.

2. The income of a factor of production can be

[3] To do this accurately we would, among other things, need to know the degree of monopoly and monopsony in each market, we would need to be able to predict the effect on oligopolists' prices and outputs of changes in their costs, and we would need to have a theory of the outcome of collective bargaining in all market situations. We would also need to know how much factor substitution would occur in response to any resulting change in relative factor prices. Finally, we would need a general equilibrium theory linking all of these markets together.

broken into two elements: (a) the price paid per unit of the factor and (b) the quantity of the factor used. The determination of factor prices and quantities is an application of the same price theory used to determine product prices and quantities.

3. The demand for any factor is *derived* from the commodities the factor is used to make. Factor demand curves slope downward because a change in a factor's price will affect the cost of production (and thus product price, quantity produced, and the need for factors) and because of the ability to substitute cheaper for more expensive factors. The formal theory of derived demand is presented in the appendix to this chapter.

4. The elasticity of factor demand will tend to be greater, (a) the greater is the elasticity of demand of the products it makes, (b) the greater is the proportion of the total cost of production accounted for by the factor, and (c) the easier it is to substitute one factor for another.

5. A profit-maximizing firm will hire units of any variable factor until the last unit hired adds as much to costs as it does to revenue. If factors are bought in a competitive market, the addition to cost will be the price of a unit of a factor. From this comes the important condition that in competitive equilibrium the price of a factor will equal its marginal revenue product. This is the marginal productivity theory of distribution.

6. The total supplies of most factors are variable over time and respond to some degree to economic influences. The most important influences are not the same for labor, arable land, natural resources, and capital.

7. The hypothesis of equal net advantage is a theory of the allocation of the total supply of factors to particular uses. Owners of factors will choose the use that produces the greatest net advantage, allowing for monetary and nonmonetary advantages of a particular employment.

8. Factor mobility (shiftability in use) is impor-

tant. Land is mobile between uses but cannot change its geographical location. Capital equipment is durable, but firms regularly replace discarded or worn out machinery with totally different machines and so change the composition of the nation's capital stock gradually but steadily. Labor mobility is greatly affected by nonmonetary considerations. The longer the period of time allowed to elapse, the more mobile is the labor force.

9. In competitive factor markets, prices are determined by demand and supply, but factor price differentials occur. Dynamic differentials in the earnings of different units of factors of production serve as signals of a disequilibrium and induce factor movements that eventually remove the differentials. Equilibrium differentials reflect differences among units of factors as well as nonmonetary benefits of different jobs; they can persist indefinitely.

10. Transfer earnings are what must be paid to a factor to prevent it from transferring to another use. Economic rent is the difference between a factor's transfer earnings and its actual earnings. Whenever the supply curve is upward-sloping, part of the factor's earnings is transfer earnings and part is rent.

11. The existence of rents in a factor's price has a potentially important policy implication: If supply is inelastic, raising the factor's price may be a relatively expensive way to induce increases in the quantity of the factor supplied.

12. The theory of distribution developed in this chapter successfully predicts changes in factor earnings that occur for particular groups in response to changes in the market conditions that affect them. However, it has little to say about changes in the broad functional distribution of income among labor, land, and capital.

Topics for Review

Factor demand as a derived demand
Marginal revenue product

The marginal productivity theory of distribution
($w = MRP$)
Factor mobility
The hypothesis of equal net advantage
Dynamic and equilibrium differentials in factor prices
Transfer earnings and economic rent

Discussion Questions

1. Other things being equal, how would you expect each of the following to affect the size distribution of after-tax income? Do any of them lead to clear predictions about the functional distribution of income?
   a. an increase in unemployment
   b. rapid population growth in an already crowded city
   c. an increase in food prices relative to other prices
   d. an increase in social insurance benefits and taxes
2. Consider the effects on the overall level of income inequality in Canada of each of the following.
   a. labor force participation of women increases sharply because many women shift from work in the home to full-time paid jobs
   b. increasing use by Western Ontario tobacco producers of foreign workers who are in Canada illegally
   c. increasing numbers of minority group members studying law and medicine
3. The demands listed below have been increasing rapidly in recent years. What derived demands would you predict have risen very sharply? Where will the extra factors of production demanded be drawn from?
   a. the demand for electric power
   b. the demand for medical services
   c. the demand for international and interregional travel
4. Can the following factor prices be explained by the marginal productivity theory of distribution?
   a. The actor James Garner is paid $25,000 for appearing in a ten-second commercial. The model who appears in the ad with him is paid $250.
   b. First prizes in a recent tennis tournament were: men's singles, $40,000; women's singles, $30,000; men's doubles, $15,000; women's doubles, $6,000; mixed doubles, $4,800.
   c. The same jockey is paid 50 percent more money for winning a ¾ mile race with a $150,000 first prize than a 1½ mile race with a $100,000 prize—on the same horse.

d. The manager of the Toronto Blue Jays is paid *not* to manage in the third year of a three-year contract.
5. Consider the large-scale substitution of jumbo jets, each with a seating capacity of about 350, for jets with a seating capacity of about 125. What kinds of labor service would you predict to have experienced an increase in demand, and what kinds a decrease? Under what conditions would airplane pilots (as a group) be made better off economically by virtue of the switch?
6. Participation in the work force in Canada as a percentage of the population aged 14 and over has risen only slightly in the last ten years, but its composition has changed substantially. For example:
   a. Almost all men between 25 and 45 years of age continue to participate in the work force.
   b. The percentage of women aged 25 and over has risen sharply.
   c. The percentage of men over 65 has dropped.
   Hypothesize about social and economic changes that might explain these conditions. How do they relate to the theory of distribution?
7. A recent study showed that after taking full account of differences in education, age, hours worked per week, weeks worked per year, etc., professionally trained people earned approximately 15 percent less if they worked in universities than if they worked in government service. Can this be accounted for by the theory of distribution?
8. Distinguish between economic rent and transfer earnings in each of the following payments for factor services.
   a. the $200 per month a landlord receives for the use of an apartment leased to students
   b. the salary of the president of the United States
   c. the $800,000 annual salary of Pete Rose
   d. the salary of a window cleaner who says, "It's dangerous, dirty work, but it beats driving a truck."
9. Which of the following are dynamic and which equilibrium differentials in factor prices?
   a. the differences in earnings of football coaches and wrestling coaches
   b. a "bonus for signing on" offered by a construction company seeking carpenters in a tight labor market
   c. differences in monthly rental changed for three-bedroom houses in different parts of the same metropolitan area

Labor Markets and the Determination of Wages

21

Why do workers in the meat-packing industry get the same pay for the same work, no matter where they work throughout Canada? Why do carpenters get different wages in different locations? Why do railway employees, who work in a declining industry, get higher rates of pay than equally skilled workers in many expanding industries? How does a worker in a plant employing 5,000 people "ask for a raise"? How does a worker let her employer know that she would be glad to trade so many cents per hour in wages for a better medical insurance scheme? Why do strikes occur?

The competitive theory of factor price determination, the subject of the preceding chapter, yields many useful and confirmed predications about factor prices, factor movements, and the distribution of income. Indeed, for the pricing of many nonhuman factors, there is little need to discard or to modify the competitive model. Much of what is observed about labor markets is also consistent with the theory. But not all of it is.

Labor is in many ways the exceptional factor of production. The factors that govern working conditions and pay are critically important to workers and their families. When employees and employers negotiate the price to be paid to the factor of production called labor, they are negotiating about something that is vital to most households. It is not surprising that people are sometimes prepared to fight over such negotiations. Considerations other than material advantage enter the relationship between employer and employee, for it is a relationship between people who look for loyalty, fairness, appreciation, and justice along with paychecks and productivity and who, if they believe these are denied them, can often respond with aggression, malice, and hatred.

Labor unions, employers' associations, and the institutions and customs that influence collective bargaining are features of the real world. They have developed in response to the exceptional conditions that govern the bargaining between free people about the terms on which one will work for another. These institutions are important because they influence the wages and working conditions that are finally agreed on.

Because labor markets are characteristically imperfectly competitive, and sometimes monopolistic, the theory of factor price determination must be extended somewhat before it can be applied to the full range of problems concerning the determination of wages.

Theoretical Models of Wage Determination

In a labor market, firms are the buyers and workers, either individually or through a labor union, are the sellers. Noncompetitive elements can enter on either or both sides of the market. The outcome of the wage bargain will be affected by the market situation.

Two extreme but relevant cases are, first, the one in which there are so many employers that no one of them can influence the wage rate by varying its own demand for labor and, second, the one in which there is a single purchaser of labor, either a single firm or an association of several firms operating as a single unit in the labor market. In the former case, labor is said to be purchased under competitive conditions; in the latter case, under monopsonistic conditions. **Monopsony** means a single buyer; it is the equivalent, on the purchasing side, of a monopoly (a single seller). What is the effect of introducing a union into each of these extreme situations?

A UNION IN A COMPETITIVE LABOR MARKET

Where there are many employers and many unorganized workers there is a competitive factor market of the kind discussed in the previous chapter. Under competitive conditions, the wage rate and level of employment are set by supply and demand.

When a union enters such a market and sets a wage for the industry above the competitive level, it is establishing a minimum wage below which no one will be allowed to work. This changes the supply curve of labor. The industry can hire as many units of labor as are prepared to work at the union wage. Each firm in the industry will have to pay that wage; the union will not let the wage rate fall. Thus the industry (and each firm) faces a supply curve that is horizontal at the level of the union wage up to a quantity of labor willing to work at that wage. This is shown in Figure 21-1. The intersection of this new supply curve and the demand curve establishes a wage rate and level of employment that differ from the competitive equilibrium.

The major effects of the union's wage setting are:

1. It will raise the wage rates of those who remain employed in the industry.
2. It will lower the actual amount of employment in the industry.
3. It will create a surplus of labor that would like to but cannot obtain jobs in the industry affected.
4. It will create an incentive for some workers to try to evade the fixed wage by offering to work at wages below the union level.

Ample evidence confirms these theoretical predictions. The unemployment that results presents a problem for the union, which is supposed to represent *all* the employees in the industry or occupation. A conflict of interest has been created between employed and unemployed union members. Pressure to cut the wage rate may develop among the unemployed, but the union must resist this pressure if the higher wage is to be maintained.

The loss of employment opportunities may well be permanent, and the unemployment may be quite long lasting. Often the actions of unions will force up the wages of those whose wages would be high in any case. This means that some displaced workers will have difficulty finding jobs that are equivalent in pay, particularly when their skills are not readily transferable to other jobs. For this reason the union jobs are likely to be prized, and many of the displaced may prefer to wait for openings caused by death or retirement rather than seek employment in other occupations.

A MONOPSONISTIC LABOR MARKET WITHOUT A UNION

Consider a labor market in which there are many unorganized workers but only a small number of firms. For simplicity, imagine a case in which the firms form an employers' hiring association in order to act as a single unit so that there is a monopsony in the labor market.

The employers' association realizes that, faced with a rising supply curve for labor, it can pick a wage rate and take the quantity of labor offered, or it can pick the quantity of labor to hire and pay the wage rate required to bring forth that quantity of labor. While the employers' association can offer any wage rate that it chooses—the laborers must either work at that rate or find a different job—the wage rate chosen will affect the profitability of its operations. For any given quantity that the monopsonist wishes to purchase, the labor supply curve shows the price per unit that it must offer; to the monopsonist, this is the *average cost curve* of the factor. In deciding how much labor to hire, however, the monopsonist will be interested in *marginal cost* because it is aware that it can bid up the wage against its own interest.

Whenever the supply curve of labor slopes upward, the marginal cost of employing extra

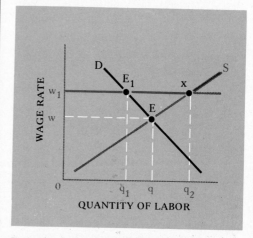

FIGURE 21-1
Union Wage Setting Above the Competitive Level

The union can raise the wages of those who continue to be employed in a competitive labor market at the expense of the level of employment. The competitive equilibrium is at E; the wage is w and employment is q. If a union enters this market and sets a wage of w_1, a new equilibrium will be established at E_1. The supply curve has become w_1xS. At the new wage, w_1, there will be q_2 workers who would like to work, but the industry only wishes to hire q_1. Employment will be q_1. The decrease in employment due to the wage increase over the competitive level is q_1q, and the level of unemployment is q_1q_2.

units will exceed the average cost.[1] It exceeds the wage paid (the average cost) because the increased wage rate necessary to attract an extra worker must be paid to everyone already employed. **[29]** The profit-maximizing monopsonist will hire labor up to the point where the marginal cost just equals the amount it is willing to pay for an additional unit of labor, which is shown by the demand curve. **[30]** This is illustrated in Figure 21-2.

[1] If, for example, 100 units of labor are employed at $2 per hour, then total cost is $200 per hour and average cost per hour is $2. If 101 units are employed and the wage rate is driven up to $2.01, then total labor cost becomes $203.01 an hour. Although average cost is only $2.01, the total cost has been increased by $3.01 as a result of hiring one more laborer. Thus the marginal cost of the extra labor is $3.01.

FIGURE 21-2
Monopsony in a Labor Market

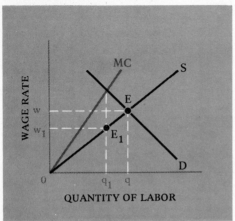

A monopsonist lowers both the wage rate and employment below their competitive levels. *D* and *S* are the competitive demand and supply curves. In competition equilibrium is at *E*, the wage rate is *w*, and the quantity of labor hired is *q*. The marginal cost of labor (*MC*) to the monopsonist is above the average cost. The monopsonistic firm will maximize profits at E_1. It will hire only q_1 units of labor. At q_1 the marginal cost of the last worker is just equal to the value to the firm of that worker's output, as shown by the demand curve. The wage that must be paid to get q_1 workers is only w_1.

FIGURE 21-3
A Wage-setting Union Enters a Monopsonistic Labor Market

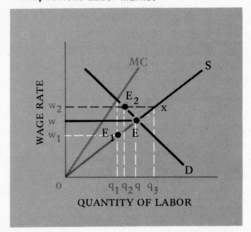

By presenting a monopsonistic employer with a fixed wage, the union can raise both wages and employment over the monopsonistic level. The monopsony position before the union enters is at E_1 (from Figure 21-2), with a wage rate of w_1 and q_1 workers hired. A union now enters and sets the wage at *w*. The supply curve of labor becomes *wES*, and wages and employment rise to their competitive levels of *w* and *q* without creating a pool of unemployed workers. If the wage is raised further, say to w_2, the supply curve will become w_2xS and the quantity of employment will fall below the competitive level to q_2 while a pool of unsuccessful job applicants of q_2q_3 will develop.

Monopsonistic conditions in the factor market will result in a lower level of employment and a lower wage rate than would rule when the factor is purchased under competitive conditions.

The common sense of this result is that the monopsonistic firm is aware that by trying to purchase more of the factor it is driving up the price against itself. It will therefore stop short of the point that is reached when the factor is purchased by many different firms, no one of which can exert an influence on the wage rate.

A UNION IN A MONOPSONISTIC MARKET

What if a wage-setting union enters a monopsonistic market and sets a wage below which

labor will not work? There will then be no point in the employer's reducing the quantity demanded in the hope of driving down the wage rate, nor will there be any point in holding off hiring for fear of driving the wage up. Here, just as in the case of a wage-setting union in a competitive market, the union presents the employer with a horizontal supply curve (up to the maximum number who will accept work at the union wage). The union raises wages above the monopsony level. This result is demonstrated in Figure 21-3.

Because the union turns the firm into a price taker in the labor market, it can prevent the exercise of the firm's monopsony power and raise

both wages and employment to the competitive levels.

The union may not be content merely to neutralize the monopsony power. It may choose to raise wages further. If it does, the argument will be exactly the same as that surrounding Figure 21-1. If the wage is raised above the competitive level, the employer will no longer wish to hire all the labor offered at that wage. The actual amount of employment will fall, and unemployment will develop. This too is shown in Figure 21-3. Notice, however, that the union can raise wages substantially above their competitive level before employment falls to a level as low as it was in the pre-union monopsonistic situation.

Labor Market Institutions

So far we have dealt with the simple case of a union that fixes a wage and allows employment to be determined by demand. Other methods of raising wages are available, and unions have goals other than high wages. Before we consider those goals, we need to review some institutional and historical details about labor markets. In the process, we shall be able to use the theory already developed to understand some past events and some present institutions.

Potential Monopsonists: Employers' Associations

A large firm has some degree of monopsony power just by virtue of its size and the number of employees with which it deals. It recognizes that its actions affect the wage rate, especially the rates received by those kinds of labor that are in some way limited to the industry in which the firm operates. This limitation will result when one large firm's need for this kind of labor represents a large fraction of the total demand for it. If steelworkers were not organized, the Steel Company of Canada would be in a position to exploit substantial monopsony power in its dealings with

them because Stelco represents a large share of the demand for whatever special talents may be required for making iron and steel.

Employers' associations are groups of employers who band together for a number of purposes, one of which may be to agree on a common policy in labor negotiations. If all steel companies offer the same terms, they can exercise even more monopsony power than any one of them could on its own. The steelworker who did not wish to accept the common conditions would have no alternative but to seek work in another industry. Today formal employers' associations that appoint official bargaining representatives exist on a local level in many industries, including the hotel, restaurant, newspaper printing, and construcion industries. There are regional or national associations in the garment manufacturing, hosiery, textile, coal mining, and furniture manufacturing industries, among others.

At least as important as formal associations are informal ones in which the several firms in an industry follow the lead set by a key firm. The industrywide pattern characterizes many manufacturing industries today. The automobile industry, for example, achieves nationwide agreement with its workers without the formal apparatus of an employers' association.

Potential Monopolists: Unions

No one bothers to define unions any more, perhaps because everyone knows what they are, or perhaps because a union is so many things: a social club, an educational instrument, a political club, one more source of withholding money from a worker's pay, a bargaining event for an individual worker, and, to some, a way of life. For the purposes of our discussion of labor markets, a **union** (or **trade union** or **labor union**) is an association of individual workers that speaks for them in negotiations with their employers.

Unions today have two different principles of organization: the craft (or trade) union and the industrial union. In the **craft union,** workers with a common set of skills are joined in a common as-

Unionism in the Public Sector

We have seen that one situation in which a union could succeed in raising both wages and employment was when a labor force faced a monopsonistic employer. Such a situation often arises in the public sector: in many cases the government has monopsony power in employing specific types of skilled labor in specific labor markets.

Whatever the reason, the scope of union activity within the public sector has expanded rapidly in the past two decades. Indeed, the rapid growth in union membership in Canada shown in Figure 21-4 arises primarily from this increase in union membership in the public sector.* In addition, because most public service unions are Canadian, their growth has diminished the role of international unions in the Canadian labor movement. (International unions today represent about one-half the organized workers in Canada, compared to a peak of three-fourths earlier in the century.)

Since 1965 public sector unions have had the right to strike, and strikes in the public sector have not been infrequent. Canadians have often been angered by interruptions in the postal service or by having to cancel holidays because of the disruption of airport services.

*Under Canadian law, municipalities are treated as private corporations and their employees governed by labor legislation applicable to the private sector. Hence the public sector in terms of labor markets refers only to provincial or federal employees.

It is often argued that such withdrawals of services are unfair because they affect large numbers of people who are not party to the labor-management dispute. They are also unfair, some argue, precisely because government often has a monopoly in the provision of the services being withheld, and hence there are no alternatives. Of course, this increases the bargaining power of the unions.

Certainly unions have been an effective force in increasing the wages of public sector employees. Not only do unions in the public sector have considerable power because of the nature of the services that strikes curtail, but public sector employers are not restrained by market forces from conceding excessive wages. Government services are not typically sold in the market place but are paid for out of general tax revenues. Further, politicians have a strong incentive to avoid unpopular strikes. Professor Morely Gunderson of the University of Toronto has estimated that during the six-year period beginning in 1965 (the year of the institution of the right to strike in the public sector) there developed a public service wage advantage of about 6 percent for males and 8 percent for females, relative to comparable jobs in the private sector. Other studies confirm the maintenance of, if not an increase in, this advantage over the next few years for all but the most senior public employees.

Many economists believe that increased

sociation, no matter where or for whom they work. The craft principle of organization was and is the hallmark of the American Federation of Labor (AFL) and its Canadian counterpart, the Trades and Labour Congress (TLC). The **industrial union** is organized along industry lines: All workers in a given plant or industry are collected into a single union. This is the pattern developed

by the member unions of the Congress of Industrial Organizations (CIO) and the Canadian Congress of Labour, which existed in the period 1940–1956. Among the prominent industrial unions are the United Automobile Workers and the United Steelworkers.

The two principles of unionism conflict. Should a carpenter employed in the steel in-public sector wages become the standard by which private sector wages are set; in this view the public sector has become a wage leader and a source of potential inflation in the economy. However, studies have called into question the evidence confirming a spillover, and the issue is still hotly contested.

Furthermore, many observers felt that a primary reason for the introduction of wage and price controls (see pages 867–873) by the federal government in 1975 was to appeal to an external force to regain control over wage settlements with their own employees. Public sector unions, in this view, had become so powerful that the federal government could not control wages in the federal civil service through the usual negotiating and bargaining procedures; hence it had to impose controls on the entire economy in order to control public sector wages.

It is useful to compare the Canadian situation with that prevailing elsewhere. In the United States, federal and state government workers are prohibited from striking and are not permitted to bargain over pay. In Britain the normal means of determining government pay levels is strict adherence to private sector comparability guidelines. Canadian public sector labor regulation policy is now among the most liberal in the world, and some believe it is too liberal. Some believe that government employees do not need collective bargaining

or the strike weapon to ensure that they are paid adequately; in the long run the supply of labor to the public sector is a function of the price paid for labor by the public employer, relative to what workers can earn elsewhere. This offers considerable insurance that public employees, with or without collective bargaining, will not long be underpaid, at least at entry job levels.

In a recent study, Sandra Christensen (formerly of Simon Fraser University and now of the Congressional Budget Office in Washington) argued that parity between public and private sector wages in comparable jobs is a desirable social objective "for reasons of equity, efficiency, and macroeconomic stability." She argued further that the introduction of collective bargaining in the public sector replaces the parity principle with the principle of "more pay to those with more power," which virtually assures a pay premium to public sector employees. She advocates that bargaining for pay in the public sector be eliminated in favor of a policy in which pay scales are set by an independent agent on the basis of comparability to the private sector. While this policy has much to recommend it, it also has obvious administrative and political drawbacks; furthermore, it rules out changes in relative wages as part of a long-run adjustment to new relative demands in the two sectors.

dustry be represented by the carpenters' union or the steelworkers' union? Disputes over which union shall have the right to *organize* (i.e., bring into their union) a particular group of workers are known as **jurisdictional disputes.** They have led to prolonged, bitter, and bloody battles of union against union, and they have played an important role in North American labor history.

Since the merger of the AFL and CIO in 1955, such disputes have become much less common in the United States.

Jurisdictional disputes often reflected the different philosophies of industrial and craft unions, for example in the trade-off between higher wages (for those who keep their jobs) and higher total employment. AFL unions tended to go for high wages for the skilled craftsman in a plant; the CIO wanted to organize the whole plant to provide employment and income to more workers even at the expense of some strategic crafts. Similar disputes occurred in Canada, but the conflict between craft and industrial unions was of less significance.

Jurisdictional disputes may involve more than mere power struggles between rival unions about who shall represent a particular group of workers. If the jurisdictional dispute concerns which occupation should do a certain job, the outcome of the dispute will affect the employment level of the workers of the two occupations —increasing the demand for the services of the winning group and decreasing demand for the losing group. (Although workers of the losing group may be able to shift unions, they will sacrifice whatever seniority they have in their union; thus, if there is excess supply, they will bear the brunt of the unemployment that is brought by a union wage above the competitive level.)

However regrettable jurisdictional disputes may seem to outsiders who are inconvenienced by them, economic analysis suggests that matters of very real importance to the welfare of the participants may be involved.

Unions in North America operate at the local level, at the national and international levels, and as a federation of unions. Typically the national officers do the bargaining, form the policies, and set the tone. Individual workers belong to a local to which they pay dues (part of which goes to the national or international headquarters). There are about 165 national or international unions in Canada with over 10,000 locals. The locals for a craft union are geographical—for example, the Toronto chapter of the carpenters' union. The locals for an industrial union are plants or companies—for example, the Ford local of the United Automobile Workers.

The **federation** is a loose organization of unions. Most international unions operating in Canada are affiliated with the single American federation, the AFL-CIO, as well as the Canadian Labour Congress (CLC). Most of the purely Canadian national unions are affiliated with either the CLC or the Quebec-based Confederation of National Trade Unions (CNTU).

Kinds of Bargaining Arrangements: Open, Closed, and Union Shops

In an **open shop** a union represents its members but does not have exclusive bargaining jurisdiction for all workers in the shop. Membership in the union is not necessary to get or to keep a job.

Unions vehemently oppose such an arrangement, and economic theory explains why. If, on the one hand, the employer yields to union demands and raises wages, the nonmembers get the benefits of the union without paying dues or sharing the risks or responsibilities. If, on the other hand, the firm chooses to fight the union, it can run its plants with the nonunion employees, thereby weakening the power of the union in the fight.

If the union succeeds in raising wages above their competitive level, there will be an excess supply of labor (see Figure 21-1). With an open shop, there is nothing to prevent unemployed nonunion workers from accepting a wage below the union wage and so undermining the union's power to maintain high wages.

If all members of an occupation must join the union in order to get a job, the union can prevent its members from accepting less than the union wage and so have the power to maintain high wages in spite of the existence of excess supply. This arrangement is called a closed shop. In a **closed shop** only union members may be employed, and the union controls its membership as it sees fit. Employers traditionally regard this as unwarranted limitation of their right to choose their employees. Its use is virtually prohibited in the United States and in most provinces in Canada.

The **union shop** is a compromise between a closed shop and an open shop. In a union shop a firm may hire anyone it chooses at the union wage, but every employee must join the union within a specified period. This leaves employers free to hire whomever they wish but gives the union the power to enforce its union wages because workers are prevented from accepting employment at lower wages.

Weapons of Conflict: Strikes, Picket Lines, Boycotts, Lockouts, Strikebreakers, Blacklists

The **strike,** the union's ultimate weapon, is the concerted refusal to work by the members of the union. It is the strike or the threat of a strike that backs up the union's demands in the bargaining process. Workers on strike are of course off the payroll, so many unions set aside a portion of the dues collected to have a fund for paying striking workers.

Picket lines are made up of striking workers who parade before the entrance to their plant or firm. Other union members will not, by time-honored convention, "cross" a picket line. Thus, if bricklayers strike against a construction firm, carpenters will not work on the project, even though they themselves may have no grievance against the firm, nor will any teamster deliver supplies to a picketed site. Pickets represent an enormous increase in the bargaining power of a small union. (Much of the bitterness against jurisdictional disputes arises from the fact that an employer may be unable to settle with either union without facing a picket line from the other union.)

A **labor boycott** is an organized attempt to persuade customers to refrain from purchasing the goods or services of a firm or industry whose employees are on strike. The boycotts organized by Cesar Chavez's United Farm Workers Union against grapes, lettuce, and most recently bananas are prominent examples.

The **lockout** is the employer's equivalent of the strike. By closing the plant the employer locks out the workers until such time as the dispute is settled. **Strikebreakers** (scabs) are workers brought in by management to operate the plant while the union is on strike. A **blacklist** is an employers' list of workers who have been fired for

playing a role in union affairs that was regarded by the employer as undesirable. Other employers are not supposed to give jobs to blacklisted workers.

Collective Bargaining

The process by which unions and employers (or their representatives) arrive at and enforce their agreements is known as **collective bargaining.** This process has an important difference from the theoretical models with which we began this chapter. There we assumed that the union set the wage and the employer decided how much labor to hire. In collective bargaining the wage is negotiated. In terms of Figure 21-3, it may be that the employer wants the wage to be w_1 and the union wants w_2. Depending on each side's market power and their bargaining strength, the final agreed wage may be anywhere in between. In collective bargaining, there is always a substantial range over which an agreement can be reached, and in particular cases the actual result will depend on the goals and strengths of the two bargaining parties and on the skill of their negotiators.

The Evolution of the Modern Union

When representatives of the United Steelworkers sit down with representatives of the Steel Company of Canada to discuss wages, contributions to pension funds, number and length of holidays, and other issues, they are engaging in what has been termed "mature collective bargaining." At the end of the negotiations, newspapers and television show the smiling representatives shaking hands. Each of the approximately 12,000 workers in the plants then knows the conditions under which he or she will work for the next year or so. Should an employee have a grievance at any time, he or she reports it to the union representative (called a **shop steward**), and a carefully designed procedure is set in motion to settle the dispute.

Unionism today is both stable and accepted. It was not always so. Within the lifetime of many of today's members, unions were fighting for their lives and union organizers and members were risking theirs. In the 1930s the labor movement evoked the loyalties and passions of people as a great liberal cause, in ways that seem quite extraordinary today. Indeed unions today often appear as conservative (even reactionary) groups of hard hats. Why the change and how did it come about?

The Urge to Organize

Trade unionism had its origin in the pitifully low standard of living of the average nineteenth century worker and his family. Much of the explanation for the low standard of living throughout the world lay in the small size of the national output relative to the population. Even in the wealthiest countries, an equal division of national wealth among all families in 1850 would have left each one in poverty by our present standards.

Poverty had existed for centuries. It was accentuated, however, by the twin processes of urbanization and industrialization. The farmer who was moderately content working the land usually became restive and discontented when the family moved into a grimy, smoky nineteenth century city, lived in a crowded, unsanitary tenement, and took a job in a sweatshop or a factory. The focus of resentment was usually the employer.

The employer set the wages, and the wages were low. The boss was often arbitrary and seldom sympathetic. And the boss was usually conspicuously better off than his employees. Unhappy workers had, of course, the right of all free people to quit their job—and starve. If they grumbled or protested, they could be fired—and worse, blacklisted, which meant no one else would hire them.

Out of these conditions and other grievances of working men and women came the full range of radical political movements. Out of the same conditions also came a pragmatic American form of collective action called **bread-and-butter unionism,** whose goals were higher wages and better working conditions rather than social and political reform.

The early industrial organizer saw that ten or a hundred employees acting together had more influence that one acting alone and dreamed of the day when all would stand solid against the employer. (The word "solidarity" occurs often in the literature and songs of the labor movement.) The union was the organization that would provide a basis for confronting the monopsony power of employers with the collective power of the workers. But it was easier to see solidarity as a solution than it was to achieve it. Organizations of workers would hurt the employer, and employers did not sit by idly; they too knew that in union there was strength. "Agitators" who tried to organize other workers were fired and blacklisted; in some cases they were beaten and killed.

REQUIREMENTS OF A SUCCESSFUL UNION

In order to realize the ambition of creating some effective power over the labor market, a union had to gain control of the supply of labor and have the financial resources necessary to outlast the employer in a struggle for strength. There was no right to organize. The union had to force an employer to negotiate with it, and few employers did so willingly. Unions started in a small way among highly skilled workers and spread slowly.

There are good theoretical reasons that help explain why the union movement showed its first real power among small groups of relatively skilled workers. First, it was easier to control the supply of skiller workers than unskilled ones. Organize the unskilled, and the employer could find replacements for them. But skilled workers—the coopers (barrelmakers), the bootmakers, the shipwrights—were another matter. There were few of them, and by controlling the conditions of apprenticeship they controlled the access to their trade. The original craft unions were in effect closed shops: One had to belong to the union to hold a job in the craft, and the union set the rules of admission.

Second, a union of a relatively few highly skilled specialists could attack the employers where they were vulnerable. Because a particular skilled occupation may be difficult to do without in an industrial process, other factors cannot easily be substituted for it. Because labor in a particular skilled occupation is likely to account for a relatively low proporiton of total costs, the effect on the employer's overall costs of giving in to a small group's demand for a wage increase is much less than the effect of giving in to an equivalent demand from the numerous unskilled workers.

In other words, the difficulty of substituting other factors and a relatively small contribution to total costs combined to create an inelastic demand for skilled labor (see page 367). This inelastic demand for their services gave the unions of skilled workers an advantage in fighting the employer not enjoyed by other groups of workers. In the early days, unions needed every advantage they could get since anti-unionism was for some a matter of principle, a crusade, and a way of life.

Even where unions gained a foothold in a strategic trade, they had their ups and downs. When employment was full and business booming, the cost of being fired for joining a union was not so great because there were other jobs. However, during periods of depression and unemployment the risks were greater. An individual worker knew that if he or she caused trouble, unemployed members of the trade would be there to take the job. Solidarity could yield to hunger. Membership in trade unions showed a clear cyclical pattern, rising in good times and falling in bad.

THE HISTORICAL DEVELOPMENT OF UNIONS IN NORTH AMERICA

The origins of the present structure of Canadian trade unionism can be traced to the latter half of the nineteenth century. Its development has been strongly dominated by the influence of what are now called international unions, which have their headquarters and an overwhelming proportion of their membership outside Canada. The creation of Canadian locals of American unions began in the 1860s, and by the end of the century a large majority of Canadian trade unionists were members of organizations chartered by the American Federation of Labor or Canadian offshoots of a competing American association called the Knights of Labor.[2] The first attempts at unifying Canadian unions into a central national organization occurred in 1873, but it was not until 1883 that the first body with nationwide representation, the Trades and Labour Congress of Canada (TLC), was formed. In 1956 the TLC merged with other groups to form the Canadian Labour Congress (CLC).

The Struggle for Autonomy and Unity

Two facets dominated the history of Canadian trade unionism in the first half of this century. One was the movement toward a single national federation; the other was the struggle to achieve autonomy in the face of American attempts to control the development of Canadian unions. The issues became intertwined when conflicts in the United States between craft and industrial unions became a disruptive force in Canada because of the TLC's ties with the American Federation of Labor. This organization, founded in 1886 by an immigrant to the United States from England, Samuel Gompers, was totally committed to organizing the skilled trades along craft lines and to pursuing the bread-and-butter goals of higher wages, better work conditions, and so on, through the control of labor supply. Until the 1930s this remained the characteristic pattern of collective action in the United States. In Canada, meanwhile, trade unionists were at-

---

[2] In 1911, the earliest date for which figures are available, international unions had 90 percent of total union membership. In recent years the proportion has been about 60 percent.

tracted to the principle of industrial unions that embraced unskilled workers as well as skilled craftsmen.

Because of the impossibility of establishing bargaining strength through the control of supply in the case of unskilled workers, the rise of industrial unionism in Canada was associated with political action as an alternative means of improving the lot of the membership. The Knights of Labor, organized in 1869, had represented an attempt to establish a single political force to advance the cause of American workers. Its influence there lasted less than twenty years, but its Canadian branch remained active much longer. The classic Canadian manifestation of revolutionary industrial unionism was the One Big Union formed by western unionists who broke away from the TLC after the Winnipeg General Strike of 1919.

In general, social and political reform were given much more emphasis by Canadian unionists than by their American counterparts. Political action here extended to the development of a viable socialist political party in the form of the Cooperative Commonwealth Federation (CCF) established in 1932 and its successor, the New Democratic Party (NDP), formed in 1961. The CLC does not have a formal affiliation with the NDP; the relationship is similar to that between the British Trades Union Congress and the British Labour Party. As interpreted by Senator Eugene Forsey, a former director of research for the CLC, "the founding of the New Democratic Party represents the triumph of the British tradition of direct political action, brought to Canada by British working-class immigrants in their baggage, over the nonpartisan AFL tradition. It is one of the marks of the independence of the Canadian labour movement from the American, with which it is otherwise, in so many ways, so closely associated."[3]

[3] Eugene Forsey, "The Influence of American Labor Organizations and Policies on Canadian Labor," in *The American Economic Impact on Canada* (Durham, N.C.: 1959).

This is probably regarded as an extreme view by many students of Canadian unionism. It is perhaps fairer to conclude that the political and economic posture of our labor movement occupies a middle ground between American adherence to the free enterprise system and the achievement of purely economic gains on the one hand, and European class consciousness and political activism on the other.

International unionism. In spite of the divergent patterns of development in the two countries, at the beginning of this century the TLC lined itself up squarely on the side of international unionism because of the greater resources made available to it through its constituent unions affiliated with the AFL. Then the rise of industrial unionism in the United States in the 1930s resulted in a severe blow to labor unity in Canada. Following the leadership of John L. Lewis of the United Mine Workers, the industrial unions in steel and automobiles split from the conservative AFL and formed the Congress of Industrial Organizations (CIO). Although the TLC had always been willing to accept both kinds of unions, in 1939 the AFL forced it to expel the Canadian branches of CIO unions under threat of the loss of AFL unions whose Canadian membership was then much larger.

The dominance of international — that is, American — unions in the Canadian labor movement continues to be a source of public concern in Canada. It is viewed as inconsistent with Canadian sovereignty and dangerous to Canadian interests. In Forsey's view, however, these fears are no longer well founded. He views the unification of the bulk of Canadian unions under the CLC in 1956 as the beginning of virtual autonomy for Canadian locals. In particular, unlike the TLC, the CLC has complete control over its qualifications for membership and has not hesitated to embrace unions expelled by the AFL-CIO or to expel unions affiliated with it.

Nevertheless agitation for greater Canadian autonomy has continued. The CLC has developed guidelines for the conduct of international unions operating in Canada, and a number of groups have severed their connection with international unions and formed independent Canadian unions. Some of the defectors have affiliated with the Confederation of Canadian Unions, a small CLC rival whose main base is in British Columbia.

Current affiliation of Canadian unions. The distribution of Canadian union membership by affiliation in 1980 is shown in Table 21-1. International unions account for 46 percent of the total, compared to about 70 percent in the mid-1950s. One factor in the increased share of national unions is the growth of membership in the two unions representing government workers, the Canadian Union of Public Employees and the Public Service Alliance. Another major component of noninternational union membership has arisen out of the distinct aspirations of French-Canadian workers. This is reflected in Table 21-1 by the 6 percent share of the Quebec-based Confederation of National Trade Unions.

TABLE 21-1
Union Membership by Type and Affiliation, 1980

Type and affiliation	Thousands of members	Percentage of total
International unions	1571	46
AFL-CIO/CLC	1305	38
CLC only	162	5
Other	104	3
National unions	1703	50
Public employee unions (CLC)	609	18
Other CLC unions	241	7
Confederation of National Trade Unions	187	6
Other	52	1
Unaffiliated unions	614	18
Directly chartered and independent local organizations	123	4
Total	3397	100

Source: Labour Canada, *Labour Organizations in Canada,* 1980.

The Development of Public Policy Toward Collective Bargaining

As shown in Figure 21-4, rapid gains in union membership occurred in the years during and immediately after World War II. This led to pressure to give Canadian unionists the legal protections provided in the United States by the Wagner Act of 1935, which guaranteed the right of workers to organize and to elect an exclusive bargaining agent. These rights were carried over into Canada through the provisions of the Wartime Labour Relations Regulations of 1944.

Government intervention in industrial disputes in Canada has a history dating back to the early years of this century. The earliest legislation applied only to public utilities and coal mining, where there was a strong public interest element; it provided that before a strike or a lockout could be initiated, the parties were required to submit any dispute to a conciliation board. This system of compulsory conciliation and compulsory delay in work stoppage was extended to a much larger segment of the economy under special emergency powers adopted by the government of Canada during World War II. In the postwar period, jurisdiction over labor policy reverted to the provinces, but principles established have been carried over into provincial legislation.

Methods and Objectives of the Modern Union

Union constitutions are extremely democratic documents. All members have one vote, officers are elected by the vote of the membership, the rights of individual workers are fully protected, and so on. In practice, however, the relation between the members of a union and its national

FIGURE 21-4
Union Membership, 1921–1980

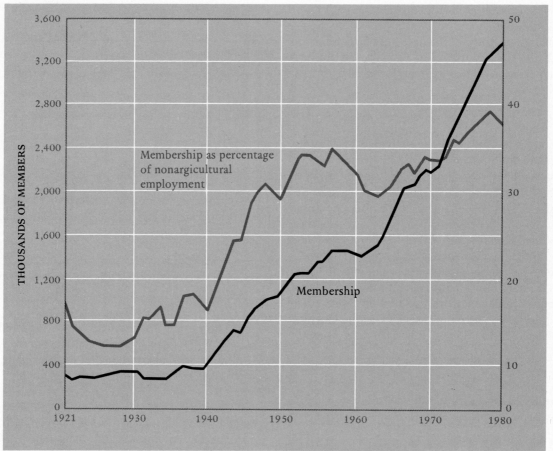

Rapid growth in unionism occurred in the period 1941–1952 and during the 1960s. The growth in union membership in recent years reflects to a large extent growth in the unions representing government employees. The figures are from Labour Canada, *Labour Organizations in Canada*, 1980.

officers is closer to that of the relationship between stockholders and managers of a giant corporation than to that of the Canadian people and their government. Unions tend toward one-party democracy in most cases. Union leaders are highly paid professionals whose business is to run the union, while the main business of union members is to earn a living on the job. The union members' indifference is understandable; they are paying dues that permit the union to pay generous salaries to union leaders to look out for the rank and file's interests—and as long as the leadership "delivers," all goes well. But delivers what and to whom?

RESTRICTING SUPPLY TO INCREASE WAGES

At the beginning of this chapter we saw that if a union raises the wage above the competitive level, it will create a pool of people eager to work at the going wage rate but unable to find employment. An alternative is to determine the quantity of labor supplied and let the wage be determined on the open market. This is illustrated in Figure 21-5. The union can restirct entry into the occupation by methods such as lengthening apprenticeshop periods and restricting openings for trainees. Such tactics make it more difficult and more expensive to enter the occupation.

Under these restrictive conditions, the quantity supplied is reduced at any given wage rate and the supply curve of labor shifts to the left. This has the effect of raising wages without anyone's ever having to negotiate a rate above what would naturally emerge from the free operation of the competitive market. Furthermore, there is no pool of unemployed wanting to work at the new higher wage but unable to find employment. Thus there is no wage-reducing pressure from unemployed persons who are trained for the occupation but are unable to find jobs.

The choice unions may face between the tactics of wage setting and supply restriction will be affected by the relative ease of enforcing one or the other kind of arrangement and the public acceptability of its tactics. In this respect unions are no different than professional groups, who may treat unions with utter disdain. Consider the professions of medicine and law. Since professional standards may be regarded as necessary to protect the public from incompetent practitioners, doctors and lawyers have found it publicly acceptable to limit supply by controlling entry into their profession.

Doctors are in short supply because of barriers to entry, including the difficulties of getting into an approved medical school, long years of low-paid internship and residency, and various certification rules. Whatever the need for high standards of entry into medical practice, there is no doubt that doctors' earnings are high *because* the barriers to entry into the profession prevent increases in the number of those admitted to medical practice. Most investigators have concluded that restrictions on entering medicine are much greater than they need be to protect the

FIGURE 21-5
Raising Wages by Restricting Entry

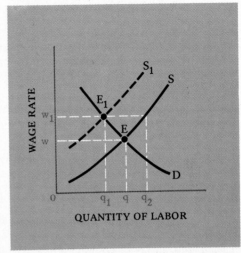

By restricting entry into an occupation, a union can shift the supply curve and raise wages. A competitive industry would be in equilibrium at E. When the supply curve shifts to S_1, the wage rises to w_1 and employment falls to q_1. Compare this to the strategy of simply imposing the wage w_1. In each case q_1 workers obtain employment at q_1. By shifting the supply curve, no pool of unsuccessful job applicants is created (as it was when a wage of w_1 was imposed without shifting the supply curve from S).

public and that earnings are substantially higher as a result.

Lawyers have been less successful in limiting entry into their profession. They have, however, usually succeeded in having their bar associations prescribe and enforce minimum fees for services such as drawing a will, probating an estate, and representing a client in court. As the theory predicts, many lawyers are underemployed in the sense that they have fewer clients than they could comfortably handle.[4] In contrast, doctors are typically overworked.

Restriction of supply will tend to raise wages. Raising wages without restricting supply will lead to unemployment or underemployment.

[4] See the discussion of barbers in Chapter 17.

COMPETING GOALS

Wages Versus Employment

A union that sets wages above the competitive level is making a choice of higher wages for some and unemployment for others. Should the union strive to maximize the earnings of the group that remains employed? If it does, some of its members will lose their jobs and the union's membership will decline. Should it instead maximize the welfare of its present members? Or should it seek to expand employment opportunities (perhaps by a low-wage policy) so that the union membership grows?

Different unions decide these questions differently. The United Mine Workers Union employed a high-wage, shrinking-employment strategy for decades, and both employment and union membership declined. The longshoremen's union has achieved high wages but chooses to ration the available jobs among its members rather than reduce its membership. It thus spreads the underemployment around. In the garment trades, the demand for labor is relatively elastic and the major unions have traditionally accepted lower wages than they could have attained in order to protect the employment of their members. The key construction unions in New York City during that city's 1975 fiscal crisis accepted a 25 percent cut in their wage rate on rehabilitation construction because of a high—30 percent—unemployment rate among their members.

Wages versus employment poses a long-term problem as well as a short-term problem. Unionization and rising wages in fruit picking have led to mechanization and a drop in the demand for labor. In the auto industry, the high-wage policy of the United Automobile Workers has encouraged the major manufacturers to increase automation. There are fewer jobs in the industry today, yet more cars are made.

Wages Versus Job Security

People who were in their teens during the Great Depression still dominate the leadership of many unions. Not surprisingly, they have a strong defensive attitude toward their jobs. They lived through a period when unemployment was above 20 percent of the total labor force and nearer 50 percent in many of the hardest hit areas. They saw people grow up, marry, and raise children on relief or part-time work.

In a period of heavy unemployment, installation of a labor-saving machine in a factory is likely to mean unemployment for those whose jobs are lost by the change. It is little wonder that new machines were opposed bitterly and that job-saving restrictive practices were adhered to with tenacity.

The heritage of this fear survived in featherbedding practices such as the standby musician at the television studio and the meticulous division of tasks in the building trades. But in the long run mechanization increases productivity—and consequently the wages and profits that are earned. After World War II the attitude of many unions slowly changed from one of resisting technological change to one of collaborating with it and trying to reduce some of its costs to individuals who are adversely affected. The return of higher unemployment rates in recent years has, however, led again to increased resistance to rapid innovation. In any event, history shows that innovation may be delayed but cannot be stopped.

Wages Versus Fringe Benefits

Today indirect or **fringe benefits**—such as company contributions to union pension and welfare funds, sick leave, and vacation pay, as well as required payments toward unemployment insurance—are estimated to make up over a quarter of the total compensation of industrial workers. During the 1970s wages and salaries grew at an average annual rate of 9.8 percent while the value of fringe benefits grew at a 14 percent annual rate. Why do unions and employers not simply agree to a wage and let it go at that? Why should an automobile worker who earned $21,000 in wages in 1980 cost the company $28,000?

Fringe benefits appeal to employees in part because many of them are not subject to income taxes. Pension funds and the like let employees provide for their future and that of their families more cheaply than they could by purchasing private insurance, and their benefits often protect them even when they lose their jobs.

There may also be advantages to employers in giving indirect or fringe benefits. One advantage is that some forms of fringe benefits, such as pension funds, tend to bind the worker more closely to the company, thereby decreasing the turnover rate among employees. If employees stand to lost part of their benefits by changing jobs, they will not be so ready to move.

Fringe benefits provide scope for bargaining. A union official may have promised the rank and file not to settle for less than $1.50, and the employer's representatives may have assured management that they would stand firm at $1.00. In negotiation they may agree on 90¢ in wage increases and 35¢ in fringe benefits. Both negotiators may claim success, whereas either would feel reluctant to accept a straight $1.25 wage increase. Collective bargaining is more successful when neither side feels it has done too badly.

Minimum Wages and Employment

An important feature of labor markets in North America is the presence of government-imposed *price floors* that establish minimum levels of compensation, called **minimum wages.** In Canada, industries under federal jurisdiction are subject to the Canadian Labour Code, which in 1979 provided for a minimum wage of $2.90 per hour. The major coverage, however, is provided by provincial legislation that in 1980 set minimum wages for adult workers ranging from $3.00 per hour in several provinces to $3.65 in Quebec and Saskatchewan.

For a very large fraction of all employment covered by the law, the minimum wage is below the actual market wage. Where this is true, the wage is said to be not "binding." But many workers are in occupations or industries where the free-market wage rate would be below the legal minimum, and there the minimum wage is said to be binding, or effective.

Whether minimum wages are effective is not always easy to determine. For example, one response of employers to minimum wage legislation might be to reduce fringe benefits so that total compensation remains constant.

Minimum wages are controversial. To the extent that they are effective, they raise the wages of employed workers. But, as our analysis in Chapter 7 indicated, an effective price floor may well lead to a market surplus—in this case, unemployment. Let us see to what extent this prediction applies to the minimum wage.[5]

The occupations and industries in which minimum wages are effective are the lowest paying in the country; they usually involve unskilled or at best semiskilled labor. In most of them the workers are unorganized. Thus the market structures in which effective minimum wages apply include both those where competitive conditions pertain and those where employers have monopsony power and can exercise it. The effects of minimum wages are different in the two cases.

EFFECTIVE MINIMUM WAGES IN A COMPETITIVE LABOR MARKET

The employment effects of an effective minimum wage are unambiguous when the labor market is competitive. By raising the wage facing employers, minimum wage legislation leads to a reduction in the quantity of labor demanded and an increase in the quantity supplied. As a result,

---

[5] One important aspect on which the analysis of minimum wages hinges is the extent of coverage. In the text we analyze the situation where coverage is comprehensive; in the box we treat the interesting case where there is a "covered" sector to which the minimum wage applies and an "uncovered" sector to which it does not.

Employment Effects of Minimum Wages with an Uncovered Sector

One argument often raised in response to the presumption that minimum wage legislation lowers employment is that such legislation is not comprehensive in its coverage: it applies to some sectors of the economy but not to all. Hence, it is alleged, those workers displaced from the covered sector are able to move to the uncovered sector and find employment. Here we consider whether total employment effects remain negative when minimum wages apply to only one sector of the economy. (Both sectors are considered to be competitive.)

We start with an economy composed of two sectors, the covered sector and the uncovered sector. The demand for labor in the two sectors is shown in the figure by the colored lines D_u and D_c. Before the introduction of minimum wage legislation, competition in the labor markets ensures that the wage rate in the two sectors is the same. (This amounts to assuming that the nonmonetary advantages of the two occupations are the same; therefore, by the hypothesis of equal net advantage, the monetary advantages must also be equal.) Accordingly, the total demand for labor—the sum of the demands in each sector for each wage rate—is shown by the black line D_A, the

horizontal sum of the two "sector" demand curves. The total supply of labor is S. Equilibrium is at E with a common wage of w in both sectors; employment in the two sectors is represented by N_c and N_u.

Now suppose a minimum wage w_m, greater than the competitive wage w, is introduced into the covered sector only. For wages above w_m, the total demand for labor is unchanged because the minimum wage is not binding. However, for wages below w_m the total demand for labor becomes the dashed black line D_A'. Since the wage in the covered sector cannot go below w_m, employment in that sector remains at N_c'. Hence decreases in wages below w_m generate additional employment only in the uncovered sector. For wages below w_m, the total demand for labor is parallel to D_u but shifted to the right by the (constant) covered sector employment of N_c. Hence the new total demand for labor is kinked at x, being steeper for wages below w_m. This is shown by the dashed line xD_A'.

As can be seen, the new equilibrium is at E' with uncovered wage w'; total employment is N_A', less than original total employment N_A. Covered sector employment falls, as predicted, from N_c to N_c'; some workers from

the actual level of employment falls and a surplus of labor (i.e., unemployment) is generated. This situation is exactly analogous to the one that arises when a union succeeds in negotiating a wage above the competitive equilibrium wage, as illustrated in Figure 21-1. The unemployment will also create incentives for people to evade the law by working below the legal minimum wage.

In a competitive labor market, the benefits of the wage increase to workers who remain employed

must be balanced against the cost to workers who become unemployed.

The Ripple Effect

The prediction from the competitive model that the employment effect of a minimum wage is unambiguously negative rests in part on the implicit assumption that all workers are the same. Some economists believe that minimum wage legislation may increase the demand for some

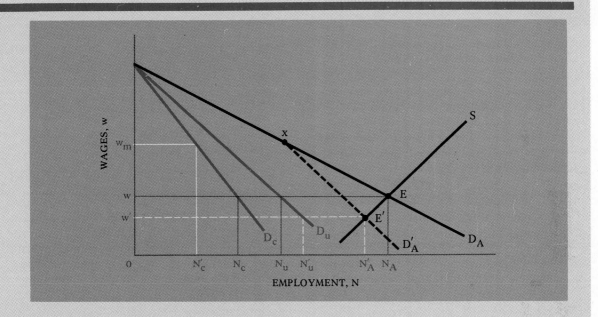

that sector move to the uncovered sector, lowering wages there and raising employment from N_u to N_u'. However, the increase in employment in the uncovered sector is less than the decrease in unemployment in the covered sector, and thus total employment still falls.

Note how the analysis rests on the assumed elasticity of the aggregate labor supply curve. If that curve were perfectly inelastic at N_A, it is obvious that total employment would remain constant. It is interesting to note that total employment would also be constant if the aggregate labor supply curve were perfectly elastic at the original wage w.

types of workers, in particular those who earn just above the minimum wage and whose skills and training do not far exceed those of workers who are directly affected by the legislation. Such workers would be substitutes for workers earning below the minimum wage, and the minimum wage legislation might cause a "ripple effect" whereby the demand for the close substitutes would actually rise. Their presence would make the demand for the sub-minimum wage workers more elastic, thereby reinforcing the reduction in

employment suffered by the latter group. Aggregate employment would still fall.

Skill Differentials and Teenage Unemployment

A further consideration arising from the ripple effect is that wage differentials between different skills might be lessened by minimum wage legislation. This might then reduce the incentives to workers to acquire skills, with serious long-run consequences for productivity in the economy.

Much skill acquisition occurs in on-the-job training. Typically, employees in occupations in which on-the-job training occurs "pay" for their education by receiving low wages in the initial stages of their employment. Minimum wage legislation rules this out. As a result, it has been argued, minimum wage legislation causes severe restrictions on the job opportunities facing teenagers. Instead of being able to "apprentice" in jobs that will lead to productive careers, many teenagers are forced into low-skill, short-term employment that has frequent and prolonged periods of unemployment.

A lot of evidence supports the notion that much of the incidence of unemployment caused by minimum wage legislation is born by teenagers. Several provinces allow for lower minimum wages for young or inexperienced workers and for workers demonstrably in a "learning period." Often such exceptions are objected to as being discriminatory.

Competitiveness

The minimum wage could also drive some firms out of business. This possibility has particular significance in an open economy in which domestic firms compete with foreign firms. An increase in the domestic minimum wage would raise domestic costs relative to foreign costs and hence lead to a reduction in the ability of domestic firms to compete. This consequence has recently been of particular concern to manufacturers in Ontario.

EFFECTIVE MINIMUM WAGES IN A MONOPSONISTIC LABOR MARKET

This case too is exactly analogous to the one in which a union facing a monopsonistic employer succeeds in negotiating a wage increase. By effectively flattening out the labor supply curve, the minimum wage law can simultaneously in-

crease wages and reduce marginal costs as perceived by the employer. Hence wages and employment may both rise. Of course, if the minimum wage is raised above the competitive wage, employment will start to fall again, as in the union case.

When set at the competitive wage, the minimum wage can protect the worker against monopsony power in the same way a union can.

This is illustrated in Figure 21-3.

Discrimination in Labor Markets

Discrimination by race, sex, and other characteristics has often occurred in the North American job market. The economic effects of discrimination against minorities and women take many forms. Discrimination does not wholly explain, but it surely contributes to, higher unemployment rates (fact: in the United States, black unemployment rates are more than twice white unemployment rates) and lower rates of pay (fact: female hourly earnings are at least 25 percent below male hourly earnings). Both lower wages and greater unemployment lead to lower incomes for the workers involved.

They may also lead to different attitudes toward the workplace and toward society. Discrimination affects not only the workers discriminated against but their children, whose aspirations and willingness to undertake the education or training required to "succeed" may be adversely affected. Indeed, it may change the definition given to success. The costs of all this are borne not only by the groups discriminated against but also by society as a whole.

Discrimination has many dimensions. Different types of discrimination (by race, by sex, by age) differ in many respects, and so do the policies needed to deal with them. With respect to the *economics* of discrimination, certain similarities that apply to all types of discrimination make it useful to look at some general features of the economics of discrimination.

A MODEL OF THE EFFECTS OF DISCRIMINATION

We begin by building a simplified picture of a world without discrimination and then introduce discrimination. While this reverses the contemporary problem (predicting the effect of removing discrimination), it provides insight into the effects of discrimination. We are concerned here with discrimination between two sets of workers who are in every sense equally qualified. Our discussion is phrased in terms of black versus white, but it applies equally to female versus male, alien versus citizen, Catholic versus Protestant, French versus English, or any other prejudicial basis for dividing workers.

Suppose there are two groups of equal size in a society. One is white; the other is black. Except for color, the groups are the same—each has the same proportion who are educated to various levels, each has identical distributions of talent, and so on. Occupation E (for elite) requires people of above average education and skills, and occupation O (ordinary) can use anyone, but if wages in the two occupations are the same, employers in occupation O will prefer to hire the above average worker. There is no racial discrimination; everyone is color-blind. The nonmonetary advantages of the two occupations are equal.

The competitive theory of distribution suggests that the wages in E occupations will be bid up slightly above those in O occupations in order that the E jobs attract the workers of above average skills. Whites and blacks of above average skill will flock to E jobs while the others, white and black alike, will have no choice but to seek O jobs. Because skills are equally distributed, each occupation will have half whites and half blacks.

Now we introduce discrimination in its most extreme form. All E occupations are hereafter open only to whites; all O occupations are open to either whites or blacks. The immediate effect is to reduce by 50 percent the supply of job applicants for E occupations (they must be *both* white and above average) and, potentially, to increase by 50 percent the supply of applicants for O jobs (this group includes all blacks and the below average whites).

Wage Level Effects

Suppose, first, that there are no barriers to mobility of labor, that everyone seeks the best job he or she is eligible for, and that wage rates are free to vary so as to equate supply and demand. The analysis is shown in Figure 21-6. Wages rise sharply in E occupations and fall in O occupations. The take-home pay of those in O occupations falls, and while the O group still includes both whites and blacks, it is now approximately two-thirds black.

Discrimination, by changing supply, can decrease the wages and incomes of a group that is discriminated against.

In the longer run, further changes may occur. Notice that total employment in E industries falls. Employers may find ways to utilize slightly below average labor and thus lure the best qualified white workers out of O occupations. While this will raise O wages slightly, it will also make them increasingly "black occupations." An important long-run effect may be that blacks will learn that it no longer pays to acquire above average skills since they are forced by discrimination to work in jobs that do not use them. Yet if they never acquire the skills they will be locked into the O occupations even if the discriminatory policy is reversed. And their children may conclude that education is for whites only.

Employment Effects

For a number of reasons, labor market discrimination may have adverse employment ef-

FIGURE 21-6
Economic Discrimination: Wage Level Effects

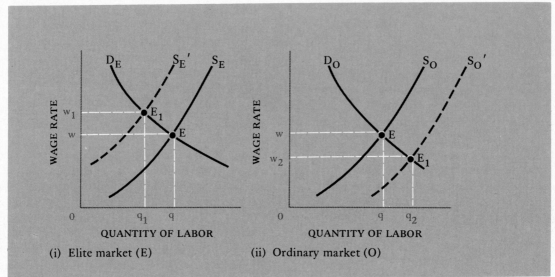

(i) Elite market (E)   (ii) Ordinary market (O)

If market E discriminates against one group and market O does not, the supply curve will shift upward in E and downward in O, and wages will rise in E and fall in O. Market E requires above average skills, while market O requires only ordinary skills. When there is no discrimination, demands and supplies are D_E and S_E in market E, and D_O and S_O in market O. Initially, the wage rate is w and employment is q in each market. When all blacks are barred from E occupations, the supply curve shifts to S_E' and the wage earned by the remaining workers, all of whom are white, rises to w_1. Blacks put out of work in the E occupation now seek work in the O occupation. The resulting shift in the supply curve to S_O' brings down the wage to w_2 in the O occupations. Since all blacks are in O occupations, they have a lower wage rate than many whites. The average white wage is higher than the average black wage.

fects that are even more important than effects on wage levels. Labor is not perfectly mobile, wages are not perfectly flexible downward, and not everyone who is denied employment in an E occupation for which he or she is trained and qualified will be willing to take a "demeaning" O job.

If wages cannot fall to the market-clearing level (say, because of minimum wage laws), the increase in supply of labor to O occupations will cause excess supply and result in unemployment of labor in O occupations. Since, in our model, blacks dominate these occupations, blacks will bear the brunt of the extra unemployment. This is illustrated in Figure 21-7(i). A similar result will occur if labor is not fully mobile between oc-

cupations, say because many of the O occupation jobs are in parts of the country to which the workers discriminated against are unable or unwilling to move. See Figure 21-7(ii). Potential O workers who cannot move to where jobs are available become unemployed or withdraw from the labor force.

A different mechanism can produce the identical result if those persons who lose their E jobs as a result of discrimination withdraw from the labor force. They may do just this if they have the skill and training to do the more respectable and more rewarding E jobs. Indeed, it may be less demeaning to accept unemployment compensation or even welfare than to accept the only jobs that the discriminatory society offers them.

FIGURE 21-7
Economic Discrimination: Employment Effects

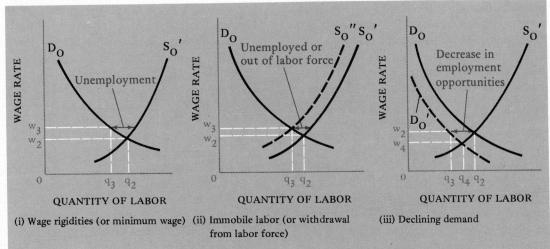

(i) Wage rigidities (or minimum wage)   (ii) Immobile labor (or withdrawal from labor force)   (iii) Declining demand

Increasing supply and/or decreasing demand in occupations in which those discriminated against are the major sources of labor can increase unemployment. In each part of the diagram, the curves D_O and S_O' are those from Figure 21-6(ii); they show the market for O workers after the discriminatory policies are put into effect. In each case the wage w_2 would clear the market and provide employment of q_2.

(i) If the wage rate cannot fall below w_3, perhaps because of a minimum wage law, employment will fall to q_3 and unemployment will occur in the amount shown by the colored arrow.

(ii) If some of the potential workers in O occupations are unable or unwilling to take employment in O jobs, the supply curve will not be S_O' but S_O''. While O wages will rise somewhat to w_3, employment will be only q_3 and a number of workers, shown by the colored arrow, will not be employed. Whether they are recorded as "unemployed" or as having withdrawn from the labor force will depend on the official definitions.

(iii) If demand is declining in O occupations over time, say from D_O to D_O', either wages and employment will fall to w_4 and q_4 or wages will be maintained but employment will fall to q_3. The colored arrow illustrates the latter case, where the fall in employment is q_2q_3.

In the long term these unemployment effects may be increased by sociological and economic forces. Children of those discriminated against may well take as role models those who have made a life outside the labor force. Technological changes in the economy tend to decrease the demand for less skilled labor of the kind required in O occupations, which become increasingly oversupplied. This possibility is sketched in Figure 21-7(iii).

All these theoretical possibilities have their counterparts in the real world. We shall discuss them briefly with respect to female/male differences in North America.

FEMALE-MALE DIFFERENTIALS IN LABOR MARKETS

Discrimination reduces a group's ability to get and keep jobs, as well as the wages earned in those jobs. Evidence from the United States suggests that discrimination against blacks results in higher unemployment rates for black workers than for white workers. But the problems of women in the labor force result more from lower wages than from unemployment.

Traditionally denied employment in many "male" occupations, adult women in the last three decades have increased their labor force participation from 30 percent in 1961 to almost 50 percent in 1980. (This is still short of the 80 percent participation rate of adult males.) Moreover, the female unemployment rate is only 1 or 2 percent higher than the rate for males. Women have steadily increased their participation in "higher status" occupations, including managerial, sales, scientific, and technical jobs.

But getting jobs is not the whole story. It has long been clear that women and men make and are offered different occupational choices, that proportionately fewer women than men reach higher paying jobs in the occupations in which both work, and that those who do, do so more slowly. As a result, average earned income of females in the labor force is well below that of males of similar ages. A number of careful studies have established that in the 1970s labor market earnings were approximately 25 percent lower for employed women than for employed men of the same age and race.

To what extent do these differences reflect discrimination against women and to what extent such other sex-linked characteristics as the voluntary choice of different lifetime patterns of labor force participation? The statistics show that, on average, women have fewer years of education, training, and work experience than men of the same age. The average working female is less mobile occupationally and geographically than her male counterpart. At least some of these facts reflect voluntary choice; for example, many women decide to withdraw from the labor force, or to work only part-time, in order to have and raise children.

Yet direct discrimination against women has been important in labor markets and continues to play a role today. Indeed, some direct discrimination by employers is vigorously defended as being "protective." A striking example came to public attention recently. Four West Virginia women told of having themselves sterilized in order to keep their well-paying jobs in a plant operated by the American Cyanamid Corporation. That company has a policy of removing women of child-bearing age from, or not hiring

them for, jobs that expose them to lead or other substances that could damage a fetus.

The extent of direct discrimination in an occupation may be measured by taking groups with similar characteristics and comparing their employment and pay status. For example, comparing starting salaries in college teaching of new Ph.D.s from the same graduate schools in a given subject and a given class of institutional employment, Professors Frank Stafford and George Johnson found the average pay of females was about 6 percent below that of males (with allowance for differences in age and prior experience). They attributed this part of a larger male-female pay differential to direct discrimination.

Women have also suffered indirect discrimination. They have been refused admission or discouraged from seeking entry into certain occupations; for example, they have traditionally been pushed into nursing rather than medicine, social work rather than law, and secretarial rather than managerial training programs. Similarly, there is ample evidence that many women in dual career marriages are under substantial pressure to put their husband's job needs first. Girls raised in a culture in which their education seems less important than that of their brothers, or where they are raised to think of themselves as potential homemakers and are urged to prepare themselves to attract and serve a husband, are less likely to acquire the skills or the opportunities for many high-paying forms of employment that are wholly within their capabilities.

Discrimination against women in job opportunities is being eliminated much more quickly than discrimination against racial minorities; the effect of Women's Liberation on attitudes—male as well as female—has been very great in a very short time. Between 1971 and 1979 the fraction of earned doctorates awarded to women in North America rose from 14 to 25 percent, and by 1980 nearly half of the new graduate enrollments were women, so this upward trend is likely to continue. In 1979, 15 percent of first professional degrees (law, medicine, etc.) were awarded to women—compared to 6.5 percent eight years earlier. Current enrollments in these fields are roughly 30 percent women. These trends reflect affirmative action on the part of schools, changed attitudes on the part of women, and brighter employment prospects for women than even ten years before.

WHO LOSES FROM DISCRIMINATION?

Obviously, the victims lose as a result of labor market discrimination. To the extent that they are denied employment or receive lower pay than they otherwise would, minorities and women are punished for their race or sex. But it would be a mistake to think that they are the only losers. Society loses too because of the efficiency losses that discrimination causes, and in other ways.

Efficiency losses arise for several reasons. If women or blacks are not given equal pay with white males for equal work, the labor force will not be allocated so as to get the most out of society's resources. When people are kept from doing the jobs at which they are most productive and must instead produce goods or services that society values less, the total value of goods and services produced is reduced. And when prejudice increases unemployment, it reduces the nation's total output.

The gainers from discrimination are those who earn the higher pay that comes from limiting supply in their occupations, those who get the jobs that blacks and women would otherwise have held, and the bigots who gain pleasure from not having to work with "them" or to consume services provided by "them." But if the total output of society is less, the net losses will have to be borne by the society as a whole.

Beyond the efficiency losses that discrimination imposes on society are further economic and social costs. Increased welfare or unemployment payments may be required, and the costs of enforcing antidiscrimination laws must be paid. The costs of discrimination also include increased crime, hostility, and violence. These things are all by-products of unemployment, pov-

erty, and frustration. Discrimination, if not attacked and rolled back, has one more cost, perhaps the most important: a sense of shame in a society that does not do what is necessary to eliminate the barriers to equal treatment.

Summary

1. A wage-setting union entering a competitive market can raise wages, but only at the cost of reducing employment and creating a pool of unsatisfied former workers who would like to work at the going wage but are unable to gain employment.

2. A wage-setting union entering a monopsonistic market may increase both employment and wages over some range. If, however, it sets the wage above the competitive level, it too will create a pool of unsatisfied workers who are unable to get the jobs they want at the going wage.

3. An employers' association is a group of employers who band together for the purpose of adopting a common policy in labor negotiations. A union is an association of workers that speaks for the workers in negotiations with the employers. Unions are subdivided into craft unions and industrial unions. In general, individual union members belong to a local union to which they pay dues (part of which goes to the national union). The local union belongs to a national or international union. A federation is a loose organization of national unions. The principal federation in Canada today is the Canadian Labour Congress.

4. Three kinds of bargaining arrangements are (a) the open shop, where, though a union represents its members, union membership is not a condition of getting or keeping a job; (b) the closed shop, where only workers who are already union members may be employed; and (c) the union shop, where the employer is free to hire anyone, but where all new employees must join the recognized union within a specified period.

5. Canadian unionism has evolved enormously since its beginnings in the latter half of the nineteenth century. International unions affiliated with the American Federation of Labor have played a major role, but almost complete autonomy is now enjoyed by Canadian locals.

6. Unions must decide on their goals. There is a basic conflict between the goals of raising wages by restricting supply (thereby reducing the union's employed membership) and preserving employment opportunities for members and potential members. Other trade-offs concern wages and job security, and wages and fringe benefits.

7. An effective minimum wage has effects similar to those of a wage-setting union. In a competitive labor market employment will fall, thereby creating incentive to violate the law. In a monopsonistic labor market minimum wage legislation can raise wages to the competitive level *and* raise employment.

8. Discrimination by race and by sex has played a role in labor markets. Direct discrimination can affect wages and employment opportunities by limiting the supply in the best-paying occupations and increasing it in less attractive occupations. Economic theory leads to the predictions that groups subject to discrimination will earn lower wages and/or suffer higher levels of unemployment than their counterparts who do not suffer discrimination. These predictions are borne out in the labor force experiences of blacks (and other minorities) and women.

9. Precisely how much of the wage and employment differentials between whites and blacks and males and females is due to discrimination is a matter of continuing research. Indirect discrimination has had an effect through limiting the opportunities for education and training available to those subject to discrimination and through lowering people's aspirations in their choices of training and of careers.

10. Discrimination imposes costs on the victims of discrimination. In addition it leads to inef-

ficiency and loss of output and is costly in other ways.

Topics for Review

Monopsony power
Union power
Collective bargaining
Goals of unions
Economic discrimination
Wage effects and employment effects of economic discrimination
Direct and indirect discrimination

Discussion Questions

1. A union that has bargaining rights in two plants of the same company in different provinces often insists on "equal pay for equal work" in the two plants. It may not always insist on equal pay for men and women in the same jobs. Can you see any economic reasons for such a distinction?

2. Predict the effect of each of the following on the wages of employees in the affected industries. What, if anything, can you say about total earnings of all employees in each case?
   a. an increase in the production of coal due to the increasing shortage of other fossil fuels
   b. passage of a law permitting public employees to bargain collectively and to strike
   c. reducing the apprenticeship period for entry into a skilled trade from five years to two years
   d. making a Ph.D. degree compulsory for all junior college teachers.

3. Since the passage of the Trade Unions Act of 1872, unions have been exempt from laws prohibiting conspiracies in restraint of trade. What do you think about this exemption? Why should wage fixing not be in violation of the law when price fixing is?

4. Why were craft unions more successful than reform-oriented industrial unions in the late nineteenth century in North America? What happened to change this in the 1930s?

5. A labor union that has a union shop contract with a particular employer is in some ways in the same position as a firm that has a monopoly of key raw materials used by the firm. Do you see any differences? Contrast the considerations that enter into the question of the best price (or wage) to charge. Who do you think is in a stronger position to bargain with General

Motors, the United Auto Workers or the Goodyear Tire and Rubber Company?

6. Suppose it is accepted that, on average, unions have raised the wages of their members. Can this be reconciled with the low and declining percentage of employees who are union members?

7. Interns and residents in many Ontario hospitals are seeking to organize in an attempt to raise their pay. If they succeed, what effect will this have on the incomes of doctors?

8. "The great increase in the number of women entering the labor force for the first time means that relatively more women than men earn beginning salaries. It is therefore not evidence of discrimination that the average wage earned by females is less than that earned by males." Discuss.

9. "One can judge the presence or absence of discrimination by looking at the proportion of the population in different occupations." Does such information help? Does it suffice? Consider each of the following examples. Relative to their numbers in the total population, there are:

   a. too many blacks and too few Jews among professional athletes

   b. too few male secretaries

   c. too few female judges

10. "Of nearly 40 million working women, 40 percent are in traditionally female occupations—secretaries, nurses, cashiers, waitresses, elementary school teachers, beauticians, maids, and sales clerks, for example. While this may result from past sex stereotyping, the notion that only a woman can do these jobs may also benefit women by preserving employment opportunities for them, given the high unemployment rates among other groups such as teenagers." Discuss this argument.

Interest and the Return on Capital

22

To many Marxists, the capitalist is a villain. To many socialists, the capitalist is at best a dispensable drone. To many liberals, capitalists are an important part of the production process, as necessary as farmers and factory workers. To many conservatives, the capitalist is a hero who steers the economy through the risky channels that lead to ever higher living standards.

A capitalist is nothing more than someone who owns capital, which we have defined as all manmade aids to further production. A key characteristic of capital is that it is durable. This means that it has two prices associated with it. The first is the price at which ownership of the capital good may be purchased. The second is the price at which its services may be hired for a period of time. This is called the rental price of capital.

At the outset let us deal with three common misconceptions.

First, capital itself is neither villain nor dispensable drone in the productive process. None but the most extreme and unrealistic members of the back-to-nature school would disagree. A primitive society in which there are no capital goods—no spear, no lever, no stone for grinding grain, no jug for carrying water—has never occurred in recorded human history.

Second, payment for the use of capital, while not necessary, serves such important functions that it would be hard to eliminate it without serious consequences. Early Communist rulers thought differently. Such payments were officially barred during the years following the Russian Revolution of 1917. The trouble with doing this, however, is that capital is scarce;

most producers would like to have more of it than they have. The available supply must somehow be allocated among the competing demands for it. The state, of course, can allocate it. But how? Any state that is interested in maximizing production will want to allocate scarce capital to its most productive uses. One effective way of doing this is to assign a "price" to capital that is meant to reflect its productivity and to allow firms to use more capital only if the capital earns enough to cover this price. Today all Communist states do this. Furthermore, their planners give a good deal of attention to setting the correct price for capital.

Third, capital does not need to be in private hands, with the price paid for capital being income for its private owners. In many Communist countries capital is owned by the state, and payments for its use go to the state rather than to private "capitalists." The desirability of private versus public ownership of the "means of production" (the term often used in socialist and Communist literature to describe capital) is still debated hotly, a matter that economic analysis has not resolved.

Capital is indispensable in any modern economy, and its efficient use requires that it be priced. When capital is privately owned, payment of its price contributes to the income of its owners; when it is publicly owned, payment of its price contributes to the revenues of the state.

The Productivity or Efficiency of Capital

In what sense is capital productive? To be productive it must lead to higher output than could be possible without it. Rarely if ever does anyone make a consumer good with the aid of only such simple tools as nature provides. Productive effort goes first into the manufacture of capital—the tools, machines, and other goods that are desired not for themselves but as aids to making other commodities. The capital goods are then used to make consumers' goods. The use of capi-

tal renders production processes roundabout. Instead of making what is wanted directly, producers engage in the indirect process of first making capital goods that are then used to make consumer goods.

In many cases production is very roundabout indeed. For example, a worker may be employed in a factory that makes machines that are used in mining coal; the coal may be burned by a power plant to make electricity; the electricity may provide power for a factory that makes machine tools; the tools may be used to make a tractor; the tractor may be used by a potato farmer to help in the production of potatoes; and the potatoes may be eaten by consumers. This kind of indirect production is worthwhile when the farmer, using a tractor, can produce more potatoes than could be produced by applying all the factors of production involved in the chain directly to the production of potatoes (using only such tools as were provided by nature). In fact, the roundabout capital-using method of production very often leads to more output than the direct method. The difference between the flows of output that would result from the two methods is called either the **productivity of capital** or the **efficiency of capital.**

The extra output, however, is not achieved without cost.

Generally speaking, a decision to increase the amount of capital available entails a present sacrifice and a future gain.

The present sacrifice occurs because resources are diverted from producing consumption goods to producing capital goods. The future gain occurs because in the long run production will be higher with the new capital than without it (even after allowing for maintenance and replacement of capital goods).

THE RATE OF RETURN ON CAPITAL

Whenever capital is productive, its use must yield a return in excess of the amounts required to cover the costs associated with all other fac-

Human Capital

While capital goods are usually discussed in terms of tangible assets such as buildings or machines, the notion of a capital asset as something that produces an increase in the stream of future output suggests another sort of capital good. Consider a high school graduate who has enough schooling to get and keep a job. Instead of taking a job, however, she elects to go to a university, and possibly to graduate or professional school. During her university career, her contribution to society's current output is small (only a summer job perhaps), but because of her education, her lifetime contribution to production may be substantially larger than it would have been had she taken a job after high school.

The choice of whether to take a job now or to continue one's education has all the basic elements of an investment decision, and it is useful to regard the student as making an investment to acquire capital. Because the capital is embodied in a person—in terms of greater skills, knowledge, and the like—rather than in a machine, this is known as acquiring **human capital.** Major elements of human capital are health and education of all sorts. An ex-

tended education program requires, for example, that resources be withdrawn from the production of goods for current consumption; the resources include materials in the school, the services of the teachers, and the time and talents of the pupils. The education is productive if the difference between the value of the lifetime output of the trained worker and the lifetime output of the untrained one exceeds the value of the resources—teachers, buildings, and so on—used up in training her. If so, education increases the value of total production of the economy.

The payoff to education as an investment in human capital has been studied extensively, and many investigators have concluded that investment in higher education pays, in the sense just defined. Of course, education also has other payoffs; it may be valued for cultural or social reasons, and it may bestow benefits or costs on individuals other than those who are educated. But the fact that it may be more than a capital investment does not prevent it from being an investment. The same is true of a painting by Rembrandt.

tors of production. This return is merely a measure of the productivity or efficiency of capital. How is it determined? Take the receipts from the sale of the goods produced by a firm and subtract the appropriate costs for purchased goods and materials, for labor, for land, and for the manager's own contributed talents. Subtract also an allowance for the taxes the firm will have to pay, and what is left may be called the **gross return to capital.**

It is convenient to divide gross return into four components.

1. **Depreciation** is an allowance for the decrease in the value of a capital good as a result of using it in production.

2. The **pure return on capital** is the amount that capital could earn in a riskless investment in equilibrium.

3. The **risk premium** compensates the owners for the actual risks of the enterprise.

4. **Economic profit** is the residual after all other deductions have been made from the gross return. It may be positive, negative, or zero.

The items in this list are related. The productivity of capital is its gross return minus its depreciation. This is also called the net return on capital, and it is composed of items 2, 3, and 4 in the list. The opportunity cost of capital is composed of the first three items. In equilibrium the gross return on capital must be just enough to cover its opportunity cost; item 4 will be zero. In a market economy, positive and negative economic profits are a signal that resources should be reallocated because earnings exceed opportunity costs in some lines of production and fall short of them in other lines. Profits are thus a phenomenon of disequilibrium.

In order to study the return to capital in its simplest form, we consider an economy that is in equilibrium with respect to the allocation of existing factors of production among all their possible uses. Thus economic profits are zero in every productive activity. This does not mean that the owners of capital get nothing; it means rather that the gross return to capital does not now include a profit element that signals the need to reallocate resources.

To simplify further at the outset, we assume that there is no risk in this economy. Consequently the gross return to capital does not include a risk premium.

We have now simplified to the point where the net return to capital is all pure return (item 2 in the list), while the gross return is pure return plus depreciation (items 1 and 2). What determines the size of the pure return on capital? Why is it high in some time periods and low in others? What causes it to change?

In discussing such questions, it is usual to deal with a rate of return *per dollar* of capital. This concept requires placing a money value on a unit of capital (the "price of capital goods") and a money value on the stream of earnings resulting from the productivity of capital. If we let X stand for the annual value of the gross return on a unit of capital, and P for the price of a unit of capital, the ratio X/P may be defined as the **rate of return on capital**. As a preliminary to understanding the determinants of the rate of return on capital, we must define two key concepts: marginal efficiency of capital and present value.

The Marginal Efficiency of Capital

It is convenient to think of society as having a quantity of capital that can be measured in physical units. The term **capital stock** refers to this total quantity of capital.[1] As with any other factor of production, there is an average and a marginal productivity of capital. The marginal productivity of capital is the contribution to output of the last unit of capital added to a fixed quantity of other factors.

Marginal productivity is a physical measure, an amount of output per unit of capital. To obtain a value measure we value the output and the capital at their market prices and express one as a ratio of the other. This gives the monetary return on the marginal dollar's worth of capital and it is called the **marginal efficiency of capital** (*MEC*).[2] A schedule that relates the rate of return on each additional dollar of capital stock to the size of the capital stock is called the **marginal efficiency of capital schedule**. The *MEC* schedule is constructed on the assumptions that the society's population is fixed and that *technology is unchanging*. These assumptions are made in order to focus on changes in the quantity of capital, other things remaining equal. As more and more capital is accumulated, with unchanging technical knowledge and population, the ratio of capital to labor increases. This is called **capital deepening**. To see why it occurs, consider the difference between a single firm and the whole economy.

When a single firm wants to expand output, it can buy another piece of land, build a factory identical to the one it now has, and hire new labor to operate the new plant. In this way the

---

[1] The idea of stock of capital being measured by a single number is a simplification. Society's stock of capital goods is made up of factories, machines, bridges, roads, and other man-made aids to further production. For expository purposes, it is useful to assume that all these can be reduced to some common unit and summed to obtain a measure of the society's *physical* stock of capital.

[2] Like the other *marginal* concepts that we have encountered, the *MEC* is the ratio of two changes. In this case, it is the change in the return of capital divided by the change in the capital stock that brought it about.

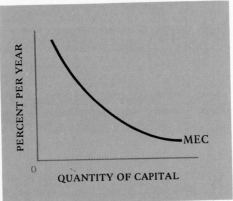

FIGURE 22-1
The Marginal Efficiency of Capital

The *MEC* curve shows the relation between the size of the capital stock and the rate of return on the marginal unit of capital. The *MEC* schedule slopes downward because of the hypothesis of diminishing returns applied to capital. Each successive unit of capital adds less to output than each previous unit. Thus the curve, which relates the value of the additional output of each additional dollar's worth of capital added to the capital stock, is downward-sloping.

firm can replicate what it already has. Since each worker in the new factory can be given the same amount of capital to work with as each worker in the old factory, output per worker and per unit of capital can remain unchanged as output rises. Increasing the quantity of capital without changing the proportions of factors used is called **capital widening.**

For the economy as a whole, capital widening is possible only as long as there are unemployed quantities of labor and other factors of production. Additional workers, for example, must be drawn from somewhere. In a fully employed economy, what one small firm can do the whole economy cannot do. If the size of the capital stock is to increase while the total labor force remains constant, the amount of capital per worker must increase. Capital deepening must occur.

What is the effect of capital deepening on the marginal efficiency of capital? Because capital is subject to diminishing returns, as are all other factors of production, the amount of output per unit of capital will fall as capital deepening occurs. Each unit of capital has, as it were, fewer units of labor to work with than previously. As more and more capital deepening occurs, the marginal return to capital declines. The *MEC* schedule when plotted graphically is thus downward-sloping (see Figure 22-1).

A Recapitulation of Terminology

The theory of capital can seem quite bewildering on first acquaintance because there are so many terms that mean almost the same thing. Let us review the standard terminology. The *productivity* and the *efficiency* of capital are the same thing; they are measured for a firm by the *return on its capital*. This return is usually measured as an amount per dollar's worth of capital, which makes it a *rate of return on capital*. This rate may be calculated as an average over all capital, in which case it is called the *average efficiency of capital* (or *average rate of return*); or it may be calculated on the last unit of capital, in which case it is called the *marginal efficiency of capital* (or *marginal rate of return*). The *MEC* schedule relates the rate of return on the marginal unit of capital to the total capital stock. It shows that as the total stock grows the marginal return on each additional unit declines.

The Present Value of Future Returns

The efficiency of capital takes the form of producing a stream of output extending into the future that, as it is sold, yields a stream of gross returns to the firm. How is the price of capital related to the efficiency of capital? To know what price a firm would be willing to pay for a piece of capital, we must be able to put a present value on the stream of gross returns that the capital will yield to the firm.

We assume first that the price level is constant; later we consider the effects of inflation.

The value of a single future payment. How much would you be prepared to pay *now* to acquire the right to receive $100 in cash in one year's time? Say the interest rate on savings accounts is 5 percent. How much would you have to deposit in a savings bank now in order to have $100 a year from now? It would surely not be profitable for you to pay more than such an amount. Alternatively, what is the most you could borrow today in return for your promise to repay $100 in one year if the interest rate is 5 percent?

Both approaches can be reduced to the question, how much money *now* is equivalent to $100 in one year's time if the interest rate is 5 percent? Letting X stand for this unknown amount, we can write $X(1.05) = \$100$. Thus $X = \$100/1.05 = \$95.24$, which tells us that the value today of $100 next year is $95.24 if the interest rate is 5 percent. That sum is said to be the present value of $100 next year. In general, the term **present value (PV)** refers to the value now of a payment, or payments, to be made in the future.

The particular numerical value depends on the interest rate used to "discount" (i.e., reduce to its present value) the $100 to be received one year hence. If the interest rate is 7 percent, the present value of the $100 receivable next year is $100/1.07 = \$93.45$. In general, the present value of X dollars one year hence at an interest rate of i per year is

$$PV = \frac{X}{(1+i)}$$

(Note that in this expression a rate of interest of 5 percent is written $i = .05$, so that $1 + i$ is 1.05.)

One hundred dollars two years hence has a present value (at an interest rate of 5 percent) of

$$\frac{\$100.00}{(1.05)(1.05)} = \$90.70$$

because $90.70 put in a savings bank now would be worth $100 in two years. In general, we may write, for the present value of X dollars after t years at i percent,

$$PV = \frac{X}{(1+i)^t}$$

The present value of a given sum will be smaller, the further away is the payment date and the higher is the rate of interest.

The value of an infinite stream of payments. So much for a single sum payable in the future; now consider the present value of a stream of income that continues indefinitely. At first that might seem very high since as time passes the total received grows without reaching any limit. Consideration of the previous section suggests, however, that a person will not value highly payments that are far in the future. To find the present value of $100 a year, payable forever, we need only ask how much money would have to be invested now at an interest rate of i percent per year to obtain $100 each year. This is simply $i \times X = \$100$, where i is the interest rate and X the sum required. This tells us that the present value of the stream of $100 forever (called an **annuity** of $100) is

$$PV = \frac{\$100}{i}$$

If the interest rate were 10 percent ($i = .10$), present value would be $1,000, which is another way of saying that $1,000 invested at 10 percent would yield $100 per year, forever. Notice that *PV* here, as above, is *inversely* related to the rate of interest. The higher the interest rate, the less is the present value of any stream of payments that goes on forever.

If you can buy an asset at its present value, the investment will yield neither gain nor loss. For example, if you buy an annuity conferring the right to receive $100 a year forever for $1,000, and borrow the capital at an interest rate of 10 percent, annual receipts ($100) and interest payments ($100) will be exactly offsetting.

THE VALUE OF AN ASSET

Many assets are valued only because of the streams of income they are expected to produce.[3]

[3] Assets can yield utilities in forms other than income streams. A painting, a house, and valuable jewelry are cases in point. They may be regarded as yielding a stream of utilities each of which could be given a monetary value.

For any such asset, its value will tend to be equal to the present value of the income stream produced. This is often called the **capitalized value** of the asset producing the income stream.

Every expected income stream can be reduced to a present value. In the previous section we considered finding the present values of amounts at specific future dates and of infinite streams of income. All actual streams of income can be treated as the sum or difference of such streams and amounts; thus the present value of *any* stream of future payments can be computed.[4] As a result, the capitalized value of an asset can always be computed.

What then determines the market price of any existing asset that will produce a stream of output over time? The asset might be a piece of land, a machine, a contract for a baseball player's services, or an apartment house. The asset produces a stream of output, and market conditions will determine the price of this output. This allows us to convert the stream of output into an equivalent stream of money. But we know how to calculate the present value of a stream of money, and this is what people will be willing to pay for it. Thus:

The equilibrium market price of the asset will be equal to the capitalized value of the asset – which is equal to the present value of the stream of gross returns associated with it.

A Theory of Interest Rate Determination

Given the concepts just discussed, we can develop a theory that relates *MEC* for the economy as a whole to the rate of interest. It is helpful to begin with the behavior of an individual firm.

---

[4] For example, receiving $100 per year for three years can be considered either as the present value of $100 next year plus the *PV* of $100 two years hence plus the *PV* of $100 three years hence, or as the *difference* between the *PV* of $100 received each year from now to infinity and the *PV* of $100 received from year four to infinity.

THE DEMAND FOR ADDITIONAL CAPITAL BY A FIRM

Suppose that for $8,000 a firm can purchase a machine that yields gross returns of $1,000 a year into the indefinite future. Also suppose that the firm can borrow (and lend) money at an interest rate of 10 percent. The present value of the stream of returns produced by the machine is $1,000/0.10 = $10,000; the present value of $8,000 now is of course $8,000. Clearly the firm can make money by purchasing the machine.

Another way to see this is to suppose that the firm has only two uses for its money: to buy the machine or to lend out the $8,000 at 10 percent interest. It will pay to buy the machine, for the firm can do so and earn $1,000 a year net, while if it lends the $8,000 at 10 percent, it will earn only $800 per year.

To restate the argument in more general terms: If X is the annual stream of gross returns produced by the machine, if P is its purchase price, and if i is the interest rate that correctly states the opportunity cost of capital to the firm, then the capital good should be purchased if

$$\frac{X}{i} > P$$

The term X/i is the present value of the stream of returns produced by the capital good; in other words, the capitalized value of the asset.

It pays to purchase a capital good whenever the present value of its future stream of gross returns is greater than the purchase price of the capital good.

This relationship can be looked at in another way by rearranging terms in the above algebraic inequality to yield

$$\frac{X}{P} > i$$

The expression X/P shows the annual gross returns produced by the capital good as a fraction of the price of the good. Earlier we defined this as the rate of return on the capital and called it *MEC*. In this form the condition is restated to say:

It pays to purchase a capital good whenever its *MEC* is greater than the interest rate that could be earned on the money invested in it.[5]

The firm will go on investing in new capital equipment as long as its rate of return, the *MEC*, exceeds the opportunity cost of capital, *i*. *MEC* declines as the firm's capital stock rises, and the firm will reach equilibrium with respect to its capital stock when *MEC* is equal to *i*.

THE ECONOMY AS A WHOLE

Assume for the moment that the interest rate is free to vary and that the only demand to borrow money is from firms seeking funds to invest in new capital equipment. The whole economy has an *MEC* schedule showing how the return on the marginal dollar of new capital declines as the capital stock grows. This *MEC* schedule represents the market demand curve for capital (since each firm will wish to acquire capital until *MEC* = *i*).

A Fixed Stock of Capital

Since the existing stock of capital can be changed only very slowly, we may take the stock as fixed over short-term periods. This stock will have an *MEC* that determines the amount that can be made by investing in a bit more capital. If the rate of interest were lower than this, there would be a rush to borrow money for profitable investment and the rate would be bid up. When the capital stock, technical knowledge — and hence the *MEC* — are given, the interest rate will tend to equal the *MEC* in equilibrium. This is illustrated in Figure 22-2.

A Growing Stock of Capital

Over time, firms and households save and invest in new capital equipment, causing the capital

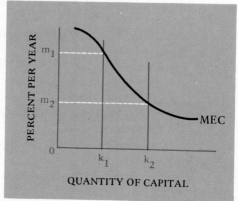

FIGURE 22-2

The Equilibrium Rate of Interest for a Fixed Capital Stock

The rate of interest tends toward the *MEC*. When the economy has a stock of capital of k_1, the rate of interest will tend toward m_1. If the stock of capital grows to k_2, the interest rate will tend to fall to m_2. Alternatively, k_1 and k_2 could be the capital stock in two otherwise similar economies. The interest rate would be higher in the economy where capital was scarce than in the economy where capital was plentiful.

stock to grow. This is shown in Figure 22-2 by a rightward shifting of the vertical line indicating the given capital stock. This has the effect of reducing both the marginal efficiency of capital and the equilibrium interest rate, as shown in Figure 22-2. In an economy with static technology and fixed supplies of land and labor, capital accumulation will tend to lower the marginal efficiency of capital and the rate of interest.

The growth of technical knowledge provides new productive uses for capital. This tends to push the *MEC* schedule outward and *ceteris paribus* will raise *MEC and* the rate of interest.

The accumulation of capital tends to lower the interest rate and the marginal efficiency of capital. The growth of technical knowledge tends to raise both rates.[6]

---

[5] In this chapter we assume that the rate of interest reflects the opportunity cost of capital to the firm. We saw on page 200 that this may not always be the case. When the market rate of interest and the firm's own opportunity cost of capital diverge, the *MEC* must be equated to the latter, not the former.

[6] Graphs illustrating the two effects will be found on page 919.

The Pure and the Market Rates of Interest

The above discussion refers to what is called the **pure rate of interest.** This is the rate of interest that would rule in equilibrium in a riskless economy when all lending and borrowing is to provide funds for investing in productive capital. The discussion allows us to isolate the influences that the size of the capital stock and the efficiency of capital exert on the interest rate.

The actual interest rate ruling at any moment of time is called the **market rate of interest.** This rate will be influenced by the pure rate, but it will diverge from the pure rate because it is influenced by additional forces that do not influence the pure rate.

FURTHER DETERMINANTS OF THE MARKET RATE OF INTEREST

Other Demands for Money to Borrow

Households borrow money to buy goods on time and to buy houses and financial assets such as stocks and bonds. Provincial and municipal governments borrow to build highways and schools. The federal government borrows to finance part of its expenditures. Each of these is a major component of the aggregate demand for funds to borrow.

Government Control of Interest Rates

Not only is the government a borrower of funds, it also affects the supply of funds available for lending. (We shall see how it does this when we study monetary policy in Chapter 38.) Governments commonly influence the rate of interest for purposes of public policy.

Bank Administration of Interest Rates

The rate of interest does not fluctuate in response to every minor fluctuation in demand and supply. As a result, the interest rate is not always determined in such a way as to equate i with MEC. Banks, for example, consider many factors when they fix the rate of interest that they charge on loans. They are reluctant to change

these rates every time changes occur in the demand for money to borrow. If there is an excess demand for loanable funds (perhaps because the MEC is much greater than the interest rate), banks, rather than raise the interest rate, will often ration the available supply of funds among their customers. In doing this they follow such criteria as the borrower's credit rating, how long the banker has known the borrower, and the amount of business the borrower does. This is called **credit rationing.** It is commonly found in lending institutions in most Western countries. When the market rate of interest is below the pure return on capital, money will appear "tight" —hard to borrow—to the typical business person.

Expectations About Business Conditions

In discussing the willingness of firms to borrow money and invest it in capital goods, we have stressed the relation between the rate of interest and the marginal efficiency of capital. Even though capital is physically productive in the sense that more can be produced with it than without it, no one will wish to invest in new equipment if there is no demand for the products produced by the capital goods. In times of severe business depression, the demand to borrow and invest money may fall to very low levels as a result of a declining demand by households for consumption goods.

Market expectations are incorporated in the marginal efficiency framework by recognizing that the efficiency of capital is measured in terms of the *values* (not the quantities) of goods it produces and that these values depend on people's willingness to buy the goods. The MEC is probably very elastic in a fully employed economy so that a small reduction in the rate of interest will lead to a large increase in investment in new capital. When a depression develops, however, and the output of existing capital cannot be sold, it might not be worth borrowing money for new investment even at very low rates of interest. In either case it is expectations about future events that matter.

The Rate of Inflation

An inflation means that the purchasing power of money is falling. When this occurs, it becomes very important to distinguish between the real rate and the money rate of interest. The **money rate of interest** is measured simply in dollars paid. If you pay me $8 interest for a $100 loan for one year, the money rate is 8 percent.

Consider further my $100 loan to you at 8 percent. The real rate that I earn depends on what happens to the overall level of prices in the economy. If the price level remains constant over the year, then the real rate that I earn will also be 8 percent. This is because I can buy 8 percent more real goods and services with the $108 that you repay me than with $100 that I lent you. However, if the price level were to rise by 8 percent, the real rate would be zero because the $108 you repay me will buy the same quantity of real goods as did the $100 I gave up. If I were unlucky enough to have lent money at 8 percent in a year in which prices rose by 10 percent, the real rate would be minus 2 percent.

The real rate of interest concerns the ratio of the purchasing power of the money returned to the purchasing power of the money borrowed, and it may be different from the money rate. The **real rate of interest** is the *difference* between the money rate of interest and the rate of change of the price level.

If lenders and borrowers are concerned with the real costs measured in terms of purchasing power, the money rate of interest will be set at the real rate they require plus an amount to cover any *expected* rate of inflation. Consider a one-year loan that is meant to earn a real return to the lender of 5 percent. If the expected rate of inflation is zero, the money rate set for the loan will also be 5 percent. However, if a 10 percent inflation is expected, the money rate will have to be set at 15 percent.

To provide a given expected real rate of interest, the money rate will have to be set at the desired real rate of interest plus the expected annual rate of inflation.

This point is often overlooked; as a result people are surprised at the high money rates of interest that exist during periods of rapid inflation. For example, when the Bank of Canada raised money rates of interest drastically in 1981, many commentators expressed shock at the "unbearably" high rates. Most of them failed to notice that with inflation running at about 13 percent, an interest rate of 18 percent represented a real rate of only 5 percent. Had the Bank given in to the heavy pressure to hold interest rates to the more "reasonable" level of 10 percent, it would have been imposing a negative real rate of interest. Lenders would then have been rewarded for lending their money by receiving back less purchasing power in interest plus principal than the purchasing power of the principal they parted with initially.

When an inflation is fully expected, the money rate can be set to give any desired real rate of interest. Problems arise, however, when the inflation rate changes unexpectedly. Consider a loan contract that the parties wish to carry a 3 percent real rate of interest. If a 7 percent inflation rate is expected, the money rate will be set at 10 percent. But what if the inflationary expectations turn out to be wrong? If the inflation rate is only 4 percent, the real rate of interest will be 6 percent. If the inflation rate is 12 percent, the real rate of interest will be minus 2 percent.

Unexpected changes in the rate of inflation cause the real rate of interest on contracts already drawn up to vary in unexpected ways. An unexpected fall in the inflation rate is beneficial to lenders; an unexpected rise is beneficial to borrowers.

The Significance of Multiple Influences

Because the market rate of interest is influenced by many factors other than the demand to borrow money for new investment, the market rate can diverge from the pure rate set by the *MEC*. If the market rate is well below the *MEC*, there will be a heavy desire to borrow and invest in new capital; the stock of capital will then grow, and the *MEC* will begin to fall toward the market rate of interest. However, if the market rate is held above the *MEC*, there will be little or no desire to borrow to invest in new capital. Capital may not even be replaced as it wears out. As the capital stock shrinks, the *MEC* will rise toward the market rate of interest.

In general there is a tendency for the interest rate and the marginal efficiency of capital to be drawn toward each other.

Since the stock of capital (and thus the *MEC*) can change only slowly, most of the short-term adjustment is done by the interest rate. However, if the interest rate were fixed, the *MEC* would change to adjust to it. One way or the other, there is a tendency for the two rates to come together.

A COMPLICATION: MANY RATES OF INTEREST

In the real world there are many different rates of interest. Speaking in terms of a single rate can be a valid simplification for many purposes because the whole set of rates *tends* to move upward or downward together. Concentrating on one "typical" rate as "the" rate of interest in such cases is quite acceptable. For some purposes, however, it is important to take into account the multiplicity of interest rates.

At the same time that you receive an interest rate of 6 or 7 percent on deposits at a trust company, you may have to pay 11 or 12 percent to borrow from that trust company to buy a house. Interest rates on consumer installment credit of 16 percent and 20 percent are observed. A small firm pays a higher interest rate on funds it borrows from banks than does a giant corporation. Different government bonds pay different rates of interest, depending on the length of the period for which the bond runs. Corporation bonds tend to pay higher interest than government bonds, and there is much variation among bonds of different companies. Considering the extreme mobility of money, why do such differences exist? Why do funds not flow between different uses to eliminate these differences? The answer is that money does flow quite rapidly between alterna-

tive assets in response to relevant interest differentials, but differences prevail because quoted interest rates are composites of many things.

Differences in risk. Corporation bonds generally have higher interest rates than Government of Canada bonds because they have a greater degree of risk. For example, in mid 1981 many corporate issues were yielding in excess of 14 percent, while federal government bonds were paying 13 percent or less. Why? Investors were sure of the ability of the government of Canada to pay both the interest and the principal on their bonds, but they were less sure about the financial condition of private corporations.

Secured loans, where the borrower pledges an asset as collateral, tend to have lower interest rates than unsecured loans, other things being equal. Loans secured by houses (mortgages) tend to have lower interest rates than loans secured by automobiles, in part because it is harder to run away with a house than with a car and in part because a car can depreciate much more rapidly and unpredictably than a house.

Differences in duration. The *term* (duration) of a loan may likewise affect its price. The same bank will usually pay a higher rate of interest on a certificate of deposit that cannot be redeemed at the bank (without penalty) for at least one year than on a straight savings account, which can be withdrawn in a matter of minutes. Yet many savers prefer savings accounts because they want to be able to withdraw their money on short notice. Except when interest rates are thought to be temporarily abnormally high, borrowers are usually willing to pay more for long-term loans than for short-term loans because they are certain of having use of the money for a longer period. Lenders usually require a higher rate of interest the longer is the time before the borrower must repay. Other things being equal, the shorter the term of a loan, the lower are the interest rates.

Differences in costs of administering credit. There is great variation in the cost of different kinds of credit transactions. It is almost as cheap (in actual dollars) for a bank to lend Pacific Western Airlines $1 million that the airline agrees to pay back with interest after one year as it is for the same bank to lend you $4,000 to buy a new car on an installment loan that you agree to pay back over two years in 24 equal installments.

The loan to you requires many more bookkeeping entries than the loan to the airline. In addition, it is easier, and therefore less costly, to check Pacific Western Airlines' credit rating than it is to check yours. The difference in the cost *per dollar* of each loan is considerable. The bank may very well make less profit per dollar on a $4,000 loan at 20 percent per year than on a $1 million loan at 10 percent per year. In general, the bigger the loan and the fewer the payments, the less the cost per dollar of servicing the loan. Why then do banks and finance companies usually insist that you repay a loan in frequent installments? They worry that if you do not pay regularly, you will not have the money when the loan comes due.

In the market for borrowed funds there will be a structure of interest rates for credit transactions of different kinds.

Individual rates will be set that take into account such factors as risk premiums, duration of loan, and costs of administration. Nevertheless, it is useful and usual to talk about movements of interest rate structures up and down as changes in "the" interest rate. This simplification is most useful when the entire structure of rates moves up or down together so that changes in a single typical rate can capture changes in all rates.

Sources of Funds for Investment

So far in this chapter we have considered financing investment only with borrowed money. But loans are just one of several sources of finance available to firms for new investment. Most firms use several sources; a profit-maximizing firm that is free to do so will obtain funds from each source until the marginal cost of the last dollar obtained from each is the same.[7] (Otherwise the firm could reduce costs by shifting from higher-cost sources of funds to lower-cost sources.) The analysis of the first part of the chapter can now be generalized. When the *MEC* exceeds the cost of obtaining funds for new investment, firms will try to raise funds not only by borrowing but by tapping their other main sources of funds. When the *MEC* is less than the opportunity cost of capital, the demand for new investment funds from all sources will be low or nonexistent.

FINANCING THE MODERN CORPORATION

The most important ways in which firms obtain funds for new investment are (1) offering shares, stocks, or equities (as they are variously called) for private or public sale; (2) borrowing by the sale of bonds; (3) borrowing from banks; and (4) reinvesting the firm's profits.

The money that a firm raises for carrying on its business is sometimes called its **money capital** as distinct from its **real capital,** the physical assets that constitute plant, equipment, and inventories. Money capital may be broken down into **equity capital,** provided by the owners, and **debt,** which consists of the funds borrowed from persons who are not owners of the firm.

The use of the term "capital" to refer to both an amount of money and a quantity of goods can be confusing, but it is usually clear from the context whether a sum of money or a stock of equipment is being referred to. The two uses are not independent of each other, for much of the money capital raised by a firm will be used to purchase the capital goods that the firm requires for production.

STOCKS AND STOCKHOLDERS

The owners of the firm are its **stockholders**—persons who have put up money to pur-

---

[7] If a firm could get all the funds it wished from each source at constant marginal costs, it would use only the cheapest source. But firms usually face rising marginal costs of funds from each source, and thus they typically obtain funds from many sources.

chase shares in the firm. They make their money available to the firm and risk losing it in return for a share in the firm's profits. Stocks in a firm often proliferate into a bewildering number of types. Basically, however, there is common stock and preferred stock.

Common stock usually carries voting rights and has only a residual claim on profits. After all other claims have been met, the remaining profits, if any, belong to the common stockholders. There is no legal limit to the profits that may be earned by the company and therefore no limit to potential dividends that may be paid out to common stockholders. Firms are not obliged by law to pay out any fixed portion of their profits as dividends, and in fact the practice among corporations as to the payout ratio varies enormously. Firms sometimes pay out a large fraction and hold back only enough to meet contingencies; at other times they pay small or no dividends in order to reinvest retained funds in the enterprise.

The basic difference between **preferred stock** and common stock is that preferred stock carries with it a right to a preference over common stock to any profits that may be available after other obligations have been met. If profits are earned, the corporation is obliged to pay a dividend to preferred stockholders, but there is a stated maximum to the rate of dividends that will be paid per dollar originally invested.

BONDS AND BONDHOLDERS

Bondholders are creditors, not owners, of the firm. They have loaned money to the firm in return for a **bond,** which is a promise to pay a stated sum of money each year by way of interest on the loan and to repay the loan at a stated time in the future (say 10, 20, or 30 years hence). This promise to pay is a legal obligation on the firm's part whether or not profits have been made. If these payments cannot be met, the bondholders can force the firm into bankruptcy. Should this happen, the bondholders have a claim on the firm's assets prior to that of the stockholders.

Only when the bondholders and all other creditors have been repaid in full can the stockholders attempt to recover anything for themselves.

A major disadvantage to the corporation of raising capital through the sale of bonds is that interest payments must be met whether or not there are profits. Many a firm that would have survived a temporary crisis had all its capital been share capital has been forced into bankruptcy because it could not meet its contractual obligations to pay interest to its bondholders.

LOANS FROM FINANCIAL INSTITUTIONS

Much of a firm's short-term and some of its long-term monetary needs are met through bank loans. This is true of giant corporations as well as of small businesses. Indeed, making commercial and industrial loans is one of the major activities of the banking system (which we shall discuss in Chapter 35). Banks, however, limit the amounts they are willing to lend companies, typically to specified fractions of the companies' total financial needs.

Many small businesses that are not well established cannot sell stocks to the public, nor can they raise all the funds they require from banks. Several government agencies, such as the Federal Business Development Bank, have been established to help such firms get access to funds at "reasonable" rates.

REINVESTED PROFITS

Another important source of funds for the established firm is the reinvesting, or plowing back, of the firm's own profits. One of the easiest ways for the firm to raise money is to retain some of its own profits rather than pay them out as dividends. Reinvestment has become an extremely important source of funds in modern times; in Canada about $10 billion per year is obtained for investment in this fashion. The shareholder who does not wish his or her profits to be reinvested can do very little about it except to sell the stock and invest in a company with a policy of paying out a larger fraction of its dividends.

SECURITIES MARKETS (STOCK MARKETS)

When a household buys shares newly issued by a company, it hands over money to the company and becomes one of its owners. The household cannot get its money back from the company except in the unlikely event that the company is liquidated. If the household wishes to get its money back, it can only persuade someone else to buy its shares in the company.

Similarly, when a household buys a bond from a company, it cannot get its money back from the company before a specified date. If I bought a 1998 bond in 1978, the bond will be redeemed by the company (i.e., the loan will be paid back) only in 1998. If I wish to get my money back sooner, all I can do is sell the bond.

An organized market where stocks and bonds are bought and sold is a **stock market** or a **securities market.** Such markets include not only the well-known New York, Toronto, and Montreal stock exchanges but also the entire network of "over-the-counter" markets handled by brokers and specialists. The selling of existing shares on the stock market indicates that the company's existing ownership is being transferred; it does not indicate that the company is raising new money from the public.

Securities markets are important because by providing for the ready transfer of corporate securities they make it possible for individuals to invest without committing themselves for long periods.

Because of the existence of securities markets, people are willing to put their savings in securities that are not themselves directly or quickly redeemable. For example, if I want to invest in a particular stock or bond that pays an attractive yield, I may do so even though I know that I will want to withdraw my money after only a year. Given a securities market, I can be confident that I can sell the stock or bond a year from now.

But while securities markets provide for the quick sale of stocks and bonds, they do not guarantee that the securities will sell at the same price at which they were bought. The price at any time is the price that equates the demand and supply for a particular security, and rapid fluctuations in stock prices are common.

Prices on the Stock Market

Figure 22-3 shows the fluctuations in two indexes of stock market prices. In October 1973 the index of Canadian industrial stocks showed the average price to be 68 percent higher than in July 1970. People who bought a representative selection of industrial stocks on the first date and held them to the later one saw the average value of their holdings rise by 68 percent (and of course they earned dividends as well).

After that prices fell. By December 1974 the index was only 58 percent of what it was in October 1973. People who bought stocks in the middle of 1970 and held them until the end of 1974 first saw their paper value rise by 68 percent and then saw all of these gains quickly disappear until they ended up holding stocks whose value was lower than it was when they were purchased. Worse, those who bought in near the top of the market saw the value of their purchases cut by 40 percent in little more than one year.

What causes such rapid gains and losses, and what do they have to do with the kind of investment we have been talking about in this chapter? When investors buy a company's stock, they are buying rights to shares in the stream of dividends to be paid out by that company. They are also buying something they can sell in the future at a gain or loss. The value of that stock depends on two things: first, what people expect the stream of future dividend payments to be and, second, what capital gain or loss people expect to realize when the stock is sold.

Both things make dealing in stocks an inherently risky operation. Will the company in which you are investing pay more or less divi-

FIGURE 22-3
Fluctuations in an Index of Stock Prices, 1965–1980

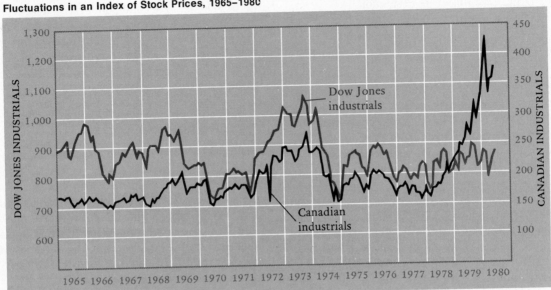

Stock market fluctuations are sharp and irregular. Shown here are monthly variations in the Dow Jones industrials index and in an index of industrial stocks traded on Canadian stock exchanges.

dends over future years? Will the company's value rise or fall so that you can sell your share in it for more or less than what you bought it for? While dividend policies of most established companies tend to be fairly stable, stock prices are subject to wide speculative swings.

A firm's earnings may rise or fall because of business conditions, the skill of its management, or for other reasons. The value of a stock derives in good part from the income stream that it is expected to confer on its owner. This might be measured by the stream of dividends the firm is expected to pay or by the firm's expected earnings. Most firms pay out only a fraction of their earnings as dividends, choosing to reinvest the undistributed profits. While these reinvested profits do not provide income directly to the stockholders, they do lead to future earnings, and by increasing the value of the company they tend to lead to increases in stock prices. It is generally believed that earnings are a better guide than dividends to understanding the prices of common stocks.

Thus one element in stock prices is the company's earnings rate. Yet companies with identical earnings per share may find their stock selling at very different prices. The ratio of price to earnings, called the **price-earnings ratio** or **PE ratio** or **P/E**, varies among companies precisely because buyers have very different expectations about the stock prices they expect to prevail in the future.

Speculative Swings

Expectations about future stock prices can be based on such factors as present earnings, careful estimates of future earnings, or the vague feelings that stock prices will be rising or falling.

In major stock market booms, people begin to expect rising stock prices and hurry to buy while stocks are cheap. This action bids up the prices of shares and creates the capital gains that justify the original expectations. This is the phenomenon of *self-realizing expectations*. Everyone gets rich on paper in the sense that the market value of their holdings rises. Money making now looks easy to others, they also rush in to buy, and new purchases push up prices still further. At this stage, attention to current earnings all but ceases. If a stock can yield, say, a 50 percent capital gain in one year, it does not matter much if the current earnings represent only a small percentage yield on the purchase price of the stocks. Everyone is "making money," so more people become attracted by the get-rich-quick opportunities. Their attempts to buy bid up prices still further, and current earnings represent an ever-diminishing percentage yield on the current price of the stocks.

Capital gains are so attractive that investors may buy stocks on margin — that is, borrow money to buy them, using the stocks themselves as security for the loans. In doing this, many investors may be borrowing money at a rate of interest considerably in excess of the rate of yield on current dividends. If $50,000 is borrowed at 10 percent (interest, $5,000 per year) to buy stocks yielding a current dividend return of only 4 percent (dividend, $2,000 per year), never mind, says the investor's logic, the stocks can be sold in a year or so for a handsome capital gain that will more than repay the $3,000 of interest not covered by dividends. Some people have the luck or good judgment to sell out near the top of the market, and they actually make money. Others wait eagerly for ever greater capital gains, and in the meantime they get richer and richer — on paper.

Eventually something breaks the period of unrestrained optimism. Some investors may begin to worry about the very high prices of stocks in relation not only to current yields but to possible future yields even when generous allowances for growth are made. Or it may be that the prices of stocks become depressed slightly when a sufficiently large number of persons try to sell out in order to realize their capital gains. As they offer their securities on the market, they cannot find purchasers without some fall in prices. Even a modest price fall may be sufficient to persuade

others that it is time to sell. But every share that is sold must be bought by someone. A wave of sellers may not find new buyers at existing prices, and prices will come down. Panic selling may now occur.

A household that borrowed $50,000 to buy stocks near the top of the market may find the paper value of its holdings sliding below $50,000. How will it repay its loan? Even if it does not worry about the loan, its broker will. The household may sell now before it loses too much, or its broker may "sell the customer out" to liquidate the loan before it is too late. All this brings prices tumbling down and provides another example of self-realizing expectations. If enough people think prices are going to come down, their attempt to sell out at the present high prices will itself create the fall in prices the expectations of which caused selling.

This is a very simple and stylized description of a typical speculative cycle, yet it describes the basic elements of market booms and busts that have recurred throughout stock market history. What was possibly the biggest boom of all began in the mid 1920s and ended on Black Tuesday, October 29, 1929. The collapse was dramatic: The average price of 50 leading U.S. stocks in November 1929 was about 50 percent below the September peak. Nor did it stop there. For three long years stock prices continued to decline, until the average value of stock sold on the New York Stock Exchange had fallen from its 1929 high of $89.10 a share to $17.35 a share by late 1933.

Are these booms and busts only ghosts from a lurid and reckless past? Until 1969, many would have said that the modern investor was too sophisticated for it ever to happen again. But look again at Figure 22-3. The index of the prices of Canadian industrial stocks tumbled by 24 percent between January 1969 and June 1970 — in just over a year. The market then recovered, and by January 1973 prices had reached an all-time high. This "boom" was followed by an even bigger "bust": In the two-year period prices fell to less than 65 percent of their January 1973 values. More recently, a sustained decline in prices from March 1977 to March 1978 took about 12 percent of the value of stocks in the index.

Stock Markets: Investment Marketplaces or Gambling Casinos?

Stock markets fulfill many important functions. It is doubtful that the great aggregations of capital needed to finance modern firms could be raised under a private ownership system without them. There is no doubt, however, that they also provide an unfortunate attraction for many naive investors whose get-rich-quick dreams are more often than not destroyed by the fall in prices that follows the occasional booms they help to create.

To some extent, public policy has sought to curb the excesses of stock market speculation through supervision of security issues. The regulatory authorities seek, among other things, to prevent both fraudulent or misleading information and trading by "insiders" (those in a company who have access to confidential information).

All in all, the stock market is both a real marketplace and a place to gamble. As in all gambling situations, those who are less well informed and less clever than the average tend to be losers in the long term.

Summary

1. Capital goods are man-made aids to production; they include machines, buildings, trucks, and human capital. When production with capital is more efficient than production without it (even when full allowance is made for the resources needed to produce and maintain the capital goods), capital is said to be *productive* or *efficient*.

2. The gross return to capital is the excess of a firm's revenue over the amount payable to factors of production other than capital, and after allowance for taxes. This can be divided into depreciation, a pure return on capital, a risk premium, and economic profits.

3. The marginal efficiency of capital schedule is downward-sloping because there are diminishing returns as more capital is added to fixed quantities of other resources with constant technical knowledge.

4. A piece of capital equipment is valued because it promises an expected stream of future income to its owners. The value of this capital equipment is the present value of the stream of gross returns it is expected to produce. A single payment of X after t years has a present value of $X/(1 + i)^t$. A stream of returns of X dollars per year in perpetuity has a present value of X/i.

5. A profit-maximizing firm will invest in a machine whenever the present value of the future stream of expected gross returns—the capitalized value of the machine—exceeds the purchase price of the machine or (what is the same thing) whenever the rate of return on the capital exceeds the rate of interest that correctly reflects the opportunity cost of capital to the firm. At equilibrium, the firm will purchase capital equipment until the marginal rate of return is equal to the rate of interest.

6. The amount of investment that firms wish to undertake will depend on the relation between the market rate of interest and the *MEC*.

7. The society as a whole will tend to acquire capital stock as long as the *MEC* is greater than the opportunity cost of money invested in capital, i. If there is competition among borrowers and lenders of money, the rate of interest will tend toward the *MEC*.

8. There are important influences on the market rate of interest other than those connected with the efficiency of capital: (a) expectations about price level changes, (b) expectations about the future state of the economy, (c) demands for funds to borrow for purposes other than investment in capital goods, (d) government control of interest rates as a tool of monetary policy, (e) bank administration of interest rates.

9. At any moment in time there is a whole struc-

ture of interest rates. Individual rates depend on the riskiness, duration, and liquidity of a loan and also on the cost to the lender of processing the loan and collecting payments of interest and principal.

10. Corporations can raise money in four main ways: by selling shares in the firm; by selling bonds; by borrowing from banks or other financial institutions; and by reinvesting (or plowing back) their own profits.

11. Securities (stock) markets allow firms to raise new capital from the sale of newly issued securities and allow the holders of existing securities to sell their securities to other investors.

12. Prices on the stock market tend to reflect the public's expectations both of firms' future earnings and of future changes in prices (for whatever reason). This necessarily puts a strong speculative dimension into security prices and large speculative swings do occur. Such swings are accentuated by the phenomenon of self-realizing expectations.

Topics for Review

The productivity or efficiency of capital
The marginal efficiency of capital and the *MEC* schedule
The gross return, the net return, and the pure return on capital
The present value of future returns and the capitalized value of assets
The inverse relationship between interest rates and the prices of assets
Reasons for the multiplicity of market interest rates
Equity capital and debt
Functions of securities markets
Self-realizing expectations

Discussion Questions

1. The Atlas Company has calculated that it has the following opportunities to invest.
   a. $20,000 to make critical replacement of an inadequate machine, with an estimated rate of return of 200 percent

   b. $100,000 in an additional machine, with an estimated return of 10 percent
   c. $50,000 for plant expansion, with a return of 25 percent
   How much would the company probably be willing to invest at an interest rate of 20 percent? of 10 percent? What assumptions are you making about risk in your answers?

2. Each of the following is sometimes described as an "investment" in everyday usage. Which represent investments in capital in the economist's sense?
   a. building of the Aswan Dam by the government of Egypt
   b. acquisition of a law degree
   c. purchase of a newly discovered Picasso painting. (Does it matter to your answer if the purchaser is the Metropolitan Museum or a private collector?)
   d. purchase by one company of the stock or assets of another company

3. The future profits of Skeeter, Inc., a going concern, are estimated by $100,000 annually for the indefinite future. What is the present value of the business at interest rates of 5 percent, 10 percent, and 25 percent? What factors will determine the appropriate rate of capitalization to use for a prospective buyer of Skeeter, Inc.?

4. Irving Fisher (1867–1947), a distinguished Yale economist, said the durability of capital goods and consumer goods was affected by the rate of interest. Assume that the more durable a house, the higher is its present cost of construction. Would you expect rising interest rates to lead to more or less durable houses being built? Would you expect rising interest rates to foster or discourage sales of mobile homes?

5. How might each of the following affect the pure rate of return on capital? How might they affect the market rate of interest?
   a. a major innovation in a specific industry
   b. an increase in the rate of inflation
   c. a wave of corporate bankruptcies
   d. a substantial increase in economic activity due to renewed confidence in the business outlook

6. Suppose you are offered, free of charge, one of each of the following pairs of assets. What considerations would determine your choice?
   a. a perpetuity that pays $20,000 a year forever; an annuity that pays $100,000 a year for only 5 years
   b. owning an oil drilling company that earned $100,000 after corporate taxes last year; owning a bond that paid $100,000 interest last year

7. Many stores, including the large mail-order chains, sell for cash or credit at the same prices. If you do not pay your bill completely within 30 days (and you are encouraged to make partial payments) a service charge of 1.5 percent per month of the unpaid balance is added to the bill. What circumstances make it desirable
   a. to pay cash
   b. to pay the bill within the next month
   c. to pay in "easy monthly installments"
   Explain whether unpaid bills by customers represent a capital investment by the firm. Is the 1.5 percent per month paid by customers on their unpaid bills a pure return on the money that the firm has tied up?

8. In 1975 interest rates on industrial bonds hit the highest levels in 45 years. Suppose you had accurately predicted this in late 1974. How might you have "cashed in" on your foresight by buying or selling bonds? Would you expect all bonds to respond in a similar way to these changes in interest rates? Would the person who owned a bond purchased in 1972, whose due date was 1986, be affected by these changes in interest rates?

9. Update Figure 22-3 on the two major stock market indexes, looking at data in recently published sources. Can you "explain" the changes that have occurred in the years since 1980? What data did you look at in attempting to explain what happened? What other data might have been useful?

Poverty, Inequality, and Mobility

23

National income divided by the total population is the average income for all Canadians. Some individuals and groups get much more than the average, and others get much less. Distribution theory attempts to explain, among other things, why this happens.

Possibly the most discussed aspect of distribution theory concerns the proportion of national income that goes to the very poor. Who are the poor? Why are they poor? What can—or should—we do about it? Poverty and the means used to prevent and alleviate it played a very large part in the political debates of the 1960s and 1970s. The intensity of the debates shows no sign of waning. We discuss the problem of poverty in the first part of this chapter; in the second part we examine the relevance of the theory of distribution for understanding income differences.

The Distribution of Income Between Rich and Poor: The Problem of Poverty

The theory of distribution offers a number of reasons for the variations in what different individuals can earn. People differ in the talents they possess and the factors they own; consequently both the quantity of factor services they can sell and the price they can receive will vary. Some factor owners are in a position to respond quickly to, and thus to take advantage of, changing opportunities. Others are immobile and will suffer when events leave them in markets where no one wants what they have to sell. To what extent do such reasons account for the continuing presence of poverty in Canada?

THE CONCEPT OF POVERTY

One possible definition of poverty is to be poorer than most of your fellow citizens. There will, of course, always be 10 percent of the population that is poorer than the other 90 percent. If poverty is regarded as a matter of low relative income, it is here to stay, for we inescapably have the (relatively) poor among us.

Clearly poverty means more than low relative income. Some minimum family income standard is required to define the **poverty level** below which a family is said to be poor. Such a standard specifies a dollar amount based on estimates of need and the cost of living. A criterion has been developed at Statistics Canada using a survey of family income and expenditures. From data on the proportion of income spent by families on the basic necessities of food, shelter, and clothing, it was estimated that families that on the average spend over 60 percent of their income on these items fall below the poverty line. This criterion implies a poverty standard for 1979 of about $5,000 for a single individual and about $8,500 for a three-person family. On this basis 12 percent of Canadian families and 34 percent of unattached individuals were suffering from poverty in 1979.

Less than 100 years ago, poverty would have been defined as the lack of the minimum amounts of food, shelter, and clothing needed to sustain life. Once this condition faced (or threatened) a large portion of the world's urban and rural masses. Total output was so low that all but a privileged minority lived at or near this level, and any flood or famine or crop failure plunged thousands into starvation. Poverty in this sense is still present in the world, even in North America. Yet in most advanced industrial countries, as in Canada, output has risen until the typical industrial worker enjoys a high material standard of living, and the provision of *subsistence requirements* of

food, shelter, and clothing is a major problem for only a small number of families. If this is so—if mere subsistence does not define the poverty level—what does it mean to say that a large number of Canadians live in poverty?

Consider the income of a member of a family just at the poverty level. Income of $8,500 for a family of four is $2,125 per person. This will not seem like a great deal to most of you, but it is above the per capita income of three-quarters of the world's population. This should not lead anyone to minimize poverty problems; the poor living and working in a large North American city need more clothes, transportation, and other basics than an Indonesian peasant. Visit the slums of any North American city and you will not lightly dismiss poverty.

But $8,500 for a family of four buys enough food, shelter, and clothing to get by. What it does not provide is enough money for the necessities and also for the full range of commodities that 90 percent of us take for granted, such as having a refrigerator, hot water, and a television set that works and attending an occasional movie. Many of the poor are understandably bitter and resentful that they and their children are outsiders looking in on the comfortable way of life shown in ads and on television. Nevertheless, they are materially better off than were many people living above the poverty line a decade ago.

Historically, the greatest source of relief from poverty has come through economic growth.

If productivity growth can be restored to even 2 percent per year, living standards will double again in the next 35 years. This will surely reduce further the number of people living in poverty. But it is a mistake to expect too much from growth, first because (as we saw in Chapter 13) productivity growth has slowed, and second because some forms of poverty seem immune to growth.

Today, after a century of rapid growth, the poor—like death and taxes—are still with us. It is safe to predict that if we rely only on growth of average income, they will be with us a century hence. For the poverty problem is no longer rooted in low *average* productivity but in the fact that particular groups have been left behind in the general rise of living standards. It is no consolation—indeed it adds to the gall—that they are poor in an increasingly affluent society.

WHO ARE THE POOR?

There are poor among people of all ages, races, and educational levels, among the working as well as the unemployed and the retired. Yet some groups have very much higher incidences of poverty than others. For example, Table 23-1 shows that you are more likely to be poor if you live in a rural area or in the Atlantic provinces, if you are a member of a large family, or if you are over 65 years old.

On the other hand, a close examination of the characteristics of the poor made by Statistics Canada in 1967 showed that poverty is by no means restricted to those groups for which its incidence is high. More than half the families who were poor lived in urban areas, were residents of Ontario or the Western provinces, had no more than one child, or were headed by a person between the ages of 25 and 65. Furthermore, 37 percent of those suffering from poverty in 1967 worked full-time during the year and 63 percent worked at least part-time. These facts may help to dispose of two superficial caricatures: the slothful father who feigns a disability because he is too lazy to do an honest day's work and the family with so many children that an ordinarily decent wage is spread so thin that the entire household is reduced to poverty. Individual households that come close to these extremes can be found, but most poor households do not.

WHY ARE THERE POOR?

To answer the question, we need to recognize that the poor come from many groups and that the causes of their poverty are various. The fact that many of the poor are over age 65 shows that age and illness force people out of the labor

TABLE 23-1

Incidence of Poverty Among Canadian Families by Selected Characteristics, 1979

Characteristic	Percentage of families falling below the poverty line
All families	11.9
Place of residence	
Metropolitan	12.1
Other urban	11.7
Rural	12.5
Region	
Atlantic	15.3
Quebec	13.4
Ontario	10.5
Prairies	12.6
British Columbia	9.5
Number of children under 16 years	
0 or 1	11.3
2 or 3	14.2
4 or more	25.1
Age of head of family	
Under 25	20.8
25–54	10.6
55–64	11.0
65 or over	17.1
Sex of head of family	
Male	8.4
Female	44.2
Employment status of head of family	
In labor force	9.2
Not in labor force	29.9

Source: Statistics Canada, 13–206.

market. Other important groups include the rural poor, who strive in vain to earn a decent living from marginal or submarginal farm lands; the urban working poor, who simply lack the skills to command a wage high enough to support themselves and their families above the poverty level; the immobile poor, who are trapped by age and outdated skills in areas and occupations where the demand for their services is declining faster than their number; and the minority poor, such as the Indian, Eskimo, and Métis peoples, who suffer the additional barriers of discrimination at many stages of their lives.

Thus there can be no simple answer to the question: What causes poverty in the midst of plenty? It is partly a result of mental and physical handicaps, partly of low motivation, and partly of the raw deal that fate gives to some—such as the children of the young father who dies unexpectedly, having been meaning to take out that life insurance policy almost any day. Partly it is a result of current and past prejudice. Partly it is a result of unwillingness or inability to invest in the kind of human capital that does pay off in the long run. Partly it is a result of the market's valuing the particular abilities that an individual does have at such a low price that, even in good health and with full-time employment, the income that can be earned leaves that person below the poverty line.

The extent of poverty is also affected greatly by the performance of the economy. A recession, with its increase in unemployment, pushes additional thousands into poverty. Inflation continually erodes the resources of those on fixed incomes, and the recent rapid inflation has far outstripped increases in welfare payments and the earnings of many families at or near the poverty level.

Fluctuations in the number classified as poor as a result of swings in the economy highlight the important distinction between the *occasionally poor* and the *persistently poor*. It is much easier to withstand six months (or even several years) of poverty due to a bout of unemployment or illness than it is to be permanently poor. For the latter condition erodes hope and warps one's entire outlook on life. While many of those officially classified as being in poverty at any time are only temporarily poor—and thus not really forced to adjust to poverty—many of the rest are virtually permanently poor.

"WAGING WAR" ON POVERTY

Eliminating poverty is easier than eliminating air pollution or cancer, for which cures are as yet unknown. For less than $2 billion per year in 1980 dollars, every family now below the poverty level could be given a sufficient income

supplement to bring it to that level. The Canadian government could, in other words, close the poverty gap. Although $2 billion is a lot of money, it represents only about two-thirds of one percent of the total income earned in the nation.[1]

Poverty, once an ineradicable scourge of humanity along with pestilence and famine, is now within the realm of control in North America. Traditionally, and currently, energies have been divided between attacking the causes of poverty and attempting to help some of the poor through payments of money to ease their poverty. Surprisingly perhaps, a good deal of the debate about attacking poverty does not concern whether we can afford it or how best to do it, but whether we *ought* to do it.

The Case Against an All-out War on Poverty

Everyone concedes that there are poor people who deserve to be helped. They are those who despite their best efforts have not been able to escape the ravages of illness, blindness, desertion, age, or obsolescence. There are as well the helpless children of the poor, who should not be made to suffer endlessly for the failings or misfortunes of their parents. But there are also the "undeserving poor," those who could work but will not as long as someone else will support them and their families.

Not only is it unnecessary and perhaps immoral to support such people, the argument says, but their number will grow rapidly if we choose to adopt more generous programs for relieving existing poverty. Even if we could afford to eliminate poverty, the attempt to do so would be self-defeating. For in doing so, the argument continues, we would destroy the incentives of those now supporting themselves just above the level at which the government would support them. They would stop working and end up on welfare

---

[1] In the United States the cost of eliminating poverty is estimated to be $20 billion—less than 20 percent of the U.S. national defence budget and less than 1 percent of the value of total U.S. annual output.

as quickly as others were raised above the poverty level.

These critics point to the decline in the work ethic that accompanies increased welfare payments, unemployment compensation, and the issuance of food stamps. There is some factual basis for this argument. Today many gladly accept unemployment compensation, welfare payments, and free goods and services — and indeed expect them, as a matter not of charity but of basic rights. Almost every program has had its scandals, and all too many people can identify others who are relying on public assistance when in fact they could support themselves.

Disincentive effects. The first part of the case against a general attack on poverty thus concerns disincentive effects. The most direct disincentive effect is on the willingness to keep working or to accept work when to do so will disqualify the person from receiving welfare or unemployment benefits.

A second such effect is on the beneficiaries of government welfare payments: Children who grow up knowing they have a welfare safety net under them may not develop the attitudes or gain the skills needed to climb above the level of the net. This effect may be particularly noticeable in those who, because of the limitations of their abilities, could never in any case hope to climb far above the level provided by the welfare safety net.

A third possible disincentive effect relates to those who will be asked to pay the extra taxes that must be levied if welfare spending increases. As more people go on welfare, fewer will be left to pay the taxes, so tax rates must rise. If, in response, taxpayers work less, the total amount of income available for redistribution will shrink.

There can be no quarrel with the logical proposition that each of these effects may occur, and each of them can be documented by case studies. Some were discussed in Chapter 20. But the important question is whether the effects are merely occasional horror stories or whether they are frequent and quantitatively significant. Oppo-

nents of an all-out attack on poverty believe that these magnitudes are, and will be proven to be, very large.

Opportunity costs. Some maintain that we cannot afford to eliminate poverty, given all the competing uses of public money. They contend that welfare spending is already at cripplingly high levels.

Advocates of the view that total government spending is already too large often argue that there are few other items over which so much discretion may be exercised. On the one hand, less could no doubt be spent on such items as hospitals or schools. Many believe, however, that significant cuts in these items are either impractical or undesirable. On the other hand, a genuine option does exist with welfare expenditures. One of the few realistic hopes of keeping government spending under control, so goes this view, lies in holding a tight rein on the expansion of welfare costs and in particular eliminating payments to the dishonest and lazy who are receiving payments without real need.

The Case for an All-out Attack on Poverty

The war on poverty has its supporters as well as its opponents. Welfare cheaters, supporters agree, should be identified, exposed, and eliminated from welfare rolls wherever possible. But the abuses should not be allowed to confuse the issue. It was one thing to put up with poverty when we had no alternative; it is another to do so when we are rich enough to spend billions on cosmetics, sports, and other frills — to say nothing of space exploration and foreign "diplomacy."

The shame of poverty, the argument says, is not that of the victim but of the society that lets it continue. One great advance of modern civilization has been to lift the stigma from those who are less able and less fortunate. It is to our credit that we have replaced the poorhouse with programs of social insurance as a matter of right, not charity. To let a few cheaters plus some unsupported fears about destruction of the will to work be the excuse for not "coming to peace with poverty" is, they say, a real immorality in modern society.

Of course, any scheme that reduces welfare payments by 65 cents or 75 cents for every dollar that the recipient earns means a 65 percent or 75 percent tax on earnings and may well provide a short-term disincentive to work. But this is the fault of the scheme, not of the people who are only responding rationally to it. Schemes that reduce this marginal disincentive feature can be designed.

Resolving the Debate?

Thus there is disagreement about the desirable direction of change in welfare expenditures. Choosing whether to expand or to contract poverty programs depends in part on value judgments of what is good and right and worth doing, and in part on positive factual assessments of what can be done and how much it will cost. Positive economic research can help to narrow the range of these uncertainties, even if it cannot dictate what we should finally do. Today a great deal of research is devoted to studying the effects of welfare expenditure on incentives—both of the recipients and of the taxpayers who must foot the bill.

THE NATURE OF CURRENT PROGRAMS

The implicit distinction between the deserving and undeserving poor has played an important part in the development of existing programs. The two underlying assumptions are, first, that the able-bodied should work and, second, that heads of households should support their families whenever possible. A three-pronged strategy has developed: (1) to provide job opportunities for all who are able to work; (2) to provide social insurance, related to work, for temporary unemployment and for retirement; and (3) to provide monetary assistance only to those poor who are unable to work for reasons of age, health, or family status.

Providing Employment Opportunities

Families with an employed member have very much less chance of being below the poverty level than those without one. One aspect of fighting poverty is to encourage economic growth and avoid general unemployment. Another is to fight discrimination that denies employment opportunities to minority group members, among whom poverty is many times more prevalent than among whites.

But nearly 40 percent of all poor families have a full-time working head; for these working poor, the problem is the lack of skills that command a decent wage, not an absence of demand for the skills they have. The current training program administered by the Department of Manpower and Immigration attacks this problem by subsidizing adult technical and vocational training and by paying living allowances to trainees who meet certain qualifications. In recent years annual expenditures have risen about $300 million, with courses being provided for about 300,000 persons per year. The department estimates that about one-half of those trained were below the poverty line. In addition, expenditures per labor force member were greater in regions with higher unemployment and poverty rates.

Social Insurance

The second prong of traditional antipoverty legislation is **social insurance.** Old age pensions have been provided by the federal government since 1927. Additional retirement income is provided by the Canada Pension Plan, which is financed through contributions of participants. However, the current level of benefits is far below that necessary to provide an income above the poverty line. Since, in 1970, nearly half of the pensioners had very limited or no other sources of income, these programs mitigate but do not eliminate poverty among the old. For those of working age, unemployment insurance provides protection against temporary loss of earnings, and the joint federal-provincial hospital and medical insurance programs make health services available to all Canadians regardless of their income.

Provincial Welfare Systems

Because of strong constitutional and political traditions, welfare payments to the poor in general—as opposed to the unemployed or retired—have generally been left in the hands of the provinces and municipalities. Because of the inadequate and varying financial resources available to the lower levels of government, the Canada Assistance Plan was introduced in 1966, giving the federal government a share in the cost of welfare programs. Effective control remains with the provinces, but 50 percent of the financing comes from the federal government. Many problems remain, however. According to the *Report of the Special Senate Committee on Poverty* (1971), "Apart from programs of social insurance, such as the Canada Pension Plan and the federal categorical programs such as Old Age Security, the welfare system really comprises the ten different provincial systems plus the welfare systems of the Territories. What they have in common is a record of failure and insufficiency, of bureaucratic rigidities that often result in the degradation, humiliation, and alienation of recipients."

The committee found that there is wide variation in benefit structures among the provinces. For example, a family of four in Hull receives $100 a month less in general welfare assistance than a similar family across the river in Ottawa. Moreover, none reaches any accepted poverty line. A bizarre example of illogical bureaucratic practices was provided to the committee by the assistant director of the Ottawa Social Planning Council:

We get a number of ladies phoning us, toothless women, some of them young women, many of them with a number of children and they had their teeth removed at public expense by the Ontario Government and then they have to apply to the municipality to have dentures put in. This is not only a silly situation from the medical point of view, but these people have to prove themselves and their need to yet another level of government. This takes time. They have to go out and

get estimates. Then at last if there is enough money made available by regional government, they will have their dental services provided.

Improvements in provincial programs appear to be hindered by three major problems. First, there is a scarcity of financial resources, particularly in the poorer provinces; second, there is no consensus about the standard of living that should be provided. The third problem involves the effects of assistance levels on work incentives and the extent to which administrative procedures are necessary to prevent abuses. These questions are under study, and definite action may still be some time off. A comprehensive proposal, the so-called negative income tax, is discussed in Chapter 25.

The Relevance of Distribution Theory

A large part of the problem of poverty is due to the pricing of the labor services that people have to offer. Factor pricing, and hence the distribution of income, is a by-product of the market-allocation system. This allocation helps to determine both the quantities of the various goods and services that are produced and the methods by which they are produced.

Does the theory of distribution studied in this part satisfactorily explain the allocation process in our economy? For the answer to be yes, it is necessary to give affirmative answers to two more basic questions. First, do market conditions of demand and supply play important roles in determining factor earnings? Second, do factors move in response to changes in factor earnings?

Some would answer no to each question. They argue that prices of products and factors bear little relation to market conditions because prices and wages are administered by oligopolies and giant unions. Such administered prices and wages are sticky downward and tend to rise annually at a bit more than the general rate of inflation. Products with above average price increases are produced by firms with above average market power, and the most powerful unions get the biggest wage increases. Entry barriers in industry and mobility barriers for factors of production, the argument continues, prevent significant movements of resources in response to product and factor price differentials that exist or develop. Thus, they argue, the theory of distribution we have studied is irrelevant to the real world.

Some of the views expressed in the previous paragraph are closely related to those discussed on pages 343–346. In the following sections of this chapter, we examine whether market forces do in fact play the roles predicted by the theories of competition and monopoly in determining factor prices and the allocation of resources.

DO MARKET CONDITIONS DETERMINE FACTOR EARNINGS?

Factors Other Than Labor

Many, if not all, nonhuman factors are sold on competitive markets. The theory predicts that changes in the earnings of these factors will be associated with changes in market conditions. Overwhelmingly the evidence supports this prediction of the theory, as shown by the examples that follow.

The market theory of factor pricing provides a good explanation of raw material prices and hence of the incomes earned by their producers. The prices of plywood, tin, rubber, cotton, and hundreds of other materials fluctuate daily in response to changes in their demand and supply. The responses of factor markets to the many shortages that seemed to characterize the Canadian economy in the 1970s provide dramatic confirmation. When the price of agricultural commodites shot up following a grain shortage, farm income soared. When oil became scarce, prices rose and oil producers and owners of oil properties found their profits and incomes rising rapidly. Not only did the relative prices of oil products rise, so also did the relative prices of

commodities, such as chemical fertilizers and air travel, that make use of petroleum products.

Land in the heart of growing cities provides another example. Such land is clearly fixed in supply, and values rise steadily in response to increasing demand for it.[2] Very high land values even make it worthwhile to destroy durable buildings in order to convert the land to more productive uses. Many historic buildings in our cities have been pulled down, to be replaced by high-rise office buildings. The skyscraper is a monument to the high value of urban land. In many smaller cities, the change from shopping downtown to shopping in outlying shopping centers has lessened the demand for land downtown and influenced relative land prices. The increase in the price of land on the periphery of every growing city is a visible example of the workings of the market.

Similar results occur in markets that are far from being perfectly competitive. In 1979 the price of power in virtually all forms rose sharply in response to the extra energy shortage caused by the change in government in Iran. Oligopolists producing key metals such as zinc, molybdenum, steel, and aluminum have not hesitated to increase prices as their costs of production rose or when demand outran their production. Further examples can be found in almost every issue of the *Financial Post* and the *Wall Street Journal,* but the point should now be clear:

The prices and earnings of nonhuman factors are successfully predicted by market theories of factor pricing.

Labor

When we apply the theory to labor, we encounter two important sets of complications. First, labor being the human factor of production, nonmonetary considerations loom large in its incentive patterns, and thus market fluctuations may have less effect. Second, the competitive and noncom-

[2] A friend is fond of saying, "Nobody buys land any more; its price is much too high because everybody wants it."

petitive elements of labor markets occur in different proportions from market to market. These complications make it harder to answer the question, Do market conditions determine factor earnings? Monopolistic elements and nonmonetary rewards, both difficult to measure, must be carefully specified if the theory that labor earnings respond to market forces is to be testable. Nevertheless, there is a mass of evidence to go on.

Market fluctuations in demand and supply. Do earnings respond to normal fluctuations of demand and supply as the theory predicts? The evidence shows that they often do. The competitive theory predicts that a decline in the demand for a product will cause a decline in the derived demand for the factors that make the product and thus a decline in their owners' incomes. A rise in the demand for a product will have the opposite effect. Cases come easily to mind.

With the advent of the automobile, many skilled carriage makers saw the demand for their services decline rapidly. Earnings fell, and many older workers found that they had been earning substantial economic rents for their scarce but highly specific skills. They suffered large income cuts when they moved to other industries. Workers who acquired skills wanted in the newly expanding automotive industry found the demands for their services and their incomes rising rapidly.

More recently there has been a large increase in the earnings of first class professional athletes in most sports. In part this has been caused by rising demand due to expansion in the number of major league teams. In part it has resulted from increased revenues to the teams and leagues from televising sports, which has increased the marginal revenue product of the athletes. And in part it has been the result of athletes' acquiring the right to offer their services to more than one employer, thereby reducing the ability of employers to hold down wages by acting as monopsonists.

Doctors as a group have also gained from an increase in demand for their services. With the rise in real incomes in the twentieth century, the typical household has spent an increasing proportion of its income on medical services. The resulting rise in demand has greatly increased the incomes of physicians relative to the incomes of many other groups in the society.

University professors are an example of a group that gained as a result of changes in labor markets during the 1960s but fell back in the 1970s. The relative earnings of a university professor were much higher by 1970 than they had been 20 years earlier. This was particularly so at the starting end of the scale, where intense competition for the scarce supply of good students who had just obtained Ph.D.s forced up their price throughout the 1960s to levels that would have seemed princely only 15 years before. In response to the higher incomes, many more university graduates went on to get advanced degrees, and a rising proportion stayed on to teach and do research in universities.

The supply of new Ph.D.s began to arrive on the market in 1969–1970, and for the first time in ten years the starting salaries of Ph.D.s hired for the fall of 1970 were not significantly higher than the salaries for those hired the previous year. By 1973 the average percentage increase in academic salaries was not only below the average percentage increase in all incomes but was insufficient even to keep pace with the increase in the cost of living. The relative downward pressure on professors' salaries continued throughout the 1970s and shows no sign of abating as additions to supply continue to outstrip additions to demand. These relative changes in factor compensation have occurred even in an occupation where nonmonetary benefits loom large. The reason is that the nonmonetary benefits exist both when demand is strong relative to supply and when it is relatively weak.

Another group that has been suffering the chill winds of the consequences of factor price determination on competitive markets is university graduates. During the 1970s the earnings of graduates fell relative to other workers, and employment opportunities dropped sharply, especially for new graduates. The downturn is explained by slackening demand due to changes in industrial structure (e.g., substituting sophisticated computers for university-trained persons) and continued growth of supply.

Price changes induced by market conditions have little to do with abstract notions of justice or merit. If you have some literary talent, why can you make a lot of money writing copy for an advertising agency but very little money writing poems? It is not because an economic dictator or group of philosophers has decided that advertising is more valuable than poetry. It is because in the Canadian economy there is a large demand for advertising and only a tiny demand for poetry.

Effects of monopoly elements in labor markets. A strong union—one able to bargain effectively and to restrict entry of labor into the field—can cause wages to rise well above the competitive level. Highly skilled plasterers, plumbers, and electricians have all managed to restrict entry into their trades and as a result maintain wages well above their transfer earnings. Many similar cases have been documented. Unions can and do succeed in raising wages and incomes when they operate in small sections of the whole economy; the high earnings attract others to enter the occupation or industry, and the privileged position can be maintained only if entry can be effectively restricted.

Not only can monopoly elements raise incomes above their competitive levels, they can also prevent wages from falling in response to decreases in demand. Of course, if the demand disappears more or less overnight, there is nothing any union can do to maintain incomes. But the story may be different when, as is more usually the case, demand shrinks slowly but steadily.

Railways and coal mining, once thriving industries, faded through the 1950s and 1960s to pale shadows of their former selves. Year by year the levels of employment in these industries shrank in response both to declining demand and to the increased use of labor-saving techniques.

What would competitive theory predict about wages? Coal mining was plainly a declining labor market from 1945 to 1960; competitive theory would predict low wages and low incomes, followed by exit of the most mobile coal miners under this forceful disincentive, and hard times for those who decide to stick it out.

Table 23-2 shows how this mechanism operated in the Canadian coal industry. During the period 1950–1969, wages rose by less than 2 percent per year while the average wage in manufacturing rose by more than 3 percent. This decline in the relative position of coal miners was accompanied by a fall in employment to less than one-third of its initial level. It is also interesting to note that the leveling off of employment that occurred in 1970 coincided with a reversal of the decline in relative wages.

The experience of the U.S. coal industry presents a striking contrast. While the level of employment went through a similar drastic adjustment, wages remained higher than the average wage in manufacturing. What happened was that powerful unions were able to prevent a relative decline in wages, but the lack of job opportunities discouraged the young from entering the industry. As workers left as a result of retirement, ill health, or death, they were not replaced. Some people argue that the "restrictive behavior" of unions in such cases has led to a more orderly, humane, and civilized phasing out than would have occurred had the adjustment been left to a free market. In the latter case, those who remained in the industry, and who were needed by it, would have suffered depressed conditions in order that the disincentive could operate on those who did leave and on those who might otherwise have entered.

During the 1970s the rapid increase in energy prices led to a renewal in demand for coal; employment and relative wages in coal mining rose in both countries.

TABLE 23-2
Employment and Hourly Wages in the Coal Industry (Selected Years)

	Canada			United States		
Year	Employment (thousands)	Hourly wages in coal industry (1971 dollars)	Average wage as a percentage of those in manufacturing	Employment (thousands)	Hourly wages in coal industry (1972 dollars)	Average wage as a percentage of those in manufacturing
1945	23	.94	136	375	1.20	118
1950	20	1.30	125	351	1.94	135
1955	14	1.48	102	205	2.47	133
1960	10	1.75	98	149	3.14	139
1965	8	1.96	92	115	3.49	134
1970	6	3.09	103	120	4.58	136
1973	7	4.62	117	139	5.41	141
1978	9	8.25	117	176	9.57	155

Source: Statistics Canada, *Review of Man Hours and Hourly Earnings,* 1945–1967, 1957–1967, 1968–1970; "Employment and Earnings: United States, 1909–1971," *Bureau of Labor Statistics, Bulletin 72–002.*

In both Canada and the United States employment in the coal industry declined sharply in the 1950s and 1960s and recovered in the 1970s. In Canada the falling demand for labor during the earlier period was reflected in a lower rate of increase in wages than occurred in manufacturing; in the United States unions were able to maintain a wage level above the average in American manufacturing.

Taken together, the competitive theory of factor markets and a bit of monopoly theory appear to explain a good deal of the variation in relative earnings of different groups in the labor force. All the above examples support the general proposition:

Earnings of labor repond to significant changes in market conditions.

DO FACTORS MOVE IN RESPONSE TO CHANGES IN EARNINGS?

The theory of factor supply says that factors will move among uses, industries, and places, taking both monetary and nonmonetary rewards into account. They will move in such a way as to equalize the net advantages to the owners of factors. Because there are impediments to the mobility of factors, there may be lags in the response of factors to changes in relative prices, but in due course adjustments will occur. We now ask, Does the world behave in the way the theory predicts?

Factors Other Than Labor

The most casual observation reveals that the allocative system works pretty much as described by the theory with respect to land, materials, and capital goods.

Land is transferred from one crop to another in response to changes in the relative profitabilities of the crops. Land on the edge of town is transferred from rural to urban uses as soon as it can earn substantially more as a building site than as a cornfield. Materials and capital goods move from use to use in response to changes in relative earnings in those uses.

This is hardly surprising. Nonmonetary benefits do not loom large for factors other than labor, and the theories of both competition and monopoly predict that quantities supplied will respond to increases in earnings generated by increased demand.

In the case of nonhuman factors, there is strong evidence that the theory is able to predict events with reasonable accuracy.

FIGURE 23-1
The Changing Composition of the Nonagricultural Labor Force

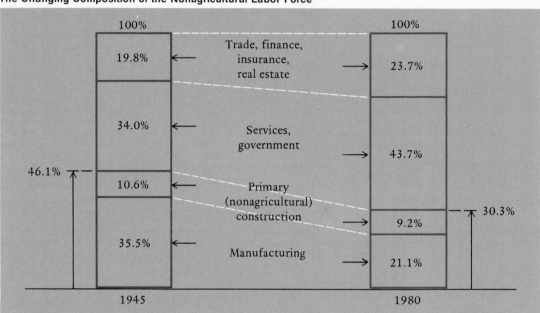

Source: Statistics Canada, 71–001.

In half a century, a major shift has occurred in labor utilization. In 1945, 46 percent of the nonagricultural labor force was in the heavy industrial (largely blue collar) sectors. As shown by the bottom two blocks, this figure had decreased to 30 percent by 1980. The shift was to the service-oriented (largely white collar) sectors of government, trade, finance, and other services.

Labor

Labor mobility can occur in many dimensions. Labor can move among occupations, industries, skill categories, and regions. These categories are not exclusive; to change occupation from a farm laborer to a steelworker, for example, a person will also have to change industries and probably towns.

Figure 23-1 illustrates one dimension of labor mobility. The shifts among sectors that have occurred in the postwar period indicate the substantial adaptability of the labor force to changing patterns of demand for the outputs of various sectors.

Table 23-3 shows the basic provincial patterns of labour mobility that have evolved. The Prairies were large net recipients of migrants in the early decades of the century, a fact largely associated with the western movement brought on by the wheat boom. The following decades saw a net outflow from the Prairies, though Alberta has recently become a net recipient primarily because of the boom in resource-based industries. The Maritimes experienced continued net out-migration until the 1970s, and except for the 1950s so has Quebec. The basic picture is one of Canada's having a very mobile population (the data in Table 23-2 show only *net* migration).

Countless studies of regional labor mobility have been made, but they do not give a simple answer to the question of whether factors move in response to monetary incentives. Substantial migrations of populations have occurred in re-

TABLE 23-3
Net Canadian Migration by Province, Thousands of Persons, 1901–1976

	1901–1910	1911–1920	1921–1930	1931–1940	1941–1950	1951–1960	1961–1970	1971–1976
Newfoundland	−9	−15	−17	−17	−17	−15	−35	−2
Prince Edward Island	−17	−14	−9	−2	−12	−11	−6	+4
Nova Scotia	−28	−37	−70	+2	−39	−34	−44	+11
New Brunswick	−30	−25	−43	−13	−42	−37	−45	+17
Quebec	−29	−99	−10	−32	−12	+205	−142	−78
Ontario	+74	+46	+129	+75	+305	+685	+236	−39
Manitoba	+111	+24	−10	−41	−61	−5	−64	−27
Saskatchewan	+283	+78	−5	−138	−199	−9	−124	−41
Alberta	+218	+85	+22	−35	−7	+127	+30	+59
British Columbia	+164	+58	+101	+72	+230	+240	+193	+92
Yukon and Northwest Territories	−31	−4	−1	0	+6	+4	+2	+3

Source: Economic Council of Canada.

sponse to differentials in returns to labor. For example, when the first decennial census was taken in 1871, more than 20 percent of the Canadian population lived in the Atlantic provinces (compared with 8 percent today). In the decade 1951–1960 net out-migration from the Atlantic provinces including Newfoundland was approximately 5 percent of the total population. Yet in spite of this, per capita income in the Atlantic provinces remains one-third below that of the rest of the country.

Although it is relatively easy to get some out-migration, it may occur more slowly than the decline of economic opportunities, in which case pockets of poverty tend to develop. Indeed, the exit itself causes further decline, for when a family migrates, both the supply of labor and the demand for labor decline—because of the reduction in demand for locally provided goods and services that the family consumed before they migrated.

Labor movement occurs, but it does not always occur rapidly enough to avoid regional pockets of extreme unemployment and poverty.

Regional Economic Policy

Non-market-oriented policies, such as the development and subsidization of transportation facilities and the redistribution of tax revenues in favor of the poorer provinces, have long been accepted as tools for reducing regional economic disparities in Canada. Since the 1960s the range of policies has been extended to include redevelopment of low-income rural areas, stimulation of capital investment in depressed areas through subsidies to firms, incentives (in the form of mobility grants) for the relocation of unemployed workers, and provision of training opportunities to permit disadvantaged members of the labor force to upgrade their skills.

One characteristic that Canada shares with many countries is the identification of industries with particular geographic regions. We readily associate the oil industry with Alberta, the automobile industry with Ontario, the textile industry with Quebec, and the fishing industry with British Columbia and the Maritimes. At a time when economic activity is high in one region of Canada, there may be recession in another region because the demand for products produced by the industries in that region is low. Using policies such as those outlined above, the federal and provincial governments attempt to stimulate depressed regions. For example, relatively larger amounts of unemployment insurance benefits are made to regions with higher unemployment rates. Or, as was done in 1978, taxes on particular goods produced or purchased in certain regions may be temporarily reduced.

Could Per Capita Incomes and Unemployment Rates Be Equalized Across Canadian Provinces?

The answer to the question posed in the title is almost certainly no—at least when we consider the kinds of policy tools likely to be available to any foreseeable Canadian government.

The reason behind this answer lies in the simple application of the hypothesis of equal net advantage stated on page 374. As long as areas differ in their nonmonetary attractiveness, there will be equilibrium differences in their per capita incomes and/or unemployment rates.

Why is this so?

Consider low levels of income. Low incomes may be the result of strong natural economic forces that will not yield to such simpleminded policy measures as raising local demand. For example, suppose that province A—despite strong physical, climatic, and social attractions—has a set of natural endowments that will not produce as high an income per person employed as province B. Relative inadequacies in economic opportunities in particular provinces might arise for many reasons: inadequate resource base, technological backwardness, slow growth in demand for one region's products, and rapid natural growth of the labor force are just a few.

Suppose that because of migration costs, cultural and language differences, climatic advantages, or other local amenities, many people would choose to live in province A despite their having lower incomes. Markets can adjust to such regional differences in two basic ways.

If wages and prices are flexible, real wages and incomes will fall in province A for those kinds of workers who are in excess supply. The cheapening real wages of some kinds of labor will give the province an advantage in new lines of production. Real wages will continue to fall until everyone who is willing to stay at the lower wage has a job and those who are not have migrated. In long-run equilibrium, province A is a low-wage, low-income province, but it has no special unemployment problem; and those who do not value its amenities as much as they value the higher incomes to be earned in province B, or who are subject to lower migration costs, will have left. What the price system does is to equalize total advantages. It does not equalize economic advantage because the noneconomic advantages of living in province A exceed those of living in province B.

The second possibility arises because we do

In addition to policies that attempt to reduce regional inequalities, the government adopts policies that attempt to eliminate the source of such inequalities. In Canada one approach has been to promote the *diversification* of industry in any one region. Governments have encouraged the entry of new firms with products whose demand does not fluctuate much, or whose fluctuations in demand are not always closely related to fluctuations in demand for products already produced in

the region. The effect of this policy is to moderate the fluctuations in overall demand for the products of the region, thereby moderating the fluctuations in the level of unemployment.

Governments attempt to accomplish this goal by many means. They offer subsidies or favorable financing to encourage firms to locate plants or other productive facilities in a particular region. Such policies lower the costs of installation of plant and equipment. Alternatively, gov-

not have these flexibilities in wages today. Such factors as minimum wage laws, national unions, and nationwide pay scales for the federal civil service put substantial restraints on possible interprovincial wage differentials. People who prefer province A remain there, yet wages do not fall to create a wage incentive to move to B. Instead unemployment rates rise until (1) the extra uncertainty of finding a job and (2) the lower life-time income expectations because of bouts of unemployment just balance both the marginal non-pecuniary advantages that A enjoys over B and the costs of moving from A to B. In the long run, those who are willing to stay in spite of the higher unemployment remain while the others leave.

In these circumstances increasing local demand, even where that is possible, will lower the rate of out-migration but will *not* lower unemployment. This is because in the long run A's unemployment rate must remain sufficiently higher than B's to balance the relative amenity and migration cost advantages that province A enjoys over B when wages are the same in both areas.

In these circumstances trade restrictions or labor market policies, such as "employ local labor only" laws or employment subsidies, will not reduce unemployment though they will increase employment. As new jobs are created, the rate of out-migration slows so that the rate of unemployment is unchanged. Unless the province's policies are sufficient to create jobs for everyone entering its labor force, all that will happen when more jobs are created is that fewer people will migrate. The local supply rises as fast as the local demand for labor, and the unemployment rate is left unchanged.

The foregoing argument does not necessarily support the view that nothing should be done for regions that have lower incomes or higher unemployment rates. There are many reasons why we might wish to make income transfers to poorer regions. However, it is important to realize that if the phenomenon is an equilibrium phenomenon, no amount of policy intervention will remove it. Policy will then have consequences that are indirect and possibly unforeseen, but policy will not succeed in equalizing incomes and unemployment rates.

If the policies continue to be increased in force as long as these differentials in income or unemployment do not disappear, expenditures will rise and rise and rise, and the ultimate goal of equalization will prove to be utterly elusive.

ernment may improve or install public capital such as roads or ports, thereby lowering the costs of transportation of goods. A third policy is to purchase goods and services from industries located in the region. All these policies have been used by the Department of Regional Economic Expansion (DREE).

An increasingly popular policy is to locate government offices in particular regions. One rationale for this is that government employment is not seasonal and is immune to changes in economic conditions. Such a presence will therefore reduce fluctuations in the level of economic activity in a region.

The overall effects of these policies have been disappointing; regional differences have hardly changed since such policies were introduced. Indeed, some argue that the unaided market would be more likely to reduce the inequalities. If demands for a region's products — and thus for its workers — were low, one would expect its prices and wages to fall. Low prices would increase demand for the region's goods, and low wages would attract new industry. Thus, if left by itself, the regional recession would cure itself and the region would become more diversified. This process has been observed in the New England region of the United States, where, in the absence of government intervention, the decaying textile industry has been substantially replaced by high-technology firms.

Regional development policies may hinder the adjustment process. When the federal government locates offices in the Maritimes and pays the same wage there that it pays in Ottawa or Vancouver, this holds up regional wages but adds to unemployment by discouraging new firms from locating in the Maritimes to gain the benefit of cheap labor.

Others believe that there is scope for public policies to reduce regional inequalities. What is required, they maintain, is merely a more determined and more expensive effort than has been mounted to far.

Summary

1. The concept of poverty involves both relative and absolute levels of income and reflects the aspirations of society as well as the income needed for subsistence alone. Today roughly 20 percent of all Canadians are classified as living in poverty. Since the aggregate poverty gap is small relative to national income, the possibility exists of eradicating poverty in Canada.

2. Economic growth, though it has led to a reduction of poverty, will by itself never eradicate it, for many of those most in need do not share directly in the fruits of growth. Thus public programs are thought to be required.

3. The incidence of poverty is higher in rural areas, in the Atlantic provinces, and among those who are old, have limited education, or are unemployed.

4. Poverty programs are a matter of lively current debate. Some people believe that it is possible and desirable to make further major reductions in poverty now. They place particular importance on an income supplement to the poor regardless of why they are poor. Others believe that further expensive attacks on poverty are undesirable both because of the additional burden they would place on the average taxpayer and because of the disincentive effects generated by welfare programs.

5. Methods used to reduce poverty include retraining programs intended to match people with available jobs; social insurance, which helps to meet the risks of such problems as ill health, unemployment, and retirement; and public assistance designed to serve those ineligible for other programs.

6. Market conditions exercise a powerful influence on factor earnings. This is most evident for nonhuman factors such as raw materials and land. For labor, the influence of nonmonetary factors is greater because the owners of labor must accompany their labor services to work. Nevertheless, market forces exert powerful influences on earnings of labor.

7. There is much evidence of the movement of factors in response to changes in earnings. Factor mobility is typically greater for nonhuman factors than it is for labor. Even where impediments to mobility exist, factors (including labor) tend to move in response to persistent differences in earnings or employment opportunities.

Topics for Review

Poverty and the poverty gap
Correlates of poverty
Occasional poverty and persistent poverty
Possible disincentive effects of alleviating poverty
Social insurance
Categorical assistance and general assistance
Regional economic policy

Discussion Questions

1. In what ways are the problems of poverty in Canada or the United States likely to be different from the problems of poverty in an underdeveloped poor country, such as Bangladesh? In what ways are they easier to solve in one place than in the other?

2. Suppose that your objectives are (first) to eradicate poverty and (second) to reduce unemployment. Evaluate the probable effectiveness of each of the following in meeting each objective.
   a. increasing welfare payments
   b. increased labor union membership
   c. creating a program of public works to hire the poor
   d. ending employment discrimination against blacks
   e. increasing the minimum wage

3. Some poor families are given "rental allowances" to help them pay their rent. What, if any, justification is there for giving the families this money instead of simply giving them extra income that they could spend on whatever they needed most?

4. Is the Sun Life Building immobile? Is the Sun Life Building more mobile among uses than the use of the land it sits on? How about the uses of the pyramids of Egypt? What resources can you think of that are immobile over a time span as long as 25 years? In general, are a factor's earnings likely to be greater or smaller if its mobility is relatively low?

5. The supply of regular New York taxicabs is rigidly controlled by a licensing system that keeps the number of cabs well below what it would be in a free-market situation. A "medallion" issued for a nominal fee by the city confers the right to operate a cab. The medallion, however, is freely salable; in 1980 its price was $68,000.

Evaluate the effect on the price of the medallion of
   a. an increase in average incomes of New Yorkers
   b. increased operation of "gypsy cabs" (cabs without medallions)
   c. increases in parking lot fees and parking violation fines in New York
   d. a new law that bans private passenger autos from midtown during business hours

6. Suppose that you had been on the margin about whether to buy a medallion and become a licensed cab operator in 1980. A 50 percent increase in taxi fares was then authorized. How, if at all, would this affect your decision? Toronto uses a similar scheme, but the price of a medallion there is only about one-half as much as it is in New York. What might account for this difference?

7. Which of the following are valid predictions of the theory of distribution? Are any of them based on misconceptions about the theory?
   a. An increase in the demand for a product will lead, *ceteris paribus*, to an increase in the wage rate of labor used to produce it.
   b. A labor-saving technological change will tend to lead to increasing wages if the quantity of output does not change.
   c. The value of a person's labor to the employer is the maximum amount the person can expect to be paid, but the wage paid may well be less than this amount.
   d. A firm selling its product in a competitive market will pay lower wages to carpenters than a monopolistic seller if both hire carpenters in the same labor market.

Part Seven

**The Market
Economy:
Problems
and Policies**

Microeconomic Policy I: Benefits and Costs of Government Intervention in the Market Economy

24

There are two caricatures of the North American economy. One pictures North America as the last stronghold of free enterprise, with millions of people in a mad and brutal race for the almighty dollar. In the other, North American business people, workers, and farmers are seen strangling slowly in a web of red tape spun by the spider of government regulation. Neither is realistic.

Many aspects of economic life, perhaps more in the United States than in Canada and more in either than in most other countries, are determined by the operation of a free-market system. In North America private preferences, expressed through private markets and influencing private profit-seeking enterprises, determine much of what is produced, how it is produced, and the incomes of productive factors.

But even casual observation makes it clear that public policies and public decisions play a very large role. Not only do laws restrict what people and firms may do, but taxes and subsidies influence their choices. Much public expenditure is not market determined, and this leads to a distribution of national product very different from what would exist in a system that relied entirely on private markets. The United States and Canada are in fact mixed economies.

Although all economies are mixed, the mixture varies greatly among economies and over time. Whether the existing mixture is wrong—and if so, in which direction—is debated sharply today. One reason for the mixture (and the debate) relates to what an unkind critic called the economists' two great insights: markets work and markets fail. A second reason is what the critic might call the political scientists' great insights: government intervention can work, and it can fail. In this chapter we discuss the role of the government in economic markets. Why is it there at all? What does it do well, and what badly? Do we need more or less government intervention?

Market Success

THE INTERDEPENDENT ECONOMY

The nation's economy consists of thousands upon thousands of individual markets. There are markets for agricultural goods, for manufactured goods, and for consumers' services; there are markets for semi-manufactured goods, such as steel and pig iron, which are outputs of some industries and inputs of others; there are markets for raw materials such as iron ore, trees, bauxite, and copper; there are markets for land and for thousands of different types of labor; there are markets in which money is borrowed and in which securities are sold.

An economy is not a series of markets functioning in isolation but an interlocking system in which an occurrence in one market will affect many others. The coordination of what occurs in the many markets is brought about by the price system. Changes in surpluses and scarcities are reflected in price and quantity changes that signal to decision makers what is happening throughout the economy. The responses to these signals cause the signals to change. Such changes trigger other changes. Like a pebble thrown into a pond, one change in one market sends ripples (and sometimes waves) through many other markets.

HOW MARKETS COORDINATE

Any change, such as an increase in demand for beef, requires many further changes and adjustments. Should production of beef change? If so, by how much and in what manner? Someone or something must decide what is to be produced, how, and by whom, and what is to be consumed and by whom. Such decisions can be made by an army of planners who sit in a central office and order more to be produced of this and less of that. Or they can be made by a large number of decentralized decision makers (households and firms), all responding to a series of economic signals given to them by the economy's markets.

How the price system gets these decisions made has been examined at several places in this book (for example, with respect to carrots and brussels sprouts in Chapter 4, agriculture in Chapter 7, and ball-point pens in Chapter 17). When shortages occur in a market, price rises and windfall profits develop; when gluts occur, price falls and windfall losses develop. These are *signals,* for all to see, that arise from the overall conditions of total supply and demand.

Individual households and firms respond to common signals according to their own best interests. There is nothing planned or intentionally coordinated about their actions, yet when (say) a shortage causes price to rise, individual buyers begin to reduce the quantities they demand and individual firms begin to increase the quantities they supply. As a result the shortage will begin to lessen. As it does, prices begin to come back down, and windfall profits are reduced. These signals in turn are seen and responded to by firms and households. Eventually, when the shortage has been eliminated, there will be no windfall profits to attract further increases in supply. The chain of adjustments to the original shortage is completed.

Notice that in the sequence of signal-response-signal-response no one had to foresee at the outset the final price and quantity. Nor did any government agency have to specify who would increase production and who would decrease consumption. Some firms responded to the signal for "more output" by increasing production, and they kept on increasing production until the signal got weaker and weaker and finally disappeared. Some buyers withdrew from the market when they thought prices were too high, and perhaps they re-entered gradually, when they wanted to, as prices became "more reasonable."

Households and firms responding to market signals, not government bureaucrats issuing orders, "decided" who would increase production and who would limit consumption. No one was forced to do something against his or her best judgment. Voluntary responses collectively produced the end result.

To say that the price system coordinates is not to imply that it is perfect. It coordinates responses even to prices "rigged" by monopolistic producers or by government controls. The signal-response process occurs in a price system even when the "wrong" signals are sent.

When an international cartel of uranium producers decided to reduce production and raise price, they created a current shortage (and a fear of worse future shortages) among those electricity utilities that depend on uranium to fuel nuclear power plants. The price of uranium shot up from under $10 per pound to over $40 in less than a year. This enormous price rise greatly increased efforts among producers outside the cartel to find more uranium and to increase their existing production by mining poorer grade ores previously considered too expensive to mine. The increases in production from these actions slowly began to ease the shortage. On the demand side, high prices and short supplies led some utilities to cancel planned nuclear plants and to delay the construction of others. Such actions implied a long-run substitution of oil or coal for uranium. (Only the fact that the OPEC cartel had also sharply raised the price of oil prevented an even more rapid reversal of the previous trend from oil to nuclear-powered generators.) With the prices of both uranium and oil quadrupling, the demand for coal increased sharply, and its price and production rose. Thus the market mechanism generated adjustments to the relative prices of different fuels, even though some prices were set by cartels rather than by the free-market forces of supply and demand. It also set in motion reactions that place limits on the power of the cartel.

This example and countless others illustrate the great discovery of the early economists.

The *unplanned* price system, like an *invisible hand* (Adam Smith's famous phrase), coordinates the responses of individual decision makers who seek only their own self interests. Because they respond to signals that reflect market conditions, their responses are coordinated without any conscious central planning of who may or must do what.

WHAT DO MARKETS DO WELL?

The free-market system has several great virtues: it provides *automatic coordination* without the need for devoting resources to central planning; it is *impersonal* in denying to any individual or firm great power over others; it leads (under well-defined circumstances) to an *efficient allocation of resources;* and it automatically sets in motion forces that *correct any disequilibrium* that may develop. We have just reviewed how markets coordinate; let us review briefly the other points.

Impersonal Decision Making

Suppose (to take an extreme example) that 10,000 families from neighboring areas decide that at existing prices they all want to move into single-family houses in the British Properties in West Vancouver, overlooking Vancouver Harbor. However, that beautiful residential area is already heavily populated. There are at most (say) 1,000 vacant houses or building sites. Obviously, not all of the present and potential residents can live there. Which ones will be able to do so, and which ones will be disappointed?

Market allocation. How would the market system make the allocation? The first impact of the great increase in demand would be a sharp rise in the asking prices of houses in the British Properties. This would persuade some British Properties residents, who probably had had no intention of moving, to sell their houses and move to other areas. The same rises in price would discourage many who had hoped to move into British Properties. The rising prices will also lead some owners of vacant lots to sell or develop them.

One way or the other—by reducing quantity demanded and by encouraging an increase in quantity supplied—the market will make the allocation. Of the 10,000 families who originally wanted to move in, 3,000 may end up living there, while 2,500 old residents move away and 500 of the vacant houses or lots become occupied. Which 3,000 moved in? Those who valued it the most. Which 2,500 moved out? Those who valued the extra money more than the privilege of staying in West Vancouver. The market has sorted them out without anyone's having to issue orders ("you go, you stay") and without the need for a court or a board to hear appeals from those who object to the orders.

Non-market allocation. Had prices not been free to rise, some other system for allocating supply would have been needed. Suppose prices had been frozen by law in order to "keep British Properties housing within the reach of the ordinary family." There would have been dozens of applicants for any house that became available. The sellers would then have had great power to decide to whom to sell (and thus whom to turn down). They might have exercised their prejudices, or they might have found ways to get a secret payoff.

Alternatively, the West Vancouver Council might set up a British Properties Authorized Waiting List (BPAWL) to determine the order in which people would be permitted to become residents. This would give some public official the duty (or perhaps the privilege) of judging the relative worthiness of potential British Property residents and ranking them accordingly. It would also provide opportunities for bribery of those with allocative authority.

Whether allocative authority rests with private individuals or with government officials, excess demand at the fixed price implies personalized power of some people over others. Many who fear the exercise of centralized or personalized power regard the avoidance of this kind of arbi-

trary power a major advantage of market allocation.

Allocative and Productive Efficiency in Equilibrium

As we saw in Chapter 14, competitive markets reach equilibrium at prices equal to both marginal costs of production and minimum average total cost. In so doing they achieve allocative and productive efficiency. (We saw in Chapter 18 that this conclusion depended on the level of costs in competitive markets being no higher than that in noncompetitive markets; we shall consider other qualifications shortly.) Early economists who believed that free markets were synonymous with perfectly competitive markets consequently believed in the efficiency of free markets.

Modern economists, aware of more qualifications concerning the possibilities of a perfectly competitive economy, nevertheless believe that free markets frequently achieve or approximate the competitive result of prices equal to marginal cost and minimum average cost. When they do this, real-world markets achieve or approximate economic efficiency.

In a market economy, market prices signal households about the relative costs *to them* of consuming different commodities. The same prices signal firms about the costs and profitability *to them* of producing the commodities by utilizing different combinations of the factors of production.

The price system links households satisfying their wants and the basic resources of the society. Firms are intermediaries that use resources to produce the commodities that satisfy households' wants.

The linkage that the price system provides will be efficient whenever three conditions are met:

1. Costs faced by firms are the opportunity costs to society of the resources required to produce commodities.

2. Prices at which firms sell their output are equal to marginal costs.
3. Entry and exit of new firms forces prices to the lowest attainable levels of average total cost.

Freely operating markets frequently (but not always) come close to satisfying these conditions.

Self-correction of Disequilibrium

The allocative efficiency discussed above, and in Chapters 14 and 18, concerned the *equilibrium* conditions of a competitive market economy. But the economic system is repeatedly thrown out of equilibrium by continual change. If in this situation the economy does not "pursue" equilibrium, there will be little comfort in saying that if only it reached equilibrium, things would be bright indeed. (We all know someone who would have been a great surgeon if only he or she had gone to medical school.)

An important characteristic of the price system is its ability to set in motion forces that tend to correct disequilibrium.

To review the advantages of the price system in this respect, imagine operating without a market mechanism. Suppose that planning boards make all market decisions. The Board in Control of Women's Clothing hears that pantsuits are all the rage in neighboring countries. It orders a certain proportion of clothing factories to make pantsuits instead of the traditional women's skirt. Conceivably the quantities of pantsuits and skirts produced could be just right, given shoppers' preferences. But what if the board misguessed, producing too many skirts and not enough pantsuits? Long lines would appear at pantsuit counters while mountains of unsold skirts piled up. Once the board saw the lines for pantsuits, it could order a change in quantities produced. Meanwhile, it could store the extra skirts for another season—or ship them to a country with different tastes.

Such a system can correct an initial mistake, but it may prove inefficient in doing so. It may

use a lot of resources in planning and administration that could instead be used to produce commodities. Further, many consumers may be greatly inconvenienced if the board is slow to correct its error. In such a system the members of the board may have no incentive to admit and correct a mistake quickly. Indeed, if the authorities do not like pantsuits, the board may get credit for having stopped that craze before it went too far!

In contrast, suppose that in a market system a similar misestimation of the demand for pantsuits and skirts was made by the women's clothing industry. Lines would develop at pantsuit counters, and inventories of skirts would accumulate. Stores would raise pantsuit prices and run skirt sales. Pantsuit manufacturers could earn large profits by raising prices and running extra shifts to increase production. Some skirt producers would be motivated to shift production quickly to pantsuits and to make skirts more attractive to buyers by cutting prices. Unlike the planning board, the producers in a market system would be motivated to correct their initial mistakes as quickly as possible. Those slowest to adjust would lose the most money and might even be forced out of business.

QUALIFICATIONS ABOUT MARKET SUCCESS

Many nineteenth century economists advocated a policy of **laissez faire**: government should not interfere with the operation of markets. They did so because they believed the price system actually achieved all of the four beneficial results we have just reviewed.

Each of the virtues of market systems that we have examined *may* occur; that does not mean that each *does* occur in every free-market situation. The price system coordinates responses, but the price system has not proved to be the only possible, or necessarily the best, system for regulating an economy. There is a difference between the word "automatic," which we have used, and the phrase "perfectly functioning," which we have not used.

The price system as it actually operates may not yield ideal results. It may not be efficient for a number of reasons, including the presence of monopoly. It may not prove impersonal, as when large firms and large unions have and exercise market power. It may not respond quickly to inefficiencies where there are impediments to the mobility of resources.

In addition, static allocative efficiency may not be a wholly satisfactory goal. One reason, examined in Chapter 18, concerns Schumpeter's insight that dynamic changes in the level of innovation can greatly affect long-run efficiency. A different reason is that a particular allocation of resources, even when it is efficient, will only by accident accord to most people's sense of what is just or fair. A free-market economy distributes output as well as produces it. There are many very different possible allocations of resources, any one of which, once achieved, would meet the test of Pareto-optimality (that no shift of resources would make someone better off without making someone else worse off). The actual distribution of income of a freely functioning competitive system reflects its past: It tends to perpetuate inequalities in the distribution of income and the ownership of assets. Executives and their children exert more influence on market allocations than do taxi drivers and their children.

When a market system "succeeds" in allocating resources efficiently but distributes income in a way that the majority consider highly unfair or unjust, the members of the society are unlikely to believe that the market has succeeded. The supporters of laissez faire focused on the virtues that a market system might achieve and neglected or played down its limitations. The more important these limitations are — in other words, the greater the failures of the market system — the greater will be the incentive to depart from laissez faire.

Market Failure

Canada does not have a laissez faire economy. What has led so many Canadians to believe that a pure private enterprise system is not the best of all possible worlds? What has led them to lessen their reliance on the unrestricted workings of the free market and, in many cases, to impose regulations on markets or to substitute collective action for individual action? What leads many Canadians today to question whether we have gone far enough — or too far — away from free markets?

Whenever market performance is judged to be faulty, it is the practice to speak of **market failure.** The word "failure" in this context probably conveys the wrong impression.

Market failure does not mean that nothing good has happened, only that the *best attainable outcome* has not been achieved.

As a result of market failure, many people believe it desirable to modify, restructure, complement, or supplement the unrestricted workings of the market. There are several major sources of market failure, and it is important to understand how they arise. As we have seen, there are two somewhat different senses in which the phrase is used. One is the failure of the market system to achieve efficiency in the allocation of society's resources, the other is its failure to serve social goals other than efficiency. We shall discuss both.

EXTERNALITIES AS A SOURCE OF INEFFICIENCY

Cost, as economists define it, concerns the value of resources used up in the process of production. According to the opportunity cost principle, value is the benefit the resources would produce in the best alternative use. But who decides what resources are used and what is their opportunity cost? When a timber company buys a forest, it perhaps regards the alternative to cutting the trees this year as cutting them next year or five years hence. But citizens in the area may value the forest as a nature sanctuary or a recreation area. The firm values the forest for the trees; the local residents may value the trees for the forest. The two values need not be the same.

These differences in point of view lead to the important distinction between private cost and social cost.

Private cost measures the value of the best alternative uses of the resources available to the producer.

As we noted in Chapter 11, private cost is usually measured by the market price of the resources that the firm uses.

Social cost measures the value of the best alternative uses of resources that are available to the whole society.

For some resources the best measure of the social cost may be exactly the same as the private cost: the price set by the market may well reflect the value of the resources in their best alternative use. For other resources, as will soon be clear, social cost may differ sharply from private cost. Discrepancies between private and social cost lead to market failure from the social point of view. The reason is that efficiency requires that prices cover social cost, but private producers, adjusting to private costs, will neglect those elements of social cost that are not included in private costs. When an element of (social) cost is not part of a private firm's profit and loss calculation, it is *external* to its decision-making process.

Discrepancies between social and private cost lead to **externalities,** which are the costs or benefits of a transaction that are incurred or received by members of the society but are not taken into account by the parties to the transaction. They are also called **third-party effects** because parties other than the two primary participants in the transaction (the buyer and the seller) are affected. Externalities arise in many different ways.

Harmful Externalities

Pollution. A major source of differences between private cost and social cost arises when firms use resources they do not regard as scarce.

This is characteristic of most examples of pollution. When a paper mill produces pulp for the world's newspapers, more people are affected than its suppliers, employees, and customers. Its water-discharged effluent hurts the fishing boats that ply nearby waters, and its smog makes many resort areas less attractive, thereby reducing the tourist revenues that local motel operators and boat renters can expect. The firm neglects these effects because its profits are not affected by the external effects of its actions, while they are affected by how much paper it produces.

This example and hundreds more concern the production of goods and services by private firms. They also concern the use of society's basic resources such as timber, coal, labor, iron ore, water, and air. The pollution connected with production is not an accidental event, as is the periodic breaking up of oil tankers off the world's beaches or the blowout of oil in the Gulf of Mexico. The pollution is the result of calculated decisions as to what and how to produce or consume.

Common-property resources. The world's oceans once teemed with fish, but today a worldwide fish shortage is upon us. There seems to be no doubt that overfishing has caused the problem. How could this happen?

Fish are one example of what is called a **common-property resource.** No one owns the oceans' fish until they are caught. Thus a fisherman can sell them only when he has caught them. Even if he realizes that doubling the catch this year will hurt next year's catch, he cannot afford to hold back unless everyone does the same.

Even if the effects of the decline in the fishing industry are regarded as problems for that industry alone (which of course they are not; unemployed fishermen and unavailable fish impose costs on all of us), the effects represent an externality to the individual act of fish production. When one fisherman takes one too many unspawned fish, he affects every other fisherman's catch next year. Yet this effect—a cost to someone else—does not play a role in the fisherman's private calculation of the cost of catching that fish. Thus there is a discrepancy between private and social cost, an externality.

Congestion. Collisions between private planes and commercial airliners are headline news when they occur. They cannot occur unless *both* planes are in the air; this is what creates the externality. Suppose that the probability of a midair plane crash is roughly proportional to the number of planes in the air. Suppose too that I have the choice of flying from Calgary to Edmonton in my own plane or on a commercial airliner that has 100 of its 150 seats filled. In choosing to fly by myself, I decide that the extra "cost" to me of taking the risk of a midair collision can be compensated for by taking out some extra life insurance.

What I have neglected is part of the social cost of my action: the increased risk for every other person in the air on my route of flight that results from one more plane in the air. Since I do not consider your increased risk, my private decision may have been the wrong social decision.

Notice that in the case of congestion no individual need be at fault. If ten planes, or cars, or people, occupy a space large enough for only nine, any one of them may be regarded as the "one-too-many."

Neglect of future consequences of present actions. When private producers ignore or undervalue future effects on others, they neglect an externality. A business facing bankruptcy tomorrow may be motivated to cheat on safety standards in order to cut costs today, even if it would hurt the firm's reputation in the long term and impose heavy future costs on others.

One dramatic example of the neglect of future effects concerns DDT. DDT was invented in 1874, but its insecticidal properties were not discovered until 1939, and it was not until World War II had moved to the mosquito-ridden Pacific three years later that its full powers were revealed.

After the war it was found to be equally effec-

tive in controlling agricultural pests, particularly the cotton boll weevil. When in 1948 the Swiss chemist Paul Mueller won the Nobel prize for his discovery of its value as a pesticide, few doubted his contributions to the world's well-being. The use of DDT great steadily until, in the peak year of 1958, 78 million pounds were used in the United States alone.

Gradually it was confirmed that DDT did more than kill unwanted insects. Once sprayed, the chemical did not break down for years. It entered the food chain and worked its way up from insects to birds and fish, to small mammals, and to larger and larger birds and mammals, including human beings. Arctic penguins, though thousands of miles from any sprayed areas, have measurable amounts of DDT in their bodies. DDT has thinned the egg shells of large birds to the point where breakage threatens many species, among them the peregrine falcon, the osprey, and the eagle.

In 1962 Rachel Carson began the public debate about DDT in her book *The Silent Spring,* in which she labeled DDT an "elixir of death." In 1969—21 years after the Nobel prize was awarded—formal attempts to ban the use of DDT began. DDT had come of age. The "future" costs that were neglected in the forties and fifties are being paid today.

Beneficial Externalities

Externalities can be for good as well as for ill. When I paint my house, I enhance my neighbors' view and the value of their property. When an Einstein or a Rembrandt gives the world a discovery or a work of art whose worth is far in excess of what he is paid to produce it, he confers an external benefit. Educating my children may make them better citizens and thus benefit third parties, even if they do not prove to be latter-day Nightingales or Mozarts. Individuals will tend to engage in too little of activities that produce beneficial externalities because they bear all of the costs but others reap part of the benefits.

Externalities, whether adverse or beneficial, make privately efficient market results socially inefficient.

MARKET IMPERFECTIONS AND IMPEDIMENTS AS A SOURCE OF INEFFICIENCY

The efficiency of the price system depends on firms and households receiving and responding to the signals provided by prices, costs, and profits. Forces that seriously change these signals or prevent the required response to them may cause a market to fail to perform efficiently. Consider a few examples.

Barriers to Mobility

One kind of market impediment is factor immobility. If increases in a factor's pay do not lead to increases in supply (for any of the reasons discussed in Chapters 21 and 23), the market will fail to reallocate resources promptly in response to changing demands. Monopoly power creates market imperfections by preventing enough resources from moving in response to the market signals of high profits. In this case, barriers to entry rather than factor immobility frustrate the flow of resources. Another kind of market imperfection is ignorance or deception; signals can work only if they are received.

Collective Consumption Goods

Certain goods and services, if they provide benefits to anyone, necessarily provide them to a large group of people. Such goods are called **collective consumption goods.** National defence is the prime example of a collective consumption good. An adequate defence establishment protects everyone in the country whether they want it or not, and there is no market where you can buy more of it and your neighbor less. The quantity of national defence provided must be decided collectively. Other examples of collective consumption goods include the beautification of a city, a levee to protect a city from a flood, and a hurricane-warning system. In general, market systems cannot compel payment for a collective consumption good since there is no way to prevent a person from receiving the services of the good if he or she refuses to pay for it.

Excessive or Prohibitive Transactions Costs

If a firm's products are not marketable, say because of an institutional barrier, they will not be produced even though people value them more than their costs. Costs of negotiating and completing a transaction, such as the costs of billing or the bad-debt cost of those who never pay, are examples of **transactions costs.** They are always present to some degree, and they are a necessary cost of doing business. If buyers cannot be made to pay for the product, for example, the producer will not be motivated to provide it. For a private firm to stay in business, it must be able to recover both production and transactions costs. If transactions costs are higher than they need to be because of imperfections in the private market, some products that it is efficient to produce will not be produced, and the market will have failed. Consider an example.

Could a private entrepreneur provide a road system for Calgary, paying for it by collecting tolls? The answer is surely no (at least with today's technology). It would be prohibitively expensive, both in money and in delays, to erect and staff a toll booth at every freeway exit. The users of a road system may be more than willing to pay the full costs of its construction and maintenance, but without an inexpensive way to make them pay, no private firm can produce the road. The government, collecting revenue by means of a gasoline tax, can do what the private market fails to do. (Whether it can do so without making a different mistake — producing more of the product than users are willing to pay for — is discussed below.)

The warning about technology merits an additional comment. Technology changes rapidly.

For example, the electronic metering of road use may make the toll booth unnecessary just as the postage meter has made licking stamps unnecessary. Thus what a private market cannot do today, it may be able to do efficiently tomorrow.

Market imperfections may lead to market failure by preventing firms and households from completing many transactions that are required for efficient resource allocation.

THE NEGLECT OF NONMARKET GOALS AS A SOURCE OF MARKET FAILURE

The two sources of market failure we have discussed—externalities and market impediments—concern the inability of the free market to achieve efficient resource allocation. Exclusive reliance on markets, even when markets are allocatively efficient, may lead to the neglect of other goals that seem important to society. The market can be said to have failed when this occurs.

Public Provision May Lead to Different Preferred Goods

Police protection, even justice, might be provided by private market mechanisms. Watchmen, Pinkerton detectives, and bodyguards all provide policelike protection. Privately hired arbitrators, "hired guns," and vigilantes of the Old West represent private ways of obtaining "justice." Yet the members of society may believe that a public police force is preferable to a private one and that public justice is preferable to justice for hire.

For another example, public schools may be better or worse than private schools, but they are likely to be different, particularly because persons other than parents, teachers, and owners influence their policies. Much of the case for public education rests on the advantages to you of having other people's children educated in a particular kind of environment that is *different* from what a private school would provide. Of course,

you can debate whether the differences make it better or worse. The market may be said to fail if the public product is better.

Protecting Individuals from the Acts of Others

People can use—even abuse—other people for economic gain in ways that the members of society find offensive. Child labor laws and minimum standards of working conditions are responses to such actions. Yet direct abuse is not the only example of this kind of market failure. In an unhindered free market, the adults in a household would usually decide how much education to buy for their children. Selfish parents might buy no education, while egalitarian parents might buy the same quantity for all their children regardless of their abilities. The members of society may want to interfere in these choices, both to protect the child of the selfish parent and to ensure that some of the scarce educational resources are distributed according to intelligence rather than wealth. All households are forced to provide a minimum of education for their children, and strong inducements are offered—through public universities, scholarships, and other means—for gifted children to consume more education than either they or their parents might voluntarily choose if they had to pay the entire cost themselves.

Paternalism: Protecting Individuals from Themselves

In a significant number of cases, members of society acting through the state seek to protect adult (and presumably responsible) individuals, not against others, but against themselves. Laws prohibiting heroin and other hard drugs and laws prescribing the installation and use of seat belts are intended primarily to protect individuals from their own ignorance or shortsightedness.

Intervention of this kind with the free choices of individuals is called **paternalism.** Whether or not such actions reflect real values of the majority of the society, or whether they simply reflect overbearing governments, there is no doubt that the market will not provide this kind of protection. Buyers do not buy what they do not want, and sellers have no motive to provide it. Thus if the members of society insist on such "protection," markets may be said to fail to provide it.

The Existence of "Social Obligations"

In a market system you can pay someone to do things for you. If you can persuade someone else to clean your house in return for $25, presumably both parties to the transaction are better off: You would prefer to part with $25 rather than clean the house yourself, and your household help prefers $25 to not cleaning your house.

Normally society does not interfere with people's ability to negotiate mutually advantageous contracts when there are no external effects. Such freedom is not allowed, however, where an activity is regarded as a social obligation. Prime examples are military service in wartime and jury duty, in which those selected are not permitted to hire substitutes. Similarly, one may not legally sell one's vote to another.

Compassion

A free-market system rewards certain groups and penalizes others. The workings of the market may be stern, even cruel; consequently society often chooses to intervene. Should heads of households be forced to bear the full burden of their misfortune if, through no fault of their own, they lose their jobs? Even if they lose their jobs through their own fault, should they and their families have to bear the whole burden, which may include starvation? Should the ill and aged be thrown on the mercy of their families? What if they have no families? Both private charities and a great many government policies are concerned with modifying the distribution of income that results from such things as where one starts, how able one is, how lucky one is, and how one fares in the free-market world.

Even if the price system allocated goods and services with complete efficiency, this would not assure market success if members of society have other goals that they wish to serve by the allocation of resources.

Responding to Market Failure

While private collective action can sometimes remedy the failures of private individual action (private charities can help the poor; volunteer fire departments can fight fires), by far the most common remedy for market failure is reliance on government intervention.

It is useful to ask several questions about possible government policies designed to correct market failure. First, what tools does the government have? Second, when and how vigorously should the tools be used? Third, under what circumstances is government intervention likely to fail?

THE TOOLS OF MICROECONOMIC POLICY

There are numerous ways in which one or another level of government can prevent, alter, complement, or replace the workings of the unrestricted market economy. It is convenient to group these methods into four broad categories:

1. *Public provision.* Goods and services may be publicly provided in addition to or instead of private provision.
2. *Redistribution.* Public expenditures and taxes may be used to provide a distribution of income and output different than that which the private market provides.
3. *Rule making.* Rules and regulations may be adopted to compel, forbid, or specify within acceptable limits the behavior that private decisions makers may engage in.
4. *Structuring incentives.* Government may alter market signals to persuade rather than force decision makers to adopt different behavior,

either by one of the above methods or in some other way.

Each of the four methods is frequently used, and each has great capacity to change whatever outcomes the unregulated market would provide. The first two will be discussed in detail in Chapter 25; the remainder of this section concerns the last two, rule making and structuring incentives.

Rule Making

Rules require, limit, or compel certain activities and market actions. It is helpful to distinguish between *proscriptive* and *prescriptive* rules.

Proscriptive rules. These regulations are like the Ten Commandments; they tell people and firms what they can and cannot do. Such rules require parents to send their children to school and to have them inoculated against measles and diphtheria. Laws that prohibit gambling and pornography attempt to enforce a particular moral code on the whole society. In Chapter 18 we discussed an important form of policy by prohibition—competition policy.

There are many other examples: Children cannot legally be served alcoholic drinks. Prostitution is prohibited in most places, even between a willing buyer and a willing seller. In most provinces you must buy insurance in case you should do damage with your private motor car. A person who offers goods for sale, including his or her own house, cannot refuse to sell because of a dislike for the customer's color or dress. There are rules against fraudulent advertising and the sale of substandard, adulterated, or poisonous foods.

Such rules only set limits to the decisions that firms and households can make; they do not replace those decisions. But the allowed limits can be changed. An important means of government regulation is to change old rules or add new ones that redefine the boundary between forbidden and permitted behavior.

Prescriptive rules. Prescriptive rule making substitutes the rule maker's judgment for the firm's or the household's judgment about such things as prices charged, products produced, and methods of production. It tends to restrict private action more than proscriptive regulation does because it replaces private decision making rather than limiting it to an acceptable set of decisions. Regulation of public utilities is an important example of prescriptive regulation (see Chapter 18). But prescriptive regulation goes far beyond the natural monopoly regulation we have discussed.

Federal regulatory commissions regularly decide such matters as who may broadcast and on what frequencies; which airlines may fly which routes; what rates bus lines and pipeline operators may charge for different kinds of services; what prices may be paid for gasoline and how much foreign textiles may be imported into Canada.

Effectiveness. The rule making appears to be a cheap, simple, and direct way of compelling desirable behavior in the face of market failure. But the simplicity is deceptive. Rules must be enforceable and enforced, and once enforced they must prove effective if they are to achieve the results hoped for by those who made them. These conditions are often difficult and expensive to achieve.

Consider the requirement for the installation of an antipollution device that will meet a certain standard in reducing automobile exhaust emissions. Such a law may be the outcome of debate in Parliament on pollution control—and having passed the bill, the government will turn to other things. Yet certain problems must be solved before the rule can achieve its purposes. It may be relatively easy to enforce the law at the manufacturers' level because they are few in number. (This is not automatically true; witness the Ford Motor Company's fine of $7 million for "rigging" pollution tests in the United States in the 1970s.) But even with perfect compliance by the manufacturer, the device will not work well unless it is kept in working order by the individual driver. And it would be expensive to inspect every vehicle regularly and to force owners to keep the devices at the standard set by law. Even a well-designed rule will work only until those regulated figure out a way to evade its intent while obeying its letter. There will be substantial incentive to find such a loophole, and resources that could be used elsewhere will be devoted to the search—and to counteracting such avoidance or evasion.

Structuring Incentives

Government can change the incentives of households and firms in a great variety of ways. It can fix minimum or maximum prices (as we saw in the discussions of agriculture and rent control in Chapter 7). It can adjust the tax system to offer many exemptions and deductions. Tax-deductible mortage interest and real estate taxes, for example, can make owned housing relatively more attractive than rental housing. Such tax treatment sends the household different signals than those sent by the free market. Scholarships to students to become nurses or teachers may offset barriers to mobility into those occupations. Fines and criminal penalties for violating the rules imposed are another part of the incentive structure.

An important means of influencing incentives is to change the prices that firms and households pay in such a way as to eliminate externalities. Because externalities are a major source of market failure, much attention has been given to means of inducing decision makers to take them into account. Charging a producing firm for the pollution it causes can motivate the firm to alter its production in a socially desirable way. Procedures that make firms take account of the extra social costs they impose are said to **internalize** the external effects of production. How exactly does this work?

First we need to define terms. The **net private benefit** (*NPB*) of a unit of production is the difference between that unit's contribution to a firm's revenue and its contribution to the firm's cost. In other words, it is the contribution to profit of that unit. If we think of each unit of production as contributing to social welfare (and call that contribution **social benefit**) and to cost (*social cost,* defined on page 456), we can define the difference between social benefit and social cost as **net social benefit** (*NSB*).

Net social benefit is the key concept in judging efficiency. A unit should be produced if, but only if, its *NSB* is greater than or equal to zero.

In general *NSB* will be equal to *NPB* plus beneficial externalities minus adverse externalities. In the following discussion, we consider an adverse externality (such as pollution) so that *NSB* is less than *NPB*.

A private firm responding only to private benefits and costs will produce up to the point at which marginal *NPB* becomes zero. But at that output marginal *NSB*, being less than *NPB*, is necessarily negative: too much has been produced from the social point of view. This market failure can be avoided by the procedure shown in Figure 24-1. Once the firm has been forced to pay for what were previously externalities, the new net private benefit is exactly the same as net social benefit. That is, *NPB* = *NSB*. Thus the firm will be motivated to produce only as long as marginal *NSB* is not negative.

Internalization avoids the market failure caused by externalities.

There are many ways to internalize external costs. Consider two. If the amount of the external cost imposed per unit of output is known, it is possible to impose an **effluent charge,** or pollution tax, that compels the producer to pay a tax on every unit of polluting production. Such a charge might lead the producer to find a way to produce without polluting. Another way to internalize external costs is to give legal standing to private citizens to sue for damages against polluters or to seek court injunctions against polluting activities. The legal action makes it costly for polluters; there will be damage payments if they lose and legal payments win or lose.

FIGURE 24-1
The Consequence and Correction of Externalities

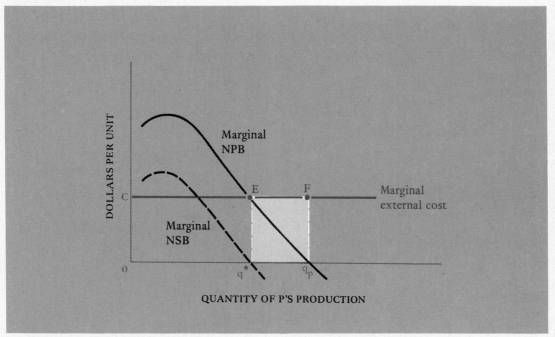

Internalizing an externality can correct market failure. The *NPB* earned by a private firm, *P,* is shown by the solid black curve. The firm is motivated to produce all units that make a positive contribution to its profits. Its equilibrium output is q_p where *NPB* is zero. This production imposes an external cost of $\$C$ *per unit* on outsiders (call them *S*), as shown by the colored line. Subtracting this additional social cost from the *NPB* yields the *NSB,* the curve shown by the dashed black line. The socially optimal output is q^* where marginal *NSB* equals zero. At this output, *NPB* is just equal to marginal external cost. (Note that the only way to avoid all the external costs is for *P* to produce nothing.) At q^* the outsiders, *S*, are still having costs inflicted on them by *P*, but *S*'s costs *plus P*'s private costs are just equal at the margin to *P*'s profit from production.

Suppose the firm is required to pay an "effluent tax" of $\$C$ per unit. Its *NPB* now becomes the dashed black line. The externality has been *internalized,* and the profit-maximizing firm reduces its output from q_p to q^*. It does this because any units produced beyond q^* would now subtract from total profits; given the tax, marginal profits are negative beyond q^*.

GOVERNMENT ATTEMPTS TO CORRECT MARKET FAILURE: BENEFITS AND COSTS

Consider the following argument: (1) The market system is working imperfectly; (2) government has the legal means to improve the situation; (3) therefore the public interest will be served by government intervention.

This appealing argument is deficient because it neglects two important considerations. First, government intervention is costly. For that reason not every market failure is worth correcting; the benefit of the correction must be balanced against the cost of achieving it. Second, government intervention may be imperfect. Just as markets sometimes succeed and sometimes fail, so government intervention sometimes succeeds and sometimes fails.

To evaluate governmental intervention it is necessary to compare the benefits and the costs of the intervention. In many cases each is large.

Avoiding Undesirable Externalities and the Coase Theorem

Look again at Figure 24-1 where a producer, P, is inflicting external costs on S. P will produce q_p instead of the socially optimal output, q^*. Consider five alternative ways the output q^* might be achieved.

I. Direct Determination of Quantity Produced

1. The government might nationalize the industry and direct it to produce q^*.
2. The government might determine q^* and then try to impose that output on the private producer. This could be attempted by either (a) fining the firm heavily if its output exceeds q^* or (b) giving the firm a subsidy if its output does not exceed q^*. To be effective, the fine or subsidy must exceed the profits resulting from producing beyond q^*.

II. Government Intervention to Internalize the Externality

3. The government can place an effluent tax on P of C per unit. This forces P to take the full social costs into account and P is then motivated to produce at q^*.
4. P can be made legally liable to compensate S. Firm P could be forced to pay C per unit (to S) in addition to its private costs of production. P would then be motivated to produce at q^*.

III. Private Agreement Between P and S

5. Even if P has no liability to compensate S, and even if the government does not levy a tax on P, the socially optimal result can still occur. This is because it will pay S to bribe P to produce at q^*. Since every unit P produces imposes a cost of C on S, it is worthwhile for S to bribe P any amount up to C for every unit by which P will reduce production. Each unit produced between q^* and q_p adds less than C to P's profits. Thus P should be prepared to stop producing those units in return for a bribe equal to or greater than its marginal profit. Thus S can bribe P to reduce output from q_p to q^*. Below q^*, however, the marginal private profit to P is greater than the cost that P's production imposes on S. Thus S cannot persuade P to produce less than q^* since at outputs less than q^* the minimum bribe P would accept is more than C.

Each scheme will produce the same socially optimal output q^*. Each, however, yields a different distribution of costs and benefits. We leave it as an exercise for the reader to discover how P and S would rank each scheme.

Each scheme will have a different cost of enforcement and a different probability of evasion. Each will also have a different degree of flexibility in the face of changing conditions. But in spite of their differences, each scheme can ensure that there is an optimal quantity of resources allocated to the production of the commodity.

Professor Ronald H. Coase of the University of Chicago once put these propositions in a most startling way. He assumed that there were no transactions costs. Then, he pointed out, it does not matter which party, P or S, is fined or made legally liable for preventing an undesirable result. Since it is in their combined interest to avoid production beyond q^*, it will pay them jointly to avoid the result. Therefore laws and court proceedings fixing legal liability for a vast range of events such as pollution damage, defective products, and so on may be irrelevant to efficient allocation of resources.

Critics of Coase have been quick to point out that in many cases transactions costs are not negligible, considerations of equity or income distribution are paramount, or one party is so much better able to identify and control adverse effects that the party should be made responsible on the grounds of efficiency. In these cases, laws still affect the allocation of resources as well as the distribution of gains and losses.

Large benefits do not justify government intervention, nor do large costs make it unwise. What matters is the relative size of benefits to costs.

The *benefits* of government intervention are the value of the market failures averted. If pollution imposes external costs of *$X,* then government action that prevents the amount of pollution will avoid *$X* of social costs. In other words, it provides public benefits of *$X.*

The *costs* of government intervention are not stated so concisely because they are of several different kinds whose *sum* is the total cost of intervention.

Government Expenditures on Corrective Activities: Internal Costs

When government inspectors visit plants to see whether they are complying with federally imposed standards of health, industrial safety, or environmental protection, they are imposing costs on the public. When regulatory bodies develop rules, hold hearings, write opinions, or have their staff prepare research reports, they are incurring costs. When the Department of Consumer and Corporate Affairs prosecutes a case on the advice of the Restrictive Trade Practices Commission, it engages lawyers, economists, technical experts, clerks, and others to prepare the case, thereby incurring costs. The costs of the judges and clerks and court reporters who hear and transcribe and review the evidence are likewise costs imposed by regulation. All these activities use valuable resources, resources that could have provided very different goods and services.

The aggregate size of federal expenditures for activities that regulate market behavior alone are large indeed. Such expenditures have grown greatly in the last several decades; they represent one cause of the growth in the size of government in the economy, described in detail in the next chapter.

Costs Imposed on Those Regulated: Direct External Costs

The nature and size of the extra costs borne by firms subject to government intervention are themselves of several kinds, and they vary with the type of regulation. A few examples are worth noting.

Changes in costs of production. Antipollution regulations forced producers not to burn high sulfur coal. As a result, extra fuel costs were imposed on many firms. Such cost increases are directly attributable to regulation.

For 50 years (since the mid 1920s) the prices of automobiles relative to other consumer goods were falling because of continuing technological advances in automobile engineering. Recent federal safety and emission standards have added so much to the cost of producing automobiles that in the 1970s Canadians had to adjust to a steadily rising trend in the relative prices of autos.

Costs of compliance. Government regulation and supervision generate a flood of reporting and related activities that are often summarized in the phrase "red tape." The number of hours of business time devoted to understanding, reporting about, and contesting regulatory provisions is enormous. Occupational safety and environmental control have greatly increased the size of nonproduction payrolls. The legal costs alone of a major corporation can run into tens of millions of dollars per year. While all of this provides lots of employment for lawyers and economic experts, it is costly because there are other tasks that such professionals could do that would add more to the production of consumer goods and services.

Losses in productivity. Quite apart from the actual expenditures, the regulatory climate may reduce the opportunity or the incentive for experimentation, innovation, and the introduction of new products. Requiring advance government clearance before a new method or product may be introduced (on grounds of potential safety hazards or environmental impact) can eliminate the incentive to develop it. (We discussed the role of regulation in productivity growth in Chapter 18.)

The requirement for advance approval by a regulatory commission before entry is permitted into a regulated industry can discourage potential competitors. The consortiums wishing to bid for the contracts to build Arctic gas pipelines found that their applications had to meet detailed and elaborate specifications laid down by the National Energy Board. Some economists believe that this sharply reduced competition for the contracts.

Costs Imposed on Third Parties: Indirect External Costs

It has been suggested that because of regulatory activities the growth rate of output per person has been decreasing. Such lost purchasing power is an externality of government intervention. It may seem paradoxical that government intervention to offset adverse externalities can create new adverse externalities, but it is plain that it can.

Consider an example. Government regulations designed to assure that all new drugs introduced are both effective and safe have the incidental effect of delaying the introduction of drugs which are both effective and safe by an average of about nine months. The benefits of these regulations are related to the unsafe and ineffective drugs kept off the market. But nothing is without cost. Here the cost includes the unavailability for about nine months of all those safe and effective drugs whose introduction was delayed.

Government Failure and the Theory of Government Intervention

All costs of intervention discussed in the previous section would be present with a government that had perfect foresight in defining goals, an unerring ability to choose the least costly means of achieving them, and intelligent and dedicated officials whose concern was to do those things — and only those things — that achieved the greatest possible efficiency of the economy.

CAUSES OF GOVERNMENT FAILURE

Government intervention usually falls short of the high standard just described. This is not because bureaucrats are worse than other people, more stupid, more rigid, or more venal. Instead, it is because they are like others, with the usual flaws and virtues. Here are six reasons why government intervention can be *imperfect* (i.e., "fail") in achieving its potential.

Imperfect knowledge or foresight. Regulators may not know enough to set correct standards. For example, natural gas prices may, with the best of intentions, be set too low. The result will be too much quantity demanded and too little quantity supplied, with no automatic correction built in. Or the automobile emission standards for 1983 may be too demanding, thereby proving unexpectedly expensive to achieve — or too lax, thereby leading to unexpected excessive pollution.

Rigidities. Regulatory rules and allocations are hard to change. Yet technology and economic circumstances change continually. Regulations that at one time protected the public against a natural monopoly may perpetuate an unnecessary monopoly after technological changes have made competition possible. Giving Bell Canada a monopoly in long-distance communication, and specifying its price structure, made sense when the technology for transmitting messages (use of cable) led to natural monopoly. After a communications satellite had been placed in orbit there was room for many competitors, but the regulatory commission was not free simply to open up the industry to anyone. Too many people had invested in the telephone industry and accepted limited profits on the expectation of continued regulation.

Inefficient means. Government may fail to choose the least costly *means* of solving a problem. It may decree a specific form of antipollution device that proves less effective and more expensive than another. A strict rule that proves all but impossible to enforce may be passed, when a milder one would have achieved higher compliance at lower enforcement cost.

Myopic regulation. Regulation may become too restricted and too narrowly defined because the regulators are forced to specialize. Specialization may lead to expertise in a given area, but the regulators may lack the breadth to relate their area to broader concerns. Officials charged with the responsibility for a healthy *railway* industry (dating from the time when railways were the dominant means of transportation) may fail to see that the encouragement of trucking, even at the expense of the railways, may be necessary for a healthy *transportation* industry.

Political constraints. Political realities may prevent the "right" policy from being adopted, even when it has been clearly identified. Suppose a technically perfect tax (or farm, or tariff) policy is designed by the experts. It will surely hurt some groups and benefit others. Lobbyists will go to work. Different cabinet ministers will argue for changes that benefit particular special interest groups. Negotiations with some or all of the provinces will take place. Eventually the law will be passed, but its final form may differ considerably from its original "technically perfect" state. This scenario occurs because the political process must respond to political realities. "After all," the official may reason as he yields to the demands of the widget lobby (against his best judgment about the public interest), "if I'm defeated for reelection (or not reappointed), I won't

be here to serve the public interest on even more important issues next year." (Next year he will have to support widgets out of a sense of consistency!)

Decision maker's objectives. Public officials almost always wish to serve the public interest. But they have their careers, their families, and their prejudices as well. Their own needs are seldom wholly absent from their consideration of the actions they will take. Similarly, their definition of the public interest is likely to be influenced heavily by their personal views of what policies are best.

A close relationship often exists between the regulators and those they regulate. Many government regulators come from industry and plan to return to it. The broadcasting official who serves five years on the Canadian Radio and Television Commission and hopes to become a network vice-president after that term of office may view the networks' case in a not wholly disinterested way. Indeed, regulators may protect an industry in ways that would be quite illegal if done from within the industry.

THE REALITY OF GOVERNMENT FAILURE

Regulation is difficult, for it requires all kinds of market decisions without the benefit of self-correcting market signals. The government regulator can decide to build a highway system and raise the money to pay for it, and once built, it will be heavily used. But would the users have been willing to pay as much for the higway as it actually cost? There is no market to answer this question.

Indeed, there is good reason to expect that the public sector will provide too much of the road network (or other public good), with the result that the marginal cost exceeds the marginal benefit. The reason is political. The beneficiaries are likely to know which politicians voted for the road network in their city, and they will reelect them, whereas taxpayers pay for so many things that they do not identify the extra taxes that the road network imposes on them.

Evaluating the costs and the probable effectiveness of government intervention requires a comparison of the unregulated economic system as it is working (not as it might work ideally) with the pattern of government intervention as it is likely to perform (not as it might perform ideally). Government failure, like market failure, is a fact of life. It can be caused by stupidity or by corruption, but those flaws are not necessary. The ordinary knowledge and skill and foresight of honest bureaucrats will not by themselves avoid the myriad problems of regulation.

THE THEORY OF GOVERNMENT INTERVENTION TO CORRECT MARKET FAILURE

Economic principles are useful in making decisions concerning the optimal correction of market failure in a particular case. In order to develop these principles, we shall look at the question of preventing pollution.

There are people who are wholly unconcerned about pollution and regard the current fuss as the troublemaking activities of a pampered generation. There are others who regard every form of pollution as a national scandal and some forms as threatening an imminent crisis of survival. A more balanced view recognizes that "pollution" covers many externalities, ranging from threats to our survival to minor nuisances. Virtually all activity leaves some waste product; to say that all pollution must be removed whatever the cost is to try for the impossible and to ensure a vast commitment of society's scarce resources to many projects that will yield a low social value. But somewhere between trying for the impossible and maintaining a callous indifference to the problem lies a middle ground. Economics helps to define it.

We approach the problem by assuming that

government intervention is perfect and imposes no indirect costs. Later we shall relax these artificial assumptions.

Costless, "Perfect" Intervention

We start with the easiest case: Government intervention is costless except for the direct costs imposed by changes in the nature of production, and government intervention is completely honest, wise, and efficient. All the government must do is identify the best form of pollution control, determine the right amount of it, and institute the appropriate means of achieving it. How should it proceed?

First it must choose among alternative antipollution strategies. Suppose a particular factory is releasing all kinds of soot and noxious gases into the atmosphere through its chimneys. The government's experts identify four ways to avoid or reduce the effects of the pollution: (1) shut down the plant or reduce its hours of operation; (2) move everyone out of the area being polluted; (3) require the company to install filters on its smokestacks in order to clean up its exhaust; (4) change the firm's method of production to one that produces cleaner discharges. After detailed study, the experts recommend the third course of action: to filter the exhausts.[1]

The next question concerns how much pollution to eliminate. The experts advise that it is easy and cheap to get rid of virtually all the soot by installing a mechanical filter. But the gases, especially sulfur dioxide (SO_2), are more of a problem. Simple recirculation of the gases would reduce the discharge of SO_2 by 50 percent; after that, the cost doubles for each further 10 percent reduction in the remaining SO_2. At most it would be possible to eliminate 99.44 percent of all SO_2, but the cost would be vast. In economic terms,

---

[1] This is not always the best solution, of course. This first-stage determination among alternative means is of prime importance in achieving the correct solution. A major source of "government failure" is choice of the wrong technique of control.

the marginal costs of removal rise sharply as the amount of SO_2 eliminated rises from 50 percent to 99.44 percent.

What percentage of the gases should be eliminated? The answer depends on the marginal benefits relative to marginal costs. The benefits of pollution control are the external effects avoided. They are not expected to rise as the amount of discharge decreases; after all, the atmosphere can handle a certain amount of discharge with no problem. The optimal amount of prevention will occur where the marginal costs of further prevention equal the marginal benefits. This is illustrated by the black curves in Figure 24-2.

The optimal amount of pollution prevention will be less than the maximum possible when pollution is costly to prevent. Thus the optimal amount of pollution is not equal to zero.

This important proposition can be generalized: The optimal amount of government intervention to avoid market failure will be lower, the greater are the costs imposed.

The Effect of Other Costs of Intervention

Next we add to our consideration the fact that government intervention brings with it enforcement costs—costs to the government, to the firm, and to third parties—of the kinds already discussed. These costs have to be added to the direct costs we have just considered.

Suppose first that the enforcement costs are known accurately and are of a lump-sum nature; that is, they are independent of whether 70 percent or 90 percent of the pollution is to be removed. Whether the intervention is now justified depends on the total size of the costs, relative to the benefits of the optimal pollution prevention policy. Say the net benefits before considering enforcement costs are estimated at $2 million. What if the enforcement costs would be $3 million? It would be better to live with the pollution than to prevent it! For prevention activities use

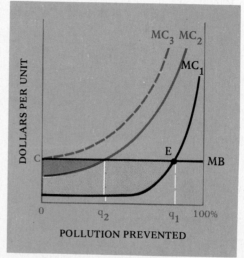

FIGURE 24-2
The Optimal Amount of Pollution Prevention

The optimal quantity of pollution prevention occurs where marginal benefits from prevention equal marginal costs of prevention. MB represents the marginal benefit achieved by pollution prevention, assumed in this example to be constant at $C per percentage point. MC_1 represents the marginal costs of preventing pollution; it rises sharply as more and more pollution is eliminated. The optimal level of pollution control is q_1, where $MB = MC_1$. Notice that not all pollution is eliminated. For all units up to q_1, marginal benefits from pollution prevention exceed marginal costs. Net benefits are shown by the total shaded area. Any further pollution elimination would add more to costs than to benefits.

If the marginal cost curve shifts upward to MC_2, due, say, to the addition of enforcement costs, the quantity of optimal prevention will decrease to q_2 and the net benefits will be reduced to the darker shaded area. If costs increase to MC_3, the optimal amount of prevention becomes zero.

up resources that the public values at $3 million to achieve benefits that the public values at only $2 million. However, if the lump-sum costs were less than the benefits—say, $500,000—it would pay to prevent the pollution, for the net gain would be $1.5 million.

What if, instead of lump-sum costs, the enforcement costs are variable, rising with the level of control sought? The marginal costs of enforcement must be added to the marginal direct costs of prevention, thereby shifting upward the marginal costs of prevention. This is shown by the colored marginal cost curves in Figure 24-2. The addition of such costs will surely decrease the amount of prevention that is optimal. If the costs are large enough, they may even make any prevention uneconomical.

The Effect of Government Failure

Finally, suppose that the government makes a mistake in regulation. Say the government mistakenly specifies a method of pollution control that is less effective than the best method. This will increase the cost of achieving any given level of prevention. If the government insists on the level of control appropriate to the correct method but requires the incorrect method, it can convert a social gain from control into a social loss. This is illustrated in Figure 24-3.

GOVERNMENT INTERVENTION IN CANADA TODAY

The theoretical principles for determining the optimal amount of intervention that we have just developed are individually accepted by virtually everyone. What they add up to, however, is more controversial.

Does government intervene too little or too much in response to market failure? This question reflects one aspect of the ongoing argument about the role of government in the economy. Much of the rhetoric of our concern with ecology urges government intervention against heartless, profit-mad, giant corporations that pervert the environment for their own crass purposes. The apparent reluctance of the Canadian public to believe in an energy shortage rests in good part on the suspicion that the oil and gas companies are somehow manipulating their supplies (and the public) for private profit. Such feelings lead to the demand for more—and more stringent—government regulation.

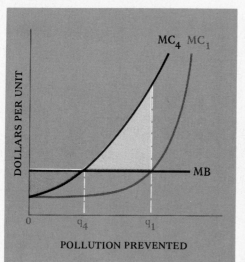

FIGURE 24-3
The Effects of Government Failure

Choice of the wrong method of control will reduce the optimal amount of intervention and may convert the gains from intervention into losses. The MB and MC_1 curves are similar to those in Figure 24-2. One common form of government failure is to specify the wrong method of intervention. Suppose the government specifies a method of pollution control that leads to the costs shown by MC_4. This is inefficient because costs at every level of pollution prevention are higher than necessary. Under such a method, the optimal level of prevention falls to q_4 with net benefits shown by the dark shaded area. Government failure reduces the appropriate amount of prevention that is optimal. The government will compound its failure if it insists on the level of prevention q_1 while requiring use of the inefficient method. The cost of every unit of pollution prevented beyond q_4 is in excess of its benefits, as shown by the light shaded area. Indeed, the result is worse than no intervention at all (the light shaded area is larger than the dark shaded area). While the best possible government intervention would have produced a net gain, government failure produces a net loss.

At the same time, the heavy hand of government regulation is seen as contributing greatly to both inflation and recession by burdening private companies with regulations that add to costs and impede innovation and by keeping prices and wages artificially high. Even perfect intervention would be costly, but imperfect intervention makes it much too costly. In this view, the deregulation of the airlines in the United States was a gift to the American consumer and it foreshadows the deregulation of motor transport, communications, and other regulated industries. In some quarters the government (rather than the oil companies or OPEC) is seen as the villain in the energy shortage: its rigid and unresponsive price controls and allocations of gasoline, oil, and natural gas are the cause of the problems that now plague us.

The Role of Analysis

Economic analysis and measurement can help to eliminate certain misconceptions that cloud and confuse the debate. We have noted one such misconception: the optimal level of pollution (or of any other negative externality) is not, as some urge, zero. Another mistake is to equate "market failure" with the greed of profit-motivated corporations. Externalities do not require callous, thoughtless, or deliberately deceptive practices of private, profit-seeking firms; they occur whenever the signals to which decision makers respond do not include social as well as private benefits and costs. Such situations are not limited to private firms in a capitalistic system. Cities and nationalized industries pollute just as much as privately owned industries when they are operated in the same way, as they typically are. A third mistake is to think that the profits of a corporation tell something about neglected externalities. It is possible for a profitable firm (such as GM) or an unprofitable one (such as Chrysler) to spend too little on pollution control or on safety, but it is also possible for it to spend too

much. The existence of profits provides no clue as to which is the case.

The Role of Ideology

While positive analysis has a role to play, there are several reasons why ideology plays a bigger role in the evaluation process here than in many other areas.

First, measuring the costs of government intervention is difficult, particularly with respect to indirect costs, because some of the trade-offs are inherently uncertain. How important and how unsafe is nuclear power? Does the ban on DDT cause so much malnutrition as to offset the gains in the ecology it brings? What cannot be readily measured can be alleged to be extremely high (or low) by opponents (or supporters) of intervention. The numerous findings by well-known scholars on both sides of each of these subjects has led one economist to the cynical conclusion that "believing is seeing."

Second, classifying the actual pattern of government intervention as successful or not is another matter touched by ideology. Has government safety regulation been (choose one) useful if imperfect, virtually ineffective, or positively perverse? All three views have been expressed and "documented."

A third difficulty arises in defining what constitutes market failure. Does product differentiation represent market success (by giving consumers the variety they want) or failure (by foisting expensive and useless variations on them)?

In Canada and the United States at the start of the 1980s it seems safe to conclude that confidence in the existing mix of free-market and government regulation is at a relatively low ebb. Not only are specific policy suggestions hotly argued, so is the whole philosophy of intervention. There is as yet no consensus as to what is wrong; the pressures for changes are strong in *both* directions.

New England and the Atlantic Provinces: A Tale of Two Regions

There are many similarities between the American New England states and the Canadian Atlantic provinces. Both have highly educated populations concentrated in relatively small areas. Both have access by waterway to foreign and domestic markets. The Atlantic provinces, however, have abundant supplies of hydroelectricity, iron, coal, and zinc that are not found in New England; thus they would seem to be more likely to be able to generate and sustain an economic boom than would New England.

Why then has just the reverse occurred? In the 1970s New England experienced a significant and sustained manufacturing investment boom; by the start of the 1980s New England had a healthy manufacturing base growing at a higher rate than the national average and an unemployment rate lower than that of most other regions in the United States. In contrast, the Atlantic provinces experienced a sharp slump in the 1970s, with manufacturing investment *falling* by 41 percent over the period 1971–1978.

At the beginning of the 1970s, New England's unemployment began to climb and per capita income began to fall. Cuts in defence spending and the aerospace program had a severe negative impact on the region. That impact was reinforced by the large oil price increases that occurred simultaneously. By 1975 the region's per capita income had been falling steadily for five years, and its unemployment rate was the worst in the nation. Consequently, the region had available a pool of relatively cheap, highly educated workers. This labor supply attracted new firms, particularly in the fields of computer and scientific technology, to the area. The result was that from 1975 to 1979 nonagricultural employ-

ment grew at a rate that was not only faster than the average for the whole nation over the same period but also faster, relative to the nation, than for any time since the end of World War II. Like a phoenix from the fire, the boom of the late 1970s arose from the recession of the early 1970s.

Superficially, the manufacturing sector in the Atlantic provinces did well during the early and mid 1970s. Wages and salaries increased faster here than they did for Canada as a whole. Yet closer examination reveals that not only did employment grow sluggishly over most of this period, but output grew more slowly than in the rest of Canada. Moreover, while manufacturing investment *decreased* in real terms by 41 percent here between 1971 and 1978, in the same period Canada had an *increase* of 108 percent. Why should a region with as many advantages as the Atlantic provinces have a performance in such an important sector that was so much worse than that of New England, when its prospects seemed so much better?

While many reasons account for the different patterns of development in the two regions, one striking difference lies in the government policies invoked to deal with the depressed economic conditions that prevailed at the beginning of the 1970s. The U.S. government essentially left the New England economy alone to adjust to its own problems. As a result, wages fell relative to those in the rest of the nation, and the region became an attractive place for new firms to locate.

At a recent conference, American economist Lester Thurow argued that

New England is a prosperous region because it got out of its old dying industries and into new growth industries. If Washington had protected New England's old dying industries, New England would still be depressed. It is correct to point out that New England went through forty years of economic pain before it made that transition, but the correct answer to this is a national policy for aiding individuals and speeding up the transition.

In contrast, the Canadian government has used many policies to support the Atlantic provinces. And these policies have been disappointingly ineffective. Many of the policies failed to recognize that much of the disparity between regions reflects regional equilibrium (see the box on pages 444–445). Many economists believe that the policy of propping up dying industries ("supporting losers") has inhibited growth by reducing the region's ability to develop new industries.

Much of the support to the region has come in the form of transfer payments. Transfers serve the intended purpose of redistributing income to the region, but they have the unintended side effect of impeding the process of regional adjustment. These policies may also have resulted in what has become known as "transfer dependency"; that is, they may have led some provinces to become increasingly dependent on government transfers for their economic well-being. In the seventies, provinces of the Atlantic region experienced current account deficits of up to *50 percent* of their gross domestic products, financed largely by intergovernmental transfers. Total government inflows in 1974 ranged from 66 percent of GNP in New Brunswick to 105 percent in Prince Edward Island.

Transfer dependency not only frustrates the market mechanism by propping up wages—thereby discouraging out-migration and new investment—it also undermines the economy in other ways. In 1973 a report prepared for the Department of Regional Economic Expansion stated:

On a broader plane, the analysis identified a more nebulous problem affecting institutional and sectoral behaviour in the Atlantic Region. The area has been dependent on assistance and support for a long period; this has left its mark on the outlook of the region. It has tended to become a part of the conventional wisdom that only government subsidies or some form of special consideration point the way to achieving prosperity. The result has been to weaken the confidence of the region in its ability to take initiatives and operate independently.

As in other regions, national and international corporate systems working within a framework of government policy provide the economic base on which local decisions and actions are made effective. Inadequacies in the functioning of these systems or in the framework or in both—weaknesses, breakdowns, obsolescence, and non-competitive effort—not only result in low levels of activity and high product costs but also inhibit the potential and dynamism of local investors and local activity. Furthermore, it cannot be assumed that government action to strengthen demand will improve performance. Increased funds made available to purchase housing, for example, may simply raise the price of new construction and increase the proportion of components imported by the region.

Will the two regions continue to develop in such different ways? Some observers believe that at the start of the 1980s the Atlantic region is on the verge of an economic boom, led by expansion in the fisheries and resource sectors, that will match and even perhaps surpass that experienced in New England. Others believe that as long as government transfers and support for declining industries remain a central part of Canadian regional policy, the Atlantic provinces will languish in transfer dependency.

Summary

1. The various markets in the economy are coordinated by the price system. Changes in prices and profits, resulting from emerging scarcities and surpluses, lead decision makers in far-flung markets to make adaptations in response to a change in any one market of the economy. Such responses tend to correct the shortages and surpluses as well as to change the market signals of prices and profits.

2. The case for the free market is that, in addition to providing automatic coordination, it often provides an impersonal, efficient, and self-correcting way of making the decisions about what to produce and how to distribute the fruits of production. Such virtues of the competitive free market led many nineteenth century economists to believe that government should not interfere in any way with the free-market determination of prices and quantities.

3. Markets do not always work perfectly. Market failure may occur for three main kinds of reasons: (a) externalities arising from differences between private and social costs and benefits, (b) market imperfections and impediments, and (c) the existence of goals that the market process neglects.

4. Pollution is an example of an externality. An important source of pollution is producers' use of water and air that they do not regard as scarce. Since they do not pay all the costs of using these resources, they are not motivated to avoid the costs. Individual use of common-property resources, congestion, and neglect of future consequences are other sources of externalities.

5. Market imperfections and impediments are anything that prevents the prompt movement of resources in response to market signals; they include monopoly, ignorance, and sources of labor immobility. They also include the inability in some situations of private firms to collect revenues for goods produced, and the existence in other situations of transactions costs of private production and sale of commodities that are much higher than costs of public provision.

6. Nonmarket goals that may lead to market failure include values placed on public provision for its own sake, on protection of individuals from themselves or from others, on recognition of social obligations, and on compassion.

7. Microeconomic policy concerns activities of the central authorities that alter the unrestricted workings of the free-market system in order to affect either the allocation of resources among uses or the distribution of income among people. Major tools of microeconomic policy include (a) public provision, (b) redistribution, (c) rule making, and (d) structuring incentives. The first two are the subject of Chapter 25. Both prescriptive and proscriptive rule making occur in a variety of forms. Incentives can be structured in a number of ways including the use of fines, subsidies, taxes, and effluent charges. All are designed to lead private decision makers to internalize externalities or to give weight to nonmarket goals.

8. There are costs as well as benefits of government intervention, and they must be considered in choosing whether, when, and how intervention is appropriate. Among these costs are the direct costs of government incurred; the costs imposed on those regulated, direct and indirect; and the costs imposed on third parties. These costs are never negligible and are often large. In addition to these costs there is the fact that government intervention may fail; if it does, the costs of intervention may be incurred without the benefits of avoiding market failure being fully realized.

9. The optimal degree of government intervention is determined by considering the magnitude of market failure, the likelihood that government intervention will correct the failure, and the costs of intervention. It is neither possible nor efficient to correct all market failure; neither is it always efficient to do nothing. Just how and where to change the proportions of free-market decision making and government intervention in that deci-

sion making is an area of continuing economic and political debate.

Topics for Review

The difference between central planning and market coordination
How the price system coordinates
Differences between private and social valuations
Causes of market failure
Externalities
Internalizing externalities
Net social benefit (*NSB*) and net private benefit (*NPB*)
Benefits and costs of government intervention
Causes of government failure
The optimal amount of pollution

Discussion Questions

1. For each of the following events, indicate how you might expect the market economy to respond.
   a. The decision of an automobile manufacturer to build a large assembly plant employing 5,000 workers near a town with only 11,000 total population, situated 40 miles from the nearest city.
   b. Discovery of a new means of making bricks that reduces their cost by 50 percent.
   c. A further doubling of the price of gasoline as a result of OPEC's latest oil summit meeting.
2. The Aswan Dam has been called Egypt's "wall against hunger," by virtue of its provision of both irrigation water and electric power to the Nile Valley. Among its less salutary side effects are:
   a. The reduced flow of water and silt in the river have allowed the Nile Delta to be overrun by sea water, leaving harmful salts.
   b. Lake Nasser, in back of the dam, has become a breeding place for malaria mosquitoes.
   c. Homes of 122,000 Nubian villagers have been inundated, along with countless antiquities for 310 miles upstream from the dam.
   Should the dam have been built? Discuss the issues involved, using the concepts of private and social costs and externalities.
3. Each of the following activities has known harmful effects: (a) cigarette smoking, (b) driving a car at 55 mph, (c) private ownership of guns, (d) drilling for offshore oil. In each case, identify whether there is a divergence between social and private costs.
4. Develop the case for (or against) government interference in the areas of education, medicine, airport construction and location, egg production, logging, electricity generation, and the location of a privately financed toll highway. Which of these do you think least suitable for government action?
5. Should the free market be allowed to determine the price for the following, or should government intervene?
   a. transit fares
   b. heating oil
   c. plastic surgery for victims of fires
   d. garbage collection
   e. postal service to newspapers and magazines
   f. fire protection for churches
   g. ice cream
6. The president of Goodyear Tire and Rubber Company complained that government regulation had imposed $30 million per year in "unproductive costs" on his company. These costs of compliance were broken down:
   a. environmental regulation, $17 million
   b. occupational safety and health, $7 million
   c. motor vehicle safety, $3 million
   d. personnel and administration, $3 million
   How would one determine whether these costs were "productive" or "unproductive"?
7. Suppose the facts asserted below are true; should they trigger government intervention? If so, what policy alternatives are available?
   a. The Concorde jet is twice as fast, twice as noisy on takeoff and landing, and carries half the passengers of jumbo jets.
   b. The cost of the average one-family house in Ottawa is now over $100,000, an amount that is out of the reach of most government employees.
   c. Cigarette smoking tends to reduce life expectancy by eight years.
   d. Saccharin in large doses has been found to cause cancer in Canadian mice.
8. Consider the possible beneficial and adverse effects of each of the following forms of government interference.
   a. Charging motorists a tax for driving in the downtown areas of large cities—and using the revenues to provide peripheral parking and shuttle buses.
   b. Prohibiting doctors from purchasing malpractice insurance.

c. Mandating no-fault auto insurance, in which the car owner's insurance company is responsible for damage to his or her vehicle no matter who causes the accident.

d. Requiring automobile manufacturers to warrantee the tires on cars they sell instead of (as at present) having the tire manufacturer be the warrantor.

9. Consider the problem of motorcycle noise pollution. What is the "optimal level of permissible noise"? How might it be determined? A given level of noise permitted might be achieved in a variety of ways; name several, including at least one that does not regulate the motorcyclist in any way. Which is the fairest way? Which is the most effective way?

10. Consider the following (alleged) facts about pollution control and indicate what, if any, influence they might have on policy determination.

a. In 1979 the cost of meeting federal pollution requirements was $61 per person.

b. More than a third of the world's known oil supplies lie under the ocean floor, and there is no known blowout-proof method of recovery.

c. Sulfur removal requirements and strip mining regulations have led to the tripling of the cost of a ton of coal used in electrical generation.

d. Every million dollars spent on pollution control creates 67 new jobs in the economy.

Microeconomic Policy II: Public Finance and Public Expenditure

25

All governments spend money, and they must raise revenue in order to do so. The Canadian federal government is no exception. Government spending and government taxation today go far beyond the minimum required to provide such essentials as a system of justice and protection against foreign enemies. Spending and taxing are also key tools of both macroeconomic and microeconomic policy.

In this chapter we look at spending and taxation as tools of microeconomic policy. Government expenditure and government taxation inescapably affect both the allocation of resources and the distribution of income. Often they are used intentionally to try to correct for market failures.

There is no simple and sharp functional distinction between expenditure and tax policies. One way to deal with polluted lakes, for example, is by public expenditure to clean them up. An alternative is to use taxes to penalize pollution or to give tax concessions to firms that install pollution-abating devices. Tax concessions that seek to induce market responses are called **tax expenditures**—that is, sacrifices of revenue by the taxing authorities that are designed to achieve purposes that the government believes are desirable.

In this chapter we are concerned both with the overall impact of public expenditure and taxation on microeconomic decisions and with the deliberate use of these tools for effecting such decisions.

TABLE 25-1
Government Tax Revenues by Source, 1980

Kind of tax	Revenue		Percentage distribution		
	Billions of dollars	Percentage	Federal	Provincial	Municipal
Income tax, persons	$31.5	37	59	41	—
Income and other taxes, corporations	11.5	14	69	31	—
General sales taxes	14.8	17	42	58	—
Customs duties	3.1	4	100	—	—
Property tax	9.4	11	—	—	100
All other taxes	14.3	17			
Total	84.6	100	52	37	11

Source: Department of Finance, *Economic Review*, 1981.

Income taxes are the major source of revenue for the federal and provincial governments. Substantial yields are also obtained from the federal manufacturer's sales tax and the provincial retail levies which make up the sales tax category. Municipal governments rely almost entirely on property taxes.

Taxation as a Tool of Micro Policy

There is a bewildering array of taxes, some highly visible (such as sales taxes and income taxes) and others all but invisible to the consumer because they are imposed on raw materials producers or manufacturers at an early stage. People are taxed on what they earn, on what they spend, and on what they own. Firms are taxed as well as households. And taxes are not only numerous, they take a big bite. Aggregate taxes amount to roughly one third of the total value of goods and services produced in Canada each year. The diversity and importance of various taxes are shown in Table 25-1.

TAXES AND THE DISTRIBUTION OF INCOME

A government that taxes the rich and exempts the poor is redistributing income. How much redistribution is achieved by Canadian taxes today?

Progressivity

Rhetoric about income distribution and tax policy often invokes the important but hard to define concepts of "equity" and "equality." Equity—fairness—is a normative concept; what one group thinks is fair may seem outrageous to another. But equality is a straightforward concept—or is it?

To tax people equality might mean several things. It might mean that each person should pay the same tax, which would be very hard on the unemployed worker and very easy on Darryl Sittler. It might mean that each should pay the same proportion of his or her income, say a flat 25 percent, whether rich or poor, living alone or supporting eight children, healthy or suffering from a disease that requires heavy use of expensive drugs. It might mean that each should pay an amount of tax such that everybody's income after taxes is the same—which would remove any incentive to earn above average income. Or it might mean none of these things.

People may not agree on what redistributions are fair, but they can agree on what redistributions actually occur. To get precise measurements of what happens, the distributional effects of taxes are usually discussed using the concept of **progressivity of taxation,** the ratio of taxes to income at different levels of income.

A **proportional tax** takes amounts of money from people in direct proportion to their income.

A **regressive tax** takes a larger percentage of income from people, the lower their income.

A **progressive tax** takes a larger percentage of income from people, the larger their income.

A tax system is said to be progressive if it decreases the inequality of income distribution and to be regressive if it increases the inequality.

It is easier to assess the progressivity or regressivity of particular taxes than of the tax system as a whole.

The Regressivity of Sales and Excise Taxes

If two families each spend the same proportion of their income on a certain commodity that is subject to a sales or an excise tax, the tax will be proportional in its effects on them. If the tax is on a commodity, such as food, that takes a larger proportion of the income of lower-income families, it will be regressive; if it is on a commodity such as jewelry, where the rich spend a larger proportion of their income than the poor, it will be progressive.

Commodities with inelastic demands provide easy sources of revenue. In many countries commodities such as tobacco, alcohol, and gasoline are singled out for very high rates of taxation. But these commodities usually account for a much greater proportion of the expenditure of lower-income than higher-income groups, and taxes on them are thus regressive.

The sales and excise taxes used in Canada today are as a whole regressive.

The Regressivity of Property Taxes

The progressivity of the property tax has been studied extensively. It is well known that the rich live in more expensive houses than the poor, but all that this establishes is that the rich tend to pay more dollars in property tax than do the poor. Because the rich tend to live in different communities than the poor and thus pay taxes at different rates, and because they tend to spend a different proportion of their income for housing, the question of the progressivity or regressivity of the property tax is difficult and controversial. Most studies have shown that the proportion of income spent for housing tends to decrease with income. Many but not all public finance experts believe that the property tax tends to be regressive in its overall effect.

The Progressivity of Personal Income Taxes

The personal tax rate is itself a function of taxable income, and it is useful to distinguish between two different rates. The **average tax rate** paid by an individual is his or her income tax divided by total income. The **marginal tax rate** is the amount of tax the taxpayer would pay on an additional dollar of income.

Table 25-2 shows the applicable rates on federal income tax in 1980. In structure, the federal personal income tax is quite progressive because the average rate rises steadily with income. However, because of the special definitions given to net income by the tax laws, the overall effect of the federal income tax is actually much less progressive than Table 25-2 suggests. To arrive at taxable income, total income is modified by certain exemptions from income, by capital gains provisions, by depletion allowances, and by permitted deductions from gross income.[1]

Despite modifications, income tax is progressive in effect as well as in structure.

The Unknown Progressivity of Corporate Income Tax

The federal corporate income tax is, for practial purposes, a flat-rate tax of 50 percent of profits as defined by the taxing authorities. It is difficult to determine its effects on income distribution, for there is great controversy over the extent to which it is "shifted" to consumers.[2] So far as the

---

[1] Until recently, most capital gains were not taxable in Canada, but beginning in 1972 taxpayers were required to include one-half of gains received in their taxable income. This change was part of the substantial revisions of the Income Tax Act made after a lengthy public debate over the far-reaching proposals of the Royal Commission on Taxation (the Carter Commission).

[2] The question of tax incidence—that is, who really pays a tax imposed on any one group—is discussed later in this chapter.

TABLE 25-2
The Rate Structure of the Personal Income Tax, 1980 (Single Taxpayer, No Dependents)

Assessed income (dollars)	Federal income tax		Provincial income tax[a]		Combined average rate on assessed income (percent)
	Tax (dollars)	Marginal rate (percent)	Tax (dollars)	Marginal rate (percent)	
7,500	389		259		9
10,000	821	17	449	8	13
12,500	1,267	18	645	8	15
15,000	1,761	20	863	9	17
17,500	2,270	20	1,098	9	19
20,000	2,794	21	1,351	10	21
25,000	3,961	23	1,915	11	24
30,000	5,285	26	2,546	13	26
50,000	11,796	33	5,410	14	34
100,000	30,565	38	13,669	17	44
200,000	73,075	43	32,373	19	53

[a] The typical provincial tax equals 44 percent of the federal tax.

Source: The National Finances.

Both marginal and average tax rates rise with income; thus the tax is progressive in structure. The combined marginal rate rises from 25 percent to a maximum of 62 percent. The combined average rate rises from 9 percent to 53 percent; it exaggerates the actual degree of progressivity because higher income taxpayers are more likely to have some income such as capital gains, which is taxed at lower rates.

tax falls on stockholders, they as a group tend to be wealthier than individuals who do not own stock, and there is thus a tendency toward progressivity. But within the stockholder group, lower-income stockholders bear a disproportionate share of the tax relative to wealthy stockholders. If a dollar were paid out in dividends instead of taxes, rich stockholders would keep a much smaller share than poorer stockholders because of their high marginal personal tax rates.

The Progressivity of the Tax System

To assess the way in which the whole tax system, as distinct from any one tax, affects income distribution is more difficult. One aspect concerns the mix of taxes of different kinds. Income taxes tend to be somewhat progressive; property and sales taxes tend to be regressive.

Assessing progressivity is even more complex than this. Is progressivity defined for the individual or for the family? When a couple with two children pays the same tax as a childless couple with the same income, is this proportional or regressive taxation? If the *family* is the relevant unit, it is proportional taxation. If the *person* is the relevant unit, equal tax rates on families of different sizes having the same income would be regressive. As it is, a household with children pays less *income* tax than a household without children but with the same income. (This does not mean, as childless people often assume, that the household with children pays less total taxes. For other taxes, such as sales taxes, tend to fall more heavily on large families than on small ones.)

One famous study by Professor Erwin Gillespie of Carleton University argued that the Canadian tax system is proportional over a middle income range but regressive for both low-income and high-income classes.

CAN PROGRESSIVITY BE INCREASED?

Many observers have argued that to achieve overall proportionality in the tax structure is in itself a significant accomplishment. Some argue that, given the enormous fraction of national income that is taxed away, more progressivity cannot be achieved. (The greater the fraction of the population's money taxed away, the harder it is to do so progressively.) Whether or not more progressivity is desirable, is more progressivity possible?

Taxes can be levied on assets, on incomes, and on expenditures. Inheritance taxes and gift taxes are taxes on assets; such taxes do not—and cannot—play a large continuing role in the overall revenue picture. Taxes on incomes are important and can be quite progressive. Taxes on expenditures—especially sales and excise taxes—are related to the dollar value of expenditures, not the incomes of those spending the money; they are known to be regressive.

Substantial progressivity in income taxes is required merely to achieve proportionality in the overall tax pattern.

Will Increasing Reliance on Income Taxes Increase Progressivity?

It may seem obvious that, since income taxes are progressive and expenditure taxes are regressive, to shift more of the tax burden to income taxes must increase progressivity. Surprisingly, some economists have argued that this is not the case. While a shift to more reliance on income taxes will raise both the average rate and the marginal rate of tax on incomes, it may or may not raise the total amount of revenue actually collected. Whether it does depends on the incentive effects of tax rates.

A graph that relates the government's income tax yield to the level of marginal tax rates has recently gained attention as the **Laffer curve,** named after the American economist Arthur Laffer. Its essential feature is that tax revenues reach a maximum at some rate of taxation well below 100 percent. The general shape of the Laffer curve is a matter of simple logic: at a zero tax rate, no revenue will be collected. Similarly, at a 100 percent tax rate, revenues will again be zero because no one will bother to earn taxable income just to support the government. For some intermediate rates, people will both earn income and pay taxes. Thus the revenue collected must reach a maximum at tax rates somewhere between zero and 100 percent. For rates higher than the rate that produces this maximum, every increase in tax rates will lead to a decrease in tax revenues. (See Figure 25-1.)

FIGURE 25-1
The Laffer Curve

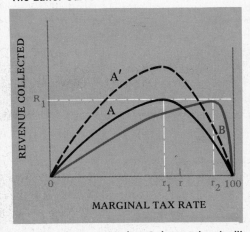

Increases in tax rates beyond some level will decrease rather than increase tax revenue. The solid black curve A shows that as tax rates are increased from zero up to r_1 tax revenues increase, but beyond r_1 further increases in rates lead to less revenue. Curve B is different; it does not reach its maximum until rate r_2. While both A and B are Laffer curves and each predicts the same maximum revenue yield, the policy implications are very different for the two curves. If actual tax rates are r and the objective is to maximize revenue, rates should be reduced if A is correct and increased if B is correct.

Structural changes in the tax laws may shift these curves. For example, by eliminating tax loopholes the A curve might be shifted to A', thereby increasing the revenue yield at every level of tax rates.

Just where this maximum occurs—whether at a tax rate of 60 percent or 80 percent or 95 percent—is an important empirical matter. Laffer and others think tax policy has already carried progressiveness too far. They believe that the United States is at or past the rate at which higher tax rates yield more revenue. As a result, they say, any attempt to increase progressivity by raising income tax rates would be self-defeating. Many other economists disagree. While they might concede that some countries (such as the United Kingdom) may have reached such a point, they argue that this has happened only because their residents can migrate to countries with lower taxes, such as Canada and the United States. They believe that the current U.S. top marginal tax rates of 50 percent on personal service income and 70 percent on other income are still short of being self-defeating in terms of tax revenue. That is, they believe that Professor Laffer has identified a potential rather than an actual problem. Less analysis has been done in Canada with explicit reference to the Laffer curve, but the consensus seems to be that our tax rates are also below the revenue-maximizing level.

Increasing Progressivity by Changing the Income Tax Structure

If the government raises income taxes for one group and lowers them for another in a way that leaves the total tax yield constant, the *structure* of the income tax will have been changed. Much repeated demand for "tax reform" relates to proposed changes in the structure of income taxes. Most economists believe that such changes can be made (whether or not they consider them desirable) and that if they were made, they would increase the progressivity of the total tax system. Here are two important and widely advocated proposals.

The negative income tax (NIT). A tax can be negative if at some level of income the government pays "the taxpayer" instead of the other way around. The so-called **negative income tax** is a policy tool designed to increase progressivity and combat poverty by making taxes negative at

very low incomes. Such a tax would extend progressivity to incomes below those where people currently have income tax liability.

There are many versions of NIT proposals; the one described here will illustrate the basic idea. The underlying belief is that a family of four is entitled to a minimum annual income—say, $3,200. The aim is to guarantee this income without eliminating the incentive to become self-supporting. This is done by combining a grant with a tax. At a break-even level the family will neither receive money from the government nor pay any tax. Below this income level the family will be paid by the government (i.e., the family pays a "negative tax"). Above this break-even level it will pay a positive tax. An example, based on a grant of $3,200 and a marginal negative tax rate of 50 percent, is given in Table 25-3.

Supporters of the negative income tax believe that it would be a particularly effective tool for

TABLE 25-3
One Version of the Negative Income Tax with a 50 Percent Marginal Tax Rate

(1) Family income	(2) Tax	(3) Family income after tax (1)−(2)
$ 0	$−3,200	$3,200
800	−2,800	3,600
1,600	−2,400	4,000
2,400	−2,000	4,400
3,200	−1,600	4,800
4,000	−1,200	5,200
4,800	− 800	5,600
5,600	− 400	6,000
6,400	0	6,400

Instead of having a zero income tax up to some level and a positive tax thereafter, the NIT has a continuous variation of tax with income. Under this plan a family with no income is entitled to $3,200. For every dollar the family earns between $0 and $6,400, its receipts from the government are reduced by 50 cents. Column 2 shows the "tax" at different levels of income. Column 3 shows the total income available for spending. The "break-even" income is $6,400, at which the family neither receives a grant nor pays a tax. On incomes above $6,400, taxes are paid.

reducing poverty. It provides a minimum level of income as a matter of right, not of charity, and it does so without removing the incentive to work of those eligible for payments. Every dollar earned adds to the after-tax income of the family. As a potential replacement for many other relief programs, it promises to avoid the most pressing cases of poverty with much less administrative cost and without the myriad exceptions that are involved in most programs. An incidental advantage is that it removes whatever incentive people might have to migrate to provinces with better welfare programs, but it does not discourage migration to places where work may be available.

The net cost of such a negative income tax scheme would depend on the level of minimum annual income and the marginal tax rate specified, on which other programs of aid to the needy were curtailed, and on the effect on the incentives of those covered.

Comprehensive income taxation (CIT). Joseph Pechman of the Brookings Institution has taken the lead in arguing that it is possible to raise more revenue from the income tax, increase its progressivity, and at the same time *reduce* the disincentive effects by reducing both average and marginal tax rates!

This sounds like magic, but it is a matter of simple arithmetic. The **tax base** is the total amount of taxable income. Under present definitions taxable income is much less than total income because there are all sorts of deductions and exemptions. If all income were taxed, regardless of source, it would be possible to raise more revenue by applying lower rates to this larger tax base. The idea of **comprehensive income taxation** is to eliminate virtually all the so-called loopholes, the deductions, and exemptions that make taxable income less than total income. By eliminating some or all personal deductions, homeowner preferences, special treatment of capital gains, and exemptions for dependents, old age, and blindness, the tax base could be increased substantially. It would then be easy to reduce tax *rates* in all income brackets.

Under these schemes it would be possible to achieve substantially more progressivity without increasing anyone's marginal tax rate. For example, imagine a definition of the CIT where comprehensive income is 150 percent of present taxable income. Rates could be left unchanged for high-income taxpayers and greatly reduced for middle- and low-income taxpayers in such amounts as to maintain the same total tax revenue but to increase progressivity.

Alternatively, some rates could be decreased by a little and others by a great deal—as long as the average decrease was one-third. Needless to say, even if everyone's tax *rates* went down under CIT, not everyone's tax *payments* would do so.

Political Barriers to Using Tax Policy to Redistribute Income

The purely political barriers to tax reform are formidable. Any single reform is likely to impose large costs on a relatively well-identified group, while the benefits it gives would be more widely diffused.

The ten people who would each lose a million dollars from a particular tax reform are much more interested in the issue than the 10 million people who would each gain a dollar. The ten, not the 10 million, would hire lobbyists and make campaign contributions. Legislators must respond to these pressures if they want long public careers. With *expenditure* programs the political pressures are reversed. The beneficiaries of a program to subsidize investment in a depressed region, to bail out a troubled firm such as Chrysler or Massey-Ferguson, or to improve the St. Lawrence Seaway are much more intensely and immediately involved than the millions of others whose taxes will rise a little bit to pay for it. The 100,000 who would gain a hundred dollars each from a particular expenditure policy are much more likely to be heard than the 10 million whose taxes would rise by a dollar each. (Even when people demand lower taxes, they vote out of office politicians who refuse to provide the services the taxes would make possible.) The result is that political pressures make redistribution by expenditures more attractive than redistribution by tax reform.

HOW MUCH PROGRESSIVITY IS DESIRABLE?

Suppose increased progressivity could be achieved; would we want it? Many say no.

One obvious objection to tax reform designed to increase progressivity is that not everyone wants more progressivity. A second is that many who want more progressivity do not want changes that make it easier for the government to raise more money. Such people fear schemes such as NIT and CIT precisely because they do not generate tax revolts. They point to the introduction of "pay as you go" (withholding) taxes in the 1940s. The argument used then to persuade people to accept withholding was that it was more convenient and less painful to have one's employer collect the taxes on income as it was earned than to have to come up with a lump sum on a date such as April 30. But, they argue, the reality has been that governments discovered they could exploit the system: they kept raising taxes until the same level of pain was suffered all year round.

A third source of opposition to increasing progressivity by means of tax reform is that every aspect of present tax policy was introduced to benefit some group whose members believe they have valid claims to special treatment. Consider some of the "loopholes" that the CIT would reduce or eliminate. Tax deductibility of charitable and educational contributions provide incentives for gifts to churches, universities, and private charities and foundations. After all, every deduction or exemption was introduced for a purpose and with some political support.

More progressivity conflicts with other goals. Further, more progressivity may conflict with what is seen as fair. Much erosion of the tax base has arisen from adjustments made in the name of equity. Special tax treatment of the aged seems fair to many. More favorable tax treatment of families with children than of childless couples seems fair to some on the basis of need but unfair to those who think population is already too high.

Finally, the case against tax policy as a means of achieving redistributive goals has some support even among those who favor more redistribution of income from rich to poor. They argue that it is misleading, unnecessary, and poor tactics politically to pay so much attention to *tax* progressivity. After all, how the money is spent is just as important, and often less controversial, than how it is collected. A regressive tax, say a sales tax, may provide funds for increasing welfare payments and thus in effect redistribute income to the poor. It is the combined overall effect of taxes and expenditures that is regarded as important, and it is easier to get governments to enact progressive expenditure programs than progressive taxes.

TAX STRUCTURE AND THE ALLOCATION OF RESOURCES

The tax system influences the allocation of resources by changing the *relative* prices of different goods and factors and the *relative* profitability of different industries and different uses of factors of production. These changes in turn affect resource movements.

While it is theoretically possible to design a *neutral* tax system—one that leaves all relative prices unchanged—Canadian tax policy, both intentionally and unintentionally, is certainly not neutral. It leads to a different allocation of resources than would occur without it.

Intended Effects

The tax structure is often used deliberately to change incentives and thus to affect resource allocation. Taxing gasoline to discourage energy consumption is one example; effluent charges on polluters are another. And tax provisions may be used as a carrot as well as a stick. One way is to allow the deduction of some expenditures from income before computing the amount of taxes payable or tax credits for some portion of expenditures. Every $100 spent by a wealthy family in the 60 percent marginal tax bracket on an item that is tax deductible costs only $40 in after-tax income. Every $100 they spend on items that are not tax deductible costs the full $100 in after-tax income. This encourages them to spend money on charitable and educational contributions.

Interest payments for a mortgage are tax deductible under the U.S. tax code, and a similar proposal was included in the budget on which the Progressive Conservative government of Joe Clark was defeated in 1978. Since payments for rental housing are not deductible, such a provision would encourge home ownership by lowering the cost of buying a house relative to the cost of renting one.

When corporations are allowed "accelerated depreciation" or "investment credits" on certain investments, it encourages them to make such investments in larger amounts. Changes in such provisions in corporation taxes are commonly used by the federal government to try to regulate investment demand, both in the aggregate and in its allocation between various sectors and industries.

Unintended Allocative Effects

Not all effects of the tax system are intended. To the extent that high income taxes discourage work, or induce people to spend money on tax avoidance, we are plainly reaping unintended and undesirable by-products of a tax system.

Consider further the tax incentives to home ownership, which were surely intended. An incidental result of providing such incentives through the income tax is that the incentive effect is much less for a poor person than for a rich one. The value of the deduction for interest is much greater to a taxpayer in the 70 percent marginal tax bracket than to someone in the 20 percent bracket. When a bank charges each of them 10 percent interest, the richer taxpayer really pays only 3 percent interest; the poorer one pays 8 percent interest if he or she itemizes deductions. For people who take the standard

deduction, the actual interest rate remains 10 percent. Thus the lower one's income, the less the incentive is to obtain a property stake in the society. This is surely an unintended effect.

The major unresolved question about taxes and allocation is empirical: Just how different is the allocation because of tax policy? Perhaps surprisingly, there is no consensus on this question. The reason is that we are not sure who really pays the taxes that are levied. This is called the problem of **tax incidence.**

TAX INCIDENCE

When a tax is imposed on a firm, does the firm pay the tax, or does it pass it on to the consumer in the form of higher prices? To see why this is a difficult question to answer, consider two examples.

Do Landlords or Tenants Pay the Property Tax?

Landlords characteristically protest that the crushing burden of property taxes makes it impossible for them to earn a reasonable living from renting buildings to tenants who abuse the property. Tenants typically reply that landlords shirk their responsibilities for building maintenance and that the whole burden of the tax is passed on to the tenants in the form of higher rents. Both sides cannot be right in alleging that they each bear the entire burden of the tax! They are arguing about the incidence of the property tax.

To examine the incidence, suppose that a city imposes a property tax. Each of the thousands of landlords in the city decides to raise rents by the full amount of the tax. There will be a decline in the quantity of rental accommodation demanded as a result of the price increase. (For one reason, higher rents will induce some renters to economize on space now that it has become more expensive.)

The decline in the quantity demanded without any change in the quantity supplied will cause a surplus of rental accommodations at the higher

FIGURE 25-2
The Incidence of a Tax on Rental Housing

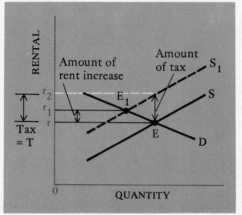

If the equilibrium rent rises by some amount less than the amount of the tax, landlords and tenants will share the burden. The supply schedule S reflects landlords' willingness to supply apartments. When a tax of T is imposed, the supply curve shifts upward, to S_1, indicating an increase of T in the price needed to call forth each quantity supplied. Equilibrium shifts from E to E_1, and rents have risen only to r_1. Of the total tax, tenants have paid rr_1 per unit and landlords r_1r_2.

high as before. This reduction in supply prevents the price from falling to its pretax level.

Eventually rentals will reach a new equilibrium at which the quantity demanded equals the quantity supplied. This equilibrium price for rental housing will be higher than the original pretax rent but lower than the rent that passes the entire tax on to the tenants. (See Figure 25-2).

The burden of the property tax is shared by landlords and tenants.

Just how it is shared by the two groups will depend on the elasticity of the demand and supply curves. If the demand curve is very flat, the landlord will pay most of the tax; if it is very steep, the tenant will.[3]

Notice that this result does not depend on who writes the check to pay the tax bill. In many European countries, the tenant rather than the landlord is sent the tax bill and pays the tax directly to the city; even in this case, however, the landlord bears part of the burden. As long as the existence of the tax reduces the quantity of rental accommodations demanded below what it otherwise would be, the tax will depress the amount received by landlords. In this way landlords will bear part of its burden.

Notice also that this result emerges even though neither landlords nor tenants realize it. Because rents are changing for all sorts of other reasons, no one will have much idea of what equilibrium rentals would be in the absence of the tax. It does not do much good just to look at what happens immediately after tax rates are changed because, as we have already seen, landlords may begin by raising rents by the full amount of the tax. Although they think they have passed it on, this creates a disequilibrium, and in the final position prices will have risen by less than the full tax.

prices. Landlords will find it difficult to replace tenants who move out, and the typical unit will remain empty longer between tenancies. Prospective tenants will find many alternative sites from which to choose and will become very particular in what they expect from landlords.

Some prospective tenants, seeing vacant apartments, will offer to pay rents below the asking price. Some landlords will accept the offer rather than earn nothing from vacant premises. Once some landlords cut their rentals, others will have to follow suit or find their properties unrented for longer periods of time.

As the rent received by landlords falls, there will be a supply reaction. There will be a movement down the supply curve when, for example, some homeowners become less willing to rent out parts of their homes. When apartment buildings are replaced (as they are continuously in a big city), it will not pay to build them quite as

---

[3] We suggest you draw a series of diagrams to see how this works. In each case, shift the supply curve up by the same vertical amount—to represent the property tax—and see what proportion of the increase is reflected in the new equilibrium price. See our discussion of the corn laws in England (pages 378-379) for another application of this analysis.

Do Taxes on Profits Affect Prices?

Economic theory predicts that a general percentage tax on pure profits will have no effect on price or output, and thus the full incidence of such a tax will fall on producers. To see this quickly, suppose that one price-quantity combination gives the firm higher profits (without considering taxes) than any other. If the government imposes a 20 percent profits tax, the firm will have only 80 percent as much profits after tax as it had before; *this will be true for each possible level of output.* The firm may grumble, but it will not be profitable for it to alter its price or output.

Notice that this argument is independent of the tax rate. [31] It applies equally whether the tax rate is 10 percent or 75 percent.

A tax on corporation income. Corporate income taxes are taxes on profits as defined by the tax laws. The definitions make them a tax on a combination of pure profits plus some of the return to capital and risk taking.

Because such a profits tax will reduce the returns to these important factors of production, it can have significant effects on the allocation of resources and on the prices and output of goods. Suppose a risky industry requires, say, a 20 percent return on its capital to make prospective owners willing to take the risk of investing in the

industry. Suppose that every firm is earning 30 percent on its investment before taxes. A 50 percent corporate income tax will reduce the return to 15 percent, below the point that makes investment attractive, and resources will leave the industry. Obviously price and output changes will occur. As firms leave the industry, and as supply decreases, prices will rise until the remaining firms can earn a sufficient level of after-tax profits so that they are once again compensated for the risks involved. Thus customers must bear part of the burden of the tax through a price increase.

A tax on profits, as defined by the taxing authorities, will have an effect on prices and outputs and thus will be shared by the consumer.

Public Expenditure as a Tool of Micro Policy

Public expenditure is large and growing. It affects both the distribution of income and the allocation of resources. In 1979 spending by federal, provincial, and municipal governments—that is, by the public sector—exceeded $100 billion, or about 40 percent of Canadian Gross National Expenditure. Table 25-4 shows

TABLE 25-4
Expenditure of All Governments by Function, 1977

Category	Billions of dollars	Percentage distribution	Average annual rate of growth, 1961–1977
Health	11.0	12	14
Social welfare	20.7	23	13
Education	13.8	15	11
Defence	3.6	4	5
Transportation and communication	7.8	9	8
Interest on the public debt	7.8	9	12
All other	26.2	28	15
Total	$90.9	100	12

Source: Statistics Canada, 68-202, and *Canada Year Book*, 1964.

Health and social services have been the fastest growing categories of government expenditure in the last two decades. The table shows combined expenditures for federal, provincial, and municipal governments. The category "All other" includes sanitation and waste removal, natural resources, general government, police and fire protection, recreation, and cultural activities.

Should Higher Education Be Subsidized?

Governments often provide goods and services that they produce at a price that is well below total costs. The case against the practice of providing free or subsidized goods and services is that the public is encouraged to consume the good or service to the point where the utility from the last unit consumed is low—indeed, in the case of a good provided free, it is zero. This means that resources are being used to produce goods whose marginal utility is less than the value of other goods that could have been produced instead.

The case for free or subsidized provision has been suggested. Some public goods are difficult or impossible to sell on a market. Thus, if they are to be provided at all, they must be provided free. In other cases, important third-party effects make it desirable to encourage a level of consumption beyond what the individual household would voluntarily choose if it had to pay the full cost itself. While there are some relatively uncontroversial cases such as providing free milk in schools attended by poor children, or general free elementary education, the case for subsidizing university education is controversial.

The facts are clear; higher education in Canada is heavily subsidized, and only a small proportion of costs is recovered from student fees. The question does not concern the need for scholarship and loan funds for poor but deserving students; instead it asks how much subsidy, independent of need, should be provided.

Supporters of heavy subsidization argue that the whole society gains from the widest possible spread of education and that it is in the general interest to encourage more educa-

tion than people would voluntarily choose on the basis of their own self-interest. The economic payoff to society of investments in human capital has been studied extensively. These studies show that education is productive in the sense of producing enough extra output later to compensate for the sacrifice of current output required to provide the education.

Critics of the present system accept the evidence but ask why the general public (a majority of whom are not university graduates) should subsidize others to obtain an investment in human capital that is a good investment from their own selfish points of view. After all, say the critics, those who get the education will earn the higher incomes their education permits. Let them borrow the money, if necessary.

Education is, of course, more than an investment in future production, and this can cut either way: a stay at a university may be valued by the student because of cultural or social reasons or because it saves the student the necessity of deciding what to do next. Each of these reasons argues against subsidy. But education may also provide the nation with a generation that is better trained and better able to cope with pressing social problems than the previous one, and this might justify a subsidy.

There is no general rule as to the appropriate degree of subsidy; the case for and against providing a commodity at less than cost varies greatly with the nature of the commodity and the externalities conferred by having more of it than the market would provide.

government expenditure by principal categories of function (or purpose) for 1977. About 40 percent of this money was spent by the federal government, the rest by provincial and municipal governments.

Types of Government Expenditures

In addition to classifying budget expenditures by function, as in Table 25-4, we may classify them by type of expenditure. This is done for the fed-

TABLE 25-5
Federal and Provincial Expenditures by Type, 1980

	Federal		Provincial	
	Billions of dollars	Percentage of total	Billions of dollars	Percentage of total
Purchases of goods and services	14.8	24	19.9	36
Transfers to persons	16.6	27	10.6	19
Interest on the public debt	9.6	16	4.0	7
Transfers to other levels of government	12.8	21	19.2	35
Other transfers	7.0	12	1.5	3
Total	$60.8	100	$55.2	100

Source: Statistics Canada, 11-003E.

eral and provincial governments in Table 25-5; Figure 25-3 shows the changing importance of different types of federal government expenditures.

Provision of goods and services. As Table 25-5 indicates, the largest type of federal expenditure until 1971, and still the dominant type for provincial and municipal governments, was the

FIGURE 25-3
The Changing Form of Major Federal Expenditures

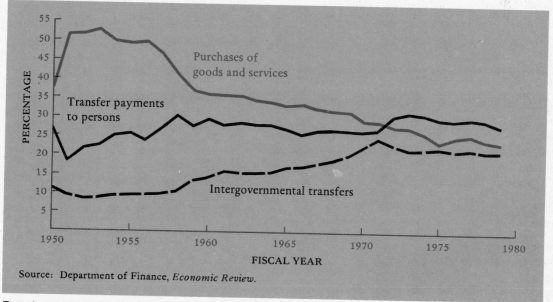

Source: Department of Finance, *Economic Review.*

Transfer payments to persons and to provincial and municipal governments have been growing steadily in importance. In 1951 one-half of all federal expenditures were for purchases of goods and services. By 1980 the fraction was less than one-fourth. Transfer payments to persons in Canada and to provincial and municipal governments have increased from less than 30 percent to more than one-half of the total. The three categories of expenditure graphed account for almost 75 percent of total federal expenditures. The largest item not shown on the graph is net interest paid by the government.

provision of goods and services. Roughly half of total expenditures at all levels of government are made for the provision of goods and services that it is assumed are desired and desirable but that the market itself would fail to provide. Among these goods and services are defence, transportation facilities, education, and municipal services. In these activities the government acts in much the same way that a firm acts, using factors of production to produce outputs. By and large these are outputs of collective consumption goods, goods with strong third-party effects, or services whose benefits are not marketable.

Transfer payments. Although government purchases of goods and services are large (about \$13 billion in 1980), they have remained roughly constant in real terms over the last 25 years. They have been overtaken by transfer payments as the largest form of federal government expenditure. Transfer payments have been steadily increasing in importance, and this has led to significant changes in both the distribution of income and the allocation of resources.

PUBLIC EXPENDITURES AND REDISTRIBUTION OF INCOME

The federal government, as Table 25-1 indicates, raises about half its revenues by income-related taxes. When these federal receipts are transferred back to individuals or to provincial and municipal governments, they have a substantial redistributive effect.

Federal Transfer Payments to Individuals

Transfer payments are defined generally as payments to private persons or institutions that do not arise out of current production activity. In 1970 a federal government white paper on income security classified transfers to individuals according to four types: demogrants, guaranteed income, social insurance, and social assistance. Old age security and family allowance payments are in the first group, guaranteed income supplements and child tax credits are examples of the

second, the Canada Pension Plan and unemployment insurance are examples of the third, and the fourth includes special programs for widows, single parents, and others who have no recourse to other support programs.

Transfers to individuals by the federal government have grown as a proportion of expenditures from about 15 percent in 1930 to about 30 percent by the mid seventies.[4] In absolute terms these transfers are intended as a form of insurance or as an incentive for individuals to redirect expenditure toward specific items such as housing or health. Many of them are part of income maintenance programs. The net effect of the transfers is to reduce inequality in the distribution of income.

There are several reasons for the growth of transfer payments. First, both the number of people eligible for them and the amounts they receive have increased. For example, there has been a general liberalization of the eligibility requirements for unemployment insurance benefits. Second, the attention to poverty (discussed in Chapter 23) has led to an increase in transfers. Third, persistent unemployment during the 1970s greatly increased unemployment compensation payments.

While some transfer payments go to people with above average incomes, most do not. Certainly transfer payments have had some tendency to redistribute income to the poor.

The percentage of all personal income received in the form of government transfer payments has increased sharply, from about 9 percent in 1965 to more than 13 percent in 1979.

INTERGOVERNMENTAL TRANSFERS AS A FORM OF REDISTRIBUTION

In addition to the federal government, there are 10 provincial governments, 2 territories, more

[4] The relative importance of the federal government in making transfers to individuals has been declining since the early 1960s while that of the provinces has been increasing. Later in this chapter we discuss the related issue of growth in intergovernmental transfers.

than 4,000 municipalities, and about 250 townships in Canada. Moreover, a large number of overlapping counties or districts are responsible for such local authorities as school boards. Each of the more than 5,000 governmental units spends public money, and each must get the money in order to spend it. Not all units have equal access to revenue, and this necessitates both the division of responsibility and intergovernmental financial flows.

The transfer of funds from higher to lower levels of government has been an important aspect of the Canadian federal system since Confederation. Transfers are also the focus of much of the current controversy over federal-provincial relations.

The scope and nature of intergovernmental grants has changed dramatically in the postwar period. Federal transfers to provincial governments expanded from $200 million in 1950 to almost $12 *billion* in 1979, a more than *fiftyfold* increase in 30 years. This represented an increase from 6.8 percent to 27.2 percent of federal revenues; for the provincial governments federal transfers as a share of their revenues increased, on average, from 20 percent to 30 percent. For some provinces federal transfers now represent more than half their total revenues. The transfers occur under four basic programs.

Revenue sharing. Under the terms of the British North America Act, the federal government may levy any tax it likes, but the provinces are restricted to *direct* taxes. This has been interpreted by the courts to mean that the provinces may levy personal and corporate income taxes, property taxes, and taxes on retail sales. Historically, most provinces have made **tax-rental arrangements** whereby the federal government collected income taxes and made a per capita payment to the provinces for that right. Today, with the exception of the Quebec personal income tax and the Ontario and Quebec corporate levies, all income taxes in Canada are collected by the federal government. Federal income tax rates are set at levels that allow substantial "tax room" to the provinces. Outside

Quebec, the provincial income tax is calculated as a percentage of the federal tax payable at rates determined by the individual provinces. A similar arrangement applies to the corporate income tax.

Equalization payments. In order to ensure that citizens in all regions of the country have access to a reasonable level of public services, **equalization payments** are made out of federal government general revenues to provinces with below average tax capacity. It is important to note that this is not a revenue-sharing program (provinces with above average tax capacity do not pay in), nor is it a conditional grants program like those discussed below. These grants are calculated by a complicated formula that involves 29 revenue sources.

Equalization payments are a relatively new phenomenon in Canada, but they have exhibited rapid growth. From their inception with the 1957 Tax-Sharing Act to the time of the 1977 Fiscal Arrangements Act, they expanded from $130 million to $2.2 billion. Equalization payments for 1980 are shown in Table 25-6. As we shall see in Chapter 27, equalization payments are inextricably entwined with the current controversy over energy policy because energy-related revenues are so unevenly distributed across provinces.

Conditional grants. Conditional grants are transfers made to the provinces to enable them to provide services in a specified area at some minimum national standard. Historically, these shared-cost programs have been a central part of federal-provincial fiscal arrangements. Their increasing number and extent was a source of considerable friction between the provinces and the federal government during the early 1970s. Participation was optional, but a province that declined to participate in a particular scheme forfeited the revenues that would otherwise have been transferred to it. This led to considerable dispute over constitutional issues and to the development of complicated schemes for compensating provinces that opt out. These programs

TABLE 25-6

Estimated Federal Payments to Provinces and Municipalities, Fiscal 1980–1981

Category	Millions of dollars
Unconditional payments	
Subsidies under the BNA Act	34
Revenue equalization	3,396
Public utilities income tax transfers	72
Other	326
Total	3,828
Conditional grants (established programs)	
Hospital insurance	2,584
Medicare	890
Post-secondary education	1,644
Total	5,118
Conditional grants (other)	
Canada Assistance Plan	1,724[a]
Municipal grants in lieu of taxes	262[a]
Other health and welfare	2,527
Total	4,513
Total payments	13,459

[a] 1979–1980 estimate.

Source: The National Finances.

The table shows the transfer of revenues from the federal government other than those arising from the income tax abatements. Equalization payments make up the bulk of the unconditional grants and are made to the lower-income provinces, that is, provinces other than Ontario, Alberta, and British Columbia.

thus became a focal point in the protracted debate over the present constitutional division of powers in Canada.

A major concern to the federal government was the open-ended nature of its commitments to shared-cost programs that were controlled by the provincial government. The provinces complained that they had initiated projects on the basis of federal sharing of the costs—often referred to disparagingly as "50¢ federal dollars"—and then faced the threat of withdrawal of federal support.

Under the Fiscal Arrangements Act of 1977, the system of relating federal contributions to provincial expenditures was discontinued in favor of a system under which federal contributions rise each year in accordance with the overall growth in the economy. The contributions are administered under a new program discussed below. The major remaining conditional grants relate to regional development programs; the projected breakdown of conditional grants for fiscal year 1979–1980 is given in Table 25-6.

Established programs financing (EPF). The 1977 Fiscal Arrangements Act placed federal financing of three major programs previously treated as conditional grants on a new basis. These are hospital insurance, medicare, and post-secondary education; they are referred to as established programs to indicate that their existence is not conditional on federal involvement. That federal contributions are independent of the costs of the programs reestablishes federal control over its own contribution. The provinces have gained, for they need not now be confined by narrowly defined federal program conditions.

The Overall Redistributive Effects of Government Expenditures

Since tax policy tends to be roughly proportional in its overall effect, the overall progressivity of governmental policies depends on the overall progressivity of government expenditures. Here the large and growing role of transfer payments and the use of many regional programs probably assure that overall there is some net redistribution of income from high-income and middle-income groups to the poor. But it is not very large.

Changes in the degree of income inequality from decade to decade are extremely small, despite growing government expenditures.

The Lorenz curve on page 364 does not look appreciably different than one based on data from 1940.

Why does government expenditure not have a bigger effect on income distribution? One view says that government programs are really less progressive than we had thought because progressive programs are offset by regressive programs. Another view is that market forces exert steady pressure toward more inequality, which government programs merely offset.

Distribution Versus Efficiency

Economists recognize that government actions can affect both the efficient allocation of resources and the distribution of income. Because it is possible to talk about *efficient* and *inefficient* allocations, but not about "better" or "worse" distributions of income, without introducing normative considerations, much of positive economics concerns efficiency and neglects redistribution of income. Many policy disagreements can be understood in terms of a difference in emphasis on these things.

From an efficiency point of view alone, the correct policy was to let domestic oil prices in all oil-importing countries rise along with the world price. Instead, many governments held the price down. For they were concerned, among other things, with the effect of rising prices on the windfall profits earned by large oil companies and on the welfare of poorer citizens. "We just cannot let the poor find their heating bills rise so much and so fast while the profits of the oil companies soar" was a common reaction.

Here is a genuine conflict for which economics cannot provide a solution—because in the end the answer must rest on value judgments. However, economics can make the consequences of various choices apparent, and it can suggest policy alternatives. The consequence of holding down the price of oil (out of concern for the effect of higher prices on the poor) in the manner discussed in Chapter 17 was an inefficient use of the countries' resources. Total production was reduced, and some new investment was misdirected into high-cost (rather than low-cost) methods of production. Thus in the long run average standards of living were reduced. Whether the reduction in the average was a reasonable price to pay for shielding the poor is an open question; yet it is unlikely that the question was ever posed or the calculations made.

Can one have both efficiency and desired redistributions? One way is to let the price system do the job of signaling relative scarcities and costs, thereby ensuring some efficiency in the allocation of resources, but at the same time use the taxes or expenditures to transfer income to achieve redistributive goals. This method does not seek to help the poor (or other underprivileged groups) by subsidizing oil or any other price. Rather, it seeks to provide these groups with sufficient income by direct income transfers. Then it leaves producers and consumers free to respond to relative prices that approximately reflect relative opportunity costs.

Advocates of this method argue that it is surer, more direct, and less costly in its side effects than the method of subsidizing the prices of particular goods. Moreover, the price-subsidy method surely ends up subsidizing some who are rich and missing some who are very poor. Subsidizing gasoline prices, for example, benefits the Cadillac owner and does nothing for those too poor to own a car. Thus even in redistribution it is haphazard.

Supporters of redistribution through the price system usually counter with one or both of two arguments. The first says that it is well and good to say we *could* let oil prices rise and simultaneously subsidize the poor and tax the rich, but the political process makes it unlikely that we *will* do so. Thus holding prices down may be the best or even the only practical way to get a fair distributive result.

The second argument claims that certain commodities such as food, heat, medical care, and housing are basic to a civilized life and should be provided to households cheaply whatever their real opportunity cost. Supporters reject the view that a minimum living standard can be provided simply by allowing a minimum income and letting the recipients spend it at market-determined prices. They believe that the inefficiencies resulting from prices that do not reflect opportunity costs are a price worth paying to ensure that everyone can afford these basics.

To understand the second view—that one must run just to stay even with inequality—imagine that the government today created complete equality in wealth and income. Inevitably market forces would produce inequality by next year, as some people and firms worked hard and long and succeeded while others took it easy or failed, as some invested wisely while others squandered their resources on a binge. Most economists agree that there is a limit to how much inequality can be eliminated; there is controversy as to how close we are to that limit. (And beyond that there is controversy as to how close it is desirable to get to "as much equality as possible," both on ethical grounds of justice and economic grounds of incentives.)

GOVERNMENT EXPENDITURE AND RESOURCE ALLOCATION

Governments spent nearly $52 billion in 1980 to provide goods and services. In these activities governmental units act like firms, using factors of production to produce outputs. They produce outputs rather than leave them to the free market because the people, acting through Parliament, the provincial legislatures, and city councils, have decided that they should. They are responding to the various sources of market failure discussed in Chapter 24. By and large these outputs are of collective consumption goods, of goods with strong externalities, or of services whose benefits are not marketable. Governments make both current consumption and investment expenditures, and thus they directly influence the economy's accumulation of capital.[5] In so doing governments are plainly changing the allocation of resources.

Under the British North American Act, Canada was established as a federal state with governing powers divided between the central authority and the provinces. Municipalities provide a third level of government whose powers are determined by the provincial legislatures. A number of economic considerations bear on the distribution of functions among governments. As we have seen, since revenue sources do not always match revenue needs at each level, a large volume of intergovernmental transfers is required. While the revenue sharing and equalization payments transfers are largely directed at income distribution, the conditional grants and EPF have perhaps their main impact on resource allocation.[6] They allow the various functions to be distributed among governments in a manner not dictated by revenue sources.

Factors Influencing the Intergovernmental Distribution of Activities

Our discussion in Chapter 24 of reasons for government intervention suggested a number of principles that ideally should determine the distribution of activities among levels of government.

Geographical extent of externalities. Because the government of a province or municipality is unlikely to be responsive to the needs of citizens outside its jurisdiction, public services that involve geographical spillovers may not be provided adequately unless responsibility for them is delegated to a higher level of government. The prime example of the collective consumption good, national defence, is a function normally delegated to the central government for this reason. Control of pollution is another obvious case, since contamination of air and water often quite literally spills over provincial and municipal boundaries. In Canada it may be gratuitous to add that the third-party effects involved in both examples are not confined within national boundaries.

Regional differences in preference. The delegation of some functions to lower levels of gov-

[5] Tax expenditures are an important force in this regard. One major tax expenditure is the program of Registered Retirement Savings Plans which allow some personal saving as a tax-deductible expense, thereby encouraging saving in the private sector.

[6] In Chapter 27 we discuss one (unintended) effect of the equalization payments scheme on resource allocation.

ernment may provide a political process that is more responsive to regional differences in preferences for public versus private goods. Some people may prefer to live in communities with higher quality schools and police protection, and they may be prepared to pay the higher taxes required. Another important issue at the local level is the extent to which industry should be attracted in order to broaden the property tax base. Individual valuations of the social costs in terms of aesthetic or environmental effects are bound to differ.

At the provincial level, the distinct aspirations of French Canada are a primary consideration in the distribution of functions between Ottawa and the provinces. Indeed, dissatisfaction with the present arrangements, not only in Quebec but in other provinces, continues to be a major political problem in Canada.

Redistribution of income. An important activity of government is the redistribution of income through taxing the relatively well off and channeling the funds to those in need by means of transfer payments. Clearly this function must be carried out by the central government unless per capita income happens to be the same in all regions. This is of course not the case in Canada; alleviating regional disparities is a major concern of the federal government.

Administrative efficiency. At a minimum, administrative efficiency demands that there be no duplication of the services provided at different levels of government and that related programs be coordinated. On the revenue side, it is desirable that a particular tax be collected by only one level of government. This consideration has led to the negotiation of federal-provincial tax agreements that provide for efficient collection and revenue sharing.

Changes in the Relative Shares of Government Expenditure

Total government expenditures multiplied by twenty-five over the period 1950–1980, representing an increase in the ratio of government expenditure to total goods and services produced in the economy from 22 percent to about 40 percent. In the period since 1960, increases in expenditure have been largest in such areas of provincial and municipal responsibility as health and education. As a result, the federal share of total government expenditures has been falling while that of provincial and municipal governments has been rising. These developments are documented in Table 25-7. Since personal and corporate income tax yields tend to rise more rapidly than income, while property and sales taxes respond less rapidly, these developments made necessary a reduction in the federal share of income tax revenues—from 60 percent in 1950 to 33 percent in 1980—that resulted in the increase in intergovernmental transfers discussed above.

TABLE 25-7
Expenditures by Level of Government, Selected Years, 1950–1980

Year	Total expenditure, all levels of government		Expenditure of government level (as a percentage of total government expenditures)[a]		
	Percentage of GNP	Millions of dollars	Federal	Provincial	Municipal
1950	22.1	4,080	51.9	26.0	22.1
1960	29.7	11,380	50.5	24.8	24.7
1970	36.4	31,148	38.3	35.6	26.0
1980	41.7	120,051	41.2	37.5	21.3

[a] Excluding transfers to other levels of government.
Source: Department of Finance, *Economic Review.*

The Political Economy of Public Health Care

Health care is an emotional and provocative issue. Almost everyone would agree that in a wealthy society, such as Canada in 1982, some minimum level of health care should be available to all citizens by right. At the same time, public outrage continues at the high current cost of medical care. Elementary economic analysis shows that these two events—the right to free medical care and the clamor over its high social cost—are not independent.

Health care has become extremely expensive. Without health insurance, a single major operation can be an enormous financial burden and a prolonged illness could impoverish even the most prudent middle-income household. Why has health care become so costly?

One reason for the growth in health costs is that health care is highly labor intensive. The wages of nurses, laboratory technicians, and other medical service personnel have risen substantially relative to their productivity (the number of temperatures taken, beds made, and meals served per employee do not increase much over time).

A second reason is that the average unit of medical care has risen in quality year by year. Health care is more expensive now than it was twenty years ago in part because it is better than it was twenty years ago. Available knowledge, techniques, equipment, and the training of new physicians all have improved over time. As a result it becomes possible not only to provide quicker, surer cures for common and recurring ailments but to prevent other less common ailments and complications as well.

Another part of the increase in costs arises from the growth in demand for health. As per capita income rises, people are prepared to consume more and better health. Health has proven to be income elastic.

Medicine and health insurance schemes are one response to increases in the costs of health. For a low monthly fee, various provincially run medical health insurance programs provide basic, and in some cases extensive, coverage against medical expenses. They also give rise to the interesting question, Are such insurance schemes themselves a reason for the expansion in medical costs?

Health insurance schemes lead to an increase in the quality of health care demanded. Unless there is some marginal charge for medical services, there will be no direct incentive to economize on health services; this is a criticism of both the public provision of services and private and public insurance. Insurance schemes generally charge the average cost of health care, not the marginal cost. An individual has no incentive to economize on his or her own elective care because doing so will not raise the average cost of total care significantly. Insurance schemes deal with this—albeit imperfectly—by means of deductible clauses where elective care gets a lower rate of coverage than a defined class of necessary treatments.

A related issue is the universality that most insurance programs provide. The price system allows individual patients to choose from a wide variety of price-quality alternative forms of health care. In contrast, public programs tend to provide the highest quality, highest cost options. If patients had to pay their own bills, and if they could make fully informed choices, many might prefer to pay less and not have the best available equipment and doctors in all circumstances. Because under insurance schemes the doctor does not have to pass along the higher costs of advanced modern techniques to patients, and therefore does not have to worry that those higher prices may cause a reduction in the demand for his or her services, doctors and hospital administrators are not highly motivated to provide low-cost alternatives.

Hence there is a bias in the public finance system for both the supplier of the services and the demander of the services: both will demand the high cost, high quality item because neither has to bear the consequences or the cost of providing the greater resources involved. In the matter of health care you may be tempted to say "nothing but the best"; yet the best medical care is costly, perhaps too costly for most buyers. Of course everyone wants the best of everything, *ceteris paribus*. But the relevant question always concerns costs: Is the extra quality worth the cost? Health insurance reduces the private cost born by individual patients, but the social cost of the resources used must still be borne by society.

A great debate has grown out of the issue of how much health care is necessary to a person's survival and how much is elective. To say that no one should starve is not to say that everybody should receive all the free food they can eat. Similarly, nonvital attention accounts for a large part of our demand for health care. If it is offered at little or no marginal cost to users, it will be consumed far beyond the point where its marginal utility is equal to the cost of providing it. The issue of the appropriateness of user cost has been very controversial in the Canadian discussion on health care.

There is also an emotional issue involved. Even when the extra cost does pay off in the increased probability of survival, we must ask how much we would pay to have, say, nine instead of ten people in one thousand die from a particular disease? Surely no one would want to spend a billion dollars per life saved; we would say that the opportunity cost of saving that life was too high. Yet doctors in hospitals often make the decision implicitly by ordering the best of everything and then pass the costs on to *society as a whole* through increased resource allocation to the health sector.

While everyone agrees that some minimum level of health care should be provided to all who need it, the definition of that minimum is a controversial and arbitrary issue. No doubt our concept of the minimum level of health care has grown over time; accordingly, we have had increasing public intervention in the health sector. A second issue is whether we should subsidize by category of individual rather than by type or seriousness of disease. For example, veterans, the very poor, and the elderly are all likely candidates for broader coverage than are middle-class families or upper-class families.

The central disadvantage of public provision is that it does not lend itself to rationing a costly commodity to uses that justify the cost. In a free market, use is rationed by each individual's decisions whether or not to pay the price. When individuals do not pay a marginal price because of government subsidy, there is no incentive to economize on use. Either the government must increase supply to meet the increased demand or it must find other ways to ration demand. In countries with national health services, such as Britain and Italy, rationing is accomplished in part by long lines at doctors' offices and in part by a reduction in the quality of medical services, which then reduces demand.

Suppose we had a consensus on the appropriate quantity of medical and hospital care, and suppose that this quantity is more than most people can afford to buy in the free market. The government might attempt to fill the gap in several ways: (1) by reimbursing part or all of medical bills, (2) by subsidizing doctors and hospitals to charge lower prices, (3) by subsidizing insurance companies to provide affordable insurance that will pay the bills, (4) by direct provision of health services, and (5) by imposing controls on the costs incurred and the prices charged. Each policy had its supporters and its opponents.

Such issues as the comprehensiveness and universality of coverage and the role of user costs continue to plague the Canadian debate. Doctors fight over the right for second billing, retired people select province-of-residence according to the comprehensiveness of medical coverage, and many other issues can be raised.

Several reasons for the changing distribution of government size can be mentioned.

The rising demand for government services. One of the reasons provincial and municipal government expenditures have been rising more rapidly than their residents' incomes is the high income elasticity of demand for city services. As societies become wealthier, their residents want more parks, more police protection, more and better schools and universities, and more generous treatment of their less fortunate neighbors. This alone, combined with the limited tax sources available, would create budgetary problems for provincial and municipal governments in a period of rising incomes and rising expectations. Taxpayers increasingly want the social services that governments provide, but they do not want to pay the taxes required to meet their cost. Elected officials arouse the people's wrath when they fail to provide wanted programs, but they do the same when they provide the services and then raise taxes.

A second and more important rise in the quantity of local government services required has to do with the changing character of central city populations and the increased demands for local government expenditures associated with these changes. The outward migration from the cities to the suburbs has been highly selective: It has consisted predominantly of the wealthier members of the community and has led to ever-increasing proportions of low-income groups in the central cities.

Among the correlates of low income are overcrowding of neighborhoods, deterioration of sanitation, unemployment, poor health, and an increase in crime. Welfare programs, police protection, sanitation, and public health by long tradition have been regarded, along with education, as primary areas of municipal government responsibility. As the cities have become poorer, the quantities required of these services have risen rapidly.

The rising relative cost of municipal government services. Government services tend to use much labor of a kind whose productivity (output per hour of work) has increased much less rapidly than its cost. Thus cost per unit of output has risen. While the national average output per hour of work in manufacturing has risen about 50 percent in the last decade, the size of the beat covered by a policeman, the number of students taught by each school teacher, the number of families that can be effectively handled by a social worker, or the number of temperatures that can be taken by one hospital nurse have not risen in proportion. Because wage levels tend to rise with national average productivity, the costs of services in the low-productivity sectors have soared. Although a rise in relative prices tends to lead to a decline in the quantity demanded in the market sector of the economy, the increased demand for government services has been so strong that government employees are not being phased out despite the rising cost of labor.

Evaluating the Role of Government

Most everyone would agree that the government has some role to play in the economy because of the myriad sources of possible market failure. Yet there is no consensus that the present level and role of government intervention is about right.

One aspect of the contemporary debate—the efficient level of government intervention—was discussed at the end of Chapter 24. There we asked when and to what degree government ought to attempt to modify private market behavior—say, by affecting the way a paper mill discharges its wastes. Other issues arise when government provides goods and services that the private sector does not and will not provide.

DO BENEFITS OF GOVERNMENT PROGRAMS EXCEED COSTS?

The federal government has developed techniques of evaluation designed to provide estimates of benefits and costs in order to determine whether the former exceed the latter. If they do, the program is said to be *cost effective,* and thus to be justified. For some government programs, such as flood control, there are well-defined benefits and costs. It is thus relatively easy to decide whether the project is justified. But consider the evaluation of a program such as the great American space adventure of the 1960s—placing a man on the moon before the end of the decade. The budgetary costs were easily defined. At its peak in 1966, the program absorbed about $6 billion per year. Unmistakably, the project succeeded; it met its stated objective. But was the "giant step for mankind" worth the billions it cost? The benefits certainly included the psychological lift that the moon walks may have given the American people and the substantial advances in technology and knowledge that the space program is known to have spawned. The real costs are those things that all that expenditure may have replaced. But what was the alternative? More arms to Vietnam? Massive urban redevelopment? A return of funds to private spenders to use as they saw fit? Most Americans will evaluate the worth of the space program very differently, depending on what they see as the alternative uses of the resources involved.

Such questions can never be answered unambiguously. As a result the evaluation of government programs is inherently political and controversial. Economic analysis of benefits and costs is involved, but it does not play the sole or even the dominant role in answering some big questions.

THE BALANCE BETWEEN PRIVATE AND PUBLIC SECTORS

When the government raises money by taxation and spends it on an activity, it increases the spending of the public sector and decreases that of the private sector. Since the public sector and the private sector spend on different things, the government is changing the allocation of resources. Is that good or bad? How do we know if the country has the right balance between the public and private sectors? Should there be more schools and fewer cars, or more cars and fewer schools?

Because automobiles and houses are sold on the market, consumer demand has a significant influence on the relative prices of these commodities, and (through prices) on the quantities produced and, thence, on the allocation of the nation's resources. This is true for all goods produced and sold on the market. But there is no market that provides relative prices for automobiles versus public schools; thus the choice between allowing money to be spent in the private sector and spending it for public goods is a matter to be decided by Parliament, the provincial legislatures, and "city hall."

John Kenneth Galbraith in a 1958 best seller, *The Affluent Society,* proclaimed the "liberal" message that a correct assignment of marginal utilities would show them to be higher for an extra dollar's worth of expenditure on parks, clean water, and education than for an extra dollar's worth of expenditure on television sets and deodorants. In this view, the political process often fails to translate preferences for public goods into effective action; thus more resources are devoted to the private sector and fewer to the public sector than would be the case if the political mechanism were as effective as the market.

The "conservative" view has a growing number of supporters who agree with Professor James Buchanan that society has already gone beyond the point where the value of the marginal dollar spent by the government is greater than the value of that dollar left in the hands of households or firms that would have spent it had it not been taxed away. Because bureaucrats, the conservatives argue, are spending other people's money, they regard a few million (or billion) dollars here or there as a mere nothing. They have lost all sense of the opportunity cost of public expenditure; thus they tend to spend far beyond the point where marginal benefits equal marginal costs.

This debate is not readily settled on a scientific basis because of the difficulty of measuring benefits when the things produced (e.g., clean air or the preservation of the Great Lakes) are not readily marketable. The so-called taxpayers' revolt, symbolized by the passage of Proposition 13 in California and similar measures intended to limit the powers of government to collect taxes, suggests that many people agree with the conservative position. The clamor for ever more public aid to help hard-pressed citizens points to the liberal position. The struggle between them continues.

WHAT IS THE ROLE OF GOVERNMENT TODAY?

We have been looking at the role of the government in the market economy throughout the microeconomic part of this book. Now, at the end, let us pause for perspective. One of the most difficult problems for the student of the North American economic system is to maintain perspective about the scope of government activity in the market economy. There are literally tens of thousands of laws, regulations, and policies that affect firms and households. Many believe that a significant amount of deregulation would be possible and beneficial.

But private decision makers still have an enormous amount of discretion about what they do and how they do it. One pitfall is to become so impressed (or obsessed) with the many ways in which government activity impinges on the individual that one fails to see that these only make changes—sometimes large but often small—in market signals in a system that basically leaves individuals free to make their own decisions. In the private sector most individuals choose their occupations, earn their livings, spend their incomes, and live their lives. In this sector firms, too, are formed, choose products, live, grow, and sometimes die.

A different pitfall is to fail to see that some, and perhaps most, of the highly significant amounts paid by the private sector to the government as taxes also buy goods and services that add to the welfare of individuals. By and large the public sector complements the private sector, doing things the private sector would leave undone or do very differently. To recognize this is not to deny that there is often waste, and sometimes worse, in public expenditure policy. Nor does it imply that whatever is, is just what people want. Social policies and social judgments evolve and change.

Yet another pitfall is failing to recognize that the public and private sectors compete in the sense that both make claims on the resources of the economy. Thus government activities are not without opportunity costs, except in those rare circumstances in which they use resources that have no alternative use.

Public policies in operation at any time are not the result of a single master plan that specifies precisely where and how the public sector shall seek to complement, help along, or interfere with the workings of the market mechanism. Rather, as individual problems arise, governments attempt to meet them by passing ameliorative legislation. These laws stay on the books, and some become obsolete and unenforceable. This is true of systems of law in general. As a result it is easy to find outrageous examples of inconsistencies and absurdities in any system. A distinguished professorship at Harvard gives its incumbent the right to graze a cow in Harvard Yard; laws still exist that permit the burning of witches.

Many anomalies exist in our economic policies; for example, laws designed to support the incomes of small farmers have created some agricultural millionaires, and commissions created to assure competition often end up creating and protecting monopolies. Neither individual policies nor whole programs are above criticism.

In a society that elects its policymakers at regular intervals, however, the majority view on the amount and type of government interference that is desirable will have some considerable influence on the interference that actually occurs. This now seems sure to be one of the major political issues of the 1980s. Fundamentally, a free-market system is retained because it is valued for its lack of coercion and its ability to do much of the allocating of society's resources. But we are not mesmerized by it; we feel free to intervene in pursuit of a better world in which to live. We also recognize, however, that some intervention has proven excessive and/or ineffective.

Summary

1. Two of the most powerful tools of microeconomic policy are taxation and public expenditure.

2. While the main purpose of taxes is to raise revenue, they represent a means of both changing incentives and redistributing income. Tax policy is potentially a powerful device for income redistribution because the progressivity or regressivity of different kinds of taxes varies greatly. Personal income tax rates are highly progressive, but their effect is modified by favorable treatment of capital gains and by other provisions of the tax law. Sales and excise taxes are likely to be regressive.

3. The total Canadian tax structure is roughly proportional except for very low income and very high income groups, for whom it is regressive. Either a negative income tax or a move in the direction of comprehensive income taxation would increase progressivity. Whether this is feasible politically, or desirable, is a subject of sharp current debate.

4. Evaluating the effects of taxes on resource allocation requires first determining tax incidence — that is, determining who really pays the taxes. For most taxes, the incidence is shared. Excise taxes, for example, affect prices and are thus partially passed on, but part is absorbed by producers. The actual incidence depends on such economic considerations as demand and supply elasticities.

5. A large part of public expenditure is for the provision of goods and services that private markets fail to provide. Direct and indirect subsidies, transfer payments to individuals, and intergovernmental transfers are all rising sharply.

6. The four major types of federal-provincial transfers are revenue sharing, equalization payments, conditional grants, and established programs financing.

7. The major redistributive activities of the federal government take the form of direct transfer payments to individuals and to provincial and local governments for economic welfare payments and regional adjustments. While the public sector has a tendency to redistribute some income from high-income and middle-income groups to the poor, the change in income inequality from decade to decade has been small.

8. Government expenditure of all kinds has a major effect on the allocation of resources. The government determines how much of our total output is devoted to national defense, education, and highways. It is also influential in areas where private provision of goods and services is common. Government subsidization of health care has led such expenditures to more than double as a fraction of total GNP in 30 years.

9. Why does the government have to intervene? How much of the subsidized commodity should be produced? What are the costs of providing it and who should pay them? What is the least inefficient form of government intervention?

10. Financial transfers to provincial and local governments are a key form of public expenditure policy; they lead to a different allocation of resources than would occur without them. The need for such transfers is dramatically revealed by regional imbalances in Canada.

11. Evaluating public expenditures involves reaching decisions about absolute merit (do benefits exceed costs?), about the relative merit of public and private expenditures, and about the desirable size of government.

12. The Canadian economy is a mixed economy and a changing one. Each generation faces anew the choice of which activities to leave to the unfettered market and which to rely on public expenditures or taxes to encourage or repress. It is clear that many people today are dissatisfied with the present role of government in the economy.

Topics for Review

Tax expenditures
Progressivity and regressivity of taxes
Tax incidence
Transfer payments to individuals
Intergovernmental transfers
Choosing between private and public expenditures

Discussion Questions

1. The Canadian taxpayer is assaulted by dozens of different taxes with different incidence, different progressivity, and different methods of collection. Discuss the case for and against using at most two different kinds of taxes. Discuss the case for a single taxing authority that would share the revenue with all levels of government.

2. "Taxes on tobacco and alcohol are nearly perfect taxes. They raise lots of revenue and discourage smoking and drinking." In this statement, to what extent are the two effects inconsistent? How is the incidence of an excise tax related to the extent to which it discourages use of the product?

3. How might each of the following affect the incidence of a real estate property tax imposed on central city rental property?
   a. The residents of the community are largely members of minority ethnic groups who face discrimination in neighboring areas.
   b. The city installs a good, cheap rapid transit system that makes commuting to the suburbs less expensive and more comfortable.
   c. Rent control is imposed; no existing building may raise the rents presently being charged.

4. The benefit principle is often used to justify excise taxes on particular commodities when their use depends on the availability of government-provided services or facilities. In such cases the tax provides a means of placing the burden of financing expenditures on those who benefit from them. Can you think of any examples where this principle applies? Can it be used to justify the use of property taxes as a major source of revenue by municipal governments?

5. Under the Canadian income tax law, capital gains are taxed at one-half the rates applicable to other income. Who benefits from this provision? What are its effects on the distribution of income and the allocation of resources?

6. Classify each of the following programs as "transfer payment to an individual," "intergovernmental transfer," "purchase of goods and services," or "none of the above." Which ones clearly tend to decrease the inequality of income distribution?
   a. payments of wages and family living allowances to soldiers serving overseas
   b. unemployment insurance payments to unemployed workers
   c. payments to provinces for support of universities
   d. a negative income tax
   e. pensions of retired Supreme Court justices
   f. an excess profits tax on oil companies

7. If governments tend to step in when markets fail, why are not similar functions performed similarly in different countries? Medical care, sport fishing rights, steel production, broadcasting, telephone service, and garbage collection are provided publicly in some Western countries and privately in others. What accounts for the diversity?

8. a. Suppose it is agreed to spend $1 billion in programs to provide the poor with housing, better clothing, more food, and better health services. Argue the case for and against assistance of this kind rather than giving the money to the poor to spend as they think best.
   b. Should federal transfers to the provinces be conditional grants or grants with no strings attached? Is this the same issue raised in the previous question or a different one?

9. Evaluate each of the following statements about the role of government in the economy.
   a. "Big government, not big business, is this country's problem. We are convinced that government should not try to perform economic functions that the marketplace performs more efficiently and more equitably. In our view, the proper and most productive role of government lies in balancing off various national needs, formulating policies, setting objectives, establishing appropriate incentives to the private sector to achieve those objectives, monitoring progress toward objectives, and, perhaps most important, providing leadership."
   b. "Government spending threatens our way of life. If such spending continues at the rate of the last 20 years, by the year 2000 half the people of this nation will be living off the other half."
   c. "It is private spending that has gone unchecked in an orgy of mindless consumption. That and so-called defence expenditures swallow our national income and make ours an overfed, overentertained, polluted, and impoverished society."

Part Eight

**Resource Allocation
in an
Open Economy**

International Trade and Protection

26

Canadians buy Volkswagens, Germans take holidays in Italy, Italians buy spice from Tanzania, Africans import oil from Kuwait, Arabs buy Japanese cameras, the Japanese depend heavily on American soybeans as a source of food, and Americans import hydroelectricity from Canada. *International trade* refers to all such exchanges of goods and services that take place across international boundaries.

The founders of modern economics were intimately concerned with foreign trade problems. The great eighteenth century British philosopher and economist David Hume, one of the first to work out the theory of the price system as a control mechanism, developed his concepts mainly in terms of prices in foreign trade. Adam Smith and David Ricardo, the two British economists who developed in full the classical theory of the functioning of the economy, were greatly concerned with trade problems. Smith in his *Wealth of Nations* (1776) attacked government restriction of trade. He was personally responsible for many reforms in the control of trade. Ricardo in 1817 developed the basic theory of the gains from trade that is studied in this chapter. The repeal of the Corn Laws—tariffs on the importation of grains into England—and the transformation of Britain in the mid nineteenth century from a country of high tariffs to one of complete free trade were to a significant extent the result of agitation by the economists whose theories of the gains from trade led them to a condemnation of all tariffs.

In this chapter we explore the fundamental question of what is to be gained by international trade, and then we deal with the pros and cons of interfering with the free flow of trade.

The Gains from International Trade

INTERPERSONAL, INTERREGIONAL, AND INTERNATIONAL TRADE

The advantages realized as a result of trade are usually called the **gains from trade.** The source of such gains is most easily studied by considering the differences between a world with trade and a world without it. Although governments often tend to regard foreign trade differently, economists from Adam Smith on have argued that the causes and consequences of international trade are simply an extension of the principles governing domestic trade. What is the advantage of trade among individuals, among groups, among regions, or among countries?

Consider trade among individuals. If there were no such trade, each person would have to be self-sufficient; each would have to produce all the food, clothing, shelter, medical services, entertainment, and luxuries that he or she consumed. Although a world of individual self-sufficiency is wildly unreal, it does not take much imagination to realize that living standards would be very low in such a world. Trade between individuals allows people to specialize in those activities they can do well and to buy from others the goods and services they cannot easily produce. A bad carpenter who is a good doctor can specialize in medicine. She can provide a physician's services not only for her own family but also for, say, an excellent carpenter without the training or the ability to practice medicine. Thus trade and specialization are intimately connected. Without trade everyone must be self-sufficient; with trade everyone can specialize in what they do well and satisfy other needs by trading.

The same principles apply to regions. Without interregional trade, each region would have to be self-sufficient. With such trade, plains regions can specialize in growing grain, mountain regions in mining and lumbering, and regions with abundant power in manufacturing. Cool regions can produce wheat and crops that thrive in temperate climates, and tropical regions can grow bananas and coconuts.

To generalize, the living standards of the inhabitants of all regions will be higher when the inhabitants of each region specialize in producing the commodities in which they have some natural or acquired advantage and obtain other products by trade, than when all seek to be self-sufficient.

The same applies to nations. A national boundary does not usually define an area that could easily be self-sufficient. Nations, like regions or persons, can gain from specialization and the international trade that must accompany it.

This preliminary discussion suggests one important possible gain from trade.

With trade, each individual, region or nation is able to concentrate on producing things in which it has an advantage while trading to obtain things that it could not produce efficiently itself.

SOURCES OF THE GAINS FROM TRADE

To concentrate on the sources of gains from trade one at a time, we begin by ruling out any gains in productivity that result from specialization. Assume that each region can produce goods at certain levels of productivity and that these levels are independent of the degree to which it specializes in the production of any good. In these circumstances, what is the gain from regional specialization?

A Special Case: Absolute Advantage

The gains from specialization are clear when there is a simple situation involving absolute advantage. **Absolute advantage** relates to the quantities of a single product that can be produced using the same quantity of resources in two different regions. One region is said to have an absolute advantage over another in the produc-

TABLE 26-1

Gains from Specialization with Absolute Advantage

	One unit of resources can produce	
	Wheat (bushels)	Cloth (yards)
Canada	10	6
England	5	10

Changes resulting from the transfer of one unit of Canadian resources into wheat production and one unit of British resources into cloth production

	Wheat (bushels)	Cloth (yards)
Canada	+10	− 6
England	− 5	+10
World	+ 5	+ 4

When there is reciprocal absolute advantage, specialization makes it possible to produce more of both commodities. The top half of the table shows the production of wheat and cloth that can be achieved in each country by using one unit of resources. The lower half shows the changes in production caused by moving one unit of resources out of cloth and into wheat production in Canada and in the opposite direction in England. There is an increase in world production of 5 bushels of wheat and 4 yards of cloth; worldwide, there are gains from specialization.

tion of commodity *X* when an equal quantity of resources can produce more *X* in the first region than in the second.

Suppose region *A* has an absolute advantage over *B* in one commodity, while *B* has an absolute advantage over *A* in another. This is a case of reciprocal absolute advantage: each country has an absolute advantage in some commodity. In such a situation the total production of both regions can be increased (relative to a situation of self-sufficiency) if each specializes in the commodity in which it has the absolute advantage.

Table 26-1 provides a simple example. Assume that, with a given quantity of resources, Canada can produce 10 bushels of wheat or 6 yards of cloth, while England (with the same quantity of resources) can produce 5 bushels of wheat or 10 yards of cloth. Suppose at first that

Canada and England were both self-sufficient, each producing wheat and cloth for home markets. Now assume that trade is opened between the two countries and that Canada moves resources out of cloth and into wheat while England moves resources out of wheat and into cloth. The gains and losses are summarized in the lower half of Table 26-1. Total world production of both wheat and cloth increases when this reallocation of production takes place; there is more wheat *and* more cloth for the same use of resources.

The potential gains from *specialization* make possible gains from *trade*. England is producing more cloth and Canada more wheat than when they were self-sufficient. Canada is probably producing more wheat and less cloth than Canadian consumers wish to buy, and England is producing more cloth and less wheat than English consumers wish to buy. If consumers in both countries are to get cloth and wheat in the desired proportions, Canada must export wheat to England and import cloth from England.

International trade is necessary to achieve the gains that international specialization makes possible.

Because specialization and trade go hand in hand — there is no motivation to achieve the gains from specialization without being able to trade the goods produced for goods desired — the term *gains from trade* is used to embrace both.

A First General Statement: Comparative Advantage

When each country has an absolute advantage over the other in one commodity, the gains from trade are obvious: if each produces the commodity in the production of which it is more efficient than the other, world production will be higher than if each tries to be self-sufficient. But what if Canada can produce both wheat and cloth more efficiently than England? In essence, this was the question David Ricardo posed over 160 years ago. His answer underlies the theory of comparative advantage that is still accepted by economists as a valid statement of the potential gains from trade.

Assume that Canadian efficiency increases above the levels recorded in the previous example, so that a unit of Canadian resources can produce either 100 bushels of wheat or 60 yards of cloth, but English efficiency remains unchanged. See Table 26-2 Now, surely Canada, which is better at producing both wheat and cloth than is England, has nothing to gain by trading with such an inefficient foreign country! It *does* have something to gain, however, as is illustrated in Table 26-2. Even though Canada is ten times as efficient as it was in the situation of Table 26-1, it is still possible to increase world production of both wheat and cloth by having Canada produce more wheat and less cloth and England produce more cloth and less wheat.

There is a gain from specialization because while Canada has an absolute advantage over England in the production of both wheat and cloth, its margin of advantage differs in the two commodities. Canada can produce 20 times as much wheat as England can by using the same quantity of resources, but only 6 times as much cloth. Canada is said to have a **comparative advantage** in the production of wheat and a comparative disadvantage in the production of cloth. (This statement implies another: England has a comparative disadvantage in the production of wheat and a comparative advantage in the production of cloth.)

A key proposition in the theory of international trade is:

The gains from specialization and trade depend on the pattern of comparative, not absolute, advantage.

A comparison of Tables 26-1 and 26-2 refutes the notion that the absolute *levels* of efficiency of two areas affect the gains from specialization. All that matters is that the margin of advantage that one area has over the other must differ between

TABLE 26-2

Gains from Specialization with Comparative Advantage

	One unit of resources can produce	
	Wheat (bushels)	Cloth (yards)
Canada	100	60
England	5	10

Changes resulting from the transfer of one-tenth of one unit of Canadian resources into wheat production and one unit of British resources into cloth production

	Wheat (bushels)	Cloth (yards)
Canada	+10	− 6
England	− 5	+10
World	+ 5	+ 4

When there is comparative advantage, specialization makes it possible to produce more of both commodities. The productivity of English resources is left unchanged from Table 26-1; that of Canadian resources is increased tenfold. England no longer has an absolute advantage in producing either commodity. Total production of both commodities can nonetheless by increased by specialization. Moving one-tenth of one unit of Canadian resources out of cloth and into wheat and moving one unit of resources in the opposite direction causes world production of wheat to rise by 5 bushels and cloth by 4 yards. Absolute advantage is not necessary for gains from trade.

commodities. As long as this margin differs, total world production can be increased when each area specializes in the production of the commodity in which it has a comparative advantage.

Comparative advantage is necessary as well as sufficient for gains from trade. This is illustrated in Table 26-3, showing Canada with an absolute advantage in both commodities and neither country with a comparative advantage over the other in the production of either commodity. Canada is ten times as efficient as Britain in the production of wheat and in the production of cloth. Now there is no way to increase the production of both wheat and cloth by reallocating resources within Canada and within England. The lower half of the table provides one example; you should try others. Absolute advan-

TABLE 26-3
Absence of Gains from Specialization Where There Is No Comparative Advantage

	One unit of resources can produce	
	Wheat (bushels)	Cloth (yards)
Canada	100	60
England	10	6

Changes resulting from the transfer of one unit of Canadian resources into wheat production and ten units of British resources into cloth production

	Wheat (bushels)	Cloth (yards)
Canada	+100	−60
England	−100	+60
World	0	0

Where there is comparative advantage, there is no reallocation of resources within each country that will increase the production of both commodities. In this example Canada has the same absolute advantage over England in each commodity (tenfold). There is no comparative advantage, and world production cannot be increased by reallocating resources in both countries. Therefore specialization does not increase total output.

tage without comparative advantage does not lead to gains from trade.

A Second General Statement: Opportunity Costs

Much of the previous argument has used the concept of a unit of resources and assumed that units of resources can be equated across countries, so that such statements as "Canada can produce ten times as much wheat with the same quantity of resources as England" are meaningful. Measurement of the real resource cost of producing commodities poses many difficulties. If, for example, England uses land, labor, and capital in proportions different from those used in Canada, it may not be clear which country gets more output "per unit of resource input." Fortunately, the proposition about the gains from trade can be restated without reference to absolute efficiencies.

To do this, we return to the examples of Tables 26-1 and 26-2 and calculate the opportunity cost of wheat and cloth in the two countries. When resources are assumed to be fully employed, the only way to produce more of one commodity is to reallocate resources and so produce less of the other commodity. Table 26-1 shows that a unit of resources in Canada can produce 10 bushels of wheat *or* 6 yards of cloth, from which it follows that the opportunity cost of producing one unit of wheat is 0.6 units of cloth while the opportunity cost of producing one unit of cloth is 1.67 units of wheat. These data are summarized in Table 26-4. The table also shows that in England the opportunity cost of one unit of wheat is two units of cloth forgone, while the opportunity cost of a unit of cloth is 0.50 units of wheat. Table 26-2 also gives rise to the opportunity costs in Table 26-4.

The sacrifice of cloth involved in producing wheat is much lower in Canada than it is in England, and world production can be increased if Canada rather than England produces wheat. Looking at cloth production, one can see that the loss of wheat involved in producing one unit of cloth is lower in England than in Canada. England is a lower (opportunity) cost producer of cloth than is Canada, and world production can be increased if England rather than Canada pro-

TABLE 26-4
The Opportunity Cost of One Unit of Wheat and One Unit of Cloth in Canada and England

	Wheat	Cloth
Canada	0.6 yards cloth	1.67 bushels wheat
England	2.0 yards cloth	0.50 bushels wheat

Comparative advantages can always be expressed in terms of opportunity costs that differ between countries. These opportunity costs can be obtained from Table 26-1 or Table 26-2. The English opportunity cost of one unit of wheat is obtained by dividing the cloth output of one unit of English resources by the wheat output. The result shows that 2 yards of cloth must be sacrificed for every extra unit of wheat produced by transferring English resources out of cloth production and into wheat. The other three cost figures are obtained in a similar manner.

TABLE 26-5
Gains from Specialization When Opportunity Costs Differ.

Changes resulting from each country's producing one more unit of a commodity in which it has the lower opportunity cost		
	Wheat (bushels)	Cloth (yards)
Canada	+1.0	−0.6
England	−0.5	+1.0
World	+0.5	+0.4

Whenever opportunity costs differ between countries, specialization can increase the production of both commodities. These calculations show that there are gains from specialization given the opportunity costs of Table 26-4. To produce one more bushel of wheat, Canada must sacrifice 0.6 yards of cloth. To produce one more yard of cloth, England must sacrifice 0.5 bushels of wheat. Making both changes raises world production of both wheat and cloth.

duces cloth. This situation is shown in Table 26-5.

The gains from trade arise from differing opportunity costs in the two countries.

The conclusions about the gains from trade in the hypothetical example of two countries and two commodities may be generalized:

1. One country has a comparative advantage over a second country in producing a commodity when the opportunity cost (in terms of some other commodity) of production in the first country is lower. This implies however that it has a comparative disadvantage in the other commodity.
2. Opportunity costs depend on the relative costs of producing two commodities, not on absolute costs. (Notice that the data in both Tables 26-1 and 26-2 give rise to the opportunity cost in Table 26-4.)
3. When opportunity costs are the same in all countries, there is no comparative advantage and no possibility of gains from specialization and trade. (You can illustrate this for yourself

by calculating the opportunity costs implied by the data in Table 26-3.)
4. When opportunity costs differ in any two countries, and both countries are producing both commodities, it is always possible to increase production of both commodities by a suitable reallocation of resources within each country. (This proposition is illustrated in Table 26-5.)

If, but only if, opportunity costs differ among countries, the specialization of each country in producing those commodities in which it has comparative advantages will make it possible to achieve gains from trade.

ADDITIONAL SOURCES OF THE GAINS FROM TRADE: LEARNING BY DOING AND ECONOMIES OF SCALE

So far we have assumed that costs are constant. With constant costs there are gains from specialization and trade as long as there are interregional differences in opportunity costs. If costs are not constant, *additional* sources of gain are possible.

Early economists placed great importance on a factor that we call learning by doing. They believed that as regions specialized in particular tasks, workers and managers would become more efficient in performing them. As people acquire expertise, or know-how, costs tend to fall. Much modern empirical work suggests that this really does happen. If it occurs in our example, output of cloth per worker will rise in England as England becomes more specialized in that commodity, and the same will happen to output of wheat per worker in Canada. This is, of course, a gain over and above that which occurs when costs are constant.

A further reason why costs might fall as regions specialize concerns economies of large-scale production. If costs fall as output increases, world output can be greater when there is one large cloth industry in England and one large wheat industry in Canada (rather than two half-size cloth industries and two half-size wheat industries, one in each country).

A Graphic Representation of the Gains from Trade

Suppose Canada has a comparative advantage in wheat and England a comparative advantage in cloth and that initially each country is self-sufficient. Each country will be operating at a point (such as E and e in the diagrams below) on its own production—and consumption—possibility curve (shown as the heavy black line). The production possibility curves are straight lines because the opportunity cost of one commodity in terms of the other is assumed to be the same, no matter what are the current levels of output of each commodity. Canada's curve (AB) is steeper because the opportunity cost of producing cloth instead of wheat is high. Canada has a comparative *advantage* in wheat and a comparative *disadvantage* in cloth.

Suppose Canada were offered the chance of obtaining cloth by trade at the English opportunity cost. It would pay Canada to produce nothing but wheat and then acquire cloth at the English opportunity cost. This would allow Canada to attain some point on AC', which is drawn through A (Canada's fully specialized output of wheat) parallel to CD.

Clearly consumption opportunities have increased: Canada could now reach a point such as E_1, which was unobtainable without trade. In these circumstances Canada would gain by trade and England would break even.

Suppose England were offered the chance of obtaining wheat at the Canadian opportunity cost in terms of cloth sacrificed. It would pay England to produce nothing but cloth and to trade along DA' (drawn parallel to AB) to reach a higher point, say e_1, than was obtainable when wheat had to be obtained at the English opportunity cost. In these circumstances England would gain by trade and Canda would break even.

But this means there is a range of "prices" of cloth in terms of wheat—lower than Canada's high opportunity cost and higher than England's low opportunity cost—at which each country gains. Represent one such relative price by the slope of the coloured line AT ($= DT$). If Canada produces only wheat and England only cloth, and they were willing to trade at this relative price, their consumption possibilities with trade are shown by the col-

TERMS OF TRADE

So far we have seen that world production can be increased when Canada and England specialize in the production of the commodity in which they have a comparative advantage and then trade with each other. How will these gains from specialization and trade be shared between the two countries? The division of the gain depends on the terms at which trade takes place. The *terms of trade* are defined as the quantity of domestic goods that must be exported to get a unit of imported goods.

The terms of trade reflect the opportunity cost of imports measured in terms of exports.

In the example of Table 26-4, the Canadian domestic opportunity cost of one unit of cloth is 1.67 bushels of wheat. If Canadians can obtain cloth by international trade at terms of trade more favorable than 1.67 bushels of wheat, they will gain by doing so. Suppose that international prices are such that 1 yard of cloth exchanges for (i.e., is equal in value to) 1 bushel of wheat. At those prices, Canadians can obtain cloth at a lower wheat opportunity cost by trade than by

ored lines AT and DT. Canada can go to some point such as E_2, which gives it more wheat and more cloth than the self-sufficiency point E, while England can go to some point such as e_2, which gives it more wheat and more cloth than at its self-sufficiency point e. Thus the central generalization of the theory of the gains from trade is graphically illustrated: Trade allows each country to have more of each commodity than it could have if each country were self-sufficient.

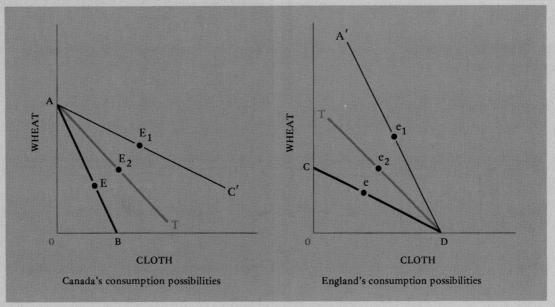

Canada's consumption possibilities   England's consumption possibilities

domestic production. Therefore the terms of trade favor selling wheat and buying cloth on international markets.

Similarly, in the example of Table 26-4, English consumers gain when they can obtain wheat abroad at any terms of trade more favorable than 2 yards of cloth per bushel of wheat, which is the English domestic opportunity cost. If the terms of trade are 1 bushel of wheat for 1 yard of cloth, the terms of trade favor English traders' buying wheat and selling cloth on international markets. Both England and Canada in this example gain from trade: each can obtain the commodity in

which it has a comparative disadvantage at a lower opportunity cost through international trade than through domestic production.

In practice an index of the terms of trade is computed as the ratio of two index numbers:

$$\text{Index of terms of trade} = \frac{\text{Index of import prices}}{\text{Index of export prices}} \times 100$$

A fall in the index is referred to as a *favorable* change in a country's terms of trade. It means that less has to be exported to pay for a unit of imports than previously. For example, when Canada's import price index rises from 100 to 120 while its export price index rises from 100 to 125, the terms of trade index falls from 100 to 96. At the new terms of trade, 96 units of exports will buy what formerly required 100 units to buy. An increase in the index of the terms of trade, called an *unfavorable* change, means the country must export more to pay for its now relatively more expensive imports.[1]

The Debate About Protectionism

There are always difficulties in conducting business in a foreign country. Differences in language, in local laws and customs, and in currency all complicate transactions. In this section our concern is not with these difficulties but with the *trade policy* by which governments intentionally erect barriers to the free flow of goods and services among nations.

Protectionism refers to the protection of domestic industries from foreign competition. Such protection may be achieved either by tariffs that raise the price of foreign goods or by nontariff barriers such as quotas or production and export subsidies that make importing difficult or impossible. **Free trade** is a situation in which no protectionism is practiced.

METHODS OF PROTECTIONISM

There are basically three means by which a country might seek to reduce the quantity of some good it imports. (1) It may place a tax on imports of the commodity, called a **tariff.** Such a tax, like any excise tax (see Chapter 25), shifts upward the supply curve of the foreign good and thus tends to raise its price. The tariff causes this

shift because it adds to the foreign producer's cost of every unit sold in the country imposing the tariff. (2) It may impose an *import quota* that limits the quantity of the commodity that may be shipped into the country in a given period. Once the quota has been reached, the effective supply curve becomes a vertical line. Until the quota has been reached there is no change in demand or supply. (3) It may take steps to reduce the demand for the imported commodity on the part of its citizens. For example, it may require potential importers to acquire a special license, or it may restrict the ability of its citizens to use their funds to purchase the foreign exchange needed to pay for the commodity. Such steps would shift the demand curve for the import to the left.[2]

The three parts of Figure 26-1 illustrate the three means. Although there are differences in the effects of the different means, almost all the issues can be raised by considering any one of them. We shall concentrate on tariffs.

Tariffs

The usual form of a tariff is a tax that is a specified percentage of the producer's price. This is called an *ad valorem* tariff. Its major purpose is to raise the price of imported goods in order to discourage imports by offsetting (to some extent at least) a cost advantage that foreign producers have over domestic producers of a particular product.[3]

To see when and how tariffs work, consider three different commodities that Canadians might import—coal, coffee, and steel. We shall make the simplifying assumptions shown in

---

[1] Statistics Canada publishes a series giving Canada's terms of trade defined inversely to the definition in the text; i.e., as the ratio on export price index to an import price index. Hence, for that series a *rise* in the terms of trade is referred to as favorable.

[2] A distinction is frequently made between tariff and nontariff barriers. The latter includes both the second and third categories mentioned here.

[3] Tariffs can also be utilized to raise revenue. In Canada customs revenues are about $4 billion per year. Although this amount is not negligible, it represents less than 15 percent of federal tax revenue. The protective function of a tariff is opposed to the revenue function because the tariff will not yield much revenue when it is effective in cutting imports. Here we concentrate on the protective feature of tariffs.

FIGURE 26-1
Alternative Means of Decreasing the Quantity of Imports of a Commodity

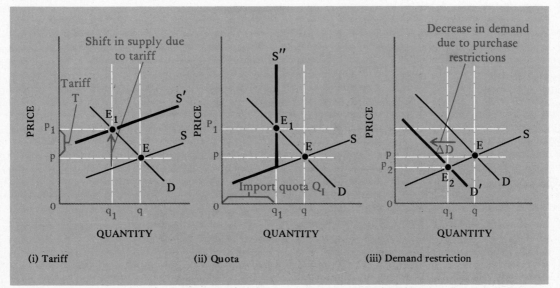

(i) Tariff   (ii) Quota   (iii) Demand restriction

The government can decrease the quantity of imports below the free-market level by policies that shift either the demand curve or the supply curve to the left or that simply regulate the quantity permitted to enter. In each diagram D and S represent the free-market demand and supply for some imported goods, with p and q being the equilibrium price and quantity. If the government wishes to achieve a smaller quantity of imports, such as q_1, it may do so in various ways.

In (i) it imposes a tariff of T per unit. This shifts the supply curve vertically by the amount of the tariff, to S', and achieves a new equilibrium at E_1.

In (ii) it imposes an import quota, Q_1, as the maximum quantity permitted to enter. This in effect changes the supply curve to the heavy kinked line S'' and leads to equilibrium at E_1.

In (iii) it causes demand to shift leftward by ΔD by a policy such as limiting importers' right to purchase the commodity or the foreign exchange needed to pay for it. In this case a new equilibrium occurs at E_2. In all three parts the equilibrium quantity imported is reduced to q_1.

Table 26-6 about the price of the commodity in Canada compared to the costs of production in a foreign country plus shipment to Canada.

There is potential demand for the importation of any commodity that can be delivered to a country at a cost lower than the cost at which it can be produced domestically. At any time there is a wide array of potentially importable commodities, some with large cost savings, some with moderate savings, and some with no advantage at all. (In the example, both coffee and steel would be candidates for importation.) A world of free trade would have no tariffs on imports. In such a world, a country would import all those commodities that it could buy from abroad at a

delivered price lower than the cost of producing them at home.

Suppose Canada wishes to protect its home industries from any foreign competition. It does not need a tariff on coal; it does need (at the assumed prices and costs) a tariff in excess of 15 percent on steel and a tariff of more than 650 percent on coffee.

Now suppose that Canada imposes a 20 percent tariff on all imports. This does not prohibit trade, but by making imported goods more expensive, it affects those items it is profitable to import. Any foreign good that enjoys a cost advantage of less than 20 percent is now effectively prohibited. This is the case of steel in the ex-

TABLE 26-6
Assumed Comparative Costs of Domestic Versus Foreign Production

Commodity	Canadian price if all production is domestic	Delivered cost of import	Percentage tariff needed to exclude	Delivered cost of imports in Canada with 20% tariff
Coal (ton)	$ 30	$ 35	none	$ 42.00
Coffee (lb.)	15	2	650+	2.40
Steel (ton)	115	100	15+	120.00

Commodities whose delivered cost to Canada is below the price of domestically produced commodities are potential imports; tariffs change the effective delivered costs of imports. In the example, foreign producers have a comparative advantage at current prices in both coffee and steel production but not in coal. To make all importation uneconomic would require a tariff of at least 15 percent on steel and 650 percent on coffee. A 20 percent tariff would exclude steel but not coffee; however, it would raise coffee prices. A tariff would not affect coal because coal imports are effectively excluded with a tariff. These data are hypothetical.

ample. A 20 percent tariff thus provides protection to domestic industries that produce at a cost disadvantage of up to 20 percent. Imported goods that enjoy cost advantages in excess of 20 percent (such as coffee) will still be in demand, but they will not be as big a bargain as previously. Because their price will be higher, a smaller quantity will be demanded than if there were no tariff.

When a country desires to prohibit trade in a specific commodity, it might do so by setting a tariff that is larger than the cost advantage of the lowest-cost foreign producer. When it desires to stimulate competition between domestic and foreign producers, it might set tariffs so as to equalize the present cost advantages. In the example of Table 26-6, a 15 percent tariff on steel would make steel produced in Canada competitive with foreign steel at current costs.

FREE TRADE VERSUS PROTECTIONISM

In today's world two facts about international trade stand out. First, there is a great deal of it. Second, virtually every government interferes to some extent with free trade.

The reasons behind these facts need to be examined.

The Case for Free Trade

We have seen that where opportunity costs differ among countries, some degree of specialization with some consequent amount of trade will raise world standards of living. Free trade allows all countries to specialize in producing commodities in which they have comparative advantages. They can then produce (and consume) more of all commodities than would be available if specialization had not taken place.

Free trade makes it possible to maximize world production and makes it *possible* for every household in the world to consume more goods than it could if free trade did not exist. Yet this does not mean that everyone will be better off with free trade than without it, for the aggregate size of the world's output and the way in which that output is divided are important considerations. It is possible that protectionism will give some people a large enough share of a smaller world output so that they will benefit from protectionism. If we ask if it is possible for free trade to be advantageous to everyone, the answer is yes. But if we ask if it is in fact always mutually advantageous to everyone, that is quite another matter.

There is abundant evidence to show that real differences in comparative costs exist and that there are potential gains from trade because of these differences. There is also ample evidence that trade occurs and that no nation tries to be self-sufficient or refuses to sell to foreigners the items it produces cheaply and well.

The case for free trade is powerful. What needs explanation is not the extent of trade but the fact that trade is not wholly free. Tariffs and nontariff barriers to trade exist 200 years after Adam Smith stated the case for free trade. Do these interferences exist merely because policymakers are ignorant of the principles of comparative advantage, or are there reasons (not included in the case for free trade) that make it sensible for a nation to enact protectionist policies? Is there a valid case for interfering with trade? If there is, how does one find the balance between the advantages of more or less trade?

The Case for Protectionism

Two kinds of arguments for protection are common. The first concerns objectives other than maximizing output; the second concerns the difference between the welfare of a single nation and that of the world.

Objectives other than maximizing output. It is quite possible to accept the proposition that production is higher with free trade and yet rationally oppose free trade because of a concern with policy objectives other than production and consumption. There are, after all, policy goals other than maximizing real national income.

For example, comparative costs might dictate that a country should specialize in producing a single commodity, say bananas. The government might decide, however, that there are distinct social advantages to encouraging a more diverse economy—one that would give citizens a wider range of occupations. The authorities might decide that the social and psychological advantages of a diverse economy more than compensate for a reduction in living standards by, say, 5 percent below what they could be with complete specialization of production.

Specializing in the production of one or two commodities, although dictated by comparative advantage, may involve risks that a country does not wish to take. One such risk is a technological advance that renders its basic product obsolete. The quartz crystal badly damaged the Swiss watch industry in just this way; between 1974 and 1979 its share of the world market dropped from 40 percent to 30 percent, and 30,000 jobs were lost.

Another risk is cyclical fluctuations in the prices of basic commodities, which may face depressed prices for years at a time, then periods of very high prices. The national income of a country specializing in the production of such commodities will be subject to wide fluctuations. Even though the average income level over a long period might be higher when there is specialization in the production of basic commodities, the serious social problems associated with a widely fluctuating national income may make the government decide to sacrifice some income in order to reduce fluctuations. Such a government might use protectionist policies to encourage the expansion of several cyclically stable industries.

Yet another reason for protectionism may be the desire to maintain national traditions. For example, many Canadians are passionately concerned with maintaining a separate nation with traditions that differ from those of the United States. Many believe that a tariff helps them to do this. They seem prepared, if necessary, to tolerate a 5 or 10 percent or larger differential in living standards in order to maintain this independence.

One frequently cited noneconomic defence of protectionism concerns national defence. It has traditionally been argued, for example, that the United States needs an experienced merchant marine in case of war and that this industry should be fostered by protectionist policies, even though it is less efficient than the foreign competition.

There is nothing irrational in a country's deciding to accept substantial costs in order to attain objectives other than maximizing living standards. Although most people would agree that, *ceteris paribus,* they prefer more income to less, economists cannot pronounce as irrational a nation that chooses to sacrifice some income in order to achieve other goals.

Protectionism as a means to higher national living standards. The most important example in this category relates to economies of scale. It is usually called the **infant industry argument.** If an industry has large economies of scale, costs and prices will be high when the industry is small, but they will fall as the industry grows. In such an industry, the country first in the field has a tremendous advantage. A newly developing country may find that its industries are unable to compete in the early stages of their development with established foreign rivals. A tariff or import quota may protect these industries from foreign competition while they grow up. When they are large enough, they will be able to produce as cheaply as can foreign rivals and thus be able to compete without protection.

A similar argument in favor of protectionism concerns learning by doing. Giving a domestic industry protection from foreign competition may enable it to learn to be efficient and give the labor force the time needed to acquire necessary skills. If so, it may pay the government to protect the industry while the learning occurs.

TRADE AND PROTECTIONISM

From what we have said it appears that there is a strong case for allowing trade in order to realize the gains from trade—and that there may also be reasons for departing from competely free trade.

It is not necessary to choose between free trade on the one hand and absolute protectionism on the other; a country can have some trade and some protectionism too.

Free Trade Versus No Trade

It would undoubtedly be possible, by using greenhouses, to grow oranges, cotton, and other now-imported raw materials and foodstuffs in Norway and to grow coffee beans in Canada. But the cost in terms of other commodities forgone

would be huge, for artificial means of production require lavish inputs of factors of production. It would likewise be possible for a tropical country currently producing foodstuffs to set up industries to produce all the manufactured products that it consumes. The cost in terms of resources used, for a small country without natural advantages in industrial production, could be very large. It is thus clear that there is a large gain to all countries in having specialization and trade. The real output and consumption of all countries would be very much lower if each had to produce domestically all the goods it consumed.

In an all-or-nothing choice, virtually all countries would choose free trade over no trade.

Some Trade Versus No Trade

Of the level of tariffs in force today, some reflect protectionism, while others reflect a use of tariffs to raise revenue. It is clear that these tariffs are not sufficient to offset widely differing cost conditions, the most dramatic of which are those associated with climate. Even the most casual observation reveals major cost differences among countries. Thus there are significant gains from trading for commodities in which a country has a large comparative disadvantage. Careful empirical measurement might put an actual numerical value on the amount of gains, but certainly production and consumption in the world, and in each major trading country, are higher with trade than they would be with no trade.

A Little More Trade Versus a Little Less Trade

Today we have trade between nations, but that trade is not perfectly free. Would we be better off if today's barriers to trade were reduced or increased a little bit? It is quite a jump from the proposition that "Some trade is better than no trade" to the proposition that "A little more trade than we have at present is better than a little less trade." Yet most arguments about commercial policy involve the latter sort of proposition, not the former. Should workers be given *some* increased protection against Japanese imports is the question debated today, not should Japan be totally excluded from the Canadian market.

Most actual policy disagreements concern the relative merits of free trade versus controlled trade with tariffs on the order of, say, 5, 10, or 15 percent. Such tariffs would not cut out imports of bananas, coffee, diamonds, bauxite, or any commodity in whose production Canada would be really inefficient. (Yet these are just the commodities that defenders of free trade sometimes use as examples when the hypothesis of the gains from trade is challenged.) When one accepts the hypothesis that some trade is better than no trade, it is not necessary to accept the hypothesis that free trade is better than controlled trade with, say, 15 percent tariffs; nor is one committed to saying that 9 percent tariffs would be better than 10 percent tariffs.

As a simplified version of the sort of argument that really does take place over commercial policy, compare the effects of a 20 percent uniform ad valorem tariff with those of free trade. As a rule, tariffs are seldom advocated to protect industries that are extremely inefficient compared to foreign industries; they are usually advocated to protect industries that can very nearly compete, but not quite. How much would be gained by removing 20 percent tariffs or how much lost by imposing 20 percent tariffs in a situation of free trade?

Tariffs of 20 percent will protect industries that are up to 20 percent less efficient than foreign competitors. If the costs of the various tariff-protected industries were spread out evenly, some would be 20 percent less efficient than their foreign competitors, and others would be only 1 percent less efficient. Their average inefficiency would be about half the tariff rate, so they would be on average about 10 percent less efficient than their foreign competitors.

Suppose that as a result of tariffs, approximately 10 percent of a country's resources are allocated to industries different from the ones to which they would be allocated if there were no tariffs. This means that about 10 percent of a country's resources would be working in certain industries only because of tariff protection. If the average protected industry is 10 percent less efficient than its foreign rival, approximately 10 percent of a country's resources are producing about 10 percent less efficiently than they would be if there were no tariffs. This causes a reduction in national income on the order of 1 percent as a result of tariff protection.

This rough-and-ready calculation is meant simply to illustrate why the gains from removing modest barriers to trade may appear small. That conclusion was established by three careful studies of the effects of tariffs in Great Britain and Europe. Professor P. J. Verdoorn estimated that the gain to the six European Common Market countries from eliminating tariffs on trade among themselves to be about .05 percent of their national incomes. Professor Harry Johnson estimated that the maximum cost to Britain of staying out of the Common Market would have been equal to approximately 1 percent of Britain's national income. Papers presented at a 1978 conference sponsored by the Economic Council of Canada suggested that the economic costs to Quebec of leaving the Canadian federation would be roughly equal to 2 percent of Quebec's total annual output.

The potential net gains from somewhat freer trade than there is today are not so large as to make it certain that the removal of all remaining barriers is desirable.

Suppose the gains from free trade would be 1 percent of national income. Is such a sacrifice of national income large or small? As a percentage it seems small, yet in 1980 prices it would be $2.6 billion *per year* in Canada. That amount every year forever could buy a lot of hospitals, schools, medical research, solar energy research —or even gasoline.

Whether free trade is better than a policy of moderate protectionism depends on the policy goals that a country is trying to attain, the magnitude of the benefits, and the costs of the actions. There is thus a highly important area for study and debate about trade and trade barriers.

There are also many claims that do not advance the debate; fallacious arguments are heard on both sides, and they color much of the popular discussion. These arguments have been around for a long time, but their survival does not make them true.

Fallacious Free Trade Arguments

Free trade always benefits all countries. This is not necessarily so. The potential gains from trade might be offset by costs such as unemployment or economic instability or by the interference with policy objectives other than maximizing income. These factors may render some interference desirable.[4]

Infant industries never grow up. It is argued that to grant protection on an infant industry basis is a mistake because infant industries seldom admit to growing up and will cling to their protection even when they are fully grown. Even if this allegation were true, it would not be a sufficient reason for avoiding protectionism. When economies of scale are realized, the real costs of production are reduced and resources are freed for other uses. Whether or not the tariff or other trade barrier remains, a cost saving has been effected by the scale economies.

Fallacious Protectionist Arguments

The exploitation doctrine. According to this view, one trading partner *must* always reap a gain at the other's expense. The principle of comparative advantage shows that it is possible for both parties to gain from trade and thus refutes the exploitation doctrine of trade. When opportu-

nity cost ratios differ in two countries, specialization and the accompanying trade make it possible to produce more of all commodities and thus make it possible for both parties to get more goods as a result of trade than they could get in its absence.

Keep the money at home. This argument says, If I buy a foreign good, I have the money and the foreigner has the money, whereas if I buy the same good locally, I have the good and our country has the money, too. Abraham Lincoln is said to have made this argument, and it is still heard today. It assumes that domestic money actually goes abroad physically when imports are purchased and that trade flows only in one direction.

The argument is based on a misconception. When Canadian importers purchase Italian-made goods, they do not send dollars abroad. They (or some financial agent) buy Italian lire (or claims on them) and use them to pay the Italian manufacturer. They purchase the lire on the foreign exchange market by giving up dollars to someone who wishes to use them for expenditure in Canada. Even if the money did go abroad physically—that is, if an Italian firm accepted a shipload of dollars—it would be because that firm (or someone to whom it could sell the dollars) wanted them to spend in the only country where they are legal tender, Canada.

Dollars ultimately do no one any good except as purchasing power. It would be miraculous if green pieces of paper could be exported in return for real goods; after all, the central bank has the power to create as much new money as it wishes. It is only because the green paper can buy Canadian commodities that others want it.

Protection against low-wage foreign labor. Surely, the argument says, the products of Oriental sweatshops will drive our products from the market, and the high Canadian standard of living will be dragged down to that of the impoverished Orient. Arguments of this sort have swayed many voters through the years.

As a prelude to considering them, stop and think what the argument would imply if taken out

[4] To see how sensitive the gains from trade are to other considerations, suppose that totally free trade led to an allocation of resources that was 1 percent more efficient than an allocation resulting from 20 percent tariffs, but led simultaneously to an average level of unemployment 1.2 percent higher. In this case, free trade would bring losses rather than gains.

of the international context and put into a local one, where the same principles govern the gains from trade. Is it really impossible for a rich person to gain from trading with a poor person? Would the local millionaire be better off if she did all her own typing, gardening, and cooking? No one believes that a rich person cannot gain from trading with those who are less rich. Why then must a rich group of people lose from trading with a poor group? "Well," you say, "the poor group will price their goods too cheaply." Does anyone believe that consumers lose from buying in a discount house or a supermarket just because the prices are lower there than at the old-fashioned corner store? Consumers gain when they can buy the same goods at a lower price. If the Koreans pay low wages and sell their goods cheaply, *Korean* labor may suffer, but we will gain because we obtain their goods at a low cost in terms of the goods that we must export in return. The cheaper our imports are, the better off we are in terms of the goods and services available for domestic consumption.

Stated in more formal terms, the gains from trade depend on comparative, not absolute, advantages. World production is higher when any two areas, say Canada and Japan, specialize in the production of the goods for which they have a comparative advantage than when they both try to be self-sufficient.

Might it not be possible, however, that Japan will undersell Canada in all lines of production and thus appropriate all, or more than all, the gains for itself, leaving Canada no better off, or even worse off, than if it had remained self-sufficient? The answer is no. The reason for this depends on the behavior of exchange rates; equality of demand and supply on the foreign exchange market ensures that trade flows in both directions.[5]

Imports can be obtained only by spending the currency of the country that makes the imports. Claims to this currency can be obtained only by exporting goods and services or by borrowing.

[5] Recall the discussion in Chapter 8, especially pages 136–141.

Thus, lending and borrowing aside, imports must equal exports. All trade must be in two directions; we can buy only if we can also sell. In the long run, trade cannot hurt a country by causing it to import without exporting. Trade, then, always provides scope for international specialization, with each country producing and exporting those goods for which it has a comparative advantage.

Exports raise national income, imports lower it. Exports add to aggregate demand; imports subtract from it. Exports thus tend to increase national income, *ceteris paribus,* and imports reduce it, *ceteris paribus.* Surely, then, it is desirable to encourage exports and discourage imports. This is an appealing argument, but it is incorrect.

Saying that exports raise national income means that they add to the value of output, but they do not add to the value of domestic consumption. In fact, exports are goods produced at home and consumed abroad, while imports are goods produced abroad and consumed at home. The standard of living in a country depends on the goods and services available for *consumption,* not on what is produced.

If exports were really good and imports really bad, then a fully employed economy that managed to increase exports without a corresponding increase in imports ought to be better off. Such a change, however, would result in a reduction in current standards of living because when more goods are sent abroad and no more are brought in from abroad, the total goods available for domestic consumption must fall.

What happens when a country achieves a surplus of exports over imports for a considerable period of time? It will accumulate claims to foreign exchange for which there are three possible uses: to add to foreign exchange reserves, to buy foreign goods, and to make investments abroad. Consider each of them.

1. Some foreign exchange reserves are required for the smooth functioning of the international payments system, as we shall see in Chapter 38. But the accumulation of reserves

over and above those required serves no purpose. Permanent excess reserves represent claims on foreign output that are never used.

2. British pounds and Indian rupees cannot be eaten, smoked, drunk, or worn. But they can be spent to buy British and Indian goods that can be eaten, smoked, drunk, or worn. When such goods are imported and consumed, they add to Canadian living standards. Indeed, the main purpose of foreign trade is to take advantage of international specialization: trade allows more consumption than would be possible if all goods were produced at home. From this point of view, the purpose of exporting is to allow the importation of goods that can be produced more cheaply abroad than at home.

3. An excess of exports over imports may be used to purchase foreign assets. Such foreign investments add to living standards only when the interest and profits earned on them are used to buy imports, or when the investment is liquidated. The essence of any investment is to permit the investor to earn profits or interest that can be used to buy goods. Foreign investments permit the later purchase of foreign goods.

The living standards of a country depend on the goods and services consumed in that country. The importance of exports is that they permit imports to be made. This two-way international exchange is valuable because more goods can be imported than could be obtained if the same goods were produced at home.

Protectionism creates domestic jobs and reduces unemployment. It is sometimes said that an economy with substantial unemployment, such as that of Canada in the 1930s or in 1980, provides an exception to the case for freer trade. Suppose that tariffs or important quotas cut the imports of Japanese cars. Korean textiles, Italian shoes, and French wine. Surely, the argument maintains, this will create more employment for Oshawa auto workers, Quebec textile workers, Ontario shoe factories, and Manitoba farm workers. The answer is that it will—initially. But the Japanese, Koreans, Italians, and French can buy from Canada only if they earn Canadian

dollars by selling goods in Canada. The decline in their sales of autos, textiles, shoes, and wine will decrease their purchases of Canadian machinery, aircraft, grain, and vacations in Canada. Jobs will be lost in our export industries and gained in those industries that formerly faced competition from imports.

The likely long-term effect is that overall unemployment will not be reduced but merely redistributed among industries. This explains why industries and unions that compete with imports favor protectionism while those with large exports favor more trade. Economists are highly skeptical about the government's ability to reduce overall unemployment by protectionism.

Subsidizing exports increases employment. Export industries do not necessarily favor free trade; they may argue instead that the government should subsidize them. This argument is closely related to the last point, though it is made by different groups. Assume that there is a rise in exports without a corresponding rise in imports, perhaps because the government pays producers a subsidy on every unit exported. According to the theory of the multiplier, this rise in exports will increase income and employment. Surely, in a time of unemployment, this is to be regarded as a good thing.

Two points may be made about such a policy. In the first place, the goods being produced by the newly employed workers in the export sector are not available for domestic consumption and so do not directly raise domestic standards of living. Surely it would be better if, instead of subsidizing exports, the central authorities subsidized the production of goods for the home market so that all goods produced—not just those produced in response to increased incomes —would contribute to a rise in domestic living standards. Or, if there is objection to the government's subsidizing private firms, the government could create new employment by building more roads, schools, and research laboratories. Consequently income and employment would go up, but there would be something more tangible to show for it in the first instance than the smoke of ships disappearing over the horizon bearing the subsidized exports to foreign markets.

The second point to be made concerns the foreign effects of a policy that fosters exports and discourages imports in a situation of general world unemployment. Although the policy raises domestic employment, it will have the reverse effect abroad, where it creates unemployment. The foreign countries will suffer a rise in their unemployment because their exports will fall and their imports rise. Not surprisingly, they may be expected to retaliate; as we will see, this has been the historical experience. If all countries try a policy of expanding exports and discouraging imports, the net effect is likely to be a large drop in the volume of international trade without much change in the level of employment in any one country.

Arguments About Barriers to Trade: A Final Word

While there are cases in which a restrictive policy has been pursued following a rational assessment of the approximate cost, it is hard to avoid the conclusion that, more often than not, such policies are pursued for flimsy objectives or on fallacious grounds, with little idea of the actual costs involved. The very high tariffs that marked the 1920s and 1930s are a conspicuous example. Clamor for the government to do something about the competition from Japan, Korea, and other countries of the East may well be another.

Canadian Trade Policy

The issue of free trade versus protectionism has been prominent throughout Canada's history because of the crucial role of external trade in the nation's economic development. According to the widely accepted "staple theory," economic growth was based on the exploitation of Canada's comparative advantage in products with a large natural resource content. The thesis, due initially to Professor Harold Innes of the University of Toronto, says that prosperity depended

on the strength of export markets for a succession of staples—fish, fur, timber, and wheat—each of which dominated a particular period of Canadian history.

After Confederation, the protective tariff as a means of fostering domestic manufacturing was adopted as a major element in the "National Policy" that emerged in the 1870s. The tariff and the transcontinental railway completed in 1885 were the key elements in a program of economic nationalism that sought to reduce the country's dependence on unstable export markets for raw materials and to promote an east-west flow of trade that would consolidate the political union of the provinces.

Current Composition of Canada's Trade

Although a century of industrialization has greatly reduced the proportion of the economy engaged in raw material production, raw and semifinished products still account for a large fraction of Canadian exports (see Table 26-7). The earlier staples have been supplanted by pulp and paper, iron ore, nonferrous metals, crude pe-

TABLE 26-7
Canadian Exports by Commodity, 1980

Commodity	Exports	
	Billions of dollars	Percentage of total
Farm and fish products	$ 8.6	11.6
Forest products	12.7	17.1
Crude petroleum and natural gas	6.9	9.3
Other minerals and metals	15.0	20.2
Chemicals and fertilizers	4.1	5.5
Motor vehicles and parts	11.1	14.9
Other manufactured goods	15.9	21.4
Total exports of domestic products	$74.3	100.0

Source: Bank of Canada Review.

Raw and semifinished products make up 60 percent of Canadian exports. Since the signing of the Automotive Products Agreement in 1965, motor vehicles and parts have become the major export industry in the manufacturing sector.

Rationalization by Formal Agreement: The Auto Pact

The Canadian automobile industry was established under tariff protection from foreign competition. The tariff caused the major U.S. automobile manufacturers to export to Canada *indirectly* by establishing branch plants within Canada to produce for the Canadian market.

By the late 1950s Canadian policymakers had become concerned about the structure of the Canadian automobile industry. It had been hoped that the protection offered by the tariff would enable the industry eventually to become efficient and to compete on its own against foreign imports. This had not happened; Canadian costs and prices remained well above their U.S. counterparts. In response to the concern, the Royal Commission on the Automobile Industry was created. Its report, the Bladen report, led to the enactment of the Automobile Products Trade Act (the Auto Pact) in 1965. The Auto Pact led to a rationalization of the Canadian automobile industry (see the discussion in the box on pages 302–303).

Prior to the enactment of the Auto Pact, a diverse range of cars was being produced and sold in Canada. Because this entailed short production runs, the industry was unable to achieve its *MES* and hence operated inefficiently. In 1964 Ford was producing 60 different models of five distinct lines at its single Canadian plant, while in its American River Rouge plant it was producing only three models of one product line. The Bladen Commission estimated that production runs of 100,000 units were necessary to achieve full productive efficiency. While this figure was easily achieved in the U.S. plant, it accounted for almost half the *total* production in the Canadian plant; hence all the production runs in the Canadian plant were significantly less than the *MES*.

The Auto Pact allowed the tariff-free importation of U.S. automobile products by Canadian *manufacturers* on a dollar-for-dollar basis with exports of Canadian products. Imports not matched by exports were subject to a "penalty" duty. As a result Canadian plants

troleum, and natural gas. The most dramatic change over the past forty years has been the decline in the proportion of exports accounted for by wheat and wheat flour from about 40 percent in 1928 to about 12 percent in the mid 1960s and 5 percent in 1971.

On the import side, Canada is highly dependent on foreign suppliers for many manufactured products, particularly durable goods such as machinery, motor vehicles, and other consumer durables (see Table 26-8). Table 26-9 shows the dramatic change that took place in the 1960s in the importance of trade in motor vehicles and parts with the United States. The Automotive Products Agreement, which went into effect in 1965, provided the opportunity for the integration of the North American auto industry by initiating free trade with respect to shipments by the manufacturers. The Canadian tariffs, ranging

TABLE 26-8
Canadian Imports by End Use, 1980

Item	Imports	
	Billions of dollars	Percentage of total
Fuels and lubricants	$ 8.3	12.0
Industrial and construction materials	16.8	24.3
Motor vehicles and parts	14.0	20.4
Producer's equipment	15.4	22.3
Food	4.1	5.9
Other consumer goods	7.0	10.1
Other imports	3.4	5.0
Total imports	$69.0	100.0

Source: Bank of Canada Review.

Manufactured goods make up a large fraction of Canadian imports. A substantial fraction of imports of manufactured goods is accounted for by motor vehicles and parts, producer's equipment, and industrial and construction materials.

specialized in particular product lines and exported most of the cars that they produced. In return, the manufacturers were able to import a wide variety of models for sale in Canada; the benefits of increased efficiency were gained without forsaking product variety in domestic consumption.

One problem with such a scheme is that the domestic economy becomes so narrowly specialized that it is vulnerable to swings in demand. In 1980 the Canadian auto industry was especially hard hit because it had specialized in large, fuel-inefficient models and in expensive specialty models, both of which were extremely vulnerable during the energy crunch. Earlier this phenomenon had worked the other way: in the 1960s Canada had specialized in smaller models. These events have caused critics of the current arrangement to ask: Did the multinationals act against Canada's interest in consciously shifting the manufacture of more energy-vulnerable lines to Canada?

In 1980, largely as a result of the adverse effect of the energy crunch, the major companies were unable to match domestic sales with domestic production and were subject to penalties under the terms of the original agreement. But the penalties appear to be unenforceable; Ottawa has declined to enforce them in the face of industry threats to curtail production further in Canadian plants.

A final problem with the Auto Pact is that the provisions for duty-free imports were granted to companies. Thus, while the country gained from the efficiency scale of production, nothing ensured that the gains would be passed along to domestic consumers in the form of lower auto prices. Instead the gains were captured by the (foreign-owned) manufacturers and to some extent by the domestic unions who negotiated for wage parity with their U.S. counterparts shortly after the pact was signed. The differential between Canadian and American consumer prices has fallen some since the pact was signed, but it has not been eliminated.

TABLE 26-9

Composition of Canada's Trade, Selected Years (percentage)

Area	Exports			Imports		
	1960	1970	1980	1960	1970	1980
United States						
Motor vehicles and parts	*	20%	13%	7%	22%	18
Crude petroleum and natural gas	2%	5	9	*	*	*
All other	55	40	41	63	49	52
Total	57	65	63	70	71	70
Britain	17	9	4	11	5	3
Other EEC	8	7	8	5	6	5
Japan	3	5	6	2	4	4
All other countries	15	14	19	12	14	18
	100%	100%	100%	100%	100%	100%

Source: Bank of Canada Review, D.B.S., Review of Foreign Trade 1960–1963, 1970.
* Less than 1 percent

The share of Canada's trade accounted for by the United States increased during the 1960s and 1970s. Increased exports of crude petroleum and natural gas and the expanded trade in automobiles were the major factors contributing to the higher American share.

Rationalization by Manufacturer's Choice: World Product Mandating

One way in which an inefficient domestic industry previously dependent on protection could survive a move to free trade would be for it to rationalize its product lines (see the box on pages 302–303). This has happened as a result of explicit policy (see the box on pages 522–523). But that is not the only way it can happen. The term "world product mandating" describes the process whereby large multinational corporations reorganize to permit foreign "branch plants" to develop particular product lines both for sale in the home market and for export into world markets. Often the strategy involves more than just specialization in production in order to exploit economies of scale; it may also involve transferring increased managerial and marketing responsibility to the former branch plant.

In Canada this phenomenon has been particularly strong in the electrical products and home appliance industries (where such firms as Westinghouse and Black & Decker have led the way) and in the relatively high-technology computer and office machine industries (where such giants as IBM, NCR, and Xerox have adopted the strategy).

For Black & Decker the experience has been highly successful. *Maclean's* magazine reported recently that in the 12 years since the local management of Black & Decker Canada persuaded its parent to grant it world rights to produce the company's orbital sander, the subsidiary has increased plant capacity five-fold, sales by nearly 25 percent a year, and staff to include 24 full-time design engineers. The company has gone on to develop several other new products for worldwide distribution —including the popular Workmate handyman's bench—and export sales now account for 45 percent of the Canadian company's production. *Maclean's* quoted the company president:

We're aiming to improve our efficiency so much that at the end of the day when tariffs come down, we will be able to compete in world markets as a way of making sure we can survive in the Canadian market as well.

The experience of Westinghouse Canada is similar. Westinghouse has had operations in this country since 1903. Until 1950, the profit ratios of the Canadian enterprise were better than those of the parent company, on the average, in three of every four years. The branch plant was aggressive, willing to take risks, and tended to innovate beyond the technology imported from the parent. Canadian innovations flowed back to the parent for adoption in its worldwide operations.

After World War II, when Canada, like

---

from 17.5 percent on finished vehicles to 25 percent on parts, were removed from imports by manufacturers who agreed to meet certain requirements regarding minimum levels of production carried on in Canada. (See the box on pages 522–523.)

Tariff Policy: The External Environment

Canada's policy options with regard to the imposition of tariffs are limited to a considerable extent by its relationships with other countries.

During the 1920s and early 1930s there were few international agreements concerning tariffs, and countries could impose any desired set of tariffs on their imports. However, when one country increased its tariffs, the action typically triggered retaliatory changes by its trading partners and frequently the situation deteriorated into a tariff war.

The General Agreement on Tariffs and Trade (GATT). One of the most notable achievements of the post-World War II world in retreating

many other countries, began lowering tariffs, Westinghouse Canada had become a mature company and had changed internally. F. H. Tyaack, the current president of Westinghouse Canada, describes what happened in the next 15 years:

Aggressiveness and risk-taking declined, defensiveness set in. Strategies became preoccupied with defending fractional points of existing market share and less concerned with new markets and strong innovational initiatives. For our firm at least, earnings declined; employment levels slipped downhill; and a number of product lines were phased out.

In this situation, the parent company sent Tyaack to Canada to take over the direction of the subsidiary operation. When he arrived in 1977, Westinghouse Canada had "many of the classic signs of a failing business entity." The parent company executives faced a choice—to make a place for Westinghouse Canada in their worldwide activities or to sell off the investment—and they chose to integrate the Canadian operation into the company's global production and marketing operations. The orientation of the Canadian operation was changed from that of a branch plant to that of a rationalized operation, with active participation in the marketing activities of the total multinational company.

Strategic planning became the responsibility of the subsidiary. It was able to work out a corporate strategy that shows early evidence of being successful even under the competitive conditions that would arise in the event of a move to free trade.

The company's exports are growing at twice the rate of domestic sales; research and development activities for specific products destined for world markets have tripled; corporate capital spending has doubled; and productivity is improving more rapidly than that of the parent company. Once again the profit ratio in Canada is better than that of the parent.

These examples show that there is much potential benefit to be gained from world product mandating. Yet the policy is not without its critics. Many believe that the narrow product specialization leaves the economy vulnerable to shifts in demand or cost conditions. Others believe that ironically, if world mandating is too successful, strong foreign subsidiaries could hinder the development of similar skills and technology by truly Canadian companies. But even critics are willing to admit that in an economy where non-Canadian companies are a fact of life, at least world product mandating is a protection against the risks of plant closures and outright colonization.

from the high-water mark of protectionism reached in the 1930s was the General Agreement on Tariffs and Trade (GATT). Under this agreement, GATT countries meet periodically to negotiate bilaterally on mutually advantageous cuts in tariffs. They agree in advance that any tariff cuts negotiated in this way will be extended to all member countries. Significant tariff reductions have been effected by the member countries.

The two most recent rounds of GATT agreements have been reduced tariffs by about one-third. The Kennedy Round negotiations were completed in 1967, and new rates were phased in over a five-year period ending in 1972. The most recent Tokyo Round negotiations began in 1975 and were completed in 1979. Final approval by the approximately 100 member nations of GATT was being secured in 1980. The reductions begin to take effect in 1981.

The enormous reductions in *tariffs* that have been the result of GATT are a bit misleading in terms of the freedom of trade because of the growing use of nontariff barriers. Perhaps the most important feature of the Tokyo Round was the agreement, for the first time, on steps to limit the growth of nontariff barriers. It is too early to tell whether these efforts will prove as successful as the tariff reductions.

Regional common markets. A common market is an agreement among a group of countries to eliminate barriers to free trade among themselves and to provide a common trading front to the rest of the world.

The most important is the so-called European Common Market. In 1957 the Treaty of Rome joined France, Germany, Italy, Holland, Belgium, and Luxembourg in the European Economic Community (EEC). The EEC is dedicated to bringing about free trade, complete mobility of factors of production, and the eventual harmonization of fiscal and monetary policies among the member countries. Tariff reductions were made according to a time schedule that eliminated all tariffs on manufactured goods among the original six before 1970. If the development continues, before the end of the century Western Europe will be a single economic community with a free movement of goods, labor, and capital among the member countries.

On January 1, 1973, despite strong divisions within each country, Great Britain, the Republic of Ireland, and Denmark joined the Community, the first two after close votes in their parliaments and the latter after a plebiscite. At the same time, Norway voted in a plebiscite to remain outside. Greece is scheduled to join in 1981 and the entry of Spain and Portugal is currently being considered.

The formation of the EEC was of great significance to Canada because it strengthened trading relations among the member countries at the expense of increased barriers to trade with nonmember countries. To offset this, Canada has attempted to negotiate special agreements with the EEC.

Other common markets have been formed, such as the Central American Common Market and the East African Community, but none has yet achieved the success of the EEC, and some have collapsed.

Tariff Policy: Options for the Future

Although Canada has participated in the general liberalization of world trade that has taken place since World War II, tariffs still have a substantial influence in the structure of the economy. The broad pattern of Canada's external trade is probably not radically different from that which comparative advantages would dictate under free trade, yet there is considerable evidence that the protection afforded to manufactured products has spawned a high-cost manufacturing sector. The tariffs promote industrial self-sufficiency, with small unspecialized firms that are unable to achieve economies of scale because of the limited size of the domestic market.

Under these circumstances, many economists believe that access to larger markets through participation in a regional free-trade area would raise Canadian productivity and living standards substantially. On political grounds, many Canadians have advocated a broad arrangement to include not only the United States but Britain, some European countries, and Japan. Political realities suggest, however, that a more feasible approach would be to promote a North American free-trade area.

Would Canadians become "hewers of wood and drawers of water" if our industry were exposed to free-trade competition from the United States? This question cannot be answered by merely observing that in most manufacturing industries costs are now higher in Canada than in the United States. To the extent that these higher costs reflect inefficiencies arising from the small Canadian market, they are the *result* of tariffs— both U.S. and Canadian—not a justification for them. The elimination of tariffs would permit Canadian producers to specialize in a limited number of lines and supply the common North American market. A narrowing in the differential between prices of cars in the United States and Canada has come about from just such specialization in the automobile industry as a result of the free-trade agreement. Canadian plants now specialize in a limited number of models and operate high-volume production runs. This issue is discussed further in the boxes on pages 522–525.

Undoubtedly, a substantial move toward free trade would cause hardships in some industries and necessitate public assistance programs to ease the adjustments in particular sectors or regions. In some instances the continuation of protection for at least a limited period may be justified on infant industry grounds. Nevertheless the question remains whether or not Canadians wish to pay the price in terms of a lower standard of living that the present tariff policy entails. If some degree of self-sufficiency is regarded as an end in itself, then economic analysis can only attempt to assess the costs involved; it cannot resolve the issue.

THE FOREIGN OWNERSHIP ISSUE

Since the mid-1950s there has been considerable controversy over the issue of foreign, and particularly U.S., ownership and control of Canadian industry. The list of firms that have been taken over by foreign investors in recent years includes such well-known corporations as Canadian Breweries, Salada Foods, British American Oil (now Gulf Canada), and McIntyre Porcupine Mines. In addition Canada has become highly dependent on foreign-controlled capital to finance the expansion of her productive capacity.

Should Canadians be concerned about this? Should new saving be channeled into buying back control of Canadian industry and/or should restrictions be place on new foreign investment? Many of the issues involve value judgments, but economists can contribute to the debate by suggesting the likely consequences of alternative courses of action.

The Statistics of Foreign Ownership

Foreign capital has played an important role in Canada's development since Confederation. Prior to World War I a large part of it came from Britain in the form of debt securities to finance railways and other large-scale investment projects. By 1926, when the first estimates of foreign capital invested were made, the United States had supplanted Britain as the major supplier. A much larger share of U.S. capital has come in the form of direct investment; the resulting increase in nonresident ownership and control of Canadian industry is shown in Table 26-10. The long-term growth has been concentrated in manufacturing, petroleum and natural gas, and mining and smelting. The substantial investment in natural resource industries reflects the large requirements of the United States for raw materials in the face of declining domestic supplies.

As can be seen in Table 26-11, the foreign-ownership ratios in terms of assets or profits vary considerably within the manufacturing sector. Nonresidents owned the tobacco industry and virtually all of the petroleum and coal products industry. Other manufacturing industries with a substantial degree of foreign control include rubber products, transport equipment (foreign control of the automobile industry is close to 100 percent), and chemicals. Outside manufacturing and the extractive industries, resident ownership predominates. In transportation and public utilities, a large fraction of the assets are accounted for by government enterprises and are therefore entirely owned and controlled within Canada.

Foreign-owned Firms and Canadian Interests

Does the Canadian economy suffer from conflicts of interest and differences in outlook between foreign-owned subsidiaries and their parent companies? Critics of foreign control argue that head-office managers may be poorly informed about or indifferent to the potential of

TABLE 26-10
Nonresident Ownership and Control of Canadian Industries, 1926–1975

Industry	Nonresident ownership (percent of total equity and debt capital)				Nonresident control (percent of total capital)			
	1926	1948	1968	1976	1926	1948	1968	1975
All residents								
Manufacturing	38	42	52	50	35	43	58	59
Petroleum and natural gas	–	–	62	51	–	–	75	75
Mining and smelting	37	39	62	57	38	40	68	57
Railways	55	45	18	20	3	3	2	2
Other utilities	32	20	19	27	20	24	5	4
U.S. residents:								
Manufacturing	30	35	44	41	30	39	46	44
Petroleum and natural gas	–	–	51	40	–	–	61	58
Mining and smelting	28	32	51	45	32	37	58	44
Railways	15	21	8	12	3	3	2	2
Other utilities	23	16	18	21	20	24	4	4

Source: Statistics Canada, 67-202.

Nonresident ownership of equity and debt capital employed in Canadian manufacturing, petroleum and natural gas extraction, and mining and smelting has increased substantially since 1948. The control ratios measure the percentage of capital invested by residents as well as nonresidents in the companies whose voting stock is controlled by nonresidents; they exceed the new ownership ratios to the extent that Canadian residents invest in companies controlled by nonresidents.

their subsidiaries. Specifically, they claim that parent companies may (1) limit the opportunities for Canadians to obtain senior positions in the subsidiaries and to play a significant role in decision making; (2) centralize research and development in the parent company and oblige Canadian scientists to look abroad for employment; and (3) prevent the subsidiary from exporting in competition with the parent and require it to buy from the parent rather than from Canadian suppliers. Since such discrimination is not consistent with profit maximization, those who believe it to be important implicitly accept the notion that corporations pursue other objectives.[6]

A study by A. E. Safarian compared the performance of foreign-owned firms to that of resident-owned firms, that of parent companies, and that of U.S. direct-investment firms elsewhere. He concluded:

Actual economic performance of subsidiary companies in Canada often does not differ greatly, however, from that of resident-owned companies. Performance is very similar between the two groups in regard to, for example, exports and research, and it is not markedly less favourable in regard to imports. When we turn to comparisons with the parent, however, we find that subsidiaries are usually less efficient. In the manufacturing sector, many subsidiaries are relatively small firms producing virtually the full range of products identical to those of the parent. Their unit costs of production exceed those of the parent in most cases. This inefficient structure of industry reflects, fundamentally, the limitations on market and firm size, and on specialization, resulting from Canadian and foreign tariffs and from lack of competition in Canada.[7]

In Safarian's view and that of many other economists, the major economic problem in Canadian industry is the inefficient size of many

[6] The issue of research and development was discussed in the box on pages 236–237.

[7] A. E. Safarian, *The Performance of Foreign-Owned Firms in Canada,* Private Planning Association, 1969, page 5.

firms, both resident and foreign owned. They argue that the specialization necessary to achieve economies of scale is inhibited by tariffs and other barriers to trade that foster local production for the relatively small Canadian market.

Extraterritoriality. Students of the foreign ownership issue have generally acknowledged that serious questions are raised by the problem of **extraterritoriality,** the application of U.S. laws and government regulations to activities carried on within Canada. A number of cases have arisen in which it was alleged that Canadian subsidiaries of American firms were prevented from exporting to certain Communist countries. As part of its foreign policy, the U.S. government restricts trade with China, North Korea, Vietnam, and Cuba, and American parent companies are responsible for ensuring that the restrictions are not circumvented through foreign subsidiaries. Since Canadian policy involves many fewer restrictions, clear conflicts of interest can arise for American subsidiaries in Canada.

Questions of extraterritoriality have also arisen in connection with the application of American antitrust laws to subsidiaries in Canada and with U.S. regulations that restrict direct investment flows from parent firms to their subsidiaries in Canada and elsewhere. Consultations between the two governments have taken place in an attempt to resolve these issues, but arrangements fully consistent with Canadian sovereignty will clearly be difficult to achieve.

Policies of the Federal Government

In response to public concern over the foreign ownership issue during the last twenty years, a number of legislative proposals dealing with it have been brought before Parliament by both Liberal and Conservative governments. The most far-reaching scheme was contained in Finance Minister Walter Gordon's budget of June 1963, which provided for a 30 percent takeover tax on acquisitions by nonresidents of resident companies listed on the Canadian stock ex-

TABLE 26-11
Nonresident Control of Canadian Industries, 1978

Industry	Percentage majority of nonresident ownership as measured by	
	Assets	Profits
Manufacturing		
Foods	47	53
Tobacco	100	100
Rubber products	95	n.a.
Leather products	32	24
Textile industries	61	53
Wood	27	30
Printing, publishing, and allied fields	15	14
Paper and allied products	41	51
Primary metals	17	41
Metal fabricating	49	53
Machinery	70	72
Transport equipment	83	91
Electrical products	67	65
Nonmetallic mineral products	77	63
Petroleum and coal products	85	88
Chemicals and chemical products	71	87
Miscellaneous manufacturing	61	57
Total, all manufacturing	58	60
Nonmanufacturing		
Mining (including mineral fuels)	48	76
Construction	13	12
Transportation	6	24
Communications	14	6
Public utilities	6	24
Wholesale trade	28	26
Retail trade	21	15
Services	25	27

Source: Statistics Canada, 61-210.

Nonresident ownership is now concentrated in a number of industries within the manufacturing sector and is also substantial in the extractive industries.

changes.[8] This proposal was abandoned as unworkable after strong protests from the financial community, but other provisions were enacted which granted preferential treatment under the corporate income tax to foreign-owned compa-

[8] The National Energy Policy and Finance Minister Allan McEachen's associated budget, presented in November 1980, are discussed in the next chapter.

nies in which Canadians held an interest of at least 25 percent.

Other legislation has focused on what have been regarded as key sectors of the Canadian economy, such as financial institutions and the communications media. For example, in view of their role in the cultural and political life of the country, broadcasting and the publishing of magazines and periodicals are subject to regulations ensuring Canadian control.

Canada Development Corporation. The idea of establishing a government holding company to promote Canadian ownership was originally proposed by Finance Minister Gordon, and legislation establishing the Canada Development Corporation was enacted in 1971. The CDC invests in Canadian enterprises, the initial capital being supplied by the government, although eventually shares in the corporation will be offered for sale to the Canadian public.

Foreign Investment Review Act. This legislation, enacted in 1973, was based on the recommendations of a task force report known as the Gray Report. It established a screening procedure for determining whether foreign takeover bids or the setting up of new foreign-owned businesses would be of "significant benefit to Canada." The criteria to be used in this evaluation are:

1. The effect on the level and nature of economic activity in Canada, including the effect on employment, on resource processing, on the use of Canadian parts, components and services, and on exports.
2. The degree and significance of participation by Canadians in the business enterprise and its affiliates.
3. The effect on productivity, industrial efficiency, technological development, product innovation, and product variety in Canada.
4. The effect on competition within any industry or industries in Canada.
5. The compatability with national industrial and economic policies, taking into consideration

industrial and economic policy objectives enunciated by provinces likely to be affected.

The major limitation of this legislation is that it has no effect on existing foreign ownership and does not apply to the expansion of existing firms unless they enter new and unrelated areas of business. On the other hand, there are those who argue that it will discourage beneficial foreign investment through cumbersome bureaucratic procedures and delays.

What Price Economic Independence?

It is generally agreed that the Canadian economy has benefited greatly from foreign investment. Productivity and the standard of living have been enhanced not only by the infusion of new capital but also by the accompanying flow of management skills and technology. At the same time, the emergence of the "multinational" firm as a dominant force in the Canadian economy has raised many questions of a noneconomic nature. While the Canadian public must decide to what extent it wishes to restrict foreign influence, economists have a duty to point out the substantial economic costs that may be involved in greater economic independence.

Summary

1. The principles governing trade between any two groups are the same—for individuals, regions, or nations.

2. One country (or region or individual) has an absolute advantage over another country (or region or individual) in the production of some commodity when, with the same input of resources in each country, it can produce more of the commodity than can the other. However, the gains from trade do not require absolute advantage on the part of each country, only comparative advantage.

3. Comparative advantage is the relative advan-

tage one country enjoys over another in various commodities. If, for example, Canada is 10 times as efficient as is England in producing commodity X and 12 times as efficient in producing commodity Y, Canada has a comparative advantage over England in Y (its margin of advantage over England is larger in Y than it is in X).

4. World production of all commodities can be increased if each country transfers resources into the production of the commodities in which it has a comparative advantage.

5. The gains from trade result from different opportunity costs in different countries, which in turn lead to differences in comparative advantage.

6. The theory of the gains from trade may be stated in this way: Trade allows all countries to obtain the goods in which they do not have a comparative advantage at a lower opportunity cost (in terms of units sacrificed of the commodities in which they do have a comparative advantage) than they would have to accept if they were to produce all commodities for themselves. This allows all countries to have more of all commodities than they could have if they made themselves self-sufficient.

7. As well as gaining the advantages of specialization arising from comparative advantage, a nation that engages in trade and specialization may realize the benefits of increasing returns to scale and learning by doing.

8. The terms of the trade refer to the quantity of imported goods that can be obtained per unit of goods exported. They show the opportunity cost of obtaining goods by trade. The terms of trade influence how the gains from trade are shared.

9. Free trade among nations may be restricted intentionally by protectionist policies in the form of tariffs, import quotas, restrictions on the purchase of foreign exchange, and in other ways.

10. The case for free trade is that world output of all commodities can be higher under free trade than when protectionism restricts regional specialization.

11. Protection can be urged as a means to ends other than maximizing world living standards. Examples of such ends are to produce a diversified economy, to reduce fluctuations in national income, to retain distinctive national traditions, and to improve national defence.

12. Protection can also be urged on grounds that it may lead to higher living standards for the protectionist country than would a policy of free trade. Such a result might come about through exploiting a monopoly position or by allowing inexperienced or uneconomically small industries to become sufficiently efficient that they can subsequently compete with foreign industries.

13. Virtually everyone would agree that free trade should be chosen if the only choice were between free trade and *no* trade. However, most real choices facing nations today are not about free trade versus no trade; rather they are about *a little more* trade (caused by a slight lowering of tariffs) versus *a little less* trade (caused by a slight raising of tariffs). Here the choice is not so obvious as that between free trade and no trade. The potential gains from small reductions in barriers to trade must be balanced against other objectives and other effects.

14. Some fallacious free trade arguments are that (a) because it is possible for free trade to be beneficial, free trade will in fact always be beneficial; and (b) because infant industries seldom admit to growing up and thus try to retain their tariff protection indefinitely, the whole country necessarily loses by protecting its infant industries.

15. Some fallacious protectionist arguments are that (a) mutually advantageous trade is impossible because one trader's gain must always be the other's loss; (b) our high-paid workers must be protected against the competition from low-paid foreign workers; (c) imports are to be discouraged because they lower national income and cause unemployment; and (d) buying abroad sends our money abroad, whereas buying at home keeps our money at home.

16. External trade has played a crucial role in Canada's economic development. Apart from the expanded trade in automobiles following the 1965 agreement with the United States, raw and semifinished products continue to dominate exports; manufactured goods account for a large proportion of imports.

17. Many economists believe that Canadian productivity and living standards are substantially reduced by tariff barriers that promote domestic production for a small domestic market and prevent the realization of economies of scale. The formation of a North American free-trade area has been advocated as a means of raising Canadian incomes.

18. Since the mid 1950s there has been considerable controversy in Canada over the increasing degree of U.S. control of Canadian industry, particularly in the manufacturing sector and the extractive industries. To a considerable extent the issue involves value judgments concerning the desirable degree of economic independence. Government policy has included restrictions on foreign ownership in key sectors, establishment of a Canada Development Corporation, and the Foreign Investment Review Act.

Topics for Review

Absolute and comparative advantage
Gains from specialization and gains from trade
Opportunity cost and comparative advantage
Terms of trade
Free trade and protectionism
The case for some protectionism
The case for free trade versus no trade
Fallacious protariff and antitariff arguments

Discussion Questions

1. Adam Smith saw a close connection between the wealth of a nation and its willingness "freely to engage" in foreign trade. What is the connection?

2. Suppose that the following situation exists. Assume no tariffs, no intervention by the government, and that labor is the only factor of production.

Country	Labor cost of production of one unit of	
	Artichokes	Bikinis
Inland	$20	$40
Outland	$20	$ X

Let X take different values—say $10, $20, $40, and $60. In each case, will there be trade? If so, in which direction?

3. The citizens of underdeveloped Atlantis can weave two feet of cloth an hour or gather one basket of coconuts. Their ministers approach the republic of Mu, whose inhabitants can weave three feet of cloth or gather two baskets of coconuts in the same period of time, and offer to trade. What possible opposition speeches do you imagine will be heard in Parliament in the capital of Mu? Appraise the validity of a few different arguments. As an economist, advise the Mu government.

4. Uruguay, formerly a significant exporter of raw beef and mutton, found it needed more exports to pay for its greatly increased imports of oil. Because the market for raw meat was limited, it decided to take advantage of a low wage rate by processing its beef, hides, and wool and then exporting these processed goods. Its exports doubled within a year with no change in exchange rates. What does this indicate about Uruguay's comparative advantages?

5. The government of Brazil, by restricting exports of coffee, has greatly improved its balance of payments and raised its national income. Is it possible that Brazil is an exception to the proposition that there are gains from trade?

6. "The only protariff argument that is likely to be valid for the whole world taken as an economic unit (rather than for a particular nation at a particular time) is the infant industry argument." Explain why you agree or disagree with this statement.

7. Some economists have taken the position that protectionist policies on the part of underdeveloped countries are apt to have little adverse effect on international trade, while the same policies on the part of economically advanced countries would serve to reduce trade. Is it possible that this is the case? Why or why not?

8. Canada recently introduced quotas on imports of

clothing. How would the effects of this differ from those on a tariff?

9. Listed below are some recent average duties paid in Canada, by industry classes.

Agricultural implements	0 %
Publishing and printing	1.4%
Sawmills	2.3%
Feed manufacturers	2.6%
Household radio and TV	19.0%
Distilleries	20.0%
Shoe factories	23.0%
Tobacco products	25.0%

What economic and political reasons can you see for duties on some commodities being above the average rate of duty charged and for others being below it? What other forms of protectionism could make some duties misleading?

10. Suppose Quebec formed a separate state, refusing to trade with the rest of Canada. What predictions would you make about the standard of living compared to what it is in Canada today? Does the fact that Canada, the United States, and Mexico are separate countries lead to a lower standard of living in the three countries than if they were united into a new country called Northica?

11. If the European Common Market caused such a rise in efficiency that the price of every good produced in Germany, France, and Italy fell below the prices of the same good manufactured in Canada, what would happen? Would Canadians gain or lose because of this?

12. Suppose each of the Canadian provinces was a separate country. If free trade were permitted among these "countries," would you expect a pattern of production to exist different from the one that does exist? If Manitoba prohibited all trade, what would be the effect on Manitoba and on the other nine countries? Suppose all ten countries prohibited all trade. What would be the result?

13. What would be the economic advantages to Canada of a North American free-trade area? The Atlantic provinces are already part of a Canadian free-trade area, yet incomes are much lower there than in Ontario. Why? Is it possible that all of Canada might become a low-income region under free trade with the United States?

14. "Canadian industry could compete in a North American free-trade area with the present lower level of wages in Canada. However, under free trade, wages would rise to the U.S. level, and without this advantage Canadian industry would collapse." Evaluate this argument.

Energy Policy: A Case Study

27

Energy is vital to our way of life. Without fuel for such "necessities" as transportation, heat, and light as well as for such "luxuries" as entertainment and recreation, life in Western societies today would be much different. Indeed, as we saw in Chapter 13, much of the rapid growth in real living standards achieved in this century can be attributed directly to the increased availability of cheap energy sources.

In Canada, energy has an additional direct impact because the energy-*producing* sector is an important part of the economy. Canada is a country rich in natural resources and especially rich in sources of energy. Canada's output of oil and natural gas, valued at world prices, equaled about 7 percent of total Canadian income in 1977. Hydroelectricity has been extensively developed in several provinces; it is available relatively inexpensively to Canadian households and firms, and it is also exported to the United States. Reserves of coal, oil, and natural gas have long been considered to be plentiful, and Canadians have enjoyed energy from these sources at a price well below that prevailing in most of the Western world. Ontario and Saskatchewan have substantial deposits of uranium that make nuclear power a viable, if controversial, alternative energy source.

Energy policy has been one of the most controversial issues of public policy in Canada during the last decade, and it promises to be even more controversial in the next decade. International developments played a central role in the energy problems that emerged in the 1970s, but domestic developments were also important. At the heart of the energy policy controversy is the so-called **two-price system.** This is the policy that keeps domestic prices of energy—in particular, oil and natural gas—below world prices.

Why is energy policy controversial? Why do we so often read about the energy "shortage"? Is there a shortage? Why did the price of energy rise so much in the 1970s? Could the increases in the price of energy have been avoided? Should they have been? Do Canadians benefit from the policy of keeping energy prices in Canada below those prevailing in world markets? Or have energy prices in fact risen too little?

These questions are complicated. Answering them involves many of the issues raised in earlier chapters of this book and also introduces some macroeconomic issues to be raised in later chapters. Since both domestic and foreign elements are involved, our analysis draws on the theory of international trade discussed in Chapter 26, and since domestic energy prices differ from world prices, aspects of tariff policy are also involved. Energy is both directly consumed by households and used as an input into production by firms, so issues of factor markets and income distribution (Chapter 20) are involved. Our discussion in Chapter 25 of government taxation policies and intergovernmental revenue flows is relevant. Finally, because energy resources are unevenly scattered throughout the country, issues of regional disparities necessarily arise.

DOMESTIC PATTERNS OF ENERGY PRODUCTION AND CONSUMPTION

Canada is a small economy rich in energy sources, rich enough to be self-sufficient. **Energy self-sufficiency** means that as much energy is produced as is used. This does not mean that Canada is not engaged in international trade in energy; much of the energy produced in Canada is exported, and much of the energy used in Canada is imported. Self-sufficiency means that energy exports are at least as large as energy imports.

Canadians are among the largest consumers of

TABLE 27-1

Per Capita Energy Consumption and Income, Selected Countries, 1978

Country	Energy consumption per capita[a]	GNP per capita (U.S. dollars)
United States	11,374	$ 9,590
Canada	9,930	9,180
Australia	6,622	7,990
West Germany	6,015	9.580
Sweden	5,954	10.210
Britain	5,212	5,030
Finland	5,205	6,820
France	4,368	8,260
Japan	3,825	7,280
Switzerland	3,690	12,100

Source: World Bank.
[a] Energy consumption per capita measured in kilograms of coal equivalent.

Canada and the United States far exceed other Western industrialized nations in energy consumption per capita. Canada ranks fifth in GNP per capita and second in energy consumption per capita. Sweden, Switzerland, and West Germany all have larger GNP per capita than Canada but consume much less energy per capita.

energy in the world. In 1978 *energy consumption per capita* was the equivalent of more than *six gallons of oil per day.* In Table 27-1 per capita energy consumption and per capita income are reported for a variety of countries. Only the United States consumes more energy on a per capita basis; Sweden, with higher average per capita income and a similar climate, consumes only 60 percent of the energy on a per capita basis that Canada consumes.

Canada's diverse energy sources are illustrated in Figure 27-1, which shows the patterns of production and consumption for the years 1965 and 1978. The near equality of production and consumption in each year reveals Canada's basic energy self-sufficiency. Total consumption of energy almost doubled over that period, while total production grew slightly more and had overtaken consumption by 1978.

While developments in all the energy sources included in Figure 27-1 are interesting, the major issues in Canada concern petroleum and natural gas. Consequently, in this chapter we focus on

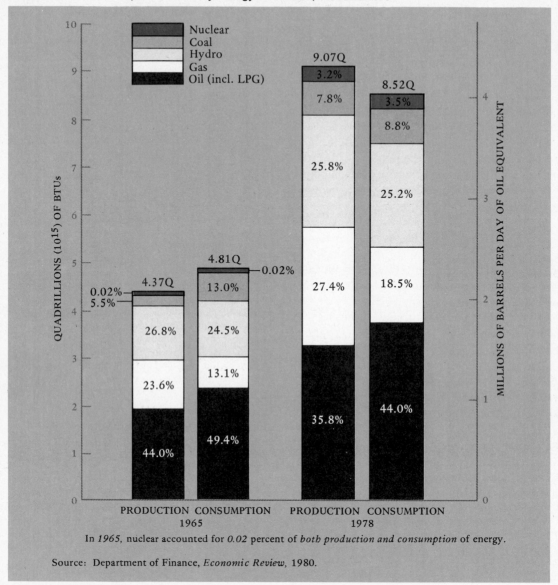

FIGURE 27-1
Production and Consumption of Primary Energy in Canada, 1965 and 1978

In *1965,* nuclear accounted for *0.02* percent of *both production and consumption* of energy.

Source: Department of Finance, *Economic Review*, 1980.

Canada is roughly self-sufficient in primary energy. In 1965 total consumption of primary energy exceeded total production; by 1978 production exceeded consumption. Oil has declined slightly in relative importance in both production and consumption, and natural gas has grown in importance. Coal production has increased while coal consumption has decreased. Nuclear power has become a significant new energy source.

issues pertaining to these two energy sources. The basic patterns of production, consumption, and trade in oil and natural gas are outlined in Table 27-2. As shown, oil and natural gas are exported (mostly from Western Canada to the United States) and simultaneously imported (mostly oil from Venezuela and the Gulf states into Eastern Canada).

Developments related to crude oil have been particularly striking. In 1960 Canada was a significant *net* importer of oil (117.3 million barrels annually, or almost 50 percent of total domestic

TABLE 27-2
Crude Petroleum, Petroleum Products, and Natural Gas Liquids: Canadian Production, Demand, Trade, Reserves (millions of barrels)

	1960	1965	1970	1971	1972	1973	1974	1975	1976	1977	1978	1979
Production	198.2	336.0	537.5	576.5	668.1	770.1	728.5	633.4	584.7	586.2	575.6	649.8
(−) Exports	45.5	117.6	271.4	308.6	412.5	491.8	404.7	321.9	236.2	193.5	180.4	192.8
(+) Imports	162.8	203.2	280.2	299.9	340.7	352.3	325.4	315.1	277.2	265.2	243.5	230.7
(−) Change in stocks	0.5	5.2	6.4	8.3	−0.8	11.6	14.6	−0.1	−12.1	11.0	−20.3	0.1
Consumption[a]	315.0	416.4	539.9	559.5	597.1	619.0	634.6	626.7	637.8	646.9	659.0	687.6
Reserves	n.a.	9,798	12,015	11,599	11,165	10,505	9,928	9,354	8,934	8,481	8,305	n.a.
Of which: Oil	n.a.	8,800	10,214	9,971	9,592	9,008	8,375	7,833	7,431	7,050	6,860	n.a.
NGL		997	1,801	1,629	1,573	1,497	1,553	1,521	1,503	1,432	1,445	n.a.

Source: Department of Finance, *Economic Review,* 1980.
[a] Excludes interproduct transfers.

Canada has moved from being a net importer of oil and natural gas in 1960 to being a net exporter in the early 1970s and again to being a net importer since 1976. Production grew through the early 1970s but has fallen off since reaching a peak in 1973. Consumption grew continually throughout the 1970s.

consumption). In 1958 the Report of the Federal Royal Commission on Energy, the Borden Report, presented an optimistic view of the prospects for a Canadian surplus of relatively low-cost energy. Upon its recommendation, in 1959 the National Energy Board was formed and in 1961 the Ottawa Valley Line was established, providing a protected market for Canadian crude oil west of that line. (From the vantage point of the 1980s, it is ironic to think of Canadian oil producers needing protection from cheap foreign supplies.) That protection, along with the rapid economic growth of the 1960s, led to a dramatic (almost fourfold) increase in Canadian production, and by 1973 Canada had *net* oil exports of almost 140 million barrels. Since 1973 output of oil has fallen—it fell by 25 percent from 1973 through 1978 before making a recovery in 1979—while consumption continued to grow. By 1976 Canada had again become a net importer, and in 1978 *net* oil imports exceeded 60 million barrels.

INTERNATIONAL DEVELOPMENTS

The postwar period, through the early 1970s, witnessed large discoveries of oil in the Middle East. These were developed chiefly by American and British oil companies, and the increased availability of oil sustained the low energy prices that formed the basis of much of the rapid postwar growth in Western economies. This economic growth carried with it rapid growth in energy demand, and in the early 1970s OPEC responded by quadrupling the price of Mideast oil.[1] While world oil prices continued to rise throughout the 1970s, during the period 1974–1978 the price increases did not keep pace with world inflation, and the relative price of oil fell slightly. However, the relative price rose sharply in 1979 when world oil prices roughly doubled.

CANADIAN ENERGY PRICES IN THE 1970s

At the start of 1973 the Canadian price of oil was about equal to the world price at roughly $3.80 a barrel. In early 1973 the National Energy Board assumed direct control of oil exports. In September 1973 domestic oil prices were frozen at $3.80 a barrel, and a special charge was levied on

---

[1] In 1973–1974 Egypt and Israel were at war, and OPEC imposed an embargo on oil exports to countries considered hostile to the Arab states. The embargo lasted six months and had its most significant impact on the United States. When the embargo was lifted, oil exports resumed at quadruple the price.

TABLE 27-3
Canadian and World Oil Prices, Selected Dates, 1973–1981 (Canadian dollars per barrel)

	Canadian wellhead price of crude oil	Canadian export charge on crude oil	Implied world price of crude oil
September 1973	$ 3.80		$ 3.80
October 1973	3.80	$ .40	4.20
April 1974	6.50	4.00	10.50
July 1975	8.00	4.25	12.25
July 1976	9.05	3.70	12.75
January 1977	9.75	3.75	13.50
July 1977	10.75	3.90	14.65
January 1978	11.75	3.80	15.55
July 1978	12.75	3.85	16.30
July 1979	13.75	9.26	23.01
January 1980	14.75	17.00	31.75
October 1980	16.75[a]	n.a.	n.a
January 1981	17.75[a]	n.a.	n.a.
July 1981	18.75[a]	n.a.	n.a.

Source: Columns 1 and 2: John F. Helliwell, "Canadian Energy Policy," *Annual Review of Energy,* 1979; and Department of Finance, *Economic Review,* 1981. Column 3 adds together columns 1 and 2.
[a] As proscribed in the National Energy Program.

World oil prices have risen almost tenfold since 1973, while domestic oil prices have risen just over fourfold. International prices are hard to measure because there are different blends and qualities of oil; moreover, there are difficulties in correlating the prices charged by different producing countries. Our estimate here is the sum of the domestic price and the export charge.

The National Energy Program introduced in October 1980 provided for a price to domestic consumers that is a blend of the domestic wellhead price and the world price. (We discuss this at the end of the chapter.)

exports to bridge the gap between the domestic price and the growing world price.[2]

This was followed a month later by the international events referred to before, which culminated in the fourfold increase in world oil prices. The embargo did not affect Canada significantly because at that time it was a *net* oil exporter.[3] However, the world price increase was important because it occurred at a time when, by historical accident, the Canadian price of oil was regulated by the Canadian government. By not raising the domestic price with the world price, the government automatically instituted the two-price system. In January 1974 the Ottawa Valley

Line was effectively removed so that the same price (except for transportation costs) was charged for oil in all parts of Canada regardless of whether domestic or imported foreign oil was used. An import-compensation scheme was introduced to subsidize refineries that used higher-cost imported oil.

At the time there was widespread belief (now proven unfounded) that the increase in oil prices was only temporary. This provided some justification for not raising domestic prices immediately, and the government also announced that it intended to raise domestic oil prices gradually until they were again equal to world prices. Thus Canadian oil prices rose substantially throughout the 1970s—by 81 percent between 1972 and 1974, and at an annual rate of 18 percent from 1974 through 1979. By the end of 1978, Canadian prices were almost 80 percent of world prices. However, domestic price increases in 1979 and 1980 were far outstripped by increases

[2] The price was frozen in response to consumer complaints that oil price rises were not matched by increased costs. The complaints led to an investigation of the oil industry by the Department of Consumer and Corporate Affairs under the Combines Investigation Act.
[3] The indirect effects were nevertheless severe, primarily because the United States, Canada's major trading partner, was so adversely affected.

FIGURE 27-2
Domestic and International Oil Prices, 1961–1980

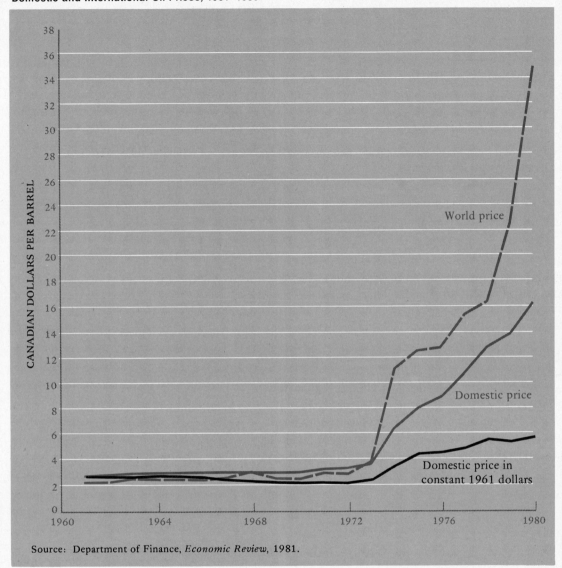

Source: Department of Finance, *Economic Review*, 1981.

The domestic price of oil rose fivefold in nominal terms over the period 1961–1980, but the world price rose by factor of 18 over the same period. The figure shows the world price of oil (the import price, c.i.f. Montreal, adjusted to domestic crude oil quality), the domestic price of oil (the wellhead price, f.o.b Edmonton, including a levy to provide the world price for synthetic crude oil), and the domestic price of oil in con-stant 1961 dollars (the wellhead price, f.o.b. Edmonton, deflated by the Consumer Price Index, 1961 = 100). The domestic price fell to one-half of the world price in 1973–1974, rose to almost two-thirds of the world price by 1979, then fell again to less than one-half of the world price. The domestic price of oil in constant 1961 dollars fell steadily from 1964 through 1972 but has been rising steadily since 1972.

in the world price, so by 1980 the Canadian price of about $15 a barrel was less than *half* the world price. These developments are shown in Figure 27-2 and Table 27-3.

Both the budget introduced by Minister of Fi-nance John Crosbie in December 1979 (which led to the defeat of Joe Clark's minority Progres-sive Conservative government) and that in-troduced by Crosbie's Liberal counterpart Allan MacEachan in October 1980 provided for gradual increases in the Canadian price of oil relative to the world price. On September 1, 1981, an energy-pricing agreement between the federal government and the Alberta government was signed, which allowed for further increases in domestic oil prices.

The Two-price System

The gap between domestic and world prices, the two-price system, is at the heart of the energy policy controversy. A related, and fundamental, issue is the desirable rate of extraction and consumption of nonrenewable resources. The question of whether this extraction rate should be decided by explicit government policy or by the private owners of the resources within the constraints imposed by market demand is addressed in the box on pages 554–555.

Let us consider a more specific question: If a country has nonrenewable energy resources that can be extracted at a cost below the world market price, should the government prevent the owners of the resources from selling them on the world market and instead force them to sell to domestic consumers at a reduced price? This is the question that Canada faced in 1974 and still faces today.

By maintaining the domestic price of oil below the world price, Canada has effectively chosen to subsidize domestic consumers and to tax the owners of oil resources. Oil produced in Canada and sold abroad is subject to a tax that makes the net price received by producers roughly equivalent to the domestic price. Oil produced abroad and purchased in Canada is subsidized by the federal government.

An Oil Export Tax

An export tax operates like a tariff in reverse. Suppose that for some good, say oil, with a given world price, Canadian production exceeds Canadian consumption. The good will be exported, as shown in Figure 8-3.[4] If a tax on the exportation of oil is introduced, the *net* price received by producers for oil exports will be less than the world price by the amount of the tax. Any given producer will now be indifferent between selling on the world market and selling to domestic consumers at the net price. Competition among producers will establish a domestic price that is equal to the world price net of the export tax. Both the price paid by domestic users and the price received by domestic producers will be less than the world price by the amount of the export tax. This is illustrated in Figure 27-3(i) for the case where oil is exported both before and after the export tax is applied.

For an oil-exporting country, an oil export tax lowers the domestic consumer and producer prices and hence leads to reduced domestic production, increased domestic consumption, and a reduced volume of exports.

An Oil Import Subsidy

Under the two-price system no imports would occur in the absence of government subsidies because the domestic price of oil is less than the world price. But as we have seen, Canada imports oil; the Canadian government has introduced an oil import subsidy. In effect, the Canadian government buys crude oil on the world market at the world price and resells it to domestic refineries at less than the world price, thereby giving a subsidy to domestic purchasers.

If the subsidy applied to all oil imports, not just imports made by refineries, and if the subsidy were the only policy used to control the price of oil, then domestic consumers would import all the oil they use while domestic refineries would export their entire oil output. Only the domestic consumer price of oil would fall; the price that domestic producers receive would remain equal to the world price. The operation of an oil import subsidy where the country is an importer both

[4] The material on pages 132 and 513 should be reviewed at this stage.

FIGURE 27-3
The Two-Price System

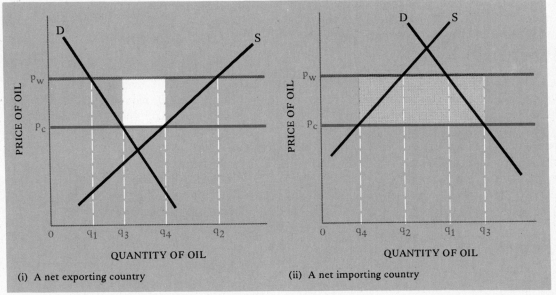

(i) A net exporting country   (ii) A net importing country

A tax on oil exports and/or a subsidy to oil imports lowers the domestic price of oil and leads to an increase in domestic consumption and a decrease in domestic production. Domestic demand and supply are given by the black lines labelled D and S. The world price is p_w; under free trade quantity demanded domestically is q_1 and domestic production is q_2. The export tax/import subsidy lowers the domestic price to p_c.

In (i) quantity $q_2 - q_1$ would be exported under free trade. The export tax reduces the net price received by producers on exports to p_c. Competition among producers drives the price facing domestic consumers down to p_c. Domestic consumption rises to q_3 and domestic production falls to q_4. The tax authority

collects revenue equal to the shaded rectangle.

In ((ii) quantity $q_1 - q_2$ would be imported under free trade. The import subsidy reduces the price paid by domestic consumers to p_c. Quantity q_3 would now be consumed. Domestic production would remain at q_2 since that amount can all be exported at the world price; domestic consumption q_2 is satisfied via imports.

In (ii) the additional imposition of an export tax would reduce the price received by domestic producers to p_c. As a result, domestic production falls to q_4 and net imports become quantity $q_3 - q_4$. The tax authorities now make payments equal to the shaded rectangle.

before and after the policy is introduced is illustrated in Figure 27-3(ii).

For an oil-importing country, an oil import subsidy lowers the price to domestic consumers; hence domestic consumption and the volume of imports rise.

A Combined Export Tax and Import Subsidy

The combined operation of an oil export tax and an oil import subsidy is readily determined be-

cause their effects are similar. When Canada was a net oil exporter, both were needed only to facilitate the fact that, because of transportation costs and for historical reasons, oil was imported into Eastern Canada and hence gross exports from Western Canada exceeded net exports for all of Canada. However, for the net importer case, as shown in Figure 27-3(ii), both policies are required in order to lower the prices facing consumers *and* producers; otherwise domestic demand would be satisfied entirely from world markets, and domestic output would be sold on world markets at world prices.[5]

For most purposes, all that matters is the *net* trade flow as explained in Figure 27-3. The relevant fact is that Canada has moved from being a net exporter of oil and natural gas into the early 1970s to being a net importer at the beginning of the 1980s so that both policies are currently required. Indeed, the National Energy Program introduced in October 1980 further complicated the relationship between the various oil prices by introducing taxes that created another wedge between the price received by producers, called the *wellhead* price, and that paid by consumers, now called the *blended* price. Related issues are taken up in the box on page 554.

Impact on Federal Revenue and Outlays

The export tax generates revenue for the federal government while the import subsidy leads to increased outlays. If exports equaled imports, revenue from the export tax would exactly equal payments for the import subsidy and there would be no effect on the fiscal position of the federal government.

Observe the different implications for the fiscal position of the government in the two situations depicted in Figure 27-3(i) and (ii). For the net exporter case in Figure 27-3(i), the federal government collects revenue from the export tax in excess of payments for the import subsidy, and the two-price system generates net revenue for the federal government. In Figure 27-3(ii), which corresponds more closely to the 1981 situation with Canada a net importer, the federal government faces additional outlays to cover payments for the import subsidy in excess of the revenue from the export tax.

The import subsidy has risen to more than $20

a barrel as of early 1981. With *net* imports of 40 million barrels, oil accounted for a net drain on federal government revenues of approximately $800 million for 1979, or approximately 6 percent of the total federal deficit projected for that year.[6]

The subsidy to oil imports is financed by Canadian taxpayers. Canadians ultimately pay the world price of oil, part of it when they purchase petroleum products and the rest when they pay their taxes. Of course the problem with doing it this way is that consumers think oil is cheap and use it lavishly; if they knew how much they were really paying—that is, if they bore the cost directly through a higher domestic price—they would use it more sparingly.

The Debate About Establishing Parity with World Prices

While low energy prices are popular with many Canadians, the fall in domestic production, the increased dependence on foreign oil, and the increased government deficit arising from the import subsidy have all become matters of concern. What then are the basic arguments for and against raising the Canadian price to *parity* with the world price?

A FALLACIOUS ARGUMENT FOR NOT MOVING TO PARITY

The policy of moving to the world price of oil is often opposed on the basis of a very simple and apparently straightforward argument. It asks: Why should Canada have the price of this important commodity dictated to it by the cartel of oil-producing nations? Why should we be forced to treat oil as being expensive simply because those countries have decided to raise the world price of

---

[5] Both policies are needed for the net importer while only one is required for the net exporter because the overall policy is to *lower* the domestic price. If the goal were to *raise* the domestic price, a net importing country would require only an import tax while a net exporter would require both an import tax and an export subsidy.

[6] The subsidy to *total consumption* is much larger because *all* oil consumed in the economy is purchased at less than world prices. Total consumption is almost 700 million barrels a year, so the annual total subsidy is about $14 billion, most of which is paid by domestic producers.

oil? Why should we let the price of such an important commodity be determined outside our boundaries and outside our own political and democratic process?

The reasoning is based on a misconception. It proceeds as though the value of oil were something Canadians could control. This is simply not the case. We Canadians can trade oil *among ourselves* at any price we decide; but the price of oil paid by the economy as a whole—the social value of oil to all of us—is the world price of oil. This point is important enough to warrant detailed argument.

The Value of Canadian Oil

From the *world's point of view,* the value of an additional barrel of Canadian oil produced today is related to what is given up in order to produce that oil in Canada; i.e., its opportunity cost measured in terms of what other goods would have been available had the barrel of oil not been produced now. (A complication in determining that opportunity cost is taken up in the box.)

From *Canada's point of view,* however, the measure is different. Canada is a small economy unable to influence the world price of oil. For example, in 1981 the world price of oil was approximately $43 per barrel. What, then, was the value to Canada of producing another barrel of oil? If one more barrel of oil were produced in Canada it could be either exported and sold at the world price or consumed at home, with one less barrel imported at a saving of the world price. In either case the gain to Canada of producing one more barrel of oil is given by the world price of that oil: it is the value of foreign goods that could be purchased with the money obtained by selling the oil (at the world price).

The value of Canadian oil to the Canadian economy is the world price of oil.

The world price of oil cannot be influenced by Canadians. It will not be influenced by the price at which Canadians trade oil among themselves. Nor will it be influenced by whether Canada remains a net importer, achieves self-sufficiency, or even becomes a net exporter. Neither is it affected by the price of producing oil in Canada.

Canadians *can* decide whether or not to set the Canadian price of oil equal to the world price. We *can* subsidize the consumption of oil and reduce the price paid by domestic consumers. We *can* tax the production of oil and reduce the price received by domestic producers. But one fact of life that must be recognized in any sensible energy program is that these subsidies and taxes do not change the value of Canadian oil to the Canadian economy as a whole; that remains equal to the world price of oil.

THE ARGUMENT FOR PARITY

The basic arguments for establishing parity with the world price of oil are those associated with the role of the price system as a mechanism for establishing an efficient allocation of resources. Figure 27-4 shows that economic waste is created by the policy of suppressing the domestic price below the world price.

The value of oil to the Canadian economy is the world price. However, the value of oil to *private* individuals and firms in Canada, and the price on which they base their own decisions concerning oil consumption and production, is the domestic price. Under the two-price system, then, the private and social values are different. The combination of the export tax and import subsidy causes Canadian producers to produce too little oil; resources are being used in other industries where they have a lower marginal product. Similarly, Canadian consumers use too much oil.[7]

Oil is expensive, this argument says, and policies that suppress the price of oil only try to pretend otherwise; for the world price of oil must be paid, whether directly or indirectly. And the average individual in the economy would be better off if Canadians were made aware of the fact.

[7] That is, "too little" and "too much" relative to a parity situation.

The Opportunity Cost of a Nonrenewable Resource

For the Canadian economy the world price of oil is given; efficient resource allocation in the Canadian economy requires that individual supply and demand decisions be based on this price. For efficient allocation of the world's resources, however, the world price of oil must accurately reflect its opportunity cost.

Whether the current world price does this is open to debate. Many believe that the current world price is artificially propped up by the cartel of oil producing nations (OPEC). Certainly the world price of oil far exceeds the direct costs of extracting the oil from the ground and refining it—this excess of price over direct costs constitutes economic rent. In the case of an ordinary good, this would be sufficient evidence to establish that the price does not reflect opportunity cost but indeed overstates it. But for oil, the opportunity cost of an extra unit of current production does exceed its "direct costs," so that some excess of market price over direct costs is desirable.

The reason for this is that oil is a nonrenewable resource. The current price of oil has to reflect not only the direct costs of extracting and refining it but also the cost of oil forgone in the future. For example, suppose oil were available "free" in the sense of having a zero cost of extraction and refining but that it was also only available in a fixed, finite amount. Then use of some oil today would still involve a cost to society because it would result in less oil being available for use in the future.

The fact that oil is a nonrenewable resource complicates greatly the relationship between the current price at which the product sells and the direct costs of producing it. If some oil is to be saved for future generations, today's price must reflect not only the direct costs but also the opportunity cost borne by future generations. This is the role played by some of the apparent economic rents in the current situation.

The cost of using oil today is not just the cost of taking it out of the ground and processing it; it is also the cost of there being less oil available for use tomorrow.

This argument is difficult and subtle, and it is hardly surprising that there should be controversy surrounding it. No doubt the difficulty in understanding the role of economic rent in *current* oil prices is at the heart of many misconceptions that lead to criticisms of "high" energy prices.

Even if one accepts the current excess of oil prices over direct costs, how could one justify the increase in these rents that would result from further increases in domestic oil prices if we were to move toward parity? The argument that market prices should exceed direct costs does not, of course, justify the particular prices set by OPEC. The answer (see page 543) is that the value of oil to the Canadian economy is the world price of oil independent of how much Canada chooses to produce or consume, and independent of how Canada prices oil internally for domestic purposes.

An increase in the domestic price of oil would lead to a shift of resources into the production of oil and out of the production of other, less valuable products. It would also induce households and industries to consume less energy by investing more in insulation, by buying smaller cars, and by making other energy-saving substitutions. The American experience with increased energy prices in the 1978–1980 period suggests that this demand elasticity is quite large.

FIGURE 27-4

The Efficiency Gains from Establishing Parity

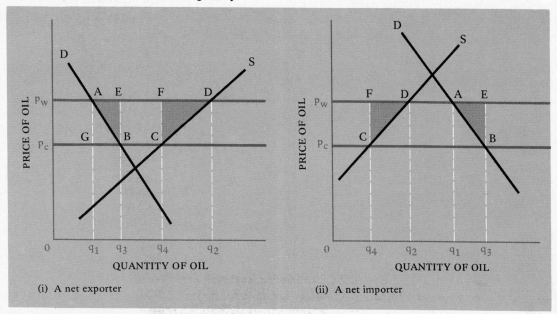

(i) A net exporter

(ii) A net importer

A movement to parity with world prices increases economic efficiency and leads to an increase in national income. Elimination of the two-price system reverses the effects shown in Figure 27-3. The domestic price rises from p_c to the world price p_w; domestic consumption falls from q_3 to q_1 and domestic production rises from q_4 to q_2. Economic rent, or producers' surplus, increases by the area of the trapezoid p_cCDP_w while consumers' surplus falls by the area of the trapezoid p_cBAP_w.

In the net exporter case shown in (i), the increase in producers' surplus exceeds the loss in consumers' surplus. The government loses its revenue from the export tax which was equal to the area of the rectangle

EBCF. Hence the net gain to society, equal to the increase in producers' surplus minus the loss in consumers' surplus and the forgone government revenue, is shown by the sum of the two shaded triangles *AEB* and *CFD.*

In the net importer case shown in (ii), the loss in consumers' surplus exceeds the gain in producers' surplus. The government gains from not having to pay the import subsidy equal to the rectangle *EBCF.* Hence the net gain to society, equal to the increase in producers' surplus plus the reduction in government outlays minus the loss in consumers' surplus, is shown by the sum of the two shaded triangles *AEB* and *CFD.*

The increase in national income that would arise from the movement to parity is illustrated in Figure 27-4. The higher are the elasticities of demand and supply, the larger will be the allocational distortions created by the two-price system, and hence the larger will be the increase in national income from moving to parity. Parity would increase the amount of economic rent generated in the economy, earned in the first instance by producers, and would also eliminate the direct subsidy to consumers that exists under

the two-price system. The impact on the government depends on whether the country is a net importer or a net exporter; in Canada's current situation as a net importer, part of the gains would accrue to the government through the elimination of its import subsidy payments.

The rise in national income means that the increase in economic rent exceeds the losses borne elsewhere in the economy. How the current and anticipated future rents are to be divided is a contentious issue; various levels of govern-

Export Taxes, Production Royalties, and Profits Taxes

Here we focus on two important aspects of the taxation of the oil and natural gas industries. First, we compare the use of an export tax with that of a production tax (often called a *royalty*) for the purpose of maintaining the Canadian producer price below the world price. Second, we examine the problems involved in taxing profits accruing to foreign owners following a move to parity.

The Two-Price System: Export Tax Versus Royalty

Consider the operation of an export tax as shown in Figure 27-4(i), the case of a net exporter. The price facing domestic consumers and producers is p_c; q_4 is produced and q_3 is consumed domestically. The rectangle $EFBC$ represents the revenue from the tax $(p_w - p_c)$ on an export volume of $(q_4 - q_3)$.

Replacing the export tax with an equal tax on all production (i.e., a royalty) would have the following effects: Since the tax is collected on all production, domestic consumers also pay the tax, and the price facing them rises to p_w. The *net* price received by producers on exports and domestic sales remains at p_c; the

production tax creates a wedge between the producer and consumer prices. Domestic demand falls to q_1 and exports rise to $(q_4 - q_1)$. Government revenue rises to the rectangle p_wFCp_c because the tax is collected on total production. The loss in consumers' surplus (see pages 162–164) is represented by the trapezoid p_wABp_c. This is because the height of the demand curve at any level of quantity demanded is a measure in money terms of the marginal utility to consumers of an additional unit of consumption. Thus the change in total utility is represented by the area under the demand curve.

Comparing the gain in revenue with the loss in consumers' surplus, we can conclude that

A royalty is superior to an export tax in the sense that the gain in revenue from changing to a royalty is greater than the loss in consumers' surplus caused by increasing the domestic price to the world level.

If the policy objective is to keep the price received by producers low, perhaps in order to tax foreign owners, then it is better to use a production tax and let the price facing domestic consumers rise to the world price than to

ment, the producing industry, and consumers all want to share. (We return to this subject below.) Nevertheless it is clear that to the extent that losses suffered by consumers are considered to be an undesirable aspect of oil price increases, movement to parity could be accomplished by some scheme to redistribute some of the rents to consumers. (A *refundable energy tax credit*, for example, was an important part of the Crosbie budget of December 1979.) Similarly, most proposals to establish parity are also accompanied by schemes to tax producers in order to redistribute the rents. Deregulation of energy prices in

the United States in 1978 was accompanied by a "windfall profits" tax on oil company revenues. The National Energy Program introduced in Canada in October 1980 also contained new tax measures aimed at the oil companies.

In order to preserve the efficiency gains from parity, these taxes must be levied in such a way that they do not distort oil production decisions; the results must be captured in such a way that the firms receive the full world price on the expensive marginal unit of oil produced. Some problems with devising such a scheme are discussed in the box.

use an export tax and keep consumer prices low. An alternative is to let producer prices also rise and tax directly the income of foreign owners.

Moving to Oil-Price Parity

We have seen that establishing oil price parity involves a loss in consumer's surplus and export tax revenue that is more than offset by the gain in producers' surplus and diminished import subsidies. A problem often noted for Canadian interests is that much of the gain in efficiency reflected by the increased producers' surplus is captured by foreign owners of the major oil companies. To the extent that it is deemed desirable to capture a larger portion of these profits for Canadians, the problem is to design a tax that will capture some of the profits yet preserve the incentives to produce the efficient quantity of output.

A profits tax would do this if profits could be measured accurately, for a tax on pure profits does not influence output decisions (see page 487). Unfortunately, actual or true costs are very hard to determine, so a profits

tax is difficult to administer. One possible reaction to a profits tax would be for the companies to inflate artificially their cost figures through increased payments to their foreign owners for parts, patents, technical advice, leasing arrangements, and overhead. This would enable them to transfer the "profits" out of the country in untaxed form.

Various proposals have been offered to deal with this problem. One would impose a net royalty tax, as is done in some mining industries; this involves allowing only notional or estimated expenses to be deducted from total revenues prior to the calculation of taxable income. A second would impose differential excise tax rates on alternative sources of supply, with the highest being applied to established conventional sources with presumably low extraction costs, and lower rates for secondary or synthetic sources that have higher extraction and refining costs. This would capture some of the rents generated by production from low-cost sources without totally discouraging production from marginal, high-cost sources. Other aspects or this problem are considered in the box on page 554.

ARGUMENTS AGAINST PARITY

If the argument for parity can be made so bluntly, how can the two price-policy be defended? Recall from Chapter 1 that most economic policies have side effects, that it is impossible to have *no* policy, and that policies must be evaluated in terms of their objectives. These aspects of moving to parity are all used as arguments for not doing so. In this section we consider two types of arguments commonly made in opposition to movement to parity. The first type raises *distributional* issues, the second raises *allocational* issues.

Distributional Arguments Against Parity

Distributional arguments concede the existence of the efficiency gains outlined. However, they emphasize that these gains are not shared evenly and indeed that some people suffer losses in spite of the overall increase in efficiency.

Foreign ownership. An increase in the Canadian price of oil will generate large "profits" (more accurately, rents) for the oil companies because most current production is from low-cost sources. As the oil companies are to a large extent foreign owned, this represents a direct transfer from Canadians to the foreign owners.[8] However, the increases in domestic oil prices will lead to increased efficiency, and one might ask whether the efficiency gains would exceed the transfers to foreigners so that Canadians would still have a net gain from parity.

The efficiency gains of a $1 increase in the price of oil have been estimated to be about 17.5 cents. Existing ownership and tax arrangements in the late 1970s led to estimates of the transfer to foreign owners in the range of 20 cents. On the basis of similar calculations, some economists have argued that until a scheme to tax rents accruing to foreigners is in place, "it is not in our national interest (broadly viewed) to raise the price of oil by one cent, let alone by ten dollars." It seems likely that developments since then, including the reduction in the share of foreign ownership and the October 1980 federal budget which reduced the share of oil revenues accruing to the oil companies, have reduced the transfer to foreigners sufficiently that a movement to parity would yield a net benefit to Canadians. Further, tax increases could accompany the move to parity so that even more of the increases in rents are captured by Canadians. Some related issues are discussed in the box on pages 546–547.

Personal income distribution. One common argument against using the price system to allocate resources is that the poor members of society are hurt more by price increases than are the rich. This argument is often used to oppose further increases in domestic oil prices.

Some economists have challenged the assumption that parity is regressive. One recent study found that the total amount spent on energy increases with income, but that, expressed as a percentage of total household current expendi-

ture, expenditure on energy shows no consistent pattern across income classes (except that of all groups, the very rich consistently consume the largest proportion of the total budget on energy). In any event, whether or not parity is regressive also depends on how the efficiency gains are redistributed.

As Figure 27-4 shows, all consumers suffer from a move to parity because the two-price system involves a subsidy to consumption. Hence some form of compensation to consumers is a likely part of any move to parity.

The assumption that movement to parity would be regressive may or may not be valid, but most economists would argue that it is inefficient to try to achieve income distribution objectives by subsidizing the consumption of particular goods. The inefficiency means a reduction in the total value of goods produced by the economy. This inefficiency need not be suffered if other, more efficient ways of directly transferring income from the rich to the poor were used to satisfy the implicit distributional objectives while keeping the domestic price of oil at a level that accurately reflects the opportunity cost of oil to the economy.

Whether or not a move to parity is regressive, there are more efficient ways of helping the poor than holding down the price of oil for everyone.

Allocational Arguments Against Parity

Arguments against parity sometimes contend that while parity offers efficiency gains of the type considered above, a movement to parity under existing arrangements will introduce distortions that may offset the original efficiency gains. In order to understand these arguments, we need to reconsider the efficiency gains from a regional perspective and then consider the possible distortions.

Clearly the most obvious and perhaps the most significant implication for Canada of the exis-

---

[8] As of the mid 1970s, approximately 80 percent of equity in oil companies operating in Canada was estimated to be held by foreigners. By early 1981 estimates of foreign ownership of the Canadian industry had fallen to below 70 percent. One aspect of the Liberal government's budget of October 1980 was to try to reduce that number by introducing incentives for Canadian ownership.

tence of OPEC is the dramatic swing in the regional terms of trade that it has brought about. The price of resource goods produced in some Atlantic and the Western provinces has risen relative to the price of the manufactured goods produced in Central and Eastern Canada, and the difference in relative prices would of course be even larger following a move to parity. Two related issues are of interest here: the regional reallocation of resources called forth by the relative price changes, and the complicated interaction between energy prices and federal-provincial fiscal arrangements.

Regional adjustment to oil price parity. Consider the efficient allocation of resources between Ontario and Alberta, which may be taken as representative of the oil-consuming and oil-producing regions. Labor is a highly mobile factor of production. Efficient allocation requires that the total labor force be divided between the two regions in such a way that the reallocation of one worker in either direction cannot increase the value of combined output. A market-determined allocation of the labor force will tend to achieve that.

Diminishing marginal productivity implies that for any firm — and hence for the aggregate of firms in each region — each additional worker will contribute less to output than did the previous worker hired. Profit-maximizing firms will employ workers up to the point where the last worker hired produces just sufficient additional output to cover his or her additional cost, that is, the wage rate. The mobility of workers will tend to equalize wage rates across firms and regions as well as the value of the product generated within any firm or region by a marginal worker. When this has occurred, further reallocation cannot increase the value of total output because the loss suffered by a firm in the region of emigration will be exactly offset by the increase in output in a firm in the region of immigration. This situation is illustrated in Figure 27-5.

The allocation of labor depicted in Figure 27-5 depends on the prices of the outputs produced in the two regions. The two labor demand curves are the respective marginal revenue product (MRP) curves. A change in the price of the output of one region would cause its demand for labor to shift; corresponding to that new price there would be a new efficient allocation of labor between the two regions.

The dependence of the allocation of labor on output prices provides an alternative view of the inefficiency inherent in the two-price system. The demand for labor in Alberta is given by the *private MRP* of labor in Alberta; it is the value to the oil industry of the output of one additional worker and it depends on the *domestic* price of oil. The *social MRP* of oil in Alberta, which is the value to the economy of the output of one additional worker, depends on the *world* price of oil. Under the two-price system the domestic price is below the world price and hence the private *MRP* of labor in Alberta is less than the social *MRP*. The two-price system thus leads to a misallocation of labor; the allocation at E_1 in Figure 27-5 is not an efficient allocation. The wage paid in Alberta is w_1, but the social value of a marginal worker's output is much higher, as shown by point Z.

The establishment of oil price parity would increase the domestic price of output in Alberta (the oil-producing region) to the world price and hence increase the demand for labor in Alberta to equal the *social* marginal revenue product of labor. Since labor is mobile, this would cause an increase in the wage rate in both regions and an increase in the share of the labor force working in Alberta. The increase in wages means a fall in the profitability in manufacturing because the output price of that sector has not risen. The associated decline in output and employment in Ontario represents one aspect of *de-industrialization,* a topic that has received considerable public attention recently.

The gain in efficiency resulting from the labor force reallocation is illustrated in Figure 27-5. For each worker who moves from Ontario to Al-

FIGURE 27-5
The Efficient Regional Allocation of Labor

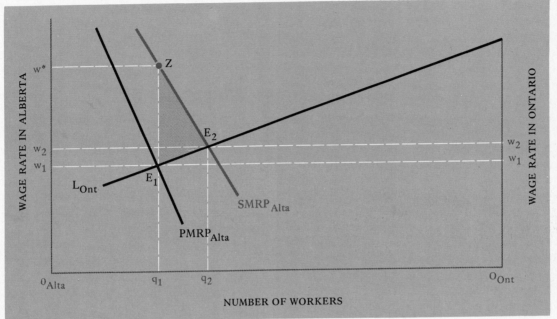

In a competitive labor market the allocation of labor will be such that the wage rate is the same in both regions. With the two-price system, the domestic price of oil is lower than the world price. Given the lower domestic price, $PMRP_{Alta}$ (the *private* marginal revenue product of labor) is the demand for labor in Alberta, drawn here with respect to the left-hand vertical axis. L_{Ont} is the demand for labor in Ontario, drawn with respect to the right-hand vertical axis. The allocation of labor is determined by the intersection of the labor demand schedules at E_1. The common wage rate is w_1 with $0_{Alta} - q_1$ units of labor in Alberta and $q_1 - 0_{Ont}$ units of labor in Ontario.

A movement to parity increases the demand for labor in Alberta. The new demand curve is given by $SMRP_{Alta}$, the *social* marginal revenue product of labor in the production of oil. The new equilibrium is at E_2. Wages rise to w_2 in both Alberta and Ontario, and $q_1 - q_2$ workers migrate from Ontario to Alberta. For each worker, output in Alberta rises by the height of $SMRP_{Alta}$ while output in Ontario due to the corresponding out-migration falls only by the height of L_{Ont}. Hence the value of the increase output in Alberta due to the in-migration exceeds the fall in the value of output in Ontario due to the corresponding out-migration by the area of the shaded triangle.

berta, total national output falls by the value of that worker's marginal product in Ontario and rises by his or her marginal product in Alberta. For all the workers who move, the latter is larger; hence total output increases. At the new equilibrium the two marginal products are equal, and no further increase in total output by reallocation of labor is possible.

While efficiency conditions would require an expansion of economic activity in Alberta at the expense of Ontario so that there is some decline of the Ontario manufacturing sector, there is no argument here for the *relocation* of the manufacturing sector.[9]

[9] You can show for yourself that a relatively inelastic *MRP* in Alberta means a relatively small labor reallocation when the price of oil changes. Expansion of the service sector in Alberta and development of the more labor-intensive synthetic production from the oil sands would of course increase the required migration from Ontario to Alberta.

Federal-provincial fiscal arrangements and regional distortions. In Canada the regional resource flows would be further complicated by existing federal-provincial fiscal arrangements. The key institutional consideration is that oil and natural gas in Alberta are in effect the property of the provincial government. Under current leasing and royalty arrangements, a large share of the oil and gas revenues accrues collectively to the residents of Alberta through their provincial government.

What are the implications of an increase in domestic oil prices in the light of this institutional factor? Given the provincial ownership of resources, the Alberta government will receive a large portion of the increased resource revenues. This will accrue indirectly to residents of Alberta in the form of improved services, reduced taxes, and the like. In effect, then, workers in Alberta are paid something in excess of their marginal product—call that excess the "fiscal benefit."

With free interprovincial migration of labor, workers will move until the marginal product of labor in Ontario is equal to the marginal product of labor *plus* the fiscal benefit in Alberta. Since economic efficiency requires that the marginal product of labor be equated between regions, there will be economic waste as a result of parity. The effect of large increases in resource revenues in Alberta will be to cause large increases in the total payments made to labor in that province without having much effect on its marginal product. This in turn will induce a flow of migrants to Alberta and thus open up a gap between the marginal products of labor in the two provinces. The economic waste is illustrated in Figure 27-6.

If parity were introduced from an initial inefficient position, such as E_1 in Figure 27-5, an efficiency gain would arise from the correct pricing of oil and an efficiency loss would arise from the fiscal distortion. Whether parity in these circumstances leads to an increase in efficiency depends on the relative magnitude of the two effects.[10]

Policies to raise the domestic price of oil to world levels under fiscal arrangements existing in 1981 can be expected to have important effects on interprovincial resource allocation in Canada. The changes in incentives related to interregional factor movements have little connection with changes in relative productivity of these factors in different parts of the country. Our analysis emphasizes the importance of federal-provincial fiscal arrangements. While some observers argue that the regional distortions introduced by those fiscal arrangements are the basis of a strong case against further increases in the price of oil, others argue that they simply demonstrate the need for a reform of current federal-provincial arrangements.[11]

Essentially our analysis suggests that there is an efficiency argument for redistributing *some* of the resource rents from Alberta to the rest of Canada. This case does not focus on the "injustice" of the distributional effects of oil price changes; it arises from the fact that under current arrangements, oil price increases are likely to lead to waste in the interprovincial allocation of factors of production.

The problem is to distribute increases in oil and natural gas rents without introducing further distortions in the allocation of resources. The

[10] An additional fiscal incentive for migration arises out of the system of equalization payments discussed in Chapter 25. Recall that essentially these use federal funds to raise selected provincial revenues to the national per capita average. The effect of an increase in Alberta's resource revenues is to increase the revenue deficiencies of the "have not" provinces, and hence to increase their equalization payments received from the federal government. Ontario has, in effect, been prohibited from being a "have-not" province even though it is relatively poor in terms of energy resources and revenues. Since the tax base in Ontario is still by far the largest single source of federal revenue, and Alberta is relatively small in this respect, Ontario bears a much greater share of the increased equalization costs than does Alberta. Hence there is a further incentive for workers to leave Ontario for provinces that are either energy rich or qualify for equalization payments.

[11] Under the present system, parity would lead to a massive increase in federal government expenditures and tax rates, while under a true revenue-sharing system it would not. Professor John Helliwell of the University of British Columbia has recently proposed an interprovincial revenue-sharing pool that would take an agreed fraction of *all* provincial revenues and distribute them as per capita grants to the provincial governments.

FIGURE 27-6
Fiscal-induced Migration and the Regional Allocation of Labor

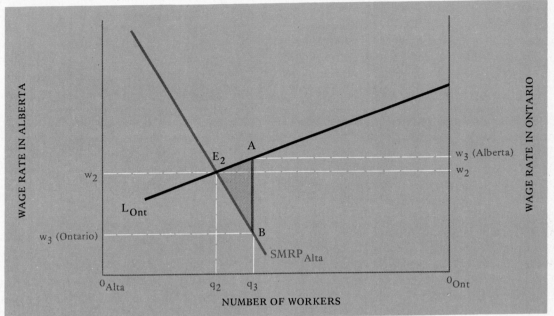

Provincial resource ownership and existing federal-provincial fiscal arrangements lead to an inefficient allocation of labor. Workers in Alberta earn a net fiscal benefit relative to those in Ontario, measured here by the distance AB. Since the net fiscal benefit is received in addition to wages, labor will migrate until the wage in Ontario exceeds that in Alberta by AB. The efficient allocation at E_2 with $0_{Alta} - q_2$ workers in Alberta and $q_2 - 0_{Ont}$ in Ontario is reproduced from Figure 27-5. As a result of the fiscal distortion in Canada, there are $q_2 q_3$ too many workers in Alberta. Migrating workers cause output in Ontario to fall by $q_2 E_2 A q_3$ while output in Alberta increases by only $q_2 E_2 B q_3$. The economic waste created by the inefficiency is measured by the shaded triangle $E_2 AB$.

ideal scheme would allow the efficiency effects illustrated in Figure 27-5 to accrue without being accompanied by the inefficiencies shown in Figure 27-6. Implicitly it would involve taxing the provinces as owners of the resources in order to redistribute. This, of course, explains why the pricing and taxing of oil resources was an integral part of the struggle between the federal government and the provinces that dominated the Canadian political scene at the start of the 1980s. It also warrants mention that the basic arguments apply equally well to all other provincially owned resources; thus any revenue-sharing scheme should also include, for example, the rents from mining and hydroelectricity sales.

Energy Prices and Export Competitiveness

Increases in the domestic price of energy influence the competitiveness of the domestic manufacturing sector in two ways. The first is the microeconomic effect of the increased factor cost on output prices, taking into account factor shares, input substitution, and output demand elasticity. The second deals with the macroeconomic consequences in terms of wages, the exchange rate, investment, and other variables that may respond to the energy price change.

On the former issue, Professor Leonard Waverman of the University of Toronto has prepared estimates which suggest that the direct cost effects of oil price parity are quite small.[12] He calculates that a 50 percent increase in *all* energy prices may lead to a cost increase ranging from 2 to 5 percent in Ontario manufacturing industries, roughly equivalent to the increases that would arise from only a 13 percent increase in wages. The effect is small because fuel costs are only a small portion of total costs for most industries, because less expensive coal could be substituted for oil and gas, and because higher energy prices induce substitution of other factors (capital and labor) for energy.

The direct effects on competitiveness do *not* provide a serious argument against moving to energy price parity. Indeed, as Canada lags behind most of its trading partners in moving toward world prices, a move to parity should not be seen as much as a reduction in competitiveness as a removal of an export subsidy.[13] Since Canadian manufacturing industries are essentially price takers in world markets, this subsidy shows up not so much in reduced prices and increased production but rather in higher profits to Canadian producers, profits earned at the expense of Canadian taxpayers who bear the cost of the subsidy. If the political consensus is that some of Canada's resource wealth is to be used to subsidize the manufacturing sector, there are more efficient ways to grant that subsidy than one which involves encouraging wasteful energy use.

Current Issues in Energy Policy: The National Energy Program

In October 1980 the federal minister of energy, mines, and resources, Marc Lalonde, announced the *National Energy Program* (NEP), a major set of policy initiatives relating to pricing and taxation in the energy sector. These policies have since been the focus of much public debate, and they will influence virtually all aspects of Canadian life for many years to come. While the NEP deals with all types of energy sources, its main focus is on oil and natural gas.

Objectives of the NEP

The NEP outlines three basic objectives:

Security of energy supply.
Opportunity for all Canadians to participate in the energy industry.
Fairness in the manner in which the benefits of the nation's rich resources are shared.

The first objective is taken to mean that Canada would ultimately become self-sufficient in oil through a combination of increased domestic supply and reduced domestic demand. The main focus of the second objective is the present foreign domination of the Canadian oil industry. The third objective relates not only to foreign ownership but also to the highly uneven regional distribution of reserves of oil and natural gas within Canada.

Specific Policies of the NEP

The NEP includes a number of specific proposals designed to meet the three objectives. These include: federally set "wellhead" and "city gate" prices for domestic producers of oil and natural gas, respectively, which rise gradually and predictably to an announced "reference" price; a "made in Canada" or blended price of oil consumed in Canada which will rise gradually and predictably to 85 percent of the world price; and a price of natural gas consumed in Canada which will rise less quickly than the blended oil price.

The increase in consumer prices relative to producer prices implied by these proposals involves increased federal taxes. The NEP establishes consumer prices that are an average of

---

[12] That the average effect is small does not mean that particular productive units will not be rendered uneconomic.

[13] For example, when American gasoline prices rose substantially in the spring of 1980, there was an outcry in Canada at Americans driving across the border to buy gasoline. However, there was no outrage at Americans buying any other of our subsidized exports. The subsidy in the export of gas was all too visible, but the subsidy provided by cheap energy consumed by export industries is equally real.

Canadianization and Nationalization of the Oil and Natural Industries

One of the main objectives of the National Energy Program (NEP) introduced in October 1980 is an increase in Canadian ownership of the oil and natural gas industries. Policies that created incentives for increased Canadian ownership of the private corporations in the industry were introduced. In addition, the activities of the government-owned Petro Canada have been expanded, perhaps most notably through the purchase of the Canadian subsidiary of Petro Fina from its Belgian parent. These developments raise a number of interesting issues.

Effects on Future Foreign Investment

Straightforward analysis suggests that there are large costs in trying to increase the Canadianization of the industry, regardless of whether it is to be held privately by Canadian residents or publicly by Petro Canada. Current policy is apparently based on the premise that if you are going to try to buy an industry, you should first tax it heavily in order to reduce its market value. But this harsh tax treatment of the income earned by foreign capital makes Canada a less favorable place for foreign capital to reside. Hence when the oil industry is ultimately bought by Canadians, it is unlikely that the foreign capital will be reinvested elsewhere in Canada; it is more likely to be moved into investments outside Canada.

As a result, Canadianization of the oil industry could reduce the amount of physical capital in place in the Canadian economy. If the funds used to purchase equity in the oil industry were instead used to finance *new* investment, more jobs and income would be created.

A Discriminatory Tax?

The imposition of discriminatory tax on income accruing to foreigners in the oil and natural gas industries raises a separate issue, not related to the self-interest of Canadians, in terms of its effects on future foreign investment in Canada. Much of the income accruing foreigners is apparently pure rent; the payment of such incomes serves no allocative function, and aside from an exploration and development issue raised, there is no efficiency argument for making such payment.

Is there a moral and/or a contractual issue

the costs of domestic and imported oil or natural gas. Unlike the situation depicted in Figure 27-3, the price paid by domestic consumers will not equal the price received by domestic producers.[14] The consumer price will be set between the world price and the (lower) price received by domestic producers. For example, in January 1981 the world price of oil was approximately $40 a barrel, the wellhead price was $17.75, and the blended oil price was $22.80.

A Petroleum Compensation Charge, equal to the difference between the blended oil price facing consumers and the wellhead oil price, is levied on domestic refiners. The revenue from that charge will offset, at least in part, the federal expenditures on the subsidy to imported oil. Similarly, the rise in the consumer price for natu-

[14] A wedge prevailed prior to the NEP because of the so-called syncrude levy and the existence of various provincial taxes. However, the NEP increases the importance of the distinction between consumer and producer prices. The NEP also allows for higher producer prices for synthetic oil, heavy oils, and tertiary reserves since they are much more expensive to extract and refine.

for making such payments? Presumably the titles to the income streams under contention were in fact purchased by bidding against other firms—including Canadian firms—for the oil rights to particular land parcels. Do the "rents" now earned not represent a legitimate, albeit high return to that investment? Is it fair to turn the rules of the game against these firms *after* their investment has turned out to be so profitable? Would we also feel compelled to "bail out" foreigners who suffered from investments that turned out to be unusually unprofitable?

These are not easy questions. They are not raised in order to introduce a simple and obvious answer, but neither are they intended to make us feel particularly easy about aspects of actual current policy. A further problem is that discriminating policies such as these invite retaliatory policies, especially in the United States.

Why Public Ownership?

One argument for a crown corporation's operating in the petroleum industry seems to rest on two issues. First, actual costs are extremely hard to identify and measure. As a result it is difficult to enforce accurately a tax on profits or rents accruing to foreigners from the oil industry; taxes that attempt to capture the rents earned by foreign-owned firms will simply result in an increased statement of costs. Thus the operation of a public firm could be justified on the grounds of increasing our knowledge about operating costs in the industry. Second, information about the true level of petroleum reserves has been unreliable. Again, the "window on the industry" argument says that the existence of a government firm may improve our knowledge of the situation.

A second argument for a crown corporation is the so-called dominant firm argument. It maintains that the petroleum industry is so vital to the economy that some control over the industry price is desirable. Further, since oil is a nonrenewable resource, current output depletes reserves for the future; thus control over the rate of extraction might also be deemed desirable. A government-owned dominant firm might achieve these goals by assuming some leadership in regulating domestic prices.

ral gas will incorporate a natural gas tax levied by the federal government.

In recognition of the increasing Canadian reserves of natural gas relative to oil, and the recent softening of the U.S. market for potential natural gas exports, the NEP attempts to encourage the domestic substitution of natural gas for oil. Not only is the price of natural gas scheduled to rise less quickly than that of oil, but a subsidy to extend a natural gas pipeline to the Maritimes and eastern Quebec is planned. Those areas, which currently meet much of their energy needs by importing oil, would then have access to domestic supplies of natural gas.

Other proposals are part of a package to encourage Canadian participation in the industry. The Petroleum and Gas Revenue Tax, applied to net operating revenues on all oil and natural gas produced in Canada, will help finance the government's planned new incentives for exploration and development by Canadian firms. The NEP also phases out *depletion allowances*. A depletion allowance permits the oil producers to write off as a current tax-deductible expense a fraction of the costs of exploration, development, and capital expenditures. Such depletion allowances shelter from income taxes a large amount of current revenues, and hence the companies are able to finance exploration and development expenditures out of current cash flows. The NEP reduces the cash flow position of the major corporations and hence encourages them to seek outside funds to finance expansion. New incentives for exploration and development, structured to encourage investment by *Canadian* companies, are introduced so that the initial objective of security of supply is not jeopardized and the induced expansion involves increased Canadian ownership.

Reactions to the NEP

It seems clear that the major impact of the NEP will be on the producing provinces (especially Alberta), on the oil companies, and on Canadian consumers. Consumers will gain relative to an immediate move to parity, but nevertheless they face a gradual and foreseeable erosion of the subsidy they now receive on the consumption of oil. Whether consumers can expect some direct compensation for the loss of their subsidy is not clear at this time. Not surprisingly, the major reaction has come from the first two groups, toward which many of the policies of the NEP were directed. It is worth looking at their reaction in detail.

The Alberta government. In direct response to the NEP, the Alberta government countered in 1981 with a series of reductions in the output of conventional crude oil. In addition, the development of expensive synthetic oil-sands projects was suspended. These actions undermined the NEP's long-run objective of security of supply and threatened to put additional pressure on the federal deficit as a result of the subsidy on the additional oil imports needed to replace the forgone Alberta production. The federal government responded by raising the Petroleum Compensation Charge and the blended price in order to finance the increased import subsidy.

On September 1, 1981, after months of negotiations, an energy pricing agreement between Alberta and the federal government was signed. This agreement accelerated the planned increase in domestic energy prices compared to what was proposed in the October 1980 NEP. Under the agreement, wellhead prices for conventionally produced oil from existing fields will rise toward a ceiling of 75 percent of world prices, a limit expected to be reached by 1986. Wellhead prices for production from new fields, oil sands plants, and frontier oil will be set at or near world prices. Natural gas prices will also rise more rapidly than provided for in the original NEP, but will still effectively be priced below oil. The agreement also contained a number of tax modifications, influencing the division of revenue between the companies and the two levels of government as well as encouraging further exploration and the development of new oil sources. As part of the agreement, the Alberta government undertook to restore current oil production and to expedite development of the oil sands project.

The oil industry. The major oil companies protested the NEP in a large number of forums and for a large number of reasons. The main issues were the squeezing of funds for exploration and development and those aspects of NEP that promoted Canadian participation in the industry at the expense of foreigners.

The most visible reaction was a rapid decline in exploration activity and a large exodus of drilling rigs and skilled labor to the United States. There is some dispute as to whether the relocation of exploration activities to the United States was a response to the "push" of the Canadian NEP or the "pull" of American deregulation; in any event, it is fair to say that the timing of the NEP in this regard was unfortunate. There is real concern in the industry that the loss of the skilled labor force will delay getting exploration back on track once the Canadian situation settles and the climate for exploration improves.

The Canadian ownership issue is addressed in the box on pages 554–555. Reaction in the industry involved not only opposition to the Canadian ownership provisions but also a scramble to qualify.[15] This led to a number of mergers or takeovers (such as Dome Petroleum's takeover of Hudson's Bay Oil and Gas in May 1981) in order to expand the stock of assets eligible for the favorable tax treatment.

Summary

1. Canada is rich in energy resources, but it is also a high consumer of energy. Production and consumption of primary energy in Canada have both grown rapidly since World War II. While Canada's energy production exceeds energy consumption in terms of total primary energy, Canada has become a net importer of petroleum.

2. The world price of oil rose rapidly throughout the 1970s, quadrupling in 1973 and almost doubling in 1979.

3. Since 1973 Canada has maintained a two-price policy that keeps the domestic price of oil below the world price. The gap between the two prices has grown in spite of a stated policy to narrow the gap. The two-price system involves an export tax and an import subsidy on oil. Since Canada is currently a net importer of oil, the two-price system requires that the federal government make payments to finance the import subsidy.

4. The opportunity cost of oil in Canada is the world price of oil. This is true regardless of whether Canada is a net importer, a net exporter, or just self-sufficient in oil.

5. A basic argument for establishing oil price parity is that economic waste is created by the two-price policy of suppressing the domestic price below the world price.

6. Two distributional arguments are often used to oppose parity. One is that much of the current profits of the oil industry are paid to foreign owners. The other is the belief that an increase in

domestic oil prices would be regressive in its effects on the personal distribution of income.

7. Parity would change the regional terms of trade in Canada, causing an expansion in such oil-producing regions as Alberta and a contraction in such oil-consuming areas as Ontario. This would eliminate the inefficient resource allocation that arises from the two-price system. Provincial ownership and the current system of equalization payments would create a distortion leading to fiscal benefits for Alberta residents and a fiscal burden for Ontario residents. This would lead to an inefficient allocation of labor between regions in the Canadian economy.

8. The National Energy Program, instituted in October 1980, introduced a number of policies designed to promote security of the energy supply, opportunity for Canadian participation in the energy industry, and fairness in the distribution of the benefits from Canada's rich resource base.

Topics for Review

Energy self-sufficiency
The two-price system
The opportunity cost of oil
The efficiency argument for oil price parity
The incidence of oil price parity
The National Energy Program

Discussion Questions

1. The National Energy Program of October 1980 reads in part:

   World oil prices are arbitrary and artificial. They do not reflect the conditions of competitive supply and demand nor the costs of production in Canada or other countries. The government is determined that the price of Canadian oil will not be linked to world prices but rather will be made in Canada, determined on the basis of Canadian circumstances and the needs of Canada's economy.

   In what sense are world oil prices arbitrary or artificial? Why do such prices not reflect the costs of production? Does the last sentence quoted provide a sound basis for the formation of energy policy?
2. Some economists have argued that OPEC, in raising

---

[15] The rules are so complex that in the case of one company it took a personal decision of the minister to determine whether the company was Canadian.

the price of oil, has done a great favor to citizens of Western economies—if not to present citizens, to future citizens—by driving home the fact that oil is a nonrenewable resource and that our use of oil today reduces the quantity available for use tomorrow. They go on to argue that, in effect, for us to vote to maintain a low price of oil now is to vote to lower the welfare of future generations. Do you agree with these arguments?

3. Suppose U.S. energy prices were to be kept low for a relatively long period to come. Would that provide a good argument for keeping Canadian energy prices low? Since the United States has in fact moved to a policy of rapidly raising energy prices to world levels, what are the implications for Canadian manufacturing and the formulation of Canadian energy policy?

4. The Alberta government has been investing 30 percent of its resource revenues in the Alberta Heritage Fund. If instead it were to return the revenues to Alberta residents as a "social dividend," how would this influence the pattern of the migration of labor from east to west? It has been proposed that the federal government tax the Alberta Heritage Fund. How might the Alberta government respond to this? Would these responses increase or decrease the existing fiscal distortion?

5. Some economists have argued that there is an efficiency basis for redistributing *some* of the rents accruing to the large reserves of oil in Western Canada.

Since all Canadians *could* access Alberta wealth, and since many *will,* it would be desirable to rearrange the current institutional framework so that they can do so without generating the rent-dissipating inefficiencies required under the current system.

How could Canadians access wealth under current (1981) institutional arrangements? Would this lead to "rent-dissipating" inefficiencies? How? What changes would lead to a redistribution without leading to rent-dissipating externalities?

6. When the Natural Energy Program was in preparation, the federal government let it be known that an export tax on natural gas was under consideration. The provinces protested. When the NEP was announced, the export tax had been replaced by the 8 percent Petroleum and Gas Revenue Tax, which was presented as a production tax. However, the provinces insisted that it was an export tax. Alberta Minister of Energy Merv Leitch said, "It is a flat out export tax. Canadian producers, consumers, and governments will pay; not American consumers."

What is the difference between a production tax and an export tax? Why would the provinces prefer one to the other? Does the Petroleum and Gas Revenue Tax correspond to either one? What about the Petroleum Compensation Charge and the Natural Gas Tax? Suppose the purpose of the tax were to limit the profits being received by foreign owners of the oil companies; which tax would be preferred for this purpose?

7. Some economists favor the establishment of parity with world prices for oil and maintenance of the two-price system for natural gas. What differences in the market conditions for the two products might lead to such a view? Do these market conditions exist today? Did they in 1981?

Part Nine

National Income
and Fiscal Policy

Aggregate Demand and Aggregate Supply

28

Inflation, unemployment, recession, and *economic growth* have become household words. Governments worry about how to reduce inflation and unemployment, how to prevent recessions, and how to increase growth. Firms are concerned with the effects of inflation on their assets and how to raise their productivity; many of them have good cause to fear recessions. Households wish to avoid the unemployment that comes in the wake of recessions and would like to protect themselves against the hazards of inflation.

What Is Macroeconomics?

As we saw in Chapter 4, the whole of economics can be divided into two main branches, micro-economics and macroeconomics.[1] Each of the concerns listed above plays a major role in macroeconomics. But what exactly *is* macroeconomics?

MICRO AND MACRO COMPARED

Microeconomics is concerned with the behavior of individual markets. A typical microeconomic problem is to explain the behavior of automobile prices. For decades car prices fell in relation to the prices of most other commodities. Recently this trend has been reversed, with automobiles becoming increasingly expensive relative to other commodities. In microeconomics we seek to understand the causes and the effects of such changes in *relative* prices.

Macroeconomics deals with the overall behavior of the whole economy. A typical macroeco-

[1] Macro and micro derive from the Greek words *makros* and *mikros*, which mean, respectively, long or large and short or small.

nomic problem is to account for the behavior of the price level as measured by the Consumer Price Index (CPI). Why is the average rate at which all prices rise quite low in some decades and quite high in others?

SOME MAJOR MACROECONOMIC ISSUES

We live in an inflationary world. Why did the pace of inflation accelerate during the early 1970s to rates never before seen in peacetime in most advanced Western nations? If Americans and Canadians thought that inflation rates in the range of 10 percent were serious, what was it like to live in Japan, Italy, or Great Britain, where inflation rates were much higher?

The economy proceeds in fits and starts rather than in a smooth upward trend. Why did the 1930s see the greatest economic depression in recorded history, with up to a fifth of the labor force unemployed in Canada and the other major countries of the world? Why were the 25 years following World War II what now appears in retrospect to have been a period of sustained secular boom with only minor interruptions from modest recessions? Why did the mid 1970s see the onset of the worst worldwide recession and slowest recovery since the 1930s?

Alternating bouts of inflationary boom and deflationary slump have caused many policy headaches in the past. Why was the recession of the mid 1970s accompanied not only by its familiar companion, high unemployment, but also by an unexpected fellow traveler, rapid inflation? Is the new disease of stagflation—simultaneous high unemployment and rapid inflation—here to stay?

The long-run trend of most advanced (and many less advanced) economies has been a rising total and per capita output accompanied by rising living standards. Does the recent slowdown of worldwide growth rates represent a change in underlying growth trends, or is it just a reflection of the prolonged cyclical downturn of the last half of the 1970s? Can governments do anything to change growth rates? If so, should they intervene

to accelerate economic growth, as one group advocates, or to slow it, as another group advocates?

KEY MACRO VARIABLES: DEFINITION AND BEHAVIOR

Many of the key variables whose behavior we study in macroeconomics are related to the price level, employment, and total output. Let us define some of these variables and see how they have behaved over the past half century.

The Price Level

The price level can be measured by any index of the economy's prices.[2] The three most common indexes are the CPI, which covers commodities bought by the "typical consumer"; the Wholesale Price Index, which covers wholesale prices; and the GNE deflator, which covers everything produced in the economy. The price level is usually denoted by the symbol P.

The annual rate of inflation is the percentage change in some price index from one year to the next. When the rate is measured by the CPI, the formula is:

$$\text{rate of inflation} = \frac{\text{this year's CPI} - \text{last year's CPI}}{\text{last year's CPI}} \times 100$$

The rate of inflation can be measured between various points in the two years. It is common to use year-end (CPI on December 31) or mid-year (CPI on July 1) figures or annual averages (average monthly CPI) in the above formula. Figure 28-1 shows the rate of inflation as measured by the rate of change of annual averages in the CPI.

Output Variables

There are several related measures of the country's total output. The one most commonly

---

[2] Price indexes are discussed on pages 33–35.

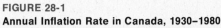

FIGURE 28-1
Annual Inflation Rate in Canada, 1930–1980

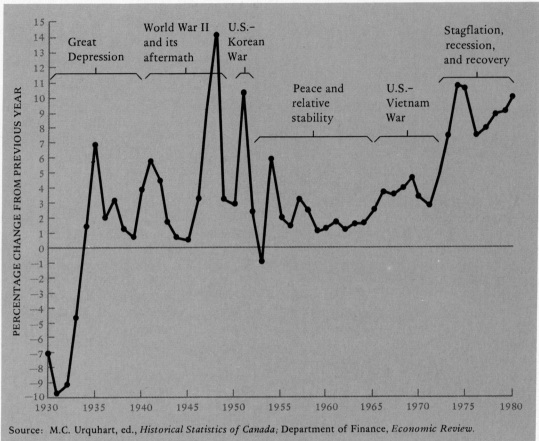

Source: M.C. Urquhart, ed., *Historical Statistics of Canada*; Department of Finance, *Economic Review*.

The rate of inflation has varied from −10 percent to +14 percent over the period since 1930. Prices fell dramatically during the onset of the Great Depression. They rose sharply during and after World War II and during the Korean War. Although variable, there was no discernible trend in the inflation rate from the end of the Korean War to the mid 1960s. The period starting in the mid 1960s, however, experienced a strong upward trend in the inflation rate, interrupted by short-term fluctuations.

used is called **gross national product (GNP)**. Its definition and calculation are discussed in the next chapter; here we merely note that it seeks to measure the total market value of the nation's output.

GNP may be measured in current dollars. This tells us the total value of the nation's output in prices ruling at the moment. It is then called **nominal GNP** or **current dollar GNP**, and its changes reflect changes both in quantities produced and in market prices.

GNP may also be measured in constant dollars. In this case the quantities produced in each year are valued in terms of prices ruling in some base year, such as 1971. It is then called **real GNP** or **constant dollar GNP**, and its changes reflect only quantity changes.

Total output is often denoted by the symbol Y.

FIGURE 28-2
Canadian GNP, 1930–1980, in Constant (1971) Dollars

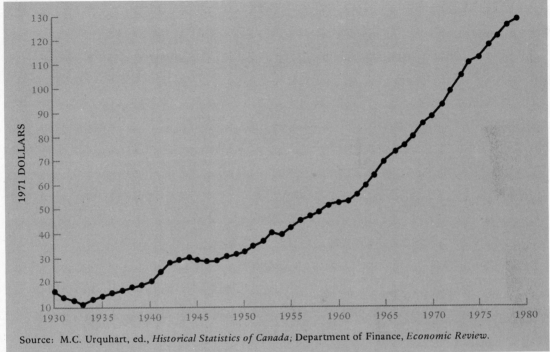

Source: M.C. Urquhart, ed., *Historical Statistics of Canada*; Department of Finance, *Economic Review*.

Constant dollar GNP measures the quantity of total output produced by the nation's economy over the period of a year. National product has risen steadily since the early 1930s, with only a few interruptions.

This represents the economic growth of the Canadian economy. Shorter-term fluctuations have occurred, but they are obscured by the long-term growth trend.

When used in this chapter, *Y* and the term *national product* refer to the nation's GNP measured in constant dollars, a measure of the total quantity of output produced in the economy.

Figure 28-2 shows real GNP produced by the Canadian economy since 1930. The series shows two kinds of movement. The major movement is a trend-increase in real output. The real output of the Canadian economy rose by over 700 percent in the half century from 1930 to 1980: this trend represents the economic growth of the Canadian economy. A secondary movement in the GNP series is that of the short-term fluctuations resulting from the cyclical behavior of the economy. The overall growth of the economy so dominates the GNP series that the cyclical behavior is

hardly visible in this figure. Cyclical patterns are more readily apparent in a series called the GNP gap.

Potential GNP and the GNP Gap

To define the GNP gap, we first need to define one new concept. **Potential GNP** or **full-employment GNP** is what the economy would produce if its productive resources were fully employed at their normal intensity of use. It may be measured either in current or in constant dollars, and it is given the symbol Y_F. *Actual GNP* is what the economy does in fact produce. When measured in current dollars it is *nominal income;* when measured in constant dollars it is

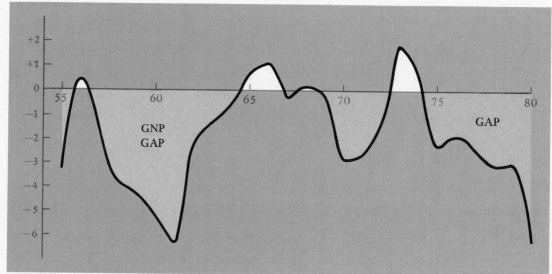

FIGURE 28-3
The GNP Gap in Canada, 1955–1980

The GNP gap measures the difference between the economy's potential output and its actual output; it is expressed here as a percentage of potential output. The cyclical behavior of the economy is clearly apparent from the behavior of the GNP gap. Slumps in economic activity cause large gaps, booms reduce the gap. The shaded area under the curve represents the deadweight loss from unemployment.

real income. The **GNP gap** is the difference between the two: potential GNP minus actual GNP. The GNP gap represents useful output—valuable goods and services—that *could have been* produced if the economy were fully employed but that actually goes unproduced. This is often referred to as the "deadweight loss" of unemployment.

Slumps in business activity are associated with large GNP gaps, booms with small ones. In a major boom the gap can even become negative, indicating that actual GNP exceeds the economy's potential GNP! This surprising result occurs because potential GNP is defined for a normal rate of utilization of factors of production, and there are many ways in which normal rates of utilization can be exceeded. Labor may work harder or work longer hours; factories may work an extra shift or not close for normal repairs and maintenance. (This is only a temporary expedient, but it is an effective one in the short term.)

Figure 28-3 shows the GNP gap for the Canadian economy expressed as a percentage of potential GNP. The fluctuations in economic activity are readily apparent from the fluctuations in the size of the gap. The deadweight loss from unemployment over any time span is indicated by the overall size of the gap over this span (i.e., by the shaded area under the curve between the two points in question).

Labor Variables

Employment denotes the number of adult workers who hold full-time civilian jobs. **Unemployment** denotes the number of persons who are not employed and are actively searching for a job. The civilian **labor force** is the total number of the employed, other than those serving in the armed services, plus the unemployed. The **unemployment rate**, usually denoted by the sym-

FIGURE 28-4
Labor Force, Employment, and Unemployment in Canada, 1930–1979

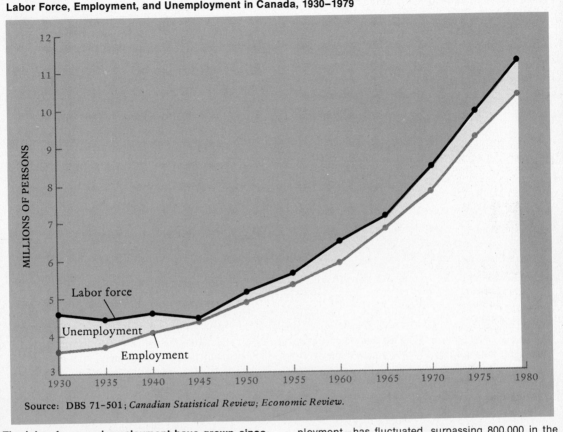

Source: DBS 71–501; *Canadian Statistical Review; Economic Review.*

The labor force and employment have grown since the 1930s with only a few interruptions. The size of the Canadian labor force has more than doubled since 1930, and so has the number of the employed. Unemployment—the gap between the labor force and em-ployment—has fluctuated, surpassing 800,000 in the 1930s and again in the late 1970s. In the 1930s the number unemployed was a much larger fraction of the labor force than it was in the late 1970s.

bol U, is unemployment expressed as a percentage of the labor force:

unemployment rate $(U) =$

$$\frac{\text{unemployed}}{\text{number in the labor force}} \times 100$$

Figure 28-4 shows labor force, employment, and unemployment in Canada. In spite of the much-discussed occurrences of business booms and slumps and inflations and deflations, the main trend of the economy has clearly been one of growth in employment that roughly matches the growth in the labor force. This is part of the economic growth of the economy. Some unemployment, however, is always present, and it fluctuates with the ebb and flow of business activity. This is part of the short-term cyclical behavior of the economy.

As with the GNP, the long-term growth trend dominates the employment figures. This unemployment *rate* graphed in Figure 28-5 gives a better picture of the effects of the shorter-term cyclical behavior of the economy on unemployment.

FIGURE 28-5
Percentage of the Labor Force Unemployed in Canada, 1930–1980

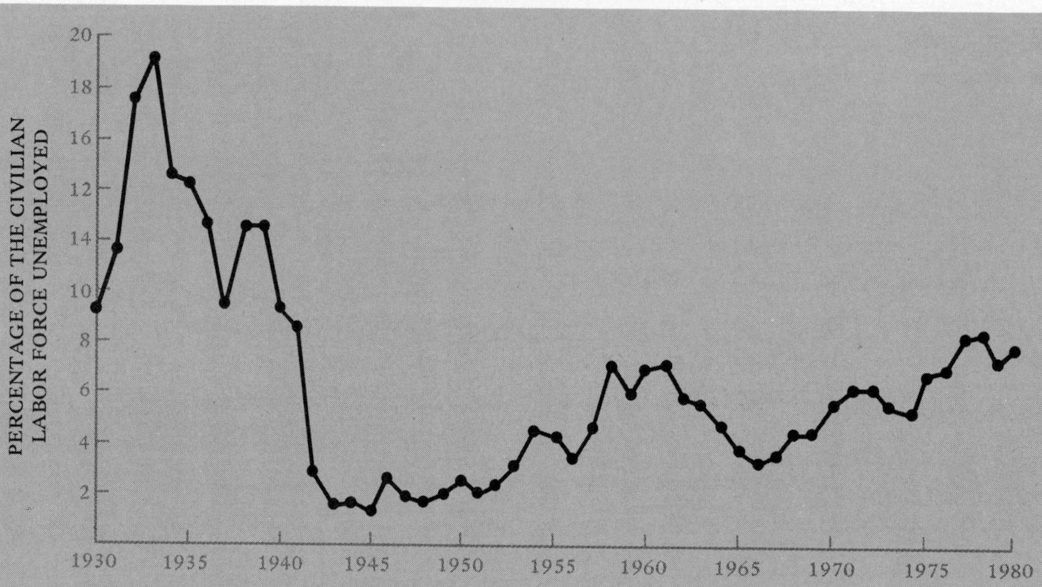

Source: DBS 71–501; *Canadian Statistical Review; Economic Review.*

The unemployment rate responds to the cyclical behavior of the economy. Booms are associated with low unemployment, slumps with high unemployment. The Great Depression of the 1930s produced record unemployment figures for an entire decade. During World War II unemployment rates fell to very low levels. The recession in the mid 1970s produced unemployment rates second only to those of the 1930s; these rates were extremely large by the standards of the post-World War II behavior of the Canadian economy.

Relations Between Output and Employment Variables

Output, employment, and unemployment are closely related to one another. If more is to be produced, either more workers must be used in production or existing workers must produce more. The first change means a rise in employment, the second a rise in output per person employed, which is called a rise in productivity. Increases in productivity are a major cause of economic growth.

A rise in unemployment will occur if output falls and some people lose their jobs as a result. It will also occur if, with the same amount of employment, the labor force grows. For example, the number of people finishing school to enter the labor force might exceed the number leaving the labor force because of retirement and death.

Changes in productivity and the labor force dominate the long-term behavior of such variables as output and employment. (They are discussed in Chapter 43, on economic growth.) But productivity and the labor force generally change only a little from one year to the next, and thus they have little effect on the short-term behavior of the economy. We assume for the time being that the labor force and productivity are constant, in order to concentrate on the shorter-term cyclical behavior. Assuming them to be constant is a reasonable approximation to reality *for purposes of analyzing* the short-term behavior of the economy.

When the labor force and productivity are constant, unemployment varies inversely with output while employment varies directly with output.

Aggregate Demand and Aggregate Supply

We want to investigate the causes of changes in the price level and in real national product (and, through national product, changes in employment and unemployment). One way to do this is by using the concepts of demand and supply.

In Chapter 5 we saw that the interaction of demand and supply in competitive markets determines prices and quantities for individual commodities. If we had a single demand curve and a single supply curve for the whole economy, we could determine the economy's price level and its total national product just as we can determine price and quantity for a single product such as wheat or breakfast cereal.

This possibility is illustrated in Figure 28-6, which assumes the existence of an aggregate demand curve and an aggregate supply curve for the entire economy. The **aggregate demand curve** (*AD*) shows a relation between the total amount of all output that will be demanded by purchasers and the price level of that output. The **aggregate supply curve** (*AS*) shows a relation between the total amount of output that will be produced and the price level of that output.

In fact, aggregate demand and aggregate supply curves can be derived, though it takes some time and care to do so. For the moment let us see what we can do with these curves if we simply assume that they exist.

THE SHAPES OF THE AGGREGATE CURVES

The aggregate demand curve typically slopes downward to the right, as shown by the *AD* curve in Figure 28-6. This shape means that, *ceteris paribus*, the higher the price level, the smaller the total quantity demanded will be; and the

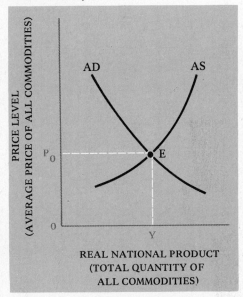

FIGURE 28-6
The Price Level and National Product for the Whole Economy

Aggregate demand and aggregate supply determine the price level and national product for the entire economy. Equilibrium is at *E* with the price level P_0 and a national product of *Y*. At higher price levels aggregate supply exceeds aggregate demand; at lower price levels aggregate demand exceeds aggregate supply.

lower the price level, the larger the total quantity demanded will be.

The aggregate supply curve shown in Figure 28-6 describes a short-term relation between the price level and national product. Its upward slope indicates that, *ceteris paribus*, the higher the price level, the greater the quantity supplied will be (at least over the short term). There are three interesting possibilities for the shape of this curve. At one time or another each of the three possibilities has been relevant. We can capture them by drawing, as in Figure 28-7, a composite aggregate supply curve with three ranges.

To the left of Y_0 the *AS* curve is horizontal. Over that range national product can be increased without any increase in the price level. This indicates that national product will vary

FIGURE 28-7
A Composite Aggregate Supply Curve

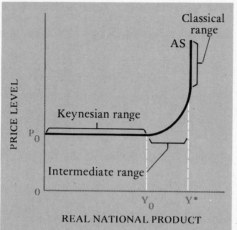

A composite aggregate supply curve can be
seen as composed of the three distinct ranges.
Over the Keynesian (horizontal) range the price
level is constant but real national product can
vary. Over the classical (vertical) range real national product is constant while the price level
can vary. Over the intermediate range real national product and the price level vary with each
other.

without significant accompanying variations in the
price level. This range may be called Keynesian because it is associated with the pioneering
work of John Maynard Keynes, who studied the
behavior of economies with heavy unemployment. This is the depression case, in which there
is substantial unemployment of all kinds of resources. Output can be increased without running into shortages and bottlenecks.

At Y^* the AS curve is vertical, indicating that
production cannot be expanded beyond Y^*, even
if prices rise. Output Y^* is the maximum that can
be produced when all of the economy's resources
are being fully utilized. The vertical portion of
AS is labeled classical because the so-called classical economists studied the economy under conditions of full utilization of all resources. They
assumed that in such circumstances no more output can be squeezed out of existing resources. If
there is an increase in aggregate demand, prices
will rise but output cannot increase.

Between Y_0 and Y^* there is an intermediate
range over which AS slopes upward. In this
range there is scope for some increase in output,
but as output rises, shortages will develop. The
excess demand for commodities that are in short
supply will force up the average of all prices
along with output. In the intermediate range of
the AS curve, therefore, prices and output vary
directly with each other.

It is important to distinguish between maximum or capacity output, Y^*, and *potential* or
full employment output defined earlier. Capacity
output represents a physical constraint on output
beyond which it is impossible to produce. Full
employment output arises when all factors of
production are employed at their *normal* intensity of use, a concept that will be given more explicit meaning later. Full employment is generally considered to occur at a level of output
below maximum capacity output, for the obvious
reason that, at least temporarily, factors can be
utilized more intensely than normal.[3] The implications of maintaining output above its full employment level are analysed in detail in Chapter
39.

It is a mistake to think that each economy has
a unique aggregate supply curve or that its shape
is always the same. The aggregate supply curve
expresses a short-term relation between the price
level and national income that is suitable for analyzing short-term fluctuations in the level of business activity. The relevant aggregate supply
curve may sometimes look like the curve in Figure 28-6 and sometimes like only one of the segments of the curve in Figure 28-7.

The composite curve of Figure 28-7 catches a
simplified essence of three situations: *depression,* where the price level is relatively constant;
full employment, where output cannot be increased; and a period of *modest slack* in the
economy, where output and the price level tend to
change together.

[3] The vertical portion of the AS curve illustrated in Figure
28-7 is labeled classical because the classical economists are
often interpreted as believing that output could not be pushed
beyond its full employment for any significant period of time.
In this interpretation, the concepts of capacity and full-
employment output merge.

SHIFTS IN THE AGGREGATE CURVES

What will happen to total output and the price level if one or both of the aggregate curves shift? Shifts in aggregate demand and aggregate supply are often called demand shocks and supply shocks respectively.

Increases in Aggregate Demand

Figure 28-8 shows how increases in aggregate demand affect the economy over the three ranges of the single composite *AS* curve. Over the Keynesian range, where there is general unemployment of resources, a rise in aggregate demand raises output without raising the price level. In this case any government (or private) policy that increases demand will increase output and employment while decreasing unemployment.

Increases in aggregate demand over the intermediate range of the *AS* curve affect both price and output. The economy is close enough to full-capacity output that increases in output can be made only at the cost of some inflation. The further one moves to the right along the *AS* curve, the steeper it becomes. As a result, the effect of successive increases in aggregate demand is felt more and more on prices and less and less on output.

Finally, in the classical range there is full utilization of all factors of production. Increases in aggregate demand leave output unchanged but cause prices to rise. This is the range of a pure demand inflation. All increases in demand in this range are inflationary and bring no offsetting gain in terms of extra output or employment.

Shifts in Aggregate Supply

Figure 28-9 shows the effects of an upward shift in the *AS* curve with no change in *AD:* the price level rises and output falls. This combination of events is now called stagflation. This rather inelegant word was derived by running together "stagnation" (less than full employment) and

FIGURE 28-8

The Effects of Increases in Aggregate Demand

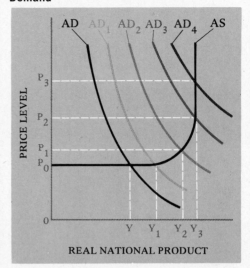

Increases in aggregate demand may cause an increase in output alone, an increase in both output and prices, or an increase in prices alone. An increase in aggregate demand from *AD* to AD_1 increases total output from *Y* to Y_1, leaving the price level unchanged. An increase to AD_2 raises output from Y_1 to Y_2 and raises the price level from P_0 to P_1. An increase to AD_3 brings a smaller increase in output (from Y_2 to Y_3) and a larger increase in the price level (from P_1 to P_2). An increase to AD_4 raises the price level from P_2 to P_3 but leaves output constant at Y_3.

"inflation" (a rise in the price level). **Stagflation** therefore refers to inflations that occur when national income is below its full-employment level. In Figure 28-9 the price level rises while national product actually falls (which implies a growing GNP gap).

AGGREGATE DEMAND AND SUPPLY IN ACTION

The tools of aggregate demand and aggregate supply can be used to give a brief overview of some of the major macro events of the last 50 years. (These events will be studied in more detail in Chapter 41.)

FIGURE 28-9

The Effect of Shifts in Aggregate Supply

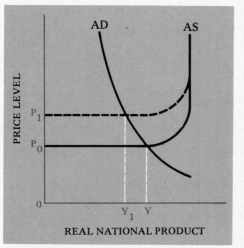

Upward shifts in aggregate supply raise prices but lower output. The original curves are AD and P_0AS. The aggregate supply curve then shifts upward to P_1AS. The shift causes output to fall from Y to Y_1 and the price level to rise from P_0 to P_1. Here a rising price level is associated with a falling level of output.

The 1930s. In the Great Depression of the 1930s, the economy could be thought of as being on the Keynesian portion of a relatively stable AS curve. The AD curve, however, was shifting. This exposed the economy to a series of demand shocks that changed national product, employment, and unemployment. Economists looked for ways in which government policy could be used to shift the AD curve to the right and thus raise output and employment.

The 1940s. During World War II the vast government purchases of war supplies increased AD and pushed the economy to full employment. After that the economy was in the classical (vertical) portion of the aggregate supply curve. Full employment and inflationary pressures prevailed. After 1941 the inflation rate was held to the low figures shown in Figure 28-1 by direct wage and price controls. When the controls were removed, the excess aggregate demand made its

presence felt in the dramatic postwar inflation that greatly increased the price level. Economists studied ways of restraining aggregate demand in order to control inflation.

1950–1965. Aggregate demand fluctuated mainly over the intermediate range on a relatively stable AS curve. Increases in aggregate demand tended to increase both national product and the price level. Because of the downward inflexibility of prices, however, decreases in aggregate demand tended to lower national product and employment while leaving the price level unchanged. Economists looked for ways to reduce the demand shocks so that output, employment, and prices could be made as stable as possible.

1965–1973. The buildup of American defense spending to finance the accelerating war in Vietnam hit the U.S. economy with a severe demand shock that took it and the Canadian economy again into the classical range of full employment and rising prices. Although there were lapses from full employment, the period was mainly one of excess demand. It culminated in the boom of 1972–1973, when excess demand throughout the world created strong worldwide inflationary pressure. The inflation rate reached 7.5 percent. Economists suggested ways in which aggregate demand could be reduced in order to alleviate the growing inflationary pressure.

1974–1980. The boom of the first part of the decade ended in 1974 with the onset of the most severe recession since the 1930s. At that time, the economy was hit with severe supply shocks. Serious crop failures combined with the sale of surplus wheat to the USSR raised food prices greatly. OPEC policies forced up not only the price of energy but the prices of fertilizer, plastics, synthetic rubber, and dozens of other products produced from petroleum. High prices and shortages of oil caused buyers to shift to such alternative energy sources as coal, and this in turn drove their prices up. All these forces pushed the aggregate supply curve upward because they increased the price level. The upward shift in the *AS* curve brought about a serious stagflation. For the first time the economy experienced simultaneously the twin "evils" of falling output and rising prices.

The mid 1970s were the first time in the last half century that a major part of the explanation of the behavior of prices and output lay in an upward-shifting aggregate supply curve. The public was so used to the behavior of the economy under the impact of demand-side shocks that behavior under severe supply-side shocks seemed incomprehensible, even paradoxical. Economists were so used to explaining observed events by demand-side shocks that many of them did not at first appreciate what was happening. Some announced the collapse of conventional macroeconomic theory; others claimed to see a complete change in all economic behavior. Although plausible at the time, such reactions can now be seen to have been excessive—once the part played by aggregate supply is appreciated.

THE SHAPES OF THE AGGREGATE CURVES EXPLAINED

Up to now we have assumed that we could draw aggregate demand and supply curves for the whole economy analogous to the curves we know we can draw for individual competitive markets. If we could simply aggregate all the demand and supply curves in individual markets to obtain aggregate demand and supply curves, there would be little left to do but to apply our aggregate tools to those aspects of macro behavior in which we were interested. Unfortunately, life is not so simple. Let us see why we cannot take such an approach.

The Fallacy of Composition

If we assumed that we could add up market demand curves for each individual commodity to obtain a downward-sloping aggregate demand curve, we would be committing the *fallacy of composition*. This is to assume that what is correct for the parts must be correct for the whole.

Consider a simple example of the fallacy. Any art collector can go into the market and add to a collection of nineteenth century French paintings provided only that he or she has enough money. But to assume that because any one person can do this, everyone could do so simultaneously is plainly wrong. The stock of nineteenth century French paintings in the world is totally fixed. All of us cannot do what any one of us may be able to do.

How does the fallacy of composition relate to demand and supply curves?

The Shape of the Aggregate Demand Curve

The demand curve for an individual commodity slopes downward for two basic reasons. First, as the price of a particular commodity rises, consumers buy less of it and more of now relatively cheaper substitutes. Second, as the price of one commodity rises, each consumer's given money income will buy a smaller total amount of goods, so a smaller quantity of the commodity in question will be bought.

The second explanation does not apply to the aggregate demand curve, and the first must be applied very cautiously; however, there are additional reasons for expecting the *aggregate* demand curve to slope downward to the right.

Why does the second reason stated above not apply to the aggregate curve, which relates total quantity demanded to the *price level?* A change in the price level means a change both in prices of commodities and in prices of factors of production, which includes wages and salaries. Thus a rise in the price level does not necessarily lead to a general loss of purchasing power. This is because it also leads to a rise in the average money incomes of households. When people have more income, they can increase their money expenditure. For example, a 10 percent rise in all prices, causing a 10 percent rise in all money incomes, might be expected to cause a 10 percent rise in money expenditure and leave the quantities of goods bought and sold unchanged. The reasons why the aggregate demand curve *does* slope downward to the right are in fact reasons why the 10 percent increase in money incomes does not lead to a 10 percent increase in money expenditure on domestically produced goods.

There are three basic reasons for expecting the aggregate demand curve to slope downward to the right.

Substitution of foreign goods. When the price level rises, domestic goods become expensive relative to foreign goods. This is true for both Canadians and foreign consumers of Canadian goods. Canadian residents will now find it advantageous to reduce their purchases of Canadian goods and to buy imported foreign goods instead. Foreign consumers will find it advantageous to reduce their purchases of Canadian exports. Since the aggregate demand curve describes the demand for Canadian goods by both foreigners and Canadians, the aggregate demand curve will slope downward.[4]

A rise in the Canadian price level, *ceteris paribus*, reduces foreign demand for Canadian exports and leads Canadians to buy foreign imports rather than increasingly expensive Canadian commodities. Thus, *ceteris paribus*, the higher the price level, the lower the quantity demanded of the nation's output.

Money and interest rate effects. The second reason why the *aggregate* demand curve slopes downward is to be found in the effects of money on interest rates and of interest rates on total purchases (topics to be discussed later in the book). The main forces are only suggested here; the logic will be apparent later when the necessary links in the argument have each been studied.

When the price of everything rises, firms need more money to finance their payrolls and other purchases of factors of production. And households need more money in the bank to cover their expenses between each payday and the next. *Ceteris paribus*, this extra need for money creates a shortage of money. When money is in short supply, interest rates tend to rise. Firms that borrow money to invest in plant and equipment and households that borrow money to buy consumer goods are responsive to rising interest rates. As rates go up they wish to spend less on capital goods, housing, and other classes of expenditure that are sensitive to interest rates. But this means a decline in the aggregate quantity demanded of the nation's output.

A rise in the price level creates a shortage of money, which drives up interest rates. This in turn discourages interest-sensitive expenditures. Thus, *ceteris paribus*, the higher the price level, the lower the quantity demanded of the nation's output.

The full explanation can be found in Chapter 38.

Direct money balance effect on expenditure. The third reason why a rise in the price level leads to a fall in aggregate demand comes from the fact that many assets that people hold as part of their wealth are denominated in terms of money. When the price level rises, the real purchasing power of these assets is reduced; consequently people holding these assets are worse off. When I hold a $1,000 bond and the price level doubles, the amount of commodities I can buy when the bond is redeemed falls by half. The bond's real value halves, and hence the real value of my net wealth falls. Thus a rise in the price level may cause a direct reduction in aggregate consumption as those who have suffered from the reduction in the value of their assets will increase their savings in order to recoup their lost wealth.

A rise in the price level lowers the real value of some assets. If as a result people spend less in order to save more, the aggregate demand for the nation's output will fall, *ceteris paribus*.

---

[4] As we saw in Chapter 8, domestic inflation will tend to lead to a depreciation of the exchange rate; thus the *relative* price of domestic goods will not rise by as much as indicated by the initial rise in the price level.

The Shape of the Aggregate Supply Curve

If we tried to derive an aggregate supply curve by adding up the changes in the quantity supplied of each commodity when its price rises, *ceteris paribus,* we would again be committing the fallacy of composition. This is because the things held constant along an individual supply curve do not remain constant when *all* prices change. The explanation of the shape of the composite aggregate supply curve turns out to be simpler than that of the aggregate demand curve.

The Keynesian portion. The horizontal shape of the *AS* curve in the Keynesian portion is a result of two forces. First, there are unemployed supplies of all resources, so output can be increased without placing *upward* pressure on prices. Second, prices are relatively rigid downward, and thus they do not fall enough to have an important influence in spite of excess supply in both labor markets and goods markets.

The absence of upward pressure on prices when there is excess supply is not surprising. But why do prices and wages not fall when firms have excess capacity and there are many unemployed workers? Why does competition among unemployed labor for the available jobs not force wages down? Why does competition among firms, all of whom would like to sell more, not force prices of commodities down?

Certainly prices would fall in perfectly competitive markets. Indeed, the prices of some basic raw materials—tin, copper, and iron, for example—do fall during a depression. But it is a matter of common observation that during a depression there is substantial *downward rigidity* in wages and in the prices of manufactured goods. In spite of a sizable excess supply of labor, money wages do not fall. Since wages are a major part of most firms' costs, this rigidity holds costs up and makes firms less likely to cut prices in the hope of gaining new sales. Further, most manufactured goods are not sold on perfectly competitive markets but are produced by large firms that set their own prices. Such firms are

reluctant to get into price wars with their rivals; instead they are inclined to hold prices relatively stable and cut production when demand for their product falls in a recession.

Of course all prices are not completely inflexible downward. Figure 28-1, for example, reveals that the price level was not constant during the Great Depression. It fell dramatically in the three years 1931–1933. After 1933, however, there were no further major reductions in the price level even in the face of an enormous GNP gap. The average change in the price level over the entire period of depression from 1933 to 1939 was a *rise* of just less than 1.5 percent per year.

The Keynesian (horizontal) portion of the aggregate supply curve is not intended, then, to be an exact description of an economy in depression. It is meant instead to capture in simple form the essential condition that has prevailed in every subsequent recession and depression: the price level does not fall significantly in the presence of those GNP gaps that the economy has actually experienced.

The classical portion. The classical (vertical) portion of the aggregate supply curve is derived from the simplifying assumption that when all resources are fully utilized, real output reaches its "full-capacity ceiling," which cannot be exceeded. As with the Keynesian portion of the *AS* curve, this is a simplification that is meant to capture a slightly more complex reality. In fact it is almost always possible to squeeze more output out of the economy. After all, three shifts a day could be worked, and every able-bodied man, woman, and child could be employed.

Although there is no absolute full-employment ceiling to output, the vertical section of the *AS* curve catches the reality that under usual conditions there is some level of output beyond which output will not respond significantly to further increases in aggregate demand. Recall that *full employment* output, which arises when all factors are employed at their *normal* level of utilization, may occur before the capacity output constraint is reached. This is discussed in detail in Chapter 39.

The intermediate portion. The intermediate portion occurs because economic growth imposes a constant need for change in the economy. This means that all sectors of the economy are never in perfect balance with each other at any moment in time. Some industries will be enjoying rapidly rising demands; they will be struggling to increase capacity in order to keep pace. Other industries will find their demands growing slowly or even declining; they will have a higher margin of extra capacity. Similarly, labor in some skill and industry classifications and geographical areas will be in very short supply while other labor will be in more abundant supply relative to the demand for it.

These inevitable imbalances in the economy mean that as production expands toward its full-employment level, shortages and bottlenecks will first appear in some but not all product and labor markets. Prices and wages will begin to rise in these markets while there is still some slack in other markets of the economy. As total output continues to increase, more and more shortages and capacity limits will be encountered, so more prices will start to rise and it will become harder and harder to obtain further increases in output. Thus the economy does not run into a capacity constraint abruptly, like a car hitting a brick wall. Instead, like a car running up an ever steepening hill, real progress becomes harder and harder to achieve as output expands further and further. Output increases by smaller and smaller amounts and more and more prices are forced up, so the *AS* curve becomes steeper and steeper the higher output is within this range.

The ratchet effect. There is a further basic and very important property of the *AS* curve that must be understood. The problem arises because the Keynesian portion of the aggregate supply curve depends on the assumption that prices are rigid downward: when demand falls, firms reduce output but do not reduce prices.

To see the importance of this downward rigidity of prices consider Figure 28-8 once again. Assume that aggregate demand shifts rightward enough to cause the price level to rise and then shifts leftward back to its original position (say, from *AD* to AD_4 and back to *AD* again). Given downward rigidity of prices, the price level cannot fall back to its original level. The original aggregate demand curve will now be associated with a higher price level. (This is not shown in Figure 28-8, which is suitable for analyzing a sequence of *increases* in aggregate demand but not decreases.)

We must now amend our aggregate supply analysis in order to deal with declines as well as increases in aggregate demand. A simplification will help: we reduce our composite aggregate supply curve to include just the Keynesian and the classical cases. This suppression of the intermediate case leaves us with the two extremes shown in Figure 28-10: depression where output can be varied at constant prices and full employment where output cannot rise but the price level can.

The change required to deal with decreases in *AD* is shown in Figure 28-10. (It should be studied carefully.) Because the price level can rise but does not normally fall by any significant amount, the Keynesian (horizontal) portion of the *AS* curve is always at the *current* price level. Whenever the price level rises, the Keynesian portion rises as well. We speak of it being "ratcheted" up, a ratchet being a device that allows a wheel to turn one way but not the other. The downward rigidity of prices requires the ratcheting up of the Keynesian portion of the *AS* curve whenever the actual price level rises.

Starting from equilibrium positions on the classical portion of the aggregate supply curve, a rise in aggregate demand will raise the price level, leaving national product unchanged. This leads to a new Keynesian portion of the aggregate supply curve so that a fall in aggregate demand will lower national product, leaving the price level unchanged.

FIGURE 28-10
The Ratchet Effect on Aggregate Supply

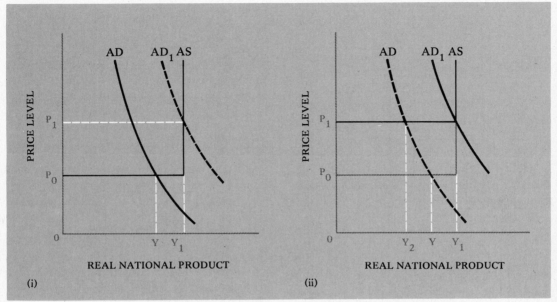

(i)

(ii)

A rise in aggregate demand raises the price level, but a fall in *AD* does not lower the price level. Suppose the economy begins in (i) on the Keynesian (horizontal) range of the aggregate supply curve, with aggregate demand *AD,* at price level P_0 and a national product of *Y.* A large demand shock then shifts aggregate demand to AD_1, the price level to P_1, and national product to Y_1. Because the price level is inflexible downward, the Keynesian portion of the aggregate supply curve now shifts upward to P_1. This indicates that once the price level has risen to P_1, prices will never again fall to P_0. The new aggregate supply curve is shown in (ii) by the heavy *AS* line, the old curve by the screened line.

Now suppose aggregate demand shifts back to *AD.* In (ii) this lowers national product to Y_2 but leaves the price level at P_1. (If the aggregate supply curve had not ratcheted upward, the fall in aggregate demand from AD_1 back to *AD* would have reduced national product only to *Y* while returning the price level to P_0.)

THE GAME PLAN

In this chapter we have only *assumed* most characteristics of the aggregate demand and supply curves. But if we are to use these tools of analysis, we need to understand their shapes more fully and what causes them to shift. For this it will be necessary to understand their components.

In Chapter 29 we consider the meaning of the basic concept of national product. In Chapters 30 and 31 we see what determines the position of the aggregate demand curve and what causes it to shift. We will then be able to study in Chapters 32 and 34 those forces that arise from private market decisions and from government fiscal policy decisions that affect the economy by shifting the aggregate demand curve. In Chapter 33 we outline the extensions to the model required by the major role of international goods in the Canadian economy, and we analyze the relationship between national income, expenditure, and the balance of trade.

In Chapters 35 to 38 we consider the role of money in the economy. In Chapter 35 we study the history and importance of money. In Chapter 36 we examine the international monetary system, and in Chapter 37 we consider the institutions in the domestic monetary sector and the determinants of the supply of money. In Chapter

38 we study the shape of the aggregate demand curve and explain more fully why it slopes downward to the right. In that chapter we also see how changes in the government's monetary policy can influence real national income and the price level by shifting the aggregate demand curve.

In Chapters 39, 40, and 41 we use the tools of aggregate demand and aggregate supply to understand more fully the causes of the macroeconomic ills of the last 10 to 15 years. We also assess some of the proposed curves for these ills. In Chapter 42 we look briefly at some of the major policy controversies whose outcome will seriously affect the economy's macro performance and the welfare of all its citizens.

Summary

1. Macroeconomics studies the behavior of such broad aggregates and averages as the price level, national product, potential GNP, the GNP gap, employment, and unemployment.

2. The dominant theme of the economy is the growth of real output and employment. In order to isolate shorter-term cyclical factors, we assume that the labor force and productivity are constant. Then we focus attention on the GNP gap and the unemployment rate.

3. Two major tools of macroeconomics are the aggregate demand and aggregate supply curves. Typically the aggregate demand curve slopes downward, indicating a lower demand for the nation's output the higher the price level.

4. Three typical situations can be captured in a composite aggregate supply curve with three sections. The first section is the Keynesian (horizontal) portion, where the price level is fixed and output can vary. The second section is the intermediate portion, over which both the price level and output can vary. The third section is the classical (vertical) portion, over which output is fixed but the price level can vary. These stylized versions are intended to capture the essence of depressionary, mild slack, and full-capacity situations without pretending to be exact descriptions of each.

5. Most of the year-to-year experience of the economy has been generated by a shifting aggregate demand curve acting on a relatively stable aggregate supply curve. This tends to associate inflations with periods of high and rising output and stable prices with periods of low and falling output.

6. Supply-side shocks that came into prominence in the 1970s tend to associate rising prices with periods of falling output. This association can be readily understood in terms of a shifting aggregate supply curve acting on a relatively stable aggregate demand curve.

7. The slope of the aggregate demand curve will be explained in full in later chapters. It arises for three basic reasons. First, when the price level rises domestic goods become expensive relative to foreign goods, and hence Canadian and foreign consumers will reduce their purchases of Canadian goods. Second, an increase in the price level, *ceteris paribus,* creates a shortage of money that drives up interest rates. Higher interest rates in turn cause firms to demand less capital goods and households to demand less new consumer goods. Both represent a fall in the demand for the nation's output. Third, a rise in the price level reduces the real value of some assets and hence may encourage increased saving and hence reduced consumption.

8. Each segment of the composite aggregate supply curve has its own explanation. The Keynesian portion arises because prices and wages do not tend to fall by significant amounts even in the face of large GNP gaps. The intermediate portion arises because as output expands, more and more capacity limitations, bottlenecks, and shortages are encountered, making further increases in output even more difficult and forcing still larger increases in prices as output does increase. The classical (vertical) portion arises from the assumption that a full-employment output hits an absolute capacity ceiling.

9. Because the price level is inflexible downward, the aggregate supply curve is subject to a ratchet effect. The Keynesian portion is always at the existing price level. Thus, if the price level rises, the Keynesian portion will move up with it. This means that in the region of full employment, increases in aggregate demand will tend to cause prices to rise while decreases in demand will tend to cause output to fall.

Topics for Review

Measures of the price level and the rate of inflation
National income, potential GNP, and the GNP gap
Employment, unemployment, and the labor force
Aggregate demand and aggregate supply
When high and rising output will be associated with rising prices
When falling output will be associated with rising prices
Keynesian, classical, and intermediate portions of an aggregate supply curve
Downward inflexibility of prices
The ratchet effect

Discussion Questions

1. Classify as micro or macro (or both) the issues raised in the following newspaper headlines.
   a. "Lettuce crop spoils as strike hits California lettuce producers."
   b. "Price of bus rides soar in Centersville as city council withdraws transport subsidy."
   c. "A fall in the unemployment rate signals the beginning of the end of the recession in the Windsor area."
   d. "Silicon chip technology brings falling prices and growing sales of minicomputers."
   e. "Wage settlements in key industries seen to pose inflationary threat."
   f. "Rising costs of imported raw materials cause most manufacturers to raise prices."
   g. "Index of Industrial Production falls by 4 points."

2. Explain each of the following by shifts in either (or both) the aggregate demand and aggregate supply curve. (Pay attention to the initial position before the shift(s) occurs.)
   a. Output and unemployment rise while prices hold steady.
   b. Prices soar but employment and output hold steady.
   c. Inflation accelerates even as the recession in business activity deepens.
   d. The inflation rate falls, but at the expense of employment.

3. Which of the following statements are examples of the fallacy of composition?
   a. "There is no real problem of unemployment today because help wanted columns are full of unfilled jobs."
   b. Because 10 percent of a random sample of the Canadian population is Asian, 10 percent of the whole Canadian population is probably Asian.
   c. There is no shortage of machinists in Plainsville— anyone who needs a machinist can get one quickly if willing to pay above market wages.
   d. If I am guaranteed a right in Canada, everyone is guaranteed that right.

4. In 1979–1980, the British government greatly reduced income taxes but restored the lost government revenue by raising excise and sales taxes. This led to a short burst of extra inflation and a fall in employment. Explain this in terms of shifts in aggregate demand and/or supply.

5. For each of the following events, indicate whether it is the cause or the consequence of a shift in aggregate demand or supply. If it is a cause, what do you predict will be the effect on the price level and on real national income?
   a. Unemployment increases in 1979 in Canada.
   b. OPEC once again raises oil prices.
   c. Country X is suffering a rapid inflation under conditions of approximately full employment.
   d. In country Y, income and employment continues to fall while the price level is quite stable.
   e. The recovery of the economy has led to a large increase in income and employment.
   f. The government decreases taxes sharply in an effort to stimulate the economy.

The Concepts of National Product and National Income

29

In the preceding chapter we saw how we could use the tools of aggregate demand and aggregate supply to explain the macro behavior of the economy. An important part of this explanation depends on the position of the aggregate demand curve. In order to understand why this curve is where it is, and what makes it shift, we need to look at the individual components of aggregate demand. In this chapter we see how the component parts of aggregate demand are defined and measured.

The aggregate demand curve, like the aggregate supply curve, relates the price level to the economy's total output, or *real national product*. This is the total market value of all goods and services produced in the economy during a year.

Closely related to real national product is the generic concept of *real national income*. This is all the income generated by the production of the national product. Clearly, much of the market value of output goes to pay the wages of workers who help to make the output; some goes as gross profit to firms that produce the commodities; and another portion goes to pay sales taxes that give governments a claim on some of the market value of production.

National Income Accounting

National income accounting is the set of rules and techniques for measuring the total flow of output (goods and services) produced and the total flow of incomes generated by this production. Let us see exactly what national income includes, how it is measured, and what it can tell us.

A standard convention of double-entry bookkeeping is that all value produced must be accounted for by a claim that someone has to it. National product is the market value of all the production in the economy over a year, while national income is the value of all the claims generated by that production. Thus it is a matter of accounting convention that these two values be equal.

National product and national income are alternative ways of looking at one magnitude: the market value of the nation's output.

Because both concepts have the same total value, we can use the terms national income and national product interchangeably whenever we are interested only in their total value. National product emphasizes the economy's output; national income emphasizes the income generated by producing that output. In Chapter 28 we spoke of national product to emphasize the quantity-of-output aspect of the aggregate demand and supply diagrams. In theoretical work the total value of output is more often referred to as national income.

Corresponding to the two concepts of national product and national income are two ways of arriving at the total value of the nation's output.

THE OUTPUT-EXPENDITURE APPROACH TO NATIONAL INCOME

Value of Expenditure and Value of Output

The output-expenditure approach to measuring the total value of output calculates the total expenditure needed to purchase the nation's output. If all production were sold directly to households, one could in theory add up all household expenditure on currently produced commodities to get the total value of the nation's output. In our complex economy, however, many groups other than households purchase the marketed part of the economy's output, while another part is not sold at all (because it is held by firms for future sale). In these circumstances, it is often simpler to calculate the market value of producers' total output directly rather than calculate the expenditure on that output by those who purchase it. Both approaches will yield the same total because they merely measure opposite sides of the same transactions. (When the bookstore sells you a book for $19.95, *its sale* and *your purchase* are each $19.95.)

The Problem of Double Counting

When we seek to arrive at the total value of output by looking at the output or sales of individual firms, we run into a complication caused by stages of production. Firms usually carry the production of something to a certain stage and then sell it to other firms. They in turn carry production further and then sell to another set of firms. From raw material to final product, many firms may be involved in the various stages of production. Under these circumstances we cannot calculate the total output of the economy by simply adding up the outputs of all firms. For the total value of sales of all firms would be greater than the total value of production available for use. Furthermore, the total value of sales depends on how many firms are involved in the stages of production of a commodity, while the value of the commodity finally produced does not.

Suppose, for example, we took the value of all farmers' sales of wheat and added to it all sales of flour by flour mills, all sales of bread by wholesale bakeries, and all sales of bread by retail stores. Our total figure would be much larger than the value of the final product, the bread produced by the economy. For we would have counted the value of the wheat four times, the flour three times, the bread produced by the bakery twice, and the service of the retail store once.

This is the problem of *double counting* (though for obvious reasons "multiple counting" would be a better term). To avoid it, national income accountants use the important concept of value added. Each firm's **value added** is the value of its output *minus* the value of the inputs that it purchases from other firms. Thus a flour mill's value added is the value of its output of flour

Value Added Through Stages of Production

Because the output of one firm often becomes the input of other firms, the total value of goods sold by all firms greatly exceeds the value of the output of final goods. This general principle is illustrated by a simple example in which firm R starts from scratch and produces goods (raw materials) valued at $100; the firm's value added is $100. Firm I purchases raw materials valued at $100 and produces semimanufactured goods that it sells for $130. Its value added is $30 because the value of the

goods is increased by $30 as a result of the firm's activities. Firm F purchases the semi-manufactured goods for $130, works them into a finished state, and sells them for $180. Firm F's value added is $50. The value of the final goods, $180, is found either by counting only the sales of firm F or by taking the sum of the values added by each firm. This value is much smaller than the $410 that we would obtain if we merely added up the market value of the commodities sold by each firm.

	Transactions between firms at three different stages of production			
	Firm R	Firm I	Firm F	All firms
A. Purchases from other firms	$ 0	$100	$130	$230 = Total interfirm sales
B. Purchases of factors of production (wages, rent, interest, profits)	100	30	50	180 = Value added
Total A + B = value of product	$100	$130	$180 = Value of final goods and services	$410 = Total value of all sales

minus the value of the grain it buys from the farmer and minus the values of any other inputs (such as electricity and fuel oil) that it buys from other firms.

In macroeconomics a firm's output is its value added; the sum of all values added is the value of all goods and services produced by the economy.

Value added is discussed further in the box.

The concept of value added suggests an important distinction between intermediate and final products. **Intermediate products** are goods and services used as inputs in a further stage of production. In the previous example, grain, flour, electricity, and fuel oil were all intermediate products used at various stages in the process that led to the production of the final product, bread. **Final products** are what the economy produces, after eliminating double counting due to stages of production. They include all con-

sumer commodities such as television sets and taxi rides, all capital goods such as factories and machine tools, plus all government production such as police protection and public parks.

Categories of Expenditure

When charting the course of total aggregate expenditure in the economy, it is useful to divide the total into several categories. Four major categories are consumption, investment, government, and net exports. Although each of these may be subdivided into finer groupings, the four-fold classification is extremely useful.

Consumption expenditure. **Consumption** covers all goods and services produced and sold to households during the year (with the exception of residential houses, which are counted as investment). It includes services such as haircuts, medical care, and legal advice; nondurable goods such as fresh food and newspapers; and durables such as cars, television sets, and air conditioners. This class of expenditure represents output of the economy that is applied directly to satisfying the wants of consumers. It is usually denoted by the symbol C.

Investment expenditure. **Investment** is the production of goods not for present consumption. Such goods are called **investment goods.** They are produced by firms, and they may be bought either by firms or by households. Most investment is done by firms, and for the present we shall concentrate solely on such investment. Firms can invest either in inventories or in capital goods such as plant and equipment.

Virtually all firms hold stocks of their inputs and their own outputs. Such stocks are called **inventories.** Inventories of inputs allow production to continue at the desired pace in spite of short-term fluctuations in the deliveries of inputs bought from other firms. Inventories of outputs allow firms to meet orders in spite of temporary fluctuations in the rate of output or sales.

Inventories are an important part of the productive process. They require an investment of the firm's money since the firm has paid for but not yet sold the goods. An accumulation of inventories counts as current investment because it represents goods produced but not used for current consumption. A drawing down—often called a decumulation—counts as *dis*investment because it reduces the stock of goods produced in the past.

All production uses capital goods: man-made aids to production such as hand tools, machines, and factory buildings. The economy's total quantity of capital goods is called the **capital stock.** The act of creating new capital goods is an act of investment.

The total investment that occurs in the economy is called **gross investment.** Gross investment may be thought of as divided into two parts, replacement investment and net investment. The amount of replacement investment required to maintain the existing capital stock intact is called the **capital consumption allowance** or simply

depreciation. Net investment is gross investment minus the capital consumption allowance. It is net investment that increases the economy's total stock of capital, while the replacement investment keeps the existing stock intact by replacing what has been used up.

Total investment expenditure is denoted by the symbol **I.**

Government expenditures on goods and services. When the government produces goods and services that households want, such as roads and air traffic control, it is engaged in useful activity. It is obviously adding to the sum total of valuable output in the same way as do private firms that produce the trucks and airplanes that use the roads and air lanes. With other government activities the case may not seem so clear. Should expenditures by the federal government to send a rocket to the moon or to pay a civil servant to file and refile papers from a now defunct department be regarded as contributions to GNP? Should payments by governments to the aged be part of national income? If so, what is the "product" produced? Everyone knows somebody who believes that many (or even most) activities "on Parliament Hill" or "down at City Hall" are wasteful if not downright harmful. But most of us also know someone else who believes that it is governments (not private firms) that are producing the really important things of life, such as pollution control.

The national income statistician avoids speculation about which government expenditures are or are not worthwhile and instead counts everything that produces goods or services and uses factors of production. Just as the national product includes, without distinction, the output of both gin and Bibles, it includes all the bombers and all the upkeep of parks, along with the services of tax collection agents, RCMP officers, and even members of Parliament. Government expenditure that is included is given the symbol **G.**

Government transfer payments. There is an important exception to the rule that all government expenditure is included in national income.

When a government agency makes welfare payments to a mother of five children whose husband has deserted her, income is transferred to the welfare recipient but the government does not receive, nor does it expect to receive, any marketable services from the deserted mother in return for the welfare payments.[1] The expenditure itself adds neither to employment of factors nor to total output. This is true whether the government raises the welfare money by taxes, by borrowing, or by creating new money. Government payments to households that are not made in return for the services of factors of production are called government transfer payments, or simply **transfer payments.** Such payments do not lead directly to any increase in output, and they are not included in the nation's national income.

The government expenditure that is part of national income does not include transfer payments.

National Income in a Closed Economy

A **closed economy** is one that does not engage in foreign trade. Of course no totally closed economy exists today. Nonetheless, for economies where foreign trade is relatively unimportant, and for problems where foreign trade is irrelevant, it is a valuable simplification to use a model of a closed economy. In such an economy the main elements of aggregate expenditure are the three already discussed.

In a closed economy national income equals the aggregate expenditure (AE) needed to purchase the output of consumption, investment, and government goods and services: GNP = AE = C + I + G.

National Income in an Open Economy

An economy that engages in foreign trade is called an **open economy.** Allowing for foreign

[1] In looking after her children the mother is performing a useful and valuable function. What she is not doing is producing a commodity that adds to total *marketed* production. The treatment of transfer payments recognizes that fact; it does not imply a value judgment that the mother's activities have a low or zero usefulness in any fundamental sense.

trade introduces a complication into the relatively straightforward procedures we have considered so far.

Net exports. One country's national product is the total value of final commodities produced in that country. If you spend $8,000 to buy a Canadian car whose synthetic rubber tires are made from Venezuelan oil, not all of that $6,000 will represent the output of Canadian producers. Because the oil was produced abroad, it is part of the national product of another country. If your cousin spends $6,000 on a Japanese car, only a small part of that value will represent expenditure on Canadian production. Some of it goes for the services of the Canadian dealers and Canadian transportation; the rest is the output of Japanese firms and expenditure on Japanese products.

Similarly, when a Canadian firm makes an investment expenditure on a Canadian-produced machine tool made partly with imported raw materials, only part of the expenditure is on Canadian production. The rest is expenditure on the production of the countries supplying the raw materials. The same is also true for government expenditures on such things as roads and dams: some of the expenditure is for imported materials, only part of it for domestically produced goods and services.

Since consumption, investment, and government expenditures all have an import content, it is necessary to subtract total domestic expenditure on imports (given the symbol **M**) to arrive at the total that goes to purchase domestically produced goods. The result, **C + I + G − M,** is domestic expenditure on domestically produced commodities.

There is a second consideration. If Canadian firms sell goods to German households, the goods are a part of German consumption expenditure as well as a part of Canadian national product. Indeed, all goods and services produced in Canada and sold abroad must be counted as part of Canadian output (they create incomes for the Canadians who produce them). To arrive at the total value of expenditure on Canadian na-

FIGURE 29-1
Two Ways of Accounting for GNP

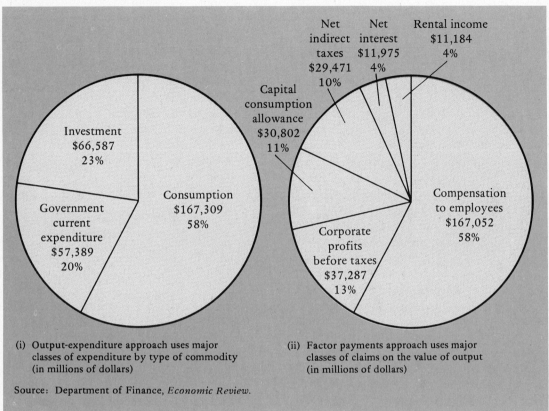

(i) Output-expenditure approach uses major
classes of expenditure by type of commodity
(in millions of dollars)

(ii) Factor payments approach uses major
classes of claims on the value of output
(in millions of dollars)

Source: Department of Finance, *Economic Review.*

Canada's 1980 GNP of $288,136 billion can be classified into expenditure or factor payment classes. Only three items are shown in the output-expenditure classification since 1980 net exports were negative at −$5,760. In the factor payments classification, compensation to employees includes wages and salaries plus employers' contributions to unemployment insurance, pensions, and other similar schemes; business profits include profits of incorporated and unincorporated business; and the capital consumption allowance is that part of the earning of business required to replace capital worn out during the year.

tional product, it is necessary to add in the value of Canadian exports. They are denoted by the symbol **X**.

From the output-expenditure approach, the total value of expenditure that measures total national income and national product in an open economy is AE = C + I + G + (X − M).

The term in parentheses is called **net exports.** It is exports, which are added to domestic expenditure, minus imports, which are subtracted from domestic expenditure. This national income measure is called **gross national product (GNP).**

We had used this term earlier; now we have seen how it is defined and constructed.

The importance of net exports. The value of net exports is usually small in relation to the total value of either **X** or **M**. Thus the correction to national income made to allow for foreign trade will not usually be large. However, a change in **X** will cause the national income to change in the same way as would a change in **C, I,** or **G.**

Figure 29-1(i) shows Canadian gross national product for 1980 calculated according to the output-expenditure approach. The box provides

Components of Income in the Output/Expenditure Approach

Personal consumption. Personal consumption includes expenditure for **durable goods** such as automobiles and appliances, **semidurable goods** such as clothing, **nondurable goods** such as food and beverages, and a wide variety of **services** such as transportation, recreation, and personal care. The one major expenditure excluded is the purchase of houses. Because houses are durable assets that provide a stream of services extending into the future, expenditure on new construction of housing is included in GNE under investment.

Housing is an important element of the expenditure of all households. National income accountants include under personal consumption both rent paid (by households that do not own their housing) and an estimated imputed value for owner-occupied housing that is the equivalent of rent. The difference between the treatment of houses and household purchases of other durable goods such as automobiles and washing machines is arbitrary. An automobile might also be viewed as an investment that produces a stream of services over several years. But the line has to be drawn somewhere, and the accountants draw it at housing.

Yet purchases of old houses, used cars, and other existing assets are excluded from GNE. A twenty-year-old house and a used car were counted as part of production in the year in which they were produced and should not be counted as part of current production whether or not their ownership has changed hands in the current year. In addition, purchases and sales of financial assets such as stocks and bonds are excluded because such transactions do not reflect current productive activity. On the other hand, the fees and commissions charged for the transfer services (e.g., commissions of real estate agents and stockbrokers) are included in GNE as payments for services provided.

Gross business capital formation. Capital formation is of two main types: investment in the form of inventory accumulation and investment in durable **fixed capital,** which yields a flow of productive services extending into the future. The latter type is broken down into residential construction, nonresidential construction (factories and commercial buildings), and machinery and equipment. Remember that "gross" means that these are total amounts spent on fixed capital whether (1) as replacement for outmoded or worn-out machines and buildings or (2) as net additions to the capital stock.

In dealing with inventories, only net changes are included because only in this way is double counting avoided. Remember that GNP aims to measure the value of goods

further details on how the various components are defined and calculated.

THE FACTOR PAYMENTS (FACTOR INCOME) APPROACH

The second approach to measuring national income and national product is usually called the factor payments approach and sometimes the factor income approach.

National income accountants distinguish four main components of factor incomes: (1) **rent,** which is the payment for the services of **land** and other factors that are rented; (2) **wages and salaries** (often referred to simply as wages), which are the payment for the services of **labor;** and (3) **interest** and (4) **profits,** both of which are payments for the services of **capital.** In order to obtain its capital goods, a firm requires money. This is made available by those who lend money to

produced but is largely computed by measuring the *sales* by firms. The accounting identity

$$\text{Sales} \equiv \begin{array}{c}\text{Opening} \\ \text{inventory} \\ \text{of goods} \\ \text{on hand}\end{array} + \begin{array}{c}\text{Production} \\ \text{for the} \\ \text{year}\end{array} - \begin{array}{c}\text{Closing} \\ \text{inventory} \\ \text{of goods} \\ \text{on hand}\end{array}$$

can be transformed into

$$\text{Production} \equiv \text{Sales} + (\text{Closing inventory} \\ - \text{Opening inventory})$$

The term in parentheses measures the net change in inventories; it must be added to sales to obtain the value of all production.

Net Exports. The reason why national accounts include only the excess of exports over imports is explained on page 582. Exports also include not only merchandise but also travel expenditures of nonresidents in Canada and investment income received from abroad. Similarly, imports include not only merchandise but travel expenditures of Canadians abroad and investment income paid to nonresidents.

Government purchases of goods and services. In principle there are many ways in which one might account for the activity of governments. They might, for example, be treated as giant firms that hire factor services and produce output that they "sell" to consumers for taxes. In fact, national income statisticians reject this approach except in the case of government enterprises such as the post office and Air Canada, which sell their output to households and firms and are treated as part of the business sector. The "output" of government departments and agencies cannot be treated in this way because there is no market price at which it can be valued. Thus the value of final product produced within the government sector is measured by the current operating expenses of federal, provincial, and local governments, including school systems and public hospitals. Expenditures on construction projects and other capital goods is included under government fixed capital formation.

It is important to remember that government expenditures as shown in the national accounts relate to purchases of goods and services only. They do not include **transfer payments** such as family allowances, old age pensions, and unemployment insurance, for these payments are not made in exchange for factor services. In addition, interest on the public debt paid to Canadians is treated as a transfer payment because it cannot be identified with the current use of factor services.

the firm and by those who put up their own money and risk its loss as the firm's owners. Interest is earned by those who lend money to the firm, and profits are earned by those who own the firm.[2] Some profits are paid out as **dividends** to the owners of the firm, the rest are retained for use by the firm. The former are called **distributed profits** and the latter **undistributed profits.**

We saw earlier that accounting practice is to account for all value produced by claims against that value. The factor payments approach to measuring national income accounts for final output in terms of the various claims to the value of that output. Owners of factors of production have claims in terms of wages, rent, interest, and

[2] The concepts of rent, wages, interest, and profits used in macroeconomics do not correspond exactly to the microeconomic concepts that go under the same names. The details of the differences need not detain us in an introductory treatment, but readers should keep in mind that differences exist.

Components of Income in the Factor Payments Approach

Wages and other labor income. Wages includes all payments to and on behalf of employees, including take-home pay, income taxes withheld, social insurance contributions, and contributions to pension funds. Obviously, only some of these payments go to households; some go to governments, some to trust funds, some to unions, and so on, but in total they represent the "labor cost" of production.

Corporation profits. All profits of corporations before taxes are treated as factor payments. Dividends become actual payments to owners for the use of their capital and for risk taking. Undistributed profits are treated as payments to owners for the same purposes, and corporate income taxes are regarded as payments to governments that must be included. Dividends paid to nonresidents are excluded because national income is defined to include the earnings of Canadian residents only.

Interest and miscellaneous investment income. Interest income received by persons (other than interest on the public debt) is treated as a transfer payment. The miscellaneous category includes profits (net of losses) of government business enterprises.

Net income of unincorporated businesses. Unincorporated enterprises such as small businesses, professions, partnerships, and farms generate income flows to their owners, and these incomes before taxes are included along with the net rental income of persons acting in a landlord capacity.

Indirect taxes. Indirect taxes are taxes levied on businesses and are therefore costs that are ultimately incorporated in the market prices of output (e.g., sales and excise taxes). Thus, to make the accounts balance, they must be included on the income side even though they are not factor costs.

Capital consumption allowances. The capital consumption allowance reflects an estimate of the depreciation of the nation's capital stock. It is a "payment" imputed out of the value of production, and its purpose is to recognize the contribution made by the nation's capital stock to current production of goods and services.

Miscellaneous adjustments. A number of small additional items are required to make the accounts balance. These include government subsidies to business (subtracted from indirect taxes); the inventory valuation adjustment (added or subtracted, depending on the nature of the adjustment); and the residual error of estimate. This last item is split between the income side and the expenditure side so that it appears in each account with opposite signs.

profits that they earned producing the output. The claims are measured before taxes. For example, total wages in the factor payments accounts include *all* wages earned, of which part will be received by suppliers of labor and part will go to the government as income taxes. A government claim on the market value of goods produced in the form of indirect taxes must, however, be entered in the accounts. If a good's sale value of $10 includes $3 of business excise taxes, only $7 will be available for payments to factors of production. The payments approach must in this case record $3 as the government's claim to part of the market value of the good.

The box describes the components of income in the factor payments approach and how they are defined. Figure 29-1 (ii) shows Canadian national income in 1980 from the factor payments approach. By virtue of accounting conventions, total national income classified by factor payment categories is the same as total national income classified by output-expenditure categories.

RELATED MEASURES OF NATIONAL INCOME

Gross national product is the most comprehensive of the several national income concepts. It measures the sum of all values added in the economy.

The next most comprehensive measure is **net national product (NNP).** This is GNP minus the capital consumption allowance (defined on page 586). NNP is thus a measure of the net output of the economy after deducting from gross output an amount necessary to maintain intact the existing stock of capital.

Two other important measures are personal income and disposable income. The interrelationship of the four measures is shown in Table 29-1.

Personal income is income earned by or paid to individuals, before allowance for personal income taxes. Some personal income goes for taxes, some for saving, and the rest for consumption. A number of adjustments to NNP are required to arrive at personal income. The most important are: (1) subtracting from NNP the business earnings retained by corporations, (2) subtracting from NNP the taxes paid by business, and (3) adding to NNP the government transfer payments and government payments of interest to households. The first two represent parts of the value of output not paid to persons; the third represents payments to households that households have available to spend or to save even though they are not part of GNP.

Disposable income is a measure of the amount of current income that households have to spend or to save. It is calculated as personal income minus personal taxes.

TABLE 29-1

Various National Income Measures, 1980 (billions of Canadian dollars)

A. Gross national product (GNP)	288.1
Less:	
1. Capital consumption allowances	30.8
2. Indirect taxes net of subsidies	29.8
B. Net national product	227.5
Less: Retained earnings	36.9
Plus:	
1. Transfer payments	30.0
2. Interest on public debt	15.5
C. Personal income	236.1
Less:	
1. Direct personal taxes	41.5
2. Misc. transfers to government	2.2
D. Personal disposable income	192.4

Sources: Bank of Canada Review, April 1981, and Statistics Canada. *National Income and Expenditure Accounts,* Fourth Quarter 1980.

Each of the four related national income measures focuses on a different aspect of the national output. GNP measures the market value of total output. NNP measures the net value of output after an allowance for maintaining the capital stock. Personal income measures income earned or received by persons, before personal income taxes. Disposable income is a measure of after-tax income of persons; it is the amount they have available to spend or to save.

For most purposes personal income is less useful than disposable income. Because disposable income measures are published only every three months, forecasters who need monthly data may use personal income instead.

The relation between GNP and disposable income is important:

Disposable income is GNP *minus* part of it that is not actually paid over to households, *minus* the personal income taxes paid by households, *plus* transfer payments received by households.

Interpreting National Income Measures

The information provided by measures of national income can be extremely useful for many

The Significance of Arbitrary Decisions

National income accounting uses many arbitrary decisions. Goods that are finished and held in inventories are valued at market value, thereby anticipating their sale even though the actual sales price may not be known. This may be justified in some cases but not in others. Clearly, practical people must arrive at some compromise between consistent definitions and measurable magnitudes. The imputation of a market value to an owner-occupied house, but not to the services of the housewife who occupies and often owns the house, probably is justified only by such a compromise.

Such arbitrary decisions surely affect the size of measured GNP. Does it matter? The surprising answer, for many purposes, is no. In any case, it is an error to believe that just because a statistical measure falls short of perfection (as all statistical measures do) it is useful. Very crude measures will often give estimates to the right order of magnitude, while substantial improvements in sophistication may make second-order improvements in these estimates.

Absolute figures mean something in general terms, although they cannot be taken seriously to the last dollar. In 1980, GNP was measured as $288.1 billion. It is certain that the market value of all production in Canada in that year was not $10 billion, nor was it $1,000 billion, but it might well have been $240 or $300 billion had different measures been defined with different arbitrary decisions built into them.

International and intertemporal comparisons, though tricky, may be meaningful when they are based on measures all of which contain roughly the same arbitrary decisions. Canadian per capita GNP is more than two times the Italian but only 75 percent of that of Switzerland. Other measures might differ, but it is unlikely that any other measure would reveal that either Canadian or Italian per capita production was higher than the per capita production in Switzerland. But the statistics also show that GNP per capita was 4 percent higher in Switzerland than in Sweden, a difference too small to have much meaning.

Canadian GNP has been growing at about 5 percent per year since World War II; it is unlikely that another measure would have indicated an 8 percent increase. Further, the Japanese GNP has been growing at about 9 percent per year, and it is inconceivable that another measure would change the conclusion that Japanese national output rose faster than Canadian national output over recent decades.

purposes, but unless it is carefully interpreted it can also be seriously misleading. Furthermore, each of the specialized measures—GNP, NNP, personal income, disposable income, and others that we shall consider shortly—gives slightly different information, so each may be the best statistic for studying a certain range of problems.

MONEY VALUES AND REAL VALUES

The GNP measures the total *money* value of final goods produced during a year. Thus it has a price and a quantity component, and a particular change in the GNP can be caused by many different combinations of price and quantity changes. A 10 percent rise in GNP might, for example, have been caused by a 10 percent rise in prices, all quantities remaining unchanged; a 10 percent rise in output, all prices remaining unchanged; or smaller increases in both prices and quantities. For some purposes the money value of national income is just the measure required. Sometimes, however, we wish to know what is happening to the *quantity* (rather than the *value*) of output. To do this we need to separate changes in the GNP caused by variations in market prices from changes caused by variations in the quantities of output. Changes of the latter kind are defined as "real" or "constant dollar" changes to distinguish them from mere "money" or "nominal" changes.

Over any long period, changes in the GNP reflect both real quantity changes and money price changes. In 1930 Canadian GNP was $5.7 billion; in 1979 it was $260 billion. When GNP is measured at prices prevailing during the same year, it is said to be measured in **current dollars.** How much of this increase resulted from a change in the volume of goods and services provided and how much from a general rise in prices?

To answer such questions, the GNP is calculated in **constant dollars;** that is, the quantities produced each year are valued at the prices ruling in an arbitrary *base year.* The resulting figures constitute a series called **real GNP** or **constant dollar GNP.** GNP measured in constant 1971 dollars means that the quantities produced in each year are each multiplied by their 1971 prices and then summed. The constant dollar figures give a measure of changes in the quantity of output because they tell what the total value of actual output would have been if prices had not changed.

Table 29-2 gives the GNP measured in both ways for selected years since 1935.[3]

[3] Comparison of the two sets of figures yields an "index number" of price changes that is called the implicit GNP deflator, or usually just the **GNE deflator.** It is defined as

$$\frac{\text{GNP in current dollars}}{\text{GNP in constant dollars}} \times 100$$

This is the most comprehensive measure of price changes available in that it covers all the goods and services produced by the entire economy. The value of the deflator in any particular year, such as 1980, is obtained by valuing 1980 output first at current prices and then at base year (say, 1971) prices. Since the former is 222.3 percent of the latter, the change must be due to the price changes between the base year and the current year: average prices have risen 122.3 percent over the period.

TABLE 29-2
GNP in Current and Constant Dollars

Year	(1) GNP in billions of current dollars	(2) GNP in billions of 1971 dollars	(3) Implicit GNE deflator 1971 = 100
1955	28.5	43.9	65.0
1965	55.4	70.0	79.1
1975	165.3	113.0	146.3
1980	288.1	129.6	222.3

Source: Statistics Canada, 13-201.

Current dollar GNP tells us about the money value of output; constant dollar GNP tells us about changes in physical output. The GNP in current dollars gives the total value of all final output in any year, valued in the selling prices of that year. The GNP in constant dollars gives the total value of all final output in any year, valued in the prices ruling in one particular year, in this case, 1971. The ratio (*GNP in curent dollars/GNP in constant dollars*) is the implicit GNE deflator. (It is in effect a price index with current-year quantity weights.)

TOTAL OUTPUT AND PER CAPITA OUTPUT

The rise in real GNP during this century has had two main causes: first, an increase in the amounts of land, labor, and capital used in production; second, an increase in output per unit of input. In other words, more inputs have been used, and each input has become more productive. For many purposes we want the measure of total output: for example, to assess a country's potential military strength or to know the total size of its market. For other purposes, however, we prefer per capita measures, which are obtained by dividing a total measure such as GNP by the relevant population.

There are many useful per capita measures. GNP divided by the total population gives a measure of how much GNP there is on average for each person in the economy; this is called **per capita GNP.** GNP divided by the number of persons employed tells us the average output per employed worker. GNP divided by the total number of hours worked measures output per

FIGURE 29-2
Disposable Income Per Capita in Canada, in Constant (1971) Dollars

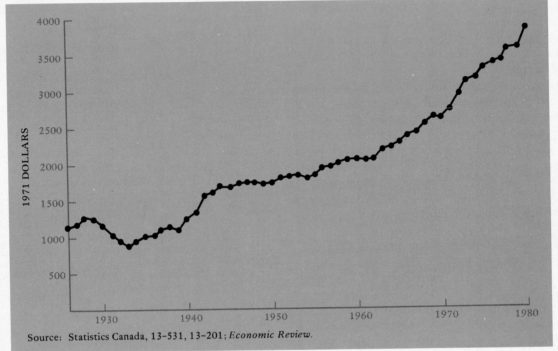

Source: Statistics Canada, 13–531, 13–201; *Economic Review*.

Disposable income per capita in constant dollars provides a measure of the real purchasing power available to the average American household. Disposable income per capita fell during the early 1930s and late 1940s but it has risen in every decade since the thirties, including the 1970s. It underestimates the average living standard because it leaves out the contribution of government expenditure to such items as police, fire, justice, defense, and recreation.

hour of labor input. A widely used measure of the purchasing power of the average person is disposable income per capita, in constant dollars. This measure is shown in Figure 29-2.

OMISSIONS FROM MEASURED NATIONAL INCOME

Finally, we come to a series of omissions from the GNP, and thus also from the NNP, disposable income, and other measures based mainly on parts of the GNP. The importance of these omissions can be judged only when we know the purpose for which the income data is to be used.

Illegal Activities

The GNP does not measure illegal activities even though many of them are ordinary business activities which produce goods and services that are sold on the market and generate factor incomes. In the United States the liquor industry during Prohibition was an important example because it accounted for a significant part of the nation's total economic activity. Today the same is true of many forms of illegal gambling, prostitution, and the illicit production and distribution of soft and hard drugs. If we want an accurate measure of the *total* demand for factors of production in the economy or of *total* marketable output—whether or not we as individuals approve of particular products—we should include these activities. Probably the main reason for leaving them out is that, because they are illicit, it would be hard to find out enough about them to include them even if we wanted to.[4]

Unreported Activities

An important source of omission from the measured GNP is the so-called underground economy. People make perfectly legal transactions such as repairing a leak in your roof but are paid in cash or in kind in order to avoid income taxes. Such transactions go unreported and hence unrecorded in the country's GNP. Their potential importance is shown by the fact that estimates of the value of income earned in the American underground economy run as high as 15 percent of American GNP. Since these are ordinary market activities, their omission is an important source of error in published GNP figures. Increases in activities that go unreported are one reason why the rate of growth of total and per capita GNP and hence of living standards may be underestimated by currently published data.

Nonmarketed Economic Activities

When a bank employee hires a carpenter to build a bookshelf in her house, the value of the bookshelf enters into the GNP; if the teller or her husband builds the bookshelf, the value of the bookshelf is omitted from the GNP. In general, any labor service that does not pass through a market is not counted in the GNP. Such omissions include, for example, the services of housewives, any do-it-yourself activity, and voluntary work

such as canvassing for a political party, helping to run a day-care center, or leading a boy scout troop.

Does the omission of nonmarketed economic activities matter? Once again, it all depends. If we wish to measure the flow of goods and services through the market sector of the economy, or to account for changes in the opportunities for employment for those households who sell their labor services in the market, most of these omissions are desirable.

If, however, we wish to measure the overall flow of goods and services available to satisfy people's wants, whatever the source of the goods and services, then all the omissions are undesirable and potentially serious.

In most advanced industrial economies the nonmarket sector is relatively small, and it can be ignored even if GNP is used for purposes for which it would be appropriate to include nonmarketed goods and services. The omissions become serious, however, when GNP or disposable income figures are used to compare living standards in very different economies. Generally, the nonmarket sector of the economy is larger in rural than in urban settings and in underdeveloped than in developed economies. Be a little cautious, then, in interpreting data from a country with a very different climate and culture. When one hears that the per capita GNP of Nigeria is $150 per year, one should not imagine living in Ottawa on that income. Certainly the average Nigerian is at a low level of real income compared to an urban North American, but the measured GNP figure does not allow for the fact that many of the things that are very costly to a North American—such as fruit and a warm house—are provided free to many Nigerians by wild fruit trees and a warm climate and by a host of nonmarketed goods and services.

Factors Affecting Human Welfare but Not Included in the Value of Output

Many things that contribute to human welfare are not included in the GNP. Leisure is one ex-

[4] Some of them do get included because people often report their earnings from illicit activities as part of their earnings from legal activities in order to avoid the fate of Al Capone. He, having avoided conviction on many counts, was finally caught for income tax evasion. Don Corleone, the godfather in Puzo's famous novel about the Mafia, undoubtedly reported part of his illegal earnings as belonging to his legal business. Thus total GNP would come closer to reflecting all income earned in the nation, but it would overstate the contribution of olive oil importing and understate the contribution of gambling and similar enterprises.

ample. In fact, although a shorter work week may make people happier, it will tend to reduce measured GNP.

GNP does not allow for the capacity of different goods to provide different satisfactions. A million dollars spent on a bomber or a missile makes the same addition to GNP as a million dollars spent on a school, a stadium, or candy bars—expenditures that may produce very different amounts of consumer satisfaction.

GNP does not measure the quality of life. To the extent that material output is purchased at the expense of overcrowded cities and highways, polluted environments, defaced countrysides, maimed accident victims, longer waits for public services, and a more complex life that entails a frenetic struggle to be happy, GNP measures only part of the total of human well-being.

WHICH MEASURE IS BEST?

We have seen that there are several distinct income measures. To ask which is *the* best is something like asking which is *the* best carpenter's tool. The answer is that it all depends on the job to be done.

The use of several measures of national income rather than one is common because different measures provide answers to different questions. GNP answers the question, What was the market value of goods and services produced for final demand? NNP answers the question, By how much did the economy's production exceed the amount necessary to replace capital equipment used up? Disposable income answers the question, How much income do consumers have to allocate between spending and saving? In addition, real (constant dollar) measures eliminate purely monetary changes and allow comparisons of purchasing power over time; per capita measures shift the focus from the nation to the average person.

Which measure we use will depend on the problem at hand. For example, if we wish to predict households' consumption behavior, dis-

posable income is what we need. If we wish to account for changes in employment, GNP is wanted (since all production requires labor inputs).

For yet other purposes, such as providing an overall measure of economic welfare, we may wish to supplement or modify conventional measures of national income.[5] Even if we do, we are unlikely to discard GNP (and its progeny) entirely in favor of such a measure. Economists and politicians interested in the ebb and flow of economic activity that passes through the market and in the rise and fall in employment opportunities for factors of production whose services are sold on the market will continue to use GNP as the measure that comes closest to telling them what they need to know.

Summary

1. National product is the total market value of goods and services produced in the economy during a year; national income is the total of all income claims generated over the same period of time. By virtue of standard accounting conventions, national product and national income have the same value.

2. National income may be calculated either by the output-expenditure approach or by the factor payments approach. Both approaches yield the same value, for they are just two ways of accounting for the total value of output.

3. The value of the output of final goods and services can be found by taking the sum of the *values added* in the economy. Value added is the market value of the firm's output minus the cost of inputs purchased from other firms.

---

[5] Measures that come closer to measuring economic welfare than GNP have been calculated. One was developed by Professors William Nordhaus and James Tobin. It tries to measure consumption of things that provide utility to households rather than total production; it gives value to such non-marketed activities as leisure and makes subtractions for such "disutilities" as pollution and congestion.

4. Using the output-expenditure approach, GNP = **AE** = **C** + **I** + **G** + (**X** − **M**). **C** represents consumption expenditures of households and **I** represents investment in capital goods such as plant equipment, residential construction, and inventory accumulation. Gross investment can be split into replacement investment (necessary to keep the stock of capital intact) and net investment (net additions to the stock of capital). **G** represents government expenditures except transfer payments. (**X** − **M**) represents the excess of exports over imports; it will be negative if imports exceed exports.

5. The factor payments approach to GNP divides total GNP according to who has a claim to the value arising from the production and sale of commodities. Wages, interest, rents, profits, taxes, depreciation (called capital consumption allowance), and indirect taxes are the major categories.

6. Several related but different national income measures are used in addition to the GNP. Net national product (NNP) measures total output after deducting an allowance for output needed to keep the capital stock intact. Personal income is income actually paid to households before any allowance for personal taxes. Disposable income gives the amount that is actually available to households to spend or to save.

7. GNP measured in constant dollars expresses the value of output measured in the prices ruling in some particular base year. Because it removes the effects of price changes, it provides a measure of real income.

8. GNP and related measures of national income must be interpreted with regard for their limitations. GNP excludes production resulting from activities that are illegal, take place in the underground economy, or do not pass through markets (such as that produced by do-it-yourself activities). Moreover, GNP does not measure everything that contributes to human welfare.

9. Notwithstanding its limitations, GNP remains the best measure available for estimating the total economic activity that passes through the markets of our economy and for accounting for changes in the employment opportunities that face housholds who sell their labor services on the open market.

Topics for Review

National income, GNP, NNP, personal income, and disposable income
Output-expenditure and factor payments approaches to measuring national income
Final goods and value added
GNP = **AE** = **C** + **I** + **G** + (**X** − **M**)
Major characteristics of GNP
Limitations of GNP as a measure of economic welfare

Discussion Questions

1. If Canada and the United States were to join together as a single country, what would be the effect on their total GNP (assuming that output in each country is unaffected)? Would any of the components in their GNPs change significantly?
2. "Every time you rent a U-haul, brick in a patio, grow a vegetable, fix your own car, photocopy an article, join a food co-op, develop film, sew a dress, avoid purchasing a convenience food, stew fruit, or raise a child, you are committing a productive act, even though these activities are not reflected in the gross national product." To what extent are each of these things "productive acts"? Are any of them included in GNP? Where they are excluded, does the exclusion matter?
3. In measuring Canadian GNE, which of the following expenditures should be included?
   a. expenditures on automobiles by consumers and by firms
   b. expenditures on Canadian flour by households, by bakers, and by French firms
   c. expenditures on food and lodging by tourists and by businessmen on expense accounts
   d. expenditures on new machinery and equipment by Canadian firms
   e. the purchase of one corporation by another corporation
   f. increases in business inventories, decreases in business inventories
4. What would be the effect on the measured value of Ca-

594   PART NINE / National Income and Fiscal Policy

nadian *real* GNP of (a) the destruction of a thousand homes by flood water; (b) passage of legislation making abortional illegal; (c) a complete cessation of all imports from South Africa; and (d) the outbreak of new Arab-Israeli hostilities in which Canadian troops became heavily involved. Speculate on the effects of each of these events on the true well-being of the Canadian people.

5. In the United States a Social Security Administration study, using 1972 data, found the "average American housewife's value" to be $4,750. It arrived at this total by adding up the hours she spent cooking, multiplied by a cook's wage, the hours spent with her children, multiplied by a babysitter's wage, and so on. Should the time a parent spends taking children to a concert be included? Are dollar amounts assigned to such activities a satisfactory proxy for market value of production? For what purposes, if any, should such values be excluded from national income?

6. What would be the effect (a) on the total value of all purchases and sales in the economy, and (b) on GNP of the integration into a single firm of GMC and all the separate firms that now supply it with components and the integration into a single firm of the Ford Motor Company and the Chrysler Corporation?

7. Use the endpaper at the back of this book to calculate the percentage increase of the most recent two decades of each of the following magnitudes: (a) GNP in current dollars; (b) GNP in constant dollars; (c) disposable income in constant dollars; and (d) disposable income per capita in constant dollars. Can you account for the relative size of these changes?

8. Consider the effect on measured GNP and on economic well-being of each of the following: (a) a reduction in the standard work week from 40 hours to 30 hours; (b) the hiring of all welfare recipients as government employees; (c) further increases in oil prices that lead to a general inflation; and (d) an increase in the salaries of priests and ministers as a result of the increased contributions of churchgoers.

What Determines National Income?

30

We saw in Chapter 28 how the interaction of the aggregate demand and aggregate supply curves determines national income, Y, and the price level, P. This is illustrated once again in Figure 30-1. Why is the aggregate demand curve where it is in that figure? It determines national income at Y, on the Keynesian portion of the aggregate supply curve; but why was it not in some other position, determining national income at, say, Y_1 or Y_2?

To provide answers to these questions, we need to develop a new relation called the **aggregate expenditure function.** This relates real national income to the aggregate real amount that all decision makers desire to spend on purchasing the nation's output. (Unless otherwise specified, real national income can be taken from now on to be measured by real GNP.)

Desired Expenditure

In the preceding chapter we discussed how national income statisticians measure actual aggregate expenditure, **AE**, and its components, consumption, **C**, investment, **I**, government, **G**, and net exports, **(X − M)**.

In this chapter we are concerned with desired expenditure. Of course, everybody would like to spend more or less unlimited amounts—if only they had the money. However, desired expenditure does not refer to what one would like to do under imaginary circumstances. It refers instead to what you and everybody else want to spend, given the resources at your, and their, command.

FIGURE 30-1
The Determination of National Income by Aggregate Demand and Aggregate Supply

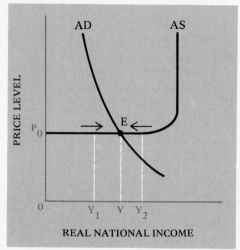

On the Keynesian portion of the aggregate supply curve, national income is determined by the aggregate demand curve. With aggregate demand and supply curves of *AD* and *AS*, national income is *Y*. If only Y_1 were produced, demand would exceed output and output would rise. If Y_2 were produced, demand would be less than output and output would fall. These forces are shown by the arrows pointing toward the equilibrium position at *E*.

Everyone who has money to spend makes expenditure decisions. It is impossible—and unnecessary—to look at each of the millions of such individual decisions. To simplify, we divide decision makers into four main groups: domestic households, firms, central authorities (called governments), and foreign purchasers of domestically produced products. Their actual purchases account for the four main categories of expenditure studied in the previous chapter: consumption, investment, government expenditure, and exports. Their desired purchases may be divided in the same fashion. As in the preceding chapter, we must allow for the fact that some of the commodities desired by each of these groups will have an import content. Thus we subtract import expenditure to obtain total desired expenditure on domestically produced goods and services:

$$AE = C + I + G + (X - M)$$

We have indicated *actual* aggregate expenditure and its components by the boldface letters **AE, C, I, G,** and **(X − M).** Now we use lightface letters to indicate *desired* amounts of expenditure in the same categories.

Desired expenditure need not equal actual expenditure, either in total or in each individual category. For example, if households want to buy commodities that firms will not or cannot produce, households will not be able to buy as much as they want. In this case, desired consumption expenditure, C, will exceed actual consumption expenditure, **C.** (One reason for this might be that because all resources are fully employed, firms cannot increase output even though the demand for more output exists.) For a second example, firms may not intend to invest in inventory accumulation this year but may nonetheless do so unintentionally. If they produce goods for sale and demand is unexpectedly low, the unsold goods that pile up on their shelves will represent undesired (and unintended) inventory accumulation. In this case actual investment expenditure, **I,** will exceed desired investment expenditure, I.

The distinction between actual and desired expenditures is important.

National income accounts measure *actual expenditures* in each of the categories, C, I, G, and (X − M). The theory of national income determination deals with *desired expenditures* in each of the categories, C, I, G, and (X − M).

To develop a theory of national income, we need to know what determines each of the components of aggregate desired expenditure. We begin in this chapter by treating all the components except consumption expenditure as constants. This allows us to study national income determination under the simplest possible conditions. In subsequent chapters we shall look at the determinants of desired I, G, and (X − M).

DESIRED CONSUMPTION EXPENDITURE

Households decide how much of their income they wish to spend on consumption, and they save the rest. **Saving** is defined as all income that is not consumed. It follows that households have to make a single decision: how to split their disposable income between consumption and saving. Household consumption expenditure is the largest single component of actual aggregate expenditure. But what determines the amount that households want to spend on goods and services for their consumption and how much they want to save? One major determinant turns out to be household disposable income. As disposable income rises, households have more money to spend on consumption—and the evidence is that they do just that. We therefore treat consumption expenditure as varying with disposable income.

The Consumption Function

The term **consumption function** describes the relationship between consumption expenditure and all the factors that determine it. It is, as we shall see, one of the most important relations in macroeconomics.[1] The macro consumption function explains the aggregate desired consumption expenditure of all households in the economy.

Consumption as a Function of Disposable Income

We have noted that one important force influencing desired consumption expenditure is household disposable income, to which we now give the symbol Y_d. Other forces, such as interest rates and inflationary expectations, also exert an

influence, but they may be set aside for the moment. In the simple theory of the consumption function, we focus on changes in disposable income to explain changes in consumption. An example of a schedule relating disposable income to desired consumption expenditure is presented in the first two columns of Table 30-1.

Average and marginal propensities to consume. To discuss the consumption function concisely, economists use some technical vocabulary.

The **average propensity to consume** (*APC*) is total consumption expenditure divided by disposable income. The calculation of *APC* for the consumption schedule illustrated in Table 30-1 will be found in the third column of the table.

The **marginal propensity to consume** (*MPC*) relates the *change* in consumption to the *change* in disposable income that brought it about. It is the change in disposable income divided into the resulting consumption change: $MPC = \Delta C/\Delta Y_d$ (where the Greek letter Δ means "a change in"). Table 30-1 shows the calculations of the *MPC* in the last column. [32]

The propensities can be calculated either for desired expenditure, as in Table 30-1, or for actual expenditure, as when national income data are used.

The shape of the consumption function. Empirical studies of year-to-year changes in disposable income and consumption (i.e., when each observation consists of income and consumption expenditure over the same year) for a period of ten years or so have found a close relation between the two. In general, years with higher than average levels of income tend to be years with higher than average levels of consumption, and vice versa. Figure 30-2 shows the general shape of such a consumption function. [33] Its essential features are:

1. There is a break-even level of income that is the level of disposable income at which households just consume all their income.

---

[1] The concept of a functional relationship is discussed on page 27.

TABLE 30-1

The Calculation of the Average Propensity to Consume (*APC*) and the Marginal Propensity to Consume (*MPC*) for a Hypothetical Economy (in billions of dollars)

Disposable income (Y_d)	Desired consumption (C)	$APC = C/Y_d$	ΔY_d (Change in Y_d)	ΔC (Change in C)	$MPC = \Delta C/\Delta Y_d$
$ 0	$ 100	0			
			$ 100	$ 80	0.80
100	180	1.80			
			300	240	0.80
400	420	1.05			
			100	80	0.80
500	500	1.00			
			500	400	0.80
1,000	900	0.90			
			1,000	800	0.80
2,000	1,700	0.85			
			1,000	800	0.80
3,000	2,500	0.83			
			1,000	800	0.80
4,000	3,300	0.83			

The *APC* measures the proportion of disposable income that households desire to spend on consumption; the *MPC* measures the proportion of any *increment* to disposable income that households desire to spend on consumption. The data are hypothetical. The *APC* calculated in the third column exceeds unity below the break-even level of income because consumption exceeds income. Above the break-even level the *APC* is less than unity and declines steadily as income rises. The last three columns are set between the lines of the first three columns to indicate that they refer to changes in the levels of income and consumption.

In this example, the *MPC* calculated in the last column is constant at 0.80 at all levels of Y_d. This indicates that 80¢ of every additional $1 of income is spent on consumption and 20¢ is used to increase saving (or decrease dissaving).

2. Below the break-even level, households consume in excess of their current disposable income. They do this by borrowing or by using up past savings, which is known as **dissaving.**[2]
3. Above the break-even level of income, households consume only part of their disposable income and save the rest.
4. Any increase in household income causes consumption expenditure to rise but by less than the rise in income. For example, every increase in household income of $1 might cause households to raise their consumption expenditure by 80¢, as is the case with the consumption function in the first two columns of Table 30-1.[3]

Using the concepts of the average and marginal propensities to consume, we can restate the four properties as two summary propositions:

---

[2] Clearly this cannot go on forever, which is one reason why dissaving cannot be a feature of long-term behavior; but it can go on for some time, and it does appear to be a feature of short-term behavior.

[3] This fourth assumption was described by John Maynard Keynes (widely regarded as the first to stress the consumption function) in his classic *The General Theory of Employment, Interest, and Money:* "The fundamental psychological law, upon which we are entitled to depend with great confidence both *a priori* from our knowledge of human nature and from the detailed facts of experience, is that men are disposed, as a rule and on the average, to increase their consumption as their income increases, but not by as much as the increase in their income."

1. There is a break-even level of disposable income at which $APC = 1$. Below this level APC is greater than unity; above it APC is less than unity.
2. MPC is greater than zero but less than unity for all levels of income.

It follows that an increase of $1 in disposable income will lead to an increase of less than $1 in both desired consumption expenditure and desired saving.

Figure 30-2 shows a graph of the consumption function plotted from the first two columns of Table 30-1. The figure makes it clear that the slope of the consumption function ($\Delta C/\Delta Y_d$) is the MPC. The upward slope of the consumption function indicates that MPC is positive. However, the slope is less than unity, indicating that MPC is less than unity.

The 45° Line

Figure 30-2 also shows a construction that will prove very useful. This is a line that connects all points where desired expenditure (measured on the vertical axis) equals disposable income (measured on the horizontal axis). Since both axes are measured in the same units, this line has an upward slope of unity, or (what is the same thing) it makes an angle of 45° with both axes. This line is called the **45° line,** and to remind us of its definition it is labeled $AE = Y_d$.

The 45° line proves handy as a reference line. For example, in Figure 30-2 it helps locate the break-even level of income at which consumption expenditure equals disposable income. Graphically, this is where the consumption line cuts the 45° line.

The Saving Function

Because households have only one decision to make on how to divide their income between consumption and saving, it follows that if we know the dependence of consumption on disposable income, we will also know the dependence

FIGURE 30-2

The Consumption and Saving Functions

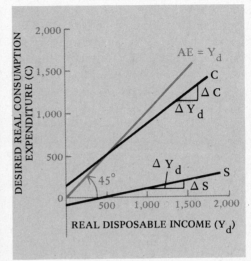

Both consumption and saving rise as income rises. This diagram plots the data from Table 30-2. The C and S lines relate desired expenditure on consumption and on saving to disposable income. The slope of the lines are $\Delta C/\Delta Y_d$ and $\Delta S/\Delta Y_d$, which are the MPC and the MPS respectively. At the break-even level of income, the consumption line cuts the 45° line and the saving line cuts the horizontal axis. Since saving is all disposable income not spent on consumption ($S = Y_d - C$), the vertical sum of the S and C lines must by definition coincide with the 45° line; that is, at each level of income, disposable income must be accounted for by the amount saved plus the amount consumed.

of saving on disposable income. Table 30-2 illustrates this.

We may define two saving concepts that are exactly parallel to the consumption concepts of APC and MPC already defined. The **average propensity to save** (APS) is the proportion of disposable income that households desire to devote to savings. It is total desired saving divided by total disposable income: $APS = S/Y_d$. The **marginal propensity to save** (MPS) relates the *change* in total desired saving to the *change* in disposable income that brought it about: $MPS =$

$\Delta S/\Delta Y_d$. Calculations from Table 30-2 will allow you to confirm for yourself that, in the example given, MPS is constant at .2 at all levels of income, while APS rises with income. For example, APS is zero at $Y = \$5,000$ and .175 at $Y = \$4,000$. [34] Figure 30-2 also graphs the saving schedule given in Table 30-2. The slope of the savings line $\Delta S/\Delta Y_d$ is the MPS.

Consumption as a Function of National Income

We have seen that desired consumption is related to *disposable* income. For a theory of the determination of national income, however, we need to know how consumption varies with national income.

The Long-term Consumption Function

The text deals with what is called a short-term consumption function. This is suitable for describing how consumption varies from year to year as income varies. It is based on empirical observations of cyclical variations in consumption and income.

Some empirical studies of the consumption function have used ten-year averages of consumption expenditure and income. Thus the time-series data used consisted of decade-by-decade averages of consumption and disposable income. When plotted on a graph, one point would relate average consumption in, say, 1900–1909 to average income in that period; another point would relate average consumption in 1910–1919 to average disposable income in that period; and so on. The characteristic of such data is that they average out the effects of cyclical fluctuations in national income and focus attention on the long-run reaction of consumption to long-run trend changes in national income.

Such studies suggest that there is a highly stable long-term division of national income between consumption and saving—in other words, that the consumption expenditure of American households tends to be a stable fraction of their disposable income. In technical terms, the APC tends to be constant over time; so too does the MPC. Further, MPC tends to be approximately equal to APC in these long-term studies. [35] The figure shows

a long-run consumption function that exhibits these properties.

Thus the consumption function described in the text is a short-term function suitable for analyzing cyclical fluctuations in the economy that take only a few years to work themselves out. The consumption function illustrated here is suitable for analyzing the behavior of the economy under long-term growth conditions over a span of many decades.

The major difference between the two functions is that the proportion of income devoted to consumption declines as income rises on the short-term function but remains constant on the long-term function.

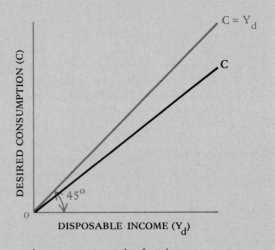

A long-term consumption function

TABLE 30–2
Consumption and Saving Schedules (millions of dollars)

Disposable income	Desired consumption expenditure	Desired saving
$ 0	$ 100	−$100
100	180	− 80
400	420	− 20
500	500	0
1,000	900	+ 100
2,000	1,700	+ 300
3,000	2,500	+ 500
4,000	3,300	+ 700

Saving and consumption account for all household disposable income. The first two columns repeat the data from Table 30-1. The third column is disposable income minus desired consumption. The three columns thus show desired consumption and desired saving at each level of income. Consumption and saving each increase steadily as disposable income rises. In this sample the break-even level of disposable income is $500 million. At an income of $100 million, $180 million is spent on consumption. Since this must involve new borrowing or the consumption of past saving, households in aggregate are dissaving. As income rises, dissaving decreases for income levels up to $500 million and saving increases above $500 million.

The transition from a relation between *consumption and disposable income* to one between *consumption and national income* is easily accomplished since, as we saw above, disposable income and national income are themselves related to each other.

The relation between disposable income and national income. We saw on pages 585 and 587 the several adjustments required to derive disposable income from GNP. Since transfer payments, the major addition, are smaller than total taxes, the major subtraction, the net effect is for disposable income to be much less than GNP. (It was just over 70 percent of GNP in 1979.)

The general relation between disposable income and national income can be approximated by assuming Y_d to be an unchanging proportion of Y. The relation might, for example, be $Y_d = .7Y$. More generally, we can write $Y_d = uY$,

where u is the proportion of national income that becomes disposable income.

Substitution of national income for disposable income in the consumption function. If we know how consumption relates to disposable income and how disposable income relates to national income, it will be an easy matter to derive the relation between consumption and national income.

To illustrate, assume that disposable income is always 70 percent of national income. Then, whatever the relation between C and Y_d, we can always substitute $.7Y$ for Y_d. Thus, if consumption were always 90 percent of Y_d, then C would always be 63 percent (70 percent of 90 percent) of y. **[36]**

This relation is further illustrated in Table 30-3. Note from the table that since we can write desired consumption as a function of Y as well as of Y_d, we can define marginal and average propensities to consume from Y as well as from Y_d.

TABLE 30–3
Consumption as a Function of Disposable Income and National Income (millions of dollars)

(1) National income (Y)	(2) Disposable income ($Y_d = .7Y$)	(3) Desired consumption ($C = 100 + .8Y_d$)
100	70	156
1,000	700	660
2,000	1,400	1,220
3,000	2,100	1,780
4,000	2,800	2,340

If desired consumption depends on disposable income, which in turn depends on national income, desired consumption can be written as a function of either income concept. The data are hypothetical. They show deductions of 30 percent of any change in national income to arrive at disposable income from national income. Deductions of 30 percent of Y imply that the remaining 70 percent of changes in Y becomes disposable income. The numbers also show consumption as 80 percent of disposable income. By relating columns 2 and 3, one sees consumption as a function of disposable income. By relating columns 1 and 3, one sees consumption as a function of national income.

The new propensities tell us the proportion of total national income that goes to desired consumption (C/Y) and the proportion of any change in national income that goes to a change in desired consumption $(\Delta C/\Delta Y)$.

We now have a function showing how desired consumption expenditure varies as national income varies. The relation is defined for real income and real expenditure (i.e., income and expenditure measured in constant prices). This means that for every given level of real income, measured in terms of purchasing power, households will spend a given fraction of that purchasing power and save the rest.

OTHER CATEGORIES OF DESIRED EXPENDITURE

Having discussed the determinants of desired consumption expenditure in some detail, we now consider briefly the categories **I, G,** and **(X − M).**

Desired Investment Expenditure

Firms plan how much to invest in new capital equipment and in inventories. In this chapter it is convenient to study how the level of national income adjusts to a fixed level of planned investment. So we assume that firms plan to make a constant amount of investment in plant and equipment each year and that they plan to hold their inventories constant. (In Chapters 31 and 32 we shall drop these assumptions and study the important effects on national income caused by changes in the level of investment.)

Desired Government Expenditure

Government expenditures on currently produced goods and services are part of aggregate expenditure on the nation's output. At the outset we take desired and actual government expenditure as a constant. Governments intend to spend, and succeed in spending, so many billions of dollars on goods and services. This amount is assumed not to change as the circumstances of the

economy change. This assumption allows us to see in this chapter how national income adjusts to a constant level of government expenditure. (In Chapter 34 we shall see how national income responds to changes in desired and actual government expenditure.)

Desired Net Exports

For purposes of our simple theory, Canadian exports may be taken as a constant because they depend on decisions taken by foreign purchasers of our goods and services. Imports, however, depend on domestic purchases. Since all categories of expenditure have an import content, imports will rise when any other category of expenditure, C, I, or G, rises. Because consumption rises with income, imports must also rise with income. Increased imports involve both increased direct purchases of foreign-produced goods (including purchases made by Canadians in the course of foreign travel) and increased indirect imports arising from imports of materials that go into the production of domestically produced consumption goods.

Since imports rise as income rises, we must expect net exports **(X − M)** to *fall* as income rises. All this says is that, with exports constant, *net* exports will fall as income rises because imports rise. This then reduces aggregate desired expenditure on domestically produced commodities below what it would be if there were no expenditure on imports. The calculation of a net export function is illustrated in Table 30-4.

THE AGGREGATE DESIRED EXPENDITURE FUNCTION

Total desired expenditure on the nation's output is the sum of desired consumption, investment, government expenditure, and net exports. How do *changes* in national income affect total desired expenditure? To answer this question, we require the **aggregate expenditure function,** which relates the level of desired expenditure to the level of income. Table 30-5 illustrates how such a function can be calculated, given the consumption function and the levels of desired investment, government expenditure, and net exports at each level of income.

The aggregate expenditure function tells how much domestic governments, firms, and households and foreigners would like to spend on purchasing final domestic output at each level of income.

The function is illustrated by the first and sixth columns of Table 30-5.

Since for the present we assume that I, G, and X are constant, C and (X − M) are the only items of AE that vary systematically with income. But this is enough to make total desired expenditure vary with national income.

Just as we could define propensities to consume and to save that accounted for all household income, so we can define propensities to spend and not to spend that account for the whole of national income. The fraction of any addition to national income that all spending units

TABLE 30-4
A Net Export Schedule (millions of dollars)

National income (Y)	Exports (X)	Imports (M = .1Y)	Net exports
1,000	240	100	140
2,000	240	200	40
2,400	240	240	0
3,000	240	300	−60
4,000	240	400	−160
5,000	240	500	−260

Net exports fall as national income rises. The data are hypothetical. They assume that exports are constant and that imports are 10 percent of national income. Net exports are then positive at low levels of national income and negative at high levels.

would like to spend is measured by $\Delta AE/\Delta Y$ and is called the economy's marginal propensity to spend. The remainder is the fraction that spending units do not wish to spend. This is the marginal propensity not to spend (or the marginal propensity to withdraw). It is measured by $1 - \Delta AE/\Delta Y$. Assume for example that decisions of all spending units cause an increase of 80¢ in

TABLE 30-5
Aggregate Expenditure and Equilibrium National Income (millions of dollars)

National income (Y)	Desired consumption (C = 100 + .6Y)	Desired investment (I = 250)	Desired government expenditure (G = 410)	Net exports (X − M = 240 − .1Y)	Desired Aggregate expenditure (AE = C + I + G + [X − M])	
$ 100	$ 160	$250	$410	$230	$1,050	Pressure on income to increase
400	340	250	410	200	1,200	
500	400	250	410	190	1,250	
1,000	700	250	410	140	1,500	
2,000	1,300	250	410	40	2,000	Equilibrium income
3,000	1,900	250	410	−60	2,500	
4,000	2,500	250	410	−160	3,000	Pressure on income
5,000	3,100	250	410	−260	3,500	to decrease

National income is in equilibrium where aggregate desired expenditure equals national income. The data are hypothetical. Aggregate desired expenditure is found by adding desired expenditures on consumption, investment, government purchases, and net exports. When national income is below its equilibrium level, aggregate desired expenditure exceeds the value of current output. This creates an incentive for firms to increase output and hence for na-

tional income to rise. When national income is above its equilibrium level, desired expenditure is less than the value of current output. This creates an incentive for firms to reduce output and hence for national income to fall. Only at the equilibrium level of national income is aggregate desired expenditure exactly equal to the value of the current output.

desired spending whenever national income rises by $1. The marginal propensity to spend is .8 (i.e., .80/1.00), while the marginal propensity to withdraw is .2 (i.e., 1.00 − .80).

Autonomous and Induced Components of Aggregate Expenditure

On page 26 we defined autonomous variables as those exerting an influence on other variables while they themselves are *not influenced* by any other variable in the theory. They are determined from outside the theory. We also defined induced variables as those that are *influenced* by other variables within the theory.

In the elementary theory of national income investment, government expenditure and exports are assumed to be autonomous while consumption expenditure and imports (and hence net exports) are assumed to be induced.

Determining Equilibrium National Income

We are now in a position to see how equilibrium national income is determined. To do this, we study the conditions that must be fulfilled if national income is to be in equilibrium. Conditions that must hold if something is to be in equilibrium are called **equilibrium conditions.**

DESIRED EXPENDITURE EQUALS NATIONAL INCOME IN EQUILIBRIUM

Table 30-5 illustrates the determination of equilibrium national income. It is based on hypothetical data where consumption is $100 + .6Y$, imports are $.1Y$, and I, G, and X are constant at values of $250, $410, and $240 respectively (all figures are in millions of dollars).

Suppose that firms are producing final output

of $1,000, and thus national income is $1,000. According to Table 30-5, total desired expenditure, $C + I + G + (X − M)$, is $1,500 at that level of income. If firms persist in producing a current output of only $1,000 in the face of aggregate desired expenditure of $1,500, one of two things must happen.[4]

One possibility is that households, firms, and governments will be unable to spend the extra $500 that they wish to spend, so shortages and lines of unsatisfied customers will appear. These provide a signal to firms that they can increase their sales if they increase their production. When they do so, national income will rise.

The second possibility is that spending units will succeed in meeting their desired expenditures by purchasing goods produced in the past. Indeed, the only way that plans to purchase more than is currently being produced can be fulfilled is by purchasing inventories of goods produced in the past. In the present case, if plans to buy $1,500 worth of commodities were fulfilled in the face of current output of only $1,000, then inventories would have to be reduced by $500. As long as inventories last, this situation could persist with more goods being sold than were currently being produced. Sooner or later, however, inventories would run out. But long before this happened, firms would take steps to increase their output. This would allow their extra sales to be made without a further decumulation of inventories, and it would increase national income. Thus the final response to an excess of aggregate desired expenditure over current output is a rise in national income.

At any level of national income at which aggregate desired expenditure exceeds total output, there will be pressure for national income to rise.

---

[4] Remember that for the moment we are operating on the Keynesian portion of the *AS* curve. This rules out, just for the moment, the possibility of increases in prices, which is another possible reaction to a shortage.

Now consider the $4,000 level of national income in Table 30-5. At this level of income, desired expenditure on domestically produced goods is only $3,000. If firms persist in producing a total output of $4,000 worth of goods, $1,000 worth must remain unsold. Therefore inventories must rise. Firms will, however, be unwilling to allow inventories of unsold goods to rise indefinitely; sooner or later they will cut back on the level of output to make it equal to the level of sales. When they do, national income will fall.

At any level of national income at which aggregate desired expenditure falls short of total output, there will be a strong tendency for national income to fall.

Now look at the national income of $2,000 in the table. At this level, and only at this level, total desired expenditure is exactly equal to national income. Purchasers are able to buy just the total value of commodities that they wish to buy without causing inventories to be depleted, and firms are just able to sell all of their current output so that their inventories are neither rising nor falling. There is no incentive for firms to change their total output. Thus national income will tend to remain steady; it is in equilibrium.

The equilibrium level of national income occurs where aggregate desired expenditure is exactly equal to total output.

Total output, or national product, is the same as national income. Thus it is an equilibrium condition that desired expenditure equal actual national income.

The results just obtained are quite general and do not depend on the numbers chosen for this specific illustration. [37] A glance at Table 30-5 will show that there is *always* a tendency for national income to be pushed in the direction of its equilibrium value. Only when aggregate desired expenditure is equal to income is there no tendency for national income to change.

A GRAPHICAL ILLUSTRATION OF EQUILIBRIUM

Figure 30-3 shows the equilibrium level of national income. The *AE* line is the graph of the aggregate expenditure function. It shows expenditure rising with income but not as much as income rises because a $1 increase in income leads to an increase in consumption expenditure of less than $1 (and also to an increase in imports). The 45° line is the graph of the equilibrium condition that aggregate desired expenditure, *AE*, should equal national income, *Y*.

The intersection of the two lines determines equilibrium income. This is the level of income where desired expenditure is just equal to total national income, which is the total value of final output.

Graphically, equilibrium occurs at the level of income at which the aggregate desired expenditure line intersects the 45° line.

We have now developed a simple but very powerful theory of the determination of equilibrium national income. It gives a general result that holds for this and for all more complex cases: national income is in equilibrium where aggregate desired expenditure is equal to national income because in that case desired purchases will exactly equal total production.

A word of caution. It is important to note that equilibrium income is not the same thing as full-employment income. The latter is the national income that would be produced if there were full employment. The former is the level of income at which desired expenditure equals total income. Nothing in our model guarantees that they will be the same, and equilibrium income may be above or below full-employment income. The relation between the two defines the GNP gap and helps to determine the amount of unemployment. The further below full-employment income is equilibrium income, the larger is the GNP gap and the more unemployment there will be at equilibrium.

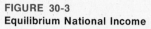

FIGURE 30-3
Equilibrium National Income

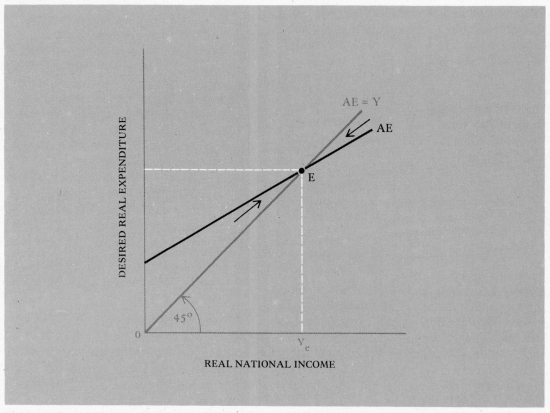

The equilibrium level of national income occurs at E, where the aggregate desired expenditure line inter-sects the 45° line. If national income is below Y_e, desired expenditure will exceed national income and production will rise. This is shown by the left-hand arrow. If national income is above Y_e, desired expenditure will be less than national income and production will fall. This is shown by the right-hand arrow in the figure.

The Relation Between Aggregate Demand and Aggregate Expenditure

We now have two important and powerful graphical tools at our command: the aggregate demand-aggregate supply diagram and the aggregate expenditure-45° line diagram. Let us call them "*AD-AS*" and "*AE*" for short. Both show the determination of equilibrium real national income. The *AD-AS* diagram relates Y to the price level while the *AE* diagram relates Y to desired expenditure. These diagrams will be used, starting in the next chapter, to shed light on the economy's macroeconomic behavior. But let us first be clear on how the two are related.

Since both diagrams have real national income on their horizontal axes, they can be stacked one above the other, as in Figure 30-4. The levels of national income determined in each can then be compared. Each graph, however, has a different vertical axis. The *AD-AS* diagram relates income to the price level, while the *AE* diagram relates income to desired expenditure.

Consider the *AE* diagram. Equilibrium national income is Y_e and, as the graph shows, lower levels of income have desired expenditure in excess of actual income while higher levels of income leave desired expenditure below actual income. The argument for why the economy moves to Y_e (see pages 604–605) assumes that firms adjust their output to demand at current prices: if desired expenditure exceeds current output, firms will produce more; if it is less than current output, firms will produce less. The equilibrium income determined by the *AE* diagram thus assumes that firms will produce whatever is demanded at the going price level, P. It assumes, therefore, that the economy is operating on the Keynesian portion of an aggregate supply curve. (Under these circumstances we say that there are no "supply constraints" on national income.)

The *AE* diagram analyzes the determination of equilibrium income on the assumption that firms are able and willing to produce whatever is demanded at the going price level.

This is in fact a demand-determined equilibrium with passive adjustment on the supply side.

The *AD* curve in Figure 30-4(ii) shows the same equilibrium income, Y_e, as in (i). In (ii) Y_e is associated with the price level P_0.

The *AD* curve shows for each price level the equilibrium income that would equate desired expenditure with actual income if firms were willing to produce that level of income at that price level.

Thus the *AD* curve shows the national income that would establish demand-side equilibrium at each price level, on the assumption that the economy is also producing that level of income at that price level.

Which diagram is most useful? When there are no supply constraints, the *AE* diagram is the more revealing way of seeing the forces that push the economy toward its equilibrium income. The *AD-AS* diagram is the more revealing when supply-side constraints are encountered. To see why, look at Figure 31-7 on page 623. If the relevant curves are AD_1, AS, and AE_1 and the price level is P_0, then national income would be in equilibrium at Y_1 *if firms were willing and able to*

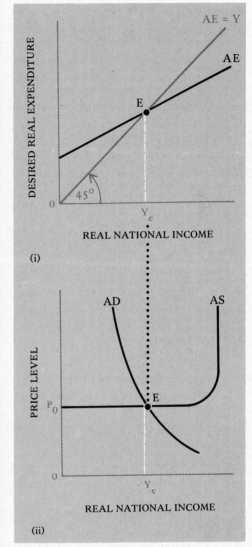

FIGURE 30-4
The *AD-AS* and *AE* Diagrams Related

(i)

(ii)

Equilibrium national income occurs where the aggregate desired expenditure function cuts the 45° line *and* where the aggregate demand and aggregate supply curves intersect. The *AE* diagram (i) shows the demand forces that drive national income to its equilibrium level when there are no supply constraints in the economy. The equilibrium income determined in the *AE* diagram yields a point on the aggregate demand curve. This curve shows for each price level the level of national income for which desired expenditure would equal income.

produce that much. But the *AD-AS* diagram shows that output Y_1 is more than the economy can produce. In other words, there is a supply-side constraint. If we had only the *AE* diagram, we would not be able to tell what would happen. The *AD-AS* diagram tells us that the price level will rise because *AD* and *AS* intersect at a price above P_0. (We defer a full analysis of this case.)[5]

In the following chapter we study the factors that can cause equilibrium to change by shifting the *AD* and *AE* curves. In beginning the analysis, it is helpful to deal with an economy that is operating on the Keynesian portion of an aggregate supply curve so that at the outset we do not have to worry about encountering supply-side constraints. Under these circumstances the *AE* diagram is our major analytical tool.

Summary

1. Desired expenditure includes desired consumption, desired investment, desired government expenditure, and desired net exports. It is the amount that decision makers want to spend on purchasing the national product.

2. With the exception of consumption and imports, the components of desired expenditure are assumed to be constant; they are determined by forces outside the simple theory of income determination.

3. Consumption expenditure is a function of disposable income with a marginal propensity to consume of less than unity. Since disposable income is a function of national income, it follows as well that consumption can be expressed as a function of national income. Both consumption and imports rise as income rises.

4. The aggregate expenditure (AE) function shows how aggregate desired expenditure varies with national income. It slopes upward with a

slope less than unity, indicating that a rise in national income of $1 leads to a rise in desired expenditure of less than $1.

5. National income is in equilibrium when aggregate desired expenditure equals national income. At that point purchasers wish to buy neither more nor less than what is being produced. At incomes above equilibrium, desired expenditure falls short of national product and output will sooner or later be curtailed. At incomes below equilibrium, desired expenditure exceeds national product and output will sooner or later be increased.

6. Graphically, equilibrium national income occurs where the aggregate expenditure curve cuts the 45° line and where the aggregate demand curve cuts the aggregate supply curve.

Topics for Review

The consumption function
Average and marginal propensities to consume and save, and to spend and not to spend
The aggregate expenditure function
The 45° line
Equilibrium national income

Discussion Questions

1. "The concept of an equilibrium level of national income is useless because the economy is never in equilibrium. If it ever got there, no economist would recognize it anyway." Discuss.
2. Interpret each of the following statements either in terms of the *shape* of a consumption function or the *values* of *MPC* and/or *APC*.
   a. "Tom Green has lost his job and his family is existing on its past savings."
   b. "The Grimsby household is so rich that they used all the extra income they earned this year to invest in a wildcat oil-drilling venture."
   c. "The widow Harris can barely make ends meet by clipping coupons on the bonds left to her by dear Henry, but she would never dip into her capital."
   d. "We always thought Hammerstein was a miser, but when his wife left him he took to wine, women, and song."

---

[5] The rise in the price level reduces demand because of the downward slope of *AD*. The reasons for the *AD* curve's sloping downward to the right were introduced in Chapter 29 and will be explained more fully in Chapter 38. The same reasons cause *AE* to *shift* vertically when the price level changes.

3. Can you think of any reasons why an individual's marginal propensity to consume might be higher in the long run than in the short run? Why it might be lower? Is it possible for an individual's average propensity to consume to be greater than unity in the short run? In the long run? Can a country's average propensity to consume be greater than unity in the short run? In the long run?

4. Along the 45° line on the basic diagram, what relationship holds between total expenditures and total income? In determining equilibrium graphically, are we restricted to choosing identical vertical and horizontal scales?

5. Explain carefully why national income changes when aggregate desired expenditure does not equal national income. Sketch a scenario that fits the cases of too much and too little desired expenditure. What factors might influence the speed with which national income moves toward its equilibrium level?

6. Explain how a sudden unexpected fall in consumer expenditure would initially cause an *increase* in investment expenditure by firms.

Changes in National Income

31

In Chapter 30 we investigated the conditions for national income to be in equilibrium. Recall that when equilibrium is obtained, there is no tendency for national income either to rise or to fall. National income does not, however, remain in a position of unchanging equilibrium; in fact, it changes continuously.

Why National Income Changes

In this chapter we study why income changes. As a preliminary to this study, we re-emphasize the important distinction between movements along curves and shifts of curves.

MOVEMENTS ALONG CURVES VERSUS SHIFTS OF CURVES

If desired expenditure rises, it makes a great deal of difference whether the rise is in response to a change in national income or to an increased desire to spend *at each level of national income* including the present one. The former change is represented by a movement along the aggregate expenditure function; it is the response of desired expenditure to a change in income. The latter change is represented by a shift in the expenditure function that occurs in response to a change in the proportion of income that people desire to spend at each level of income. It is the type of change that can itself disturb an existing equilibrium and cause national income to move from one equilibrium level to another. Figure 31-1 illustrates this important distinction.

The response of expenditure to a change in income is indicated by a movement along the expenditure function and is shown graphically by the slope of the expenditure curve.

The response of any expenditure to a change in income is called a **marginal propensity.** In Chapter 30 we defined the marginal propensities to save, consume, and spend out of national income as the changes in saving, in consumption, and in total spending that were brought about by a change in national income: $\Delta S/\Delta Y$, $\Delta C/\Delta Y$, and $\Delta AE/\Delta Y$. Graphically, marginal propensities are shown by the *slopes* of the relevant curves.

Marginal propensities relate to movements along curves and tell us how much a particular component of desired expenditure responds to a change in income.

Flows of expenditure can change for a second reason: the curves *themselves* may shift, indicating a new level of expenditure for *each* level of national income. One such shift is illustrated in Figure 31-1(ii).

The main causes of upward shifts in the aggregate expenditure function are:

1. An increase in the amount that firms wish to spend on investment at each level of income.
2. An increase in the amount that governments wish to spend on currently produced goods and services at each level of income.
3. An increase in the amount that households wish to spend on consumption at each level of disposable income. This is the same thing as a decrease in the amount that households wish to save at each level of disposable income.
4. Anything that shifts the function relating disposable income to national income in such a way that households get a larger disposable income at each level of national income—for example, a reduction in tax rates.
5. An increase in exports, X, so there is more foreign expenditure on domestically produced output at each level of national income.
6. A decrease in imports, M, causing a shift of consumption, investment, or government ex-

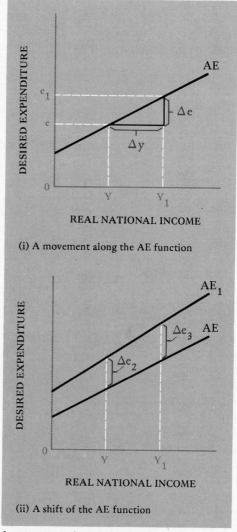

FIGURE 31-1
Movements Along Curves and Shifts of Curves

(i) A movement along the AE function

(ii) A shift of the AE function

A movement along the aggregate expenditure function occurs in response to a change in income; a shift of the *AE* function indicates a different level of desired expenditure at each level of income. In (i), a change in income of ΔY, from Y to Y_1, changes expenditure by Δe, from e to e_1. In (ii), a shift in the expenditure function itself raises the amount of expenditure associated with *each* level of income. At Y, for example, AE is increased by Δe_2; at Y_1, AE is increased by Δe_3. (If the shift is a parallel one, then $\Delta e_2 = \Delta e_3$.)

penditure away from foreign produced goods and toward goods produced domestically.

Ceteris paribus, either (5) or (6) will increase net exports, $X - M$.

What effects will each of these shifts have on equilibrium national income?

SHIFTS IN THE DESIRED EXPENDITURE FUNCTION

The desired expenditure function shifts directly when one of its components shifts, indirectly when something else shifts and that in turn causes a component of desired expenditure to shift.

Direct Shifts in Aggregate Expenditure

What will happen to national income if there is a shift in the consumption expenditure of households, in the investment expenditure of private firms, in government expenditure, or in exports? What will happen if, say, households permanently increase their levels of consumption spending at each level of income? if the Ford Motor Company of Canada increases its rate of annual investment by $25 million in order to meet the threat of small car imports? if the Canadian government increases its defence spending? or if Canadian exports of prefabricated housing soar? Fortunately, the same analysis can be used to study all four changes.

Each of the changes shifts the entire aggregate expenditure function upward.[1] A constant shift, indicating the same additional expenditure at all levels of income, shifts AE parallel to itself. Such shifts are illustrated in Figure 31-2. A change in the propensity to consume out of disposable or national income, however, changes the slope of the AE line. (Recall that the slope is the marginal

propensity to spend out of national income.) Such a shift is illustrated in Figure 31-3.

All upward shifts in AE increase equilibrium national income. After the shift, at the original level of income desired expenditure exceeds income, and this causes income to rise. As income rises, expenditure rises, but by less than the rise in income that induced it. The rise in income continues until expenditure is once again equal to (the now higher level of) income. In other words, the upward shift of the expenditure function induces a movement along the new function until the flow of desired expenditure is again equal to national income.

What will happen to national income if there is a fall in consumption, investment, exports or government spending? What will happen if, say, households permanently decrease their rate of spending at each level of income? if a loss of markets to foreign cars causes the North American automobile industry to reduce their investment expenditure permanently? if exports of refrigerators to Mexico fall because of increases in Mexican tariffs? or if the government drastically reduces expenditure on urban transport? Each of these changes shifts the aggregate expenditure function downward. A constant shift, indicating the same reduction in expenditure at all levels of income, shifts AE parallel to itself. A fall in the propensity to consume out of national income reduces the slope of the AE function. Figures 31-2 and 31-3 show that both kinds of shifts cause national income to fall.

We have now derived two important predictions of the theory of national income.

1. **A rise in the amount of desired consumption, investment, government, or export expenditure associated with each level of income will increase equilibrium national income, other things being equal.**
2. **A fall in the amount of desired consumption, investment, government, or export expenditure associated with each level of income will lower equilibrium national income, other things being equal.**

---

[1] It is extremely important to remember that we are dealing with continuous flows measured as so much per period of time. An upward shift in the expenditure function means that *in each period* expenditure is more than it was previously.

FIGURE 31-2

Parallel Shifts in the Aggregate Expenditure Function

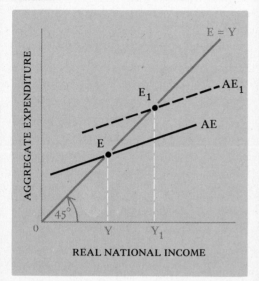

Parallel upward shifts in the *AE* function in-crease equilibrium income; parallel downward shifts decrease equilibrium income. Initially the aggregate expenditure function is *AE*, with na-tional income *Y*. A parallel upward shift in *AE*, say to *AE*₁, increases equilibrium income to *Y*₁. A downward shift in the function from *AE*₁ to *AE* lowers equilibrium income from *Y*₁ to *Y*.

Such parallel shifts mean that the same change in desired expenditure takes place at each level of national income.

Indirect Shifts in Aggregate Expenditure

So far we have considered the effects of direct changes in components of aggregate expenditure, consumption, investment, government expendi-ture, and exports. However, there are other flows that exert an indirect effect on expenditure. Consider the effects of changes in saving, taxes, and imports.

Increases in saving. What will happen to na-tional income if domestic households go on a saving kick? Perhaps they just do not like this year's models of gas-guzzling cars, and they elect to save the money they originally intended to

FIGURE 31-3

Changes in the Slope of the Aggregate Expenditure Function

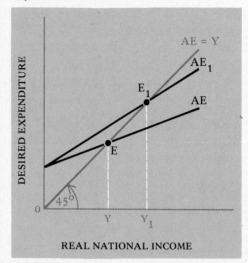

Increases in the slope of the aggregate expen-diture function increase equilibrium income; decreases in the slope decrease equilibrium income. Initially the aggregate expenditure function is *AE,* with national income in equilib-rium at *Y*. The propensity to spend out of na-tional income then increases, shifting the ex-penditure function to *AE*₁. Equilibrium income increases to *Y*₁. The opposite change, a fall in the propensity to spend out of national income, is shown by a shift of the expenditure function from *AE*₁ to *AE* and of equilibrium income from *Y*₁ to *Y*.

The shift from *AE* to *AE*₁ can be caused by a rise in the propensity to consume or a fall in tax rates that raises the proportion of national in-come going to disposable income. The shift from *AE*₁ to *AE* can be caused by a fall in the propen-sity to consume or a rise in tax rates.

spend on car purchases. A rise in saving means a fall in consumption. This causes a downward shift in the aggregate expenditure function and, as we have seen, that causes a fall in national in-come.

Increases in imports. What will happen if, in-stead of saving the money they do not spend on

TABLE 31-1
Shifts in the Function Relating Consumption to National Income

(1) National income (Y)	Disposable income equal to 70 percent of national income			Disposable income equal to 60 percent of national income		
	(2) Disposable income ($Y_d = .7Y$)	(3) Consumption ($C = .9Y_d$)	(4) Consumption ($C = .8Y_d$)	(5) Disposable income ($Y_d = .6Y$)	(6) Consumption ($C = .9Y_d$)	
100	70	63	56	60	54	
500	350	315	280	300	270	
1,000	700	630	560	600	540	

The consumption function shifts if either the propensity to consume out of disposable income changes, or the relation between disposable and national income changes. The table is based on simplified hypothetical data where C is always a constant fraction of Y_d and Y_d is always a constant fraction of Y. Initially, $Y_d = .7Y$ and $C = .9Y_d$. This yields a schedule relating consumption to national income that is given in columns 1 and 3. An increased saving propensity is indicated in column 4, where C falls to $.8Y_d$. This yields the new consumption schedule given in columns 1 and 4. In- creased tax rates, which lower the proportion of national income passing into disposable income, are illustrated in column 5. With the initial consumption function of $.9Y_d$, this yields the consumption schedule given in columns 1 and 6. Comparison of columns 3 and 4 shows that a fall in the propensity to consume shifts the schedule rating consumption to disposable income and to national income down- ward; comparison of columns 3 and 6 shows that a rise in tax rates shifts the schedule relating consumption to na- tional income downward.

Canadian-made cars, domestic households turn increasingly to gas-saving foreign cars? Or if firms and governments buy from abroad com- modities they formerly purchased at home? Any of these changes causes a fall in aggregate expen- diture on domestic production. The result is a fall in equilibrium national income.

Increases in tax rates. Finally, what will be the effect of a rise in tax rates? Suppose rates are raised so as to take an extra 10 percent of na- tional income at all levels of income in taxes. This will reduce the disposable income associ- ated with each level of national income. If 80 percent of disposable income is consumed, con- sumption expenditure will fall by 8 percent of na- tional income at each level of national income. This will shift the consumption schedule in Table 31-1 from that shown by columns 1 and 3 to that shown by columns 1 and 6.

Reductions in saving, imports, and tax rates. Not surprisingly, the opposite changes have the opposite effects. A fall in desired saving

at each level of income means more consumption expenditure at each level of income. A fall in im- ports means more spent on home production at each level of income. A fall in tax rates means more disposable income and hence more expen- diture at each level of income. All these changes raise the aggregate expenditure function, either by shifting it parallel to itself or by changing its slope. They thus cause an increase in equilibrium national income, as shown in Figures 31-2 and 31-3.

We have now derived two additional predic- tions of the theory of national income.

3. **A rise in tax rates, saving, or imports will lower the level of national income, other things being equal.**

4. **A fall in tax rates, saving, or imports will raise the level of national income, other things being equal.**

These predictions translate directly into predic- tions about unemployment and employment: anything that raises national income raises em- ployment and lowers unemployment; anything that lowers national income has the opposite effect.[2]

The Paradox of Thrift

These predictions have one important and rather surprising application. It is frequently assumed by analogy with the individual household that for the whole economy thrift is always good and prodigality always bad; that the former leads to increased wealth and prosperity and the latter to eventual bankruptcy. But is a penny saved really as good as a penny earned?

Prediction 3 (above) tells us what we should expect to happen if all households try simultaneously to increase the amount that they save. *The increase in thriftiness will decrease the equilibrium level of national income!* The upward shift in the savings schedule causes a fall in the aggregate expenditure function, which reduces national income.

The contrary case, a general decrease in household thriftiness and an increase in consumption, causes an upward shift in the aggregate expenditure function, which increases national income.

We have now derived the predictions of the so-called paradox of thrift.

Other things being equal, the more frugal and thrifty are spending units, the lower will be the level of national income and total employment. The more prodigal and spendthrift are spending units, the higher will be the level of national income and employment.

The prediction is not in fact a paradox. It is a straightforward, and important, corollary of prediction 3 that in turn follows logically from the theory of the determination of national income. It seems paradoxical to those who expect the way in which a single household should act if it wishes to raise its wealth and its future ability to consume ("save, save, and save some more") to

be directly applicable to the economy as a whole. Indeed, the expectations that lead to the "paradox" are based on the fallacy of composition (see page 571), the belief that what is true for the parts is necessarily true for the whole.

The paradox of thrift applies to governments as well as to households. If governments decide to save more, they must raise taxes or cut expenditure. Both alternatives will shift the aggregate expenditure function downward and reduce equilibrium national income. If governments decide to save less (that is, to become more spendthrift), they must lower taxes and/or raise spending. This will shift the expenditure function upward and raise equilibrium national income.

The policy implication of this prediction is that substantial unemployment is correctly combated by encouraging governments, firms, and households to *spend* more, not by encouraging them to save more. In times of unemployment and depression, frugality and parsimony will only make things worse. This prediction goes directly against the idea that we should tighten our belts when times are tough. The idea that it is possible to spend one's way out of a depression touches a very sensitive point in the consciences of people raised in the belief that success is based on hard work and frugality and not on prodigality; as a result, the idea often arouses great emotional hostility.

The implications of the paradox of thrift were not generally understood during the Great Depression of the 1930s. Country after country adopted policies that were, in the light of today's knowledge, disastrously misguided. In Canada, Prime Minister R. B. Bennett was quoted as saying in 1932. "We are now faced with the real crisis in the history of Canada. To maintain our credit we must practise the most rigid economy and not spend a single cent." His government that year brought down a budget based on the principle of trying to balance revenues and expenditures, and it included *increases* in income, corporation, and sales taxes.

U.S. President Franklin D. Roosevelt, in his first inaugural address (1933), urged:

---

[2] This assumes, as we did on page 566, that the labor force and productivity are constant.

Our greatest primary task is to put people to work . . . [this task] can be helped by insistence that the Federal, State, and local governments act forthwith on the demand that their costs be drastically reduced. . . . There must be a strict supervision on all banking and credits and investments.

Across the Atlantic, King Georg V told the House of Commons in 1931 that, "The present condition of the national finances, in the opinion of His Majesty's Ministers, calls for the imposition of additional taxation, and for the effecting of economies in public expenditure." At the time, unemployment in Canada was over 19 percent, while in both North American and Britain it was above 20 percent.

You should not read on until you are sure that you know what national income theory predicts to be the outcome of the policies recommended in the 1930s. The suffering and misery of that unhappy decade would have been greatly reduced if those in authority had known even as much economics as is contained in this chapter.

Assumptions Underlying the Paradox of Thrift

The striking prediction of the paradox of thrift depends critically on two basic assumptions.

The first assumption is that the economy is on the Keynesian portion of an aggregate supply curve so that output varies directly with aggregate demand and aggregate desired expenditure. However, if the economy is on the classical portion of an aggregate supply curve, a fall in saving will increase aggregate demand, but this will not increase output and employment.

The second assumption is that the volume of investment is at least partly independent of the volume of saving. There is no reason, according to the theory, why the amount that firms spend on investment at any level of income should bear any particular relation to the amount that households save. If the Smiths and the Greens save more, the theory assumes that there is no reason why the Johnsons or Acme, Inc., should decide to increase their investment expenditure to offset

the effects of their neighbors' saving. Under these circumstances, an increase in saving necessarily reduces aggregate desired expenditure.

If this second assumption is incorrect, none of the predictions of the paradox of thrift need hold. If changes in household saving cause changes in investment, there would be offsetting shifts in *both* consumption and investment whenever the desire to save changed. If, for example, households saved an extra $1 billion, their consumption expenditure would fall; but they might lend the money to firms that would spend the extra $1 billion on investment. Thus, while the composition of expenditure would change, there would be no change in total expenditure and hence no downward pressure on national income.

The predictions of the paradox of thrift, and most other predictions of the elementary theory of national income, depend critically, then, on the assumptions that saving and investment decisions are made to a great extent by different groups in society and that there is no mechanism whereby a change in the amount that is desired to be saved at a particular level of income will cause a change in the amount that is desired to be invested at the same level of income.

The Multiplier: A Measure of the Magnitude of Changes in Income

We have seen the direction of the effect on national income of various changes in the aggregate expenditure function. What can we know about the *magnitude* of these changes?

What if there is an upward shift in any of the elements of autonomous expenditure? Say government expenditure or private investment increases by $2 billion; by how much will national income change?

Economists must know the answer to this question in order to determine the effects of changes in expenditures in both the private and the public sectors. At the beginning of the 1980s, those wishing to balance the federal budget called for cutting as much as $4 billion from federal expenditure. To predict the effect of this policy on unemployment, one had to know by how much national income would decrease as a result.

During a depression, government measures are often taken to stimulate the economy. If these measures have a larger effect than estimated, demand may rise too much and full employment may be achieved with demand still rising. This will have an inflationary effect because no further increase in output can occur to meet further increases in demand. If, on the other hand, the government greatly overestimates the effect of its measures, much time will have been wasted. There is also a danger that the policy will be discredited as ineffective, even though the correct diagnosis is merely that too little of the correct thing was done.

DEFINITION OF THE MULTIPLIER

A central prediction of national income theory is that an increase in autonomous expenditure, whatever its source, will cause an increase in national income that is greater than the initial increase in expenditure. The change in autonomous expenditure might come, for example, from an increase in private investment, from new government spending, or from additional exports. The **multiplier** is the ratio of the change in national income to the initial change in expenditure that brings it about.

The importance of the multiplier in national income theory makes it worthwhile to use more than one approach to develop it and to show why its value exceeds unity.

THE MULTIPLIER: AN INTUITIVE STATEMENT

What would happen to national income if the government increased its expenditure on road building by $1 million per year with no corresponding rise in taxes (so that initially the other components of aggregate expenditure were left unaffected)?[3]

National income will initially rise by $1 million because of the increase in government spending. The road program will create $1 million worth of new income and a corresponding amount of employment for those households and firms on which the money is spent. Yet that is not the end of the story. The increase in national income of $1 million will cause an increase in disposable income, which will cause an induced rise in consumption expenditure. Owners of factors of production that gain new income directly from the government's road program will spend some of it on food, clothing, entertainment, cars, television sets, and other consumption commodities. When output expands to meet this demand, employment will increase in all the affected industries. When the owners of factors that are newly employed to produce consumption commodities spend their extra incomes, output and employment will rise further; more income will then be created and more expenditure induced. Indeed, at this stage we might begin to wonder whether the increase in income will ever come to an end. This question will be more easily answered if we look at a second way to describe the process of income expansion.

THE MULTIPLIER: A GRAPHICAL ANALYSIS

Figure 31-4 illustrates the multiplier graphically. The increase in autonomous expenditure of ΔA initially raises national income by that amount. Then the increase in national income induces more consumption expenditure, and this further raises national income. As income rises, consumption expenditure rises by less than income. Income will stop rising when desired aggregate expenditure is once again equal to national income.

A high marginal propensity to spend means a

---

[3] For simplicity we assume that there is no import content to road building.

FIGURE 31-4
The Multiplier

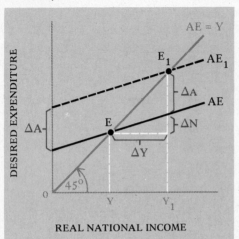

An increase in autonomous expenditure increases national income by a multiple of the initial increase. Initial equilibrium income is Y, where the expenditure function AE cuts the 45° line. Autonomous expenditure now increases by ΔA, taking the new expenditure function to AE_1 and equilibrium income to Y_1. The increase in income of ΔY is equal to the increase in autonomous expenditure of ΔA plus the increase in induced expenditure of ΔN. Since ΔN is positive, ΔY exceeds ΔA. The multiplier, which is the ratio $\Delta Y/\Delta A$, is thus greater than one.

steep AE curve. The resulting induced consumption expenditure caused by the initial increase in income is large, with the result that the final rise in income is correspondingly great. A low marginal propensity to spend means a relatively flat AE curve. The resulting induced consumption expenditure caused by the initial increase in income is small. The result is that the final rise in income is not much larger than the initial rise in autonomous expenditure that brought it about. Both cases are shown in Figure 31-5.

The multiplier is given the symbol K. It is defined as the final change in income divided by the change in autonomous expenditure that brought it about. In symbols,

$$K = \frac{\Delta Y}{\Delta A}$$

Using the symbols of Figure 31-4, we can break up ΔY, the change in Y, into the change in autonomous expenditure, ΔA, and the induced change in expenditure, ΔN. Substituting $\Delta Y = \Delta A + \Delta N$ in the above expression yields

$$K = \frac{\Delta A + \Delta N}{\Delta A}$$

This shows that it is the induced change in expenditure, ΔN, that makes the multiplier greater than unity. As the induced component to expenditure becomes smaller (the AE line becomes flatter), the multiplier becomes smaller. Indeed, if ΔN were zero, the multiplier would be one. The common sense of this is that if there were no induced expenditure, those who initially received the government's expenditure of \$1 million per year would spend none of their extra income. There would then be no repercussions; income would rise by the \$1 million of ΔA but no further.

The size of the induced component depends, *ceteris paribus*, on the marginal propensity to spend. If it is high, people who receive the initial \$1 million of extra income will in turn raise their spending a lot. If it is low, they will raise their spending only a little.

The larger is the marginal propensity to spend (the steeper the aggregate expenditure function), the larger is the value of the multiplier.

THE SIZE OF THE MULTIPLIER

We have seen that the multiplier depends on the slope of the aggregate expenditure function. It turns out that the precise relation is

$$K = \frac{1}{1-n}$$

where n is the slope of the expenditure function, that is, the marginal propensity to spend. **[38]** The term $1-n$ is the marginal propensity not to spend, or what we called the marginal propensity to withdraw (see page 603). For example if 80¢ of every \$1 of new national income is spent ($n = .8$), then 20¢ (1.00 − .80) is the amount not spent of every \$1 of new income. If we refer to $1-n$ as

w, we can write the size of the multiplier as

$$K = \frac{1}{w}$$

The multiplier is the reciprocal of the marginal propensity to withdraw (or not to spend).

If w is very small, the multiplier will be very large (because extra income induces much extra expenditure). The large possible value of w is unity, indicating that all extra income is not spent. In this case, as we have already argued, the multiplier has a value of unity, indicating that the increase in income is confined to the initial increase in autonomous expenditure.

HOW LARGE IS THE MULTIPLIER IN CANADA?

The predictions and the policy implications of a multiplier of 1.5 or 2 are very different from those of a multiplier of 5 or 10. Will $10 billion of new investment expenditure increase national income by $15 billion or by $50 billion? Clearly this is an important question.

If the marginal propensity to spend out of national income is known or can be estimated, the magnitude of the effect on income of a shift in any component of aggregate expenditure can be estimated.

A number of studies of the Canadian economy have been made to determine the effects on equilibrium income of shifts in the aggregate expenditure function. The theory of income determination developed in this and the preceding chapter is utilized in a more complex form that takes account of much more detail concerning the workings of the economy. The technique used is to construct an econometric model; that is, a set of mathematical relationships among economic variables is derived from an examination of historical data. Such models have been constructed by a number of economic research groups in Canada, including the Research Department of the Bank of Canada, the Economic Council of Canada, and the Institute for Policy Analysis at the University of Toronto.

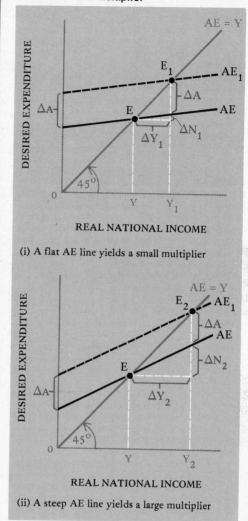

FIGURE 31-5
The Size of the Multiplier

(i) A flat AE line yields a small multiplier

(ii) A steep AE line yields a large multiplier

The steeper the expenditure function, the larger the marginal propensity to spend and the larger the multiplier. In both parts of the figure national income, initially at Y, is disturbed by an increase in autonomous expenditure of ΔA.

In (i), the aggregate expenditure function is flat (a low marginal propensity to spend) and there is only a small increase in induced expenditure of ΔN_1. The increase in national income of ΔY_1 is only slightly larger than the increase in autonomous expenditure that brought it about. The multiplier is small.

In (ii), the AE function is steep (a high marginal propensity to spend) and there is a large increase in induced expenditure of ΔN_2. The increase in national income of ΔY_2 is much larger than the increase in autonomous expenditure that brought it about. The multiplier is large.

The Multiplier: A Numerical Approach

Suppose that the economy behaves in this simple way: whenever national income rises by $1, disposable incomes rises by 60¢, induced consumption expenditure on domestically produced goods and services rises by 50¢, and induced import expenditures and savings each rise by 5¢. This economy's marginal propensity to spend out of national income is .5.

Now suppose that autonomous expenditure increases because the government spends an extra $1 million a year on new roads. National income initially rises by $1 million. But that is not the end of it; there is a second round of spending. The factors of production involved directly and indirectly in road building receive an extra $600 thousand as disposable income, and then spend an extra $500 thousand each year on domestically produced goods and services. This $500 thousand generates $300 thousand of new disposable income and $250

thousand of new consumption expenditure (the remaining $50 thousand goes to increased imports and savings), which is a third round of additions to aggregate expenditure.

And so it continues, each successive round of new income generating 50 percent as much in new expenditure. Each additional round of expenditure creates new income and yet another round of expenditure.

The table below carries the process through ten rounds. Students with sufficient patience (and no faith in mathematics) may compute as many rounds in the process as they wish; they will find that the sum of the rounds of expenditures approaches $2 million, which is twice the initial injection of $1 million. [39] The multiplier is thus 2, given these numerical assumptions about the relations between national income and disposable income and induced expenditure.

	Increases in disposable income	Increases in expenditure
	(thousands of dollars per year)	
		$1,000.00
Assumed increase in government expenditure per year		
2nd round (increase in disposable income and expenditure)	$600.00	500.00
3rd round (increase in disposable income and expenditure)	300.00	250.00
4th round (increase in disposable income and expenditure)	150.00	125.00
5th round (increase in disposable income and expenditure)	75.00	62.50
6th round (increase in disposable income and expenditure)	37.50	31.25
7th round (increase in disposable income and expenditure)	18.75	15.63
8th round (increase in disposable income and expenditure)	9.38	7.81
9th round (increase in disposable income and expenditure)	4.69	3.91
10th round (increase in disposable income and expenditure)	2.34	1.95
Sum of 1st 10 rounds		1,998.05
All other rounds		1.95
Total		$2,000.00

As an example of the complexity of the theory required, consider the treatment of imports. In the simple theory used here, we assume that the same fixed proportion of all components of expenditures is spent on imports. In reality this is not the case, and it is particularly important in calculating multipliers to take account of the differences in important components among the various categories of expenditure. If, for example, there is an increase in government expenditures resulting from increased employment of civil servants, there will be an immediate dollar-for-dollar increase in national income, and imports will increase only as a result of the induced increase in consumption expenditures.

On the other hand, an increase in government purchases of goods from the private sector will involve some import component so that the immediate increase in domestic production and income will be less than the increase in expenditures. In fact, it is possible that the multiplier will be less than one when it is calculated as the ratio of the increase in equilibrium income to the increase in autonomous expenditure if this increase involves a large import component. However, this possibility does not seem to be of much practical importance in the light of the multiplier estimates that have been made. For example, the Economic Council of Canada has estimated the multiplier to be 2.1 for an increase in government expenditures in the form of capital formation. But that is after the *full* round of induced changes illustrated in the box have worked themselves out — a process that may take several years. The Economic Council calculates that the multiplier that occurs after one year is only 1.6.

Other studies of the Canadian economy have been made that caution that as a rough order of magnitude the GNP multiplier is between 1.5 and 2.5. This may not sound very precise. But only about three decades ago economists thought the multiplier might be as high as 5 or 10. Today we are confident that an increase in autonomous expenditure of $10 million per year will lead to an increase in GNP of roughly $15 to $25 million — maybe only $14 million, or maybe as much as $27 million — but we are certain that (other things remaining approximately equal) it will not increase GNP by so much as $50 million or so little as only $11 million. For practical purposes, this acquired knowledge makes an enormous difference in our ability to control the economy.

Inflationary and Deflationary Gaps

Up to now we have considered equilibrium positions on the Keynesian portion of the aggregate supply curve. Now we want to look at situations in which the price level can rise. This will take us to positions off the Keynesian portion of the *AS* curve. To simplify matters at the outset, we employ the version of the aggregate supply curve introduced in Figure 28-10, on page 575.

The *kinked aggregate supply curve* contains only a Keynesian portion and a classical portion, as shown by the *AS* curves in Figures 31-6 and 31-7. National income, Y_F, at which the kink occurs, can be identified as full-employment national income.

The kinked aggregate supply curve makes a sharp distinction between situations of unemployment, where the price level is fixed and real national income is variable, and situations of full employment, where real national income is fixed at its full-employment level while the price level is variable.

In analyzing situations of unemployment and full employment, three gaps are used by policy analysts such as the Council of Economic Canada. These are considered below.

Situations of Unemployment

When national income is below its full-employment level, two gaps may be calculated. The first gap, which we encountered in Chapter

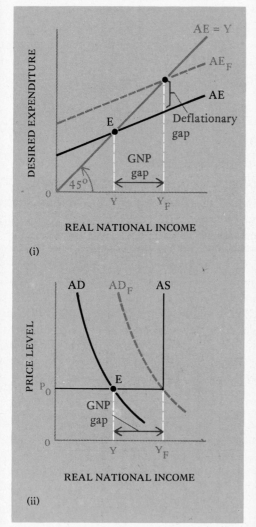

FIGURE 31-6
The GNP Gap and the Deflationary Gap

(i)

(ii)

The GNP gap measures the shortfall of equilibrium national income below full-employment national income; the deflationary gap measures the shortfall of aggregate desired expenditure below full-employment income. Aggregate expenditure and aggregate demand, AE and AD, produce equilibrium income of Y, which falls short of full-employment income, Y_F. The GNP gap is $Y_F - Y$. The deflationary gap is the amount by which the aggregate expenditure function would have to be shifted upward to create full employment. This would require shifting AE to AE_F, which would shift AD to AD_F.

28, measures the extent of the shortfall in national income.

The extent to which actual national income is below its full-employment level is called the GNP gap.

This can be shown in both an *AD-AS* diagram and an aggregate expenditure diagram, such as in the two parts of Figure 31-6. The GNP gap measures the lost output that could have been produced if full employment had been achieved.

The second gap measures the extent of the shortfall in desired expenditure. When national income is in equilibrium at less than full employment, a sufficiently large upward shift in the aggregate expenditure function would raise national income to its full-employment level.

The extent to which the aggregate expenditure schedule would have to shift upward to produce the full-employment level of national income is called the deflationary gap.

Because this gap refers to a shortfall of autonomous expenditure, it can be shown only in part (i) of Figure 31-6.

Situations of Full Employment

Now consider inflationary situations. If aggregate desired expenditure exceeds the economy's full-employment output at the current price level, there will be inflationary demand pressure in the economy. Such a situation is shown in Figure 31-7 when the aggregate expenditure curve has shifted to AE_1 in part (i) and the aggregate demand function to AD_1 in part (ii) while the price level is still at P_0.

If aggregate desired expenditure exceeds output at the full-employment level of income, there is inflationary pressure. Enough output to satisfy demand at current prices cannot be produced.

The extent to which the aggregate expenditure schedule would have to shift downward to pro-

duce the full-employment level of national income without inflation is called the **inflationary gap**.

This gap is shown in part (i) of Figure 31-7.[4]

USING THE CONCEPTS OF THE "GAPS"

The modern theory of income determination is an elaboration of the original model put forward by John Maynard Keynes in *The General Theory of Employment, Interest and Money*, first published in 1936. In the original Keynesian model, the emphasis was on situations of unemployment rather than full employment. This was not surprising since Keynes was concerned to find cures for the Great Depression, which had had disastrous consequences for the tens of millions of workers who made up the massive armies of unemployed in Western industrial nations. Indeed, the Depression was helping to undermine the very social fabric of Western democracies; finding a cure for it was then the most pressing social problem.

The extension of the theory to cover problems of full employment and demand inflation did not come until World War II, when those problems replaced the nightmare of persistent, massive unemployment in the minds and consciences of people. The concept of the inflationary gap proved the vehicle for extending the theory beyond the conditions that it was originally designed to explain.

The concepts of both inflationary and deflationary gaps prove useful in discussing policy questions of how to achieve stability in the economy. That discussion can be foreshadowed by noting that one way to combat unemployment is to estimate the size of the deflationary gap and

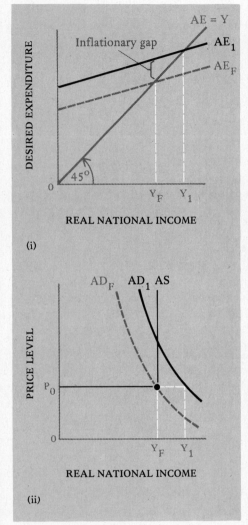

FIGURE 31-7
The Inflationary Gap

(i)

(ii)

The inflationary gap is the amount by which the aggregate expenditure curve must be shifted downward to produce equilibrium at full-employment income at the present price level. Aggregate expenditure and aggregate demand are AE_1 and AD_1 and the price level is P_0. At full-employment income, aggregate desired expenditure exceeds income by the amount of the inflationary gap. To produce equilibrium at Y_F and P_0, the aggregate expenditure curve would have to be shifted downward to AE_F (which would shift the aggregate demand curve to AD_F).

---

[4] There is a fourth gap, shown in Figure 31-7. When the price level is P_0 but aggregate expenditure is AE_1, there is enough desired expenditure to purchase Y_1 of national output if only it could be produced. The gap $Y_1 - Y_F$ measures the inability of current full-employment capacity to produce the level of output that would yield an equilibrium (desired expenditure equals income) at the current price level. This gap does not play any great part in current policy discussion because the amount that could be bought, if only it could be produced, is of no great importance to any macro policy.

attempt to eliminate it by policies that shift the aggregate expenditure curve upward. Similarly, one way to combat inflation is to estimate the size of the inflationary gap and attempt to eliminate it by policies that shift the aggregate expenditure curve downward. Such policies are discussed in detail in Chapter 34.

Summary

1. A movement along an expenditure curve represents an induced change in expenditure in response to a change in national income. A shift of an expenditure function represents a change in expenditure associated with each level of national income.

2. Movements along curves are described by marginal propensities. They give the change in expenditure as a proportion of the change in income that brought it about. The marginal propensity gives the slope of the expenditure function over the range for which it is measured.

3. Equilibrium national income is increased by an upward shift in the consumption, investment, government, or export expenditure associated with each level of national income. National income is decreased by the opposite changes.

4. Equilibrium national income is decreased by an increase in saving, imports, or taxes associated with each level of income. National income is increased by the opposite changes.

5. The above predictions have an important counterintuitive application: the paradox of thrift. What is true for the individual is not true for the nation. If everyone reduces consumption and increases saving, national income will fall. Leading governments demonstrated ignorance of this by their economic policies during the Great Depression, when they tried to fight the Depression by cutting their expenditures because their tax revenues had fallen.

6. The magnitude of the effect on national income of shifts in autonomous expenditure (such as I, G, and X) is given by the multiplier. This is defined as $K = \Delta Y/\Delta A$, where ΔA is the change in autonomous expenditure. The elementary theory of national income gives the value of the multiplier as $1/(1 - n) = 1/w$, where n is the marginal propensity to spend and w is the marginal propensity to withdraw (or not to spend). Thus the larger the propensity to spend, the larger the multiplier.

7. It is a basic prediction of national income theory that the multiplier is greater than unity. Its actual size is an important magnitude. As a rough order of magnitude for Canada today, the GNP multiplier is taken to be about 2. (An increase in autonomous expenditure of $\$X$ million will tend to lead to an increase in GNP of about $\$2X$ million.)

8. The GNP gap is the difference between actual national income and full-employment or potential national income. It represents a waste in terms of lost production because all of the nation's resources are not fully employed.

9. The inflationary and deflationary gaps measure the level of aggregate desired expenditure relative to the level required to achieve full employment. An inflationary gap means that aggregate desired expenditure is more than sufficient to produce full-employment national income at constant prices. A deflationary gap means that it is insufficient to do so.

Topics for Review

Shifts of and movements along expenditure curves
The effect on national income of changes in the amounts of I, G, X, S, T, and M associated with each level of income
The paradox of thrift
The multiplier
The relation between the size of the multiplier and the slope of the expenditure schedule
The kinked aggregate supply function
The GNP gap
Inflationary and deflationary gaps

Discussion Questions

1. In what direction would each of the following change national income, *ceteris paribus?* Which expenditure flows would be affected first? Would other elements of expenditure also change? Be sure to distinguish between movements along curves and shifts of curves.
   a. the production and sale of an atomic reactor
   b. a decrease in personal income tax withholding for low-income taxpayers
   c. the institution of a new federal program of $20 million of payments to the elderly
   d. a spurt in consumer spending for video recorders accompanied by a reduction in savings
   e. a reduction in spending on foreign travel accompanied by an equivalent increase in saving
   f. a decision to reduce provincial spending on hospital construction

2. The fallacy of composition is defined as a fallacy in which what is true of a part is inaccurately assumed to be true also of the whole. Can the "paradox" in the paradox of thrift be explained by applying this point of logic? Explain.

3. Predict whether each of the following events will, *ceteris paribus,* increase, decrease, or leave unchanged the size of the multiplier:
   a. a shift from foreign travel to holidays at home
   b. an expansion of expenditures on highways
   c. decisions by corporations to pay out a smaller percentage of their earnings in dividends and to increase their bank balances whenever national income falls
   d. widespread adoption by cities of a city income tax

4. If you were running a country's economic stabilization program, would you prefer the country to have a large or a small multiplier?

5. The president of the Chamber of Commerce of Southeastern Connecticut commented on the effects in his area of a 22-week strike at a shipyard where the lost payroll was $2 million per week: "You don't just figure $2 million a week times 22 weeks, you have to multiply that by four or five. That shipyard is the prime source of money in this region. Money comes into the region from Washington and then the shipyard worker's wife takes it to the grocery, and the grocery clerk takes it to the gas station, and so on until it leaves the area in taxes or some other way." Interpret his statement in terms of the analysis of this chapter.

6. Homer Hardcrust, chairman of the Economic Council of Canada, proposes that because of the economic situation the government should prepare an austerity program and cut down government expenditures to set an example for private households. Under what economic conditions might Hardcrust's advice make sense? Under what conditions would it worsen the situation?

7. "We now have approximately 70 percent of our industrial capacity being used; which means that 30 percent or so is not being used. With eight million people unemployed, that's another tremendous untapped reservoir of workers and capacity that can be tapped before you have pressures of an inflationary type." Does the speaker (President Carter, at a news conference) express views consistent with the kinked aggregate supply curve?

Cycles and Fluctuations in National Income

32

Changing, always changing; this is the dominant characteristic of the GNP for as far back as records exist. Long-term growth and short-term fluctuations are the two major components of the GNP changes that we observe. Long-term growth is seen in the steady upward trend in the potential GNP—the GNP that can be produced when the economy is at full employment. (Long-term growth will be studied in Chapters 43 and 44.) Shorter-term fluctuations are seen in oscillations of actual GNP around the level set by potential GNP. Such oscillations are related to changes in aggregate demand and aggregate supply. They lead to changes in what is actually produced, and these changes in turn cause variations in the amount of employment and unemployment. Short-term fluctuations in GNP are the subject of the present chapter.

THE HISTORICAL RECORD

Figure 32-1 shows the year-to-year changes in real GNP. What produces such changes? If, on the one hand, aggregate demand shifts to the left because of decreases in desired consumption, investment, government expenditure, or net exports without a compensating change in any of the other components, aggregate expenditure will fall. Total output will soon be reduced in response, and employment and actual GNP will fall. If, on the other hand, aggregate demand shifts to the right, aggregate expenditure will rise. This will cause a rise in real output, and employment and real GNP will rise—at least until all

FIGURE 32-1
Annual Changes in Real GNP

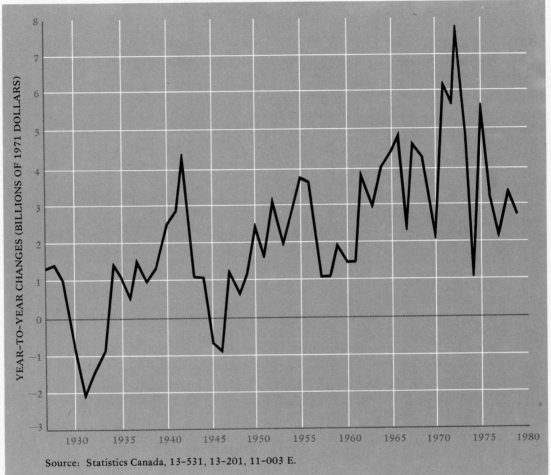

Source: Statistics Canada, 13-531, 13-201, 11-003 E.

Real national income changes continually from one year to the next. Despite a strong upward trend shown by the fact that most changes are increases, real national income does not rise steadily year after year. Generally, two or three years of very rapid increase tend to be followed by two or three years of slow increase, or even decline, in GNP.

available factors of production become fully employed.

Fluctuations in aggregate demand have usually been the major reason for short-term fluctuations in GNP. Events of the mid 1970s, however, have made the citizens of advanced industrial countries acutely aware of supply-side causes. If supplies of such critical raw materials as oil or iron ore are drastically reduced, output will fall and unemployment will rise even though there is enough demand to buy the whole of the economy's potential GNP. If goods cannot be produced, they cannot be sold.

In Chapter 31 we developed a theory of how national income changes in response to changes in the various components of aggregate expendi-

FIGURE 32-2
Three Indicators of Economic Activity in Canada, 1926–1979

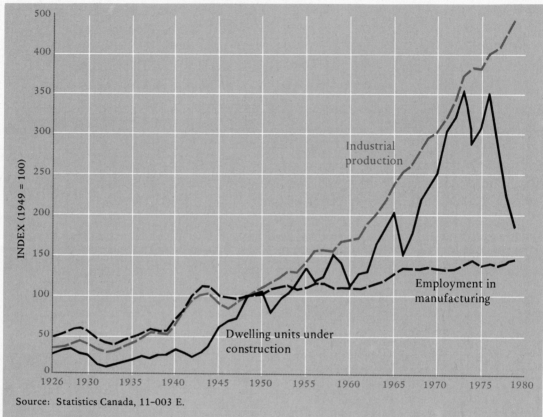

Source: Statistics Canada, 11–003 E.

Short-term variability and a long-term upward trend characterize many indexes of Canadian economic activity. All three series are index numbers with 1949 = 100, so all pass through 100 at 1949. All series exhibit differing degrees of short-term variability and differing trend rates of growth. Dwelling starts under construction vary greatly from year to year, and fell continually over the last five years in the figure. Employment in manufacturing does not fluctuate greatly because even a large change in unemployment, say from 4 percent to 8 percent of the labor force, makes a relatively small percentage change in employment.

ture. If there were merely occasional sharp shifts in these components, we would expect national income to show occasional sharp changes followed by long periods of little or no change. This is not, however, the picture suggested by Figure 32-1; instead the short-term situation is one of continual change but at a varying rate. Evidently there are factors at work causing the economy to display continual short-term fluctuations around its long-term rising growth trend.

The short-term behavior of the economy cannot be fully caught by a single statistic. Figure 32-2 shows three important economic series; each series, as well as each of a dozen other widely used series, tells us something about the general variability of the economy. It is obvious that some series vary more than others and that they do not all move together.

Fluctuations such as those in Figure 32-1 have traditionally been called **business cycles.**

There is a fairly general consensus among students of economic fluctuations that:

1. There is a common pattern of variation that more or less pervades all economic series.
2. There is substantial difference from cycle to cycle in duration and in amplitude.
3. There are differences among economic series in their particular patterns of fluctuation.

When economic time series are observed at monthly or quarterly intervals rather than annually, many exhibit marked seasonal patterns. This is illustrated by the monthly unemployment rates shown in Figure 32-3. For purposes of analyzing cyclical movements in economic activity it is common to make use of **seasonally adjusted** series. For example, between June and October 1979, the unadjusted unemployment rate fell from 7.0 to 6.4 percent. However, according to the calculations of Statistics Canada based on observation of past seasonal variation, this was a smaller fall than is usual at this time of the year. Thus, when seasonal influences have been removed, the seasonally adjusted rate remained unchanged at 7.4 percent.

IS THERE A PRINCIPAL CAUSE OF CYCLES?

Professor Alvin Hansen, one of the most distinguished American students of business cycles, once reported that in the U.S. economy between

FIGURE 32-3
Monthly Unemployment Rate, 1978 and 1979

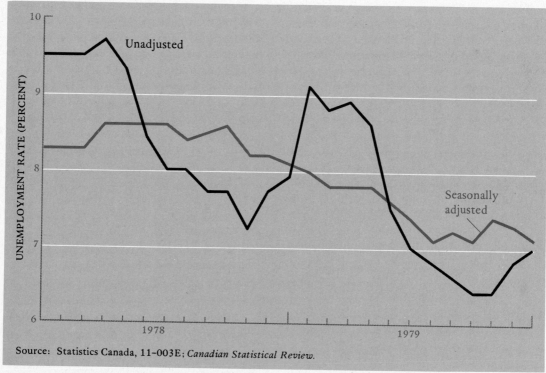

Source: Statistics Canada, 11–003E; *Canadian Statistical Review.*

Most of the month-to-month variation in unemployment is attributable to seasonal factors. The unadjusted rate typically rises sharply in the winter, when employment falls in industries such as construction, fishing, and tourism. These influences are removed in the calculation of the seasonally adjusted rate.

1795 and 1937 there were 17 cycles, of an average duration of 8.35 years. A shorter "inventory cycle" of 40 months' duration was also found, as well as longer cycles associated with building booms (15 to 20 years). The Russian economist Kondratieff identified long waves of 40 to 50 years associated with the introduction of major innovations. Some economists have recently argued for the existence in many Western democracies of a political business cycle associated with the pattern of elections.

Why does the economy undergo business fluctuations? It seems apparent from the behavior of the economy that some elements of aggregate expenditure must be changing continuously. Such a situation causes the equilibrium level of national income to be changing continuously as well and causes the actual level of national income to be moving in pursuit of this equilibrium income.

What are the possible sources of these continuous disturbances? The theory of income determination suggests four main candidates—shifts in each of the four main components of aggregate expenditure. Each can shift in response to outside exogenous shocks, to endogenous forces within the economy, and to government policy measures.

Shifts in Consumption

About two-thirds of total expenditure in Canada is made up of consumption expenditures. If households were to reduce their consumption expenditure by 3 percent, this would amount to a reduction of 2 percent in total expenditure. Combined with a multiplier of 2, this would cause GNP to decline by 4 percent. Perhaps this does not sound like very much, but if employment were to change merely in proportion to income, this could change a situation of 4 percent unemployment (a level considered to be full employment or even above full employment and one not achieved since 1967), to one of 8 percent, which was exceeded only very recently, in 1977 and 1978. Clearly, even relatively small percentage fluctuations in consumption can have big effects

on the economy. Such fluctuations have occurred in the past. What causes them?

In discussing the effects of shifts in the consumption function on GNP, it is useful to distinguish between factors that change the function relating household consumption to household disposable income, and factors changing the relation between disposable income and GNP. (We first encountered the distinction on page 614.)

SHIFTS IN THE RELATIONSHIP BETWEEN CONSUMPTION AND DISPOSABLE INCOME

From time to time tastes change; when they do, consumption levels and patterns may change. A large number of households may decide that they do not take to this year's car models and elect to save the money they were expected to spend on a new car this year. If this happens, the consumption function will shift downward this year. Incomes earned in Oshawa (and many other places) will fall, and unemployment will rise. The unemployed auto workers will cut their spending on other products, and a multiplier process will be set up that will magnify and spread the original cut in spending on new automobiles into a general fall in income and employment.

While the demand for an individual commodity (such as cars) often shifts sharply from year to year, the aggregate proportion of consumer income going to current expenditure tends to be relatively more stable. The division between consumption and saving does however shift. What are some of the reasons for this?

Expectations About the Future

Many kinds of consumer expenditures—such as food, clothing, and automobile repair—are hard to postpone. Many others are discretionary. The latter include purchases of durable goods such as television sets and new cars and luxuries such as restaurant meals and long vacation trips. It is now well known that consumers' discretionary expenditures respond to the general economic and political climate. If consumers are apprehensive about the economic future, particularly about the possibility of unemployment, they tend to postpone purchases and increase savings. Generally, when consumers are optimistic, they are willing to buy and to dissave by extending their credit purchases.

Inflationary expectations have proven very troublesome to consumers. On the one hand, if households expect prices to rise rapidly, they may rush to buy new goods they know they will have to purchase sometime in the relatively near future. In such circumstances purchases at today's prices may be an attractive use of accumulated savings. However, inflationary expectations also cause insecurity about the adequacy of the household's future income and may lead to a decrease in purchases in order to increase savings.

If many consumers are led to postpone durable purchases—which on average account for about 15 percent of all consumer expenditures—this will lead to sharp downward shifts in consumption expenditures and leftward shifts in the aggregate demand function. When such postponements occur, the age of the existing stock of durables grows. Once the end of the period of pessimism comes, there is likely to be a sudden outburst of expenditures out of accumulated savings. The consumption function may shift sharply upward for a year or two until the backlog of demand is exhausted.

Terms of Credit

Most durable consumer goods and many nondurable ones are purchased on credit, which may range from a few months to pay for a stereo or a new suit to up to five years to pay for an automobile. If credit becomes more difficult or more costly to obtain, many households will postpone their planned, credit-financed purchases. If the amount of the typical down payment rises, or if monthly carrying charges rise, some consumers will postpone replacing a television set or do without the recreational vehicle they had planned to buy. Instead they may add the purchase price to their savings deposit at the bank (which is probably advertising new, higher rates of interest).

Notice here that government policymakers can, by controlling the cost and availability of credit, shift the consumption function and thereby affect aggregate demand.

Changes in Income Distribution

Because the consumption function relates *aggregate* consumption expenditures of the nation's households to their aggregate disposable income, the consumption function can change without the habits of any individual changing. For example, if income is transferred from a rich family that saves 40 percent of its marginal income to a poor family that spends every dollar it gets, the consumption function will shift up, indicating more consumption and less saving at the same level of aggregate disposable income.

More generally, since different households have different marginal propensities to consume, aggregate consumption depends not only on aggregate income but also on the distribution of this income among households. Thus a change in the distribution of income will cause a change in the aggregate *level* of consumption expenditure that is associated with any given *level* of national income. In other words, there will be a shift in the consumption function.

Here too the government can have a significant role, either through its transfer payments to households or through changes in the structure of taxes.

SHIFTS IN THE RELATIONSHIP BETWEEN DISPOSABLE INCOME AND NATIONAL INCOME

Even if the relationship between disposable income and consumption does not change, a change in the relationship of Y_d to GNP will shift the consumption function relating consumption to GNP. For example, if households consume 90 percent of their disposable income and if disposable income is 70 percent of GNP, then consumption will be 63 percent of GNP. Suppose that with no change in the 90 percent propensity to consume out of Y_d, personal income tax reductions increase disposable income from 70 to 80 percent of GNP. Consumption is thereby increased from 63 to 72 percent of GNP. This shift in consumption will increase aggregate demand.

An increase in tax rates lowers the aggregate demand function by lowering the ratio of disposable income to national income. A decrease in tax rates has the opposite effect.

If the government cuts taxes during an election year, in order to win votes, the effect will be to shift the consumption function upward. This may well trigger a cyclical boom.

Shifts in Exports

A country like Canada, in which foreign trade plays such a large role, is subject to destabilizing influences from foreign demand. Since about one-half of all goods produced in Canada are exported, fluctuations in the national income of other countries can be transmitted to our economy through fluctuations in their demand for our exports. As Figure 32-4 shows, changes in merchandise exports played an important role during the Great Depression. The fall in export demand triggered by the depression in the economies of our major trading partners led to a fall in our exports, thereby reinforcing the early stages of the recession in Canada. Similarly, during World War II exports boomed at the same time that the domestic economy was expanding.

Similar influences of exports on the domestic economy can be seen throughout the period. Perhaps the most notable episode was the boom in the early 1970s followed by the post-OPEC decline in the economy. Exports rose sharply from 1971 to 1973 and then fell sharply in the years 1973–1975.

This period warrants further examination. As we saw in Chapter 27, Canada was a net exporter of petroleum in 1973. Hence the increase in world oil prices brought on by OPEC should

translate into an *increase* in foreign demand for Canadian petroleum products. However, Canadian exports of this kind are regulated by the National Energy Board, and they did not in fact increase. Also the OPEC shock caused a major recession in countries—particularly the United States—that purchase nonpetroleum exports from Canada. The recession abroad led to a reduction in the level of Canadian exports, which in turn led to a reduction in the growth of Canadian GNP. From 1974 to 1975, exports fell by more than 4 percent while growth in GNE fell by 4 percent relative to the growth in GNE achieved in the previous two-year period.

Factors other than foreign incomes also affect Canadian exports. One of the most important is the ability of Canadian firms to compete in international markets, as influenced in the short-run by changes in the exchange rate and more directly by changes in domestic costs relative to foreign costs. Labor costs as reflected in wages are important, as are the costs of material inputs and energy.

In an open economy, fluctuations in exports play a key role in the theory of cyclical fluctuations.

Investment and Its Determinants

An important source of disturbance is investment expenditure. Consider the period 1929–1932. In 1929 total investment expenditure of firms and households in the Canadian economy was $1.2 billion, almost double the amount of expenditure needed to replace the capital goods that we used up that year in the process of producing a GNP of $6.1 billion. The Canadian economy in 1929, then, was adding rapidly to its stock of capital equipment. Four years later, in 1933, total investment expenditure was $145 million. This was less than one-third of the amount needed merely to keep the stock of capital intact. The Canadian economy in 1933, with its GNP reduced to $3.5 billion, was rapidly reducing its stock of capital equipment.

FIGURE 32-4
Changes in GNP and Selected Components, 1927–1979

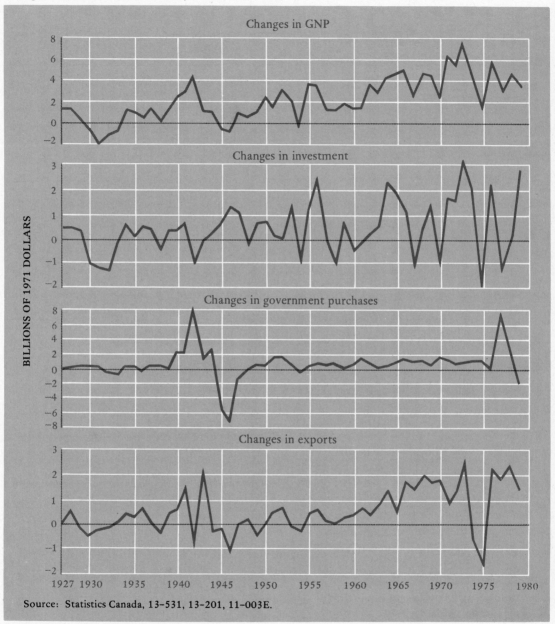

Source: Statistics Canada, 13–531, 13–201, 11–003E.

Changes in GNP have been closely related to changes in investment expenditure. The year-to-year fluctuations in GNP correlate closely to changes in investment except during World War II and its aftermath, when changes in government expenditures were the dominant influence. Changes in merchandise exports have reinforced the destabilizing influence of the other two expenditure categories.

TABLE 32-1
Fixed Investment and GNP During the 1974 American Recession (billions of 1972 U.S. dollars)

Quarter	Total		Quarter-to-quarter change	
	Gross private fixed domestic investment	GNP	Gross private fixed domestic investment	GNP
1973: 4th	$188	$1,241		
1974: 1st	184	1,230	$— 4	$—11
2nd	179	1,221	— 5	— 9
3rd	171	1,213	— 8	— 8
4th	161	1,192	—10	—21
1975: 1st	150	1,161	—11	—31
2nd	147	1,177	— 3	+16
3rd	150	1,209	+ 3	+32
4th	152	1,219	+ 2	+10

There is a close correlation between changes in fixed investment and changes in GNP. Investment expenditure, although only a small fraction of total expenditure, is a volatile component of it. The data in the last two columns lend support to the theory that a decline in investment expenditure was a major cause of the 1974 American recession.

Investment expenditure is both volatile and closely correlated with changes in GNP. This is shown in Figure 32-4.

Investment expenditures play a key role in most theories of cyclical fluctuations.

Consider the severe recession that beset the U.S. economy between the end of 1973 and the middle of 1975. Table 32-1 shows that while fixed investment was only about 15 percent of GNP over this period, *changes* in such investment were about one-third as large as changes in GNP, and in seven of the eight quarters they moved in the same direction. In Canada during the same period, changes in investment were much less marked and much less closely tied to changes in GNP; movements in Canadian GNP, as noted before, were caused primarily by fluctuations in exports, which in turn were associated with changes in investment abroad.

WHY DOES INVESTMENT CHANGE?

It is useful to know that changes in investment are one of the prime causes of short-term fluctuations, but we do not have the whole story unless we know why investment fluctuates. In discuss-

ing the theory of income determination in Chapters 30 and 31 we talked simply of shifts in investment, not of the underlying causes of such shifts. It would be quite possible for two economists to accept all that has been said so far in this chapter and yet believe in different causes of cyclical fluctuations.

One theory might be that investment depends mainly on business firms' anticipations of the future state of their markets. When there is confidence in the future, investment will be high; when there is pessimism, investment will be low. To go further in understanding fluctuations we would have to appeal to psychology to explain variations in business attitudes. The economist alone could not go beyond studying the consequences of exogenous, unexplained shifts in the investment function.

A second theory might be that monetary factors provide the major explanation of fluctuations in investment.[1] When credit is easily obtainable, interest rates are low and banks and other financial institutions are eager to lend money to investors; when credit is tight, interest rates are high and loans are hard to obtain. The first theory is close to that advocated by Keynes;

[1] The monetary sector is studied in detail in Part Ten.

the second is close to the one advocated by many monetarists.

While each dollar of investment has the same consequences for aggregate demand, different types of investment respond to different sets of causes. Thus it is useful to discuss separately the determinants of business fixed investment (machinery, equipment, and nonresidential construction), changes in inventories, and residential construction.

INVESTMENT IN INVENTORIES[2]

Inventory changes represent only a small fraction of private investment in a typical year. Their average size is not an adequate measure of their importance because, as Figure 32-5 shows, they are one of the more volatile elements of total investment and therefore contribute importantly in shifts in the investment schedule.

Firms characteristically hold substantial inventories of raw materials, goods in process, and goods already produced but unsold. It is almost impossible to imagine a manufacturing firm doing business successfully without some minimum holdings of inventories. In fact, most firms choose to hold inventories well above the necessary minimum level. They do this for many reasons; for one, it is usually cheaper to hold production constant in the face of daily, weekly, or even monthly fluctuations in sales than to adjust levels of production frequently. Although many things can influence the desired size of a firm's inventory holdings, the two most important factors are the size of a firm's sales and the rate of interest.

Empirical studies show that the stock of inventories held tends to rise as a firm's rate of production and sales rises. But while the size of invento-

ries is related to level of sales, the *change* in inventories (which is a form of investment) is related to the *change* in the level of sales.

A firm may wish to hold inventories of 10 percent of its sales: if sales are $100,000, it will wish to hold inventories of $10,000; if its sales increase to $110,000, it will want to hold inventories of $11,000. When a firm with $10,000 in inventories wishes to increase its inventories by 10 percent, it will require an additional $1,000 in inventories. *Over the period during which the stock is being increased,* there will be a total of $1,000 new inventory investment.

The higher the level of production and sales, the larger the desired stock of inventories. Changes in the rate of production and sales cause temporary bouts of investment (or disinvestment) in inventories.

When a firm has money tied up in inventories, that money cannot be doing something else. The rate of interest represents the cost of borrowing this money, and obviously the higher is the rate of interest, the higher will be the cost of holding an inventory of a given size. Suppose a firm holds the level of inventories it desires, given its level of sales and the cost of holding inventories. Now suppose the rate of interest rises from 8 percent to 18 percent. As it does, the cost of holding inventories rises and, *ceteris paribus,* firms would be expected to hold smaller inventories. Producers can do this by letting their rate of output fall temporarily below their rate of sales. Alternatively, a fall in interest rates makes it less costly to have funds invested in inventories, and then firms are expected to let inventories expand somewhat.

By causing firms to change the level of inventories that they desire to hold, a change in the rate of interest can lead to a flurry of investment or disinvestment as firms adjust their inventory levels to the new levels they plan to hold.

The higher the rate of interest, the lower the desired stock of inventories. Thus changes in the rate of interest cause temporary bouts of investment (or disinvestment) in inventories.

[2] As we saw in Chapter 28, there are two kinds of changes in inventories. Intended changes are a *cause* of cyclical fluctuations and are discussed here. Unintended changes are a *consequence* of fluctuations due (for example) to firms' finding their inventories rising in a recession because they do not have customers for their current production and thus their goods pile up in warehouses. Because it is impossible to isolate these changes in the statistics, we have excluded changes in inventories from Table 32-1.

FIGURE 32-5
Components of Gross Private Investment, 1926–1979

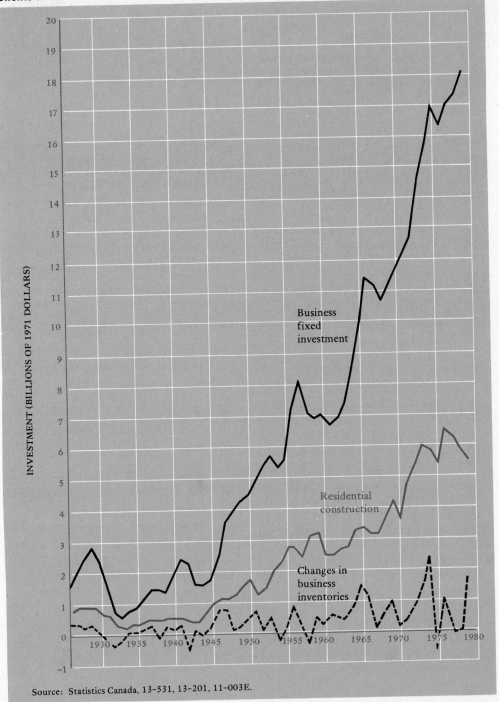

Source: Statistics Canada, 13–531, 13–201, 11–003E.

The components of investment fluctuate substantially from year to year. While changes in business inventories are typically a small fraction of gross private investment in any given year, such changes vary considerably from year to year and hence account for a substantial part of year to year changes in gross investment.

INVESTMENT IN RESIDENTIAL CONSTRUCTION

In recent years the value of expenditures on residential structures has varied between one-fifth and one-third of all gross private investment in Canada and has accounted for 4 to 5 percent of GNP. Figure 32-5 shows the course of residential construction in Canada since 1926. Notice the substantial fluctuations from year to year. Because expenditures for housing construction are both large and variable, they exert a major impact on the economy.

To what does residential construction respond? Many of the influences on residential construction are noneconomic, dependent on demographic or cultural considerations such as new family formation. A rapidly expanding population will require more new construction than will a static population. Changes in marriage age also affect the demand for housing: if marriages are postponed, as during World War II, so too is family formation—and the demand for new housing units declines. But while demographic and cultural considerations affect people's hopes for housing, households must not only want to buy houses, they must be able to do so. Thus periods of high employment and high average family earnings tend to lead to increases in house building, and unemployment and falling earnings to decreases in such building.

The vast majority of houses are purchased with money borrowed on mortages that run 20, 25, or even 30 years. Interest on the borrowed money typically accounts for over one-half of the purchaser's annual mortgage payments (the rest being repayment of principal). A rise in the rate of interest charged on mortages from 10 percent to 16 percent can lead to an increase of more than 40 percent in the monthly payment necessary to buy a given house. It is for this reason that sharp variations in interest rates exert a substantial effect on the demand for housing.

Expenditures for residential construction tend to vary directly with changes in average income and inversely with interest rates.

BUSINESS FIXED INVESTMENT

Investment in machinery, equipment, and nonresidential construction is the largest components of domestic investment. Why does a business firm decide to build a new factory? Why does a firm decide to engage in major modernization this year rather than next?

Successful firms invest in plant and equipment not only because they like being surrounded by impressive pieces of hardware but because they want to sell at a profit the goods that the equipment can produce. But profitability—and thus the level of investment in plant and equipment—depends on a variety of economic variables. One is the rate of innovation. New innovations typically require new plant and equipment, and in some instances (e.g., the basic changes that followed the introduction of railways) innovation brings fundamental changes in the nature of the capital stock and leads to vast amounts of new investment.

Expectations also play a role. The decision to invest *now* is to a great extent an act of faith in the future. If businesses guess wrong, the penalties can be great. Business managers do their best to predict the extent of their firms' markets, but many things can influence those markets other than the tastes of households. A new government may adopt different taxing and spending policies that affect a business profoundly. An increase in the price of oil can shift the demand for large and small cars, for coal, for skis, for stay-at-home recreational activities, and for a host of other goods and services. Particularly in the short run, expectations can have a decisive influence on the timing of business investments. Sometimes a form of group psychology takes over and general optimism (or pessimism) can lead to a burst of investment spending (or cutbacks in investment). If such expectations prove false, corrective adjustments will occur later; meanwhile, voltaile investment behavior will be observed.

Some economists, and many business analysts, lay great stress on the effect of profits on investment. It is assumed that business firms are

The Cost of Buying a House on Time

Few people who buy a house can pay cash, and most purchases are financed by borrowing money on a *mortgage*. A mortgage is a loan to the house purchaser (sometimes of as much as 85 or 90 percent of the purchase price, but 60 to 75 percent is common). In return, the borrower promises to make fixed monthly payments that cover interest on the money borrowed and repay the amount borrowed over some agreed period, commonly 20 years. (The monthly payments often include an amount to cover insurance and taxes, but this is ignored in what follows.) The house itself acts as security for the loan. Loans of this type are said to be *amortized,* which means that fixed payments cover the interest on the principal outstanding *and* repay the principal over a stated period.

Because the loan stretches over a long period, a great deal of the total amount paid by the borrower is interest on the outstanding loan. For example, on a 20-year mortgage for $10,000 at a nominal annual interest rate of 8 percent per year (a monthly rate of 8/12 of 1 percent), a total of $20,075 would be paid in 240 monthly installments of $83.65 each. This is $10,000 to repay the principal of the loan and $10,075 of interest. At a 12 percent nominal annual rate (a monthly rate of 1 percent) the total payments would be $26,426, making $16,426 total interest as well as $10,000 to repay the principal.

Because interest is such a large part of the total payments on a mortgage, small changes in the rate of interest cause relatively large changes in the annual payments. For instance, a rise in the rate of interest from 8 percent to 10 percent increases the monthly payments on a 20-year mortgage by nearly 15.4 percent (from $8.37 to $9.66 per thousand dollars borrowed).

The interest on a mortgage is calculated on the amount of the loan still outstanding. After each payment the amount outstanding is reduced so that, with fixed annual payments, most of the total amount paid goes to paying interest in the early years and to repaying principal in later years. It follows that the purchaser's equity in the house builds up slowly at first, then more and more rapidly as the terminal date approaches.

Note in the table that when half the life of the mortgage has passed, only about a quarter of the principal has been repaid. In the first year of the mortage, $993 goes as interest and only $165 to reduce the principal on the loan. In the last year, only $60 is interest and $1,098 goes to repay the principal.

Breakdown of payments in selected years on a 20-year mortge for $10,000 at 10 percent (all figures to the nearest dollar)

Year	Payments made over the year	Interest paid over the year	Principal (amount of loan) repaid over the year	Equity (amount of loans repaid over all previous years)
1	$1,158	$993	$ 165	$ 165
2	1,158	975	183	349
5	1,158	912	246	1,020
10	1,158	753	405	2,698
15	1,158	491	667	5,458
19	1,158	164	994	8,902
20	1,158	60	1,098	10,000

not able (or do not wish) to borrow all the funds they require, but that they may use their own funds to finance their investment projects. Profits thus become a key explanatory factor in investment because retained profits provide an important source of investable funds.

Many economists believe that the two major influences on the level of business fixed investment are the rate of interest and *changes* in the level of national income.

Business Fixed Investment and the Rate of Interest

It will pay a business firm to borrow money to finance its investment projects as long as the return on the investment (including an allowance for the riskiness of the project) exceeds the rate of interest. Thus a particular investment in a new machine becomes more attractive (other things being equal) the lower the rate of interest. To go from this conclusion to a prediction about how actual aggregate investment in plant and equipment responds to changes in the interest rate is more complicated.

The aggregate quantity of a society's capital goods is called its capital stock. Changes in the potential profitability of plant and equipment will lead to desired changes in capital stock, but capital goods cannot be produced (or worn out) overnight. Investment concerns actual expenditures for investment goods, not the desired level of the stock of capital. A desired increase in capital goods generates investment when the capital goods are actually produced. Suppose, for example, that in response to a fall in interest rates there is an increase of $2 billion in the desired capital stock. If the capital stock is raised by $2 billion within a year, net investment will rise to $2 billion for a year and then fall to zero. In this case a fall in the interest rate will lead only to a one-year increase in the amount of investment.

But the timing of investment will depend on how fast the stock of capital can be built up to its new desired level. The actual volume of invest-

ment in plant and equipment that takes place each year is limited by the capacities of the capital-goods and the construction industries.

Assume that in response to a fall in interest rates the firms in the economy decide that they want a total of 30,000 newly built and equipped factories in operation next year, but that factories can only be built and equipped at the rate of 10,000 a year. It will take three years before the desired addition to the capital stock is achieved. If, at the end of the first year, a rise in the rate of interest decreases the desired overall addition to the capital stock from 30,000 to 20,000 factories, this new change will have no effect on investment in year 2 because the capital-goods industries would still have to work to capacity to fill back orders.

Thus, while we expect the capital stock (and thus investment) to be related to long-term changes in the level of interest rates, we cannot make precise predictions about the relationship of investment in a particular year in response to a change in the interest rate.

Substantial variations in the interest rate can have a major effect on the length of the backlog of orders for capital equipment rather than on the level of investment in a particular year.

Changes in National Income[3]

The need for plant and equipment is obviously influenced by the demand for the goods the plant and equipment are designed to produce. If there is a rise in demand that is expected to persist and that cannot be met by increasing production with existing industrial capacity, then new plant and equipment will be needed. The production of such plant and equipment is investment. Once

---

[3] It is not the *level* of national income but the year-to-year change in income that we discuss here. A big increase in income can occur at either a high or a low level of income. The level of income too plays a role in determining the level of investment — through the effect of the level of income on expectations and on profits.

the new plants have been built and put into operation, however, the rate of new investment will fall. This further illustrates an important characteristic of investment already encountered in the case of inventories: if the desired stock of capital goods increases, there will be an investment boom while the new capital is being produced. But if nothing else changes, and even though business conditions continue to look rosy enough to justify the increased stock of capital, investment in new plant and equipment will cease once the larger capital stock is achieved. This aspect of investment leads to the accelerator theory of investment, which requires a close look.

THE ACCELERATOR THEORY OF INVESTMENT

Because changes in the desired stock of capital goods lead to spurts in investment activity, the pattern of investment from year to year may prove quite changeable. According to the accelerator theory (usually called the **accelerator**), investment is related to the rate of change of national income. When income is increasing, it is necessary to invest in order to increase the capacity to produce consumption goods; when income is falling, it may not even be necessary to replace old capital as it wears out, let alone to invest in new capital.

The main insight which the accelerator theory provides is the emphasis on the role of net investment as a *disequilibrium* phenomenon—something that occurs when the stock of capital goods differs from what firms and households would like it to be. Net investment will not occur when the desired quantities of inventories, buildings, or equipment has been achieved. Anything that changes the desired quantities can generate investment. The accelerator focuses on one such source of change, changing national income. This gives the accelerator its particular importance in connection with *fluctuations* in national income. As we shall see, it can itself contribute to those fluctuations.

How the Accelerator Works: A Numerical Example

To see how the theory works, it is convenient to make the simplifying assumption that there is a particular capital stock needed to produce a given level of an industry's output. (The ratio of the value of capital to the annual value of output is called the **capital-output ratio**.). Given this assumption, suppose that the industry is producing at capacity and the demand for its product increases. If the industry is to produce the higher level of output, its capital stock must increase. This necessitates new investment.

Table 32-2 provides a simple numerical example of the accelerator that, worked through step by step, leads to three conclusions:

1. Rising rather than high levels of sales are needed to call forth net investment.
2. For net investment to remain constant, sales must rise by a constant amount per year.
3. The amount of net investment will be a multiple of the increase in sales because the capital-output ratio is greater than one.[4]

The data in Table 32-2 are for a single industry, but if many industries behave in this way, one would expect aggregate net investment to bear a similar relation to changes in national income. This is what the accelerator theory predicts. **[40]**

The accelerator theory says nothing directly about replacement investment, but it does have implications for such investment. When sales are constant (no net investment required), replacement investment will be required to maintain the capital stock at the desired level. When sales are increasing from a position of full capacity, both net investment and replacement investment will

[4] In the example in the table the capital-output ratio is 5. Why should anyone spend $5 on capital stock to get $1 of output? It is not unreasonable to spend $5 to purchase a machine that produces only $1 of output *per year*, provided that the machine will last enough years to repay the $5 plus a reasonable return on this investment.

TABLE 32-2
An Illustration of the Accelerator Theory of Investment

(1) Year	(2) Annual sales	(3) Change in sales	(4) Required stock of capital, assuming a capital-output ratio of 5/1	(5) Net investment: increase in required capital stock
1	$10	$0	$ 50	$ 0
2	10	0	50	0
3	11	1	55	5
4	13	2	65	10
5	16	3	80	15
6	19	3	95	15
7	22	3	110	15
8	24	2	120	10
9	25	1	125	5
10	25	0	125	0

With a fixed capital-output ratio, net investment occur only when it is necessary to increase the stock of capital in order to change output. Assume that it takes $5 of capital to produce $1 of output per year. In years 1 and 2, there is no need for investment. In year 3, a rise in sales of $1 requires investment of $5 to provide the needed capital stock. In year 4, a further rise of $2 in sales requires an additional investment of $10 to provide the needed capital stock. As columns (3) and (5) show, the amount of net investment is proportional to the *change* in sales. When the increase in sales tapers off in years 7–9, investment declines. When, in year 10, sales no longer increase, net investment falls to zero because the capital stock of year 9 is adequate to provide output for year 10's sales.

be required. When sales are falling so that the desired capital stock is below the actual capital stock, not only will net investment be zero but there will be a tendency to postpone replacement investment as well until the capital stock falls to the desired levels.

Limitations of the Accelerator

Taken literally, the accelerator posits a mechanical and rigid response of investment to changes in sales (and thus, aggregatively, to changes in national income). It does this by assuming a proportional relationship between changes in income and the size of the desired capital stock, and by assuming a fixed capital-output ratio. Each assumption is invalid to some degree.

Changes in sales that are thought to be temporary in their effect on demand will not necessarily lead to new investment. It is usually possible to increase the level of output for a given capital stock by working overtime or extra shifts. While this would be more expensive per unit of output

in the long run, it will usually be preferable to making investments in new plant and equipment that would lie idle after a temporary spurt of demand had subsided. Thus expectations about what is required capital stock may lead to a much less mechanistic response of investment to income that the accelerator suggests.

A further limitation of the accelerator theory is that it takes a very limited view of what constitutes investment. The fixed capital-output ratio emphasizes investment in what economists call **capital widening,** the investment in additional capacity that uses the same ratio of capital to labor as existing capacity. It does not explain **capital deepening,** which is the kind of increase in the amount of capital per unit of labor expected in response to a fall in the rate of interest. Neither does the theory say anything about investments brought about as a result of new processes or new products. Furthermore, it does not allow for the fact that investment in any period is likely to be limited by the capacity of the capital-goods industry.

For these and other reasons, the accelerator does not by itself give anything like a complete explanation of variations in investment in plant and equipment, and it should not be surprising that a simple accelerator theory provides a relatively poor overall explanation of changes in investment. Yet accelerator-like influences do exist, and they play a role in the cyclical variability of investment.

Government and Cyclical Fluctuations

Governments frequently alter their revenues and expenditures in an intentional response to cyclical swings in the economy. In Chapter 34 we shall consider such use of government expenditure and tax policies for the purpose of stabilizing the economy. In Chapter 38 we shall look at use of monetary policy for the same purpose. Such policies play important roles in the actual pattern of cyclical fluctuations observed.

Government expenditures and taxes are also altered for many other reasons, since public officials respond to all of the groups in our society that look to governments to provide goods, services, and wealth transfers to them. When this happens, changes in government expenditures can become the initiating cause of cyclical fluctuations.

GOVERNMENT EXPENDITURES ON GOODS AND SERVICES

As Figure 32-4 shows, World War II brought a rapid expansion of economic activity, and government spending was a major contributing factor. Wars always result in an enormous increase in federal governmental expenditures as men and materials are shifted from civilian to military purposes, a shift that is then reversed in the postwar period. For example, federal government purchases of goods and services rose from $683 million in 1939 to $4,978 million in 1944 and fell back to $1,541 million by 1947. Changes in government purchases of goods and services during 1940–1946 were the dominant influence on GNP, and they had a substantial effect during the Korean War at the beginning of the 1950s.

Aside from periods of major wars, government expenditures have not often actually been destabilizing. For peacetime periods before 1940, government expenditures were both small and relatively stable. Since 1955 they have been large and stable and growing rather steadily. Thus, whatever their potential for being a major source of cyclical instability, they have not proven to be such except during wars. Indeed, many economists believe that the growth in the size of the government sector in the last half century has been an important source of added stability in the economy, since public expenditures tend to be less volatile than private expenditures and therefore tend to stabilize the economy.

GOVERNMENT TRANSFER PAYMENTS

Large as the government's purchases of goods and services are, its transfer payments to individuals are larger yet, amounting to roughly one-eighth of personal income. Sharp fluctuations in such transfer payments too could theoretically be a highly destabilizing factor via their effects on personal consumption and investment. Here the empirical evidence suggests that expenditures of these kinds tend to be sharply *counter-cyclical*, rising relative to national income when national income is falling. The reason is clear: many of these expenditures, such as those for unemployment insurance and welfare, rise when unemployment rises and fall when unemployment declines.

Elements of a Theory of Fluctuations

We have seen that the components of aggregate demand such as consumption and investment may be influenced by factors such as expectations, interest rates, and government policies. If any of these factors change, investment or consumption may change, and if investment or consumption change, national income will change as well. This might be the end of the story if we were trying to explain occasional erratic changes in national income. Most economic time series, however, display more or less continuous upswings and downswings. The evidence suggests that, whatever the initiating cause of a disturbance, the movements of the economy, up or down, tend to acquire a momentum of their own. After a while such cumulative movements appear to run their course and generate the seeds of their own reversal. Not all cycles are alike in duration or intensity, but each appears to have tendencies toward cumulative movements that

eventually reverse themselves. This was true long before governments attempted to intervene and stabilize the economy, and it is true still. In the following discussion we consider the cyclical tendencies in an economy where government is not actively intervening.

THE TERMINOLOGY OF BUSINESS FLUCTUATIONS

Although recurrent fluctuations in economic activity are neither smooth nor regular, a vocabulary has developed to denote their different stages. Figure 32-6 shows a stylized cycle that will serve to illustrate some terms.

FIGURE 32-6
A Stylized Business Cycle

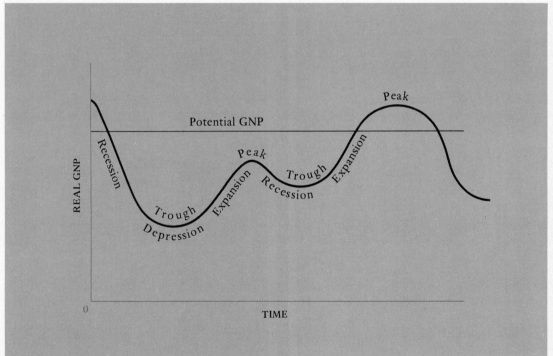

While the phases of business fluctuations are described by a series of commonly used terms, no two cycles are the same. Starting from a lower turning point, or trough, a cycle goes through a phase of expansion, reaches an upper turning point, or peak, and then enters a period of recession. Cycles differ from one another in the severity of their troughs and peaks and in the speed with which one phase follows another. Severe troughs are called depressions. Peaks are called inflations when a rapidly rising price level is a dominant symptom.

Trough. The trough is, simply, the bottom. If the trough is sufficiently severe, it may be called a **depression.** A trough is characterized by unemployment of labor and a level of consumer demand that is low in relation to the capacity of industry to produce goods for consumption. There is thus a substantial amount of unused industrial capacity. Business profits will be low, and in many individual cases they will be negative. Confidence in the future will be lacking and, as a result, firms will be unwilling to take risks in making new investments. Banks and other financial institutions will have surplus cash that no one whom they consider to be a reasonable credit risk wishes to borrow.

Expansion or recovery. When something sets off a recovery, the lower turning point of the cycle has been reached. The symptoms of an expansion are many: worn-out machinery will be replaced; employment, income, and consumer spending all begin to rise; expectations become more favorable as a result of increases in production, sales, and profits. Investments that once seemed risky may now be undertaken as the climate of business opinion begins to change from pessimism to optimism. As demand expands, production will be expanded with relative ease merely by reemploying the existing unused capacity and unemployed labor.

Peak. The peak is the **upper turning point.** At the peak there is a high degree of utilization of existing capacity, labor shortages begin to occur, particularly in certain key skill categories, and shortages of certain key raw materials develop. Bottlenecks appear with increasing frequency. It now becomes difficult to increase output because the supply of unused resources is rapidly disappearing; output can be raised further only by means of investment that increases capacity. Because of such investment expenditure, investment funds will be in short supply. Because such investment takes time, further rises in demand are now met more by increases in prices than by increases in production. As shortages develop in more and more markets, a situation of general

excess demand for factors develops. Costs rise but prices rise also, and business remains generally very profitable.

Losses are infrequent because a money profit can be earned merely by holding on to goods whose prices are rising and selling them later at higher prices. Expectations of the future are favorable, and more investment may be made than is justified on the basis of current levels of prices and sales alone.

Recession. Beyond the upper turning point, the economy turns downward. When the contraction is sustained, it is called a **recession.** Suppose that for some reason demand falls off and as a result production and employment fall. As employment falls, so do households' incomes; falling income causes demand to fall further, and more and more firms get into difficulties. Prices and profits fall. New investments that looked profitable on the expectation of continuously rising demand and prices suddenly appear unprofitable; investment is reduced to a low level, and it may not even be worth replacing capital goods as they wear out because unused capacity is increasing steadily.

CUMULATIVE MOVEMENTS AND TURNING POINTS

Many events occur in the economy at once, and all may contribute to rises and falls in national income. Our purpose at the moment is to show how it is that cumulative self-reinforcing and self-reversing movements can occur. This may be done concisely by putting together two now-familiar concepts—the multiplier and the accelerator. A simple theory emerges that, while not a complete theory of cyclical fluctuations, emphasizes many important interactions.

The Interaction of the Multiplier and the Accelerator

The combination of the multiplier and the accelerator can cause upward or downward movements in the economy to be cumulative. Imagine that the economy is settled into a depression with heavy unemployment and that there then occurs a revival of investment demand. Orders are placed for new plant and equipment, and this creates new employment in the capital-goods industries. The newly employed workers spend most of their earnings; this creates new demand for the consumer goods that they buy. A multiplier process is now set up with new employment and incomes created in the consumer goods industries.

The spending of the newly created incomes in turn causes further increases in demand. At some stage the increased demand for consumer goods will create, through the accelerator process, an increased demand for capital goods. Once existing equipment is fully employed in any industry, extra output will require new capital equipment—and the accelerator theory takes over as the major determinant of investment expenditure. Such investment will increase or at least maintain demand in the capital-goods sector of the economy. So the process goes on, the multiplier-accelerator mechanism continuing to produce a rapid rate of expansion in the economy.

The Upper Turning Point

A very rapid expansion can continue for some time, but it cannot go on forever because eventually the economy will run into bottlenecks (or ceilings) in terms of some resources. For example, investment funds may become scarce, and as a result interest rates will rise. Firms now find new investments more expensive than anticipated, and thus some will be unprofitable to make. Or suppose that what limits the expansion is exhaustion of the reservoir of unemployed labor. Once this has happened, further expansion of the economy requires growth of the labor force or growth of labor productivity. The full-employment ceiling guarantees that any sustained rapid growth rate of real income and employment will eventually be slowed. At this point the accelerator again comes into play. A

slowing down in the rate of increase of production leads to a decrease in the investment required in new plant and equipment. This causes a fall in employment in the capital-goods industries and, through the multiplier, a fall in consumer demand. Once consumer demand begins to fall, investment in plant and equipment will be reduced to a low level because firms will already have more productive capacity than they can use. Unemployment begins to mount, and the upper turning point has been passed.

The Lower Turning Point

A rapid contraction, too, is eventually brought to an end. Consider the worst sort of depression you can imagine, one in which every postponable expenditure of households, firms, or governments is postponed. Even then aggregate demand will not fall to zero. For there is a minimum level of consumption expenditure that households will be obliged to make to sustain life. Even if aggregate demand consisted only of consumption, it would not fall to zero because households can and will use up savings, or go into debt, to buy the necessities of life. Moreover, transfer payments to households in the form of unemployment compensation and welfare payments will increase and will provide the funds to support consumption expenditures.

Nor is consumption the only element of aggregate demand. Government expenditure will not fall to zero. Civil service salaries and national defence expenditures will continue. Moreover, the political pressure for governments to increase their expenditures will surely grow and may be effective. Even business investment, in many ways the most easily postponed component of aggregate demand, will not fall to zero. In our most severe depression, between 1930 and 1932, investment fell drastically, but at the depth of the Depression it was still nearly $150 million. In the industries providing food, basic clothing, and shelter, demand may remain fairly high in spite of quite large reductions in national income. These industries will certainly be carrying out some investment to replace equipment as it wears out, and they may even undertake some net investment.

Taken together, the minimum levels of consumption, investment, and government expenditure will assure a minimum equilibrium level of national income that, although well below the full-employment level, will not be zero. There is a floor! (This may be small comfort, however; it is possible for the economy to settle into a period of heavy unemployment for a long time, and if it does, many will suffer great hardship.)

Sooner or later, though, an upturn will begin. If nothing else causes an expansion of business activity, there will eventually be a revival of replacement investment because as existing capital wears out the capital stock will eventually fall below the level required to produce current output. At this stage new machines will be bought to replace those that are worn out.

The rise in the level of activity in the capital-goods industries will cause, by way of the multiplier, a further rise in income. The economy has turned the corner. An expansion, once started, will trigger the sort of cumulative upward movement already discussed.

THE VARIETY OF CYCLICAL FLUCTUATIONS

The previous section suggests why an economy that is subjected to periodic external shocks will tend to generate a continuously changing pattern of fluctuations, as first cumulative and then self-reversing forces come into play. But no two cycles are the same. In some the recession phase is short; in others a full-scale period of stagnation sets in. In some cycles the peak phase develops into a severe inflation; in others the pressure of excess demand is hardly felt and a new recession sets in before the economy has fully recovered from the last trough. Some cycles are of long duration, some are very short.

Our discussion of cumulative movements, floors and ceilings, and turning points only hints

at what happened in actual cyclical movements; this is as far as the theory can be carried without the use of complex dynamic models. But this type of theory can fit either a very modest fluctuation such as the recession of 1960–1961, a bigger fluctuation such as that of 1973–1975, or the massive disaster that was the 1930s. Cycles differ from one another in terms of the origin and the magnitude of the initiating shock. Sometimes, but not always, economists can identify the initiating causes. (The causes of the Great Depression remain shrouded in controversy despite nearly four decades of study.) Inventories are believed by many economists, and housing by some, to lead to their own special patterns of fluctuation. Governments bent on reelection may affect the course of a cycle by timing expenditures or tax cuts in order to create a favorable economic climate at election time.

Inventory Cycles

There are, as we have seen, good reasons to suppose that the required size of inventories is related to the level of firms' sales, and sales are related to the level of national income. If firms maintain anything like a rigid inventory-to-sales ratio, this will cause an accelerator-like linkage between investment in inventories and *changes* in national income.

Look back at the fluctuating investment in business inventories shown in Figure 32-5. Many observers believe that these sharp and somewhat periodic fluctuations lead to an "inventory cycle" of roughly 40 months' average duration.

A Building Cycle?

Economists have noted some long-run, wavelike movements of roughly 20 years' duration in the statistics for expenditures on residential construction. These are sometimes referred to as "building cycles." Some economists suggest an accelerator-like explanation that runs from external events to demographic changes, to changes in the demand for housing and other buildings, and thence to changes in construction activity.

A major war, by taking males away from home, tends to retard family formation and thereby tends to depress the demand for private housing. After the conclusion of the war there is typically a great increase in marriages and household formation, a large increase in the demand for housing, and a boom in the construction industry. Typically, too, there are the postponed babies and an increase in the birth rate.

Depending on the capacity of the building industry, the boom may last many years before the desired increases in the stock of buildings of various kinds are achieved, but eventually the demand will taper off and the construction boom will have ended. Then, approximately 20 years after the end of the war that triggered the boom, there is likely to be a further boom in the number of marriages and births as the new generation starts its process of family formation. Wars are not the only source of such population-induced cycles; a severe depression will lead to a similar postponement of family formation.

The evidence concerning construction expenditures over the past century is thought by many economists to provide support for the theory just outlined, a theory very much like the accelerator, though with changes in demographic factors (rather than changes in income) providing the impetus.

FLUCTUATIONS: A CONSENSUS VIEW?

Economists once argued long and bitterly about which was the best explanation of the recurrent cyclical behavior of the economy. Today most agree that there need not be one cause or one class of causes for business cycles. In an economy that has tendencies for both cumulative and self-reversing behavior, any sort of large shock, whether from without or within the system, can initiate a cyclical swing. Wars are important; so, too, are major technical inventions. A major automobile strike could curtail production and bring on a recession. A sharp increase in interest rates and a general tightening of credit can cause a sharp decrease in investment. Expectations can be changed by a political campaign or a development in another part of the world. The list of possible initial impulses, autonomous or induced, is long. It is probably true that the characteristic cyclical pattern includes many outside shocks that initiate, sometimes reinforce, and sometimes dampen the cumulative tendencies that exist within the economy.

Cycles differ also in terms of their internal structure. In some, full employment of labor may be the bottleneck that determines the ceiling. In others, high interest rates and shortages of funds for business expansion may nip an expansion and turn it into a recession while unemployment of labor is still an acute problem. These and other differences occupy the attention of economists concerned with understanding the cyclical economy.

An important part of controlling cycles is to anticipate correctly when a turning point is near. Control requires more than understanding; it requires countercyclical policies. Into this picture we must now bring the central authorities, who seek to influence the pattern of business fluctuations. The federal government tries both to prevent extremes of expansion and contraction from developing and to mitigate the most undesirable effects of those peaks and troughs that do occur.

Summary

1. Short-term fluctuations in GNP are usually, though not always, the result of variations in aggregate demand. Overall, these fluctuations show a fairly clear pattern that is sometimes described as cyclical. In spite of the overall pattern, the evidence is that the cycles are irregular in amplitude, in timing, in duration, and in the way they affect particular industries and sectors of the economy.

2. In an open economy like that of Canada, an important source of fluctuations is changes in the level of exports. These changes are often due to changes in the level of income in trading partners' economies, and thus they are an important mechanism by which business cycles are transmitted internationally.

3. An important source of fluctuations is shifts in the consumption function due to changes in income distribution, availability of credit, stocks of durable goods, and expectations about the future course of the economy. Even if the relation of consumption to disposable income does not change, the government can shift the consumption function related to GNP by changing personal tax rates. An increase in personal taxes lowers disposable income relative to GNP and can decrease the level of consumption at every level of GNP.

4. Investment is large enough and volatile enough to cause fluctuations in aggregate demand. Most economists regard shifts in investment as a major cause of business fluctuations. Saying that, however, does not commit one to a particular theory of *why* aggregate demand and investment fluctuate. The three principal components of private investment are changes in business inventories, residential construction, and business fixed investment. Each responds to somewhat different influences.

5. Changes in business inventories, the smallest of the three major components of investment expenditure, often account for an important fraction of the year-to-year changes in the level of investment. They are thought to respond both to changes in the level of production and sales and to the rate of interest.

6. Residential construction, a major component of investment, shows a wavelike motion of its own. House building responds to economic (as well as noneconomic) influences, varying directly with the level of national income and inversely with the rate of interest. The rate of interest is important because interest payments are a large fraction of the mortgage payments that greatly affect a household's ability to purchase a house.

7. Business fixed investment depends on a number of variables—among them innovation, changes in the level of national income, expectations about the future, the level of profits, and the rate of interest.

8. The accelerator theory relates net investment to changes in the level of national income on the assumption of a fixed capital-output ratio. Its central prediction is that rising income is required to maintain a positive level of investment. Its central insight is that net investment is a disequilibrium phenomenon that occurs when the capital stock is different from the desired capital stock.

9. The acclerator does not provide a complete theory of investment. It neglects capital deepening and the influence of variables other than the rate of change of national income. Moreover, the actual world is not one with a fixed capital-output ratio. Nevertheless, an accelerator-like mechanism may help explain some of the fluctuations in total investment, in inventory changes, and in construction activity.

10. Government expenditure, both on goods and services and on transfer payments, can have a large effect on aggregate demand and thus can affect cyclical fluctuations. Government purchases of goods and services tend to be dramatically destabilizing during wartime but relatively stable during peacetime. Transfer payments tend to be countercyclical.

11. Economists break down a stylized cycle into four phases—trough, expansion, peak, and recession—which have certain characteristic features, although no two real-world cycles are exactly the same.

12. The elements of a theory of fluctuations are summarized in terms of a set of tendencies for *cumulative movements* and a set of ceilings or floors that lead to *turning points*. A theory that predicts cumulative but eventually reversing movements is a theory of fluctuations. Such a theory explains some characteristics of all cy-

cles, but it fails to explain the great variety among cycles, which differ from one another in the nature of the initiating shock, in their internal structure, and, as a consequence, in their duration and amplitude.

Topics for Review

Business cycles and business fluctuations
International transmission of fluctuations through exports
Causes of shifts in the consumption function
Components of investment
The accelerator
Phases of the cycle
Cumulative upward and downward movements in economic activity
The interaction of the multiplier and the accelerator
Different kinds of cycles

Discussion Questions

1. "In most years changes in government expenditures are larger than changes in inventories, and consumption is larger than investment in both plant and equipment and housing combined. Therefore, the theorists who say that investment is the main culprit in causing cycles are neglecting the facts of our economy." Reply to this charge.

2. How and in what direction might each of the following shift the function relating consumption expenditure to disposable income?
   a. introduction of free dental care
   b. a change in attitudes so that we become a nation of conspicuous conservers rather than conspicuous consumers, taking pride in how little we eat or spend for housing, clothing, and so on
   c. increases in income taxes
   d. news that due to medical advances everyone can count on more years of retirement than ever before
   e. a spreading belief that all-out nuclear war is likely within the next ten years
   f. sharp increases in the down payments required on durable goods.

3. Suppose the government wished to reduce private investment in order to reduce an inflationary gap. What policies might it adopt? If it wished to do so in such a way as to have a major effect on residential housing and a minor effect on plant and equipment expenditures, which measures might it use?

4. What effect on total investment—and on which category of investment—would you predict as a result of each of the following?
   a. widespread endorsement of ZPG (zero population growth) by young couples
   b. a sharp increase in the frequency and duration of strikes in the transportation industries
   c. forecasts of record levels of real national income over the next five years
   d. tax reform that eliminated deductions for property taxes in computing taxable personal income

5. Recently, when interest rates rose sharply, home construction fell dramatically but sales of mobile homes increased. How does the rise in the sale of mobile homes relate to the notion that investment responds to the rate of interest?

6. Empirical studies show that as the volume of a firm's sales increases, the size of its inventories of raw materials tends to increase in proportion. It is common for business firms to speak of such inventories in terms of "a 20-day supply of coal" rather than "52,000 tons of coal" or "$280,000 worth of coal." Why should relative size be more important than absolute quantity or dollar value?

7. Over the course of a cycle, why are some series more variable than others? Which of the following would you predict to exhibit the most variation, and which the least?
   a. purchases of food
   b. purchases of automobiles
   c. purchases of new housing
   d. purchases of luxury goods
   Check your predictions about (a) and (b) using the national income accounts as published by Statistics Canada.

8. Predict the cyclical behavior of the following series:
   a. unemployment insurance payments
   b. business failures
   c. birth rates
   d. government expenditures
   e. investment in capital equipment
   Check your predictions against the facts for the period 1965–1972.

National Income, International Trade, and the Balance of Payments

33

International trade plays an important role in virtually all modern economies. Chapter 26 focused on the microeconomic aspects of international trade: exports and imports arise out of the incentive to *specialize* in production in order to exploit comparative advantage. This chapter focuses on some macroeconomic aspects of international trade, that is, on macroeconomics in an open economy. In an open economy, as we saw in the previous chapter, exports are an important source of demand for domestically produced goods while imports are a component of domestic expenditure that does not correspond to demand for domestically produced goods.

In Chapter 26 it was convenient to assume that the values of exports and imports were equal. In the first half of this chapter we shall relax this assumption and examine both the causes of trade imbalances and the implications of such imbalances for the domestic economy. The **balance of trade** (or the trade balance) is the difference between the dollar value of exports and imports in a given year. An excess of exports over imports is referred to as a *surplus* in the balance of trade, and an excess of imports over exports is called a *deficit*. A situation where exports are just equal in value to imports is a situation of *balanced trade*.

Any balance-of-trade surplus or deficit creates the need for financial flows between the countries involved. A balance-of-trade surplus represents an excess of receipts over expenditures in foreign markets; a balance-of-trade deficit means that expenditures exceed receipts. These imbalances are then reflected in the transfer of ownership of various financial assets. The relationship between trade imbalances and international financial flows is summarized in the balance-of-payments accounts, which we discuss in the second half of the chapter.

THE HISTORICAL RECORD

Canada is a very open economy. It is rich in natural resources and raw materials that it exports to many other countries which are less favorably endowed. Further, Canada's manufacturing sector is very specialized and export oriented: more than 30 percent of the goods manufactured in Canada in 1979 were exported. As we saw in the preceding chapter, fluctuations in exports play a key role in explaining fluctuations in the level of economic activity in the Canadian economy.

Similarly, imports play an important role in the Canadian economy; Canadian households typically consume a wide range of imported goods, and Canadian industry utilizes imported parts and components. A large segment of the Canadian economy is involved in foreign trade, primarily—but not exclusively—with the United States.

Figure 33-1 shows merchandise exports and imports as a percentage of GNP for the years 1947–1979. As can be seen, both ratios have consistently been in the 20 to 30 percent range. Both exhibit slight upward trends, reaching their historical peaks in the last year in the figure, 1979.

The data in Figure 33-1 underestimate the international exposure of the Canadian economy in two important ways. First, the figures represent

FIGURE 33–1

Exports and Imports as a Percentage of GNP, 1947–1979 (figures for fourth quarter of year)

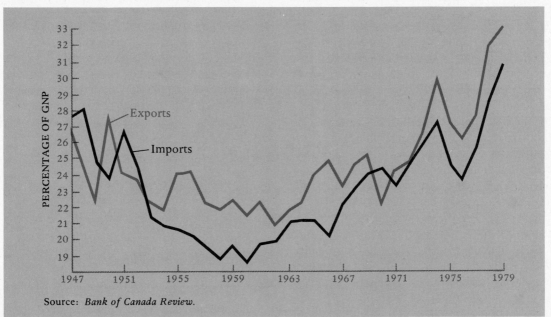

Source: *Bank of Canada Review.*

Exports and imports have each been a relatively constant fraction of GNP in the post-World War II period. Exports and imports are plotted as a percentage of national income. Although exports, imports, and GNP all fluctuate considerably, the three series tend to be fairly closely correlated, and thus their ratios are relatively stable. Fluctuations in exports cause fluctuations in GNP, so the two series tend to move together. Fluctuations in GNP cause fluctuations in expenditure on imports, so these two series tend to move together as well.

those goods actually imported and exported. Many imported goods face competition in domestic markets from close substitutes produced in Canada, called import-competing goods. Similarly, goods identical or very similar to those exported are also produced and consumed in Canada. Hence the fractions of *importables* and *exportables* are much larger than the fractions of actual imports and exports. Second, because government expenditure accounts for more than 30 percent of Canadian GNP, exports represent virtually one-half of the total production of goods in the private sector.

National Income and the Balance of Trade

INTERNATIONAL TRANSMISSION OF BUSINESS CYCLES: THE EXPORT MULTIPLIER

Exports are an important source of demand for domestically produced goods. A key determinant of exports is the level of activity in the country's major trading partners. When the United States experiences a boom, as it did in the period 1968–1970, there is a large American demand for Canadian exports. In turn, via the multiplier process, the increase in exports will cause an expansion in Canadian national income, as shown in Figure 30-4 on page 607. Similarly, when the United States experiences a recession, as it did in 1973–1975, American demand for Canadian goods will be low. We documented this in the preceding chapter. Again the change in exports causes a multiplier effect, this time leading to a reduction in Canadian national income.

As a result of the export multiplier, the business cycles of major trading partners are likely to be closely correlated.

Exports provide a key link between trading partners so that the level of activities in each tend to move together.

This prediction is borne out by Figure 33-2,

which shows the movements in American and Canadian GNP from 1946 to 1980. The two countries have extensive bilateral trade, and the figure shows that movements in national income in the two countries are indeed very similar.

Imports and the Multiplier

As we saw in Chapter 30, expenditure on imports will grow as domestic national income grows. Expenditure on imports does not represent a demand for Canadian goods; such expenditure leads to a reduction in the value of the multiplier. [41] Of course this has both desirable and undesirable consequences. It is undesirable because it reduces the effectiveness of domestic policies that attempt to change the level of domestic income. It is desirable because it reduces the impact on national income of fluctuations in such autonomous expenditure items as investment and exports.

The consequence of the latter effect is that imports act as a **built-in-stabilizer.** A built-in-stabilizer is anything that increases the marginal propensity to withdraw and hence reduces the size of the multiplier. (We encounter other built-in stabilizers in the next chapter in our analysis of the government sector and the role of fiscal policy.)

THE NET EXPORT FUNCTION

The balance of trade, which is the difference between exports and imports, $X - M$, is also referred to as *net exports*. (See page 583.) The **net export function** relates the value of $X - M$ to national income.

The value of exports depends on the level of foreign demand for our goods and services. This in turn depends on the level of foreign income and on the *terms of trade* (the price of Canadian goods relative to foreign goods). Differences in foreign and domestic inflation rates and changes in the exchange rate are the main reasons why the terms of trade change.

FIGURE 33-2
The Relation Between Canadian and American GNP, 1946–1980

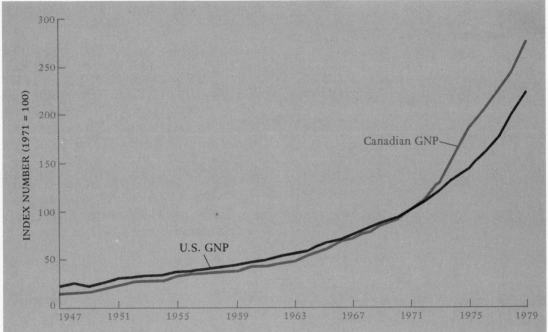

The GNPs of Canada and the United States corre-lated closely over the post-World War II period. Both series are calculated as an index number with 1971 = 100 and hence pass through that common point in 1971. Fluctuations in GNP in the United States lead to fluctuations in the American demand for Canadian ex-ports. Because of the export multiplier, fluctuations in Canadian GNP will correlate closely with fluctuations in GNP in the United States.

For the moment, let us consider an economy operating on the Keynesian portion of its aggregate supply curve and maintaining a fixed exchange rate. In this case the value of exports depends only on conditions external to the economy—foreign income and inflation. Hence exports are *exogenous*.

If exports were constant, national income could still fluctuate in response to changes in other components of autonomous expenditure. Fluctuations in national income will cause imports to fluctuate. As a result, with exports constant the balance of trade will fluctuate with the level of national income. Net exports will vary inversely with the level of national income because expenditure on imports is directly related to the level of national income.

For given levels of foreign income and other de-terminants of exports, the balance-of-trade sur-plus will be inversely related to national income.

This inverse relationship is illustrated in Figure 33-3, which is based on the hypothetical data of Table 30-4 on page 603.

Shifts in the Net Export Function

Shifts in the net export function are important because they lead to shifts in the aggregate ex-penditure function. As we shall see, this relation-ship is important for our understanding the role of net exports in determining national income and the formulation of policy in an open econ-omy. As we noted, net exports depend on foreign

FIGURE 33-3
The Derivation of the Net Export Function

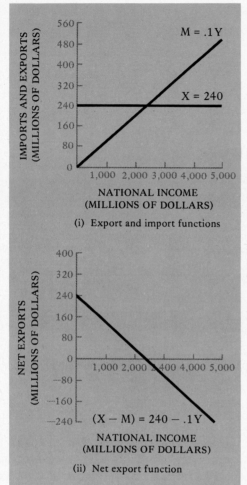

(i) Export and import functions

(ii) Net export function

Net exports, defined as the difference between exports and imports, are inversely related to the level of national income. In (i) exports are constant at $240 million while imports rise with national income. Therefore net exports, shown in (ii), decline with national income. The figure is based on the hypothetical data in Table 30-5. With national income equal to $2,400 million, imports are equal to exports at $240 million and net exports are zero. For levels of national income below $2,400 million, imports are less than exports and hence net exports are positive. For levels of national income above $2,400 million, imports are greater than exports and hence net exports are negative.

income and the terms of trade as well as on national income. Let us see how changes in these entities might lead to shifts in the net export function.

Foreign income. An increase in foreign income, *ceteris paribus*, will lead to an increase in the quantity of Canadian goods demanded by foreign countries. This will lead to an upward shift in the net export function. A fall in foreign income leads to a downward shift in the net export function. These shifts are shown in Figure 33-4.

Foreign prices. An increase in foreign prices, *ceteris paribus*, will lead both foreign and domestic agents to substitute cheaper Canadian goods for the now more expensive foreign goods. As a result, exports will rise, imports at any level of national income will fall, and the net export function will shift upward. A fall in foreign prices has the reverse effect, with substitution away from Canadian goods in favor of foreign goods and the net export curve shifting downward. These shifts are shown in Figure 33-5.[1]

Domestic prices. An increase in domestic prices, *ceteris paribus*, leads both foreign and domestic agents to substitute foreign goods for the now more expensive Canadian goods. This leads to an increase in imports and a fall in exports—and thus to a downward shift in the net export function. A fall in domestic prices leads to substitution in favor of Canadian goods and an upward shift in the net export function. These shifts are illustrated in Figure 33-5.

The exchange rate. A depreciation of the Canadian dollar shifts expenditure away from foreign goods and toward Canadian goods. (The mechanism by which this happens is analyzed in the box.) Hence Canadians will import less and foreigners will buy more of our goods for export. The net export function shifts upward. An appre-

---

[1] Figure 33-5 illustrates the shifts that arise in the particular case where the *marginal* propensity to import remains constant but the *average* propensity to import falls.

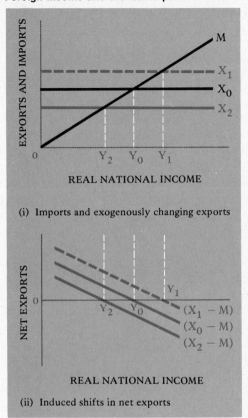

FIGURE 33-4
Foreign Income and the Net Export Function

(i) Imports and exogenously changing exports

(ii) Induced shifts in net exports

Changes in the level of foreign income cause the level of exports to change and lead to a shift in the net export function. In (i) a rise in foreign income causes the level of exports to rise to X_1. The level of income at which there is balanced trade rises from Y_0 to Y_1, and in (ii) the net export function shifts upward from $X_0 - M$ to $X_1 - M$.

A fall in foreign incomes causes the level of exports to fall to X_2 in (i). The level of income at which there is balanced trade falls to Y_2, and in (ii) the net export function shifts downward to $X_2 - M$.

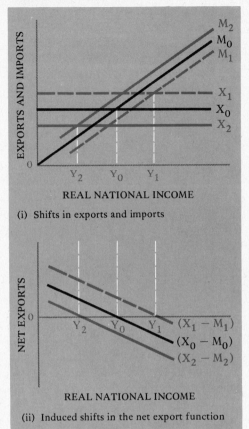

FIGURE 33-5
Relative Prices and the Net Export Function

(i) Shifts in exports and imports

(ii) Induced shifts in the net export function

Decreases in the relative price of domestic goods shift the net export function upward, and increases shift it downward. In (i) the initial levels of exports and imports are shown as the solid black lines X_0 and M_0. In (ii) the corresponding net export function is the solid black line $X_0 - M_0$.

A fall in the prices of Canadian goods relative to foreign goods, whether due to foreign inflation, Canadian deflation, or a devaluation of the Canadian dollar, causes exports to increase to the level of the dashed colored line X_1 in (i) and imports as a function of Canadian income to fall to the level of the dashed colored line M_1. As a result, the level of income that corresponds to balanced trade rises from Y_0 to Y_1, and the net export function shifts upward to $X_1 - M_1$ in (ii).

A rise in the relative prices of Canadian goods, whether due to Canadian inflation, foreign deflation, or an appreciation of the Canadian dollar, causes exports to fall, imports to rise, and the net export function to shift downward, to the solid colored lines X_2, M_2, and $X_2 - M_2$.

ciation of the Canadian dollar has the opposite effect, causing substitution of foreign for Canadian goods and shifting the net export function downward. This is also shown in Figure 33-5.

Alternative Approaches to the Analysis of Devaluation

We have said that a devaluation of the domestic currency leads to a shift of expenditure away from foreign goods and toward domestic goods. Thus a devaluation causes the net export function to shift upward to the right. The exact mechanism by which devaluation influences net exports depends on some key specific assumptions. Alternative assumptions will lead to different views of the effectiveness of devaluation. Here we explore three models of devaluation. Which one is appropriate in any given situation will depend on the conditions prevailing in the particular country at the time of the devaluation.

The small open economy model. In Chapter 8 we analyzed the effects of devaluation in a small open economy, that is, one which is too small in world markets to influence world prices. In such an economy a devaluation simply means that the prices of all traded goods rise proportionately in terms of the domestic currency. For example, if the pound sterling price of steel is given and fixed, a 10 percent devaluation of the Canadian dollar (which means a 10 percent increase in the number of Canadian dollars required to buy one pound) will lead to a 10 percent increase in the Canadian dollar price of steel. This increase applies to domestic prices of both imports and exports; in this model the terms of trade do not change.

If the relative price does not change, how does a devaluation succeed in shifting the net export function?

As we saw in Chapter 8, the mechanism works as follows: Domestic spending on imports falls because of the higher prices, and the reduction in quantity demanded causes a reduction in the quantity of imports. Domestic residents also reduce their consumption of exportables, and this leads to an increase in the excess supply of exportables in the domestic economy. Since a small economy can sell all it wants of its exportables at given world prices, the increase in the domestic excess supply leads directly to an increase in the quantity of exports. (See Figure 8-5.) This establishes the shift in the net export function.

In terms of the absorption approach, the increased prices led to a reduction in *total* expenditure so that at a given level of income net exports increased. The increase in total domestic absorption due to the increase in the price level follows from the monetary mechanism (see page 572).

The nontradeable goods model. A second model arises as an extension of the preceding model. We maintain the small open economy assumption but abandon the assumption that all goods are traded. And we draw a distinction between internationally tradeable and nontradeable goods. **Tradeables** are bought and sold on world markets at a fixed world price in terms of foreign currency. **Nontradeables** do not enter directly into international trade, either because they cannot be transported (services such as haircuts, maid services, restaurant meals) or because the cost of transport is prohibitively high (cement). The price of nontradeable goods is determined not on world markets but by domestic supply and demand.

A devaluation now causes the price of *traded* goods to rise. The change in the relative prices of traded and nontraded goods is often referred to as a change in the *internal terms of trade*. Domestic production of traded good rises as resources shift from the lower priced nontraded goods sector. Domestic demand shifts away from traded goods and toward the lower-priced nontraded goods. Excess demand for imports falls and excess supply of exports rises, as in Figure 8-6. This gives rise to the predicted shift in the net export function.

The focus is now on the relative price of tradeables to nontradeables, but it is still true that for net exports to rise, domestic absorption must fall relative to national income. By definition, expenditure on domestic nontradeable goods equals income received from sales of nontradeable goods. Therefore the difference between total expenditure (absorption) and total income equals the balance-of-trade deficit.

The Keynesian model. A very different view of devaluation arises from the Keynesian model employed in this chapter. In an economy on the horizontal portion of its aggregate supply curve, the price of its output is fixed in terms of its own currency. A devaluation reduces the foreign exchange value of the home currency and thereby also lowers the price of the home good in terms of the foreign currency. Similarly, a devaluation raises the domestic price of imported goods. Hence in the Keynesian model a devaluation is associated with a change in the *external terms of trade* (the relative price of imports to exports), and thus it causes a shift of expenditure on the part of both domestic and foreign consumers away from the now relatively expensive foreign good and toward the now relatively inexpensive Canadian good. Nevertheless, it is still true that net exports will rise only if national income rises relative to domestic absorption.

Note that in this model, domestic residents buy less foreign goods but at a higher price; *expenditure* on foreign goods falls only when domestic import demand is elastic. The possibility of inelastic demand raises the potential for a devaluation to lead to a worsening of the trade balance, an issue that has been at the center of a long-standing controversy about the effectiveness of devaluation. It is shown in the theory of international trade that if domestic prices are unaffected by variations in foreign demand, the perverse case can occur only if the sum of the elasticities of demand for imported goods in the two countries is less than one. In other words, quite highly inelastic demands are required to produce this case. If this situation were commonly encountered, the case for freely fluctuating rates would be dealt a crippling blow, because far from improving matters, currency depreciations in the face of balance-of-payments deficits and currency appreciations in the face of surpluses would make matters worse. Most economists today dismiss the perverse case as a theoretical curio of little practical importance. For simplicity, we assume that the domestic demand for imports is elastic.

The Keynesian assumptions are most compatible with the analysis of Figure 33-8. In Figure 33-8 the shift in the aggregate demand curve induced by the shift in the net export function leads to an increase in real domestic national income with unchanged domestic prices. The small open economy model with its assumption of flexible domestic prices is more compatible with the analysis of Figure 33-9. In Figure 33-9 the shift in the aggregate demand curve leads to an increase in domestic prices at unchanged real domestic income.

FIGURE 33-6
Domestic Absorption, Aggregate Expenditure, and National Income

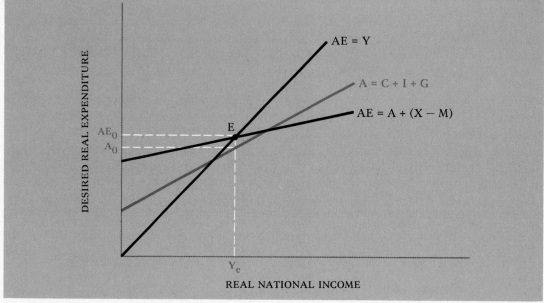

Equilibrium national income occurs at *E*, where the aggregate desired expenditure line, *A* + (*X* − *M*), intersects the 45° line. Domestic absorption, *A* (equal to *C* + *I* + *G*), is given by the colored line *A*. Aggregate desired expenditure is given by the black line *AE*. At any level of income, the vertical distance from *AE* to *A* is, by construction, equal to net exports, *X* − *M*. The *AE* line is flatter than the *A* line since, as shown in Figure 33-3, net exports fall as national income rises. At the equilibrium level of national income, Y_0, domestic absorption is less than national income and net exports are positive, equal to $AE_0 − E_0$.

NET EXPORTS AND DOMESTIC ABSORPTION

The model of national income determination outlined in the preceding three chapters can be summarized in an equation that links actual output of domestic goods and services to total desired expenditure on domestically produced goods and services. That is,

$$Y = C + I + G + (X − M)$$

The sum of $C + I + G$ corresponds to total expenditure on all goods and services (domestic and foreign) for use *within* the economy; this total is often referred to as **domestic absorption.** Denoting this by the symbol A, the basic relationship can be rewritten as

$$Y = A + (X − M)$$

The right-hand side of this equation is desired aggregate expenditure on Canadian goods and services, represented as the sum of expenditure for *internal* use (domestic absorption) plus expenditure due to *external* demand (net exports).

In an open economy, equilibrium national income equals domestic absorption plus net exports.

This is illustrated in Figure 33-6 for an economy on the Keynesian portion of its aggregate supply curve.[2]

Rearranging the previous equation by subtracting A from both sides, we get

$$X − M = Y − A$$

[2] If Figure 33-6 were drawn using the hypothetical data in Table 30-5, equilibrium national income would occur at $2,000 million with net exports equal to $40 million.

FIGURE 33-7
A Fall in Exports and the Level of National Income

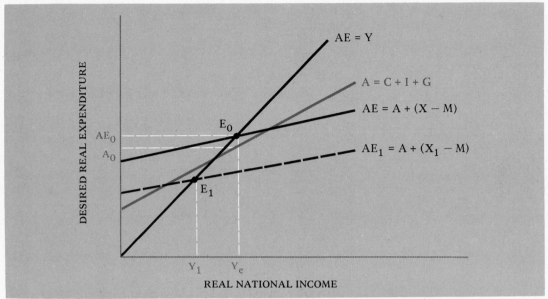

An exogenous reduction in the level of exports leads to a fall in equilibrium national income. The original equilibrium at E_0 replicates that shown in Figure 33-6. A fall in the level of exports causes AE to shift downward to the dashed line AE_1 while leaving A unchanged. This shift in AE relative to A occurs because the net export function shifts downward, as shown previously in Figure 33-4.

The new equilibrium is at E_1. National income falls from Y_0 to Y_1. Note that at the new equilibrium, national income is less than domestic absorption, so net exports are negative. The reduction in net exports reflects both the exogenous reduction in exports and the (smaller) induced reduction in imports.

This makes it clear that net exports can be positive only if national income exceeds domestic absorption. That is, only if total demand for goods and services to be used in Canada is less than total output of goods and services in Canada can net exports of goods from Canada be positive. And if net exports are positive, it must be the case that national income exceeds the absorption of goods and services within Canada.[3]

Similarly, it is evident that a balance-of-trade deficit occurs when absorption of goods and services within Canada exceeds national income.

The relationship between domestic absorption, net exports, and aggregate expenditure is apparent in Figure 33-6.

---

[3] Note that foreigners can influence the demand for Canadian goods and services in two ways: by demanding exports and by investing in Canada.

Absorption versus Component Approaches to the Trade Balance

The simple relationship between net exports and the gap between national income and absorption suggests a useful way of grouping categories of expenditure in an open economy. Organizing the model of income determination in this way has led most economists to view the trade balance as an aggregate phenomenon: it must equal the difference between two aggregates, national income and domestic absorption.

The trade balance, by definition, is also equal to the *sum* of all exports minus the *sum* of all imports. Since this is true, it is often tempting to try to *explain* changes or trends in the trade account by "counting" the changes or trends in particular exports and imports. Since both this "component" definition and the absorption definition are

Is Canada's Current Account a Cause for Concern?

Some observers have expressed alarm at recent trends in Canada's balance of payments, which shows a large current account deficit matched by a large capital account surplus. Here we address two sources of this alarm.

IS CANADA HEADED FOR FINANCIAL RUIN?

Concern over the balance of payments arises from the belief that Canada is borrowing abroad to finance a current account deficit that arises mainly from the invisibles account. Tourist expenditures of Canadians traveling abroad and interest payments to service past debts are commonly singled out as "causes" of Canada's heavy foreign borrowing. Two contentions are involved; first, that the country is borrowing abroad to help cover a current account deficit; second, that the policy of financing investment by foreign borrowing is in some way unsound.

The first contention mixes up cause and effect. The various items in the balance of payments represent unrelated decisions by many individuals, firms, and governments, each of whom seeks his or her own best possible economic position. The coordination and reconciliation of these independent actions is accomplished by the foreign exchange market. No one *decides* to borrow in the United States

in order to finance an excess of current account payments over receipts. If Canada is to have capital imports, there *must* be a deficit on current account. The exchange rate will rise until the necessary deficit occurs. The causal sequence runs, therefore, from the capital imports to the current account deficit.

If there had been less foreign borrowing during the period, the Canadian dollar would have depreciated, with the result that the foreign exchange required to finance Canadian travel abroad and the payment of interest and dividends to foreign investors would have been acquired in some other way. There would have been higher exports or lower imports or less travel abroad or more foreigners visiting Canada or some combination of these and other changes in individual balance-of-payments items.

The second contention is more easily dealt with. The relevant question to ask when assessing the economic implications of rapidly rising debt, whether foreign or domestic, is whether the funds raised are being used to finance new investment that will generate sufficient returns in the future to compensate for the burden of interest payments. If Canada's capacity to produce and export is being adequately enhanced by the investment, there is no reason to suppose the country is headed for financial ruin.

The current account deficit reflects the ex-

correct as *definitions* of the trade balance, either is valid as a framework that can be used to organize information in order to *analyze* the trade account. The component approach tends to lead the analyst to ignore the interactions between the items included in the trade balance and other variables such as national income. The absorption approach tends to draw attention to such interactions, and for this reason most economists prefer the absorption approach.

In order to compare the approaches, consider

the effect on the trade balance of an exogenous increase in the foreign demand for one particular Canadian export. As we saw in Chapter 31, an increase in a particular export, *ceteris paribus*, will lead to an increase in national income. This increase in national income will lead in turn to increased expenditure on some imports. If one takes the component approach to analyzing the trade account, one will miss this induced effect. For example, if exports of wheat rose by $20 million in a given year, the components approach

cess of current domestic spending over current income. If absorption is high in part because investment is high, then the deficit does not mean that Canada is "living beyond her means." High current consumption expenditure is justified by the high expected *future* income arising from the current investment. When that income is being earned, the debts accruing due to current borrowing can be repaid, and there will be a current account surplus.

STRUCTURAL PROBLEMS AND THE BALANCE OF TRADE

It is commonly alleged that the chronic current account deficit reflects serious structural problems in the Canadian economy. This means essentially that Canada produces the wrong combination of goods so that exports are too low and imports too high.* In this view, one of the problems arising from the deficit is that the high propensity to import frustrates expansionary policy from having its desired impact on domestic output and employment. The implied policy remedies in-

* A related contention is that our exports are concentrated on raw materials rather than manufacturing goods. For 1979 the merchandise trade balance was a surplus of about $4 billion, composed of a $20 billion surplus in raw materials and a $16 billion deficit in manufactured goods.

clude the encouragement of domestic production of import substitutes through the use of tariffs and other forms of protection.

One response to the claim that structural problems cause the deficit follows immediately from the absorption approach. If it is true that Canada is not allocating resources properly to exploit its comparative advantage — and hence is producing the "wrong" mix of output — this will be reflected in a reduced value of total output produced. But this reduction in real income will carry with it a reduction in expenditure. A balance-of-trade deficit will arise only if the reduction in real income is greater than the reduction in domestic absorption. To put it another way, correction of the structural problem will lead to higher real domestic income *and* therefore higher real domestic absorption. The current account deficit will be improved only if income rises by more than absorption.

Professor Neil Bruce of Queen's University has recently challenged the view that structural changes have led to the increased deficit. His research showed fairly constant long-term shares of raw materials and manufactures in Canada's trade. The facts of the Canadian case are that its raw materials base is so broad and varied that *at the aggregate level* there are only relatively moderate changes in the division of total output between the raw materials and manufacturing sectors.

would lead to the conclusion that in that year the trade balance would improve by $20 million because of wheat exports. But the increased wheat exports would be reflected in higher incomes for farmers and the producers of transportation services who ship the wheat. These groups will spend some of their increased incomes on imports and some on domestic goods. The latter will lead to a multiplier effect on national income and result in further increases in spending on imports.

Clearly the net effect on the trade balance of the increased wheat exports must include the induced increases in imports. By relating the trade balance to the difference between total income and total spending in the domestic economy, this is exactly what the absorption approach does. [42] This is discussed further in the box and is illustrated in Figure 33-7 (page 659), which shows that the change in net exports differs from the reduction in the level of exports that caused the change.

NET EXPORTS AND AGGREGATE DEMAND

A shift in the net export function, *ceteris paribus,* also indicates a shift in the aggregate demand function. For example, as Figure 33-5 shows, a devaluation leads to an upward shift in the net export function and hence in the aggregate expenditure function. The change in aggregate expenditure leads to an upward shift of the aggregate demand curve.

Keynesian case. Suppose the economy were in an unemployment situation operating on the horizontal portion of the aggregate supply curve, as in Figure 33-8. The shift in aggregate demand then leads to an increase in national income and no change in domestic prices. Since there is no further change in the terms of trade, the response of the trade balance occurs as a movement along the *new* net export function. The effect of the devaluation on the trade account can be read off the new net export function at the new higher income level.

Classical case. Suppose the economy is already in a situation of full employment and is operating on the vertical portion of the aggregate supply curve, as in Figure 33-9. The increase in *AE* implied by the devaluation would lead to no change in national income and an increase in domestic prices. The increase in domestic prices, as we saw in Figure 33-5, causes a downward shift in the net export function.[4]

Internal and External Balance

If full employment occurs at a level of national income that exceeds the level that is consistent with a balance of trade, then achieving full employment will lead to a balance-of-trade deficit. On the other hand, if full employment occurs at a

---

[4] In both the Keynesian and classical cases, there are competing effects operating on the trade balance. The relative strengths of these competing effects are the source of considerable debate that involves arguments too advanced for a first-year textbook. Figure 33-8 and 33-9 show the "standard" case where net exports rise. [43]

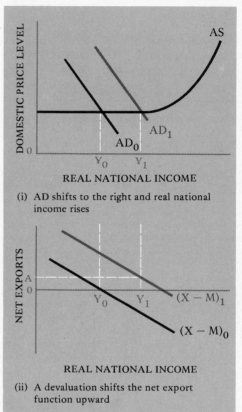

FIGURE 33-8

Currency Devaluation in an Unemployment Situation

(i) AD shifts to the right and real national income rises

(ii) A devaluation shifts the net export function upward

A currency devaluation with domestic prices constant leads to an increase in real national income and an improvement in the trade account surplus. The devaluation shifts the net export function from $(X-M)_0$ to $(X-M)_1$ in (ii). This leads to a shift in aggregate demand in (i) from AD_0 to AD_1. Real national income rises both absolutely, as shown in (i), and relative to domestic absorption. The combined effect is an increase in net exports. Before the devaluation, net exports were zero at the initial level of national income Y_0. After the devaluation, net exports equal $0A$ at the new level of national income Y_1.

level of income below that consistent with a balance of trade, the achievement of full employment will lead to a balance-of-trade surplus. Since over the long run a balance of trade might

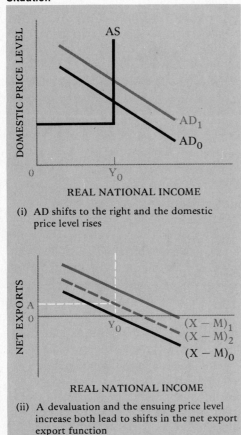

FIGURE 33-9

Currency Devaluation in a Full-employment Situation

(i) AD shifts to the right and the domestic price level rises

(ii) A devaluation and the ensuing price level increase both lead to shifts in the net export function

A currency devaluation with real domestic output constant leads to an increase in the domestic price level and an improvement in the trade account. The devaluation shifts the net export function from $(X - M)_0$ to $(X - M)_1$ in (ii). This leads to a shift in aggregate demand in (i) from AD_0 to AD_1. Since aggregate supply is vertical, there is a rise in the domestic price level but no increase in real national income. The rise in domestic prices causes the net export function to shift downward to $(X - M)_2$. Because it also causes a reduction in domestic absorption, net exports remain higher than they were initially. The increase in net exports, $0A$, equals the reduction in domestic absorption.

itself by a desirable policy objective, there is a potential for conflict between the internal target of full employment and the external target of balanced trade. Policies to achieve full employment must be combined with policies to alter relative prices, thereby shifting the net export function so that full employment and balanced trade are compatible. Appropriate ways to combine such policies are analyzed in Chapter 40.

Canada's Balance of International Payments

THE NATURE OF BALANCE-OF-PAYMENTS ACCOUNTS

In order to know what is happening to the course of international trade, governments keep track of the actual *transactions* among countries. The record of such transactions is made in the **balance-of-payments accounts.** Each transaction, such as the shipment of exports or the arrival of imported goods, is classified according to the payments or receipts that would typically arise from it.

Any transaction that is expected to lead to a payment to other nations is classified as a debit $(-)$ item because, *ceteris paibus,* it subtracts from our foreign exchange reserves. Canadian imports and outflows of Canadian capital to purchase foreign assets are debit items. (An outflow of capital is really an *import* of the foreign assets purchased.) Any transaction that is expected to lead to a payment by foreigners to Canada or its residents is classified as a credit $(+)$ item because, *ceteris paribus,* it adds to our foreign exchange reserves. Canadian exports and capital flows into Canada are credit items.

Any item that typically gives rise to the acquisition of foreign exchange is recorded as a credit; any item that typically gives rise to the sale of foreign exchange is recorded as a debit.

When an American firm purchases Canadian newsprint, the transaction appears as a credit in the Canadian balance of payments because when the newsprint is paid for, Americans dollars are sold (and Canadian dollars purchased). Canada thus gains foreign exchange on the deal. However, when a Canadian shipping firm insures with Lloyds of London a cargo destined for Alexandria, Egypt, this represents a debit in the Canadian balance of payments because when the insurance premium is paid, the shipping firm must pay Lloyds in sterling. Because the firm purchases sterling (by selling Canadian dollars), Canada's stock of foreign exchange is diminished. Of course, a credit item to one country is a debit item to the other, and vice versa. Thus the newsprint transaction is a debit in the American balance of payments because it depletes foreign exchange, and the insurance transaction is a credit in the British balance of payments because it earns foreign exchange.[5]

Because it is generally possible to measure only those movements of goods and services that correspond to transactions in foreign exchange, it is necessary to make a number of assumptions, some of them quite arbitrary. How, for example, should gifts of goods to foreigners be recorded? If the goods had been sold, they would have given rise to earnings of foreign exchange, but when they are given away, they do not. For another example, what should be done about an export to a foreign firm that subsequently defaults on the debt it incurred when it bought the good on credit? These and many related problems are important both to the statistician who attempts to measure the balance of payments and to the careful observer who attempts to account for detailed movements in the flows of trade and payments. For more general purposes, it can be assumed that the balance of payments measures the actual flow of payments between nations.

The first thing to notice about the record of international transactions is that the balance of payments refers to actual transactions, not desired transactions. We have seen that at some exchange rate between dollars and pounds it is

quite possible for holders of sterling to want to purchase more dollars in exchange for pounds than holders of dollars want to sell in exchange for pounds. In this situation quantity demanded exceeds quantity supplied. But it is not possible for sterling holders to buy more dollars than dollar holders will sell; every dollar that is bought must have been sold by someone, and every dollar that is sold must have been bought by someone.

Because the amount of dollars bought must equal the amount of dollars actually sold, the balance of payments always balances.

In the balance-of-payments accounts, an attempt is made to record the reasons for which payments are made. These accounts show what volume of payments is (or will be) made by foreigners to Canadians for such purposes as the purchase of Canadian goods; the use of Canadian services (shipping, tourist facilities, etc.); the lending of money to Canadian households, firms, or governments; and the investment of money in Canada. The acounts should also show what volume of payments is (or will be) made by Canadians to foreigners for the purchase of foreign goods; the use of foreign services; the lending of money to foreign households, firms, or governments; and the investment of money abroad.

Although the total number of Canadian dollars bought on the foreign exchange market must equal the total number sold, this is not true of purchases and sales for a particular purpose. It is quite possible, for example, that more dollars are sold for the purpose of obtaining foreign currency to import foreign cars than are bought for the purpose of buying Canadian cars for export to other countries. In such a case, Canada has a balance-of-payments deficit on the "car account": the value of Canadian imports of cars exceeds the value of Canadian exports of cars. For most general purposes, economists are not interested in the balance of payments for single commodities but are instead interested in larger classes of transactions.

[5] As we shall see, there is nothing *inherently* good about "credits" or bad about "debits." The purpose of earning foreign exchange (gaining a credit) is to be able to use it (incurring a debit).

TABLE 33-1
Canadian Balance of International Payments, 1980 (billions of dollars)

Current Account			
Merchandise exports	+76.1		
Merchandise imports	−68.1		
Balance of trade (visibles)		+8.0	
Services	−10.7		
Transfers	+ 1.2		
Invisible Balance		−9.5	
Balance on Current Account			−1.5
Capital Account			
New direct investment	−2.1		
Other long-term capital flows	+3.5		
Total long-term capital flows		+1.4	
Short-term capital flows		−1.4	
Balance on Capital Account			0.0
Balance on Current plus Capital Accounts			−1.5
Use of Official Reserves			
(increase −, decrease +)			+1.5
Overall Balance of Payments			Always zero[a]

[a] In balance-of-payments accounts there is a "statistical discrepancy" item that results from the inability to measure accurately some industrial items. For example, many capital transactions are not recorded. In this table the discrepancy is included in the short-term capital flows item.

The overall balance of payments always balances, but the individual components do not have to. The principal categories of greatest interest are shown in color. In the table, drawn from the Canadian experience for 1980, there is a positive (surplus) balance on merchandise trade but a larger negative (deficit) balance on trade in invisibles, so the current account is in deficit. There is a zero balance on the capital account; capital imports equaled capital exports. The capital *plus* current accounts surplus of −$1.5 billion is what is commonly referred to as the "balance of payments." It is exactly matched by the change in official reserves.

MAJOR CATEGORIES IN THE BALANCE-OF-PAYMENTS ACCOUNTS

Table 33-1 presents a typical balance-of-payments account that shows divisions that are of particular interest.

Current Account

The balance of payments on *current account* includes all payments made because of current purchases of goods and services. There is no automatic reason why current account payments should balance (any more than the automobile account should). It is quite possible for more dollars to be sold in order to purchase imports than are bought in order to allow foreigners to purchase our exports. If so, the dollars must have come from somewhere, and the excess of sales over purchases on current account must be exactly matched by an excess of purchases over sales on the capital account or a decline in the reserves of gold and foreign exchange held by the central authorities.

The current account is often divided in a number of different ways. One common division is into trade balances on visible and invisible items. **Visibles** are goods—all those things such as cars, pulpwood, aluminum, coffee, and iron ore that can be seen and touched when they cross international borders. **Invisibles** are services—all those things that cannot be seen or touched, such as insurance, freight haulage, and tourist expenditures. When a Canadian firm buys insurance from Lloyds of London for a shipment of goods consigned to Egypt, the firm consumes a British export just as surely as if it purchased and used a British-made automobile or sent its president on a vacation to Scotland. Payment for the insurance services, for the automobile, and for the vacation must be made in pounds; each is thus a Canadian import and a British export.

The terminology used to describe the current account is not standardized and can be confusing. We use the term *current account* to include *both* visible and invisible items in the balance-of-payments accounts. The term *balance of trade,* sometimes called the *merchandise trade balance,* is also used to refer to the narrower concept of the balance of trade on visible items.[6]

The current account balance is given by the difference between the dollar value of exports and imports in a given year. In Table 33-1, merchandise exports exceeded imports in the year reported, and thus there was a *surplus* in the merchandise trade balance. In other years imports exceed exports and there is a *deficit,* and in some years the balance of trade is virtually zero.

Note that the balance of trade relates only to the *difference* between exports and imports, not to the *volume* of trade. Thus one could have a $30 million excess of exports over imports on a volume of exports of $300 million or on a volume of $50 million. In either case the same pressure on the exchange rate would be exerted. But the effect of foreign trade on the nation's economy would be very different because such things as the gains from trade depend on the volume of trade.

The gains from trade depend on the volume of trade, not the balance of trade. The effect on foreign exchange markets depends on the balance of trade, not the volume of trade.

An important invisible item for Canada is the payment of interest and dividends on foreign loans and investments in Canada. When an American corporation owns a subsidiary in Canada, it receives dividend payments in Canadian

dollars. If the American owners wish to spend these dividends at home, they will need to exchange Canadian for American dollars. Interest and dividends paid to foreigners thus use up foreign exchange and are entered as debit items on the balance of payments. In the table, the deficit on invisibles (due to debt servicing) exceeds the merchandise trade surplus, and hence the overall current account is in deficit.

Capital Account

The *capital account* records transactions related to international movements of financial capital. The main items here are capital transfers. Consider an American citizen who wishes to invest abroad by lending money to a Canadian industry; he is exporting capital to Canada from the United States. Suppose that he buys newly issued bonds being sold in Toronto by an expanding Canadian firm. In order to do this, he needs to obtain Canadian dollars. He is a supplier of foreign exchange and a demander of Canadian dollars; therefore his transaction is a credit item in the Canadian balance-of-payments accounts.

An important distinction is often made between short-term and long-term capital movements. The distinction is important because short-term capital movements tend to be much more volatile than long-term ones and thus are more likely to cause sudden sharp changes in the capital account balance.

Short-term capital is held for many reasons. The mere fact of international trade forces traders to hold money balances because their receipts and expenditures are not perfectly synchronized. It usually does not matter where such funds are held. The funds can easily be moved from one currency to another in response to small changes in incentives or because of real or imaginary fears of all sorts. When short-term capital is transferred from one country to another, purchases and sales of foreign exchange tend to occur and are entered in the balance-of-payments accounts.

The two major subdivisions of the long-term

---

[6] An alternative usage assigns the term *balance of trade* to encompass all current account items, thereby reserving the term *merchandise trade balance* solely for the visible items.

component are **direct investment** and **portfolio investment.** Direct investment is the item in the balance-of-payments accounts that records changes in nonresident ownership of domestic firms and resident ownership of foreign firms. Thus direct investment in Canada is capital investment in a branch plant or subsidiary corporation in Canada in which the investor has voting control. Alternatively, it may be in the form of a takeover in which a controlling interest is acquired in a firm previously controlled by residents. Portfolio investment, on the other hand, is investment in bonds or a minority holding of shares that does not involve legal control.

Why do international capital movements occur? Allowing for risk and other such factors, investors will seek to invest where the return is highest. Just as capital moves from industry to industry within one country in search of its most productive uses, so capital tends to move from country to country in search of the highest rates of return. Such capital movements mean that the households and firms of one country are making investments in another country.

Capital movements often seem baffling to beginners, who find it puzzling that the export of capital is a debit item and the export of a good is a credit item. But the apparent contradiction can be resolved. Consider the export of Canadian capital to invest in a British bond. The capital transaction involves the purchase, and hence the *import,* of a British bond, and this has the same effect on the balance of payments as the purchase, and hence the import, of a British good. Both items involve payments to foreigners and use foreign exchange, and they are thus debit items in the Canadian balance of payments.

Official Reserves

The final major element of the balance-of-payments accounts is the change in gold and foreign exchange reserves held by the central authorities. Central authorities of most countries hold supplies of gold and foreign exchange in order that they may intervene in the foreign exchange market to influence their country's rate of exchange. When a country has a payments deficit on all other counts—that is, when it uses more foreign currency than it obtains—the deficit must be made up by an equivalent reduction in its reserves of gold and foreign exchange. Canadian reserves are held mainly in the form of gold and U.S. dollars. At the end of 1980, U.S. dollars accounted for about one-half of the total.

THE RELATION AMONG CURRENT, CAPITAL, AND OFFICIAL ACCOUNTS

The relation among the three divisions of accounts follows from the fact that their sum must be zero.

A deficit on current plus capital accounts must be matched by a net surplus on the official financing accounts—which entails the government's borrowing abroad or decreasing its exchange reserves. A surplus on current plus capital accounts implies a deficit on the official financing accounts. Similarly, deficits on current account can be offset by surpluses on capital account, and vice versa.

To illustrate these relationships, consider a situation in which the value of Canadian imports exceeds the value of Canadian exports. This involves a current account deficit, which has been the characteristic situation in the years since World War II. In such a situation Canadian export sales will not earn all the foreign currency that Canadians need in order to buy the imports. Thus the excess of imports over exports can be paid for only if Canadians obtain foreign currency from other sources.

There are several possibilities. First, foreign currency may be provided by foreign investors eager to obtain Canadian dollars so that they can buy Canadian stocks, bonds, and real estate. In this case the current account deficit is balanced by a surplus on capital account. Second, Canadian governments, rather than Canadian firms or citizens, may have borrowed from foreign governments to finance their expenditures. This too causes a capital account surplus. Third, the Canadian government may have depleted its reserves of foreign currency. One way or another, the current account deficit can occur only when someone provides the foreign currency needed to pay for the excess Canadian imports.

Our reasoning starting from the existence of a current account deficit and showed that, in the absence of government financing from its foreign exchange reserves, it implied a capital account surplus. However, this does not mean that the current account deficit caused the capital inflow. Our reasoning could just as easily have started with the capital account surplus and deduced the existence of the current account deficit.

BALANCE-OF-PAYMENTS DEFICITS AND SURPLUSES

Meaning of the Concepts

We have already noted that when all the uses to which foreign currency is put and all the sources from which it came are added up, the two amounts are necessarily equal, and thus the overall accounts of all international payments necessarily balance.

Yet it is common to speak of a country as having a balance-of-payments deficit or surplus. What does this mean? These terms usually refer to the account *excluding* changes in official financing. A **balance-of-payments surplus** means that the authorities are reducing liabilities to foreigners or else adding to their holdings of official reserves in such forms as gold and foreign exchange. A **balance-of-payments deficit** means that the authorities are adding to liabilities to foreigners or else reducing their stocks of official reserves.

The statement, for example, that Canada had a balance-of-payments deficit of $1.5 billion in 1980 means that official reserves fell by $1.5 billion because all other transactions combined were in deficit by that amount.

A balance-of-payments deficit means that the reserves of the central authorities are being run down; a surplus means that reserves are rising.

Consequences of Deficits and Surpluses

People sometimes act as though deficits were bad and surpluses good. A balance-of-payments deficit means that in the aggregate debit items exceed credit items; it says nothing about whether this is beneficial or harmful. For example, an investment by a Canadian firm in foreign countries that will yield future profits for Canadian owners is a debit item that will increase a balance-of-payments deficit, yet there is nothing necessarily bad about the investment. On the opposite side, the transfer of ownership of Canadian firms to foreigners is a credit item that will decrease a balance-of-payments deficit, but such loss of control over Canadian firms is not necessarily desirable.

There is nothing inherently good about a balance-of-payments surplus or inherently bad about a balance-of-payments deficit.

When a balance-of-payments deficit is caused by something considered undesirable (such as heavy dependence on Mideast oil), it may be that the government will seek a way to decrease such imports. When the same deficit is caused by something considered desirable (such as contributions to underdeveloped nations to foster their economic development), the government may be willing to draw down its reserves for the purpose.

Whether desirable or undesirable, permanent deficits on the balance-of-payments accounts cannot be maintained, for the official reserves that are needed to finance such deficits are sure to be exhausted.

It might seem that a permanent surplus could be tolerated, but this is not the case either. If we have a permanent balance-of-payments surplus, some of our trading partners must have a permanent deficit. Unless we are prepared to give them the money, or allow them to increase their debts to us without limit, that too must be ended.

In the long term, when the balance of payments on current plus capital accounts is out of balance in either direction, something must be done. One approach is to maintain the exchange rate and adopt policies to shift the demand and supply curves in the foreign exchange market to the point where the balance of payments is approximately zero. The government might do this through import or export restrictions, changes in interest rates, policies to alter the level of national income, or a variety of other methods.

Another approach is to allow exchange rates to change. Suppose the United States has a balance-of-payments surplus with respect to Britain. Holders of sterling are trying to make more payments in dollars than holders of dollars wish to make in sterling. If exchange rates are free to vary, the dollar will appreciate and the pound depreciate until the balance of payments is in equilibrium.

If exchange rates are completely free to vary, balance-of-payments deficits and surpluses will be eliminated through exchange rate adjustments.

The concern of economists and policy officials with "the balance-of-payments problem" is largely a carryover from the fact that for most of the hundred years before 1972 the world operated under a regime of fixed exchange rates.

In today's world, while no country need have a balance-of-payments problem, many still have them. As long as governments intervene in foreign exchange markets, there will be balance-of-payments deficits and surpluses. Surpluses will occur whenever the currency is held below its equilibrium value, deficits whenever it is held above its equilibrium value. Persistent deficits will cause persistent loss of reserves; they are evidence that the government is trying to resist longer-term trends.

But there is one great difference between this kind of balance-of-payments problem and that under fixed exchange rates. The central bank always has an available solution to its balance-of-payments problem: it can stop intervening in the market and let the exchange rate find its equilibrium level. This will not only end its balance-of-payments problem, it will end its loss of foreign exchange reserves.

Canada's Balance-of-Payments Experience

Figure 33-10 charts the movements in the major items in Canada's balance of payments over the period 1951–1980. The 1950s were characterized by a high level of capital inflow, particularly in the form of direct investment induced by the attractive opportunities available in Canada, especially in the natural resource industries. The high demand for Canadian dollars associated with this inflow kept the external value of the Canadian dollar at historically high levels, and it remained well above one U.S. dollar until 1961 (see Figure 8-10 on page 148). The high value of our currency provided a stimulus to imports and reduced demand for our exports, so there was a trade deficit during most of this period.

In contrast, the 1960s were characterized by surpluses on merchandise trade stimulated by the pegging of the Canadian dollar below one U.S. dollar at 92.5 U.S. cents. The upward pressure on our currency disappeared as the capital account surplus fell and a large deficit on invisibles emerged. The latter reflected to a large extent the growing burden of dividend and interest payments arising out of the accumulated amount of past foreign investment.

In the early 1970s the trade surplus rose to very high levels while the capital account surplus continued to decline and the invisibles deficit continued to increase. By the middle of the decade an entirely new picture had emerged. The capital account returned to a large surplus position but, in contrast with the 1950s, capital inflows were in the form of portfolio investment, and Canada became a net exporter of direct investment capital. The major component of the inflow was borrowing by provinces and provincially owned corporations such as Ontario Hydro. At the same time, the deficit on invisibles

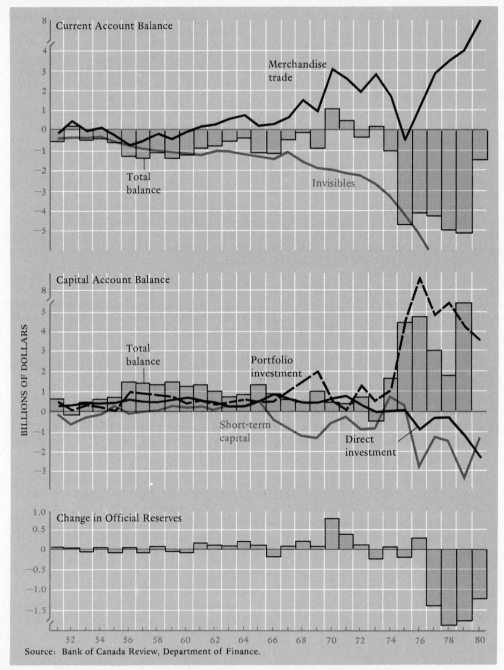

FIGURE 33-10
Canada's Balance of Payments, 1951–1980

Source: Bank of Canada Review, Department of Finance.

Canada has typically experienced a capital account surplus offset by a current account deficit. Although the merchandise trade balance has consistently been in surplus, debt servicing payments on past international borrowing have led to an overall current account deficit. On the capital account, direct investment has recently become negative while a surplus on portfolio investment has emerged. Errors and omissions are included in the short-term capital account.

FIGURE 33-11

Canada's Current Account Deficit as a Percentage of National Income, 1951–1980

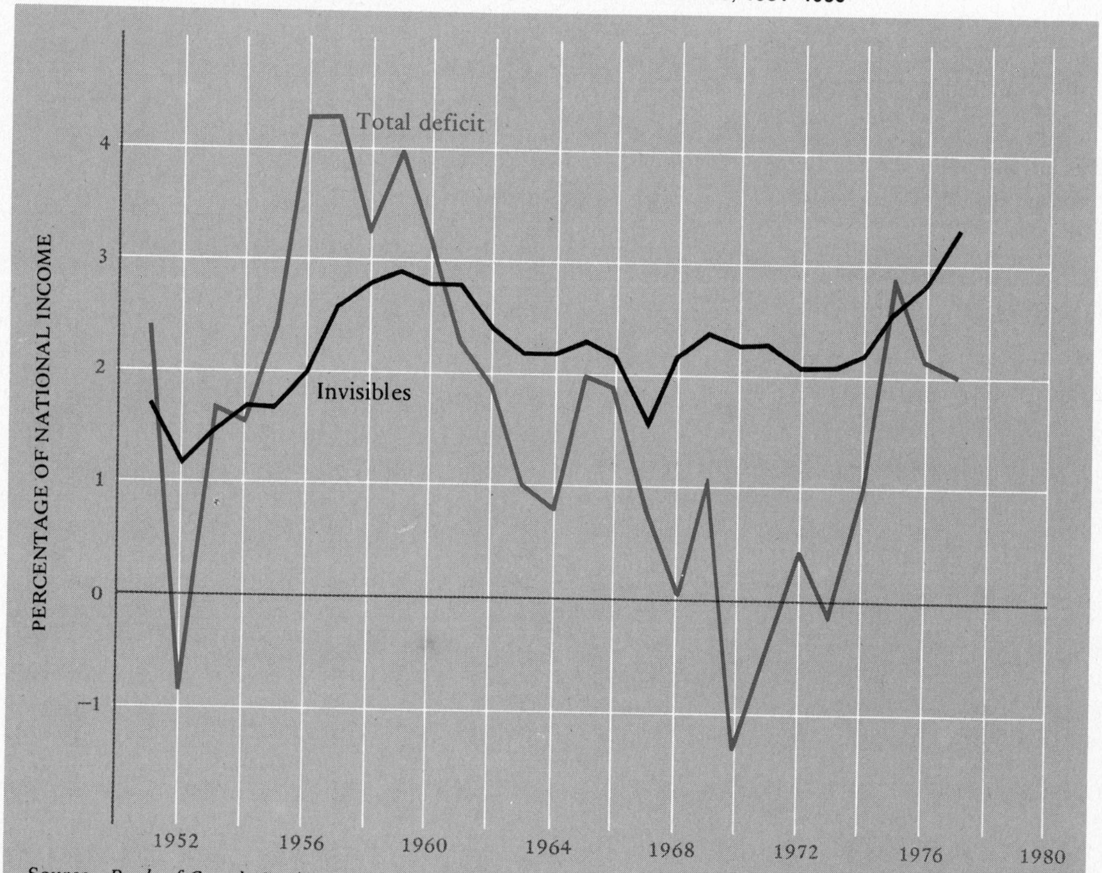

Source: *Bank of Canada Review.*

Canada's current account deficit as a percentage of national income has been lower in recent years than it was in the late 1950s. Net outpayments of interest and dividends, as reflected in the deficit on invisibles, have remained a relatively constant percentage of national income.

reached very high levels, reflecting not only large payments of interest and dividends but a substantial deficit in travel.

The specific figures for 1980 are shown in Table 33-1. The merchandise surplus was very large by historical standards, and the overall current account deficit was correspondingly small in spite of the continued growth in the invisibles deficit.

To put the recent figures in perspective, it is useful to consider them in relation to the growth in Canada's total national income (see Figure 33-11). For example, the current account deficit reached nearly $5 billion in 1975, compared with a peak level in the 1950s of about $1.5 billion in 1957. However, as a fraction of national income, the deficit actually declined. While the deficit was more than three times as high as the figure recorded eighteen years earlier, national income was nearly five times as large.

Summary

1. A balance-of-trade surplus occurs when the value of exports exceeds the value of imports. A balance-of-trade deficit occurs when the value of imports exceeds the value of exports.

2. Fluctuations in income in one country will be transmitted to its trading partners via the export multiplier.

3. Imports act as an automatic stabilizer by reducing the size of the multiplier.

4. The net export function indicates an inverse relationship between the balance of trade and the level of national income.

5. Domestic absorption corresponds to total expenditure on all goods and services for use within the economy. Net exports equal the excess of national income over domestic absorption.

6. The balance-of-payments accounts record international transactions. A debit item is a transaction that leads to a depletion of foreign exchange reserves; a credit item is one that earns foreign exchange reserves.

7. The current account is the sum of the merchandise trade balance plus the balance of trade on invisibles. A current account surplus must be matched by either a capital account deficit or an increase in official reserves. A current account deficit must be matched by either a capital account surplus or a decrease in official reserves.

8. A balance-of-payments deficit means that reserves of the central authorities are being run down; a surplus means that reserves are rising.

9. Canada typically has run a current account deficit due to debt service payments in excess of a merchandise trade surplus. Rising debt servicing reflects a long period of foreign borrowing, but debt service payments have actually fallen as a fraction of GNP.

Topics for Review

Balance of trade, net export function
Domestic absorption
Internal and external balance
Balance-of-payments accounts
Current account, merchandise trade balance, visibles and invisibles
Capital account, short-term and long-term capital, direct and portfolio investment
Balance-of-payments surplus or deficit

Discussion Questions

1. Since the North Sea discovery of large oil fields belonging to Great Brtain, the British economy has experienced a substantial balance-of-trade surplus. What does this imply about expenditure in Britain? How would you explain this? There is currently a high level of unemployment in Britain. Would policies to correct this worsen the trade account problem?

2. In discussing the Canadian balance of payments, and in particular the recurring current account deficit, Prime Minister Trudeau has argued that "Canada is living beyond her means." What is the truth in this view? What is wrong with this view? Canada's deficit on tourist account is often cited, and it is argued that Canadians should stop holidaying in Florida. Of what relevance is the balance on tourist account? Would Canadians be helped by reducing their holidays abroad?

3. What would happen to the balance of trade following a devaluation in a Keynesian model where both foreign and domestic import demands were completely inelastic? What would happen to the trade account over the course of two or three years if those elasticities were small in the short-run but larger in the long-run? For countries that import a lot of oil, would this be a reasonable scenario to expect?

4. It is often argued that Canada historically has run a trade deficit because we do not export enough manufactured goods. Analyze this contention using (a) the components approach, and (b) the absorption approach, to the trade balance.

Fiscal Policy

34

Fiscal policy involves using government expenditure and tax policy to shift the aggregate demand and aggregate expenditure functions toward desired positions. Since government spending increases aggregate expenditure and taxation decreases it, the *directions* of the required shifts are easily established in most circumstances. But, as we shall see, the *timing* and the *magnitude* of changes in tax and expenditure policies pose more difficult issues.

Any policy that attempts to stabilize national income at or near a desired level (usually full-employment national income) is called **stabilization policy**. This chapter deals first with the theory of fiscal policy as a tool of stabilization policy and then with the actual experience of using it.

There is no doubt that the government can exert a major influence on the circular flow of income. Prime examples occur during major wars when governments engage in massive military spending and abandon fiscal caution. As more and more money is spent, both GNP and employment tend to rise to unprecedented heights. Government of Canada defence expenditure rose, for example, from $70 million, or 1.2 percent of the GNP, in 1939, to $4,299 million, or 36 percent of the GNP, in 1944. At the same time the unemployment rate fell from 11.4 to 1.4 percent. Economists agree that the increase in the government's aggregate expenditure caused the rise in the GNP and the fall in unemployment. Similar experiences occurred during the rearmament of most European countries before, or just following, the outbreak of World War II in 1939.

When used appropriately, fiscal policy can be an important tool for influencing the economy. In the heyday of fiscal policy in the 1940s, 1950s, and 1960s, many economists thought that the economy could be regulated adequately by varying the size of the government's taxes and expenditures. That day is now past. Today most economists are aware of the limitations of fiscal policy, and there is much discussion of other tools of stabilization that can complement fiscal policy or possibly even replace it.

In this chapter we ask what might be expected from fiscal policy under the most favorable circumstances. The limitations of fiscal policy and the choices among alternative policies are studied in later chapters.

The Theory of Fiscal Policy

Not so many years ago people generally accepted, and indeed many still fervently believe, the argument that prudent government should always balance its budget. The argument is based on an analogy with what seems prudent behavior for the individual. It is a foolish individual whose current expenditure consistently exceeds his or her current revenue so that he or she goes steadily further into debt. From this observation it is argued that if avoiding a steadily rising debt is good for the individual, it must also be good for the nation.

But the paradox of thrift, discussed in Chapter 31, suggests that analogy between the government and the household may be misleading. When a government follows a balanced budget policy, as most governments tried to do even during the Great Depression of the 1930s, it must restrict its expenditure during a recession because its tax revenue will necessarily be falling at that time. During a recovery, when its revenue is high and rising, it increases its spending. In other words, it rolls with the economy, raising and lowering its expenditure in step with everyone else.

By the mid 1930s, many economists had concluded that the government, by going along with the crowd, was not making the most of its poten-

tial to control the economy in a beneficial manner. Why, they asked, should not the government try to stabilize the economy by doing just the opposite of what everyone else was doing—by increasing its demand when private demand was falling and lowering its demand when private demand was rising? This policy would hold aggregate demand constant even though its individual components were fluctuating.

When Milton Friedman said, "We are all Keynesians now," he was referring to (among other things) the general acceptance of the view that the government's budget is much more than just the revenue and expenditure statement of a very large organization. Whether we like it or not, the sheer size of the government's budget inevitably makes it a powerful tool for influencing the economy.

THE BUDGET BALANCE

The **budget balance** refers to the difference between all government revenue and all government expenditure. For this purpose government expenditure includes both purchases of currently produced goods and services and transfer payments. Thus the budget balance is the difference between all the money the government takes in as revenue and all the money it pays out.

There are three possibilities for the relation between these two flows. If current revenue is exactly equal to current expenditure, the government has a **balanced budget;** if revenues exceed expenditures, there is a **budget surplus;** if revenues fall short of expenditures, there is a **budget deficit.**

If the government raises its spending without raising taxes, its extra expenditure may be said to be *deficit financed.* If the extra spending is accompanied by an equal increase in tax revenue, we speak of a *balanced budget change in spending.*

Financial Implications of Budget Deficits and Surpluses

When the government spends more than it raises, where does the money come from? If the government raises more than it spends, where does the money go? The difference between expenditure and current revenue shows up as changes in the level of the government's debt. When expenditures exceed revenues, the balance must be borrowed from someone; when revenues exceed expenditures, the balance pays off some of the loans made in the past.

A deficit requires an increase in borrowing, for which there are two main sources: the central bank and the private sector of the economy—banks and other financial institutions, firms, and households.[1] The government borrows money from these sources by selling treasury bills or bonds to them. A **treasury bill** is a promise to repay a stated amount 90 days from the date of issue. It is sold in return for a smaller amount paid to the government now. The difference between the two sums represents the interest on the loan. A government bond is also a promise to pay a stated sum of money in the future, but in the more distant future than a bill—possibly as much as 25 years from now.

A surplus allows the government to reduce its outstanding debt. Treasury bills and bonds may be redeemed from tax revenue when they fall due rather than from money raised by selling new bills and bonds.

When the government makes new loans from or repays old loans to the private sector, this action merely shifts funds between the two sectors. When the government "borrows" from the central bank, however, the central bank creates new money. Since, unlike the private sector, the central bank can create as much money as it wishes, there is no limit to what the government can "borrow" from the central bank.

FISCAL POLICY WHEN PRIVATE EXPENDITURE FUNCTIONS DO NOT SHIFT

A relatively easy problem faces fiscal policy-makers when private-sector expenditure func-

tions for consumption, investment, and net exports are given and unchanging. What is needed then is a once-and-for-all fiscal change that will remove any existing inflationary or deflationary gap.

Changes in either expenditure or tax rates. The necessary policies were established in Chapter 31: a reduction in tax rates or an increase in government expenditure shifts the aggregate expenditure function upward; an increase in tax rates or a cut in government expenditure will shift the aggregate expenditure function downward.

The key proposition in the theory of fiscal policy follows these results.

Government taxes and expenditure can be used to remove inflationary and deflationary gaps by shifting the aggregate expenditure and aggregate demand functions.

The necessary policies are described and illustrated in Figures 34-1 and 34-2.

Balanced budget changes in expenditure and tax rates. The changes analyzed so far would move government expenditure and tax rates in opposite directions. Another policy available to the government is to make a balanced budget change in both expenditures and taxes.

Consider a balanced budget increase in expenditure. Say the government increases personal income tax rates enough to raise an extra $1 billion that it then spends on purchasing goods and services. Aggregate expenditure will be unaffected by this change only if the $1 billion that the government takes from the private sector would have been spent by the private sector in any case. If this is the case, the government's policy will reduce private expenditure by $1 billion and raise its own expenditure by $1 billion. Aggregate expenditure, and hence national income and employment, will remain unchanged.

But this is not the usual case. When an extra $1 billion in taxes is taken away from households, they usually reduce their spending on domestically produced goods by less than $1 billion. If, say, the marginal propensity to con-

---

[1] In Canada the central bank is the Bank of Canada, which will be described and discussed in Chapter 37.

FIGURE 34-1
Policies to Eliminate a Deflationary Gap

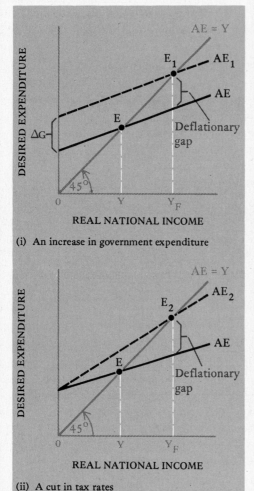

(i) An increase in government expenditure

(ii) A cut in tax rates

FIGURE 34-2
Policies to Eliminate an Inflationary Gap

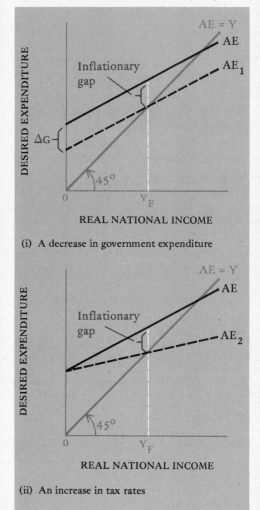

(i) A decrease in government expenditure

(ii) An increase in tax rates

Policies that shift the aggregate expenditure function upward can be used to eliminate deflationary gaps. In each part the original aggregate expenditure function, AE, produces the deflationary gap shown by the braces. In (i) an increase in government expenditure, ΔG, shifts AE to AE_1. This eliminates the deflationary gap and raises equilibrium income from Y to Y_F.

In (ii) a cut in tax rates raises the percentage of national income that goes to disposable income. This causes a corresponding increase in the amount of consumption expenditure associated with each level of national income and thus pivots AE to AE_2. That eliminates the deflationary gap and raises equilibrium income from Y to Y_F.

Policies that shift the aggregate expenditure function downward can be used to eliminate inflationary gaps. In each part the original aggregate expenditure function, AE, produces the inflationary gap shown by the braces. In (i) a cut in government expenditure, ΔG, shifts AE to AE_1 and removes the inflationary gap.

In (ii) a rise in tax rates reduces the proportion of national income that goes to disposable income. This causes a corresponding decrease in the amount of consumption expenditure associated with each level of national income and thus pivots AE to AE_2. That eliminates the inflationary gap.

sume out of disposable income is .75, consumption expenditure will fall by only $750 million. If the government spends the entire $1 billion on domestically produced goods, aggregate expenditure will increase by $250 million. In this case the balanced budget increase in government expenditure has an expansionary effect because it shifts the aggregate expenditure function upward.

A balanced budget increase in government expenditure will have an expansionary effect on national income, and a balanced budget decrease will have a contractionary effect.

The **balanced budget multiplier** measures these effects. It is the change in income divided by the balanced budget change in government expenditure that brought it about. Thus, if the extra $1 billion of government spending financed by the extra $1 billion of taxes causes national income to rise by $500 million, the balanced budget multiplier is .5; if income rises by $1 billion, it is 1.

In general, the balanced budget multiplier is much lower than the multiplier that relates the change in income to a deficit-financed increase in government expenditure with tax rates constant. For with a deficit-financed increase in expenditure, there is no increase in taxes and hence no consequent decrease in consumption expenditure to offset the increase in government expenditure. With a balanced budget increase in expenditure, however, the offsetting increase in taxes and decrease in consumption does occur.

FISCAL POLICY WHEN PRIVATE EXPENDITURE FUNCTIONS ARE SHIFTING

Thus far we have considered fiscal policy intended to remove an inflationary or deflationary gap when the expenditure function was given (and unchanged by anything other than the fiscal policy itself). But as we saw in Chapter 32, private expenditure functions change continually. Investment expenditure shifts a great deal with business conditions, and consumption functions sometimes shift upward as the public

goes on a spending spree or downward as people become cautious and increase their saving. This makes stabilization policy much more difficult than it would be if it were necessary only to identify a stable inflationary or deflationary gap and then take steps to eliminate it once and for all.

What can the government reasonably expect to achieve by using fiscal policy when private expenditure functions are shifting continually? Fiscal policy might be altered often in an effort to stabilize the economy completely, or it might be altered less frequently as a reaction to gaps that appear to be large and persistent.

Fine Tuning

In the heyday of Keynesian fiscal policy in the 1950s and 1960s, many economists advocated the use of fiscal policy to remove even minor fluctuations in national income around its full-employment level. Fiscal policy was to be altered frequently, and by relatively small amounts, to hold national income almost precisely at its full-employment level. This is called **fine tuning** the economy.

The feasibility of fine tuning depends on, among other things, the length of the so-called **decision lag**, the period of time between perceiving a problem and making the desired reaction to it. Many things contribute to the length of this lag. Experts must study the economy and agree among themselves on what fiscal changes are most desirable; they must then persuade the government to initiate the action they endorse.

In countries where political institutions keep the decision lag short, fine tuning has been attempted. Careful assessment of the results shows that their successes, if any, fell far short of what was hoped for them. The basic reason for this lies in the complexity of any economy. Although economists and policymakers can identify broad and persistent trends, they do not have detailed knowledge of what is going on at any moment in time, of all the forces that are operating to cause changes in the immediate future, and of all the short-term effects of small changes in the various government expenditures and tax rates. Because of these imperfections in detailed knowledge, efforts at fine tuning often did as much as encourage minor fluctuations in the economy as to remove them. As a result of these experiences, fine tuning is out of favor at present.

The Removal of Persistent Gaps

In addition to more or less continuous fluctuations, the economy occasionally develops severe and persistent inflationary or deflationary gaps. One such inflationary gap developed in the late 1960s. A deflationary gap developed after 1973 when Canada, along with many other Western countries, experienced the deepest and longest-lasting recession since the 1930s. Another one opened up in 1980. Gaps such as these persist long enough for their major causes to be studied and understood and for fiscal remedies to be carefully planned and executed.

Many economists who do not believe in fine tuning believe that fiscal policy can aid in removing persistent gaps.

Tools of Fiscal Policy

The major fiscal tools that governments can use can be classified in many ways; one important classification is based on the division between automatic and discretionary tools.

AUTOMATIC TOOLS OF FISCAL POLICY: BUILT-IN STABILIZERS

As a result of factors discussed in Chapter 32, the aggregate demand and aggregate expenditure functions are continually fluctuating. A stabilization policy for fine tuning the economy would thus require a policy that was itself ever changing. If such a conscious fine tuning policy is impossible, must we through up our hands and say that nothing can be done through fiscal policy except in the face of major and long-lived inflationary or deflationary gaps?

Fortunately, this is not the case. Much of the

adjustment of fiscal policy to an ever-changing economic environment is done automatically by what are called built-in stabilizers. A **built-in stabilizer** is anything that reduces the marginal propensity to spend out of national income and hence reduces the value of the multiplier (see page 618). Built-in stabilizers thus reduce the magnitude of the fluctuations in national income caused by autonomous changes in such expenditures as investment. Furthermore, they do so without the government's having to react consciously to each change in national income as it occurs.

Three built-in stabilizers are taxes, government expenditure on goods and services, and government transfer payments; a fourth, considered in the previous chapter, is expenditure on imports.

Taxes

Direct taxes act as a built-in stabilizer because they reduce the marginal propensity to consume out of national income. Consider an example. If there were no taxes, every change in national income of $1 would cause a change in disposable income of nearly a dollar.[2] With a marginal propensity to consume out of Y_d of (say) .8, consumption would change by 80¢. With taxes, however, disposable income changes by less than $1; hence consumption expenditure will change by *less than* 80¢ when national income changes by $1 (even though the *MPC* out of Y_d is still .8).

Direct taxes reduce the fluctuations in disposable income associated with a given fluctuation in national income. Hence, for a given *MPC* out of disposable income, they reduce the *MPC* out of national income.

This is illustrated in Table 34-1. The lower is the *MPC* out of national income, the lower will be

---

[2] Undistributed profits and other minor items would still hold disposable income below national income. We ignore these in the text because taxes are the major source of the discrepancy between Y_d and Y.

TABLE 34-1
The Effect of Tax Rates on the Marginal Propensity to Consume Out of National Income

Marginal rate of tax	National income changes by $1,000 million (The *MPC* out of disposable income is .8)				
	Change in national income (millions) ΔY	Change in tax revenue (millions) ΔT	Change in disposable income (millions) ΔY_d	Change in consumption (millions) ΔC	Marginal propensity to consume out of national income $\Delta C/\Delta Y$
.2	$1,000	$200	$800	$640	.65
.4	1,000	400	600	480	.48

The higher is the marginal rate of tax, the lower is the marginal propensity to consume out of national income. When national income changes by $1,000, disposable income changes by $800 when the tax rate is 20 percent and by $600 when the tax rate is 40 percent. Although the *MPC* out of disposable income is the same in both examples, consumption changes by $640 in the first case and by only $480 in the second. These calculations illustrate that households' *MPC* out of their disposable income is unchanged. An increase in tax rates will lower the *MPC* out of national income on which the size of the multiplier depends.

the multiplier (as we saw on pages 618–619). Thus higher tax rates will reduce the fluctuations in national income associated with autonomous shifts in expenditure functions.

Tax rates have increased greatly over this century. Although citizens complain about the burden of high taxes—perhaps with good reason—few are aware that the high taxes help to stabilize the economy and reduce the large swings in national income and employment that once plagued all industrial economies.

To see the common sense of this, consider the extreme case in which the marginal tax rate is 100 percent. If there is an autonomous rise of $1 billion in investment expenditure, none of the $1 billion will reach households as disposable income. There are no induced rounds of secondary expenditure; the rise in national income is limited to the initial $1 billion in new investment, and the multiplier is unity. Similarly, a drop in investment expenditure of $1 billion reduces incomes earned in the investment industry by $1 billion and hence reduces government tax revenue by $1 billion. But it does not affect disposable income. Thus there are no secondary rounds of induced contractions in consumption experience to magnify the initial drop in national income caused by the investment decline.

Government Expenditure

Government expenditure on goods and services tends to be relatively stable in the face of cyclical variations in national income. Much expenditure is already committed by earlier legislation, so only a small proportion can be varied at the government's discretion from one year to the next. And even this small part is slow to change.

In contrast, private consumption and investment expenditure tend to vary with national income. The consumption function is an expression of the tendency for consumption expenditure to rise and fall as national income rises and falls. And as we saw in Chapter 32, investment expenditure tends to vary with national income; it is high in booms and low in slumps.

The twentieth century rise in the importance of government in the economy may have been a mixed blessing. One benefit, however, has been to put a large built-in stabilizer into the economy. It has transferred expenditure from the private sector (which it varies cyclically) to the public sector (where it does not). The value of the multiplier has been reduced as a result.

Steady government expenditure acts as a built-in stabilizer by reducing the marginal propensity to spend out of national income.

Two Case Studies of American Fiscal Policy

The 1960s saw two major experiments with fiscal policy in the United States. In terms of achieving their objectives, the first was a success and the second a failure.

Fiscal Drag and the 1964 Tax Cuts

Fiscal drag, first diagnosed in the early 1960s, is the problem of a rising full-employment surplus produced by economic growth acting on stable government expenditure and fixed tax rates. President Kennedy's Council of Economic Advisers proposed a major cut in tax rates to deal with it.

Throughout the 1950s full-employment GNP was rising 2 to 3 percent per year because of economic growth. This increased aggregate supply, as illustrated in the figure by the shift of AS to AS_1. But since higher output means higher income earned, aggregate demand was also shifting outward. With both demand and supply increasing, it might seem that maintaining full employment would be no problem. There was a problem, however, and it lay with the tax system.

With tax rates constant, rising national income causes rising tax revenues. These revenues are money that does not become disposable income for households. If the government spent all its extra tax revenue, aggregate demand would not be depressed. With a rela-

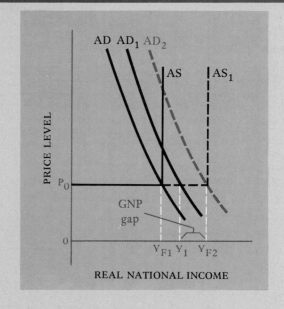

tively stable level of government expenditure, however, rising tax revenues exert a drag on the growth of aggregate demand by taking income away from households that would have spent it and transferring it to governments that do not. This is shown in the figure: AD shifts only to AD_1, there is an increased full-employment surplus, and a GNP gap is created.

To prevent an ever stronger depressing effect being exerted on national income by a

Transfer Payments

Social insurance and welfare services. All welfare payments tend to rise in times of falling national income with its accompanying unemployment and hardship. Many welfare schemes are financed by taxes based on payrolls or earnings, and these taxes tend to yield less when income is low. Thus welfare schemes tend to add

to aggregate expenditure in times of slumps. They also tend to reduce aggregate expenditure in times of booms and full employment, when payments are low and revenues high. These net deficits and surpluses on welfare expenditures tend to stabilize the economy just as though the money were used to build dams or bridges.

The Canada Pension Plan is financed by taxes (contributions) on both employers and employ-

growing full-employment surplus, it is necessary to reduce the surplus periodically either by increasing government spending or by reducing tax rates.

The full significance of the long-term problem of fiscal policy in a growing economy was not appreciated until the 1960s. When it was, the Kennedy and Johnson administrations advocated a large cut in tax rates to remove the fiscal drag. Their concern was not with cyclical stabilization of the economy but with solving a problem associated with long-term economic growth.

When the 1964 tax cut was enacted, the predicted effects occurred. The tax cuts increased disposable income, causing an increase in consumption expenditure which in turn caused an increase in national income and employment.

The Vietnam Inflation and the 1968 Tax Surcharges

By the time the full effects of the 1964 tax cut were felt, the large increases in military expenditures due to the escalation of the war in Vietnam were also exerting a substantial expansionary effect on the economy. With GNP already at the full-employment level, the large 1967 budget deficit produced a large inflationary gap in 1968.

By mid 1968 a temporary tax surcharge bill was approved by Congress. This bill raised effective tax rates for a period of about 18 months and produced a substantial budget surplus. The object was to slow inflation by removing the inflationary gap. The restraining effect was disappointingly small; inflation hardly slowed its trend toward ever higher rates.

The apparent failure of the contractionary budgetary policy of 1968–1969 caused much debate among economists. The general judgment, after long discussions, seem to be that the "failure" of the 1968–1969 tax surcharges to restrain inflation revealed the shortcomings of the fine tuning but did not show fiscal policy to be generally impotent. Numerous factors had offset the effects of the surcharge, and the knowledge that the tax surcharge was temporary may have caused households to make only small downward revisions in their expected permanent incomes and hence only very small reductions in their consumption.* Another factor, understood now but unappreciated then, is that inflationary expectations, once entrenched, are not easily shaken—especially by a transitory tax surcharge.

* For further discussion, see the appendix to this chapter.

ees; the rate in 1981 was 1.8 percent each on the first $13,300 of annual income in excess of an exemption of $1,352. Unemployment insurance is financed by a tax on covered payrolls shared by employers and employees. During periods of depression, tax collections decrease while payments to individuals under these programs rise. Thus both the payments and the receipts serve as built-in stabilizers.

Agricultural support policies. When there is a slump in the economy, there is a general decline in the demand for all goods, including agricultural produce. The free-market prices of agricultural goods fall, and government agricultural supports come into play. This means that government transfers which support agricultural disposable income will rise as national income falls.

Transfer payments act as built-in stabilizers; they tend to stabilize disposable income, and hence consumption expenditure, in the face of fluctuations in a national income.

Assume a reduction in autonomous expenditure of $10 billion that, in the absence of transfer payments, would reduce disposable income by $6 billion. With an *MPC* out of disposable income of .8, this $6 billion reduction would cause an initial induced fall in consumption expenditure of $4.8 billion. Now assume instead that the fall in national income is accompanied by an increase in transfer payments of $4 billion. Instead of falling by $6 billion, disposable income now falls by only $2 billion. With the *MPC* out of Y_d still at .8, the initial induced fall in consumption expenditure is only $1.6 billion instead of $4.8 billion.

The smaller is the induced fall in consumption expenditure, the smaller will be the multiplier and hence the smaller the final reduction in national income as it responds to the initial fall in autonomous expenditure.

The Origin of Built-in Stabilizers

Most built-in stabilizers are fairly new phenomena in this country. Fifty years ago high marginal rates of taxation, high and stable government expenditures, farm stabilization policies, and large unemployment and other transfer payments were unknown in Canada. Each of these built-in stabilizers was the unforeseen by-product of policies originally adopted for other reasons. The progressive income tax arose out of a concern to make the distribution of income less unequal. The growth of the government sector has been the result of many factors other than a desire for cyclical stability. Social insurance and agricultural support programs were adopted more because of a concern with the welfare of the individuals and groups involved than with preserving the health of the economy. But unforeseen or not, they work. (Even governments can be lucky.)

The Partial Nature of the Job Done by Built-in Stabilizers

No matter how lucky governments have been in finding built-in stabilizers, these forces cannot reduce fluctuations to zero. Stabilizers work by producing stabilizing reactions to changes in income. But until the income change occurs, the stabilizer is not even brought into play.

The evidence of the Canadian economy as reviewed in Chapter 32 suggests two important conclusions. First, fluctuations have been less extreme since 1945 than they were earlier. This is due in part to the operation of power built-in stabilizers not on the scene before World War II. Second, the magnitude of the post-1945 fluctuations has nonetheless been sufficient to cause policymakers serious concern.

Fiscal Drag

High and stable government expenditures combined with high marginal tax rates not only act as built-in stabilizers, they also lead to **fiscal drag** in periods of sustained economic growth. Fiscal drag is a rising government budget surplus produced by growth in the level of full-employment income acting on stable government expenditure and fixed tax rates. The American experience with fiscal drag during the high growth era of the early 1960s is discussed in the box on pages 680–681.

DISCRETIONARY FISCAL POLICY

Short-term, minor fluctuations that are not removed automatically by built-in stabilizers cannot, with present knowledge and techniques, be removed by consciously fine tuning the economy. We have already noted, however, that larger and more persistent gaps sometimes appear. In these cases there is time for the government to operate a **discretionary fiscal policy**, that is, to institute changes in taxes and expenditures that are designed to offset gaps. To do this effectively, the government needs to make periodic conscious decisions to alter fiscal policy. The government's economic advisers must study current economic trends and predict the probable course of the economy. If the predicted course is unsatisfactory, the cabinet must be persuaded to adopt the necessary fiscal changes.

In considering discretionary fiscal policy, we shall deal with three main questions. First, does it matter whether government expenditure or government tax revenue is varied to achieve the desired budget deficit or surplus? Second, why is it important that the fiscal change be easily reversible? Third, does it matter whether households and firms regard the government's fiscal changes as being temporary or as being long-lived?

The Choice Between Changes in Tax Rates and Changes in Government Expenditures

There is often sharp debate on whether taxes or expenditures or both should be used to achieve any stabilizing changes that are thought to be desirable. What issues are involved in these debates? What factors affect the choice between changes in government expenditure and changes in tax rates?

Location of effects. The multiplier effects of an increase in aggregate expenditure tend to spread over the whole economy, causing a rising demand for virtually every commodity. If a slump is general, with widespread unemployment, this will be an advantage. If, however, a slump is severely localized, with a major depression in a particular industry (such as automobiles) or area (such as the Maritimes), then it may be desirable to achieve a disproportionate effect in the depressed industry or area. In this case, raising government expenditure has a distinct advantage over cutting taxes. A tax cut would have its initial impact on the entire economy, but by careful choice of projects much of the initial effect of extra expenditure can be channeled into the depressed industry or area. Thus, if specific impact effects are important, increased government expenditure will have an advantage over tax cuts.

Time lags. We have discussed the decision lags of discretionary fiscal policy. There is no reason why they should be of significantly different lengths for changes in government expenditure and in tax rates.

However, there is a second type of lag, one that may differ for changes in taxes and changes in expenditure. After a fiscal change has been authorized, there will necessarily be some lag before it actually goes into effect. This is an **execution lag.** Once the cabinet has approved appropriations for a new road-building program, for example, it will be some time before substantial income payments are made to private firms and households. Routes must be surveyed; land must be acquired, often by condemnatory procedures; public protests must often be heard; bids must be called for and contracts let. All this can take considerable time. However, the execution lag can be very short for tax cuts. Once tax reductions are decided, rates of withholding can be reduced quickly. Only a few weeks after the tax cut wage earners may find themselves with more take-home pay.

The Need for Reversibility

To see what is involved in the issue of reversibility, assume that national income is *normally* at or near full-employment income. Then a *temporary* slump in private investment opens up a large deflationary gap. The gap persists. Eventually the government decides to adopt some combination of tax cuts and expenditure increases to push the economy back toward full employment. If this policy is successful, private investment can be expected to recover to its pre-slump level. If the government does not then reverse its policy, an inflationary gap will open up as the combination of recovered investment expenditure and continuing fiscal stimulus takes national income into the inflationary range. This is illustrated in Figure 34-3.

Alternatively, assume that starting from the same situation of nearly full employment, an *abnormal* investment boom opens up an infla-

FIGURE 34-3
Effects of Fiscal Policies That Are Not Reversed

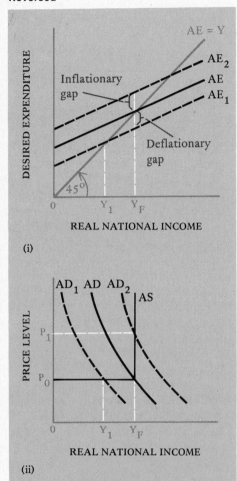

(i)

(ii)

Fiscal policies that are initially appropriate may become inappropriate when the private expenditure function shifts. The normal levels of the aggregate demand and aggregate expenditure functions are assumed to be AD and AE, leaving income normally at Y_F.

First, a persistent slump in private investment shifts aggregate demand to AD_1 and aggregate expenditure to AE_1, producing income of Y_1 and the deflationary gap indicated by the brace. The government now cuts taxes and raises expenditures to restore aggregate demand and aggregate expenditure to AD and AE and national income to Y_F. Later, private investment recovers to its original level, pushing aggregate demand and aggregate expenditure to AD_2 and AE_2. Unless the fiscal policy is quickly reversed, an inflationary gap (indicated by the brace) will open up and the price level will rise to P_1.

Second, starting from income Y_F, a persistent investment boom takes AD and AE to AD_2 and AE_2. In order to stop the price level from rising in the face of the inflationary gap, the government raises taxes and cuts expenditure, thereby shifting the curves back to AD and AE. Eventually, however, the investment boom comes to a halt and the curves shift down to AD_1 and AE_1. Unless the fiscal policy can be rapidly reversed, a deflationary gap (indicated by the brace) will open up and equilibrium income will settle down at Y_1.

tionary gap. Rather than let the inflation persist, the government reduces expenditure and raises taxes to remove the gap. Then, when the investment boom is over, investment expenditure will return to its original level. If the government does nothing, a deflationary gap will open up and a serious slump ensue. This too is illustrated in Figure 34-3.

Fiscal policies designed to remove persistent inflationary or deflationary gaps resulting from abnormally high or low levels of private expenditure will destabilize the economy unless they can be fairly rapidly reversed once private expenditure returns to its more normal level.

The Choice Between Changes Seen by Households as "Temporary" or as "Longlasting"

Consider the attempt to remove a persistent inflationary or deflationary gap through changes in tax rates. Such a gap, though persistent, is unlikely to be regarded as a permanent feature of the economy. The tax changes might therefore be advocated only for "the duration," that is, for as long as it is thought the gap would persist without the tax changes. Fiscal policy designed to remove an inflationary gap could take the form, say, of a surcharge on income taxes for a two-year period, while a recession could be fought with "temporary" tax rebates.

Such tax changes cause changes in household disposable income and, according to the Keynesian theory of the consumption function, would cause changes in consumption expenditure. Consumption expenditure would increase as tax rebates rose in times of deflationary gaps and would decrease as tax surcharges rose in times of inflationary gaps. This theory of the effects of short-term tax changes relies on the assumption that household consumption depends on current disposable income.

Permanent-income theories. Many recent theories of the consumption function have emphasized what is called a household's expected *lifetime income* or *permanent income* as the major determinant of consumption. According to such theories, households have expectations about their lifetime incomes and adjust their consumption to those expectations. When temporary fluctuations in income occur, households maintain their long-term consumption plans and use their stocks of wealth as a buffer to absorb income fluctuations. Thus when there is a purely temporary rise in income, households will save all the extra income; when there is a purely temporary fall in income, households will maintain their long-term consumption plans by using up part of their wealth accumulated through past saving. The two most important theories of this type are the *life-cycle* and the *permanent-income* hypotheses. The first is associated principally with Franco Modigliani and the second with Milton Friedman.[3]

To the extent that this kind of influence is at

[3] Professor Friedman was awarded the 1976 Nobel Prize in economics for his work on the theories of money and stabilization policy.

work, it may have serious consequences for short-lived tax changes. A temporary rebate raises a household's disposable income, but households, recognizing it as temporary, might not revise their expenditure plans and instead save the extra money. Thus the hoped-for increase in aggregate expenditure would not occur. Similarly, a temporary rise in tax rates reduces disposable income, but that may merely cause a fall in saving. Thus total expenditure is again unchanged, and a temporary surcharge fails to reduce the inflationary gap.

If households' consumption is more closely related to lifetime income than to current income, tax changes that are known to be of short duration may have relatively small effects on current consumption.[4]

The advantage of having households perceive as permanent any tax cut or tax surcharge conflicts with the need for the reversibility of cuts and surcharges if they are not to destabilize the economy at a later date. This problem reduces the effectiveness of changes in tax rates as a stabilizing tool.

Fiscal Policy in Action

We have seen that governments inevitably have a major impact on GNP through their fiscal behavior. The very size of a government's budget guarantees that. However, the conscious use of the budget to influence GNP that constitutes fiscal policy is by no means inevitable. Fiscal impact is unavoidable, but fiscal policy is a matter of choice.

Before we look at some of the experience of fiscal policy, let us consider how we are to assess the direction of current fiscal policy.

[4] The permanent-income theory is not as immediately applicable to fiscal policy as it may seem. This is because fiscal policy seeks to affect *expenditure* (on consumption and investment goods) while permanent-income theories seek to explain the consumption of goods and services—which in the case of durables is spread over the whole life of the durable. This important matter is discussed further in the appendix to this chapter.

JUDGING THE STANCE OF FISCAL POLICY

Governments seek to shift aggregate demand by consciously changing their fiscal policy stance. The "stance" of fiscal policy refers to its expansionary or contractionary effects on the economy. An expansionary fiscal policy is one that increases aggregate demand and thus tends to increase national income; a contractionary fiscal policy reduces aggregate demand and thus tends to lower national income. Now, how can we judge changes in the stance of fiscal policy from one year to the next?

In popular discussion, a change in the government's current deficit or surplus is often taken as an indicator. When the deficit rises (i.e., tax yields fall and/or government expenditure rises), this is widely taken to indicate an expansionary change in fiscal policy. When the deficit falls (i.e., tax yields rise and/or government expenditure falls), this is widely taken to indicate a contractionary policy. This argument is based on a comparison of government expenditure and tax revenue.

But tax revenues are the result of the interaction of tax rates, which the government does set, and the level of national income, which is influenced by many forces that are beyond the government's control. Thus to judge changes in the government's budget deficit or surplus can be very misleading. It confuses endogenous changes due to changes in national income with exogenous changes due to changes in the stance of fiscal policy.

The major tools of fiscal policy are government expenditure and *tax rates*. The budget deficit or surplus is the relation between government expenditure and *tax revenues*.

The distinction between the two causes of changes in the budget balance is easily seen in what is called the government's **budget surplus function**. This function, which relates the surplus (government revenue minus government expenditure) to national income, is graphed in Figure 34-4. Endogenous changes in the government's budget balance due to changes in national income are shown by movements *along* a given surplus function. Changes in the budget balance due to policy-induced changes in government expenditure or in tax rates are shown by *shifts* in the surplus function. Such shifts indicate a different budget balance at *each* level of national income.

When measuring changes in the stance of fiscal policy, it is common to calculate changes in the estimated budget balance at some base level of national income. Holding income constant ensures that measured shifts in the budget balance are due to policy-induced shifts of the surplus function rather than income-induced movements along the function. The base most commonly used is full-employment national income, and the measure calculated is called the **full-employment surplus** (*FES*). This is an estimate of government tax revenues minus government expenditures, not as they are actually are, but as they would be if full-employment national income had obtained (i.e., if the GNP gap had been zero). In this usage a full-employment budget deficit (expenditures exceed revenues) is regarded as a negative full-employment surplus.

Changes in the full-employment surplus are an indicator of changes in the stance of fiscal policy.[5]

Figure 34-4 analyzes the use of the full-employment surplus, as well as the errors that can arise from use of the current surplus as an indicator of the stance of fiscal policy.

THE GREAT DEPRESSION AND WORLD WAR II

The 1930s saw massive unemployment that was not eliminated until the outbreak of war. This experience has left many with the misconception that wars, but not discretionary fiscal policy, can solve an unemployment problem. A review of

---

[5] The full-employment surplus is the simplest adequate measure, and it is vastly superior to the current surplus for estimating year-to-year changes in the stance of fiscal policy. More sophisticated measures exist and are often used in detailed empirical work.

FIGURE 34-4
The Budget Surplus Function

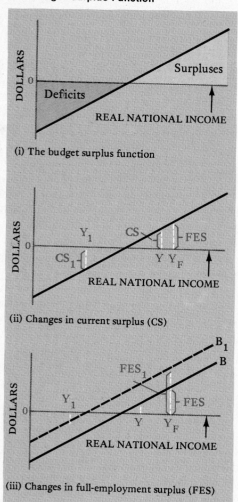

(i) The budget surplus function

(ii) Changes in current surplus (CS)

(iii) Changes in full-employment surplus (FES)

Changes in national income cause changes in the current surplus by moving the economy along its surplus function; changes in the stance of fiscal policy shift the surplus function. The budget surplus function expresses the difference between government's tax revenues and its expenditures at each level of national income. The curve shown in (i) assumes that as income fluctuates tax revenues fluctuate more than expenditure. Thus deficits are associated with low levels of income and surpluses with high levels.

In (ii) a fall in national income from Y to Y_1 causes the budget to go from a current surplus of CS to a current deficit of CS_1 with no change in government expenditure or tax rates—that is, the fiscal policy stance is unchanged. The unchanged fiscal stance is correctly measured by the constant full-employment surplus, FES.

In (iii) there is a contractionary change in the stance of fiscal policy; a government expenditure cut and/or a tax rate increase shifts the surplus function from B to B_1, indicating that there is a larger budget surplus *at each level of national income*. This change is correctly measured by the rise in the full-employment surplus from FES to FES_1. The misleading effects of judging changes in the policy stance from changes in the current surplus can be seen by noting that if national income had fallen from Y to Y_1 at the same time that the surplus function shifted from B to B_1, the current balance would have gone from surplus to deficit in spite of the rise in the full-employment surplus.

the facts shows that fiscal policy contributed little to recovery from the Depression, not because it failed to work but because it was not used.

Between 1929 and 1933, GNP in Canada fell by more than $2.5 billion, a drop of over 40 percent from the 1929 level of $6.2 billion. During the period the federal deficit reached a peak of $160 million; this was clearly a drop in the bucket even when augmented by a deficit at the provincial and municipal level of approximately the same magnitude. Indeed, during the entire decade of the 1930s the aggregate federal deficit

was about $850 million—less than one-third of the deficit recorded in the single year 1944.

The data for the United States shows a similar pattern. Although the administration that took office in 1933 was committed to fighting the depression with a program known as the "New Deal," the level of government expenditures remained far below the level necessary to provide an adequate stimulus. The average deficit of the U.S. government during the 1930s was $2.5 billion, but the GNP was $103 billion in 1929 and fell to $56 billion in 1933.

Once the massive, war-geared expenditure of the 1940s began, income responded sharply and unemployment all but evaporated. Total government expenditure on goods and services, which during the 1930s had been running well below $1 billion and about 20 percent of the Canadian GNP, jumped to $5 billion and accounted for over 40 percent of the GNP. Although the federal deficit averaged more than $2 billion per year from 1942 to 1945, the financing of Canada's war effort was an outstanding success compared either to Canada's performance in World War I or to any other country's fiscal performance in World War II. The inflationary gap was reduced by a variety of tax measures including increased excises, increased corporate and personal income taxes, higher customs duties, and an excess profits tax. The increase in the cost of living between 1939 and 1945 was held to 18 percent, compared with a rise of 74 percent that occurred during World War I. In the United States prices rose by almost one-third during 1940–1945.

THE POSTWAR PERIOD

The most pressing economic problem of 1946 was the inflationary gap arising from the relaxation of wartime controls and the release of pent-up consumer demand. People rushed to spend their wartime savings on new cars and other goods that had not been available during the war. Between 1945 and 1948, prices rose more than they had risen during the war.

The New Status of Fiscal Policy

An important legacy of World War II was a radically altered view of the role of government expenditures and taxes as instruments of government policy. The 1945 White Paper on Employment and Income established the principle that the federal government had a responsibility to maintain high and stable levels of employment and income.

The implementation of this policy was greatly complicated by the unsettled state of federal-provincial relations. As early as 1940 a proposal to widen federal jurisdiction had been made by the Rowell-Sirois commission, but the division of powers has continued to be a contentious issue to the present day. Through a succession of temporary agreements (see Chapter 25) the federal government has retained sufficient power to operate a flexible fiscal policy, and consideration of the desired degree of fiscal stimulus or restraint has become an important element in the budgets presented to Parliament.

An effort to improve the input of economic analysis into policy formation was made in 1963 through the establishment of the Economic Council of Canada. The council's *Annual Reviews* and other publications have served to quantify and add perspective to policy issues.

In comparison with earlier eras, the postwar period has been one of prosperity and steady growth. The first prolonged slump occurred during the years 1958–1963 when the unemployment rate reached a peak of 7.1 percent (see Figure 28-5 on page 566). By 1965 this margin of unused resources had been virtually eliminated, but in retrospect it appears that policymakers misjudged the situation. Rising income had tended to move the federal budget into a surplus position, but some of the restraining effects of the built-in stabilizers were offset by tax cuts introduced in the budget of April 1965. Tax increases and some expenditure cuts were imposed in the years 1966–1968, but fiscal restraint came too late to prevent the entrenchment of inflationary forces. For a discussion of the American experience during the early 1960s, see the box on pages 680–681.

Budgetary Policy in the 1970s

As the Canadian economy entered the 1970s the federal government shifted to an expansionary policy in view of the steep rise in unemployment that had occurred. With an unemployment rate in excess of 6 percent during most of 1971 and 1972, the federal budget was maintained in a def-

FIGURE 34-5

The Budget Balance (National Accounts Basis), 1955–1980

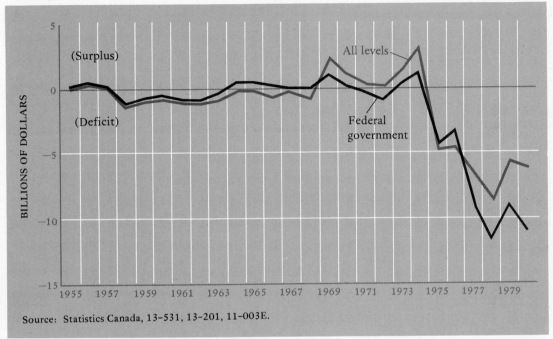

Source: Statistics Canada, 13–531, 13–201, 11–003E.

The budget balance exhibits substantial short-term fluctuations and a recent trend toward increased deficits. The federal government is the largest deficit unit; in 1979 its deficit was more than $9 billion, while the deficits of all levels of government combined totaled less than $6 billion.

icit position. In 1974 the emphasis shifted to moderating the inflationary pressures that were again building up. At midyear the unemployment rate was down around 5 percent and the Consumer Price Index was rising at a rate in excess of 10 percent. However, toward the end of the year there was a significant worsening of the outlook. Slower growth and rising unemployment occurred in Canada, while the United States experienced a substantial *decline* in real GNP. In view of these conditions, an expansionary budget was brought down late in the year which provided for a reduction in personal income taxes of about $1.5 million in 1975.

As Figure 34-5 shows, the federal budget moved to a substantial deficit position in 1975 and has remained there, reaching $10.7 billion by 1980. In part, this reflects discretionary fiscal policy because, as shown in Table 34-2, the full employment budget also moved into a substantial deficit. However, the actual deficit also reflects automatic responses to the economic conditions of the 1975–1980 period, which tended to depress government revenues relative to expenditures. First, the relatively low levels of economic activity over that period caused tax revenues to be low relative to outlays on unemployment insurance benefits. Second, the relatively high rate of inflation caused outlays to grow rapidly—because many federal transfer payments such as old-age pensions were indexed to inflation—and at the same time did not lead to increased tax revenues because the income tax system had to be indexed to prevent inflation-induced increases in real tax payments. (See the box on pages 690–691 for further discussion.)

Inflation Indexing of Income Taxes

Marginal tax rates rise quite steeply in Canada, as Table 25-2 shows. This means that as individuals' incomes grow, they pay in taxes an increasing fraction of the *additional* income they earn. Many economists believe that high marginal tax rates provide strong disincentives to the supply of effort: a steelworker with a high marginal tax rate is less inclined to work overtime in periods of boom, and a lawyer or a highly trained technical consultant is less likely to accept one more case, the higher is his or her marginal tax rate. Further, since the marginal tax rate is not only rising but is above the average tax rate, the average tax rate rises with income; therefore, the higher is total income, the higher is the fraction of *total* income paid in taxes.

In inflationary situations, when an individual's money income rises, the purchasing power of this income does not necessarily rise. For example, a secretary who gets a 10 percent raise is no better off when the prices of everything she purchases also rise by 10 percent *and* the fraction of income she pays in taxes does not change. However, with marginal tax rates that rise with money income, the fraction of income she pays in taxes will rise; as a result, her *after-tax money income* will rise by less than 10 percent. Even though her *before-tax real income* remains unchanged (prices and before-tax money income both rise by 10 percent), her *after-tax real income* will fall because she now pays in taxes a larger fraction of her income.

With rising marginal tax rates in terms of money income, inflation will cause after-tax real income to fall unless before-tax real income grows substantially.

This is because inflation, by increasing the dollar value of the taxpayer's money income, moves the taxpayer into a tax bracket with a higher marginal tax rate. Unless the growth of before-tax nominal (money) income exceeds the rate of inflation, the increase in taxes will necessarily reduce after-tax real income.

The indexation of income tax prevents this automatic increase in tax rates in response to inflation. When a tax system is indexed, the rate of taxation at any given level of *real* income remains constant: the tax schedule — that is, the tax bracket at which a particular marginal rate applies — is adjusted each year to allow for the effects of inflation on nominal incomes. If inflation has averaged 10 percent in the economy but average real income is unchanged, the average person's nominal income will go up by 10 percent. If before the inflation there was a $30,000 cutoff for a 40 percent marginal tax rate, that cutoff would now move up by 10 percent to $33,000. People whose initial incomes were under $30,000 and whose real income remained unchanged would now have money income under $33,000 and would not move to a higher tax bracket. People whose income before the inflation was $30,000 and whose *real* income grew would, by definition, have nominal incomes that grew in excess of the 10 percent inflation rate; hence they would move to a higher tax bracket. Similarly, people whose real income fell would move to a lower tax bracket.

In an indexed tax system, average and marginal tax rates depend only on real income.

In his 1973 budget John Turner, then Minister of Finance, indexed the Canadian income tax system. It was still indexed in 1981, though there were suggestions that the indexing might be removed. In the very high inflation of the 1970s indexation reduced the tax burden of Canadians quite considerably, compared to what it would have been had the tax schedule of 1972 remained in force in terms of money income. By the same token it has reduced the tax revenues of the federal government over the same period.

There are arguments against indexing the tax system. For example, people think that indexation is inflationary because it reduces the public's resistance to inflation. With an unindexed tax system, inflation leads to higher taxes and people will therefore resist inflation; indexation of the tax system, it is argued, reduces public opposition to inflation and thus makes it easier for governments to justify inflationary policies. Others argue that indexation will reduce inflation because it reduces the payoff to governments from pursuing inflationary policies. The increased tax bite that arises from an unindexed tax system in the presence of inflation provides a great incentive for governments to follow inflationary policies; real resources can be transferred from the private sector to the public purse simply by inflating people into higher tax brackets. Hence, whether indexation leads to more or less inflationary policies is not clear.

Politicians do not necessarily like inflation-indexed tax systems. In the United States the tax system has not been indexed. However, since 1975 the U.S. Congress has passed a number of tax cuts. The main purpose of these tax cuts was to undo the automatic increases in taxes that would have resulted from the American inflation. Politicians were in reality indexing the tax system each year, and they were doing it in a manner that gave them political credit for passing tax cuts. This option is not available to Canadian politicians; apparently all the political credit accrued to the person who initially indexed the tax system. Thus many Canadian politicians would like to de-index the tax system so that they too could get the credit for passing tax cuts each year. (Ironically, in 1981 the Reagan administration committed itself to indexation of the U.S. tax system by 1984.)

One important aspect of an indexed tax system can be seen by comparing the American and Canadian experiences in the "great stagflation" of 1974–1976. The fall in real incomes caused by the recession also led to a fall in Canadian government tax revenues, thereby mitigating the fall in aggregate demand. The United States did not have an indexed tax system, and as a result the automatic stabilizer aspect of the income tax due to falling *real* income was in part offset by the increased tax revenues due to rising *money* income. An inflation-induced fiscal drag served to exacerbate the fall in aggregate expenditure. In Canada, with its indexed tax system, the automatic stabilizer aspect of the income tax operated without any offsetting inflation-induced tax increases; a large government deficit resulted, and the initial fall in aggregate demand was mitigated automatically.

TABLE 34-2
Actual and Full-employment Budget Balances for the Federal Government (billions of dollars)

Year	Actual budget surplus[a]	Full-employment budget surplus[a] FES
1969	1.0	0.7
1970	0.3	0.5
1971	−0.1	0.0
1972	−0.7	−0.6
1973	0.4	−0.5
1974	1.1	0.0
1975	−3.8	−3.2
1976	−3.4	−3.3
1977	−7.7	−6.5
1978	−11.4	−9.7
1979	−9.2	−7.6
1980	−10.7	−6.5

Source: Statistics Canada, 13-001, and Department of Finance.
[a] A minus indicates a deficit.

Changes in the full-employment surplus in the 1970s indicate changes in the stance of fiscal policy. Because the economy operated at less than full employment during most of the 1970s, actual budget surpluses were less than full-employment surpluses in most years. The stance of fiscal policy was relatively stable during the first half of the seventies. The very large actual deficits in the late 1970s were partly an endogenous response to high inflation and low levels of national income and partly, as shown by the large negative *FES,* a change in the stance of fiscal policy. Fiscal policy was most expansionary at the end of the decade and most contractionary at the beginning.

Tax cuts were introduced in 1977 and 1978 in response to the worsening recession, but policy decisions were complicated by the emergence of two major dilemmas. First, by the time of the October 1980 budget, the federal government deficit was so large that, according to Minister of Finance Allan McEachen in his budget address, it was necessary to reduce the deficit to allow the government "flexibility to meet future needs and to slow growth of our interest payments." However, cuts in government spending and increases in taxes in order to reduce the deficit would also lead to a further contraction in the level of economic activity. The second dilemma was that the

rate of inflation was unacceptably high, despite a rate of unemployment of 8 percent in 1980. The direction, not simply the extent, of desired government policy was at issue. The coexistence of high unemployment and a high inflation rate has come to be called *stagflation,* and the question of its causes and cures is taken up in Chapter 40.

Can Fiscal Restraint Cure Inflation?

A restrictive fiscal policy that raises taxes and lowers government expenditure can lower the aggregate expenditure function. This can remove an inflationary gap or create a deflationary gap. If the inflation is due to excess demand, a restrictive fiscal policy can control the inflation by removing the excess demand. The inflation of the last half of the 1970s and the early 1980s, however, proceeded without excess demand. Much of the blame seemed to lie with an upward-shifting aggregate supply curve rather than with the aggregate demand curve. Since fiscal policy works through the demand side of the economy, its scope for controlling the current supply-side inflation is limited.

PROPOSALS CONCERNING THE BUDGET BALANCE

Although few people see a restrictive fiscal policy as the solution to the present inflation, many argue that governments should not add to inflationary pressures by spending more than they raise in taxes. Thus the call has gone out for fiscal restraint as one, possibly small, part of a more general anti-inflationary package.

An Annually Balanced Budget?

Much current rhetoric of fiscal restraint calls for a balanced budget. Some people would make an annually balanced budget an object of policy; in the United States there are some who would even make it an obligation enforced by an act of Congress.

The discussion earlier in this chapter suggests

that an annually balanced budget would be extremely difficult—and perhaps impossible—to achieve. With fixed tax rates, tax revenues fluctuate endogenously as national income fluctuates. We have seen that much government expenditure is fixed by past commitments and that most of the rest is hard to change quickly. Thus an annually balanced budget may be quite unfeasible. But suppose an annually balanced budget, or something approaching it, were feasible. What would its effects be? Would they be desirable?

We saw earlier that a large government sector whose expenditures on goods and services are not very sensitive to the cyclical variations in national income is a major built-in stabilizer. To insist that annual government expenditure be tied to annual tax receipts would be to abandon the present built-in stability provided by the government. Government expenditure would then become a major *destabilizing* force. Tax revenues necessarily rise in booms and fall in slumps; an annually balanced budget would force government expenditure to do the same. Changes in national income would then cause induced changes not only in household consumption expenditure but also in government expenditure. This would greatly increase the economy's marginal propensity to spend and hence increase the value of the multiplier.

An annually balanced budget would accentuate the swings in national income that accompany changes in such autonomous expenditure flows as investment and exports.

A Cyclically Balanced Budget?

Annually balanced budget proposals are aimed at two major problems: first, to avoid the alleged inflationary consequences of chronic budget deficits; second, to prevent stabilization policy from leading to a continual increase in the size of the government sector. How could the growth in the public sector occur? During a slump the government increases expenditures to stimulate the economy, but during a boom the government allows inflation to occur rather than cut expenditure. In the next slump, government expenditure is raised once again. The more ready willingness to follow an expansionary fiscal policy in slumps than to follow a contractionary policy in booms can lead to a long-term increase in the size of the government sector.

The annually balanced budget would prevent both these occurrences—but at the cost, as we have seen, of destabilizing the economy.

An alternative policy, one that would prevent continual deficits and could inhibit the growth in the size of the government sector, would be to balance the budget over a number of years, say, over a five-year or a seven-year period. This would be more feasible than the annually balanced budget, and it would not make government expenditure a destabilizing force. The policies are illustrated in Figure 34-6.

Although more attractive in principle than the annually balanced budget, a cyclically balanced budget would carry problems of its own. Government might well spend in excess of revenue in (say) 1982, leaving an obligation to spend less than current revenue in 1983 and 1984. Could such an obligation to balance over a period of several years be made binding? What the government commits itself to in one year does not necessarily restrict what it or its successor does the next year.

The problems of achieving a cyclically balanced budget or a budget balanced over any reasonable time span remain unsolved. Clearly, however, the cyclically balanced budget is both more feasible and more desirable than the annually balanced budget.

Yet there is serious doubt that the idea of a balanced budget over any time period is a sensible one. Many economists believe that a superior alternative to insisting on a precise balance is to pay attention to the balance without making a fetish of never adding to the national debt. We shall see in the next section that there is no reason why a country cannot live satisfactorily forever with a growing national debt.

FIGURE 34-6
Balanced and Unbalanced Budgets

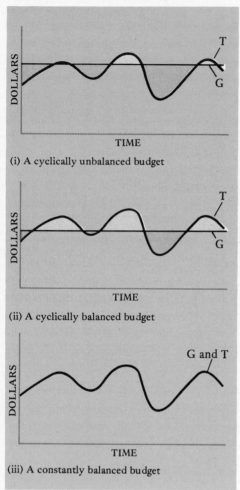

(i) A cyclically unbalanced budget

(ii) A cyclically balanced budget

(iii) A constantly balanced budget

An annually (constantly) balanced budget is a destabilizer; a cyclically balanced budget is a stabilizer. The flow of tax receipts is shown varying over the business cycle while government expenditure is shown at a constant rate.

In (i) deficits (dark areas) are common and surpluses (light areas) are rare because the average level of expenditure exceeds the average level of taxes. This policy will tend to stabilize the economy against cyclical fluctuations, but the average fiscal stance of the government is expansionary. This has been the characteristic federal budgetary position over the last several decades.

In (ii) government expenditure has been reduced until it is approximately equal to the average level of tax receipts. The budget is now balanced cyclically. The policy still tends to stabilize the economy against cyclical fluctuations because of deficits in slumps and surpluses in booms. But the average fiscal stance is neither strongly expansionary nor strongly contractionary.

In (iii) an annually balanced budget has been imposed. Deficits have been prevented, but government expenditure now varies over the business cycle, tending to destabilize the economy by accentuating the cyclical swings in aggregate expenditure.

THE NATIONAL DEBT

We may worry about the impact on inflation of the government's deficit or surplus in any one year. Should we also worry about the cumulative effect of decades of budget deficits that have outweighed budget surpluses? The cumulative effect shows up in a rising national debt.

Does an increasing debt matter? Would an ever-increasing debt lead to an ultimate collapse of the free enterprise economy? Does the debt represent a burden we are passing on to our heirs? It is to these and related questions that we now turn.

The national debt represents money that the federal government has borrowed by selling bonds to households, firms, and financial institutions. In this sense, the national debt is owed by all of us to some of us.

The Size of the Debt

The national debt in March 1980 was $105 billion, more than $4,400 for every man, woman, and child in the country. Just over 20 percent of the debt was held by the government itself and by the Bank of Canada.[6] Interest payments on this part of the debt are only bookkeeping transactions. The debt actually held by the private sector is about $80 billion, or more than $3,300 per person.

These "per person" figures are often quoted in an attempt to shock the reader, but they require interpretation. For a government, as for a household, the significance of debt depends on what it represents and on whether the income is available to pay the interest. No one would be shocked, for example, to find that an average family of four had a mortgage of $35,000 on a $60,000 home.

Consider the actual size of the public debt. Figure 34-7 shows the growth of national debt in Canada; the trend of the debt has been steadily upward. But as national income grows, the scale of government activity can be expected to grow. Just to maintain its relative share of the GNP, government spending would have to increase at the same rate as the GNP. If a constant proportion of government expenditures was financed by borrowing, government debt would be growing at the same rate as the GNP. This suggests that debt statistics should be looked at in the perspective of national income data.

How large is the debt as a fraction of the total value of the economy's annual production? How large are interest payments as a fraction of GNP? What proportion of the tax load is incurred because interest has to be paid on the national debt? Figure 34-8 shows these data.

As Figure 34-8 reveals, national debt as a function of GNP declined steadily during the postwar period. (National debt had grown rapidly throughout World War II, and total debt actually exceeded GNP in 1946.) In the past three years we have seen a slight reversal in this trend, but in 1980 the ratio was still below its 1966 level. Interest payments on the debt have be-

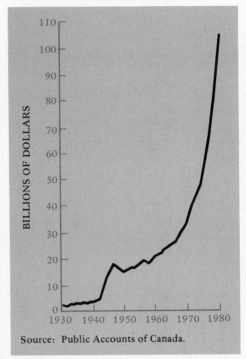

FIGURE 34-7
Trends in the National Debt Since 1932

Source: Public Accounts of Canada.

The trend in the national debt has been upward at least since 1932. The national debt has risen in most years since 1932. The rise has been relatively gradual except during World War II and since 1972. Since that time the rise has been very rapid when measured in current dollars.

haved similarly, declining from a peak of 2.9 percent of GNP in 1947 to hover around 1 percent throughout the 1970s. Such interest payments, which comprised about a quarter of all government expenditure at the end of the 1930s, have been relatively stable in the 4 to 7 percent range for the past quarter century.[7] Clearly the picture of a spendthrift government adding recklessly to the burden of the national debt is wrong.

---

[6] The Bank of Canada buys government bonds in the course of operating monetary policy (see Chapter 38).

[7] Figures for the level of this debt and interest charges on it have been calculated on a net basis, allowing for earning assets held in the public sector.

FIGURE 34-8
The Relative Significance of the National Debt

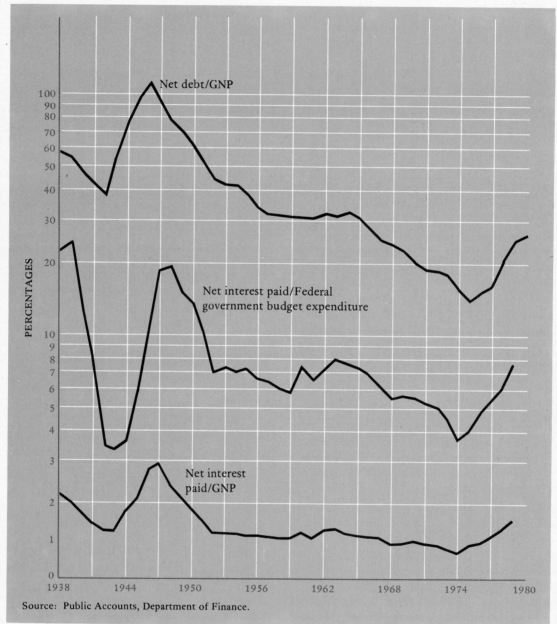

Source: Public Accounts, Department of Finance.

The national debt itself and interest payments on it have not risen in proportion to the GNP since the end of World War II. Three significant ratios are plotted here on a ratio scale. The national debt, after rising sharply through World War II, was a declining fraction of GNP until 1975, after which there was a slight rise. Interest payments reached 2.9 percent of GNP in 1948, but for the last 25 years they have remained at under 1.5 percent. Such interest payments required the use of over 20 percent of all federal budget receipts during the late 1930s but now require less than 7 percent. Clearly the picture of a spendthrift government adding recklessly to the burden of the national debt is wrong.

Is There a Limit to the Size of the Debt?

The Keynesian view. To the extent that the money raised by borrowing is spent on items that add to national income, the borrowing creates the extra income out of which extra taxes can be raised to pay the interest. To the extent that the money is spent on items that do not add to national income, it will be necessary to increase existing taxes in order to provide funds to meet the interest payments. Up to a point, this will not cause serious problems because the process of paying interest on the debt involves only a transfer from some citizens (taxpayers) to other citizens (holders of government bonds).

If, however, the national debt grew so fast that the interest payments on the debt took up an ever larger proportion of national income, there would be an ever-increasing tax burden to finance the interest payments. Clearly, then, there is a grain of truth in the worry over the size of the interest payments on the national debt. Yet this worry applies only to those expenditures that do not themselves help to create the extra income out of which interest payments can be met. And the worry becomes significant only if such new non-income-creating debt is a large fraction of current national income.

Such a situation existed in Canada during the crisis period of World War II, a period by historical standards very short. Since then, as shown in Figure 34-8, the trend has been for national income to grow faster than the national debt so that total debt has been declining as a percentage of national income. Only with the large deficits of the past three years has this trend been reversed.

A good measure of whether the size of the debt is approaching dangerous levels is the willingness of borrowers to hold government bonds at various rates of interest.

Well before a government reaches an absolute debt limit (in terms of its ability to raise the money to pay the interest on its bonds) the public would lose confidence in its debt. The price of bonds would fall and interest rates would rise as borrowers asked a premium for risk. The fact that government bonds are regarded as the least risky type of investment available provides compelling evidence that the financial community is not concerned about the size of the debt.

The basic points of the Keynesian view of the national debt are that (1) the size of the debt is of no great practical importance and (2) the debt should be increased or decreased according to the needss of full-employment policy.

A non-Keynesian view. An alternative view is based on what has come to be called *fiscal conservatism.* Fiscal conservatives think that many parts of the Keynesian view are correct but irrelevant. The conservatives believe that deficits have important harmful effects that are not recognized by Keynesians.

The main premise of this alternative theory is that governments are not passive agents who do what is necessary to create full employment and maximize social welfare. Instead, governments are composed of individuals, such as elected officials, legislators, and civil servants, who, like everyone else, seek mainly to maximize their own well-being. And their welfare is best served by government's having a big role and a satisfied electorate. Thus they tend to favor spending and to resist tax increases. This creates a persistent tendency toward deficits that is quite independent of any consideration of a sound fiscal policy.

In the conservative view, the government is an irresponsible body by economists' standards because it seeks to increase its own welfare by creating a large budget deficit. The theory of national income predicts that whenever the economy is at or near full-employment income, the large-deficit policy will be undesirable because it will create an inflationary gap.

The non-Keynesian theory takes a broad historical perspective. It says that in the eighteenth century, spendthrift European rulers habitually spent more than their tax revenues and so created inflationary gaps. The resulting inflations were harmful because they reduced the purchasing power of savings and disrupted trade. By the end of the nineteenth century, the doctrine was well established that a balanced budget is the citizen's only protection against profligate government spending and consequent wild inflation. Thus the balanced budget doctrine was not silly and irrational, as Keynes made it out to be. Instead, it was the symbol of the people's victory in a long struggle to control the spendthrift proclivities of the nation's rulers.

The Keynesian revolution swept away that view. Budget deficits became, according to Keynesians, the tool by which benign and enlightened central authorities sought to ensure full employment. But, say the anti-Keynesians, deficit spending let the tiger out of the cage. Released from the nearly century-old constraint of balancing the budget, governments went on a series of wild spending sprees. Inflationary gaps, deflationary gaps, or full employment notwithstanding, governments spent and spent and spent. Deficits accumulated, national debts rose, and inflation became the rule.

Inflation robbed the people of the real value of their savings by lowering the purchasing power of money saved. In the end, the inflations even defeated the full-employment goal; when governments were finally forced to reduce inflation, they imposed massive deflationary gaps in order to reduce inflations that had developed a momentum of their own. Today we see the legacy of these disastrous policies: the simultaneous occurrence of high inflation, high unemployment rates, and large budget deficits.[8]

The debate reflects deeply held views about the role of government, the nature and motivation of public officials, and the desirability of stabilization. Keynesians tend to regard government officials as well-meaning and substantial government intervention as essential to an effective and humane society. Fiscal conservatives regard public officials as self-serving and of limited competence and see public intervention, however well motivated, as probably inept and ultimately destabilizing. Both recognize that an interventionist government will play a large role in economic affairs. Conservatives regard that prospect with concern, Keynesians with relative equanimity.

Summary

1. Fiscal policy uses government expenditure and tax policies to influence the economy by shifting the aggregate expenditure function. When private expenditure functions are fixed, it is a relatively simple matter to increase expenditure, to cut tax rates, or to make a balanced budget increase in expenditure in order to remove a deflationary gap (and to make the opposite changes to remove an inflationary gap).

2. Fiscal policy is more difficult when, as is almost always the case, private expenditure functions are continually shifting. Fine tuning, the attempt to hold the aggregate expenditure function virtually constant by offsetting even small fluctuations in private expenditure, has been largely discredited. Yet large and persistent gaps can be offset by fiscal policy.

3. Short-term stabilization by fiscal policy works largely through such automatic stabilizers as tax revenues that vary directly with national income, expenditures on goods and services that do not vary directly with national income, and transfer payments that vary inversely with national income.

4. Discretionary fiscal policy is used to attack large and persistent gaps. The choice between tax and expenditure changes turns, among other things, on the nature of the decision and execution lags and on the need for generalized or localized impact effects.

5. Fiscal stabilization policy needs to be reversible. Otherwise the economy may overshoot its target once private investment recovers from a temporary slump or falls back from a tempo-

---

[8] The pro-Keynesian view can be found in almost any modern textbook on macroeconomics. The view of the fiscal conservatives is well presented in J. M. Buchanan, J. Burton, and R. E. Wayne, *The Consequences of Mr. Keynes* (London: Institute of Economic Affairs, 1978).

rary boom. Also without full reversibility, fiscal policy may cause a secular upward shift in the proportion of the GNP accounted for by government as expenditure is raised in recessions and not cut in expansions. Tax changes also need to be perceived as relatively long-lived if they are to induce major changes in household spending patterns. (Temporary changes may merely affect the current saving rate and not expenditure.) This possibility is further discussed in the appendix to this chapter.

6. Changes in the stance of fiscal policy may be reasonably judged by changes in the full-employment surplus. This is the balance between revenues and expenditures as they would be if full employment prevailed.

7. The evidence of the 1930s is that fiscal policy did not end the depression—because it was not really used. Government deficits and expenditures were far too small to overcome the massive deficiencies in aggregate demand.

8. World War II generated the conditions that made people willing to accept government expenditures large enough to overcome the deflationary gap. Indeed, these expenditures created an inflationary gap as war needs grew more urgent and more demanding.

9. After World War II, it became generally accepted that fiscal policy should be used to stabilize the economy. The evolution of active fiscal policy in Canada was complicated by problems in federal-provincial relations, but the federal government has retained sufficient power through special agreements with the provinces.

10. Fiscal policy was relatively stable during the first half of the 1970s and then became more expansionary from 1976 to 1980.

11. An annually balanced budget would be virtually unfeasible; even if it were possible, it would destabilize the economy. A cyclically balanced budget would act as a stabilizer while also curbing the secular growth of the government sector. However, there is no reason why a healthy economy cannot live with a national debt that is steadily growing (e.g., by keeping its ratio to national income constant) and thus with a secularly unbalanced budget.

12. The national debt and debt service have risen and fallen as a percentage of national income, but those percentages have not shown a long-term trend to grow inexorably.

13. Keynesians take a relatively sanguine view of the national debt. As long as it does not grow wildly as a proportion of national income, they view its short-term fluctuations and its long-term upward trend in absolute terms as a stabilizing device. Fiscal conservatives mistrust government and view insistence on a balanced budget as the only effective means of curtailing reckless government spending that wastes scarce resources and feeds the fires of inflation.

Topics for Review

Fiscal policy
Budget balance, balanced and unbalanced budgets, surpluses and deficits
Fine tuning
Built-in stabilizers
Discretionary fiscal policy
Decision lags and execution lags
The stance of fiscal policy
The actual budget balance and the full-employment surplus
The Keynesian and the fiscal conservative views of budget deficits

Discussion Questions

1. "Fiscal policy has been a relatively weak instrument in Canada because of our heavy dependence on foreign trade and because of the wide regional disparities in employment opportunities." Discuss.
2. On presidential economics:
   a. President Carter in 1977 said, "There will be no new programs implemented under my administration unless we can be sure that the cost of those programs is compatible with my goal of having a

balanced budget before the end of that term." Does this mean President Carter rejected fiscal policy? What might it mean?

b. President Ford in 1975 maintained that his proposed package of $28 billion cut in federal expenditure and a $28 billion tax cut "as a short-term measure would not affect the economy in any significant way." Does this mean that President Ford believed the balanced budget multiplier was zero? If so, why then might he have proposed the package? If not, what might he have meant?

c. Why is it so much easier for presidential candidates to advocate balanced budgets than it is for incumbent presidents to achieve them?

3. Arrange in order the following in terms of the expected size of their effect on aggregate demand and employment:

a. government subsidies to farmers of $100 million, financed by an increase in income taxes of $100 million

b. government deficit expenditure of $100 million during a recession

c. government deficit expenditure of $100 million near the end of a recovery

d. a general tax cut, costing $100 million in lost revenue to the treasury

4. J. K. Galbraith said, about coping with a deflationary gap by means of a tax rebate: "Those who advocate a tax cut do so in deeply conditioned disregard of its economic ineffectiveness, its demonstrated political disutility, and its patently reactionary social effects." What might Professor Galbraith have had in mind by his statement?

5. Consider how each of the following ways of dealing with poverty might affect the stability of the economy.

a. a negative income tax (see page 482)

b. an increase in unemployment insurance payments

c. a Food-for-the-Needy program that channels surplus food products to any family that has no employed member

6. When the government subsidizes particular industries or regions rather than industry in general, is this a sure sign of "playing politics" with fiscal policy?

7. During the 1930s governments generally believed in the doctrine of "sound finance"—that the government's budget should always be balanced. However, between 1929 and 1932 tax revenues fell faster than expenditures, and deficits resulted. What would have been the consequences for employment of keeping the budget balanced by raising tax rates?

8. In addition to full employment, stable prices are generally regarded as an objective of economic policy. Can fiscal policy affect the price level as well as the level of employment?

9. How does growth in full-employment income produce fiscal drag? How may inflation produce fiscal drag? Is not fiscal drag just another name for a built-in stabilizer?

10. Wars involve a massive shift of the nation's resources from the production of consumer goods to the production of military goods. In this sense the wartime generation "pays" for the war. In what sense might postwar generations also pay? How might the method the government uses to finance its wartime expenditure influence who pays for wars?

11. Consider the typical annual expenditures and revenues of the organizations listed below. Comment on the appropriate debt policy for each, taking into account their respective goals, life spans, and resources.

a. family household (consider its life cycle)

b. federal government

c. private corporation (differentiate between a rapidly growing and a mature firm)

d. a village of 5,000 inhabitants

e. the local Home and School Association

12. The national debt is essentially the net result of past and present fiscal policy; that is, the net debt increases when the government runs a budget deficit. Does increasing the national debt make a nation poorer? What effect, if any, does the national debt have on the distribution of income?

13. A late 1979 *Financial Post* article heralded "How a slump may fuel the deficit." Why do deficits rise in slumps? Does this signal a change in the stance of fiscal policy?

Part Ten

Money, Banking, and Monetary Policy

The Nature and Importance of Money

35

Everyone understands the importance of money, or the lack of it, to his or her own welfare. Most people believe that money is one of the more important things in life and that there is never enough of it. Money gives an individual command over goods, but increasing the world's money supply would not change the quantity of goods available. Inflation is on all our minds these days, and everyone knows that inflation and money are somehow related to one another.

What, then, is the significance of money to the economy as a whole, and why are economists concerned about it? Indeed, what is money, and how did it come to play its present role?

The Nature of Money

Inflation is a monetary phenomenon in the sense that a rise in the general level of prices is the same thing as a decrease in the purchasing power of money. But what exactly *is* money? There is probably more folklore and general nonsense believed about money than about any other aspect of the economy. In this section of the chapter we describe the functions of money and outline the history of money. One purpose of this account is to remove some misconceptions.

WHAT IS MONEY?

Traditionally in economics **money** has been defined as any generally accepted medium of exchange—anything that will be accepted by virtually everyone in exchange for goods and services.

Money has several different functions: to act as a medium of exchange, as a store of value, and as a unit of account.

Different kinds of money vary in the degree of efficiency with which they fulfill these functions, and different definitions of money may be required for different purposes.

A Medium of Exchange

An important function of money is to facilitate exchange. Without money the economic system, which is based on specialization and the division of labor, would be impossible, and we would have to return to primitive forms of production and exchange. It is not without justification that money has been called one of the great inventions contributing to human freedom.

If there were no money, goods would have to be exchanged by barter, one good being swapped directly for another. We discussed this cumbersome system in Chapter 4; the major difficulty with barter is that each transaction requires a *double coincidence of wants*. For an exchange to occur between A and B, not only must A have what B wants, but B must have what A wants. If all exchange were restricted to barter, anyone who specialized in producing one commodity would have to spend a great deal of time searching for satisfactory transactions.

The use of money as a generally accepted **medium of exchange** removes these problems. People can sell their output for money and subsequently use the money to buy what they wish from others. The double coincidence of wants is unnecessary when money is used as a medium of exchange. Efficient production demands specialization, and this in turn requires that people satisfy most of their desires by consuming goods produced by others. In any complex economy, such exchanges entail the use of some kind of money.

The difficulties of barter force people to become more or less self-sufficient. With money as a medium of exchange, everyone is free to specialize; with specialization in the direction of one's natural talents and abilities, the production of all commodities can be increased.

To serve as an efficient medium of exchange, money must have a number of characteristics: it must be readily acceptable; it must have a high value for its weight (otherwise it would be a nuisance to carry around); it must be divisible because money that comes only in large denominations is useless for transactions having only a small value; and it must not be readily counterfeitable because if money can be easily duplicated by individuals, it will lose its value.

The nature of what serves as a medium of exchange changes over time. Recently there has been considerable talk about a chequeless society. In this society, one's salary is fed into the memory of a giant computer. Purchases are paid for by inserting an identity card into the seller's recording device, which immediately tells the central computer to reduce the credit in the buyer's account and increase the credit in the seller's account. Such a society would dispense with cash and cheques but not with money. Credit in the computer constitutes each individual's medium of exchange. Call it what you like, for all practical purposes it is money.

During the 1970s there was a sharp rise in barter transactions. One week a gasoline station might supply gasoline to another, only on the promise of the receiver to pay back the same number of gallons of gasoline out of its next week's allotment. And there were such offers as, I'll paint your house if you'll fix my daughter's teeth. These examples do not represent a reversal of the forces that led to the need for and the convenience of using money. The first example reflects only the belief that in a period of gasoline shortage and rationing, dollars may not be as satisfactory a medium of exchange for gasoline as the promise of gasoline at another time. The second example, and the widely reported development of barter clearing houses, almost surely indicates the desire to avoid or evade taxation. If you hire me (a painter) to paint your house, and I hire you (a dentist) to do orthodonture, Revenue Canada's taxation department will surely find out about it. If we engage in barter, Revenue Canada will still want to know about it, for the transaction is legally subject to tax, but it is much less likely to find out.

A Store of Value

Money is a handy way to store purchasing power when the price level is relatively stable. With barter, some other good must be taken in exchange; with money, goods may be sold today and money stored until it is needed. This provides a claim on someone else's goods that can be exercised at a future date. The two sides of the transaction can be separated in time with the obvious increase in freedom that this confers.

To be a satisfactory store of value, however, money must have a relatively stable value. When prices are stable, it is possible to know exactly how much command over real goods and services has been stored up when a certain sum of money has been accumulated. When prices change rapidly, there is no way of knowing how many goods can be bought when previously accumulated money is spent. This reduces the usefulness of money as a store of value.

Although money can serve as a satisfactory store of accumulated purchasing power for a single individual, it cannot do so for the society as a whole. If a single individual accumulates a pile of dollars, he or she will, when the time comes to spend it, be able to command the current output of some other individual. The whole society cannot do this. If all individuals were to save their money and then retire simultaneously to live on their savings, there would be no current production to purchase and consume. The society's ability to satisfy wants depends on goods and services being available; if some of this want-satisfying capacity is to be stored up

for the whole society, goods that are currently producible must be left unconsumed and carried over to future periods.

A Unit of Account

Money may also be used purely for accounting purposes without having a physical existence of its own. For instance, a government store in a truly communist society might say that everyone had so many "dollars" to use each month. Goods could then be assigned prices and each consumer's purchases recorded, the consumer being allowed to buy until the allocated supply of dollars was exhausted. These dollars need have no existence other than as entries in the store's books, yet they would serve as a perfectly satisfactory unit of account. Whether they could also serve as a medium of exchange between individuals depends on whether the store would agree to transfer dollar credits from one customer to another at the customer's request. Banks will transfer dollars credited to demand deposits in this way, and thus a bank deposit can serve as both a unit of account and a medium of exchange. Notice that the use of *dollars* in this context suggests a further sense in which money is a unit of account. People think about values in terms of the monetary unit with which they are familiar.

A further but related function of money is sometimes distinguished: that of a "standard of deferred payments." Payments that are to be made in the future, on account of debts and so on, are reckoned in money. Money is used as a unit of account with the added dimension of time because the account will not be settled until some time in the future.

DO WE NEED MONEY?

Many radical social reformers have seen money as the root of society's evils and have dreamed of the day when the institution of money would be eradicated. Whenever this hope has been combined with a "back to the land" social program and the simple, self-sufficient life for everyone, the goals are at least consistent. For the self-sufficient community that is small enough to base all transactions on barter can dispense with money.

Sometimes the dream of abandoning money is combined with the ideas of a modern industrial socialist state that enjoys a high standard of living without private ownership. Here the goals are contradictory: efficient production demands a specialization of tasks, and this requires that people satisfy most of their wants by consuming goods produced by others. A sophisticated economy also requires that people be able to consume on a different time path than they produce, that is, to borrow now and repay later, or to save now for later needs. In any complex economy, such exchanges require that some kind of money be used.

THE ORIGINS AND GROWTH OF METALLIC MONEY

The origins of money are lost in antiquity; most primitive tribes known today make some use of it. The ability of money to free people from the cumbersome necessity of barter must have led to its early use as soon as some generally acceptable commodity appeared. All sorts of commodities have been used as money at one time or another, but gold and silver proved to have great advantages. They were precious because their supply was relatively limited, and they were in constant demand by the rich for ornament and decoration. They had the additional advantage that they do not easily wear out. Thus they tended to have a high and stable price. They were easily recognized and generally known to be commodities that, because of their stable price, would be accepted by most people. They were also divisible into extremely small units (gold, to a single grain).

Precious metals thus came to circulate as money and to be used in many transactions. Before the invention of coins it was necessary to carry precious metals around in bulk. When a purchase was to be made, the requisite quantity of the metal would have to be weighed carefully on a scale. A sack of gold and a highly accurate set of scales were the common equipment of the merchant and trader.

Such a system, though better than barter, was cumbersome. Coins eliminated the need to weigh the metal at each transaction. The prince or ruler weighed the metal and made a coin out of it to which he affixed his own seal to guarantee the amount of precious metal it contained. A certain coin was stated on its face to contain exactly 1/16 of an ounce of gold. If a commodity was priced at 1/8 of an ounce of gold, two coins would be given over without weighing the gold. This was clearly a great convenience as long as traders knew that they could accept the coin at its "face value." The face value itself was nothing more than a guarantee that a certain weight of metal was contained therein.

The prince's subjects, however, could not let a good opportunity pass. Someone soon had the idea of clipping a thin slice off the edge of the coin. If he collected a coin stamped as containing half an ounce of gold, he could clip a slice off the edge and pass the coin off as still containing half an ounce of gold. ("Doesn't the stamp prove it?" he would argue.) If he got away with this, he would have made a profit equal to the market value of the clipped metal.

Whenever this practice became common, even the most myopic traders noticed that things were not what they seemed in the coinage world. It became necessary to weigh each coin before accepting it at its face value; out came the scales again, and most of the usefulness of coins was lost. To get around this problem, the idea arose of minting the coins with a rough edge. The absence of the rough edge would immediately be apparent and would indicate that the coin had been clipped. The practice, called milling, survives on some coins as an interesting anachronism to remind us that there were days when the market value of the metal in the coin (if it were melted down) was equal to the face value of the coin.

Not to be outdone by the cunning of his subjects, the prince was quick to seize the chance of getting something for nothing. Because he was empowered to mint the coins, he was in a very good position to work a *really* profitable fraud. When he found himself with bills that he could not pay and that it was inexpedient to repudiate, he merely used some suitable occasion—a marriage, an anniversary, an alliance—to remint the coinage. The subjects would be ordered to bring their gold coins into the mint to be melted down and coined afresh with a new stamp. The subjects could then go away the proud possessors of one new coin for every old coin that they had brought in. Between the melting down and the recoining, however, the prince had only to toss some inexpensive base metal in with the molten gold to earn a handsome profit. If the coinage were debased by adding, say, one pound of new base metal to every four pounds of old coins, five coins would be made for every four turned in. For every four coins brought in, the prince could return four and have one left for himself as profit. With these coins he could pay his bills.

The result was inflation. The subjects had the same number of coins as before and hence could demand the same quantity of goods. When the prince paid his bills, however, the recipients of the extra coins could be expected to spend some or all of them, and this would represent a net increase in demand. The extra demand would bid up prices. Debasing the coinage thus led to a rise in prices. It was the experience of such inflations that led early economists to propound the *quantity theory of money and prices*. They argued that there was a relation between the average level of prices and the quantity of money in circulation, such that a change in the quantity of money would lead to a change in the price level in the same direction. We shall have more to say about this theory later in the chapter.

The early experience of currency debasement led to a famous economic "law" that has stood the test of time. The hypothesis is that "bad money drives out good." It has come to be known as **Gresham's law** after the Elizabethan financial expert Sir Thomas Gresham, who first explained the workings of the law to Queen Elizabeth.

To see how the law works, assume there are two kinds of gold coins, Royals and Sovereigns. Royals have not been debased—the gold in the coin is actually worth its face value. Sovereigns have been debased to the point that the gold in the coin is worth only 80 percent of its face value. If you possessed one of each type of coin, each with the same face value, and had a bill to pay, what would you do? Clearly, you would pay the bill with the debased Sovereign and keep the the undebased Royal. You part with less gold that way. If you wanted to obtain a certain amount of gold bullion by melting down the gold coins (as was frequently done), which coins would you use? Clearly, you would use Royals because you would part with less "face value" that way—for according to face value, five Sovereigns are equal to five Royals, but if you melt them down it takes only four Royals to get the same amount of gold as is contained in five Sovereigns. The debased coins would thus remain in circulation and the undebased coins would disappear. Whenever people got hold of an undebased coin, they would hold on to it; whenever they got a debased coin, they would pass it on.

THE EVOLUTION OF PAPER MONEY

Another important step in the history of money was the evolution of paper currency. Artisans who worked with gold were called goldsmiths. Naturally they kept very secure safes in which to store their gold.[1] Among the public the practice grew up of storing gold with the goldsmith for safekeeping. In return, the goldsmith would give the depositor a receipt promising to hand over the gold on demand. If the depositor wished to make a large purchase, he or she could go to the goldsmith, reclaim the gold, and hand it over to the seller of the goods. Chances were that the

---

[1] All the basic ideas about paper money can be explained by concentrating on the goldsmiths, though there were earlier sources of paper money in various negotiable evidences of debt.

seller would not require the gold but would carry it back to the goldsmith for safekeeping.

Clearly, if people knew the goldsmith to be reliable, there was no need to go through the cumbersome and risky business of physically transferring the gold. The buyer need only transfer the goldsmith's receipt to the seller, who would accept it, secure in the knowledge that the goldsmith would pay over the gold whenever it was needed. If the seller wished to buy a good from a third party who also knew the goldsmith to be reliable, this transaction too could be effected by passing the goldsmith's receipt from the buyer to the seller. The convenience of using pieces of paper instead of gold is obvious.

Thus, when it first came into being, paper money was a promise to pay on demand so much gold, the promise being made first by goldsmiths and later by banks. Banks too became known for their vaults ("safes") where the precious gold was stored and protected. As long as the institutions were known to be reliable, their pieces of paper would be "as good as gold." Such paper money was *backed* by precious metal and was *convertible* on demand into this metal. When a country's money is convertible into gold, the country is said to be on a *gold standard*. For the fifty years prior to World War I many countries were on a gold standard; the operation of that system is discussed in the next chapter.

In nineteenth century Canada, private banks operating under charters granted initially by the provincial legislatures and after Confederation by the federal government commonly issued paper money nominally convertible into gold. **Bank notes** represented banks' promises to pay. They remained an important part of the money supply in Canada well into the current century, and they were not completely supplanted by government-issued paper until 1950.

Fractionally Backed Paper Money

For most transactions individuals were content to use paper currency. It was soon discovered that it was not necessary to keep an ounce of gold in the vaults for every claim to an ounce circulating as paper money. It was necessary to keep some gold on hand because, for some transactions, paper would not do. If a man wished to make a purchase from a distant place where his local bank was not known, he might have to convert his paper into gold and ship the gold. Further, he might not have perfect confidence in the bank's ability to honor its pledge to redeem the notes in gold at a future time. His alternative was to exchange his notes for gold and store the gold until he needed it.

For these and other reasons, some holders of notes demanded gold in return for their notes. However, some of the bank's customers received gold in various transactions and stored it in the bank for safekeeping. They accepted promises to pay (i.e., bank notes) in return. At any one time, then, some of the bank's customers would be withdrawing gold, others would be depositing it, and the great majority would be trading in the bank's paper notes without any need or desire to convert them into gold. Thus the bank was able to issue more money redeemable in gold than the amount of gold held in its vaults. This was good business because the money could be profitably invested by purchasing securities that yielded a return and granting interest-earning loans to households and firms.

This discovery was made by the early goldsmiths. From that time to the present, banks have had many more claims to pay outstanding against them than they actually had in reserves available to pay those claims. In such a situation we say that the currency is *fractionally backed* by the reserves.

In the past the major problem of a fractionally backed, convertible currency was that of maintaining its convertibility into the precious metal by which it was backed. The imprudent bank that issued too much paper money found itself unable to redeem its currency in gold when the demand for gold was even slightly higher than usual. This bank would then have to suspend payments, and all holders of its notes would suddenly find them worthless. The prudent bank, which kept a reasonable relation between its note issue and its gold reserve, found that it could meet the normal everyday demand for gold without any trouble.

It was always the problem with fractionally backed currency that if all noteholders demanded gold at once, they could not all be satisfied. Thus, if the public ever lost confidence and en masse demanded redemption of their currency, the banks would be unable to honor their pledges and the holders of their notes would lose everything. The history of nineteenth and early twentieth century banking on both sides of the Atlantic is replete with examples of banks ruined by "panics," sudden runs on their gold reserves. When this happens, the bank's depositors and the holders of its notes would find themselves holding worthless pieces of paper.

The so-called central bank was a natural outcome of this sort of banking system. For where were the commercial banks to keep *their* reserves? Their own vaults, although safer than those of their customers, were not safe against a really determined attempt at robbery. Where were the commercial banks to turn when they had good investments but were in temporary need of cash? If they provided loans for the public against reasonable security, why should not some other institution provide loans to them against the same sort of security? Central banks evolved in response to these and other needs.

The Development of Fiat Currencies

As time went on, note issue by private banks became less common and central banks took control of the currency. Central banks in turn became governmental institutions. In time *only* central banks were permitted to issue notes. Originally the central banks issued currency that was fully convertible into gold. In those days, gold would be brought to the central bank, which would issue currency in the form of "gold certificates" that asserted the gold was there on demand. The gold supply thus set some upper limit on the amount of currency. But central banks

could issue (as bank notes) more currency than they had gold because not all of the currency was presented for payment at any one time. Thus even under a gold standard central banks had substantial discretionary control over the quantity of currency outstanding.

During the period between World Wars I and II, virtually all the countries of the world abandoned the gold standard. The reasons for this need not be gone into here (they will be mentioned in Chapter 36). The result of abandoning the gold standard was that currency was no longer convertible into gold—or anything else. Money that is not convertible by law into anything valuable depends upon its acceptability for its value. Money that is declared by government order (or fiat) to be legal tender for settlement of all debts is called a **fiat money.**

Today virtually all currency is fiat money.

Some countries (including the United States until 1968) preserve the fiction that their currency is backed by gold, but no country allows its currency to be converted into gold on demand. The gold reserve held as backing for Canadian currency was eliminated in 1940, although note issues continued to carry the traditional statement "will pay to the bearer on demand" until 1954. The holder of a $20 bill who took this seriously and demanded $20 could hand over the $20 bill and receive in return a different but identical $20 bill! Today's Bank of Canada notes simply say "this note is legal tender."

The meaning of the phrase **legal tender** is that if you are offered something that is legal tender in payment for a debt and you refuse to accept it, the debt is no longer legally collectible.

Not only is our currency fiat money, so is our coinage. Modern coins, unlike their historical ancestors, rarely contain a value of metal equal to their fact value; indeed, the value of the metal is characteristically a minute fraction of the value of the coin. Modern coins, like modern paper money, are merely tokens.

Limits on the Issue of Currency by the Central Bank

The gold standard imposed an upper limit on the quantity of convertible currency that could be issued. Now that this system has been abandoned, does it matter that there is no longer any such constraint on the central bank?

Gold derived its value because it was scarce relative to the demand for it (the demand being derived from both its monetary and its non-monetary uses). Tying a currency to gold meant that the quantity of money in a country was determined by such chance occurrences as the discovery of new gold supplies. This was not without advantages, the most important being that it provided a check on governments' ability to cause inflation. Gold cannot be manufactured at will; paper currency can. There is little doubt that in the past, if the money supply had been purely paper, many governments would have attempted to pay their bills by printing new money rather than by raising taxes. Such increases in the money supply, in periods of full employment, would lead to inflation in the same way that the debasement of metallic currency did. Thus the gold standard provided some check on inflation by making it difficult for the government

to change the money supply. Periods of major gold discoveries, however, brought about inflations on their own. In the 1500s, for example, Spanish gold and silver flowed into Europe from the New World, bringing inflation in their wake.

A major problem caused by a reliance on gold is that it is usually desirable to increase the money supply when real national income is increasing. This cannot be done on a gold standard unless, by pure chance, gold is discovered at the same time. The gold standard took discretionary powers over the money supply out of the hands of the central authorities. Whether or not one thinks this is a good thing depends on how one thinks the central authorities would use this discretion. In general, a gold standard is probably better than having the currency managed by an ignorant or irresponsible government, but it is worse than having the currency supply adjusted by a well-informed and intelligent one. "Better" and "worse" in this context are judged by the criterion of having a money supply that varies adequately with the needs of the economy but does not vary so as to cause violent inflations or deflations.

Why is Fiat Money Valuable?

In the early days of the gold standard, paper money was valuable because everyone believed it was convertible into gold on demand. Experience during periods of crisis, when there was often a temporary suspension of convertibility into gold, and of panic, when there were bank failures, served to demonstrate that the mere *promise* of convertibility was not sufficient to make money valuable. Gradually the realization grew that neither was convertibility necessary.

Fiat money is valuable when it will be accepted in payment for goods and for debts and is not valuable when it will not be accepted.

Today our paper money and our coinage is valuable because it is generally accepted. Because everyone accepts it as valuable, it *is* valuable; the fact that it can no longer be converted into anything has no effect on its functioning as a medium of exchange.

Many people are disturbed to learn that present-day paper money is neither backed by, nor convertible into, anything more valuable—that it is nothing but pieces of paper whose value derives from common acceptance and from confidence that it will continue to be accepted in the future. People believe their money should be more substantial than that; after all, what of "dollar diplomacy" and the "bedrock solidity" of the Swiss franc? But money is in fact only pieces of paper. There is no point in pretending otherwise.

If paper money is acceptable, it is a medium of exchange; if its purchasing power remains stable, it is a satisfactory store of value; and if both of these things are true, it will also serve as a satisfactory unit of account.

DEPOSIT MONEY

By the twentieth century private banks had, by law, lost the authority to issue money by issuing bank notes. Yet they did not lose the power to create money in the form of deposit money. Just *how* this is done will be discussed in Chapter 37; here we ask what is deposit money?

Banks' customers frequently deposit coins and paper money with the banks for safekeeping, just as in former times they deposited gold. Such a deposit is recorded as an entry on the customer's account. If the customer wishes to pay a debt, he or she may come to the bank and claim the money in dollars, then pay the money over to another person. This person may then redeposit the money in a bank.

Like the gold transfers, this is a tedious procedure, particularly for large payments. It is more convenient to have the bank transfer claims to this money on deposit. The common "cheque" is an instruction to the bank to make the transfer. As soon as such transfers became easy and inexpensive, and cheques became widely accepted in payment for commodities and debts, the deposits became a form of money called **deposit money**.

When individual A deposits $100 in a bank, his account is credited with $100. This is the bank's promise to pay $100 cash on demand. If A pays B $100 by giving her a cheque that B then depos-

its in the same bank, the bank merely reduces A's account by $100 and increases B's by the same amount. Thus the bank still promises to pay on demand the $100 originally deposited, but it now promises to pay it to B rather than to A. What makes all of this so convenient is that B can actually deposit A's cheque in any bank, and the banks will arrange the transfer of credits.

Cheques are in some ways the modern equivalent of old-time bank notes issued by commercial banks. The passing of a bank note from hand to hand transferred ownership of a claim against the bank. A cheque on a deposit account is similarly an order to the bank to pay the designated recipient, rather than oneself, money credited to the account. Cheques, unlike bank notes, do not circulate freely from hand to hand; thus cheques themselves are not currency. The balance in the demand deposit *is* money; the cheque transfers money from one person to another. Because cheques are easily drawn and deposited, and because they are relatively safe from theft, they are widely used.

Thus, when commercial banks lost the right to issue notes of their own, the form of bank money changed but the substance did not. Today banks have money in their vaults (or on deposit with the central banks) just as they always did. Once it was gold, today it is the legal tender of the times—paper money. It is true today, just as in the past, that most of the bank's customers are content to pay their bills by passing among themselves the bank's promises to pay money on demand. Only a small proportion of the transactions made by the bank's customers is made in cash.

Today, just as in the past, banks can create money by issuing more promises to pay (deposits) than they have money available to pay out.

Demand Deposits

A customer's deposit in a bank can be kept in one of two basic forms, as a demand deposit or as a term deposit in a savings account. A **demand** deposit means that the customer can withdraw the money on demand (i.e., without giving any notice of intention to withdraw). Demand deposits are transferable by cheque. Such a cheque instructs the bank to pay without a delay a stated sum of money to the person to whom the cheque is made payable.

Term Deposits

A **term deposit** is an interest-bearing deposit that is legally withdrawable only after a certain amount of notice. In practice such term deposits are quickly convertible into medium-of-exchange. Until quite recently it was impossible to pay a bill by writing a cheque on a term deposit. A depositor wishing to use a term deposit to pay a bill had to withdraw money from a savings (term) account and then either pay the bill in cash or deposit the funds in a demand account and write a cheque on the demand account.

The Disappearing Distinction Between Demand and Term Deposits

When interest rates on time deposits amounted to only a few percent, people were content to keep their savings in term deposits and their reserves of cash for ordinary transactions in demand deposits. Then, as interest rates available on term deposits and other safe liquid investments grew, it became more and more expensive (in terms of lost interest) to keep cash in demand deposits, even for a week or two. Starting in the early 1970s, a series of devices were invented that tended to make it easier to convert interest-bearing deposits into demand deposits transferable by cheque. Chequable savings accounts are now common, and some banks even offer a service whereby fixed sums are automatically transferred from a customer's savings account to his or her demand account at regular intervals. The effective distinction is no longer between demand and term accounts but rather between a multitude of types of accounts each offering different combinations of interest pay-

ments, service provided, and service charges levied.

NEAR MONEY AND MONEY SUBSTITUTES

Over the past two centuries what has been accepted by the public as money has expanded from gold and silver coins to include, first, bank notes and then bank deposits subject to transfer by cheque. Until recently, most economists would have agreed that money stopped at that point. No such agreement exists today, and an important debate centers on the definition of money appropriate to the present world.

The two major functions of money are to act as a medium of exchange and to be a temporary store of value to bridge the gap between receiving and making payments. The problem of deciding what is money stems from the fact that anything that can fulfill the first function can also fulfill the second one, but many things that can fulfill the second do not fulfill the first.

Near Money

Assets that fulfill adequately the store-of-value function and are readily converted into a medium of exchange but are not themselves a medium of exchange are sometimes called **near money**. Deposits at a trust company are a characteristic form of near money. When you have a savings deposit at a trust company, you know exactly how much purchasing power you hold (at today's prices) and, given modern banking practices, you can turn your deposit into a medium of exchange — cash or a chequing deposit — at a moment's notice. Additionally, your deposit will earn some interest during the period that you hold it. Why then does not everybody keep their money in such deposits instead of in chequing deposits or currency? The answer is that the inconvenience of continually shifting money back and forth may outweigh the interest that can be earned. One week's interest on $100 (at 10 percent per year) is only about 20¢, not enough to cover carfare to the bank or the cost of mailing a letter. For money that will be needed soon, it would hardly pay to shift it to a savings deposit.

In general, whether it pays to convert cash or chequing deposits into interest-earning savings deposits for a given period will depend on the inconvenience and other transactions costs of shifting funds in and out and on the amount of interest that can be earned.

There is a wide spectrum of assets in the economy that pay interest and also serve as reasonably satisfactory temporary stores of value. The difference between these assets and savings deposits is that their capital values are not quite as certain as are those of savings deposits. If I elect to store my purchasing power in the form of a government bond that matures in 30 days, its price on the market may change between the time I buy it and the time I want to sell it—say 10 days later. If the price changes, I will suffer or enjoy a change in the purchasing power available to me. But because of the short horizon to maturity, the price will not change very much. (After all, the government will pay the bond's face value in a few weeks.) Such a security is thus a reasonably satisfactory short-run store of purchasing power. Indeed, any readily salable capital asset whose value does not fluctuate significantly with the rate of interest will satisfactorily fulfill this short-term, store-of-value function.

Money Substitutes

Things that serve as a temporary medium of exchange but are not a store of value are sometimes called **money substitutes.** Credit cards are a prime example. With a credit card many transactions can be made without cash or a cheque. The evidence of a credit, the credit slip you sign and hand over to the store, is not money because it cannot be used to make further transactions. Furthermore, when your credit card company sends you a bill, you have to use money in (delayed) payment for the original transaction.

The credit card serves the short-run function of a medium of exchange by allowing you to make purchases even though you have no cash or bank deposit currently in your possession. But this is only temporary; money remains the final medium of exchange for these transactions when the credit account is settled.

CHANGING CONCEPTS OF WHAT IS MONEY

What is an acceptable enough medium of exchange to count as money has changed and will continue to change over time. New monetary assets such as certificates of deposit are continuously being developed to serve some, if not all, the functions of money, and they are more or less readily convertible into money. There is no single, timeless definition of what is money and what what is only near money or a money substitute. Indeed, as we shall see, our monetary authorities use several different definitions of money, and these definitions change from year to year.

The Importance of Money

THE "REAL" AND MONEY PARTS OF THE ECONOMY

Very early in the history of economics changes in the quantity of money were seen to be associated with changes in the price level. Eighteenth and nineteenth century economists developed the first comprehensive theories of the functioning of the economy, with money playing a special part in those theories. The economy was conceived of as being divisible into a "real part" and a "monetary part."

The allocation of resources is determined in the real part of the economy by demand and supply. This allocation depends on the structure of *relative* prices. Whether a lot of beef is produced relative to pork depends on the relation between the prices of the two commodities. If the price of beef is higher than the price of pork and both commodities cost about the same to produce, the incentive exists to produce beef rather than pork. This argument depends on the relationship between the prices of the two commodities, not on the money price of each. At prices of 50¢ a pound for pork and $1.50 for beef, the *relative* incentive will be the same as it would be at $1 for pork and $3 for beef. As with beef and pork, so with all other commodities: the allocation of resources between different lines of production depends on relative prices.

According to the early economists, the price *level* was determined in the monetary part of the economy. An increase in the money supply led to an increase in all money prices. In the beef and pork example, an increase in the total money available might raise the price of pork from 50¢ to $1 a pound and the price of beef from $1.50 to $3, but in equilibrium it would leave relative prices unchanged. Hence it would have no effect on the real part of the economy, that is, on the amount of resources allocated to beef and to pork production (and to everything else). If the quantity of money were doubled, the prices of everything bought would double; and money income would also double, so everyone earning an income would be made no better or worse off by the change. Thus, in equilibrium, the real and the monetary parts of the economy were believed to have no effect on each other.

Because early economists believed that the most important questions—How much does the economy produce? What share of it does each group in the society get?—were answered in the real sector, they spoke of money as a "veil" behind which occurred the real events that affected material well-being. The doctrine that the quantity of money influences the level of money prices but has no effect on the real part of the economy is called the doctrine of the **neutrality of money.**

Modern economists still accept the insights of the early economists that relative prices are a major determinant of the real allocation of resources and that the quantity of money has a lot to do with determining the absolute level of prices. They do not however accept the neutrality of money, as we shall see in Chapter 38.

In this section of the chapter we look at the experience of price level changes—one aspect of the importance of money.

THE EXPERIENCE OF PRICE LEVEL CHANGES

Figure 35-1 shows the course of Canadian prices from 1867 to 1980. Considerable year-to-year fluctuations are apparent. However, no trend is evident over the period 1867–1939. Both world wars were associated with sharp inflations, and World War I was followed by a sharp deflation. In spite of the major fluctuations that occurred from Confederation until World War II, the price trend during the entire period was neither upward nor downward. The period following World War II, however, is unique in North American history because no major deflation has accompanied it. The price level rose rapidly until the end of the Korean War in 1952. It then became relatively stable for a while, rising by only 34 percent between 1952 and 1967, an average of 2 percent per year. During the last dozen years we have experienced a significant new round of inflation, one that began gradually but quickly accelerated. Wholesale prices rose 140 percent between 1967 and January 1980.

Long as it is, a century may still not be long enough to give a clear perspective of long-term price fluctuations. Indeed, 1867–1939 was not a typical period in the history of price levels. The experience of the period since 1946 looks much more dramatic and unusual when compared only with the post-Confederation experience than when considered in longer perspective. An indication of the course of price levels in England over seven centuries is given in Figure 35-2. The figure shows that there was an overall inflationary trend but that it was by no means evenly spread over the centuries. Some further idea of the variability of price levels can be obtained from Table 35-1, which looks at the same price

FIGURE 35-1
Index of Canadian Wholesale Prices, 1867–1980

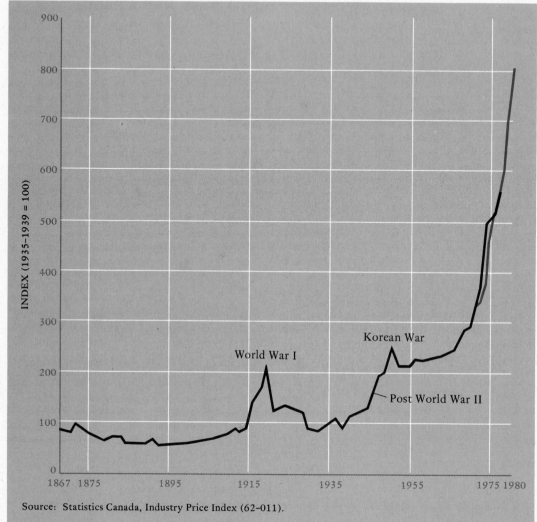

Source: Statistics Canada, Industry Price Index (62–011).

Persistent peacetime inflation is only a recent problem in Canada. Although the price level has fluctuated throughout Canadian history, no long-term trend was visible during the period from Confederation to 1940. From the time of World War II to the present, the price level has shown a consistent upward trend.

level over various periods within the seven centuries.

The period since World War II has seen fairly general inflationary tendencies throughout the world. Table 35-2 shows the average rate of change in the price level of 20 countries over 15 years. Notice the great range and variability of experience from country to country; notice too that the rate of inflation increased in most countries. While OPEC is often identified as a major

FIGURE 35-2
A Price Index of Consumables in Southern England, 1275–1959

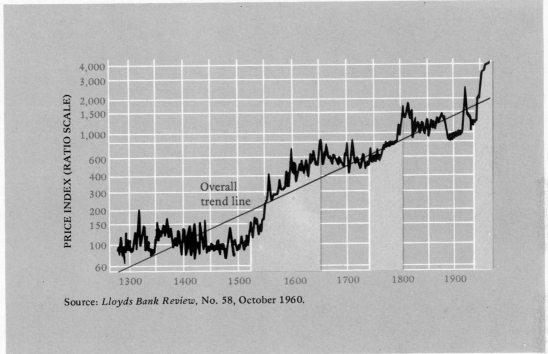

Source: *Lloyds Bank Review*, No. 58, October 1960.

Over the last seven centuries long periods of stable prices have alternated with long periods of rising prices. This remarkable price series shows an index of the prices of food, clothing, and fuel in southern England from 1275 through 1959. The trend line shows that the average change in prices over the whole period was .5 percent per year. The shaded areas indicate periods of unreversed inflation. The series also shows that even the perspective of a century can be misleading because long periods of stable or gently falling prices tended to alternate with long periods of rising prices.

source of the worldwide inflationary trend, note that the current increase in inflation started in most countries before 1973 and the OPEC embargo.

WHY INFLATIONS MATTER

Modern economists have devoted much effort to identifying and measuring the consequences of inflation. Even the early economists, with their strict division between the economy's real and monetary sectors, were strongly opposed to rapid inflations or deflations because of the harm that could be done during the transition from one price level to another. Indeed, it may take years

to move from one equilibrium price level to another, and in the course of the movement many people may be hurt. The consequences of an inflation depend significantly on whether or not it is anticipated.

The Effects of Unanticipated Inflations

Unanticipated inflations cause more upset than do anticipated inflations. Contracts freely entered into when the price level was expected to remain constant will yield hardships for some and unexpected gains for others once the unanticipated inflation begins.

A first effect of a continuing inflation is to in-

TABLE 35-1
Seven Centuries of English Prices

Period	Number of years in period	Percentage change in price level over whole period	Average annual percentage change over period
1275–1525	250	+ 29	+ 0.12
1526–1650	125	+550	+ 4.40
1651–1744	94	− 38	− 0.40
1745–1813	69	+263	+ 3.81
1814–1893	80	− 51	− 0.64
1894–1920	27	+183	+ 6.78
1921–1932	12	− 59	− 4.92
1933–1960	28	+322	+11.50

Source: Lloyds Bank Review, No. 58, October 1960.

Long periods of relatively stable prices have alternated with long periods of continuous inflation. The table shows percentage changes in the price level over selected time periods. (The data come from the series graphed in Figure 35-2.) Notice, first, the very long periods during which the change in the price level averaged less than 1 percent per year. Most of the unreversed rises in the price level before 1960 occurred in three periods: 1526–1650, when Spanish gold and silver flowed into Europe; 1750–1800, when banking spread from London into the English provincial cities, greatly increasing the supply of bank money; and 1939–1950, when there was massive deficit financing of World War II and its aftermath. The recent period of inflation (since 1960) is not included in the data.

TABLE 35-2
Inflation Rates of Selected Countries, 1963–1978

Country	Average annual rate of increase of consumer prices		
	1963–1968	1968–1973	1973–1978
Argentina	25.5	33.4	170.2
Canada	3.1	4.6	9.2
Chile	28.1	74.6	199.1
China (Nationalist)	4.0	4.8	12.5
Denmark	6.3	6.4	11.0
Ecuador	3.8	8.1	14.7
France	3.2	6.1	10.7
Iran	1.6	5.1	15.3
Italy	3.5	5.7	16.4
Japan	5.1	7.2	11.3
Mexico	3.1	6.3	20.1
Netherlands	4.7	6.9	7.8
Norway	4.2	6.9	9.5
South Korea	14.9	9.9	17.9
Switzerland	3.5	5.6	4.0
Syria	3.2	5.5	11.8
United Kingdom	3.8	7.5	16.1
United States	2.6	5.0	8.0
West Germany	2.5	4.6	4.8
Yugoslavia	15.7	14.2	17.0

Source: Computed from IMF, *International Statistics Yearbook* 1979.

Inflation rates vary greatly among countries, yet the worldwide trend is one of increased inflation. Annual rates of increase in prices, of the size shown in the table, cause substantial changes in price levels over five-year periods. In Chile between 1973 and 1978, prices on average tripled every year. In West Germany prices rose 27 percent in five years. In Canada prices were roughly 55 percent higher in 1978 than in 1973. The trend to increasing inflation of the 1970s afflicted most countries.

fluence the allocation of resources by changing *relative* prices (including *relative* wages), often in haphazard fashion. In a market economy, changes in relative prices are supposed to signal resource shifts in response to changing patterns of demand and supply. In an inflationary period other influences may play a major (and potentially distorting) role.

For example, workers in occupations with strong unions will be able to keep their wages rising as fast as prices; they may even be able to do better than they would have done if prices had never risen. In other occupations, wages and salaries will be very slow to adjust. Employees in these occupations will lose substantially because of the inflation. Schoolteachers often find themselves in this group. Not only do these individu-

als suffer, but the change in relative wages will affect the allocation of resources. For example, the fall in the real income of teachers relative to that of plumbers is likely to reduce the supply of new entrants into the teaching profession below what it would have been in the absence of inflation.

A second effect of unanticipated inflations is to redistribute wealth from lenders to borrowers, whereas unanticipated deflations do the opposite. To see why this is true, suppose that Mr.

Jones lends Ms. Smith $100 at 5 percent interest for one year. If the price level rises by 10 percent over the year, Jones will actually earn a negative rate of interest on the loan. The $105 Jones gets back from Smith can buy fewer goods than the $100 Jones originally parted with. As well as doing without the money for a year, Jones is worse off in terms of purchasing power at the end of the year than at the beginning.

Jones' loss, however, is Smith's gain. Smith did not even have to use the $100 in any productive business enterprise to show a gain. All she needed to do was to buy and hold goods whose prices rose merely by the average rate of inflation. At the end of the year Smith can sell the goods for $110, pay back the $100 she borrowed plus $5 interest, and show a gain of $5 for having done nothing more than hold goods instead of money. This sort of redistribution occurs not just on borrowing and lending contracts but on any form of contract that is stated in terms of monetary units.

A third effect of inflation, whether anticipated or unanticipated, is to reduce the living standards of those on fixed incomes. Consider the case of Mr. and Mrs. Prudent, who invested in an annuity designed to provide them with a fixed annual dollar income after retirement. The Prudents saved enough throughout their working years to give themselves a retirement income of $10,000 a year. They figured that with the children no longer at home and with their durable goods already purchased, $10,000 would allow a good standard of living for their retirement years. However, if the price level doubles just before the Prudents retire, the purchasing power of their money income will be halved. They will still get $10,000 a year, but it will buy only half as many goods as they had expected it to buy.

Furthermore, if the price level continues to rise slowly, say at 3 percent per year, the Prudents will have to cut their real purchases of goods and services by a steady 3 percent each year. If they should live for 23 years after retirement, their living standard will have been halved once again. By that time they will be able to buy only as many goods per year as if they had saved just enough to provide themselves an income of $2,500 a year. Instead of having a modest but satisfactory living standard, the Prudents will have been made progressively worse off, until finally they will have been reduced to poverty.

This kind of situation was not far from the experience of those who saved during the years before World War II and then retired into the creeping inflation of the 1950s and 1960s. It understates the plight of retirees facing the sharp inflation that characterized the 1970s. As the 1980s begin—with double-digit inflation—the nightmare of inflation eroding retirement incomes affects not only the Prudents but the Welloffs.

The reduction in the purchasing power of money savings is one of the most dramatic and obvious effects of an inflation. It helps to explain the hostility to inflation felt by anyone who has suffered seriously from one.

The Effects of Anticipated Inflations

To the extent that inflations are anticipated, some of the haphazard effects can be avoided by drawing up contracts in real terms or with "escalator clauses" or "indexing" that build changes in average price levels into such things as social insurance benefits and specific wage and price contracts. Escalator contracts are common in labor agreements, in long-term raw material contracts, and in many government procurement agreements.

Even without a formal contract in real terms, it is possible to allow for the effects of an inflation. Wage and price contracts are major examples. If, say, a 10 percent inflation is expected over the next year, a money wage that rises by 10 percent over that period may represent the minimum demand of a union intent on preserving or increasing the purchasing power of its members. A banker will demand 9 percent interest for the use of money if 3 percent is the real rate of interest and 6 percent is the anticipated rate of inflation.

While some people may be able to avoid the ef-

Hyperinflation

Can a sharp inflation continue year after year without triggering an explosive inflation that wholly destroys the value of a currency? The answer appears to be yes—at least some of the time. Inflation rates of 50, 100, and even 200 percent or more a year have occurred year after year and proven quite manageable as people adjust their contracts to real terms. While there are strains and side effects, the evidence shows such situations to be possible without hyperinflation.

Does this mean there is nothing to fear from rapid inflation? The historical record is not entirely reassuring. There have been a number of so-called hyperinflations in which at some point prices began to rise at an ever-accelerating rate until the nation's money ceased to be a satisfactory store of value even for the short period between receipt and expenditure. Consider the index of wholesale prices in Germany during and after World War I:

Date	Wholesale price index (1913 = 1)
Jan 1913	1
Jan 1920	13
Jan 1921	14
Jan 1922	37
July 1922	101
Jan 1923	2,785
July 1923	74,800
Aug 1923	944,000
Sept 1923	23,900,000
Oct 1923	7,096,000,000
15 Nov 1923	750,000,000,000

The index shows that a good purchased with one 100 mark note in July 1923 would have required *ten million* 100 mark notes for its purchase only four months later!

While Germany had experienced substantial inflation during World War I, averaging more than 30 percent per year, the immediate postwar years of 1920 and 1921 gave no sign of an explosive inflation. Indeed, during 1920 price stability was experienced. But in 1922 and 1923 the price level exploded. On November 15, 1923, the mark was officially repudiated, its value wholly destroyed. How could this happen?

When an inflation becomes so rapid that people lose confidence in the purchasing power of their currency, they rush to spend it. But people who have goods become increasingly reluctant to accept the rapidly depreciating money in exchange. The rush to spend money accelerates the increase in prices until people finally become unwilling to accept money on any terms. What was once money then ceases to be money.

The price system can then be restored only by official repudiation of the old monetary unit and its replacement by a new unit. This destroys the value not only of monetary savings but of all contracts specified in terms of the old monetary units.

There are approximately a dozen documented hyperinflations in world history, among them the collapse of the *continental* during the American revolution, the *ruble* during the Russian revolution, the *drachma* during and after the German occupation of Greece in World War II, the *pengo* in Hungary during 1945 and 1946, and the Chinese national currency during 1946–1948. Every one of these hyperinflations was accompanied by great increases in the money supply; new money was printed to give governments purchasing power they could not or would not obtain by taxation. And every one occurred in the midst of a major political upheaval in which grave doubts existed about the stability and future of the government itself.

Is hyperinflation likely in the absence of civil war, revolution, or collapse of the government? Most economists think not. And it is clear that inflation rates of 5 or 10 or 20 percent per year—which many Canadians find so upsetting—do not mean the inevitable or likely onset of a disastrous hyperinflation, however serious their distributive and social effects may be.

fects of inflation when they see it coming, many people can not do so much of the time. One of the most troubling aspects of the rapid increase in the inflation rate at the start of the 1980s was the unavailability to ordinary people of "inflation proof" havens for their savings. Thus many of those who correctly anticipated a continued inflation were unable to protect themselves against it.

Even a fully foreseen inflation has real effects. Many practices—such as business accounting conventions, definitions of allowable expenses given in tax laws, and many private pension schemes—make use of money definitions that cannot be altered even in the face of an inflation that is fully foreseen. In addition, not everyone can find a way to adjust to an anticipated inflation without incurring substantial transactions costs—for example, paying commissions for buying and selling property. These transactions costs may be particularly high for those with relatively small amounts to protect.

Does Everyone Lose by Inflations?

Contrary to popular opinion, inflation does not generally make everyone or even the vast majority worse off. This is because inflation does not normally have major effects on the economy's total output.

The popular image of the average person's being slowly impoverished as money prices rise steadily faster than his or her money income is mistaken. This is in sharp contrast to the overall effects of a serious recession. A recession typically will lower average living standards because many of the country's resources—its labor, factories, and raw materials—lie idle.

The main undesirable domestic effects of inflation, whether foreseen or unforeseen, are distributive: contracts stated in money terms do not have the effects in terms of real purchasing power that was expected of them. Since contracts are two-sided, one person's losses are another's gains.

Thus *typical* households and firms are wrong when they say that inflation is pricing everything out of their reach.[2] When income-earning households and firms say that inflation is ruining them, what they are probably thinking is how much better off they would be if they had this year's money income to spend at the prices ruling several years ago. But this is impossible, for that much output is not available. Few would prefer the prices of, say, ten years ago and their money incomes of the same period because real income rose over the decade, inflation notwithstanding. Of course, some groups are seriously hurt by inflation, but the *average* household and the *average* firm are not hurt because in most years money income rises significantly faster than money prices.

In saying that the main effects of inflation are redistributional, we do *not* say that inflation is unimportant. Redistributions of income can be very important. After all, the causes of the distribution of income among social classes were *the* major problem faced by the classical economists. The call for a major redistribution from capitalists to workers was, and still is, an important part of Marxian economics. Rapid inflations cause major, arbitrary, and socially destructive redistributions. The continual erosion of the purchasing power of fixed money incomes is tragic to those who suffer it, and such erosion is only one of the many serious negative redistributive effects of inflation.

Other effects of inflation may also be serious. For example, social and personal tensions arise from the race to keep up with the rise in prices and from the knowledge that some gain from inflation at the expense of others.

Some goods may go nearly out of reach if their *relative* prices rise. For example, the rise in the relative price of prime cuts of beef over the last 20 years (because of rapidly rising demand as real income has risen) certainly has been dramatic, yet this has not been due to inflation, but rather to a change in relative prices. Even if the overall price level had remained constant, prime cuts of beef would have risen in price. Householders would have found it just as expensive to buy a steak *relative to their overall budget* as they do in today's inflationary world.

The Classical Quantity Theory

The oldest theory of the relation between money and the price level is the **quantity theory of money,** which predicts a proportional relation between the two. This theory, in modernized form, is still with us today.

As a first step in showing the links between the supply of money and the price level, it is necessary to understand why firms and households choose to hold money balances (that is, cash and demand deposits). There is a cost in holding any money balance because the money held could have been used to purchase bonds instead and would then have earned interest as a return. It could, for example, be deposited in a savings account or used to buy a 30-day treasury bill.

The opportunity cost of holding each dollar of money balances in the rate of interest that could have been earned if the money had been used to purchase bonds.

Clearly, then, money will be held only if it provides services to the holders that are at least as valuable as the opportunity cost of holding it.

The total amount of money balances that everyone wishes to hold for all purposes is called the **demand for money.**[3]

THE TRANSACTIONS DEMAND FOR MONEY

The reason for wanting to hold money originally stressed in the quantity theory is the so-called transactions motive. It is still thought to be important, though it is no longer believed to be the only major motive for holding money.

Virtually all transactions in an economy require money. Money is passed from households to firms to pay for the goods and services produced by firms, and money is passed from firms to households to pay for the factor services supplied by households to firms. These transactions force both firms and households to hold money balances called **transactions balances.**[4]

Consider, for example, the balances held because of wage payments. Assume that firms pay wages every Friday and that households spend all their wages on the purchase of goods and services, with the expenditure being spread out evenly over the week. Thus on Friday morning firms must hold balances equal to the weekly wage bill; on Friday afternoon households will hold these balances. During the week households' balances will be drawn down as a result of purchasing goods and services. Over the same period, the balances held by firms will build up as a result of selling goods and services until, on the following Friday morning, firms will again have amassed balances equal to the wage bill that must be met on that day. On the average over the week, firms will hold balances equal to half the wage bill, and so will households; thus total money balances held will be equal to the total weekly wage bill.

The size of these transactions balances depends, therefore, on the size of the wage bill. If the wage bill doubles, either because twice as many people are employed at the same rate or because the same number is employed at twice the wage rate, transactions balances held must also double. The argument has been conducted in terms of the wage bill, but a similar analysis holds for payments for all factor services.

Transactions balances must be held because payments and receipts are not perfectly synchronized. The more often that wages are paid, the more nearly synchronized payments and receipts will be and the smaller will the balance held need to be. Changes in social institutions such as the

---

[3] Notice that the quantity of money is a stock and that the demand for it is a demand for a stock: People wish to hold so many dollars in cash or deposits. This makes the demand for money different from the demand for goods, which is (usually) a flow demand. When we say, for example, that the demand for carrots is 7 million tons, we must say over what time·period this is measured. If we specify "per month," then the demand is to purchase a flow of carrots of 7 million tons each month.

[4] The phrase "transactions balances" is a shorthand way of saying "*transactions* motive for holding money *balances.*" The money itself is not earmarked for a particular purpose. In Chapter 38 we discuss the transactions motive in more detail and introduce other motives considered important in explaining money demand.

pattern of paying bills will thus affect the transactions balances required. Assume—an extreme example—that wages are paid daily instead of weekly. On the average, the total balances required will be equal to the total *daily* wage bill, which is of course only a fraction of the weekly wage bill, and thus a change to a shorter pay period should lead to a lower transactions demand for money.

A change in the pay period is only one example of an institutional change that can alter the transactions demand for money. A current example is the growth of short-term money substitutes such as credit cards. With short-term consumer credit you can come much closer to synchronizing your payments with your receipts. If, for example, you can charge all of your purchases and then pay the charge accounts on payday, you do not need transactions balances except during the small interval between receiving your pay and paying your bills.

In most societies perfect synchronization of payments and receipts is not possible and transactions balances must be held. For given social institutions these balances will tend to vary directly with national income measured in current dollars.

ASSUMPTIONS OF THE QUANTITY THEORY

The demand for money. The quantity theory assumes that the demand for money changes directly and in strict proportion to the level of national income—an assumption that is not unreasonable if the transactions demand is the only source of the desire to hold money balances.

To express this assumption in symbolic terms, let M_d stand for the demand for money, let Y stand for real national income, and let P stand for the average price at which goods and services are sold in the markets of the economy.[5] Then we

can write the assumed relationship as

$$M_d = kPY$$

where k is a constant showing desired money balances as a fraction of the value of annual national income. If firms and households hold money balances equal to the value of two weeks' sales and purchases, k would be $1/26$ and the demand for money could be expressed as $M_d = 0.038PY$.

The supply of money. For the moment we assume that the overall quantity of money, M, can be set at any amount desired by the Bank of Canada operating in its capacity as the nation's central bank.[6] Within broad limits, as we shall see in Chapter 37, privately owned banks can exercise considerable control over the money supply. The limits themselves are determined by the central bank, which has the ultimate power to control major changes in the supply of money.

The Demand for Money and Aggregate Demand

The link between money and aggregate demand for commodities is provided in the classical quantity theory by the assumption that when firms and households do not hold the amount of money that they would like to hold, they try to alter their money holdings by altering their expenditures on commodities. If they have more money than they wish to hold, they will raise their expenditures above their receipts so as to spend their unwanted money balances. This raises aggregate demand. If they have less money than they wish to hold, they will cut their spending below their receipts so as to increase their holdings. This lowers aggregate demand.[7]

---

[5] Up to now we have let Y stand for national income without distinguishing money and real income, since we had assumed constant prices. We now relax that assumption and need a more complex notation in which Y is real (constant-dollar) national income and PY is money national income.

[6] The symbol M, used in this chapter to designate the supply of money, was used in earlier chapters to indicate the quantity of imports. However, no confusion should arise since the context will make clear which usage is intended.

[7] One important difference between the classical quantity theory and modern theories is this link between money and aggregate demand. Modern quantity theorists, along with other modern economists, recognize that the link will usually be indirect—from money to interest rates to expenditure—rather than direct from money to expenditure. This is developed in more detail in Chapter 38.

The Quantity Theory of Money and the Velocity of Circulation

The basic quantity theory of money can be set out formally in terms of the following four equations. Equation 1 states that the demand for money balances depends upon the value of transactions as measured by nominal income, given by the product $P \cdot Y$.

$$M_d = kPY \tag{1}$$

Equation 2 states that the supply of money is a given, M, set by the central bank at whatever level it desires.

$$M_s = M \tag{2}$$

Equation 3 states the equilibrium condition that the demand for money must equal its supply.

$$M_d = M_s \tag{3}$$

Substitution produces the basic relation among P, M, and Y as shown in equation 4.

$$M = kPY \tag{4}$$

National income, PY, is proportional to the money supply, as shown by the aggregate demand curve in Figure 35-3.

The original form of the Classical quantity theory assumes that k is a constant given by the transactions demand for money and that Y is constant because full employment is maintained. Thus M and P move proportionally; see Figure 35-4. Increases or decreases in the money supply lead to proportional increases or decreases in prices.

Often the quantity theory is presented using the concept of the velocity of circulation, V, instead of the proportion of the money income that people wish to hold in cash, k. The **veloc-ity of circulation** is defined as national income divided by the quantity of money, as given in equation 5.

$$V = PY/M \tag{5}$$

Rearranging, the quantity theory can be written in terms of the equation of exchange, equation 6.

$$MV = PY \tag{6}$$

Velocity may be interpreted as showing the average amount of "work" done by a unit of money while acting as a medium of exchange for the transactions that produce the country's national income. Thus, if the annual national income is $1,200 billion and the stock of money is $300 billion, then each dollar's worth of money is used on average four times to effect the exchanges required in producing national income.

Fortunately, there is a simple relation between k and V. One is the reciprocal of the other, as may be seen immediately by comparing equations 4 and 6. Thus it makes no difference whether we choose to work with k or V. An example may help to illustrate the interpretation of each. Assume that the stock of money people wish to hold is equal to one-fifth of the value of total transactions. Thus k is 0.2 and V, the reciprocal of k, is 5. This indicates that if the money supply is to be one-fifth of the value of annual transactions, the average unit of money must account for $5 worth of transactions—that is, each dollar must be used on average 5 times in order to bring about an aggregate value of national income 5 times as large as the stock of money.

When firms and households hold cash balances just equal to their desired holdings—that is, when the actual supply of money equals the demand for money—money national income must be at that level which multiplied by k yields the actual money supply. In the example above, if firms and households held money balances equal to the value of two weeks' sales and purchases, k would be $1/26$ and money national income would be 26 times the money supply. Given the value of k, in equilibrium any particular money supply is said to be able to *support* a particular level of money income.[8]

Rearranging the demand for money equation and setting that demand equal to the actual money supply, we can write

$$PY = M/k$$

Thus, for a given money supply, nominal income is also given. A larger level of real national income can be sustained only if the price level falls to keep the demand for transactions balances constant. This can be interpreted as an aggregate demand relationship. If real output were to increase without a compensating fall in the price level, the demand for money would exceed the existing supply. Households and firms would then reduce expenditure in an attempt to reattain equilibrium in their holdings of money balances. The higher real output will also equal desired expenditure only if the price level falls to maintain money demand equal to money supply. Hence, for a given money supply, the aggregate demand for goods is inversely related to the price level, as illustrated in Figure 35-3.

Changes in the Money Supply

We can now ask how an increase in the money supply would affect aggregate demand. We start from a position where money demand equals the initial money supply; at that value of prices and real income, households and firms will not wish to hold the additional money, and hence they will try to spend it. The increase in the money supply thus causes the aggregate demand curve to shift upward and to the right, as shown in Figure 35-4. Along the new aggregate demand curve nominal income (PY) is constant at a new higher level such that firms and households are willing to hold the increased money supply.

[8] In the language of the box, a given value of k means a given velocity of circulation, so that a particular money supply is consistent with only a certain amount of transactions.

FIGURE 35-3
The Classical Quantity Theory and Aggregate Demand

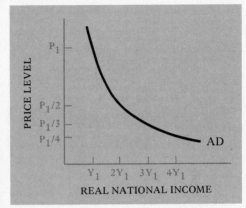

The classical quantity theory implies an aggregate demand curve that slopes downward to the right when drawn for a given stock of money. Given the transactions demand for money, $M_d = kPY$, nominal income (the product PY) must be constant if the money supply is constant. Real output is measured on the horizontal axis. Each increase in real output can be sustained only if the price level falls proportionately. If the price level does not fall, households and firms will desire money balances in excess of the existing supply, and they will reduce expenditure below income in order to accumulate new money balances. The resulting aggregate demand curve, a rectangular hyperbola, exhibits unitary elasticity of demand.

MONEY, PRICES, AND OUTPUT IN THE CLASSICAL QUANTITY THEORY

We have seen that in the classical quantity theory, an increase in the money supply leads to an increase in aggregate demand. In order to determine the individual effect on output and the price level, aggregate supply must be specified.

Assume for the moment, as did most economists of 70 years ago, that full employment is the natural state of the economy, that any lapses from this state will be temporary and self-correcting, and that full-employment income, Y_F, changes only slowly. Total output will thus usually be full-employment output and the aggregate supply curve will be vertical, as in Figure 35-4.

FIGURE 35-4
The Effects of an Increase in the Money Supply

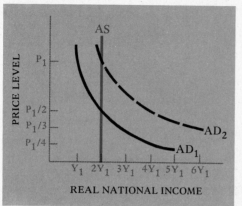

An increase in the money supply leads to a proportional increase in aggregate demand. For monetary equilibrium, an increase in the money supply must be matched by an equal increase in the demand for money. For this to happen we require an equal increase in the product PY. In the diagram, the product PY along the dashed line AD_2 is double that along the solid line AD_1 and hence corresponds to a doubled money supply. If output is fixed at its full-employment level, $2Y_1$ say, as shown by the colored vertical line AS, then the doubling of the money supply will lead to a doubling of the price level, from $P_1/2$ to P_1.

In such a situation, changes in aggregate demand cannot cause changes in total output. If quantity produced is constant at the full-employment level, variations in aggregate demand can cause variations only in prices. If there is excess aggregate demand, prices must rise until the money value of aggregate output is made equal to aggregate demand measured in money terms. If aggregate demand is not sufficient to purchase full-employment output valued at existing prices, the price level will fall until once again the value of total output is equal to the value of aggregate demand.

Now suppose that in this sort of situation there is an increase in the supply of money. Firms and households do not wish to hold this additional money, so they spend it. This adds to aggregate demand at full employment and bids up prices. As prices rise, more money is required for transactions purposes. Eventually the price rise will be sufficient so that all of the extra money will be absorbed into transactions balances. When this happens, aggregate desired expenditure will no longer exceed income and the pressure for further price rises will be gone.

Now assume a drastic fall in the money supply. According to the quantity theory, firms and households will try to cut their spending in order to build up their holdings of cash. This reduces aggregate demand below income and in turn causes prices to fall (assuming output remains at the full-employment level). As prices fall, smaller transactions balances are required. Eventually prices will fall sufficiently so that the existing supply of money will be enough to satisfy everyone's transactions needs. People will then no longer be trying to hold their spending below their income in order to add to their cash balances, and the downward pressure on prices will cease.

The classical quantity theory predicts a positive relationship between the price level and the money supply.

Given the assumption that both K and Y are constant, the predicted relationship is one of *proportionality*. [44] Since real income does not change in response to changes in the money supply, the real value of money balances is constant (at a value equal to kY), and changes in the nominal money supply lead to equal percentage changes in the price level.

Many economists believe that this is a valid description of the relationship between money, prices, and output in the very long run. In trying to explain the difference between the current price level and that prevailing, say a century ago, they would first look to changes in the money supply. But few economists think of the classical quantity theory as being applicable to the relationship between money, prices, and output over periods as short as a month or even a year or two. This is so for two reasons. First, the aggregate supply curve is not likely to be vertical (at least in the short run), so monetary induced fluctuations in aggregate demand lead to fluctuations in the price level *and* output.[9] Second, k is likely to vary significantly in the short run, thereby making the relationship between the money supply and aggregate demand much less simple than the classical quantity theory suggests.

A more general view of the role of money in the economy, one that is in accord with modern economics and that takes these two factors into account, is developed beginning in Chapter 38. First, however, we discuss in the next two chapters some international and domestic institutional aspects of money.

Summary

1. Traditionally in economics, money has referred to any generally accepted medium of exchange. A number of functions of money may, however, be distinguished—the major ones are the medium of exchange, the store of value, and the unit of account.

2. Money arose because of the inconvenience of barter, and it developed in stages from precious metal to metal coinage, to paper money convertible to precious metal, to token coinage and paper money fractionally backed by precious metals, to fiat money, and to deposit money. Societies have shown great sophistication in developing monetary instruments to meet their needs.

3. Today there is debate about what constitutes money. Concentrating on the medium-of-exchange function, money is restricted to notes, coins, and deposits subject to transfer by cheque. It is difficult, however, to separate the medium-of-exchange function from the function of providing a temporary store of purchasing power between the selling and the buying of goods. Any readily salable asset that has a secure capital value can be a satisfactory store of purchasing power. In an inflationary world, any asset that does not increase in value will be a poor store of value. When the asset earns an interest return, it has an advantage over cash and demand deposits (as long as the interest earned exceeds the costs and trouble of transferring into and out of the asset).

4. The question of what is money is further complicated by the existence of money substitutes. For example, credit cards allow purchases and sales to be made without the use of currency or cheques. While credit cards substitute for money at the time of purchase, the accounts must eventually be settled using money.

5. Early economic theory regarded the economy as being divided into a real part and a money part. The real part was concerned with production, the allocation of resources, and the distribution of income—determined only by relative prices. The monetary part merely determined the level of prices at which real transactions took place. This was determined by the quantity of money. Double the quantity of money, and in the new equilibrium all money prices would double but relative prices and the entire real sector would be left unaffected.

6. Inflation has been a common but by no means constant state of affairs in world history. Although inflation is widespread in the world today, the rate of inflation varies greatly from country to country.

7. Three of the major effects of unanticipated inflations are (1) to influence the allocation of resources and the distribution of income by haphazardly changing relative prices and wages, (2) to influence the real outcome of borrowing and lending agreements and other contracts expressed in money terms, and (3) to reduce the living standards of people living on fixed incomes. Some but not all of these adverse effects may

---

[9] If output rises so that the demand for money in real terms rises, the price level need not change in proportion to the money supply.

be avoided if the rate of inflation is accurately anticipated.

8. The quantity theory of money provided early economists with the link between the money supply and the price level. They assumed that the transactions motive was the sole source of the demand for money — and that the demand for money was directly proportional to the level of national income.

9. Other assumptions of the quantity theory were that the supply of money was determined by the central bank and that when households and firms have more (or less) money than they wish, they increase (or decrease) their expenditures on goods and services to restore the desired money balances. An increase in the money supply leads to an increase in aggregate demand; a decrease in the money supply leads to a decrease in aggregate demand. Given full employment (which the classical economists assumed to be the natural state of affairs), changes in the money supply lead to proportional changes in the price level with no changes in real output.

Topics for Review

Functions of money
Gresham's.law
The gold standard and convertible money
Fully backed, fractionally backed, and fiat money
Legal tender
Deposit money and the use of cheques
Demand and time deposits
Near money and money substitutes
Real and monetary parts of the economy
Effects of anticipated and unanticipated inflations
The classical quantity theory of money
The modified quantity theory

Discussion Questions

1. "For the love of money is the root of all evil" (I Timothy 6:10). If a nation were to become a theocracy and money were made illegal, would you expect the level of national income to be affected? How about the productivity of labor? Might classical economists have answered this question differently than modern ones?

2. Which of the following groups, if any, might be expected to *benefit* from a rapid unforeseen inflation: (a) landlords, (b) storekeepers with large inventories, (c) printers of price lists, (d) homeowners with mortgages, (e) old-age pensioners, (f) tenants, (g) a government whose tax revenue comes mostly from a progressive income tax, (h) bondholders.

3. Consider each of the following with respect to its potential use as a medium of exchange, a store of value, and a unit of account. Which would you think might be regarded as money? (a) a $100 Bank of Canada note, (b) an American Express credit card, (c) a painting by Picasso, (d) one share of Bell Canada stock, (e) a Government of Canada bond payable in three months, (f) a savings account at Montreal Trust, (g) a lifetime pass to Montreal Canadiens hockey games.

4. We often read that money serves three purposes: (a) as a medium of exchange, (b) as a unit of account, and (c) as a store of value. Does something that serves as a country's medium of exchange necessarily serve as a unit of account? Is any one of the three absolutely essential?

5. When in 1976 the Austrian government minted a new 1,000 schilling gold coin — worth $59 face value — the one-inch diameter coin came into great demand among jewelers and coin collectors. By law, the number of such coins to be minted each year is limited. Lines of people eager to get the coins formed outside the government mint and local banks.

   "There is exceptional interest in the new coin," said a Viennese banker. "It's a numismatic hit and a financial success." It has disappeared from circulation, however. Explain why.

6. In Canada, American and Canadian coins often circulate side by side, exchanging at their face values, even though notes often are of unequal value. Someone who receives a U.S. coin has the option of spending it at face value or taking it to the bank and converting it to Canadian money at the going rate of exchange. When the rate of exchange was near "par," so that $1 Canadian was within plus or minus 3¢ of $1 U.S., the two monies circulated side by side. When the Canadian dollar fell to $0.83 U.S., predict which money disappeared from circulation according to Gresham's law. Why did a 2¢ differential not produce this result?

7. Some years ago a strike closed all banks in Ireland for several months. What do you think happened to

money, near money, and money substitutes during the period?

8. During hyperinflations in several foreign countries after World War II, American cigarettes were sometimes used in place of money. What made them suitable?

9. During inflations, money is not a perfect store of value and many people seek to buy other assets better suited to that purpose. From January 1979 to March 1980, the purchasing power of the Canadian dollar declined by 14 percent. In January 1979 silver was selling for about U.S. $10 an ounce and gold for U.S. $270 an ounce. In March 1980 an ounce of silver sold for U.S. $20 and gold for U.S. $480 an ounce. Are gold and silver better stores of value than dollars? Before you answer, you should take into account the fact that silver reached U.S. $50 an ounce and gold U.S. $950 in January 1980.

10. Take some five-year period during the last ten years and (using library sources) calculate which of the following was the best store of value over that period: (a) the dollar, (b) the Dow Jones industrial average, (c) gold, (d) a Quebec Hydro bond. How confident are you that the one that was the best store of value over those five years will be the best over the *next* 18 months?

International Monetary Systems

36

We have seen, in the context of a single economy, that money serves as a medium of exchange, a unit of account, and a store of value. It is an asset that can be held to bridge the gap between receipts and expenditures, one that eliminates the need for trade in the form of direct barter. At the international level there is an analogous role for money in facilitating international flows of goods and factors. For example, there is the need for a medium of exchange that countries can accumulate when their balance of payments shows a surplus and can run down when there is a deficit.

The nations of the world have tried several different systems of international monetary management. No system has been fully satisfactory, and periods of crisis have alternated with periods of stability. Changes have usually occurred during or after a crisis. The gold standard, the Breton Woods system, the International Monetary Fund, the Smithsonian agreements, the European snake—all are part of the history of the international monetary systems of the twentieth century.

The issues involved in determining whether and how well international payments schemes work affect ordinary citizens and their standard of living even though the issues are understood by only a small number of international traders, bankers, financiers, and economists. In this chapter we review the principal systems and indicate when and why they ran into trouble. Our study is of more than historical interest, for the realization of our hope for a better, more smoothly functioning system than we have today lies in learning the lessons of the historical experience.

The century began with a system of fixed exchange rates under the gold standard which encountered periodic crises in the post-World War I years but did not collapse until the onset of the Great Depression. The 1930s were a period of unsuccessful experimentation with flexible, market-determined exchange rates. This phase was ended by World War II, when governments fixed exchange rates and managed international payments with the successful waging of war as their main policy objective.

In 1944 an era of fixed exchange rates in peacetime was again instituted, this time by international agreement at a conference in Bretton Woods, New Hampshire. The system lasted for over a quarter of a century, until its shortcomings and periods of crisis seemed to prevail over its advantages and periods of stability. After several attempts to patch up the system in the 1970s, it finally broke down and was abandoned as countries turned one by one to market-determined, flexible exchange rates.

Neither the fixed rates of the gold standard or the Bretton Woods system nor the flexible rates of the 1930s or the 1970s have avoided problems. Yet they had different problems, and it is worth examining each of the major episodes.

Before World War II

THE GOLD STANDARD IN THEORY

The gold standard was not *designed*. Like the price system, it just happened. It arose out of the general acceptance of gold as the commodity to be used as money. In most countries, paper currency was freely convertible into gold at a fixed rate.

The gold standard is an example of a fixed exchange rate system. Rates of exchange between the standard units of currency of various countries were fixed by their values in terms of the standard unit, gold. In 1914 the U.S. dollar

was covertible into .053 standard ounces of gold, while the British pound sterling was convertible into .257 standard ounces. This meant that the pound was worth 4.86 times as much as the dollar in terms of gold, thus making one pound worth U.S. $4.86. (In practice, the exchange rate fluctuated within narrow limits set by the cost of shipping gold.)

As long as all countries were on the gold standard, a person in any one country could be sure of being able to make payments to a person in any other country. Someone who was unable to buy or sell claims to the foreign currencies on the foreign exchange market could always convert currency into gold and then ship the gold.

The Gold Flow, Price Level Mechanism

The gold standard was supposed to work to maintain a balance of international payments by forcing adjustments in price levels within individual countries. Consider a country that had a balance-of-payments deficit because the value of what its citizens were importing (i.e., buying) from other countries exceeded the value of what they were exporting (i.e., selling) to other countries. The demand for foreign exchange would exceed the supply on this country's foreign exchange market. Some people who wished to make foreign payments would be unable to obtain foreign exchange. No matter; they would merely convert their domestic currency into gold and ship the gold. Therefore, some people in a surplus country would secure gold in payment for exports. They would deposit this to their credit and accept claims on gold—in terms of convertible paper money or bank deposits—in return. Thus deficit countries would be losing gold while surplus countries would be gaining it.

Under the gold standard, the whole money supply was linked to the supply of gold (see pages 705–707). The international movements of gold would therefore lead to a fall in the money supply in the deficit country and a rise in the surplus country. If full employment prevails, changes in the domestic money supply—according to the classical quantity theory studied in the previous chapter—will cause changes in domestic price levels. Deficit countries would thus have falling price levels while surplus countries would have rising price levels. The exports of deficit countries would become relatively cheaper, while those of surplus countries would become relatively more expensive. The resulting changes in quantities bought and sold would move the balance of payments toward an equilibrium position.

ACTUAL EXPERIENCE OF THE GOLD STANDARD

The half century before World War I was the heyday of the gold standard; during this relatively trouble-free period, the automatic mechanism seemed to work well. Subsequent research has suggested, however, that the gold standard succeeded during the period mainly because it was not called on to do much work. Trade flowed between nations in large and rapidly expanding volume, and it is probable that existing exchange rates and price levels were never far from the equilibrium ones. No major trading country found itself with a serious and persistent balance-of-payments deficit, so no major country was called upon to restore equilibrium through a large change in its domestic price level.

Inevitably there were short-run fluctuations, but they were ironed out either by movements of short-run capital in response to changes in interest rates or by changes in national income and employment.

Problems in the 1920s

In the 1920s the gold standard was called on to do a major job. It failed utterly, and it was abandoned. How did this come about? During World War I, most belligerent countries had suspended convertibility of currency (i.e., they went off the gold standard). Most countries suffered major

inflations, but the degree of inflation differed from country to country. As we have seen, this will lead to changes in the equilibrium exchange rates.

After the war, countries returned to the gold standard (i.e., they restored convertibility of their currencies into gold). For reasons of prestige, many insisted on returning at the prewar rates. This meant that some countries' goods were overpriced and others' underpriced. Large deficits and surpluses in the balance of payments inevitably appeared, and the adjustment mechanism required that price levels should change in each of the countries in order to restore equilibrium. Exchange rates were not adjusted, and price levels changed very slowly. By the onset of the Great Depression, equilibrium price levels had not yet been attained. The financial chaos brought on by the Depression destroyed the existing payments system.

Major Disabilities of a Gold Standard

While inflationary policies combined with an overly rigid adherence to pre-World War I exchange rates led to the downfall of the gold standard, one may ask whether an altered gold standard, based on more realistic exchange rates, might not have succeeded. While some modern economists, notably Robert Mundell of Columbia University, think it would, most believe the gold standard suffered from key disabilities.

Like any other fixed exchange rate system, it required a mechanism for orderly adjustment to changes in the supply and demand for a nation's currency. The price adjustment process worked too slowly and too imperfectly to cope with large and persistent disequilibrium.

Furthermore, gold as the basis for an international money supply suffered several special disadvantages. They included a limited supply that could not be expanded as rapidly as increases in the volume of world trade required, an uneven distribution of existing and potential new gold supplies among the nations of the world, and a large and frequently volatile speculative demand for gold during periods of crisis. These factors could cause large, disruptive variations in the supply of gold available for international monetary purposes.

THE 1930s: EXPERIMENTATION WITH FLUCTUATING RATES

It is doubtful that any fixed exchange rate system could have survived the Great Depression, for the changes in the demand and supply of foreign exchange were large and sudden. The speculative demand for gold rose sharply, as it always does during periods of major uncertainty, and one by one nations simply suspended convertibility of their currencies into gold, thereby abandoning gold as the medium of exchange at home and abroad.

Following the abandonment of the gold standard, various experiments were tried with both fixed and fluctuating rates. Often a rate would be allowed to fluctuate on the free market until it had reached what looked like equilibrium, and then it would be fixed at that level. Sometimes, as with the British pound, the rate was left to be determined by a free market throughout the period.

But the overriding feature of the decade was that considerations of massive unemployment came to dominate economic policies in virtually every country, and all devices, including exchange rate manipulations, seemed fair game for dealing with them. Many governments adopted policies that were acts of desperation and that made long-term sense only if other countries were not also in crisis. They tended not to consider the long-term effects on trade, or on their trading partners, of the policies they adopted, hoping to gain short-term advantages before their policies provoked the inevitable reaction from others.

The use of devaluations to improve domestic unemployment rested on a simple and superficially plausible line of analysis: if a country has unemployed workers at home, why not substitute home production for imports and thus give jobs to one's own citizens instead of to foreigners? One way to do this is to urge people to "buy Canadian." Another, probably more effective way is to lower the prices of domestic goods relative to those of imports. The devaluation of one's currency does this by making foreign goods that much more expensive. (A 10 percent devaluation, *ceteris paribus,* means that it will take 10 percent more domestic money to buy the same imports; this is equivalent to a 10 percent rise in the prices of all foreign goods.)

Of course, if this policy works, other countries will find *their* exports falling and unemployment rising as a consequence. Because such policies attempt to solve one country's problems by inflicting them on others, they are called **beggar-my-neighbor policies** and are sometimes described as attempts to "export one's unemployment."

In a situation of inadequate world demand, a beggar-my-neighbor policy on the part of one country can work only in the unlikely event that other countries do not try to protect themselves. A situation in which all countries devalue their currencies in an attempt to gain a competitive advantage over one another is called a situation of **competitive devaluations.**

Precisely this happened during the 1930s. One country would devalue its currency in an attempt to reduce its imports and stimulate exports. But because other countries suffered the same kinds of problems of unemployment, they did not sit idly by. Retaliation was swift, and devaluation followed devaluation.

The effect was both futile and perverse, futile because the simultaneous attempts of all countries to cut imports without suffering a comparable cut in exports is bound to be self-defeating.

When unemployment is due to insufficient world aggregate demand, it cannot be cured by measures designed to redistribute among nations the fixed and inadequate total of demand.

And it was perverse because the net effect of restrictions on trade was to decrease the volume of trade and thereby sacrifice the gains from trade without raising worldwide employment.[1]

These policies, along with other restrictive trade policies such as import duties, export subsidies, quotas, and prohibitions, led to a declining volume of world trade and brought no relief from the worldwide depression. Moreover, they contributed to a loss of faith in the economic system and in the ability of either economists or politicians to cope with economic crises.

The Rise and Fall of the Bretton Woods System, 1944–1972

The one lesson that everyone thought had been learned from the competitive devaluations of the 1930s was that neither a system of freely fluctuating exchange rates nor a system of fixed rates with easily accomplished devaluations could prevent disaster in international affairs. In order to achieve a system of orderly exchange rates that would be conducive to the free flow of trade following World War II, representatives of most countries that had participated in the alliance against Germany, Italy, and Japan convened to agree on a system of international payments for the postwar world. The international monetary system that developed out of the agreements reached at Bretton Woods consisted of a large body of rules and understandings for the regulation of international transactions and payments imbalances.

The object of the Bretton Woods system was to create a set of rules that would maintain fixed exchange rates in the face of short-term fluctuations; to guarantee that changes in exchange rates would occur only in the face of long-term, persistent deficits or surpluses in the balance of payments; and to ensure that when such changes did occur they would not spark a series of competitive devaluations.

The basic characteristic of the Bretton Woods system was that U.S. dollars held by foreign monetary authorities were made directly convertible into gold at a fixed price (of approximately $35 an ounce) by the U.S. government while foreign governments fixed the prices at which their currencies were convertible into U.S. dollars. It was this characteristic that made the system a **gold exchange standard:** gold was the ultimate reserve, but the currencies were held as reserves because directly or indirectly they could be *exchanged* for gold.

The rate at which each country's currency was convertible into dollars was pegged. The pegged rate could be changed from time to time in the face of a "fundamental disequilibrium" in the balance of payments. A system with a rate that is pegged against short-term fluctuations but that can be adjusted from time to time is called an **adjustable peg system.**

In order to maintain convertibility of their currencies at fixed exchange rates, the monetary authorities of each country had to be ready to buy and sell their currency in foreign exchange markets to offset imbalances in demand and supply at the pegged rates.[2]

In order to be able to support the exchange market by buying domestic currency, the monetary authorities had to have reserves of acceptable foreign exchange to offer in return. In the Bretton Woods system, the authorities held reserves of gold and claims on key currencies—mainly the American dollar and the British pound sterling. When a country's currency was in excess supply, its authorities would sell dol-

---

[1] It was perverse in a second way as well. Under a paper currency system, a simultaneous equal devaluation of all currencies would have no effect, beneficial or harmful. If all countries devalue their currencies in the same proportion, they will all be right back where they started, with no change in the relative prices of goods from any country and hence no change in relative prices from the original situation. In a gold standard world such as existed at the start of the 1930s, however, each country devalues by lowering the gold content of its currency. Thus a full round of competitive devaluations of X percent leaves relative exchange rates unchanged, but it raises the price of gold (measured in all currencies) by X percent. The effect of this is to enrich those producing gold and those holding stocks of it and thus to increase their claims on the world's output.

[2] The exchange rates were not quite fixed; they were permitted to vary by 1 percent on either side of their par values. Later the bands of permitted fluctuation were widened to 2.25 percent on either side of par.

lars, sterling, or gold. When a country's currency was in excess demand, its authorities would buy dollars or sterling. If they then wished to increase their gold reserves, they would use the dollars to purchase gold from the United States, thereby depleting the U.S. gold stock.

The problem for the United States was to have enough gold to maintain fixed-price convertibility of the dollar into gold as demanded by foreign monetary authorities. The problem for all other countries was to maintain convertibility (on a restricted or unrestricted basis, depending on the country in question) between their currency and the U.S. dollar at a fixed rate of exchange.

The Bretton Woods international payments system was an adjustable peg, gold exchange standard where the ultimate international money was gold. Countries held much of their exchange reserves in the form of U.S. dollars, which they could convert into gold, and British pounds sterling, which they could convert into dollars.

THE INTERNATIONAL MONETARY FUND

The International Monetary Fund (also called the IMF and the Fund) was created to manage the system. It had several tasks. First, it tried to ensure that countries kept their exchange rates pegged in the short run. Second, it made loans—out of funds subscribed by member nations—to governments that needed them to support their exchange rates in the face of temporary payments deficits. Third, the Fund was supposed to consult with countries wishing to alter their exchange rates to ensure that the rate was really being changed to remove a persistent payments disequilibrium and that one devaluation did not set off a self-canceling round of competitive devaluations.

PROBLEMS OF AN ADJUSTABLE PEG SYSTEM

Three major problems of the Bretton Woods system, which will recur with any adjustable peg system, were (1) providing sufficient reserves to iron out short-term fluctuations in international receipts and payments while keeping exchange rates fixed; (2) making adjustments of the rates to long-term trends in receipts and payments; and (3) handling speculative crises.

Since many people advocate a return to an adjustable peg system, it will be worth examining each of these problems to learn what must be guarded against if a similar system were to be adopted.

Reserves to Accommodate Short-term Fluctuations

We have seen that each country's monetary authorities had to be prepared to buy or sell foreign exchange to offset imbalances at the fixed exchange rates. To be able to sell, one must have reserves. Even when the exchange rate is an equilibrium rate over several years, there may be considerable imbalances over shorter periods of time.

The amount of reserves that the authorities hold depends on their estimate of the maximum amount of foreign exchange they might have to sell to stabilize the exchange rate in the face of a particularly unfavorable period of excess demand. If the authorities run out of reserves, they cannot maintain the pegged rate, so they will want to hold some safety margin over the maximum they expect to use. It is generally believed that the absolute size of any gap they may have to fill with their own foreign exchange sales will increase as the volume of international payments increases.

Since there was a strong upward trend in the volume of overall international payments, there was also a strong upward trend in the demand for foreign exchange reserves.

The crisis in gold reserves. The ultimate reserve in the Bretton Woods gold exchange standard was gold. The use of gold as a reserve caused two serious problems during the 1960s and early 1970s. First, the world's supply of monetary gold did not grow fast enough to provide adequate reserves for an expanding volume of trade. During the 1960s, as a result of a fixed price of gold, rising costs of production, and rising commercial uses, the world's stock of monetary gold was rising at less than 2 percent per year while trade was growing at nearly 10 percent per year. Gold, which had been 66 percent of the total monetary reserves in 1959, was only 40 percent in 1970 and had fallen to 30 percent by 1972; over this period, reserve holdings of dollars and sterling rose sharply. Clearly, the gold backing needed to maintain convertibility of these currencies was becoming increasingly inadequate.

Second, the country whose currency is convertible into gold must maintain sufficient reserves to ensure convertibility. During the 1960s the United States lost substantial gold reserves to other countries that had acquired dollar claims through their balance-of-payments surpluses with the United States. By the late 1960s the loss of U.S. reserves had been sufficiently large to undermine confidence in America's continued ability to maintain dollar convertibility.

By 1970 there was an inadequate world supply of gold for monetary uses, and the United States had too small a proportion of the supply that did exist.

Problems for nations whose currency is held as a reserve. Under the Bretton Woods system the supply of gold was augmented by reserves of key currencies, the U.S. dollar and the British pound sterling. Because the need for reserves expanded much more rapidly than the gold stock in the period since World War II, the system required nations to hold an increasing fraction of their reserves in dollars and sterling. They would be willing to do this only as long as they had confidence in the convertibility of these currencies, but maintaining confidence was made difficult by a continually declining percentage of gold backing for the dollar.

While it is prestigious to have one's currency held as a reserve currency — and even advantageous as long as other countries are willing to increase their holdings of one's paper money without making claims on current output — there are both disadvantages and hazards for the country whose currency is involved.

Such a country is placed under great pressure not to devalue its currency. If it does devalue, owing to a severe balance-of-payments deficit, all countries holding that currency will find the value of their reserves diminished. If it tries to avoid devaluation, the fear that it may be unable to do so will impair the usefulness of the currency as a reserve because other countries will become reluctant to hold it.

The result may well be that too much of the domestic policy of the country whose currency is the reserve becomes subservient to the overriding need to maintain its exchange rate and its gold reserves. These considerations make it more difficult for the country to deal with its own unemployment and inflation. This was the case of Britain throughout much of the Bretton Woods era and of the United States during the early seventies.

Search for a new type of reserves. The desire to provide a supplementary reserve not tied to the currency of a particular country led to the development in 1969 of **special drawing rights** (SDRs) at the IMF. SDRs were designed to provide a supplement to existing reserve assets by setting up a Special Drawing Account kept separate from all other operations of the Fund. Each member country of the Fund was assigned an SDR quota that was guaranteed in terms of a fixed gold value and that it could use to acquire an equivalent amount of convertible currencies from other participants. SDRs could be used without prior consultation with the Fund, but only to cope with balance-of-payments difficulties.

SDRs might have gone a long way toward alleviating the system's difficulties if the system had not been overwhelmed by much more fundamental problems in the early 1970s. In any case SDRs have outlasted the Bretton Woods system that they were first designed to assist.

Adjusting to Long-term Disequilibria

The second characteristic problem of a fixed rate system is the adjustment to changing trends in trade. With fixed exchange rates, long-term disequilibria (what the IMF used to call *fundamental disequilibria*) can be expected to develop because of secular shifts in the demands for and supplies of foreign exchange.

There are three important long-term causes of shifts in demands and supplies in the foreign exchange market. First, different trading countries have different rates of inflation. Persistent differences will cause continuing changes in the equilibrium rates of exchange, as we saw earlier. If exchange rates are maintained at a fixed level, this will inevitably lead to cumulating excess demands or supplies of particular currencies. Second, changes in the demands for and supplies of imports and exports are associated with long-term economic growth. Because different countries grow at different rates, their demands for imports and their supplies of exports would be expected to be shifting at different rates. Third, structural changes, such as major new innovations or a rise in the price of oil, cause major changes in the pattern and balance of imports and exports among nations.

The associated shifts in demand and supply on the foreign exchange market imply that, even when starting from a current account equilibrium with imports equal to exports at a given rate of exchange, there is no reason to believe that equilibrium will exist at the same rate of exchange 10 or 20 years later (any more than equilibrium relative prices would be expected to remain unchanged over 20 years within any one country).

The rate of exchange that will lead to a balance-of-payments equilibrium will tend to change over time; over a decade the change can be substantial.

Governments may react to long-term disequilibria in at least three ways.

1. The exchange rate can be changed whenever it is clear that a balance-of-payments deficit or surplus is a result of a long-term shift in the demands and supplies in the foreign exchange market, rather than the result of some transient factor. This was the solution envisaged by the framers of the IMF when they allowed member countries, after consultation with the IMF, to change their exchange rates in the face of a "fundamental disequilibrium." During the period of the Bretton Woods system, there were three major rounds of exchange rate adjustments. The first two were led by a devaluation of sterling, the second of the world's two reserve currencies; the third round was led by the devaluation of the U.S. dollar in December 1971.

2. Domestic price levels can be allowed to change in an attempt to establish an equilibrium set of international prices. Changes in domestic price levels have all sorts of domestic repercussions (e.g., reductions in aggregate demand intended to lower the price level are more likely to raise unemployment than to lower prices), and one should have expected governments to be more willing to change exchange rates—which can be done by a stroke of a pen—than to try to change the price level. A deflation is difficult to accomplish, while an inflation is thought to be accompanied by undesirable side effects.

3. Restrictions can be imposed on trade and foreign payments. Imports and foreign spending by tourists and governments can be restricted, and the export of capital can be slowed or even stopped. Surplus countries were often quick to criticize such restrictions on international trade and payments. As long as exchange rates were fixed and price levels proved difficult to manipulate, the deficit countries had little option but to restrict the quantity of foreign exchange their residents were permitted to obtain so as to equate it to the quantity available.

Speculative Crises

The third characteristic problem of a fixed rate system is the handling of speculation in the foreign exchange market. When enough people begin to doubt the ability of the central authorities to maintain the current rate, speculative crises develop. The most important reason for such crises is that equilibrium exchange rates change, and over time they tend to get further and further away from any given set of fixed rates. When the disequilibrium becomes obvious to everyone, traders and speculators come to believe that a realignment of rates cannot long be delayed. Since the *direction* of required adjustments is not in doubt, speculators can earn large profits with virtually no risk. If somehow changes in rates are not made, all they will lose is the interest on their money.

At such a time there will be a rush to buy currencies expected to be revalued and a rush to sell currencies expected to be devalued. Even when the authorities take dramatic steps to remove the payments deficit, there may be doubt as to whether these measures will work before the exchange reserves are exhausted. Speculative flows of funds can reach very large proportions, and it may be impossible to avoid changing the exchange rate under such pressure.

Speculative crises are one of the most intractable problems of any adjustable peg system. The impact of such crises might be reduced if governments had more adequate reserves. When a speculative crisis precedes an exchange rate adjustment, however, more adequate reserves may just mean that speculators will make larger profits since more of them will be able to sell the currency about to be devalued and to buy the currency about to be revalued before the monetary authorities are forced to act.

During the Bretton Woods period, governments tended to resist changing their exchange rates until they had no alternative. This made the situation so obvious that speculators could hardly lose, and their actions set off the final crises that forced exchange rate readjustments. More frequent and surprise changes made before they had become inevitable might have diminished the occurrence of speculative crises. However, they would have removed the day-to-day certainty associated with the system of fixed exchange rates that was its chief advantage.

Moreover, a surprise change might lead to suspicion that a devaluation was made to gain a competitive advantage for a country's exports rather than to remove a fundamental disequilibrium. After all, governments were not supposed to devalue until it was *clear* that they were faced with a fundamental disequilibrium. If this was clear to them, it was also likely to be clear to ordinary traders and speculators.

COLLAPSE OF THE BRETTON WOODS SYSTEM

The Bretton Woods system worked reasonably well for nearly 20 years. Then it was beset by a series of crises of ever-increasing severity that reflected the system's underlying weaknesses.

Speculation Against the British Pound

Throughout the 1950s and 1960s the British economy was more inflation prone than the U.S. economy, and the British balance of payments was generally in a less satisfactory state. Holders of sterling thus had reason to worry that the British government might not be able to maintain its pledge to keep sterling convertible into dollars at a fixed rate. When these fears grew strong, there would be speculative rushes to sell sterling before it was devalued. The crises in the 1960s were of this kind. By the mid 1960s it was clear to everyone that the pound was seriously overvalued. Finally, in 1967 it was devalued in the midst of a serious speculative crisis. Many other countries with balance-of-payments deficits followed, bringing about the first major round of adjustments in the pegged rates since 1949.

Speculation Against the American Dollar

The U.S. dollar was not devalued in 1967. The lower prices of those currencies that were devalued in 1967 plus the increasing Vietnam War expenditures combined to produce a growing deficit in the American balance of payments. This deficit led to the belief that the dollar itself was becoming seriously overvalued. People rushed to buy gold because a devaluation of the U.S. dollar would take the form of raising its gold price.[3]

The first break in the Bretton Woods system came when the major trading countries were forced to stop pegging the free-market price of gold. Speculative pressure to buy gold could not be resisted, and the market price was allowed to go free in 1968. From that point there were two prices of gold: one was the official price at which monetary authorities could settle their debts with each other by transferring gold; the other was the free-market price, determined by the forces of private demand and supply independent of any intervention by central banks. The free-market price quickly rose far above the official U.S. price of $35 an ounce.

Once the free-market price of gold was allowed to be determined independently of the official price, speculation against the dollar shifted to those currencies that were clearly undervalued relative to the dollar.[4] The German mark and the Japanese yen were particularly popular targets, and during periods of crisis billions and billions of dollars flowed into speculative holdings of these currencies. The ability of central banks to maintain pegged exchange rates in the face of such vast flights of funds was in question; on several occasions all exchange markets had to be closed for periods of up to a week.

Devaluation of the American Dollar

The need for agreement. By 1971 the American authorities had come to the conclusion that

the dollar would have to be devalued. This uncovered a problem, inherent in the Bretton Woods system, that had so far gone virtually unnoted. Because the system required that each foreign country fix its exchange rate against the dollar, the American authorities could not independently fix their exchange rate against other currencies.[5] This system had worked reasonably well while the American price level was relatively stable. Countries that were inflating a bit too fast could occasionally devalue their currencies, and countries that were inflating even more slowly than the United States could occasionally revalue theirs. Occasional upward and downward readjustments relative to the dollar served to keep the system near equilibrium.

But if the United States began to inflate rapidly (or to do anything else that put it in a serious payments deficit with most other countries), it would become necessary to devalue the U.S. dollar relative to most (or even conceivably all) other currencies. Any other country in this situation would merely unilaterally devalue its currency relative to the U.S. dollar. But the only way that the required U.S. devaluation could be brought about was for all other countries to agree to revalue their currencies relative to the dollar.

Under the Bretton Woods system any country other than the United States could devalue its currency by a unilateral decision, but a U.S. devaluation required the cooperation of all countries against whose currency the dollar was to be devalued.

Speculation and negotiated devaluation. Prompted by continuing speculation against the dollar, President Nixon announced the suspension of the gold convertibility of the dollar in August 1971. He also made known the intention of the United States to achieve a de facto devaluation of the dollar by persuading

---

[3] Under a Bretton Woods type of system, the dollar is devalued by raising the official price at which the Fed will convert dollars into gold.

[4] When the free-market price of gold was held the same as the official price, a devaluation of the dollar entailed a rise in the free-market price—and hence profit for all holders of gold. Once the free-market price was left to be determined by the forces of private demand and supply independent of any central bank intervention, there was no reason to believe that a rise in the official price of gold would affect the (much higher) free-market price. Speculators against the dollar then had to hold other currencies whose price was sure to rise against the dollar in the event of the dollar's being devalued.

[5] If, for example, the British authorities pegged the pound sterling at $2.40, as they did in 1967, then the dollar was pegged at £0.417 and the United States could not independently decide on another rate. Similar considerations applied to all other currencies.

those nations whose balance of payments were in surplus to allow their rates to float upward against the dollar.

By ending the gold convertibility of the dollar, the U.S. government brought the gold exchange standard aspect of the Bretton Woods system officially to an end.

The fixed exchange rate aspect of the system lasted a little longer.

The immediate response to the announced intention of devaluing the dollar was a speculative run against that currency. The crisis was so severe that for the second time in the year foreign exchange markets were closed throughout Europe. When the markets reopened after a week, several countries allowed their rates to float. The Japanese, however, announced their intention of retaining their existing rate. In spite of severe Japanese controls, $4 billion in speculative funds managed to find its way into yen in the last two weeks of August, and the Japanese were forced to abandon their fixed rate policy by allowing the yen to float upward.

After some very hard bargaining, an agreement between the major trading nations was signed at the Smithsonian Institution in Washington, D.C., in December 1971. The main element of the agreement was that all countries consented to a 7.9 percent devaluation of the dollar against their currencies.

The De Facto Dollar Standard

Following the Smithsonian agreements, the world was on a de facto **dollar standard.** This arrangement still had fixed exchange rate features as long as the dollar was regarded as a safe and stable currency. Foreign monetary authorities held their reserves in the form of dollars and settled their international debts with dollars. But the dollar was not convertible into gold or anything else. The ultimate value of the dollar was given not by gold but by the American goods, services, and assets that dollars could be used to purchase.

One major problem with such a dollar system

is that the kind of American inflation that upset the Bretton Woods system is no less upsetting to a dollar standard because the real purchasing power value of the world's dollar reserves is eroded by such an inflation.

The Final Breakdown of Fixed Exchange Rates

The Smithsonian agreements did not lead to a new period of international payments stability. This doomed the hope that a de facto dollar standard could provide the basis for an international payments system free of major rounds of crisis and devaluation.

The U.S. inflation continued unchecked, and the U.S. balance of payments never returned to the relatively satisfactory position that had been maintained throughout the 1960s. Within a year of the agreements, speculators began to believe that a further realignment of rates was necessary. In January 1973 heavy speculative movements of capital once again began to occur. In February the United States proposed a further 11 percent devaluation of the dollar. This was to be accomplished by raising the official price of gold to $42.22 an ounce and not keeping other currencies tied to the dollar at the old rates. Needless to say, intense speculative activity followed the announcement.

Five member countries of the European Common Market then decided to stabilize their currencies against each other but to let them float together against the dollar. This joint float was called the **snake.** Norway and Sweden later became associated with this arrangement. The other EEC countries (Ireland, Italy, and the United Kingdom) and Japan announced their intention to allow their currencies to float in value. In June 1972 the Bank of England had abandoned the de facto dollar standard with the announcement that it had "temporarily" abandoned its commitment to support sterling at a fixed par value against the U.S. dollar. The events of 1973 led "temporarily" to become "indefinitely."

Fluctuations in exchange rates were severe.

By early July the snake currencies had appreciated about 30 percent against the dollar, but by the end of the year they had returned nearly to their February values.

The dollar devaluation formally took effect in October 1973. Most industrialized countries maintained the nominal values of their currencies in terms of gold and SDRs, thereby appreciating them in terms of the U.S. dollar by 11 percent. The devaluation quickly became redundant, for in spite of attempts to restore fixed rates, the drift to flexible rates had become irresistible by the end of 1973.

The Present System: Its Nature and Its Problems

A DIRTY FLOAT

By 1974 many industrial countries—Austria, Canada, Italy, Japan, Switzerland, the United Kingdom, and the United States—were no longer maintaining rates for exchange transactions within announced margins, while other industrial countries—Belgium, Denmark, France, Germany, Luxembourg, the Netherlands, Norway, and Sweden—maintained fixed bands for exchange transactions among their currencies but not against the dollar.[6] A large proportion of the remaining countries maintained stable rates of exchange for their currencies in terms of *one* of the three major currencies (the U.S. dollar, pound sterling, or the French franc). This implied that such a country's rate fluctuated against the major currencies to which its national currency was not tied.

Although such exchange rates are determined on the free market, there is nevertheless substantial intervention in these markets by central banks. Central banks try to reduce short-term fluctuations in rates and sometimes try to resist longer-term trends. The difference between the present system and the previous one is that central banks no longer have announced values for their exchange rates (values that they are committed to in advance to defend even at heavy cost). Central banks do not need to say what their targets are; they may change them with complete flexibility as circumstances change. Sometimes they leave the rate completely free from their own intervention while at other times quite heavy intervention occurs with the object of altering the exchange rate from what its value would be on the free market. Such a system is called a **managed float** or a **dirty float.** The rate floats because it is not pegged at any publicly announced par value. The floating rate, however, is managed (or dirty) because the central bank does intervene in the foreign exchange market to influence the rate.

To manage exchange rates, central banks still hold reserves in the form of gold, foreign exchange, and SDRs (see Table 36-1). The relatively fixed stock of monetary gold is an important part of the total. Dollars continue to play a large role in the reserves of many countries. SDRs and reserves at the IMF, while a small

TABLE 36-1
Changing Composition of International Reserves (year-end data)

Type of reserve	Billions of U.S. dollars		Percentage of total	
	1970	1979	1970	1979
Gold[a]	$39.5	$360.1	41.2	57.2
SDRs and reserves at IMF	10.8	24.2	11.3	3.9
Foreign exchange				
U.S. dollars[b]	34.3	154.7	35.9	24.5
All other	11.1	91.0	11.6	14.4
Total reserves	$95.7	$630.0	100.0	100.0

[a] Valued at market prices. The number of ounces of monetary gold was 1.1 billion in 1970, 0.9 billion in 1979.
[b] Official claims on dollars plus identified holdings. This number greatly underestimates foreign total dollar holdings.

The U.S. dollar, though declining in importance, is still a major part of international reserves. The rise in the importance of gold is purely a price effect due to the peak in gold prices reached in 1979 and 1980. The dollar figures do not include vast unofficial holdings of dollars by private persons and firms. The *total* foreign dollar holdings in 1979 was estimated to be above $700 billion.

---

[6] Canada had in fact abandoned fixed exchange rates in June 1970, well before the Smithsonian agreement.

part of the total, raise the possibility that in the future the ultimate real reserve may become the SDR, which is a genuine international paper money. If this happens, the system will have become an "international paper money standard."

The present international monetary system is a dollar standard with managed exchange rate flexibility.

The experiences of the period of managed intervention have been mixed. On the one hand, short-term movements in exchange rates have been more volatile than advocates of flexible rates would perhaps have hoped; on the other, exchange rates have been managed without any rounds of competitive devaluation and have been allowed to change to compensate for substantial national differences in inflation rates.

SURVIVAL OF THE IMF IN A WORLD OF FLOATING EXCHANGE RATES

Although the IMF bitterly resisted the drift toward floating exchange rates, it has now accommodated itself to them and promises to be as effective a means of securing international financial cooperation under a system of managed floating rates as it was under fixed rates.

The changing position of the IMF is illustrated by amendments to its charter that were agreed to in 1976. These amendments, while allowing for the possible return to fixed rates at some possible future date, have legalized floating rates within the framework of the IMF system.

1. With the concurrence of the IMF, any country may adopt a floating exchange rate.
2. The exchange rate management of a floating currency must be subject to IMF surveillance and must not be conducted so as to disadvantage other countries.
3. The agreed practices with respect to floating rates will operate until such time as a general return to par values is attained. If new par values are ever fixed, they will be set in terms of SDRs rather than gold or U.S. dollars.

The acceptance by the IMF of the reality of floating exchange rates is perhaps the best indication that such rates are not a mere transition to a new period of pegged rates.

CURRENT PROBLEMS

The shift from fixed rates to a system of managed flexible rates has not ended the sense of recurring crises in international trade and payments problems—for several reasons.

The Loss of Confidence in the Dollar as a Reserve Currency

Historical background. Balance-of-payments deficits are nothing new to the U.S. economy. In the 1950s and 1960s the United States ran frequent deficits on the sum of current and capital accounts. Much of this was due to American loans, investments, and contributions to other nations who were rebuilding their economies after World War II. As long as other nations were willing to accumulate dollar holdings, this caused no problem; indeed, the buildup of dollars in foreign exchange reserves provided the growth in reserves that was needed to finance the steadily growing volume of world trade.

As Table 36-1 shows, the number of dollars grew sharply over the decade of the 1970s as governments, banks, corporations, and even individuals held dollars without using them to exercise claims on U.S. output. But every dollar held is a potential dollar offered for sale if the holders decide to reduce their holdings.[7]

The effect of the dollar devaluations of the early 1970s. The two devaluations of the dollar in 1971 (7.9 percent) and 1973 (11 percent) automatically reduced the value of the exchange reserves of everyone who held dollars. Had ev-

---

[7] Nor could the American economy expand quickly enough to provide goods should the holders attempt to buy American products. Any attempt to spend these large holdings of dollars would have caused massive inflation in the United States.

FIGURE 36-1
The Decline of the U.S. Dollar During the 1970s

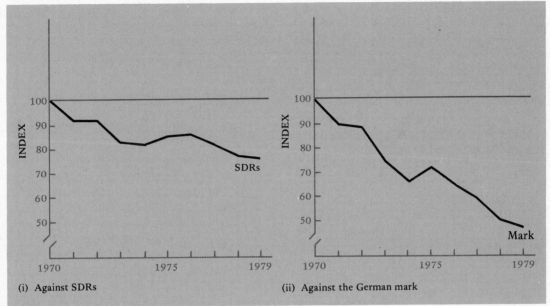

(i) Against SDRs   (ii) Against the German mark

The dollar depreciated sharply on the world's foreign exchange markets during the 1970s. In each part the curve is an index number (1970 = 100) that reflects the price of the U.S. dollar (at year-end) relative to other forms of foreign exchange. The price of the SDR in (i) is an average of 16 key currencies and is the best measure of the average devaluation of the dollar. The German mark, shown in (ii), proved the strongest of the world's currencies over the decade. The dollar depreciated 25 percent relative to SDRs and more than 50 percent relative to the mark.

eryone believed this was a once-and-for-all adjustment, they might well have licked their wounds and gone on as before. But nothing in American policy indicated that the trade deficits and the inflationary problems that caused the dollar problem were at an end. Thus many believed that the past devaluations were but prelude to inevitable future devaluations.

Fears of further devaluation not only made holders of dollars reluctant to increase their dollar holdings year by year (as it was necessary to do to finance the American balance-of-payments deficits without devaluation), but actually led many prudent holders of dollars to want to decrease their reliance on such a shaky reserve. As people tried to get rid of dollars, the dollar's value in terms of other currencies began to fall (see Figure 36-1). Between 1970 and 1973

the American dollar declined 22 percent against the yen and 30 percent against the mark. From 1973 to early 1980 it dropped an additional 23 percent against the yen and 31 percent against the mark.

As the dollar lost value, everyone who held large quantities of dollars became uncomfortable. The decreasing value of the dollar reduced the adequacy of most countries' reserves and threatened their financial stability.

Attempts to flee from the dollar. Had the dollar been but a small part of the reserve picture, it could have been replaced (as the pound was largely replaced in the late 1960s). But dollars were a key part of the world's foreign exchange reserves, and the system could not have functioned without them or some substitute.

While one country (or one bank) could readily reduce its holdings of dollars by buying gold or other currencies, the whole world could not do so unless an alternative source of international reserves was available. One source of the incredible rise in the price of gold in 1979–1980 from $250 to over $900 an ounce was the attempt of many holders of dollars to flee to gold. Since the monetary gold supply was in fact declining, this merely bid up the price of gold and depressed the price of the dollar. And this shrunk the size of the dollar reserves without letting their holders escape to a safer source of reserve. The volatile price of gold, shown in Figure 36-2, does not make it a very safe reserve.

Such attempted flights from the dollar will end only if the causes of the dollar's decline in price are eliminated, or if an adequate alternative international reserve is created to replace it. Neither has occurred. Periodically over the 1970s the discomfort or concern with the dollar edged into panic. Only the concerted willingness of France, Germany, Japan, and Britain to increase their dollar holdings has prevented a major crisis. They have done so in order to support an orderly monetary system, not out of faith in the stability of the dollar.

Continuing causes of the decline of the dollar. A major continuing cause of the decline of the dollar during the late 1970s was the unwillingness or inability of Americans to decrease their dependence on imported oil. In addition, the inflation rate in the U.S. rose more rapidly than did that of many of its trading partners, because of a series of relatively expansionary monetary and fiscal policies. With other nations unwilling to increase their dollar holdings, these factors together put the dollar under continuous downward pressure. In late 1980 and early 1981 the dollar recovered substantially, but as of March 1981 its value in terms of other major currencies was still well below its level of a decade earlier.

The Lack of an Alternative to the Dollar as a Reserve Currency

Governments operating dirty floats need reserves, just as do governments operating adjustable pegs. The search for an adequate supply of reserves has continued unabated since the demise of the Bretton Woods system. In January 1976, agreement was reached for a 30 percent average increase in the quotas of funds that member countries must provide to the IMF and from which the IMF can make loans to countries wishing to support their exchange rates. But increases of that quantity have not done more than keep up with the growth in the volume of world trade. They have certainly not provided a substitute for the enormous role of the dollar. As the dollar's role as a reserve currency became less popular, several other currencies—first the mark, then the yen—gained temporary prominence as potential reserve currencies.

While it is possible that some other national

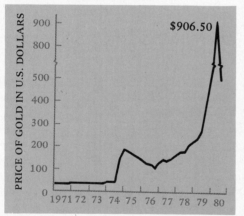

FIGURE 36-2
The Price of Gold, 1970–1980

Gold soared in value and proved highly volatile after convertibility of the dollar was ended. The two devaluations of the U.S. dollar under the gold exchange standard can be seen in the early 1970s, but they are barely visible. The course of gold speculation is seen in the subsequent experience. (Note that the vertical axis is interrupted between $500 and $800.) Gold does not exhibit the sort of price stability desired in an international source of reserve assets.

currencies will take over the reserve currency role played by the dollar, this is not likely. First, such a replacement of the dollar would require a massive shift out of dollars and into the new currency. Unless this were carefully managed, it would result in a sharp depreciation of the dollar that would hurt the United States and all other holders of dollars. Second, no other country is likely to accept for its currency the role of major international reserve. We have seen that the reserve currency role results in major problems and limits the scope of domestic policy action. The American experience has not gone unnoticed.

Why does the world not turn to an international paper reserve system based on SDRs or some similar creation? Such a solution has much support from academic economists, who see an appropriate international institution managing the supply of international currency to accommodate growth and to avoid inflation.

Critics—among them most of the world's central bankers—distrust the concept of an international paper currency and can point to the fact that few countries have managed their own money supplies in an effective way. However difficult the task of the Bank of Canada or the U.S. Federal Reserve System may be, the task of a World Reserve Board would be more difficult.

Some who are skeptical of an international paper monetary standard have urged a return to the gold standard. We have seen that this approach has critical disadvantages. In fact, the IMF and the U.S. government have at various times taken the lead in the attempt to "demonetize" gold completely. The violent fluctuations in gold prices in 1979–1980 have done nothing to decrease the opposition to a return to the gold standard.

For the moment at least, the world cannot agree on an international monetary reserve. Until it does, there will be crises whenever there is a desire to shift from one to another of the multiple sources of reserves: dollars, gold, SDRs, marks, francs, and yen. The speculative opportunities inherent in such a system remain large.

The Changing Pattern and Volume of Trade

Growing world interdependence. As the volume of international trade increases each year, countries quite naturally become more dependent on other countries to supply them with goods and provide them with markets. This situation has a number of favorable consequences in terms of gains from trade, but it is not an unmixed blessing.

One undesirable consequence is that a major shock to one economy quickly spreads to a large fraction of the world. This was the case with the cutoff of Iranian oil in 1979. It is much easier to resolve a crisis in one country than to resolve a simultaneous crisis in a large fraction of the world. Indeed most of the emergency powers of the IMF contemplated only isolated emergencies.

A second aspect of the growing world interdependency is the tighter connection between world and domestic economic policies. It was once possible for a major country such as the United States to be regarded as a closed economy, one little disturbed by foreign developments. This is no longer true of any major country of the free world. Countries cannot pursue policies designed to solve unemployment, inflation, or lagging growth on the assumption that other countries will be unaffected. Yet the political and economic mechanisms for achieving a mutually consistent set of economic policies on the part of different nations do not exist.

The Impact of OPEC

The most serious event affecting the future payments system—and indeed the whole of international economic relations—was the tenfold increase in the price of oil in the decade following the formation of the OPEC cartel. The price rises have generated an unprecedented imbalance in the form of a massive payments surplus for the oil producers and a corresponding deficit for the oil-importing countries. The excess purchasing power in the hands of oil producers has come to be called **petrodollars.** The size of this excess has been put in the neighborhood of $75 billion to $100 billion *per year* at the start of the 1980s. The cumulative stock of petrodollars may well exceed $500 billion. Petrodollars cause several different kinds of current problems, some of them short term, others long term in nature.

Short-term problems of industrialized countries. In the long term many and perhaps most petrodollars will be used for the purchase of both consumption goods and services and investment goods from industrialized countries. In time these countries will thus find their exports to the oil producers rising to meet their imports from them. But the oil-producing countries cannot spend their oil revenues on goods and services fast enough.[8] Nor can the industrialized oil-consuming countries produce the goods and services at the necessary rate for all the oil revenues to be spent without creating enormous inflationary pressures.[9]

Thus in the short term the OPEC countries have excess dollars. And they have an understandable desire to earn a return on those funds. One way is to invest their surplus revenues in the advanced industrialized nations, thereby returning on capital account the purchasing power extracted from the current accounts of the oil-importing nations. This situation raises many serious problems. One of the most important arises from the potential havoc brought to foreign exchange markets when surplus oil funds are invested in liquid assets and switched between currencies in response to changes in interest rates and expected capital gains arising from possible exchange rate alterations. This happened in both 1979 and 1980.

The world seeks but has not yet found some means for placing the funds in less liquid investments and/or creating sufficient central bank cooperation to allow the funds to be moved without upsetting foreign exchange markets completely.

Another use of surplus petrodollars is speculative, and many observers believe that a good part of the wild rise and sudden fall in gold prices in 1979–1980 was due to just such a use of petrodollars.

Short-term problems of the underdeveloped countries. Consider a country like Kenya for which the OPEC price increase turned a small trade surplus into a massive deficit overnight. The country was unable to generate revenues quickly enough to pay its oil bill, yet it could sharply decrease its use of oil only at the cost of a great slowdown in its domestic economy.

Although there were many dire predictions following the 1973–1974 oil price rise that the international monetary system could not cope with this new challenge, they were proved wrong. The IMF stepped in with loan arrangements to help those countries most severely affected by the rising oil prices, the repayments of maturing loans were deferred, and the OPEC nations established a fund for short-term loans to such countries. The purely short-term problems can be and were solved through international cooperation and recognition of the need for accommodation on the part of creditor nations.

Longer-term problems of the changing terms of trade for underdeveloped countries. For a country such as the United States, Japan, or West Germany the higher price of oil will eventually be recovered in the higher price of the goods that that country sells to oil producers. But many of the less-developed countries of the world have no export commodities that will loom large enough to owners of petrodollars to offset the rising cost of oil imports. More Saudi Arabians will visit Kenyan game parks and buy more Kenyan coffee, but not enough more. It is probable that the price of what residents of many oil-importing countries must buy has risen perma-

---

[8] There is a limit to the speed with which any country can absorb foreign goods, and many oil-producing countries are at that limit. Ships wait months to unload for want of dock capacity, unloaded goods sit in wharfside stockpiles for months — even years — for want of transportation capacity, and so on.

[9] Production of the goods produces factor incomes and thus adds to domestic demand, while export of the goods removes them from domestic markets and thus reduces domestic supplies.

nently relative to the price of what they can hope to sell. In other words, there has been a change in the terms of trade to their long-term disadvantage. This sort of disadvantage is likely to be greatest in countries that are already among the poorer nations of the world. Any decrease in their relative standard of living seems unfortunate to them—and to many observers.

However, this is not an international *payments* problem at all; rather, it concerns the distribution of world wealth. It can be dealt with by gifts or grants to these countries, and some such increases in world contributions have occurred. To attempt to solve this problem as though it were a payments problem, by artificially supporting the currency of the country above its equilibrium value, is undesirable. It implies an indirect subsidy that prevents the efficient use of the country's resources. This occurs because maintaining the exchange rate at a disequilibrium level distorts the price signals of foreign goods relative to domestic goods. Consequently, trade will not follow patterns of comparative advantage.

The Challenge for the 1980s

The 1970s witnessed the replacement of a system of managed fixed exchange rates by a system of managed flexible rates. The problems of the latter have been well defined by the events of the decade, but they cannot be said to have been solved. Officials understand the need both to develop an adequate reserve unit not tied to any national currency and to devise workable guidelines for managing flexible rates.

AN INTERNATIONAL RESERVE CURRENCY

Many and perhaps most economists believe that a controlled international money supply based on SDRs and expanded to keep pace with the volume of world trade is the best answer to the reserve problem. But an international paper currency, like a national currency, cannot work until there is confidence in it. The turmoil of the last two decades did nothing to create the climate of confidence required for the complete demonetization of gold and the dollar as international media of exchange. Flawed though either gold or the dollar is, each seems better (at this date) to many of the world's bankers than SDRs or similar "pieces of paper."

THE MANAGEMENT OF EXCHANGE RATES

The managed aspect of managed floating rates poses several potential problems for the international monetary system. They include the possibilities of mutually inconsistent exchange rate stabilization policies, competitive exchange rate depreciation, and instability of exchange rates in the face of speculative pressures. To help avoid these problems, the IMF issued guidelines for exchange rate management in June 1974. The guidelines emphasized the point that exchange rate policy is a matter for international consultation and surveillance by the IMF and that intervention practices by individual central banks should be based on three principles: (1) exchange authorities should prevent sudden and disproportionate short-term movements in exchange rates and ensure an orderly adjustment of exchange rates to longer-term pressures; (2) in consultation with the IMF, countries should establish a target zone for the medium-term values of their exchange rates and keep the actual rate within that target zone; (3) countries should recognize that exchange rate management involves joint responsibilities.

The experiences of the 1970s have underlined one of the most important problems not yet solved: coping with the massive volume of short-term funds that can be switched very rapidly between financial centers. Short-term capital flows forced the abandonment of exchange rates that were agreed on in 1971, and they have caused violent fluctuations in floating rates as recently as 1979.

Various attempts have been made to limit such flows. Italy has adopted a "two-tier" foreign exchange market with one price for foreign exchange to finance current account transactions and another price (and another set of controls) for foreign exchange to finance capital movements. Germany has used direct controls on overseas borrowing. There has also been a considerable extension of arrangements under which central banks in surplus countries lend the funds they are accumulating back to central banks in deficit countries, thereby enhancing the ability of banks to maintain stable exchange rates in the face of short-term speculative flights of capital.

The major problem in managing speculative flows is to identify them accurately. Experience suggests that exchange rate management can smooth out temporary fluctuations but cannot resist underlying trends in equilibrium rates caused by relative inflation rates, structural changes, and persistent nonspeculative capital flows. In the day-to-day management it is not always easy to distinguish among them.

THE NEED FOR COOPERATION

One of the most impressive aspects of the international payments history of the last 30 years has been the steady rise of effective international cooperation. When the gold standard collapsed and the Great Depression overwhelmed the countries of the world, "every man for himself" was the rule of the day. Rising tariffs, competitive exchange rate devaluations, and all forms of beggar-my-neighbor policies abounded.

After World War II the countries of the world cooperated in bringing the Bretton Woods system and the IMF into being. The system itself was far from perfect, and it finally broke down as a result of its own·internal contradictions. But the international cooperation that was necessary to set the system up survived the collapse of the system itself. The joint cooperative actions of central banks allowed them to weather in the 1970s speculative crises that would have forced them to devalue their currencies in the 1950s.

Thus the collapse of Bretton Woods did not plunge the world into the same chaos that followed the breakdown of the gold standard. The world was also better able to cope with the terrible strains caused by the sharp rise in oil prices in the 1970s. Enormous oil-related problems remain, and they are matters for continuing international dialogue.

Whatever the problems of the future, the world has a better chance of coping with them — or even just learning to live with them — when its countries cooperate through the IMF and other international organizations than when each country seeks its own selfish solution without concern for the interests of others.

Summary

1. Under the gold standard, the central authorities of each country kept their paper currency convertible into gold at a fixed rate, and the "gold content" of each currency established fixed rates of exchange between all the currencies. Because all currencies were freely convertible into gold, they were also freely convertible into each other.

2. The gold standard was supposed to work through changes in national price levels and from them to changes in the prices of imported and exported commodities. A deficit country would lose gold, its money supply would shrink, its price level would fall; thus imports would become relatively more expensive while exports became relatively cheaper, and both changes would tend to reduce the deficit. A surplus country would gain gold, expand its money supply, experience an inflation that would make its imports relatively cheap and its exports relatively inexpensive, and thus find its surplus being reduced.

3. Before 1914 this system was not required to remove major disequilibria in the balance of payments. In the 1920s the gold standard was required to do so and failed. The major disabilities of a gold standard in the 1920s were that price levels adjusted too slowly and the authorities were unwilling to adopt realistic exchange

rates. Any gold standard system suffers from the serious difficulties of a rigid supply and a large and volatile speculative demand for gold.

4. The gold standard was abandoned and many experiments were tried throughout the 1930s. The use of exchange rates and trade restrictions to increase local employment in the face of inadequate aggregate world demand was discredited as a means of dealing with a worldwide unemployment problem.

5. The international payments system existing between 1944 and the early 1970s was called the Bretton Woods system. It put the world on an adjustable peg, gold exchange standard. To maintain their rates of exchange vis-à-vis the U.S. dollar, foreign monetary authorities bought and sold reserves of gold and of the two reserve currencies, the British pound sterling and the U.S. dollar. Exchange rates were only to be changed in the face of a fundamental disequilibrium in the balance of payments.

6. The International Monetary Fund (IMF) was the major institution of the Bretton Woods system. It tried to ensure that countries pegged their exchange rates and changed them only in the face of fundamental disequilibrium. To this end it made loans of foreign exchange to countries trying to weather temporary balance-of-payments deficits.

7. Three major problems with any adjustable peg system are (1) to provide sufficient international reserves, (2) to adjust to long-term trends in receipts and payments, and (3) to handle periodic speculative crises. The SDR is a relatively new international paper money meant to provide adequate international reserves not linked to gold or the U.S. dollar.

8. The Bretton Woods system broke down under a series of speculative crises that stemmed from the failure of the system to provide sufficient international reserves, and the need to accommodate devaluations of the U.S. dollar.

9. The two major events in the transition from

the Bretton Woods system to the present one were the abandonment of gold convertibility of dollars held by foreign central banks in 1971 and the drift toward flexibility of exchange rates that occurred mainly during 1972 and 1973.

10. The present system is a dollar standard with managed flexibility of exchange rates, often called a dirty float. The system is under very heavy strain because of the current account deficits of so many of the oil-importing countries, because of the enormous supplies of short-term foreign investment held by the oil exporters, and because of the loss of confidence in the dollar as a reserve currency.

11. Current problems are the need to find an adequate reserve not tied to a national currency, the accommodation to both the short-term and the longer-term impact of OPEC, and the development of rules for managing flexible exchange rates. The spirit of international cooperation is a constructive step toward finding solutions.

Topics for Review

The gold standard
The Bretton Woods system
A dollar standard
Kinds of foreign exchange reserves
Pegged exchange rates and adjustable pegs
Freely floating exchange rates
Dirty or managed floats
Petrodollars

Discussion Questions

1. What role in international payments does or did gold play under (a) the gold standard, (b) the adjustable peg Bretton Woods system, (c) the present system? In 1974 *Barron's* had an editorial headed, "Monetary Reform and Gold: You Can't Have One Without the Other." Does the gold price experience of the 1970s bear out this editorial opinion?
2. For a traditional gold standard to work successfully, why must there be free import and export of gold?
3. The U.S. dollar is no longer convertible into gold

because of a change in U.S. policy. Does this lack of conversion make the dollar any less useful as an international medium of exchange? And does it mean that one could now treat gold as just another metal, such as copper, stockpiled by the United States?

4. Might a person who regards inflation as the number one economic danger favor a return to the pre-1914 gold standard? Would you predict noninflationary results if in order to restore the gold standard, the price of gold had to be set at $1600 per ounce, either all at once or gradually?

5. "Under a flexible exchange rate system no country need suffer unemployment, for if its prices are low enough there will be more than enough demand to keep its factories and farms fully occupied." The evidence suggests that flexible rates have not generally eliminated unemployment. Can you explain why? Can changing exchange rates ever cure unemployment?

6. It is sometimes said that a fixed rate system subject to periodic crises is a speculator's heaven, for the speculator can make a fortune with no risk. Was this true under the gold exchange standard?

7. The OPEC oil price increase has caused grave problems in international payments and increased the need for IMF loans. Why has the market adjustment of exchange rates failed to solve the problem?

The Banking System and the Supply of Money

37

The total stock of money in the economy at any moment is called the **money supply** or the **supply of money.** This total may be defined in different ways. The most commonly used measure in Canada is **M1,** which includes currency and demand deposits.

M1 is a narrowly defined concept of money that concentrates on the medium of exchange function. Funds held in **demand deposits** can be transferred by cheque or withdrawn on demand (i.e., without prior notice being given). The two forms of demand deposit offered by the chartered banks are current accounts and personal chequing accounts.

Broader definitions of money add in savings accounts and term deposits that serve the temporary store of value function and are in practice quickly convertible into a medium of exchange at a known and completely secure price ($1 on deposit in a savings account is always convertible into a $1 demand deposit or $1 in currency). Table 37-1 shows the various definitions of the money supply used in Canada.

In our economy the quantity of money is affected both by the private banking system and by the actions of the central bank. The private banks affect the money supply as an incidental but very important feature of how they do business. In so doing, they respond to what is happening in the economy—to the level of business activity, to interest rates, and to the demands of their customers for currency and for loans. The central bank, which in Canada is the Bank of

Canada, influences the money supply as a matter of deliberate monetary policy.

The Chartered Banks

Modern banking systems are of two main types. In one system, there is a small number of banks, each with a very large number of branch offices; in the other system, there are many independent banks. The banking systems of Britain and Canada are of the first type, with only a few banks accounting for the overwhelming bulk of the business. In the United States there are approximately 15,000 independent banks, some (such as the Bank of America) with hundreds of branches and others with only a single office. Branch banking in the United States is governed

TABLE 37-1

The Supply of Money in Canada, June 1980 (billions of dollars)

Currency	$ 9.3
Plus Demand deposits	14.3
Equals M1	23.6
Plus Chequable savings deposits	7.4
Equals M1B	31.0
Plus Personal savings deposits	63.5
Nonpersonal notice deposits	2.1
Equals M2	96.6
Plus Nonpersonal term deposits	35.5
Foreign currency deposits	10.8
Equals M3	$142.9

Source: Bank of Canada Review.

The money supply can be defined in a variety of ways; M1, M1B, M2, and M3 figures are all published regularly by the Bank of Canada. M1 is the narrowly defined money supply that includes items that serve directly as a medium of exchange. M1B also includes the relatively new category of chequable savings deposits. M2 includes additional categories of bank deposits that serve the store of value function and can be readily converted into demand deposits or currency. M3 adds in bank term deposits that cannot be converted easily because the funds must remain on deposit for a fixed term and foreign currency deposits whose value in terms of Canadian dollars is not fixed but varies with the exchange rate.

by state law. Interstate branching is not allowed, and in some states only "unit banks" with a single office are permitted.

The Canadian banking system consists of eleven **chartered banks,** which are privately owned, profit-seeking institutions. As Table 37-2 shows, the five largest together hold 90 percent of total bank assets, and each has more than 900 branches. All the banks have certain common attributes: they hold deposits for their customers; they permit certain deposits to be transferred by cheque from an individual account to other accounts held in any bank branch in the country; they make loans to households and firms; and they invest in government securities.

Chartered banks are by no means the only financial institutions in the country. Many other institutions, such as trust companies, mortgage loan companies, and credit unions, accept savings deposits and grant loans for specific purposes. Finance companies make loans to households for practically any purpose—sometimes at very high effective interest rates. The post office and the telegraph system will transfer money, and credit card companies will extend credit so that purchases can be made on a buy-now, pay-later basis.

What distinguishes banks from the other members of the financial system, each of which does some of the things that banks do? The chartered banks are unique in one basic way. They accept demand deposits upon which cheques may be drawn, and they will transfer funds from one person's deposit to another's when ordered to do so by a customer's cheque. Other financial institutions offer chequable savings accounts, but they do not have facilities to transfer funds to accounts in other institutions and must use the banking system to clear cheques.[1] In any event, only a small fraction of the dollar volume of cheques issued is accounted for by cheques drawn on nonbank institutions.

---

[1] Revisions to the Bank Act, passed in 1980, provide for nonbank access to the clearing system via the formation of the Canadian Payments Association. However, just how the new system will function is as yet unclear.

TABLE 37-2
Assets and Branches of the Chartered Banks

Bank	Number of branches	Assets	
		Millions of dollars	Percentage of total
Royal Bank of Canada	1522	51,722	23.5
Canadian Imperial Bank of Commerce	1716	45,995	20.9
Bank of Montreal	1255	38,180	17.3
Bank of Nova Scotia	994	34,869	15.8
Toronto Dominion Bank	1006	28,209	12.8
National Bank of Canada	757	15,475	7.0
Mercantile Bank of Canada	14	3,109	1.4
Bank of British Columbia	45	2,000	*
Other	12	685	*

*Less than 1 percent.
Source: The Financial Post Survey of Industrials, 1980.

Although there are eleven chartered banks operating in Canada, the industry is dominated by the big five, who between them hold more than 90 percent of the industry's total assets. The National Bank of Canada was formed in 1979 by the amalgamation of the Banque Canadienne Nationale and the Banque Provinciale de Canada. Included in "other" are the Continental Bank, the Northend Bank, and the Canadian Commercial and Industrial Bank.

Cheque Clearing and Collection

Bank deposits are an effective medium of exchange only because banks accept each other's cheques. If you keep your account at the Royal Bank and receive a cheque drawn on the Bank of Montreal, you are likely either to cash it or to deposit it in the Royal Bank. If the rules of the banking business were different, so that you had to present a cheque to the bank on which it was drawn, you would be so inconvenienced that you would be unwilling to accept cheques for most transactions. Fortunately, banks accept one another's cheques. But the problem of presenting cheques for payment remains. If a depositor in bank A writes a cheque to someone who deposits it in bank B, bank A now owes money to bank B.

There are, of course, millions of such transactions in the course of a day, resulting in an enormous sorting and bookkeeping job. Multibank systems make use of a **clearing house** where interbank debts are settled. At the end of the day, all the cheques drawn by bank A's customers and deposited in bank B are totaled and set against the total of all the cheques drawn by bank B's customers and deposited in bank A. It is necessary only to settle the difference between the two sums. The actual cheques are passed through the clearing house back to the bank on which they were drawn. Both banks are then able to adjust the individual accounts by a set of book entries; a flow of cash between banks is necessary only when there is a net transfer of cash from the customers of one bank to those of another. This flow of cash is accomplished by a transfer between banks of deposits in the Bank of Canada.

Credit Cards

A relatively new form of interbank cooperation is the bank credit card. Visa and Master Card are the most commonly used credit cards in Canada; each is run by a group of chartered banks. Either card permits the holder to charge purchases of goods and services. The participating banks promptly pay the merchants and bill the credit card holder, who has the option of paying at once or paying later at the cost of a prespecified rate of interest. Banks find this highly profitable because it provides "instant" loans with a small amount of paperwork and a high rate of interest, typically around 20 percent per year.

BANKS AS PROFIT-SEEKING INSTITUTIONS

Banks are private firms that start with invested capital and seek to "make money" in the same sense as do firms making neckties or bicycles. Banks do not set out to "make money" in the literal sense; nonetheless they do so as a by-product of their attempt to make profits for their owners.

A chartered bank provides a variety of services to its customers: a relatively safe place to store money; the convenience of demand deposits that can be transferred by personal cheque; a safe and convenient place to earn a guaranteed return on savings; and often financial advice and estate management services. The bank earns some revenue by charging for these services, but such fees are a small part of the bank's total earnings. The largest part (typically about five-sixths) of a bank's earnings is derived from the bank's ability to invest profitably the funds placed with it.

Principal Assets and Liabilities

Tables 37-3 and 37-4 show the major items that make up the consolidated balance sheet of the chartered banks. The bulk of a bank's liabilities are deposits that are owed to its depositors. The principal assets of a bank are the *securities* it buys, including government bonds, and the *loans* it makes to individuals, businesses, and provincial and municipal governments. A bank loan is a liability to the borrower (who must pay it back) but an asset to the bank. The bank expects not only to have the loan repaid but to receive interest that more than compensates for the paperwork involved and the risk of nonpayment.

Most money deposited with banks is "at work," having been invested in loans or securities. Banks earn money by lending and investing

TABLE 37-3

Major Assets of the Chartered Banks, November 1980 (billions of dollars)

Liquid assets	
Bank of Canada notes and deposits	$ 6.8
Treasury bills	7.4
Government of Canada bonds	2.7
Other liquid assets	1.3
Less liquid assets	111.5
Loans	7.8
Canadian securities	7.8
Total major assets	$137.5

Source: *Bank of Canada Review*, December 1980.

Both highly liquid assets and long-term assets appear in the balance sheets of the chartered banks. Banks hold a relatively small fraction (usually about 15 percent) of total assets as liquid assets; the bulk is held in longer-term assets on which a larger interest yield can typically be earned.

the money left with them so as to earn more than it costs them to attract the deposits. Deposits are the lifeblood of a chartered bank. Without them, the bank has nothing to lend or invest except the small amount of its initial capital.

Most bank services are designed to attract or keep deposits. On some categories of deposits, it pays the depositor an interest rate in the expectation that it can earn more than that by reinvesting the money. For example, in December 1980 banks were paying 13 percent on nonchequable

TABLE 37-4

Canadian Dollar Deposit Liabilities of the Chartered Banks, November 1980 (billions of dollars)

Personal savings deposits	$ 74.5
Nonpersonal term and notice deposits	33.4
Demand deposits	15.9
Total privately held deposits	$123.8
Government of Canada deposits	3.2
Total Canadian dollar deposits	$127.0

Source: *Bank of Canada Review*, December 1980.

The liabilities of the chartered banks are typically much more liquid than their assets. Bank liabilities are typically very short-term; deposits are much greater than reserves, as given in Table 37-3.

personal savings deposits and 17.5 percent on 90-day term deposits. In the case of demand deposits, the bank must earn more by investing them than the excess of the cost of providing the services its depositors expect over the service charges it collects.

Liquid assets. In 1980 less than one-sixth of total major assets of the chartered banks consisted of cash and interest-earning assets that could readily be converted into cash. Cash reserves are held in the form of deposits in the Bank of Canada and notes. All banks need to keep some reserves of cash to satisfy their depositors' day-to-day requirements. Indeed, all banks are forced by law to hold such cash reserves. A bank's **cash reserve ratio** is the fraction of its deposits that it holds as reserves either as currency in its vaults or as deposits with the central bank. Those reserves that the banks are required to hold under the Bank Act are called **required cash reserves.** Any reserves that it holds over and above required reserves are called **excess cash reserves.** Since 1968 the required cash reserve ratios have been 12 percent for demand deposits and 4 percent for term deposits; revisions to the Bank Act in 1980 reduced the former to 10 percent.

The bulk of earning liquid assets is held in the form of bonds and treasury bills (government securities with usual terms to maturity of three or six months) issued by the government of Canada. These assets generally yield a lower rate of return than loans, but they act as **secondary reserves** that can be used to replenish cash holdings should they be run down.

The Creation and Destruction of Money

The banking system can create money because at any moment of time most of the banks' depositors do not require their deposits to be redeemed in currency. Just as the goldsmiths discovered that only a fraction of the gold they held was ever withdrawn, and just as banks discovered that only a fraction of convertible bank notes was actually converted, so too have banks discovered that only a fraction of their deposits will be withdrawn in cash at any one time. Most deposits of any individual bank remain on deposit with it; thus an individual bank need only keep fractional reserves against its deposits.

Many funds withdrawn by a depositor from one bank do not leave the banking system even though they leave the bank. When Ms. Jones withdraws $4,000 from her bank to buy a new car, chances are the car dealer will deposit Ms. Jones' cheque in its account. Thus the banking system as a whole will have merely transferred its deposit liabilities from one depositor to another and from one bank to another. For this reason, the banking system as a whole may operate with fewer reserves than would any one bank standing alone. A fractional reserve system creates the leverage by which chartered banks can create new money.

If banks can increase their reserves, they can increase their deposits even more. Since deposits are money, banks can thus increase the money supply.

In a real sense, that is all there is to money creation. Yet the process is worth examining in some detail. We shall limit our attention to chartered banks and their creation of demand deposits.

Some Simplifying Assumptions

To focus on the essential aspects of how banks create money, assume that the banks can invest in only one kind of asset, loans, and that there is only one kind of deposit, a demand deposit.

Three other assumptions listed below are provisional; later, when we have developed the basic ideas concerning the bank's creation of money, these assumptions will be relaxed.

Fixed required reserve ratio. It is assumed that all banks have the same required reserve ratio, which does not change. In our numerical illustration we shall assume that the required reserve ratio is 20 percent, that is, that banks must have at least $1 of reserves for every $5 of deposits.

No excess reserves. It is assumed that all banks want to invest any reserves they have in excess of the legally required amount. This implies that they always believe there are safe investments to be made when they have excess reserves.

No cash drain from the banking system. It is assumed that the public holds a fixed amount of currency in circulation, an amount that will not change with changes in the total money supply. Thus changes in the money supply will take the form of changes in deposit money. If extra money is created, the money will be deposited in a bank; if money is destroyed, bank deposits will be decreased.

Armed with these assumptions, we shall now examine money creation, starting with the simplest possible situation and progressing to two more complex but more realistic ones. The three situations are: (1) a single new deposit in a system that has only one bank, (2) a single new deposit in a system with many banks, and (3) many new deposits in a many-bank system. Surprisingly, perhaps, the results are exactly the same in all three cases.

A MONOPOLY BANK, A SINGLE NEW DEPOSIT

Suppose that the entire country is served by a single multibranch bank, called a *monopoly bank* because it has no competitors. The balance sheet of this monopoly bank appears in Table 37-5.

The monopoly bank's assets consist of $200 of reserves, held partly as currency and partly as deposits with the central bank, and $900 of loans outstanding to its customers. Its liabilities are $100 to those who intially contributed capital to start the bank and $1,000 to current depositors. The bank's ratio of reserves to deposits is 200/

TABLE 37-5
The Monopoly Bank's Initial Balance Sheet

Assets		Liabilities	
Cash and other reserves	$ 200	Deposits	$1,000
Loans	900	Capital	100
	$1,100		$1,100

The monopoly bank has a reserve of 20 percent of its deposit liabilities. The bank earns its money by finding profitable investments for much of the money deposited with it. In this balance sheet, loans are the earning assets of the bank.

1,000 = .20, exactly equal to its minimum requirement.

An immigrant arrives in the country and opens an account by depositing $100 with the monopoly bank. This is a wholly new deposit for the bank, and it results in a revised balance sheet (Table 37-6). As a result of the immigrant's new deposit, both cash assets and deposit liabilities have risen by $100. More important, the reserve ratio has increased from .20 to 300/1,100 = .27. The monopoly bank now has excess reserves— with $300 in reserves it could support $1,500 in deposits.

The monopoly bank knows that any new deposit it creates will remain in the system. It is in a

TABLE 37-6
The Monopoly Bank's Balance Sheet After an Immigrant Deposits $100

Assets		Liabilities	
Cash and other reserves	$ 300	Deposits	$1,100
Loans	900	Capital	100
	$1,200		$1,200

The immigrant's deposit raises deposit liabilities and cash assets by the same amount. Since both cash and deposits rise by $100, the cash reserve ratio, formerly .20, now increases to .27. The bank has more cash than it needs to provide a 20 percent reserve against its deposit liabilities.

position to say to the next business executive who comes in for a loan, "We will lend your firm $400 at the going rate of interest." The bank does so by adding that amount to the firm's deposit account. The bank does not care how the executive spends the money, for whoever receives the firm's cheques will deposit them in the same bank (since there is no other).

Table 37-7 shows what happens when the new deposits are created. The immigrant's deposit initially raised cash assets and deposit liabilities by $100. The new loans create an additional $400 of deposit liabilities. This restores the reserve ratio to its legal minimum (300/1,500 = .20), and no further expansion of deposit money is possible. As the bank's customers do business with each other, settling their accounts by cheques, the ownership of the deposits will be continually changing. But what matters to the bank is that its total deposits will remain constant.

The extent to which the bank can increase its loans *and thus its deposits* and thus the money supply depends on the reserve ratio. Because in this case the ratio is 1/5 (= .20), the bank is able to expand deposits to five times the original new acquisition of money. In general, if the reserve ratio is r, a monopoly bank can increase its deposits by $1/r$ times any new reserves. This general relationship proves true of a banking system whether or not there is a monopoly bank. **[45]**

The "multiple expansion of deposits" that has just been worked through applies in reverse to a withdrawal of funds. Suppose a depositor in a monopoly bank withdraws $50 (in the form of a $50 bill) and spends it in a new shop, whose owners decide to frame the bill and display it on their wall. The bank has lost both cash and a deposit. Its revised balance sheet is shown in Table 37-8. As a result of the loss of $50 cash and $50 deposits, the bank's reserve ratio has fallen to 250/1,450 = .17. This is below the legal minimum, and the bank will have to take steps to restore the required ratio.

Say that the bank calls for the repayment of some loans made to its customers and repayable at short notice, hoping thereby to raise its cash position to restore the required ratio. What happens, however, is that the loans are not repaid by cash but by the customers' drawing cheques on their accounts in favor of the bank. This means that deposit liabilities are reduced by the repayment of the loan, but cash is unchanged. To restore the correct reserve ratio, it will be necessary to reduce deposits — by calling in loans and not making new ones until deposits are once again only five times reserves.

The revised balanced sheet when this has been achieved appears in Table 37-9. The bank lost $50 in cash from the initial withdrawal of funds. To maintain a reserve ratio of .20, it was necessary that deposits fall by $250. The initial withdrawal trimmed deposits by $50, but the remain-

TABLE 37-7
The Monopoly Bank's Balance Sheet After Making a $400 Loan

Assets		Liabilities	
Cash and other reserves	$ 300	Deposits	$1,500
Loans	1,300	Capital	100
	$1,600		$1,600

The loan restores the reserve ratio of .20. By increasing its loans by a multiple of its new cash deposit, the bank restores its reserve ratio of .20.

TABLE 37-8
The Monopoly Bank's Balance Sheet After a $50 Withdrawal

Assets		Liabilities	
Cash and other reserves	$ 250	Deposits	$1,450
Loans	1,300	Capital	100
	$1,550		$1,550

A withdrawal lowers the bank's reserve ratio. The withdrawal of currency reduces both cash assets and deposit liabilities by the same amount. The reserve ratio, which was .20 before the withdrawal, is now only .17.

TABLE 37-9

The Monopoly Bank's Balance Sheet After the Reserve Ratio Has Been Restored

Assets		Liabilities	
Cash and other			
reserves	$ 250	Deposits	$1,250
Loans	1,100	Capital	100
	$1,350		$1,350

A multiple contraction of loans is necessary to restore the reserve ratio after a withdrawal. A withdrawal of $50 in currency reduces deposits by $50. A further contraction of $200 in loans and deposits is necessary to cause deposits to fall by five times the fall in cash. This restores the reserve ratio of .20.

TABLE 37-10

The Initial Balance Sheet of the Canadian Immigrants Bank of Commerce (CIBC)

Assets		Liabilities	
Cash and other			
reserves	$ 200	Deposits	$1,000
Loans	900	Capital	100
	$1,100		$1,100

The initial position is the same as that of the monopoly bank in Table 37-5. Although the balance sheet of the CIBC is initially the same as that of the monopoly bank, the crucial difference is that the CIBC is one of many banks in a multibank system, while the monopoly bank was itself the whole banking system.

ing $200 cut had to be effected by reducing outstanding loans. The new position restored the reserve ratio to $250/$1,250 = .20.

The result of the withdrawal of $50 is that the quantity of deposit money shrinks by $250 and the volume of loans available to the bank's customers shrinks by $200.

MANY BANKS, A SINGLE NEW DEPOSIT

Deposit creation is more complicated in a multibank system than in a single-bank system, but *the end result is exactly the same.* It is more complicated because, when a bank makes a loan, the recipient of the loan may pay the money to someone who deposits it not in the original bank but in another bank. How this works is most easily seen under the extreme assumption that every new borrower immediately withdraws the borrowed funds from the lending bank and pays someone who then deposits the money in another bank or banks.

Suppose that the Canadian Immigrants Bank of Commerce is initially in the position of the monopoly bank (shown in Table 37-5), which is repeated in Table 37-10. Now suppose that, as before, an immigrant makes a wholly new deposit of $100. The bank's position after the deposit is shown in Table 37-11. This is exactly the same position given in Table 37-6, when the mo-

nopoly bank received the immigrant's deposit. The reserve ratio is once again 300/1,000 = .27, but here the similarity to the monopoly bank ends.

The Immigrants Bank cannot use its excess reserves to support $400 of new loans. When the bank makes new loans to its customers, they will make payments to other persons who will deposit the cheques in their own banks. Because of this, the Immigrants Bank will suffer an *adverse clearing;* that is, the cheques drawn against it will not be offset by deposits of cheques drawn against other banks, and it will lose cash to the other banks. But even though it cannot expand loans and deposits by as much as the monopoly bank, it can do something. It has more reserves

TABLE 37-11

The Balance Sheet of the CIBC After a $100 Deposit

Assets		Liabilities	
Cash and other			
reserves	$ 300	Deposits	$1,100
Loans	900	Capital	100
	$1,200		$1,200

The immigrant's deposit raises deposit liabilities and cash assets by the same amount. Since both cash and deposits rise by $100, the cash reserve ratio, formerly .20, now increases to .27. The bank has more cash than it needs to provide a 20 percent reserve against its deposit liabilities.

than required, and even on the extreme assumption that every dollar that it lends will be withdrawn and deposited in another bank, there is an opportunity to make some profitable loans with the excess reserves on hand.

With its present level of deposits at $1,100, the bank needs only $220 of reserves (.20 × $1,100 = $220), so it can lend the $80 excess that it has on hand. Table 37-12 shows the position after this has been done and after the new deposit has been withdrawn to be deposited to the account of a customer of another bank. The Immigrants Bank once again has a 20 percent reserve ratio.

So far deposits in the CIBC have increased by only the initial $100 of new immigrant's money with which we started, as shown in Table 37-11. (Of this, $20 is held as cash reserve against the deposit and $80 has been lent out to a customer.) But other banks have received new deposits of $80 as the persons receiving payment from the initial borrower deposited those payments in their own banks. The receiving banks (sometimes called "second-generation banks") receive new deposits of $80, and when the cheques clear, they have new reserves of $80. Because they require an addition to their reserves of only $16 to support the new deposit, they have $64 of excess reserves. They now increase their loans by $64. After this money is spent by the borrowers and has been deposited in other, third-generation

TABLE 37-12

The CIBC Balance Sheet After a New Loan and a Loss of Cash

Assets		Liabilities	
Cash and other			
reserves	$ 220	Deposits	$1,100
Loans	980	Capital	100
	$1,200		$1,200

The bank lends its surplus cash and suffers an adverse clearing. The bank keeps $20 as a reserve against the new deposit of $100. It lends $80 to a customer who writes a cheque to someone who deals with another bank. When the cheque clears, CIBC has suffered an $80 cash drain, has increased its loans by $80, and has restored its reserve ratio to .20.

TABLE 37-13

Changes in the Balance Sheets of Second-generation Banks

Assets		Liabilities	
Cash and other			
reserves	+$16	Deposits	+$80
Loans	+ 64		
	+$80		+$80

Second-generation banks receive deposits and expand loans. The second-generation banks gain new deposits of $80 as a result of the loan granted by the CIBC, which is used to make payments to customers of the second-generation banks. These banks keep 20 percent of the cash they acquire as their reserve against the new deposit, and they can make new loans using the other 80 percent. When the customers who borrowed the money make payments to the customers of third-generation banks, the CIBC suffers an adverse clearing.

banks, the balance sheets of the second-generation banks will have changed, as in Table 37-13.

The third-generation banks now find themselves with $64 of new deposits. Against these they need only hold $12.80 in cash, so they have excess reserves of $51.20 that they can immediately lend out. Thus there begins a long sequence of new deposits, new loans, new deposits, and new loans. The stages are shown in Table 37-14. The series in the table should look familiar, for it is the same converging series we met when dealing with the multiplier.

The banking system has created new deposits and thus new money, though each banker can honestly say, "All I did was invest my excess reserves. I can do no more than manage wisely the money I receive."

If r is the reserve ratio, the ultimate effect on the deposits of the banking system of a new deposit will be $1/r$ times the new deposit. [46] This is exactly the same result reached in the monopoly bank case.[2]

---

[2] Indeed, the process might have been the same. Look again at Table 37-6. If the monopoly bank had merely loaned its excess reserves of $80, it would have soon received a new deposit of $80 in one of its branches. This in turn would give it excess reserves of $64, which it could loan—and so on.

TABLE 37-14
Many Banks, a Single New Deposit

Bank	New deposits	New loans	Addition to reserves
Immigrants Bank	$100.00	$ 80.00	$ 20.00
Second-generation bank	80.00	64.00	16.00
Third-generation bank	64.00	51.20	12.80
Fourth-generation bank	51.20	40.96	10.24
Fifth-generation bank	40.96	32.77	8.19
Sixth-generation bank	32.77	26.22	6.55
Seventh-generation bank	26.22	20.98	5.24
Eighth-generation bank	20.98	16.78	4.20
Ninth-generation bank	16.78	13.42	3.36
Tenth-generation bank	13.42	10.74	2.68
Total first 10 generations	446.33	357.07	89.26
All remaining generations	53.67	42.93	10.74
Total for banking systems	$500.00	$400.00	$100.00

The banking system as a whole can create deposit money whenever it receives new reserves. The table shows the process of the creation of deposit money on the assumptions that all the loans made by one set of banks end up as deposits in another set of banks (called the "next-generation banks"), that the required reserve ratio (*r*) is .20, and that there are no excess reserves. Although each bank suffers a cash drain whenever it grants a new loan, the system as a whole does not, and the system ends up doing in a series of steps what a monopoly bank would do all at once; that is, it increases deposit money by 1/*r*, which in this example is five times the amount of any increase in reserves that it obtains.

MANY BANKS, MANY DEPOSITS

The two cases discussed before, the monopoly bank and the single new deposit in a many-bank situation, serve this purpose: they show that under either set of opposite extreme assumptions, the result is the same. So it is, too, in intermediate situations where banks suffer some, but less than a total, loss of cash to other banks. A far more realistic picture of the process of deposit creation is one in which new deposits (or new withdrawals) tend to accrue simultaneously to all banks, perhaps because of changes in the monetary policy of the government. Say, for example, that the community contains ten banks of equal size and that each receives new deposits of $100 in cash. Now each bank is in the position shown in Tables 37-6 and 37-11, and each can begin to expand deposits based on the $100 of excess reserves. (Each bank does this by granting loans to customers.)

Because each bank does one-tenth of the total banking business, an average of 90 percent of any newly created deposit will find its way into other banks as the customer pays other people in the community by cheque. This will represent a loss of cash from the lending bank to the other banks. However, 10 percent of each new deposit created by every other bank should find its way into this bank. All banks receive new cash and all start creating deposits simultaneously; no bank should suffer a significant loss of cash to any other bank.

Thus all banks can go on expanding deposits without losing cash to each other; they need only worry about keeping enough cash to satisfy those depositors who will occasionally require currency. The expansion can go on with each bank watching its own ratio of cash reserves to deposits, expanding deposits as long as the ratio exceeds 1/5 and ceasing when it reaches that figure. The process will come to a halt when each bank has created $400 in additional deposits, so that for each initial $100 cash deposit, there is now $500 in deposits backed by $100 in cash. Now *each* of the banks will have entries in its books similar to those shown in Table 37-7.

The general rule, if there is no currency drain, is that a banking system with a reserve ratio of *r* can change its deposits by 1/*r* times any change in reserves.

EXCESS RESERVES AND CURRENCY DRAINS

Two of the simplifying assumptions made earlier can now be relaxed.

Excess reserves. If banks do not choose to invest excess reserves, the multiple expansion discussed will not occur. Turn back to Table 37-6. If the monopoly bank had been content to hold 27 percent reserves, it might well have done nothing more. Other things being equal, banks will choose to invest excess reserves because of the profit motive. But there may be times when they believe the risk is too great. It is one thing to be offered 12 percent or even 24 percent interest on a loan, but if the borrower defaults on the payment of interest and principal, the bank will be the loser. Similarly, although a bank can always acquire liquid assets such as treasury bills or short-term government of Canada bonds, it may not always consider it profitable to do so because of the transactions cost involved. A bank that receives an inflow of cash and accumulates excess reserves may decide not to acquire earning assets if it expects the inflow to be reversed in the near future, for the transactions costs in and out may exceed the interest that can be earned.

There is nothing automatic about credit expansion; it rests on the decisions of bankers. If banks do not choose to use excess reserves to expand their investments, there will not be an expansion of deposits.

The significance of relaxing this assumption

about excess reserves is that it cuts the automatic link between the creation of excess reserves and money creation. Excess reserves make it *possible* for the banks to expand the money supply, but only if they want to do so. However, the upper limit of deposits is determined by the required reserve ratio and by the reserves available to the banks, both of which are under the control of the central bank.

Currency drain. Suppose firms and households find it convenient to keep a fixed *fraction* of their money holding in currency (say 5 percent) instead of a fixed *amount* of dollars. In that case an extra $100 in money supply will not all stay in the banking system; only $95 will remain on deposit, while the rest will be added to currency in circulation. In such a situation any multiple expansion of bank deposits will be accompanied by a currency drain to the public that will reduce the maximum expansion below what it was when the public was content to hold all its new money as bank deposits. Table 37-15 shows the position of a monopoly bank after a credit expansion of $400 and a currency drain of $20.

The story of deposit creation when there is a currency drain to the public might go like this: Each bank starts creating deposits and suffers no significant loss of cash to other banks. But because approximately 5 percent of newly created deposits is withdrawn to be held as currency,

TABLE 37-15
The Monopoly Bank's Balance Sheet After a Credit Expansion and a Currency Drain

Assets		Liabilities	
Cash reserves	$ 280	Deposits	$1,480
Loans	1,300	Capital	100
	$1,580		$1,580

The maximum possible deposit expansion is reduced by a currency drain. This example differs from that shown in Table 37-7 because, after a new deposit of $100 and a new loan of $400, 5 percent of the newly created money is withdrawn as currency to be held by the public. Cash and deposits each fall by $20 and the reserve ratio falls below 20 percent.

each bank suffers a currency drain to the public. The expansion continues, each bank watching its own ratio of cash reserves to deposits, expanding deposits as long as the ratio exceeds 1/5 and ceasing when it reaches that figure. Because the expansion is accompanied by a currency drain, it will come to a halt with a smaller deposit expansion than in the no currency drain case.[3]

Central Banks

All advanced free-market economies have, in addition to private banks, a central bank that is responsible for control of the money supply and that exerts a strong influence over major financial markets. The central bank is an instrument of the government, whether or not it is in fact publicly owned. The Bank of England – the "Old Lady of Threadneedle Street" – is one of the oldest and most famous central banks; it began to operate as the central bank of England in the seventeenth century. In the United States the central bank is called the Federal Reserve System, and in this country it is the Bank of Canada.

The similarities of central banks in the functions they perform and the tools they use are much more important than their differences in organization. Although our attention is given to the operations of the Bank of Canada, the basic situation is not different for the Bank of England, the Bank of Greece, or the Federal Reserve System.

Organization of the Bank of Canada

The Bank of Canada is a publicly owned corporation; all profits accruing from its operations

are remitted to the government of Canada. The responsibility for the bank's affairs rests with a board of directors composed of the governnor, the senior deputy governor, the deputy minister of finance, and twelve directors. The governor is appointed by the directors, with the approval of the cabinet, for a seven-year term. The present governor is Mr. Gerald Bouey, who was appointed in 1973, and reappointed for a second term in 1980.

BASIC FUNCTIONS OF A CENTRAL BANK

A central bank serves four main functions: as a banker for private banks, as a bank for the government, as the controller of the nation's supply of money, and as a supporter of financial markets.

The first three functions are revealed by a study of the balance sheet of a central bank. Table 37-16 is such a balance sheet.

Banker to the Chartered Banks

The central bank accepts deposits from the chartered banks and will, on order, transfer them to the account of another bank. In this way the central bank provides the chartered banks with the equivalent of a chequing account and with a means of settling debts to other banks. The deposits of the chartered banks with the central bank appear in Table 37-16. Notice that the cash reserves of the chartered banks deposited with the central bank are *liabilities* of the central bank (because it promises to pay them on demand), just as the money reserves of an individual or corporation deposited with a chartered bank are the liabilities of the chartered bank.

Historically, one of the earliest services provided by central banks was that of "lender of last resort" to the banking system. Central banks would lend money to private banks that had sound investments (such as government securities and safe loans to individuals) but were in urgent need of cash. If such banks could not obtain ready cash, they might be forced into insol-

---

[3] It can be shown algebraically that the percentage of currency drain must be added to the reserve ratio to determine the maximum possible expansion of deposits. [47] Thus if r is the reserve ratio and v the currency drain, the banking system can increase its deposits by $1/(r + v)$ times any new money received by it, instead of by the $1/r$ derived in math note 45 (see page 755). If $r = .20$ and $v = .05$, the expansion will be limited to 4 (= $1/.25$) instead of 5 (= $1/.20$) times the new reserves.

TABLE 37-16

Assets and Liabilities of the Bank of Canada, December 1980 (millions of dollars)

Assets			Liabilities		
Government of Canada securities		$15,794	Notes in circulation		$11,108
Held outright	$15,678		Deposits of Government of		
Held under purchase			Canada		59
and resale agreements	116		Deposits of chartered banks		5,466
Advances to banks		16	Foreign currency liabilities		58
Foreign currency assets		284	Other liabilities and capital		622
Other assets		1,219			$17,313
		$17,313			

Source: Bank of Canada Review, February 1981.

The balance sheet of the Bank of Canada shows that it serves as banker to the chartered banks and the government and as issuer of our currency; it also suggests the Bank's role as regulator of money markets and the money supply. The principal liabilities of the Bank are the basis of the money supply. Bank of Canada notes are currency, and the deposits of the chartered banks give them the reserves they use to create deposit money. The Bank's holdings of Government of Canada securities arise from its operations designed to regulate the money supply and financial markets.

vency because they could not meet the demands of their depositors, in spite of their being basically sound. Today's central banks continue to be the lender of last resort, but Canadian banks seldom use their borrowing privileges at the central bank.

U.S. banks borrow extensively from the Federal Reserve System in order to build up their reserves, but the corresponding institutional arrangement that Canadian banks use is somewhat more complicated. It is reflected in Table 37-16 by Bank of Canada holdings of government securities under **purchase and resale agreements (PRA)**. Rather than rely on advances from the Bank of Canada, the chartered banks meet their immediate cash requirements by varying the amount of **day-to-day loans** they make available to a group of investment dealers who carry inventories of government of Canada securities. When necessary, these dealers can obtain financing from the Bank of Canada under PRA; that is, they can sell securities to the Bank of Canada and agree to buy them back at a later date. Thus, when the chartered banks reduce their day-to-day loans, they induce an increase in PRA. The result is the same as if the banks had borrowed from the Bank of Canada directly.

Banker to the Government

Governments, too, need to hold their funds in an account into which they can make deposits and on which they can write cheques. The government of Canada keeps its chequing deposits at the Bank of Canada, replenishing them from much larger accounts kept at the chartered banks. When the government requires more money, it too needs to borrow, and it does so by printing bonds. Most are sold directly to the public, but occasionally the government raises funds by selling securities (mostly short-term) to the central bank, which "buys" them by crediting the government's account with a deposit for the amount of the purchase. In December 1980 the Bank of Canada held over $15 billion in government of Canada securities. These securities play an important role in the monetary system.

Controller and Regulator of the Money Supply

One of the most important functions of a central bank is to control the money supply. From Table 37-16 it is clear that the overwhelming proportion of a central bank's liabilities (its promises to pay) are either notes (money) or the reserves of the chartered banks, which underlie the deposits (money) of households and firms.

The central bank can affect the levels of its assets and liabilities in many ways, and as its liabilities rise and fall, so does the money supply. Consider a single example. Suppose the central bank buys $100 million worth of newly printed bonds from the government of Canada. The bank's assets (government bonds) rise by $100 million, and so do its liabilities (government of Canada deposits). The government has an extra $100 million of purchasing power to spend. As easy as printing money, you say. Indeed, it is the same thing.

Regulator and Supporter of Money Markets

Central banks usually assume a major responsibility to support the country's financial system and to prevent serious disruption by wide-scale panic and resulting bank failures. Various institutions are in the business of borrowing on a short-term and lending on a long-term basis. To some extent the chartered banks do this when they take in demand (or savings) deposits and lend money for various terms. But trust and mortgage loan companies are the major institution for this kind of transaction. They receive deposits from the public and lend the money on long-term mortgages. Large, unanticipated increases in interest rates tend to squeeze these institutions. The average rate that they earn on their investments rises only slowly as old contracts mature and new ones are made, but they must either pay higher rates to hold onto their deposits or they must accept wide-scale withdrawals that could easily bring about their insolvency. To prevent such financial disasters, central banks often buy and sell government bonds either to slow the rate of change in interest rates or to narrow the range over which the rates are allowed to fluctuate.

Conflicts Among Functions

The several functions of the central bank can each be performed, but they are not always mu-

tually compatible. When the Bank of Canada seeks to bring about a tight money supply and causes interest rates to rise, it is causing the credit squeeze that makes life uncomfortable for banks and other financial institutions and makes borrowing expensive for the government. When the Bank of Canada chooses to ease those problems, say by lending money to banks, it is relaxing its tight-money policy.

The central bank must strive to balance these conflicting objectives. When it wishes to raise interest rates to control the money supply, it must do so by an amount and on such a timetable as to prevent financial panic or disasters in money markets. While in theory there is a compromise that is the ideal balance of all the objectives, there is a major debate about whether an actual central bank can find and follow it. Many critics think that it cannot, that periodically central banks cause problems by their monetary mismanagement.

Control of the Money Supply

The Bank Act requires each chartered bank to maintain reserves in the form of Bank of Canada notes and deposits at the Bank of Canada, and it permits the central bank to buy and sell various financial assets. The provisions enable the central bank to vary the amount of cash reserves available to the banking system and thus to regulate the money supply.

OPEN MARKET OPERATIONS

The most important tool that the central bank has for influencing the supply of money is the purchase or sale of government securities on the open market. At the end of 1980 the Bank of Canada held $15 billion in government securities. In 1962 it held less than $3 billion. In a typical year the Bank of Canada buys and sells over $500 million worth of government securities. What is the effect of these purchases and sales?

Purchases and sales by the central bank of government securities in financial markets are known as **open market operations.** There are active and well-organized markets for government securities, just as there is a stock market. You or I, or General Motors, or the Bank of Montreal, or the Bank of Canada can enter this market and buy or sell negotiable government securities at whatever price supply and demand establishes. When the Bank of Canada buys or sells securities, it does not know from whom it buys or to whom it sells them. The effect on the money supply depends only on whether the transaction is with a chartered bank or with an individual firm, or nonbank financial institution.

Purchases on the Open Market

When the Bank of Canada buys a security from a holder in the nonbank private sector, it pays for it with a cheque drawn on the central bank and payable to the seller. The seller deposits this cheque in its own bank. The chartered bank presents the cheque to the Bank of Canada for payment, and the central bank makes a book entry increasing the deposit of the chartered bank at the central bank. At the end of these transactions, the central bank has acquired a new asset in the form of a security and a new liability in the form of a deposit by the charterd bank. The seller has reduced its security holdings and increased its deposits. The chartered bank has a new deposit equal to the amount paid for the security by the central bank. The chartered bank's reserves and its deposit liabilities have increased by an equal amount.

When the central bank buys securities on the open market, the reserves of the chartered banks are increased. These banks in turn can expand deposits, thereby increasing the money supply.

Table 37-17 shows the changes in the balance sheets of the several parties in response to a central bank purchase of $100 in government securities from the nonbank private sector. After these transactions, the chartered banks have excess reserves and are in a position to expand their loans and deposits. Indeed, the chartered banks

TABLE 37-17

Balance Sheet Changes Caused by an Open Market Purchase from the Nonbank Private Sector

Nonbank Private Sector		
Assets		Liabilities
Bonds	−$100	No change
Deposits	+ 100	

Chartered Banks		
Assets		Liabilities
Reserves (deposits) with central bank)	+$100	Demand deposits +$100

Central Bank		
Assets		Liabilities
Bond	+$100	Deposits of chartered banks +$100

The money supply is increased when the central bank makes an open market purchase from the nonbank private sector. When the Bank of Canada buys a $100 bond, the seller gains money and gives up a bond, and the chartered banks gain a new deposit of $100. Chartered banks can now engage in a multiple expansion of deposit money of the sort analyzed in the chapter.

are in precisely the position studied on page 754. (See Table 37-6.) The new deposit made by an immigrant might just as well have been made by someone who had sold a security to the Bank of Canada.

What if the seller of the security is a chartered bank instead of a private individual? It trades one asset (a security) for another asset (an increased deposit with the central bank). Table 37-18 summarizes the changes that would take place. The chartered banks again find themselves with excess reserves, and they can expand the money supply by expanding loans and deposits or by purchasing securities.

If the central bank buys many securities in the open market, the entire banking system will gain new reserves. Whether the seller is a household, a firm, or a bank, the purchase by the Bank of Canada of securities on the open market sets in motion a series of book transactions that in-

TABLE 37-18

Balance Sheet Changes Caused by an Open Market Purchase from a Chartered Bank

Chartered Banks		
Assets		Liabilities
Reserves	+$100	No change
Bonds	− 100	

Central Bank		
Assets		Liabilities
Bonds	+$100	Deposits of chartered banks +$100

The money supply is increased when the central bank makes an open market purchase from a chartered bank. When the Bank of Canada buys a $100 bond directly from a chartered bank, there is no change in the assets or liabilities of the nonbank sector, but chartered banks gain reserves of $100. They can now engage in a multiple expansion of deposit money of the sort analyzed earlier in the chapter.

crease the banking system's reserves and thus make possible a multiple expansion of credit.[4]

Sales on the Open Market

When the central bank sells securities to a nonbank holder, it receives in return the buyer's cheque drawn against its own deposit in a chartered bank. The central bank presents the cheque to the chartered bank for payment. Payment is made by a book entry reducing the chartered bank's deposit at the central bank.

Now the central bank has reduced its assets by the value of the securities it sold and reduced its liabilities in the form of money owed to the chartered banks. The nonbank private sector has increased its holding of securities and reduced its cash on deposit with a chartered bank. The char-

tered bank has reduced its deposit liabilities and reduced its reserves (on deposit with the central bank) by the same amount. Each of the asset changes is balanced by a liability change. Indeed, everything balances!

But the chartered bank finds that by suffering an equal change in its reserves and deposit liabilities, its ratio of reserves to deposits falls. The changes are the opposite of those shown in Table 37-16. If the reserve ratio was previously at the minimum acceptable level, the chartered bank will have to take immediate steps to restore its reserve ratio. The necessary reduction in deposits can be effected by not making new investments when old ones are redeemed (e.g., by not granting a new loan when old ones are repaid) or by selling (liquidating) existing investments.

To understand this, set up the balance sheet changes that correspond to the verbal description of this case and work through what would have happened if the central bank had sold the securities directly to a chartered bank. In this case there should be a reduction in the chartered bank's reserves by the value of the securities sold by the central bank and (if reserves are pushed below acceptable levels) pressure to liquidate assets in order to reestablish an acceptable reserve ratio.

When the central bank sells securities on the open market, the reserves of the chartered banks are decreased. These banks in turn are forced to contract deposits, thereby decreasing the money supply.

The question arises, What if the public does not want to play ball? How can the central bank force the public to buy securities? The answer, of course, is that there is always a price at which the public will buy. The central bank in its open market operations must be prepared to have the price of the securities fall if it insists on suddenly selling a large volume of them. As we shall see, a fall in the price of securities is the same thing as a rise in interest rates, so if the Bank of Canada wishes to curtail the money supply by selling bonds, it may well drive up interest rates.

---

[4] The effect of an open market purchase on *bank reserves* is the same regardless of the identity of the seller. However, a purchase from a nonbank holder involves an immediate effect on the money supply in the form of increased bank deposits, while a purchase from a chartered bank does not. This can be seen by comparing Tables 37-17 and 37-18.

Notice in Table 37-16 that the Bank of Canada's holdings of government securities are large relative to the reserves of the chartered banks. By selling securities it can contract those reserves very sharply if it chooses. Similarly, by buying securities it can expand them. In its open market operations the central bank has a potent weapon for affecting the size of bank reserves — and thus for affecting the money supply.

OTHER CENTRAL BANK POLICIES

A central bank controls the money supply with the ultimate objective of influencing key macroeconomic variables such as unemployment and inflation. How the money supply influences such targets is the subject of Chapter 38, where we focus attention on the relationship between the money supply and the level of interest rates. Besides using open market operations to control the money supply, the central bank has a number of methods of exerting influence on the economy.

Changes in Required Reserves

An alternative method of controlling bank reserves is to vary the required reserve ratios. Such variations can have very sharp effects on the money supply and thus on the economy. For example, a decrease in the required reserve ratio from 20 percent to $16^2/_3$ percent results in a potential increase in deposits from five times the quantity of reserves available to six times reserves, an increase of 20 percent. Of course, if banks choose not to increase their loans, they need not respond in any way to a decrease in required legal reserves. Therefore a decrease in the required reserve ratio is only permissive, but in normal times the profit motive will lead most banks to respond by increasing loans and deposits.

Increasing the required ratio when the banking system is fully "loaned up" is the opposite side of this picture. Banks that were at the legal reserve ratio will be forced to cut their loans and deposits until they reach the new higher ratio. This causes the money supply to shrink and credit to become tight.

This method of controlling the money supply has been used in the United States but not in Canada. Given the small margin of excess reserves held by the chartered banks, increases in the required reserve ratios would force abrupt adjustments in bank assets. An equivalent contraction in the money supply can be brought about by using the more flexible tool of open market operations, which can be spread out over time to induce a more orderly adjustment. Changes in reserve requirements are occasionally made, but this is usually done for purposes other than stabilizing the economy. For example, reforms of the Bank Act proposed in the late seventies and passed in 1980 reduced the reserve requirement on demand deposits from 12 percent to 10 percent.

Changes in the Bank Rate

The rate of interest at which the central bank makes advances to the chartered banks is called the **bank rate** (or **discount rate** in the United States). In principle, an increase in the bank rate can affect the money supply by raising the banks' demands for excess cash reserves. Banks might be induced to maintain a larger cushion in view of the higher cost of borrowing if they suffer a loss of cash and are forced to seek accommodation from the central bank to meet their reserve requirements. Although this mechanism may operate in the United States, it is not likely to be of importance in Canada because the chartered banks rarely borrow from the Bank of Canada.[5]

Since March 1980 the bank rate has been a "market rate," being set automatically at a premium of one-fourth of one percent over the average rate determined in the weekly Thursday auction of three-month treasury bills. Until that

---

[5] As we have seen, when the chartered banks need cash to meet reserve requirements, they usually obtain it by varying the amount of day-to-day loans they make to investment dealers.

change, the bank rate played an important role as a signal of the central bank's views concerning the appropriate level of interest rates and its intentions with regard to monetary tightness or ease. The "announcement effects" of bank rate changes were frequently used to reinforce the effects of changes in monetary policy.

Most observers believed that a market-determined bank rate would lessen the role played by the bank rate by eliminating the announcement effect; however, the financial press now gives considerable attention to changes in the bank rate, and it is not at all clear that it is less important as a signal about monetary policy.

Secondary Reserve Requirements

At times when the central bank attempts to restrain inflationary forces, it may wish to dampen expenditures not only through higher interest rates but also through some form of direct control over the expansion of bank loans. Restricting the supply of cash reserves will not restrain the banks from extending credit if they have substantial quantities of liquid assets that can be sold off to finance new loans. The Bank of Canada is empowered to restrict the ability of the chartered banks to expand their loans through the imposition of a required minimum secondary reserve ratio within the range of 0 to 12 percent of deposits. Secondary reserves are defined as holdings of treasury bills, day-to-day loans, and excess cash reserves. A required minimum ratio of 8 percent was in effect from the end of 1971 until the end of 1974 when it was lowered to 7 percent. Further reductions were made during 1975 and 1977 so that at the beginning of 1978 the required ratio was 5 percent.

Moral Suasion

The term "moral suasion" is generally used to describe attempts by the central bank to enlist the cooperation of private financial institutions in the pursuit of some objective of monetary policy. In a country such as Canada where there are only a few banks, the central bank can easily communicate its view to the chartered banks. In some cases moral suasion involves general discussions aimed at improving understanding of the current financial situation and the objectives of policy. In other cases specific requests have been issued to the banks, For example, on a number of occasions in recent years the Bank of Canada has attempted to restrain the growth of term deposits by requesting the observance of ceilings either on the interest rates offered or on the volume of deposits.

Summary

1. There are various definitions of the money supply; today the most commonly used measure is M1, which defines money narrowly as currency plus demand deposits. M1 was over $23 billion in 1980.

2. The banking system in Canada consists of eleven chartered banks. The five largest account for 90 percent of total bank assets, and each of them has more than 900 branches.

3. The chartered banks are profit-seeking institutions that allow their customers to transfer deposits from one bank to another by means of cheques. They create and destroy money as a by-product of their operations—by making or liquidating loans and various other kinds of investments.

4. Because most customers are content to pay their accounts by cheque rather than with currency, the banks need keep only a small cash reserve against their deposit liabilities. Consequently, banks can create deposit money. When the banking system receives a new deposit, it can create new deposits to some multiple of this amount. The amount of new deposits created depends on the legal minimum reserves the Bank of Canada enforces on the banks, the amount of currency drain to the public, and whether the banks are motivated to hold excess reserves.

5. All advanced free-market economies have a central bank that serves as banker for private banks, banker for the government, controller and regulator of the money supply, and regulator and supporter of money markets.

6. The major tool the central bank uses to control the supply of money is open market operations. Purchases of bonds on the open market expand the money supply because they create new deposits that permit (but do not force) a multiple expansion of bank credit. Sales on the open market reduce bank reserves and force a multiple contraction of bank credit on the part of all banks that do not have excess reserves.

Topics for Review

The banking system
Assets and liabilities of a chartered bank
The creation and destruction of deposit money
Cash reserve ratio, required cash reserves, and excess
  cash reserves
Functions of a central bank
Open market operations

Discussion Questions

1. Chartered banks in Canada are no longer allowed to issue their own bank notes. How do they now create money? (Explain the process carefully.) How do they make profits? Is it possible for them to create money without being aware of it?
2. In some countries there are no legal reserve requirements. At what level would you expect banks to hold reserves? Would you predict lower reserve ratios in these countries than in Canada?
3. What useful functions do their deposits with the Bank of Canada perform for the chartered banks? Why would the banks usually prefer to keep their cash reserves at or near the legal minimum? Mention several ways in which a chartered bank might build up deficient reserves to the required amount.

4. If all depositors tried to turn their deposits into cash at once, they would find that there are not sufficient reserves in the system to allow everyone to do this at the same time. Why then do we not have panicky runs on the banks? Would a 100 percent reserve requirement be safer? What effect would such a reserve requirement have on the banking system's ability to create money? Would it preclude any possibility of a panic?

5. The reciprocal of the required reserve ratio indicates the maximum multiple expansion of demand deposits that can take place with an increase in bank reserves. Why is the actual expansion likely to be less than the maximum?

6. What would be the effect on the money supply of each of the following?
   a. a decline in the public's confidence in the banks
   b. a desire on the part of banks to increase their levels of excess reserves
   c. the monopolizing of the banking system into a single super bank
   d. the increased use of credit cards

7. During the Christmas and the summer holiday seasons, the level of household spending rises and so does the amount of currency held by the public. Does the rise in the amount of currency cause the rise in spending, or vice versa? Predict the effects of a law passed in October prohibiting the public from withdrawing extra currency from the banks until after the Christmas season.

8. How would you expect the following to change the relative size of M1, M1B, M2, and M3?
   a. allowing interest payments on demand deposits
   b. setting the same maximum interest rate on time deposits in trust companies as in chartered banks (trust companies are now higher)
   c. printing twice as much currency as now printed annually

38

The Macroeconomic Role of Money and the Theory of Monetary Policy

At one time or another most of us have known the surprise of opening our wallet or purse to discover that we had either more or less money than we thought. There can be as much pleasure in deciding how to spend an unexpected windfall in the first case as there can be pain in deciding what intended expenditure to eliminate in the second case.

What determines how much money people hold in their purses and wallets and how much they keep in the bank? What happens when everyone discovers that they are holding more, or less, money than they believe they need to hold?

These turn out to be key questions for our study of the influence of money on output and prices. The answers will help us to establish links between the money supply and the aggregate expenditure and aggregate demand functions; such links are the major topic of the first half of this chapter.

In the preceding chapter we saw that the Bank of Canada can regulate the quantity of money; the second half of this chapter examines the Bank's use of such control in order to influence the economy.

The Demand for and the Supply of Money

KINDS OF ASSETS

At any moment in time households have a given stock of wealth. This wealth is held in many forms. Some of it is money in the bank or in the wallet; some is in short-term securities such as CDs and treasury bills; some is in long-term bonds; and some is in real capital, which may be held directly (in the form of family businesses) or indirectly (in the form of shares of stock that indicate ownership of a corporation's assets). All these ways of holding wealth may be grouped into three main categories: (1) assets that serve as a medium of exchange, that is, paper money, coins, and bank chequing deposits; (2) other financial assets, such as bonds earning a fixed rate of interest, that will yield a fixed money value at some future *maturity* date and that can usually be sold before maturity for a price that fluctuates on the open market; and (3) claims on real capital, that is, physical objects such as factories and machines.

In this chapter we are concerned with the amount of wealth everyone in the economy wishes to hold in the form of money balances. This total is called the **demand for money**, a concept we encountered in Chapter 35 in the discussion of the classical quantity theory of money and prices. We can discover what determines this important magnitude by looking at the division of wealth between the holding of money on the one hand and the holding of other financial assets and real capital on the other. The amount of many balances held in the economy is a *stock* quantity. It is so many millions of dollars. (It is *not* a flow of so much per unit of time.)

"Money" and "Bonds"

There are many different kinds of financial assets. They differ from each other in the rate of interest they yield and in their **liquidity**: the degree of ease and certainty with which an asset can be turned into a given amount of the economy's medium of exchange. The spectrum of financial assets reaches from perfectly liquid currency that earns no interest at one end to relatively illiquid long-term bonds that earn a substantial interest rate at the other end.

To simplify our discussion, it is helpful to assume that only kinds of financial assets exist: *money*, which is perfectly liquid but earns no in-

terest return, and *bonds*, which are less liquid but earn an interest return. Here the term *bonds* stands for all interest-earning financial assets plus claims on real capital such as equities.

The Rate of Interest and the Price of Bonds

A bond is a promise by the issuer to pay a stated sum of money as interest each year and to repay the face value of the bond at some future "redemption date," often many years distant. The time until the redemption date is called the **term to maturity** or often simply the **term** of the bond. Some bonds, called perpetuities, pay interest forever and never repay the principal.

The price of any bond reflects the value of the stream of future payments that its owner will receive.

The relationship between interest rates and bond prices is most easily seen in the case of a perpetuity. Assume that such a bond will pay $100 per year to its holder. The *present value* of this bond depends on how much $100 per year is worth, and this in turn depends on the rate of interest. (The discussion of the concept of present value in Chapter 22, pages 417–418, may profitably be read at this time.)

A bond that will produce a stream of income of $100 a year forever is worth $1,000 at 10 percent interest because $1,000 invested at 10 percent per annum will yield $100 interest per year forever. But the same bond is worth $2,000 when the interest rate is 5 percent per year because it takes $2,000 invested at 5 percent per annum to yield $100 interest per year. The lower the rate of interest obtainable on the market, the more valuable is a bond paying a fixed amount of interest.

Similar relations apply to bonds that are not perpetuities, though the calculation of present value must allow for the lump-sum repayment of principal at maturity. In general, the present value of any asset that yields a stream of money over time is inversely related to the interest rate.

This proposition has two important implications: (1) if the rate of interest falls, the value of an asset producing a given income stream will rise; and (2) when the market price of an asset producing a fixed income is forced up, this is equivalent to a decrease in the rate of interest earned by the asset.

Thus a promise to pay $100 one year from now is worth $92.59 when the interest rate is 8 percent and only $89.29 when the interest rate is 12 percent. For $92.59 at 8 percent interest ($92.59 × 1.08) and $89.29 at 12 percent interest ($89.29 × 1.12) are both worth $100 in one year's time.

The rate of interest and bond prices vary inversely with each other.

A redeemable bond differs from a perpetuity in that its present value becomes increasingly dominated by the fixed redemption value as the redemption date approaches. Take an extreme case: if a bond will be redeemable for $1,000 in a week's time, its present value will be very close to $1,000 no matter what the interest rate. Thus its value will not change much even if the rate of interest leaps from 5 percent to 10 percent during that week.

The closer to the present date is the redemption date of a bond, the less the bond's value will change with a change in the rate of interest.

For example, a rise in the interest rate from 8 to 12 percent will lower the value of $100 payable in one year's time by 3.6 percent, but the same rise will lower the value of the same sum payable in ten years time by a full 37.9 percent.[1]

WHAT DETERMINES THE SUPPLY OF MONEY?

As used in this chapter, the supply of money is M1: the quantity of currency plus demand de-

posits with the chartered banks. In January 1981, M1 was approximately $25 billion. We saw in the preceding chapter that deposit money is created by the chartered banks, but only within limits set by their reserves, which are under the control of the Bank of Canada. Thus the ultimate control of the money supply is in the Bank of Canada's hands. Later in this chapter we shall look at the degree to which the Bank of Canada can in fact control the money supply with a view to manipulating the economy. For now we shall simplify by assuming that the money supply can be precisely controlled by the Bank of Canada. This makes it an exogenous variable, to be determined by the Bank's policy decisions.

Let us see first how the economy adjusts to a given money supply.

WHAT DETERMINES THE DEMAND FOR MONEY?

When we say that on January 2, 1981, the demand for money was $25 billion, we mean that on that date everyone wished to hold money balances that totaled $25 billion. But why do firms and households wish to hold money balances at all?

There is a cost in holding any money balance. The money could instead be used to purchase bonds; it would then earn interest as a return. The opportunity cost of holding any money balance is the rate of interest that could have been earned if the money had instead been used to purchase bonds.

Clearly money will be held only when it provides services that are valued at least as highly as the opportunity cost of holding it. The services provided by money balances are, first, to finance purchases and sales; second, to provide a cushion against uncertainty about the timing of cash flows; and third, to provide a hedge against uncertainty over the prices of other financial assets. The desire to hold money to obtain each of these services is summarized by the so-called **transactions motive, precautionary motive,** and **speculative motive** for holding money. We may now see

---

[1] The example assumes annual compounding. The first case is calculated from the numbers of the previous example: $(92.58 - 89.29)/92.58$. The ten-year case uses the formula present value = the principal/$(l + r)^n$, which gives $46.30 with 8 percent and $28.75 with 12 percent. The fall in value is thus $(46.30 - 28.75)/46.30 = 0.379$.

how these motives together determine the demand for money.

The Demand for Money and National Income I: The Transactions Motive Once Again

The transactions demand for money, which played a key role in the argument of the quantity theorists, is one element (among several) in contemporary theories. Keynesians expect, as did the quantity theorists, that the transactions demand will take the form of currency and demand deposits and will rise and fall directly with the level of national income.

In an imaginary world, where the receipts and disbursements of households and firms were perfectly synchronized, it would be unnecessary to hold transactions balances. If every time a household spent $10 it received $10 as part payment of its income, no transactions balances would be needed. In the real world, however, receipts and disbursements are not perfectly synchronized. As a result, households and firms will hold money balances in order to finance transactions. The need for transactions balances depends on the money value of all kinds of transactions. This in turn depends on the money value of national income.[2] If money national income doubles, the money value of transactions will tend to double, as will the demand for money to finance the transactions.

The Demand for Money and National Income II: The Precautionary Motive

Many goods and services are sold on credit. The seller can never be certain when payment for those goods will be made, and the buyer can never be certain of the day of delivery and thus on the day on which payment will fall due. In order to operate without a series of cash crises caused by receipts being abnormally low and/or disbursements being abnormally high, firms and households carry money balances as a precaution. The larger are the precautionary balances, the greater is the degree of protection against running out of money because of temporary fluctuations in cash flows.

How serious this risk is depends on the penalties for being caught without sufficient money balances. A firm is unlikely to be pushed into insolvency, but it may have to incur considerable costs if it is forced to borrow money at high interest rates for short periods in order to meet a temporary cash crisis.

The transactions motive arises because a firm knows that payments and receipts will not synchronize perfectly. The precautionary motive arises because the firm is uncertain about the *degree* to which payments and receipts will synchronize.

The protection provided by a given quantity of precautionary balances depends on the volume of payments and receipts. A $100 precautionary balance provides a large cushion (50 percent) for a person whose volume of payments per month is $200, and a very small cushion (1 percent) for a firm whose monthly volume is $10,000. Haphazard fluctuations of the sort that give rise to precautionary balances may be expected to vary directly with the firm's cash flow. To provide the same degree of protection as the value of transactions rises, more money is necessary. Thus the firm's precautionary demand for money will rise as national income rises.[3]

The transactions and precautionary motives cause the demand for money to vary directly with the value of national income measured at current prices.

---

[2] The difference between total transactions and national income arises from the problem of "double counting" (see page 579). In economies where both magnitudes have been estimated, the value of total transactions runs from five to ten times as large as national income.

[3] Institutional arrangements affect the precautionary demands. In the past, for example, a traveler would have had to carry a substantial precautionary balance in cash, but today a credit card covers most unforeseen expenses that may arise while traveling.

The Demand for Money and Wealth: The Speculative Motive

Households that hold bonds will have to sell some if they wish to consume in excess of their current income or if some temporary excess of payments over receipts exceeds their money holdings. At one extreme, if a household or firm held all its wealth in bonds, it would earn interest on all that wealth, but it would have to sell some bonds the first time its payments exceeded its receipts. At the other extreme, if a household or firm held all its wealth in money, the money would earn no interest, but the household or firm would never have to sell bonds to meet excesses of payments over current receipts. Wealth holders usually do not adopt either extreme position; instead, they hold part of their wealth as money and part as bonds. (Do not forget that "bonds" are here defined to include such interest-earning assets as deposits in savings accounts, certificates of deposit, and treasury bills.)

A household that holds bonds and money runs the risk that an unexpected gap between its receipts and its payments will force it to sell some bonds. If the price of bonds were fixed, there would be no risk in selling. But the price of bonds fluctuates from day to day on the open market. A household that may have to sell bonds to meet a need for money takes the risk that the price of bonds may be unexpectedly low at the time it sells them. Of course, if the household is lucky, the price may be unexpectedly high. But because no one knows in advance which way the price will go, firms and households must accept a risk whenever they hold in the form of bonds wealth that they may need to spend. Many firms and households do not like risk—economists say they are *risk averse*. This leads them to hold more money than they otherwise would, in order to reduce the risk of having to sell bonds in the future at a price that cannot be predicted in advance.

The motive that leads firms to hold more money in order to avoid the risks inherent in a fluctuating price of bonds was analyzed first by Keynes, who called it the **speculative motive.** The modern analysis of this motive, sketched in the preceding paragraph, is the work of Professor James Tobin of Yale University, winner of the 1981 Nobel prize in economics.

Firms and households tend to insure against this risk by holding some fraction of their wealth in money and the rest in earning assets. Thus the demand for money depends on wealth and varies directly with wealth. For example, Ms. B. O'Reiley might elect to hold 5 percent of her wealth in money and the other 95 percent in bonds. If Ms. O'Reiley's wealth is $50,000, her demand for money will be $2,500. If her wealth increases to $60,000, her demand for money will rise to $3,000. Although an individual's wealth may rise or fall rapidly, the total wealth of a society changes only slowly. For the analysis of short-term fluctuations in national income, the effects of changes in wealth are fairly small, and we shall ignore them for the present. (Over the long term, however, variations in wealth can have a major effect on the demand for money.)

A second important aspect of the speculative demand for money leads to the extremely important relation discussed in the next section.

The Demand for Money and the Rate of Interest

An important force acting on the decision of how to divide wealth between bonds and money is the cost of holding money. Wealth held in cash earns no interest; hence the reduction in risk involved in holding more money also carries a cost in terms of interest earnings forgone.

The speculative motive leads a household or firm to add to its money holdings until the reduction in risk obtained by the last dollar added is just balanced (in the wealth holder's view) by the cost in terms of the interest forgone on that dollar.

Because the cost of holding money balances is the interest that could have been earned if wealth had been held in bonds instead, the demand to hold money will vary inversely with the interest rate. When the rate of interest falls, the cost of holding money falls. This leads to more money being held both for precautionary motives (to reduce risks caused by uncertainty about the flows of payments and receipts) and for speculative motives (to reduce risks associated with fluctuations in the market price of bonds). When the rate of interest rises, the cost of holding money rises. This leads to less money being held for speculative and precautionary motives.

The transactions demand for money is also related to the rate of interest because wealth held as money is not earning interest for its owners. Thus, other things being equal, people are motivated to reduce their balances of idle cash to a minimum. One way to do this is to make frequent switches between money and other assets.

Consider a man who is paid monthly. He can hold all unspent income in a demand deposit at his bank, in which case he will have an average transactions balance equal to half his monthly salary. Or, dividing the month into four quarters, he could keep a quarter of his salary in cash at payday and invest the other three quarters in interest-yielding assets. At the start of the second quarter, he would cash in a third of his assets and obtain enough cash to finance the second quarter's expenditure. He would do the same at the start of the third quarter, and at the start of the fourth quarter he would cash in the last of his assets. In this way he reduces his average transactions holding to one-eighth of a month's income (at the start of each quarter of the month he has one-fourth of a month's income as a balance, and by the end of the quarter he is down to nothing) and correspondingly increases his average holding of interest-earning assets.

Similar calculations would show that if the same man made *daily* transfers of funds, he could reduce his transactions balances even further. Obviously, the sensible arrangement will depend on how much interest can be earned and how costly (in terms of trips to the bank, inconvenience, and brokerage fees) it is to switch assets. Since these transactions costs are certainly not negligible, balances held to meet transactions demands will not be negligible.

The higher the rate of return on interest-earning assets, the greater is the inducement to invest available funds rather than to hold money to bridge the gaps between receipts and payments. Yet in order to hold a smaller quantity of transactions balances, one must make more frequent switches between money and other assets and thereby incur higher costs. The modern theory of transactions balances predicts that these costs will be less of an inhibition the higher is the rate of interest, and thus that the amount of money held for transactions purposes will be lower the higher is the rate of interest.

There is an important general conclusion of this analysis:

The demand for money varies inversely with the rate of interest.

The Total Demand for Money: Recapitulation

The demand for money is defined as the total amount of money balances that everyone in the economy wishes to hold. Our discussion of the motives for holding money leads to the conclusion that the demand for money, which is the demand to hold a stock of money balances, varies directly with national income and wealth, and inversely with the rate of interest.

Variations in wealth are an important influence on variations in the demand for money in the long term; they are relatively unimportant in the short term, however, because society's total wealth changes only slowly.

Figure 38-1 shows the influences of national income and rate of interest, the two variables that account for most of the short-term variations in the quantity of money demanded. Following Keynes, the function relating money demand to the rate of interest is called the **liquidity preference (LP) function.** Since this function merely shows how the demand for money varies with the rate of interest, it is often labeled M^D, for money demand, rather than LP, for liquidity preference. Whichever name is used the relation

FIGURE 38-1
The Demand for Money as a Function of Income and Interest Rates

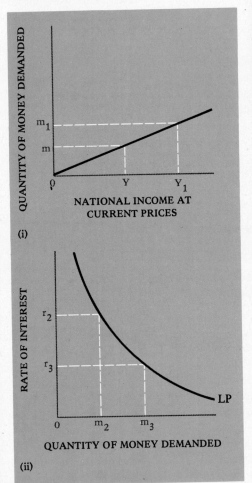

(i)

(ii)

The quantity of money demanded varies directly with national income and inversely with the rate of interest. In (i) the demand for money varies directly with money national income. As income rises from Y to Y_1, firms and households increase their demand for money from m to m_1.

In (ii) the demand for money varies inversely with the rate of interest along the liquidity preference function. As the rate falls from r_2 to r_3, firms and households increase their demand for money from m_2 to m_3.

(Note that the quantity of money is a variable in both parts of this figure but that it appears once on the horizontal axis and once on the vertical axis.)

is clear: how the quantity of money people wish to hold varies as the rate of interest varies.

The Determination of Monetary Equilibrium: The Transmission Mechanism

A **monetary disequilibrium** is a situation where the demand for money does not equal the supply of money. A **monetary equilibrium** is a situation where the two magnitudes are equal. In Chapter 5 we saw that when there is disequilibrium in a competitive market for some commodity such as carrots, the price will change to bring about an equilibrium. What will do the same job with respect to money demand and money supply?

The answer is that the rate of interest will change to eliminate the excess demand for money. But as we saw in Chapter 32, desired investment expenditure is sensitive to the interest rate. Here, then, is a link between monetary factors and real expenditure flows.

The mechanism by which excess demand for or supply of money affects the aggregate expenditure function is called the transmission mechanism. In the next two sections we study its two parts, first, the link between monetary disequilibrium and the interest rate and, second, the link between the interest rate and the aggregate expenditure function.

FROM MONETARY DISEQUILIBRIUM TO CHANGES IN THE RATE OF INTEREST

To study how monetary disequilibrium affects the rate of interest, we look separately at situations of excess demand and excess supply.

An Excess Demand for Money

We saw that firms and households must decide how much of their wealth to hold as money and how much to hold as bonds. When a single household or firm finds that it has less money than it wishes to hold, it need only sell some bonds and add the proceeds to its money holdings. This transaction simply redistributes given stocks of bonds and money between two individuals; it does not change the total supply of either money or bonds. Now assume that everyone in the economy has an excess demand for money balances. All try to sell bonds to add to their money balances. But what one person can do, everyone cannot do. At any moment in time, the society's total stocks of money and bonds are fixed; there is just so much money and so many bonds in existence. If everyone tries to sell bonds, there will be no one to buy them. The price of bonds will fall.

We saw earlier that a fall in the price of bonds is the same thing as a rise in the rate of interest. (For example, if a "bond" offering a single payment of $100 in one year's time falls in price from $95 to $90, this implies a rise in the rate of interest from 5.3 to 11.1 percent.) As the interest rate rises, people will economize on money balances because the opportunity cost of holding them is rising; that is, money balances move upward along the liquidity preference curve in response to a rise in the rate of interest. Eventually the interest rate will rise high enough that people will no longer try to add to their money balances by selling bonds. When there is no longer an excess supply of bonds, the interest rate will stop rising. The demand for money again equals the supply.

The net effect of the original excess demand for money will have been an increase in the rate of interest, as illustrated in Figure 38-2.

An excess demand for money causes firms and households to try to sell bonds to add to their money balances. This raises interest rates and lowers the quantity of money demanded until it equals the fixed money supply.

In other words, because the money supply is fixed by the Bank of Canada, the rate of interest will fluctuate until people are willing to hold that fixed supply. If they want to hold more, their attempts to get it by selling bonds will drive up the interest rate. If they want to hold less, their attempts to buy bonds with their unwanted holdings will drive down the interest rate.

FIGURE 38-2

The Effects of Monetary Disequilibrium on the Interest Rate

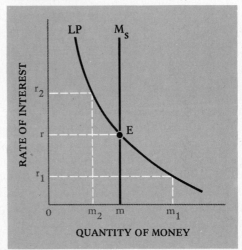

The interest rate rises when there is an excess demand for money and falls when there is an excess supply of money. The fixed quantity of money, m, is shown by the completely inelastic supply curve M_S. The demand for money is LP. Equilibrium is at E with a rate of interest of r.

If the interest rate is r_1, there will be an excess demand for money of $m_1 m$. Bonds will be offered for sale in an attempt to increase money holdings. This will force the rate of interest up to r (the price of bonds falls), at which point the quantity of money demanded has fallen to equal the fixed quantity supplied of m.

If the interest rate is r_2, there will be an excess supply of money of $m m_2$. Bonds will be demanded in return for excess money balances. This will force the rate of interest down to r (the price of bonds rises), at which point the quantity of money demanded has risen to equal the fixed supply of m.

An Excess Supply of Money

Assume now that firms and households hold larger money balances than they would like. A single household or firm would purchase bonds with its excess balances; it would then reach monetary equilibrium by reducing its money holdings and increasing its bond holdings.

But what one household or firm can do, all cannot do. When all households enter the bond market and try to purchase bonds with unwanted stocks of money, they bid up the price of existing bonds—which entails a fall in the interest rate. As the rate falls, households and firms become willing to hold larger quantities of money; that is, the quantity of money demanded moves downward along the liquidity preference curve in response to a fall in the rate of interest.

This rise in the price of bonds continues until firms and households stop trying to convert bonds into money. It continues, then, until everyone is content to hold the existing supplies of money and bonds. Thus the whole economy arrives at equilibrium because the price of bonds rises (the rate of interest falls) until the quantities of money and bonds demanded equal their fixed supplies. This is also shown in Figure 38-2.

An excess supply of money causes firms and households to try to buy bonds. This lowers interest rates until the quantity of money demanded equals the constant money supply.

Monetary Equilibrium

We have discussed the two cases of monetary disequilibrium, excess monetary demand and excess monetary supply. Clearly the condition for monetary equilibrium is that the rate of interest be such that everyone is willing to hold the existing supplies of money and bonds. While a single individual can reach equilibrium holdings of money and bonds by adjusting the quantities held at existing market prices, the whole economy can reach equilibrium only by having bond prices (i.e., the rate of interest) adjust so that people are willing to hold the existing fixed quantities of money and bonds.

FROM CHANGES IN THE RATE OF INTEREST TO SHIFTS IN AGGREGATE EXPENDITURE

The second link in the transmission mechanism from money to aggregate expenditure is one that relates interest rates to expenditure. We saw in Chapter 32 that investment, which includes ex-

penditure on inventory accumulation, residential construction, and plant and equipment, responds to changes in the rate of interest. Other things being equal, a decrease in the rate of interest makes borrowing cheaper and will set off a bout of new investment expenditure.[4]

Economists hypothesize an inverse relation between the rate of interest and the quantity of investment. This relation is shown by a downward-sloping curve, indicating that the lower is the rate of interest, the higher will be investment expenditure. This relation between investment and the rate of interest is called the **marginal efficiency of investment (MEI) function.** A graph of it is shown in Figure 38-3(ii).

THE TRANSMISSION MECHANISM SUMMARIZED

The transmission mechanism provides a connection between monetary forces and real expenditure forces. A monetary disequilibrium sets up a chain of events that will eventually cause the aggregate expenditure function to shift. The working of this mechanism may be summarized:

The transmission mechanism works from an excess demand or excess supply of money, to changes in the demand or supply of bonds, to changes in bond prices and interest rates, to changes in investment expenditure, to shifts in the aggregate expenditure function.

Because a change in the money supply changes interest rates—and thereby changes investment and national income—the influence of money spreads throughout the whole economic system. The money supply is linked to aggregate demand and aggregate expenditure by the interest rate.

The Theory of Monetary Policy

Monetary policy attempts to influence the economy by altering the money supply and interest

---

[4] In Chapter 32 we saw that purchases of durable consumer goods also respond to changes in interest rates. In this chapter we concentrate on investment expenditure, which may be taken to stand for *all interest-senstive expenditure.*

FIGURE 38-3

The Effects of Changes in the Money Supply on Investment Expenditure

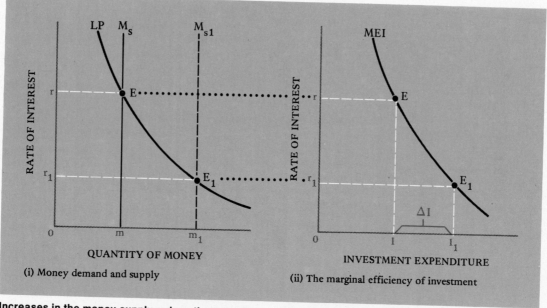

(i) Money demand and supply

(ii) The marginal efficiency of investment

Increases in the money supply reduce the rate of interest and increase desired investment expenditure. The economy is in equilibrium at E with a quantity of money of m (yielding inelastic money supply curve, M_S), an interest rate of r, and investment expenditure of I. The Bank of Canada then increases the money supply to M_{s1}. This forces the rate of interest down to r_1

and increases investment expenditure by ΔI, to I_1. This is the effect of an expansionary monetary policy.

A contractionary monetary policy reduces the money supply from M_{S1} to M_S. This raises interest rates from r_1 to r and lowers investment expenditure by ΔI, from I_1 to I.

rates. Monetary policy is administered by the country's central bank, which in Canada is the Bank of Canada. When the Bank changes the money supply, it creates the type of monetary disequilibrium whose effects we have just studied.[5]

POLICY-INDUCED MONETARY DISEQUILIBRIUM

Say that the economy is in equilibrium, with desired aggregate expenditure equal to income at less than full-employment national income and

with the demand for money equal to its supply. Then the Bank of Canada increases the money supply, which creates an excess supply of money. Firms and households now hold larger money balances than they require, and they will try to buy bonds with the extra money balances. This action forces up the price of bonds, which means a fall in the rate of interest. Desired investment rises along the MEI curve. These changes, shown in Figure 38-3, are merely an application of the transmission mechanism.

The increase in desired investment expenditure shifts the AE and AD functions. The aggregate expenditure curve shifts upward, indicating more desired expenditure at each level of national income. The aggregate demand curve shifts rightward, indicating a higher demand for output at each price level. These shifts raise

[5] As we shall see, the Bank of Canada can in principle affect the money supply or interest rates; it cannot, however, expect to have an independent influence on both.

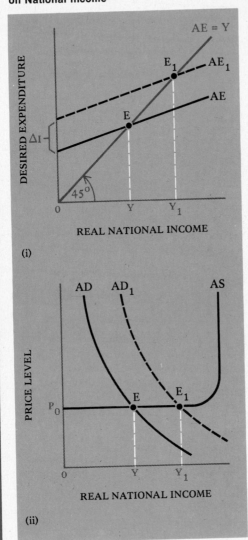

FIGURE 38-4
The Effects of Changes in the Money Supply on National Income

(i)

(ii)

Changes in the money supply cause shifts in the aggregate expenditure and aggregate demand functions. An expansionary monetary policy increases the money supply. In Figure 38-3 it increased desired investment expenditure by ΔI. Here it raises the aggregate expenditure function by ΔI (which is the same as ΔI in Figure 38-3), from AE to AE_1. It also shifts the aggregate demand curve outward from AD to AD_1. Equilibrium income rises from Y to Y_1.

A contractionary monetary policy decreases the money supply. When the supply of money falls (from M_{S1} to M_S in Figure 38-3), investment falls by ΔI thereby shifting aggregate expenditure from AE_1 to AE. This reduces equilibrium income from Y_1 to Y.

equilibrium national income, as shown in Figure 38-4.

What happens when the Bank of Canada decreases the money supply? This creates an excess demand for money because firms and households no longer have the money balances they wish to hold at the existing level of interest rates. In an effort to replenish their inadequate holdings of money, firms and households will seek to sell bonds. But all cannot succeed in doing this; their efforts to sell will drive the price of bonds down, which means an increase in the interest rate. The increased interest rate will cause a reduction in investment expenditure. This in turn shifts the aggregate expenditure function downward and the aggregate demand curve leftward. These shifts lower equilibrium income.[6]

Monetary policy seeks to create a monetary disequilibrium that will work through the transmission mechanism to shift the aggregate expenditure and aggregate demand functions and so change equilibrium national income. An increase in the money supply is expansionary, a decrease is contractionary.

THE STRENGTH OF MONETARY POLICY

So far we have seen that increases in the quantity of money tend to increase national income, while decreases in the quantity of money tend to decrease national income. How strong is this relation? If, for example, the Bank of Canada engineers an immediate 10 percent increase in the money supply, by how much will income rise?

The magnitude of the changes in national income caused by changes in the money supply

---

[6] Since the demand for money in general will depend upon the level of national income, as shown in Figure 38-1(i), our analysis at this stage is incomplete. The induced change in equilibrium national income will lead to a shift in the liquidity preference function in Figure 38-2. For simplicity we assume in the analysis in the text that the liquidity preference function does not shift in response to a change in national income. The appendix to this chapter presents a formal analysis in which this effect is allowed for and in which equilibrium levels of the interest rate and national income are determined simultaneously.

depends on the shapes of the schedules for liquidity preference and marginal efficiency of investment. The influences of the shapes of the two schedules may be summarized:

1. A change in the money supply will have a larger effect on interest rates, the steeper (less interest elastic) is the *LP* function.[7]
2. A change in the rate of interest will have a larger effect on investment, and hence on national income, the flatter (more interest elastic) is the *MEI* function.[8]

The combination that produces the largest effect on national income for a given change in the money supply is a steep *LP* function and a flat, *MEI* function. This combination makes monetary policy a powerful means of influencing the economy.

The combination that produces the smallest effect is a flat *LP* function and a steep *MEI* function. This combination makes monetary policy relatively ineffective. All this is illustrated in Figure 38-5.

Not surprisingly, much of the controversy about the effectiveness of monetary policy as a means for influencing national income has centered on the shapes of these two functions. We shall discuss this controversy further in Chapter 42.

Changes in the Price Level

With what we know now, we can begin to study the theory of inflation systematically. Here we confine that study to certain basic points, leaving the full story to be taken up in Part Eleven. Our ultimate goal is to discover the *causes* of changes in the price level. The best place to start, however, is with some *consequences* of changes in the price level.

THE SHAPE OF THE AGGREGATE DEMAND CURVE

Our first task is to see the effects on aggregate expenditure and hence on equilibrium income of changes in the price level. In Chapter 28 we mentioned three ways that the price level influences aggregate demand: it changes the relative price of domestic to foreign goods, it alters the real value of existing monetary assets, and it creates a monetary disequilibrium. In this chapter we focus on the third.

The chain of causes that links changes in the price level to changes in the aggregate expenditure function, though long, is already largely familiar. In brief, a rise in the price level creates monetary disequilibrium, then the process of the transmission mechanism links monetary disequilibrium to a shift in the aggregate expenditure function. Let us follow the steps in detail.

We begin at a position of equilibrium, where at the current price level, P, aggregate desired expenditure equals income, Y, and the demand and supply of money are equal. P and Y yield one point on the aggregate demand curve.

Now let the price level rise to some higher level, P_1. For any given *real* national income, the money value of total sales must rise in proportion to the rise in the price level. If real income is constant while the price level rises by, say, 10 percent, then the market value of national income must rise by 10 percent.

The rise in the money value of all transactions leads to an increase in the quantity of money needed for transactions purposes. This causes a rise in the demand for money.

A rise in the demand for money, with an unchanged supply of money, creates an excess demand for money. This monetary disequilibrium sets the transmission mechanism in operation. The excess demand for money leads to (1) an attempt to sell bonds to replenish money balances, (2) a fall in bond prices, which entails a

---

[7] The elasticity of this function is defined as the percentage change in the quantity of money demanded, divided by the percentage change in the rate of interest.

[8] The elasticity of this function is defined as the percentage change in investment, divided by the percentage change in the rate of interest.

FIGURE 38-5
The Strength of Monetary Policy

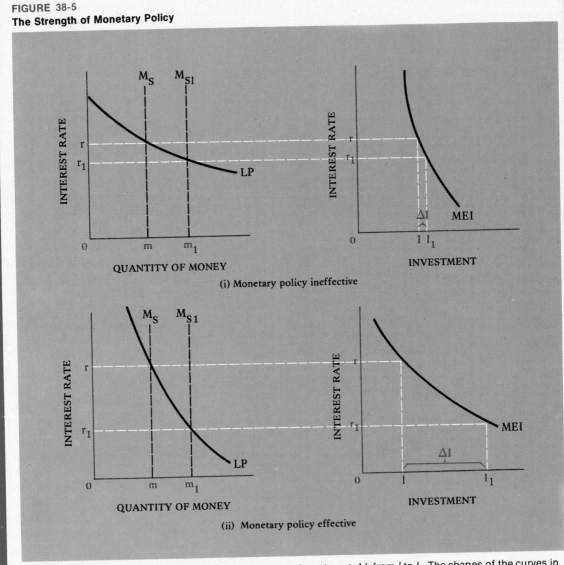

(i) Monetary policy ineffective

(ii) Monetary policy effective

Monetary policy is most effective when the *LP* curve is very inelastic and the *MEI* curve is very elastic. In both (i) and (ii) the same increase in the money supply from M_S to M_{S1} lowers the rate of interest from r to r_1. This fall in the rate of interest leads to an increase in investment, ΔI, from I to I_1. The shapes of the curves in (i) cause monetary policy to have a small effect on investment—and thus on aggregate expenditure; the shapes of the curves in (ii) cause monetary policy to have a large effect.

rise in interest rates, and (3) a fall in desired investment, which means a downward shift in the aggregate expenditure function. This process is described further in Figure 38-6.

The new equilibrium national income that results from these changes is less than the original equilibrium income. The higher price level, P_1, and the lower income, Y_1, yield a second point in

A Common Error in Explaining the Shape of the Aggregate Demand Curve

Beginners sometimes offer a plausible but erroneous argument to account for the slope of the *AD* function. They argue that a rise in the price level will obviously lower the aggregate expenditure function because people will be able to buy less with their money incomes as prices rise. Thus the *AD* curve will slope upward to the left.

This appealing argument confuses real and nominal values. The aggregate expenditure function is expressed in real units; it shows how real expenditure (measured in constant prices) is related to real national income (measured in constant prices). An inflation that raises the money value of prices also raises the money value of most incomes. If both money prices and money incomes rise in the same proportion, the aggregate expenditure function will remain unchanged. Inflation does not shift the aggregate expenditure function through its effects on the purchasing power of money incomes that are fixed for the whole economy. (Of course, some unfortunate people are on incomes fixed in money terms, but the vast majority of income earners find the prices of what they sell to earn their incomes rising along with the prices of what they buy to spend their incomes.)

Perhaps the easiest way to see that inflation does not necessarily shift the aggregate expenditure function downward by reducing real expenditure directly is to note that if *real* national income is constant everyone cannot be worse off. Since total real income is fixed at any point in the aggregate expenditure function, one person's loss must be someone else's gain. Thus inflation will *not* directly shift the aggregate expenditure function downward, because a given level of *real* income (and a given interest rate) will be associated with a given level of *real* desired expenditure whatever the price level.*

The correct reason why a rise in the price level lowers aggregate expenditure is that it raises interest rates, and this lowers investment expenditure.

* Inflation will shift the aggregate expenditure function downward through its effects on money incomes only if it redistributes income systematically from people with higher marginal propensities to consume to people with lower propensities. (We ignore this redistributive effect here because there is no evidence that it exerts a systematic and continuous force on the expenditure function in one direction or the other.)

an aggregate demand function that slopes downward to the right. The slope of the *AD* curve is explained further in Figure 38-7 and again in the appendix to this chapter.

The inverse relation between the price level and equilibrium real income shown by the *AD* curve occurs because *ceteris paribus* a rise in the price level raises the demand for money, and this shifts the aggregate expenditure function downward and lowers equilibrium national income.

Notice the qualification, "Other things being equal." It is important for this argument that the nominal money supply remain constant. The monetary disequilibrium occurs because the demand for money increases when the price level rises *while the money supply is held constant.* The attempt to add to money balances by selling bonds is what drives the interest rate up and reduces desired expenditure, thereby reducing equilibrium national income.

FIGURE 38-6
The Effects of Changes in the Price Level on Investment Expenditure

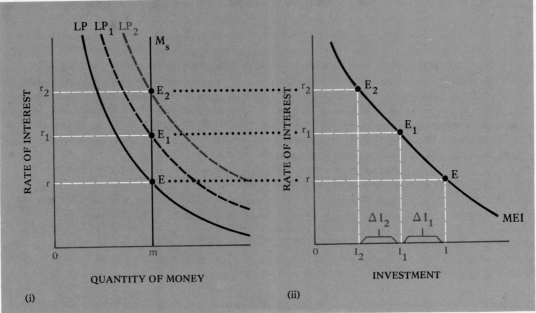

An increase in the price level raises the rate of interest and lowers investment expenditure. The economy is in equilibrium at E, with a liquidity preference schedule and money supply of LP and M_s, a rate of interest of r, and investment expenditure of I. An increase in the price level raises the money value of transactions and increases the demand for money to LP_1. This raises interest rates to r_1 and lowers investment expenditure by ΔI_1, to I_1.

A further increase in the price level shifts the liquidity preference function to LP_2, raises the interest rate to r_2, and lowers investment expenditure by ΔI_2, to I_2.

EQUILIBRIUM NATIONAL INCOME AND THE PRICE LEVEL

The aggregate demand curve shows points where desired expenditure equals income and the demand for money equals its supply. If firms are willing and able to produce whatever is demanded at some price level, the aggregate demand curve will determine the equilibrium level of national income at that price level. This is the case on the perfectly elastic Keynesian portion of the aggregate supply curve.

What if an *upward-sloping AS* curve lies to the left of the *downward-sloping AD* curve at the current price level, as shown at P_1 in Figure 38-8? This situation is not an equilibrium. When firms produce all they are willing to produce at the going price level, aggregate desired expenditure exceeds output. Thus there is excess demand, and the price level will rise. As this happens, aggregate quantity supplied increases along the *AS* curve while aggregate quantity demanded decreases along the *AD* curve (for the reasons just analyzed). This will continue until an equilibrium is reached.

THE PRICE LEVEL AND THE MONETARY ADJUSTMENT MECHANISM

The foregoing analysis has a very important but subtle implication for the theory of inflation:

A sufficiently large rise in the price level will eliminate any inflationary gap, provided the nominal money supply is held constant.

FIGURE 38-7
The Slope of the Aggregate Demand Curve

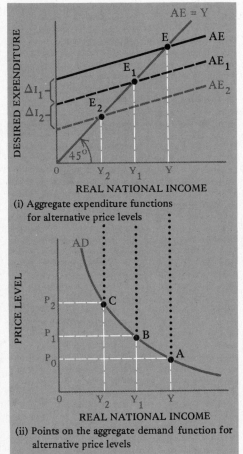

(i) Aggregate expenditure functions
   for alternative price levels

(ii) Points on the aggregate demand function for
     alternative price levels

The aggregate demand curve's slope occurs because an increase in the price level lowers aggregate expenditures and hence lowers equilibrium income. Initially the price level is P_0, the aggregate expenditure function is AE, and equilibrium income is Y. This yields point A on the AD curve in (ii).

A rise in the price level to P_1 shifts the aggregate expenditure function downward by ΔI_1 (see Figure 38-6), to AE_1. Equilibrium national income is now Y_1. This yields point B on the AD curve.

A rise in the price level to P_2 shifts the aggregate expenditure function downward by ΔI_2 (see Figure 38-6), to AE_2. Equilibrium income is now Y_2. This yields point C on the AD curve.

Repeating the process for every price level traces out the curved line of the aggregate demand function shown in (ii).

FIGURE 38-8
Determination of National Income and the Price Level

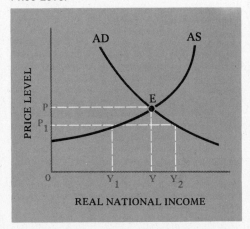

When the *AD* curve slopes downward and the *AS* curve slopes upward, they jointly determine national income and the price level. The initial price level is P_1. The level of income that would leave desired expenditure equal to national income is Y_2. Suppose, however, the output Y_1 is all that firms are willing to produce at a price level of P_1. But at that level of national income aggregate desired expenditure exceeds total output, and the excess demand will cause the price level to rise. As this occurs, the aggregate quantity supplied increases along AS while aggregate quantity demanded decreases along AD. Equilibrium is reached at a price level of P and a national income of Y, where aggregate demand equals aggregate supply.

To see this, it is convenient to use the kinked aggregate supply curve used earlier and now shown in Figure 38-9.[9] Assume that an expenditure boom has created an inflationary gap. Under the impact of excess aggregate demand, the price level will rise. The shortage of money caused by the rise in the money value of transactions raises interest rates so that at any level of real income, desired real expenditure will be reduced. The falling desired real expenditure as the price level rises is shown by a movement upward to the left

[9] The kinked aggregate supply curve is used because it gives rise to a precise and explicit level of real national income corresponding to full employment.

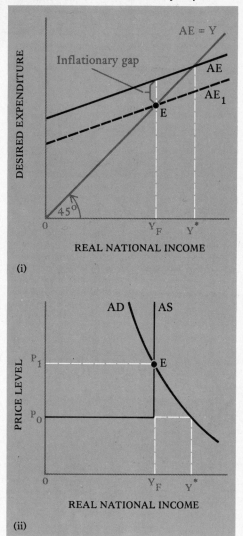

FIGURE 38-9

The Elimination of an Inflationary Gap

A rise in the price level will eliminate an inflationary gap. The economy's curves are AE, AD, and AS: the price level is P_0. Income would be in equilibrium if Y^* could be produced. But full employment output is only Y_F, so there is an inflationary gap in (i) and excess aggregate demand of $Y^* - Y_F$ in (ii).

The inflationary gap causes the price level to rise to P_1. The monetary adjustment mechanism (working through a rising demand for money, a falling price of bonds, a rising interest rate, and falling investment) lowers aggregate expenditure to AE_1, eliminating the inflationary gap and producing equilibrium at Y_F.

The same process is shown in (ii): the economy moves upward along its AD curve until at price level P_1 aggregate demand equals aggregate supply at full-employment income. The excess aggregate demand has been eliminated.

along the AD curve. This reduces the inflationary gap. Eventually, when the price level is high enough, the inflationary gap disappears and the price level stops rising.

This mechanism, described further in Figure 38-9, may be called a *monetary adjustment mechanism*. It works through the monetary transmission mechanism described previously.

The monetary adjustment mechanism will eliminate any inflationary gap, provided that the money supply is held constant.

The reason is that the ensuing inflation causes a shortage of money that will sooner or later cause interest rates to rise enough to eliminate the excess demand.

The theory just outlined shows that inflationary gaps tend to be self-correcting. They will cause the price level to increase, but those increases set in motion a chain of events in the markets for financial assets that will eventually remove the inflationary gap. (If this were not so, there would be no automatic mechanism to stop any demand inflation once it had begun.)

The self-correcting mechanism is the reason why price levels and the money supply have been linked for so long in economics. Many things can cause the price level to rise for some time. Yet whatever the reason for the rise, unless the money supply is expanded, the price level increase itself sets up forces that will reduce the aggregate expenditure function. Sooner or later these forces will remove any initial inflationary gap and so bring any demand inflation to a halt.

Inflations that are caused by upward shifts in the aggregate supply curve may continue after the inflationary gap is removed. If so, the monetary adjustment mechanism will continue to operate, producing falling aggregate expenditure, falling national income, and rising unemployment.[10]

[10] This possibility was first discussed on page 570 (see Figure 28-9). By explaining the slope of the aggregate demand curve, the monetary adjustment mechanism explains why, *ceteris paribus*, inflations that are caused by upward shifts in the aggregate supply curve are associated with falling national income and rising unemployment.

FRUSTRATION OF THE MONETARY ADJUSTMENT MECHANISM

The self-correcting mechanism for removing an inflationary gap can be frustrated indefinitely if the money supply is increased at the same rate that prices are rising. Say that the price level

is rising 10 percent a year under the pressure of a large inflationary gap. Demand for money will also be rising at about 10 percent per year. Now suppose that the Bank of Canada increases the money supply at 10 percent per year. No excess demand for money will develop, for the extra money needed to meet the rising demand will be

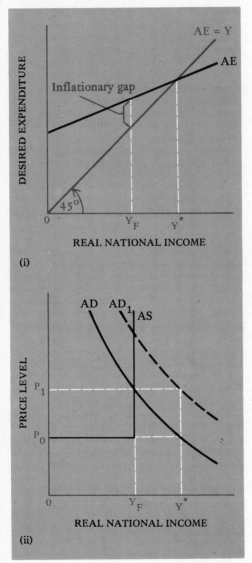

FIGURE 38-10
Frustration of the Monetary Adjustment Mechanism

(i)

(ii)

An inflationary gap can persist forever if the money supply increases as fast as the price level rises. Initially the aggregate curves are AE, AD, and AS and the price level is P_0. National income would be in equilibrium at Y^* if that quantity could be produced. But full-employment income is only Y_F, so there is an inflationary gap, shown in (i). The price level now rises, but the Bank of Canada increases the money supply, so no excess demand for money develops. The real interest rate does not rise, so aggregate desired expenditure remains unchanged in real terms. Since the AE curve does not shift, the inflationary gap remains unchanged in spite of the rise in the price level.

The same process is shown in (ii). The rise in the price level tends to shift the economy upward to the left along any given AD curve, thereby tending to reduce the excess aggregate demand. But the increase in the money supply shifts the aggregate demand curve outward, thereby tending to increase excess aggregate demand. If the two forces just balance each other, by the time the price level has risen to P_1 the aggregate demand curve will have shifted to AD_1, leaving the excess aggregate demand unchanged.

forthcoming. The real interest rate will not rise, and the inflationary gap will not be reduced.[11] This process is analyzed in Figure 38-10 (page 785).

If the money supply increases at the same rate that the price level rises, no excess demand for money will emerge, and the monetary adjustment mechanism that automatically removes an inflationary gap will be frustrated.

An inflation is said to be *validated* when the money supply is increased as fast as the price level so that the monetary adjustment mechanism is frustrated. A validated inflation can go on forever.[12]

A FEW IMPLICATIONS

There is tremendous debate about the relevance of the monetary adjustment mechanism for policy. A group of economists called monetarists make it the centerpiece of their policy recommendations. They maintain that central banks can and should hold the money supply constant in the face of increases in the price level and that this behavior is both necessary and sufficient to control inflation.

Opponents of the monetarist view are divided into several groups. A few say that it is not within the power of central banks to control the money supply. (This denies the analysis of the control of the money supply presented in Chapter 37.) Others say that, given the government's political and economic objectives, it is quite unrealistic to expect the Bank of Canada to attempt to hold the money supply constant in the face of an inflation even though it is able to do so.

Still others say that while an inflation might be stopped by the monetary adjustment mechanism, the economic and social costs of doing so would be too great. Therefore, say the last group, the central bank *should* frustrate the monetary adjustment mechanism, and the government should find other ways of bringing inflation under control. We shall return to these very important debates in Part Eleven.

Instruments and Objectives of Monetary Policy

The Bank of Canada conducts monetary policy in order to influence aggregate expenditure in the economy and thereby influence output, unemployment, and inflation. These variables that the Bank is ultimately concerned with influencing—the objectives of its policy—are called **policy variables.** The variables that it controls *directly* in order to achieve these objectives are called its **policy instruments.** Sometimes it is also useful to identify variables which are neither directly controlled nor for which there is an ultimate desired attainable value but which nevertheless play a key role in the execution of monetary policy. These variables are called the central bank's **intermediate targets;** their importance lies in the influence they exert on the policy variables.[13]

Policy Variables

The major policy variables that we shall consider in this chapter are the level of real national income and the rate of change of the price level. The Bank of Canada can seek to remove inflationary and deflationary gaps by its monetary policy and thus seek to influence national income.

Other major policy variables that are sometimes important are the rate of interest and the

---

[11] With a continuing inflation we need to distinguish between the real and nominal rates of interest (see pages 421–422). The real rate (on which expenditure depends) will be unchanged, but the nominal rate will rise by the rate of inflation. Thus, if the real rate of interest is 3 percent, the nominal rate will be 3, 5, and 10 percent when the inflation is expected to continue at a rate of 0, 2, and 7 percent respectively.

[12] As we shall see in the next chapter, once the inflation comes to be expected, it can persist even in the absence of an inflationary gap *so long as* the actual and expected inflation continue to be validated by increases in the money supply.

[13] In addition, there exist variables that serve as *policy indicators* by which the current thrust of monetary policy might be judged.

exchange rate. For a number of reasons the Bank of Canada may be concerned about the rate of interest quite separately from any effects that the rate may have on national income. First, the higher is the rate of interest, the higher will be the cost of servicing the national debt. The government thus has an obvious concern to keep the interest rate it pays as low as possible. Second, the Bank may want to prevent interest rates from changing too rapidly and thereby causing severe financial strain on those who are vulnerable to rapid changes in interest rates. (The reasons why this may be a matter of serious concern are discussed on page 791.)

The exchange rate is an important variable in an open economy such as that of Canada; changes in it will influence inflation and the demand for Canadian goods. Monetary policy might therefore be explicitly guided by the desire to control the exchange rate. This in turn would place additional emphasis on the interest rate because changes in the interest rate may elicit changes in the exchange rate. If Canadian interest rates are high relative to those in the rest of the world, there may be an influx of foreign capital to take advantage of the high domestic rates. If Canadian rates are low relative to those in the rest of the world, there may be a large outflow of capital to foreign financial centers. Rapid movements of international funds and the resultant changes in the exchange rate can be upsetting to the economy (as we shall see in Chapter 40). Thus the Bank may desire to control interest rates in order to influence international capital flows and the exchange rate; in this event the exchange rate would be a policy variable while the interest rate would be either a policy instrument or an intermediate target.

Policy Instruments

Having selected its policy variables and formulated goals for their behavior, the Bank of Canada must decide how to achieve these objectives. How can the policy variables be made to perform in the way that the Bank wishes?

Since the Bank cannot control income or inflation directly, it must employ its policy instruments, which it does control directly, to influence aggregate expenditure in the desired manner. The primary instrument available to the Bank of Canada is open market operations.

The Bank may choose to *set the price* at which it sells or buys bonds on the open market (thereby setting the yield on the bonds) and allow the quantity of sales or purchases to be determined by market demand. This approach is called *interest rate control,* and here the interest rate is properly viewed as a policy instrument.

Alternatively, the Bank may choose to *set the quantity* of open market sales or purchases and allow the price — and hence the interest rate — to be determined by market demand. This approach is called *base control.* When the Bank of Canada makes an open market transaction, it causes a change in its own monetary liabilities of an equal amount (see Tables 37-17 and 37-18). These monetary liabilities equal the sum of currency plus reserves of the chartered banks; that sum forms the potential base on which the credit expansion process studied in Chapter 37 operates, and it is often called the **monetary base.** When the Bank of Canada chooses to control directly the *quantity* of its open market operations, it is choosing to control the size of the monetary base.

Because of the liquidity preference function, which relates the quantity of money to the rate of interest, the central bank cannot expect to be able to control both the interest rate and the monetary base independently.[14]

Intermediate Targets

Since the central bank cannot normally expect to influence its policy variables directly, it uses its policy instruments to achieve target levels of variables that it can control closely and that in

---

[14] Recall from Chapter 37 that the Bank has available to it a number of other policies that influence indirectly both interest rates and the money supply.

Can Monetary Policy Be Destabilizing?

In the real world the full effects of monetary policy occur only after quite long time lags. Lags that occur after the decision is made to implement the policy are called *execution lags*. Execution lags can arise from several sources, and they can have important implications for the conduct of monetary policy.

Sources of Execution Lags

1. Open market operations affect the reserves of the chartered banks. The full increase in the money supply occurs only when the banks have granted enough new loans and made enough investments to expand the money supply by the full amount permitted by existing reserve ratios. This process can take quite a long time.

2. The division of all assets into money and bonds was useful for seeing the underlying forces at work in determining the demand for money. In fact, however, there is a whole series of assets—from currency and demand deposits to term deposits, to treasury bills and short-term bonds, to very long-term bonds and equities—that offer alternative ways of holding wealth. When households find themselves with larger money balances than they require, a chain of substitution occurs, with short-term and long-term interest rates falling as households try to hold less money and more interest-earning assets. The change in longer-term interest rates will in turn affect interest-sensitive expenditures. This process of adjustments along a chain of assets and interest rates can take considerable time to work out.

3. It takes time for new investment plans to be drawn up, approved, and put into effect. It may easily take up to a year before the full increase in investment expenditure builds up in response to a fall in interest rates.

4. The increased investment expenditures will set off a multiplier process that increases national income by some multiple of the initiating increase in investment expenditure. This too takes some time to work out.

Similar considerations apply to contractionary monetary policies that seek to shift the aggregate expenditure function downward. Furthermore, although the end result is fairly predictable, the speed with which the entire

turn influence the ultimate objectives. The two major intermediate targets are the money supply and the rate of interest. As we have stressed, the two are not independent of each other. Hence it is important that the central bank not choose inconsistent targets for them. By the same token, since the two are closely related, it appears not to matter much which one is used (we take up this point below). Table 38-1 illustrates some possible operating regimes for the central bank.

If the Bank chooses the interest rate as its intermediate target, it can achieve that target directly by using interest rate control as its in-

struments. In this case the distinction between intermediate target and policy instrument is redundant. If the Bank chooses the money supply as its intermediate target, it must achieve its target indirectly by means of either base control or interest rate control.

CONTROLLING NATIONAL INCOME THROUGH MONETARY POLICY

Suppose that the Bank of Canada wishes to make real national income or the inflation rate its main policy variable. The Bank must then work

expansionary or contractionary process works itself out can vary from time to time in ways that are hard to predict.

Monetary policy is capable of exerting expansionary and contractionary forces on the economy, but it operates with a time lag that is long and unpredictably variable.

Implications of Execution Lags for Fine Tuning

To see the significance of execution lags for the conduct of monetary policy, assume that the execution lag is 18 months. If on December 1 the Bank of Canada decides that the economy needs stimulus, it can be increasing the money supply within days, and by the end of the year a significant increase may be registered.

But because the full effects of this policy take much time to work out, the policy may prove to be destabilizing. Perhaps by the fall of next year a substantial inflationary gap will have developed. The Bank may then call for a contractionary policy, but the full effects

of the monetary expansion initiated nine months earlier is just being felt—so an expansionary monetary stimulus is adding to the existing inflationary gap.

If the Bank now applies the monetary brakes by contracting the money supply, the full effects of this move will not be felt for another 18 months. By that time a contraction may have already set in because of the natural cyclical forces of the economy. If so, the delayed effects of the monetary policy may turn a minor downturn into a major recession.

The long execution lag of monetary policy makes monetary fine tuning difficult, and it may make it destabilizing.

If the execution lag were known with certainty, it could be built into the Bank's calculations. But the fact that the lag is highly variable makes this nearly impossible. Of course, when a persistent gap has existed and is predicted to continue for a long time, the full effects of monetary policy may be in the appropriate direction even when they occur after their usual long time lag.

through its policy instruments to achieve its objectives in terms of the policy variables.

Assume that in pursuit of an expansionary policy the Bank wishes to increase aggregate demand. It will enter the open market and buy bonds. This expands the reserves of the chartered banks and leads to an increase in the money supply in the manner analyzed on pages 762–765. The increase in the money supply forces the rate of interest down and leads to an increase in investment expenditure. This shifts the aggregate expenditure function upward, which is the result desired.

A contractionary policy would be achieved by reversing the process: the Bank would sell bonds, thereby reducing the money supply, raising interest rates, and shifting the aggregate expenditure function downward.

TARGETS OF MONETARY POLICY: MONEY SUPPLY VERSUS INTEREST RATES

We have seen that the central bank can use its instruments to vary both the money supply and interest rates. Since the two variables are not in-

TABLE 38-1
Assignment of Variables Under Alternative Operating Regimes of Monetary Policy

Regime	Policy instrument	Intermediate target	Policy variables
1. Monetary targeting: base control	Open market operations; regulate volume of open market sales and purchases	Quantity of money (M1) via money supply process	GNP Inflation Unemployment
2. Monetary targeting: interest rate control	Open market operations; regulate price at which open market sales and purchases are made (i.e., regulate interest rate)	Quantity of money (M1) via liquidity preference	GNP Inflation Unemployment
3. Interest rate targeting	Open market operations; regulate intermediate target directly	Interest rates	GNP Inflation Unemployment

Even with a given set of policy variables, there is a variety of operating regimes that central banks might adopt. The central bank could use either the quantity of money (in current Canadian policy, M1) or the interest rate as its intermediate target.

When the central bank opts for monetary targeting, it can influence its target only indirectly. Through its open market operations it can control directly either the size of the monetary base or the level of interest rates. If it controls the monetary base (Regime 1), the quantity of money is influenced via the money supply process while the interest rate is determined via monetary equilibrium as in Figure 38-2. If the central bank controls the interest rate (Regime 2),

the influence on the quantity of money operates via the liquidity preference function.

Should the central bank choose to use the interest rate as an intermediate target (Regime 3), it can achieve its target directly by using open market operations to control the interest rate. Although this appears to be a simpler process (and in terms of operation, it is simpler), many economists favor monetary targeting.

Other variables, such as the interest rate and the exchange rate, might also appear as policy variables. The interest rate could then appear as a policy instrument, an intermediate target, or a policy variable, depending on the policy regime.

dependent of each other, it might not seem to matter which of the two the central bank selected as primary target variable. Broadly similar results might be expected if either the money supply or interest rates were chosen as an intermediate target.

If, for example, the central bank wishes to remove a deflationary gap by driving down interest rates, it will purchase securities, driving up the prices and thus driving down interest rates. These open market purchases will also expand the money supply through the mechanism described earlier. Thus it is largely immaterial whether the central bank seeks first to drive down interest rates or to expand the money supply, for doing one will accomplish the other. Similarly, driving up interest rates by open mar-

ket sales of government securities will tend to contract the money supply as the public gives up money in return for securities. The transmission mechanism by which monetary policy influences aggregate expenditure is not essentially altered by the Bank's choice of operating regime.

In spite of the interrelation between these two possible target variables, many economists have argued that it is important that the money supply be used as the intermediate target. It is much easier, they say, to assess the trends of the economy and to assess the current thrust of monetary policy when the money supply is used as the intermediate target rather than the rate of interest. The argument proceeds in three steps.

1. In times of business expansion, both interest rates and the money supply will be rising. In-

terest rates rise because of a heavy demand to borrow money and an increasing shortage of loanable funds. The money supply expands because banks expand their loans to meet the pressing demands from firms and households.

2. A restrictive monetary policy requires that the central bank increase the rate of interest and reduce (or slow the rate of expansion of) the money supply. Thus, if the central bank seeks to restrain a business expansion that is threatening to get out of hand and produce a serious inflationary gap, it will wish to *accentuate* the rising trend in interest rates but to *reverse* the rising trend in the money supply. By selling bonds in the open market it does both.

3. It is easier to discover whether current policy is contractionary, expansionary, or neutral if it is working through the money supply rather than interest rates. If a typical rate of interest rises to 15 percent during an expansion, we may be uncertain how much of this is due to the tightening of monetary policy and how much of it would have happened anyway. Indeed, the more rapid the expansion, the more rapidly will interest rates tend to rise without assistance from the central bank. But if the annual rate of increase in the money supply is, say, 20 percent, this is unambiguously expansionary and it clearly shows that a much more restrictive policy is required to restrain the business expansion.

THE SHIFT FROM INTEREST RATES TO THE MONEY SUPPLY AS THE PRIMARY TARGET VARIABLE

Prior to the 1970s, monetary policy was formulated in terms of target levels of interest rates and other measures of the cost and availability of credit. Many economists were highly critical of the Bank of Canada for this, and indeed by 1973 the Bank itself had indicated some dissatisfaction with this strategy.

Many argued that by acting to stabilize interest rates, the Bank in effect had been increasing the amplitude of fluctuations in income and employ-

TABLE 38-2

Inflation and Money Supply (M1) Growth in Canada, 1960–1980

| Years | Annual percentage rates of change | |
	Consumer Price Index	Money supply (M1)
1960–1965	1.6	5.2
1965–1970	3.9	6.2
1970–1975	7.3	12.9
1975–1980	8.7	8.0
1970–71	2.8	12.7
1971–72	4.8	14.3
1972–73	7.5	14.5
1973–74	10.9	9.6
1974–75	10.7	13.6
1975–76	7.5	8.0
1976–77	8.0	8.4
1977–78	9.0	10.2
1978–79	9.1	7.0
1979–80	10.1	6.4

Monetary growth was abnormally high during the early 1970s; since 1975 the Bank of Canada has embarked on a policy of gradually reducing the rate of monetary expansion. The acceleration in money growth that occurred in the early 1970s was followed by an increase in inflation. The gradual reduction in monetary growth in the second half of the 1970s has so far resulted in only limited success in reducing inflation.

ment. Demand booms, it was believed, were being reinforced by increases in the money supply aimed at the interest rate increases that would otherwise result from the demand boom. Similarly, recessions were being reinforced by contraction of the money supply.

Others noted that the rapid increase in inflation rates that occurred in the early 1970s was associated with rapid increases in the money supply. As shown in Table 38-2, during the first five years of the seventies the annual growth in the money supply exceeded 12 percent four times and averaged almost 13 percent.

The Bank began to move toward greater emphasis on control of the money supply. In November 1975 the Bank announced that it was adopting the practice of formulating policy in terms of explicit target ranges for the rate of growth of the narrowly defined money supply

Implementing the Strategy of Monetary Gradualism

In November 1975 the Bank of Canada announced that it was adopting the strategy of monetary gradualism: controlling and gradually reducing the rate of growth of the money supply. In adopting the quantity of money as its intermediate target, the Bank was explicit both in its belief of the need for control of the money supply for the *long-term* control of inflation and in its concern for the *short-term* destabilizing potential of monetary fine tuning. Several aspects of this strategy have continued to be controversial.

Which Monetary Aggregate Should Be Controlled?

The Bank has opted to focus on the narrowly defined money supply, M1. It also controls interest rates in order to achieve its M1 target; in terms of Table 38-1, it has opted for Regime 1. The choice of M1 as intermediate target and the use of interest rate control are not really independent; since M1 is more responsive to interest rate changes than are broader monetary aggregates, it is only natural to focus on M1 when interest rate control is used. For example, an increase in interest rates causes agents to reduce their demand deposits and move into interest-bearing deposits and securities: in this event, M1 will fall by the amount of the reduction in demand deposits

while M2 will fall by much less because some of the reduction goes into term deposits, which are included in the definition of M2. Therefore M1 tends to exhibit a much higher interest elasticity of demand than does M2, and interest rate control is more effective in controlling M1.

Nevertheless, many critics believe that the Bank should be focusing on a broad aggregate such as M2. What criteria could be used to choose between these alternatives as the Bank's intermediate target?

Link to aggregate expenditure. As the ultimate purpose of monetary policy is to stabilize national income by influencing aggregate expenditure, the choice of a monetary aggregate might depend on which one is more closely related to expenditure. Although the historical evidence is inconclusive, many of the Bank's critics sense that M1 is becoming increasingly irrelevant. As control on M1 has been exerted, innovations in financial management have created alternatives to demand deposits. Attempts to curtail demand by restricting the growth of M1 simply leads to adjustments that economize on M1 holdings and have little or no influence on aggregate demand. (One example is the switch from using demand deposits to using interest-bearing chequing deposits.) The critics believe that aggregate demand will fall only if growth of *all* liquid assets is curtailed, and for this reason

(M1) and that it intended to make these targets public.

The first target range was set at 10 to 15 percent per year with an indication that the Bank intended to bring about a series of gradual reductions in the target range in an effort to put downward pressure on the rate of inflation. The first reduction, to a range of 8 to 12 percent, came in

August 1976, and a lower range of 7 to 11 percent was adopted in October 1977. Successive steps further reduced the range; in mid February 1981 the target range was 4 to 8 percent. As Figure 38-11 shows, the Bank has been quite successful at keeping actual money growth inside the target range, although there has been considerable movement within that range.

they favor the use of a broader monetary aggregate such as M2.

Controlability. The strategy of controlling a given monetary aggregate is feasible only when the particular targets can be achieved. The high interest elasticity of demand for M1 means that interest rate changes can be used to control M1, and for this reason the Bank prefers to target on M1. Control of M2 would require far more variation in interest rates, and from this viewpoint it would be less desirable. However, interest rate control is not the only possibility; advocates of M2 targeting are often advocates of base control rather than interest rate control.

Other Aspects of Monetary Gradualism

Interest rate versus base control. The decision between interest rate control and base control is in part dependent on which monetary aggregate is adopted as an intermediate target. In addition, some critics think that the policy of interest rate control adopted by the Bank is too complex and depends too crucially on a stable relationship between interest rates and desired holdings of liquid deposits. Increasing levels of competition in the financial sector and rapid developments in computer-assisted funds-transfer mechanisms lead many observers to be skeptical about this relation-ship's potential for being a dependable base for policy.

The merits of gradualism. The Bank adopted a gradualist strategy on the grounds that it wished to avoid the extreme unemployment problems that a more severe restriction in monetary growth might entail. However, gradualism itself may well undermine confidence in the use of monetary policy. Since the reduction in monetary growth is so gradual, any influence it exerts on inflation is relatively minor in the short run. Other things also influence the current inflation rate, and it is possible for "bad luck" to offset the effects of gradualist policy for significant periods of time. Indeed, this may well have happened in Canada. As Table 38-2 shows, the Bank has been relatively successful in meeting its monetary targets, yet over the period 1978–1981 inflation continued to rise. Thus many critics have been able to claim that monetary policy has failed; others simply say it has been "too gradual" and has been offset by specific factors such as OPEC's doubling of world oil prices in 1979. Further, the reduction in the target growth rate has been so gradual that, over substantial periods of time, movements within the allowable range of monetary growth have dominated reductions in the actual target (see Figure 38-11), thereby prompting the view that "monetary policy has not failed; it has not actually been tried."

A Monetary Rule?

The record of monetary policy in the 1970s lends force to the monetarist economists' persistent criticisms of monetary fine tuning.

The monetarists argue that (1) monetary policy is a potent force of expansionary and contractionary pressures; (2) monetary policy works with lags that are both long and variable; and (3) central banks are often given to sudden and strong reversal of their policy stance. Consequently monetary policy has a destabilizing effect on the economy, the policy itself accentuating rather than dampening the economy's natural cyclical swings.

Monetarists argue from this position that the

FIGURE 38-11
The Money Supply and Target Growth Ranges (seasonally adjusted)

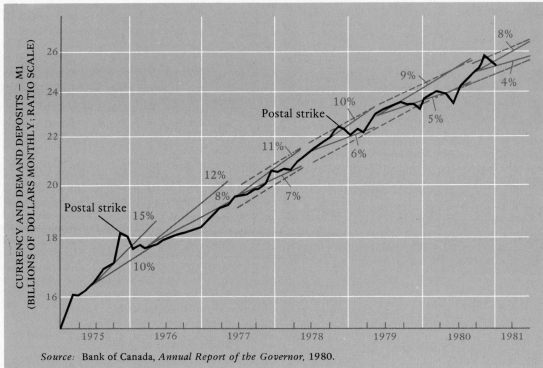

Source: Bank of Canada, *Annual Report of the Governor*, 1980.

Announced targets for monetary expansion have been gradually reduced since their inception in 1975. When the Bank of Canada announces targets for the rate of growth of M1, it allows for a 2 percent error on either side of the target. The solid colored lines fan out from the initial supply at the upper and lower bounds of the tolerance from the target growth rate. The parallel dashed colored lines give the limits for the 4 percent spread around the midpoint in the period for which the targets apply. The solid black line gives the actual money supply.

The Bank of Canada has been reasonably successful in staying within its announced target range of growth for M1. However, considerable fluctuation within the range has occurred. For example, although the target range of M1 growth was reduced in August 1976 and again in November 1977, the actual rate of growth of M1 was higher during 1977 than during 1976 and higher during 1976 than during 1975.

During postal strikes money liquidity problems arise because bills cannot always be paid. To compensate, the Bank allows the measured money supply to grow.

stability of the economy would be much improved if the central bank stopped trying to stabilize it. What then should the authorities do? Since growth of population and productivity leads to a rising level of output, the central bank ought to provide the extra money needed to allow the holding of additional transactions, precautionary, and speculative balances as real income and wealth rise over time.

According to the monetarists, the central bank should expand the money supply year in and

year out at a constant rate equal to the rate of growth of real income. When the growth rate shows signs of long-term change, the Bank could adjust its rate of monetary expansion, but it should not alter this rate with a view to stabilizing the economy against short-term fluctuations.

Theorists have conducted a long debate over this monetarist recommendation. The outcome is that, at least in many standard models of the economy, cyclical fluctuations can be made smaller with the *best* fine tuning policy than they are with a constant-rate rule. However, many economists believe that a constant-rate rule would be superior to actual policies that have been or are likely to be followed.

In fact the Bank of Canada's policy does not correspond to a monetarist constant-rate rule. First, the target range itself is adjusted periodically and gradually reduced. Second, as Figure 38-11 shows, the *actual* growth rate of money fluctuated considerably within the target range in response to current economic events. Third, a major aspect of the announced targets is that they indicate the broad intentions of the central bank for the *future* course of the money supply; as we shall see in Chapter 39, this is intended to influence expectations in a manner consistent with current policy. Nevertheless the current policy pursued by the Bank of Canada is heavily influenced by the monetarist contention that monetary fine tuning can be destabilizing.

Some Problems of Expansionary Monetary Policy

There are many situations in which an expansionary monetary policy can fail to have the intended effects. It has already been shown (page 780) that if the liquidity preference schedule is very flat, the purchase of securities will have little effect on the rate of interest. Assume that the price of bonds is already quite high and that the public feels that it cannot long remain so high. People will be inclined to hold demand or savings deposits instead of bonds both because they expect to be able to buy bonds later at a more favorable price and because they fear capital losses if they buy bonds now.

If the central bank enters this market and offers to buy bonds, only a small increase in price will be needed to persuade the public to sell their bonds, which they already believe to be unusually high in price. When prices rise further, the public will become even more convinced that they should sell bonds now and hold money, hoping to buy back the bonds for a large gain when prices fall. In these circumstances, open market operations will succeed in increasing the money

supply, but they need not drive the interest rate down much.

A second unfavorable situation occurs if the marginal efficiency of investment schedule is very interest inelastic. For example, the presence of substantial excess capacity in existing capital equipment combined with unfavorable expectations about future sales would make businessmen reluctant to engage in new investment on any terms. In such circumstances the amount of investment they are prepared to make would not be likely to change much in response to variations in interest rates.

In a severe depression a highly inelastic marginal efficiency of investment schedule is likely to occur, and both unfavorable circumstances may occur simultaneously. A relatively elastic liquidity preference schedule means that even large open market purchases will not drive the interest rate down very far. A highly inelastic marginal efficiency of investment schedule means that any reduction in interest rates will have only a negligible effect in inducing an increase in investment expenditure. In such circumstances even quite large increases in the money supply will have little effect in increasing aggregate demand.

Some Problems of Contractionary Monetary Policy

Most economists believe that contractionary monetary policy will not face the same problems as expansionary policy, principally because it is not likely to be applied in recessionary periods when liquidity preference is very elastic and the investment schedule is inelastic. Hence contractionary monetary policy is likely to be effective in reducing aggregate demand.

Nevertheless, problems arise in connection with contractionary monetary policy. The central bank must be willing to accept the higher interest rates that accompany monetary contraction even though they will no doubt prove unpopular; the contractionary policy is effective only because of the increase in interest rates. Furthermore, higher interest rates are likely to attract foreign capital, thereby causing an appreciation of the domestic currency; these exchange rate developments, to be discussed in Chapter 40, will also be unpopular, especially with the export industries. Finally, while the monetary contraction will be effective in lowering aggregate demand, its effects on real output and inflation individually are uncertain. It may be that contractionary policy aimed at reducing inflation has its major impact by increasing unemployment; this issue is taken up in the next few chapters.

MONETARY POLICY: SOME INTERIM CONCLUSIONS

There is general agreement among economists that rapid changes in the money supply have major effects on the economy and particularly on the price level. Thus most economists agree that control of the money supply is a necessary condition for avoiding rapid inflations.

Many economists also hold that changes in the money supply could be used, if we knew enough, to help in the government's efforts to stabilize the economy by avoiding the extremes of large inflationary and deflationary gaps.

There is disagreement, however, on a number of important issues that we summarize here and discuss in more detail in Part Eleven.

1. Is control of the money supply a sufficient means of controlling inflation? Some economists answer yes; others think not and look to causes of inflation in addition to excessive monetary expansion.

2. How important is monetary policy as a potential tool of stabilization policy? Most economists give some potential role to monetary policy, but opinions vary greatly on how important its role should be. At one extreme some economists give it a relatively minor role as a supplement to fiscal policy; at the other extreme some economists give it the exclusive role, arguing that "fiscal policy" is effective only insofar as it causes changes in the money supply.

3. Should monetary policy be used as a stabilization device? Although many economists would answer "of course," some who believe that monetary policy is potentially very powerful argue against its use. They believe that we know so little about the precise timing of the important effects of monetary policy that we are likely to do—and in the past have done—more harm than good by using such policies. They argue for a constant rate of monetary expansion directed at a zero trend in the price level in the face of a positive trend rate of growth in real output. However, they would not vary the rate of monetary expansion in an attempt to remove short-term inflationary or deflationary gaps.

These major areas of disagreement will be studied in more detail in Part Eleven.

Summary

1. For simplicity, we divide all forms of holding wealth into money, which is a medium of exchange and earns no interest, and bonds, which earn an interest return but can be turned into money only by selling them at a price that is determined on the open market.

2. The price of bonds varies inversely with the rate of interest. A rise in the rate of interest lowers the prices of all bonds. The longer its term to maturity, the greater the change in the price of a bond for a given change in the interest rate.

3. The reasons for holding money balances in spite of the opportunity cost of bond interest forgone are described by the transactions, precautionary, and speculative motives. They have the effect of making the demand for money vary *directly* with national income valued in current dollars and with wealth, and *inversely* with the rate of interest.

4. Monetary disequilibrium causes the interest rate to change. When there is an excess demand for money balances, people try to sell bonds. This pushes the price of bonds down and the interest rate up. When there is an excess supply of money balances, people try to buy bonds. This pushes the price of bonds up and the rate of interest down. Monetary equilibrium is established when people are willing to hold the fixed stocks

of money and bonds at the current rate of interest.

5. A change in the interest rate causes desired investment to change along the *MEI* function. This shifts the aggregate desired expenditure function and causes equilibrium national income to change.

6. Points (4) and (5) together describe the transmission mechanism that links money to national income. An excess demand for money tends to reduce national income; an excess supply of money tends to increase it.

7. The appendix to this chapter presents a formal analysis in which equilibrium levels of the interest rate and national income are determined simultaneously and their equilibrium response to monetary and fiscal policy are derived.

8. Monetary policy seeks to influence national income through the transmission mechanism. An increase in the supply of money creates downward pressure on the interest rate; this is expansionary. A decrease in the money supply creates upward pressure on the interest rate; this is contractionary.

9. A given change in the money supply will have larger effects on national income, the steeper is the *LP* function and the flatter is the *MEI* function.

10. A rise in the price level raises the demand for money. The resulting monetary disequilibrium causes the interest rate to rise and aggregate expenditure to fall. This lowers equilibrium national income.

11. *Ceteris paribus,* each price level is associated with an equilibrium real national income such that desired expenditure equals income and the demand for money equals the supply. Each price level and its corresponding equilibrium real national income gives one point on the aggregate demand curve.

12. The whole aggregate demand curve slopes upward to the left because the higher the price level, the lower is equilibrium national income.

The explanation lies with the monetary adjustment mechanism: the higher the price level, the higher the demand for money, the higher the rate of interest, the lower the aggregate expenditure function, and thus the lower equilibrium income.

13. The monetary adjustment mechanism that causes the aggregate demand curve to slope upward to the left means that a sufficiently large rise in the price level will eliminate any inflationary gap. However, this mechanism can be frustrated if the Bank of Canada increases the money supply as fast as the price level is rising.

14. The ultimate objectives of monetary policy are called policy variables. Both real national income and the inflation rate are policy variables. Interest rates and the exchange rate may also be policy variables. Where the authority cannot influence its policy variables directly, it must work through policy instruments that it can control and that will in turn influence intermediate target variables that are closely related to policy variables. The money supply and the rate of interest are the principal intermediate targets.

15. To reduce national income, the Bank of Canada sells bonds on the open market, thereby driving up the rate of interest and reducing the quantity of money. To increase national income, the Bank of Canada buys bonds on the open market, thereby driving down the rate of interest and increasing the quantity of money.

16. The monetary authority cannot have wholly separate policies with respect to national income and the interest rate because the two are related. For example, a policy of stabilizing interest rates will accentuate fluctuations in national income.

17. The Bank of Canada has moved away from the interest rate and toward growth in the money supply as its primary policy target. Since 1975 it has been announcing upper and lower bounds for future money growth rates, and the bounds have gradually been reduced. On the whole, the Bank has been successful in meeting these targets.

18. It is generally agreed that rapid changes in the money supply and interest rates can have large effects on the economy. There is disagreement, however, on how much monetary policy can and should be used as a device for stabilizing the economy or coping with temporary bouts of rising prices.

Topics for Review

Interest rates and bond prices
Transactions, precautionary, and speculative motives for holding money
Monetary disequilibrium and equilibrium
The transmission mechanism
The liquidity preference (*LP*) function
The marginal efficiency of investment (*MEI*) function
The strength of monetary policy
The shape of the aggregate demand function
The monetary adjustment mechanism and its frustration
A validated inflation
Policy variables, policy instruments, and intermediate targets
Monetary policy as a destabilizing force

Discussion Questions

1. Describing a possible future "cashless society," a public report recently said: "In the cashless society of the future, a customer could insert a plastic card into a machine at a store and the amount of the purchase would be deducted from his 'bank account' in the computer automatically and transferred to the store's account. No cash or cheques would ever change hands." What would such an institutional change do to the various motives for holding money balances? What functions would remain for chartered banks and for the central bank if money as we now know it disappeared in this fashion? What benefits and disadvantages can you see in such a scheme?
2. What motives would explain the following holdings?
    a. the currency and coins in the cash register of the local supermarket at the start of each working day.
    b. the payroll account of the Ford Motor Company in the local bank.
    c. certificates of deposit that mature after one's retirement
    d. the holdings of government bonds by private individuals
3. Which of the holdings in the previous question would you expect to change significantly if interest rates rose from 7 percent to 15 percent?

4. What would happen to the economy if Parliament were to vote a once-and-for-all universal social dividend of $5,000 paid to every Canadian over the age of 17, to be financed by the creation of new money?
5. What sort of situation might lead a society to have a very flat liquidity preference schedule and a very steep marginal efficiency of investment schedule? Is this a good combination for those who wish to affect the level of income by changing the money supply?
6. One relationship encountered in this chapter and elsewhere is the inverse one between bond prices and interest rates. Be sure that you can explain just why this occurs. Is this a special feature of bonds, or does it apply to the value of other earning assets as well?
7. Suppose you are sure that the Bank of Canada is going to engage in policies that will decrease the money supply sharply starting next month. How might you make speculative profits by purchases or sales of bonds now?
8. What do you expect to happen to interest rates if the Bank of Canada reduces the money supply? What would happen if, starting from a situation of 10 percent rates of inflation and of monetary expansion, the Bank of Canada cut the rate of monetary expansion to 5 percent?
9. Trace out the full sequence of events by which the monetary adjustment mechanism would work if, in the face of a constant money supply, workers and firms insisted on actions that raised prices continually at a rate of 10 percent per year. "Sooner or later in this situation something would have to give." What possible things could "give"? What would be the consequences of each "giving"?
10. If the monetary adjustment mechanism is always present in any economy, why has it not prevented the inflations of the 1970s and 1980s?
11. Describe the chief weapons of monetary policy available to the Bank of Canada and indicate whether, and if so how, they might be used for the following purposes:
    a. to create a mild tightening of bank credit
    b. to signal that the Bank of Canada favors a sharp curtailment of bank lending
    c. to permit an expansion of bank loans with existing reserves
    d. to supply banks and the public with a temporary increase of currency for Christmas shopping
12. It is often said that an expansionary monetary policy is like "pushing on a string." What is meant by such a statement? How does this contrast with a contractionary monetary policy?

Part Eleven

Macroeconomic Policy

The Nature of Unemployment and Inflation

39

There is general agreement that the four major goals of macroeconomic policy are (1) to maintain a low and stable level of unemployment, (2) to maintain a stable price level, (3) to maintain a satisfactory balance of payments position, and (4) to sustain a high rate of growth. Sometimes these policy objectives will conflict; when they do, painful choices may have to be made.

Policymakers' problems are further complicated by disagreement among economists over their diagnoses of the causes of the economy's present ills. Indeed, many believe that macroeconomics itself is in a genuine crisis.

A decade or so ago there was consensus that the macro behavior of the economy was fairly well understood and that policy goals could be achieved by using the available tools. Policy conflicts might arise from the nature of the economy, at times making it impossible to achieve all goals simultaneously. Hard choices among alternative goals might then be necessary, but once the choices were made, policymakers thought they had sufficient knowledge to achieve their chosen goals through the use of macro policy.

Today this consensus no longer exists.[1] There is disagreement over the causes of the severe inflations that hit Western countries in the 1970s. Ten years ago economists spoke confidently about the choice *between* unemployment and

---

[1] The disagreements among economists are serious, and their outcome will profoundly affect the average citizen. Many issues go well beyond introductory economics; while they can be outlined here, their full nature cannot well be appreciated without the benefit of intermediate and perhaps advanced courses in macroeconomics and monetary theory.

inflation; today high unemployment *and* high rates of inflation often exist simultaneously.

In this chapter we concentrate on the twin policy objectives of low unemployment and stable prices. We begin by considering unemployment and the inflation rate separately, asking why each is a cause for concern, why it changes, and how it can be controlled by the central authorities. Our discussion will bring together material that has been introduced in widely separated parts of this book, and we shall conclude the chapter with a consideration of what happens when conflicts develop between price stability and full employment—in particular, what happens when a desirable reduction can be made in unemployment only at the cost of an undesirable increase in inflation.

The balance of payments objective is the subject of Chapter 40. In Chapter 41 we shall deal with the experience of inflation and unemployment over the last half century. In Chapter 42 we shall consider some of the policy issues and debates concerning the control of inflation and unemployment in Canada today. Economic growth is then the topic of the final part of the book, Part Twelve.

Unemployment

Keynes distinguished between voluntary and involuntary unemployment. Voluntary unemployment occurs when there is a job available but the unemployed person is not willing to accept it at the going wage rate for that job. Involuntary unemployment occurs when a person is willing to accept a job at the going wage rate but no such job can be found. Clearly when we are concerned about the undesirable social effects of unemployment in terms of lost output and human suffering, it is involuntary unemployment that concerns us most.

WHY POLICYMAKERS ARE CONCERNED

The social and political importance of the unemployment rate is enormous. It is widely reported in newspapers and on television; the government is blamed when it is high and takes credit when it is low; it is often a hot issue in elections; and few macroeconomic policies are formed without some consideration of their effect on it. No other summary statistic, with the possible exceptions of the exchange rate and the Consumer Price Index, carries such weight as both a formal and an informal objective of policy as does the percentage of the civilian labor force unemployed.

There are two main reasons for worrying about unemployment: it produces economic waste and it causes human suffering. The economic waste is fairly obvious. Human services are the least durable of economic commodities. If a fully employed economy with a constant labor force has 10 million people willing to work in 1980, their services must either be used in 1980 or wasted. When the services of only 9 million are used because 10 percent of the labor force is unemployed, the potential 1980 output of 1 million workers is lost forever. In an economy characterized by scarcity, where there is not nearly enough output to meet everyone's needs, this waste of potential output seems undesirable to most people.

Then there is the human cost of unemployment. The severe hardship and misery that can be caused by prolonged periods of unemployment were discussed earlier; they are heavy costs. Yet it is wrong to think that if the number of unemployed rises by, say, 100,000, this means that 100,000 workers join the ranks of the permanently unemployed. Modern research has shown that short-term variations in the unemployment rate, at or near the full-employment level, reflect, to a great extent, changes in the duration of short-term unemployment. Moreover, some people decide to stay unemployed rather than accept a job at a lower pay level than the one they lost because they believe that the difference between what they could earn and their unemployment benefits is too small. Such people choose the alternative of unemployment.

However, when a deep recession is followed by a long trough and a relatively slow recovery, as was the case in the mid 1970s, long-term unemployment increases. People begin to exhaust their unemployment insurance and must fall back on savings, welfare, or charity. When this happens, the human suffering caused by unemployment increases.

Before we can make a value judgment about the human costs of a rise in unemployment, we need to know how the increase is distributed both between long-term and short-term unemployment and between those for whom there is no work alternative and those for whom there is a nonpreferred employment alternative.

CAUSES OF UNEMPLOYMENT

In discussing the causes of unemployment, it is helpful to distinguish among several kinds of unemployment.

Frictional Unemployment

Unemployment associated with normal labor turnover is called **frictional unemployment.** This is the amount of unemployment that occurs when full-employment income, Y_F, is being produced.

People leave jobs for all sorts of reasons and then take time to find new jobs; old persons leave the labor force and young persons join it, but new workers may not fill the jobs vacated by those who have left. All this movement takes time. The result is a pool of persons who are frictionally unemployed in the process of finding new jobs.

Frictional unemployment is unavoidable in any free society; it may run as high as 3 or 4 percent of the labor force.

National income theory seeks to explain the causes of, and cures for, unemployment in excess of unavoidable frictional unemployment.

Structural Unemployment

Structural changes in the economy can be a cause of unemployment. As economic growth proceeds, the mix of required inputs changes, as do the proportions in which final goods are demanded. These changes require considerable re-adjustments in the economy. **Structural unemployment** occurs when the adjustments do not occur fast enough, so that severe pockets of unemployment occur in areas, industries, and occupations in which the demand for factors of production is falling faster than is the supply. In Canada today, for example, structural unemployment exists in the Atlantic provinces and in the automobile industry.

Structural unemployment can increase either because the pace of change accelerates or because the rate of adjustment to change slows down. Examples of the former are the increased adjustments required by the rapid increases in energy prices occurring in recent years. Examples of the latter would be government policies that increasingly discourage movement among regions, industries, and occupations. Policies that prevent firms from replacing some labor with new machines may protect employment in the short term. However, if they lead to the decline of an industry that cannot then compete with more innovative foreign competitors, the policies can in the end cause pockets of severe structural unemployment.

Structural unemployment may be said to exist when there is a mismatching between the unemployed and the available jobs in terms of regional location, required skills, or any other relevant dimension.

As with many distinctions, the one between structural and frictional unemployment becomes blurred at the edges. In a sense, structural unemployment is really long-term frictional unemployment. Consider a change that requires a reallocation of labor. When the reallocation occurs quickly, we call the unemployment frictional while it lasts; when the reallocation occurs slowly—possibly only after the person who has lost a job dies or retires from the labor force and has been replaced by a new person with different and more marketable skills—we call the unemployment structural.

One useful measure of the total of frictional *plus* structural unemployment is the percentage of the labor force unemployed when the number of unfilled job vacancies is equal to the number of persons seeking jobs. When the two magnitudes are equal, there is a job opening to match every person seeking a job. The unemployment that then occurs must be either frictional or structural.

Deficient-demand Unemployment

Unemployment that occurs because there is insufficient aggregate demand to purchase full-employment output is called **deficient-demand unemployment.** One useful measure of this kind of unemployment is the difference between the number of persons seeking jobs and the number of unfilled job vacancies (i.e., total unemployment *minus* frictional and structural unemployment) expressed as a percentage of the labor force. This measure shows the excess of the supply of workers looking for jobs over the number of jobs available. It will be positive when there is deficient aggregate demand and negative when there is excess aggregate demand.

Deficient-demand unemployment refers to the unemployed who would have jobs if the economy were producing its full-employment output.

At a time of heavy unemployment, frictional, structural, and deficient-demand causes will all be operative. It is not usually possible to say that one particular worker is unemployed because of deficient demand and another for structural reasons, nor is it possible to say what proportion of the total unemployment is accounted for by each cause. Nonetheless, all three causes can operate and contribute to the total volume of unemployment.

Search Unemployment

We have seen that national income theory is concerned with the causes of and cures for involuntary unemployment in excess of unavoidable frictional and structural unemployment. Unfortunately, in practice it is not easy to draw lines between the several types of involuntary unemployment or between those who are voluntarily unemployed and those who are involuntarily unemployed.

How should we classify an unemployed woman who refuses to accept a job at a lower skill level than the one for which she feels she is qualified? What if she turns down a job for which she is trained because she hopes to get a higher wage offer for the same job from another firm? People who could find work of the type for which they are fitted yet remain unemployed in order to search for a better offer are said to be in **search unemployment.**

In one sense they are voluntarily unemployed because they could find some job; in another sense they are involuntarily unemployed because they have not yet succeeded in finding a job for which they are suited at a rate of pay that they believe exists somewhere. Those in search unemployment can be said to have been frictionally unemployed if they find an acceptable job within a reasonable period of time; they can be said to be in structural unemployment if a long search reveals that there are not enough jobs to employ everyone with their particular training and experience.

Search unemployment occurs in a grey area between voluntary and involuntary unemployment and between frictional and structural unemployment. It exists when workers who could take jobs remain unemployed in order to look for something better.

Workers do not have perfect knowledge of all available jobs and rates of pay, and they may be able to gain information only by searching the market. In the face of this uncertainty, it may be quite sensible to refuse a first job offer, for it may prove to be a poor offer in the light of further market information. How long it will pay to remain in search unemployment depends on the economic costs of being unemployed.

Sufficient search unemployment to allow unemployed people time to find an available job that best uses their talents and training is socially desirable. Too much search—for example, holding off, to be supported by others, in the hope of stumbling into a job better than that for which one is really suited — is clearly undesirable and an economic waste. Here again search unemployment is a grey area: some is useful and some is wasteful.

Two recent developments apparently have increased the amount of search unemployment in many Western economies. First, there has been a large increase in the number of households with more than one income earner. When both husband and wife work, it is possible for one to support both while the other looks for "a really good job" rather than accept the first job offer. Second, unemployment insurance reduces the income loss caused by being unemployed and may enable a person to prolong the search for the "right job." Some observers argue that the 1971 liberalization of Canada's unemployment insurance benefits had a significant impact on the unemployment rate, perhaps causing it to rise by as much as one or two percentage points.

MEASURED AND NONMEASURED UNEMPLOYMENT

The number of unemployed persons is estimated from a sample survey conducted each month by Statistics Canada. Persons who are currently without a job but who say they have actively searched for one during the sample period are recorded as unemployed. The total number of estimated unemployed is then expressed as a percentage of the labor force (employed plus unemployed) to obtain the figure for percentage unemployment.

This measured figure for unemployment may not reflect the number of people who are truly unemployed. *It may overestimate or underestimate the number who would accept the offer of a job for which they are qualified if one were forthcoming at the wage rate presently being paid to those who are employed.*

On the one hand, the measured figure may overstate unemployment by including people who are not involuntarily unemployed. For example, unemployment compensation provides protection against genuine hardships, but it also induces some to stay out of work and collect unemployment benefits for as long as they last. Such people have in fact voluntarily withdrawn from the labor force, but they will usually show up in the statistics as being the ranks of the unemployed because, for fear of losing their benefits, they tell the person who surveys them that they are actively looking for a job.

On the other hand, the measured figure may understate involuntary unemployment by omitting people who would accept a job if one were available. For example, if a slump lasts long enough that jobs cannot be found even when unemployment benefits are exhausted, some people will become discouraged and stop seeking work. These people have voluntarily withdrawn from the labor force and will not be recorded as unemployed; they are, however, truly unemployed in the sense that they would willingly accept a job if one were available.

TOOLS FOR THE CONTROL OF UNEMPLOYMENT

Reducing Unemployment

Frictional unemployment is inevitable in any changing economy. A certain minimum amount of unemployment must be accepted as being "in the nature of things." Yet any policy measure that makes it easier or quicker to move between jobs can reduce the volume of frictional unemployment somewhat.

Structural unemployment may be attacked by policies for retraining and relocating labor. These can be used as part of a general effort to increase the speed with which the supplies of various types of labor adjust to the changing pattern of demands.

Unemployment that is due to deficient aggregate demand can be attacked by increasing aggregate demand. This may be done by any of the expansionary fiscal and monetary policies discussed in Parts Nine and Ten.

Genuine search unemployment may be reduced, first, by making it easier for individuals to locate job openings and, second, by increasing the chance that individuals will accept an offer received early in their search period. The first can be done, for example, by providing market information on job availability; the second requires increasing the cost of search to the unemployed individual. A reduction in the unemployment benefits, for example, would increase the income loss associated with continued search and make it more likely that individuals will reduce the time they spend in search unemployment. This may not always be desirable; as we have observed, a certain amount of search unemployment is useful in ensuring that people find a job for which they are well suited. Phony (no intention of accepting a job) and unreasonable (looking for too good a job) search unemployment might be reduced by more careful screening of persons before they are allowed to collect unemployment benefits.

Coping with Unemployment

Unemployment can never be reduced to zero. Frictional unemployment is inevitable; some deficient-demand unemployment will always exist at the troughs of business cycles; some structural unemployment must exist as the structure of the demand for labor changes faster than the supply of labor can adapt to it. All kinds of unemployment have costs in terms of the output that could have been produced by the unemployed workers. Yet reducing unemployment is also costly. For example, retraining and reallocation schemes designed to reduce structural unemployment will use scarce resources.

It would be neither possible nor desirable to reduce unemployment to zero. The causes could never be removed completely, and to reduce the amount of unemployment stemming from those causes is a costly process.

Unemployment insurance is one method of helping people to live with the unemployment that is inevitable. Certainly unemployment insurance has benefits in reducing significantly the human costs of the bouts of unemployment that are inevitable in a changing society. Nothing, however, is without cost. While alleviating the suffering from some kinds of unemployment, unemployment insurance itself contributes to other kinds of unemployment by encouraging voluntary and search unemployment.

Supporters of unemployment insurance emphasize its benefits. Critics emphasize its costs. As with any policy, a rational assessment of the value of unemployment insurance requires a balancing of its undoubted benefits against its undoubted costs. Most Canadians seem convinced that, when this calculation is made, the benefits greatly exceed the costs.

EXPERIENCE OF UNEMPLOYMENT

Figure 28-5 (see page 566) shows the behavior of the unemployment rate since 1930. Until 1970 the rate fluctuated cyclically but showed no clear trend. During the 1950s the average unemployment rate was 4 percent; the average rose to 6.1 percent during the first five years of the 1960s but fell again to 4 percent during the second half of that decade. During the 1970s, however, the cyclical fluctuations appeared to be superimposed on a rising trend. From 1970 to 1976 the *low* figure for unemployment of 5.3 percent was above the *average* for the two decades of the 1950s and 1960s of 4.5 percent.[2] This low of 5.3 percent was achieved during 1974; the rate then rose steadily until it peaked at 8.4 percent in 1978. At the beginning of the new decade it stood at 7.5 percent.

Clearly the level of unemployment that will persist when all deficient-demand unemployment is removed has risen in recent years. Just how much deficient-demand unemployment remains when the overall rate is 8 percent is a matter of current debate. While some believe the answer is almost none, others believe it may be as much as 2 or 3 percent.

---

[2] Figures in this section are based on annual averages of unemployment.

Employment and Unemployment in the 1970s

Although stagflation was the prevalent experience of most industries in the 1970s, the decade started with a significant economic boom in 1972–1973. In many countries the force of this boom was not fully appreciated. Until quite late in the expansion, most governments thought that their problem was to reduce slack in the economy rather than to contain excess demand. This mistaken diagnosis was to a great extent caused by a shift in the relation between the recorded unemployment rate and the pressure of excess demand. The shift reflected a rise in the amount of unemployment associated with full-capacity output, often called the *natural rate of unemployment*. This rise had occurred more or less unnoticed by policymakers; as a result heavy inflationary pressures were allowed to build up before policymakers realized that the economy was suffering from an inflationary gap rather than a deflationary gap.

In Canada a major cause of the shift was the change in regulations governing unemployment insurance made in the early 1970s: benefits were raised, making unemployment much less unattractive relative to work than it had been. Coverage was greatly increased to include, for example, seasonal workers such as fishermen and lumberjacks, whose normal labor pattern would be to work only part of the year. And accessibility was increased (e.g., benefit cheques could now be mailed, making surveillance of the allegedly unemployed person much harder than it had been). But these changes were not the only cause of the shift; other important factors included increases in legal minimum wages and changes in age and sex composition of the labor force.

Two Canadian economists, Pierre Fortin and Keith Newton, estimated the Canadian natural rate of unemployment (which they defined as the non-accelerating inflation rate of unemployment, NAIRU) to be as shown in the figure. Accustomed to booms being indicated by unemployment figures of 3 percent and normal capacity output by 4 percent, the government watched actual unemployment rise steadily to over 6 percent in 1972 and then come down only slightly to 5.6 percent in 1973. It is not surprising that some policymakers were misled into thinking there was substantial excess capacity in the economy in 1972 and even 1973, for at the time there was no consensus among economists that the natural rate of unemployment had risen.

In an independent study, Frank Reid and Noah Meltz of the University of Toronto argued that structural and frictional unemployment rose by about 3 percent from the mid 1960s to the mid 1970s. They cite these main causes:

(i) the continuing shift from agricultural to nonagricultural employment contributed approximately 0.2 percentage points; (ii) the 1971 change in the Unemployment Insurance Act contributed about 1.9 percentage points of which 0.7 percentage points resulted from the higher benefit-wage ratio and 1.2 percentage points from revisions in the regulations of the Act; (iii) demographic changes contributed about 1.2 percentage points by increasing structural unemployment. The demographic changes have resulted partly from exogenous factors such as the increased fraction of youth in the population and partly by other factors such as changes in the Unemployment Insurance Act and changing social attitudes.

One important policy implication of our analysis is that the 1971 revision of the U.I. Act substantially changed the meaning of the unemployment rate as an indicator of excess demand in the labor market between the mid-1960s and mid-1970s, with the result that a higher target rate of unemployment for monetary and fiscal policy is appropriate. . . . It is possible that as a result of this change the government was led to adopt an overexpansionary monetary and fiscal policy during the early 1970s, producing an acceleration of inflation in that period.

This shift in labor market conditions helps to reconcile two competing views of the performance of the Canadian economy in the 1970s, one based on unemployment, the other based on employment.

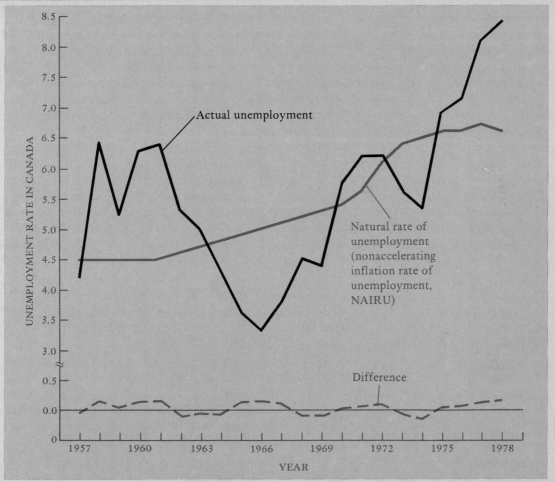

View 1. Canadian economic performance was terrible. In 1975 and 1976 the Canadian inflation rate was above 10 percent, whereas in the late 1960s it was always below 5 percent. Yet in the late 1960s unemployment never rose beyond 4.5 percent while in the early 1970s it never fell below 5.3 percent (1974), and in fact it rose to 6.9 percent by 1975.

View 2. Canadian economic performance was good. Sure, inflation was higher, but Canada achieved a remarkable growth in employment. The highest employment growth in Canada in the late 1960s was 3.1 percent, achieved in 1969. Yet between 1971 and 1978 the *lowest* was 3 percent, achieved in 1972. In 1973 employment grew an incredibly high 5 percent. The high inflation rate was well worth the extremely high employment growth.

The apparent conflict between these two views arises because it seems inconsistent that unemployment and employment should both grow rapidly. But in light of the evidence of the increase in the natural rate of unemployment, there was nothing paradoxical in the Canadian experience of a rise in unemployment accompanying a rise in employment. The rise in the labor force, combined with rising aggregate demand, permitted more employment; the rise in the structural and frictional forces led to a higher proportion of the labor force being unemployed.

Expressed as percentage points, these may not seem like big differences, but a reduction of one percentage point in the unemployment rate means about one hundred thousand more people in jobs rather than in the ranks of the unemployed. It is important to settle the issue of how much deficient-demand unemployment exists because to apply the cure of raising aggregate demand when there is no deficient-demand unemployment would add greatly to inflationary pressure while doing little to reduce unemployment. Influencing aggregate demand in order to lower the overall unemployment rate is a desirable policy goal, yet it is not the only one. Another pressing policy problem is to reduce the pockets of very high unemployment that persist in various regions and among various groups even when national income is at or near its full-employment level.

Inflation

THE DEFINITION OF INFLATION

In 1965 an article in the authoritative *Encyclopedia of Social Sciences* defined inflation in the way economists had always defined it, as a rise in the price level. Then, in the early 1970s, a new distinction was adopted by many economists: a rise in the price level that did not go on continuously was called *a rise in the price level;* the term *inflation* was reserved for a rise in the price level that went on continuously. Today there is confusion in communication. More or less half the economics profession and virtually all the general public use the old definition of inflation as a rise in the price level. The other half of the economics profession (and almost no one else) uses the more restrictive definition of inflation as covering only a *sustained* or *continuous* rise in the price level.

In this book we use the older definition and talk about inflations that are fast or slow, short-lived or long-lived, or that have any other set of characteristics. There is of course no right or

wrong about definitions, which are to be judged instead on whether or not they are convenient. There is some value in using the continuous definitions in theoretical work. When talking to the public, however, using the monetarist definitions would cause confusion. We would have to keep saying, for example, that "only some of the current rise in prices is an inflation, while the rest is merely a rise in the price level," and "we won't know if the current rise in the price level is an inflation or not until we see if it is sustained."

No matter of substance depends on the terms that we select to refer to clearly defined concepts. When we point out that, where we use the terms "sustained inflation" and "nonsustained inflation" (or their equivalents), others use the terms "inflation" and "a rise in the price level," our purpose is only to guard against your being confused when you encounter the different usages. Our selection of terms reflects only a desire to keep our language as close as possible to common usage.

WHY POLICYMAKERS ARE CONCERNED[3]

By and large, governments do not have policies about the price level per se. No one feels that the price level ruling in Canada in 1867 was intrinsically better or worse than that ruling in 1967. Standards of living depend on the purchasing power of money income, and if all money incomes and all prices doubled overnight, the living standards of income earners would be left unchanged. What does matter is what happens while the price level is changing—that is, the process of inflation or deflation. Whatever the present level of prices, there will be many economic consequences if it rises or falls sharply over the course of the next few years. Since sustained deflations have not occurred in the twentieth century, we confine our attention to in-

---

[3] This matter is discussed at greater length in Chapter 35, pages 715–719.

creases in the price level, that is, to periods of *inflation.*

There is a very strong belief among the general public that inflation is seriously eroding the average Canadian's living standards. There is, however, no evidence that this is so. If inflation is to lower living standards over the long term, it has to lower either the level or the rate of growth of potential national income or else raise the GNP gap. Many economists have studied the effects of inflation, but no one has yet established any of these alleged effects.[4]

Since inflation seems neither to affect the level or the rate of growth of full-employment national income nor to raise the average GNP gap, it follows that inflation does not reduce *average* living standards. A main consequence of inflation is the *redistribution* of income, benefiting some people and hurting others.

The redistributions of income caused by inflations are often large and haphazard, and they produce serious social tensions.

This is one major reason for avoiding inflations.

Many people whose real incomes fell during the late 1970s are skeptical of the proposition that inflation does not lower total income. The problem is that the proposition refers to the effects of inflation *ceteris paribus*, while in the real world many things are changing at once. Of course, inflation may accompany a fall in living standards—as, for example, when the price level rises during a recession. Yet here the cause of the fall in living standards is the drop in real output associated with the downturn in the business cycle, not the rise in the price level.

A rise in prices may also be the mechanism by which a fall in living standards due to some other cause is accomplished. When, for example, OPEC increased oil prices enormously, the living standards of major oil-importing nations had to fall. The mechanism by which this was brought about in most countries was a rise in

prices relative to earnings. But other mechanisms are possible, and the cause of the fall in living standards was in fact the rise in the price of oil imports, not the inflation that accompanied it. The rise in oil prices was bad news, but the inflation was merely the bearer of that news, not the news itself.

Perhaps the most telling point against the general perception that inflation is lowering average living standards is made by the figures for per capita real disposable income. In spite of those things that were not constant in the 1970s—in spite of OPEC, agricultural price rises, and other supply shocks—the per capita disposable income measured in 1971 dollars rose every year during the 1970s. At the end of the decade, the average Canadian had 53 percent more real purchasing power in the form of disposable income than he or she had had at the beginning.

CLASSIFICATION OF THE CAUSES OF INFLATION

Most economists agree that there are at least two senses in which inflation is a monetary phenomenon. First, very rapid inflations in many countries, particularly those of South America, have been caused by rapid expansions of the money supply. Such expansions have been due to large and persistent government budget deficits that were often incurred to finance development projects that governments could not or would not pay for out of tax receipts. Second, whatever its causes, inflation cannot continue for a sustained period without increases in the money supply.

Beyond this agreement, there is serious controversy over the causes of the mild inflations experienced by the countries of North America and Western Europe in the 1950s and 1960s and of the somewhat more rapid inflations of the 1970s. Several theories—demand-pull, wage cost-push, import cost-push, price-push, structural rigidity, expectational, and inertial—have been advanced as explanations.

---

[4] But it can raise the GNP gap temporarily, as we shall see later.

The Public's and the Economist's Perceptions of Inflation

Ask someone on the street what is the economic public enemy number one and the odds are that the answer will be "inflation." Inflation, you will be told, is eroding our living standards and adding in many ways to life's uncertainties. Yet real per capita disposable income rose continuously through the 1970s.

Of course different people have different inflationary experiences. The person you asked might be living on the Canada Pension Plan; it certainly does not provide a princely income, but being fully indexed, it is not eroded by inflation. A similar situation would hold if the respondent were living on a fully indexed public sector pension. Indeed, there are reasons for believing that people who live on incomes that are fully tied to the CPI actually benefit from inflation. (Being a fixed weighted index, the CPI makes no allowance for the quantity adjustments that people make when relative prices change. See page 34.)

If the respondent were living on a fixed-income private sector pension, he or she would be right in saying that inflation was hurting very much.

But what of the typical wage earner? The fact is that over the decade money wages have risen faster than many prices, so workers are better off. Why then are so many ordinary working people's perceptions so far wide of the facts? We do not know, but we can see some interesting possibilities.

1. It is possible that people confuse the messenger with the message. For example, the rise in OPEC prices in 1979 meant that to pay for the same amount of oil imports, more goods and services had to be exported and hence less goods and services were available for home consumption. But the rise in the price level was only the means by which the fall in real living standards was effected. If the price level had been held constant, the same real fall would have to have occurred through other means (such as a fall in money wages or a rise in unemployment).

2. People may think that they could have this year's money incomes and last year's prices. An inflation raises money prices and money incomes; if real output has risen, it will raise the latter more than the former. Many people do not understand the link between incomes and prices. They welcome their 12 percent rise in money incomes but deplore the 10 percent rise in money prices that makes their real income rise by a mere 2 percent. They do not realize that if prices had risen by only 4 percent, their money incomes would have risen by only 6 percent, leaving the real income rise unchanged at 2 percent. Thus when many people deplore the rise in prices, they may be thinking—quite erroneously—that if prices had risen by less this year, they could have preserved the same increase in their money incomes. The fundamental relations in the economy are real relations. Average real incomes can rise only by as much as average per capita output rises. If with a given real increase in output we reduce the rate at which money prices increase, so will we reduce the rate at which money incomes increase.

3. Discrete income increases and continuous price increases may create an erroneous impression of trend reductions in real incomes. Individual money incomes are adjusted discretely, often only once a year, while the CPI rises more or less continuously. A typical pattern of money income, shown in the top figure, gives rise to the pattern of real income shown in the lower figure.

Although the trend of real income is upward and on average people's real incomes rise each year, the short-term comparisons are very different. Comparing each week with the previous week, we find that real income falls (a bit) 51 weeks out of 52 while real incomes rise (a lot) only one week in 52—when the annual

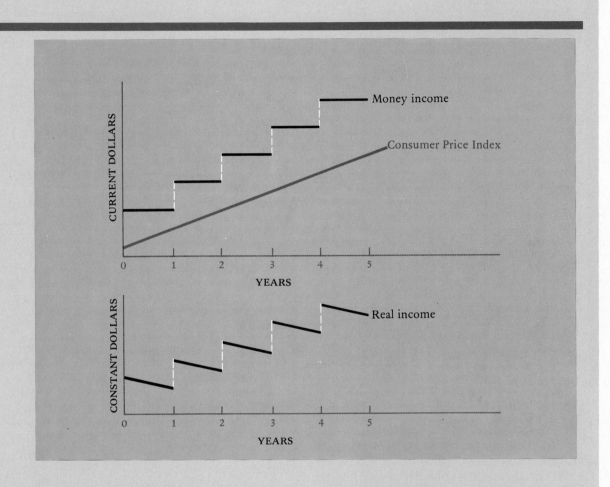

wage adjustment occurs. Thus it is quite possible that the correct perception that inflation is making one gradually worse off (comparing one week with the next) may lead to the mistaken perception that inflation is ultimately making one worse off (comparing one year with the next).

Many economists would agree with Yale's James Tobin when he wrote, " 'Inflation' has become the national obsession, the catchall scapegoat for individual and societal economic difficulties, the symptom that diverts attention from the basic maladies."* Other economists believe, contrarary to Tobin, that inflation itself has serious long-term effects on the structure of society. Most economists agree, however, that the public's perception of the immediate consequences of inflation on their real living standards is seriously distorted.

*Brookings Papers on Economic Activity, 1980, page 70.

FIGURE 39-1
Demand-side Inflation

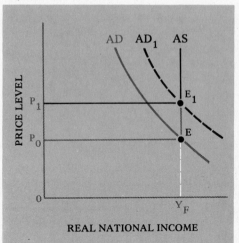

REAL NATIONAL INCOME

Increases in aggregate demand can cause inflationary gaps that in turn cause the price level to rise. With the aggregate demand curve *AD* and the aggregate supply curve P_0AS, the economy is in equilibrium at *E* with price level P_0 and national income Y_F. A rise in aggregate demand to AD_1 creates an inflationary gap. The price level then rises to P_1, at which point the economy is in equilibrium at E_1 on its new aggregate supply curve, P_1AS.

The theories fall into three main groups: (1) those that find the initiating forces of inflation in shifts of the aggregate demand curve, (2) those that find it in shifts of the aggregate supply curve, and (3) those that find it in endogenous shifts of aggregate supply induced by shifts in aggregate demand. We call the three groups demand-side theories, supply-side theories, and demand-supply theories. Although some supporters speak as though these theories were in inevitable conflict, this is not necessarily so. More than one cause may be operating, and the issues dividing advocates of different theories are often ones of emphasis among the various causes.

Different theories of inflation are not necessarily competing theories of inflation; the causes that several theories emphasize may all be operating at the same time.

DEMAND-PULL THEORIES OF INFLATION

The usual collective name for all demand-side theories is the **demand-pull** theory. This theory explains price level changes by inflationary and deflationary gaps. It says that price level changes are accounted for by changes in aggregate demand. A rise in aggregate demand in a situation of more or less full employment will create excess demand in many individual markets, and prices will be bid upward. The rise in demand for goods and services will cause a rise in demand for factors, and their prices will be bid upward as well. Thus inflation in the prices both of consumer goods and of factors of production is caused by a rise in aggregate demand when the economy is at full employment.

Virtually all economists agree that excess aggregate demand can be, and often has been, a major cause of inflation.

Demand-pull theories are illustrated in Figure 39-1.

All demand-pull theories agree in finding the immediate cause of inflation to be shifts in aggregate demand that cause inflationary gaps. They differ, however, on just what it is that causes the aggregate demand curve to shift. Monetarists see the main cause as increases in the money supply. Neo-Keynesians accept monetary expansion as one major cause but also hold that temporary bouts of demand inflation can be caused by shifts in the consumption, investment, or government expenditure functions without the money supply necessarily having to increase.

SUPPLY-SIDE THEORIES OF INFLATION

Supply-side theories look to shifts in the aggregate supply curve as the initiating cause of inflation. The resulting inflations are also called cost-push or supply-shock inflations. As the aggregate supply curve shifts upward, equilibrium moves upward and to the left along the given aggregate demand curve. Thus the price level rises while real national income falls, as shown in Figure 39-2.

FIGURE 39-2
Supply-side Inflation

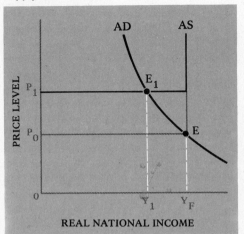

Supply-side inflation causes upward shifts in the aggregate supply curve; this raises the price level and lowers real income. The economy is in equilibrium with aggregate demand curve *AD*, aggregate supply curve P_0AS, equilibrium price level P_0, and national income Y_F. An upward shift in the aggregate supply curve to P_1AS raises equilibrium to E_1. The price level then rises to P_1 while national income falls to Y_1.

The various theories of supply-side inflation differ from one another in what they assume to be the main cause of the upward shift in the aggregate supply curve: wages, domestic prices, import prices, or structural rigidities.

Wage Cost-push Inflation

The **wage cost-push** theory of inflation says that rises in wage costs not themselves associated with excess demand are the *initiating* cause of inflation. Powerful unions are seen as demanding increases in wages even when there is no excess demand for labor. Employers, the theory says, generally accede to these demands and pass the increased wage costs on to the consumer through higher prices. Thus the root cause of the inflation is union power combined with weak employer resistance to labor's demands. Consequently the upward push to prices originates from the cost side rather than from the demand side of the economy.

Price-push Inflation

The **price-push,** or administered price theory of inflation, is similar to the wage cost-push theory. The price-push theory predicts the same sequence of events as does the wage cost-push theory, but with firms rather than unions as the main culprits. The theory says that sellers have monopoly power and would like to raise prices but are restrained from doing so for fear of antitrust action, adverse public opinion, or regulatory review of their prices. Under these circumstances, cost increases can provide the necessary excuse for price increases. During wage negotiations, for example, sellers grant wage increases and then use them as an excuse to raise prices by more than is required to offset the rise in wage costs.

Import Cost-push Inflation

An **import cost-push** inflation is a rise in a country's price level due to a rise in the prices of important imports. The theory relies on linkages among countries that arise from international trade. A demand-pull inflation in country A raises all its prices, including those of its exports. If country B uses country A's exports, A's demand-pull inflation becomes B's import cost-push inflation. A's export prices may also rise for reasons other than a general inflation in A. When OPEC increased the price of oil, this caused significant import cost-push inflations in the oil-importing countries.

Except for unusual disturbances, such as those created by OPEC, this theory does not account for world inflation. Basically all it does is to place the initiating cause of an inflation in some other country. Country B can import country A's inflation through a rise in its import prices; but why did A have an inflation in the first place? The import cost-push theory explains the transmission of inflation from initiating countries to receiving countries, but it does not explain the cause of inflation in the initiating countries.

Structural Rigidity Inflation

The **structural rigidity** theory of inflation assumes that resources do not move quickly from one use to another, and that it is easy to increase money wages and prices but hard to decrease them. Given these conditions, when patterns of demand and costs change, real adjustments occur very slowly. Shortages appear in potentially expanding sectors and prices rise because the slow movement of resources prevents these sectors from expanding rapidly enough. Contracting sectors keep factors of production on part-time employment or even in full unemployment because mobility is low in the economy. Because their wages and prices are rigid, there are no significant wage and price reductions in these potentially contracting sectors. Thus the mere process of adjustment in an economy with structural rigidities causes inflation to occur. Prices in expanding sectors rise, and prices in contracting sectors stay the same; on average, therefore, prices rise.

Many economists believe that the structural rigidity theory explains why the inflation rate, instead of falling to zero in the face of a persistent deflationary gap in the late 1950s and early 1960s, remained in the 1 to 3 percent range. Although this theory cannot be a major part of the explanation of the very high inflation rates of the 1970s and early 1980s, it suggests that a zero inflation rate may be an unachievable target. If there is anything in the structural rigidity theory, then the minimum inflation rate compatible with a changing economy may be 1 to 2 percent rather than zero.

DEMAND-SUPPLY THEORIES OF INFLATION

Theories in this group see inflation as being initiated by aggregate demand shifts but persisting because of aggregate supply shifts long after the aggregate demand curve has been stabilized. The

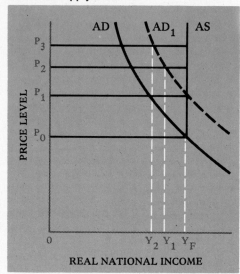

FIGURE 39-3
Demand-Supply Inflations

Demand-pull inflations that produce entrenched inflationary expectations can turn into supply-side inflations once demand increases come to a halt. Suppose increases in aggregate demand have been shifting the aggregate demand curve continually to the right, causing a continuing demand inflation with output constant at Y_F. When the aggregate demand curve has increased from AD to AD_1, taking the price level from P_0 to P_1, the curve is then stabilized so that further demand inflation does not occur. If inflationary expectations are firmly entrenched, firms and unions may continue to raise prices and wages, shifting the horizontal portion of the aggregate supply curve upward to P_2 and eventually to P_3. This causes a supply-side inflation with prices rising, while output falls from Y_F to Y_1 to Y_2 along the fixed aggregate demand curve AD_1.

process is analyzed in Figure 39-3.

There are two main theories of this type, the expectational and inertial theories.

Expectational Inflation

The **expectational** theory of inflation depends on a general set of expectations of price and wage increases. Suppose, for example, that both unions and firms expect that a 10 percent inflation will occur next year. Unions will tend to start negotiations from a *base* of a 10 percent increase in money wages (which would hold their real wages constant). They will argue that firms will be able to meet the extra 10 percent on the wage bill out of the extra revenues that will arise because product prices will go up by 10 percent. *Starting from this base,* unions will then negotiate in an attempt to obtain some desired increase in their real wages. Firms will also be inclined to begin bargaining by conceding at least a 10 percent increase in money wages, since they expect that the prices at which they sell their products will rise by 10 percent. The real substance of the debate between unions and employers will thus center on how much money wages can rise in excess of 10 percent. Here such factors as profits, productivity, and bargaining power will be important.

Since both labor and management expect an inflation of 10 percent (or any other figure), their behavior in wage and price setting will tend to bring that rate of inflation about, whatever the state of monetary and fiscal policy.

Expectational inflation does not break out all by itself, for expectations do not arise out of thin air. It is possible, however, that an expectational inflation may take over from a demand-pull inflation once excess demand is reduced or eliminated. Say, for example, that the government has been generating a demand-pull inflation of 10 percent per year for two or three years as a result of spending well in excess of its tax revenue and creating new money to finance its budget deficit. Firms and unions may now expect this rate to continue; if so, they will grant 10 percent wage and price increases at a minimum. Suppose then that the government eliminates its budget deficit and stabilizes the money supply but that the expectations of 10 percent inflation persist. Wage and price increases of at least 10 percent will occur in the *expectation* of continuing inflation. At this point what was a demand-pull inflation becomes an expectational inflation.

The danger of expectational inflation is that it may cause a demand-pull inflation (or any other kind) that has lasted for several years to persist long after the original causes of the inflation have been removed.

Once inflationary expectations become established, it may not be an easy matter to force decisions makers to revise these expectations downward notwithstanding changed government fiscal and monetary policies.

Expectational inflation depends on forward-looking comparisons. Wage and price setters form expectations about what they expect the general price level will be and then set their own money price or wage in relation to the price level they expect to exist over their planning horizon.

An appropriate way for the government to attack expectational inflation, therefore, is to take action that lowers people's expectations about a future rise in the price level.[5]

One major difference between expectational inflation and wage cost-push inflation is that the former can only sustain an ongoing inflation while the latter can initiate a new one. If the economy were settled in a period of stable prices, an expectational inflation would not break out spontaneously. The theory of wage cost-push inflation says that labor can force up wages (and hence costs and prices) even in the absence of excess demand. Thus wage cost-push (if it exists) could turn a period of stable prices into one of rising prices, forcing up wage rates and hence prices spontaneously.

Inertial Inflation

Expectational inflation tends to be emphasized by monetarists. Neo-Keynesians emphasize a similar but by no means identical theory. **Inertial inflation** is the tendency for an inflation rate, once established, to persist on its own inertia even when the original cause has been removed. The forces of inertia are somewhat wider than mere expectations of further inflation.

---

[5] The two major policy attempts to influence expectations have been wage and price controls and monetary gradualism. They are discussed in Chapter 41.

According to the inertial theory, firms and workers are concerned with relative wages and prices. They look at what has happened to closely related wages and prices when determining their own. If they see that closely related prices and wages have risen by 6 percent, they will tend to use 6 percent as a base for negotiating their own increases. If everyone does the same when setting wages and prices, an inflationary spiral will be hard to break once it has begun. The inflation rate will come down only when a recession becomes so severe that a majority of wage and price setters are willing to cut their wages and prices relative to those closely related wages and prices to which they pay most attention. If enough people try to do this, the overall rate of wage and price inflation will slow.

According to such advocates of the inertial theory as James Tobin of Yale University, a large and persistent deflationary gap must be present before much impact can be made on inertial inflation. Even then, they argue, the rate will come down only very slowly because wage and price setters are cautious about cutting their relative wages and prices even when markets are slack.

Inertial inflation depends on backward-looking comparisons. Wage and price setters look at recent wage settlements and price decisions for closely related labor groups and products when setting their own wages and prices.

Slowing inertial inflation requires more than just changing people's expectations of the general rate of inflation. Market conditions must be created where wage and price setters wish to lower their own wages or prices relative to closely related wages and prices that have already been set.

The differences between expectational and inertial inflation are relatively minor under the older theory of how expectations are formed. This theory, which is called the theory of **adaptive expectations,** assumes that people's expectations of the future inflation rate are based on observed inflation rates in the recent past. This puts substantial inertia into the formation of expecta-

tions concerning the future inflation rate, and makes the expectational and inertial theories of inflation quite similar.

The newer theory of expectations formation, however, gives rise to a sharp distinction between the two. This theory, which is called **rational expectations,** assumes that people look to monetary and fiscal policy and the general state of the economy to predict the future inflation rate. On average, people get their predictions correct. Of course mistakes are made, but these are random errors, not the sort of systematic errors that would occur if people predicted the future merely by projecting past rates of inflation.

With rational expectations, expectational inflation is substantially different from inertial inflation. A change in government policy that is anti-inflationary will lead people's expectations of inflation to fall and they will correspondingly moderate their own price and wage increases, the sum of which determines the actual inflation rate. Thus with rational expectations, expectational inflation is appropriately countered by anti-inflationary fiscal and monetary policy. But inertial inflation depends on comparisons with other existing wages and prices. If recent price and wage contracts were in the 6 to 8 percent inflation range, new contracts will tend to follow along—and so will the earlier contracts when they come to be renegotiated. Inertial inflation is not easily broken by a mere change in macroeconomic policy. Firms and unions looking back at recently set wages and prices will continue their inflationary behavior even though the central bank adopts a significant anti-inflationary monetary policy.

A Dominant Cause?

Few economists would rule out all structural influences, but virtually no one believes the structural rigidity theory to be the major explanation of today's inflation. Many economists believe that all significant inflations have their initiating causes in excess aggregate demand. Others believe that some of the mild inflations of the 1950s, 1960s, and early 1970s were initiated through wage cost-push or price-push. Most agree that in many countries import cost-push inflation contributed to the more rapid inflation rates of the 1970s and early 1980s. Most economists agree that an inflation once started often generates inflationary expectations and inertias that can cause the inflation to persist for some time after the initiating causes have been removed.

Debate continues among economists who accept the demand-pull explanation. Monetarists place most emphasis on increases in the money supply as the cause of the excess aggregate demand. Neo-Keynesians look to other contributory causes, such as temporary bursts in investment and government spending.

When explaining why inflation persists when there is neither demand-pull nor import-price inflation, monetarists stress expectational inflation while neo-Keynesians stress inertial inflation. The monetarist view makes this type of inflation responsive to anti-inflationary policy since, according to the theory of rational expectations, people will lower their inflationary expectations when they see government policy become more anti-inflationary. The Keynesian view is more gloomy. Inertial inflation may drive up the price level (and reduce national income) from the aggregate supply side long after the government's anti-inflationary policies have stopped the outward movement of the aggregate demand curve.

Of course there does not have to be a single cause of inflation, and certainly the weight of different causes can vary from time to time and place to place. For this reason people who look for a single dominant cause of inflations *may* be missing the real issue, the balance between various causes at different times and places.

THE CONTROL OF INFLATION: VALIDATED AND UNVALIDATED INFLATION

When inflation is allowed to persist because the government permits the money supply to expand at the same rate as the inflation, economists speak of the inflation as being *validated* by increases in the money supply. When an inflation occurs that is not accompanied by an increase in the money supply, it is *unvalidated*. The consequences of validated and invalidated inflation were discussed on pages 784–786; this discussion should now be reviewed. The earlier discussion established that:

A continuing inflation not validated by increases in the money supply moves the economy upward to the left along its aggregate demand curve, first removing any inflationary gap and then producing ever-falling levels of output and ever-rising levels of unemployment.

The distinction between validated and unvalidated inflation has an important consequence for controlling inflation. Demand-pull inflations caused by increases in the money supply (such as the government's financing a budget deficit by creating new money) can go on indefinitely because they bring their own monetary validation with them. However, all other kinds of inflation will eventually lead to falling output and rising unemployment *if* the money supply is held constant. Sooner or later, output will become low enough and unemployment high enough that prices and wages will stop rising.

In summary, the initial consequences of bringing a cost-push, price-push, or expectational inflation to a halt by refusing to increase the money supply will be a fall in output and a rise in unemployment. If the push or expectational factors prove stubborn, the inflation may persist for some time in the face of these undesirable consequences.

Rising prices and rising unemployment present policymakers with a serious dilemma. Should they let the recession persist, knowing that if it is deep enough and sufficiently long-lasting, it will break the inflationary spiral? Or should they validate the inflation by increasing the money supply and so remove the disincentives provided by the recession to making further increases in wages and prices? Neither alternative is attractive to politicians whose constituents expect them to reduce inflation *and* unemployment.

Is the CPI Overworked?

Cost of living allowance (COLA) clauses have become a standard part of many collective agreements, and this clause has been a major issue in some strikes. For many Canadians, monetary compensation for the rising "cost of living" forms part of their daily lives: taxes, pensions, social assistance payments, and some wages rise as prices rise. The key to these increases is the consumer price index (CPI); cost of living adjustments are almost invariably linked with the CPI. Every time the cost of the basket of goods and services that constitutes the CPI moves upward, a host of payments are increased as well.

The CPI is a convenient measure. It is published monthly, just a few weeks after the end of the period it covers, thereby allowing changes in indexed payments to be made quickly. Publication of the index provides a consistent series for calculating adjustments built into "cost of living" changes.

But the index has disadvantages. One major flaw is the CPI's failure to incorporate substitutions made by consumers as prices change. COLA clauses are generally intended to preserve "real income" in terms of consumer welfare or utility. However, indexing to the CPI preserves purchasing power in terms of a *fixed bundle* of commodities. Since some prices always rise faster than others, and thus relative prices change, individuals substitute some commodities for others. By ignoring this substitution effect, COLA adjustments often cause real income to change.

Assume, for example, that the price of an

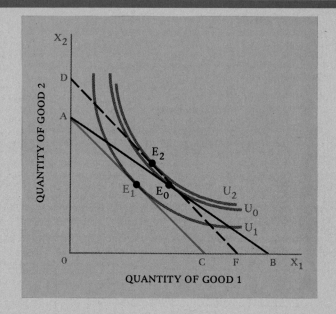

item with a 20 percent weight in the CPI rises by 50 percent while all other prices remain constant. The CPI will rise by 10 percent, and a worker with a COLA clause will receive a 10 percent increase in money income. It would appear that real income has been held constant. But if that worker reduces his or her consumption of the item whose price rose by 50 percent and turns to an only slightly less satisfactory substitute, a 10 percent increase in money incomes will not be needed to restore real income to its original level. This is shown in the figure where the individual is initially at point E_0 with utility level U_0. The rise in price of good 1 shifts the budget line from

EXPERIENCE OF INFLATION

Figure 28-1 (see page 562) shows the inflation rate over the last 50 years, as measured by the Consumer Price Index. Like the unemployment figures, inflation rates showed no tendency to increase until the late 1960s. The average rate of inflation in the 1950s was 2.4 percent, and from 1960 to 1967 it was 2.2 percent. The dramatic rise in the inflation rate began with the accelera-

AB to the colored line *AC*. With no change in money income, consumption moves to E_1 with a lower utility level of U_1. Increasing money income by the fixed-weight cost of living change means that the individual could again consume the original bundle at E_0; that is, a COLA adjustment shifts the budget line to the dashed line *DF*, which is parallel to *AC* (and therefore reflects the increased relative price of good 1) but which passes through E_0. However, the individual now chooses to consume at E_2, substituting away from the expensive good 1. Adjusting money income by the fixed-weight CPI allows the individual to raise utility from U_0 to U_2.

There are other drawbacks to using the CPI. The CPI is not a cost of living index because many items that affect real income are not recorded in the CPI. Changes in income taxes and the cost of services paid out of tax revenue are not in the index even though changes in them could affect what else the consumer buys. There is also the problem that improvements in the quality of a good may not be reflected accurately, though Statistics Canada does try to allow for such improvements.

A particularly acute problem is the CPI's treatment of owner-occupied housing. In order to approximate the average cost of using a house, the CPI is calculated as though 20 percent of all houses were bought and sold each year. When the price of housing goes up, the new housing prices enter the CPI and cause it to rise regardless of the actual volume of transactions. It is further assumed that 20 percent of existing houses are refinanced each year at current interest rates, so when interest rates rise, the increased cost of financing a house also enters the CPI. This of course may be an accurate reflection of costs for some Canadians but it is not valid for all, and using the CPI for making adjustments can generate serious inequities. For example, increases in the CPI are often used to index pensions; pensioners who own their own houses and hence earn capital gains when housing prices rise are compensated again by receiving an increased pension. Short-term fluctuations in interest rates also lead to erratic month-to-month movements in the CPI, thereby making it difficult to determine changes in the underlying trend rate of inflation.

While the CPI is clearly a very useful summary measure, it is only that. In the inflation-conscious atmosphere of the 1980s, we clearly try to use it too much, to apply it to situations where it is not really appropriate. A study recently prepared for the Economic Council of Canada cautioned against the increasing use of the CPI.* The authors argued that the CPI should be used in conjunction with other measures such as the implicit price index of gross national expenditures and the industrial selling price. The CPI is one tool for gauging price shifts and changes in the cost of living, but it is not necessarily the best tool, and it is certainly not the only one.

* M. C. McCracken and E. Ruddick, *Towards a Better Understanding of the Consumer Price Index.*

---

tion of U.S. government expenditures for the Vietnam War, when the inflation rate rose to 4 percent in 1968 and to 4.6 percent in 1969. The rate subsided substantially in the recession year 1970, but the rate of 2.9 percent in 1971 still exceeded the average rate of each of the previous two decades. Then the inflation rate jumped to 7.9 percent in 1973 and to almost 11 percent in both 1974 and 1975.

In the course of 1975 the economy encountered an upper turning point and passed from boom to recession. As the slump developed the inflation rate fell to 7.5 percent in 1976. Even in the depths of the most serious trough in business activity since the Great Depression of the 1930s, however, the inflation rate remained stubbornly above the rate achieved in the previous trough and well above the average rate for the previous two decades. As the economy slowly recovered, the inflation rate rose steadily, reaching 10.1 percent in 1980.

These inflation figures are based on year-to-year increases in the Consumer Price Index. Recently economists have become aware of the extent to which short-term changes in the CPI are dominated by changes in the money prices of a few commodities whose *relative* prices are temporarily rising. Concentration on such short-term changes in the CPI can muddle assessments of the efficacy of anti-inflationary policies.

Government fiscal and monetary policy that is directed at the control of inflation can be expected to influence the trend of all prices. However, it cannot influence cyclical and short-term fluctuations in relative prices. From one year to the next, these relative price effects can be the dominating influence on movements in the CPI.

From decade to decade, however, short-term movements are unimportant because greater-than-average rises due to temporary shortages cancel out less-than-average rises due to temporary surpluses. Yet, as we have seen, this is not so from one year to the next. As a result, a successful government anti-inflationary policy that reduces the trend rate of inflation may be discredited when the measured rate rises because of a temporary fluctuation in a few prices such as those for food or energy.

To get a better measure of the impact of policy on the inflation rate, economists sometimes omit from the price index certain prices that cannot be affected by monetary and fiscal policy. Changes in the amended index are then said to measure the underlying rate of inflation. Two common omissions are food and energy prices.

The rationale for removing food prices is that

in the short term they are dominated by demand and supply fluctuations that have nothing to do with inflationary forces, while over the long term they follow the rest of the CPI. The rationale for excluding energy prices is that they are determined in part by local shortages and in part by OPEC policy over which the government has no control. Yet long-term trend changes in energy prices are a contributory force to inflation, and their omission is thus more debatable than that of food in calculating the underlying rate of inflation.

A Link Between Inflation and Unemployment

So far in this chapter we have considered inflation and unemployment separately. Until the 1960s most economists and policymakers viewed them as independent policy goals and accepted the twin objectives of full employment *and* stable prices. The early Keynesian policies for achieving full employment without inflation were based on the kinked aggregate supply curve shown in Figures 39-1 and 39-2. We have seen that this curve creates a sharp distinction between how the economy reacts to a rise in aggregate demand when there is unemployment (real national income rises and prices remain constant) and when there is full employment (real national income remains constant and prices rise).

Throughout the 1950s, however, evidence accumulated that when the economy expanded out of a slump, the price level and real national income would *both* rise. Furthermore full-employment income, Y_F, did not appear to be the absolute barrier to further output of the kind suggested by the kinked aggregate supply curve. Indeed, it always seemed possible to squeeze a little more output from the economy by sufficiently large increases in aggregate demand. This is true because factories can be run at more than normal capacity and labor can work at more than normal hours. But such increases in output *above* Y_F always seemed to be associated with inflations.

This experience suggested that, when the economy is close to full employment, shifts in aggregate demand affect *both* output and prices.

THE INTERMEDIATE SECTION OF THE AGGREGATE SUPPLY CURVE

Economists sought to capture this behavior by introducing an intermediate section into the aggregate supply curve. We first saw this section in Chapter 28; it is shown again in Figure 39-4. When the intermediate section is introduced, full-employment income, Y_F, is no longer defined as the maximum output the economy can produce.

Full-employment or potential national income must be redefined as *normal* capacity output. At this output there is no upward *demand* pressure on prices. Instead there is just enough demand to employ plant and equipment at normal capacity and to employ a normal-size labor force at normal hours.

Over the intermediate portion of the aggregate supply curve, the initial effect of a rise in aggregate demand is a rise in both prices and output. This is shown in Figure 39-4.

In Figure 39-4 full-employment national income, Y_F, occurs at the end of the Keynesian segment of the aggregate supply curve. When increases in aggregate demand cause the economy to expand out of a slump, the price level may in some circumstances start to rise *before* full-employment income is reached, thus placing Y_F somewhere in the intermediate section of *AS*. However, for our purposes the important facts are (1) that the maximum level of output, Y_M, exceeds Y_F, and (2) that when heavy aggregate demand pushes the economy *beyond* Y_F, inflationary pressure ensues. Hence in what follows we do not introduce the added complication that an expansion of aggregate demand might cause prices to rise before Y_F is reached. We continue instead with the simpler case in which Y_F is located at the end of the Keynesian segment of

FIGURE 39-4
Simultaneous Changes in Output and Prices

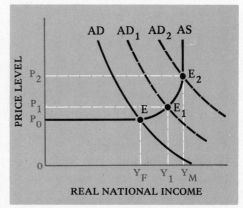

Over the intermediate section of the aggregate supply curve, the initial effect of any increase in aggregate demand is an increase in both output and prices. A rise in aggregate demand from AD to AD_1 to AD_2 takes national income from Y_F to Y_1 to Y_M and the price level from P_0 to P_1 to P_2. National income, Y_M, is the absolute maximum output that can be squeezed from the economy when everyone is working well beyond normal capacity. However, these effects on output and prices are only the initial or impact effects; they do not represent stable equilibrium positions.

the aggregate supply curve: demand inflation only occurs when the economy is pushed beyond its full employment level of income.

Upward Shifts in Aggregate Supply

Yet this is not the end of the story. If it were, a once-and-for-all rise in the price level of a few percentage points would be the only penalty for a permanent increase in the flow of output. However, Figure 39-4 shows only the *initial* effects of an increase in aggregate demand that puts the equilibrium position on the intermediate portion of the aggregate supply curve. The full effects follow because *whenever the economy comes to rest on the intermediate portion of the aggregate supply curve, the curve itself starts to shift upward.*

FIGURE 39-5

An Upward-shifting Aggregate Supply Curve

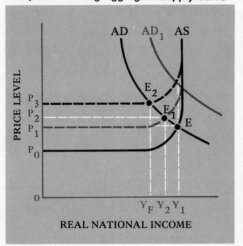

When equilibrium lies in the intermediate por- tion of the aggregate supply curve, the curve itself shifts upward. An increase in aggregate demand to AD has taken national income to Y_1 and the price level to P_1 on the intermediate por- tion of the aggregate supply curve P_0AS. The aggregate supply curve then shifts to P_1AS, reducing national income to Y_2 and raising the price level to P_2. This shifts the aggregate supply curve to P_2AS. As long as national income ex- ceeds Y_F, the price level goes on rising and the aggregate supply curve goes on shifting up- ward. The final equilibrium is at Y_F with a price level of P_3.

If the aggregate demand curve were shifted outward by monetary policy, reaching AD_1 when the aggregate supply curve reached P_3AS, na- tional income would be held constant at Y_1 in spite of the rise in the price level. Since the aggregate supply curve goes on shifting upward as long as Y exceeds Y_F, holding income at Y_1 requires continued upward shifts in aggregate demand and continued inflation.

Why do the upward shifts in aggregate supply occur? One major reason lies in the way that markets adjust to excess demand. When the aggregate demand curve rises sufficiently to take equilibrium income above Y_F, manufacturing firms raise their output and seek to get more labor inputs by working their existing work force longer hours and hiring new workers. They also increase their demand for raw materials and other inputs. This expansion of output creates excess demand in some markets for labor and raw materials. Excess demand in turn causes input prices to rise. Manufacturing firms find their cost curves shifting upward, so they must raise prices to cover the extra costs. The initial increase in output and prices is represented by a movement along the aggregate supply curve into its intermediate range. The continuing rise in costs and prices *shifts* the whole aggregate sup- ply curve upward.

As long as firms are producing beyond normal capacity, however, there will be *continued* upward pressure on wage and material costs that will force the aggregate supply curve continually upward. The upward-shifting aggregate supply curve is shown in Figure 39-5. (The significance of the aggregate demand curve in the figure will be explained later.) Notice that the upward shifts in the aggregate supply curve occur whenever equilibrium is on the intermediate portion of the curve.

The Phillips Curve

The tendency for the price level to *continue* to rise whenever national income exceeds Y_F is more easily seen on a new diagram showing what is called a **Phillips curve,** which is named after its modern discoverer, the late Professor A. W. Phillips of the London School of Economics.[6] This curve is shown in Figure 39-6. The AS curve relates national income to the *price level*. The Phillips curve relates national income to the *rate of change of the price level*.

[6] Phillips drew graphs of British data from 1862 to 1958, showing the rate of change of *money wages* and the percent- age of *unemployment*. Figure 39-6 shows the rate of change of prices and the level of national income. This has the effect of making the curve slope upward to the right instead of upward to the left as did Phillips' original curve. The basic be- havior being described by the two curves is, however, iden- tical. (Unemployment and national income are inversely related, while the rate of increase of money wages and money prices are directly related to each other.)

The slope of the curve to the left of Y_F indicates the same downward inflexibility of the price level as is shown by the horizontal position of the aggregate supply curve. The aggregate supply curve is horizontal at the current price level while the Phillips curve, which measures inflation, is horizontal on the income axis (i.e., at a zero rate of inflation). These are two ways of showing that the price level does not fall even though national income is below Y_F.

The shape of the Phillips curve to the right of Y_F shows that the inflation rate will be positive for incomes above Y_F. This is of course the same as saying that the AS curve relating income to the price level will be shifting upward continually for national incomes in excess of Y_F. The increasing height of the Phillips curve as national income rises further above Y_F indicates the further hypothesis that the greater is the inflationary gap, the more rapidly will the price level be rising.

In summary:

1. The downward inflexibility of the price level in the face of deflationary gaps is shown both by a horizontal AS curve at the current price level and by a horizontal Phillips curve lying on the income axis (inflation = zero) when national income is less than Y_F.

2. The tendency for prices to rise continually in the face of inflationary gaps is shown both by the tendency for the aggregate supply curve to shift upward and by the position of the Phillips curve above the income axis (thus showing positive inflation rates) when national income exceeds Y_F.

Unvalidated Demand Inflation: National Income Tends to Full-employment Income

The effects of an inflation caused by excess demand but unvalidated by further increases in the money supply are shown in Figure 39-5. An increase in aggregate demand has taken national income into the intermediate portion of the aggregate supply curve so that current income exceeds full-employment income. As long as an inflationary gap persists, the continued upward

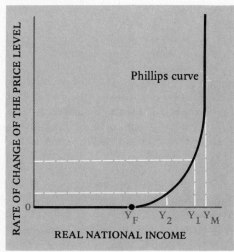

FIGURE 39-6
The Phillips Curve

The Phillips curve relates national income to the rate of change of the price level rather than to the price level itself. Here the vertical axis represents the rate of change of the price level, not the price level itself (as it would be in an aggregate supply diagram). The Phillips curve lies on the axis for national incomes below Y_F, indicating the same downward inflexibility of prices as shown by the Keynesian portion of the AS curve. To the right of Y_F the Phillips curve rises ever more steeply, indicating that more output can be obtained only at the cost of an increasingly rapid inflation rate. National income of Y_M is the absolute maximum that can be squeezed out of the economy.

When aggregate demand and aggregate supply intersect to yield national income Y_1 (see Figure 39-5) the inflation rate is given by the height of the Phillips curve at that income. As the rising price level reduces national income, income falls first to Y_2 (which produces a lower but still positive rate of inflation) and then to Y_F. At Y_F there is no further demand inflation and the price level remains constant.

pressure on prices continues to shift the aggregate supply curve upward. But the inflation is not validated, so the upward-shifting aggregate supply curve moves the economy upward and to the left along its fixed aggregate demand curve, as shown in the figure. Prices rise and output falls. The rise in the price level halts when national income has returned to normal capacity output at Y_F, and the inflationary gap is eliminated.

When the process comes to a halt, the economy is back at full-employment national income, Y_F, but with a higher price level, as shown in Figure 39-5.

Increases in *output* caused by a movement into the intermediate section of the aggregate supply curve are transitory.

In Figure 39-6 the same process is shown by movements along the Phillips curve. The original rise in aggregate demand took national income to Y_1. At this point on the Phillips curve the price level is rising at a fairly fast rate. Equilibrium national income falls back toward Y_F (passing through Y_2 when the aggregate supply curve is P_1AS in Figure 39-5). As income falls, the inflationary pressure is reduced until finally, when income reaches Y_F, the inflationary gap has been removed and the price level becomes stable.

The Long-run Aggregate Supply Curve: National Income and a Constant Price Level

The analysis just conducted means that the upward-sloping aggregate supply curve is a *short-run curve*. It shows how output and the price level can vary together under the impact of a rise in aggregate demand. We have seen, however, that when the economy comes to rest at a point on the intermediate portion of the aggregate supply curve, prices will go on rising and that this will lead to an upward *shift* in the whole short-run aggregate supply curve.

A *long-run* aggregate supply curve shows combinations of national income and the price level that can persist. The long-run aggregate supply curve is vertical at full-employment income, indicating that a stable price level cannot be achieved at higher levels of income. There is also a short-run aggregate supply curve that allows national income to rise temporarily above Y_F. The relationship is shown in Figure 39-7.

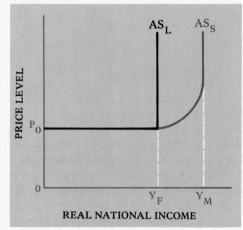

FIGURE 39-7

Short-run and Long-run Aggregate Supply Curves

The long-run aggregate supply curve is kinked at full-employment national income. In the long run, the aggregate supply curve is the heavy black curve AS_L, where P_0 is the current price level. This means that any output up to full-employment national income, Y_F, is possible, but no more. In the short run, the aggregate supply curve is P_0AS_s, where the intermediate portion indicates that it is possible to produce more than Y_F.

When output exceeds Y_F, the pressure of excess demand causes the price level to rise continuously, thereby shifting AS_s upward. A stable price level is not therefore consistent with output in excess of Y_F.

VALIDATED DEMAND INFLATION: AN UNEMPLOYMENT-INFLATION TRADE-OFF?

The Phillips curve suggested a permanent trade-off between the rate of inflation and the amount of national income. If, for example, equilibrium national income exceeds Y_F, the price level will be rising. We saw earlier (Figure 39-5) that the rise in the price level will shift the economy upward to the left along its fixed aggregate demand curve until national income falls back to Y_F, at which point all demand pressures will be removed from the price level.

However, if the Bank of Canada increases the money supply as fast as the price level is rising, that will shift the aggregate demand curve to the right. It can hold national income constant at some value in excess of Y_F, as shown by the screened curve in Figure 39-5. This keeps national income at Y_1 in spite of the rising price level. On the Phillips curve the economy remains at the point on the curve corresponding to national income Y_1. National income is stabilized at a level in excess of full employment and the inflation rate is constant.

The Phillips curve thus suggests a long-term trade-off between national income and the rate of inflation. If the central bank increases the money supply as fast as the price level is rising, the aggregate demand curve will shift upward as fast as the aggregate supply curve is shifting upward. Equilibrium national income will thus remain constant and, according to the Phillips curve, a constant rate of inflation will be the price paid for holding national income above Y_F.

VALIDATED DEMAND INFLATION AND ACCELERATING INFLATION

Most economists who accept the expectational theory of inflation—that expectations of future inflation are an important cause of current inflations—deny the existence of the long-term trade-off between inflation and national income just described. They argue that the economy could not be held at some point on the Phillips curve of Figure 39-6, with a constant rate of inflation and national income greater than Y_F, unless people did *not* expect that rate of inflation. Once they do come to expect it, wages and prices will rise in response to *both* the general excess demand and inflationary expectations.

To illustrate, assume that (with no inflationary expectations) the general excess demand associated with Y_1 in the figure makes all sellers decide to raise their relative prices by 5 percent. Since they expect the general price level to remain constant, they all raise their money prices by 5 percent. But because everyone's money prices actually do rise, no one succeeds in raising relative prices; they have instead generated a 5 percent inflation.

Now everyone tries again and all they do once more is to generate a further 5 percent inflation. Sooner or later, if this process continues, everyone comes to expect a continuing 5 percent inflation. When this happens sellers who want to raise their relative prices by 5 percent must increase their money prices by 10 percent—5 percent to keep abreast of the general inflation and 5 percent to raise relative prices. But this round of increases only generates a 10 percent inflation. Once people become adjusted to the 10 percent figure, they will raise their money prices by 15 percent in a vain effort to raise their relative prices. (The effort is vain because *every* price cannot rise relative to the average of all prices.)

According to this theory—often called the Phelps-Friedman theory—the general excess demand created when national income exceeds Y_F leads everyone to try to raise relative prices. This generates a general inflation, and once this comes to be expected, prices will rise ever faster in an effort to keep ahead of the general price rise. According to this theory, the attempt to hold national income above Y_F leads to an ever-accelerating rate of inflation.

THE PHELPS-FRIEDMAN THEORY: ACCELERATING INFLATION AND AN UNSTABLE PHILLIPS CURVE[7]

In the late 1960s Professors Milton Friedman of the University of Chicago and Edmund Phelps of Columbia University began to mount an attack on the theoretical underpinnings of the theory of a stable Phillips curve. They argued that the curve describes a transitory relationship that cannot exist over the long term.

According to their theory, the economy could not remain in a position to the right of Y_F on the Phillips curve shown in Figure 39-6. Any position with income in excess of Y_F implies substantial continued inflation. But sooner or later people would come to realize that the inflation was permanent. Unions would then demand even

---

[7] The remainder of this chapter may be omitted without loss of continuity.

larger wage increases, and others would revise their own expectations of continued inflation. This new behavior would accelerate the inflation. When people came to accept the new higher rate as permanent, they would again revise their behavior, and this would accelerate the inflation still further. Extensive empirical research over the first half of the 1970s has given support to the view that the Phillips curve would not remain stable if the economy were to operate at a low level of unemployment and a high rate of inflation for a sustained period.

This theory is a mixture of demand-pull and expectational inflation, and it has a number of important aspects that we will study in detail.

The Short-term Phillips Curve for Zero Expected Inflation

In the Phelps-Friedman theory a critical role is played by inflationary expectations. We shall use the symbol P_e to refer to the rate of inflation that decisions makers *expect* will rule over their planning period—say, the next year.

The pure demand-pull element of the Phelps-Friedman theory is illustrated in Figure 39-8 by the Phillips curve labeled $PP(P_e = 0)$. *This particular Phillips curve is drawn on the assumption that people expect a zero rate of inflation.* (This is indicated by the notation $P_e = 0$.) The curve shows that the higher is the level of national income (i.e., the higher is the level of aggregate demand), the higher will be the associated rate of inflation.[8] The point where the PP curve for zero expected inflation cuts the axis, labeled Y_F, indicates the level of national income at which there is no significant demand-pull inflation. The

percentage of the labor force unemployed at Y_F is the **natural rate of unemployment.** Because of frictional unemployment, the natural rate of unemployment will certainly be positive; it may well be as high as 5 or 6 percent in Canada today.

Why does the Phillips curve for zero expected inflation cut the axis at Y_F? When national income is at its full-employment level, the Phelps-Friedman theory envisages all markets in the economy being in equilibrium, with demands equal to supplies. Thus there is no market pressure on any price either to rise or to fall. In these circumstances all prices, and hence the price level, will remain stable.

Why does the Phillips curve for zero expected inflation show prices rising when national income exceeds its full-employment level and falling when national income is less than its full-employment level? Let the economy begin at full-employment income. Consider, first, the effects of a rise in aggregate demand. All individual demand curves shift outward, creating excess demands in all markets. Decision makers will respond in two ways: (1) they will increase their outputs (working overtime, extra shifts, etc.), and (2) they will raise their money prices, seeking thereby to raise their relative prices. Since this happens in all markets, the first response leads to an increase in national income while the second response causes a rise in the price level. Now consider what happens when there is a fall in aggregate demand with national income initially at its full-employment level. Decision makers respond by reducing output and by cutting money prices, seeking thereby to lower their relative prices. Since this happens in all markets, there is a fall in national income combined with some downward movement in the price level.

Why does the price level continue to change as long as national income remains unequal to its full-employment level? We have seen that when there is excess demand in all markets, all decisions makers raise their money prices,

---

[8] The Phillips curve in Figure 39-6 was drawn with a horizontal flat portion to the left of Y_F to indicate that prices do not fall when output is below its full employment level. In Figure 39-8 the portion left of Y_F is drawn negatively sloped; this allows for the possibility that prices might fall at levels of output below full employment. However, in Figure 39-8 the slope to the left of Y_F is flatter than to the right, thus preserving the key *asymmetry* property that increases in the price level when Y exceeds Y_F can be much more rapid than decreases in the price level when Y is less than Y_F.

FIGURE 39-8
The Phelps-Friedman Theory of the Phillips Curve

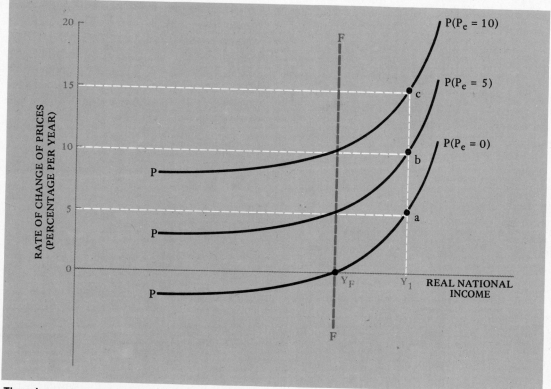

There is a separate Phillips curve for each expected rate of inflation. The Phillips curve of Figure 39-6, shown here as $PP(P_e = 0)$, relates national income to inflation on the assumption that the price level is expected to remain stable. The actual rate of inflation depends on national income and the expected rate of inflation. Thus for each expected rate of inflation the associated short-run Phillips curve lies above the $P_e = 0$ curve by the amount of the expected rate of inflation. Consider, for example, an inflationary gap with national income at Y_1. The actual rate of inflation will be 5 percent when the expected rate is zero (point *a*), 10 percent when the expected rate is 5 percent

(point *b*), and 15 percent when the expected rate is 10 percent (point *c*).

In long-term equilibrium the actual rate of inflation must remain equal to the expected rate (otherwise expectations would be revised). This can only occur at the full-employment level of income Y_F, that is, along *FF*. At Y_F there is no demand pressure on the price level; hence the only influence on actual inflation is expected inflation. Any stable rate of inflation (provided it is validated by the appropriate rate of monetary expansion) is compatible with Y_F and its associated natural rate of unemployment.

seeking thereby to raise their relative prices. But by definition *all* relative prices cannot rise. (It is impossible, for example, for rye whiskey to become more expensive relative to Scotch while at the same time Scotch becomes more expensive relative to rye.) Thus at least some decision makers will be frustrated in their attempts to

raise their *relative* prices. Take a simple example: if all raise their money prices by 5 percent, seeking thereby to raise their relative prices by 5 percent, a 5 percent inflation will be generated; but no one will have succeeded in raising his or her own prices relative to other prices. As long as the excess demand persists, people will go on raising their money prices, trying unsuccessfully to raise their relative prices. (Some may succeed, but everyone cannot.) Thus general excess demand will be associated with a level of national income above its full-employment level and a *continuing* rise in prices.

An exactly parallel argument shows that when there is general excess supply, decreases in money prices by all decision makers, in an attempt to cut relative prices, will lead to a fall in the general price level, but many *relative* prices will not be decreased. Decision makers, therefore, will cut prices further. Because of these vain attempts to cut relative prices, national income below its full-employment level will be associated with a *continuing* downward pressure on prices.

In summary, the Phelps-Friedman theory holds, first, that general excess demand in the economy will be associated with national income above its full-employment level and with continuing inflation; and second, that general excess supply will be associated with national income below its full-employment level and with a continuing downward pressure on prices. In other words, the Phillips curve for zero expected inflation is upward sloping, and it cuts the axis at Y_F.

The Actual Inflation Rate

The foregoing discussion of upward and downward pressure on the price level relied on the desire to raise relative prices when national income exceeded Y_F and to lower them when national income fell short of Y_F. Since each decision maker's relative price is the relation between their own price and the general price level,[9] it follows that any decision to change relative prices means changing one's money price *relative* to what one *expects* the price level to be (over the time for which one's own price is being set). If a decision maker wishes to raise his or her

relative price by 5 percent, this requires a 5 percent increase in the money price when no inflation is expected, a 10 percent increase in the money price when a 5 percent inflation is expected, and so on. If, on the other hand, the decision maker wishes to reduce his or her relative price by 2 percent, this requires a 2 percent reduction in the money price when no inflation is expected, a 3 percent *increase* in the money price when a 5 percent inflation is expected, and so on. In general, a decision to change a relative price by x percent requires a change in the money price by an amount equal to x percent *plus* the expected rate of inflation.

The above discussion explains what determines the actual rate of inflation in this theory.

According to the Phelps-Friedman theory, the actual rate of inflation is given by the demand-pull element *plus* the expected rate of inflation.[10]

Thus, for example, if everyone expects a 5 percent inflation, prices and wages will be raised by 5 percent *plus* the amount due to the pull of excess demand, which is shown by the Phillips curve for $P_e = 0$.

Another way of making the same point is to say that there is a separate Phillips curve relating actual inflation to national income for each expected rate of inflation. Each curve is defined for a particular expected rate of inflation, and each is called a short-run Phillips curve. (Each curve is short-run in the sense that the Phillips curve on which the economy is located will be given at any moment of time but will change whenever P_e changes.) This point is illustrated for three levels of expected rates of inflation in Figure 39-8.

The Relation Beween Actual and Expected Inflation

Since actual inflation is equal to expected inflation *plus* an allowance for demand pressure, it

[9] That is, a relative price is p/P where p is the individual price in question and P is the general price level (which is an average of the economy's prices).

[10] In symbols: $P_a = PD + P_e$ where P_a is the actual rate of inflation, PD is the inflation rate caused by demand pressure, and P_e is the expected rate of inflation.

follows that actual inflation exceeds expected inflation when national income exceeds Y_F because demand pressures are then positive.[11] When national income equals Y_F, demand pressures are zero, and actual inflation will equal expected inflation. When actual national income is less than Y_F, demand pressures are negative, and actual inflation will be less than the expected rate.[12]

People are assumed to base their expectations about the inflation rate in the immediate future on the actual rates that have occurred over the previous two or three years. Thus whenever actual rates of inflation exceed expected rates, expectations will catch up—but with a lag. For example, if people are expecting a 5 percent inflation but continue to experience a 7 percent inflation, sooner or later they will revise their expectations upward and come to expect a 7 percent inflation. Conversely, if people expect a 7 percent inflation but experience only a 5 percent inflation, sooner or later they will revise their expectations downward and come to expect only a 5 percent inflation.

IMPLICATIONS OF THE PHELPS-FRIEDMAN THEORY

Accelerating Inflation

A first important implication of the Phelps-Friedman theory is that if national income is *kept* above Y_F, the rate of inflation will accelerate continuously. Say the economy starts in full-employment equilibrium at stable prices—that is, at the point where the Phillips curve for $P_e = 0$ cuts the axis. Now let aggregate demand increase. Excess demand is created; national income increases; and the economy moves up its short-run Phillips curve to a higher level of na-

tional income and, say, a 5 percent inflation. This is shown by point *a* in Figure 39-8. The inflation occurs because people are trying to adjust their *relative* wages and prices upward in response to excess demand. No one expects an inflation. If the inflation persists, however, it will eventually come to be expected. People will then add a catch-up factor of 5 percent to any wage and price change they plan to make. When they do this, the rate of inflation will accelerate to 10 percent (point *b*). Sooner or later this will come to be expected, and the rate of inflation will then accelerate to 15 percent (point *c*), of which 10 percent is to keep ahead of expected inflation and 5 percent is a response to excess demand.

According to the Phelps-Friedman theory, whenever the economy has a level of national income above full-employment income (or, the same thing, a level of unemployment below the natural rate of unemployment), the actual rate of inflation will eventually accelerate. How fast it accelerates depends on how fast current inflationary expectations adjust to past actual rates.

It follows that if the government tries to maintain excess aggregate demand in the mistaken view that it can increase real national income above Y_F (i.e., lower unemployment below its natural rate) at the cost of a stable rate of inflation, it will be in for a nasty shock. For a while people may not expect the inflation to continue; as a result inflation will proceed at a stable pace. Sooner or later, however, people will come to expect the inflation to continue; they will revise their inflationary expectations upward, and this will cause the inflation rate to accelerate. Later the new higher rate will come to be accepted; expectations of future inflation will be revised upward, and the actual rate of inflation will once again accelerate.[13]

---

[11] The allowance is positive when Y exceeds Y_F and negative when Y falls short of Y_F.

[12] This is easily seen when we look at the relation $P_a = PD + P_e$ given in footnote 10 before. It immediately follows that when $PD > 0$, $P_a > P_e$; when $PD = 0$, $P_a = P_e$; and when $PD < 0$, $P_a < P_e$.

[13] As we have seen, the government will have to induce ever more rapid rates of monetary expansion to validate an ever-accelerating inflation rate. But if the government does try to hold national income above Y_F, it will induce, according to this theory, an ever-accelerating rate of inflation that will *have to be validated* by ever-increasing rates of monetary expansion.

The Long-run Phillips Curve Is Vertical

When national income equals Y_F in the Phelps-Friedman theory, there is no excess demand pressure on inflation. *Thus the only inflation that can occur when $Y = Y_F$ is expectational inflation.* If everyone expects a 5 percent inflation, all prices will be raised by 5 percent and an actual inflation rate of 5 percent will occur. If the money supply is increased by 5 percent to validate this inflation, then full-employment income and the natural rate of unemployment can be maintained indefinitely with a 5 percent expected and a 5 percent actual inflation. But the same argument could be repeated for 10 percent or for any other rate of inflation (or deflation).

In general, since at the natural rate of unemployment there is neither upward nor downward pressure on prices due to excess demand, the only cause of inflation arises from attempts to try to keep up with whatever rate of inflation is expected.[14] Thus full-employment national income and its associated natural rate of unemployment are compatible with *any* actual rate of inflation, provided that, first, the inflation is expected and, second, it is accompanied by the appropriate rate of monetary expansion.

The long-run Phillips curve that relates national income to a stable rate of inflation is vertical at full-employment income.

Policy Implications

The Phelps-Friedman theory has a number of implications for economic policy. If the theory turns out to be substantially correct, these policy implications will be extremely important. A first implication has already been discussed.

Attempts to reduce unemployment below its natural rate will eventually cause the rate of inflation to accelerate.

[14] The basic Phelps-Friedman relation is $P_a = PD + P_e$. When $Y = Y_F$, there is no excess demand inflation, so $PD = 0$. It follows immediately that we must have $P_a = P_e$ when $Y = Y_F$.

A second implication concerns the natural rate of unemployment.

It is essential to discover the natural rate of unemployment because it is the only acceptable target for long-run stabilization policy.

To see why knowing the natural rate of unemployment is so important, assume that the economy has functioned satisfactorily for some time at an average unemployment rate of 5 percent and that the inflation rate has shown no tendency to accelerate. Policymakers will conclude that 5 percent is the natural rate of unemployment. Now assume that unbeknown to the policymakers the natural rate of unemployment rises to 7 percent. If they go on trying to stabilize the economy around a 5 percent unemployment rate, the first indication they will have that something has gone wrong is that the inflation rate will begin to accelerate. It may take some time before policymakers conclude that the acceleration is not due to some transient cause but represents a genuine tendency for continual acceleration. By the time they reach that conclusion and decide to stabilize the economy around a higher level of unemployment, a very rapid inflation may already exist and may have been built into people's expectations. Thus, if the Phelps-Friedman theory is correct, quick and accurate determination of the natural rate of unemployment must be an important part of any effective anti-inflationary policy.

Once an expectational inflation is under way, policymakers may have to take account of a third important policy implication.

A period of excess demand and accelerating inflation will lead to accelerating inflationary expectations. A prolonged period with unemployment above the natural rate may be required before inflationary expectations are revised downward sufficiently to permit the actual inflation rate to fall.

This implication is illustrated in Figure 39-9. An increase in inflationary expectations moves the economy to a higher short-term Phillips curve. This increases inflationary pressures. To offset

FIGURE 39-9
Falling Real National Income and Rising Inflation (Stagflation)

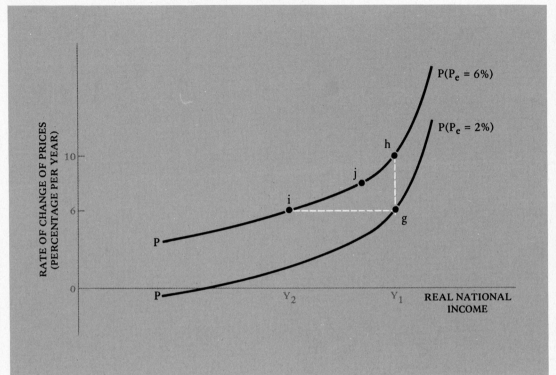

When the expected rate of inflation is rising, a fall in national income can easily be associated with a rise in the actual rate of inflation. The economy is at point *g* with a level of national income of Y_1, an expected rate of inflation of 2 percent, and an actual rate of 6 percent. Since the actual rate exceeds the expected rate, expectations will be revised upward. Suppose people come to expect a 6 percent inflation in the next period. If national income is held constant at Y_1, the economy will move to point *h* and the actual rate of inflation will accelerate to 10 percent. In order to offset this increase in inflationary expectations and hold inflation to 6 percent, national income must be reduced all the way to Y_2 (point *i*). If national income *falls* to any amount less than Y_1 but greater than Y_2 the economy will move to some point such as *j* where *falling* real national income is associated with *rising* inflation.

this a decline in national income is required, which moves the economy downward and to the left along any given short-term Phillips curve. This decreases inflationary pressure. In the early stages of a contraction in national income that is designed to bring an *accelerating* inflation under control, the effect of accelerating expectations may dominate the effect of declining demand and output. As a result, falling national income and rising unemployment may be associated with constant or even rising rates of inflation. When this occurs, the economy is suffering a stagflation — the coexistence of high rates of inflation and high rates of unemployment.

An Inflation-Unemployment Cycle

The way in which changes in unemployment and inflation may work out over the longer period of a full cycle is illustrated in Figure 39-10.

FIGURE 39-10
An Inflation-Unemployment Cycle

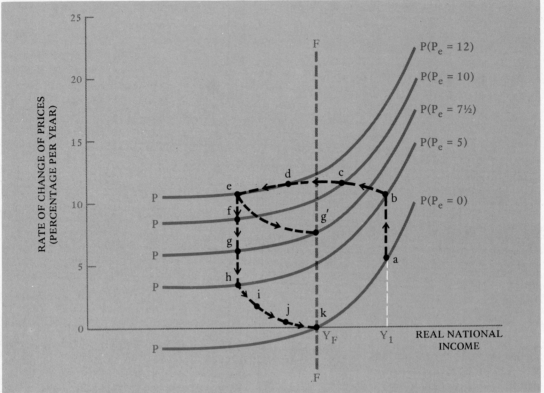

Removing entrenched inflationary expectations may require a prolonged bout of low national income combined with high rates of inflation. An economy with an inflationary gap (actual income in excess of Y_F) may build a head of steam in terms of rising rates of actual and expected inflation. (See the path from point a to point b.) If aggregate demand (and hence national income) is then reduced in order to restrain the inflation, a period may ensue in which the inflationary effects of rising inflationary expectations more than offset the deflationary effects of falling national income.

(See the path from b to d.) Sooner or later, however, the deflationary effects of falling national income will predominate and the actual rate of inflation will begin to fall. (See the path from d to e.) Inflationary expectations will now be revised downward and the actual rate will fall without further reductions in national income. (See the path from e to h.) Once inflationary expectations are low enough, a cautious expansion toward full-employment income should be possible without setting off a new bout of demand-pull or expectational inflation. (See the path from h to k.)

Consider what happens (according to the Phelps-Friedman theory) when the government first expands aggregate demand to induce a higher degree of resource utilization and then slams on the brakes by sharply lowering aggregate demand in an attempt to eliminate the resulting inflation. The type of path that this se-

quence of events produces is shown in black in Figure 39-10.

In this example the economy starts at point k with full-employment national income and stable prices. An expansion of aggregate demand then takes the economy to point a with national income of Y_1 and a 5 percent inflation rate. As long as people expect a zero inflation rate (i.e., they do not expect the existing 5 percent rate to persist) the economy will remain at *a*. When inflationary expectations are revised upward, the relevant Phillips curve will shift upward. The actual rate of inflation accelerates. When the expected rate of inflation reaches 5 percent, the economy is at point *b* with a 10 percent actual rate of inflation.

Suppose that at this stage the government decides to do something. Perhaps the monetary authorities refuse to increase the money supply enough to validate the inflation fully. Actual *Y* now falls, but the expected rate of inflation goes on accelerating and the two opposing forces take the economy to point *c* with a 10 percent expected inflation and an actual rate of 12 percent. The continuing nonvalidation of the inflation causes national income to fall further, and if the expected rate rises to 12 percent, the economy will move to poind *d*. If the expected rate of inflation now holds constant at 12 percent, the nonvalidation of the actual inflation will force the economy down the $P_e = 12$ percent Phillips curve to some point such as *e*. At last the actual rate of inflation is falling; more important, it is below the expected rate.

The period of rising prices and rising unemployment may finally be at an end. The expected rate will now be revised downward, and if the government keeps the rate of monetary expansion in line with the actual rate of inflation, the economy can move through points *f*, *g*, and *h* as the expected rate falls to 10, 7.5, and 5 percent. Indeed if the government is careful, it can at some point begin stimulating aggregate demand again. As long as the inflationary effects of increases in demand are less than the deflationary effects of decreases in expectations, the economy can move through points *h*, *i*, and *j* back toward point *k*, where both full-employment income and a stable price level are achieved.

Note however that if the economy is restimulated too quickly, say from *e* to *g'*, it may reach the full-employment level of income when there are still substantial inflationary expectations in the system. The government then has the choice of validating the inflation to hold *Y* at Y_F or allowing another recession to occur to lower the actual rate of inflation and, after a lag, causing a lowering of inflationary expectations.

Summary

1. At one time or another four major goals of macroeconomic policy have been important: a satisfactory balance of payments position, a high rate of growth, and low levels of unemployment and inflation.

2. Unemployment may be voluntary or involuntary. Involuntary unemployment is a serious social concern both because it causes economic waste measured in terms of lost output and because it is a source of human suffering.

3. There are several kinds of unemployment: frictional unemployment, due to the time taken in moving from job to job as a result of normal labor turnover; structural unemployment, caused by the need to reallocate resources between occupations, regions, and industries as the structure of demands and supplies changes; deficient-demand unemployment, caused by too low a level of aggregate demand; and search unemployment, caused by the need to discover the state of the labor market by searching for alternative employment opportunities.

4. Unemployment can be reduced by raising aggregate demand, by making it easier to move between jobs, and by raising the cost of staying unemployed.

5. Unemployment insurance helps to alleviate the human suffering associated with inevitable unemployment. It also increases unemployment by encouraging voluntary and search unemployment.

6. Control of inflation is a major goal of macroeconomic policy. Inflation redistributes income in haphazard ways, and this is sufficient to make it a matter of serious concern. There is no strong evidence that mild inflations change the average living standard of the population.

7. Inflation has many alleged causes. Demand-pull inflation occurs when there is an inflationary gap. Wage cost-push and price-push inflations occur when unions and price-setting firms raise wages and prices independently of the state of aggregate demand. Import cost-push inflation occurs when rising prices of major imports pushes up the domestic price level. Expectational inflation occurs when wages and prices rise in the expectation that a current inflation will continue. Inertial inflation occurs when wage and price setters look to other wages and prices in making their own decisions and are cautious about reducing their relative wages or prices.

8. A validated inflation, one in which the money supply increases in step with the rise in prices, can go on indefinitely with no necessary fall in output. An unvalidated inflation will be accompanied by rising rates of interest and falling levels of output. Sooner or later output will fall and unemployment will rise to levels sufficient to bring the unvalidated inflation to a halt.

9. Some prices fluctuate greatly in the short run for causes that cannot be influenced by macroeconomic policy. To obtain a more reliable indication of the effects of anti-inflation policy, some of these prices are sometimes removed from the CPI.

10. When aggregate demand increases enough to take national income above Y_F, that is, into the intermediate portion of the aggregate supply curve, the initial effect is a rise in national income and a rise in the price level. However, the excess demand causes the price level to go on rising, and this causes an upward shift in the aggregate supply curve. If the aggregate demand curve is constant, this process will continue until national income falls back to Y_F.

11. The tendency for the price level to rise continuously when national income exceeds Y_F is shown by the Phillips curve, which relates national income to the rate of inflation. The curve suggests a trade-off: higher levels of national income are achievable at the cost of higher rates of inflation. To hold income above Y_F, the central bank will have to increase the money supply at the same rate as the price level is rising.

12. The Phelps-Friedman or accelerationist theory combines the demand-pull and expectational theories of inflation. It denies the existence of a stable trade-off between national income and the rate of inflation. It says instead that whenever the authorities take action to hold national income above Y_F, the rate of inflation will accelerate continuously.

13. The percentage of the labor force that is unemployed when the economy is at full employment is labeled the natural rate of unemployment.

14. The Phelps-Friedman theory also predicts that a prolonged period of demand-pull inflation will cause inflationary expectations to become entrenched. Even after the excess demand is removed, an expectational inflation may persist and a prolonged period of slump, with national income below Y_F, may be necessary before expectations are revised downward sufficiently that the economy can return to full employment and a low or zero rate of inflation.

Topics for Review

Frictional, structural, deficient-demand, and search unemployment
Voluntary and involuntary unemployment; measured and unmeasured unemployment
Demand-pull, wage cost-push, import cost-push, price-push, structural rigidity, expectational, and inertial inflations
Validated and unvalidated inflation
The natural rate of unemployment
The Phillips curve and the accelerationist theory

Discussion Questions

1. To what extent is today's unemployment a serious social problem? If people could vote to choose between 10 percent unemployment combined with zero inflation and 2 percent unemployment combined with 10 percent inflation, which alternative do you think would win? Which groups might prefer the first alternative and which groups the second?

2. It is often argued that the true unemployment figure for Canada is much higher than the officially reported figure. What are possible sources of "hidden unemployment"? On the other side, are there reasons for expecting some exaggeration of the number of people reported as unemployed? Would the relative strength of these opposing forces change over the course of the business cycle? What would you expect if a short recession turned into a long and deep depression?

3. On what source or sources of unemployment do the following statements focus their attention?
   a. "We can reduce unemployment without increasing inflation by targeting unemployment programs toward those groups and to those geographical areas where unemployment is especially high."
   b. "We have never had full employment in this country and never will have. Even during World War II the unemployment rate was nearly 2 percent."
   c. "If people on unemployment compensation were required to take a job when it is offered to them, the unemployment rate would drop 30 percent within three months."
   d. "The cure for unemployment is spending. Public spending or private spending, foolish spending or shrewd spending, it doesn't really matter. Spend, spend, spend. Employ, employ, employ."

4. On what source or sources of inflation do the following statements focus their attention?
   a. "The one basic cause of inflation is the government's spending more than it takes in. The cure is a balanced budget."
   b. "The breaking out of major labor negotiations in steel, autos, and other basic industries will lead to double-digit wage increases and a serious inflationary effect."
   c. "Wage settlements are high. The widespread publicity they are receiving will make it difficult to wind down inflation."
   d. "While the CPI rose by 7 percent last month, most of the increase was in a very few sectors where bottlenecks are developing."

5. "Inflations cannot long persist, whatever their initiating causes, unless the inflations are validated by increases in the money supply." Why is this so? Does it not imply that control of inflation is merely a matter of not allowing increases in the money supply to rise faster than the rate of increase of real national income?

6. Look at the rate of increases of the money supply and the CPI over the last three years and decide whether or not the current inflation is being validated.

7. Discuss the following views on the effects of inflation.
   a. "Now the beast [of inflation] is easily visible, a luminescent specter, a killer, a threat to society, public enemy No. 1"—Robert D. Hersy Jr., 1979.
   b. "Inflation—has become the national obsession, the catchall scapegoat for individual and societal economic difficulties, the symptom that diverts attention from the basic maladies."—James Tobin, 1980.

8. William Nordhaus of Yale University recently described inflation as an "inertial process like people standing up at a fooball game. When some people jump up to see better, other people can't see unless they stand up, too. When everybody is up, people as a group can't see as well as they did when they were all sitting; in fact, they probably see worse and are more uncomfortable. But the problem is how to get them all to sit down together." What view of inflation is Professor Nordhaus embracing?

9. In an article on the harmful effects of inflation, a reporter wrote, "with the rise in mortgage interest rates to 10 percent heaven only knows the price of what was once idealized as 'the $100,000 house.'" At the time the inflation rate was 9 percent. Did the 10 percent interest rate represent a heavy burden of inflation on the new home owner? What do you think the mortgage interest rate would have been if the inflation rate had been zero? What would have been a heavier real burden on the purchaser of a new house?

10. "On the Rise, A New Breed of Debtors," a recent newspaper article, suggested that because of the ravages of inflation many people were going into debt to make ends meet. What would be a rational debt policy—to borrow or to lend—if you thought the rate of inflation was going to be at least as high as the current rate of interest? Does your answer suggest possible reasons for the "rise in the new breed of debtors" other than an inability to make ends meet?

Macroeconomic Policy and the Balance of Payments

40

In Chapter 33 we considered some macroeconomic aspects of an open economy, focusing on both the current account, arising from international trade in goods and services, and the capital account, arising from international trade in financial assets. In this chapter we explore the implications of these open economy relationships for macroeconomic policy.

We consider first the possible conflicts between the objectives of full employment and a balanced current account that might arise because of the inverse relationship between net exports and national income. We then turn to the broader issues of the balance of payments and the exchange rate. These issues involve both current and capital accounts. Concern about the balance of payments arises whenever the authorities are committed to maintaining a fixed value of the exchange rate or to limiting the variations in the exchange rate. With a flexible exchange rate, a balance-of-payments disequilibrium is avoided automatically. The authorites need not be concerned with the balance of payments. Between the two extremes is the case of a managed or "dirty" float under which the authorities seek to control the exchange rate but are not committed to a publicly announced value. This system, used in Canada in the 1970s, is discussed at the end of the chapter.

Macroeconomic Policy and the Current Account

The major item in the current account is the balance of trade. As we saw in Chapter 26, the purpose of international trade is to take advantage of international comparative advantage: Goods are exported in order to import other goods that are cheaper to obtain than to produce at home. *Capital flows aside,* either a large import or a large export surplus is regarded as undesirable, and a country will seek a situation in which imports equal exports.

An enlightened government will regard an export surplus as being less undesirable than an import surplus. An export surplus means that foreign exchange is accumulating, and the accumulation can go on more or less indefinitely as far as the surplus country is concerned. In this situation the country is producing without consuming to the extent of its export surplus. Although this depresses living standards below what they could be, it is not a cause of any crisis.

Of course, when one country has an export surplus, some other country must be suffering an import surplus, and that country may be forced to take steps to remove it. An import surplus can continue only as long as foreign exchange reserves last. A monthly important surplus equal to, say, 5 percent of the total exchange reserves can last only for 20 months, and long before that there will most likely occur a speculative flight of capital in expectation of a devaluation of the currency.

Causes of Persistent Current Account Problems

Persistent balance-of-trade problems arise whenever there occur over time economic changes that tend to create a widening gap between receipts and payments. Three major causes are worth mentioning.

The first is changes in consumption patterns that occur in the course of economic growth because of differing income elasticities of demand. Consider two countries with identical rates of growth; the first has a comparative advantage in commodities with low income elasticities, while the second has comparative advan-

tages in commodities with high income elasticities. The first country will have persistent balance-of-trade problems at a fixed exchange rate because the demand for its exports will rise less rapidly than its own demand for imports.

The second cause of disequilibrium is changes in comparative advantage over time. For example, the rapid growth and growing technological sophistication of the Japanese economy has enabled Japan to obtain an increasing share of the world market for a variety of manufactured goods. As a result, Japan has experienced trade surpluses and created problems for her trading partners, who have had to contend with trade deficits.

A third source of trade balance problems is inflation of the domestic price level. As we saw in Chapter 33, an increase in Canadian prices relative to foreign prices causes exports to fall and imports to rise. As a result the net export function shifts downward, as shown in Figure 33-5 on page 655, so that a given level of national income is associated with a deteriorating trade balance. An analysis of inflation and the trade account appears in the box.

THE CURRENT ACCOUNT AND DOMESTIC POLICY OBJECTIVES

As we noted in Chapter 33, there is potential for conflict between the objectives of internal and external balance, where external balance is defined in terms of a balanced current account. Policies used to achieve one objective will also affect the other. When this "side" effect moves the economy further from the other objective, the objectives are said to be in conflict.

The use of monetary or fiscal policy to eliminate an inflationary or deflationary gap will also influence the balance of trade by causing a *movement along* the net export function. Whether there is a conflict between the objectives of internal and external balance depends on whether the initial situation is one of a surplus or a deficit on

Inflation, the Current Account, and the PPP Exchange Rate*

Today's international economy is characterized by high and persistent inflation. Inflation differentials between trading partners have important implications for their exchange rates and their current accounts.

The PPP rate. In order to focus on the role of relative prices, we use the concept of the purchasing power parity exchange rate, the PPP rate. The PPP rate between two countries' currencies adjusts so that the *relative price levels of the two countries remain constant when measured in a common currency.*

For example, if the United States incurs a 20 percent inflation while Canada inflates by only 5 percent over the same period, the PPP value of the Canadian dollar will appreciate by 15 percent. If the actual exchange rate had changed by that amount, then over the period the price of goods in either country would have risen by 5 percent in terms of Canadian dollars and by 15 percent in terms of U.S. dollars. If the inflation experience of the two countries were reversed, the PPP value of the Canadian dollar would depreciate by 15 percent.

Using the analysis outlined in Figure 33-5, the PPP rate can also be understood as follows. An inflation differential shifts the net export function; the change in the PPP exchange

*The discussions of exchange rate determination (pages 136–142) and the role of relative prices in influencing the current account (page 654) should be reviewed.

rate is defined as that exchange rate change that would cause the net export function to return to its original position.

Of course, the actual exchange rate prevailing at any moment can differ from the PPP rate (see, for example, the discussion in the box on page 850). Here we consider the effects on the PPP rate and the current account for three cases that correspond to the three possible relationships between domestic and foreign inflation.

Equal rates of inflation in all countries. Suppose that the price levels in Canada and in our trading partners are rising at a 10 percent rate. At a given exchange rate the prices of Canadian exports expressed in foreign currencies will be rising at 10 percent, but the prices of foreign-produced goods will also be rising at 10 percent. Thus the competitive position of our exports will be unaffected. Similarly, Canadian residents will find that the Canadian dollar prices of both imports and domestically produced goods are rising at 10 percent, so there will be no inducement for demand to shift between imports and domestic goods. It follows that at a given exchange rate, equal rates of inflation in the domestic and foreign economies will have no effect on the balance of trade.

Ceteris paribus, if the domestic rate of inflation is the same as the foreign rate, the net export

the trade account and whether there is an inflationary gap or a deflationary gap. Four combinations can occur.

1. A trade account *deficit* combined with a *deflationary gap* poses a conflict because the expansion of national income to eliminate the deflationary gap leads to an increase in expen-

ditures on imports and hence a worsening of the trade deficit.

2. A trade account *deficit* combined with an *inflationary gap* poses no conflict because the contraction of national income to eliminate the inflationary gap leads to a reduction in imports and hence reduces the trade deficit.

3. A trade account *surplus* combined with a

function and the PPP exchange rate will be unaffected.

Thus no policy problem arises in this case.

Higher domestic inflation. Suppose that the price level in Canada is rising by 10 percent while our trading partners are experiencing inflation at a 4 percent rate. At a given exchange rate domestic exports will fall and imports will rise, as shown in Figure 33-5.

If the domestic rate of inflation is higher than the foreign rate, the net export function will be shifting downward, so the PPP value of the domestic currency will be falling.

Under these circumstances Canada would have basically two policy options. It could allow its currency to depreciate continuously at a rate of 6 percent. This would keep the exchange rate at the equilibrium PPP level and stop the net export function from shifting. Alternatively, policies could be introduced to reduce inflation to an average annual rate of 4 percent. This may be the preferred policy since reducing inflation is likely to be desirable for other reasons.

Nevertheless it is important to bear in mind that a *continuous* depreciation will be required as long as the inflation rate remains above the rate in the rest of the world. If a country on a fixed exchange rate finds that its price level has been rising more rapidly than that of its trad-

ing partners, a *one-shot* devaluation will provide only a temporary solution unless the domestic inflation rate is subsequently brought down.

Lower domestic inflation. Suppose that the situation is reversed, that the inflation rate in Canada is 4 percent compared with 10 percent in the rest of the world. In this case the relative price of Canadian goods will be falling, exports will rise, and imports will fall, as shown in Figure 33-5.

If the domestic rate of inflation is lower than the foreign rate, the net export function will be shifting upward and to the right, so the PPP value of the domestic currency will be rising.

Here the policy option is either to allow the Canadian dollar to appreciate or to raise the domestic rate of inflation to 10 percent.

This case is symmetrical with the previous one, but there is one important difference. Solving the balance-of-payments problem by expansionary monetary policy involves a conflict with the goal of stable prices. It would seem to be foolish to increase the domestic rate of inflation simply for the purpose of avoiding an appreciation of the currency. Nevertheless it has been argued that in the early 1970s Canada responded to the sharp increase in inflation rates in other countries in exactly this way.

deflationary gap poses no conflict because the expansion of national income to eliminate the deflationary gap increases imports and hence reduces the trade surplus.
4. A trade account *surplus* combined with an *inflationary gap* poses a conflict because the contraction of national income to eliminate the inflationary gap leads to a reduction

in imports and hence an increase in the trade balance surplus.

Conflicts Between Balanced Trade and Full Employment

In case 1 the deficit calls for a decrease in national income but the deflationary gap calls for an increase. In case 4 the surplus calls for an increase in national income but the inflationary gap calls for a decrease.

A conflict arises between the objectives of balanced trade and full employment when the two call for opposite changes in the level of national income.

While both case 1 and case 4 involve a conflict, case 1 has traditionally attracted the most attention, perhaps because a trade deficit is generally viewed as being a more serious problem than a trade surplus and—at least in the past—unemployment has been considered a more serious problem than inflation. Case 1 is often referred to as a situation in which there is a "balance-of-payments constraint" on domestic stabilization policy. This was discussed in the box on pages 660–661.

The absorption approach outlined in Chapter 33 is useful in suggesting policies to deal with situations where there is a conflict between the objectives of internal and external balance. Basically, the conflicts arise from *movements along* the net export function; resolution of the conflicts arises from *shifts in* the net export function.

EXPENDITURE-CHANGING AND EXPENDITURE-SWITCHING POLICIES

Recall that aggregate desired expenditure is equal to domestic absorption plus net exports. It is useful to distinguish between two types of policies that might be used to maintain internal and external balance. Policies that maintain the level of aggregate desired expenditure but influence its composition between domestic absorption and net exports are called **expenditure-switching** policies. Policies that change aggregate desired expenditure are called **expenditure-changing** policies.

Both types of policies operate by influencing domestic absorption, but an expenditure-switching policy also involves an offsetting shift in the net export function. Policies that change the price of domestic goods relative to foreign

goods would lead to such a shift, as shown in Figure 33-5. Domestic inflation or deflation relative to foreign conditions, a devaluation or revaluation of the domestic currency, or restrictions on international trade such as tariffs or quotas are all expenditure-switching policies.[1]

The conflict between the objectives of internal and external balance arises as a result of the use of expenditure-changing policies. These policies involve moving along a given net export function, so changes in the trade balance and national income must be inversely related. If the initial situation calls for them to move together, the use of expenditure-changing policies necessarily involves a conflict. However, expenditure-switching policies cause the net export function to shift, and as shown in Figure 33-5 this can lead to positively related changes in the trade balance and national income.

It is useful to consider specific policies for dealing with a current account deficit.

Policies to Deal with a Balance-of-trade Deficit

As we have seen, a balance-of-trade deficit means that national income is below domestic absorption. Now consider policies to eliminate the trade account deficit; to be successful, the policies must raise national income relative to domestic absorption.

If the economy already has an inflationary gap, national income should not be increased further. The trade deficit indicates that domestic absorption is above the current level of national income and hence, by virtue of the inflationary gap, above the full-employment level. To eliminate the deficit, absorption must be lowered. In other words, if net exports are to rise, resources must

---

[1] When restrictions on internation trade such as tariffs or quotas are used in this manner, they are referred to as *commercial policy*. Commercial policy may in some circumstances be useful for macroeconomic purposes, but it is never the case that commercial policy *must* be used, for there are other expenditure-switching policies that will have the same macroeconomic effects.

be released through a reduction in domestic usage. This calls for *expenditure-reducing* policies such as reductions in the money supply, cuts in government expenditure, and increases in taxes. No conflict for expenditure-changing policies arises in this case because the expenditure reduction reduces the inflationary gap and improves the trade balance by inducing a movement along the net export function.

When national income is below its full-employment level, it can be expanded. But an expansion in national income with a fixed net export function would worsen the trade balance, so expenditure-increasing policies are not appropriate. A reduction in national income to reduce the deficit would worsen unemployment, so expenditure-reducing policies are not appropriate. Policies that induce a *switch* of some expenditure from foreign goods to domestic goods—thereby shifting the net export function and raising national income while maintaining domestic absorption—will be successful. Such policies will reduce both the deflationary gap and the trade deficit; they include devaluation of the currency and the institution of protective measures such as tariffs and quotas.[2]

To achieve internal and external balance, a combination of policies is required. Expenditure-increasing policies are called for to achieve full employment, and expenditure-switching policies are required to achieve balanced trade. This is illustrated in Figure 40-1.

Macroeconomic Policy and the Capital Account

The capital account of the balance of payments records international movements of investment funds. When foreign investors buy securities issued by Canadian corporations or govern-

---

[2] Note that devaluation may be appropriate in the presence of unemployment, but if it is used in a situation of full employment *without accompanying expenditure-reducing policies,* it may lead to inflation and little improvement in the balance of trade. This point was illustrated in Figure 33-8.

ments, or make investments in Canadian industry, this capital inflow is recorded as a receipt item in the balance of payments because it gives rise to an increase in the amount of foreign currency offered for Canadian dollars in the foreign exchange market. Conversely, the acquisition of foreign assets by Canadians represents a capital outflow and is recorded as a payment because foreign currency is used up by such transactions.

The primary means by which capital flows can be influenced by the policy authorities is the manipulation of domestic interest rates. International traders hold transactions balances just as do domestic traders. These balances are often lent out on a short-term basis rather than being left idle. Naturally enough, holders of these balances will tend to lend them, other things being equal, in those markets where interest rates are highest. If short-term interest rates are raised in Canada, this will induce an inflow of short-term capital to take advantage of the higher Canadian rates. A lowering of Canadian interest rates will have the opposite effect as capital moves elsewhere to take advantage of relatively higher foreign rates.

Long-term capital flows are typically less sensitive to interest rate differentials, but they are nevertheless likely to show some response. In particular, Canadian corporations and governments attempt to minimize the cost of long-term borrowing by selling bonds in foreign markets when the foreign interest rate is lower than the Canadian rate.

In discussing the current account we did not distinguish between the effects of monetary and fiscal policy. However, capital flows respond to interest rates, and monetary and fiscal policies that have the same influence on income have opposite effects on interest rates. As we saw in Chapter 38, expansionary monetary policy exerts its influence on income by *reducing* interest rates. Fiscal policy influences aggregate demand directly, and fiscal policy induced increases in national income create an excess demand for money, which causes interest rates to rise. In discussing capital flows, then, it is nec-

FIGURE 40-1
Expenditure-changing and Expenditure-switching Policies

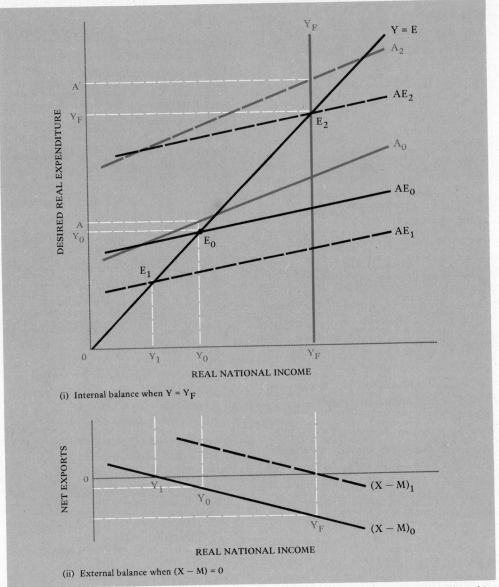

(i) Internal balance when $Y = Y_F$

(ii) External balance when $(X - M) = 0$

A combination of domestic unemployment and a trade balance deficit poses a conflict between the objectives of internal and external balance. Initial equilibrium is at E_0 in (i) where the AE_0 curve intersects the 45° line. In (ii) the net export function is the solid line $(X - M)_0$. At the initial equilibrium there is a deflationary gap and a trade balance deficit.

An expenditure-reducing policy aimed at eliminating the trade balance deficit shifts AE_0 downward to AE_1. (As net exports are zero at the new equilibrium level of income Y_1, it is evident that the A_1 line would intersect AE_1 at the new equilibrium point, E_1.) The conflict is apparent since net exports are zero but the deflationary gap has increased.

An expenditure-increasing policy designed to eliminate the deflationary gap shifts AE_0 upward to AE_2 by shifting the domestic absorption line to A_2. The conflict arises in this instance because the trade deficit increases.

It is evident that to achieve internal and external balance, expenditure-switching policies must be used to cause the net export function to be in balance at Y_F, as shown by the dashed line $(X - M)_1$ in (ii), and expenditure-changing policies must be used to set domestic absorption equal to full-employment income. The AE line must remain at AE_2, but A_2 must shift to pass through the new equilibrium, E_2.

essary to distinguish between the operation of monetary and fiscal policies.

Fiscal Policy and the Capital Account

Fiscal policies such as increases in government expenditure and tax cuts, which are intended to raise the level of national income, also cause interest rates to rise. Fiscal policies that are intended to lead to a contraction in national income will cause a reduction in interest rates. The effect of fiscal policy on the capital account can be summarized:

An expansionary fiscal policy will raise domestic interest rates and lead to an inflow of foreign capital, thereby improving the capital account surplus. A contractionary fiscal policy will have the opposite effects.

These effects can be understood in terms of expansionary fiscal policy leading to increased government deficits and therefore increased government borrowing. This forces other domestic borrowers to import their capital requirements from foreign financial centers. In many cases provincial governments finance their deficits by borrowing abroad themselves, thereby giving rise directly to a capital account surplus.

Monetary Policy and the Capital Account

Since capital flows respond to changes in interest rates, monetary policy will also influence the capital account.

An expansionary monetary policy will lower domestic interest rates and lead to an outflow of capital, thereby moving the capital account toward a deficit position. A contractionary monetary policy will have the opposite effects.

AN ALTERNATIVE CONCEPT OF EXTERNAL BALANCE

So far we have used the term *external balance* to mean zero net exports. In many circumstances this is not appropriate; a country may have a target level other than zero for the current ac-

count.[3] It may be, however, that it wishes to preserve its stock of international reserves. In that case, external balance would mean zero overall balance of payments so that any current account imbalance is exactly offset by capital account transactions. Let us see how monetary and fiscal policy might be combined to achieve internal and external balance in this circumstance.

Combining Monetary and Fiscal Policy

Consider an attempt to increase employment with expansionary monetary policy that reduces interest rates and thereby stimulates investment and other interest-sensitive expenditure. The decline in domestic interest rates makes it more attractive to invest short-term capital abroad rather than at home. The outflow of short-term capital to be invested at more attractive rates in foreign financial centers worsens the balance of payments on the short-term capital account. Of course, if the expansionary policy succeeds in raising income, there will be additional strain on the balance of payments on current account as a consequence of the increased expenditure on imports caused by the rise in income.

In principle, the conflict can be removed by an appropriate combination of monetary and fiscal policy. Consider the country with full employment and a balance-of-payments deficit. It could eliminate the deficit by following a tighter monetary policy to increase domestic interest rates and attract short-term capital. At the same time, the contractionary effect of tight money on domestic expenditure and employment could be offset by raising government expenditures or cutting taxes. Thus both goals can be achieved through a combination of tight monetary policy and expansionary fiscal policy.

Although this strategy may be workable in the

[3] For example, a nation with a large undeveloped natural resource base may have a low current national income yet anticipate a high national income in the future when the resource base is developed. Any attempt to raise domestic consumption in the present—that is, to consume some of the future income now—will raise present domestic absorption above present national income, leading to a *desired* balance-of-trade deficit.

short run, it is unlikely to be a satisfactory solution to a persistent balance-of-payments problem. A country that is unable to maintain full employment because of an overvalued currency will find it increasingly difficult to maintain its exchange rate by importing short-term capital. Short-term international capital flows are extremely volatile, and they are particularly sensitive to shifts in expectations concerning exchange rates. If investors lose confidence in a country's ability to maintain its existing parity, capital outflows will build up and ultimately a devaluation will be required to reduce the deficit and restore confidence.

Macroeconomic Policy Under Fixed Exchange Rates

The responsiveness of capital flows to interest rates has important implications for the ability of fiscal and monetary policy to achieve full employment. As we have seen, changes in interest rates that may be desirable to influence the level of aggregate demand will also have an effect on the capital account of the balance of payments. Indeed, if the interest elasticity of capital flows is very high, the maintenance of a fixed exchange rate will virtually immobilize monetary policy but enhance fiscal policy for the purposes of domestic stabilization. To see why this is so, it is useful to examine the relationship between the money supply and the balance-of-payments deficit.

The Balance of Payments and the Money Supply

Suppose that Canada is experiencing a balance-of-payments deficit and that the Bank of Canada intervenes in the foreign exchange market in order to maintain the value of the Canadian dollar. The Bank will be selling foreign currency in exchange for Canadian dollars and thereby running down the stock of official reserves. Payment for the foreign currency acquired by private participants in the market will normally be made

TABLE 40-1

Balance Sheet Changes Caused by a Sale of Foreign Currency by the Central Bank

Nonbank private sector		
Assets		Liabilities
Foreign currency (equivalent value in Canadian dollars)	+100	
Deposits	−100	

Chartered banks		
Assets		Liabilities
Reserves (deposits with central bank)	−100	Demand deposits −100

Central bank		
Assets		Liabilities
Foreign currency	−100	Deposits of chartered banks −100

The money supply is reduced when the central bank sells foreign currency to maintain a fixed exchange rate when there is a balance-of-payments deficit. A deficit of 100 leads to an excess demand for foreign currency of 100, which is met by a reduction of official reserves by this amount. When the central bank receives payment in the form of a cheque drawn on a chartered bank, bank reserves fall by 100. There will then be a multiple contraction of deposit money through the process analyzed in Chapter 37.

in the form of a Canadian dollar cheque drawn on one of the chartered banks. This cheque will be cleared by reducing the deposits of the chartered bank at the Bank of Canada. These transactions are summarized in Table 40-1.

If there are no offsetting transactions, a balance-of-payments deficit will lead to a decrease both in bank reserves and in bank deposits equal to the amount of foreign exchange sold by the central bank. A surplus will lead to an increase in bank reserves and deposits.

Thus a balance-of-payments deficit will lead to a contraction of the money supply. Of course, the central bank has the option of preventing this from happening by undertaking other offsetting transactions. For example, the decrease in bank reserves can be offset by an open market purchase of bonds, which will have the effect of increasing bank reserves. This procedure of insulating the domestic money supply from the effects of balance-of-payments deficits or surpluses is known as **sterilization.**

Monetary Policy Under Fixed Exchange Rates

To see the limitations of monetary policy under a fixed exchange rate, consider the following sequence of events. Suppose that interest rates in Canada are at levels similar to those in the rest of the world, and thus there is no inducement for large international movements of capital. Suppose now that the Bank of Canada, faced with a high domestic unemployment rate, seeks to stimulate demand through an expansionary monetary policy. The Bank buys bonds in the open market, thereby increasing bank reserves and the money supply and reducing interest rates.

Lower interest rates stimulate an outflow of capital from Canada and thus a deficit on the capital account. To maintain the fixed exchange rate, the Bank will have to intervene in the foreign exchange market and sell foreign currency. *This will have the effect of reducing the money supply and thus reversing the increase brought about by the open market operation.* If no other transactions are initiated by the Bank of Canada, the money supply will fall until it returns to its initial level and domestic interest rates will rise to their initial level. Thus the deficit will be self-correcting, and the Bank's expansionary policy will be nullified.

Suppose now that the Bank of Canada attempts to sterilize the impact on the money supply of the balance-of-payments deficit. The difficulty with this strategy is that it can be continued only as long as the Bank has sufficient reserves of foreign exchange. If capital flows are highly sensitive to interest rates, as is likely to be the case, these reserves will be run down at a rapid rate and the Bank will be forced to abandon its expansionary policy.

Under a fixed exchange rate, there is little scope for the use of monetary policy for domestic stabilization purposes because of the sensitivity of international capital flows to interest rates. The central bank will be forced to maintain domestic interest rates close to the levels existing in the rest of the world, and it will not be able to bring about substantial changes in the domestic money supply.

Fiscal Policy Under Fixed Exchange Rates

Consider now the effectiveness of fiscal policy under fixed exchange rates. Suppose again that Canadian interest rates are in line with those of the rest of the world when an expansionary fiscal policy is introduced, aimed at reducing a high domestic unemployment rate. The fiscal expansion raises the level of domestic interest rates and national income.

Higher interest rates stimulate a flow of capital into Canda, thereby leading to a surplus on the capital account. If the capital flows are large enough, as they are likely to be in Canada because of our close integration with U.S. capital markets, the surplus on capital account will be larger than the current account deficit arising from the increased national income. Hence there will be an overall balance-of-payments surplus.

To maintain the fixed exchange rate, the Bank of Canada will have to intervene in the foreign exchange market and buy foreign currency. This will have the effect of increasing the money supply, *thus reinforcing the initial fiscal stimulus.*

Under a fixed exchange rate, interest-sensitive international capital flows stabilize the domestic interest rate and enhance the effectiveness of fiscal policy.

Macroeconomic Policy Under Flexible Exchange Rates

A major advantage of a flexible exchange rate is that it removes any conflict between domestic stabilization objectives and the balance of payments because deficits or surpluses are automatically eliminated through movements in the exchange rate. In addition, a flexible rate cushions the domestic economy against cyclical variations in economic activity in other countries. If, for example, the U.S. economy goes into a recession, the decline in U.S. income will lead to a reduction in demand for goods exported from Canada. The fall in exports will reduce income in Canada through the multiplier effect, but if the value of the Canadian dollar is allowed to respond to market forces, there will also be a depreciation. This fall in the external value of our currency will stimulate demand for our exports and encourage the substitution of domestically produced goods for imports. Thus the depreciation will provide a stimulus to demand in Canada that will at least partially offset the depressing effect of a U.S. recession.

FISCAL POLICY UNDER FLEXIBLE RATES

Suppose the government seeks to remove a deflationary gap by expansionary fiscal policy. An increase in government expenditures and/or a reduction in taxes will increase income through the multiplier effect and reduce the size of the gap. There will also be an increase in imports as a result of the increase in income, which will cause the domestic currency to depreciate. This will provide an additional stimulus to demand because it will increase demand for our exports and encourage the substitution of domestically produced goods for imports. Thus the effect of a flexible exchange rate operating through the current account is to add to the potency of fiscal policy. However, this is not the whole story, for there will also be repercussions on the capital account.

Capital Flows and the Crowding-out Effect

Expansionary fiscal policy causes domestic interest rates to rise. This causes interest-sensitive private expenditures to fall, thus partially offsetting the initial expansionary effect of the fiscal stimulus. This is called the *crowding-out effect*

and plays an important role in the monetarist criticism of fiscal policy studied in Chapter 42. In an open economy, this crowding-out effect will be magnified by the influence of interest rates on international capital flows.

Highest domestic interest rates will induce a capital inflow and cause the domestic currency to appreciate. If capital flows are highly interest elastic, this effect will swamp the depreciation induced by the current account effect so that on balance the external value of the currency is likely to rise substantially. This will depress demand by discouraging exports and encouraging the substitution of imports for domestically produced goods.

We thus conclude that under flexible exchange rates there will be a strong crowding-out effect that will greatly reduce the effectiveness of fiscal policy. However, it is possible to eliminate the crowding-out effect by supporting the fiscal policy with an accommodating monetary policy. Suppose that the central bank responds to the increase in the demand for money induced by the fiscal expansion by increasing the supply of money so as to maintain domestic interest rates at their initial level. There will then be no capital inflow and no tendency for the currency to appreciate. Income will expand by the multiplier process and there will be an additional stimulus from a depreciation of the currency.

The effectiveness of fiscal policy under flexible exchange rates depends on an accommodating monetary policy that permits the money supply to expand so as to prevent an increase in interest rates.

MONETARY POLICY UNDER FLEXIBLE RATES

We have seen that there is little scope under fixed exchange rates for the use of monetary policy for domestic stabilization purposes. Under flexible exchange rates, the situation is reversed and monetary policy becomes a very powerful tool.

Suppose the Bank of Canada seeks to stimulate demand through an expansionary monetary policy. The Bank buys bonds in the open market, thereby increasing bank reserves and the money supply and reducing interest rates. Lower interest rates will cause an outflow of capital from Canada and thus a deficit on the capital account.

Under a fixed rate, the Bank may be forced to reverse its policy in order to stem the loss of foreign exchange reserves. Under a flexible rate, however, the Canadian dollar can be allowed to depreciate, and this will stimulate exports and discourage imports so that the deficit on the capital account will be offset by a surplus on the current account.

Domestic employment will be stimulated not only by the fall in interest rates but also by the increased demand for domestically produced goods brought about by a depreciation of the currency. (See Figure 40-2.) Indeed if capital flows are highly interest elastic, a small fall in Canadian interest rates will induce a large depreciation of the Canadian dollar.

Under flexible exchange rates, monetary policy is a powerful tool for stabilizing domestic income and employment. If capital flows are highly interest elastic, the main channel by which an increase in the money supply increases demand for domestically produced goods is a depreciation of the currency.

CANADIAN EXPERIENCE WITH FLEXIBLE EXCHANGE RATES

The foregoing arguments suggest that the adoption of a flexible exchange rate can improve the effectiveness of stabilization policy. It is instructive to examine the behavior of the Canadian economy during the two periods since World War II when Canada operated under this system.

Experience with a Flexible Rate, 1955–1961

Canada operated under a flexible exchange rate from 1950 to 1961. The one major cyclical fluctuation of the economy in this period began with the recovery from the mild recession of 1954.

As Figure 40-3 shows, the Canadian economy experienced large capital inflows during the period 1955 to 1961 in response to the attractive investment opportunities that existed in Canada. As a result the value of the Canadian dollar remained above one U.S. dollar and at times rose as high as 105 U.S. cents. This had the effect of reducing exports and increasing imports, so there was a deficit on merchandise trade.

During the period 1955 to 1957 there was an investment boom, and national income remained close to the full-employment level. The flexible exchange rate served as a stabilizer since the resulting trade deficit had a desirable dampening effect on demand. By the end of 1957, however, the economy had turned down and the unemployment rate rose sharply. Depressed conditions remained throughout the period 1958 to 1961, with the unemployment rate at or above 7 percent for three of the four years.

How did monetary policy respond to this serious recession? Although the money supply had expanded at a rapid rate during 1958, this trend was reversed in 1959 and 1960, and the average rate of growth over the three years was under 3 percent. This was well below the growth in real output, and as a result interest rates rose sharply in 1959 and until the second half of 1961 remained above the levels prevailing in 1958. In short, the period 1959 to 1961 was characterized by a very restrictive monetary policy in spite of a clear need for the opposite strategy.

As the theory outlined before indicates, what was needed was an expansionary policy that would have reduced interest rates and discouraged capital inflows. This would have caused the Canadian dollar to depreciate and stimulated the economy by moving the trade account toward a surplus position. Unfortunately, the advantages of a flexible exchange rate were not utilized to help deal with a serious unemployment problem, and the hoped for depreciation of the Canadian dollar did not occur until 1961.[4]

[4] The tight money policy followed during this period was a subject of considerable public discussion. In 1960 a group of academic economists called on the minister of finance to dismiss the governor of the Bank of Canada. An acrimonious confrontation between the minister and the governor ensued, and the latter was finally replaced in July 1961. This is discussed further on page 860.

The Period of Rising Inflation Rates, 1965–1975

The origins of the inflation problem of the 1970s can be traced to the second half of the 1960s. At

that time the U.S. economy was experiencing boom conditions to a considerable extent as a result of expenditures related to the Vietnam War. The U.S. inflation rate increased almost continuously until 1971. Prior to May 1970,

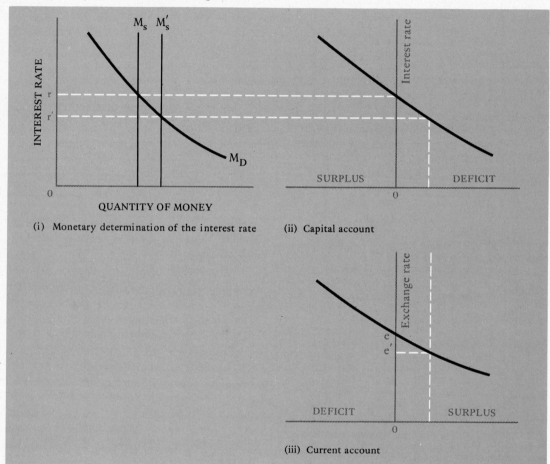

(i) Monetary determination of the interest rate

(ii) Capital account

(iii) Current account

Under flexible exchange rates, monetary policy affects domestic income through its effect on the exchange rate. In (i) the interest rate is determined by the condition of money market equilibrium. The interest sensitivity of international capital flows is shown in (ii), where an increase in domestic interest rates increases the capital account surplus. The dependence of the current account on the exchange rate is shown in (iii), where the results of the analysis in Figure 33-8 are used to indicate that a depreciation of the domestic currency (a rise in e, the price of foreign exchange) leads to an increase in the current account surplus. We begin with a money supply M_S and an interest rate r at which the capital account is in balance. The current account must therefore be in balance, and this will occur at an exchange rate e. If the money supply is increased to M_S', the interest rate will fall to r', stimulating a capital outflow and a capital account deficit. As a result the exchange rate rises to e', where there is an offsetting current account surplus.

FIGURE 40-3
The Canadian Experience with a Flexible Exchange Rate, 1955–1961

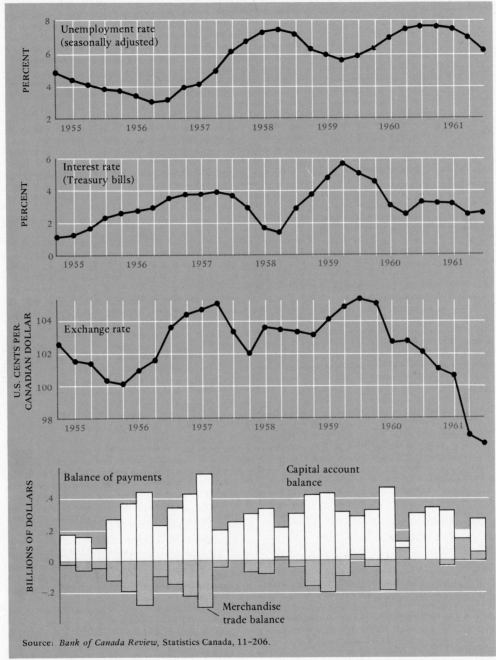

Source: *Bank of Canada Review*, Statistics Canada, 11-206.

The flexible exchange rate acted to dampen the investment boom that occurred in 1955–1957, but tight monetary policy worsened the recession in 1958–1960. High interest rates in 1958–1960 stimulated a large capital account surplus. This maintained a high external value of the Canadian dollar despite high unemployment. Only after a crisis over responsibility during 1960 were interest rates lowered, and then the value of the dollar fell.

The Canadian Dollar's Slide in 1977–1978: Was It a National Crisis?*

From the third quarter of 1976 to the first quarter of 1979, the value of the Canadian dollar fell steadily from more than $1.05 U.S. to less than 85 U.S. cents. News commentators and others viewed this as a national problem of crisis proportions.

Such hysteria was also evident a few years ago when sterling went through a similar adjustment. Just as the panic soon passed and predictions of dire consequences were soon forgotten in Britain, they will soon pass and be forgotten in Canada. In the meantime, an observer can only wonder how it is that we sat relatively passively when the real disease of inflation ravished the country in the mid 1970s and then hit the panic button at a delayed symptom that has relatively little substance in itself.

The PPP Rate

The underlying trend in the value of the dollar, the purchasing power parity exchange rate

*Adapted from an article by R. G. Lipsey in the *Financial Post*, April 22, 1978.

(the PPP rate), changes as the Canadian price level changes relative to the price level in the United States, our major trading partner. (See the box on pages 838–839.) Other factors can affect the *actual* exchange rate, causing it to diverge from its PPP value.

The American inflation of the late 1960s was not matched in Canada, and as a result the PPP rate rose from about 93 cents in 1967 to close to parity by 1971. Since that time the Canadian inflation rate has exceeded the American rate, and the PPP rate has fallen steadily, reaching the range 89–91 cents at the beginning of 1978.

During the 1970s, large capital inflows held the actual rate well above its PPP rate – in fact, the unprecedented foreign borrowing in 1976 held the rate well over parity. By then it was clear to most observers that the gap between the actual rate and the PPP rate was widening. The actual rate had to come down to restore our international competitiveness. The only questions were "when?" and "how much?"

Canada was committed to maintaining a fixed exchange rate, and as a consequence inflation inevitably spilled over into Canada.

The fixed value of the Canadian dollar, combined with inflation in the United States and other countries, resulted in a large trade surplus and a high level of demand in Canada. In order to maintain the fixed exchange rate, the Bank of Canada was obliged to *validate* the rising inflation rate in Canada by allowing the Canadian money supply to grow at a faster rate.[5] In 1967

[5] See page 817 for a discussion of the validation of inflation by money supply increases after the fact.

the rate of growth of M1 was nearly 10 percent, compared with the average of about 5 percent between 1960 and 1964.

The freeing of the Canadian dollar in 1970 provided the Bank of Canada with an opportunity to stem the inflationary pressures. The rate of growth of the money supply was sharply curtailed, and the inflation rate eased thereafter. As would be expected, there was a substantial appreciation of the Canadian dollar. However, shortly after the Bank of Canada had freed itself from the shackles of a fixed exchange rate and made substantial progress in bringing inflation under control, it appears to have gotten cold feet.

Help for Exports

The slide began at the end of 1976 and continued through 1977 and 1978. Instead of the outcry that accompanied it, a more appropriate reaction would have been: "At last help has arrived to encourage exports and discourage imports, reversing the forces set in motion by our excessive inflation of the previous few years."

Rather than reacting with panic and dismay, we should be congratulating ourselves on an extremely orderly, if long overdue, adjustment; an adjustment well supervised by the Bank of Canada and *not* accompanied by wild swings of private speculation (such as accompanied similar adjustments in the 1930s).

But will the decline in the Canadian dollar itself cause another burst of inflation that will nullify any competitive advantage conferred by the fall in the exchange rate? The answer is no, though there will be a one-time rise in the Consumer Price Index due to increased import prices.

Everyone understands that the two events, a local Canadian inflation and a fall in the actual exchange rate to match the fall in the PPP rate, offset each other. Yet when the two events are separated in time, people seem to lose sight of their offsetting nature and overreact to the fall in the value of the Canadian dollar. The rapid Canadian inflation improved the competitive position of imports into the Canadian market and hurt that of our exports to foreign markets.

The delayed fall in the value of the Canadian dollar restored the pre-inflation competitive positions, and merely completes the great inflation of 1973–1976. This suggests that we should concentrate our attention on the underlying Canadian inflation rate. The rate is still disturbingly high and coming down painfully slowly, if at all. Inflation is the enemy that destroys the real value of our money; the change in the exchange rate is merely the inevitable completion of the inflation; it realigns the prices of imported goods with the already increased prices of domestic goods.

Its subsequent policy indicated a reluctance to exploit fully the benefits of a flexible rate.

First the Bank of Canada attempted to resist the appreciation of the Canadian dollar in 1970 and 1971 by intervening heavily in the foreign exchange market. This is reflected in the large increase in official reserves shown in Figure 33-10 on page 670. As we have seen, a country that is attempting to hold its inflation rate below that of its trading partners must allow its currency to appreciate freely. If the exchange rate is held down, the central bank will eventually be forced to raise the rate of growth of the money supply and to allow the domestic rate of inflation to rise.

The second error in policy was the sharp turnaround in monetary policy that occurred in 1971. In response to the rising unemployment rate, the Bank of Canada shifted to an expansionary policy, but *in retrospect* it is clear that the pendulum was allowed to swing too far. With the inflation rate again rising in the United States, the rate of growth of the money supply was allowed to rise sharply in Canada. Following this the inflation rate increased sharply and in fact rose substantially above the U.S. rate. During the period 1971 to 1976 the inflation rate measured in terms of the GNE deflator averaged about 10 percent in Canada, compared with about 7 percent in the United States. Consequently the Canadian dollar became overvalued in relation to the U.S. dollar, and a sharp depreciation occurred in 1977 and early 1978.

In summary, Canada appears to have missed an opportunity to avoid at least some of the inflation that plagued the world economy in the 1970s. Monetary policy was immobilized in the late 1960s by a commitment to a fixed exchange rate at a time when inflation rates began to rise in other countries. In the early 1970s the full benefits of a flexible rate were not realized because the Bank of Canada resisted the appreciation of the Canadian dollar and permitted excessively high rates of growth of the money supply.

What are the reasons for this failure of policy? Undoubtedly a full explanation would be quite complex, but it is possible to identify two factors. First, the importance of operating monetary policy so as to maintain independent control of the money supply was not recognized until inflationary forces had become entrenched. As we pointed out in Chapter 38 (see page 792), it was not until 1973 that the Bank of Canada began to move toward greater emphasis on control of the money supply, and explicit target rates of growth were not adopted until late 1975.

A second factor was the Bank's reluctance to permit wide swings in the exchange rate. It was clearly influenced by a concern for the effect of an appreciation on the competitive position of Canada's export industries. In effect the Bank of Canada operated a "dirty float" rather than a flexible exchange rate after the fixed rate was abandoned. In 1972 and 1973 it did not intervene heavily in the foreign exchange market to prevent a further appreciation of the Canadian dollar; instead it permitted a rapid rate of growth in the money supply, which had the same effect.

The experience of this period illustrates dramatically the futility of trying to protect Canada's export industries by holding the exchange rate below its equilibrium level. This could only be done by increasing the rate of growth of the money supply, *which had the effect of raising the domestic rate of inflation.* Whatever was gained by Canada's export industries from a lower exchange rate was subsequently lost through a higher rate of inflation. Their competitive position in world markets depends on their costs of production relative to those of other countries measured in terms of the same currency. The cost of production in Canada, measured in terms of, say, U.S. dollars, will rise as a result of either an appreciation of the Canadian dollar or an increase in domestic wages and prices. In view of the other undesirable effects of inflation, it seems clear that an appreciation of the Canadian dollar would have been less harmful to the Canadian economy.

Controlling Monetary Aggregates, 1975–1980

In 1975 the Bank of Canada began to follow policies that utilized the monetary independence created by flexible exchange rates. The Bank started announcing target rates of growth for the money supply. During the period 1976 to 1978 the value of the Canadian dollar fell sharply. As the box emphasizes, that fall was largely in response to factors occurring prior to the policy of targeting monetary growth. Since 1978 the value of the Canadian dollar has fluctuated in the range of 87 to 81 U.S. cents.

While on the surface this policy appears to meet some of the earlier objections to the use of monetary policy under flexible exchange rates, most economists believe nevertheless that the policy is still one of a "dirty float." Two examples are especially noteworthy.

In 1978–1979 a large number of wage contracts, following the unwinding of wage and price controls, were coming up for renewal. At the same time, the Canadian dollar was under substantial pressure. The Bank of Canada, worried that an inflationary surge coming from a depreciation would trigger an unacceptable increase in wages, intervened to support the dollar. However, many economists are skeptical of the importance of the direct influence of the exchange rate on wages; they believed that the harmful disruptions to financial markets caused by the uncertainty arising from the Bank's departure from its independent monetary stance were likely to be larger than any possible gains on the wage front.

More recently a problem for Canadian monetary and exchange rate management has arisen from the volatile behavior of interest rates in the United States. A rise in foreign interest rates leads to large outflows of short-term capital and a depreciation of the domestic currency. Hence a rise in foreign interest rates such as occurred in the United States in February 1980, December 1980, and May 1981 must be matched by a rise in Canadian rates, a depreciation of the Canadian dollar, or some combination of the two. In the 1980 episodes, Canadian interest rates rose but by less than those in the United States. As a result the Canadian dollar fell from a peak of 87 U.S. cents in July to 82.5 U.S. cents in December. When the next round of U.S. interest rate increases occurred in 1981, Canadian interest rates rose virtually as high as their U.S. counterparts and the dollar remained relatively stable at around 83 U.S. cents. Again, the Bank of Canada was criticized for pursuing a "dirty float."

Summary

1. A commitment to a fixed exchange rate forces the policy authorities to be concerned about the balance of payments.

2. Expenditure policy can be used to control the trade balance by influencing income and thereby imports. There will be a conflict of objectives if there is a balance-of-payments deficit and a deflationary gap at the same time. Expenditure-switching policies can be used to deal with conflict situations.

3. The capital account will be influenced by both fiscal and monetary policy because both influence domestic interest rates.

4. Under a fixed exchange rate, there is little scope for the use of monetary policy for domestic stabilization purposes. Because of the sensitivity of international capital flows to interest rates, the central bank will be forced to maintain domestic interest rates close to the levels in the rest of the world, and it will not be able to bring about substantial changes in the domestic money supply.

5. Under a fixed exchange rate, capital flows will act to reinforce the effectiveness of fiscal policy.

6. Under a flexible exchange rate, fiscal policy actions will be offset by a crowding-out effect unless they are accompanied by an accommodating monetary policy that prevents changes in interest rates.

7. Under a flexible exchange rate, monetary policy is a powerful tool. When capital flows are highly interest elastic, the main channel by which an increase in the money supply increases demand for domestically produced goods is a depreciation of the exchange rate.

8. During the period 1958 to 1961, Canada was on a flexible exchange rate but the authorities failed to use monetary policy effectively to deal with a serious unemployment problem. In the late 1960s Canada was on a fixed exchange rate that prevented the authorities from avoiding the rising inflation rates experienced by other countries.

9. The floating of the Canadian dollar in 1970 did not remove the inflationary pressure because the Bank of Canada permitted excessively high rates of growth of the money supply during the period 1971 to 1975.

10. Since 1975 the Bank of Canada has been following a policy of controlling the rate of growth of the money supply. Nevertheless there have been episodes in which a "dirty float" has

occurred, for policies to stabilize the exchange rate were also pursued.

Topics for Review

Expenditure-changing and expenditure-switching policies

Monetary and fiscal policy under fixed exchange rates

Sterilization

Monetary and fiscal policy under flexible exchange rates

Dirty float

Discussion Questions

1. Explain how a country can influence the external value of its currency by (a) direct intervention in the foreign exchange market, (b) fiscal policy, (c) monetary policy.

2. In his annnual report for 1977, Bank of Canada Governor Gerald Bouey said: "If we in Canada continue our progress towards better control of our prices and costs we shall unquestionably benefit from higher levels of employment and output than would otherwise be possible. Better price performance will improve the competitive position of Canadian suppliers in foreign markets and in relation to foreign goods in Canadian markets." Why should Canada be concerned with its competitive position under a flexible exchange rate? In what other ways might a lowering of the rate of inflation lead to increased employment?

3. Which of the following pairs of policy goals can be reached simultaneously using an appropriate macroeconomic policy, and which involve conflicting objectives? Indicate the policies you would advocate in each case.
   a. lower rate of inflation and a reduced trade-deficit
   b. elimination of an inflationary gap and a trade deficit
   c. lower rate of unemployment and a reduced trade deficit
   d. lower rate of unemployment and a reduced overall balance-of-payments deficit.

4. Explain why the use of monetary policy for domestic stabilization is limited under a fixed exchange rate.

5. A country that maintains a fixed exchange rate will have to allow its inflation rate to adjust to the level occurring in the rest of the world. Is this inconsistent with the theories of demand-pull and expectational inflation discussed in the previous chapter?

6. In a speech in December 1980, Bank of Canada Governor Gerald Bouey stated that "the rapid run-up of U.S. short-term [interest] rates is bound to have a major impact on Canada through increases in interest rates here or through a fall in the foreign exchange value of the Canadian dollar, or some combination of the two." Why must one of these responses occur? What policies can the Bank of Canada follow in order to influence which of the possible responses occurs? Which is preferable?

Macroeconomic Experience

41

The problems of the present are rooted in the events of the past. With the tools at our command we can now examine, and understand at least in broad outline, the experience of the last half century.

THE 1930s: DEPRESSION ECONOMICS

The late 1920s were a boom period in Canada and much of the rest of the world. Employment was high, output was high and rising—the North American automobile industry, for example, was in a strong growth period—and optimism was the rule of the day. Then came the great American stock market crash of 1929, dashing many hopes for unlimited prosperity.

Much more important to the average citizen was the economic collapse that by 1932 had taken the economy to the depths of the most serious depression in history, the Great Depression. Unemployment became a grave social problem in the aggregate and a personal tragedy for those most seriously affected by it. At its peak in 1933, unemployment reached 20 percent of the labor force! In 1933 real GNP per capita had fallen to less than two-thirds of its 1929 value, and at no time during the 1930s did it regain its 1929 value.

The price level fell somewhat from 1928 to 1933 in the face of a heavy excess supply of labor and capital; it then rose slowly during the gradual recovery of the late 1930s. Nevertheless, it is a fair approximation to characterize the period from 1932 to 1939 as one of stable prices and heavy unemployment.

FIGURE 41-1
Depression Macroeconomics

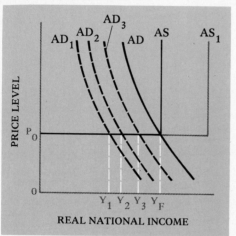

When there is a substantial GNP gap, fluctuations in aggregate demand determine fluctuations in national income. With aggregate demand and supply of AD and AS, the late 1920s were a period of more or less full employment. The Great Depression caused a sharp drop in aggregate demand (to AD_1 in the figure) and opened the large GNP gap ($Y_F - Y_1$). The slow recovery through the 1930s took aggregate demand to positions such as AD_2 and AD_3, thereby narrowing the GNP gap (to $Y_F - Y_2$ and $Y_F - Y_3$).

In these circumstances equilibrium income is said to be demand determined. An increase in full-employment national income, shown by the rightward shift of the aggregate supply curve to AS_1, has no effect on equilibrium income.

In short, the economy was operating on the Keynesian portion of its aggregate supply function. In fact, it was the experience of that troubled decade that led Keynes to develop his model of the behavior of the economy under conditions of excess supply and downwardly rigid prices. In such circumstances, changes in national income are determined by aggregate demand alone, as shown in Figure 41-1.

Under these depressionary conditions, an increase in capacity that raises full-employment output by extending the horizontal portion of the aggregate supply curve has no effect on equilibrium national income. Because there is not enough demand to employ existing capacity, the creation of additional capacity serves no current purpose.

For this reason many early Keynesians paid little attention to the long-term effect of investment on aggregate supply. Although not an unreasonable thing to do when analyzing severe deflationary conditions, the neglect was serious when the economy was operating at full employment. When national income is already at full employment, income cannot be increased by raising aggregate demand. What is needed is a rightward extension of the aggregate supply curve. A major long-term cause of such extensions is investment.

The early 1930s saw aggregate demand at a low level, with a very large GNP gap. In the course of the decade, demand recovered and income rose slowly. There was a further setback in the recession of 1937, but by the end of the decade the GNP gap had narrowed substantially.

The main problem facing the economy throughout the decade of the 1930s was a deficiency of aggregate demand.

In these circumstances, any policy that increased demand would have helped to alleviate the depression. This was Keynes' great insight.

THE 1940s: FULL EMPLOYMENT AND INFLATION

With the outbreak of World War II, governments threw fiscal caution to the winds as they spent huge amounts that were much in excess of their tax receipts. Aggregate demand rose steadily, first eliminating the GNP gap and then opening a large inflationary gap, as shown in Figure 41-2. Price controls and rationing were used to slow the inflation that resulted from the excess demand.

Price controls, which were becoming increasingly difficult to enforce, were removed when the war ended. The inflationary gap then made its full effects felt, and the price level rose by 39 percent in three years. But by the end of the decade prices once again appeared to be fairly steady, and the period of demand inflation seemed to be at an end.

The experience of the 1940s suggested several conclusions that are illustrated in Figure 41-2. First, the quick recovery to full employment during World War II convinced most observers that Keynes was right. A major depression caused by deficient aggregate demand had been cured by measures that increased aggregate demand. This

conclusion led the federal government in 1945 to issue a White Paper on *Employment and Income*. In it the government proclaimed that high employment was a major aim of government policy and that fiscal policy would be used to achieve that goal.

A second conclusion drawn by most economists was that excess demand at full-employment income was a major cause of inflation. (This had been known before, but the experience of World War II reconfirmed it.) Demand inflation was recognized as a major concern whenever aggregate demand threatened to exceed aggregate supply at full-employment national income.

The third lesson that many economists learned was that price controls designed to suppress a demand-pull inflation were a temporary expedient at best. As time passed controls became increasingly hard to enforce; when they were removed, the excess aggregate demand took the price level to where it would have been had the controls never existed. Figure 41-3 demonstrates this.

The conclusion from World War II experience was that price controls might postpone a demand inflation, but they would have no long-term effect on the price level when the inflationary pressure originated in excess demand.

This was a recognition that price controls attack the symptoms but not the cause of demand-pull inflation. (Note that a demand-pull inflation is often simply called a demand inflation.)

THE 1950s: THE GOAL OF FULL EMPLOYMENT WITHOUT INFLATION

The governments of most Western countries entered the postwar period committed to the goals of full employment and stable prices. Aggregate demand was to be manipulated in order to keep demand equal to full-employment aggregate supply at the prevailing price level (see Figure 41-4). Fluctuations in private-sector demand were to be offset by compensating fluctuations in the public

FIGURE 41-2
Wartime Demand Inflation

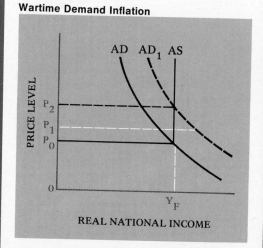

When there is sufficient aggregate demand, real national income is determined by full-employment aggregate supply while aggregate demand determines the equilibrium price level. Government expenditures during World War II quickly took aggregate demand to AD, which restored full employment. As expenditures increased further, they took aggregate demand to AD_1, opening up a substantial inflationary gap. Once aggregate demand was sufficient to purchase the economy's full-employment output, real national income was determined by the position of the aggregate supply curve. Further increases in aggregate demand could then affect only the price level.

The inflationary gap was contained by wartime price controls, so the price level rose only a little, to P_1. When controls were removed after the war, the price level rose to its equilibrium at P_2, changing the aggregate supply curve to P_2AS.

FIGURE 41-3
Wage and Price Controls and Excess Demand

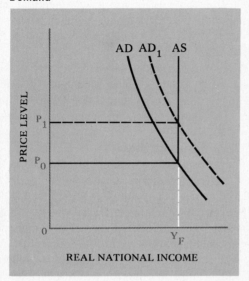

PRICE LEVEL

REAL NATIONAL INCOME

Wage and price controls can delay a demand inflation only for as long as they are in place. When aggregate demand rises from AD to AD_1, an inflationary gap develops. In the absence of controls the price level would rise from P_0 to P_1. Effective controls hold the price level at P_0 but do not eliminate the inflationary gap. Once the controls are removed the price level rises to its equilibrium value, P_1. The controls have delayed but not altered the final response of the price level to the excess aggregate demand.

FIGURE 41-4
Full Employment and Relatively Stable Prices

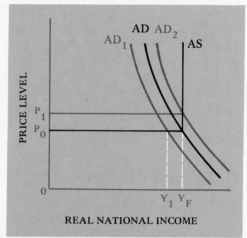

PRICE LEVEL

REAL NATIONAL INCOME

If aggregate demand and supply can be held at AD and AS, the goals of full employment and stable prices can both be achieved. From the end of the Korean War to the end of the 1950s, full employment and stable prices seemed to be within grasp. Inevitably there were some fluctuations, making aggregate demand oscillate—say between AD_1 and AD_2. This led to fluctuations in national income between Y_1 and Y_F and to unreversed increases in the price level when an inflationary gap appeared. This caused a slow upward drift in the horizontal part of the aggregate supply curve. One such upward shift is shown from P_0 to P_1.

sector in order to hold aggregate demand approximately constant at its full-employment level. This was the policy of fine tuning the economy, discussed on page 677. Many Western countries including Canada pursued an active stabilization policy in which both fiscal and monetary changes were made frequently in an effort to fine tune.

The 1950s opened with a major bout of demand inflation brought on by heavy expenditures in the United States associated with the Korean War. The U.S. price level rose about 10 percent in two years. This was a wartime demand inflation similar to that experienced during and after World War II; although its consequences might be disturbing, its causes were well understood.

The expansion in the U.S. economy led to an increase in demand for Canadian exports and to a balance-of-payments surplus. In an attempt to insulate the Canadian economy from the inflationary pressures arising in the United States, Canada broke from the Bretton Woods agreement to maintain a system of fixed exchange rates and allowed the foreign exchange value of the Canadian dollar to be determined freely in the foreign exchange market. This floating exchange rate was maintained until May 1962, when the rate was again fixed.

After this inflation had run its course, the economy settled down at an average performance that seemed (particularly in retrospect) to come quite close to the twin goals of full employment and stable prices. The average rate of unemployment in 1953–1959 was 4.7 percent, while the average rate of inflation was around 1.2 percent per year.

The fluctuations in demand caused some mild fluctuations in income and employment. They also caused a slow upward shift in the price level. Although a worry at the time, this price experience would be regarded as virtual stability by today's standards.

Toward the end of the decade, one new problem was causing concern. There was a tendency for the price level to rise despite a significant GNP gap. Thus, for example, when aggregate demand was at AD_1 in Figure 41-4, the price level might be rising at 1 to 2 percent per year. This seemed to imply a spontaneous upward shift in the horizontal portion of the aggregate supply curve (say from P_0 to P_1 in the figure) *not associated with any excess demand.*

Various explanations were put forward. The most commonly given were the structural rigidity and the wage cost-push hypotheses (discussed on pages 813–814). The inflation was very mild and the debate on its causes inconclusive. However, this was the first real evidence of a force that later became a plaguing policy problem: inflations originating in shifts in the aggregate supply curve.

THE 1960s: INFLATION-UNEMPLOYMENT TRADE-OFFS AND MORE DEMAND INFLATION

The Trade-off Relation

As the 1950s wore on, it became increasingly evident that the view of the economy given by the kinked aggregate supply curve in Figure 41-4 was inadequate. With such an aggregate supply curve, increases in aggregate demand affect only national income when Y is less than Y_F and only the price level when Y equals Y_F. Full employment and stable prices are attainable simultaneously provided only that the aggregate demand

curve can be made to intersect the aggregate supply curve at the latter's kink.

The experience of the late 1950s forced economists to regard the kinked aggregate supply curve as an inadequate description of the supply side of the economy. An intermediate section was suggested, over which the price level and national income could vary simultaneously, as shown in Figure 39-4 on page 821. However, the realization that the aggregate supply curve would continue to shift upward when equilibrium was on its rising portion and that the aggregate demand curve would have to be shifted right by monetary policy to prevent national income from falling, led to the formulation of the Phillips curve, shown in Figure 39-6 on page 823.

The Phillips curve is often called a trade-off curve because it shows an apparent trade-off between income and inflation: a higher level of real national income can be obtained, but at the cost of more inflation. (Since a rise in national income entails a fall in unemployment, the trade-off was often expressed in terms of an unemployment-inflation trade-off rather than an income-inflation trade-off. But the two relations are interchangeable over the short term because national income and unemployment vary inversely with each other.)

The 1960s were the era of the Phillips curve trade-off. Economists sought to measure the inflation-unemployment trade-off curve for various economies while policymakers discussed which point on the curve the economy should be made to operate at. Table 41-1 shows the trade-off for the Canadian economy that existed on the basis of data for the 1950s and 1960s. In general, conservatives favored points close to Y_F, where the inflation rate was very low, while liberals favored points further to the right along the curve, where higher output and lower unemployment were obtained at the cost of a higher inflation rate.

Inflation-Unemployment Experience

The 1950s ended with a high level of unemployment and a current account deficit in Canada.

TABLE 41-1

Employment, Unemployment, and Inflation in Canada, 1947–1970

Unemployment[a]	Number of years	Average unemployment[a]	Average employment[a]	Average annual rate of inflation of CPI (percent)
Less than 4.0	11	3.1	96.9	4.8
4.0–4.9	6	4.5	95.5	2.4
5.0 or more	7	6.3	93.7	1.7

Source: Department of Finance, *Economic Review*, 1977.
[a] As a percentage of the civilian labor force.

On average, inflation and unemployment were negatively related over the years 1947–1970. During this period higher levels of unemployment tended to be associated with stable or only slowly rising prices. Lower levels of unemployment tended to be associated with higher rates of inflation. The data are plotted in Figure 41-5.

Part of the problem was that the U.S. economy was in a mild recession. Several Canadian academic economists maintained that the Canadian recession, and in particular Canadian unemployment, was in fact being aggrevated by the restrictive monetary policy pursued by the Bank of Canada. They argued that if monetary policy were loosened, aggregate demand would increase and unemployment would be reduced. They also argued that the current account deficit was primarily due to unusually low levels of exports caused by the U.S. recession; when the American recession ended, they contended, the current account would improve.

The governor of the Bank of Canada, James Coyne, argued that the current account deficit indicated that the Canadian economy was living beyond its means, financed by unusually large capital inflows. He defended the Bank's tight monetary policy on the grounds that if the money supply grew and interest rates fell, capital inflows would *increase*. This would lead to an appreciation of the dollar and a further worsening of the unemployment problem. Moreover, the increased current account deficit could be financed only by even larger capital inflows. Thus, in Coyne's view, an expansionary monetary policy would only exacerbate the problem, and contractionary policy was needed to restrain demand and eliminate the current account deficit.

After considerable controversy in academic and political arenas, the Bank of Canada's policies were repudiated. It was decided that expansionary policies were needed. Since he could not agree with these policies, Coyne was replaced as governor in July 1961, establishing the important precedent that in circumstances of fundamental disagreement the governor of the Bank of Canada, an appointed official, must either agree to pursue the policies of the elected government as put forward by the minister of finance or resign.

The money supply began to expand. We saw in Chapter 40 that expansionary monetary policy under flexible exchange rates will lead to a capital outflow, a currency depreciation, and effective expansion of aggregate demand. These predictions were all borne out by developments during this period. Unemployment began to fall almost immediately, and the recession was quickly ended. Downward pressure was put on the Canadian dollar, and in May 1962 the government pegged the Canadian dollar at 92.5 U.S. cents, lower than it had been throughout the previous ten years.

The next four years witnessed an economic boom in Canada. Devaluation had improved the competitive position of the Canadian export sector, and the American economy, stimulated in part by a massive tax cut passed in 1964, was booming, thereby further stimulating Canadian exports. Moreover, from 1962 to 1965 the Canadian federal government cut taxes and increased expenditure. We saw in Chapter 40 that fiscal policy is expected to be effective under fixed exchange rates; the actual result supported this prediction.

The result of a large increase in government expenditure, unmatched by an increase in taxes, was just what economic theory predicts: aggregate demand rose greatly; full employment was restored quickly; and a serious inflationary gap opened up.

By 1966 unemployment was low and price increases were beginning to accelerate. To fight inflation, the government cut its spending and increased taxes in order to reduce aggregate demand. But the American government was still running a deficit in order to finance the Vietnam War. As a result, economic activity in the United States remained at a very high level, as did the demand for Canadian exports. In turn, this maintained the high level of aggregate demand in Canada. Throughout the period 1965–1969 inflation in Canada rose steadily from an annual rate of 2.4 percent to one of 4.6 percent; the U.S. inflation rate rose from 1.9 percent to 6.1 percent over the same period.

The experience of the 1960s seemed to confirm the notion of a stable trade-off between inflation and unemployment and to establish confidence in the role of macroeconomic policy to influence the economy in a predictable manner.

THE 1970s: INFLATION, STAGFLATION, AND THE "FAILURE OF CONVENTIONAL WISDOM"

At the end of the 1960s the Canadian government decided that the control of inflation was Canada's most important policy objective. The problem was attacked with all the means at the government's disposal, with the strongest role in the anti-inflation battle being assigned to contractionary monetary policy. The restriction in aggregate demand had the desired domestic result; by 1970 inflation had been lowered to 3.3 per-

cent. But unemployment had risen to 5.7 percent.

A Return to Floating Exchange Rates

As the analysis in Chapter 40 predicts (see pages 845–847), tight monetary policy via high interest rates and low import demand caused the balance of payments to move into surplus. The Bank of Canada accumulated foreign exchange rapidly; it tried to sterilize the effects that its purchases of foreign exchange would otherwise have had on the domestic money supply, but it had only limited success. In the end, faced with the alternative of accepting a rapid rate of domestic monetary expansion or dropping the fixed exchange rate, the Bank chose the latter. On May 31, 1970, the Bank announced that it would no longer maintain the Canadian dollar at a fixed par value. Canada had reverted to a floating exchange rate.

The attempt to inflate at a slower rate than the United States was incompatible with fixed exchange rates; in the face of a high balance-of-payments surplus, either the economy had to be allowed to expand faster or the exchange rate had to be freed. The latter course was chosen.

Once it was freed, the Canadian dollar rose rapidly to virtual par with the U.S. dollar. The stage was now set for Canada to continue to pursue its policy of striving for a lower rate of inflation than that in the United States. If Canada were to achieve this goal, it would be necessary that the value of the Canadian dollar *continue to rise* at a rate approximately equal to the excess of the U.S. inflation rate over the Canadian inflation rate.[1]

However, the Bank of Canada, after adopting a flexible exchange rate in order to be able to pursue its anti-inflation policy consistently, simultaneously adopted a more expansionary posture. In particular, it embarked on a policy commonly

[1] The discussion of the PPP exchange rate in the boxes on pages 838 and 850 could usefully be reviewed at this stage.

referred to as a **dirty float.** A dirty float prevails when a central bank operates so as to regulate closely the foreign exchange value of the domestic currency without undertaking an explicit commitment to maintain it at or near a publicly announced value.

There are two ways to manage a dirty float. One method is to intervene directly in the foreign exchange market to stabilize the exchange rate. A balance-of-payments surplus such as Canada was experiencing at the time would mean that the Bank of Canada would have to buy foreign exchange to keep the Canadian dollar from appreciating. Of course, the purchase of foreign exchange by the Bank of Canada would have meant that the supply of Canadian dollars would be rising. This was precisely the problem that had arisen under a fixed exchange rate and had led to the adoption of a flexible exchange rate. Not surprisingly, the Bank of Canada did not actively engage in this direct intervention approach to managing the dirty float.

The second method of managing a dirty float is to set domestic monetary conditions (rates of interest and rates of monetary expansion) so that the exchange market clears at the desired exchange rate without substantial government intervention in the foreign exchange market. Essentially, this means adopting the monetary policy that would be consistent with fixed rates (and hence might better be termed a *dirty fix*). The Bank of Canada chose this method, and it led to a more rapid expansion of the money supply than would have been consistent with the goal of reducing inflation. Indeed, it led predictably to a rate of inflation roughly equal to that in the United States and higher than the target rate which led to the monetary contraction of the late 1960s and the adoption of a flexible exchange rate in 1970. Indirectly, by maintaining policies consistent with a stable exchange rate, inflation was imported from the United States.

In introspect, it appears that during this period Canada missed a golden opportunity to avoid the take-off into accelerated inflation that so many other countries experienced. By mid 1970 the ef-fects of the 1968–1970 tight monetary policy had worked their way through the economy. Inflation was low and falling. The necessary price of increased unemployment had been paid, and most economists now agree that not only were no further increases in unemployment necessary, but in fact as expectations of inflation fell, the level of unemployment could also fall. (This possibility is discussed on pages 832–833.) Thus the stage was set for continued low inflation as long as the exchange rate was allowed to continue to adjust. Instead the exchange rate was stabilized and Canada reverted to a high inflation path. Why?

One reason often put forward to explain this apparent policy mistake was discussed in Chapter 8 (see especially pages 144–145). Canadian export industries had a significant competitive advantage during the period of the late 1960s, when Canada was maintaining a fixed exchange rate and inflating more slowly than the United States, and this competitive advantage was reflected in the current account surplus experienced over that period. The revaluation that followed the floating of the exchange rate in June 1970 eroded much of the competitive advantage because the rise in the exchange rate also increased Canadian costs in terms of U.S. dollars. As a result, further appreciation of the Canadian dollar was opposed on the grounds that it would further harm the competitive position of the export sector. As the box on page 850 emphasized, this is not the case when the appreciation arises from a low domestic inflation rate relative to the foreign rate. Stabilizing the exchange rate merely led to increased domestic inflation with no gain in competitive advantage for the domestic export sector; their costs in terms of U.S. dollars still rose, not as a result of a rise in the exchange rate but rather as a result of increased domestic factor costs, especially wages.

An alternative explanation of the policy error, put forward by the late Harry Johnson, is that the Bank of Canada's operating procedures were geared to maintaining the historical near equality between Canadian and U.S. interest rates. In doing this, the Bank also maintained — perhaps inadvertently — the historical close relationship between the two inflation rates because Canadian monetary policy merely mimicked U.S. monetary policy. Consequently little or no movement in the exchange rate was required to maintain equilibrium in the foreign exchange market.

A third explanation or justification for the dirty float was that by the middle of 1970 unemployment had become so high that the government had decided that it was the most important problem. Accordingly, from 1970 through 1973 fiscal policy and monetary policy became expansionary. To the surprise and consternation of the policymakers, while inflation and the level of economic activity increased sharply between 1970 and 1973, the unemployment rate barely fell at all. What had happened to the Phillips curve?

The Elusive Trade-off

By the early 1970s a major doctrine of macroeconomic policy, the existence of a stable inflation-income or inflation-unemployment trade-off, was being seriously questioned. Toward the end of the 1960s and during the early 1970s the Phillips curves of most countries began to shift upward, and the phenomena of higher inflation and higher unemployment were being felt all over the world. In other words, any level of national income and unemployment was associated with a higher rate of inflation than previously. For example, in Canada the recession at the beginning of the 1970s left the inflation rate at just over 3 percent, a rate that before the 1960s had been associated only with peaks of business activity and large inflationary gaps, while unemployment stood at 5.7 percent. A decline in 1971 followed by a recovery in 1972–1973 saw the unemployment rate rise to 6.2 percent and then fall back to 5.5 percent, but the recovery saw the inflation rate jump to 7.5 percent in 1973.

The breakdown of the Canadian Phillips curve

relation is shown in Figure 41-5. The colored curve shows the relatively stable inflation-income trade-off as it appeared to policymakers in the late 1960s. The dots show the 1970s. They show that the decade's experience was always above the earlier curve, indicating unprecedented high inflation associated with any given level of pressure or demand.

It was clear by the early 1970s that something was very wrong with the simple theory of the stable Phillips curve trade-off. As so often happens, a newer theory was at hand to explain the failure of the similar Phillips curve. In 1968 Professor Edmund S. Phelps of Columbia University and Professor Milton Friedman of the University of Chicago had mounted a major attack on the Phillips curve trade-off, an attack based on the expectational theory of inflation (explained in Chapter 39). Their argument said that an attempt to hold national income *above* its full-employment level would lead not to a stable rate of inflation but to an ever-accelerating rate. They called the rate of unemployment associated with full-employment income the *natural rate of unemployment*. An alternative statement of their theory's major prediction was that an attempt to hold unemployment *below* its natural rate would lead to an accelerating rate of inflation.

The Phelps-Friedman theory is important for at least two reasons. First, it produced a major change in the way macro policy problems are viewed. It suggested that the trade-off between unemployment and inflation was merely transitory. Attempts to hold output above Y_F (and hence unemployment below its natural rate), while leading to temporary gains in employment output, are likely to lead to ever-accelerating rates of inflation. The puzzle posed by Figure 41-5 is resolved at least in part by the prediction of the Phelps-Friedman theory that the short-run Phillips curve would shift upward in response to continued inflation that got built into expectations.[2]

[2] This effect was likely reinforced in the early 1970s by an increase in the natural rate of unemployment, as discussed in the box on pages 860–861.

FIGURE 41-5
Canadian Stagflation in the 1970s

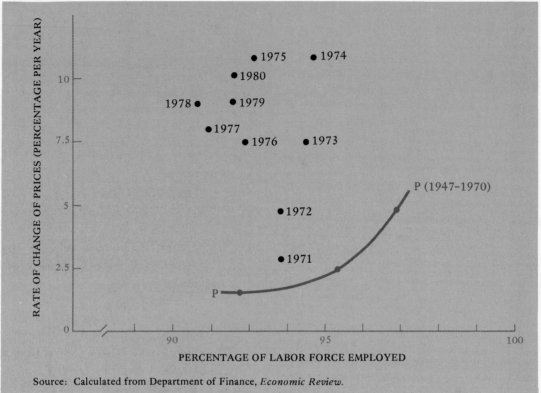

Source: Calculated from Department of Finance, *Economic Review.*

The 1970s were unusual in combining high rates of unemployment with high rates of inflation. The three colored dots are plotted from Table 41-1. They show the average rates of inflation associated with the indicated rates of employment between 1947 and 1970. The colored curve is thus a rough Phillips curve for the economy of that period. The black dots show the rates of employment and inflation for each of the years 1971 to 1979. The years 1974–1975 saw the most extreme stagflation. The employment rate fell from 94.5 to 93.1 percent while the rate of inflation rose from 7.5 to 10.8 percent. In 1978 the employment rate fell to its all-time low since World War II of 91.6 percent while the inflation rate rose steadily.

Second, the theory provided an explanation for bouts of stagflation: strong inflationary expectations can sustain the inflation rate and rising expectations can even increase it temporarily in the face of declining demand and output and hence rising unemployment.

1974–1975: Stagflation and Supply Shocks

Before 1973 the major force driving economic fluctuations had always been aggregate demand. When demand was high, output would be high, unemployment low, and strong inflationary pressures would exist. When aggregate demand was low, output would be low, unemployment high, and inflationary pressures weak or nonexistent. These associations had become the conventional wisdom about how the economy must behave. They were so widely accepted as the natural state of things that ordinary citizens, most policymakers, and many economists were mystified when quite a different association of events occurred.

In 1974 and 1975 the economies of all Western countries fell into the deepest recession since the Great Depression. Unemployment rose from under 5.5 percent in 1973 to over 7 percent in 1976. The economy encountered the new economic disease of stagflation: falling output and rising unemployment combined with high and sometimes rising inflation rates. Inflation reached an annual rate of 10.8 percent in 1975.

Aggregate supply shifts. For the first time in recent history the economy was being affected significantly by shifts in *aggregate supply* not caused by excess aggregate demand. The most severe of the shifts in aggregate supply—often called supply-side shocks—came with the OPEC oil embargo in 1973, which was followed by major increases in OPEC's prices. Not only fuel but a host of other petroleum-based products from plastics to fertilizers suddenly rose in price. The rising prices of these vital materials meant rising costs for many firms. Rising costs were passed on by raising the prices of finished goods, which in turn caused an upward shift in the aggregate supply curve.

The other major supply-side shock that hit the economy at this time came from the agricultural sector. A series of crop failures drove up many food prices. At the same time, the sale to the USSR of large stocks of North American wheat and other agricultural commodities removed the depressing effect on prices that large buffer stocks had exerted, and this too led to price rises. Again the price level rose for causes associated with supply rather than demand shifts.

Aggregate demand shifts. In the United States, the supply-side shocks were reinforced by severe contractionary shifts in aggregate demand. The effect of OPEC was to transfer large amounts of income from American purchasers to sellers of petroleum products. Had the sellers spent the money in the same way that Americans would have, aggregate demand would have been unaffected. But much of the new oil income was spent on short-term financial securities, gold, and land rather than on currently produced goods and services. Thus the effect on aggregate demand was the same as if the American propen-

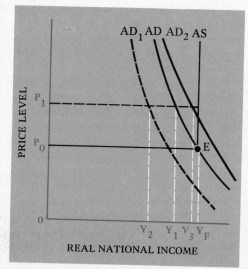

FIGURE 41-6
Stagflation

Upward shifts in aggregate supply cause rising prices and falling output. Initially aggregate demand is *AD* and aggregate supply is $P_0 AS$, producing equilibrium at *E*. The aggregate supply curve now shifts upward to $P_1 AS$. This reduces national income from Y_F to Y_1 and raises the price level from P_0 to P_1 along the given aggregate demand curve, *AD*. If aggregate demand shifts simultaneously to AD_1, the fall in output will be even larger than it would otherwise have been (from Y_F to Y_2). This is roughly what happened in the United States from 1973 to 1975. In Canada, policy was more expansionary and the *AD* curve shifted to AD_2.

sity to save had risen: there was a reduction in the amount of income spent on current production. This caused a leftward shift in the aggregate demand curve (or, the same thing, a downward shift in the aggregate expenditure curve).

The net stagflationary effects of this upward shift in aggregate supply and fall in aggregate demand are shown in Figure 41-6.

In Canada there were also contractionary forces operating on aggregate demand, mostly due to the decline in export demand caused by the American recession. However, they were offset by the expansionary monetary and fiscal policies employed by the federal government. And as noted in the box on pages 690–691, the

TABLE 41-2
Canadian and U.S. Macroeconomic Performance, 1974–1980

	U.S. unemployment *minus* Canadian unemployment	U.S. inflation rate *minus* Canadian inflation rate (CPI excluding food)	Canadian price level (CPI)[a] over U.S. price level (1967 = 100)
1974	0.1	2.4	0.97
1975	1.6	−2.9	0.99
1976	0.6	−3.2	1.01
1977	−1.1	−1.5	1.02
1978	−2.4	2.1	1.04
1979	−1.3	1.7	1.05
1980	−0.2	−0.1	1.05

[a] All items.

The United States experienced a deeper recession in 1974–1975 and a stronger recovery in 1976–1978 than did Canada. By sustaining aggregate demand, Canada had less unemployment during the 1974–1976 recession yet had more rapid inflation. The Canadian price level relative to the U.S. price level rose continuously over the 1974–1978 period.

Canadian income tax was inflation indexed, thus eliminating the inflation-induced fiscal drag experienced in the United States. Moreover, provincial governments ran large deficits, and investment projects such as the James Bay Hydro development were just getting under way. Consequently, unemployment in Canada was kept relatively low and the path of real output growth was sustained relatively close to its pre-1973 path. But the low rate of unemployment was accompanied by a high rate of inflation.

Table 41-2 compares Canada and the United States. In 1974, with almost the same unemployment rate, the United States had 2.5 percent more inflation. In 1975 the U.S. unemployment rate was 1.6 points above the Canadian rate, but the U.S. inflation rate was a dramatic 2.9 points below the Canadian rate. The deeper recession and lower inflation rate in the United States continued for another year, to be followed by a stronger and more rapid recovery. By 1978 the U.S. recovery had led to a substantially lower unemployment rate and a higher inflation rate. The third column of the table shows that Canadian prices had now risen as much above American prices as they had been held below them in the period of monetary restraint in 1969–1970.

There is no mystery about the differences when one looks at the change in the rate of monetary expansion and the comparative aggregate demands in the two countries.

American neo-Keynesians such as Alan Blinder and James Tobin have criticized the U.S. authorities for exacerbating the recession by not accommodating the supply-side shocks of 1974–1975 with a corresponding monetary expansion. They argue that the price rises were going to occur in any case because of the supply shock; monetary restraint only served to ensure falling output and rising unemployment as well.

Some monetarists argue that monetary accommodation would have been felt mainly in a higher rate of inflation with no gain on the output side. More extreme monetarists even deny the possibility that relative price supply shocks (such as the rise in oil prices) can drive up the price level — and so they deny the existence of the problem. They maintain that the aggregate price level is determined by aggregate monetary conditions alone, and hence that supply shocks that cause some prices to rise must also lead some other prices to fall so that the price index remains constant.

It is instructive to contrast the experiences of

the Canadian and American economies during the great stagflation of 1974–1975. Both economies were subject to the external demand shock of world recession and to the supply-side shock of rapid increases in world prices of oil and agricultural products. Yet the two economies were subjected to very different domestic policies: the rate of monetary expansion remained high in Canada and fell drastically in the United States. Canadian real output and employment remained much higher, suggesting that the Keynesians are right in saying that positive real effects will result from the accommodation or nonaccommodation of supply-side shocks. But the Canadian inflation rate also held much higher for over a year, suggesting that the moderate monetarists are right in arguing that at least part of the monetary accommodation of supply shocks will come out in a higher inflation rate.

1975–1978: Wage and Price Controls and Monetary Gradualism

The combination of persistently high inflation and rising unemployment, even though it looked favorable by international standards, was regarded as serious by Canadian policymakers. Although unemployment was high and rising, estimates of changes in the national rate of unemployment (discussed in the box on pages 860–861) now suggest that in fact the Canadian labor market had *excess demand* on average through 1974 and only modest slack in 1975.

By the summer of 1975 Canadian policymakers clearly anticipated an accelerating rate of inflation. Wage settlements seemed to be increasing rather than decreasing, at least according to the perception of Ottawa policymakers who were watching the individual settlements come in. Policymakers thought they perceived an *accelerating* wage-push inflation in a time of world recession. In an atmosphere of crisis thought to require desperate moves, wage and price controls were initiated in the autumn of 1975. An Anti-Inflation Board (AIB) was set up

with power to control wages and prices for three years.

At roughly the same time, the Bank of Canada began to focus on the rate of growth of the money supply, and it announced its intention to wind down the rate of monetary expansion very slowly. (We discussed this policy of *monetary gradualism* in Chapter 38.)

Wage and price controls and monetary gradualism were to be used to force down the inflation rate at the same time. Whether it was a conscious act of policy to use the two together is not clear, but the use of both policies simultaneously may have helped to avoid partially the sustained increases in unemployment usually required to wind down an inflation. An initial increase in unemployment normally occurs when aggregate demand is curtailed while inflationary expectations remain high. Since inflation does not usually fall immediately in response to the adoption of anti-inflationary policies, the economy normally follows what is called a "stagflationary loop."

The approach of trying to avoid stagflation by combining restrictive monetary policy with wage and price controls had been advocated by Professor John Young in 1970. Professor Young believed that a public campaign to convince people of the government's commitment to reducing inflation would reduce expectations of inflation. At that time the Prices and Incomes Commission sought, but failed to get, labor's voluntary cooperation in running an incomes policy.

The Anti-Inflation Board

The policy of wage and price controls invoked a political storm. Under the Canadian constitution, the British North America Act, control of all labor matters clearly lies with the provinces. Until the fall of 1975 it was the general opinion among lawyers that peacetime wage and price controls were unconstitutional. Nonetheless, Ottawa invoked these policies, presumably hoping that their perceived need would justify them. Several challenges were then brought before the

A View from the Outside of the Inside of Upside Down*

On the 18th of October, 1971, I assumed responsibility for the Price Commission in the conduct of Phase II of President Nixon's Wage and Price Control program. . . . I want to relate something about my view of policy-making at the national level. I want to explain why it is inherently a confused sort of occupation and I want to imbue the reader with a healthy skepticism for the ability of central control to solve economic problems.

One of the main reasons why the policy-making process in general and wage and price controls in particular are inherently difficult is because they are attempting to regulate the most sophisticated information system that the world has ever seen—namely the North American market economy. . . . The information system is the network formed by free people buying and selling, and the signals are the variations in and the levels of wages, prices, interest rates, rents and, unfortunately, taxes.

. . . most of the products and services that we take for granted in our everyday lives can be taken for granted only because there is a functioning price system. A system that, despite its imperfections, delivers just the right quantity of California lettuce to Montana or Alberta, Canada; and decides the relationship between raw log prices in California and the price of furnished lumber in Boston. As we discovered when we tampered with, and effectively suspended, the operation of the price system, we could no longer rely on the system itself and were forced to get more and more involved with what were, before controls, essentially automatic functions.

The problem that policy-makers must cope with, if they are determined to control the system, is the endless detail that is involved in the operation of the system. To control the system and yet keep it running smoothly, the authorities must intercept all of the signals coming from the system (and there are hundreds of millions), interpret them, appropriately change them (assuming they know how) and retransmit them.

What we at the Price Commision continuously found was that everything is related to everything else and there was, accordingly, no such thing as one intervention. We were drawn inevitably and progressively deeper into the system, and the temptation to limit the necessity for our involvement by arbitrarily changing the system was very great. Herein lies the real danger from centralized control, that is, that an inability to handle the overload of signals, both incoming and outgoing, may produce attempts to simplify the system and hence jeopardize its survival.

The difficulty of taking over the wage-price signalling mechanism is indicated by the fact that during the first three weeks of Phase II there were nearly 400,000 inquiries about the program. In terms of getting down to the nitty gritty, had the Dow Chemical Company and the Commission not agreed to an across the board increase of 2 percent, we would have had to examine nearly 100,000 submissions on different products for that company alone.

. . . Wage and price controls are, by nature, a bureaucratic nightmare. There is no easy way to proceed, no escape from the remorseless tide of detail that is the inevitable consequence of attempting to interrupt the normal current of economic affairs. There is also no escape from the conclusion that detailed regulation breeds a restiveness in those being regulated that eventually must lead either to the collapse of the controls or the adoption of more coercive measures.

*Excerpted from an article of the same title by Jackson Grayson, dean of the School of Business, Southern Methodist University, in M. Walker, ed., *The Illusion of Wage and Price Control*, Vancouver, B.C., The Fraser Institute, 1976.

TABLE 41-3
Output and Inflation Rates in Canada, 1973–1980

	GNP gap as a percentage of potential GNP	Annual percentage change in Consumer Price Index			Annual percentage change in GNE deflator	Wage settlements, excluding construction
		All items	Excluding food	Excluding food and energy		
1973	−1.9[a]	7.9	5.1	4.7	9.1	10.5
1974	0.8	10.9	8.8	8.3	15.3	14.8
1975	2.3	10.8	10.1	9.6	10.8	17.4
1976	1.4	7.5	9.4	8.8	9.5	10.4
1977	2.4	8.0	7.9	7.3	7.0	7.6
1978	3.1	8.9	6.4	6.2	6.3	7.0
1979	2.9	9.2	7.9	8.0	10.3	8.2
1980	n.a.	10.1	10.0	9.4	10.5	10.2

[a] Minus indicates a negative GNP gap (actual national income exceeded potential income).

The overall inflation rate in the 1970s responded to both demand and supply shocks. The presence of stagflation is most obvious in 1974–1975 and 1977–1979, when extremely high inflation rates coexisted with a high and rising GNP gap. The impact of supply shocks on the inflation rate can be seen by comparing the different inflation rates in the table. In 1979, for example, the inflation rate of 9.2 percent would have been only 8 percent had it not been for the supply shocks of rising food and energy prices.

The GNE deflator, which is an index of prices of goods produced in Canada, rose sharply in the 1973–1974 period and responded more obviously to the post-1975 disinflation policies than did the CPI.

Wage settlements have risen steadily since the end of wage and price controls in 1978. Whether this is a typical post-controls bubble or it can be explained by other factors (such as excess demand) is the subject of much current controversy and research.

courts, the major one coming from the Canadian Labour Congress. The government referred the matter directly to the Supreme Court of Canada.

The government stood first on its general powers to control the economy (the national dimension test) and second on the Peace, Order, and Good Government (POGG) clause in the British North America Act. The latter in effect gives the federal government the power to do anything it believes is required in circumstances of national emergency. Therefore the issue became whether or not there was an emergency in 1975 sufficient to justify suspending the normal division of powers within the Constitution.

In a hotly contested and precedent-setting decision, the Supreme Court upheld the validity of the Anti-Inflation Act but only as emergency or crisis legislation of temporary duration. Clearly this decision will make it difficult for a government of Canada to institute wage and price controls at some future date, although tax-based incomes policies (TIPs), discussed in Chapter 42, might be possible, for they could be interpreted as an amendment to existing tax laws.

Most economists now believe that the first year of the gradualist policy was "too gradual." The panic concerning an accelerating wage and price spiral turned out to be unfounded; the evidence indicates that weakening market conditions would have brought down inflation in any case, as had happened in other countries. As Table 41-3 shows, national income was below its full-employment level in 1975. The Canadian slowdown might have been less marked because of the relatively strong demand and expansionary monetary conditions in Canada in 1974–1975, but by autumn of 1975 a slowdown in wage and price inflation was clearly evident.

The AIB's targets for wage increases were 10 percent in 1976, 8 percent in 1977, and 6 percent in 1978. The very modest targets for reduction in wage inflation given by the AIB in its first year were probably at or above the rates that the market would have produced in any case. There was even some fear that the controls would

International Experience with Wage and Price Controls

In spite of the continued advocacy of incomes policy by some economists, there is much evidence that casts doubt on the effectiveness of such policies as a device for the long-term control of inflation.

European experience. European countries have tried many variants of incomes policies. In a study of the European experience, Professor David Smith of Queen's University concluded that incomes policies could not be judged an effective control of inflation. At best, a really determined policy might decelerate the rate of inflation by one-half to one percentage point per year. Even then there is evidence that the policy becomes progressively more difficult to administer as time passes. Professors Robert Flanagan and Lloyd Ulman of the University of California reached similar conclusions in reviewing European experiences a few years after Smith's study.

One of the main problems associated with attempts to control labor costs in Europe can be expressed in terms of the very different behavior of the *wage rate,* which is the amount workers get per hour, and *wage earnings,* which is the amount they get per week. It was observed that earnings tended to vary with aggregate demand, even though wage rates were held down by an incomes policy. The consequent widening spread between rates and earnings was christened *wage drift.*

Consider an incomes policy that will allow a rise in wage rates of only 10 percent. The average wage is then raised from, say, $10 to $11 per hour. However, in order to attract labor, firms can offer other inducements such as bonuses and guaranteed overtime pay (whether or not the overtime is worked). If by these devices they can raise average earnings 20 percent—from say, $350 to $420 per week —the rise in earnings will greatly exceed the

rise in output, and inflation will occur in spite of the effective control over wage rates.

British experience. Several times during the decades of the 1950s and 1960s successive British governments tried incomes policies in attempts to control inflation. A large number of empirical studies have credited these attempts with "success" ranging from almost nothing to less than nothing.

Undaunted by these experiences, the British government drew the conclusion not that incomes policies were ineffective but that they had been pursued with sufficient severity. In 1972 the British had one of the largest budget deficits in their history, and at the same time they allowed the money supply to increase by nearly 25 percent in one year! The result was fully predictable on the basis of standard theory: a rapid inflation. But the government, encouraged by a surprising number of academic economists, clung to its cost-push theory that inflation was due solely to union power and had little to do with fiscal and monetary matters. The government attempted to suppress the enormous inflationary forces that it had let loose by using direct controls on wages and prices. A head-on battle with the unions was precipitated. Strikes in key industries forced the adoption of a three-day work week, power cuts closed down television at 10:30 P.M., and a large portion of the population was driven to use candles for much of the day and night. In the end a general election was called, and the Conservative government was defeated. The new Labor government had little option but to give in to the strikers' demands, and the incomes policy collapsed.

The net effect on controlling inflation was negligible or zero, and the cost in terms of social stress was enormous. Nevertheless the Labor government failed to control the budget deficit and money supply growth, and again it resorted to an incomes policy in the face of an accelerating rate of inflation. A voluntary scheme to restrain wage increases was instituted in 1974 and was replaced by statutory controls the following year. By 1977 the inflation rate at last began to fall. Some gave the credit to incomes policies, but this was not an obvious conclusion, for at about this time the Bank of England finally began to reduce the rate of growth of the money supply.

U.S. experience. The first major use of incomes policies in the United States occurred in 1971 when that country was clearly suffering a demand-pull inflation. The program was implemented in several stages. Phase I (which lasted for two months) imposed a complete freeze on virtually all wages and prices in the economy. Phase II (fourteen months) attempted to hold wage increases to 5.5 percent per year and price increases to no more than was necessary to cover any increase in costs. Phase III (five months) began in mid January 1973. At that time the economy was expanding rapidly and a need was recognized for a more flexible program that would permit substantial changes in relative prices.

When it became apparent that Phase III was not restraining inflation, a new freeze was introduced in June 1973 with the announcement that it was to be followed by a further set of Phase IV controls. During Phase IV a number of sectors were "decontrolled" as an initial stage of returning to free markets. Phase IV controls proved ineffective, however, and they gradually petered out. By April 1974, when the control authority expired, its later phases were acknowledged failures.

Extensive research into the effects of this experiment with wage and price controls suggests that the entire costly effort had little or no effect on wages but that it did hold down price inflation by perhaps as much as two per-

centage points. The restraint on prices was achieved by forcing a narrowing of profit margins. Not surprisingly, once the controls were lifted, profit margins were restored. Thus the episode had little or no lasting effect on the price level.

What Can We Conclude?

The major conclusions that can be drawn from the experience of other countries are that (1) the great majority of incomes policies that have been tried to date have had little or no lasting effect on price levels and (2) those policies that are pursued with real vigor and determination can be costly in terms of strikes, slowdowns, lost output, and general social upheaval.

Commenting on this last point, the late Harry Johnson concluded that

An incomes policy is an exercise in the futile wasting of social and national loyalty, is bound to get mired in detailed microeconomic questions of income distribution, . . . and in the long run may (as it seems it already has in Britain) turn national loyalty such as it is into bitter class conflict and social disintegration.*

Of course there can be no finality on any social issue, and some observers will continue to draw the lesson that the failure of incomes policies so far means only that they have been pursued with too little vigor and determination. Others, however, will accept the view of the vast majority of economists who have studied the evidence from many countries: that while wage and price controls can have a temporary restraining effect on prices, they are an ineffective method of executing long-term control over the price level.

*H. G. Johnson, "Inflation, Unemployment and the Floating Rate," *Canadian Public Policy,* Spring 1975, page 183.

become floors instead of ceilings and serve to accelerate rather than decelerate inflation. In 1977–1978, however, the targets were reduced on schedule and there seemed little doubt that some restraint on wages was exercised. Inevitably figures have varied among researchers, but something like an average of 2.5 percentage points appears to be the agreed number for the average annual restraint on wages over the three years of controls.

When the AIB was introduced in the autumn of 1975, inflation as measured by the rate of change of the CPI was 10.2 percent. By the end of 1976 that rate had fallen to 5.9 percent. However, much of the reduction was due to a moderation of food price increases. As discussed on page 820, many economists feel that the short-run fluctuations in food prices should be excluded when assessing the underlying inflation trend in the economy, and during 1976 the fall in the rate of change of the CPI *excluding food* was much more modest, from 10.1 percent to 9.4 percent, as shown in Table 41.3. In the next year the AIB targets were reduced and the rate of change of the CPI excluding food continued to fall gradually; however, food prices shot up and overall inflation as measured by the change in the total CPI in fact *rose* steadily throughout 1977.

These factors greatly complicate the assessment of the AIB. It seems clear that the AIB cannot take credit for the sharp fall in the rate of inflation in 1976. How much of the steady decline in the underlying rate of inflation as measured by the CPI *excluding food* can be attributed to the AIB is also debatable since the severe recession that occurred in 1976 and 1977, with falling aggregate demand and rising unemployment and plant capacity, would itself have led to some moderation of inflation even in the absence of AIB.

When controls were lifted in 1978, the rate of inflation measured by the CPI, excluding food, rose from 6.4 percent in the last year of controls to 7.9 percent in 1979. This apparent post-controls bubble is still being studied. The tentative verdict is that the AIB succeeded in retarding wage increases somewhat more than would have occurred in its absence but that most of the gains were lost in the post-control wage bubble evident in Table 41-3. This is consistent with the analysis presented in Figure 41-3.

The AIB had perhaps its clearest and strongest impact on the rate of increase of wages in the public sector. During the mid 1970s the government had found it extremely difficult to restrain public sector wages, which had accelerated particularly since the growth of unionization in that sector over the late 1960s. Many economists thought that public sector wage increases had led to increased pressure on private sector wages and thus had been a force in contributing to the acceleration of inflation in the 1970s. In any event, the AIB is generally credited with slowing the rate of increase of wages in the public sector. In the private sector some wage restraint was also clearly achieved, although less than in the public sector and perhaps in part in response to the public sector slowdown.

The AIB was unable to control prices directly, though it did try to influence them indirectly by monitoring profits. AIB officials apparently adopted the view that prices are primarily cost determined, a view often described as a neo-Keynesian view of inflation. By restraining wages, the AIB believed it would automatically restrain prices rather than merely widen markups and thus redistribute income from wages to profits. But markups did widen. The controls served to redistribute income from wages to profits, and thus they did less to restrain prices than to restrain wages. Among other things, this result guarantees that unions will be even more hostile to a future experiment with wage and price controls than they were to this one.

In 1978 the wage and price controls were removed. Inflation, measured in terms of the CPI, excluding food, had been reduced from 10.1 percent in 1975 to 6.4 percent in 1978, as shown in Table 41-3. Controls were used, apparently successfully, as part of a package to counter the explosive double-digit inflation of the 1974–1975 period. It seems probable, however, that the rapid rates of inflation of around 10 percent did not persist long enough to build up strongly felt or uniformly held expectations of continued inflation at those rates. The underlying or *core* rate of the economy was still widely perceived to be in the 6 to 7 percent range that had persisted throughout most of the decade. The rise in inflation above this core rate was fairly easily reversed. The real problem for continued anti-inflationary policy is reducing the rate of inflation below the underlying core rate. The wage and price controls imposed by the AIB never got to the point of attempting to do this.

Monetary Gradualism

Following its conversion in 1975 to a policy of controlling the money supply according to a pre-announced target range, the Bank of Canada has been one of the most successful central banks in achieving its monetary targets. The targets for M1 growth were met most of the time and have been successively reduced, as shown in Figure 38-2. Inflation at first appeared to be responding, though slowly. The rate measured by the CPI, excluding food, fell in successive years starting in 1975 from 10.1 to 9.4 to 7.9 to 6.4 percent. Then, in 1979, it rose to 7.9 percent, and in 1980 it rose to 10 percent, taking it all the way back to where it had been at the peak of the 1975 "crisis." Developments in early 1981 were no more encouraging; inflation stood at 10.4 percent on an annual basis as of September 1981. Had five years of gradualism accomplishing nothing?

The inflation bubble in 1980 did not appear to be a supply-side shock. The rates just quoted excluded food, and Canada's national energy policy held the price of petroleum products at less than half of the world price. The rate of inflation of the energy price component of the CPI was 11 percent in 1980, only one percentage point above the overall rise in the CPI, excluding food. However, wage costs have increased, as Table 41-3 shows.

By 1978 there was some evidence of excess demand in the economy in spite of the high rates of unemployment. The Canadian dollar, which had been held at a 2 to 3 cent premium over the U.S. dollar by heavy capital inflows, fell continuously over the period 1976–1978. Since then it has fluctuated in the range of 82 to 87 U.S. cents. This has resulted in a major export boom. Until relative capacities adjust, the export sector may hit capacity constraints while other parts of the economy exhibit significant excess capacity.

Assessment of the contribution of fiscal policy is less straightforward. On the one hand, actual and full-employment budget deficits have been large. On the other hand, the government seems to have had little trouble financing these deficits in the bond market, so the deficits have not led to major monetary expansion. However, many of the bonds are sold abroad (or crowd out private issues domestically, thereby forcing them abroad). These government deficits have also occurred at a time when it is hard to argue that the government demand was obviously fueling excess demand in the rest of the country.[3]

In his 1980 annual report, the governor of the Bank of Canada, Gerald Bouey, commented on fiscal policy.

During the last half of the 1970s fiscal policy, as measured by the spending of the Government of Canada and the provinces, was much less expansionary than it was in the first half. . . . The Government of Canada, however, has experienced a large and growing over-all deficit, and in the last few years its net borrowing requirements have been of the order of 4 percent of Gross National Expenditure. From the point of view of dealing with inflation, this was an uncomfortably large deficit for the Government of Canada to have at a time when the level of economic activity relative to the economy's demonstrated capacity was as high as it then was. I am pleased that in the last budget the Government recognized the need to reduce its over-all deficit in the years ahead.

[3] There is the question of whether borrowing abroad to finance current deficits does not seriously reduce the living standards of future Canadians (see pages 669–671). But this question is separate from that of the contribution of the deficit to current inflation.

What If the Strategy of Gradualism Fails?
A Neo-Keynesian Alternative

Since 1975 the fight against inflation in Canada has centered on the Bank of Canada's policy of gradually reducing the rate of growth of the money supply. Neo-Keynesians are pessimistic about our ability to reduce the inflation rate by restricting demand, whether this is done through monetary or fiscal measures. Keynesian theory predicts that inflation rates will be resistant to downward pressures and that the main effect of depressing demand will be to lower output and employment.

This pessimism arises because of inflationary inertias. The Keynesian explanation of such inertias is as follows: Once a given inflation rate is established, individual wage setters are reluctant to be the first to lower their own rates of increase because they will lose out relatively to other wages set in the recent past. It is easy enough to persuade wage setters to take more than they see being earned around them; it is more difficult to persuade them to be the first to take less. Because of this behavior, the rate of decline in the inflation rate that can be induced by depressing demand may be so gradual that it will be swamped by occasional "supply-side shocks" that drive up prices because of such factors as crop failures and OPEC price increases.

What if after several years of gradualist policy the inflation rate seems just as firmly entrenched as it is now, so that the neo-Keynesian pessimism appears to be supported by the evidence?

One alternative, in the style of Margaret Thatcher, is to induce a large enough recession to do the job: a really fierce restrictive monetary and fiscal policy to sustain a 1930s-style recession until inflation subsides. Neo-Keynesian theory is pessimistic on this policy; it predicts that the cumulated loss in output would be very large indeed.

A second alternative is to try some form of incomes policy. Many economists opposed wage and price controls in 1975 because the government had not yet tried traditional monetary and fiscal policies and because they thought controls would be an excuse, as they had been in the United Kingdom, for doing little else by way of anti-inflationary policy. But if present policies do not work, there will be increased pressure to try controls again.

A third alternative is to try "supply-side" incentives—tax reductions, cuts in unemployment insurance benefits, and the like. Many economists believe that any effects such policies will have on output and productivity will occur only in the long run, and hence there is little hope for much help on the current anti-inflation battle from these policies.

One appealing alternative raises from the possibility that while no one policy alone can be expected to be successful in reducing inflation at an acceptable cost in terms of unemployment, a combination of policies might well be successful. Just as an incomes policy cannot be effective when other policies continue to fuel demand in an inflationary manner, so too may it be unreasonable to expect a policy of monetary gradualism operating on its own to stop inflation in the short run.

A Neo-Keynesian Package

The center piece of the neo-Keynesian package is a tight monetary policy: the rate of monetary expansion would be reduced rapidly over two to three years to levels consistent with a low rate of inflation.

The second policy is increased fiscal restraint. This would be partly psychological, for there is not much evidence that current budget deficits are fueling current inflationary fires. But psychology is an important element of inflationary inertia. The government must be seen to be willing to bear its share of the burden. The government would be saying, "This time it is an emergency, and we are prepared to take drastic fiscal measures rather than merely use wage and price controls as an excuse for doing nothing else, as we did last time." The reduction of government expenditure would also make possible the tax cuts referred to below. Expenditure cuts would help monetary policy by putting some modest downward pressure on interest rates.

Third, wage and price controls could then be used to cut through the inflationary inertias and accomplish what the Keynesian view says the free market cannot easily do—to get wage inflation down *rapidly* in line with the much lower inflation rate that is all that is being validated by monetary and fiscal policy.*

Fourth, once-and-for-all measures such as

cutting indirect taxes and abolishing some agricultural marketing boards could be used to give downward supply-side shocks at the outset. This would lend credence to the view that the policy is really working.

Fifth, some supply-side incentive measures should also be a part of the package. They will not have a large moderating effect on the current inflation rate, but anything that aids productivity growth will help matters a few years down the line.

Finally, the package should include some post-controls policies to counter any rebounding of inflationary expectations. Wage and price guidelines should be used with the warning that their violation risks a continued imposition of controls. Some supply-side measures should also be held in reserve to counter the burst of structural inflation that occurs when distorted relative prices and wages are adjusted in the post-controls period.

Such a package would not operate like magic; inflation has built up over a long period of time, and it will be eliminated only over time. But neo-Keynesians argue that it is a preferable reaction to that of people who, in the summer of 1981, when interest rates rose above 20 percent and the Canadian dollar fell below 81 cents U.S., were advocating the abandonment of the only anti-inflationary policy then being pursued—monetary gradualism—and replacing it with one or another type of control. Using controls as a *substitute* for demand reduction is a proven recipe for disaster; using them as a *complement* to demand reduction is an option that some believe is worth trying.

---

* There might, of course, be constitutional problems, and labor's hostility, understandably, would be strong. There is some evidence that the AIB was more effective in redistributing incomes from wages to profits than in restraining price inflation. Given this experience, price and profit controls should perhaps accompany wage controls. It should be made clear that the controls are solely an anti-inflationaly device and are not intended to alter the distribution of income between wages and profits.

THE CONTROL OF AGGREGATE DEMAND AND THE CONTROL OF INFLATION

The experience of the 1970s reinforced a lesson that had become increasingly obvious in the 1960s. Armed with the tools of economic theory, policymakers are able to influence aggregate demand. Some details remain to be settled regarding the relative powers of fiscal and monetary policy, but there is no doubt that, using a mixture of the two, governments can manipulate aggregate demand. Modern economic theory is not the irrelevant white elephant some commentators would make it out to be; it is a potent tool — far more potent than any current rival — for understanding and controlling the macro behavior of the economy.

If this is the case, why does macro policy encounter so many problems? The difficulty is not in manipulating demand; this we know how to do, at least within a reasonable margin of error. The grave uncertainty lies in how the impact of a change in aggregate demand will be divided between quantity changes and price changes.

Say that the government engineers a 10 percent increase in aggregate expenditure. At one time this might lead to a 10 percent increase in real output with prices constant; at another time it might lead to a 10 percent increase in prices with real output constant; at still other times it might lead to any number of different combinations of price and output changes that combine to make up a 10 percent increase in national income valued at current prices.

The great problem of macroeconomics in the 1980s arises from the fact that, while governments can cause changes in aggregate demand, they are uncertain about how the effects of such changes will be divided between quantities and prices.

It is on this issue that current controversies turn. Our present inability to understand fully and to predict accurately the division of effects between real and monetary variables lies at the root of policymakers' failure to control the inflation rate as readily as they can control aggregate demand.

Thus we still ask: Why did the inflation rate not fall below 6 percent in the recession of the late 1970s? Why did the rate accelerate at the end of the decade? Will the recession engineered in 1980 slow the inflation rate? What is wrong? What can be done? These current policy debates are the subject of the next chapter.

Summary

1. The 1930s were the decade of the Great Depression, when Keynesian economics was born. Declining aggregate demand and the relative downward inflexibility of prices (after the first shock of recession had passed) combined to create a problem of massive unemployment.

2. During World War II, massive deficit-financed government expenditure first restored full employment and then opened a serious inflationary gap whose effects were partially masked by price controls. After the war, price controls were removed and inflation took the price level to its new and higher equilibrium.

3. In the 1950s governments sought to produce both full employment and stable prices. Although their policies were not completely successful, the unemployment rate and the inflation rate were both very modest by the standards of the 1970s and 1980s.

4. The 1960s were the era of the Phillips curve trade-off: policymakers thought they could reduce the unemployment rate more or less to any desired level if they were willing to accept the associated stable inflation rate. The decade opened with unemployment and a deflationary gap that was remedied by the 1964 U.S. tax cut. The worldwide economic expansion of the late 1960s then opened up an inflationary gap. The decade closed with the unsuccessful attempt to dampen inflationary forces through temporary tax increases in 1968–1969.

5. The 1970s saw a series of shocks to the world economy that were to a large extent offset by Canadian policymakers. The decade began with a policy-induced recession. Canada came out of the recession in the mid 1970s into inflation, which was attacked by wage and price controls and increasingly restrictive monetary policies.

6. The experience of the last 50 years shows that policymakers have impressive ability to manipulate aggregate demand. Where we lack understanding and control, however, is in knowledge of how the effects of a change in aggregate demand will be distributed between changes in output, real income, and employment on the one hand and changes in prices on the other.

Topics for Review

The effects on the economy of demand-side shocks
The effects on the economy of supply-side shocks
Causes of stagflation
Monetary gradualism
The effects of price controls in inflationary gap situations

Discussion Questions

1. "We have nothing to fear but fear itself" — Franklin Roosevelt, Inaugural Address, 1933. With hindsight might Roosevelt had been said, "We have nothing to fear but the fear of spending"?

2. In a recent issue of *Business Week* MIT economist Franco Modigliani was quoted as saying, "The view that saving is a nuisance that threatens full employment is dead. As far as I am concerned it should have been dead in the mid 1950s." Under what circumstances might increased savings threaten full employment? Under what circumstances might they help the economy to reach full employment?

3. What theory or theories of inflation are suggested by each of the following quotations?
   a. "February Producer Prices Up a Sharp 1.5 Percent — Rise in Costs of Energy Largest in 6 Years" — newspaper report, 1979.
   b. "From the point of view of dealing with inflation, this [deficit equal to 4 percent of GNE] was an uncomfortably large deficit for the government of Canada to have at a time when the level of economic

activity relative to the economy's demonstrated capacity was as high as it was." — Annual Report of the Governor of the Bank of Canada, 1980.
   c. ". . . inflation was the almost inevitable outgrowth of the enormous international stresses during this period. . . . As attempts [to maintain real income growth] were essentially incompatible with the real constraints of the situation, they resulted in higher inflation. . . ." — Department of Finance, *Economic Review*, 1981.
   d. "The nation's spiraling inflation reflects a global depletion of physical resources and therefore cannot be cured by traditional fiscal and monetary tools" — a study issued in 1980 by the Worldwatch Institute.

4. A recent newspaper article on inflation warned, "It is a mistake to think that every higher price is due to inflation." Give some examples of higher prices that have increased the CPI without being a part of a general inflationary process.

5. A recent newspaper discussion of inflation gave the following arguments *for* and *against* reductions in specific taxes.

For:
   a. "Cuts in payroll taxes would reduce employment costs, thereby helping to slow down price inflation."
   b. "Faster depreciation write-offs would provide greater incentives for new equipment and technology investments, thus boosting productivity."

Against:
   c. "Pumping more money and more purchasing power into the economy through a tax cut without cutting federal spending would do little to restrain inflation [indeed it would increase it]."
   d. "A better approach would be to achieve a budget surplus and pay off the federal debt."

Match each one of the above statements with the following theoretical category that best describes it.
   (i) Shift the aggregate demand curve to the right.
   (ii) Shift the aggregate supply curve downward.
   (iii) Shift the aggregate demand curve to the left.
   (iv) Shift the kink on the aggregate supply curve outward to the right.

6. Interviewed at the end of 1978, Fred Kahn, President Carter's newly appointed "anti-inflation czar," answered the question "Will President Carter's new [anti-inflation] program succeed?" with a resounding, "It has got to succeed." Taking, say, a two-year time horizon, did it succeed?

Current Issues in Macroeconomic Policy

42

In this chapter we consider the controversies over some alleged causes of and cures for our present macroeconomic ills. In the current disagreement over aspects of macroeconomic policy two extreme views can be seen.[1]

In the first view, held by many monetarists, the free-market economy has strong self-regulating tendencies: if a satisfactory general climate is maintained, the economy will tend naturally toward full employment and a relatively stable price level. At the same time, private initiative, spurred on by the profit motive, will yield a satisfactory growth of real national income.

In this view the government's attempts to stabilize the economy will usually be perverse. They will cause larger recessions on the downside, and bigger inflations on the upside, than would have occurred had government policy been passive. Instead of trying to stabilize the economy, government policy should take a very stable stance. The fiscal stance should be one of low and stable government expenditure and a budget that is balanced cyclically if not annually. The monetary stance should be one of a constant rate of growth of the money supply, say 3 percent annually, year in and year out, to accommodate the increased demand for money associated with a growth of wealth and full-employment income. Against this stable backdrop, the natural

[1] "Extreme" implies only the descriptive statement that the view lies at one end or the other of a spectrum of views. It does not imply a judgmental statement that the view is wrong, subversive, or otherwise undesirable. The history of ideas is full of examples where extreme views proved correct and moderate views wrong (and vice versa).

corrective forces of the economy can be relied on to prevent the extremes of serious recessions and serious inflation.

The second view, held by many Keynesians, maintains that the free enterprise economy has weak self-regulatory powers. Fluctuations in autonomous expenditure, especially investment, will give rise to fluctuations in national income and unemployment. As a result of the restrictive practices of monopolies and the tendency of large corporations to avoid risks and adopt safe and cautious policies, the income growth rate will be low. Further, the enormous power of large unions and corporations may cause wage cost-push inflations that cannot be blamed on monetary mismanagement.

In this view, active government intervention is vital. Without such efforts the economy will sometimes undergo wide cyclical fluctuations, with alternating bouts of inflation and unemployment; at other times it will settle into prolonged stable periods of heavy unemployment. To avoid these situations, government must use its instruments of fiscal policy supplemented by monetary policy.

In this chapter we look first at controversies over the control of inflation, then at disputes over stabilization policy in general. We shall consider the two major groups of theories that command widest support and a third that, though less widely accepted among economists, is probably the most popular of the three among the general public!

The first theory, called monetarism, points to variations in the money supply as the major cause of recessions and inflations. The second theory is called neo-Keynesian: "Keynesian" because it derived from the Keynesian theory of income determination, "neo" because it has been developed and amended by much theoretical and empirical work done in the half century since Keynes wrote. The third theory is called post-Keynesian: "Keynesian" since it finds its roots in Keynesian economics, "post" because it really goes beyond Keynesian theory as it is now understood. It emphasizes things that Keynes dis-

cussed at length but which did not find their way into the subsequent formal development of Keynes' model: power structures and institutional rigidities.

In this chapter we give our attention primarily to monetarism and neo-Keynesianism, but we will speak of post-Keynesian theories from time to time. (Note that neo-Keynsians are often referred to as just Keynesians.)

Control of Inflation in the 1980s

As the 1980s began the control of inflation seemed to many to be the major macroeconomic problem. There was much agreement among monetarists and neo-Keynesians on the causes of inflation, but there was considerable disagreement on how to control it.

CAUSES OF INFLATION

The consensus on causes is illustrated in Figure 42-1. The inflation of the last half of the 1970s and the early 1980s was occurring in the face of a substantial GNP gap. The inflation was generated by aggregate supply curve shifts and was being validated by monetary policy. By increasing the money supply, the Bank of Canada allowed the aggregate demand curve to shift upward at about the same speed as aggregate supply. Aggregate supply was shifting upward in part because of import cost-push inflation and in part because of expectational and inertial forces. Monetarists and neo-Keynesians more or less agree on this much. Post-Keynesians also agree, except that they see upward-shifting aggregate supply as a chronic problem associated with the power of trade unions and oligopolistic firms rather than a transitory problem associated with expectations and inertia.

While all agree that monetary policy contributed to the great inflation of the 1970s and early 1980s, agreement stops there. Monetarists are

FIGURE 42-1
Inflation in the 1970s and Early 1980s

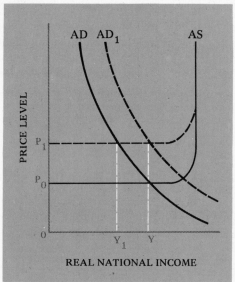

Aggregate supply shifts generated the inflation, and a validating monetary policy permitted accommodating shifts in aggregate demand. Shifts in aggregate supply such as that from P_0AS to P_1AS generated an inflation that would have reduced national income from Y to Y_1 if the aggregate demand curve were fixed. However, the Bank of Canada expanded the money supply about as fast as prices rose, so by the time the aggregate supply curve reached P_1AS, the aggregate demand curve had shifted to AD_1. This produced an inflation with a constant GNP gap.

inclined to blame fluctuations in monetary policy for the fluctuations in the inflation rate. Neo-Keynesians see monetary policy as contributing to the underlying rate but point to nonrecurring supply shocks as a major cause of short-term variations in the inflation rate over the last decade.

There is also disagreement over the role played by wage cost-push. Monetarists dismiss it as of no importance and so do many neo-Keynesians. Other neo-Keynesians, and most post-Keynesians, think wage cost-push important; their view of inflation is thus the most pes-

simistic. In existing circumstances they see inflation as more or less inevitable, given powerful corporations and unions and the existing wage-bargaining arrangements. Even if inflation could be halted temporarily, they believe, it would break out again spontaneously because of continued wage cost-push.

AN APPROPRIATE TARGET RATE OF INFLATION

One major debate centers on the dimensions of a cure for the inflation problem. Must we be satisfied with 2, 3, or 4 percent inflation? Or can we aim at the zero rate that would signal a truly stable price level?

The problem of choosing an appropriate rate lies in the economy's need for continued relative price adjustments. For example, the price of imported oil is being raised periodically by OPEC, and the rising oil price is inevitably taking other energy prices up with it. And in any changing economy, expanding sectors will find their money wages and prices rising in response to their need to expand. When many prices are rising, a zero rate of inflation overall would require compensating reductions in many other prices.

Some monetarists believe there is enough downward flexibility in money wages and prices that the price level—which is after all merely an appropriate average of all prices—can be held constant in spite of increases in some money prices and money wages. Some monetarists and most Keynesians (neo and post) argue that this downward flexibility does not exist. If the money supply were held constant in the face of import cost-push inflation, they believe, other prices would not fall but real income and output would fall. Upward shifts in the aggregate supply curve caused by an increasing price level would shift the economy's equilibrium upward and to the left along its fixed aggregate demand curve. Thus, they argue, the attempt to target for a zero inflation rate would produce a positive inflation rate caused by import cost-push and structural inflation, and this would be accompanied by a growing GNP gap. These economists call for a target rate equal to import cost-push and structural inflation – say, a rate between 2 and 4 percent. They would have the Bank of Canada validate this much inflation, which they hope could be combined with full-employment national income.

Whether or not a zero rate of inflation is possible, most people would settle for the 2 to 4 percent rate that is consistent with import cost-push and structural inflation – at least as an interim target.

POSSIBLE CURES FOR INFLATION

What everyone wants to know is, How can the existing inflation be slowed? What are the available cures?

All the major theories agree that monetary restraint is a *necessary condition* for slowing inflation. If monetary policy allows the aggregate demand curve to shift rightward each year, an inflation will be virtually assured. Even if cost-push forces do not raise the aggregate supply curve, the rising aggregate demand curve will soon generate an inflationary gap that will force the price level upward.

Successful control of inflation requires enough monetary restraint to prevent the aggregate demand curve from shifting rapidly upward year after year.

Monetarist Cures

Monetarists believe that control of the money supply is a sufficient as well as a necessary condition for controlling inflation. They advocate having the Bank of Canada sharply reduce the rate of monetary expansion to one consistent with the target rate of inflation.

This policy is illustrated in Figure 42-2. (For simplicity, the rate of import cost-push and structural inflation is taken as zero.) The money supply is held constant so that the aggregate demand curve is fixed at *AD*. Expectational inflation causes prices to rise, but now the economy moves up its fixed aggregate demand curve with

FIGURE 42-2
The Monetarist Cure for Inflation

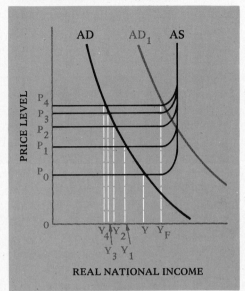

When inflation is being generated by an upward-shifting aggregate supply curve, fixing the aggregate demand curve will cause national income to fall and will eventually bring the inflation to a halt. An ongoing expectational inflation shifts the *AS* curve upward from P_0AS to P_1AS, P_2AS, and so on. If the money supply is held constant, the aggregate demand curve will not shift upward. National income will then fall from Y to Y_1 to Y_2 to Y_3. As the depression worsens, expectations of further inflation weaken and in each period the rate of price rise slackens. Finally the price level comes to rest at P_4, with the corresponding low level of national income at Y_4.

Aggregate demand may then be cautiously expanded toward AD_1 and, if the inflation was mainly expectational, income will rise toward Y_F, with the price level relatively stable at P_4.

a rising price level and falling national income.[2] As national income continues to fall, unemployment and the GNP gap grow. Expectations of

---

[2] The mechanism operating here is the monetary adjustment mechanism described on page 783. As prices rise and the money supply is held constant, a shortage of money develops. This forces up interest rates and causes investment and other interest-sensitive expenditures to be curtailed.

further inflation are weakened as the recession deepens. Eventually people come to expect no further price rises, and the inflation comes to a halt.

Evidence from the recent past suggests that the downward revision of inflationary expectations is slow to occur in response even to severe slumps in economic activity. However, monetarists believe that this may be misleading because governments have been so timid and so quick to abandon their policies. They argue that a really sharp recession, with the government demonstrating that it is determined to keep to a policy of monetary restraint, would cause firms and unions to revise their inflationary expectations downward very quickly. Then perhaps a recession involving 8 to 10 percent unemployment for only one or two years would be enough. Although high unemployment is a heavy cost, it is one worth paying, monetarists argue, if inflation can again be brought back to the 0 to 4 percent range.

Once expectational inflation has been removed, the money supply can be expanded cautiously to reduce the severe money shortage. This move will bring interest rates down and increase investment expenditure, thereby shifting the aggregate demand curve outward. National income will rise, and if the original inflation really was expectational, it should be possible to approach full employment without a further outburst of inflation.

Neo-Keynesian Cures

Neo-Keynesians agree that the monetarists' scenario is possible. However, they argue that the cure would be much slower and therefore much more painful than monetarists think. They stress existing evidence that inflationary expectations and inertias are hard to alter. If indeed rising unemployment can do the job, statistical studies based on past experience suggest that four "percentage-point years" of unemployment are needed to force inertial and expectational inflation down by one percentage point; that is, a rise in unemployment of four percentage points for one year or two percentage points held for two years is required to force inflationary expectations and inertia down from, say, 10 percent to 9 percent.

To appreciate the gloomy implications of these figures, assume that with a labor force of 10 million, unemployment is currently 6 percent and that the actual and the expected inflation rates are 10 percent. In order to force expectational and inertial inflation down to 4 percent, there would have to be 24 "percentage-point years." This means 10 percent unemployment (400,000 more unemployed persons) for six years or 12 percent unemployment (600,000 more unemployed persons) for four years! This, the neo-Keynesians say, would represent a colossal loss in GNP and heavy suffering among the unemployed.

Many neo-Keynesians seek to avoid the lost output by creating a policy package that includes the same monetary restraint that the monetarists advocate but adds to it temporary policies designed to slow the rise in the aggregate supply curve directly. Such a policy package is illustrated in Figure 42-3.

The policies advocated by the Keynesians are called **income policies.** These are any form of direct or indirect intervention by the government into wage and price formation with a view to influencing the rate of inflation (and sometimes the distribution of income as well). Incomes policies vary from direct controls on wages and prices, to tax incentives, to mere "jawboning," which is setting guidelines and relying on voluntary cooperation from the private sector in adhering to them.

Wage and price controls. The most obvious instrument for slowing the upward shift of the aggregate supply curve is direct controls over wages and prices. The rate of monetary expansion would be slowed gradually to validate an inflation rate that fell by, say, two percentage points each year. Wage and price controls would *force* that falling rate of inflation on the economy. Over three years the controls would force the rate down from, say, 10 to 8 to 6 to 4 percent, and the rate of monetary expansion would be slowed correspondingly. Once the target rate of inflation has been achieved and stabilized, the controls can be removed. If everyone then expects the new lower rate to persist, expectational and inertial inflation will have been broken without the recession required by the monetarists' policy that would use monetary restraint alone.

TIPs. Past experience of wage and price controls has made many economists and administrators very reluctant to resort to them. As a result, many Keynesians advocate new methods to achieve the same purpose. The most important are the so-called **tax-based incomes policies (TIPs)**. They provide a tax incentive for management and labor to conform to government established wage and price guidelines. Increases in wages and prices in excess of the guideline rates would be heavily taxed, thereby making firms and unions reluctant to engage in inflation-producing behavior.

TIPs rely on tax incentives to secure voluntary conformity with the guidelines; wage and price controls try to force conformity by legal means.

Consider the neo-Keynesian scenario for using TIPs to slow a 10 percent inflation. Each year the Bank of Canada slows the rate of growth of the money supply so as to validate, say, 2 percent less inflation than last year at the same level of national income. Each year the government's guidelines are lowered to follow the Bank of Canada's monetary policy. The TIPs encourage conformity of wage and price setting with the guidelines so that the inflation rate falls year by year from, say, 10 to 8 to 6 to 4 percent without a reduction in national income.

If it could be initiated without significant cost, the Keynesian package would be superior to that of the monetarists because it avoids the fall in

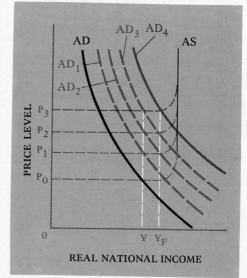

FIGURE 42-3

The Neo-Keynesian Cure for Inflation

When inflation is being generated by aggregate supply shifts, a restrictive monetary policy combined with an incomes policy might halt the inflation without lowering output. An ongoing expectational inflation is met by only a gradual reduction in the rate of monetary expansion so that aggregate demand shifts from *AD* to AD_1 to AD_2 and finally comes to a halt at AD_3. At the same time, incomes policies slow the upward shift in aggregate supply by direct order (wage and price controls) or by incentives (TIPs) so that it shifts upward from P_0AS to P_1AS to P_2AS and comes to a halt at P_3AS. The inflation is slowed and finally halted with no reduction in output.

Once expectations have been stabilized, aggregate demand can be expanded cautiously to AD_4, taking the economy back to full employment at the stable price level P_3.

output and the corresponding rise in unemployment. Critics argue, however, that the TIPs would prove to be little different from wage and price controls. They would be a nightmare to design, costly to administer, ineffectual in restraining wages and prices, and they would have similar distorting effects on the economy. These issues are taken up in the box.

TIPs: Tax-based Incomes Policies

Tax-based incomes policies (TIPs) were originally advanced in 1971 by American economists Henry Wallich and Sidney Weintraub. Advocates of TIPs argue that inflation is not only a demand-pull phenomena but is also the result of cost push. Though they have been advanced in numerous forms, all TIPs programs are basically modifications of the original Wallich-Weintraub proposal.

The Wallich-Weintraub plan. The original proposal called for the imposition of a surtax on any corporation that granted wage increases in excess of some nationally defined guideline. By biting into profits, such a plan would "stiffen the backs of management" against granting excessive wage settlements to workers. Although the basic TIPs plan focused on wage restraint, it was not intended to penalize labor. Because real wage growth is determined by productivity growth, the growth of money wages in excess of productivity growth leads to inflation, eroding any perceived gain by workers. Eventually the wage guidelines would be reduced until they matched the growth rate in national productivity, that is, to a noninflationary rate of wage increase.

Extension to prices. The effectiveness of the original plan depends critically on the assumption that most of the burden of the tax will be absorbed by firms and not shifted to consumers, that is, that firms will not exploit lower wage settlements to increase their profit margins. Advocates of TIPs have argued that competition from smaller firms not subject to the plan and from imports would keep price rises to a minimum. Historical evidence showing price markup over unit labor costs remaining relatively constant is also often cited as proof that corporations will not use TIPs as an excuse to increase their profit margins.

It seems dubious that the constancy of markups experienced during the pre-control period would still prevail after controls are imposed. This has led some economists to suggest that the plan be extended to include prices. This would involve tax penalties for those firms that raise prices in excess of the guidelines. However, a tax penalty that depends on *average* price increases for particular firms raises measurement and index number problems so insurmountable that most analysts are persuaded that this approach is impracticable.

Carrot or stick? Instead of merely punishing firms for failing to maintain the guidelines, rewards in the form of tax rebates could be given to those firms that grant wage increases that fall below the guidelines. Labor could also be involved by means of a payroll tax that places a surtax on workers who hold out for wage increases in excess of the guidelines and awards tax reductions to those who settle for less.

Under the penalty approach a TIPs program could be limited to, say, the top 200 firms, which produce more than 50 percent of GNP and provide most of the employment. These firms already have sophisticated accounting departments that could readily provide most of the information needed to imple-

Post-Keynesian Cures

A third position is that of the post-Keynesians. They contend that the upward shift in the aggregate supply curve is caused by wage cost-push, price-push, and various structural rigidities. Unlike inertia and expectations, these causes will not go away merely because the inflament such a plan. Few if any of the smaller firms would clamor to be included in the scheme if inclusion only raised the possibility of being penalized for granting excessive wage settlements. Under a penalty-reward approach, however, all firms, and possibly labor, would demand to be included because they stand to gain from reaching settlements that more than satisfy the wage guidelines. The administrative burden of implementing a penalty-reward scheme would be much greater than that of a penalty only scheme.

Administrative problems. Despite the apparent simplicity of a TIPs program on paper, there are numerous practical problems that would have to be surmounted before such a policy could be implemented. Few if any of the supporters of TIPs have gone beyond a general description of how the program would operate.

For example, what should constitute the basic accounting unit over which wage increases are to be measured—the plant, the corporation, or the large vertically integrated industry? It may not be feasible to measure average wage increases for economic units in a manner appropriate for a tax-based penalty or subsidy. The unit for tax accounting purposes often bears little resemblance to the unit that negotiates wages with its workers.

For a second example, should a TIPs program be temporary or permanent? Under the former, labor and management might agree to defer settlements until after the program ceases, thereby evading the controls and rendering them ineffective. Under the latter,

workers who were not able to adjust their settlements to an equitable level before the program was implemented may suffer permanently.

Another administrative detail not specifically addressed by most advocates is: How would nonmonetary benefits fit into a TIP program? Should pensions, unemployment insurance, health insurance, and other programs contributed to by employers be included in the measurement of overall wage increases? Most economists would say yes, for to omit them would allow employers to evade the guidelines by increasing the size of the workers' benefit package. Yet measurement of these benefits may be administratively impossible. Separating increases in the wage rate from increases in overall labor income would be an administrative nightmare; wage drift like that which plagued the European experience with incomes policies (see page 870) might become a problem.

Of necessity the rules governing wage settlement behavior would be arbitrary, yet the means to evade them are innumerable. It would be impossible to cover every eventuality under the rules, and to try to do so would only further increase the administrative burden. It is difficult to determine in detail how a particular TIPs would work until someone has tried it. In the meantime, some believe that in spite of the cost TIPs would be worth their price because they would slow inflation. Others believe TIPs would be extremely costly because of the nightmarish web of rules and regulations they would eventually spin and because they would not in the end restrain inflation significantly.

tion rate is forced to a low level for a year or two. Instead, inflationary pressure will always be present when the economy is anywhere near full employment. Post-Keynesians thus advocate

permanent wage and price controls or TIPs as the only way to achieve anything approaching full employment and relatively stable prices.

At the moment there is little evidence to sup-

Supply-side Economics

Toward the end of the 1970s a new cry was frequently heard in popular discussion and in serious debate: supply-side economics. Supply-side economics is not new. Indeed, it is what Adam Smith's *Wealth of Nations* was all about. In its modern version, like many general but catchy terms, it sometimes means all things to all people.

1. In explaining inflation and stagflation, for one group it means an emphasis on the aggregate supply curve. As we have seen at length in these chapters, "supply-side shocks" are now a major part of most explanations of what happened in the 1970s.
2. In controlling inflation, for a second group it means an emphasis on pushing the aggregate supply curve outward rather than reining the aggregate demand curve inward. This proposition concerns short-run stabilization policy.
3. In concern over living standards, for a third group it means an emphasis on pushing the aggregate supply curve out to the right rather than manipulating aggregate demand. The motto here might be, "It is more important to increase full-employment national income than to try to reduce the temporary deviations from it that the market economy produces." This proposition concerns long-run growth policy.

   Point (1) is a diagnosis of our past ills; for a

discussion of the role of aggregate supply shifts in explaining past events, see pages 864–867. Points (2) and (3) are policy prescriptions for improving things in the future. Both require pushing the aggregate supply curve outward in the manner shown in Figure 41-1 on page 856. The key idea is to provide the appropriate *incentives* for the private sector to do the job. How might this be done?

a. *By encouraging saving.* Keynes emphasized the negative effect of saving on aggregate demand. Supply-side economics emphasizes its positive effect—that of encouraging investment in order to increase productive capacity and hence full-employment national income.
b. *By encouraging labor force participation.* Reducing taxes, the argument says, will make people work more, and increasing the labor supply will increase full-employment output.
c. *By encouraging risk taking.* Cutting taxes and regulations will make businesses more willing to invest and to innovate. Risking capital to introduce new products and new methods is historically one of the great mechanisms for economic growth. If we can encourage more of it, full-employment national income will grow faster.
d. *By encouraging labor mobility.* Stop lavish welfare schemes that encourage the unem-

port the post-Keynesian view of the causes of inflation. Therefore their extreme solution, which would take Canada significantly closer to having a command economy, does not seem to many economists to be appropriate.

Post-Keynesians also stress the political causes of inflation. They study political circumstances that lead governments to adopt policies

that either cause or validate inflations. They argue, for example, that whenever a democratic government persistently follows inflationary policies, it is because a coalition of groups believes that, whatever the public rhetoric, it is actually gaining from inflation. Thus post-Keynesians predict that inflation will not be controlled until these political circumstances are changed. Some

ployed to stay in depressed regions. In the absence of state support, they should be forced to move to regions where they could earn their living productively.

e. *By getting people back to producing goods rather than tax loopholes*. Millions of high-powered lawyers, accountants, and entrepreneurs are currently employed solely in finding loopholes to protect high-income individuals and firms from heavy tax liabilities. If we eliminate high marginal tax rates, it will not be worthwhile for the rich to pay for these expensive services and to devote so much time to tax affairs. The resources will then be freed to produce goods and services that contribute to people's want satisfaction.

The number of proposals is myriad. All have the intended effect of increasing full-employment income by increasing the supply of capital or labor or by increasing the rate of technical change.

If even a small increase in the growth rate of full-employment income could be achieved, the long-term effects on living standards would be enormous (as Table 43-1 on page 911 illustrates). Thus policy (3) is a viable objective. Increasing the growth rate of full employment *will* raise living standards.

The second objective, however, is more debatable. It would, however, be an enormous

achievement to raise the growth rate by one-half of one percentage point, but the effect on the *level* of income two years down the line would only be 1 percent more full-employment output. In the face of an inflationary gap of, say, 10 percent (aggregate demand is 10 percent greater than full-employment aggregate supply at current prices), increasing aggregate supply by 1 percent is not going to do much to the inflation rate. Even the conservative economist Herbert Stein of the American Enterprise Institute, who could be expected to be sympathetic to many supply-side measures, warned in early 1980:

Despite the tone of much of the current argument, the propositions of supply-side economics are not matters of ideology or principle. They are matters of arithmetic. So far one must say that the arithmetic of any of the "newer" propositions is highly doubtful. Supply-side economics may yet prove to be the irritant which, like the grain of sand in the oyster shell, produces a pearl of new economic wisdom. But up to this point the pearl has not appeared.*

Whether or not its potential for controlling inflation is overstated—certainly supply effects are important—there is no doubt that supply-side economics in one form or another is here to stay.

*The AEI Economist, April 1980, published by American Enterprise Institute.

people believe that, in looking for the political roots of inflation, post-Keynesians are on stronger ground than when they present their wage cost-push and price-push theory of the immediate economic causes of inflation.

Some ideas on control of inflation that cut across monetarist and Keynesian camps are covered by *supply-side economics*. These are discussed in the box, which notes that supply-side economics focuses on increasing the level of output forthcoming at full employment.

Controversies over Stabilization Policy

Stabilization policy, as we have seen, involves the use of monetary and fiscal policy to shift the aggregate demand and expenditure functions in order to avoid the extremes of large inflationary and deflationary gaps. Differences between monetarists and neo-Keynesians on this subject have narrowed somewhat over the past 15 years, yet significant differences remain.

CAUSES OF CYCLICAL FLUCTUATIONS

Monetarist Views

Monetarists believe that monetary causes are the major source of serious fluctuations in national income.[3] The modern interpretation of business cycles as having mainly monetary causes relies heavily on the evidence advanced by Milton Friedman and Anna Schwartz in their monumental *A Monetary History of the United States, 1867–1960.* They establish a strong correlation between changes in the money supply and changes in the level of business activity. Major recessions are found to be associated with absolute declines in the money supply, and minor recessions with the slowing of the rate of increase in the money supply below its long-term trend.

The correlation between changes in the money supply and changes in the level of business activity is now accepted by virtually all economists. But there is controversy over how this is to be interpreted; do changes in the money supply cause changes in the level of business activity, or vice versa?

Friedman and Schwartz maintain that changes in the money supply cause changes in business activity. They argue, for example, that the severity of the Great Depression was due to a major

contraction in the money supply. Their analysis runs along the following lines.

The stock market crash of 1929, and other factors associated with a moderate downswing in business activity during the late 1920s, led to a reduction in the public's desire to hold demand deposits and an increase in its desire for cash. The banking system could not meet this increased demand for liquidity without help from the central bank.[4] The American Federal Reserve System had been set up to provide just such emergency assistance to basically sound banks that were unable to meet sudden demands by their depositors for currency. However, the Fed refused to extend the necessary help, and successive waves of bank failures followed. During each wave, literally hundreds of banks failed, ruining many depositors and worsening an already severe depression. In the last half of 1931, almost 2,000 American banks were forced to suspend operations! One consequence of this was a sharp drop in the money supply; by 1933 the money supply was 35 percent below the level of 1929.

For monetarists, fluctuations in the money supply cause fluctuations in national income.

Neo-Keynesian Views

The neo-Keynesians' view on the causes of cyclical fluctuations in the economy has two parts. First, it emphasizes variations in investment as a cause of business cycles and stresses nonmonetary causes of such variations. Many pre-Keynesian economists also took this view.[5]

---

[3] The view that fluctuations often have monetary causes is not new. The English economist R.G. Hawtrey, the Austrian Nobel laureate F. A. von Hayek, the Swedish economist Knut Wicksell are prominent among those who earlier gave monetary factors an important role in their explanations of the turning points in cycles and/or the tendency for expansions and contractions, once begun, to become cumulative and self-reinforcing. Modern monetarists carry on this tradition.

[4] As we saw in Chapter 37, banks are never able to meet from their own reserves a sudden demand to withdraw currency on the part of a large fraction of their depositors. Their reserves are always inadequate to meet such a demand.

[5] Like the monetarists, the neo-Keynesians are modern advocates of views that have a long history. The great Austrian (and later American) economist Joseph Schumpeter stressed such explanations early in the present century. The Swedish economist Wicksell and the German Speithoff both stressed this aspect of economic fluctuations before the emergence of the Keynesian school of thought.

Second, neo-Keynesians believe that the economy lacks natural corrective mechanisms that will always force it easily and quickly back to full employment. They believe that the economy may settle into an *underemployment equilibrium,* where it may stay for a long time unless it is forced out by an active stabilization policy. If investment opportunities seem unattractive, the equilibrium national income (where aggregate desired expenditure equals income) may leave a large GNP gap. Monetarists charge that there are strong forces, omitted from the Keynesian model, that will drive income back to its full-employment level.[6] Keynesians respond that these forces are weak or nonexistent (and are thus omitted from their model of the determination of national income).[7]

Neo-Keynesians reject what they regard as the extreme monetarist view that only money matters in explaining cyclical fluctuations. Many believe that both monetary and nonmonetary forces are important in explaining the behavior of the economy. Although they accept serious monetary mismanagement as one potential source of economic fluctuations, they do not believe that it is the only or even the major source of such fluctuations. Thus they deny the monetary interpretation of business cycle history given by Friedman and Schwartz.

As for the 1930s, neo-Keynesians accept the argument that the Federal Reserve System's behavior was perverse. However, they argue that the cyclical behavior of investment and consumption expenditure was the major cause of the Great Depression. In support of this view, they point out that in Canada, where the central bank came to the aid of the banking system, bank failures were trivial during the Great Depression,

and as a consequence the money supply did *not* shrink drastically as it did in the United States. In spite of these markedly different monetary histories, the behavior of the GNP gap, investment expenditure, and unemployment in Canada was very similar to that in the United States.[8]

Neo-Keynesians accept the correlation between changes in the money supply and changes in the level of economic activity, but their explanation reverses the causality suggested by the monetarists: the neo-Keynesians argue that changes in the level of economic activity tend to cause changes in the money supply. They offer several reasons for this, but only the most important need be mentioned.

Neo-Keynesians point out that from 1945 to the early 1970s most central banks tended to stabilize interest rates as the target variable of monetary policy. To do this they had to increase the money supply during upswings in the business cycle and decrease it during downswings. This created the positive correlation on which the monetarists rely. The central bank followed this monetary policy when an expansion got under way because the demand for money tended to increase, and when there was no increase in the money supply, interest rates would rise. The central bank might prevent this rise in interest rates (by buying bonds offered for sale at current prices), but in so doing it would increase banks' reserves and thereby inject new money into the economy. Similarly, in a cyclical contraction interest rates would tend to fall unless the central bank stepped in and sold bonds to keep interest rates up. And if it did so, this would decrease the money supply.

For neo-Keynesians, fluctuations in national income cause fluctuations in the money supply.

This argument applies to relatively mild cyclical swings; most neo-Keynesians agree that major changes in the money supply induced by

---

[6] The two main forces are a fall in the rate of interest, which encourages investment, and a fall in the price level, which encourages consumption by the so-called Pigou effect.

[7] Keynesians believe that the interest elasticity of investment is very low, especially in recessions, when the ability to sell goods at all over the next few years is the main determinant of investment. They also point to evidence that the price level does not fall significantly, so whatever the effects of a fall might be, they are not felt in practice.

[8] Of course it can be argued that the recession in the United States was the *cause* of the depression in Canada via the export multiplier process outlined in Chapter 33.

the central bank can be a cause of changes in national income.

CONTROL OF CYCLICAL FLUCTUATIONS: MONETARY VERSUS FISCAL POLICY[9]

Monetarists believe that national income can be influenced strongly by monetary policy and only weakly by fiscal policy. Keynesians believe that fiscal policy may be more potent than monetary policy. The difference in views turns partly on the slopes of two relations that both groups agree do exist. The different views are illustrated in Figure 42-4.

The Effect of Changes in the Money Supply

The demand for money. The first relation is the demand for money. Monetarists believe it is insensitive to interest rates; Keynesians think it is sensitive to interest rates because money is a near substitute for a whole range of short-term, interest-earning assets.

An expansionary monetary policy creates an excess supply of money. Firms and households seek to buy bonds with their surplus money, and this lowers the rate of interest. The rate falls until everyone is prepared to hold the increased supply of money. If the monetarists are right, this will require a large fall in the interest rate; if the Keynesians are right, there need be only a small fall.

A contractionary monetary policy creates excess demand by lowering the supply of money. Firms and households seek to restore their money balances by selling bonds, and the rate of interest rises until everyone is satisfied to hold only the reduced money supply. If the monetarists are right, this will require a large rise in the interest rate; if the Keynesians are right, there need be only a small rise.

Investment expenditure. The second relation is the marginal efficiency of investment function. A

rise in the rate of interest lowers investment expenditure, and a fall in the rate of interest raises it. Monetarists hold that investment expenditure is highly sensitive to interest rates. Keynesians believe that it is influenced mainly by sales, profits, and expectations and that it does not respond greatly to the rate of interest, at least over the short term.

Implications for the Effectiveness of Fiscal and Monetary Policy

The shapes just discussed have direct implications for the effectiveness of monetary policy, as illustrated in Figure 42-5.

According to the monetarists, changes in the money supply cause large changes in interest rates that in turn cause large changes in expenditure. According to the Keynesians, changes in the money supply cause small changes in interest rates that in turn cause small or negligible changes in expenditure.

The same assumptions about sensitivities to interest rates cause monetarists and Keynesians to disagree over the potency of fiscal policy, as illustrated in Figure 42-6. Consider an increase in government expenditure. This raises national income and creates excess demand for money because of a rise in the demand for transactions balances. The rate of interest rises until everyone is content to hold the existing stock of money. The rise in the interest rate lowers private investment expenditure. (A parallel analysis applies to a decline in government expenditure.)

According to the monetarists, changes in government expenditure will induce large changes in interest rates that in turn cause large offsetting changes in private investment expenditure, leaving a small net effect on aggregate demand. According to the neo-Keynesians, changes in government expenditure cause only small changes in interest rates that in turn cause small or negligible offsetting changes in investment expenditure.

[9] This section may be omitted without loss of continuity.

FIGURE 42-4
Monetarist and Neo-Keynesian Views on Interest Sensitivities

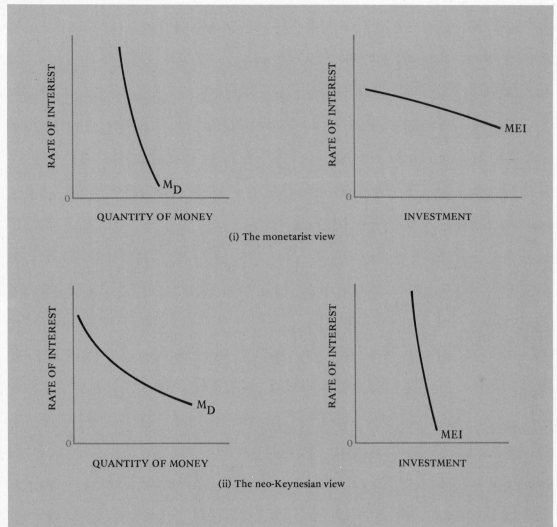

(i) The monetarist view

(ii) The neo-Keynesian view

Monetarists and neo-Keynesians disagree about the interest sensitivities of the demand for money and the marginal efficiency of investment functions. M_D is the demand for money and *MEI* is the marginal efficiency of investment function that relates investment expenditure to the rate of interest. Monetarists hold that the demand for money does not respond much to changes in the rate of interest, while investment expenditure is very sensitive to such changes. Neo-Keynesians hold that the demand for money is very sensitive to changes in interest rates, while investment expenditure is insensitive to such changes.

The tendency just discussed is called the **crowding out effect.** It may be defined as the offsetting reduction in private investment that follows an expansionary fiscal policy due to a rise in interest rates. Monetarists believe the crowding out effect is large, so that an increase in government expenditure will crowd out almost as much private expenditure and thus have only a small

FIGURE 42-5
Monetarist and Neo-Keynesian Views on Monetary Policy

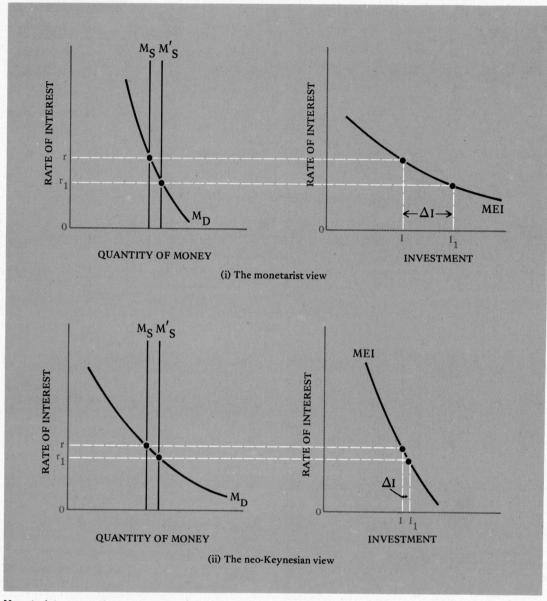

(i) The monetarist view

(ii) The neo-Keynesian view

Monetarist assumptions make monetary policy very effective; neo-Keynesian assumptions make it relatively ineffective. Initially the economy is in equilibrium with an interest rate of r and investment expenditure of I. In both parts the expansionary monetary policy of the central bank shifts the money supply to M'_s. The rate of interest falls to r_1, and this causes an increase in investment expenditure of ΔI (from I to I_1).

(i) In the monetarist view, ΔI is large. Monetary policy is effective.

(ii) In the neo-Keynesian view, ΔI is small. Monetary policy is ineffective.

FIGURE 42-6
Monetarist and Neo-Keynesian Views on Fiscal Policy

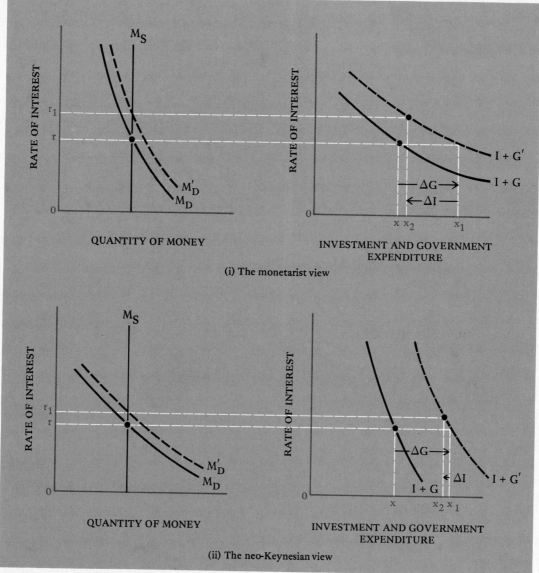

(i) The monetarist view

(ii) The neo-Keynesian view

Neo-Keynesian assumptions make fiscal policy very effective; monetarist assumptions make it relatively ineffective. Initially the economy is in equilibrium with an interest rate of r and investment plus government expenditure of X. Suppose the government increases its expenditure by $\Delta G = X_1 - X$. The effect on national income is given by the multiplier formula (see page 618) if the interest rate remains at r. But when expenditure rises, the transactions demand for money rises. This shifts M_D to M'_D, and leads to an increase in the rate of interest to r_1. The rise in interest rates leads to a reduction in interest-sensitive investment expendi-

ture by $X_1 - X_2$. This "crowding out" of private investment expenditure, caused by a rise in interest rates brought about by the expansionary fiscal policy, reduces the multiplier because the decline in investment partially offsets the rise in government expenditure. The net effect of the two changes is an increase of $G + I$ from X to X_2.

(i) In the monetarist world, the crowding-out effect is large so fiscal policy is relatively ineffective.

(ii) In the neo-Keynesian world, the crowding-out effect is small so fiscal policy is relatively effective.

net expansionary effect on income. Keynesians believe the crowding out effect is small when the economy is suffering from a substantial GNP gap, which is when one would wish to use an expansionary fiscal policy. In this case only a small part of any rise in government expenditure will be offset by a fall in private expenditure. Thus there will be a large net increase in aggregate expenditure and hence a large increase in equilibrium national income.

Policy Preferences

When policy intervention is called for, monetarists have a strong preference for monetary policy. Keynesians tend to be less strong in their preferences. They believe that monetary policy can influence national income through its effects on interest rates. Thus they tend to deny that there is serious conflict between monetary and fiscal policies; they see the policies as complements to each other.

Neo-Keynesians tend to place heavier emphasis on fiscal policy. They do this because they believe that monetary policy may prove weak in major depressions, when it is particularly important to have some policy intervention. In addition, they are disturbed by the uneven effects of monetary policy. A restrictive monetary policy, for example, tends to fall particularly heavily on potential home owners, small businesses, and rapidly expanding firms specializing in new products.

When monetary restraints are applied, home building tends to be seriously affected because interest costs are a major part of the total expense of buying a house. Thus a restrictive monetary policy hits at potential home owners, particularly those with modest means who would have the most difficulty in raising a mortgage.

Small firms usually have more trouble getting credit than do large firms. It can be argued that the continual use of monetary policy reinforces the already strong tendency for large firms to dominate the economy. The reason is that new products are often manufactured by small, new, rapidly expanding firms. Since the costs of production must be met before goods are sold, rapidly expanding firms usually find themselves in constant need of credit to meet the gap between paying their costs and receiving money from the sale of their goods. New firms are the source of much economic growth, yet they are the firms that are hardest hit, and sometimes driven into insolvency, by restrictive monetary policies that make it impossible for them to obtain the credit they need.

For all these reasons, neo-Keynesians call for an active stabilization policy with fiscal policy playing a major role and monetary policy playing, at most, a supporting part.

The Micro Foundations of Monetarism and Neo-Keynesianism[10]

Keynes made a vast advance in our study of the overall behavior of the economy by concentrating on a few aggregated functions such as consumption and investment. For a long time Keynesian economics seemed to work well both in explaining the overall behavior of the economy and in suggesting successful policies for controlling inflation and unemployment. As long as it worked reasonably well, few were interested in just how it worked. Then, as control of the economy by means of traditional fiscal and monetary tools seemed to become more and more difficult during the late 1960s and the 1970s, the question of the foundations of the Keynesian theory became more pressing. This concern took the form of asking: What behavior in individual markets for products and factors of production is implied by the Keynesian aggregate relation-

---

[10] This section (to page 902) may be omitted without loss of continuity.

ships? The question involves the *micro foundations* or *micro underpinnings* of macro models.

In the late 1960s and early 1970s the monetarist model made its serious challenge as an alternative model for understanding the macro behavior of the economy and predicting appropriate policies. The explanations of observed events and the prediction of policies for changing them that were suggested by the monetarist model were very different from those of the Keynesian model.

The micro underpinnings are at the heart of the debate between monetarism and neo-Keynesianism. Consequently they are at the frontier of much modern research. The issues are important, but they are also difficult; we need to be aware of them in broad outline if not in detail.

ONE MONETARIST MICROECONOMIC MODEL

Many economists accept the main monetarist view that monetary forces are the most important cause acting on inflation and unemployment. These economists differ among themselves on many other matters concerning the behavior of the economy. Thus there is no single accepted monetarist microeconomic model of the economy. Many monetarists, however, follow the leads of Milton Friedman in his 1968 Presidential Address to the American Economics Association and Professor Edmund Phelps in his classic attack on the theory of the stable Phillips curve, also published in 1968. These economists view the markets of the economy as competitive. They realize, of course, that perfect competition does not exist everywhere in the economy, but they believe that the forces of competition are strong — strong enough so that a model based on the theory of perfect competition will be closer to the real behavior of the economy than one based on the theory of oligopoly to which many neo-Keynesians appeal.

According to this prototype model, markets behave more or less as if they were perfectly competitive. In particular, prices and wages are flexible and they adjust to establish equilibrium at all times. When a competitive market is in equilibrium (see Chapter 5), the market is said to have *cleared,* which means that every purchaser has been able to buy all he or she wishes to buy and every seller has been able to sell all he or she wishes to sell at the going price.[11] When each and every market is in equilibrium, there is full employment of all resources. The prices that clear markets are called **market clearing prices.**

According to the monetarists, departure from full-employment equilibrium occurs mainly because people make mistakes. How does this happen?

Assume that each of the economy's markets is in equilibrium; there is full employment, prices are stable, and the actual and expected rates of inflation are zero. Now let the government increase the money supply at some constant rate, say 5 percent per year. People find themselves with unwanted money balances, which they seek to spend. For simplicity, assume that this leads to an increase in desired expenditure on all commodities: the demand for each commodity shifts to the right, and competitively determined prices rise. Individual decision makers see their selling prices go up and mistake the increase for a rise in their own relative price (because they expect the overall rate of inflation to be zero). Firms will produce more and workers will work more because both groups think they are getting an increased relative price for what they sell. Thus total output and employment rise.

Sooner or later both groups will realize that all prices are rising and that their own relative prices are in fact unchanged. Since relative prices determine behavior, and since relative prices are unchanged, output and employment will fall back to their initial level. The extra output and em-

---

[11] Competitive markets clear only at the equilibrium price. At any other price there are either unsatisfied would-be purchasers (excess demand) or unsatisfied would-be sellers (excess supply).

ployment occurred only while people were being fooled; when they realized that all prices were rising at 5 percent, they reverted to their initial behavior. The only difference is that now the actual and expected rate of inflation is 5 percent.

Now assume that the government wishes to continue to have the extra output and employment that was achieved while people were being fooled. To do this, it doubles the rate of increase in the money supply. This increases demand, and prices begin to rise by 10 percent. As long as people expect the overall rate of inflation to be 5 percent, they will make the same mistake they made before. Thinking their own relative price has risen by 5 percent, workers will work harder and firms will produce more. Thus the extra output and employment will be restored, but only because everyone is again being fooled.

Sooner or later people will see that all prices are rising by 10 percent and realize that their own relative price has never changed. Their behavior will then revert to what it was originally. The extra output and employment is lost once more, and now the actual and expected inflation rate is 10 percent. To achieve the higher output and employment again, the government must now raise the rate of monetary expansion to 15 percent!

If the government tries to maintain the position of higher output, it will have to expand the money supply ever faster to validate an *accelerating* inflation rate. If it does not do so, people will soon realize that relative prices are not changing, and their behavior will revert to what it was originally.

Now return to the initial equilibrium with no monetary expansion and stable prices. Then let the government reduce the money supply at a constant rate so that demand falls off. Prices begin to fall. Firms and workers mistakenly think their own relative prices are falling; firms voluntarily produce less, and laborers voluntarily work less. Output falls and a deflation occurs. Sooner or later people will notice that *all* prices are falling and realize that they have been fooled—their relative price has not changed. Output and em-

ployment revert to their original levels, but now the actual and expected rate of "inflation" is −5 percent.

To restore the cut in output and employment, the rate of monetary contraction must be raised to 10 percent. Once again people will be fooled for a while, workers will work less and firms produce less, and sooner or later they will discover the real situation and their behavior will revert to what it was—only now the actual and expected rate of "inflation" is −10 percent!

According to the monetarist theory of the economy, deviations from full employment occur only because people make mistakes that cause markets to clear at more or less than full-employment output. People are not prevented from selling as many commodities or as much labor as they wish; the contraction or expansion in output is *voluntary*.

The major conclusion following from this part of the model is that there is no long-term trade-off between inflation and national income. An attempt to hold income above its full-employment level will lead not to a constant rate of inflation, but to a continuously accelerating inflation. Most economists now accept one version or another of this view that inflation will tend to accelerate if income is held permanently below its full-employment level. Most neo-Keynesians do not accept, however, that increases in output above Y_F occur only because workers and firms make mistakes.

The other part of the model is more contentious. The downward flexibility of prices in the competitive model leads to the prediction that as long as national income is below its full-employment level the price level should *fall* at an ever-accelerating rate. Neo-Keynesians say that the observed downward inflexibility of the price level totally refutes this view even as a prototype explanation. Neo-Keynesians also reject the prediction that the main cause of GNP gaps is voluntary reductions in employment and output due to errors in reading the signals provided by the price system.

The Theory of Rational Expectations

This monetarist model has recently been augmented by the addition of the theory of *rational expectations,* first discussed in Chapter 39. According to this theory, people learn fairly quickly from their mistakes; while random errors can be made, systematic and persistent errors are not made.

Not all monetarists accept the full theory of rational expectations. For those who do, however, the contrast with the neo-Keynesians is extreme. Not only is there no long-term trade-off between output and employment on the one hand and inflation on the other (with which many neo-Keynesians would agree), but there is no chance for fiscal or monetary policy to stabilize the economy in the face of small or large inflationary or deflationary gaps. Government policy can do harm but cannot do good (except by random chance). Thus even in the face of major recessions, laissez-faire is the best stabilization policy conceivable. Let us see how this argument proceeds.

The theory says that people learn and will alter their behavior when they find they are making systematic mistakes. Suppose, for example, you always thought that next year's inflation rate would be the same as this year's rate but in fact it always increased by two percentage points over what it was last year. When this year's rate was 2 percent, you expected next year's rate to be 2 percent, but it would turn out to be 4 percent. You then expected the following year's rate to be 4 percent, but it would turn out to be 6 percent. And so it went, with you constantly underpredicting the rate by 2 percent. According to the theory of rational expectations, you would soon notice this and revise your expectations to remove the error. You would then look for the rate to rise by two points each year, and as long as the pattern continued, your expectations would be right on target.

According to the theory of rational expectations, people do not make persistent, systematic errors in predicting the overall inflation rate; however, they may make unsystematic errors.

What are the implications of combining the monetarist micro foundations with the theory of rational expectations? (1) According to the monetarists' micro foundations, deviations from full employment occur only because of errors in predicting the price level (which allows workers and firms to mistake changes in the price level for changes in relative prices). (2) According to the theory of rational expectations, errors in predicting the price level are only random. (3) It follows from (1) and (2) that the economy's deviations from full employment must be random. (4) It follows from (3) that there is no room for systematic stabilization policy; although governments can identify and offset systematic deviations from full employment, it is the essence of random fluctuations that they cannot be predicted well enough to be offset by planned stabilization policy.

The strongest monetarist attack on stabilization policy has two parts. The first is a model of an economy where deviations from full employment occur because of errors. The second is a theory of people's expectations that predicts that persistent systematic errors—and hence persistent systematic deviations from full employment—will not occur.

According to this view there is no room for active government policy to stabilize the economy. The causes of fluctuations are random (although because of long lags the behavior of the economy may be systematically cyclical). It is in the nature of random fluctuations that they cannot be foreseen and offset. Thus there is no room for stabilization policy to reduce the fluctuations in the economy by offsetting the disturbances that emanate from the private sector.

THE NEO-KEYNESIAN MICRO FOUNDATIONS

The neo-Keynesian micro foundations emphasize the oligopolistic nature of the economy. Large firms are seen as price setters, not price takers. Their short-run cost curves tend to be

The Progress of Economics

In this chapter we have discussed a number of current controversies about the behavior of the economy and the evidence relating to them that is now available. General acceptance of the view that the validity of economic theories should be tested by confronting their predictions with the mass of all available evidence is fairly new in economics. At this point you might reread the quotation from Lord William Beveridge given on page xxix of this book. The controversy that Beveridge describes was the one that followed the 1936 publication of Keynes' *The General Theory of Employment, Interest and Money.* Keynes' work gave rise to the macroeconomics discussed in Part Nine and used so often in subsequent sections of this text. The question of how various parts of macroeconomic theory have been or could be tested has been raised at many points in this book: you might reflect on how very different this approach to the problem of accepting or rejecting theories is from the approach described by Beveridge.

Since 1936 great progress has been made in economics in relating theory to evidence. This progress has been reflected in the superior ability of governments to achieve their policy objectives. The financial aspects of World War II were far better handled than those of World War I. When President Roosevelt tried to reduce unemployment in the 1930s, his efforts were greatly hampered by the failure even of economists to realize the critical importance of budget deficits in raising aggregate demand and in injecting newly created money into the economy. When the Vietnam War caused the U.S. government to adopt expansive fiscal and monetary policies, economists

had no trouble in predicting the outcome: more involvement abroad was obtained at the cost of heavy inflationary pressure at home.

Such important policy areas as the running of wars, the curing of major depressions, and coping with inflations are where the general tone of theories is tested, even if all their specific predictions are not. In some general sense, then, economic theories have always been subjected to empirical tests. When they were wildly at variance with the facts, the ensuing disaster could not but be noticed, and the theories were discarded or amended in the light of what was learned. Our current inability to avoid the twin problems of inflation and unemployment is a case in point—and it is leading to intensive new research.

The advances of economics in the last 40 years reflect economists' changed attitudes toward empirical observations. Today economists are much less likely to dismiss theories just because they do not like them and to refuse to abandon theories just because they do like them. Economists are more likely to try to base their theories as much as possible on empirical observation and to accept empirical relevance as the ultimate arbiter of the value of theories. As human beings, we may be anguished at the upsetting of a pet theory; as scientists, we should try to train ourselves to take pleasure in it because of the new knowledge gained thereby. It has been said that one of the great tragedies of science is the continual slaying of beautiful theories by ugly facts. It must always be remembered that when theory and fact come into conflict, it is theory, not fact, that must give way.

fairly flat, and they set prices by adding a relatively inflexible markup to their costs.[12] They then sell what they can at the going price. This is not a model of market clearing; firms will usually be able and willing to sell more than their current sales at the going price. Cyclical fluctuations in aggregate demand cause cyclical fluctuations in the demand for each firm's products, which in turn cause individual firms to make cyclical variations in *output and employment* rather than in *price*.

While in the monetarist model fluctuations in aggregate demand have their impact on mainly prices, in the neo-Keynesian model their main impact is on output and employment.

The same is true for labor markets in the neo-Keynesian model. Wages are set with the price level and productivity in view, but they are relatively insensitive to short-term cyclical fluctuations in demand.

Let us see how this short-term wage inflexibility may stem from rational behavior on the part of workers. If wage rates fluctuate to clear labor markets, wages will fluctuate over the cycle. *All* workers will then bear the uncertainty associated with the cyclical fluctuations in wages. However, if wages are set in response to long-term considerations but do not vary cyclically so as to clear labor markets, the cyclical fluctuations in demand will cause employment to fluctuate. Since much hiring and firing is done by seniority, employment fluctuations are borne by the 10 or 20 percent of workers who are least senior. The majority of workers will then have little uncertainty in the face of cyclical fluctuations in demand, all the uncertainty having been placed on the *minority* with low seniority. Thus contracts that fix wages over the cycle and allow employment to vary may be preferable to the ma-

jority of workers over contracts that allow wages to vary in order to clear the labor market continually and thus prevent unemployment.[13]

In the Keynesian microeconomic view of the world, the economy does not have a unique short-term equilibrium. Because markets do not clear (firms would like to sell more and some workers would work more at current prices), fluctuations in aggregate demand cause output and employment (rather than prices) to fluctuate in the short term.

The Keynesian micro model leaves room for systematic disturbances that cause prolonged deflationary or inflationary gaps. Because of this, there is room for stabilization policy to offset at least those GNP gaps that are large and persistent. Such policies seek to alter aggregate demand using both fiscal and monetary tools.

DIFFERENCES IN THE TWO MODELS

There are many differences in the micro behavior implied by the two models. Let us consider two of them.

Voluntary Versus Involuntary Unemployment

In the monetarist model, all unemployment and output below capacity is voluntary. Workers decide to be unemployed and firms decide to produce less than capacity output as a result of errors they make in predicting the general price level (and therefore the relative price of what they sell).

In the Keynesian model, prices and wages do not fluctuate so as to clear markets. Unemployment and production below capacity is involuntary in the sense that unemployed workers would

---

[12] Complete cyclical inflexibility of markup is not necessary. What matters is that firms do not adjust prices continually so that they are always unwilling to sell further units at the same price.

[13] Such contracts may be acceptable even to the least senior employees, who know that they bear the uncertainty early in life but realize that when they move up the seniority ladder they will be relatively secure against normal cyclical fluctuations in employment.

Reaganomics and the "McDonalds-isation" of America

Since 1973 the *nature* of employment in America has changed dramatically. Between 1973 and 1979, total nonagricultural employment grew by 11 million, but 70 percent of those jobs were provided not in the goods-producing sectors but in the service sector, which includes retail trade, business and personal services, and state and local government offices. By 1979, 43 percent of all total non-agricultural employment was in services and retail trade. Employment in these two sectors has risen three times faster than total employment and sixteen times faster than in the goods-producing sector, with the growth concentrated in three areas: eating and drinking places, health services, and business services. *Total employment in manufacturing today is less than the increase in employment in eating and drinking places over the past decade.* Preliminary data show that many of the same trends have occurred in Canada. For example, total nonagricultural employment grew by 25.6 percent between 1972 and 1979, but employment in the goods-producing sector grew by only 17.5 percent.

These structural changes were accompanied by significant changes in the behavior of key economic aggregates. During the last decade the major macroeconomic trends stood in sharp contrast to the rapid growth, rising productivity, low unemployment, and virtually nonexistent inflation which characterized the period from World War II to the late 1960s. It is perhaps understandable that many politicians view the economic environment of that time as a goal to which we should be attempting to steer our economies today. Since the growth in our standard of living be-

tween 1945 and 1970 was spearheaded by rapidly rising industrial output and productivity, authorities have been led to consider policies that they hope will initiate a revival of growth in industrial capacity and output.

The government of the United Kingdom has attempted to increase the competitiveness and efficiency of British industry through the stringent application of conservative economic principles that include tight monetary policy and massive permanent cuts in spending. In the United States the Reagan administration has embarked on a program designed to restore America's economic might by slashing income and business taxes to encourage investment, by increasing military spending to boost vital segments of the economy, and by reducing the burden of government through reductions in bureaucratic regulations. In Canada we hear tentative talk of an "industrial strategy" designed to secure our economic future by reviving productivity and industrial output. No one is quite certain yet what such a "strategy" entails, but it is probably the opposite of Reaganomics, for it is based on increased government involvement in the private sector of the economy.

Despite its apparent appeal, however, a return to the "good old days" may be neither desirable nor possible. Some economists have begun to question the conventional wisdom of an industry-led economic recovery. In her article "Reagan and the Real America," Emma Rothschild argues that the structural changes of the 1970s (outlined in the first paragraph of this box) make Reagan policies obsolete. She believes that the application of traditional policies "could lead to an economic crisis and a level of unemployment in comparison with which the events of 1975 and 1980 will appear as the merest disturbance of the compassionate state." Hardly an optimistic outlook, but it is one that she believes is supported by the facts.

It is the goods-producing sector that Reagon hopes will spearhead America's economic revival, yet its share of total employment has declined rapidly since the late 1960s. Given its declining importance in economic life, a dramatic growth rate in that sector wou'd be required to reduce inflation and unemployment substantially and to increase overall productivity. Thus there are doubts about the effectiveness of Reaganesque policies. By the end of the 1970s, both Canada and the United States had very small proportions of total employment in manufacturing: 20 and 23 percent respectively, compared to 25 percent in Sweden, 27 percent in France, and 35 percent in West Germany.

The nature of employment has also changed as a result of the changing composition of output. The role of women in the work force has increased, and women are concentrated in the sectors of greatest growth. Women's participation in the Canadian work force is now 40 percent of total employment, with 43 percent in business services, 78 percent in health services, and only 27.5 percent in manufacturing. (Similar figures apply in the United States.) Hours of work also tend to be shorter in the growth sectors: 27 hours per week in eating and drinking places, compared to 37.6 hours in the economy as a whole and 37.7 hours in manufacturing. Many of these jobs tend to be poorly paid; real wages in services fell slightly

between 1972 and 1979, while manufacturing pay has shown a slight upward trend over the same time period. In addition, these new positions offer minimal job security and little chance of advancement. In Rothschild's words, the economy has been "moving towards a structure of employment evermore dominated by jobs that are badly paid, unchanging, and unproductive."

Reagan's policies are aimed at rejuvenating the manufacturing sector of the economy, which is dominated by middle-class, male, industrial workers. This is a dubious strategy in view of the changes in the labor force outlined before because manufacturing is ill-suited to provide employment for part-time, temporary, young, female, or older workers. Any policy, to be effective, cannot ignore the dramatic structural changes that have occurred in the economy. Yet any policy that recognizes the trends and is designed to encourage growth in the retail trade and service industries is unlikely to increase aggregate productivity, for productivity in these sectors has traditionally been very low. This presents a real dilemma for policymakers.

These trends raise questions about the appropriateness of policies oriented toward the goods-producing sector. President Reagan has his mandate, and he intends to exercise it. Whether or not he is misguided, as Rothschild contends, will be known for certain only as his policies face the test of time. How Canada will respond to these developments is even less clear.

like jobs at the going wage rate but cannot find them, and firms would like to sell more at going prices but customers are not forthcoming.

Response to Errors Versus Response to Correctly Understood Signals

In the monetarist model, deviations from full-employment income occur only when the price level is being mistakenly predicted. In boom conditions, people are on average underpredicting the price level and consequently mistaking rises in their own money prices for rises in their relative prices. In recessionary conditions, people are overpredicting the price level and thus mistaking reductions in their own money prices for reductions in their relative prices.

In the Keynesian model, deviations from full employment do not imply errors, one way or the other, in predicting the price level. Labor groups and firms set their money prices with longer-run considerations in mind and then sell all they can sell at the going price as demand varies over the cycle.

Current Debate

Major current debate centers on these two prototype models and some of their subtler offshoots. Much of our view on how the economy behaves both at the micro and at the macro level will be influenced by the progress of the debate. So will our views on the place of fiscal and monetary policy as possible measures for alleviating inflationary and deflationary gaps.

How Much Unemployment at Full Employment?

Another example of the current interest in microeconomic underpinnings of macro concepts is the concern over the unemployment that occurs at "full employment." The uncritical macroeconomic approach just *defines* that amount of un-

employment as "full employment" and stops worrying about it. But why is it that amount and not a higher or a lower amount? What could be done to change it?

Let us see how this issue arises in a macro model. Everyone, including those who maintain that all recent inflations have been cost-push inflations, agrees that demand inflations can occur. Thus they agree that national income cannot be held above Y_F indefinitely without causing inflation. The goal of stable prices requires that the maximum target for national income be set at Y_F.

The amount of unemployment occurring at Y_F is often called the natural rate of unemployment, a term that is misleading to the extent that it implies that the unemployment is unavoidable.

Look again at Figures 39-1 and 39-2 on pages 812 and 813. There is evidence that the natural rate of unemployment has been rising in many countries since the late 1960s. Even if it is not rising, it is still disturbingly high; when the overall level of unemployment is judged to be at its "natural" rate, some groups will be suffering unemployment rates of 20 to 30 percent! If these unsatisfactory performances in individual labor markets are to be changed, even pure demand-pull inflation theorists will have to find instruments other than aggregate demand stimulation to lower unemployment levels.

Raising aggregate demand will cure unemployment only if there are unemployed supplies of *all* resources ready to work when there is demand for their potential outputs. If firms do not have unused productive capacity, unemployed labor will not be put to work merely because people have more money to spend.

Demand stimulation can cure deficient-demand unemployment, but it does not provide the major cure for structural unemployment.

Economic theory predicts that to the extent that high unemployment is structural, an attempt to cure it by stimulating aggregate demand will only cause inflation without reducing unemployment. The best that aggregate demand stimulation can do is to raise national income to its full-capacity level, that is, make Y equal to Y_F. It cannot lower the amount of unemployment that is associated with Y_F, that is, frictional and structural unemployment.

An attempt to arrest rising structural unemployment by increasing aggregate demand will lead only to an inflation accompanying the rising level of unemployment.

There is nothing inevitable about the unemployment that occurs at full-employment income. It has frictional and structural causes; it can be reduced by measures to speed up the reallocation of labor among geographical regions, skill categories, industries, and occupations.

THE COMPOSITION OF MACRO VARIABLES

We have seen that macroeconomic policy is concerned with the behavior of key averages and aggregates such as the average level of all prices and the overall level of unemployment. We have also seen that current research is looking at the micro underpinnings of many assumed macro relations. In fact, we care about more than just the macro averages and aggregates—we also care about their composition.

Consider unemployment once again. We worry about more than just the country's overall rate of unemployment. Is the overall rate of unemployment made up of very unequal rates of unemployment, such as those among industries, occupations, or areas? Or is it made up of rates that are very similar across all classifications? We would assess a 6 percent overall unemployment rate in Canada very differently if we knew that it resulted from 6 percent unemployment in all industries, occupations, and geographical areas than if we knew that it resulted—as it actually does—from 25 percent unemployment in some industries, occupations, and areas and only 1 to 2 percent unemployment in others.

Levels of unemployment of 15 to 20 percent are very serious matters indeed. They imply levels of social and personal upheaval that just do not accompany unemployment rates of the order of 4 to 5 percent. The degree of regional and occupational inequality in unemployment rates in Canada has remained quite high throughout the postwar period. While policymakers could be satisfied that the overall rate in Canada was held at a very low level from 1945 until the mid 1970s, there was always reason to be disturbed at the high rates that persisted in some sectors.

Why did these localized high rates occur? How is it that in the midst of the "fully employed" society we had persistent pockets of poverty that would not respond to the cure of raising aggregate demand? Why does the market not adjust to bring about approximate equality in unemployment rates?

Does this market mechanism work at all? How fast does it work? Does the shifting pattern of economic growth continue to disturb markets so that the adjustment mechanism can never catch up? Would things be better if we interfered more in the market mechanism? What government policies would reduce labor market disequilibria? Would things be better if we interfered less with the market mechanism? How much do restrictive practices and the resistance of unions to the introduction of new technologies contribute to structural unemployment?

A similar set of "disaggregated observations" could be produced for any macro variable, and each would provide a similar set of questions. But to state just one set is enough to show that we have now gone full circle and are back at the *micro*economics with which we began our study in Chapter 5.

There is no sharp distinction between microeconomics and macroeconomics. There are merely higher and lower levels of aggregation and a series of questions appropriate to each level of aggregation, with each series shading into the other.

Summary

1. The consensus is that the inflation of the late 1970s and early 1980s was caused by supply shocks due to expectational, inertial, and import cost-push inflation that was then validated by the Bank of Canada.

2. Some monetarists believe there is enough downward flexibility of money prices to allow a target rate of zero inflation. Other monetarists and most neo-Keynesians believe that the target rate must be in the range of 2 to 4 percent to allow for necessary price increases where money prices are relatively inflexible downward.

3. Almost everyone agrees that a necessary condition for the reduction of inflation is a reduction in the rate of monetary expansion.

4. Monetarists would stop inflation solely by reducing the rate of monetary expansion. Neo-Keynesians say this would lead to a large depression. They seek to avoid the loss of output associated with the monetarist cure by adding a policy of wage and price controls or TIPs that would slow the inflation rate directly and so avoid the temporary loss of output associated with the monetarist cure.

5. Post-Keynesians believe the inflation is caused by wage cost-push and price-push and thus that it can be controlled only by permanent wage and price controls. They believe all contemporary attempts to control inflation are doomed to failure.

6. Monetarists believe that cyclical fluctuations in the economy stem mainly from monetary causes. Neo-Keynesians tend to emphasize fluctuations in expenditure flows not themselves caused by monetary factors.

7. Monetarists tend to believe that stabilization policy is unnecessary. Neo-Keynesians believe it is essential. Where government intervention is called for, monetarists tend to believe that monetary policy has a large effect while fiscal policy has only a small effect. Neo-Keynesians hold the opposite view. These views are elaborated in a formal model in the appendix to this chapter.

8. The monetarists' macro model is based on a microeconomic model of competitive, fully clearing markets. The only equilibrium of all markets is one of full employment. Departures from this norm occur (voluntarily) only because people make mistakes in predicting the price level.

9. The neo-Keynesian model assumes that wages and prices are relatively rigid over the cycle and are certainly not market clearing. Fluctuations in demand cause fluctuations in employment and production because prices are fixed and firms and labor groups will sell what they can at the going price.

10. The theory of rational expectations says that people make only random errors in predicting the price level. Combined with the monetarist theory that deviations from equilibrium occur only because of errors, this predicts that the source of deviation will be random, not systematic. This leaves no place for systematic stabilization policy. Neo-Keynesians reply that even the most casual observations of the economy conflict with this view.

11. The amount of unemployment occurring at full-employment income has been called the natural rate. The economy's aggregate natural rate of 5 to 6 percent conceals vast differences in unemployment by occupational, industrial, educational, racial, and age classifications.

12. Macroeconomic theory is a valuable tool, but it conceals many important microeconomic relations concerned with the dispersion of micro figures around a macro average.

Topics for Review

The appropriate target rate of inflation

Wage and price controls and TIPs

Explanations of the correlation between the quantity of money and national income

Underemployment equilibrium

Keynesian and monetarist micro foundations
The theory of rational expectations
The natural rate of unemployment

Discussion Questions

1. In its 1979 report the Joint Economic Committee of the Congress urged the U.S. administration to fight inflation and combat unemployment by encouraging private sector saving and investment. How might expanded saving and investment help to reduce inflation and/or combat unemployment?

2. Suppose the following "facts" are accepted. Would any of them give substantial support to either the monetarists or the neo-Keynesians in their debate?
   a. Recessions have always been accompanied by a decrease in the money supply.
   b. Expanding the money supply during a recent deep depression led to falling interest rates and increasing excess reserves, but aggregate spending continued to fall.
   c. The recovery phases of each of the four most recent business cycles came to a halt shortly after the central bank slowed the rate of monetary expansion.

3. The quantity equation of exchange, $MV = PY$, is used as part of the quantity theory of money (see Chapter 35). This theory says that the quantity of money, M, times the velocity of circulation, V, equals the value of money national income. Could both monetarists and neo-Keynesians accept this equation as accurate? How might one use it to discuss the differing roles given by the two groups of economists to monetary and fiscal policy in achieving full-employment national income at stable prices?

4. Neo-Keynesian and Nobel laureate Paul Samuelson recently quoted a "conservative economist friend" as saying in mid 1980, "If you're contriving a teensy-weensy recession for us, please don't bother. It won't do the job. What's needed is a believable declaration that Washington will countenance *whatever* degree of unemployment is needed to bring us back on the path to price stability, and a demonstrated willingness to *stick* to that resolution no matter how politically unpopular the short-run joblessness, production cutbacks, and dips in profit might be." Discuss the "conservative friend's" view of inflation. Does experience since 1980 suggest that his advice was followed? If so, what was the consequence?

5. In 1979 in Britain, the newly elected conservative government of Prime Minister Margaret Thatcher embraced the monetarist view of inflation and decided to follow the advice of Professor Samuelson's "conservative friend" quoted in the previous question. Check unemployment and inflation rates and money supply figures in Britain since 1977 to see whether she stuck to the advice and whether the inflation rate moderated.

6. A recent ad in the *New York Times* has this to say about inflation. "First [our politicians] blamed wage increases and price hikes for inflation. Then when 'voluntary guidelines' were established, the blame shifted to OPEC oil prices. Both explanations were wrong. Government policy is responsible for inflation—paying for deficit spending by 'creating money out of thin air.'" What theories of inflation are rejected and accepted by the writers of this ad?

7. Relate each of the following to the shapes of the *LP*, *MEI*, and *AD* functions.
   a. There is so much uncertainty about the future that a fall in interest rates does not lead to increased spending on goods and services.
   b. Buying of houses, cars, and consumer goods on credit is greatly stimulated by new government policies providing loan insurance to lenders.
   c. A reduced need for transactions balances is due to the development of a chequeless society.

8. "Whether or not the monetarists are correct in their criticism of neo-Keynesians depends critically on the size of the crowding out effect." To what extent is this correct? To the extent that it is correct, does it imply a simple empirical test that should solve the debate about relevant policies once and for all?

Part Twelve

Economic Growth and Comparative Systems

Growth in Developed Economies

43

In Chapter 32 we saw that investment can be the cause of economic fluctuations ranging from mild disturbances to major upheavals. Investment has been even more important as the major reason for the economic growth that has raised living standards so rapidly since about 1800. Eightfold or tenfold increases in material living standards have occurred over a single lifetime.

Investment affects growth because it affects the economy's ability to *produce* goods by changing both the quantity and the quality of the capital stock available.

Investment increases the economy's potential, or full-employment, national income.

The theory of economic growth concentrates on the effect of investment on full-employment national income. Contrast this with the theory of fluctuations, which concentrates on the effects of investment expenditure on aggregate demand and hence on the degree to which actual current national income falls short of, or exceeds, potential national income. See Figure 43-1. Put another way, the theory of fluctuations is concerned with the degree of utilization of existing productive capacity, while the theory of growth is concerned with the growth of productive capacity, or full-employment national income.

The Nature of Economic Growth

Economic growth has been a dominant force in industrial nations for 200 years. It has been the source of industrialization's greatest triumph: the raising of the ordinary person's living standards to levels where leisure, travel, and luxury goods are within reach. It has produced standards of living in industrial nations that are the envy of the rest of the world and has led many other nations—with varying degrees of success—to strive to copy that performance. Economic growth has also been the source of spectacular adverse complications such as pollution of the air, water, and land by chemicals, heat, and noise.

Members of developed societies have come to accept growth. Even when they worry about pollution and other undesirable concomitants of growth, they ask, How can we remove this or that harmful side effect of growth? Few people ask, How can we stop growth? and even fewer take those few seriously.

Yet growth, which seems inevitable to most of us, has not always been present, nor is it present everywhere today. During human history there have been periods of increases in living standards followed by long periods with no change. One of the latter was documented by Professor Phelps-Brown of the London School of Economics, who showed that there was no significant increase in the real income of English building-trade workers between 1215 and 1798, a period of almost six centuries. Peasants in many under-developed countries today enjoy a living standard probably little different from that of their ancestors a thousand or more years ago.

Recent data show that world output has doubled in the last 15 years. Despite dramatic population growth, worldwide output per person has increased sharply; it was twice as high in 1975 as in 1950.

These figures provide impressive evidence of the mastery of aspects of our environment, but they are enormously misleading in one respect: most of the growth in output has occurred in countries that make up only about one-fifth of the world's population, while much of the population growth has occurred in countries that have not experienced economic growth.

For many countries, and for much of history, the phenomenon of growth has been absent.

In this chapter and the next we ask, Why are there large differences among countries in their growth rates?

THE DEFINITION OF ECONOMIC GROWTH

In a country such as Canada where GNP has increased tenfold in half a century, and where personal consumption expenditures per capita have doubled in real terms in about 30 years, it is easy to recognize the phenomenon of growth. It is harder to measure it because of several potential confusions. Because each is found in some contemporary discussions, it is worth bearing them

---

FIGURE 43-1
Short-run and Long-run Effects of Investment

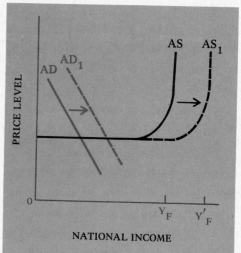

Investment affects aggregate demand in the short run and aggregate supply in the long run. An increase in investment expenditure increases aggregate demand from say AD to AD_1 and is thus an important part of the theory of fluctuations. Such an effect is shown by the colored curves. Over the long run, net investment increases the productive capacity of the economy. This leads to an increase in the level of full-employment income and involves a rightward shift in the aggregate supply curve from say AS to AS_1, as shown by the black curves.

in mind as you read of any country's spectacular achievements.

Capacity versus utilization. The increase in an economy's national income over three or four years reflects changes both in its productive capacity and in the percentage of utilization of this capacity.

If there have been large decreases in unemployment, high rates of increase in national income may be observed. But such increases will not be sustainable once full employment is reached. For example, Canadian GNP increased by nearly 50 percent between 1933 and 1937, but this reflected almost entirely the reduction in the GNP gap from the depths of the Great Depression, not growth in full-employment national income.

A great deal of confusion would be avoided if the term "growth rate" were used to refer only to the growth rate of full-employment national income and if comparisons of national income figures for one country over several years were divided into two parts: changes due to such growth and changes due to variations in the GNP gap.

Money versus real output. Part of any increase in the money value of full-employment output may be due to a rise in prices rather than in output. Constant-dollar measures are essential to measure growth, and they are now commonly used by all major statistical agencies in reporting growth rates.

Output, output per person, and output per hour of labor. To determine a nation's growth in the context of its ability to wage war or pollute its environment, we must look at total output. To measure living standards, per capita output is important; a country's average material living standard depends on output per person. (As an example of the relations between these concepts, a doubling of national output combined with a doubling of population would mean no change in per capita output. As will be seen in Chapter 44, population growth is a problem plaguing many countries.)

Output per person may grow at a different rate than the economy's productive capacity per person. As an economy grows, many people choose to spend a shorter portion of their days and lives at work. As standards of living rise, entry into the labor force tends to be delayed by increased schooling, work weeks are shortened to permit greater leisure, and the size of the older non-working population rises because of earlier retirement and longer life spans. To offset this, there may be increases in the labor force participation of women and of men who worked previously in nonmarket sectors of the economy.

In theoretical discussions of growth, it is useful to have an indicator of the ability of an economy to convert its resources into goods and services. A widely used summary measure of this is output per hour of labor, often called simply **productivity.** Obviously, productivity depends not only on labor effort but also on the amount and kind of machinery used, the raw materials available, and so on. The focus of this measure is explained by the special emphasis that human beings place on human labor.

THE CUMULATIVE NATURE OF GROWTH

A growth rate of 2 percent per year may seem insignificant, but if it is continued for a century, it will lead to more than a sevenfold increase in real national income!

The cumulative effect of small annual growth rates is large.

To appreciate the cumulative effect of what seem like very small differences in growth rates, examine Table 43-1. Notice that when one country grows faster than another, the gap in their living standards widens progressively. If two countries start from the same level of income, and if country A grows at 3 percent while B grows at 2 percent per year, A's income per capita will be twice B's in 69 years. You may not think it matters much whether the economy

TABLE 43-1
The Cumulative Effect of Growth

Year	Percentage rate of growth per year				
	1%	2%	3%	5%	7%
0	100	100	100	100	100
10	111	122	135	165	201
30	135	182	246	448	817
50	165	272	448	1,218	3,312
70	201	406	817	3,312	13,429
100	272	739	2,009	14,841	109,660

Small differences in growth rates make enormous differences in levels of potential national income over a few decades. Assume that potential national income is 100 in year zero. At a rate of growth of 3 percent, it will be 135 in 10 years, 448 after 50 years, and over 2,000 in a century. Compound interest is a powerful force!

grows at 2 percent or 3 percent, but your children and grandchildren will!

Students of the 1960s were taught that, if the then current growth trends continued, America would not long remain the world's richest nation, for Sweden, Canada, Japan, and many others were growing at a much faster rate. Many students of that era rejected the notion; deep down they *knew* that the material standard of living of the United States was and would remain the highest the world had ever known. But by 1980 several industrial countries, including Sweden and Canada, had passed the United States in terms of per capita national income and several more were within 10 percent of the U.S. level. In addition, Kuwait and several other oil producers reported higher average incomes.

BENEFITS OF GROWTH

Growth in Living Standards

A country whose per capita output grows at 3 percent per year doubles its living standards about every 24 years. (A helpful approximation device is the "rule of 72." Divide any growth rate into 72 and the resulting number approximates the number of years it will take for income to double.) [48]

A primary reason for desiring growth is to raise general living standards.

The extreme importance of economic growth in raising income can be illustrated by comparing the real income of a father with the real income of the daughter who follows in her father's footsteps. If the daughter neither rises nor falls in the relative income scale compared with her father, her share of the country's national income will be the same as her father's. If the daughter is 30 years younger than her father, she can expect to have a real income nearly twice as large as that which her father enjoyed when her father was the same age. These figures assume that the father and daughter live in a country such as Canada or the United States where the growth rate has been 2 or 3 percent per year. If they live in Japan, where growth has been going on at a rate of about 8 percent per year, the daughter's income will be about 10 times as large as her father's.

For those who share in it, growth is a powerful weapon against poverty. A family earning $5,500 today can expect $8,200 within ten years (in constant dollars) if it just shares in a 4 percent growth rate. The transformation of the life style of blue-collar workers in North America as well as in Germany and Japan in a generation provides a notable example of the escape from poverty that growth makes possible.

Of course, not everyone benefits equally from growth. Many of the poorest are not even in the labor force and thus are least likely to share in the higher wages that, along with profits, are the primary means by which the gains from growth are distributed. For this reason, even in a growing economy redistribution policies will be needed if poverty is to be averted.

Growth and Income Redistribution

Economic growth makes many kinds of redistributions easier to achieve. For example, a rapid

An Open Letter to the Ordinary Citizen from a Supporter of the Growth-Is-Good School

Dear Ordinary Citizen:

You live in the world's first civilization that is devoted principally to satisfying *your* needs rather than those of a privileged minority. Past civilizations have always been based on leisure and high consumption for a tiny upper class, a reasonable living standard for a small middle class, and hard work with little more than subsistence consumption for the great mass of people. In the past, the average person saw little of the civilized and civilizing products of the economy, except when he or she was toiling to produce them.

The continuing Industrial Revolution is based on mass-produced goods for you, the ordinary citizen. It ushered in a period of sustained economic growth that has raised consumption standards of ordinary citizens to levels previously reserved throughout history for a tiny privileged minority. Reflect on a few examples: travel, live and recorded music, art, good food, inexpensive books, universal literacy and a genuine chance to be educated. Most important, there is leisure to provide time and energy to enjoy these and thousands of other products of the modern industrial economy.

Would any ordinary family seriously doubt the benefits of growth and prefer to be back in the world of 150 or 500 years ago, in its same relative social and economic position? Most surely the answer is no. But we cannot say the same for those with incomes in the top 1 or 2 percent of the income distribution. Economic growth has destroyed much of their privileged consumption position: they must now vie with the masses when visiting the world's beauty spots and be annoyed, while lounging on the terrace of a palatial mansion, by the sound of charter flights carrying ordinary people to inexpensive holidays in far places. The rich resent their loss of exclusive rights to luxury consumption. Some complain bitterly, and it is not surprising that they find their intellectual apologists.

Whether they know it or not, the antigrowth economists—such as Harvard's Ken Galbraith, Cambridge's Joan Robinson, and the LSE's Ed Mishan—are not the social revolutionaries they think they are. They are counterrevolutionaries who would set back the clock of material progress for the ordinary person. They say that growth has produced pollution and wasteful consumption of all kinds of frivolous products which add nothing to human happiness. But the democratic solution to pollution is not to go back to where so few people consume luxuries that pollution is trivial; it is to accept pollution as part of a transitional phase connected with the ushering in of mass consumption, to keep the mass consumption, and to learn to control the pollution it tends to create.

It is only through further growth that the average citizen can enjoy consumption standards (of travel, culture, medical and health care, etc.) now available to people in the top 25 percent of the income distribution—which includes the intellectuals who earn large royalties from the books they write denouncing growth. If you think that extra income confers little real benefit, just ask those in that top 25 percent to trade incomes with the average citizen. Or see how hard *they* struggle to reduce their income taxes.

Ordinary citizens, do not be deceived by disguised elitist doctrines. Remember that the very rich and the elite have much to gain by stopping growth—and even more by rolling it back—but you have everything to gain by letting it go forward.

Onward!

I. Growthman

growth rate makes it much more feasible politically to alleviate poverty. If existing income is to be redistributed, someone's standard of living will actually have to be lowered. However, when there is economic growth, and when the increment in income is redistributed (through government intervention), it is possible to reduce income inequalities without actually having to lower anyone's income. It is much easier for a rapidly growing economy to be generous toward its less fortunate citizens – or neighbors – than it is for a static economy.

Growth and Life Style

A family often finds that a big increase in its income can lead to a major change in the pattern of its consumption – that extra money buys important amenities of life. In the same way, the members of society as a whole may change their consumption patterns as their average income rises. Not only do markets in a country that is growing rapidly make it profitable to produce more cars, but the government is led to produce more highways and to provide more recreational areas for its newly affluent (and mobile) citizens. At yet a later stage, a concern about litter, pollution, and ugliness may become important, and their correction may then begin to account for a significant fraction of GNP. Such "amenities" usually become matters of social concern only when growth has assured the provision of the basic requirements for food, clothing, and housing of a substantial majority of the population.

National Defence and Prestige

When one country is competing with another for power or prestige, rates of growth are important. If our national income is growing at 2 percent, say, while the other country's is growing at 5 percent, the other country will only have to wait for our relative strength to dwindle. Moreover, a country will find the expenses of an arms race or a program of foreign aid easier to bear, the faster its productivity is growing.

More subtly, growth has become part of the currency of international prestige. Countries that are engaged in persuading other countries of the might or right of their economic and political systems point to their rapid rates of growth as evidence of their achievements.

COSTS OF GROWTH

The benefits discussed above suggest that growth is a great blessing. It is surely true that, *ceteris paribus*, most people would regard a fast rate of growth as preferable to a slow one, but other things are seldom equal.

Social and Personal Costs of Growth

Industrialization, unless carefully managed, causes deterioration of the environment. Unspoiled landscapes give way to highways, factories, and billboards; air and water become polluted; and in some cases unique and priceless relics of earlier ages – from flora and fauna to ancient ruins – disappear. Urbanization tends to move people away from the simpler life of farms and small towns and into the crowded, slum-ridden, and often darkly evil life of the urban ghetto. Those remaining behind in the rural areas find that rural life, too, has changed. Larger-scale farming, the decline of population, and the migration of children from the farm to the city all have their costs. The stepped-up tempo of life brings joys to some but tragedy to others. Accidents, ulcers, crime rates, suicides, divorces, and murder all tend to be higher in periods of rapid change and in more developed societies.

When an economy is growing, it is also changing. Innovation leaves obsolete machines in its wake, and it also leaves partially obsolete people. No matter how well trained you are at age 25, in another 25 years your skills may well be partially obsolete. Some will find that their skills have become completely outdated and unneeded. A rapid rate of growth requires rapid adjustments, which can cause much upset and misery to the individuals affected. The decline in the number

An Open Letter to the Ordinary Citizen from a Supporter of the Growth-Is-Bad School

Dear Ordinary Citizen:

You live in a world that is being despoiled by a mindless search for ever higher levels of material consumption at the cost of all other values. Once upon a time, men and women knew how to enjoy creative work and to derive satisfaction from simple activities undertaken in scarce, and hence highly valued, leisure time. Today the ordinary worker is a mindless cog in an assembly line that turns out ever more goods that the advertisers must work overtime to persuade the worker to consume.

Statisticians and politicians count the increasing flow of material output as a triumph of modern civilization. Consider not the flow of output in general, but the individual products that it contains. You arise from your electric-blanketed bed, clean your teeth with an electric toothbrush, open with an electric can opener a can of the sad remnants of a once-proud orange, you eat your bread baked from super-refined and chemically refortified flour, and you climb into your car to sit in vast traffic jams on exhaust-polluted highways. And so it goes, with endless consumption of high-technology products that give you no more real satisfaction than the simple, cheaply produced equivalent products used by your great-grandfathers: soft woolly blankets, natural bristle toothbrushes, real oranges, old-fashioned and coarse but healthy bread, and public transport that moved on uncongested roads and gave its passengers time to chat with their neighbors, to read, or just to day-dream.

Television commercials tell you that by consuming more you are happier. But happiness lies not in increasing consumption but in increasing the ratio of *satisfaction of wants* to *total wants*. Since the more you consume the more the advertisers persuade you that you want to consume, you are almost certainly less happy than the average citizen in a small town in 1900 whom we can visualize sitting on the family porch, sipping a cool beer or a lemonade, and enjoying the antics of the children as they play with scooters made out of old crates and jump rope with pieces of old clothesline.

Today the landscape is dotted with endless factories producing the plastic trivia of the modern industrial society. They drown you in a cloud of noise, air, and water pollution. The countryside is despoiled by strip mines, petroleum cracking plants, and dangerous nuclear power stations that produce the energy that is devoured insatiably by modern factories and motor vehicles.

Worse, our precious heritage of natural resources is being fast used up. Spaceship earth flies, captainless, in its senseless orgy of self-consuming consumption.

Now is the time to stop this madness. We must stabilize production, reduce pollution, conserve our natural resources, and seek justice through a more equitable distribution of existing total income.

A long time ago Malthus taught us that if we do not limit population voluntarily, nature will do it for us in a cruel and savage manner. Today the same is true of output: if we do not halt its growth voluntarily, the halt will be imposed on us by a disastrous increase in pollution and a rapid exhaustion of natural resources.

Citizens, awake! Shake off the worship of growth, learn to enjoy the bounty that is yours already, and reject the endless, self-defeating search for increased happiness through ever-increasing consumption.

Upward!

A. Nongrowthman

of unskilled jobs makes the lot of untrained workers much more difficult. When they lose jobs, they may well fail to find others—particularly if they are over 50.

It is often argued that costs of this kind are a small price to pay for the great benefits that growth can bring. Even if that is true in the aggregate (which is a matter of debate), these personal costs are very unevenly borne. Indeed, many of those for whom growth is most costly (in terms of jobs) share least in the fruits of growth. Yet it is also a mistake to see only the costs—to yearn for the good old days while enjoying higher living standards that growth alone has made possible.

The Opportunity Cost of Growth

In a world of scarcity, almost nothing is free. Growth requires heavy investments of resources in capital goods as well as in activities such as education. Often these investments yield no *immediate* return in terms of goods and services for consumption; thus they imply sacrifices by the current generation of consumers.

Growth, which promises more goods tomorrow, is achieved by consuming fewer goods today. For the economy as a whole this is the primary cost of growth.

An example will suggest the magnitude of this cost. Suppose the fictitious economy of Adanac has full employment and is experiencing growth at the rate of 2 percent per year. Its citizens consume 85 percent of the GNP and invest 15 percent. The people of Adanac know that if they are willing to decrease immediately their consumption to 77 percent, they will produce more capital and thus shift at once to a 3 percent growth rate. The new rate can be maintained as long as they keep saving and investing 23 percent of the national income. Should they do it?

Table 43-2 represents the choice in terms of time paths of consumption. How expensive is the "invest now, consume later" strategy? On the assumed figures, it takes ten years for the actual

TABLE 43-2
The Opportunity Cost of Growth

In year	(A) Level of consumption at 2% growth rate	(B) Level of consumption at 3% growth rate	(C) Cumulative gain (loss) in consumption
0	85.0	77.0	(8.0)
1	86.7	79.3	(15.4)
2	88.5	81.8	(22.1)
3	90.3	84.2	(28.2)
4	92.1	86.8	(33.5)
5	93.9	89.5	(37.9)
6	95.8	92.9	(40.8)
7	97.8	95.0	(43.6)
8	99.7	97.9	(45.4)
9	101.8	100.9	(46.3)
10	103.8	103.9	(46.2)
15	114.7	120.8	(28.6)
20	126.8	140.3	19.6
30	154.9	189.4	251.0
40	189.2	255.6	745.9

Transferring resources from consumption to investment goods lowers current income but raises future income. The example assumes that income in year zero is 100, and that consumption of 85 percent of national income is possible with a 2 percent growth rate. It is further assumed that to achieve a 3 percent growth rate, consumption must fall to 77 percent of income. A shift from (A) to (B) decreases consumption for 10 years but increases it thereafter. The cumulative effect on consumption is shown in (C); the gains eventually become large.

amount of consumption to catch up to what it would have been had no reallocation been made. In the intervening ten years a good deal of consumption was lost, and the cumulative losses in consumption must be made up before society can really be said to have broken even. It takes an additional nine years before total consumption over the whole period is as large as it would have been if the economy had remained on the 2 percent path. [49]

A policy of sacrificing present living standards for a gain that does not begin to be reaped for a generation is hardly likely to appeal to any but the altruistic or the very young. The question of how much of its living standards one generation is prepared to sacrifice for its heirs (who are in any case likely to be richer) is troublesome. As one critic put it, Why should we sacrifice for them? What have they ever done for us?

Many governments, particularly those seeking a larger role in world affairs, have chosen to force the diversion of resources from consumption to investment. The Germans under Hitler, the Russians under Stalin, and the Chinese under Mao Tse-tung adopted four-year and five-year plans that did just this. Many less-developed countries are using such plans today. Such resource shifts are particularly important when actual growth rates are very small (say, less than 1 percent), for without some current sacrifice there is little or no prospect of real growth in the lifetimes of today's citizens. The very lowest growth rates are frequently encountered in the very poorest countries. This creates a cruel dilemma, discussed in Chapter 44 as the vicious circle of poverty.

GROWTH AS A GOAL OF POLICY: DO THE BENEFITS JUSTIFY THE COSTS?

Suppose that the members of a society want to increase their output of goods by 10 percent in one year. There are many ways they can do this.

1. They may be able to find idle and unutilized resources and put them to work.
2. They may be able to schedule extra shifts and overtime labor.
3. They may, by exhortation or by an appropriate incentive system, induce people to work much harder.
4. They may (if they have time) increase the supply of machines and factories.
5. They may utilize new techniques that permit them to get more output from the same inputs.

In the short run, the first three approaches seem the more promising; in fact, when nations face such crises as wars, these devices are used to achieve rapid increases in output. But the gains to be achieved by utilizing unemployed resources, extending the hours of use of employed ones, or "working harder" are limited. Eventually they will be used up. When there are

no longer unutilized resources or underutilized capacity, further increases in output become more difficult to achieve.

In the long term, it is the last two approaches that bring the sustained increases in living standards that have eliminated the 14-hour day and the six-day work week and made possible both leisure and high material standards of living.

But do the developed countries need yet more growth? Most people think they do. Poverty is now a solvable problem in North America as a direct result of enhanced average living standards. Clearly, people in the top quarter of the present income distribution have more opportunities for leisure, travel, culture, fine wines, and gracious living than have persons with much lower incomes. Most of those now in the bottom half of the income distribution would like these opportunities too. Only growth can give it to them.

Today, many countries that have not yet—or have only newly—undergone sustained periods of economic growth in modern times are urgently seeking to copy those that have in order to obtain the benefits of growth.

Most nations and most people today wish to pursue the goal of growth for the benefits it brings, despite its costs.

How seriously the costs are taken depends in part on how many of the benefits of growth have already been achieved. With mounting population problems, the poor countries are increasingly preoccupied with creating growth. With mounting awareness of pollution, the rich countries are devoting ever more resources to overcoming the problems caused by growth—at the same time that they are understandably reluctant to give up further growth.

Indeed, a similar conflict can often be seen within the same country at one time: a relatively poor community fights to acquire a new paper mill for the employment and income it will create; another, relatively affluent community deplores the ruin of its beaches and its air by an existing mill.

Theories of Economic Growth

Economists today recognize that many different factors may contribute to—or impede—economic growth. Although our present knowledge of the relative importance of these factors is far from complete, modern economists look at the problems of growth more optimistically than did the classical economists of a century and more ago. Of particular importance is the nature and source of the investment opportunities that, when utilized, lead to growth. The differences between the classical and contemporary points of view can best be understood by considering a revealing though unrealistic case.

GROWTH IN A WORLD WITHOUT LEARNING

Suppose that there is a known and fixed stock of projects that might be undertaken; suppose nothing ever happens to increase either the supply of such projects or knowledge about them. Whenever the opportunity is ripe, some of the investment opportunities are utilized, thereby increasing the stock of capital goods and depleting the reservoir of unutilized investment opportunities. Of course, the most productive opportunities will be used first.

Such a view of investment opportunities can be represented by a fixed marginal efficiency of capital schedule of the kind met in Chapter 22. Such a schedule is graphed in Figure 43-2; it relates the stock of capital to the productivity of an additional unit of capital. The productivity of a unit of capital is calculated by dividing the annual value of the additional output resulting from an extra unit of capital by the value of that unit of capital. Thus, for example, a marginal efficiency of capital of .2 means that $1 of new capital adds 20¢ per year to the stream of output.

The downward slope of the *MEC* schedule indicates that, with knowledge constant, increases in the stock of capital bring smaller and smaller increases in output per unit of capital. That is,

FIGURE 43-2
The Marginal Efficiency of Capital Schedule

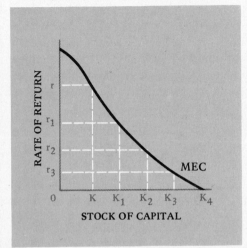

A declining **MEC** schedule shows that successive increases to the capital stock bring smaller and smaller increases in output and thus a declining rate of return. A fixed *MEC* schedule can represent the theory of growth in an economy with some unutilized investment opportunities but no learning. Increases in investment that increase the capital stock from K to K_1 to ... K_4 lower the rate of return from r to r_1 to ... zero. Because the productivity of successive units of capital decreases, the capital-output ratio rises.

the rate of return on successive units of capital declines. This shape is a consequence of the law of diminishing returns.[1] If, with land, labor, and knowledge constant, more and more capital is used, the net amount added by successive increments will diminish and may eventually reach zero. Given this schedule, as capital is accumulated in a state of constant knowledge the society will move down its *MEC* schedule.

In such a "nonlearning" world, where new investment opportunities do not appear, growth occurs only so long as there are unutilized opportunities to use capital effectively to increase output. Growth, in a nonlearning world, is a transitory phenomenon that occurs as long as the

[1] This hypothesis was discussed on pages 212–213.

society has a backlog of unutilized investment opportunities.

So far we have discussed the *marginal* efficiency of capital. The *average* efficiency of capital refers to the average amount produced in the whole economy per unit of capital employed. It is common in discussions of the theory of growth to talk in terms of the *capital-output ratio*, which is the reciprocal of output per unit of capital. In a world without learning, the capital-output ratio is increasing.

In a world without learning the growth in the capital stock will have two important consequences:

1. **Successive increases in capital accumulation will be less and less productive, and the capital-output ratio will be increasing.**
2. **The marginal efficiency of new capital will be decreasing and will eventually be pushed to zero as the backlog of investment opportunities is used up.**

GROWTH WITH LEARNING

The steady depletion of growth opportunities in the previous model resulted from the fact that new investment opportunities were never discovered or created. However, if investment opportunities are created as well as used up with the passage of time, the *MEC* schedule will shift outward over time and the effects of increasing the capital stock may be different. This is illustrated in Figure 43-3. Such outward shifts can be regarded as the consequences of "learning" either about investment opportunites or about the techniques that create such opportunities. When learning occurs, what matters is how rapidly the *MEC* schedule shifts relative to the amount of capital investment being undertaken. Three possibilities are shown in Figure 43-3.

Gradual Reduction in Investment Opportunities: The Classical View

If, as in Figure 43-3(i), investment opportunities are created but at a slower rate than they are

used up, there will be a tendency toward a falling rate of return and an increasing ratio of capital to output. The predictions in this case are the same as those given above (in color) for the world without learning, though the cause is different: too slow, rather than no, discovery of new investment opportunities.

This figure illustrates the theory of growth held by most early economists. They saw the economic problem as one of fixed land, a rising population, and a gradual exhaustion of investment opportunities. These conditions, they believed, would ultimately force the economy into a static condition with no growth, very high capital-output ratios, and the marginal return on additional units of capital forced down toward zero.

Constant or Rising Investment Opportunities: The Contemporary View

The pessimism of the classical economists came from their failure to anticipate the possibility of really rapid innovation—of technological progress that could push investment opportunities outward as rapidly or more rapidly than they were used up, as shown in parts (ii) and (iii) of Figure 43-3.

In a world with rapid innovation:

1. **Successive increases in capital accumulation may prove highly productive, and the capital-output ratio may be constant or decreasing.**
2. **In spite of large amounts of capital accumulation, the marginal efficiency of new capital may remain constant or even increase as new investment opportunities are created.**

The historical record suggests that outward shifts in investment opportunities over time have led to the reality of sustained growth. Evidently modern economies have been successful in generating new investment opportunities at least as rapidly as old ones were used up. Modern economists devote more attention to understanding the *shifts* in the *MEC* schedule over time and less to its shape under a nonlearning situation.

FIGURE 43-3
Shifting Investment Opportunities: Three Cases

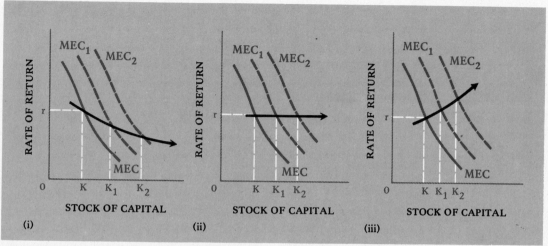

When both knowledge and the capital stock grow, the actual marginal efficiency of capital depends on their relative rates of growth. In each case, the economy at period 0 has the MEC curve, a capital stock of K, and a rate of return of r. In period 1 the curve shifts to MEC_1 and there is investment to increase the stock of capital by KK_1. In period 2 the curve shifts to MEC_2 and there is new investment of K_1K_2. It is the relative size of the shift of the MEC curve and the additions of the capital stock that are important.

In (i) investment occurs more rapidly than increases in investment opportunities and r will fall along the black curve. In (ii) investment occurs at exactly the same rate as investment opportunities and r is constant. In (iii) investment occurs less rapidly than increases in investment opportunities and r will rise.

A CONTEMPORARY VIEW OF GROWTH

The classical economists had a relatively simple theory of growth because they viewed a single mechanism—capital accumulation—as decisively important. Contemporary theorists begin by recognizing a number of factors that influence growth, no one of which is necessarily dominant.

The Quantity of Capital per Worker

Human beings have always been tool users. It is still true that more and more tools tend to lead to more and more output. As long as a society has unexploited investment opportunities, productive capacity can be increased by increasing the stock of capital. The effect on output per worker of "mere" capital accumulation is so noticeable that it was once regarded as virtually the sole source of growth.

But if capital accumulation were the only source of growth, it would lead to movement down the MEC schedule and to a rising capital-output ratio and a falling rate of return on capital. The evidence does not support these predictions. The facts suggest that investment opportunities have expanded as rapidly as investments in capital goods, roughly along the pattern of Figure 43-3(ii). While capital accumulation has taken place and has accounted for much observed growth, it cannot have been the only source of growth.

The Quality of Capital

New knowledge and inventions can contribute markedly to the growth of potential national income, even without capital accumulation. In order to see this, assume that the proportion of the society's resources devoted to the production of capital goods is just sufficient to replace capi-

The Productivity Slowdown in Canada

Productivity is the measure of the efficiency with which the inputs into the production process—labor, capital, and raw resources—are combined to produce the goods and services that we consume.* Rising productivity is the primary source of our increasing standard of living, and any slowing of the productivity growth trend is a cause for concern.

In recent years the statistics have shown a marked decline in labor productivity growth over the period 1973–1979, compared to the previous 25 years. The average annual growth rate in labor productivity from 1947 to 1972 of 2.7 percent accounted for one-half of the growth in real GNE over the period. Since 1973 labor productivity has grown, on average, only 0.3 percent per year.

Although the evidence suggests that productivity follows closely the cyclical path of growth in GNE, in the opinion of the federal Department of Finance the post-1973 downturn in GNE cannot fully explain the slowdown in labor productivity in the same period. Their research suggests that the dramatic drop in productivity is indicative of major structural changes in the economy.

Some observers have argued that the causes of the productivity slowdown are specific to Canada, and they look for a dramatic single solution, perhaps one new "magic product," to put Canada back on track. But the evidence is overwhelming that the slowdown is world-wide, and most studies suggest that it has many small causes. Hence the problem is not likely to yield to a single dramatic solution.

Intersectoral shifts of the labor force have been an important source of aggregate labor productivity growth in recent decades. The rapid growth in productivity in the 1950s and 1960s was in part the result of labor moving from the low-productivity agricultural sector to the high-productivity manufacturing sector. This trend has slowed recently, yet no sharp break to account for the sudden decline in productivity growth can be observed. The recent tendency for labor to move from the highly productive manufacturing industries to the less productive service industries probably accounts for some of the recent decline, but again no sharp break with earlier patterns is evident.

In a recent report, the Canadian Department of Finance delved more deeply into two areas that they believed accounted for approximately 50 percent of the recent decline in Canadian productivity growth. First, since 1973 productivity in the energy sector of the economy has fallen 9.2 percent, reflecting both falling output and accelerating employment. Output has fallen both as a result of the depletion of easily accessible oil reserves and the influence of the National Energy Board, which gained control over the rate of depletion in 1973.

The second area was the declining capital/labor ratio, which became evident in the 1970s. A growing capital/labor ratio has long

*As in Chapter 13 (see page 232), we use labor productivity as a convenient approximation for total factor productivity.

tal as it wears out. Thus, if the old capital were merely replaced in the same form, the capital stock would be constant and there would be no increase in the capacity to produce. But if there is a growth of knowledge so that as old equipment wears out it is replaced by different, more productive equipment, national income will be growing.

Increases in productive capacity that are intrinsic to the form of capital goods in use are

been associated with secular increases in output per person. Any decline in this ratio would therefore be associated with a decline in productivity. The report found that a slowing of the trend rate of growth of the capital/labor ratio in some important sectors of the economy has contributed up to 25 percent of the productivity slowdown. The declining rate of growth of the capital/labor ratio can be accounted for in part by:

1. Increased employment in energy-related industries.
2. A cutback in investment in the late 1970s by major utilities as a result of having earlier overestimated demand and built up excess capacity.
3. Later hours of operation by retail stores, resulting in more employment for the same capital outlay.
4. Rising energy prices, which lead naturally to a decline in the capital/labor ratio because energy and capital are complements. *

Other areas that have often been cited as causes for declining productivity (such as the increasing costs of complying with government regulations and the changing age and sex composition of the labor force) were explored and found to be either minor or insignificant;

---

* A rapid rise in energy prices has, understandably, altered the optimal input mix of capital and labor in industry. Higher prices for energy have made some machinery obsolete or expensive; this has led to the hiring of more labor, which in turn reduces productivity.

the major trends in these factors were evident before the current slowdown began.

Reversing Canada's productivity slowdown is important because productivity ultimately influences our standard of living. Some of the policies that have been advocated are:

1. The dropping of tariffs and other barriers to trade to force Canadian industry to become more competitive and hence more productive.
2. Government encouragement for new high-productivity industries as opposed to its support for old low-productivity industries.
3. More vocational and on-the-job training to increase the overall level of education of Canadian labor, since education is a major source of increased productivity.
4. Reducing the number of regulations with which industry has been forced to comply.

It is also possible that the current slowdown is largely a statistical artifact, the result of measurement errors. Some economists believe that inflation distorts conventional accounting practices in such a way as to lead to underestimates of output and overestimates of cost. Others believe that high energy prices have rendered obsolete much of the capital stock that still appears on the books so that the effective capital stock is much smaller than current measures indicate. These errors lead to underestimates of current productivity; according to this view, we will experience an equally illusory productivity boom when corrections in the measures are made.

---

called **embodied technical change.** The historical importance of embodied technical change is clearly visible: the assembly line and automation transformed much of manufacturing, the airplane revolutionized transportation, and electronic de-

vices now dominate the communications industries. These innovations plus less well-known but no less profound ones—for example, improvements in the strength of metals, the productivity of seeds, and the techniques for recovering basic raw materials from the ground—create new investment opportunities.

Less visible but nonetheless important changes occur through **disembodied technical change.** These concern innovations in the organization of production that are not embodied in the form of the capital goods or raw materials used. One example is improved techniques of managerial control.

Most innovations involve both embodied and disembodied changes: new processes require new machines, which make yet newer processes economical. Computerization promises many such changes in the years ahead. One of them, which many regard with a mixture of awe and apprehension, is a cashless society in which banks become parts of vast information networks that receive one's pay, pay one's bills, and invest one's savings. But whatever the form of innovation, the nature of the goods and services consumed and the way they are made changes continually as innovations occur. Major innovations of the past century have resulted from the development of the telephone, the linotype, the automobile, the airplane, plastics, the assembly line, coaxial cable, xerography, computers, transistors, and silicon chips. It is hard for us to imagine life if we had none of them.

The Quality of Labor

The "quality" of labor—or human capital—has several aspects. One involves improvements in the health and longevity of the population. Of course, these are desired as ends in themselves, yet they have consequences for both the size of the labor force and its productivity. There is no doubt that they have increased productivity per worker-hour by cutting down on illness, accidents, and absenteeism. At the same time, the extension of the normal life span with no comparable increase in the working life span has created a larger group of nonworking aged that exercises a claim on total output. Whether health improvements alone have increased output per capita is not clear.

A second aspect of the quality of human capital concerns technical training, from learning to operate a machine to learning how to be a scientist. Training is clearly required to invent, operate, manage, and repair complex machines. More subtly, there are often believed to be general social advantages to an educated population. It has been shown that productivity improves with literacy and that, in general, the longer a person has been educated, the more adaptable he or she is to new and changing challenges—and thus, in the long run, the more productive. But education may also increase feelings of alienation in a society that is thought to be arbitrary or unjust.

The Quantity of Labor

The size of a country's population and the extent of participation in the labor force are important in and of themselves, not merely because they affect the quantity of a factor of production. For this reason, it is less common to speak of the quantity of people available for work as a source of, or detriment to, growth than it is to speak of the quantity of capital or iron ore in the same way. But, clearly, for any given state of knowledge and supplies of other factors of production, the size of the population can affect the level of output per capita. Every child born has both a mouth and a pair of hands; over a lifetime, each person will be both a consumer and a producer. Thus, on average, it is perfectly possible to speak of overpopulated or underpopulated economies, depending on whether the contribution to production of additional people would raise or lower the level of per capita income.

Because population size is related to income per capita, it is possible to define a theoretical concept, *optimal population,* that maximizes income per capita.

Many countries have had, or do have, conscious population policies. North America in the nineteenth century sought immigrants, and Canada still does today. So did Australia until very recently. Germany under Hitler paid bonuses for additional Aryan children and otherwise offered incentives to create Germans. Greece in the 1950s and 1960s tried to stem emigration to Western Europe. All are examples of countries that believed they had insufficient population, though the motives were not in every case purely economic. In contrast, many underdeveloped countries of South America, Africa, and Asia desire to limit population growth.

Institutional Considerations

Almost all aspects of a country's institutions can foster or deter the efficient use of a society's natural and human resources. Social and religious habits, legal institutions, and traditional patterns of national and international trade are all important. So too is the political climate. In Chapter 44 many of these institutions will be discussed as potential barriers to development.

Is There a Most Important Source of Growth?

The modern theory of growth tends to reject a dominant source of growth and to recognize that several different influences singly and in interaction affect the growth rate.

Among the major contributors to rapid economic growth are a capital stock that is steadily growing and improving in quality, a healthy and well-educated labor force, and a rate of population growth that is small enough to permit per capita growth in capital.

These factors are more likely to be utilized effectively in some institutional settings than in others.

A complete theory of growth would do more than list a series of influences all of which affect the growth rate. It would include assessments of (1) their relative importance, (2) the trade-offs involved in having more of one beneficial influence and less of another, and (3) the interactions among the various influences. This poses a formidable empirical challenge to research that is just beginning to be accepted.

While much remains to be learned, an important tentative conclusion of such scholars as E. F. Denison and Robert Solow is that improvements in the *quality* of capital, human as well as physical, have played a larger role than increases in the *quantity* of capital in the economic growth of the United States since 1900. Whether quality rather than quantity of capital is also the more important source of growth for countries with very different cultural patterns, more acute population problems, or more limited natural resources is a matter of continuing research.

ARE THERE LIMITS TO GROWTH?

Those opposed to growth argue that sustained growth for another century is undesirable; some even argue that it is impossible. Of course all terrestrial things have an ultimate limit. Astronomers predict that the solar system itself will die as the sun burns out in another 6 billion or so years. To be of practical concern a limit must be within some reasonable planning horizon. Best-selling books of the 1970s by Jay Forrester [*World Dynamics* (1973)] and D. H. Meadows et al. [*The Limits to Growth* (1974)] predicted the imminence of a growth-induced doomsday. Living standards were predicted to reach a peak about the year 2000 and then, in the words of Professor Nordhaus, a leading critic of these models, to "descend inexorably to the level of Neanderthal man." What can be said about this debate?

The Uncontroversial Fact of Increasing Pressure on Natural Resources

The years since World War II have seen a rapid acceleration in the consumption of the world's resources, particularly fossil fuels and basic minerals. World population has increased from under 2.5 billion to over 4 billion in that period, and this alone has increased the demand for all the world's resources. But the single fact of population growth greatly understates the pressure on resources.

A Case Study of Rapid Growth: Japan, 1953–1971

The real national income of Japan was 5.4 times as large in 1973 as it was in 1953. Japan's economic growth rate was more than double the average rate in ten North American and European countries and greatly exceeded the rate in any of them. What accounts for the extraordinarily rapid growth of Japan's economy? To answer that question, two economists, Edward F. Denison and William K. Chung, analyzed and measured the sources of economic growth in Japan from 1953 to 1971 and compared the results with those for ten Western countries. They also measured the difference between levels of output per worker in the United States and Japan in 1970 and identified its sources and magnitude. The results were published in 1976.*

They find that no single factor was responsible for Japan's high postwar growth rate. Rather, the Japanese economy benefited from several major sources of growth: an increase in quantity of labor, an increase in quantity of capital, improved technology in production, and economies of scale. Japan gained more in each of these respects than did any of the ten other countries studied. In addition, Japan had the greatest reallocation of labor from agriculture to industry of all the countries studied except Italy. Since productivity is generally higher in industry than in agriculture, a shift of this kind raises average productivity and thereby contributes to growth even without an increase in output per person in either sector.

The overall growth record of Japan is as good as it is partly because of a low *level* of productivity. It is easier to improve from a low base than a high one. At the end of the period productivity was still more than 40 percent lower in Japan than in the United States, even after eliminating the effects of differences between the countries in working hours, in composition and allocation of the labor force, in amounts of capital and land, in size of markets, and in the cyclical positions of the two economies. There is thus an obvious potential for still further Japanese growth relative to the United States or Canada.

Can Japan's growth rate be sustained? The authors stressed the probability of a declining growth rate as various ways of securing fast growth by "catching up" are successively exhausted. Nevertheless, they considered a fairly high rate of long-term growth in Japan—between 5 and 8 percent per year—likely for the rest of this century. (This prediction proved accurate for the 1970s.) By the year 2000 Japan may well be enjoying the highest standard of living of any industrialized country in the world.

* Edward F. Denison and William K. Chung, *How Japan's Economy Grew So Fast: The Sources of Postwar Expansion* (Washington, D.C.: Brookings, 1976).

Calculations by Professor Nathan Keyfitz of Harvard, and others, focus on the resources used by those who can claim a life style of the level enjoyed by 90 percent of American families. This so-called middle class, which today includes about one-sixth of the world's population, consumes 15 to 30 times as much oil per capita and, overall, at least five times as much of the earth's scarce resources per capita as do the other "poor" five-sixths of the population.

The world's poor are not, however, content to remain forever poor. Whether they live in the USSR, Brazil, Korea, or Kenya, they have let their governments understand that they expect policies that generate enough growth to give *them* the higher consumption levels that all of *us* take for granted. This upward aspiration is being fulfilled to a degree. The growth of the middle class has been nearly 4 percent per year—twice the rate of population growth—over the postwar period. The number of persons realizing middle-class living standards is estimated to have increased from 200 million to 700 million between 1950 and 1980.

This growth is a major factor in the recently recognized or projected shortages of natural resources: the increases in demand of the last three decades have outstripped discovery of new supplies and caused crises in energy and mineral supplies as well as food shortages. Yet the 4 percent growth rate of the middle class, which is too fast for present resources, is too slow for the aspirations of the billions who live in underdeveloped countries and see the fruits of development all around them. Thus the pressure on world resources of energy, minerals, and food is likely to accelerate even if population growth is reduced.

Another way to look at the problem of resource pressure is to note that present technology and resources could not possibly support the present population of the world at the standard of living of today's average North American family. Such a shift in level of living, if made overnight, would more than double the world's demand for resources. The demand for oil would increase fivefold or tenfold. Since these calculations (most unrealistically) assume no population growth anywhere in the world and no growth in living standards for the richest sixth of the world's population, the fact of insufficient resources is plain.

Doomsday Predictions

Those most opposed to growth combine the undoubted acceleration of resource utilization with a series of assumptions: first, that there is no technical progress; second, that no new resources are discovered or rendered usable by new techniques; and third, that there is no substi-

tution of more plentiful resources for those that become scarce. Under these circumstances, exhaustion of one or more key resources is predictable. If, in addition, population growth continues at historical rates, this exhaustion will occur relatively quickly—certainly within the next century. And if the increasing production continues to pollute the atmosphere faster than the pollutants can be absorbed, the capacity to produce will be diminished and the quality of life further damaged.

These are the basic assumptions of the doomsday models. Doom can come in several ways (or in any combination of them): natural resource depletion, famine due to overpopulation, or an increasing and ultimately fatal pollution of the earth and its atmosphere.

The many possible routes to disaster mean that no single restraint will suffice to prevent it. If both natural resource usage and pollution are controlled, doom will result from overpopulation. Population control will prove self-defeating because it leads to an increase in the per capita food supply and in the standard of living—which in turn generates forces to trigger a resurgence in population growth.

The only way to prevent disaster, some doomsday models suggest, is to stop economic growth at once through a comprehensive plan to curtail drastically natural resource use (by 75 percent), pollution generation (by 50 percent), investment (by 40 percent), and the birth rate (by 30 percent). Since the countries of the world are not likely to agree on the stern measures needed to meet these targets, a descent down the slippery slope of declining living standards during our own lifetimes is inevitable—and disaster looms for our grandchildren.

A Reply to Doomsday

Critics reply that predictions of an imminent doomsday are as old as human life itself and about as reliable as predictions of the arrival of universal peace and goodwill on earth. They recognize the pressures on the world's resources, and they concede that at present rates of utilization we would clearly run out of specific resources—particularly oil, gas, and certain minerals—in the foreseeable future.

But, they argue, all economic history shows the key assumptions of the doomsday models to be invalid. Nothing could be clearer than that technology changes. People are ingenious in finding ways not only to economize on the use of scarce resources but to substitute materials that are common for those that become scarce. Just as ample taconite replaced scarce iron ore in making steel, just as ample coal replaced scarce charcoal in making iron and steel, and just as synthetic rubber replaced natural rubber in making tires, so it is reasonable to expect new energy sources to be developed to replace fossil fuels. The potential supplies of nuclear and solar energy are inexhaustible, and one day we will be able to harness them.

Can it be doubted, they ask, that a society that has developed birth control pills and explored Mars can solve the problems of overpopulation and control of pollutants?

A Tentative Verdict

Most economists agree that conjuring up absolute limits to growth based on the assumptions of constant technology and fixed resources is not warranted. Yet there is surely cause for concern. Most agree that any barrier can be overcome by technological advances—but not in an instant, and not automatically. Clearly there is a problem of timing: how soon can we discover and put into practice the knowledge required to solve the problems that are made ever more imminent by growth in population, growth in affluence, and by the growing aspirations of the billions who now live in poverty? There is no guarantee that a whole generation may not be caught in transition, with social and political consequences that promise to be enormous even if they are not cataclysmic. The nightmare conjured up by the doomsday models may have served its purpose if it helps to focus our attention on these problems and their imminence.

Summary

1. Investment that causes short-term fluctuations in national income by affecting aggregate demand also makes possible long-term economic growth by increasing a nation's capacity to produce. Such growth is frequently measured using rates of change of potential real national income per person or per hour of labor.

2. The cumulative effects of even small differences in growth rates become large over periods of a generation or more.

3. The most important benefit of growth lies in its contribution to the long-run struggle to raise living standards and escape poverty. Growth also makes more manageable the policies that would redistribute income among people. Economic growth can likewise play an important role in a country's national defense or in its struggle for international prestige.

4. Growth, while often beneficial, is never costless. The opportunity cost of growth is the diversion of resources from current consumption to capital formation. For some individuals who are left behind in a rapidly changing world the costs are higher and more personal. The optimal rate of growth involves balancing benefits and costs. Few wish to forgo the benefits growth can bring, but few wish to maximize growth at any cost.

5. Understanding growth involves understanding both the utilization of existing investment opportunities and the process of creating new investment opportunities. The source of economic growth was once thought to be almost entirely capital accumulation and the utilization of a backlog of unexploited investment opportunities. Today most economists recognize that many investment opportunities can be *created,* and much attention is given to the sources of outward shifts in the *MEC* schedule.

6. In addition to mere increases in quantity of capital per person, any list of factors importantly affecting growth includes the extent of innovation, the quality of human capital, the size of the working population, and the whole institutional setting.

7. The critical importance of increasing knowledge and new technology in sustaining growth is highlighted by the great drain on existing natural resources of the explosive growth of the last two or three decades. Without continuing new knowledge, the present needs and aspirations of the world's population cannot be met.

Topics for Review

The role of investment in increasing potential national income

The cumulative nature of growth

Benefits and costs of growth

Effects of capital accumulation with and without new knowledge

Embodied and disembodied technical change

Factors affecting growth

Limits to growth

Discussion Questions

1. We usually study and measure economic growth in macroeconomic terms. But in a market economy who makes the decisions that lead to growth? What kind of decisions and what kind of actions cause growth to occur? How might a detailed study of individual markets be relevant to understanding economic growth?

2. Why is rising productivity a more significant contributing factor for economic growth than simply increasing the quantity of productive resources? Define *productivity*. List all the factors that increase the productivity of labor and the productivity of capital. Comment on the differences and similarities of the two lists.

3. *Family Weekly* recently listed (among others) the following "inventions that have changed our lives": microwave ovens, digital clocks, bank credit cards, freeze-dried coffee, tape cassettes, climate-controlled shopping malls, automatic toll collectors, soft contact lenses, tubeless tires, and electronic word processors.

Which of them would you hate to do without? Which, if any, will have a major impact on life in the twenty-first century? If there are any that you believe will not, does that mean they are frivolous and unimportant?

4. The Overseas Development Council, in 1977, introduced "a new measure of economic development based on the physical quality of life." Its index, called PQLI, gives one-third weight to each of three indicators: literacy, life expectancy, and infant mortality. While countries such as the United States and the Netherlands rank very high on either the PQLI or on an index of per capita real national income, some relatively poor countries, such as Sri Lanka, rank much higher on the PQLI index than much richer countries such as Algeria and Kuwait. Discuss the merits or deficiencies of this measure.

5. "The case for economic growth is that it gives man greater control over his environment, and consequently increases his freedom." Explain why you agree or disagree with this statement by Nobel laureate W. Arthur Lewis.

6. Growth in income per capita is a necessary condition for a rising standard of living in a country. Is it also a *sufficient* condition for making everyone better off? Why may not everyone benefit from economic growth?

7. GNP in real terms in Canada doubled between 1965 and 1980. Over this period the annual percentage rate of increase in GNP in constant dollars was 4.8 percent per year. Evaluate this measure of growth with respect to how well it reflects changes in (a) the material well-being of the average resident of Canada and (b) the nation's capacity to produce goods and services. In each case suggest what additional information you would like to know.

8. You discover that a particular economy has achieved a rapid increase in the size of its capital stock over several decades with no appreciable change in the rate of return to capital. What, if anything, can you conclude about its rate of innovation? Its rate of growth?

9. Consider a developed economy that decides to achieve a zero rate of growth for the future. What implications would such a "stationary state" have for the processes of production and consumption?

10. Suppose solar energy becomes the dominant form of energy in the twenty-first century. What changes will this make in the comparative advantages and growth rates of Africa and Northern Europe?

Growth and the Less-developed Countries

44

In our civilized, comfortable urban life, most of us lose sight of the fact that, in terms of the life span of the earth, it is a very short time since human beings lived as other animals, scratching an existence as best they could. It is only about 10,000 years since human beings became food producers rather than food gatherers. It is only within the last few centuries that a significant proportion of the world's population could look forward to anything but a hard struggle to wrest an existence from a reluctant nature. The concept of leisure combined with high consumption standards as a right to be enjoyed by all is new in human history.

The Uneven Pattern of Development

Table 44-1 repays careful study. It shows how few people have made the transition from poverty to relative comfort. There are more than 4.5 billion people alive today, but the wealthy parts of the world, where people work no more than 40 or 50 hours per week and enjoy substantial leisure and a level of consumption at or above half of that attained by the residents of North America, contain only about 20 percent of the world's population. Many of the rest struggle for subsistence. About 2 billion exist on a level at or below that enjoyed by peasants in ancient Egypt or Babylon.

Data of the sort shown in Table 44-1 cannot be

TABLE 44-1
Income and Population Differences Among Groups of Countries, 1977

Classification (based on GNP per capita in 1976 U.S. dollars)[a]	Number of countries (1)	GNP (billions) (2)	Population (millions) (3)	GNP per capital (4)	Percentage of the world's GNP (5)	Percentage of the world's population (6)	Growth rate[b] (7)
I Less than $175	22	$ 130	968	$ 135	1.7	23.1	1.5
II $175–349	19	84	347	242	1.1	8.3	4.8
III $350–699	22	481	1254	384	6.4	29.9	5.2
IV $700–1,399	25	478	442	1,081	6.4	10.5	4.0
V $1,400–2,799	19	416	183	2,276	5.4	4.4	4.7
VI $2,800–5,599	12	2,314	574	4,028	30.6	13.7	3.5
VII $5,600 or more	18	3,669	426	8,606	48.4	10.1	4.6
Totals	137	$7,572	4194	$1,805	100.0	100.0	

Source: U.S. Arms Control and Disarmament Agency, *World Military Expenditures 1968–1977; International Financial Statistics; Statistical Abstract*
[a] The groups represent arbitrary groupings in which real GNP per capita doubles with each progression.
[b] Average annual percentage rate of growth of real GNP per capita, 1968–1977.

Over half of the world's population live in poverty; many of the very poorest are in countries that have the lowest growth rates and thus fall ever farther behind. The unequal distribution of the world's income is shown in columns 5 and 6. Groups I–III, with over 60 percent of the world's population, earn less than 10 percent of world income. Groups VI–VII, with 24 percent of the world's population, earn 79 percent of world income. Column 7 shows that the poorer countries are not closing the gap in income between rich and poor countries.

accurate down to the last $100.[1] Nevertheless, the *development gap*—the discrepancy between the standards of living in countries at the two ends of the distribution—is real and large.

There are many different ways to look at the inequality of income distribution among the world's population. Consider Figure 44-1, which plots the Lorenz curve of the world's income distribution alongside that for Canada. Clearly the distribution of income in Canada is much closer to equality than the world distribution.

Another approach is to look at the geographic distribution of income per capita, as shown in Figure 44-2. Recent political discussions of income distribution have distinguished between richer and poorer nations as "North" versus "South." The map reveals why.

The Consequences of Underdevelopment

The human consequences of very low income levels can be severe. Someone studying the effect of rainfall variations would find that for a rich country such as Canada the variations would be reflected in farm output and farm income: for each inch of rainfall below some critical amount, farm output and income would vary in a regular way. In poor countries such as India, variations in rainfall are reflected in the death rate. Indeed, many live so close to subsistence that slight fluctuations in the food supply bring death by starvation to large numbers. Other less dramatic characteristics of poverty include inadequate diet, poor health, short life expectancy, illiteracy, and—very important—an attitude of helpless resignation to the caprice of nature.

[1] There are many problems in comparing national incomes across countries. For example, home-grown food is vitally important to living standards in underdeveloped countries, but it is excluded—or at best imperfectly included—in the national income statistics of most countries. So is a warm climate. But these data do reflect enormous real differences in living standards that no statistical discrepancies can hide.

FIGURE 44-1

Lorenz Curves Showing Inequalities Among the Nations of the World and Within Canada

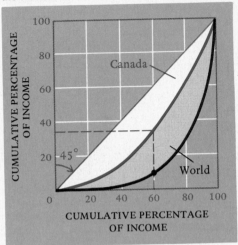

The inequality in the distribution of income is much less within Canada than it is among all the nations of the world. In a Lorenz curve, a wholly equal distribution of income would be represented by the 45° line: 20 percent of the population would have 20 percent of the income, 50 percent of the population would have 50 percent of the income, and so on. The very unequal distribution of world income is shown by the black curve. For example, 60 percent of the world's population live in countries that earn only 10 percent of the world's income, as shown by the black dot.

Contrast this with the distribution of income within Canada: the poorest 60 percent of the Canadian population earn 33 percent of the nation's income. This is not equality, but it is much less unequal than the differences between rich and poor countries.

These facts make the problems of economic growth very much more pressing in poor countries than in rich ones. Reformers in underdeveloped countries—often called **less-developed countries (LDCs)**—feel a sense of urgency not felt by their counterparts in rich countries. Many now living at the bare subsistence margin can look forward to improvements in their lot only if their country experiences an immediate and rapid rate of economic growth. Yet, as the first row of Table 44-1 shows, the development gap

for the very poorest countries has been widening. As will be seen, this is a problem of both output and population. It is also an international political problem.

Incentives for Development

Obviously "underdevelopment" is nothing new.[2] Concern with it as a remediable condition, however, is recent; it has become a compelling policy issue only within the present century. Probably the dominant reason for this newfound concern has been the apparent success of planned programs of "crash" development in the Soviet Union (see the box) and China. Leaders in other countries ask, If they can do it, why not us?

In the last 35 years there have been many examples of rapid and more or less planned economic development. In a world that each year is made smaller by communication and transportation improvements, these developments are visible to all. It is bad enough to be poor, but to be poor when others are escaping poverty is intolerable. Suddenly people see that it is possible to achieve better lives for themselves and their children.

A second push toward development has come from the developed countries, with their policies to aid less-developed countries. We shall discuss such programs and their motivation later.

A third pressure for development results from the emergence of a relatively cohesive bloc of LDCs within the United Nations. The bloc is attempting to utilize its political bargaining power to achieve economic ends.

Both from within and from without the LDCs the passive acceptance of underdeveloped status has ended. LDCs want to achieve major increases in living standards within a generation.

[2] The terminology of development is often confusing. "Underdeveloped," "less developed," and "developing" do not mean the same thing in ordinary English, yet each has been used to describe the same phenomenon. For the most part we shall refer to the underdeveloped countries as the less-developed countries, the LDCs for short. Some of them are making progress, that is, developing; others are not. All of these are terms used by development economists, and should be understood as such.

FIGURE 44-2
Countries of the World, According to Per Capita GNP, 1976

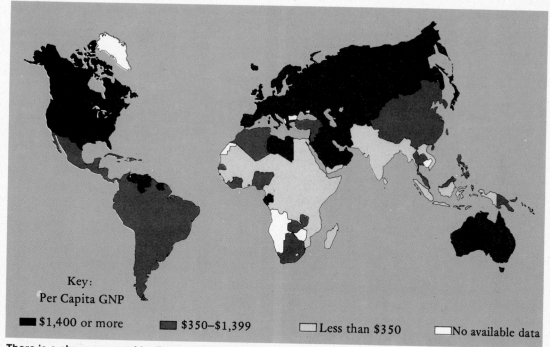

Key:
Per Capita GNP

■ $1,400 or more   ■ $350–$1,399   ☐ Less than $350   ☐ No available data

There is a sharp geographic division between North and South in the level of income per capita. The nations of the world are classified here according to three levels of measured per capita GNP. The poorest, shown in light gray, represents 31 percent of the world's population. The middle group, shown in dark gray, represents about 41 percent of world population. The wealthiest group, shown in black, includes all of North America, Europe, the Soviet Union, and Japan yet includes only 28 percent of the world's people. Areas shown in white are those for which data are unavailable. See Table 44-1 for more detail.

What are the causes of underdevelopment, and how may they be overcome?

Barriers to Economic Development

When income per head is taken as an index of the level of economic development, a country may develop by any set of devices that causes its aggregate income to grow faster than its population. However, there are many impediments to such growth.

POPULATION GROWTH

Today many LDCs have more national income than before, but they also have more mouths to feed. Thus their standard of living is no higher than it was a hundred or even a thousand years ago. The average Burmese and the rural Ethiopian are as hungry today as their great-grandparents were. The growth problem faced by underdeveloped countries is how to get off the treadmill and onto the escalator. Will modest gains in the capital stock eventually add up to enough to produce sustained growth? Not necessarily; it is the amount of output *per person* that determines whether living standards will rise. There is all too often a losing race between output and population.

Population growth is a central problem of economic development. If population expands as fast as national income, per capita income will not increase. A country may by great effort raise the quantity of capital only to find that a corre-

TABLE 44-2
The Relation of Population Growth to Per Capita GNP, 1968–1977 (percentages)

Classification of countries (GNP per capita, 1976 U.S. dollars)			Average annual rate of growth of			Population growth as a percentage of real GNP growth
Group[a]	Average income level	Percentage of population	Real GNP	Population	Real GNP per capita	
I	less than $175	23.1	4.0	2.6	1.4	65
II–IV	$175–1,399	48.7	6.8	2.1	4.7	30
V–VII	$1,400 or more	28.2	4.4	0.5	3.9	10

Source: Calculated from sources in Table 44-1.
[a] Groups from Table 44-1.

Growth in per capita real income depends on the difference between growth rates of real national income and population. The very poorest countries have *both* a relatively low growth rate of income and a relatively high growth rate of population. The middle group shows rising living standards despite large population growth by virtue of a high growth rate of income. The wealthiest countries owe much of their growth in living standards to a low rate of population increase.

sponding rise in population has occurred, so that the net effect of its "growth policy" is that a larger population is now maintained at the original low standard of living. Much of the problem of the very poorest countries is due to population growth. They have made appreciable gains in income, but most of the gains have been eaten up (literally) by the increasing population. Table 44-2 shows this.

The population problem has led economists to talk about the "critical minimum effort" that is required not merely to increase capital but to increase it fast enough so that the increase in output outraces the increase in population. The problem arises because population size is not independent of the level of income. When population control is left to nature, nature solves it in a cruel way. Population increases until many are forced to live at a subsistence level; further population growth is halted by famine, pestilence, and plague. This grim situation was perceived early in the history of economics by Thomas Malthus.

In some ways, the population problem is more severe today than it was even a generation ago because advances in medicine and in public health have brought sharp and sudden decreases in death rates. It is ironic that much of the compassion shown by wealthier nations for the poor and underprivileged people of the world has traditionally taken the form of improving their health, thereby doing little to avert their poverty. We praise the medical missionaries who brought modern medicine to the tropics, but the elimination of malaria has doubled population growth in Sri Lanka. Cholera, once a killer, is now largely under control. No one argues against controlling disease, but other steps must also be taken if the child who survives the infectious illnesses of infancy is not to die of starvation in early adulthood.

Figure 44-3 illustrates actual and projected world population growth. The population problem is not limited to underdeveloped countries, but about seven-eighths of the expected growth in the world's population is in Africa, Asia, and Latin America, those areas where underdevelopment is the rule rather than the exception.

NATURAL RESOURCES

A country with ample fertile land and a large supply of easily developed resources will find growth in income easier to achieve than one poorly endowed with such resources. Kuwait has an income per capita above that of the United States because by accident it sits on top of the world's greatest known oil field. Oil is transforming living standards in Kuwait. But a lack of oil

FIGURE 44-3
World Population Growth, 1400–2000

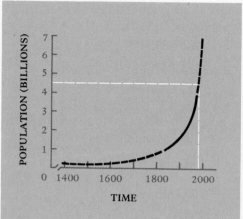

The current growth in the world's population is explosive. The solid line reflects present measurements. The dashed line involves projections from observed trends. It took about 50,000 years from the emergence of modern human beings for the world's population to reach 1 billion. It took 100 years to add a second billion, 30 years to add the third billion, and 15 years to add the fourth billion. If present trends continue, the 1975 population of 4 billion will double by 2005.

proved a devastating setback to many LDCs when the OPEC cartel increased oil prices tenfold during the 1970s. Without oil their development efforts would be halted, but to buy oil took so much scarce foreign exchange that it threatened to cripple their attempts to import needed capital goods.

Natural resource endowments can be the product of people as well as of nature. In fact, a nation's supplies of land and natural resources are often readily expandable in their effective use, if not in their total quantity. Badly fragmented land holdings may result from a dowry or inheritance system. For example, when farm land is divided into very small parcels, it may be much more difficult to achieve the advantages of modern agriculture than it is when the land is available in huge tracts for large-scale farming.

Lands left idle because of a lack of irrigation or

spoiled by excessive irrigation or lack of crop rotation are well-known examples of barriers to development. Ignorance is another. The nations of the Middle East sat through recorded history alongside the Dead Sea without realizing that it was a substantial source of potash. Not until after World War I were these resources utilized; now they provide Israel with raw materials for its rapidly growing fertilizer and chemical industries.

INEFFICIENCY IN THE USE OF RESOURCES

Low levels of income and slower than necessary growth rates may result from the inefficient use of resources as well as the lack of key resources.

It is useful to distinguish between two kinds of inefficiency. An hour of labor would be used inefficiently, for example, if a worker, even though working at top efficiency, were engaged in making a product that no one wanted. Using society's resources to make the wrong products is an example of **allocative inefficiency.**

In terms of the production possibility boundary encountered in Chapter 1, allocative inefficiency represents operation at the wrong place on the boundary. Allocative inefficiency will occur if the signals to which people respond are distorted—both monopoly and tariffs are commonly cited sources of distortions—or if market imperfections prevent resources from moving to their best uses.

A second kind of inefficiency has come to be called X-inefficiency, following Professor Harvey Leibenstein. **X-inefficiency** arises whenever resources are used in such a way that even if they are making the right product, they are doing so less productively than is possible. One example would be workers too hungry or too unmotivated to concentrate on their tasks.

All economies suffer from X-inefficiency because all are to some extent captives of their customs, their institutions, and their histories. But LDCs may be particularly vulnerable because of such factors as illiteracy, poor health, and lack of skills. They may also have cultural attitudes that give greater weight to friendship, loyalty, and tradition than to productivity. However admirable those qualities may be, they may not promote the most efficient use of resources.

INADEQUATE HUMAN RESOURCES

A well-developed entrepreneurial class, motivated and trained to organize resources for efficient production, is often missing in underdeveloped countries. This lack may be a heritage of a colonial system that gave the local population no opportunity to develop; it may result from the fact that managerial positions are awarded on the basis of family status or political patronage; it may reflect the presence of economic or cultural attitudes that do not favor acquisition of wealth by organizing productive activities; or it may simply be due to the nonexistence of the quantity or quality of education or training that is required.

Poor health is likewise a source of inadequate human resources. When the labor force is healthy, less time is lost and more effective effort is expended. The economic analysis of medical advances is a young field, however, and there is a great deal to be learned about the size of the drag of poor health on the growth of an economy.

INSTITUTIONAL AND CULTURAL BARRIERS

The progress of economic development is reflected in the increasing flow of goods and services from a nation's farms and factories to its households. Yet the ability to sustain and expand these flows depends on many aspects of economic and social organization.

Infrastructure

Certain key supporting services—sometimes called the **infrastructure**—such as a transportation and communications network are necessary to efficient commerce. Roads, bridges, railways, and harbors are needed to transport people, materials, and finished goods. The most dramatic confirmation of their importance comes in wartime, when belligerents always place high priority on destroying each other's transportation facilities.

Reasonable phone and postal services, water supply, and sanitation are essential to economic development. The absence, whatever the reason, of a dependable infrastructure can impose severe barriers to economic development.

Financial Institutions

The lack of an adequate and trusted system of financial institutions is often a barrier to development. Because investment has a key role in growth, banks are needed to help overcome the shortage of funds for investment. It may take as much as $10 of capital to increase full-employment national income by $1 per year. If this is so, it will take $66 *billion* of capital to raise average income per year by $100 in a country of 66 million—such as Mexico in 1980.

One source of funds for investment is the savings of households and firms. When banks and banking do not function well and smoothly, the link between private saving and investment may be broken and the problem of finding funds for investment greatly intensified.

Many people in LDCs do not trust banks, sometimes with good reason, more often without. Either they do not maintain deposits or they panic periodically, drawing them out and seeking security for their money in mattresses, in gold, or in real estate. The tendency to flee from money is made stronger when, as in recent years, a sharp inflation threatens the value of money holdings. When this happens, increases in savings do not become available for investment in productive capacity. When banks cannot count on their deposits being left in the banking system, they cannot engage in the kind of long-term loans needed to finance investments.

Developing countries must not only create

banking institutions, they must create enough stability and reliability that people will trust their savings to those who wish to invest.

Cultural, Social, and Religious Barriers

Traditions and habitual ways of doing business vary among societies, and not all are equally conducive to productivity. Max Weber argued that the "Protestant ethic" encourages the acquisition of wealth and is consequently more likely to encourage growth than is an ethic that directs activity away from the economic sphere.

Often in the LDCs personal considerations of family, of past favors, or of traditional friendship or enmity are more important than market signals in explaining behavior. One may find a too-small firm struggling to survive against a larger rival and learn that the owner prefers to remain small rather than expand because expansion would require use of nonfamily capital or leadership. To avoid paying too harsh a competitive price for built-in inefficiency, the firms' owners may then spend half their energies in an attempt to influence the government to prevent larger firms from being formed or to try to secure restrictions on the sale of output—and they may well succeed. Such behavior is very likely to inhibit economic growth.

When people believe that who your father is is more important than what you do, it may take a generation to persuade employers to change their attitudes and another generation to persuade workers that times have changed. Structuring incentives is a widely used form of policy action in market-oriented economies, but this may be harder to do in a personalistic society than in a market economy. If people habitually bribe the tax collector rather than pay taxes, they will not be likely to respond to policies that are supposed to work by raising or lowering taxes. All that will change is the size of the bribe.

In a society in which children are expected to stay in their fathers' occupations, it is more difficult for the labor force to change its characteristics and to adapt to the requirements of growth than in a society where upward mobility is itself a goal.

There is lively current debate on how much to make of the significance of differing cultural attitudes. Some believe that traditional and cultural considerations dominate peasant societies to the exclusion of economic responses; others suggest that any resulting inefficiency may be relatively small.

If it is true that social, religious, or legal patterns make growth more difficult, this need not mean that they are undesirable. Instead it means that the benefits of these patterns must now be weighed against the costs, of which the effect on growth is one. When people derive satisfaction from a religion whose beliefs inhibit growth, when they value a society in which every man owns his own land and is more nearly self-sufficient than in another society, they may be quite willing to pay a price in terms of growth opportunities forgone.

Whether a society's customs reflect cherished values or only such things as residual influences of a colonial history or an oligarchical political structure is important to the policymakers who must decide whether the cost in terms of efficiency should be paid. In any case, cultural attitudes are not easily changed.

THE CHALLENGE TO DEVELOPMENT POLICY

The many barriers to economic development—population growth, lack of natural and human resources, inefficient use of resources, and institutional and cultural restraints—singly or in combination can keep a country poor.

Economic development policy involves identifying the particular barriers to the level and kind of development desired and then devising policies to overcome them. Planners can seek funds for investment, and they can attempt to identify cultural, legal, social, and psychological barriers to growth. They can undertake the programs of ed-

The Economy of the Soviet Union

The modern *economic* history of the Soviet Union is usually taken to have begun in 1928, eleven years after the Bolshevik revolution. By the late 1920s Joseph Stalin had emerged as an effective strong man, ready to undertake the economic task of lifting Russia from an underdeveloped giant to a major industrial power. Basically, Stalin's economic policy had three strategies.

1. To consolidate management over all economic resources to ensure that they would respond to the needs of the regime.
2. To constrict consumption to an absolute minimum so that the maximum possible rate of capital accumulation, and thus growth, could be achieved.
3. To channel growth into the areas of heavy industrial development required for a major military power.

The famous five-year plans (see the box on page 944) began the rapid industrial development that was to transform the Soviet Union into a major world power. The tenth five-year plan, covering the period 1976–1980, was only the second to put major emphasis on production of consumer goods, and the Russian economy is to this day plagued by serious shortages of consumer goods, perhaps most notably food.

Ownership. With certain limited exceptions, the central government—the state—owns all land, all natural resources, all capital goods, all business enterprises, and most urban housing. Private enterprise is profitable where it is permitted, and illegal black markets have arisen in response to the restricted supply of officially available goods.

The organization of production. Industrial production is organized predominantly around individual plants. However, production decisions are made in a highly organized pyramidal bureaucracy.

The industrial firm's targets include output quotas. A firm is often given maximum levels of inputs (such as number of employees, tons of coal). The wages a firm can offer are fixed by the government, and there is no open market on which the firm's manager can acquire scarce commodities. Within limits, workers are free to choose any job they are offered—except that workers on collective farms have not been allowed to leave them at will.

Clearly, industry is governed by the rules of a command economy. Within the guidelines of the plan, the firm is encouraged to be efficient and, where possible, to make "above-plan profits," part of which may be retained in the firm and used for the benefit of the employees.*

---

*Because prices are specified by the state and are spelled out in the directive, the firm can earn above-plan profits only by exceeding output quotas. Many critics both outside and inside the system have noticed an over-concentration on physical output—on technological rather than economic efficiency.

ucation, legal reform, resource development, negotiation of trade treaties, or actual investment that smooth the way to more rapid growth.

All this is more easily said than done. Further, as the dozens of "development missions" sent out by the World Bank and other international, national, and private agencies have discovered, the problems and strategies vary greatly from country to country. Economic development as a field of expertise is in its infancy. However, there are common basic choices that all developing countries must face, and there are a number of alternative development strategies that may be pursued.

Observers have often noted that many microeconomic inefficiencies result from the command principle. Among them are stockpiles, shortages, and poor product quality. Despite inefficiencies, the Soviet system clearly works. It has produced a growing flow of armaments, goods, machines, and space vehicles.

Agricultural production (which in 1928 absorbed 80 percent of the Soviet labor force and today absorbs about 25 percent) is almost as centralized as manufacturing. Collective farms were designed to provide cheap and adequate food supplies. Collective farmers do not receive wages; rather, they share in the income of the farm. But the government's policy, designed to keep food prices down by keeping farm prices low, has kept farm income low, too. Agricultural production has been a chronic trouble spot in the Soviet economy.

The distribution of goods and household incentives. Both the nature and the quantity of the goods to be produced are specified by the central planners. Households are free to spend their incomes on these goods. Here individual choice rather than "command" is at work, but the function of a market is restricted. If too many consumers want a particular item, for instance, it runs out; no price rise signals producers that there is a higher demand. The shortage is not an effective signal because producers are not motivated to respond to it. There is no automatic feedback of what consumers *want* that has an effect on the goods and services actually produced.

Until the consumer riots in Poland in 1970, Soviet planners were reluctant to respond to such clear consumer signals as shortages of particular goods. After that Soviet planners began to take account of shortages and surpluses of particular consumer goods at existing prices in setting new production targets.

Household incomes come from the state principally in the form of wages and salaries. "To each according to his need" was the Marxian ideal, but in the Soviet Union scientists and engineers, ballet dancers, and athletes apparently need more than do laborers and teachers. Wage *differentials* are in fact very much larger than in North America.

But wages are not the only determinant of the distribution of income. Many goods and services such as medical care, higher education, and old age pensions are provided free to those who qualify. State housing is provided at low cost. Large families receive special money allowances and special housing. Thus standards of living in the Soviet Union are somewhat less unequal than wage differentials suggest. There are fewer extreme incomes at either end but a somewhat greater spread in the incomes of the middle and upper middle income groups.

Some Basic Choices

HOW MUCH GOVERNMENT CONTROL?

How much government control over the economy is necessary and desirable? Practically every shade of opinion from "The only way to grow is to get the government's dead hand out of everything" to "The only way to grow is to get a fully planned, centrally controlled economy" has been seriously advocated. The extreme views are easily refuted by historical evidence. Many economies have grown with very little government assistance; Great Britain, Holland, Singapore, and Hong Kong are all examples. Others, such as the Soviet Union and Poland, have sustained growth with a high degree of centralized control. In other countries there is almost every conceivable mix of government and private initiative in the growth process. Many possible combinations of state and private initiative have been used successfully. On the question of what will prove the best mix at a particular time and in a particular place, there is likely to be much disagreement.

The Case for Planning

Active government intervention in the management of a country's economy often rests on the real or alleged failure of market forces to produce satisfactory results. The major appeal of such intervention is that it is expected to accelerate the pace of economic development.

Any of the barriers to development may be lowered by enlightened actions of the government. Consider, for example, how the central authorities might seek to ease a shortage of investment funds. In a fully employed free-market economy, investment is influenced by the quantity of savings households and firms make, and thus the division of resources between consumption and saving is one determinant of the rate of growth.

When living standards are low, people have urgent uses for their current income. When savings decisions are left to individual determination, savings tend to be low, and this is an impediment to investment and growth. In a variety of ways, central authorities can intervene and force people to save more than they otherwise would. Compulsory saving has been one of the main aims of most development plans of centralized governments such as those of the USSR and China.

The goal of such plans is to raise savings and thus lower current consumption below what it would be in an unplanned economy. While forced savings plans are largely associated with totalitarian regimes, a frequent subject of planning in less centrally controlled societies is in-

creasing the savings rate through tax incentives and monetary policies. The object is the same: to increase investment in order to increase growth, and thus to make future generations better off.

Central governments of an authoritarian sort can be particularly effective in overcoming some of the sources of X-inefficiency. A dictatorship may suppress social and even religious institutions that are barriers to growth, and it may hold on to power until a new generation grows up that did not know and does not value the old institutions. It is much more difficult for a democratic government, which must command popular support at each election, to do currently unpopular things in the interests of long-term growth. Whether the gains in growth that an authoritarian government can achieve are worth the political and social costs is, of course, an important value judgment.

The Case for Laissez Faire

Most people would agree that government must play an important part in any development program and especially in education, transportation, and communication. But what of the sectors usually left to private enterprise in advanced capitalist countries?

The advocates of laissez faire in these sectors place great emphasis on human drive, initiative, and inventiveness. Once the infrastructure has been established, an army of entrepreneurs will do vastly more to develop the economy than will an army of civil servants. The market will provide the opportunities and direct their efforts, and individuals will act energetically within it once their self-interest is understood. People who seem irretrievably lethargic and unenterprising when held down by lack of incentives will show amazing bursts of energy when given sufficient self-interest in economic activity.

Furthermore, the argument goes, individual capitalists are far less wasteful than civil servants of the country's capital. A bureaucrat investing capital that is not his own (raised perhaps from the peasants by a state marketing board that buys cheap and sells dear) may choose to enhance his own prestige at the public's expense by spending too much money on cars, offices, and secretaries and too little on truly productive activities. Even if the bureaucrat is genuinely interested in the country's well-being, the incentive structure of a bureaucracy does not encourage creative risk taking. If his ventures fail, his head will likely roll; if they succeed, he will receive no profits—and his superior may get the medal.

WHAT SORTS OF EDUCATION?

Most studies of underdeveloped countries suggest that undereducation is a barrier to development and often urge increased expenditures on education. This poses a choice: whether to spend educational funds on erasing illiteracy and increasing the level of mass education or on training a small cadre of scientific and technical specialists. The problem is serious because education is expensive and does not pay off quickly.

To improve basic education requires a large investment in school building and in teacher training. This investment will result in a visible change in the level of education only after ten or more years, and it will not do much for productivity over that time span.

The opportunity cost of basic education expenditures always seems high. Yet it is essential to make them because the gains will be critical to economic development a generation later.

A great many developing countries have put a large fraction of their educational resources into training a small number of highly educated men and women—often by sending them abroad for advanced study—because the tangible results of a few hundred doctors or engineers or Ph.D.s are relatively more visible than the results from raising the school-leaving age by a year or two, say, from age 10 to age 12. It is not yet clear whether this policy pays off, but it is clear that it has some drawbacks.

Many of this educated elite are recruited from the privileged classes on the basis of family position, not merit; many regard their education as the passport to a new aristocracy rather than as a mandate to serve their fellow citizens; and an appreciable fraction emigrate to countries where their newly acquired skills bring higher pay than at home. Of those who return home, many seek the security of a government job, which they may utilize to advance their own status in what is sometimes a self-serving and unproductive bureaucracy.

WHAT POPULATION POLICY?

The race between population and income has been a dominant feature of many underdeveloped countries. There are only two possible ways for a country to win this race. One is to make such a massive push that it achieves a growth rate well in excess of the rate of population growth. The other is to control population growth. The problem *can* be solved by restricting population growth. This is not a matter of serious debate, though the means of restricting it are, for there are considerations of religion, custom, and education involved.

The consequences of different population policies are large. Sweden and Venezuela have similar death rates. Yet the birth rate in Sweden is 12 per thousand, and in Venezuela it is 42. These variations in birth rates have economic consequences. In Venezuela the net increase of population per year is 33 per thousand (3.3 percent), but it is only 3 per thousand (0.3 percent) in Sweden. If each country were to achieve an overall rate of growth of production of 3 percent per year, Sweden's living standards would be increasing by 2.7 percent per year while Venezuela's would be falling by 0.3 percent per year. In 1977 Sweden's income per capita ($8,400) was three times as high as Venezuela's ($2,600) —and Venezuela is the wealthiest country in South and Central America. The gap will widen rapidly if present population trends continue.

Different countries have adopted very different positions with respect to population. Kenya, with a birth rate of 50 per thousand, until very recently rejected any serious national policy of population control. Mexico, with nearly as high a birth rate in the early 1970s, began to dispense free contraceptives and family planning information and has seen its annual rate of population growth drop from 3.2 percent to 2.5 percent in less than five years.

The Chinese — today a quarter of the world's population — have reduced their rate of population increase from more than 3 percent to 1.2 percent in the last 25 years by promoting later marriages and exhorting parents to value daughters as well as sons and thus to be content with fewer children. In 1980 China began more aggressive steps in an announced attempt to achieve zero population growth by the year 2000. It has introduced new regulations to limit families to one or at most two children. Those that comply will receive bonuses and preferential treatment in housing and education for their offspring. (Housing space will be allocated to all families as though they had two children.) Families that do not comply with the policy will have their salaries decreased and will be promoted more slowly.

Aggressive population control policies do not always work. Indira Gandhi, in her first term as prime minister of India, imposed male surgical sterilization in the mid 1970s. It succeeded in the short run — at its peak nearly 1 million vasectomies per month were being performed — but failed in the longer run because a political storm of opposition toppled her government. Consequently, any national program of population control has become a liability too heavy for the leading Indian political parties to support.

Positive economics cannot decide whether population control is desirable, but it can describe the consequences of any choice. Economic development is much easier to achieve with population control than without it.

HOW TO ACQUIRE CAPITAL?

A country can raise funds for investment in three distinct ways: from the savings (voluntary or forced) of its domestic households and firms, by loans or investment from abroad, and by contributions from foreigners.

Capital from Domestic Saving: The Vicious Circle of Poverty

If capital is to be created at home by a country's own efforts, resources must be diverted from the production of goods for current consumption. This means a cut in present living standards. If living standards are already at or near the subsistence level, such a diversion will be difficult. At best, it will be possible to reallocate only a small proportion of resources to the production of capital goods.

Such a situation is often described as *the vicious circle of poverty:* because a country has little capital per head, it is poor; because it is poor, it can devote only a few resources to creating new capital rather than to producing goods for immediate consumption; because little new capital can be produced, capital per head remains low, and the country remains poor.

The vicious circle can be made to seem an absolute constraint on growth rates. Of course it is not; if it were, we would all still be at the level of Neanderthal man. The grain of truth in the vicious circle argument is that some surplus must be available somewhere in the society to promote saving and investment. In a poor society with an even distribution of income, where nearly everyone is at the subsistence level, saving may be very difficult. But this is not the common experience. Usually there will be at least a small middle class that can save and invest if opportunities for the profitable use of funds arise. Also in most poor societies today the average household is usually above the physical subsistence level. Even the poorest households will find that they can sacrifice some present living standards for a future gain. After all, presented with a profitable opportunity, villagers in Ghana planted cocoa plants at the turn of the century even though there was a seven-year growing period before any return could be expected!

The last example points to an important fact: in underdeveloped countries one resource that is often *not* scarce is labor hours. Profitable home or village investment that requires mainly labor inputs may be made with relatively little sacrifice in current living standards. However, this is not the kind of investment that will appeal to planners mesmerized by large, spectacular, and symbolic investments such as dams, nuclear power stations, and steel mills.

Imported Capital

Another way of accumulating the capital needed for growth is to borrow it from abroad. When a poor country, A, borrows from a rich country, B, it can use the borrowed funds to purchase capital goods produced in B. Country A thus accumulates capital and needs to cut its current output of consumption goods only to pay interest on its loans. As the new capital begins to add to current production, it becomes easier to pay the interest on the loan and also to repay the principal out of the increase in output. In this way income can be raised immediately and the major sacrifice postponed until later, when part of the increased income that might have been used to raise domestic consumption is instead used to pay off the loan. This method has the great advantage of giving a poor country an initial increase in capital goods far greater than it could possibly have created by diverting its own resources from consumption industries.

However, many countries, developed or undeveloped, are suspicious of foreign capital. They fear that foreign investors will gain control over their industries or their government. The extent of foreign control depends on the form that foreign capital takes. When foreigners buy bonds in domestic companies, they do not own or control anything; when they buy common stocks, they own part or all of a company, but their control over management may be small. If a foreign company (perhaps a multinational corporation) establishes a plant and imports its own managers and technicians, it will have much more control. Finally, if foreign firms subsidize an LDC government in return for permission to produce, they may feel justified in exacting political commitments.

Whether foreign ownership of one's industries carries political disadvantages sufficiently large to outweigh the economic gains is a subject of debate. In Canada, for example, there is serious political opposition to having a large part of Canadian industry owned by U.S. nationals. Many other countries suppress these fears and actively seek more foreign investment than they are getting.

The economic choices are quite clear:

Accumulating a given amount of capital through domestic saving requires greater current sacrifice but later pays a higher return. Foreign financing requires small present sacrifices but involves holding down living standards later in order to make the interest payments to foreign investors.

When both ways of financing are equally possible, the choice between them raises an important intergenerational question: to what extent should the sacrifices required to pay for growth be met now rather than ten years from now? One suspects that, political considerations aside, most people would prefer to postpone the cost by using borrowed capital.

Getting foreign capital is easier said than done in the early stages of development. Canada and America were once underdeveloped in the sense of being underpopulated, with many unused resources, but they were latent giants that promised rich returns to foreign investors. It is harder to see similar investment opportunities in Pakistan, say, where overpopulation has been a problem for centuries and where the soil has been severely salt-damaged by centuries of irrigation without proper drainage. The ability of such a country to borrow from private sources is small. Foreign capital plays a role, but it is capital provided by foreign governments and international agencies, not by private investors.

Contributed Capital

From the viewpoint of the receiving country, contributed capital might seem ideal. It has the advantage of enabling the country to shift to more rapid growth without either sacrificing consumption now or having to repay later. Investment funds for development are being received

"Aid," "Trade," or "Restitution"

The motivations behind international giving have become the subject of debate. Do developed nations give aid for humanitarian reasons, because it serves their political objectives, or because it is economically self-serving? Obviously all three motives can play a role, but which one dominates? Should LDCs demand aid, accept it gratefully, or reject it?

LDCs more or less chronically lack capital and lack wealth. Typically they have large and mounting foreign debts as a result of past borrowing. In these circumstances, one might think that foreign aid, whether from a single country or from an international forum, would be eagerly sought and gratefully received. This is not always so; there is some significant resistance to accepting aid.

The slogan "Trade, not aid" reflected political opposition to economic aid in certain recipient countries in the 1950s. Yugoslavia turned down much aid proffered by the Soviets after 1948, and China accepted no foreign aid after 1960. In 1975 Colombia made the decision to forgo further U.S. aid on the grounds that it bred an unhealthy economic dependency.

The primary explanation of this attitude lies in a country's noneconomic goals. It may suspect the motives of the givers and fear that hidden strings may be attached to the offer. Independent countries prize their independence and want to avoid either the fact or the appearance of being satellites. Pride—a desire to be beholden to no one—is also a factor.

One response was to do without aid, no matter how badly it was needed. Another, increasingly the pattern in the 1970s, was to reject "aid" but to demand "wealth transfers," not as a matter of charity but as a matter of "restitution" or redress for past sins by colonial powers against their former colonies. The obvious problem of asserting such claims against noncolonial powers such as the United States and the USSR has been no deterrent. There is a generalized sense that the inhabitants of the "North" exploited the nations of the "South" in past centuries and that present generations should redress the balance. The paradoxical aspect of this is that while "restitution, not charity" makes LDCs willing to accept aid, precisely that claim decreases the willingness of developed countries to offer it.

What *are* the motives of givers of aid? The Scandinavian Nobel Prize winning economist Gunnar Myrdal has argued that humanitarian considerations have played a large role. The evidence for the existence of humanitarian motives is in part the success of voluntary appeals in developed countries for food, funds, and clothes for persons in stricken areas of the world. As per capita incomes have risen in the Western world, so have contributions, private as well as public. It is the policy of the governments of most of the so-called Western democracies to devote some resources to alleviating poverty throughout the world.

Professor Edward S. Mason, among others, has argued that such aid can best be understood by looking to political and security motives. He points to the substantial U.S. congressional preference for military assistance over economic assistance, the denial of aid to countries such as Sri Lanka that traded with Communist countries, the fostering of Tito's Yugoslavia *because of* its anti-Soviet stand—all of which reveal a strong political motive. Many critics of OPEC think its contributions are designed to quiet opposition among LDCs to the oil price hikes that have proved so profitable to the oil producers and so painful to oil users, LDCs and developed countries alike.

Should motives and attitudes, either of givers or of receivers, matter? After all, it is economically beneficial to receive aid when you are poor. Economists cannot say that fears, aspirations, pride, and "face" are either foolish or unworthy; they can only note that they do have their cost.

today by underdeveloped countries from the governments of the developed countries acting both unilaterally (as in the U.S. Agency for International Development and a similar Soviet program) and through international agencies such as the World Bank, the Export-Import Bank, and the OPEC Fund established in January 1980.

Contributed capital has played a significant role in post-World War II economic development. For example, American foreign aid expenditures in the decade after the war were $90 billion, and even today they amount to more than $3 billion per year. The $3 billion is more than 1 percent of the GNP of the 2 billion people who live in the most underdeveloped nations of the world. The OPEC Fund started with an initial capital of $4 billion and is expected to grow rapidly.

The Soviet Union has given substantial aid to less-developed countries. Russian aid to China in the 1950s was essential to that country's development of heavy industry. In addition to funds, the USSR transported capital in the form of more than 150 complete plants and sent thousands of technician specialists to China to help plan, build, and run factories. China today is itself a significant donor to a few ideologically sympathetic countries, including Tanzania and Albania.

Alternative Development Strategies

In the search for development, individual LDCs have a number of policy options. The choice among them is in part a matter of what the planners believe will work, in part a question of the nature of the society that will be created once development has occurred.

The noneconomic aspects of the choice of a development strategy may be illustrated by the Greek government's explicit decision in the mid 1960s to change the direction of its growth. At that time Greece was achieving rapid growth in

income per capita largely because of a booming tourist trade and the emigration of many young Greeks to West Germany to work in factories there. The emigrants had been earning incomes in Greece that were substantially below the Greek average, and their remittances home to their families increased both domestic income and foreign exchange reserves. Although it was helpful to the Greek rate of growth to continue to rely on tourism and emigration as bulwarks of the economy, this policy threatened an image of life that visualized "Greece for the Greeks." Even at the prospect of some loss in growth, Greek planners recommended the restriction of emigration, the moderation of the size of the tourist role in the economy, and the development of new industry for the Greek economy.

There may be economic reasons for choosing a different pattern of growth than the free market would provide. One role of planning is to direct growth in a different direction, one that the planners guess will have the greatest chance of long-run success.

Unplanned growth will usually tend to exploit the country's present comparative advantages; planners may choose a pattern of growth that involves trying to change the country's future comparative advantage.

One reason for doing so is the belief that planners can evaluate the future more accurately than the countless individuals whose decisions determine market prices. A country need not passively accept its current comparative advantages. Many skills can be acquired, and fostering an apparently uneconomic domestic industry may, by changing the characteristics of the labor force, develop a comparative advantage in that line of production.

The Japanese had no visible comparable advantage in any industrial skill when Commodore Matthew Perry opened that feudal country to Western influence in 1854, but they became a major industrial power by the end of the century. Their continuing gains relative to the United States in fields such as steel, automobile manu-

Planning in the Soviet Union

Five-year plans. Five-year plans are, roughly, blueprints for later detailed implementation. They contain no orders to individual plants and no detailed quotas of goods to be produced, but they do prescribe both the level of aggregate income that is to be achieved and the *structure* of the economy by major sectors and industries.

Every five-year plan has included decisions about how drastically to curtail consumption in order to release resources for investment. Each has also decided how much effort is to be devoted to developing educational and technical resources that will be needed in the future. Decisions are also required about such matters as the form capital investment should take, and the state-controlled banking system lends only to those enterprises whose expansion the planners want to encourage.

One-year plans. Planning details are spelled out in the one-year plans. They are extremely complex exercises that work out the myriad microeconomic implications of certain broad objectives. By and large, the one-year plans translate the objectives of the five-year plans into detail sufficient to enable individual plants (or farms) to meet them and to ensure that the required supplies of needed resources are made available.

There is obviously an enormous coordinating job here. Tentative plans are sent to lower bureaucratic levels for comments and suggestions before being issued as final orders. Actual quotas are to some degree negotiated between the directors at the operating levels, who have a strong desire to hold down the quotas expected of them, and the higher-level planners, who must achieve apparent miracles to satisfy overall growth objectives.

Prices in the Planning Process

Factor pricing. For internal productive use, "prices" of commodities or resources are designed to measure the scarcity value of the resources, compared to alternative uses. If the efficient use of resource is to occur, the charge for using, say, the services of a carpenter any-

---

facture, and communications do not need to be called to anyone's attention today. Soviet planners in the 1920s and 1930s chose to create an industrial economy out of a predominantly agricultural one and succeeded in vastly changing the mix between agriculture and industry in a single generation (see the discussion in the box).

These illustrations suggest why the big choice may be that of a development strategy. Governments must choose between agricultural and industrial emphases; between different kinds of industrial development; and between more or less reliance on foreign trade. Several possibilities have been widely advocated, and each has been tried. None is without difficulties.

AGRICULTURAL DEVELOPMENT

Everyone needs food. An LDC may choose to devote a major portion of its resources to stimulating agricultural production, say, by mechanizing farms, irrigating land, and utilizing new seeds and fertilizers. If successful, the country will stave off starvation for its current population, and it may even develop an excess over current needs and so have a crop available for export. A food surplus can earn foreign exchange to buy needed imports.

Among the attractions of the agricultural strategy are that it does not require a great deal of technical training or hard-to-acquire know-how,

where should reflect the value of his or her marginal product elsewhere.

But the state may wish to pay carpenters a higher wage than this, either because it has embarked on a program of income redistribution in which carpenters are to be favored or because the state wishes to denote carpentry as a "prestige" occupation. To avoid productive inefficiency, the planners assign *two* wage rates for carpenters. One is charged as a cost of production; the other (which may be higher or lower) is actually paid out to carpenters and becomes the source of their income.

With one important exception, this dual treatment of factor prices has long been part of the Soviet planning procedure. The exception concerns the cost of capital. Because "interest" is traditionally a payment to private owners of capital in capitalist societies, interest rates were odious to Marx and to early Marxist planners. Soviet planners were reluctant to assign a real scarcity-value interest rate to funds allocated for investment until a series of studies showed that investment allocation was among the least efficient aspects of Soviet planning. Today a number very much like an interest rate is used to measure the cost of capital.

Consumer prices and the turnover tax. Consumer prices are made up of two parts: the full cost of the good produced, using the correct internal accounting prices for factors, plus the **turnover tax.** The tax is in form an excise tax, and it varies tremendously from commodity to commodity.

The size of the turnover tax is determined by the planners' idea of what goods people should be encouraged or discouraged to consume. In part this is a means for redistributing income; goods consumed by low-income groups may have very low turnover taxes.

Revenue from the turnover tax is used by the state for new investment. By changing the average rate of the turnover tax, the planners can affect the relative size of consumption and investment. By varying the tax rate on different kinds of commodities, the state affects the relative sacrifice in consumption among different kinds of consumers.

---

nor does it place the country in direct competition with highly industrial countries.

India, Pakistan, Taiwan, and other Asian countries have achieved dramatic increases in food production by the application of new technology—and new seed—to agricultural production. Increases of up to 50 percent have been achieved in grain production, and it has been estimated that with adequate supplies of water, pesticides, fertilizers, and modern equipment, production could be doubled or even tripled. This has been labeled the "green revolution." When the Nobel Prize Committee gave the 1970 *peace* prize to the American plant pathologist Norman Borlaug, it recognized the potential importance of these developments in alleviating, for at least a generation, the shortage of food that the population explosion was expected to bring.

The possibilities of achieving such dramatic gains in agricultural output may seem almost irresistible at first glance, yet many economists think they should be resisted—and they point to a series of problems.

One problem is that a vast amount of resources is required to irrigate land and mechanize production, and these resources used alternatively could provide industrial development and industrial employment opportunities. Thus there is a clear opportunity cost. Critics of the agricultural strategy argue that the search for a generation free from starvation will provide at best only a temporary solution because population will surely expand to meet the food supply. Instead, they argue, underdeveloped countries should start at once to reduce their dependence on agriculture. Let someone else grow the food; industrialization should not be delayed.

A second problem with the agricultural strategy is that the great increases in world production of wheat, rice, and other agricultural commodities that the "green revolution" makes possible could depress their prices and not lead to increased earnings from exports. What one agricultural country can do, so can others, and there may well be a glut on world markets. This is the heart of the argument of the distinguished Latin American economist Raúl Prebisch. He maintains that underdeveloped countries, overspecialized in the production of agricultural commodities, are sure to suffer steadily worsening terms of trade relative to manufacturing outputs. Prebisch believes that current market prices fail to anticipate fully this worsening in the terms of trade for agriculture and thus that planners should intervene and shift the country out of what is sure to be a long-run overreliance on agriculture.

A third problem has arisen (most acutely in India and Pakistan) where increasing agricultural output has been accompanied by decreasing labor requirements in agricultural production without a compensating increase in employment opportunities elsewhere. Millions of tenant farmers—and their bullocks—have been evicted from their tenant holdings by owners who are buying tractors to replace them. Many have found no other work.

Where there is already large-scale unemployment, devoting resources to labor-saving innovations makes little sense unless at the same time new jobs are developed for the displaced labor.

Despite the worldwide need for food, the agriculture strategy of development has not proven to be a surefire path to economic development.

SPECIALIZATION IN A FEW COMMODITIES

Many LDCs have existing unexploited resources such as copper, uranium, or opportunities for tourism. The principle of comparative advantage provides the traditional case for the desirability of relying on such resources. By specializing in producing those products in which it has the greatest comparative advantage, the country can achieve the most rapid growth in the short run. To neglect these opportunities will result in a lower living standard than would result from specialization accompanied by increased international trade.

These are cogent reasons in favor of *some* specialization. But specialization involves risks, and the risks may be worth reducing even at the loss of some income. Specialization here, as with agriculture, makes the economy highly vulnerable to cyclical fluctuations in world demand and supply. When a recession in developed countries decreases overseas travel, an LDC that has relied on tourism for needed foreign exchange is in immediate trouble.

The problem is not only cyclical. When technological or taste changes render a product partially or wholly obsolete, a country can face a major calamity for generations. Just as individual firms and regions may become overspecialized, so too may countries.

IMPORT SUBSTITUTION INDUSTRIALIZATION

International trade may bring great benefits, but it also entails risks. During the Great Depression the collapse in world agricultural prices caused the value of the exports of agricultural countries to decline drastically relative to the prices of goods those countries imported. During World War II many countries found that the manufactured goods they wished to import were simply unavailable. In each of those situations dependence on foreign trade for necessities did not seem wholly attractive. More recently, the rising prices of fuel and other imports have created enormous balance-of-payments problems for many LDCs. Such countries must either reduce imports or increase exports.

In order to conserve scarce foreign exchange reserves (and protect itself from interruptions in supply), a country can attempt to reduce its reliance on foreign trade by using its resources to produce domestic substitutes for some of the goods presently imported.

Much of the industrialization by LDCs in the 1950s and 1960s was directed toward **import substitution industry (ISI),** which is producing for sale in the home market goods that were previously imported. Because countries characteristically suffer from a significant comparative disadvantage when they produce goods for the first time, it proved necessary both to subsidize the home industry and to restrict imports to allow the infant ISI time to develop.

Implementing an import substitution policy is relatively easy. It can be done by imposing import quotas and raising tariffs. Such actions provide incentives for the development of domestic industry by carving out a ready-made market and by providing a substantial price umbrella that promises high profits to successful local manufacturers and to foreign investors who might enter with both capital and know-how. Subsidies, government loans, and other forms of encouragement have also been used in many cases. A study of import substitution industries in seven countries found that the effective rate of protection or subsidy varied from 25 to more than 200 percent.

The ISI strategy also has problems. It may well foster *inefficient* industries by virtue of the amount of protection granted, and in the long run countries do not become rich by being inefficient. It may well aggravate inequalities in income distribution by raising the prices of manufactured goods relative to agricultural goods and by favoring profits over wages. Another difficulty with the ISI strategy is that the opportunities for import substitution are limited; once the country runs out of imports to substitute for, what then?

The success of ISI is now in question. Taiwan followed it and has come to be one of the great successes of economic development of the recent past. Its income per capita has averaged a rate of increase of over 6 percent during the whole of the last two decades. Yet in India, Pakistan, Mexico, and Argentina it has not been a success. Mexico has succeeded, but largely by shifting from ISI to an export-oriented strategy.

ISI is now regarded as a strategy of limited promise unless it can lead to the ultimate establishment of efficient industries.

INDUSTRIALIZATION FOR EXPORT

Most development economists believe that industrialization ought to be encouraged only in areas where, once the protected phase of the development period is past, the country will have a reliable and efficient industry that can compete in world markets.

Obviously, if Tanzania or Peru could quickly develop steel, shipbuilding, and manufacturing industries that operated as efficiently as those of Japan or West Germany, they too might share in the rapid economic growth enjoyed by those industrial countries. Indeed, if a decade or two (or even three) of protection and subsidization could give infant industries time to mature and become efficient, the price might be worth paying. After all, both Japan and Russia were underdeveloped countries within living memory.

The greatest problem with such a strategy is that there is a good chance of failure. Even when the country has the basic natural resources, it may be backward enough that it is unlikely it will have the labor or managerial talent to achieve success within a reasonable time. India may create a steel industry and have its productivity increase year by year, but it must do more: it must catch up to the steel industries of other countries in order to compete in world markets.

The catch-up problem is a race against a moving target. Suppose you are committed to making a given industry competitive in ten years. In such a situation, it is not sufficient to make gains in productivity; they must be made at a rate fast enough to overcome a present disadvantage against an improving opponent. Suppose you must improve by 50 percent to achieve the present level of a competitor who is improving at *r* percent per year. If you want to catch up in ten years, you must improve at *r* + 4 percent per year. [50] If *r* is 6 percent, you must achieve 10 percent. To achieve 6 percent or 7 percent may be admirable, but you will lose the race just the same.

Thus, while this route to development is available, it depends both on having the required resources and on overcoming the difficulties that contribute to *X*-inefficiency. This often means devoting resources for a long period to education, training, development of an infrastructure, and overcoming the various cultural and social barriers to efficient production.

While this is hard, it is not impossible. Indeed, there have been some spectacular success stories: Brazil, Korea, Hong Kong, and Taiwan are charter members in a new category, "newly industrializing countries" that are providing vigorous competition in manufactured goods in world markets. Their success has led to a further (and bitterly resented) problem for the industrialization strategy. When an LDC succeeds, it is likely to find the developed countries trying to protect *their* home industries from the new competition.

The greatest success in development has been achieved by nations that have succeeded in developing efficient industrial export industries.

Having recognized this fact, it is easy to be led astray by it. LDCs sometimes pursue certain lines of production on a subsidized basis either for prestige purposes or because of a confusion between cause and effect. Because most wealthy nations have a steel industry, the leaders of many underdeveloped nations regard their countries as primitive until they develop a domestic steel industry. Because several LDCs have succeeded in producing consumer durables, many others as-

sume that they should try to do so. However if a country has a serious comparative disadvantage in steel or in making consumer durables, fostering such industries will make that country poor.

COMMODITY PRICE STABILIZATION AGREEMENTS

When all or most producers of a commodity can agree on price and output levels, they can achieve monopoly profits not available in competitive markets. Many LDCs are heavily committed to the production and export of one or more basic commodities such as bananas, bauxite, cocoa, coffee, copper, cotton, iron ore, jute, manganese, meat, oil, phosphates, rubber, sugar, tea, tropical timber, and tin. Why not get together and create an effective cartel that gives producers the enormous profits that are potentially available? This has been tried many times in history; until OPEC, it has always failed. Yet everyone knows that OPEC's success transformed a handful of formerly poor LDCs into the wealthiest of nations.[3]

OPEC's success has not been easy to copy because the special conditions of demand and supply that apply to oil do not apply equally to most other primary commodities. In the case of oil there are few large producing countries, supply is quite inelastic outside those countries, demand is relatively inelastic in the short and middle run, and the largest producers are Arab nations that find discipline in political and religious unity and in a common hatred of Israel. Perhaps equally important, the largest producer —Saudi Arabia—has been prepared to put up with a good deal of cheating by its partners.

Wheat, coffee, cocoa, tin, rubber, and copper have all been suggested as potential targets for similar joint marketing strategies, but none has

[3] This has added to the terminological confusion. It was once fashionable to speak of a nonaligned *third world* as another term for LDCs, the first two "worlds" being the developed capitalist and developed socialist countries. Now some commentators divide the LDCs into a richer (oil-producing) *third world* and a still poor *fourth world*.

the right combination of attributes, and only copper has supply and demand situations that are remotely similar to those of oil. The inability to utilize "commodity power" more widely through cartelization has not led to its total abandonment, as we will see in the final section of this chapter.

A NEW INTERNATIONAL ECONOMIC ORDER (NIEO)?

In May 1974 the General Assembly of the United Nations adopted (over the objections of the developed countries) a Declaration on the Establishment of a New International Economic Order. This represented an attempt on the part of LDCs to utilize collective *political* power to achieve a larger share of the world's goods.[4]

NIEO had its origin in the emergence within the United Nations of a political bloc of LDCs that goes back at least to 1964. These nations, economically weak but numerous, were targets of the struggle between the United States and the USSR for allegiance. They agreed to remain "nonaligned" with either of the two major power groups. At an Algiers summit conference of more than 100 nonaligned nations in September 1973, the importance of *economic* goals was expressed by the slogan, "Poor of the world, unite!"[5]

The NIEO proposals are aimed basically at wealth transfers instead of wealth creations; they are concerned with a more equal distribution of existing wealth rather than economic development.

Principal Economic Proposals of NIEO

In the many international meetings since 1974, the LDCs have offered dozens of specific demands and proposals covering trade, unilateral

[4] An excellent introduction to this development is Rachel McCulloch's *Economic and Political Issues in the NIEO* (International Institute for Economic Research, 1979). Professor McCulloch's analysis is heavily relied on here.

[5] Despite the similarity to the Communist slogan, "Workers of the world, unite!" this movement has been directed with equal vigor against both socialist and capitalist developed countries.

and multinational aid, investment, and technology transfers from developed to underdeveloped countries. Three proposals are important.

Primary commodities, buffer stocks, and the common fund. Because many LDCs depend on exports of primary commodities (i.e., raw materials) as their source of foreign exchange, their share of the world's wealth depends crucially on the prices of those commodities. The NIEO Integrated Programs for Commodities was designed to "raise and stabilize" the prices of 18 products by creating a "common fund" to which both producers and consumers would contribute. The fund was to be used to buy up surplus supplies and thus create "buffer stocks" of the commodities.

Even if stabilization were the only goal, this kind of buffer stock policy would have grave difficulties, such as those associated with national agricultural stabilization programs. (See Chapter 7.) However, *increasing* prices (not mere stabilization) was a major part of the proposal. This would involve accumulating ever larger inventories of the commodities in order to keep prices above the free-market levels. The wasteful accumulation of inventories would be one of the real resource costs of this proposal, and the need for continuing contributions to the common fund would be considerable.

To expect consuming countries to contribute to a fund whose purpose is to permit producers to restrict sales and raise prices sounds like a triumph of hope over reason. Nevertheless, in the context of the OPEC embargo, many developed countries indicated a willingness to discuss the proposal, presumably to prevent the formation of similar cartels in other commodities. As of 1980, nothing more substantial than talk has resulted.

Preferential treatment of LDC manufactures. Newly industrializing LDCs sought preferential tariff and quota treatment for commodities subject to tariff and nontariff barriers. It is all right, the argument said, for the United States to limit textile imports, but the LDCs should be given preference over developed countries in fighting for shares of the full quota.

One of the demands of the NIEO was for a Generalized System of Preferences. After more than a decade of opposition, followed by detailed negotiation, most major industrialized nations, including the United States, have granted some such treatment. The effects have been relatively smaller than the LDCs expected, owing to the exclusion from preferential treatment of commodities that are highly labor intensive and that thus create unemployment problems in the developed countries. Unfortunately, these commodities—such as textiles—are precisely those in which the LDCs have the greatest comparative advantage.

Debt renegotiation and forgiveness. LDCs were major borrowers in international markets well before the OPEC price increases. Total LDC debt grew from less than $40 billion in 1965 to $100 billion in 1973. Five years later the debt was $250 billion, largely because of oil price increases. Combined with current account deficits due to oil imports, both LDCs and their creditors feared the inability of LDCs to repay on schedule the loans that had been made.

Demands of the LDCs at various United Nations conferences on trade and development (known, like super bowl games, by Roman numerals—e.g., UNCTAD IV) ranged from debt cancellation and a moratorium on payments for a few years to milder suggestions for case-by-case renegotiation of scheduling and interest payments. Not surprisingly, the general proposals were rejected by developed nations—and were even opposed by some borrowers who feared that if debts were canceled, their future ability to borrow would be diminished.

The so-called debt problem has two aspects. The first, faced by resource-rich LDCs such as Zaire, is a crisis of meeting current payments of interest and principal. Here an adjustment of terms has proven feasible and has been undertaken. The second aspect is one of reduced real income due to rising costs of the LDCs' imports. Here it is an increase in contributed aid to those who have large debts that has been sought. But if aid of, say, $50 billion is appropriate, should it be given in the form of debt forgiveness? Why, critics ask, should those LDCs who have paid their debts be discriminated against?

An Evaluation of NIEO

NIEO succeeded in stimulating discussion for at least three reasons. First, an effective political bloc gradually emerged within the United Nations that was capable of standing firm against divide-and-conquer strategies. Both capitalist and socialist countries wanted the political allegiance of the LDCs, so they were prepared to talk and to listen. Second, the commodity boom of the early 1970s and the remarkable success of OPEC made threats of cartel action frightening (at least temporarily) and made proposals for a common fund for buffer stocks seem moderate in contrast. Third, many developed countries were genuinely willing to consider wealth transfers from rich to poor as morally and politically desirable.

Thus far the major accomplishments of NIEO demands have been small. The issues and proposals have been discussed extensively, but little major redistribution of wealth has resulted.

Why has the talk proven unpersuasive? The main answer is that the political and economic threats made by the LDCs against the developed countries are no longer regarded as substantial. NIEO's future rests on persuasion rather than coercion of the developed countries. Here the very stridency that unified the "South" in their demands has brought forth a unified resistance on the part of the "North."

From an economic point of view NIEO has two major flaws. First, it focuses too much on redistribution and too little on seeking real growth in world output. Second, it puts its faith in bureaucratic allocations of wealth, trade, and natural resources rather than in market mechanisms. Nothing in the world's experience to date suggests that this will increase total world output. Many modern development economists would share the view of Professor McCulloch that the developed countries should be adopting policies to expand rather than contract world wealth. If that is so, the major proposals of NIEO will not prove attractive.

Some Controversial Unresolved Issues

The economics of development, like most fields of economics, is in a state of change. The view presented in this chapter is perhaps the mainline view of economists in developed economies such as our own. Problems look different when viewed from the inside out, and they look different from the perspective of socialist nations than they do from our sort of market-oriented economy.

Yet even within the group of Western economists studying development there are important current controversies.

The Pace of Development

Reformers in underdeveloped countries often think in terms of transforming their economies within a generation or two. The sense of urgency is quite understandable, but unless it is tempered by some sense of historical perspective, totally unreasonable aspirations may develop—only to be dashed all too predictably.

Many underdeveloped countries are probably in a stage of development analogous to that of medieval England, having not yet achieved anything like the commercial sophistication of the Elizabethan era. It took 600 years for England to develop from the medieval stage to its present one. Such a change would be easier now, for much of the needed technology can be imported rather than invented. But what is the proper pace? To effect a similar growth within 50 or 100 years would require a tremendous achievement of the kind accomplished by America, Japan, and a handful of other countries; to aspire to do it in 20 or 30 years may be to court disaster—or to invite an extraordinarily repressive political regime. But to urge patience may be to keep the downtrodden poor, and perhaps exploited, and it may be a cover for failing to do what is required for growth.

The View of Population Policy

The view (presented in this chapter) of population growth as a formidable barrier to development is neo-Malthusian and constitutes what is probably the current conventional wisdom on underdevelopment. However, there are opposing views.

This view allows no place for the value of children in parents' utility functions. Critics point out that the psychic value of children should be included as a part of the living standards of their parents. They also point out that in rural societies even quite young children are a productive resource because of the work they can do; and fully grown children provide old-age security for their parents in societies where state help for the aged is negligible.

The neo-Malthusian theory is also criticized for assuming that people breed blindly, as animals do. Critics point out that traditional methods of limiting family size have been known and practiced since the dawn of history. Thus they argue that large families in rural societies are a matter of choice. The population explosion came not through any change in "breeding habits" but as a result of medical advances that greatly extended life expectancy (which surely must be counted as a direct welfare gain for those affected). Critics argue that once an urban society has developed, family size will be reduced voluntarily. This was certainly the experience of Western industrial countries; why, critics ask, should it not be the experience of the developing countries?

The Cost of Creating Capital

Is it true that LDCs must suffer if they wish to grow? A recent criticism of the conventional wisdom questions the alleged heavy opportunity cost of creating domestic capital. Production of consumption and capital goods are substitutes only when factor supplies are constant. But, critics say, the development of a market economy will lead people to substitute work for leisure.

For example, the arrival of Europeans with new goods to trade led the North American Indians to collect furs and other commodities needed for exchange. Until they were decimated by later generations of land-hungry settlers, the Indians' standard of living rose steadily with no immediate sacrifice. They created the capital needed for their production — weapons and means of transport — in their abundant leisure time. Thus their consumption began to rise immediately.

This too, the argument says, could happen in underdeveloped countries if market transactions were allowed to evolve naturally. The spread of a market economy would lead people to give up leisure in order to produce the goods needed to buy the goods that private traders are introducing from the outside world. In this view it is the pattern of development chosen, rather than development itself, that imposes the need for heavy sacrifices.

Summary

1. Sustained economic development is relatively recent in history and has been highly uneven. About one-fourth of the world's population still exists at a level of bare subsistence, and nearly three-fourths are poor by North American standards. The gap between rich and poor is very large and is keenly felt.

2. The pressure for economic development comes in part from the LDCs. The transformation in less than half a century of Soviet Russia from a backward peasant economy to a major industrial power has had a powerful demonstration effect on the quest for economic development. Moreover, as the LDCs have become a cohesive political bloc within the United Nations, they have come to demand economic assistance in their development efforts.

3. Much of the effective push toward more rapid development of the third world has come from the efforts of the World Bank and the development agencies of the developed countries.

4. There are many impediments to economic development; merely to want economic growth and development is not enough to assure it. Population growth, resource limitations, and the inefficient use of resources are among the formidable barriers to economic development in particular underdeveloped countries. So too are a series of institutional and cultural barriers that make economic growth more difficult.

5. A series of basic (and controversial) choices face LDCs as they contemplate development. How much should they intervene in the economy, and how much should they rely on the free market? History has demonstrated that growth is possible with almost any conceivable mixture of free market and central control. Centralized planning can change both the pace of economic development and its direction; it can also prove highly wasteful and destroy individual initiative.

6. Educational policy, while vitally important to the long-run rate of economic development, yields its benefits only in the future. As a result, the improvement of basic education is sometimes bypassed in the search for more immediate results.

7. A population policy is an important and volatile issue in most LDCs. The race between output and population is a critical aspect of development efforts in many countries. Different countries have chosen very different attitudes toward limiting population growth.

8. Acquiring capital for development is invariably a major concern in development. One source is domestic savings, but here the vicious circle of poverty may arise: a country that is poor because it has little capital cannot readily forgo consumption to accumulate capital because it is poor. Importing capital rather than using domestic savings permits heavy investment during the early years of development, with much smaller sacrifices of current living standards. But im-

ported capital is available only when the under-developed country has opportunities that are attractive to foreign investors. Much foreign capital for underdeveloped countries in the last three decades has been in the form of contributions by foreign governments and international institutions.

9. Selecting a development strategy involves a number of difficult choices. A country need not simply accept its current comparative advantages; there are reasons for not pushing specialization according to current comparative advantage too far, including the risks of fluctuations or declines in the demand for one's principal product and the overdependence on foreign trade. There may also be noneconomic reasons for preferring a different pattern of development. All considerations must be tempered by knowledge of what will in the end be likely to work.

10. Much current debate about development concerns a choice among (a) agricultural development, (b) exploitation of natural resources, (c) development of import substitution industries, and (d) development of an industrial capacity that will create new export industries. None of the strategies is without problems and risks.

11. Collective rather than individual development efforts became more common in the 1970s. OPEC's success renewed interest in commodity price stabilization cartels, but without notable success. A political initiative calling for a New International Economic Order seems to have achieved little more than discussion over this period.

12. The major thrust of NIEO has been for wealth transfers from developed to less-developed countries (as opposed to wealth creation). Of its major proposals, only the granting of some preference to LDC manufactures has occurred.

13. The view of economic development presented in this chapter is subject to criticism for neglecting to discuss – or misconceiving – important problems. One is the perhaps unrealistic haste that underlies most development efforts. A second is the overemphasis on population growth as a barrier to development. A third is an exaggeration of the opportunity cost of creating capital. Economic development is today a field in ferment.

Topics for Review

The gap between LDCs and developed economies
Barriers to development
Infrastructure
The role of planning in development
Alternative development strategies
Wealth creation versus wealth transfers

Discussion Questions

1. Each of the following is a headline from a recent story in the *New York Times*. Relate them to the problem of economic development.
   a. Africa: Ferment for a Better Life
   b. Black Africa: Economies on the Brink of Collapse because of OPEC
   c. Hungary Reforming Economy to Attract Tourists
   d. Goodyear to Build Plant in Congo for $16 Million
   e. Algeria's 4-Year Plan Stresses Industrial Growth
   f. India: Giant Hobbled by Erratic Rainfall
   g. Foreign Banks to Finance New Guinea Copper Mine
   h. Not All Benefit by Green Revolution
   i. OPEC Nations Provide Loans to Undeveloped Nations to Pay for Oil Imports
2. If you were a member of a foreign aid team assigned to study needed development projects for a poor recipient country, to which of the following would you be likely to give relatively high priority, and why?
   a. birth control clinics
   b. a national airlines
   c. taxes on imported luxuries
   d. better roads
   e. modernization of farming techniques
   f. training in engineering and business management
   g. primary education
   h. scholarships to students to receive medical and legal training abroad

3. China requires 5 million tons more grain each year just to keep up with its annual population growth of 17 million people. This is about five times Canada's wheat supply at present. What policy choices do these facts pose for the Chinese government? How should it resolve those choices?

4. "This natural inequality of the two powers of population and of production in the earth . . . form the great difficulty that to me appears insurmountable in the way to perfectability of society. All other arguments are of slight and subordinate consideration in comparison of this. I see no way by which man can escape from the weight of this law which pervades all animated nature. No fancied equality, no agrarian regulations in their utmost extent, could remove the pressure of it even for a single century" (T. R. Malthus, *Population: The First Essay*, Chapter 1, page 6). Discuss Malthus' "insurmountable difficulty" in view of the history of the past 100 years.

5. To what extent does the vicious circle of poverty apply to poor families living in developed countries? Consider carefully, for example, the similarities and differences facing a poor black family living in Arkansas and one living in Ghana, where per capita income is less than $400 per year.

6. How might each of the following affect a country's economic development?
   a. a tradition that a man's land be divided equally among all his children
   b. a very unequal distribution of national income
   c. specialization in a commodity in which it has a virtual world monopoly
   d. a decision to be entirely self-sufficient

7. The president of Venezuela said recently: "The decision of OPEC members to raise petroleum prices should be applauded by all third world countries. It represents the irrevocable decision to dignify the terms of trade, to revalue raw materials and other basic products of the third world." Which underdeveloped countries might be expected to have agreed? Which to have disagreed?

8. "High Coffee Prices Bring Hope to Impoverished Latin American Peasants" reads the headline. Mexico, Kenya, and Burundi, among other underdeveloped countries, have the right combination of soil and climate to increase greatly their coffee production. Discuss the benefits and risks to them if they pursue coffee production as a major avenue of their development efforts.

Appendixes

More on Functional Relations

Appendix to Chapter 2

The idea of relations among variables is one of the basic notions behind all science. Such relations can be expressed as functional relations.

FUNCTIONAL RELATIONS: THE GENERAL EXPRESSION OF RELATIONS AMONG VARIABLES

Consider two examples, one from a natural science and one from economics. The gravitational attraction of two bodies depends on their mass and on the distance separating them, attraction increasing with size and diminishing with distance; the amount of a commodity that people would like to buy depends on (among other things) the price of the commodity, purchases increasing as price falls. When mathematicians wish to say that one variable depends on another, they say that one variable is a function of the other. [51][1]

Thus gravitational attraction is a function of the mass of the two bodies concerned and the distance between them, and the quantity of a product demanded is a function of the price of the product.

One of the virtues of mathematics is that it permits the concise expression of ideas that would otherwise require long, drawn-out verbal statements. There are two steps in giving compact symbolic expression to functional relations. First, each variable is given a symbol. Second, a symbol is designated to express the idea of one variable's dependence on another. Thus, if G equals gravitational attraction, M equals the mass of two bodies, and d equals the distance between two bodies, we may write

$$G = f(M, d)$$

where f is read "is a function of" and means "depends

[1] Reference numbers in color refer to Mathematical Notes, which begin on page M-1.

on." The whole equation defines a hypothesis and is read "gravitational attraction is a function of the mass of the two bodies concerned and the distance between them." The same hypothesis can be written as

$$G = G(M, d)$$

This is read in exactly the same way and means the same thing as the previous expression. Instead of using f to represent "a function of," the left-hand symbol, G, is repeated.[2]

The hypothesis about the variables desired purchases and price can be written

$$q = f(p)$$

or

$$q = q(p)$$

where q stands for the quantity people wish to purchase of some commodity and p is the price of the commodity. The expression says that the quantity of some commodity that people desire to purchase is a function of its price. The alternative way of writing this merely uses different letters to stand for the same functional relation between p and q.

FUNCTIONAL FORMS: PRECISE RELATIONS AMONG VARIABLES

The expression $Y = Y(X)$ merely states that the variables Y and X are related; it says nothing about the form that this relation takes. Usually the hypothesis to be expressed says more than that. Does Y increase as X increases? Does Y decrease as X increases? Or is the relation more complicated? Take a very simple example, where Y is the length of a board in feet, and X is the length of the same board in yards. Quite clearly, $Y = Y(X)$. Further, in this case the exact form of the function is known, for length in feet (Y) is merely three times the length in yards (X), so we may write $Y = 3X$.

This relation is a definitional one, for the length of something measured in feet is defined to be three times its length measured in yards. It is nonetheless useful to have a way of writing relationships that are definitionally true. The expression $Y = 3X$ specifies the

exact form of the relation between Y and X and provides a rule whereby, if we have the value of one, we can calculate the value of the other.

Now consider a second example. Let C stand for consumption expenditure, the total amount spent on purchasing goods and services by all Canadian households during a year. Let Y_d stand for the total amount of income that these households had available to spend during the year. We might state the hypothesis that

$$C = f(Y_d)$$

and, even more specifically,

$$C = 0.8Y_d$$

The first expression gives the hypothesis that the total consumption expenditure of households depends on their income. The second expression says, more specifically, that total consumption expenditure is 80 percent of the total available for spending. The second equation expresses a very specific hypothesis about the relation between two observable magnitudes. There is no reason why it *must* be true; it may be consistent or inconsistent with the facts. This is a matter for testing. However, the equation is a concise statement of a particular hypothesis.

Thus the general view that there is a relation between Y and X is denoted by $Y = f(X)$, whereas any precise relation may be expressed by a particular equation such as $Y = 2X$, $Y = 4X^2$, or $Y = X + 2X^2 + 0.5X^3$.

If Y increases as X increases (e.g., $Y = 10 + 2X$), we say that Y is an *increasing function* of X or that Y and X *vary directly* with each other. If Y decreases as X increases (e.g., $Y = 10 - 2X$), we say that Y is a *decreasing function of X* or that Y and X *vary inversely* with each other.

Y varying inversely with X merely means that Y changes in the opposite direction from X. This should not be confused with the mathematical special case called "the inverse function" where $Y = 1/X$.

ERROR TERMS IN ECONOMIC HYPOTHESES

Expressing hypotheses in the form of functions is misleading in one respect. When we say that the world behaves so that $Y = f(X)$, we do not expect that knowing X will tell us *exactly* what Y will be, but only that it will tell us what Y will be *within some margin of error.*

---

[2] Any convenient symbol may be used on the right-hand side before the parenthesis to mean "a function of." The repetition of the left-hand symbol may be convenient in reminding us of what is a function of what.

This error in predicting Y from a knowledge of X arises for two quite distinct reasons.

First, there may be other variables that also affect Y. When, for example, we say that the demand for butter is a function of the price of butter, $D_b = f(p_b)$, we know that other factors will also influence this demand. A change in the price of margarine will certainly affect the demand for butter, even though the price of butter does not change. Thus we do not expect to find a perfect relation between D_b and p_b that will allow us to predict D_b exactly from a knowledge of p_b.

Second, variables can never be measured exactly. Even if X is the only cause of Y, measurements will give various Ys corresponding to the same X. In the case of the demand for butter, errors of measurement might not be large. In other cases, errors might be substantial—as, for example, in the case of a relation between the total consumption expenditure of all Canadian households and their total income. The measurements of consumption and income may be subject to quite wide margins of error, and various values of consumption associated with the same measured value of income may be observed, not because consumption is varying independently of income but because the error of measurement is varying from period to period.

When we say Y is a function of X, we appear to say Y is completely determined by X. Instead of the deterministic formulation

$$Y = f(X)$$

it would be more accurate to write

$$Y = f(X) + \epsilon$$

or

$$Y = f(X, \epsilon)$$

where ϵ, the Greek letter epsilon, represents an **error term**. Such a term indicates that the observed value of Y will differ from the value predicted by the functional relation between Y and X. Divergences will occur both because of observational errors and because of neglected variables. While economists always mean this, they usually do not say so.

The deterministic formulation is a simplification; an error term is really present in all assumed and observed functional relations.

This is true, by the way, not only of economics and other subjects dealing with human behavior, but of physics, chemistry, geology, and all other sciences. The old-time dichotomy between "exact" and "inexact" sciences is now abandoned; all theories and all measurements are subject to error.

Graphing Economic Magnitudes

Appendix to Chapter 3

The popular saying "The facts speak for themselves" is almost always wrong when there is a large number of facts. Theories are needed to explain how facts are linked together, and summary measures are needed to assist in sorting out what it is that facts show in relation to theories. The simplest means of providing compact summaries of a large number of observations is through the use of tables and graphs. Graphs play important roles in economics by representing geometrically both observed data and economic theories. Here both uses will be discussed.

GRAPHING ECONOMIC OBSERVATIONS

Because the surface of a piece of paper is two-dimensional, a graph may readily be used to represent pictorially the interrelation between two variables. Flip through this book and you will see dozens of examples. Figure 3A-1 shows more generally how a coordinate grid can permit the representation of any two measurable variables.

Economics is very often concerned only with the positive values of variables, and in such cases the graph is confined to the upper right-hand (or "positive") quadrant. Whenever either or both variables take on a negative value, one or more of the other quadrants must be included.

The Scatter Diagram

The scatter diagram provides a method of graphing any number of observations made on two variables. In Chapter 3 data for income and meat purchases for a large number of households were studied. To show these data on a scatter diagram, income was measure on the horizontal axis and meat purchases on the vertical axis. Any point in the diagram represents a particular income combined with a particular quantity of meat purchased. Thus each household for which there

FIGURE 3A-1
A Coordinate Graph

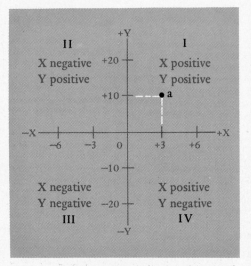

The axes divide the total space into four quadrants according to the signs of the variables. The upper right-hand quadrant is one in which both *X* and *Y* are greater than zero; it is usually called the *positive quadrant*. Point *a* in the figure has *coordinates Y* = 10 and *X* = 3 in the coordinate graph. These coordinates *define* point *a*.

are observations can be represented on the diagram by a dot, the coordinates of which indicate the household's income and the amount of beef it purchases.

The scatter diagram is useful because if there is a simple relation between the two variables, it will be apparent to the eye once the data are plotted.

The scatter diagram in Chapter 3, for example, made it apparent that more meat tends to be bought as income rises (see page 39). It also made it apparent that this relation is only approximately linear. As income rises above $10,000 a year, beef purchases seem to rise less and less with further equal increases in income. The diagram also gives some idea of the strength of the relation: If income were the only determinant of beef purchases, all of the dots would lie on a line; as it is, the points are all somewhat scattered and particular incomes are often represented by several households, each with different quantities of beef purchased. The data used in this example are **cross-sectional data.** The incomes and beef purchases of different households are compared over a single period of time.

Scatter diagrams may also be drawn of a number of observations taken on two variables at successive

periods of time. Thus, if one wanted to know whether there was any simple relation between personal income and personal consumption in Canada between 1950 and 1979, data would be collected for the levels of personal income and expenditure per capita in each year from 1950 to 1979, as is done in Table 3A-1. This information could be plotted on a scatter diagram with income on the *X* axis and consumption on the *Y* axis to discover any systematic relation between the two variables. The data are plotted in Figure 3A-2, and they do indeed suggest a systematic linear relation. In this exercise a scatter diagram of observations taken over successive periods of time has been used. Such data are called **time-series data,** and plotting them on a scatter diagram involves no new technique. When cross-sectional data are plotted, each point gives the values

TABLE 3A-1
Income and Consumption, 1950–1979 (1971 dollars)

Year	Disposable personal income per capita	Personal consumption expenditures per capita
1950	$1,583	$1,487
1951	1,635	1,467
1952	1,696	1,520
1953	1,735	1,584
1954	1,682	1,594
1955	1,771	1,685
1956	1,877	1,769
1957	1,878	1,776
1958	1,905	1,789
1959	1,925	1,845
1960	1,949	1,869
1961	1,921	1,851
1962	2,030	1,898
1963	2,084	1,954
1964	2,141	2,033
1965	2,262	2,118
1966	2,365	2,187
1967	2,427	2,251
1968	2,491	2,325
1969	2,571	2,398
1970	2,596	2,419
1971	2,779	2,579
1972	3,001	2,742
1973	3,233	2,891
1974	3,406	3,001
1975	3,555	3,105
1976	3,704	3,250
1977	3,761	3,324
1978	3,858	3,387
1979	3,927	3,439

Source: Statistics Canada, 13-531, 13-201.

FIGURE 3A-2

A Scatter Diagram Relating Consumption and Disposable Income

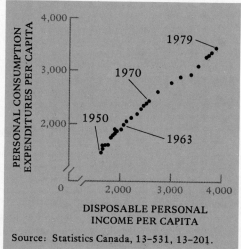

Source: Statistics Canada, 13-531, 13-201.

A scatter diagram shows paired values of two variables. The data of Table 3A-1 are plotted here. Each dot shows, for a particular year, the values of per capita personal consumption and per capita disposable personal income. They show a close, positive, linear relationship between the two variables.

FIGURE 3A-3

A Time Series of Consumption Expenditures per capita, 1950–1979

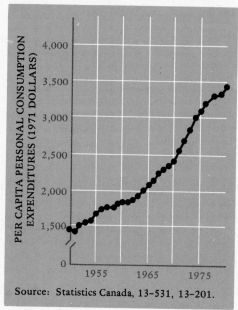

Source: Statistics Canada, 13-531, 13-201.

A time series plots values of a single variable in chronological order. The graph shows that, with only minor interruptions, consumption per capita measured in 1971 dollars rose from 1950 to 1979. The data are shown in the last column of Table 3A-1.

of two variables for a particular unit (say a household); when time-series data are plotted, each point tells the values of two variables for a particular year.

Time-series Graphs

Instead of studying the relation between income and consumption suggested in the previous paragraph, a study of the pattern of the changes in either one of these variables over time could be made. In Figure 3A-3 this information is shown for consumption. In the figure, time is one variable, consumption expenditure the other. But time is a very special variable: the order in which successive events happen is important. The year 1965 followed 1964; they were not two independent and unrelated years. (In contrast, two randomly selected households are independent and unrelated.) For this reason it is customary to draw in the line segments connecting the successive points, as has been done in Figure 3A-3.

A chart such as this figure is called a time-series graph or, more simply, a time series. This kind of

graph makes it easy to see if the variable being considered has varied in a systematic way over the years or if its behavior has been more or less erratic.

Ratio (Logarithmic) Scales

If *proportionate* rather than absolute changes in variables are important, it is more revealing to use a ratio scale rather than a natural scale. On a **natural scale** the distance between numbers is proportionate to the absolute difference between those numbers. Thus 200 is placed halfway between 100 and 300. On a **ratio scale** the distance between numbers is proportionate to the absolute difference between their logarithms. Equal distances anywhere on a ratio scale represent equal percentage changes rather than equal absolute changes. On a ratio scale the distance between 100 and 200 is the same as the distance between 200 and 400, between 1,000 and 2,000, and between any two numbers that stand in the ratio 1:2 to each other. For

TABLE 3A–2
Two Series

Time period	Series A	Series B
0	$10	$ 10
1	18	20
2	26	40
3	34	80
4	42	160

Series A shows constant absolute growth ($8 per period) but declining percentage growth. Series B shows constant percentage growth (100 percent per period) but rising absolute growth.

obvious reasons a ratio scale is also called a **logarithmic scale.**

Table 3A-2 shows two series, one growing at a constant absolute amount of 8 units per period and the other growing at a constant rate of 100 percent per period. In Figure 3A-4 the series are plotted first on a natural scale, then on a ratio scale. The natural scale makes it easy for the eye to judge absolute variations, and the logarithmic scale makes it easy for the eye to judge proportionate variations.[1]

GRAPHING FUNCTIONS

Functions were discussed in the Appendix to Chapter 2. Simple functions can be represented in the same two-dimensional space in which data can be graphed. When this is done, we obtain a geometrical expression of the functions. Since economic theory is often expressed in terms of functions, graphing these functions is a way of providing a graphical representation of the theory.

Linear Functions

Consider the functions

$$Y = 0.5X$$

$$Y = X$$

$$Y = 2X$$

[1] Graphs with a ratio scale on one axis and a natural scale on the other are frequently encountered in economics. In the cases just illustrated there is a ratio scale on the vertical axis and a natural scale on the horizontal (or time) axis. Such graphs are often called *semi-log* graphs. In scientific work graphs with ratio scales on both axes are frequently encountered. Such graphs are often referred to as *double-log* graphs.

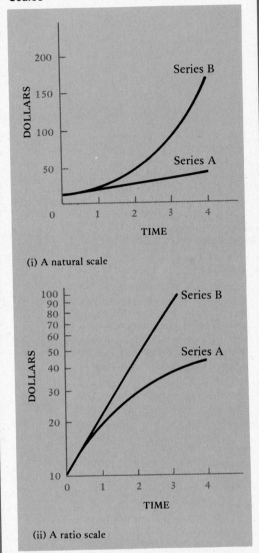

FIGURE 3A-4
The Difference Between Natural and Ratio Scales

(i) A natural scale

(ii) A ratio scale

On a natural scale, equal distances represent equal amounts; on a ratio scale, equal vertical distances represent equal percentage changes. The two series in Table 3A-2 are plotted in each chart. Series A, which grows at a constant absolute amount, is a straight line on a natural scale but a downward-bending curve on a ratio scale because the same absolute growth is decreasing percentage growth. Series B, which grows at a rising absolute but a constant percentage rate, is upward-bending on a natural scale but is a straight line on a ratio scale.

FIGURE 3A-5
Straight Lines Through the Origin

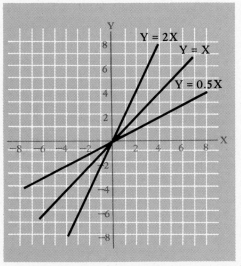

These straight lines differ only in their slopes.
Each is a special case of *Y = bX.*

These are graphed in Figure 3A-5. All of the Y functions are straight lines through the origin, because if $X = 0$ in each of the above relations, Y also becomes 0. The straight lines differ only because of their slopes; each is a special case of $Y = bX$.

The symbol Δ is used to indicate a change in a variable. Thus ΔX means the value of the change in X, and ΔY means the value of the change in Y. In the first equation, if $X = 10$, then Y is 5, and if X goes up to 16, Y goes to 8. Thus, in this exercise, $\Delta X = 6$ and $\Delta Y = 3$.

Now consider the ratio $\Delta Y/\Delta X$. In the above example it is equal to 0.5. For any change made in X in the first equation, $\Delta Y/\Delta X$ is always 0.5. In the second the ratio is unity, and in the third it is always 2. In general, if we write $Y = bX$, then the ratio $\Delta Y/\Delta X$ is always equal to b.

This ratio defines the slope of a straight line. The greater the slope, the steeper the line. For example, the slopes of the three functions in Figure 3A-5 are 2, 1, and 0.5.

Now consider the equations

$$Y = 2X$$

$$Y = 10 + 2X$$

$$Y = -5 + 2X$$

These are graphed in Figure 3A-6. All three lines are parallel, that is, they have the same slope; they differ only in their intercepts. Each is a special case of $Y = a + 2X$. Apparently the addition of a (positive or negative) constant does not affect the slope of the line.

In general, the equation of a straight line may be written

$$Y = a + bX$$

where X and Y are variables while a and b are parameters that determine respectively the intercept and the slope of the line. (The intercept is the value of Y when X is zero.) Changing a shifts the curve upward or downward parallel to itself while leaving its slope unchanged.

Each of the straight lines that has been drawn is upward-sloping—it has a positive slope. A function such as $Y = 10 - 2X$, or, more generally, $Y = a - bX$, will slope downward.

Figures 3A-5 and 3A-6 provide both the numerical grids which were used to plot the functions and the equations of the lines. Functions are often represented graphically, however, primarily in order to compare their general shapes. In such a situation both the numerical grid and the precise equation are often suppressed.

FIGURE 3A-6
Straight Lines with Slope of + 2

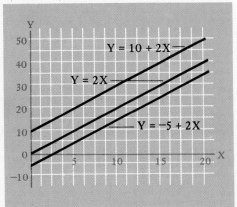

**Parallel straight lines have the same slope but
different intercepts.** These straight lines differ
only in their intercepts. Each is a special case of
Y = a + 2X.

FIGURE 3A-7
Three Rectangular Hyperbolas

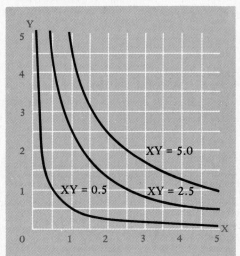

A rectangular hyperbola is an example of a nonlinear relation between two variables. Each of these hyperbolas is one member of the family $XY = a$. If a is also taken as a variable, the family of curves shows the interrelations among the three variables X, Y, and a.

Nonlinear Functions

Many of the relations encountered in economics are nonlinear. A nonlinear relation is expressed graphically by a curved line and algebraically by some expression more complex than that for a straight line. Two common examples of nonlinear relations are expressed by the equations

$$Y = \frac{a}{X}$$

$$Y = a + bX + cX^2$$

The first equation describes what is called a rectangular hyperbola. Three examples are plotted in Figure 3A-7. The second equation describes a parabola that takes on various positions and shapes depending on the signs and magnitudes of a, b, and c. One example of such a parabola is given in Figure 3A-8.

Unlike a straight line, which has a constant slope, a variable slope is the essence of a nonlinear function. The slope changes from point to point, but it may be evaluated at any point. The slope of a curve at a point is defined to be the slope of the tangent to the curve at that point. For example, in Figure 3A-8 the slope of

FIGURE 3A-8
A Parabola

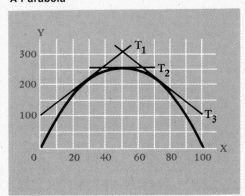

A parabola is an example of a nonlinear relation between two variables. The slope of a parabola, as with any nonlinear function, is not constant. The slope—how Y is tending to change as X changes—can be measured at any point on the function as the slope of a line that is tangent to the function at that point.

the function at $X = 30$ is the slope of the line T_1 that *is tangent to* (just touches) the function at that point. Line T_2 gives the slope of the same function at $X = 50$ and line T_3 at $X = 70$. When the curve is rising, the slope is positive; when the curve is falling, the slope is negative. When the slope is zero (as at $X = 50$), the function is neither rising nor falling.

Functions of Three Variables

Often in economics it is desirable to represent three variables on a two-dimensional graph. Consider the function $XY = a$, where X, Y, and a are all variables. Now look at Figure 3A-7, which plots this function for three different values of a. The variables X and Y are represented on the axes. The variable a is represented by the labels on the curves. A more familiar example of this sort of representation is the contour map of a mountain, where the vertical axis represents latitude, the horizontal axis longitude, and the contour lines are labeled to represent points of equal altitude. The important characteristic of such a map is that a *three-dimensional* mountain can be shown in a two-dimensional graph. Several examples of this kind of procedure occur throughout the book. (See, for example, indifference curves in Chapter 9 and isoquants in the appendix to Chapter 13.)

Elasticity: A Formal Analysis

Appendix to Chapter 6

In Chapter 6 we defined elasticity as

$$\eta = \frac{\Delta p}{\Delta q} \times \frac{\text{average } q}{\text{average } p}$$

where the averages are over the arc of the demand curve being considered. This is called **arc elasticity,** and it measures the average responsiveness of quantity to price over an interval of the demand curve.

Most theoretical treatments use a different but related concept called **point elasticity.** This is the responsiveness of quantity to price at a particular point on the demand curve. The precise definition of point elasticity uses the concept of a derivative, which is drawn from differential calculus.

In this appendix we first study an approximation to point elasticity that uses high school algebra. Then we will replace this approximate definition with the exact definition.

Before proceeding, we should notice one further change. In the chapter text we multiplied all our calculations of demand elasticities by -1, thereby defining elasticity of demand as a positive number. In theoretical work it is more convenient to retain the concept's natural sign. Thus normal demand curves will have negative signs, and statements about "more" or "less" elastic must be understood to refer to the absolute, not the algebraic value of demand elasticity.

The following symbols will be used throughout.

$\eta \equiv$ elasticity of demand
$\eta_s \equiv$ elasticity of supply
$q \equiv$ the original quantity
$\Delta q \equiv$ the change in quantity
$p \equiv$ the original price
$\Delta p \equiv$ the change in price

POINT ELASTICITY ACCORDING TO THE APPROXIMATE DEFINITION

Point elasticity measures elasticity at some point (p,q). In the approximate definition, however, the respon-

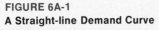

FIGURE 6A-1
A Straight-line Demand Curve

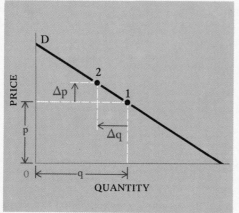

Because *p/q* varies with *Δq/Δp* constant, the elasticity varies along this demand curve, being high at the left and low at the right.

siveness is measured over a small range starting from that point. For example, in Figure 6A-1 the elasticity at point 1 can be measured by the responsiveness of quantity demanded to a change in price that takes price and quantity from point 1 to point 2. The algebraic formula for this elasticity concept is

$$\eta = \frac{\Delta q/q}{\Delta p/p}$$

This is similar to the definition of arc elasticity used in the text except that, since elasticity is being measured at a point, the *p* and *q* corresponding to that point are used (rather than the average *p* and *q* over an arc of the curve).

Let us first try a little manipulation of the above expression. Inverting the denominator and multiplying will result in

$$\eta = \frac{\Delta q}{q} \times \frac{p}{\Delta p}$$

Since it does not matter in which order multiplication is done (i.e., $q \times \Delta p = \Delta p \times q$), the order of the two terms in the denominator may be reversed and written

$$\eta = \frac{\Delta q}{\Delta p} \times \frac{p}{q} \qquad [1]$$

Equation [1] splits elasticity into two parts: $\Delta q/\Delta p$, the ratio of the change in price, which is related to the

slope of the demand curve, and *p/q*, which is related to the *point* on the curve at which the measurement is made.

Figure 6A-1 shows a straight-line demand curve. To measure the elasticity at point 1, take *p* and *q* at that point and then consider a price change, say, to point 2, and measure Δ*p* and Δ*q* as indicated. The slope of the straight line joining points 1 and 2 is Δ*p/*Δ*q*. The term in equation [1] is Δ*q/*Δ*p*, which is the reciprocal of Δ*p/*Δ*q*. Therefore the first term in the elasticity formula is the reciprocal of the slope of the straight line joining the two price-quantity positions under consideration.

Although point elasticity of demand refers to a point (*p,q*) on the demand curve, the first term in [1] still refers to changes over an arc of the curve. This is the part of the formula that involves approximation and, as we shall see, it has some unsatisfactory results. Nonetheless some interesting results can be derived using this formula as long as we confine ourselves to straight-line demand and supply curves.

1. The elasticity of a downward-sloping straight-line demand curve varies from zero at the quantity axis to infinity (∞) at the price axis. First notice that a straight line has a constant slope, so the ratio Δ*p/*Δ*q* is the same everywhere on the line. Therefore its reciprocal, Δ*q/*Δ*p*, must also be constant. The changes in *η* can now be inferred by inspecting the ratio *p/q*. Where the line cuts the quantity axis, price is zero, so the ratio *p/q* is zero; thus *η* = 0. Moving up the line, *p* rises and *q* falls, so the ratio *p/q* rises; thus elasticity rises. Approaching the top of the line, *q* approaches zero, so the ratio becomes very large. Thus elasticity increases without limit as the price axis is approached.

2. Where there are two straight-line demand curves of the same slope, the one farther from the origin is less elastic at each price than the one closer to the origin. Figure 6A-2 shows two parallel straight-line demand curves. Pick any price, say *p,* and compare the elasticities of the two curves at that price. Since the curves are parallel, the ratio Δ*q/*Δ*p* is the same on both curves. Since elasticities at the same price are being compared on both curves, *p* is the same, and the only factor left to vary is *q*. On the curve farther from the origin, quantity is larger (i.e., $q_1 > q$), and hence p/q_1 is smaller than *p/q;* thus *η* is smaller.

It follows from theorem 2 that parallel shifts of a straight-line demand curve lower elasticity (at each price) when the line shifts outward and raise elasticity when the line shifts inward.

FIGURE 6A-2
Two Parallel Straight-line Demand Curves

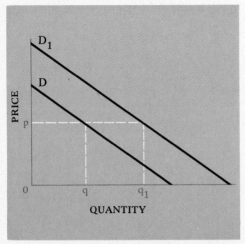

For any given price the quantities are different on the two curves; thus the elasticities are different on the two parallel curves, being higher on *D* than on *D₁*.

$$p \overset{\iota}{=} \bar{p} + b^*q$$
$$p \overset{\iota}{=} \bar{p} + b^{**}q$$

Take any common price $\hat{p}$ on both curves and solve for the associated (different) quantities, q_1 on the first curve and q_2 on the second:

$$\hat{p} = \bar{p} + b^*q_1 = \bar{p} + b^{**}q_2$$

$$q_2 = \frac{b^*}{b^{**}}q_1$$

The elasticity on the second curve at the common price $\hat{p}$ is

$$\frac{\Delta q_2}{\Delta p} \times \frac{\hat{p}}{q_2}$$

Substituting $\Delta q_2/\Delta p = 1/b^{**}$ and $q_2 = (b^*/b^{**})q_1$ yields

$$\frac{1}{b^{**}} \times \frac{\hat{p}}{\left(\dfrac{b^*}{b^{**}}\right)q_1}$$

which reduces to

$$\frac{1}{b^*} \times \frac{\hat{p}}{q_1}$$

which is the elasticity of the first demand curve at $\hat{p}$.

3. The elasticities of two intersecting straight-line demand curves can be compared at the point of intersection merely by comparing slopes, the steeper curve being the less elastic. In Figure 6A-3 there are two intersecting curves. At the point of intersection, p and q are common to both curves and hence the ratio p/q is the same. Therefore η varies only with $\Delta q/\Delta p$. On the steeper curve, $\Delta q/\Delta p$ is smaller than on the flatter curve, so elasticity is lower.

4. If the slope of a straight-line demand curve changes while the price intercept remains constant, elasticity at any given price is unchanged. This is an interesting case for at least two reasons. First, when more customers having similar tastes to those already in the market enter the market, the demand curve pivots outward in this way. Second, when more firms enter a market that is shared proportionally among all firms, each firm's demand curve shifts inward in this way.

Many different approaches are possible. (A geometric proof could easily be given.) The algebraic proof is as follows. Consider two straight-line demand curves with the same price intercept $\bar{p}$ but different slopes b^* and b^{**}:

FIGURE 6A-3
Two Intersecting Straight-line Demand Curves

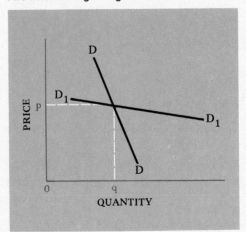

Elasticities are different at the point of intersection because the slopes are different, being higher on *D* than on *D₁*.

FIGURE 6A-4
A Straight-line Supply Curve Through the Origin

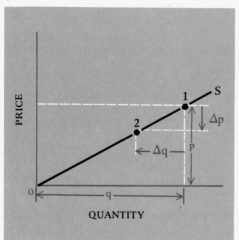

At every point on the curve, *p/q* equals $\Delta p/\Delta q$; thus elasticity equals unity at every point.

FIGURE 6A-5
Point Elasticity of Demand Measured by the Approximate Formula

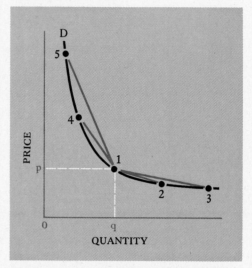

When the approximation of equation [1] is used, there are many elasticities measured from point 1. This is because the slope of the chord between 1 and every other point on the curve varies.

5. *Any straight-line supply curve through the origin has an elasticity of one.* Such a supply curve is shown in Figure 6A-4. Consider the two triangles with the sides *p, q,* and the *S* curve, and $\Delta p, \Delta q,$ and the *S* curve. Clearly these are similar triangles. Therefore the ratios of their sides are equal; that is,

$$\frac{p}{q} = \frac{\Delta p}{\Delta q} \qquad [2]$$

Elasticity of supply is defined as

$$\eta_s = \frac{\Delta q}{\Delta p} \times \frac{p}{q} \qquad [3]$$

which, by substitution from [2], gives

$$\eta_s = \frac{q}{p} \times \frac{p}{q} \equiv 1 \qquad [4]$$

6. *The elasticity measured from any point* p, q, *according to equation [1] above, is in general dependent on the direction and magnitude of the change in price and quantity.* Except for a straight line (for which the slope does not change), the ratio $\Delta q/\Delta p$ will not be the same at different points on a curve. Figure 6A-5 shows a demand curve that is not a straight line. To measure the elasticity from point 1, the ratio $\Delta q/\Delta p$

—and thus η—will vary according to the size and the direction of the price change.

Theorem 6 yields a result that is very inconvenient and is avoided by use of a different definition of point elasticity.

POINT ELASTICITY ACCORDING TO THE PRECISE DEFINITION

To measure the elasticity at a point exactly, it is necessary to know the reaction of quantity to a change in price *at that point,* not over a range of the curve.

The reaction of quantity to price change at a point is called *dq/dp,* and this is defined to be the reciprocal of the slope of the straight line tangent to the demand curve at the point in question. In Figure 6A-6 the elasticity of demand at point 1 is the ratio *p/q* (as it has been in all previous measures), now multiplied by the ratio of $\Delta q/\Delta p$ measured along the straight line, *T,* tangent to the curve at 1, that is, by *dq/dp.*

Thus the exact definition of point elasticity is

FIGURE 6A-6
Point Elasticity of Demand Measured by the Exact Formula

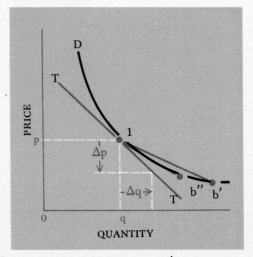

When the exact definition $\eta = \dfrac{dq}{dp} \times \dfrac{p}{q}$ is used, there is only one elasticity measured from point 1. This is because there is only one tangent to the demand curve at point 1.

$$\eta = \frac{dq}{dp} \times \frac{p}{q} \qquad [5]$$

The ratio dq/dp, as defined, is in fact the differential calculus concept of the *derivative* of quantity with respect to price.

This definition of point elasticity is the one normally used in economic theory. Equation [1] is mathematically only an approximation to this expression. It is obvious from Figure 6A-6 that arc elasticity will come closer to the point elasticity the smaller the price change used to calculate the arc elasticity. The $\Delta q/\Delta p$ in equation [1] is the reciprocal of the slope of the chord connecting the two points being compared. As the chord becomes shorter, its slope gets closer to that of the tangent T. (Compare the chords connecting point 1 to b' and b'' in Figure 6A-6). Thus the error in using [1] as an approximation to [5] diminishes as the size of Δp diminishes.[1]

---

[1] That the statement in the text is true over every range of price change is an accident of the way the curve in Figure 6A-6 is drawn. The fundamental theorem of differential calculus shows, however, that if the demand curve is differentiable, the text statement must be true in the neighborhood of the point in question.

Elements of Dynamics

Appendix to Chapter 7

Our method of analysis so far in this book has been that of comparative statics. To predict the effects of some change in market data, for example, we started from a position of equilibrium and then introduced the change to be studied. We determined the new equilibrium position and compared it with the original position: The differences between the two positions of equilibrium had to be due to the changes in the data that were introduced. This method of analysis is called comparative statics because it compares two positions of static equilibrium.

The Limited Usefulness of Comparative Statics

Theories based on comparative statics are of most interest when one is concerned with predicting where a market will settle down after all the effects of some change have been worked out. Since in an ever-changing world such a final settling down will never be observable, it might appear that comparative statics is useless, but this is not the case. If, in response to some change, the relevant variables move in the direction of their equilibrium values (in what has been called *pursuit of equilibrium*), then statements such as "in response to an increase in demand, price will rise" will be predictions and will be testable.

Further, in comparing two different situations such as two industries with different demand elasticities, it is not necessary that the two industries actually be in equilibrium, but only that they do not depart from it in a systematic manner. Remember, theories have "error terms." As long as errors are not systematic, the procedures of statistical analysis will permit testing the validity of the hypothesis that the two situations differ from one another in the systematic manner predicted by the static theory even though they will also differ because of nonsystematic errors.

Although comparative statics thus has a substantial range of relevance, it can *never* give predictions about how price, quantity bought and sold, and any other variables included in the theories will behave *as they move from one position of equilibrium to another.* We might wish to predict, for example, how price and output of rubber would change from year to year in response to a change in demand where the final equilibrium could not be reached until 10 or 15 years after the original demand shift occurred. In such cases, as we will see, the market may never settle down in a position of equilibrium, and in these cases, predictions derived from static equilibrium theory are likely to be contradicted by the actual behavior of the market.

Therefore, although theories based on the technique of comparative static analysis are adequate for dealing with many problems, they cannot be used to handle two important classes of problems. First, they cannot be used to predict the path that the market will follow when moving from one equilibrium to another. Second, they cannot predict whether a given equilibrium position will ever be attained. Indeed, when an equilibrium is not attained, predictions based on the assumption that it will be are likely to turn out to be empirically false.

Dynamic analysis must be used to study behavior in situations other than equilibrium. Dynamic analysis, or **dynamics,** can be defined as the study of the behavior of systems (single markets or whole economies) in disequilibrium situations.

LAGS IN ADJUSTMENT OF SUPPLY

The method of comparative statics is based on the hypothesis that a change in the equilibrium market price will induce a fairly rapid adjustment of the *actual* price to the new equilibrium level. However, this assumption is unrealistic when applied to the markets for many agricultural commodities, and that fact is another source of short-run instability in those markets.

In particular, given a shift in demand, the movement of price to the new equilibrium will be delayed to the extent that the induced changes in the desired level of production require some interval of time to be implemented. It takes five years for newly planted rubber trees to reach maturity and begin to yield latex. It takes several months for new plantings of carrots and brussels sprouts to be ready for harvesting. It takes five months for a newly hatched chicken to reach maturity and begin to produce eggs. The gap between a change in the desire to produce goods and a change in actual production is called a **supply lag.**

Every commodity has its own characteristic, and often quite complex, supply lag. For example, farmers can meet an increase in the demand for milk to some extent almost immediately by diverting milk from other uses such as cheese making; to a greater extent within 27 months by not slaughtering calves at birth but waiting and letting them breed and produce milk; and to an ever-increasing extent as the larger number of heifers give birth to their calves.

Figure 7A-1 shows the fluctuations in the price of hogs and the number of hogs slaughtered that occurred over the period 1950–1979. Note that peaks (troughs) in the supply of hogs tend to coincide with troughs (peaks) in the price of hogs and that turning points in the supply tend to occur two years after turning points in the price. A model with a supply lag can explain this behavior.

The effect of a shift in demand. Consider the market for hogs as shown in Figure 7A-2. The curve S is an ordinary supply curve for hogs, and the demand curve is assumed to shift from D to D_1 so that the new equilibrium price and quantity are p_1 and q_1 respectively. When the increase in demand occurs, however, it is not possible to produce more hogs until more litters can be raised. In the intervening period, the whole effect of the rise in demand will have to be taken out in a price increase.

Until the rate of output begins to increase, supply will continue to come onto the market at the rate of q per period. This complete inelasticity of supply is shown by drawing a vertical supply line at the output of q and labeling it S_1. Since the demand for hogs has shifted from D to D_1, the market price will rise to p_2, which is the level at which the new demand is equated to the unchanged supply. If price reacts quickly, it may rise to p_2 within a week or two after this rise in demand and stay there until more hogs can be raised.

But if p_2 is to be the market price of hogs, farmers would like to produce at the rate of q_2. They are likely to plan to increase output to that rate, for there is as yet no signal to tell them that a lower rate, q_1, is the "correct" rate of output at which to produce.

When the newly bred hogs reach maturity, the rate of production will suddenly expand to q_2, and price will fall drastically. Indeed, the price that will clear the market is now p_3. But once the price stabilizes at p_3,

FIGURE 7A-1
The Hog Market

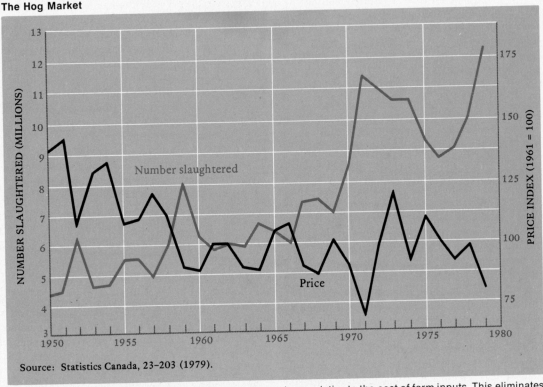

Source: Statistics Canada, 23–203 (1979).

Because of a supply lag, peaks in the number slaughtered tend to coincide with troughs in the price. The price index plotted here shows the price of hogs relative to the cost of farm inputs. This eliminates the upward trend that has dominated both prices and costs in recent years.

farmers will wish to produce and sell a quantity much less than q_2. They will cut back on next year's breeding not only to a level below q_2 but to a level below the equilibrium level of q_1; when the new crop is slaughtered, the quantity supplied will fall drastically. At this point we may well begin to wonder whether the market will ever reach equilibrium.

The cobweb. Figure 7A-3 shows the time path by which the price and quantity of hogs adjust to the new equilibrium. In the market described by Figure 7A-2, they will oscillate around their equilibrium values in cycles of diminishing amplitude. Thus if nothing further disturbs the market, they will eventually approach their equilibrium levels. If continual shifts in demand and supply are imposed on this system, the less regular pattern shown in Figure 7A-1 could result.

The market in Figure 7A-3 has a **stable equilibrium.**

A stable equilibrium is one that will be restored if it is disturbed; thus the actual price and quantity will tend toward their equilibrium levels. An **unstable equilibrium** is one that will not be restored if it is disturbed; thus the actual price and quantity will tend away from their equilibrium levels. Such a case is shown in Figure 7A-4.

The difference between the two markets is in the relation between the slopes of the demand and supply curves. In Figure 7A-3 the demand curve is flatter than the supply curve. The absolute quantity demanded changes more as price changes than does the absolute quantity supplied. An excess demand or supply can be eliminated with only a small price change, and the price change in turn causes only a very small change in the quantity supplied in the following year. Hence this change has only a small effect on next year's price.

FIGURE 7A-2
The Effect of a Supply Lag

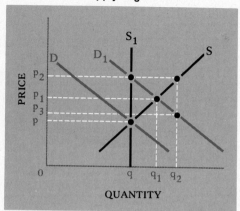

A supply lag can create oscillations in price in response to a change in demand. The shift in demand from D to D_1 causes an initial rise in price to p_2, above the equilibrium price p_1, because of the lag in the adjustment of supply. In the next period output will be q_2 and price will fall to p_3, which is below the equilibrium price.

FIGURE 7A-4
An Unstable Cobweb

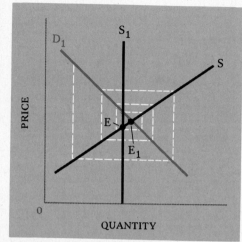

Price and quantity oscillate increasing'y in response to an increase in demand. Original equilibrium is at E. The increase in demand to D_1 creates a new equilibrium at E_1. However, the oscillations are explosive; price and quantity do not converge on the new equilibrium values.

In Figure 7A-4 the supply curve is flatter than the demand curve: The quantity supplied responds more to price changes than does the quantity demanded. When there is excess supply, a large price fall is necessary to induce purchasers to take up the additional quantity. This price fall causes a large reduction in the

FIGURE 7A-3
The Cobweb

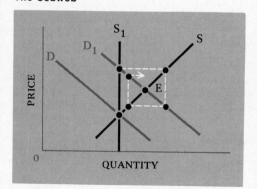

Price and quantity oscillate and trace out a cobweb as they approach their equilibrium values.

quantity supplied next year (because supply is very responsive to price). Next year there is a large shortage, and a big price increase is necessary to reduce the quantity demanded to the level of the quantity available. Inevitably, this price rise causes a very large increase in the quantity supplied in the following year. Thus there are alternating periods of ever-increasing surplus and shortage.

In the case of the unstable equilibrium, the oscillations become bigger and bigger. Nothing in the theory so far prevents these oscillations from becoming infinitely large. In practice, however, this would not be expected to happen; the oscillations would probably tend to reach limits. A full theory of such a market would require an analysis of these limits. What has been established is that, in the unstable case, the operation of the competitive price system does not tend to remove a disequilibrium; rather, it tends to accentuate it.[1]

The simple cobweb model introduces dynamic

[1] The fluctuations in prices in agricultural goods have led to the development of extensive commodities markets in which traders speculate about future prices. It is a matter of some debate as to whether, in the context of a hog cycle, such speculation would dampen price fluctuations or not.

theory, illustrates its ability to suggest theoretical explanations of fluctuations in prices and quantities, and emphasizes that there may be problems for which a satisfactory explanation cannot be found in static theory.

THE RELEVANCE OF STATICS AND DYNAMICS IN EVALUATING THE PRICE SYSTEM

The price system is a control system. How well does this control system work? Static theory can give us some idea, but it will not allow us to make a complete and detailed evaluation.

To evaluate any control system it is necessary to know how it corrects errors (disequilibrium situations), how many incorrect decisions it causes because it produces the wrong signals for considerable periods of time (e.g., continually displaying disequilibrium prices to farmers), and the extent to which an alternative control system might do better. These questions belong to dynamics.

Consider another application of static theory that is revealing but does not offer sufficient basis for a complete judgment. We have examined the proposition that the competitive price system allocates scarce commodities by price rather than by sellers' preferences. In equilibrium in a competitive market, everyone who wants to buy at the prevailing price can buy, and everyone who wants to sell can sell. Since there are neither unsatisfied sellers nor unsatisfied buyers, there is no scope for either group to exercise arbitrary power over the other. This proposition is often used as an argument in favor of a free-market economy unhampered by intervention by the central authorities. The value of the impersonal aspect of the price system is a matter of opinion, but it is a matter of economics to decide whether the hypothesis of impersonality is correct.

The proposition that the competitive price system provides an impersonal method of rationing the available supply—a method free from the arbitrary influence of individual buyers and sellers—is correct in equilibrium but incorrect in disequilibrium.

Consider disequilibrium situations. First, when the market price is below the equilibrium price, the quantity demanded exceeds the quantity supplied. There will be unsatisfied buyers who would like to purchase at the going price but are unable to do so. Suppliers must decide to whom they will sell. Thus there is allocation of the available supplies according to sellers' preferences. Second, when the market price is above the equilibrium level, the quantity supplied exceeds the quantity demanded. Now the shoe is on the other foot. There will be unsatisfied sellers who would like to sell at the going price but are unable to find buyers. In this situation the buyers have the power to decide which sellers shall earn an income by selling their goods and which shall earn nothing by being unable to sell.

Thus the positive proposition that a free-market economy produces an impersonal rationing system free from the power of individual buyers and sellers is true only so long as markets are normally at or near equilibrium. If markets are often out of equilibrium, and if many transactions take place at disequilibrium prices, conditions conducive to the exercise of power by buyers or sellers will in fact exist. Thus the evaluation of this argument by a person trying to make up his or her mind in as objective a fashion as possible depends both on the person's beliefs about the value of impersonality and on the factual question of the extent to which most real transactions take place at or very near equilibrium prices.

Dynamics is important both to an understanding of the behavior of systems out of equilibrium and to an evaluation of the significance of equilibrium situations. Many issues look very different in dynamic terms. Often they can be ignored—but you should always be aware of the possible error in so doing. The present appendix should provide a warning against coming to firm and final conclusions about the efficacy of the price system on the basis of static analysis alone.

The Derivation of the Demand Curve from Indifference Curves

Appendix to Chapter 9

In this appendix we use indifference theory to study the slope of the demand curve. Taking up the discussion of demand curves from where we left it at the end of Chapter 9, we derive a result that has been important in the history of economics: some demand curves may slope upward rather than downward. The conditions that could give rise to this perverse result are also studied.

DERIVATION OF DEMAND CURVES

To use indifference theory to derive the household demand curve introduced in Chapter 5, it is necessary to depart from the world of two commodities that we used for purposes of illustration in Chapter 9.

What happens to the household's demand for some commodity, say carrots, as the price of that commodity changes, *all other prices being held constant?* In Figure 9A-1 a new type of indifference map is plotted in which the quantity of carrots is represented on the horizontal axis and the value of all other goods consumed is represented on the vertical axis. The indifference curves give the rate at which the household is prepared to swap carrots for money (which allows it to buy all other goods) at each level of consumption of carrots and of other goods. Given the money price of carrots and the household's income, a budget line can be obtained showing all those combinations of carrots and other goods that the household can consume for its given level of money income and the given price of carrots. Now assume a change in the money price of carrots. By joining the points of equilibrium, we can trace a price-consumption line between carrots and all other commodities in the same way that such a line was traced for food and clothing in Figure 9-13.

Note that Figure 9A-1 is similar to Figure 9-13. The axes are labeled differently and the price-consumption line in Figure 9A-1 is crowded into the upper part of the diagram, indicating that whatever the price of carrots, the household does not spend a large part of its income on them. Every point on the price-consump-

FIGURE 9A-1
The Derivation of a Demand Curve

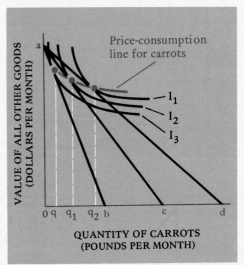

Every point on the price-consumption line corresponds to both a price of the commodity and a quantity of the commodity demanded; this is the information required for a demand curve. The household has a of income; if it buys no carrots, it can consume a worth of all other goods. For each price of carrots there is a single budget line. As the price of carrots falls, the budget line pivots from ab to ac to $ad,$ and the quantity of carrots demanded rises from q to q_1 to q_2. This leads to a downward-sloping demand curve for carrots.

tion line corresponds to one price and one quantity of carrots demanded. In the figure the quantity of carrots consumed increases as their price falls. These pairs of price-quantity values can be transferred to a new figure and used to plot a conventional downward-sloping demand curve.

THE SLOPE OF THE DEMAND CURVE

We have derived from the indifference curve analysis of household behavior the information needed to plot a demand curve for a commodity—carrots in the example just considered. If plotted on a conventional price-quantity diagram, the demand curve would be downward-sloping: the lower the price of carrots, the larger the quantity purchased. We now ask if that was an accidental or a necessary result.

The possibility that a commodity might have an upward-sloping demand curve has been discussed at length in demand theory. A good with such a demand curve is called a **Giffen good,** after the Victorian economist who is thought to have observed such a case.

We must make a careful distinction between two concepts: the so-called **income** and **substitution effects.** A fall in the price of one commodity has something of the effect of a rise in income because it makes it possible for the household to have more of all goods. In indifference theory, the income effect is removed by reducing the household's income *until it can just attain its original level of satisfaction at the new set of prices.*

This is illustrated in Figure 9A-2. The original budget line is at ab and a fall in the price of carrots takes it to aj. The original equilibrium is at E with q of carrots consumed and the final equilibrium is at E_2 with q_2 of carrots consumed. To remove the income effect, imagine reducing the household's income until it is just able to attain its original indifference curve. In other words, shift the line aj inward toward the origin, parallel to itself, until it just touches the indifference curve that passes through E. In the figure, the new budget line is a_1j_1 and the household would be in equilibrium on it at E_1, consuming q_1 of carrots and attaining the same level of satisfaction that it did at E.

It follows immediately from the convex shape of the indifference curves that more carrots are consumed at E_1 than at E. Thus the substitution effect is necessarily negative: price and quantity move in opposite directions, so a fall in the price of carrots increases the quantity consumed.

We have said that the fall in the price of carrots would cause the household to move from E to E_1 on the *same* indifference curve. But this, of course, is not what happens when the price of carrots falls in the real world. No economic dictator reduces everyone's money income to ensure that they get no increase in utility from the price change. Instead, the budget line in Figure 9A-2 pivots from ab to aj and the equilibrium goes directly from E to E_2. To get from the intermediate position E_1 to the final position E_2, we restore the household's income, keeping prices constant. This shifts the budget line outward parallel to itself from a_1j_1 to aj. As long as carrots are a normal good this increases their consumption—in the figure, the increase is from q_1 to q_2. This increase is an *income effect* since real income rises with relative prices constant.

In the actual world, when the price of carrots falls, the budget line moves directly from ab to aj and the consumption of carrots goes from q to q_2. It was seen,

FIGURE 9A-2
The Income Effect and the Substitution Effect in Indifference Theory

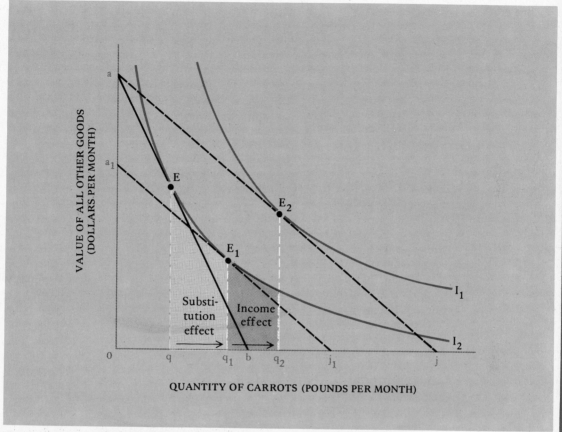

QUANTITY OF CARROTS (POUNDS PER MONTH)

The substitution effect is defined by sliding the budget line around a fixed indifference curve; the income effect is defined by a parallel shift of the budget line. The original budget line is ab with equilibrium at E. A fall in the price of carrots takes the budget line to aj and equilibrium to E_2. The intermediate point E_1 divides the quantity change into a substitution effect qq_1 and an income effect q_1q_2. The intermediate budget line a_1j_1 just allows the household to attain its original level of satisfaction at the new prices.

however, that this movement can be broken up into a substitution effect that takes consumption from q to q_1 and an income effect that takes it from q_1 to q_2.

The change in quantity demanded for one commodity in response to a change in its price can be thought of as a composite of the income and the substitution effects. The theory predicts that the substitution effect is negative; thus a fall in the relative price of a commodity, with the level of satisfaction held constant, leads to a rise in the demand for the commodity. Unless an increase in income is expected to lead to a reduction in consumption of the commodity, because it is an inferior good, the theory gives the unambiguous prediction

that more of the commodity will be demanded when its price falls.

A normal income effect (the good is not inferior) is sufficient to ensure that the demand curve slopes downward. A decrease in price will then lead to an increase in quantity demanded because of both the substitution effect and the increase in real income.

In the case of an inferior good, however, a definite prediction about what will happen cannot be made. Quantity demanded is increased by the substitution effect but decreased by the income effect. Thus the final result depends on the relative strengths of the two op-

Figure 9A-3
Negative Income Effects of a Fall in Prices in Indifference Theory

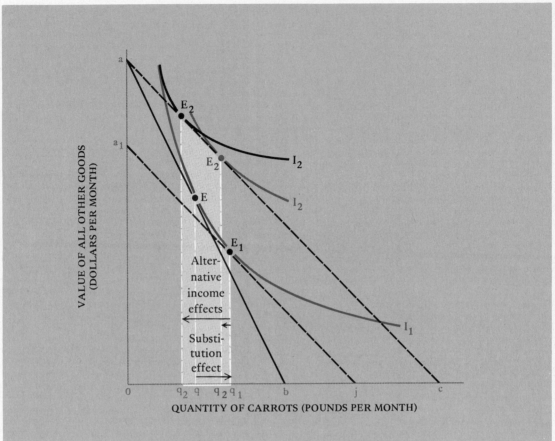

A large enough negative income effect can outweigh the substitution effect and lead to a decrease in consumption in response to a fall in price. Suppose the consumer is in equilibrium at E and the price of carrots decreases. The budget line shifts to ac. With inferior goods, the income effect is in the opposite direction from the substitution effect. Thus it is possible that the new equilibrium at E_2 will involve a smaller quantity of carrots than it did before the price decrease. Two cases are shown. The colored indifference curve I_2 leads to an increase in carrot consumption and thus a downward-sloping demand curve. The black I_2 leads to the black E_2 and an upward-sloping demand curve in which the quantity purchased decreases despite the price decrease. This is the so-called Giffen good case. Note that the two curves labeled I_2 are *alternatives;* they cannot exist simultaneously.

posing effects. Two cases of a negative income effect are shown in Figure 9A-3. The Giffen good case (which leads to an upward-sloping demand curve) occurs only when the negative income effect is large enough to outweigh the substitution effect.

We conclude from this analysis that the Giffen case of an upward-sloping demand curve for a commodity is a theoretical possibility. For this to happen the good must be inferior. But that is not enough; the change in price must have a negative income effect *strong enough* to offset the substitution effect. A combination of circumstances that makes this possible is not often expected, and therefore an upward-sloping market demand curve must be expected to be an infrequent exception to the general prediction that demand curves will slope downward to the right.

Balance Sheets, Income Statements, and Costs of Production: Two Views

Appendix to Chapter 11

Accounting is a major branch of study in and of itself. Many students of economics will want to study accounting at some stage in their careers. It is not our intention to give a short course in accounting in this appendix, but rather to acquaint you with the kinds of summary statements that are used by both economists and accountants. **Balance sheets** report the picture of a firm *at a moment in time*. They balance in the sense that they show the assets (or valuable things) owned by the firm on one side and the claims against those assets on the other side. **Income statements** refer to a *period of time* (e.g., a year) and report in summary fashion the flows of resources through the firm in the course of its operations. Balance sheets thus measure a stock; income statements measure a flow.

In order to illustrate what balance sheets and income statements are, the same example will be treated from two points of view: that of the accountant and that of the economist.

AN EXAMPLE

Late in 1980, James Maykby, the second vice-president of the Acme Artificial Flower Corporation (at a salary of $50,000 per year), decided he would go into business for himself. He quit his job and organized the Maykby Leaf Company. He purchased suitable plant and equipment for $160,000 and acquired some raw materials and supplies. By December 31, 1980, he was in a position to start manufacturing. The funds for his enterprise were $80,000 raised as a bank loan on the factory (on which he is obligated to pay interest of $10,000 per year) and $110,000 of his own funds, which had previously been invested in common stocks. He also owed $10,000 to certain firms that had provided him with supplies.

Maykby, who is a trained accountant, drew up a statement of his company's position as of December 31, 1980 (see Table 11A-1).

Maykby showed this balance sheet to his brother-in-

TABLE 11A-1
Maykby Leaf Company, Balance Sheet, December 31, 1980

Assets		Liabilities and equity	
Cash in bank	$ 10,000	Owed to suppliers	$ 10,000
Plant and equipment	160,000	Bank loan	80,000
Raw materials and supplies	30,000	Equity	110,000
Total assets	$200,000	Total liabilities and equity	$200,000

law, an economist, and was very pleased and surprised to find that he agreed that this was a fair and accurate statement of the position of the company as it prepared to start operation.[1]

During 1981, the company had a busy year hiring factors, producing and selling goods, and so on. The following points summarize these activities of the 12-month period.

1. The firm hired labor and purchased additional raw materials in the amount of $115,000, of which it still owed $20,000 at the end of the year.[2]
2. The firm manufactured artificial leaves and flowers whose sale value was $200,000. At year's end it had sold all these goods and still had on hand $30,000 worth of raw materials.
3. The firm paid off the $10,000 owed to suppliers at the beginning of the year.
4. At the very end of 1981 the company purchased a new machine for $10,000 and paid cash for it.
5. The company paid the bank $10,000 interest on the loan.
6. Maykby paid himself $20,000 "instead of salary."

AN ACCOUNTANT'S BALANCE SHEET AND INCOME STATEMENT

Taking account of all these things and also recognizing that he had depreciation on his plant and equipment,[3] Maykby spent New Year's Day 1982 preparing three financial reports (see Tables 11A-2, 11A-3, and 11A-4).

These accounts reflect the operations of the firm as described before. The bookkeeping procedure by which these various activities are made to yield both the year-end balance sheet and the income statement need not concern you at this time, but you should notice several things.

First, note that some transactions affect the balance sheet but do not enter into the current income statement. Examples of these are the purchase of a machine, which is an exchange of assets—cash for plant and equipment—and which will be entered as a cost in the income statements of some future periods as depreciation is charged; and the payment of past debts,

TABLE 11A-2
Maykby Leaf Company, Accountant's Balance Sheet, December 31, 1981

Assets		Liabilities and equity	
Cash in bank	$ 65,000	Owed to suppliers of factors	$ 20,000
(See Exhibit 1)		(See Exhibit 4)	
Plant and equipment	146,000	Bank loan	80,000
(See Exhibit 2)		Equity	141,000
Raw materials and supplies	30,000	(See Exhibit 5)	
(See Exhibit 3)		Total liabilities and equity	$241,000
Total assets	$241,000		

[1] He usually finds that he and his brother-in-law disagree about everything.
[2] In this example all purchased and hired factors are treated in a single category.

[3] The tax people told him he could charge 15 percent of the cost of his equipment as depreciation during 1981, and he decided to use this amount in his own books as well. No depreciation was charged on the new machine.

TABLE 11A-3

Maykby Leaf Company, Exhibits to Balance Sheet of December 31, 1981

Exhibit 1. Cash

Balance, January 1, 1981	$ 10,000	
+Deposits		
Proceeds of sales of goods	200,000	$210,000
−Payments		
Payments to suppliers (1981 bills)	10,000	
Payments for labor and additional raw materials	95,000	
Salary of Mr. Maykby	20,000	
Purchase of new machine	10,000	
Interest payment to bank	10,000	−145,000
Balance, December 31, 1981		65,000

Exhibit 2. Plant and Equipment

Balance, January 1, 1981	$160,000	
+New machine purchased	10,000	170,000
−Depreciation charged		− 24,000
Balance, December 31, 1981		146,000

Exhibit 3. Raw Materials and Supplies

On hand January 1, 1981	$ 30,000	
Purchases in 1981	115,000	145,000
Used for production during 1981		−115,000
On hand December 31, 1981		30,000

Exhibit 4. Owed to Suppliers

Balance, January 1, 1981	$ 10,000	
New purchases, 1981	115,000	125,000
Paid on old accounts	10,000	
Paid on new accounts	95,000	−105,000
Balance, December 31, 1981		$ 20,000

Exhibit 5. Equity

Original investment	$110,000
+Income earned during year	31,000
(See income statement)	
Balance, December 31, 1981	$141,000

which entered the income statements in the period in which the things purchased were used in production.[4]

Second, note that the net profit from operations increased the owner's equity, since it was not "paid out" to him. A loss would have decreased his equity.

Third, note that the income statement, covering a year's operation, provides a link between the opening

[4] Beginning students often have difficulty with the distinction between *cash* flows and *income* flows. If you do, analyze item by item the entries in Exhibit 1 in Table 11A-3 and in Table 11A-4, the income statement.

TABLE 11A-4

Maykby Leaf Company, Accountant's Income Statement for the Year 1981

Sales		$200,000
Costs of operation		
Hired services and raw materials used	$115,000	
Depreciation	24,000	
Mr. Maykby	20,000	
Interest	10,000	−169,000
Profit		$ 31,000

TABLE 11A-5
Maykby Leaf Company, Economist's Balance Sheet, December 31, 1981

Assets		Liabilities and equity	
Cash	$ 65,000	Owed to suppliers	$ 20,000
Plant and equipment	134,000	Bank loan	80,000
Raw materials, etc.	30,000	Equity (see Exhibit)	129,000
	$229,000		$229,000

balance sheet (the assets and the claims against assets at the beginning of the year) and the closing balance sheet.

Fourth, note that every change in a balance sheet between two dates can be accounted for by events that occurred during the year. (See the exhibits to the balance sheet, Table 11A-3.)

After studying these records, Maykby feels that it has been a good year. The company has money in the bank, it has shown a profit, and it was able to sell the goods it produced. He is bothered, however, by the fact that he and his wife have felt poorer than in past years. Probably the cost of living has gone up!

AN ECONOMIST'S BALANCE SHEET AND INCOME STATEMENT

When Maykby's brother-in-law reviews the December 31, 1981, balance sheet and the 1981 income statement, he criticizes them in three respects. He says:

1. Maykby should have charged the company $50,000 for his services, since that is what he could have earned outside.
2. Maykby should have charged the company for the use of the $110,000 of his funds. He computes that had Maykby left these funds in the stock market he

TABLE 11A-6
Exhibit to Balance Sheet, December 31,1981:
Equity of Mr. Maykby

Original investment		$110,000
New investment by Mr. Maykby		
Salary not collected	$30,000	
Return on capital not collected	11,000	41,000
		151,000
Less loss from operations		22,000
Equity		$129,000

TABLE 11A-7
Maykby Leaf Company, Economist's Income Statement for the Year 1981

Sales		$200,000
Cost of operations		
Hired services and raw materials	$115,000	
Depreciation[a]	36,000	
Interest to bank[b]	10,000	
Imputed cost of capital	11,000	
Services of Maykby	50,000	−222,000
Loss		$(22,000)

[a] Market value on January 1 less market value on December 31.
[b] Because the bank loan is secured by the factory, its opportunity cost seems to the economist as properly measured by the interest payment.

would have earned $11,000 in dividends and capital gains.
3. Maykby's depreciation figure is arbitrary. The plant and equipment purchased for $160,000 a year ago now has a *market value* of only $124,000. (Assume he is correct about this fact.)

The brother-in-law prepared three *revised* statements. (See Tables 11A-5, 11A-6, and 11A-7.)

It is not hard for Maykby to understand the difference between the accounting profit of $31,000 and the reported economist's loss of $22,000. The difference of $53,000 is made up as follows:

Extra salary	$30,000
Imputed cost of capital	11,000
Extra depreciation	12,000
	$53,000

What Maykby does *not* understand is in what sense he *lost* $22,000 during the year. In order to explain this his brother-in-law prepared the report shown in Table 11A-8.

TABLE 11A-8
Maykby's Situation Before and After

	(1) As second vice-president of Acme Flower Company	(2) As owner-manager of Maykby Leaf Company	Difference (2) − (1)
Salary paid	$ 50,000	$ 20,000	− $30,000
Earnings on capital, invested in stocks	11,000	0	− 11,000
Assets owned	110,000 (stocks)	129,000 (equity in Maykby Leaf Co.)	+ 19,000
Net change			−$22,000

Although Maykby spent the afternoon muttering to himself and telling his wife that his brother-in-law was not only totally lacking in any business sense but unpleasant as well, he was observed that evening at the public library asking the librarian whether there was a good "teach-yourself" book on economics. (We do not know her answer.)

The next day, Maykby suggested to the economist that they work out together the expected economic profits for next year. "After all," he said, "dwelling on what might have been doesn't really help decide whether I should continue the Leaf Company next year." The economist agreed. Because of expected sales increases, they concluded, the prospects were good enough to continue for at least another year. They dipped deep in the bowl of New Year's cheer to toast those stalwart pillars of society, the independent business person and the economist.

Summary

1. The balance sheet reports the assets and the claims against those assets at a moment in time. Balance sheets always balance because the equity of the owners is *by definition* the amount of the assets less the claims of the creditors of the company.

2. How large the "total assets" figure is depends on the valuations placed on them, and these can differ. The valuation problem arises over and over again—in the matter of inventories, patents, properties, and so forth, owned.

3. In order to avoid arbitrary, misleading, and even deliberately deceptive manipulation of accounts, accountants have developed certain normal and usual procedures of valuation. These may not in all cases reflect the economist's definition of the value of the resources.

4. The income statement reports the revenues and the costs that arise from the firm's use of inputs to produce outputs. It always covers a specified period of time. It also crucially involves the valuation problem: What is the value of the inputs used and outputs produced? Here again there are conventional accounting principles that may or may not be satisfactory for purposes of economic analysis.

5. The income statement of a firm may be important for several different purposes, and different principles of valuation may be required. For determining its income tax liability, the firm must use the valuations specified as permissible by the tax authorities. For determining its comparative performance compared to other companies, or to itself in other periods, it must use a consistent set of procedures, whatever the principle that governs them. For determining whether it has made the best use of the resources under its control, it must use valuations based on the alternative use of these resources. The economist's concept of opportunity cost is designed to do this job.

6. In general, it is the principles of valuation used and not the form of these statements that are important and decisive in interpreting the operations of the firm. Students of the firm who use reported financial data as an aid to their analysis must be prepared to examine in detail whether the principles of valuation used are appropriate for their purpose and to adjust, correct, or recompute in cases where they are not appropriate.

More on Long-run Competitive Equilibrium

Appendix to Chapter 14

In Chapter 14 we showed how the forces of entry and exit in a competitive industry forced firms to an equilibrium position with zero profits. Here we consider further implications of this process and some complications of long-run equilibrium.

LONG-RUN EQUILIBRIUM IMPLIES MINIMUM ATTAINABLE COSTS

A competitive industry will not be in long-run equilibrium as long as any firm can increase its profits by changing its output or its method of production. A firm might change its profits by (a) increasing or decreasing output from an existing plant, (b) opening or closing additional identical plants, or (c) changing the size of the plants it operates.

We saw in Chapter 14 that if a firm is to be in long-run equilibrium, condition (a) implies that price, p, equals short-run marginal cost ($SRMC$) and that (b) implies that price equals short-run ATC. These two conditions were met by firms in the position of Figure 14-6(ii), page 258.

The additional condition (c) means that each existing firm must be producing at the lowest point on its long-run average cost curve. Taken together, these conditions mean that all firms in the industry should be in the position illustrated in Figure 14A-1.[1]

---

[1] We assume that all existing firms and all new entrants face identical $LRATC$ curves. This merely means that all firms face the same set of factor prices and have the same technology available to them. There are some apparent complications when different units of the same factor have different efficiencies; these complications are necessarily left to an intermediate level course. Here we may assert simply that the assumption that total costs are the same for all producing firms in a competitive industry is a consequence of the opportunity cost principle. It does not deny the fact that there are differences among firms; it says only that these differences will be included in the total costs of production because a superior factor owned by one firm could be leased or sold to another firm.

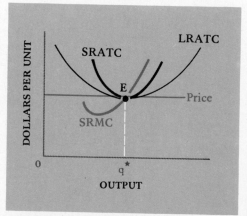

FIGURE 14A-1

The Equilibrium of a Firm When the Industry Is in Long-run Equilibrium

In long-run competitive equilibrium the firm is operating at the minimum point on its *LRATC* curve. In long-run equilibrium each firm must be: (i) maximizing short-run profits, $SRMC = p$; (ii) earning profits of zero on its existing plant, $SRATC$ = price; and (iii) unable to increase its profits by altering the size of plant. These three conditions can only be met when the firm is at the minimum point on its *LRATC* curve, *E*.

To see why this is so, we shall assume that it is not the case and show how firms may increase their profits. (If they can do so, they were not originally in long-run equilibrium.) Figure 14A-2 shows two firms that have $SRMC = SRATC$ = price. Each of these firms can, however, increase its profits by discarding its present plant when it wears out and building a plant of different size. The smaller firm should increase its plant size, thereby lowering its average total costs. The larger firm should build a smaller plant, thereby lowering its ATC. Since each firm is a price taker, each of these changes will increase the firm's profits.

The only way in which a price-taking firm can be in long-run equilibrium with respect to its size is by producing at the minimum point on its *LRATC* curve.

Each firm must be producing at minimum $LRATC$ (at a point such as q^* in Figure 14A-2). Since for an industry to be in long-run equilibrium each firm must be in long-run equilibrium, it follows that in long-run com-

petitive equilibrium all firms in the industry will be selling at a price equal to minimum $LRATC$.

In long-run equilibrium, the firm's cost is the lowest attainable cost, given the limits of known technology and factor prices.

LONG-RUN RESPONSES TO CHANGES IN DEMAND

Suppose a competitive industry is in long-run equilibrium as shown in Figure 14A-1. Now suppose that the demand for the product increases. Price will rise to equate demand with the industry's short-run supply. Each firm will expand output until its short-run marginal cost once again equals price. Each firm will earn profits as a result of the rise in price, and the profits will induce new firms to enter the industry. This shifts the short-run supply curve to the right and forces down the price. Entry continues until all firms are once again just covering average total costs. To recapitulate: The short-run effects of the rise in demand are a rise in price and output; the long-run effects are a further rise in output and a fall in price.

Now consider a fall in demand. The industry starts with firms in long-run equilibrium as shown in Figure 14A-1, and the market demand curve shifts left and price falls. There are two possible consequences.

First, the decline in demand forces price below ATC but leaves it above AVC. Firms are then in the position shown in Figure 14-6(i), page 258. The firms can cover their variable costs and earn some return on their capital, so they remain in production for as long as their existing plant and equipment lasts. But it is not worth replacing capital as it wears out. Exit will occur as old capital wears out and is not replaced. As firms exit the short-run supply curve shifts left and market price rises. This continues until the remaining firms in the industry can cover their total costs. At this point it will pay to replace capital as it wears out, and the decline in the size of the industry will be brought to a halt. In this case the adjustment may take a very long time, for the industry shrinks in size only as existing plant and equipment wears out.

The second possibility occurs when the decline in demand is so large that price is forced below the level of AVC. In this case firms cannot even cover their variable costs, and some will shut down immediately. Thus the reduction in capital devoted to production in

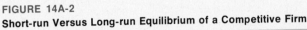

FIGURE 14A-2
Short-run Versus Long-run Equilibrium of a Competitive Firm

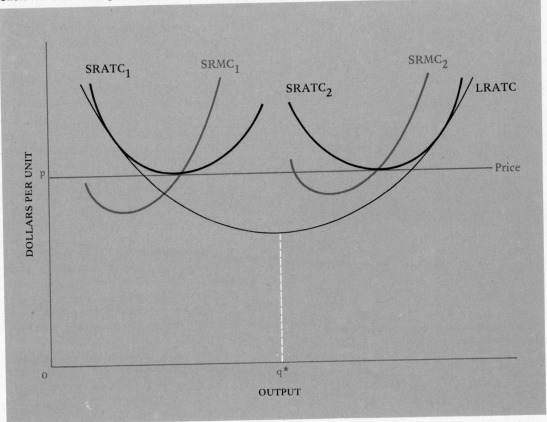

A competitive firm that is not at the minimum point on its _LRATC_ curve cannot be in long-run equilibrium. Suppose two firms have identical _LRATC_ curves but one firm has too small a plant, with costs $SRATC_1$, while the other firm has too large a plant, with costs of $SRATC_2$. Both firms are in short-run equilibrium at price $p = MC = ATC$, but neither is in long-run equilibrium. Firm 1 can increase its profits by building a larger plant (thereby moving downward to the right along its _LRATC_ curve). Firm 2 can increase its profits by building a smaller plant (thereby moving downward to the left along its _LRATC_ curve).

the industry occurs rapidly because some existing capacity is scrapped or sold for other uses. Once sufficient capital has been withdrawn so that price rises to a level that allows the remaining firms to cover their AVC, the rapid withdrawal of capital will cease. Further exit occurs more slowly, as described above.

THE LONG-RUN INDUSTRY SUPPLY CURVE

Adjustments to long-run changes in demand do not necessarily leave the _level_ of long-run costs unchanged. The response of costs to such long-run changes in required equilibrium output is shown by the **long-run industry supply curve _(LRS)_**. This curve shows the relation between equilibrium price and the output firms will be willing to supply after all desired entry or exit has occurred.

The long-run supply curve connects positions of long-run equilibrium after all demand-induced changes have occurred.

When induced changes in factor prices are considered,

it is possible for *LRS* to rise, to fall, or to remain constand. Figures 14A-3, 14A-4, and 14A-5 illustrate the three possibilities.

Constant Costs (Constant *LRS*)

The long-run supply curve in Figure 14A-3 is horizontal. This indicates that the industry, given time, will adjust its size to provide whatever quantity may be demanded at a constant price. Such conditions obtain if factor prices do not change as the output of the whole industry expands or contracts. An industry with a horizontal long-run supply curve is said to be a **constant-cost industry**. While conditions of constant *LRS* may exist, such conditions are not necessary.

Increasing Long-run Costs (Increasing *LRS*)

Short-run cost curves rise because of the existence of fixed factors and the law of diminishing returns to variable factors. A different explanation must apply in the long run, since there are no fixed factors.

When an industry expands its output, it needs more inputs. The increase in demand for these inputs may bid up their prices. Such growth-induced changes in prices may be expected whenever rapid growth occurs. The reason for this is that a large industry demands large quantities of certain key materials and certain kinds of skilled labor. As the industry grows larger and larger these become increasingly scarce. Thus growth of the steel industry increases the demand of steel producers for iron ore, for coking coal, and for blast furnace operators, none of which is in perfectly elastic supply. Increasing scarcity of these inputs will tend to raise their price, and this in turn will raise the cost of producing steel.

If costs rise with increasing levels of industry output, so too must the price at which the producers are willing to supply the market. The common sense of this result is that if firms were just covering their costs before the increase in demand, the price they receive will have to rise enough to cover any increases in factor prices they must pay.

To see more specifically why this result occurs, remember that an increase in the price of inputs will shift the marginal cost (and average cost) curves of all firms upward. This shift in the marginal cost curves of all firms shifts the industry short-run supply curve to the left.

The effect on *LRS* of growth in industry output may be thought of for analytic purposes as occurring in

FIGURE 14A-3

A Long-run Supply Curve Under Conditions of Constant Cost

The long-run supply curve connects equilibrium points after the demand-induced shifts in the supply curve. The shift in demand from *D* to D_1 first raises the price to p_1 as industry output expands along the short-run supply curve. Firms will be earning profits and entry will thus occur. This induces a shift in the short-run supply curve from *S* to S_1. The long-run supply curve is *LRS*. In the case illustrated the increase in supply is just sufficient to keep the price at *p*. Thus output has been "at constant cost" in the long run.

two stages: an increase in the number of firms with no increase in factor prices and an induced increase in factor prices. Figure 14A-4 shows how these two stages lead to an upward-sloping *LRS* curve.

In reality the two stages occur simultaneously. In recent years the very rapid increase in the demand for electric power has led to a large increase in the number of electric generating plants. This in turn has led to sharp increases in the demand for inputs—and hence to increases in their price. This development has been particularly marked with the prices of coal and oil, the key fuels in electricity generation. Indeed, one of the aspects of what is today called the "energy crisis" is that greatly increased demands for energy have bid up the prices of basic fuels. As one commentator said, "talk of the energy crisis is mood music for higher fuel

FIGURE 14A-4
A Rising Long-run Supply Curve

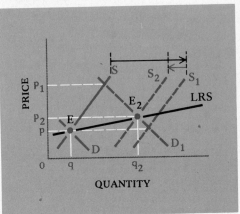

If growth in industry size increases factor prices, the *LRS* will be upward-sloping. Suppose an industry is in equilibrium at *E*. Then demand increases from *D* to D_1. In the short run price will rise to p_1. In the long run this increases the number of firms, thereby shifting the supply curve from *S* to S_1 (as shown by the black arrow). This is the supply curve that would pertain with an expanded number of firms if input prices did not change. But the increase in industry production bids up the prices of factors used, thereby shifting the supply curve leftward from S_1 to S_2 (as shown by the colored arrow). Equilibrium E_2 is at price p_2. Price has risen from *p* to p_2 because firms must recover the costs imposed by the higher input prices.

prices." Higher fuel prices in turn lead to higher prices of the things the fuel is used to make.

Rising *LRS* — **rising supply price** as it is sometimes called — is often a characteristic of sharp and rapid growth. A competitive industry with rising long-run supply prices is often called a **rising-cost industry.**

Decreasing Long-run Costs (Decreasing *LRS*)?

So far we have suggested that the long-run supply curve may be constant or rising. Could it ever decline, thereby indicating that higher outputs were associated with lower prices in long-run equilibrium?

It is tempting to answer yes because of the opportunities of more efficient scales of operation using

greater mechanization and more effective specialization of labor. But this answer would not be correct for perfectly competitive industries because each firm in long-run equilibrium must already be at the lowest point on its *LRATC* curve. If a firm could lower its costs by building a larger, more mechanized plant, it would be profitable to do so without waiting for an increase in demand. Since any single firm can sell all it wishes at the going market price, it will be profitable to expand the scale of its operations as long as its *LRATC* is falling.

There is a reason, however, why the long-run supply curve might slope downward: the expansion of an industry might lead to a fall in the prices of some of its inputs. If this occurs, the firms will find their cost curves shifting downward as they expand their outputs.

As an illustration of how the expansion of one industry could cause the prices of some of its inputs to fall, consider the early stages of the growth of the automobile industry. As the output of automobiles increased, the industry's demand for tires grew greatly.

FIGURE 14A-5
A Declining Long-run Supply Curve

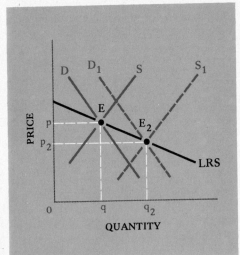

If growth in industry size reduces factor prices, the *LRS* will be downward-sloping. From an original equilibrium at *E*, an increase in demand to D_1 leads to an increase in supply to S_1 and a new equilibrium at E_2. Price p_2 is below the original price *p* because lower factor prices allow firms to cover their total costs at the lower price.

This, as suggested earlier, would have increased the demand for rubber and tended to raise its price, but it also provided the opportunity for Goodyear, Firestone, and other tire manufacturers to build large modern plants and reap the benefits of increasing returns in tire production. At first these economies were large enough to offset any factor price increases, and tire prices charged to manufacturers of automobiles fell. Thus automobile costs fell because of lower prices of an important input.

To see the effect of a fall in input prices caused by the expansion of an industry, suppose that the demand for the industry's product increases. Price and profits will rise and new entry will occur as a result. But when expansion of the industry has gone far enough to bring price back to its initial level, cost curves will be lower than they were initially because of the fall in input prices. Firms will thus still be earning profits. A further expansion will then occur until price falls to the level of the minimum points on each firm's new, lower *LRATC* curve. (This case is illustrated in Figure 14A-5.) An industry that has a declining long-run supply curve is often called a **falling-cost industry**.

THE EXISTENCE OF LONG-RUN COMPETITIVE EQUILIBRIUM

The greatest limitation on the usefulness of the model of perfect competition is that it may not be a suitable yardstick for evaluating real-world markets because it may be that perfect competition cannot exist in some circumstances that commonly occur in the real world.

The Problem Caused by Declining Costs

A necessary condition for a long-run competitive equilibrium to exist is that any economies of scale that are available to a firm should be exhausted at a level of output that is small relative to the whole industry's output. We have seen that a competitive firm will never be in equilibrium on the falling part of its *LRATC* — if price is given and costs can be reduced by expanding scale, profits can also be increased by doing so. Thus firms will grow in size at least until all scale economies are exhausted. Provided the output that yields the minimum *LRATC* for each firm is small relative to the industry's total output, there will be a larger number of firms in the industry and the industry will remain competitive. If, however, reaching the mini-

mum *LRATC* makes firms so large that they have significant market power, they will cease to be price takers and perfect competition will cease to exist.

In an industry with declining costs, the market may be too small relative to technology to be compatible with perfect competition. Indeed, if scale economies exist over such a large range that one firm's *LRATC* would still be falling if it served the entire market, a single firm may come to monopolize the market. This is what the classical economists called the case of *natural* monopoly; it is considered in Chapter 18.

The Problem of Constant Costs

Constant long-run costs also create problems for the competitive theory. Only if the firm's *LRATC* curve is U-shaped will there be a determinate size of the firm in a competitive industry. To see why, assume instead that *LRATC* falls to a minimum at some level of output and then remains constant for all larger outputs. All firms would have to be at least the minimum size, but they could be just that size or much larger since price would equal *LRATC* for any output above the minimum efficient size. In other words, there would then be no unique size for the firm. Are there reasons to believe the curve may not be U-shaped?

U-shaped plant curves. There are very good reasons why the *LRATC* curve for a single-plant firm may be expected to be U-shaped. There is a great deal in modern technology that results in lower average costs for large, automated factories compared with smaller factories in which a few workers use relatively unsophisticated capital equipment. As a single plant becomes too large, however, costs may rise because of the sheer difficulty of planning for, and controlling the behavior of, a vast integrated operation. Thus we have no problem accounting for a U-shaped cost curve for the *plant*.

U-shaped firm cost curve. What of the U-shaped cost curve for the *firm*? A declining portion will occur for the same reason that the *LRATC* for one plant declines when the firm is so small that it operates only one plant. Now, however, let the firm be operating one plant at the output where its *LRATC* is a minimum. Call that output q^*. What if the firm decides to double its output to $2q^*$? If it tries to build a vast plant with twice the output of the optimal size plant, the firm's average total cost of production may rise (because the vast plant has higher costs than a plant of the optimal size). But the firm has the option of *replicating* its first plant in a physically separate location. If the firm obtains a second parcel of land, builds an identical second plant, staffs it identically, and allows its production to be managed independently, there seems no reason why the second plant's minimum *LRATC* should be different from that of the first plant. *Because the firm can replicate plants and have them managed independently, there seems no reason why any firm faced with constant factor prices should not face constant LRATCs at least for multiples of the output for which one plant achieves the lowest plant LRATC.*

In the modern theory of perfect competition a U-shaped *firm* cost curve is merely *assumed*. Without it — although a competitive equilibrium may exist for an arbitrary number of firms — there is nothing to determine the equilibrium size of the firm and hence the number of firms in the industry. The basic point is that for perfect competition to persist, there must be something that stops firms, not just plants, from increasing in size indefinitely.

The Derivation of the Demand for Factors

Appendix to Chapter 20

We have said that factor demand is a derived demand. Precisely how is the demand for the factor derived from the demand for the product?

In Chapter 20 we saw that all profit-maximizing firms will hire units of the variable factor up to the point at which the marginal cost of the factor equals the marginal revenue produced by the factor. For a firm that is a price taker in factor markets, this means that it hires a factor up to the point at which the factor's price equals its marginal revenue product.

The Demand Curve for a Profit-maximizing Firm

Consider a single firm with only one variable factor, labor, and one fixed factor, capital. Assume that the average and marginal revenue products of the labor are those shown in Figure 20A-1. The firm wishes to hire the quantity of labor that will maximize its profits.

The demand curve for a factor is the downward-sloping portion of the marginal revenue product curve where it is below the average revenue product curve.

To see why this statement is correct, let us ask a number of questions.

Why do points on the downward-sloping portion of MRP, such as a and b in the figure, belong on the demand curve? If the wage rate (the price of the variable factor) is w_2, the profit-maximizing firm will hire the factor up to the point where $w = MRP$, that is, up to q_3. This is point a. If the wage rate is w_1, the firm will hire up to q_4. This is point b. Points a and b are thus on the firm's demand curve for the factor.

What is the maximum wage rate the firm will pay? What is the *maximum* wage rate at which the firm will still hire workers? We saw in Chapter 14

FIGURE 20A-1
The Relation of the Demand for a Factor and *MRP*

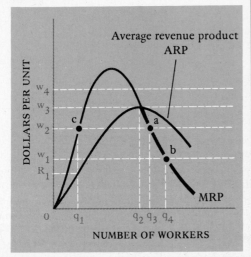

The derived demand curve for a factor is the downward-sloping portion of *MRP* below *ARP*. The heavy black portion of *MRP* is the firm's demand curve for the factor.

that it will never pay to produce a product when its price is below the level of average variable cost. We also saw (see page 216) that where average product is a maximum, average variable cost is a minimum. For any wage rate above w_3 — such as w_4 — the average revenue generated by a unit of labor (shown by *ARP*) would be less than the variable cost of the unit of labor (its wage rate). For such a wage rate it does not pay the firm to hire any workers. In other words w_3, where average revenue product is a maximum, is the highest factor price a firm could pay and still cover variable costs.

Why is the downward-sloping, not the upward-sloping, portion of MRP the demand curve? Consider the wage rate w_2. Here $w = MRP$ at both q_1 (point c) and q_3 (point a). We have already seen that point a is on the demand curve; what about point c? For every unit of labor hired up to q_1, *MRP* is less than the wage rate. In other words, each unit of labor is contributing

less to revenue than to cost. Thus a profit-maximizing firm would be better off hiring zero units than q_1 units. For every unit of labor from q_1 to q_3, *MRP* exceeds the wage rate. Thus, if a firm were hiring q_1 units, it would find each additional unit beyond q_1 (up to q_3) worth hiring. Point c (where *MRP* is rising when it equals the wage rate) is a point of *minimum* profit, not maximum profit. [52] A firm at point c would improve its profitability by moving in either direction, to hiring zero workers or to hiring q_3 workers. (We already know that q_3 is better than zero because at that quantity *ARP* is greater than the wage rate.)

Only points where *MRP* cuts the wage rate from above, that is, where *MRP* is downward-sloping, are possible profit-maximizing quantities.

Will There Be a Downward-sloping Portion of *MRP*?

Having shown that only downward-sloping portions of *MRP* are relevant to the demand curve for the factor, we may ask whether we have any reason to believe *MRP* will slope downward. The presence of diminishing returns is sufficient to assure this result, as can be easily shown. Marginal revenue product depends on two things: (1) the physical increase in output that an additional unit of the variable factor makes possible, multiplied by (2) the increase in revenue derived from that extra output. The first of these is called the **marginal physical product** (*MPP*); the second is the by now familiar concept of marginal revenue:

$$MRP = MPP \times MR$$

The hypothesis of diminishing marginal returns was introduced in Chapter 12. This hypothesis says that *MPP* has a declining section over some range of output. If marginal revenue is constant (as it is in perfect competition), *MRP* will have the same shape as *MPP* and must also decline.

Marginal revenue, however, may not be constant. If *MR* declines as output increases (as it does in monopoly and in any other situation in which the firm's demand curve declines), *MRP* must decline even more sharply. The hypothesis of diminishing marginal productivity thus implies diminishing *MRP* and a downward-sloping demand curve for the factor.

The Permanent-income Hypothesis and the Life-cycle Hypothesis

Appendix to Chapter 34

In the Keynesian theory of the consumption function, current consumption expenditure is related to current income—either current disposable income or current national income. Recent attempts to reconcile the apparently conflicting empirical data on short-term and long-term consumption behavior have produced a series of theories that relate consumption to some longer-term concept of income than the income that the household is currently earning.

The two most influential theories of this type are the **permanent-income hypothesis (PIH),** developed by Professor Friedman, and the **life-cycle hypothesis (LCH),** developed by Professors Modigliani and Ando and the late Professor Brumberg. Although there are many significant differences between these theories, their similarities are more important than their differences, and they may be looked at together when studying their major characteristics. In doing this it is important to ask: What variables do these theories seek to explain? What assumptions do the theories make? What are the major implications of these assumptions? How do the theories reconcile the apparently conflicting empirical evidence? And what implications do they have for the overall behavior of the economy?

VARIABLES

Three important variables need to be considered: consumption, saving, and income. Keynesian-type theories seek to explain the amounts that households spend on purchasing goods and services for consumption. This concept is called *consumption expenditure.* Permanent-income theories seek to explain the actual flows of consumption of the services that are provided by the commodities that households buy. This concept is called *actual consumption*.[1] With services and non-durable goods, expenditure and actual consumption occur more or less at the same time and the distinction between the two concepts is not important. The consumption of a haircut, for example, occurs at the time it is purchased, and an orange or a package of corn flakes is consumed very soon after it is purchased. Thus, if we knew purchases of such goods and services at some time, say last year, we would also know last year's consumption of those goods and services. But this is not the case with durable consumer goods. A screwdriver is purchased at one point in time, but it yields up its services over a long time, possibly as long as the purchaser's lifetime. The same is true of a house and a watch and, over a shorter period of time, of a car and a dress. For such products, if we know purchases last year, we do not necessarily know last year's consumption of the services that the products yielded.

Thus one important characteristic of durable goods is that *expenditure* to purchase them is not necessarily synchronized with consumption of the stream of services that the goods provide. If in 1970 Mr. Smith buys a car for $4,000, runs it for six years, and then discards it as worn out, his expenditure on automobiles is $4,000 in 1970 and zero for the next five years. His consumption of the services of automobiles, however, is spread out at an average annual rate of $666 for six years. If everyone followed Mr. Smith's example by buying a new car in 1970 and replacing it in 1976, the automobile industry would undergo wild booms in 1970 and 1976 with five intervening years of slump even though the actual consumption of automobiles would be spread more or less evenly over time. This example is extreme, but it illustrates the possibilities, where consumers' durables are concerned, of quite different time paths of *consumption expenditure*, which is the subject of Keynesian theories of the consumption function, and *actual consumption*, which is the subject of permanent-income type theories.

Now consider saving. The change in emphasis from consumption expenditure to actual consumption im-

plies a change in the definition of saving. Saving is no longer income minus consumption expenditure; it is now income minus the value of actual consumption. When Mr. Smith spent $4,000 on his car in 1970 but used only $666 worth of its services in that year, he was actually consuming $666 and saving $3,334. The purchase of a consumers' durable is thus counted as saving and only the value of its services actually consumed is counted as consumption.

So much for consumption and saving. The third important variable in this type of theory is the income variable. Instead of using current income, the theories use a concept of long-term income. The precise definition varies from one theory to another, but basically it is related to the household's expected income stream over a fairly long planning period. In the LCH it is the income that the household expects to earn over its lifetime.[2]

Every household is assumed to have a view of its expected lifetime earnings. This is not as unreasonable as it might seem. Students training to be doctors have a very different view of expected lifetime income than those training to become high school teachers. Both expected income streams—for a doctor and for a high school teacher—will be very different from that expected by an assembly-line worker or a professional athlete. One possible lifetime income stream is illustrated in Figure 34A-1.

The household's expected lifetime income is then converted into a single figure for *annual* **permanent income.** In the life-cycle hypothesis this permanent income is the maximum amount the household could spend on consumption each year without accumulating debts *that are passed on to future generations*. If a household were to consume a constant amount equal to its permanent income each year, it would add to its debts in years when current income was less than permanent income and reduce its debt or increase its assets in years when its current income exceeded its permanent income; however, over its lifetime it would just break even, leaving neither accumulated assets nor debts to its heirs. If the interest rate were zero, permanent income would be just the sum of all expected incomes divided by the number of expected

---

[1] Because Keynes' followers did not always distinguish carefully between the concepts of consumption expenditure and actual consumption, the word "consumption" is often used in both contexts. We follow this normal practice, but where there is any possible ambiguity in the term we will refer to "consumption expenditure" and "actual consumption."

[2] In the PIH the household has an infinite time horizon and the relevant permanent-income concept is the amount the household could consume forever without increasing or decreasing its present stock of wealth.

FIGURE 34A-1
Current Income and Permanent Income

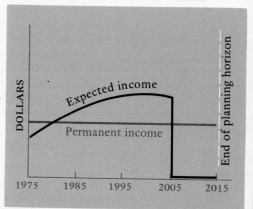

Expected current income may vary greatly over a lifetime, but expected permanent income is defined to be the constant annual equivalent. The graph shows a hypothetical expected income stream from work for a household whose planning horizon was 40 years from 1975. The current income rises to a peak, then falls slowly for a while, and finally falls sharply on retirement. The corresponding permanent income is the amount the household could consume at a steady rate over its lifetime by borrowing early against future earnings (as do most newly married couples), then repaying past debts, and finally saving for retirement when income is at its peak without either incurring debt or accumulating new wealth to be passed on to future generations.

years of life. With a positive interest rate, permanent income will diverge somewhat from this amount because of the costs of borrowing and the extra income that can be earned by investing savings.

ASSUMPTIONS

The basic assumption of this type of theory, whether PIH or LCH, is that the household's actual consumption is related to its permanent rather than to its current income. Two households that have the same permanent income (and are similar in other relevant characteristics) will have the same consumption patterns even though their current incomes behave very differently.

IMPLICATIONS

The major implication of these theories is that changes in a household's current income will affect its actual consumption only so far as they affect its permanent income. Consider two income changes that could occur to a household with a permanent income of $10,000 per year and an expected lifetime of 30 more years. In the first, suppose the household receives an unexpected extra income of $2,000 *for this year only*. The increase in the household's permanent income is thus very small. If the rate of interest were zero, the household could consume an extra $66.66 per year for the rest of its expected lifespan; with a positive rate of interest, the extra annual consumption would be more because money not spent this year could be invested and would earn interest.[3] In the second case, the household gets a totally unforeseen increase of $2,000 a year for the rest of its life. In this event the household's permanent income has risen by $2,000 because the household can actually consume $2,000 more every year without accumulating new debts. Although in both cases current income rises $2,000, the effect on permanent income is very different in the two cases.

Keynesian theory assumes that *consumption expenditure* is related to current income and therefore predicts the same change in this year's consumption expenditure in each of the above cases. Permanent-income theories relate *actual consumption* to permanent income and therefore predict very different changes in actual consumption in each case. In the first case there would be only a small increase in actual annual consumption; in the second there would be a large increase.

In permanent-income theories, any change in current income that is thought to be temporary will have only a small effect on permanent income and hence on actual consumption.

Implications for the Behavior of the Economy

According to the permanent-income and the life-cycle hypotheses, actual consumption is not much affected by temporary changes in income. Does this mean that

---

[3] If the rate of interest were 7 percent, the household could invest the $2,000, consume an extra $161 a year, and just have nothing left at the end of 30 years.

aggregate expenditure, $C + I + G + (X - M)$, is not much affected? *Not necessarily.* Consider what happens when households get a temporary increase in their incomes. If actual consumption is not greatly affected by this, then households must be saving most of the temporary increase in their incomes. But from the point of view of these theories, households save when they buy a durable good just as much as when they buy a financial asset such as a stock or a bond. In both cases actual current consumption is not changed.

Thus spending a temporary increase in income on bonds or on new cars is consistent with both the PIH and the LCH. But it makes a great deal of difference to the short-run behavior of the economy which is done. If households buy stocks and bonds, aggregate expenditure on currently produced final goods will not rise when income rises temporarily;[4] if households buy automobiles or any other durable consumer good, aggregate expenditure on currently produced final goods will rise when income rises temporarily. Thus the PIH and the LCH leave unsettled the question that is critical in determining the size of the multiplier: What is the reaction of household *expenditures* on currently produced goods and services, particularly durables, to short-term, temporary changes in income?

The PIH and LCH theories leave unanswered the critical question of the ability of short-term changes in fiscal policy to remove inflationary and deflationary gaps.

Assume, for example, that a serious deflationary gap emerges and that the government attempts to stimulate a recovery by giving tax rebates and by cutting tax rates—both on an announced temporary basis. This will raise households' current disposable incomes by the amount of the tax cuts, but it will raise their permanent incomes by only a small amount. According to the PIH, the flow of actual current consumption should not rise much. Yet it is quite consistent with the PIH that households should spend their tax savings on durable consumer goods, the consumption of which can be spread over many years. In this case, even though actual consumption this year would not respond much to the tax cuts, expenditure would respond a great deal. Since current output and employment depends on expenditure rather than on real

consumption, the tax cut would be effective in stimulating the economy. However, it is also consistent with the PIH that households spend only a small part of their tax savings on consumption goods and seek to invest the rest in bonds and other financial assets. In this case the tax cuts may have only a small stimulating effect on the economy. It is important to note that the PIH and the LCH do *not* predict unambiguously that changes in taxes that are announced to be only short-lived will be ineffective in removing inflationary or deflationary gaps.

A Reconciliation of the Data

The PIH and the LCH are able to reconcile the observation that the MPC appears to be equal to the APC in long-period data while it is less than the APC in short-period and cross-sectional data.[5] They do this by relating changes in observed income to changes in permanent income.

Long-term time-series data using decade-by-decade averages remove the effects of temporary fluctuations in income. The observed changes in Y mainly represent permanent increases in real income because of economic growth. Long-term time-series studies will thus tend to measure accurately the propensity to consume out of permanent income.

Now consider short-term data. A study covering 10 or 15 years at the most and using annual observations of C and Y will use an income series dominated by temporary changes caused by cyclical fluctuations. When a household loses employment because of a business recession, it does not expect to remain unemployed forever; neither does it expect the extra income that it earns from heavy overtime work during a period of peak demand to persist. It may therefore be assumed that households expect these cyclical changes in current income to be temporary and that they will thus have little effect on permanent income. Since consumption is assumed to depend on permanent income, it follows that the observed relation between consumption and cyclical changes in income will tend to be

---

[4] Except for any indirect effect through changes in interest rates.

[5] The short-run and long-run time-series data are described in Chapter 30 (see especially pages 597–602). Cross-section data are for a number of households at one point in time, and they show for that point in time how household consumption varies with household income. The data yield a consumption function similar to that obtained from short-term time-series data but with an even lower MPC.

smaller than the relation shown by the long-term time-series data. What this shows, then, is the lack of relation between changes in consumption and temporary changes in income, not a lack of relation between changes in consumption and changes in permanent income.

A similar analysis shows that cross-section studies are strongly influenced by the behavior of households whose incomes have temporarily departed from their permanent levels. Thus cross-section studies should be expected to yield a much lower observed marginal propensity to consume than that yielded by long-term time-series studies.

CONCLUSION

While permanent-income type theories succeed in reconciling various empirical observations of consumption functions, they leave ambiguous the multiplier effects of temporary increases in income. They are consistent with a constancy in both the *MPC* and the *APC* when *permanent income* changes. They also suggest a high degree of stability of the actual flow of consumption in the face of temporary fluctuations in current income. This is consistent with an *APC* out of *current income* that varies inversely with current income, falling as income rises and rising as income falls.

Money in the National Income Model

Appendix to Chapter 38

We have studied the interaction between money, interest rates, and national income in terms of the apparatus in Figures 38-3, 38-4, and 38-5. A loose end that arises in that model can best be seen by considering the impact of a change in the money supply. This leads to a fall in interest rates as shown in Figure 38-3(i), to increases in expenditure as shown in Figure 38-3(ii), and to increased national income as shown in Figure 38-4. But increased national income in turn leads to an increased need for transactions balances. This increased demand for money must then be added to the liquidity preference schedule in Figure 38-3. How is the increase in demand satisfied? Does accounting for it radically alter the conclusions of the analysis of Chapter 38?

The answer to the last question is no. This appendix provides a model that integrates monetary and expenditure factors and shows how they jointly determine the interest rate and the level of national income. The approach is that first suggested by the British economist Sir John Hicks (awarded the Nobel Prize in economics in 1972) in his famous review of Keynes' *General Theory,* "Mr. Keynes and the Classics: A Suggested Interpretation." This approach involves identifying the relationship between income and interest rates that is imposed first by goods market equilibrium and then by money market equilibrium. We then bring the two together to determine the one combination of real national income and interest rate that satisfies both equilibrium conditions simultaneously. Finally we use the model to examine monetary and fiscal policy.

THE INTEREST RATE AND AGGREGATE EXPENDITURE: THE *IS* CURVE

As we saw in going from Figure 38-3(ii) to Figure 38-4(i), a fall in the rate of interest is associated with a rise in the level of real national income due to increased investment expenditures. Figure 38A-1 depicts this relationship between interest rates and national income as the negatively sloped *IS* curve. The negative relationship is derived for *given* values of the other variables influencing the aggregate expenditure function of Figure 38-4(i). The *IS* curve shows the combinations of national income and the rate of interest for which aggregate expenditure just equals total production in the economy.

For given settings of the relationships underlying the aggregate expenditure function, the condition of goods market equilibrium, $Y = AE$, means that the level of national income will vary inversely with the interest rate.

Fiscal Policy

Increases in the level of government expenditure raise the total level of aggregate expenditure *for any given interest rate;* as Figure 34-1 shows, this in turn leads to a multiplier effect on national income. In terms of the present model, an increase in government expenditure causes the *IS* curve to shift upward to the right as shown in Figure 38A-1. Combinations of national income and the interest rate that were on the original *IS* curve and hence were initially positions of equilibrium in the goods market are now positions of excess demand due to the increase in autonomous government demand. Hence output must rise to satisfy the increased demand (in the process leading to the now familiar mutliplier effect), or interest rates must rise to reduce investment demand, or as *IS'* in Figure 38A-1 shows, some combination of both must occur.[1]

Expansionary fiscal policy causes the *IS* curve to shift upward and to the right, creating a new locus of points for which aggregate expenditure equals national income.

By similar reasoning, cuts in government spending or tax increases shift the *IS* curve down to the left. [53]

[1] A reduction in taxes, by altering the relationship between national income and disposable income, would also lead to a rightward shift in the *IS* curve.

FIGURE 38A-1
Goods Market Equilibrium: The *IS* Curve

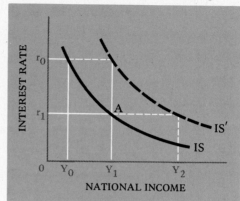

The locus of combinations of national income and the interest rate for which aggregate expenditure equals output is called the *IS* curve. The *IS* curve slopes downward to the right, indicating that a fall in the interest rate from r_0 to r_1 leads, via increased investment, to an increased level of national income from Y_0 to Y_1. Expansionary fiscal policy creates excess demand for output and causes the *IS* curve to shift right to *IS'*; from an initial position at *A*, the interest rate must rise to r_0, or national income must rise to Y_2, or some combination of both along *IS'* must occur.

LIQUIDITY PREFERENCE AND NATIONAL INCOME: THE *LM* CURVE

When the money supply is held constant, if the demand for and the supply of money are to be equal, the *total* demand for money arising from the transactions, speculative, and precautionary motives must also be constant. As we have seen, the demand for money can be expected to vary directly with the level of national income and inversely with the rate of interest. Hence if the money market is to be in equilibrium with a given money supply, any increase in national income must be accompanied by an increase in the interest rate so as to keep total money demand constant. This is depicted by the positively sloped *LM* curve in Figure 38A-2. The *LM* curve shows the combinations of national income and the rate of interest for which total money demand is constant at the level of a given money supply.

FIGURE 38A-2

Money Market Equilibrium: The *LM* Curve

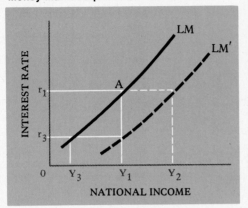

The locus of combinations of national income and the interest rate for which total money demand equals a given money supply is called the *LM* curve. The *LM* curve slopes upward to the right, indicating that a fall in the rate of interest from r_1 to r_3, which causes the demand for money to rise, must be accompanied by a fall in income, say from Y_1 to Y_3, in order to keep money demand equal to the constant money supply. An open market purchase creates an excess supply of money and causes the *LM* curve to shift right to *LM'*; from an initial position at *A*, the interest rate must fall to r_3, or national income must rise to Y_2, or some combination of both along *LM'* must occur.

For a given money supply, the condition of money market equilibrium means that the level of national income will vary directly with the interest rate.

Monetary Policy

An increase in the supply of money resulting from an open market purchase by the central bank causes the *LM* curve to shift downward to the right, as in Figure 38A-2. The combinations of national income and interest rate that were on the original *LM* curve and hence that were initially positions of money market equilibrium now correspond to excess supply due to the increase in the supply of money. To reestablish equilibrium, the demand for money must increase to match the larger money supply; hence national income

must rise, or the interest rate must fall, or as *LM'* in Figure 38A-2 shows, some combination of both must occur.

An increase in the money supply causes the *LM* curve to shift downward to the right, creating a new locus of points for which total money demand equals the money supply.

By similar reasoning, a decrease in the money supply causes the *LM* curve to shift upward to the left. [54]

MACROECONOMIC EQUILIBRIUM DETERMINATION OF NATIONAL INCOME AND THE INTEREST RATE

The model is shown in Figure 38A-3. The intersection of the two curves indicates the only combination of national income and the rate of interest for which aggregate expenditure equals national income *and* the demand for money is equal to the supply.

The intersection of the *IS* and *LM* curves gives the equilibrium levels of national income and the rate of interest in a model that combines both expenditure and monetary influences.

Figure 38A-3 shows the effects of particular shifts in the *IS and LM* curves. This analysis leads to four general predictions.

1. A rightward shift of the *IS* curve raises national income and the rate of interest.
2. A leftward shift of the *IS* curve lowers national income and the rate of interest.
3. A rightward shift of the *LM* curve raises national income and lowers the rate of interest.
4. A leftward shift of the *LM* curve lowers national income and raises the rate of interest.

The Effects of Fiscal and Monetary Policy

Given our analysis of the effects of government expenditure on the *IS* curve and the effects of the money supply on the *LM* curve, we can summarize the analysis in our four basic predictions about the effects of monetary and fiscal policy.

FIGURE 38A-3
The Effects of Shifts in the *IS* and *LM* Curves

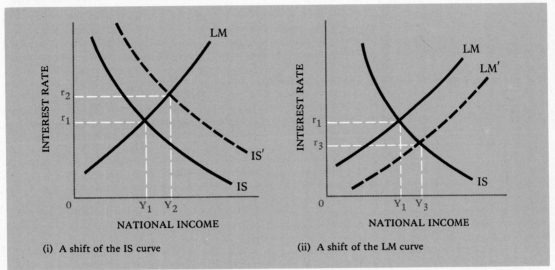

(i) A shift of the IS curve   (ii) A shift of the LM curve

Similar shifts in the *IS* and *LM* curves have similar effects on national income and opposite effects on the rate of interest. The initial levels of income and the rate of interest are Y_0 and r_0 in both parts of the figure. In (i) a rightward shift in the *IS* curve from *IS* to *IS'* raises national income from Y_0 to Y_1 and raises the rate of interest from r_0 to r_1. In (ii) a rightward shift in the *LM* curve from *LM* to *LM'* raises national income from Y_0 to Y_2 and lowers the rate of interest from r_0 to r_2. Part (i) shows the effect of an increase in government expenditure; (ii) shows the effect of an increase in the money supply.

1. An increase in G raises national income and raises the rate of interest.
2. An increase in the money supply raises national income and lowers the rate of interest.
3. A decrease in G lowers national income and lowers the rate of interest.
4. A decrease in the money supply lowers national income and raises the rate of interest.

These results represent what may be called the neo-Keynesian synthesis, in which both monetary and fiscal policies have an effect on national income and interest rates. [55]

THE PRICE LEVEL AND AGGREGATE DEMAND

So far we have treated the price level as given and presumed that all changes in national income were changes in *real* output. Consider now what would happen to the analysis if the price level were allowed to vary.

Changes in the Price Level

As Figure 38-6 shows, an increase in the price level leads to an increase in liquidity preference. In order for money market equilibrium to be preserved, the interest rate must rise (as in Figure 38-6), or the level of income must fall, or, since either leads to a reduction in money demand, some combination of both must occur—that is, the *LM* curve must shift upward to the left.

A fall in the price level reduces liquidity preference and the *LM* curve shifts down and to the right.

Increases in the price level cause the *LM* curve to shift upward to the left; decreases in the price level cause the *LM* curve to shift downward to the right.

FIGURE 38A-4
The Derivation of Aggregate Demand

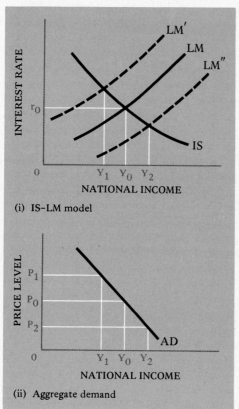

(i) IS–LM model

(ii) Aggregate demand

Changes in the price level shift the *LM* curve and thus change the equilibrium level of income. An increase in the price level increases the demand for money. Alternatively, it can be seen as reducing the real value of the existing money stock. The excess demand for money leads to a leftward shift of the *LM* curve to *LM'* and a fall in national income. A fall in the price level creates an excess supply of money and a rightward shift of the *LM* curve to *LM''*. The price level and national income are inversely related, as shown by the *AD* curve in (ii).

But from the previous section we know that the effect in the first case is to reduce national income while the effect in the second case is to increase national income. This is illustrated in Figure 38A-4.

Equilibrium in the money and goods markets combined implies that the price level and national income are inversely related, as summarized in the downward-sloping aggregate demand curve.

The relationship summarized in the aggregate demand curve is a straight forward extension of the transmission mechanism running from liquidity preference to the rate of interest to aggregate expenditure, as illustrated in Figure 38-6.

Shifts in the Aggregate Demand Curve

The *AD* curve was derived on the basis of a given money supply and given relationships underlying the *IS* curve; it is a straightforward exercise to demonstrate that fiscal and monetary policies, by influencing the *IS* and *LM* curves, cause the *AD* curve to shift. [56] The mechanism by which monetary and fiscal policy causes the shift in *AD* is illustrated in Figure 38-4.

An increase in the money supply means that the *LM* curve corresponding to any particular price level shifts downward to the right. Hence that price level now corresponds to a higher level of real national income; that is, the aggregate demand curve shifts to the right as a result of an increase in the money supply.

An increase in government expenditure causes the *IS* curve to shift upward to the right as before; it now intersects any given *LM* curve at a higher level of national income. Again, any given price level now corresponds to a larger real national income; that is, the aggregate demand curve shifts to the right as a result of an increase in government expenditure.

More on Monetary Versus Fiscal Policy

Appendix to Chapter 42

Much of the debate between the monetarists and the neo-Keynesians about stabilization policy can be summarized by using the *IS* and *LM* curves introduced in the appendix to Chapter 38.[1] This is merely a more succinct way of summarizing the points of controversy analyzed in Chapter 42; anyone who has mastered the *IS-LM* apparatus can follow the argument in Chapter 42 using the formal analysis sketched in this appendix.

THE RELATIVE EFFECTIVENESS OF MONETARY AND FISCAL POLICY

Although the neo-Keynesian synthesis holds that both monetary and fiscal policy can influence national income, many neo-Keynesians believe that monetary policy tends to be relatively ineffective compared to fiscal policy. Many monetarists hold the opposite view. Much of the debate turns on the assumed shapes of the *IS* and *LM* curves.

The Shape of the *IS* Curve

The monetarist case arises if investment is very sensitive to changes in the rate of interest. Then a rise in income that creates a given excess supply of goods need only be accompanied by a *small* fall in the rate of interest in order to generate the increase in investment expenditure required to offset the initial excess supply. In this case the *IS* curve is relatively flat.

The neo-Keynesian case occurs if investment is relatively interest inelastic. Then a *large* fall in interest rates is necessary to induce the increase in investment expenditure to offset an excess supply of goods caused

[1] Much of the debate also depends on points of theory and measurement that are too advanced for the discussion in an elementary textbook.

FIGURE 42A-1
The Relative Efficacies of Fiscal and Monetary Policy

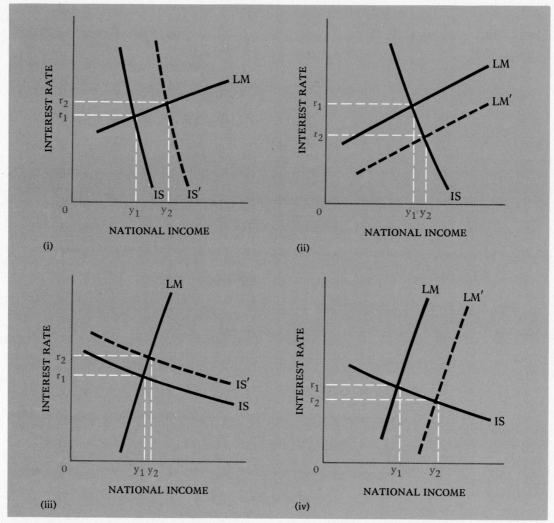

A neo-Keynesian view makes fiscal policy more effective than monetary policy; a monetarist view finds monetary policy more effective than fiscal policy. In each of the four parts of the figure, the initial levels of national income and the interest rate are y_1 and r_1. The curve that shifts is indicated by a prime mark, and the new levels of income and the interest rate are y_2 and r_2.

A neo-Keynesian view is shown in (i) and (ii). A relatively flat *LM* curve means that a shift in the *IS* curve

has a large effect on income and only a small effect on interest rates. A relatively steep *IS* curve means that a shift in the *LM* curve has a large effect on interest rates and only a small effect on income.

A monetarist view is shown in (iii) and (iv). A steep *LM* curve means that a shift in the *IS* curve has a large effect on the interest rate and only a small effect on income. A flat *IS* curve means that a shift in the *LM* curve has a large effect on income and only a small effect on interest rates.

by a rise in income. This makes the *IS* curve relatively steep.

The Shape of the *LM* Curve

Both sides agree that the demand for money can respond to the level of income; for a given money supply and interest rate, an increase (decrease) in the level of income raises (lowers) the demand for money and hence causes an excess demand for (supply of) money. But they disagree on the response to changes in the interest rates.

The monetarist case arises when the demand for money is relatively unresponsive to the interest rate. In this event an increase in the demand for money caused by a rise in national income calls forth a large rise in the rate of interest in order to keep the overall demand for money constant. This makes the *LM* curve very steep.

In the neo-Keynesian case the demand for money is interest elastic. When income rises and the transactions demand for money rises with it, only a small rise in interest rates is needed to restore the overall demand to its original level. This makes the *LM* curve relatively flat.

Fiscal Versus Monetary Policy

The implications for fiscal and monetary policy of the assumed shapes in the *IS* and *LM* curves are analyzed in Figure 42A-1. The figure shows the basic monetarist and neo-Keynesian predictions of the effects of these policies.

The effectiveness of fiscal policy. An attempt to stabilize the economy through the use of discretionary fiscal policy shows up in this model as a shift in the *IS* curve. For example, an expansionary fiscal policy shifts the *IS* curve to the right, thereby raising both the interest rate and national income.

Given the neo-Keynesian view that the *IS* curve is relatively steep and the *LM* curve is relatively flat, expansionary policy has only a slight effect on the interest rate and a strong effect on national income. Given the monetarist view that the *IS* curve is relatively flat and the *LM* curve is relatively steep, expansionary fiscal policy will put strong upward pressure on the interest rate; this in turn leads to a crowding out of private sector investment expenditure, and hence the policy will have only a small effect on national income.

The effectiveness of monetary policy. An attempt to stabilize the economy through the use of monetary policy shows up in this model as a shift in the *LM* curve. For example, an expansionary monetary policy shifts the *LM* curve to the right, thereby lowering interest rates and raising national income.

Given the neo-Keynesian view that the *IS* curve is relatively steep and the *LM* curve is relatively flat, expansionary monetary policy will not be very effective in lowering the interest rate. Any interest rate reduction that occurs will not stimulate much of an increase in investment expenditure. Hence monetary policy will not be very effective in influencing national income.

Given the monetarist view that the *IS* curve is relatively flat and the *LM* curve is relatively steep, expansionary monetary policy will lead to a sharp reduction in interest rates and a large increase in investment expenditure. Hence monetary policy will be effective in influencing national income.

Neo-Keynesian and Monetarist Views: A Recapitalition

Given the neo-Keynesian view of the shapes of the *IS* and *LM* curves, the effects of fiscal policy are mainly felt in relatively large changes in national income and relatively small changes in the rate of interest, while the effects of monetary policy are mainly felt in relatively small changes in national income and relatively large changes in the rate of interest.

Given the monetarist view of the shapes of the *IS* and *LM* curves, the effects of fiscal policy are mainly felt in relatively small changes in national income and relatively large changes in the rate of interest, while the effects of monetary policy are mainly felt in relatively large changes in national income and relatively small changes in the rate of interest.

THE MONETARY MECHANISM AND AGGREGATE DEMAND

The differing views about the shapes of the *IS* and *LM* curves can be interpreted as differing views about the shape of the aggregate demand curve and its responsiveness to monetary and fiscal policy.

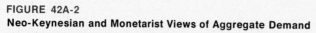

FIGURE 42A-2
Neo-Keynesian and Monetarist Views of Aggregate Demand

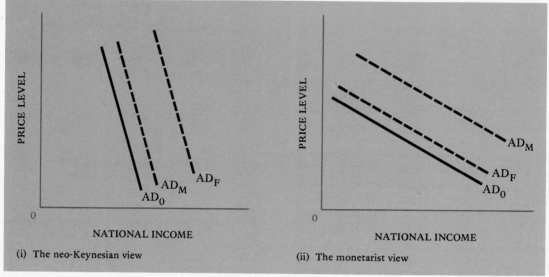

(i) The neo-Keynesian view   (ii) The monetarist view

The Neo-Keynesian view is that aggregate demand is relatively price inelastic and responsive to fiscal policy but not to monetary policy; the monetarist view is that aggregate demand is relatively elastic with respect to price and responsive to monetary policy but not to fiscal policy. In both parts the black line AD_0 is initial aggregate demand, the dashed line AD_M is aggregate demand that arises when expansionary monetary policy is introduced, and the dashed line AD_F is aggregate demand that arises when expansionary fiscal policy is introduced. In (i) the steep AD curve shifts less in response to monetary policy than in response to fiscal policy. In (ii) the flat AD curve shifts more in response to monetary policy than in response to fiscal policy.

Neo-Keynesian Views About Aggregate Demand

As we demonstrated in the Appendix to Chapter 38, by shifting the LM curve, changes in the price level influence the level of national income that is demanded. Given the neo-Keynesian view, such shifts have little influence in the level of national income. Hence the neo-Keynesian view implies that the aggregate demand curve will be relatively steep.

Shifts in the aggregate demand curve arise when national income changes at a given price level. The above analysis shows that in the neo-Keynesian view fiscal policy leads to large shifts in national income while monetary policy leads only to very small changes. The neo-Keynesian view thus implies that fiscal policy will lead to large shifts in the aggregate demand curve while monetary policy will lead only to small shifts in aggregate demand.

This is illustrated in Figure 42A-2(i).

Monetarist Views About Aggregate Demand

Since monetarist views imply that shifts in the LM curve lead to large shifts in national income they imply that the aggregate demand curve must be relatively flat.

For a given price level, monetarist views hold that fiscal policy is ineffective while monetary policy is effective. Hence fiscal policy leads only to small shifts in the aggregate demand curve while monetary policy leads to large shifts.

This is illustrated in Figure 42A-2(ii).

Mathematical Notes

1. It may not be immediately obvious that calculating the ratio of the cost of purchasing a fixed bundle of commodities in two periods is the same thing as calculating the percentage change in each price and then averaging these by weighting each price by the proportion of total expenditure devoted to the commodity. The following expression, however, illustrates the equivalence of these two procedures for the two-commodity case:

$$\frac{q^A p_1^A + q^B p_1^B}{q^A p_0^A + q^B p_0^B} = \frac{p_1^A}{p_0^A}\left(\frac{q^A p_0^A}{q^A p_0^A + q^B p_0^B}\right)$$

$$+ \frac{p_1^B}{p_0^B}\left(\frac{q^B p_0^B}{q^A p_0^A + q^B p_0^B}\right)$$

The qs are fixed quantity weights while the ps are prices; A and B refer to two commodities; 0 and 1 refer respectively to the base period and some subsequent time period. The expression on the left is the fixed bundle q^A and q^B valued at given year prices divided by its value in base year prices. The first term in the expression on the right gives the ratio of the price of good A in the given and the base year multiplied by the proportion of total expenditure in the base year devoted to good A. The second term does the same for good B. Simple multiplication and division reduces the right-hand expression to the left-hand one.

2. Many variables affect the quantity demanded. Using functional notation, the argument of the next several pages can be anticipated. Let Q^D represent the quantity of a commodity demanded and

$$T, \overline{Y}, N, Y^*, p, p_j$$

represent, respectively, tastes, average household income, population, income distribution, its price, and the price of the jth other commodity.

The demand function is

$$Q^D = D(T, \overline{Y}, N, Y^*, p, p_j), j = 1, 2, \ldots, \text{n}$$

The demand schedule or curve looks at

$$Q^D = q(p) \Big|_{T,\bar{Y},N,Y^*,p_j}$$

where the notation means that the variables to the right of the vertical line are held constant.

This function is correctly described as the demand function with respect to price, all other variables held constant. This function, often written concisely $q = q(p)$, shifts in response to changes in other variables. Consider average income. If, as is usually hypothesized, $\dfrac{\partial Q^D}{\partial \bar{Y}} > 0$, then increases in average income shift $q = q(p)$ rightward and decreases in average income shift $q = q(p)$ leftward. Changes in other variables likewise shift this function in the direction implied by the relationship of that variable to the quantity demanded.

3. Quantity demanded is a simple, straightforward, but frequently misunderstood concept in everyday use, but it has a clear mathematical meaning. It refers to the dependent variable in the demand function from note 2 above:

$$Q^D = D(T,\bar{Y},N,Y^*,p,p_j)$$

It takes on a specific value, therefore, whenever a specific value is assigned to each of the independent variables. A change in Q^D occurs whenever the specific value of any independent variable is changed. Q^D could change, for example, from 10,000 tons per month to 20,000 tons per month as a result of a *ceteris paribus* change in any one price, in average income, in the distribution of income, in tastes, or in population. Also it could change as a result of the net effect of changes in all of the independent variables occurring at once. Thus a change in the price of a commodity is a sufficient reason for a change in Q^D but not a necessary reason.

Some textbooks reserve the term *change in quantity demanded* for a movement along a demand curve, that is, a change in Q^D as a result of a change in p. They then use other words for a change in Q^D caused by a change in the other variables in the demand function. This usage gives the single variable Q^D more than one name, and this is potentially confusing.

Our usage, which corresponds to that in all intermediate and advanced treatments, avoids this practice. We call Q^D *quantity demanded* and refer to *any* change in Q^D as a *change in quantity demanded*. In this usage it is correct to say that a movement along a demand curve is a change in quantity demanded. But it is incorrect to say that a change in quantity demanded can occur only because of a movement along a demand curve (since Q^D can change for other reasons, e.g., a *ceteris paribus* change in average household income).

4. Continuing the development of note 2, let Q^S represent the quantity of a commodity supplied and

$$G,X,p,p_j,w_i$$

represent, respectively, producers' goals, technology, price, price of the jth other commodity, and costs of the ith factor of production.

The supply function is

$$Q^S = S(G,X,p,p_j,w_i), \quad j = 1, 2, \ldots, n \\ i = 1, 2, \ldots, m$$

The supply schedule and supply curve looks at

$$Q^S = s(p) \Big|_{G,X,p_j,w_i}$$

This is the supply function with respect to price, all other variables held constant. This function, often written concisely $q = s(p)$, shifts in response to changes in other variables.

5. Continuing the development of notes 2 and 4, equilibrium occurs where

$$Q^D = Q^S$$

which *for specified values of all other variables* requires $q(p) = s(p)$. This condition is met only at the point where demand and supply curves intersect. Thus supply and demand curves are said to determine equilibrium price. A shift in any of the variables held constant in the q and s functions will shift the demand or supply curve and lead to a different equilibrium.

6. The definition in the text uses finite changes and is called *arc elasticity*. The parallel definition using derivatives is

$$\eta = \frac{dq}{dp} \cdot \frac{p}{q}$$

and is called *point elasticity*. Further discussion appears in the Appendix to Chapter 6.

7. The propositions in the text are proven as follows. Letting TR stand for total revenue we can write:

$$TR = pq$$

$$dTR/dp = q + p\,\frac{dq}{dp} \tag{1}$$

But from the equation in note 6

$$q\eta = p\frac{dq}{dp} \qquad [2]$$

which we can substitute in [1] to obtain

$$\frac{dTR}{dp} = q + q\eta = q(1 + \eta) \qquad [3]$$

Because η is a negative number, the sign of [3] is negative if the absolute value of η exceeds unity (demand elastic) and positive if it is less than unity (demand inelastic).

8. The "axis-reversal" arose in the following way. Marshall theorized in terms of "demand price" and "supply price" as the prices that would lead to a given quantity being demanded or supplied. Thus he wrote

$$p^d = D(q) \qquad [1]$$

$$p^s = S(q) \qquad [2]$$

and the condition of equilibrium as

$$D(q) = S(q) \qquad [3]$$

When graphing the behavioral relations [1] and [2], Marshall naturally put the independent variable, q, on the horizontal axis.

Leon Walras, whose formulation of the working of a competitive market has become the accepted one, focused on quantities demanded and supplied *at a given price*. That is

$$q^d = q(p) \qquad [4]$$

$$q^s = s(p) \qquad [5]$$

and for equilibrium

$$q(p) = s(p) \qquad [6]$$

Walras did not go in for graphic representation. Had he done so he would surely have placed p (his independent variable) on the horizontal axis.

Marshall, among his other influences on later generations of economists, was the great popularizer of graphic analysis in economics. Today we use his graphs, even for Walras' analysis. The "axis-reversal" is thus one of those accidents of history that seem odd to people who did not live through the "perfectly natural" sequence of steps that produced it.

9. The distinction made between an incremental change and a marginal change is the distinction for the function $Y = Y(X)$ between $\frac{\Delta Y}{\Delta X}$ and the derivative $\frac{dY}{dX}$.

The latter is the limit of the former as ΔX approaches zero. Precisely this sort of difference underlies the distinction between arc and point elasticity, and we shall meet it repeatedly—in this chapter in reference to marginal and incremental *utility* and in later chapters with respect to such concepts as marginal and incremental *product, cost,* and *revenue*. Where Y is a function of more than one variable—for example, $Y = f(X, Z)$—the marginal relationship between Y and X is the partial derivative $\frac{\partial Y}{\partial X}$ rather than the total derivative.

10. The hypothesis of diminishing marginal utility requires that we be able to measure utility of consumption by a function $U = U(X_1, X_2, \ldots, X_n)$, where $X_1, \ldots, X_n$ are quantities of the n goods consumed by a household. There are now two utility hypotheses. First, $\frac{\partial u}{\partial X_i} > 0$ which says that the consumer can get more utility by increasing consumption of the typical, i^{th}, commodity. Second, $\frac{\partial^2 u}{\partial X_i^2} < 0$ which says that the marginal utility of additional consumption is declining.

11. The relationship of the slope of the budget line to relative prices can be seen as follows. In the two-commodity example a change in expenditure (ΔE) is given by the equation

$$\Delta E = \Delta C p_C + \Delta F p_F \qquad [1]$$

Along a budget line, expenditure is constant, that is, $\Delta E = 0$. Thus, along such a line,

$$\Delta C p_C + \Delta F p_F = 0 \qquad [2]$$

whence

$$-\frac{\Delta C}{\Delta F} = \frac{p_F}{p_C} \qquad [3]$$

The ratio $-\Delta C/\Delta F$ is the slope of the budget line. It is negative because, with a fixed budget, to consume more F one must consume less C. In words, equation [3] says that the negative of the slope of the budget line is the ratio of the absolute prices (i.e., the relative price). While prices do not show directly in Figure 9-8, they are implicit in the budget line: its slope depends solely on the relative price, while its position, given a fixed money income, depends on the absolute prices of the two goods.

12. Because the slope of the indifference curve is negative, it is the absolute value of the slope that declines as one moves downward to the right along the curve. The algebraic value of course increases. The phrase diminishing marginal rate of substitution thus refers to the absolute, not the algebraic, value of the slope.

13. Assume that changes in tastes are not related to changes in price. Now if tastes change, there is an even chance that they will offset the effect of a rise in p causing a fall in q. Thus there is a .5 chance in any one week that taste changes will cause Δp and Δq to move together. Twenty-six weeks gives 25 changes in p and q and thus $(\frac{1}{2})^{25} =$ one chance in 33,554,432 that taste changes accounted for the observations. Clearly an upward-sloping demand curve is the odds-on favorite compared to the explanation that a coincidence of chance *shifts* in demand and supply produced the observations.

14. Marginal product as defined in the text is really "incremental product." A mathematician would distinguish between this notion and its limit as ΔL approaches zero. Technically, MP measures the rate at which total product is changing as one factor is varied. The marginal product is the partial derivative of the total product with respect to the variable factor. In symbols,

$$MP = \frac{\partial TP}{\partial L}$$

Economists often use the term marginal product interchangeably with incremental product.

15. We have referred specifically both to diminishing *marginal* product and to diminishing *average* product. In most cases, eventually diminishing marginal product implies eventually diminishing average product. This is, however, not necessary, as the following figure shows.

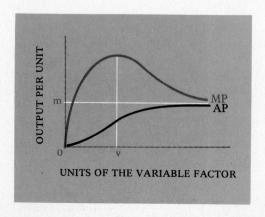

UNITS OF THE VARIABLE FACTOR

In this case, marginal product diminishes after v units of the variable factor are employed. Because marginal product falls toward, but never quite reaches, a value of m, average product rises continually toward, but never quite reaches, the same value.

16. Let q be the quantity of output and X the quantity of the variable factor. In the short run,

$$TP = q = f(X) \qquad [1]$$

We now define

$$AP = \frac{q}{X} = \frac{f(X)}{X} \qquad [2]$$

$$MP = \frac{dq}{dX} \qquad [3]$$

We are concerned about the relation between these two. Whether average product is rising, at a maximum, or falling is determined by its derivative with respect to X.

$$\frac{d\frac{q}{X}}{dX} = \frac{X\frac{dq}{dX} - q}{X^2} \qquad [4]$$

This may be rewritten:

$$\frac{1}{X}\left(\frac{dq}{dX} - \frac{q}{X}\right) = \frac{1}{X}(MP - AP) \qquad [5]$$

Clearly, when MP is greater than AP, the expression in [5] is positive and thus AP is rising. When MP is less than AP, AP is falling. When they are equal, AP is at a stationary value.

17. The mathematically correct definition of marginal costs is the rate of change of total cost, with respect to output, q. Thus $MC = dTC/dq$. From the definitions, $TC = TFC + TVC$. Fixed costs are not a function of output. Thus we may write $TC = K + f(q)$, where $f(q)$ is total variable costs and K is a constant. From this, we see that $MC = df(q)/dq$. MC is thus independent of the size of the fixed costs.

18. This point is easily seen if a little algebra is used:

$$AVC = \frac{TVC}{q}$$

but

$$TVC = L \times w$$

and

$$q = AP \times L$$

where L is the quantity of the variable factor used and where w is its cost per unit. Therefore

$$AVC = \frac{L \times w}{AP \times L} = \frac{w}{AP}$$

Since w is a constant, it follows that AVC and AP vary inversely with each other, and when AP is at its maximum value, AVC must be at its minimum value.

19. Strictly speaking, the marginal rate of substitution refers to the slope of the tangent to the isoquant at a particular point while the calculations in Table 13-1 refer to the average rate of substitution between two distinct points on the isoquant. Assume a production function

$$Q = Q(K, L) \qquad [1]$$

Isoquants are given by the function

$$K = I(L, Q) \qquad [2]$$

derived from [1] by expressing K as an explicit function of L and Q. A single isoquant relates to a particular value at which Q is held constant. Define Q_K, and Q_L as an alternative, more compact notation for $\partial Q/\partial K$ and $\partial Q/\partial L$, the marginal products of capital and labor. Also let Q_{KK} and Q_{LL} stand for $\partial^2 Q/\partial L^2$ and $\partial^2 Q/\partial K^2$ respectively. To obtain the slope of the isoquant, totally differentiate [1] to obtain

$$dQ = Q_K dK + Q_L dL$$

Then, since we are moving along a single isoquant, set $dQ = 0$ to obtain

$$\frac{dK}{dL} = -\frac{Q_L}{Q_K} = MRS$$

Diminishing marginal productivity implies Q_{LL}, $Q_{KK} < 0$ and hence, as we move down the isoquant of Figure 13-1, Q_K is rising and Q_L is falling, so the absolute value of MRS is diminishing. This is called the hypothesis of diminishing marginal rate of substitution.

20. Formally the problem is to maximize $Q = Q(K, L)$ subject to the budget constraint

$$p_K K + p_L L = C$$

To do this, form the Lagrangean

$$Q(K, L) - \lambda(p_K K + p_L L - C)$$

The first-order conditions for finding the saddle point

on this function are

$$Q_K - \lambda p_K = 0; \; Q_k = \lambda p_K \qquad [1]$$

$$Q_L - \lambda p_L = 0; \; Q_L = \lambda p_L \qquad [2]$$

$$-p_K K - p_L L + C = 0 \qquad [3]$$

Dividing [1] by [2] yields

$$\frac{Q_K}{Q_L} = \frac{p_K}{p_L}$$

that is, the ratio of the marginal products, which is (-1) times the MRS, is equal to the ratio of the prices, which is (-1) times the slope of the isocost line.

21. For this note and the next two it is helpful first to define some terms. Let

$$\pi_n = TR_n - TC_n$$

where π_n is the profit when n units are sold.

If the firm is maximizing its profits by producing n units, it is necessary that the profits at output q_n are at least as large as the profits at output zero. If the firm is maximizing its profits at output n, then

$$\pi_n \geq \pi_0 \qquad [1]$$

The condition says that profits from producing must be greater than profits from not producing. Condition [1] can be rewritten

$$\begin{aligned} TR_n - TVC_n - TFC_n \\ \geq TR_0 - TVC_0 - TFC_0 \end{aligned} \qquad [2]$$

But note that by definition

$$TR_0 = 0 \qquad [3]$$
$$TVC_0 = 0 \qquad [4]$$
$$TFC_n = TFC_0 = K \qquad [5]$$

where K is a constant. By substituting [3], [4], and [5] into [2], we get

$$TR_n - TVC_n \geq 0$$

from which we obtain

$$TR_n \geq TVC_n$$

On a per unit basis, it becomes

$$\frac{TR_n}{q_n} \geq \frac{TVC_n}{q_n} \qquad [6]$$

where q_n is the number of units.

Since $TR_n = q_n p_n$ where p_n is the price when n units are sold, [6] may be rewritten

$$p_n \geqslant AVC_n$$

This proves rule 1.

22. Using elementary calculus, rule 2 may be proved

$$\pi_n = TR_n - TC_n$$

each of which is a function of output q. To maximize π it is necessary that

$$\frac{d\pi}{dq} = 0 \qquad [1]$$

and that

$$\frac{d^2\pi}{dq^2} < 0 \qquad [2]$$

From the definitions

$$\frac{d\pi}{dq} = \frac{dTR}{dq} - \frac{dTC}{dq} = MR - MC \qquad [3]$$

From [1] and [3], a necessary condition of maximum π is $MR - MC = 0$, or $MR = MC$, as is required by rule 2.

23. Not every point where $MR = MC$ is a point of profit maximization. Continuing the equations of the previous footnote,

$$\frac{d^2\pi}{dq^2} = \frac{dMR}{dq} - \frac{dMC}{dq} \qquad [4]$$

From [2] and [4], a necessary condition of maximum π is

$$\frac{dMR}{dq} - \frac{dMC}{dq} < 0$$

which says that the slope of MC must be greater than the slope of MR. Taken with the previous result, it implies that, for q_n to maximize π, $MR_n = MC_n$ at a point where MC cuts MR from below.

24. Mathematically, marginal revenue is the rate of change of total revenue with output dTR/dq. Incremental revenue is $\Delta TR/\Delta q$. But the term marginal revenue is loosely used to refer to both concepts.

25. To prove that, for a downward-sloping demand curve, marginal revenue is less than price, let $p = p(q)$. Then

$$TR = p \times q = p(q) \times q$$

$$MR = \frac{dTR}{dq} = q\frac{dp}{dq} + p$$

For a downward-sloping demand curve, dp/dq is negative by definition, and thus MR is less than price for positive values of q.

26. These propositions are easily proved using calculus. Let $p = a - bq$, which is the general equation for a downward-sloping straight line ($b > 0$)

$$TR = pq = aq - bq^2$$

and

$$MR = \frac{dTR}{dq} = a - 2bq$$

Comparison with the demand equation shows that the proof is complete.

27. The monopolist that produces in a single plant but sells in two or more markets will equate the marginal revenue in each market with its marginal cost. Thus $MC = MR_1 = MR_2$ is an equilibrium condition for a monopolist selling in two markets. But the ratio of price to marginal revenue is a function of elasticity of demand: the higher the elasticity, the lower the ratio. Thus equal marginal revenues imply a higher price in the market with the less elastic demand curve.

28. Using the expression for MR given in math note 25, it can be seen that, at the kink in the demand curve, q and p are unambiguously determined. But dp/dq, the slope of the demand curve, is very different in the upward and downward directions. Thus the level of MR must be different for increases and decreases in price at the same quantity.

29. The proposition that the marginal labor cost is above the average labor cost when the average is rising is essentially the same proposition proved in math note 16. But let us do it again, using elementary calculus. The quantity of labor depends on the wage rate: $L = f(w)$. The marginal cost of labor is $d(wL)/dL = w + L(dw/dL)$. But w is the average cost of labor, and as long as the supply curve slopes upward, $dw/dL > 0$, and thus $MC > AC$.

30. The condition defined for profit-maximizing behavior by a monopsonist is to hire the factor up to the point where demand equals marginal cost. This condition ($MC = MRP$) is defined by equation [1] on page

368. To see why, note that a firm's demand curve for a factor reflects the factor's contribution to the firm's revenue. Let Q be output, R revenue, and L the number of units of labor hired. The contribution to revenue of additional labor is $\frac{\partial R}{\partial L}$. This in turn depends on the contribution of the extra labor to output $\frac{\partial Q}{\partial L}$ (the marginal product of the factor) and $\partial R/\partial Q$, the firm's marginal revenue from the extra output. Thus

$$\frac{\partial R}{\partial L} = \frac{\partial Q}{\partial L} \times \frac{\partial R}{\partial Q}$$

or, $MRP = MP \cdot MR$

31. Let t be the tax rate applied to the profits, π, of the firm. The profits after tax will be $(1 - t)\pi$. If profits are maximized at output q^*, then by definition

$$\pi(q^*) > \pi(q_i)$$

where q_i is any other output.

Now multiply each side by $(1 - t)$. Since $(1 - t)$ is positive for any tax rate less than 100 percent, the direction of the inequality does not change. Thus

$$(1 - t)\pi(q^*) > (1 - t)\times(q_i)$$

This shows that q^* is the profit maximizing output no matter what the tax rate.

32. In the text we define MPC as an incremental ratio. For mathematical treatments it is more convenient to define all marginal concepts as derivatives: $MPC = dC/dY_d$, $MPS = dS/dY_d$, and so on.

33. The graph shows a linear consumption function, $C = a + bY_d$, where $a > 0$ and $0 < b < 1$. The $MPC = dC/dY_d = b$. The $APC = C/Y_d = (a + bY_d) /Y_d = a/Y_d + b$. This declines as Y_d rises, and clearly $APC \to b$ as $Y_d \to \infty$. The break-even level of income is $C = Y_d$ or $a + bY_d = Y_d$, which solves as $Y_d = a/(1 - b)$.

34. Since $S = Y_d - C$, there is a simple relation between the propensities to consume and to save:

$$APC = \frac{C}{Y_d} = \frac{Y - S}{Y_d} = 1 - \frac{S}{Y_d} = 1 - APS$$

and

$$MPC = \frac{\Delta C}{\Delta Y_d} = \frac{\Delta Y - \Delta S}{\Delta Y_d} = 1 - \frac{\Delta S}{\Delta Y_d}$$
$$= 1 - MPS$$

Therefore, $APC + APS = 1$ and $MPC + MPS = 1$, where the propensities are measured out of disposable income.

35. A constant APC necessarily implies the equality of APC and MPC:

$$APC = \frac{C}{Y}$$

If $\frac{C}{Y} = k$

then $C = kY$

and $\frac{\Delta C}{\Delta Y} = k = MPC$

36. This involves using functions of functions. We have $C = c(Y_d)$ and $Y_d = f(Y)$. So by substitution $C = c[f(Y)]$. In the linear expressions used in the text, $C = a + bY_d$ and $Y_d = \mu Y$, so $C = a + (b\mu)Y$.

37. The elementary theory of national income can be described by the following set of equations (or model).

$$Y = AE \qquad \text{(equilibrium condition)} \quad [1]$$
$$AE = C + I + G + (X - M) \quad \text{(definition of } AE\text{)} \quad [2]$$
$$C = A + bY \qquad \text{(consumption function)} \quad [3]$$
$$M = mY \qquad \text{(import function)} \quad [4]$$

where I, G, and X are all treated as constant. Substituting [3] and [4] and collecting terms in Y, we can obtain the aggregate expenditure function relating desired expenditure to income.

$$AE = (a + I + G + X) + (b - m)Y$$

where the first term (in parentheses) is autonomous expenditure and the second term is induced expenditure. Using [1], the equilibrium level of income can be derived by solving

$$Y = (a + I + G + X) + (b - m)Y$$

to obtain

$$Y = \frac{1}{(1 - b + m)} (a + I + G + X) \qquad [5]$$

The example in Table 30-5 has these values: $a = 100$, I

$= 250, G = 410, X = 240, b = .6$, and $m = .1$. Substituting into [5] yields

$$Y = \frac{1}{(1 - .6 + .1)}(100 + 250 + 410 + 240)$$

$$= \frac{1}{(.5)}(1000) = 2000.$$

38. National income, Y, is divided into autonomous expenditure, A, and induced expenditure, N:

$$Y = A + N$$

Any change in Y must be accounted for by changes in these components.

$$\Delta Y = \Delta A + \Delta N \qquad [1]$$

Changes in induced expenditure depend on changes in Y.

$$\Delta N = n\Delta Y \qquad [2]$$

where $0 < n < 1$ is the marginal propensity to spend out of national income.

Substituting [2] into [1], manipulating it, and letting $w = 1 - n$ yields

$$\Delta Y = A + n\Delta Y$$
$$\Delta Y - n\Delta Y = A$$
$$\Delta Y(1 - n) = A$$

$$\frac{\Delta Y}{\Delta A} = \frac{1}{1 - n} = \frac{1}{w} = K$$

which are the expressions in the text.

39. The total expenditure over all rounds is the sum of an infinite series. Letting J stand for the initiating expenditure and r for the marginal propensity to spend, the total expenditure for n rounds can be written

$$\Delta J (1 + r + r^2 + r^3 + \cdots + r^n)$$

If r is less than 1, the series in brackets converges to $1/(1 - r)$ as n approaches infinity. Total expenditure is thus $\Delta J/(1 - r)$. In the example in the box, $r = .5$; therefore total expenditure is 2 times ΔJ.

40. The accelerator may be stated as a general macroeconomic theory. Define I_n as the volume of net investment this year and ΔY as the increase in national income from last year to this year. The accelerator theory is the relationship between I_n and ΔY.

Assume that the capital-output ratio is a constant.

$$\frac{K}{Y} = \alpha$$

or

$$K = \alpha Y$$

If Y is to change, K must be changed accordingly:

$$\Delta K = \alpha\Delta Y$$

But the change in the capital stock (ΔK) *is* net investment, so

$$\Delta K \equiv I_n = \alpha\Delta Y$$

41. As we saw in math note 38, the multiplier, K, is equal to the reciprocal of the marginal propensity to withdraw, w.

$$K = \frac{1}{w}$$

In an open economy the marginal propensity to withdraw is equal to the sum of the marginal propensity to save $(1 - b)$ plus the marginal propensity to import, m. Hence the multiplier in an open economy

$$K_0 = \frac{1}{(1 - b) + m}$$

is less than that in a closed economy

$$K_c = \frac{1}{(1 - b)}$$

if the two economies had a common marginal propensity to consume, b. Note that the denominator of K_0 can be written as $[1 - (b - m)]$ where $(b - m)$ is the marginal propensity to consume *home goods*.

42. Using the multiplier derived in math note 41, we see that an autonomous increase in exports leads to an increase in national income given by

$$\Delta Y = \frac{1}{(1 - b) + m}\Delta X$$

The resulting increase in imports is given by the marginal propensity to import times the change in national income

$$\Delta M = m\Delta Y$$

Combining, we can calculate the change in the trade balance, $\Delta T = \Delta X - \Delta M$, as

$$\Delta T = \frac{(1 - b)}{(1 - b) + m}\Delta X = (1 - b)\,\Delta Y$$

which is positive since b is less than one.

43. In the Keynesian case where real national income rises, the change in net exports can be calculated using the absorption approach. The change in net exports is given by

$$\Delta(X - M) = \Delta(Y - A) = \Delta Y - \Delta A \qquad [1]$$

Using the fact that A equals $C + I + G$,

$$\Delta A = \Delta C = b\Delta Y \qquad [2]$$

where b is the marginal propensity to consume. Hence substituting equation [2] into [1], we get

$$\Delta(X - M) = \Delta Y - b\Delta Y$$
$$= (1 - b)\Delta Y > 0, \qquad [3a]$$

which is the same as the result in math note 42. (As an exercise, you should calculate the change in imports, M.)

In the classical case, real income is constant so the change in domestic in net exports equals minus the change in domestic absorption. Devaluation causes the domestic price *level* to rise and hence, via the monetary mechanism discussed in Chapter 28, absorption falls.

$$\Delta(X - M) = -\Delta A > 0. \qquad [3b]$$

These unambiguous results, however, can be reversed if the change in the terms of trade exerts a positive influence on domestic absorption.

44. Reproducing equation (4) from the box on page 722, we have the basic relationship between the nominal money supply and nominal income.

$$M = kPY \qquad [1]$$

Further, the vertical aggregate supply curve gives

$$Y = Y_F \qquad [2]$$

Solving [1] and [2] for P yields

$$P = M/kY_F \qquad [3]$$

Since k and Y_F are constant, the change in P resulting from a change in M is

$$\Delta P = (1/kY_F)\Delta M \qquad [4]$$

Hence changes in the money supply lead to proportional price level changes where the factor of proportion is $(1/kY_F)$; the real value of money balances, (M/P), is thus constant at kY_F.

45. This is easily proved. In equilibrium, the banking system wants sufficient deposits (D) to establish the legal ratio (r) of deposits to reserves (R). This gives $R/D = r$. Any change in D of ΔD has to be accompanied by a change in R of ΔR of sufficient size to restore r. Thus $\Delta R/\Delta D = r$, so that $\Delta D = \Delta R/r$, and $\Delta D/\Delta R = 1/r$.

46. Proof: Let r be the reserve ratio. Let $z = 1 - r$ be the excess reserves per dollar of new deposit. If X dollars are deposited in the system assumed in the text, the successive rounds of new deposits will be X, zX, z^2X, z^3X. . . . The series

$$X + zX + z^2X + z^3X \cdots = X[1 + z + z^2 + z^3 + \ldots]$$

has a limit

$$X\frac{1}{1 - z} = X\left[\frac{1}{1 - (1 - r)}\right] = \frac{X}{r}$$

47. Suppose the public desire to hold a fraction, v, for any new deposits in cash. Now let the banking system receive an initial increase in its reserves of ΔR. It can expand deposits by an amount ΔD. As it does so, the banking system suffers a cash drain to the public of $v\Delta D$. The banking system can only increase deposits to the extent the required reserve ratio, r, makes possible. The maximum is:

$$r\Delta D = \Delta R - v\Delta D$$

The left-hand side gives the required reserves, the right-hand side the actual reserves after the cash drain. From this

$$r = \frac{\Delta R}{\Delta D} - v$$

or

$$\frac{\Delta D}{\Delta R} = \frac{1}{r + v}$$

48. The "rule of 72" is an approximation derived from the mathematics of compound interest. Any measure X_t will have the value $X_t = X_0 e^{rt}$ after t years at a continuous growth rate of r percent per year. Because $X_1/X_0 = 2$ requires $r \times t = 0.69$, a "rule of 69" would be correct for continuous growth. But 69 is an awkward number that is easily divisible only by 3 and 23. The number 72 is very close to 69 and is divisible by the integers 2, 3, 4, 6, 8, 9, 12, 18, 24, and 36. Thus it is convenient to use a "rule of 72" instead of 69. Probably the original reason for the use of 72 is that the rule was developed in the context of compound interest, and if interest is compounded only once a year the product of $r \times t$ for X to double is approximately .72.

49. The time taken to break even is a function of the *difference* in growth rates, not their level. Thus, in the example, had 4 percent and 5 percent or 5 percent and 6 percent been used, it still would have taken the same number of years. To see this quickly, recognize that we are interested in the ratio of two growth paths: $e^{r1t}/e^{r2t} = e^{(r1 - r2)t}$.

50. The derivation of this result is as follows. Let X be your level and Y your competitor's.

$$X_0 = \frac{2}{3} Y_0 \qquad [1]$$

$$Y_{10} = Y_0 e^{10r} \qquad [2]$$

$$X_{10} = X_0 e^{10(r + a)} \qquad [3]$$

If $X_{10} = Y_{10}$ then

$$Y_0 e^{10r} = X_0 e^{10(r + a)} \qquad [4]$$

and

$$\frac{Y_0}{X_0} = \frac{3}{2} = e^{10a} \qquad [5]$$

for which $a = 0.04$.

51. Modern mathematicians distinguish between a correspondence and a function. There is a *correspondence* between Y and X if each value of X is associated with one or more values of Y. Y is a *function of X* if there is one and only one value of Y associated with each value of X. Mathematicians of an older generation described both relations as functional relations and then distinguished between single-valued functions (in modern language, functional relations) and multi-valued functions (in modern language, relations of correspondence). In the text we adopt the older, more embracing usage of the term functional relation.

52. The condition that for profit maximization MRP be downward-sloping at the point where $w = MRP$ is just an application of the proposition (proved in math notes 22 and 23) that for profit maximization MC must cut MR from below. Consider the output added by the last unit of the variable factor. Its marginal cost is w, and its marginal revenue is MRP. Thus w must cut MRP from below. Since w is a horizontal line, MRP must be falling.

Putting the matter in standard mathematical terms,

$$w = MRP \qquad [1]$$

is a first order condition of *either* maximizing or mini-

mizing. The second order condition for maximization is

$$\frac{dw}{dq} > \frac{dMRP}{dq} \qquad [2]$$

Since

$$\frac{dw}{dq} = 0 \qquad [3]$$

the slope of MRP must be negative to satisfy [2], that is, it must be declining.

53. The equation for the IS curve is given by

$$y = c(y - T) + I(r) + G \qquad [1]$$

where $c'(y - T) > 0$ is the marginal propensity to consume $(c'(y - T) = b)$, $I_r < 0$ is the response of investment to a change in the interest rate, and T is taxes. Substituting $T = T_0 + ty$ into [1], and differentiating, we get

$$wdy = -b(dT_0 + ydt) + I_r dr + dG \qquad [2]$$

where w is equal to $[1 - b(1 - t)]$, the marginal propensity not to spend. The IS curve is drawn for $dT_0 = dt = dG = 0$. Its slope is therefore

$$\left.\frac{dr}{dy}\right|_{IS} = \frac{w}{I_r} < 0 \qquad [3]$$

The horizontal shift in the IS curve due to a change in any of the exogenous variables (T_0, t, or G) can be calculated from [2] by setting $dr = 0$. For example, a change in h shifts the IS curve by

$$\left.\frac{dy}{dG}\right|_{dr = 0} = \frac{1}{w} > 0$$

while a change in tax rates causes a shift of

$$\left.\frac{dy}{dt}\right|_{dr = 0} = \frac{-by}{w} < 0$$

54. The equation for the LM curve is given by

$$M = PL(y, r) \qquad [1]$$

where $L(y, r)$ represents the demand for real money balances which depends positively on income ($L_y > 0$) and negatively on the interest rate ($L_r < 0$). Differentiating [1] we get

$$dM = L(y, r)dP + PL_y dy + PL_r dr \qquad [2]$$

The LM curve is drawn for $dM = dP = 0$. Its slope is therefore

$$\frac{dr}{dy}\Big|_{LM} = -\frac{L_y}{L_r} > 0 \qquad [3]$$

The horizontal shift in the *LM* curve due to a change in the money supply can be calculated from [2] by setting $dr = 0$.

$$\frac{dy}{dM}\Big|_{dr=0} = \frac{1}{PL_y} > 0 \qquad [4]$$

55. Equation [2] from each of the two previous math notes can be combined to give two relationships between dy and dr. Solving them simultaneously we can derive the following expressions for the effects of monetary and fiscal policy on national income and interest rates. Restricting our analysis of fiscal policy to the effects of government expenditure (so $dT = dt = 0$), and holding $dP = 0$, these are as follows:

$$\frac{dy}{dM} = \frac{-I_r}{D} > 0 \qquad\qquad \frac{dr}{dM} = \frac{-w}{D} < 0$$

$$\frac{dy}{dG} = \frac{-PL_r}{D} > 0 \qquad\qquad \frac{dr}{dG} = \frac{PL_y}{D} > 0$$

where $D \equiv -(I_r PL_y + wPL_r) > 0$.

56. The aggregate demand curve can be written by solving equations [1] from each of the math notes 53 and 54 to eliminate the interest rate, thus leaving a relationship between P and y. The relationship between *changes* in P and y can be written

$$Ddy = I_r L(y, P)dP - PL_r dG - I_r dM \qquad [1]$$

where D is as defined in note 55.

The *AD* curve is drawn from $dG = dM = 0$, so its slope is given by

$$\frac{dP}{dy}\Big|_{AD} = \frac{I_r L(y, P)}{D} < 0 \qquad [2]$$

The horizontal shift in *AD* can be calculated from equation [1] by setting $dP = 0$, so that the effects of monetary (dM) and fiscal (dG) policy can be written as follows:

$$\frac{dy}{dM}\Big|_{dP=0} = \frac{-I_r}{D} > 0$$

$$\frac{dy}{dG}\Big|_{dP=0} = \frac{-PL_r}{D} > 0$$

which, of course, are as in math note 55.

Glossary

absolute advantage One nation has an absolute advantage over another nation in the production of a commodity when the same amount of resources will produce more of the commodity in the one nation than in the other.

absolute cost advantages Existing firms have absolute cost advantages when their average cost curves are significantly lower over their entire range than those of firms that are potential entrants into the industry.

absolute price A price expressed in money terms.

accelerator The theory that relates the level of investment to the rate of change of national income.

actual GNP The gross national product that the economy in fact produces.

adaptive expectations The theory that people form expectations about the future behavior of some variable on the basis of its behavior in the recent past. With respect to inflation the *expected* future inflation rate depends on past *actual* inflation rates.

adjustable peg system A system in which monetary authorities peg (i.e., fix) the price of their domestic currency on the foreign exchange market but in which the price at which the currency is pegged can be adjusted (i.e., changed) from time to time.

administered price A price set by conscious decision of the seller rather than by the impersonal forces of demand and supply.

ad valorem tax See *excise tax*.

AE In boldface, the term represents actual aggregate expenditure; in lightface, desired aggregate expenditure.

AE = C + I + G Indicates the three main components of aggregate expenditure in a closed economy: consumption expenditure, investment expenditure, and government expenditure.

AE = C + I + G + (X − M) Indicates the four main components of aggregate expenditure in an open economy: consumption expenditure, investment expenditure, government expenditure, and net exports (exports *minus* imports).

aggregate demand (AD) curve A relation between the total amount of all output that will be demanded by purchasers and the price level of that output. It shows the combination of real national income and the price level that makes aggregate desired expenditure equal to national income and the demand for money equal to the supply of money.

aggregate expenditure (AE) function The function that relates aggregate desired expenditure to national income.

aggregate supply (AS) curve A relation between the total amount of output that will be produced and the price level of that output.

allocation of resources The distribution of the available factors of production among the various uses to which they might be put.

allocative efficiency An allocation of resources in which price equals marginal cost in all industries and which is thus Pareto-optimal; it is often treated as a goal of economic organization.

allocative inefficiency The absence of allocative efficiency. Some consumers could be made better off by producing a different bundle of goods, without any consumers being made worse off.

annuity A specific sum of money, paid at stated intervals, that continues to be paid indefinitely.

antitrust laws See *combines laws*

appreciation of the exchange rate A rise in the free-market value of domestic currency in terms of foreign currencies.

a priori Literally, "at a prior time" or "in advance"; knowledge that is prior to actual experience.

arbitrage The purchase of any commodity in markets where it is cheap in order to sell it in markets where it is dear, with the consequent effect of eliminating intermarket differentials.

arc elasticity Elasticity of demand, for discrete changes in price and quantity. For analytical purposes, it is usually defined by the formula

$$\eta = \frac{\Delta q/q}{\Delta p/p}$$

An alternative formula often used where computations are involved is

$$\eta = -\frac{(q_2 - q_1)/(q_2 + q_1)}{(p_2 - p_1)/(p_2 + p_1)}$$

autarky The absence of international trade.

autarky price The price of a traded commodity that would have prevailed domestically if there were no international trade.

automatic transfer service (ATS) A savings deposit from which funds are transferred automatically to the depositor's demand deposit to cover cheques as they are drawn.

autonomous expenditure In macroeconomics, elements of expenditure that do not vary systematically with other variables such as national income and the interest rate, but which are determined by forces outside of the theory. Also called *exogenous expenditure*.

autonomous variables See *exogenous variables*.

average cost (AC) Some measure of cost divided by the number of units of output.

average fixed costs (AFC) Total fixed costs divided by number of units of output.

average product (AP) Total product divided by the number of units of the variable factor used in its production.

average propensity to consume (APC) The proportion of income devoted to consumption: total consumption expenditure divided by income. The income variable may be disposable income, in which case $APC = C/Y_d$, or it may be national income, in which case $APC = C/Y$.

average propensity to save (APS) The proportion of income devoted to saving: total saving divided by income. The income variable may be disposable income, in which case $APS = S/Y_d$, or it may be national income, in which case $APS = S/Y$.

average revenue (AR) Total revenue divided by quantity. Where a single price prevails, $AR = p$.

average tax rate The ratio of total tax paid to total income earned.

average total cost (ATC) Total cost divided by the number of units of output; the sum of average fixed costs and average variable costs. Also called *cost per unit, unit cost, average cost (AC)*.

average variable costs (AVC) Total variable costs divided by the number of units of output. Also called *direct unit costs, avoidable unit costs*.

balanced budget A situation in which current revenue is exactly equal to current expenditures.

balanced budget multiplier The change in income divided by the tax-financed change in government expenditure that brought it about.

balanced growth policy Simultaneous growth in all sectors of the economy; a growth experience suitable to a closed economy.

balanced trade A situation in which the value of total imports exactly equals the value of total exports.

balance-of-payments accounts A summmary record of a country's transactions that typically involve payments or receipts of foreign exchange.

balance-of-payments deficit A situation in which a country's receipts on current and capital account fall short of its payments (ignoring transactions by monetary authorities).

balance-of-payments surplus A situation in which a country's receipts on current and capital account exceed its payments (ignoring transactions by monetary authorities).

balance of trade The difference between the value of exports and the value of imports of visible items (goods).

balance sheet A report showing a firm's assets and the claims against those assets at a moment in time. Balance sheets always balance because the owners' equity is defined as the amount of the assets less the claims of the creditors.

bank notes Paper money issued by banks.

bank rate The rate of interest at which the Bank of Canada is prepared to lend cash reserves to the chartered banks. The comparable rate in the United States is called the *discount rate*.

barriers to entry Legal or other impediments to entry into an industry. Patents, franchises, economies of scale, and established brand preferences may each lead to such barriers.

barter A system in which goods and services are traded directly for other goods and services.

base period A year or other point in time chosen for comparison purposes in connection with expressing or computing *index numbers* or *constant dollars*.

beggar-my-neighbor policies Policies designed to increase a country's prosperity (especially by reducing its unemployment) at the expense of reducing prosperity in other countries (especially by increasing their unemployment).

blacklist An employer's list of workers who have been fired for union activity.

black market A situation in which goods are sold illegally at prices above a legal maximum price.

bond An evidence of debt carrying a specified amount and schedule of interest payments as well as a date for redemption of the face value of the bond.

bondholders Creditors of the firm, whose evidence of debt is a bond issued by the firm.

boycott A concerted refusal to buy (buyers' boycott) or to sell (producers' or sellers' boycott) a commodity.

bread-and-butter unionism A union movement whose major objectives are wages, hours, and conditions of employment rather than political or social ends.

budget balance The difference between total government revenue and total government expenditure.

budget deficit The shortfall of current revenue below current expenditure.

budget line (isocost line) A line on a diagram showing all combinations of commodities that a household may obtain if it spends a given amount of money at fixed prices of the commodities.

budget surplus The excess of current revenue over current expenditure.

budget surplus function A function relating the size of the government's budget surplus (revenue minus expenditure) to the level of national income. (Deficits are shown as negative surpluses.)

built-in stabilizer Anything that tends to adjust government revenues and expenditures automatically (i.e., without an explicit policy decision) so as to reduce inflationary and deflationary gaps whenever they develop.

business cycles More or less regular patterns of fluctuations in the level of economic activity.

C In boldface, the term represents actual consumption expenditure; in lightface, desired consumption expenditure.

C + I + G − M Indicates the main components of domestic expenditure on domestically produced commodities.

capacity The level of output that corresponds to the minimum level of short-run average total costs. Also called *plant capacity*.

capital A factor of production defined to include all man-made aids to further production.

capital consumption allowance An estimate of the amount by which the capital stock is depleted through its contribution to current production. Often called *depreciation*.

capital deepening Adding capital to the production process in such a way as to increase the ratio of capital to labor and other factors of production.

capitalized value The value of an asset measured by the present value of the income stream it is expected to produce.

capital flows Purchases by foreigners of assets previously owned or newly issued by domestic citizens and governments, or vice versa.

capital-output ratio The ratio of the value of capital to the annual value of output produced by it.

capital stock The aggregate quantity of a society's capital goods.

capital widening Adding capital to the production process in such a way as to leave factor proportions unchanged.

cartel An organization of producers designed to limit or eliminate competition among its members, usually by agreeing to restrict output in an effort to achieve noncompetitive prices.

cash reserve ratio See *reserve ratio.*

ceiling price A maximum permitted price.

central authorities All public agencies, government bodies, and other organizations belonging to or under the control of government.

central bank A bank that acts as banker to the banking system and often to the government as well. In the modern world the central bank is usually the sole money-issuing authority.

certificate of deposit (CD) A negotiable time deposit carrying a higher interest rate than that paid on ordinary time deposits.

ceteris paribus Literally, "other things being equal"; usually used in economics to indicate that all variables except the ones specified are assumed not to change.

change in demand An increase or decrease in the quantity demanded at each possible price of the commodity, represented by a shift of the whole demand curve.

change in supply An increase or decrease in the quantity supplied at each possible price of the commodity, represented by a shift of the whole supply curve.

chartered bank A financial institution licensed by Parliament under the Bank Act which regulates its operations and its relationship with the government and the Bank of Canada. It accepts deposits from customers, which it agrees to transfer when ordered by a cheque, and it makes loans and other investments. An equivalent term used in some other countries is *commercial bank.*

civilian labor force The total number of employed, other than persons serving in the armed forces, plus the number of unemployed.

cleared market A market in which buyers have been able to buy all they wish and sellers have been able to sell all they wish at the going price; a competitive market in equilibrium.

clearing house An institution where interbank indebtednesses arising from transfer of cheques between banks are computed, offset against each other, and net amounts owing are calculated.

closed economy An economy that does not engage in foreign trade.

closed shop A bargaining arrangement in which only union members can be employed. Union membership precedes employment.

coefficient of determination (r^2 or R^2) The coefficient showing the fraction of the total variance of the dependent variable that can be associated with the independent variables in the regression equation; r^2 is used for two variables and R^2 for three or more variables.

collective bargaining The whole process by which unions and employers arrive at and enforce agreements.

collective consumption goods Goods or services that, if they provide benefits to anyone, necessarily provide benefits to a large group of people or a community.

collusion An agreement among sellers to set a common price and/or to share a market. Collusion may be overt or secret. It may be explicit or tacit.

combine laws Laws prohibiting acquisition and exercise of monopoly power, conspiracy in restraint of trade, and restrictive trade practices. Called *antitrust laws* in the United States.

command economy An economy in which the decisions of the central authorities exert the major influence over the allocation of resources.

commercial bank See *chartered bank.*

commodities Marketable items produced to satisfy wants. Commodities may be either *goods,* which are tangible, or *services,* which are intangible.

common-property resource A natural resource that is owned by no one and may be used by anyone.

common stock A form of equity capital usually carrying voting rights and a residual claim to the assets and profits of the firm.

comparative advantage (1) Country A has a comparative advantage over country B in producing a commodity, X, when it can do so at a lesser opportunity cost in terms of other products forgone. (2) As distinguished from absolute advantage: Comparing two countries, A and B, and two commodities, X and Y, country A has a comparative advantage in X when its margin of absolute advantage is greater in X than in Y.

comparative statics Comparative static equilibrium analysis; the derivation of predictions by analyzing the effect of a change in some exogenous variable or parameter on the equilibrium position.

competitive devaluations A round of devaluations of exchange rates by a number of countries, each trying to gain a competitive advantage over the other and each failing to the extent that other countries also devalue.

complement A commodity that tends to be used jointly with the original commodity. Technically, a complement to a commodity is another commodity for which the cross elasticity of demand is non-negligible and negative.

comprehensive income taxation (CIT) A proposal to expand the tax base from the presently defined concept of taxable income, to include income from most sources and to eliminate most exemptions and deductions. CIT can be defined in many different ways, depending on what is added to taxable income.

concentration ratio The fraction of total market sales (or some other measure of market occupancy) made by a specified number of the industry's largest firms. Four-firm and eight-firm concentrations ratios are the most frequently used.

conglomerate merger See *merger*.

conscious parallel action See *tacit collusion*.

constant-cost industry An industry in which costs of the most efficient size firm remain constant as the entire industry expands or contracts in the long run.

constant dollar GNP Gross national product valued in prices prevailing in some base year; year-to-year changes in constant dollar GNP reflect changes only in quantities produced. Also called *real GNP*.

constant dollars A series expressed in terms of the level of prices prevailing in a specified *base period*. Constant dollars are thus free of inflationary or deflationary trends. Used in contrast to *current dollars*.

constant returns A situation in which output increases proportionately with the quantity of inputs as the scale of production is increased.

consumerism A movement that asserts a conflict between the interests of firms and the public interest.

Consumer Price Index (CPI) A measure of the average percentage change in the prices of commodities commonly bought by households; compiled monthly by Statistics Canada.

consumers' durables See *durable good*.

consumers' surplus The difference between the total value consumers place on all units consumed of a commodity and the payment they must make to purchase the same amount of the commodity.

consumption The act of using commodities to satisfy wants.

consumption function The relationship between consumption expenditure and all of the factors that determine it. In the simplest consumption function, consumption depends only on current income.

consumption possibility set The bundle of goods available for domestic consumption. International trade allows this bundle of goods to differ from the bundle of goods produced within a country.

corporation A form of business organization with a legal existence separate from that of the owners, in which ownership and financial responsibility are divided, limited, and shared among any number of individual and institutional shareholders.

cost (of output) To a producing firm, the value of factors of production used up in producing output.

cost minimization Achieving the lowest attainable cost of producing a specified output. It is an implication of profit maximization that the firm will choose the least costly method available of producing any specific output.

CPI See *Consumer Price Index*.

craft union A union organized according to a specified set of skills or occupations.

credit rationing Rationing of available funds among borrowers in a situation in which there is excess demand for loans at prevailing interest rates.

cross elasticity of demand A measure of the extent to which quantity of a commodity demanded responds to changes in price of a related commodity. Formula:

$$\frac{\text{percentage change in quantity of } x}{\text{percentage change in price of } y}$$

cross-sectional data Data referring to a number of different observations at the same point in time.

current dollar GNP Gross national product valued in prices prevailing at the time of measurement; year-to-year changes in current dollar GNP reflect changes both in quantities produced and in market prices. Also called *nominal GNP*.

current dollars A measurement expressed in terms of the prices prevailing at the time of measurement.

day-to-day loan Loan made by a chartered bank to an investment dealer. Such loans make up part of the *secondary reserves* of the chartered banks.

debt Amounts owed to one's creditors, including banks and other financial institutions.

decision lag A lapse of time between obtaining relevant information about some problem and reaching a decision on what to do about it.

decreasing returns A situation in which output increases less than in proportion to inputs as the scale of production increases. A firm in this situation, with fixed factor prices, is an *increasing cost* firm.

deficient-demand unemployment Unemployment that is due to insufficient aggregate demand and that can be reduced by measures that raise aggregate demand.

deflationary gap The amount by which the aggregate demand schedule must be increased to achieve full-employment income.

demand There are several distinct but closely related concepts: (1) *quantity demanded;* (2) the whole relationship of the quantity demanded to variables that determine it, such as tastes, household income, distribution of income, population, price of the commodity, and prices of other commodities; (3) the *demand schedule;* (4) the *demand curve.* The phrase increase (decrease) in demand means a shift of the demand curve to the right (left), indicating an increase (decrease) in the quantity demanded at each possible price.

demand curve The graphic representation of the *demand schedule.*

demand deposit A bank deposit that is withdrawable on demand and transferable by means of a cheque.

demand for money The total amount of money balances that the public wishes to hold for all purposes.

demand-pull inflation Inflation arising from excess aggregate demand.

demand schedule The relationship between the quantity demanded of a commodity and its price, *ceteris paribus.*

deposit money Money held by the public in the form of demand deposits with commercial banks.

depreciation (1) The loss in value of an asset over a period of time; includes both physical wear and tear and obsolescence. (2) The amount by which the capital stock is depleted through its contribution to current production.

depreciation of the exchange rate A fall in the free-market value of domestic currency in terms of foreign currencies.

depression A period of very low economic activity with very high unemployment and high excess capacity.

derived demand The demand for a factor of production that results from the demand for products it is used to make.

devaluation of the exchange rate A downward revision in the value at which a country's currency is pegged in terms of foreign currencies.

differentiated products Products sufficiently distinguishable within an industry that the producer of each has some power over its own price; the products of firms in monopolistically competitive industry.

diminishing marginal rate of substitution The hypothesis that the marginal rate of substitution changes systematically as the amounts of two commodities being consumed vary.

direct investment Foreign investment in the form of a *takeover* or capital investment in a branch plant or subsidiary corporation in which the investor has voting control.

dirty float Although foreign exchange rates are left to be determined on the free market, monetary authorities intervene in this market so as to influence exchange rates, but they are *not* publicly committed to holding their country's exchange rate at any announced "par value." Also called *managed float.*

discount rate (1) In banking, the rate at which the central bank is prepared to lend cash reserves to the chartered banks. (2) More generally, the rate of interest used to discount a stream of future payments to arrive at their *present value.*

discretionary fiscal policy Fiscal policy that is a conscious response (not according to any predetermined rule) to each particular state of the economy as it arises.

disembodied technical change Technical change that raises output without the necessity of building new capital to embody the new knowledge.

disequilibrium The state or condition of a market that exhibits excess demand or excess supply.

disequilibrium price A price at which quantity demanded does not equal quantity supplied.

disposable income The income that households have available for spending and saving.

dissaving Negative saving; a situation in which household consumption expenditure exceeds disposable income.

distributed profits Earnings of a firm distributed as dividends to the owners of the firm.

dividends That part of profits paid out to shareholders of a corporation.

division of labor The breaking up of a task (e.g., making pins) into a number of repetitive operations, each one done by a different worker.

dollar standard (for international payments) International indebtedness between monetary authorities is settled in terms of U.S. dollars, which are not necessarily backed by gold or any other ultimate monetary base.

domestic absorption Total expenditure on all goods and services (domestic and foreign) for use within the economy; the sum of $C + I + G$.

dumping In international trade, the practice of selling a commodity at a lower price in the export market than in the domestic market.

duopoly An industry that contains only two firms.

durable good A good which yields its services only gradually over an extended period of time; often divided into the subcategories *producers' durables* (e.g., machines and equipment) and *consumers' durables* (e.g., cars, appliances).

dynamic (or disequilibrium) differential A difference in factor prices caused by disequilibrium that will tend to lead to corrective movements of resources. In equilibrium these differentials will be eliminated. Observed because it often takes considerable time for equilibrium to be reached.

dynamics Dynamic analysis is the study of the behavior of systems in disequilibrium situations.

economic efficiency (in production) A method of producing some quantity of output is economically efficient when it is the least costly method of producing that output.

economic profits or losses (often simply **profits**) The difference in the revenues received from the sale of output and the opportunity cost of the inputs used to make the output. Negative profits are losses.

economic rent That part of the payment to a factor in excess of its *transfer earnings*.

economies of scope Economies achieved by a large firm through multiproduct production, large-scale distribution, advertising, etc. They are an advantage of such firms in addition to economies of scale in production.

economy A set of interrelated production and consumption activities.

efficiency of capital See *productivity of capital*.

effluent charge A fee, fine, or tax on a producer for polluting activity, usually on a per unit basis.

elastic demand The situation existing when for a given percentage change in price there is a greater percentage change in quantity demanded; elasticity greater than 1.

elasticity of demand A measure of the responsiveness of quantity of a commodity demanded to a change in market price. Formula:

$$\frac{\text{percentage change in quantity demanded}}{\text{percentage change in price}}$$

Conventionally expressed as a positive number, it is a pure number ranging from zero to infinity.

embodied technical change A technical change that can be utilized only when new capital, embodying the new techniques, is built.

employment The number of workers 16 years of age and older who hold full-time civilian jobs.

endogenous expenditure See *induced expenditure*.

endogenous variables Variables explained within a theory. Also called *induced variables*.

energy self-sufficiency A country is self-sufficient in energy when it produces as much energy as it uses. If it imports energy, its energy exports will be at least as large as its energy imports.

envelope curve Any curve that encloses, by just being tangent to, a series of other curves. In particular, the *envelope cost curve* is the *LRAC* curve; it encloses the *SRAC* curves by being tangent to them but not cutting them.

equalization payments Transfers of tax revenues from the federal government to the lower-income provinces to compensate them for their lower potential per capita tax yields.

equilibrium condition A condition that must be fulfilled for some economic variable, such as price or national income, to be in equilibrium.

equilibrium differentials Differences in factor prices that would persist in equilibrium, without any tendency for them to be removed. These differences may be associated with differences in the factors themselves or with the nonmonetary advantages of different employments.

equilibrium price The price at which quantity demanded equals quantity supplied.

equity capital Capital provided by the owners of a firm.

error term An expressed or implied variable in a functional relationship to allow for (1) omitted variables and (2) errors in measurement.

excess capacity (1) Production at levels below the output at which *ATC* is a minimum. (2) The difference between such actual output and capacity output.

excess capacity theorem The proposition that equilibrium in a monopolistically competitive industry will occur where each firm has excess capacity.

excess (cash) reserves Reserves held by a chartered bank in excess of the legally required amount.

excess demand A situation in which, at the given price, quantity demanded exceeds quantity supplied. Also called *shortage*.

excess supply A situation in which, at the given price, quantity supplied exceeds quantity demanded. Also called *surplus*.

exchange rate The price in terms of one currency at which another currency, or claims on it, can be bought and sold.

excise tax A tax on the sale of a particular commodity. A *specific tax* is a fixed tax per unit of the taxed commodity. An *ad valorem tax* is a fixed percentage of the value of the commodity.

execution lag A lapse of time between the decision to do something and its actually being done.

exogenous expenditure See *autonomous expenditure*.

exogenous variables Variables that influence other variables within a theory but that themselves are determined by factors outside the theory. Also called *autonomous variables*.

expectational inflation Inflation that occurs because decision makers raise prices (so as to keep their relative prices constant) in the expectation that the price level is going to rise.

expenditure-changing policies Policies that change the level of aggregate desired expenditure.

expenditure-switching policies Policies that maintain the level of aggregate desired expenditure but change the relative proportions of its components, domestic absorption, and net exports.

externalities (also called **third-party effects**) Effects, either good or bad, on parties not directly involved in the production or use of a commodity.

exports Goods and services sent out of a country in the course of international trade.

extraterritoriality The application of the laws of one country to activities carried on within another country.

factor markets Markets in which households sell the services of the factors of production that they control.

factor mobility The ease with which factors can be transferred between uses.

factors of production Resources used to produce goods and services to satisfy wants. Land, labor, and capital are three frequently used basic categories of factors of production.

falling-cost industry An industry in which the lowest costs attainable by a firm fall as the whole scale of the industry expands.

federation In respect to labor unions, a federation is any loose organization of national unions.

fiat money Paper money or coinage that is neither backed by nor convertible into anything else yet is legal tender.

final products The economy's output of goods and services after all double counting has been eliminated.

fine tuning The attempt to maintain national income closely at its full-employment level by means of frequent changes in fiscal or monetary policy.

firm The unit that makes decisions regarding the employment of factors of production and the production of goods and services.

fiscal drag The tendency for a deflationary gap to open up at full-employment income because tax revenues rise faster than government expenditure as full-employment income rises due to economic growth.

fiscal policy The deliberate use of the government's revenue-raising and spending activities in an effort to influence the behavior of such macro variables as the GNP and total employment.

fixed capital Capital invested in goods that are used repeatedly or continually before wearing out, such as machinery or buildings.

fixed costs Costs that do not change with output. Also sometimes called *overhead cost*.

fixed exchange rate An exchange rate that is fixed or pegged within very narrow bands by the action of monetary authorities.

fixed factors Factors that cannot be increased in the short run.

flexible or **floating exchange rate** An exchange rate that is left to be determined on the free market without any attempt by monetary authorities to determine its value.

foreign exchange (foreign media of exchange) Actual foreign currency or various claims on it such as bank balances or promises to pay.

45° line In macroeconomic graphs, the line that joins all those points at which expenditure equals income.

fractional reserve system In contrast to a 100 percent reserve system, a banking system in which banks are required to keep only a fraction of their deposits in cash or on deposit with the central bank.

freedom of entry and exit The absence of legal or other

artificial barriers to entering into production or withdrawing assets from production.

free good A commodity for which no price needs to be paid because the quantity supplied exceeds the quantity demanded at a price of zero.

free-market economy An economy in which the decisions of individual households and firms (as distinct from the central authorities) exert the major influence over the allocation of resources.

free trade A situation in which all commodities can be freely imported and exported without special taxes or restrictions being levied merely because of their status as "imports" or "exports."

frictional unemployment Unemployment caused by the time taken for labor to move from one job to another.

fringe benefits Payments (other than wages) for the benefit of labor. They may include company contributions to pension and welfare funds, sick leave, paid holidays.

full-cost pricing Pricing according to average total cost plus a fixed markup. Usually the costs are standard costs as defined by good accounting practice.

full-employment GNP See *potential GNP*.

full-employment national income (Y_F) See *potential GNP*.

full-employment surplus (FES) An estimate of government tax revenues less government expenditures as they would be at full-employment national income.

function Loosely, an expression of a relation between two or more variables. Precisely, Y is a function of the variables $X_1, \ldots, X_n$ if for every set of values of the variables $X_1, \ldots, X_n$ there is associated a unique value of the variable Y.

functional distribution of income The distribution of income by major factors of production.

G In boldface, the term represents actual government expenditure; in lightface, desired government expenditure.

gains from trade The increased production that results from specialization and trade as opposed to a situation of self-sufficiency. It can be applied to persons, regions, or nations.

Giffen good An inferior good for which the negative income effect outweighs the substitution effect and leads to an upward-sloping demand curve.

given period A year or other point in time for which an *index number* measures a change in some variable

that has occurred since some earlier point in time (*base period*).

GNP deflator See *gross national product deflator*.

GNP gap Output that could have been produced if the economy were fully employed but that instead goes unproduced; *potential GNP* minus *actual GNP*.

gold exchange standard A monetary system in which some countries' currencies are directly convertible into gold while other countries' currencies are indirectly convertible by being convertible into the gold-backed currencies at a fixed rate. Under the Bretton Woods version only the U.S. dollar was directly convertible into gold.

goods Tangible commodities such as cars or shoes.

Gresham's law The theory that "bad," or debased, money drives "good," or undebased, money out of circulation because people will keep the good money and spend the bad money.

gross investment The total value of all investment goods produced in the economy during a stated period of time.

gross national product (GNP) The sum of all values added in the economy. It is the sum of the values of all final goods produced and, which is the same thing, the sum of all factor incomes earned.

gross national product deflator An index number derived by dividing GNP measured in current dollars by GNP measured in constant dollars and multiplying by 100. It is in effect a price index with current-year quantity weights measuring the average change in price of all the items in the GNP. Also called the *implicit GNP deflator*.

gross return to capital The receipts from the sale of goods produced by a firm less the cost of purchased goods and materials, labor, land, the manager's talents, and taxes.

homogeneous product (1) identical products; (2) a product similar enough across an industry that no one firm has any power over price; (3) the product of a firm in perfect competition.

horizontal merger See *merger*.

household All the people who live under one roof and who make, or are subject to others making for them, joint financial decisions.

human capital The capitalized value of productive investments in persons. Usually refers to investments resulting from expenditures on education, training, and health improvements.

hypothesis of equal net advantage The hypothesis that owners of factors will choose the use of their factors that produces the greatest net advantage to themselves and therefore will move their factors among uses until net advantages are equalized.

hypothesis of diminishing returns The hypothesis that if increasing quantities of a variable factor are applied to a given quantity of fixed factors, the marginal product and average product of the variable factor will eventually decrease. Also called *hypothesis of diminishing returns, law of diminishing returns, law of variable proportions.*

I In boldface, the term represents actual investment expenditure; in lightface, desired investment expenditure.

identification problem The ambiguity introduced by attempting to use observations of prices and quantities actually exchanged to draw inferences about either supply curves or demand curves when shifts in both curves have occurred.

implicit GNP deflator See *gross national product deflator.*

import cost-push inflation Inflation caused by increases in the prices of a country's major imports.

imports Goods and services brought into a country in the course of international trade.

import substitution industry (ISI) Domestic production for sale in the home market of goods previously imported; usually involves some form of protection or subsidy.

imputed costs The costs of using in production factors already owned by the firm, measured by the earnings they could have received in their best alternative employment.

income-consumption line A line connecting the points of tangency of a set of indifference curves with a series of parallel budget lines, showing how consumption of a good changes as income changes, with relative prices held constant.

income effect The effect on quantity demanded of a change in real income.

income elasticity of demand A measure of the responsiveness of quantity demanded to a change in income. Formula:

$$\frac{\text{percentage change in quantity demanded}}{\text{percentage change in income}}$$

income statement A financial report showing the revenues and costs that arise from the firm's use of inputs to produce outputs, over a specified period of time.

incomes policy Any attempt by the central authorities to influence wage and price formation. The instruments vary from voluntary guidelines at one extreme to legally enforced wage and price controls at the other.

increasing returns A situation in which output increases more than in proportion to inputs as the scale of a firm's production increases. A firm in this situation, with fixed factor prices, is a *decreasing cost* firm.

incremental cost See *marginal cost.*

incremental product See *marginal product.*

incremental revenue See *marginal revenue.*

indexing The automatic increasing of money values as the average level of all prices rises during an inflation.

index numbers Averages that measure changes over time of variables such as the price level and industrial production. They are conventionally expressed as percentages relative to a base period assigned the value 100.

indifference curve A curve showing all combinations of two commodities that give the household equal amounts of satisfaction and among which the household is thus indifferent.

indifference map A set of indifference curves, each indicating a constant level of satisfaction derived by the household concerned, and based on a given set of household preferences.

induced expenditure In macroeconomics, elements of expenditure that are explained by variables within the theory, such as national income and interest rates. Also called *endogenous expenditure.*

industrial union A union organized to include all workers in an industry, regardless of skills.

industry A group of firms producing similar products.

inelastic demand The situation in which for a given percentage change in price there is a smaller percentage change in quantity demanded; elasticity less than unity.

inertial inflation Inflation that persists only because decision makers raise prices (so as to maintain their desired relative prices) when they see that closely related prices have risen.

infant industry argument for tariffs The argument that new domestic industries with potential economies of scale need to be protected from competition from established low-cost foreign producers so that they can grow large enough to reap their own economies of scale and achieve costs as low as those of foreign producers.

inferior goods Goods for which income elasticity is negative.

inflation A rise in the average level of all prices. Sometimes restricted to only prolonged or sustained rises.

inflationary gap The extent to which aggregate desired expenditure exceeds national income at full-employment national income.

infrastructure The basic installations and facilities (especially transportation and communications systems) on which the growth of a community depends.

injections Income earned by domestic firms that does not arise out of the spending of domestic households and income earned by domestic households that does not arise out of the spending of domestic firms.

innovation The introduction of inventions into methods of production.

inputs Materials and factor services used in the process of production. It includes the services of factors of production plus intermediate products.

interest (i) In microeconomics, the payment for borrowed money, (ii) in macroeconomics, the total income paid for the use of borrowed capital.

interest rate The price paid per dollar borrowed per year. Expressed either as a fraction (e.g., .06) or as a percentage (e.g., 6 percent).

intermediate products All goods and services that are used as inputs into a further stage of production.

intermediate targets Variables that the central authorities cannot control directly and do not seek to control ultimately yet have an important role in monetary policy.

internalization A process that results in a producer's taking account of a previously external effect.

international trade The exchange of goods and services across national boundaries.

internalization A process that results in a producer's taking account of a previously external effect.

invention The discovery of something new, such as a new production technique or a new product.

inventories Stocks of raw materials, or of finished goods, held by firms to mitigate the effect of short-term fluctuations in production or sales.

investment Expenditures on the production of goods not for present consumption.

investment goods Capital goods such as plant and equipment plus inventories; production that is not sold for consumption purposes.

invisibles All those items of foreign trade that are intangible; services as opposed to goods.

isocost line The graphic representation of alternative combinations of factors that a firm can buy for a given outlay.

isoquant A curve showing all technologically efficient factor combinations for producing a specified output; an iso-product curve.

isoquant map A series of isoquants from the same production function, each isoquant relating to a specific level of output.

jurisdictional dispute Dispute between unions over which has the right to organize a group of workers.

kinked demand curve A demand curve with a corner, or "kink," at the prevailing price. The curve is more elastic in response to price increases than to price decreases.

labor A factor of production usually defined to include all physical and mental contributions to economic activity provided by people.

labor boycott An organized boycott to persuade customers to refrain from purchasing the products of a firm or industry whose employees are on strike.

labor force The number of people either employed or actively seeking work. See also *civilian labor force*.

labor union See *union*.

Laffer curve A graph relating the revenue yield of a tax system to the marginal or average tax rate imposed.

laissez faire Literally, "let do"; a policy implying the absence of government intervention in a market economy.

land A factor of production usually defined to include all gifts of nature, including raw materials as well as "land" conventionally defined.

law of diminishing returns See *hypothesis of diminishing returns*.

law of variable proportions See *hypothesis of diminishing returns*.

legal tender Anything that by law must be accepted for the purchase of goods and services or in discharge of a debt, and thus money.

less-developed countries (LDCs) The underdeveloped countries of the world, most of which are in Asia, Africa, and South and Central America. They are also called "undeveloped," "developing," and the "South."

life-cycle hypothesis (LCH) The hypothesis that relates

the household's actual consumption to its expected lifetime income rather than, as in early Keynesian theory, to its current income.

limited liability The limitation of the financial responsibility of an owner (shareholder) of a corporation to the amount of money he or she has actually made available to the firm by purchasing its shares.

limited partnership Partnership with limited liability for partners not participating in management.

limit price The minimum price at which a new firm can enter a market without incurring a loss; equal to its minimum average cost. Existing lower-cost firms may be able to discourage new entrants by setting the price below this limit.

liquidity The degree of ease and certainty with which an asset can be turned into a given amount of the economy's medium of exchange.

liquidity preference (LP) function The function that relates the demand for money to the rate of interest.

lockout The employer's equivalent of a strike, in which he temporarily closes his plant.

logarithmic scale A scale in which equal proportional changes are shown as equal distances. Thus 1 inch may always represent doubling of a variable, whether from 3 to 6 or 50 to 100. Contrasted with *natural scale*. (Also called *log scale* or *ratio scale*.)

long run The period of time long enough for all inputs to be varied, but in which the basic technology of production is unchanged.

long-run average cost curve (LRAC) The curve relating the least-cost method of producing any output to the level of output. Sometimes called *long-run average total cost* (*LRATC*).

long-run industry supply (LRS) curve The curve showing the relation of the quantity supplied to prices with quantities of all factors freely variable, and allowing time for firms to achieve long-run equilibrium.

Lorenz curve A graph showing the extent of departure from equality of income distribution.

M In boldface, the term represents actual imports; in lightface, desired imports.

M1 A narrow definition of the money supply: currency in circulation plus demand deposits.

M1B A less narrow definition of the money supply: M1 plus chequable savings deposits.

M2 A broader definition of the money supply: M1B plus personal savings deposits and nonpersonal notice deposits.

M3 The broadest definition of the money supply in wide use; M2 plus nonpersonal term deposits and foreign currency deposits.

macroeconomics The study of the determination of economic aggregates, such as total output, total employment, and the price level.

managed float See *dirty float*.

marginal cost (MC) The increase in total cost resulting from raising the rate of production by 1 unit; mathematically, the rate of change of cost with respect to output. Also called *incremental cost*.

marginal efficiency of capital (MEC) The marginal rate of return on a nation's capital stock. It is the rate of return on one additional dollar of net investment, i.e., an addition of \$1 to capital stock.

marginal efficiency of capital schedule A schedule relating *MEC* to the size of the capital stock.

marginal efficiency of investment (MEI) function The function that relates the quantity of investment to the rate of interest.

marginal physical product (MPP) See *marginal product*.

marginal product (MP) The increase in quantity of total output that results from using 1 unit more of a variable factor; mathematically, the rate of change of output with respect to the quantity of the variable factor. Also called *incremental product* or *marginal physical product* (*MPP*).

marginal productivity theory of distribution The implication from profit maximization that the use of a factor should be expanded until its marginal revenue product equals its price.

marginal propensity The ratio of the change of any flow to the change in income that brought it about.

marginal propensity to consume (MPC) The change in consumption divided by the change in income that brought it about (mathematically, the rate of change of consumption with respect to income). The income variable may be disposable income, in which case $MPC = \Delta C/\Delta Y_d$, or it may be national income, in which case $MPC = \Delta C/\Delta Y$.

marginal propensity to save (MPS) The change in saving divided by the change in income that brought it about (mathematically, the rate of change of saving with respect to income). The income variable may either be disposable income, in which case $MPS = \Delta S/\Delta Y_d$, or it may be national income, in which case $MPS = \Delta S/\Delta Y$.

marginal rate of substitution (MRS) (1) In consumption the slope of an indifference curve, showing how much more of one commodity must be provided to compensate for the giving up of one unit of another commodity if the level of satisfaction is to be held constant. (2) In production, the slope of an isoquant, showing how much more of one factor of production must be used to compensate for the use of one less unit of another factor of production if production is to be held constant.

marginal revenue (MR) (incremental revenue) The change in a firm's total revenue arising from the sale of 1 unit more; mathematically, the rate of change of revenue with respect to output.

marginal revenue product (MRP) The addition of revenue attributable to the last unit of a variable factor. $MRP = MPP \times MR$; mathematically, the rate of change of revenue with respect to quantity of the variable factor.

marginal tax rate The fraction of an additional dollar of income that is paid in taxes.

marginal utility The additional satisfaction obtained by a buyer from consuming 1 unit more of a good; mathematically, the rate of change of utility with respect to consumption.

margin requirement The fraction of the price of a stock that must be paid in cash, while putting up the stock as security against a loan for the balance.

market A concept with many possible definitions. (1) An area over which buyers and sellers negotiate the exchange of a well-defined commodity. (2) From the point of view of a household, the firms from which it can buy a well-defined product. (3) From the point of view of a firm, the buyers to whom it can sell a well-defined product.

market-clearing prices Prices at which quantity demanded equals quantity supplied so that there are neither unsatisfied buyers nor unsatisfied sellers. The equilibrium price in a perfectly competitive market.

market economy A society in which people specialize in productive activities and meet most of their material wants through exchanges voluntarily agreed upon.

market failure Failure of the unregulated market system to achieve socially optimal results. Its sources include externalities, market impediments and imperfections, and nonmarket goals.

market rate of interest The actual interest rate in effect at a given moment.

market sector That portion of an economy in which commodities are bought and sold and producers must cover their costs from the proceeds of their sales.

market structure Characteristics of market organiza-

tion likely to affect behavior and performance of firms, such as the number and size of sellers, the extent of knowledge about each other's actions, the degree of freedom of entry, and the degree of product differentiation.

markup The amount added to cost to determine price.

medium of exchange Anything that is generally acceptable in return for goods and services sold.

merger The purchase of either the physical assets or the controlling share ownership of one company by another. In a *horizontal* merger both companies produce the same product; in a *vertical* merger one company is a supplier of the other; if the two are in unrelated industries, it is a *conglomerate* merger.

microeconomic policy Activities of the central authorities that alter resource allocation and/or income distribution.

microeconomics The study of the allocation of resources and the distribution of income as they are affected by the workings of the price system and by some government policies.

minimum efficient scale (MES) The smallest size of firm required to achieve the economies of scale in production and/or distribution. Also called *minimum optimal scale (MOS)*.

minimum wages Base rates of worker compensation, established by federal or provincial legislation.

mixed economy Economy in which some decisions are made by firms and households and some by central authorities.

monetarists A group of economists who stress monetary causes of cyclical fluctuations and inflations, who believe that an active stabilization policy is not normally required, and who stress the relative efficacy of monetary over fiscal policy.

monetary base The sum of currency in circulation plus the reserves of the chartered banks; the monetary liabilities of the Bank of Canada.

monetary disequilibrium A situation in which the demand for money does not equal the supply of money.

monetary equilibrium A situation in which the demand for money equals the supply of money.

monetary policy An attempt to influence the economy by operating on such monetary variables as the quantity of money and the rate of interest.

money Any generally accepted medium of exchange.

money capital The funds used to finance a firm. Money capital includes both equity capital and debt.

money flow The flow of money payments from buyers to sellers in return for goods and services received.

money income A household or firm's income in the form of some monetary unit.

money rate of interest A rate of interest expressed in current dollars.

money substitute Anything such as a credit card or a charge account that permits the holder to purchase goods and services whether or not he or she possesses legal tender at the time.

money supply The total quantity of money existing at a point in time.

monopolistic competition A market structure of an industry in which there are many sellers and freedom of entry, but in which each firm has a product somewhat differentiated from the others, giving it some control over its price.

monopoly A market structure in which the output of an industry is controlled by a single seller or a group of sellers making joint decisions.

monopsony A market situation in which there is a single buyer or a group of buyers making joint decisions. Monopsony and monopsony power are the equivalent on the buying side of monopoly and monopoly power on the selling side.

multiple regression analysis See *regression analysis*.

multiplier The ratio of the change in national income to the change in autonomous expenditure that brought it about.

national debt The current volume of outstanding federal government debt.

national income accounting The set of rules and techniques for measuring the total flows of outputs produced and inputs used by the economy.

natural monopoly An industry characterized by economies of scale sufficiently large that one firm can most efficiently supply the entire market demand.

natural rate of unemployment The rate of unemployment (due to frictional and structural causes) consistent with full-employment national income, Y_F. In the Phelps-Friedman theory this is the rate of unemployment at which there is neither upward nor downward pressure on the price level.

natural scale A scale in which equal absolute amounts are represented by equal distances.

near money Liquid assets easily convertible into money without risk of significant loss of value. They can be used as short-term stores of purchasing power but are not themselves media of exchange.

negative income tax (NIT) A tax system in which households with incomes below taxable levels receive payments from the government based on a percentage of the amount by which their income is below the minimum taxable level.

neo-Keynesians Sometimes called Keynesians; a group of economists who stress changes in both aggregate expenditure and the money supply as causes of cyclical fluctuations and inflations, who believe that an active government stabilization policy is called for, and who stress the relative efficacy of fiscal policy over monetary policy.

net export function The function that relates the balance-of-trade surplus to the level of national income.

net exports Total exports *minus* total imports $(X - M)$.

net investment Gross investment *minus* replacement investment.

net national product (NNP) Gross national product *minus* a capital consumption allowance.

net private benefit (NPB) The difference between private benefits and private costs.

net social benefit (NSB) The difference between social benefits and social costs. Where private production produces externalities, it is net private benefit plus external benefits and minus external costs.

neutrality of money The doctrine that the money supply affects only the absolute level of prices and has no effect on relative prices and hence no effect on the allocation of resources or the distribution of income.

nominal GNP See *current dollar GNP*.

nondurable goods Goods, such as food, that are consumed in the same period in which they are purchased and do not have a useful life that extends into the future.

nonmarket sector That portion of an economy in which commodities are given away and producers must cover their costs from some source other than the proceeds of sales.

nonprice competition Competition by sellers for sales by means other than price cutting. Advertising, product differentiation, trading stamps, and other promotional devices are examples.

nontariff barriers to trade Restrictions, other than tariffs, that may reduce the flow of international trade.

nontradeables Goods and services that are produced in the domestic economy but are not traded in international markets.

normal goods Goods for which income elasticity is positive.

normal profits A term used by some economists for the imputed returns to capital and risk taking just necessary to keep the owners in the industry. They are included in what the economist, but not the businessman, sees as *total costs*.

normative statement A statement about what ought to be.

oligopoly A market structure in which a small number of rival firms dominate the industry. The leading firms are aware that they are interdependent.

open economy An economy that engages in foreign trade.

open market operations The purchase and sale on the open market by the central bank of securities (usually short-term government securities).

open shop A bargaining arrangement whereby a union represents its members but does not have exclusive jurisdiction. Membership in the union is not a condition of getting or keeping a job.

opportunity cost The cost of using resources for a certain purpose, measured by the benefit or revenues given up by not using them in their best alternative use.

organization theory In economics, a set of hypotheses in which the decisions of an organization are a function of its size and form of organization.

outputs The quantities of goods and services produced.

paradox of value The apparent contradiction in the observed fact that some absolute necessities to life are cheap in price while some relatively unimportant luxuries are very expensive.

Pareto-efficiency See *Pareto-optimality*.

Pareto-optimality An allocation of resources in which it is impossible by reallocation to make some consumers better off without simultaneously making others worse off. Also called *Pareto-efficiency*.

partnership A form of business organization with two or more joint owners, each of whom is personally responsible for all of the firm's actions and debts.

paternalism Protection of individuals against themselves.

P/E or PE ratio See *price-earnings ratio*.

per capita GNP GNP divided by total population. Also called *GNP per person*.

perfect competition A market form in which all firms are price takers and in which there is freedom of entry into and exit from the industry.

permanent income The maximum amount that a household can consume per year into the indefinite future without reducing its wealth. (A number of similar but not identical definitions are in common use.)

permanent-income hypothesis (PIH) The hypothesis that relates actual consumption to permanent income rather than (as in the original Keynesian theory) to current income.

personal income Income earned by individuals before allowance for personal income taxes paid or payable.

petrodollars The excess purchasing power held by the oil-producing countries.

Phillips curve Originally a relation between the percentage of the labor force unemployed and the rate of change of money wages. It can also be expressed as a relation between the percentage of the labor force employed and the rate of price inflation, or between actual national income as a proportion of potential national income and the rate of price inflation.

picket lines Striking workers parading at the entrances to a plant or firm on strike. A picket line is a symbolic blockade of the entrance.

point elasticity Elasticity calculated at a point, i.e., over an interval where changes in the variables approach zero. The formula for point elasticity of demand is

$$\eta = \frac{dq}{dp} \times \frac{p}{q}$$

The minus sign is often dropped so *n* is expressed as a positive number.

point of diminishing average productivity The level of output at which average product reaches a maximum.

point of diminishing marginal productivity The level of output at which marginal product reaches a maximum.

policy instruments The variables that the central authorities can control directly to achieve their policy objectives.

policy variables The variables that the government ultimately seeks to control; the variables in whose behavior it is ultimately interested.

political business cycle Cyclical swings in the economy generated by fiscal and monetary policy for the purpose of winning elections.

portfolio investment Foreign investment in bonds or a minority holding of shares that does not involve legal control. Contrasted with *direct investment*.

positive statement A statement about what is, was, or

will be, as opposed to a statement about what ought to be.

potential GNP The gross national product the economy could produce if its productive resources were fully employed at their normal intensity of use. Also called *full-employment GNP* or *full-employment national income (Y_F)*.

poverty gap (or **income gap**) The number of dollars required to raise everyone whose income is below the poverty level to that level.

poverty level A measure of the minimum amount of annual income required to avoid poverty; approximately $5,000 for a single individual and about $8,500 for a three-person family in 1979.

precautionary motive The desire to hold money balances for protection against the uncertainty of the timing of cash flows.

preferred stock A form of equity capital with a preference over common stock to receipt of dividends up to a stated maximum amount; may be voting or nonvoting.

present value (PV) The value *now* of a sum payable at a later date or of a stream of income receivable at future dates. *PV* is the discounted value of future payments.

price ceiling A maximum permitted price.

price-consumption line A line connecting the points of tangency between a set of indifference curves and a set of budget lines where one absolute price is fixed and the other varies, money income being held constant.

price discrimination The sale by a single firm of the same commodity to different buyers at two or more different prices for reasons not associated with differences in cost. It may be systematic or unsystematic.

price-earnings ratio (PE ratio) Ratio of the price of a share of stock to the earnings per share of that stock, often written as *price/earnings* or simply *P/E*.

price floor A minimum permitted price.

price index A number that shows the average percentage change that has occurred in some group of prices over some period of time.

price-push inflation Inflation caused by increases in prices brought about by the monopoly power of sellers and not associated with excess aggregate demand.

price taker A firm that acts as if it could alter its rate of production and sales without affecting the market price of its product.

price theory The theory of how prices are determined; competitive price theory concerns the determination of prices in competitive markets by the interaction of demand and supply.

principle of substitution The proposition that the proportions in which various inputs are used will vary as the relative prices of these inputs vary.

private cost The value of the best alternative use of resources used in production as valued by the producer.

private sector That portion of an economy in which principal decisions are made by private units such as households and firms.

producers' association An organization of producers of a commodity usually formed to serve as a joint selling organization for the producers and often operated as a cartel.

producers' durables See *durable good*.

product differentiation The existence of similar but not identical products sold by a single industry such as the breakfast food and the automobile industries.

production The act of making commodities.

production function A functional relation showing the maximum output that can be produced by each and every combination of inputs.

production possibility boundary A curve on a graph that shows which alternative combination of commodities can just be obtained if all available productive resources are used. It is the boundary between attainable and unobtainable output combinations.

productive efficiency Production at the lowest attainable level of long-run average total cost.

productivity Output produced per unit of input; frequently used to refer to *labor productivity*, measured by output per hour worked.

productivity of capital (efficiency of capital) The increase in production resulting from the use of capital, after allowance for the maintenance and replacement of the capital.

product markets Markets in which firms sell their outputs of goods and services.

profit (1) In ordinary usage, the difference between the value of outputs and the value of inputs. (2) In microeconomics, the value of inputs, which includes the opportunity cost of capital, so that profits are *economic profits*. (3) In macroeconomics, profits exclude interest on borrowed capital but do not exclude the return to owner's (or equity) capital. Profits in macroeconomics are thus the return available to owner's capital—that is, the sum of the microeconomic concepts of the opportunity cost of owner's capital plus economic profits.

progressive tax A tax that takes a larger percentage of income the higher the level of income.

progressivity of taxation The ratio of taxes to income as income increases. If the ratio decreases, the tax is *regressive;* if it remains constant, *proportional;* if it increases, *progressive.*

proportional tax A tax that takes a constant percentage of income at all levels of income and is thus neither progressive nor regressive.

protectionism The partial or complete protection of domestic industries from foreign competition in domestic markets by use of tariffs or such nontariff barriers to trade as import quotas.

proxy A document authorizing the holder to vote one's stock in a corporation.

proxy fight A struggle between competing factions in a corporation to obtain the proxies for a majority of the outstanding shares.

public sector That portion of an economy where production is under control of the central authorities or bodies appointed by them, including all production by governments and nationalized industries.

public utility regulation Regulation of prices and services of industries that have been deemed to be natural monopolies.

purchase and resale agreement (PRA) An arrangement by which the Bank of Canada makes short-term advances as a lender of last resort to investment dealers. Government securities are sold to the Bank with an agreement to repurchase them.

pure rate of interest The rate of interest that would rule in equilibrium in a riskless economy where all lending and borrowing is for investment in productive capital.

pure return on capital The amount capital can earn in a riskless investment; hence the transfer earnings of capital in a riskless investment.

quantity actually bought The amount of a commodity that households succeed in purchasing in some time period.

quantity actually sold The amount of a commodity that producers succeed in selling in some time period.

quantity demanded The amount of a commodity that households wish to purchase in some time period. An increase (decrease) in quantity demanded refers to a movement down (up) the demand curve in response to a fall (rise) in price.

quantity exchanged The identical amount of a commodity that households actually purchase and producers actually sell in some time period.

quantity supplied The amount of a commodity producers wish to sell in some time period. An increase (decrease) in quantity supplied refers to a movement up (down) the supply curve in response to a rise (fall) in price.

quantity theory of money A theory that predicts that the money value of national income (PY) changes in proportion to changes in the money supply. (The change will be in all prices, P, if national income, Y, is at its full-employment level, Y_F.)

random sample A sample chosen from a group or population in such a way that every member of the group has an equal chance of being selected.

rate base The total allowable investment to which the rate of return allowed by a regulatory commission is applied. The public utility may build into its prices the amount of profits so determined.

rate of return The ratio of profits earned by a firm to total investment capital.

rate of return on capital (Sometimes used synonymously with *rate of return.*) Frequently used to refer to a specific capital good; the annual net income produced by a capital good, expressed as a percentage of the price of the good.

rational expectations The theory that people learn quickly from their mistakes, that while random errors may be made, systematic and persistent errors are not made.

ratio scale See *logarithmic scale.*

real capital (or **physical capital**) Physical assets, including plant, equipment, and inventories.

real flow The flow of goods and services from sellers to buyers.

real GNP See *constant dollar GNP.*

real income A household's income expressed in terms of the command over commodities that the money income confers; money income corrected for changes in price levels, thus the purchasing power of money income.

real rate of interest A rate of interest expressed in constant dollars. It is the money rate of interest corrected for the change in the purchasing power of money.

recession In general, a downswing in the level of economic activity. The U.S. Department of Commerce defines a recession as occurring when real GNP falls for two successive quarters.

regression analysis (sometimes called *correlation analysis*) A quantitative analysis of the systematic interrelationships between two or more variables.

Simple regression concerns the relation between Y and a single independent variable, X_1; *multiple* regression concerns the relation between Y and more than one indendent variables, $X_1, \ldots, X_n$.

regression equation The mathematical equation describing the statistically determined equation of best fit between variables in regression analysis.

regressive tax A tax that takes a larger percentage of income at lower levels of income.

relative price The ratio of the price of one good to the price of another good; a ratio of two absolute prices.

rent (1) In macroeconomics, the proportion of national income going to the owners of the factor of production, land. (2) In microeconomics, a shorthand for *economic rent*. (3) In everyday usage, the payment for rental housing.

required (cash) reserves In banking, the amount of reserves a bank must, by law, keep either in currency or in deposits with the central bank.

reserve ratio In banking, the fraction of deposits of the public that a bank holds in reserves.

resource allocation The allocation of an economy's scarce resources among alternative uses.

return to capital The total amount available for payments to owners of capital; the sum of pure returns to capital, risk premiums, and economic profits.

revaluation of the exchange rate An increase in the value at which a country's currency is pegged in terms of foreign currencies; the opposite of *devaluation*.

rising-cost industry An industry in which the minimum cost attainable by a firm rises as the scale of the industry expands.

rising supply price A rising long-run supply curve, caused by increases in factor prices as output is increased, or by diseconomies of scale.

risk premium The return to capital necessary to compensate owners of capital for the risk of loss of their capital.

sample A small number of items, chosen from a larger group or population, that is intended to be representative of the larger entity.

satisficing A hypothesized objective of firms, in contrast to maximizing behavior, whereby firms set target levels of satisfactory performance (e.g., profits) rather than seek to maximize some objective (e.g., profits).

saving Household saving is disposable income not spent on domestically produced or imported consumption goods and services. Firm saving is profits not distributed to owners.

scarce good A commodity for which the quantity demanded would exceed the quantity supplied if its price were zero.

scatter diagram A graph of statistical observations of paired values of two variables, one measured on the horizontal and the other on the vertical axis. Each point on the coordinate grid represents the values of the variables for a particular unit of observation.

seasonal adjustment The adjustment of monthly or quarterly time series to remove variation due to seasonal influences.

secondary reserves Interest-earning liquid assets held by banks. For purposes of the minimum ratio to deposits imposed by the Bank of Canada, secondary reserves are defined as holdings of *treasury bills, day-to-day loans,* and *excess cash reserves.*

sectors Parts of an economy.

securities market See *stock market.*

selective credit controls Controls on credit imposed through such means as margin requirements, installment buying, and minimum down payments on mortgages.

sellers' preferences Allocation of scarce commodities by decision of those who sell them.

semidurable goods Goods, such as clothing, that are intermediate between *durable* and *nondurable* goods.

services Intangible commodities such as haircuts or medical care.

shop steward The representative of a local union in the shop or plant.

short run The period of time over which the quantity of some inputs cannot, as a practical matter, be varied.

short-run equilibrium Generally, equilibrium subject to fixed factors; for a competitive firm, the output at which market price equals marginal cost; for a competitive industry, the price and output at which industry demand equals short-run industry supply and all firms are in short-run equilibrium. Either profits or losses are possible.

short-run supply curve The curve showing the relation of quantity supplied to prices, with one or more fixed factors; the horizontal sum of marginal cost curves (above the level of average variable costs) of all firms in an industry.

single proprietorship A firm consisting of one owner, where the single owner is solely responsible for the firm's actions and debts.

size distribution of income The distribution of income by size class, without regard to source of income.

small open economy An economy that engages in foreign trade but has no influence on the world prices of traded goods.

snake The agreement among several Western European countries to fix exchange rates among their own currencies and then to let them fluctuate in common against the U.S. dollar. Also called the *joint float*.

social benefit The contribution an activity makes to the society's welfare.

social cost (social opportunity cost) The value of the best alternative use of resources available to society, as valued by society.

social insurance Programs, such as pensions, unemployment insurance, and medical insurance, that provide payments to eligible persons who have had their income impaired by unemployment, retirement, ill health, etc.

special drawing rights (SDRs) Established in 1968, the Special Drawing Account of the International Monetary Fund provides additional international reserves for member countries. Subject to certain repayment provisions, members are able to treat SDRs in the same way as their own holdings of international currencies for financing balance-of-payments surpluses or deficits.

specialization of labor An organization of production in which individual workers specialize in the production of particular goods or services (and satisfy their wants by trading) rather than produce for themselves everything they consume (and thus be self-sufficient).

specific tax See *excise tax*.

speculative motive The desire to hold money balances as a hedge against the uncertainty of the prices of other financial assets.

stabilization policy Any policy designed to reduce the economy's cyclical fluctuations. Attempts by the central authorities to remove inflationary and deflationary gaps when they appear.

stable equilibrium An equilibrium that if disturbed will be restored. A pendulum at rest is in stable equilibrium.

stagflation The coexistence of high rates of unemployment with high, and sometimes rising, rates of inflation.

sterilization Operations undertaken by the central bank to offset the effects of the money supply of balance-of-payments surpluses or deficits.

stockholders The owners of a corporation.

stock market (securities market) An organized market where stocks and bonds are bought and sold.

strike The concerted refusal of the members of a union to work.

strikebreakers Nonunion workers brought in by management to operate the plant while a union is on strike. (Derisively called "scabs" by union members.)

structural rigidity inflation The theory that downward inflexibility of money prices means that the adjustment of *relative* prices necessary in any changing economy will cause a rise in the average level of all prices (i.e., an inflation).

structural unemployment Unemployment due to a mismatching between characteristics required by available jobs and characteristics possessed by the unemployed labor. (The sum of frictional plus structural unemployment may be measured by the number of unemployed when the total number of jobs available is equal to the total number of persons looking for acceptable jobs.)

substitute A commodity that satisfies similar needs or desires as the original commodity; technically, a substitute for a commodity is another commodity for which the cross elasticity of demand is non-negligible and positive.

substitution effect The change in quantity of a good demanded resulting from a change in its relative price, eliminating the effect on real income of the change in price.

supply There are several distinct but closely related concepts: (1) *quantity supplied;* (2) the whole relationship of the quantity supplied to variables that determine it, such as producers' goals, technology, price of the commodity, prices of other commodities, and prices of factors of production; (3) the *supply schedule;* (4) the *supply curve.* The phrase increase (decrease) in supply means a shift of the supply curve to the right (left), indicating an increase (decrease) in the quantity supplied at each possible price.

supply curve The graphic representation of the *supply schedule*.

supply lag The time interval between a change in a market price and the date at which the change in production it induces comes onto the market.

supply of effort (or total supply of labor) The total number of hours of work that the population is willing to supply.

supply of money See *money supply*.

supply schedule The relationship between the quantity supplied of a commodity and its price, *ceteris paribus.*

surplus function See *budget surplus function.*

tacit collusion See also *collusion.* The adoption, without explicit agreement, of a common policy by sellers in an industry. Sometimes also called *conscious parallel action.*

takeover bid See *tender offer.*

tariff A tax applied on imports.

tax base The aggregate amount of taxable income.

tax-based incomes policies (TIPs) Tax incentives for labor and management to encourage them to conform to wage and price guidelines.

tax expenditures The name given to exemptions and deductions from taxable income and to tax credits, which amount to subsidies or preferences to taxpayers.

tax incidence The location of the ultimate burden of a tax; the identity of the ultimate bearer or bearers of the tax.

tax-rental arrangements An agreement by which the federal government makes a per capita payment to the provinces for the right to collect income taxes.

tax expenditures The name the Treasury Department gives to exemptions and deductions from taxable income and to tax credits, which amount to subsidies or preferences to taxpayers.

tax incidence The location of the ultimate burden of a tax; the identity of the ultimate bearer or bearers of the tax.

technological efficiency (sometimes called *technical efficiency*) A method of production is technologically efficient if the same output cannot be produced with fewer real resources.

tender offer (takeover bid) An offer to buy directly some or all of the outstanding common stock of a corporation from its stockholders at a specified price per share, in an attempt to gain control of the corporation.

term See *term to maturity.*

terms of trade The relation between the average price of a country's exports and the average price of its imports.

term to maturity The period of time from the present to the redemption date of a bond. Often simply the *term* of the bond.

third-party effects See *externalities.*

time deposit An interest-earning bank deposit, legally subject to notice before withdrawal (in practice the notice requirement is not normally enforced) and not transferable by cheque.

time series A series of observations on the values of a variable at different points in time.

time-series data Data on variables where measurements are made for successive periods (or moments) of time. Contrasted with cross-sectional data.

total cost (TC) Fixed costs plus variable costs at a given level of output; the sum of the opportunity costs of the factors used to produce that output.

total product (TP) The total amount produced during some period of time by all the factors of production employed over that time period.

total revenue (TR) The total receipts from the sale of a product; price times quantity.

total utility The total satisfaction resulting from the consumption of a given commodity by a buyer in a period of time.

tradeables Goods that are traded in international markets.

trade deficit The excess of imports over exports.

trade surplus The excess of exports over imports.

trade union See *union.*

transactions balances Money held for day-to-day needs because the receipts and payments of firms and households are not perfectly synchronized.

transactions costs Costs that must be incurred in effecting market transactions (such as negotiation costs, billing costs, bad debts).

transactions motive The desire to hold money balances in order to finance purchases and sales.

transfer earnings That part of the payment to a factor in its present use that is just enough to keep it from transferring to another use.

transfer payment A payment to a private person or institution that does not arise out of current productive activity; typically made by governments, as in welfare payments, but also made by businesses and private individuals in the form of charitable contributions.

treasury bill The characteristic form of short-term government debt. A bill is a promise to pay a certain sum of money at some time in the early future (often one, three, or six months). It carries no interest payment; the lender earns interest because the price at which he or she buys the bill is less than its future redemption value.

trigger prices In U.S. trade policy, prices for imported commodities set by the U.S. government on the basis of average total cost of the low-cost producing nation. A foreign country that sells below a trigger price is subject to proceedings under antidumping laws.

turnover tax An excise tax levied on commodities, commonly used in socialist countries.

two-price system The Canadian energy policy that sets domestic prices of oil and natural gas below world prices.

unbalanced growth policy Growth in only a few sectors of the economy with remaining needs met by international trade.

undistributed profits Earnings of a firm not distributed as dividends but retained by the firm.

unemployment The number of persons who are not employed and are actively searching for a job.

unemployment rate Unemployment expressed as a percentage of the labor force.

union An association of workers authorized to represent them in bargaining with employers. Also called *trade union* or *labor union.*

union shop A bargaining arrangement in which the employer may hire anyone, but every employee must join the union within a specified period of time (often 60 days).

unstable equilibrium An equilibrium that is not stable. A book standing on edge is in unstable equilibrium.

utility The satisfaction that results from the consumption of a commodity.

value added The value of a firm's output *minus* the value of the inputs that it purchases from other firms.

variable A magnitude (such as the price of wheat) that can take on a specific value but whose value will vary among times and places.

variable costs Costs whose total varies directly with changes in output. Also called *direct costs.*

variable factors Factors whose quantity used in production can be varied in the short run.

velocity of circulation National income divided by the quantity of money. Sometimes called the *income velocity of circulation.*

vertical merger See *merger.*

very long run The period in which even the technological possibilities open to a firm are subject to change.

visibles All those items of foreign trade that are tangible; goods as opposed to services.

wage and price controls Direct government intervention into wage and price formation with legal power to enforce the government's decisions on wages and prices.

wage cost-push inflation Inflation caused by increases in labor costs that are not themselves associated with excess aggregate demand.

wages and salaries Payments made for the use of labor services. Also called *wages.*

windfall profits Profits that bear no relation to current or historical costs, arising usually from a sudden increase in demand or reduction in supply.

withdrawals Income earned by households and not passed on to firms in return for goods and services purchased, and income earned by firms and not passed on to households in return for factor services purchased.

X In boldface, the term represents actual exports; in lightface, desired exports.

X − M In boldface, the term represents actual net exports (which is the difference between total exports and total imports); in lightface, the term represents desired net exports.

X-inefficiency When resources are used less productively than is possible so that society is at a point *inside* its production possibility boundary.

Index

Absolute advantage, 505–506
Absolute cost advantage, 300
Absolute price, 166
Accelerating inflation
  and unstable Phillips Curve,
    825–833
  and validated demand inflation,
    825
Accelerator, and multiplier,
    644–645
Accelerator theory of investment,
    640–642
Accountant, balance sheet and
    income statement, A-26–A-28
Actual consumption, A-40
Actual GNP, 563
Adaptive expectations, 816
Adjustable peg system, 732,
    733–736
Administered prices, under
    oligopoly, 297
Administration costs, and many
    interest rates, 422–423
Ad valorem tariff, 512
Adverse clearing, 756
Advertising
  as firm-created barrier entry,
    301–302, 304
  misleading, 334
The Affluent Society (Galbraith),
    499
AFL-CIO, 392, 393
After-tax real income, vs. after-tax
    money income, 690
Agency for International Develop-
    ment (U.S.), 943
Aggregate curves, shifts in, 569
Aggregate demand, 567–576
  in action, 569–571
  and aggregate expenditure,
    606–608

Aggregate demand (*Continued*)
  and demand for money, 721–723
  increases in, 569
  and inflation, 812, 876
  and monetary mechanism,
    A-51–A-52
  and national income, 596,
    606–608
  and net exports, 662–663
  in 1930s, 856
  and price level, A-47–A-48
  and stagflation, 865–867
Aggregate demand curve, 153,
    567–568
  error in explaining, 781
  and price level, 779–781
  shape, 571–572
  shifts in, 569
  slope, 783
Aggregate desired expenditure
    function, 602–604
Aggregate expenditure
  and aggregate demand, 606–608
  direct vs. indirect shifts in,
    612–614
  and interest rate, 776, 777,
    A-44–A-45
  and monetary gradualism,
    792–793
Aggregate expenditure function,
    595, 602–604
Aggregate supply, 567–576
  and national income, 596
  and stagflation, 865
  upward shifts, 821–822
Aggregate supply curve, 567–568
  intermediate section, 821–824
  kinked, 621
  shape, 573–574
  shifts in, 569
  short-run and long-run, 824
Agricultural Products Marketing
    Act (1972), 119
Agricultural support policies, as
    built-in stabilizer, 681–682
Agriculture, 110–111
  Canadian policy, 118–121
  development, 944–946
  long-term trends, 111–112
  short-term fluctuations, 112–114
  stabilization and support plans,
    114–118, 681–682
Air Canada, 58

Airlines, deregulation, 339
Akerloff, George, 185
Alberta government, reaction to
    NEP, 556
Alcan, 345
Alchian, Armen, 341
Allocation. *See also* Resource
    allocation
  of commodity in short supply,
    100–102
  market vs. non-market, 452–453
Allocative efficiency
  in equilibrium, market, 453–454
  and perfect competition,
    265–267
Allocative inefficiency, 933
  monopoly, 277–278
American Automobile Association,
    44
American Cyanamid Corp., 408
American Federation of Labor, 390,
    395, 396
American Motors Corp., 207, 359
American Telephone and
    Telegraph Co., 348
American Tobacco Co., 332n
Amortization, mortgage, 638
Analysis
  of data, 39–41
  extending, 41–42
  and government intervention, 471
Ando, Professor, A-39
Annual Review, Economic Council
    of Canada, 13
Annuity, 417
Anticipated inflations, 717–719
Anti-Dumping Act (1968), 283
Anti-Dumping Tribunal (ADT), 283
Anti-Inflation Act, 869
Anti-Inflation Board, 99, 867–873
Antitrust policy, 331
Antonelli, Giovanni, 165n
Appreciation, 135
A priori, 23
Arbitrage, 139
Arc elasticity, A-11
Assets
  banks, 752–753
  financial, 768–770
Asset value, 417–418
Assumptions
  PIH and LCH, A-41
  and theory, 25, 26–27

Aswan Dam, 429, 475
Atlantic Provinces vs. New England,
    government intervention,
    472–473
Atlas Co., 429
Attainable combination, 7
Attitude survey, and utility, 161
Autarky price, 132
Automobile industry
  and Auto Pact, 303, 522–523
  oligopoly in, 296
  and perfect competition, 251
  production and costs in short
    run, 207–208
Automotive Products Agreement
    (1965), 522
Automotive Products Trade Act
    (1965), 303, 522–523
Autonomous components,
    aggregate expenditure, 604
Autonomous variable, 26
Auto Pact (1965), 303, 522–523
Average cost, 215
Average cost curve, 217
  and labor market, 387
  long run, 223; vs. short run, 25
Average fixed costs, 216
Average product, 210
Average product curve, 211
  shape, 212–214
Average propensity to consume,
    597
  calculation, 598
Average propensity to save, 599
Average revenue, 254
  monopolist, 273, 274
Average tax rate, 479
Average total cost, 215–216
Average variable costs, 216
Averch, Harvey, 337
Avoidable costs, 215

Bain, Joe S., 280
Baker, Russell, 18
Balanced budget, 674
  annually, 692–693
Balanced budget multiplier, 677
Balanced trade, 131
Balance of payments. *See also*
    Exchange rate
  Canada, 663–671
  current account, 660–661

and money supply, 844–845
Balance-of-payments accounts, 663–665
  categories, 665–667
Balance-of-payments deficit, 668–669
Balance-of-payments surplus, 668–669
Balance of trade, 135, 650–652
  absorption vs. component approach, 659–661
  and full employment, 839–840
  and national income, 652–663
  problems, 661, 837
Balance-of-trade deficit, 840–841
Balance sheet, A-25–A-29
  bank, and international trade, 134
  Bank of Canada, 761
  central bank, and open market purchases, 763, 764
  central bank, and sale of foreign currency, 844
  many banks, single new deposit, 756, 757
  monopoly bank, 754, 755, 756, 759
  second-generation bank, 757
Ball, J. A., 332n
Ball Point Pen Co., 314
Ball-point pens, patent monopoly, 314–315
Bank(s). See also Bank of Canada; Central banks
  administration of interest rates, 420
  balance sheet, and international trade, 134
  chartered, 750–753
  currency drains, 759–760
  excess reserves, 759
  many, and many deposits, 758–759
  many, and single new deposit, 756–757
  monopoly, and single new deposit, 754–756
  as profit seekers, 752–753
Bank Act, 340, 750n, 753, 765
Bank notes, 707
Bank of Canada, 15, 50, 421, 619, 695, 749–750, 762, 765, 766, 777, 787, 795, 798, 854. See

  also Bank(s); Central banks
  balance sheet, 761
  and flexible exchange rates, 850–852
  and floating exchange rates, 861–862
  organization, 760
Bank of Canada Review, 45
Bank of England, 738, 760, 871
Bank of Greece, 760
Bank rate, changes in, 765–766
Bargaining, collective, 393, 397
Bargaining arrangements, unions, 392–393
Barriers to entry
  monopoly, 275
  oligopoly, 300–305
Barron's, 747
Barter, 703–704
  and market economy, 47
  vs. metallic money, 705
Base control, 787
  vs. interest rate, 793
Base period, price index, 33
Baumol, William, 351
Beggar-my-neighbor policies, 731
Behavior, group vs. individual, 23–24
Behavioral rules, profit-maximizing firm, 250–251
Bell Canada, 288, 291, 345
Beneficial externalities, 457
Bennett, R. B., 615
Berle, A. A., 350
Beveridge, Lord William, 901
Biased sample, 35
Bishop, R. L., 292
Black & Decker Canada, 524
Black economy, and tax rates, 372
Blacklist, 393
Black market, and ceiling price, 100, 101–102
Blinder, Alan, 866
Bond, 424
  and money, 769
  price, and interest rate, 769–770
Bondholders, 424
Borlaug, Norman, 945
Bouey, Gerald, 760, 854, 873
Boycott, labor, 393
Brady, Robert, 345n
Brand proliferation, as firm-created barrier to entry, 303–304

Bread-and-butter unionism, 394
Brechez, Phillipe, 354
Bretton Woods system, 732–739
British Columbia Milk Board, 120
B.C. Sugar Refining Co., 333
British Columbia Telephone, 291
British North America Act, 491, 494, 867, 869
Bruce, Neil, 661
Brumberg, Professor, A-39
Buchanan, James, 499, 698n
Budget
  annually balanced, 692–693
  cyclically balanced, 693
Budgetary policy, in 1970, 688–692
Budget balance, 674–675, 689
  actual, and full-employment, 692
  proposals on, 692–693
Budget deficit, 674
Budget line
  and household choice, 165–168
  and household satisfaction, 171, 172
Budget surplus, 674
Budget surplus function, 686, 687
Buffer stocks, and NIEO, 949
Building cycle, 646–647
Built-in stabilizer, 678–682
Burnham, James, 345n
Burton, J., 698n
Business
  capital formation, 586–587
  expectations, and interest rates, 420
Business cycles, 626–629
  causes, 629–630
  defined, 628
  and export multiplier, 652
  government and fluctuations in, 642
  stylized, 643
  terminology, 643–647
  variety, 646–647
Business fixed investment, 636, 637–640
Business Week, 877
Butcher, Willard, 339

Campaign GM, 347
Canada. See also Government
  balance of payments, 663–671
  competition policy, 332–334

Canada (*Continued*)
  concentration ratios in manufac-
    turing, 291–292, 293
  current account, 660–661
  and flexible exchange rates,
    847–853
  foreign investment and R&D
    expenditure, 236–237
  GNP, 653
  macroeconomic performance,
    1974–1980, 866
  multiplier, 619–621
  productivity growth, 233–234
  productivity slowdown, 920–921
  promoting R&D expenditure in,
    238–239
  trade policy, 521–530
Canada Assistance Plan, 437
Canada Cement Ltd., 291
Canada Development Corp., 530
Canada Pension Plan, 436, 490
Canadian Breweries Ltd., 333
Canadian Broadcasting Corp., 58,
  335
Canadian Cancer Society, 51
Canadian Congress of Labour, 390
Canadian Dairy Commission, 119
Canadian Egg Marketing Agency,
  118, 119
Canadian Industries Ltd., 291
Canadian Labour Congress, 392,
  395, 396, 869
Canadian National Railways, 58
Canadian Pacific Railroad, 345
Canadian Payments Association,
  750n
Canadian Radio and Television
  Commission, 336
Canadian Transport Commission,
  291, 335, 336
Canadian Union of Public
  Employees, 397
Canadian Wheat Board, 115, 121
Canadian Wheat Board Act (1935),
  120
Capacity
  defined, 217–218
  vs. utilization, 910
  utilization level, and innovation,
    240–241
Capital, 197, 585. *See also* Interest
  rate; Money
  acquired, and development,
    940–943
  cost of creating, 951–952

fixed vs. growing stock, 419
human, 414
labor, costs, and, 216
labor, output, and, 210
mobility, 375
and productivity, 234
productivity or efficiency,
  413–418
quality, 919–922
quantity per worker, 919
rate of return on, 413–417
total supply, 373
Capital account, 666–667
  vs. current and official accounts,
    667–668
  and macroeconomic policy,
    841–844
Capital consumption allowance,
  581, 584
Capital deepening, 415, 641
Capital flows, 137
  and crowding-out effect, 846
Capital formation, gross business,
  586–587
*Capitalism, Socialism, and
  Democracy* (Schumpeter), 329
Capitalist economies, 51n
Capitalized value, 418
Capital-output ratio, 640, 918
Capital stock, 415, 581
Capital widening, 416, 641
Carroll, Lewis, 83
Cartel, 310
  OPEC as, 319
Carter, Jimmy, 18, 340, 625,
  699–700
Carter Commission, 13
Cash flow, vs. income flow, A-27
Cash reserve ratio, 753
Caves, Richard, 236
CBC television, 18
Ceiling prices, 100, 102
  and rent controls, 103
Central American Common
  Market, 526
Central authorities. *See*
  Government
Central banks, 760–762. *See also*
  Bank(s); Bank of Canada
  and control of money supply,
    761–766
  exchange rate management,
    142–147
  limits on issue of currency, 709
  open market operations, 762–765

Ceteris Paribus, 68
Chamberlin, Edward, 292
Chamber of Commerce of South-
  eastern Connecticut, 625
Change in demand, 53–54, 73
Change in supply, 54–55, 78
Charities, as decision makers, 51
Chartered banks, 750–753
  central bank as banker to,
    760–761
Chateau Lafite-Rothschild, 190
Chavez, Cesar, 393
Cheating, and producers' associa-
  tion instability, 310–311
Cheques, clearing and collection,
  751
China, population policy, 940
Choice, 7
  and marginal utility, 154
  nonmaximization by, 353–356
  and opportunity cost, 7–8
  and production possibilities, 8–9
Christensen, Sandra, 391
Chrysler Corp., 207, 359, 594
Chung, William K., 924
Circular flow, 55–57
Civil Aeronautics Board (U.S.),
  339
Clark, Joe, 539
Clark, John Bates, 369
Classical portion, aggregate supply
  curve, 573–574
Clearing house, 751
Closed economy, 129, 392
  national income, 582
Closed shop, 392
Coal industry, employment and
  wages, 440, 441
Coase Theorem, 464
Cobb-Douglas production function,
  213
Cobweb, and supply lag, A-18–A-20
Coca-Cola Co., 279
Coefficient of determination, 40
Collective bargaining, 393
  public policy on, 397
Collective consumption goods, and
  market inefficiency, 458
Collusion, tacit, 280
Combines Investigation Act, 332,
  333–334, 538n
Combines laws, 330–334
Command economy, 51–52
Command system, 59–60
Commercial policy, 840n

Commodities
defined, 6–7
primary, and NIEO, 949
and resources, 6–7
in short supply, allocation of,
100–102
Commodities demand, and elasticity
of factor demand, 366
Commodity price stabilization
agreements, and development,
948–949
Common fund, NIEO, 949
Common markets, 526, 533, 738
Common-property resources, and
harmful externalities, 456–457
Common stock, 424
Communist party, 18
Comparative advantage, 131,
506–508
Comparative statics, 80–81
limited usefulness, A-16–A-17
Compassion, as nonmarket goal,
460
Competition. See also Perfect
competition
of few, 296–306
innovation under, 328–329
vs. monopoly, 324–330
public policy on, 331, 332–334
Competitive devaluations, 731
Competitive firm, short-run vs.
long-run equilibrium, A-32
Competitive industries, 290
Competitive labor market
minimum wage in, 401–404
unions in, 386–387
Competitive market
equilibrium exchange rate in,
138–140
factor prices in, 376–382
Competitiveness, and minimum
wage, 404
Complements, and demand curve
shifts, 64
Compliance with government
regulation, costs of, 465
Composition, fallacy of, 571
Comprehensive income taxation,
483
Concentration ratios, 280
in manufacturing, 291–292, 293
Conditional grants, 491–492
Confederation of Canadian Unions,
397
Confederation of National Trade

Unions, 392, 397
Congestion, as harmful externality,
457
Congress of Industrial
Organizations, 390, 396
Conscious parallel action, 280
Consolidated Mining and Smelting
Co., 291
Conspicuous consumption goods,
183
Constant cost(s)
and long-run competitive
equilibrium, A-35–A-36
and long-run industry supply
curve, A-33
Constant-cost industry, A-33
Constant dollar GNP, 562, 589
Constant dollars, 589
Constant elasticity, and demand
curve, 91
Constant returns, 225
Consumer and Corporate Affairs
Department, 333, 334
Consumer Association of Canada,
118
Consumer information, product
quality, and demand, 184–185
Consumerism, 347–348
Consumer Price Index (CPI), 33,
561
and cost-of-living allowances,
818–819
in 1970s, 689
Consumer prices and turnover tax,
Soviet Union, 945
Consumers' surplus
and allocative efficiency, 267
and utility, 162–164
Consumption, 580
defined, 7
desired expenditure, 597–602
and disposable income, 597–599,
630–631
energy, 535–537
of goods and services, 9
and national income, 600–602,
630–632
Consumption and saving schedules,
601
Consumption expenditure, 580–581,
A-39
Consumption function, 597
long-term, 600
and saving function, 599
Consumption possibility set,

128–129
expansion through trade,
129–131
Consumption quantity, goods and
services, 10
Continental Pen Co., 314
Contractionist monetary policy,
795–796
Contributed capital, and
development, 941–943
Control. See also Rent control;
Wage and price controls
of aggregate demand and
inflation, 876
and development in LDCs,
937–939
of firm, 348–351
of government by firm, 347
of inflation, 817, 876, 879–887
of monetary aggregates, 852–853
of money supply, 761–766
of national income through
monetary policy, 788–789
of resource allocation, 124–125
separation of ownership from,
350–352
of unemployment, 804–805
Control of entry, and haircut
prices, 312–314
Cooperative Commonwealth
Federation, 396
Coordinate graph, A-6
Corn Laws (England), 524
Corporate income tax
and prices, 487
unknown progressivity, 479
Corporation, 193, 194–195
financing, 423
profits, 584
Cost. See also Inflation, Marginal
cost; Opportunity cost;
Production costs
administration, and many interest
rates, 422–423
of buying house on time, 638
capital, labor, and, 216
of creating capital, controversy
over, 951–952
and factor prices, 231
of government attempts to
correct market failure,
463–466
of growth, 913–916
and long-run equilibrium, 259,
A-30–A-31

Cost (*Continued*)
  long-run vs. short-run, 225–226
  and market structure, 326–328
  minimization in long run, 221–222
  of money, 201
  and monopolization of competitive industry, 326
  and natural monopoly regulation, 336–337
  and perfect competition, 268
  of production, and exchange rates, 141
  and profit to firm, 197–204
  purpose of assigning, 199
  and quantity produced, 325–326
  and resource allocation, 123
  and returns, 223–225
  short-run variations, 214–218
Cost curves
  long-run, 223–225
  shifts, 226–227
  short-run, 216–217
Cost effectiveness of government programs, 498–499
Cost minimization, and isoquants, 229–230
Cost-of-living allowances, and consumer price index, 818–819
Council of Economic Advisers (U.S.), 13, 339
Countercyclical expenditures, 642
Cournot, A. A., 297
Cournot-Nash equilibrium, 297–298
Coyne, James, 860
Craft union, 389–390
Credit, terms, and consumption, 631
Credit cards, 751–752
Credit rationing, 420
Crosbie, John, 539
Cross-classification table, 40, 41
Cross elasticity of demand, 94, 179
Cross-sectional data, A-6
Cross-subsidization, 338
Crowding-out effect, 891
  and capital flows, 846
Cultural barriers to development, 935
Cumulative movements, business cycle, 644–646
Currency, limits on issue by central bank, 709

Currency drains, banks, 759–760
Current account, 665–666
  balance of payments, 660–661
  vs. capital and official accounts, 667–668
  and domestic policy objectives, 837–840
  and expenditure-changing vs. expenditure-switching policies, 840
  inflation, PPP exchange rate, and, 838–839
  and macroeconomic policy, 836–837
Current dollar GNP, 562, 589
Current dollars, 589
Current income, and permanent income, A-40–A-41
Curves, movement along vs. shifts of, 610–612
Cycles. *See* Business cycles; Cyclical fluctuations
Cyclical fluctuations
  agricultural prices and incomes, 112–114
  causes, 888–890
  and government, 642

Dacca, Bangladesh, pedicabs in, 245
Data analysis, in testing economic theories, 39–41
Day-to-day loans, 761
DDT, as harmful externality, 457
Debt, 423
  renegotiation and forgiveness, and NIEO, 950
Decision, to accept or reject hypothesis, 43
Decision makers
  central authorities as, 50–51
  firms as, 50
  households as, 48–50
  objectives, and government failure, 467
Decision making
  and economic system, 59–60
  market, 452–453
  time horizons for, 208–210
Declining competitive industry, demand in, 261–264
Declining costs, and long-run competitive equilibrium, A-35

Decreasing costs, and returns, 223–224
Decreasing long-run costs, and long-run industry supply curve, A-34–A-35
Decreasing returns, 225
Decumulation of inventory, 581
Deduction and measurement, interaction, 28
De facto dollar standard, 738
Deficient-demand unemployment, 803
Deficit, in balance of trade, 650
Deflationary gap, 621–624
  and current account, 838–839
  and fiscal policy, 675–676
De jure floating exchange rate, 145
Demand. *See also* Factor demand; Supply
  agriculture, 111
  change in, 53–54, 73
  cross elasticities of, 179
  declining competitive industry, 261–264
  for dollars, 137
  firm manipulation of, 344–345
  for government services, 498
  and identification problem, 180–181
  income elasticities of, 178–179
  and innovation, 241–242
  and labor earnings, 439–441
  law of, 80–81
  long-run responses to changes in, A-31–A-32
  measurement, 177–181
  and price, 68–69, 78–83; of gasoline, 318, 319
  price elasticities, 177–178
  product quality, consumer information, and, 184–185
  and quantity demanded, 67–68
  for rental housing, 107
  and rent controls, 108
  shift, and supply lag, A-17–A-18
  theory of, 66–67
  and wheat production, 122, 123
Demand curve
  and constant elasticity, 91
  and demand schedule, 69–73
  derivation, A-21–A-22
  for dollars, 137
  and elasticity, 253, A-12–A-13
  for factor, 365–366

firm vs. market, 250
household, 158–159; vs. market, 153
perfectly competitive firm, 253–254
perfectly inelastic, 183, 186
shape, 87
shifts, 70–73; vs. movements along, 72–73
slope, A-22–A-24
straight-line, elasticity along, 90
Demand deposit, 710–711, 749
Demand elasticity, 86–94
defined, 89
determinants, 92
for factors, 366–369
and farm prices, 112, 113
firm vs. market, 252
monopolist, 273–274
and price elasticity, 88–92, 177–178
and total utility, 159–160
Demand for additional capital, by firm, 418–419
Demand for money, 720, 721.
See also Demand; Money
and aggregate demand, 721–723
and cyclical fluctuations, 890
defined, 769
determinants, 770–778
excess, 774–775
and interest rates, 420, 772–773
and money supply, 768–774
Demand inflation, and inflation-unemployment trade-offs of 1960s, 859–861
Demand-pull inflation, 812
Demand schedule, and demand curve, 69–73
Demand theory
criticisms, 181–188
and national household decision making, 181–182
and predictions of what can happen, 182–188
Denison, E. F., 923, 924
Depletion allowance, 555–556
Deposit, and bank reserve ratio, 754
Deposit money, 710–711
Depreciation, 135, 201–202, 414, 581
Depression
and aggregate supply curve, 568

business cycle, 644
Derived demand, 365
Desired expenditure, 595–604
aggregate, 602–604
consumption, 597–602
shifts in function, 612–616
Determination
coefficient of, 40
of interest rates, 418–423
Devaluation
analysis of, 656–657
competitive, 731
of currency, 143
and full employment, 663
and unemployment, 662
of U.S. dollar, 737–738, 740–741
Development. See also Economic growth
agricultural, 944–946
alternative strategies, 943–951
barriers to, 931–936
and capital acquisition, 940–943
choices in LDCs, 937–943
and commodity price stabilization agreements, 948–949
and education, 939
and government control, 937–939
and human resources, 934
by import substitution industrialization, 946–947
incentives for, 930–931
and industrialization for export, 947–948
and inefficiency in resource use, 933–934
and natural resources, 932–933
and New International Economic Order (NIEO), 949–951
pace of, 951
and population growth, 931–932
and population policy, 939–940
and specialization in few commodities, 946
uneven pattern, 928–931
Development gap, 929
Differentials, in factor prices, 377–378
Differentiated product, 293
and oligopolistic behavior, 298
Diminishing marginal rate of substitution, 170
Diminishing marginal utility,

hypothesis of, 154–155
Diminishing returns, 212–213
vs. decreasing returns, 225n
Direct costs, 215
Direct external costs of government attempts to control market failure, 465–466
Direct investment, 667
Dirty float, 739–740, 852, 853, 862–863
Discount rate, 765
Discretionary fiscal policy, 682–685
Discrimination, in labor market, 404–409
Disembodied technical change, 922
Disequilibrium, 80
market's self-correction of, 454
and net investment, 640
Disequilibrium price, 80
Disincentive effects of war on poverty, 435
Disinvestment, in inventory, 581
Disposable income, 586–587.
See also Income
and consumption, 597–599, 630–631
and national income, 601, 631–632
per capita, 590
Dissaving, 598
Distributed profits, 585
Distribution of income, 362–365.
See also National income distribution
Disutility, marginal, 156
Dividends, 194
Division of labor, 213–214
Adam Smith on, 49
and factor services, 47–48
Dollar(s) (Canadian). See also Dollar(s) (U.S.); Exchange rate; Interest rate; Money
demand for, 137
exchange rate, 147–149
slide, 1977-1978, 850–851
supply of, 138
Dollar(s) (U.S.)
devaluation, 737–738, 740–741
as reserve currency, 740–743
speculation against, 736–737
Dollar standard, 738
Domestic absorption, 658
and net exports, 658–661

Domestic prices, and net export function, 654
Domestic saving, and development, 940–941
Donner Foundation, 51
Doomsday predictions, 925–926
Double counting, 579–580, 771n
Double taxation, of corporate income, 195
Downward rigidity, wages and prices, 573
Dumping, and price discrimination, 282–283
Duopoly, 297
Du Pont, 84
Durable goods, 586
  housing as, 103
Duration, and many interest rates, 422
Dynamic analysis, 112n
Dynamic differentials, factor prices, 377
Dynamics, A-17
  and price system, A-20

Earnings, labor, and market conditions, 438–441
East African Community, 526
East India Co., 195
Eastman, Harry, 302
Eastman-Stykolt hypothesis, MES, and industry rationalization, 302–303
Eaton (T.) Co., 348
Economic analysis, and economic policy, 12–15
Economic Council of Canada, 5, 13, 333, 618, 621, 688
Economic development.
  See Development; Economic growth
Economic efficiency
  of firm, 197
  vs. technological, 198
Economic growth. See also Development
  arguments pro and con, 912, 914
  benefits, 911–913
  costs, 913–916
  cumulative nature, 910–911
  defined, 908–910
  and innovation, 240
  in Japan, 924
  as policy goal, 916

and production possibility boundary, 11
  in world with and without learning, 917–918
Economic observations, graphing, A-5–A-8
Economic policy
  and economic analysis, 12–15
  economists' roles in, 12–15
  regional and factor earnings, 443–446
Economic problems
  classification, 9–12
  defined, 6
  energy, 3–4
  growth, 4–5
  inflation, 3
  pollution, 5
  poverty, 5–6
  productivity, 4–5
  unemployment, 3
  wealth, 5–6
Economic profits, 203, 414
Economic relations
  evaluating evidence, 42–43
  measurement and testing, 36–43
Economic rent, and transfer earnings, 378–380
Economics
  defined, 6, 12
  as developing science, 29
  of Great Depression, 855–856
  and positive vs. normative statements, 22
  progress of, 898
  and scientific approach, 22–23
  of superstar salaries, 370
  supply-side, 886–887
Economic series, 628–629
Economic systems
  differences, 58–60
  and ends and means, 61–62
  and incentive systems, 61
  and values, 60–61
Economic theory
  firm in, 195–197
  statistical testing, 38–42
Economies of scale, 327, 509
Economies of scope, 327
Economists
  balance sheet and income statement, A-28–A-29

disagreement among, 16–17
  roles in economic policy, 12–15
Economy. See also Business cycles; Development; Economic growth; Fiscal policy; Monetary policy
  Canadian, 290–296
  and circular flow, 55–57
  decision makers, 48–51
  fine tuning, 677–678
  government's role in, 6
  implications of PIH and LCH for behavior of, A-41–A-42
  interdependent, 451
  and interest rates, 419–420
  market, 46–48
  and markets, 51–55
  and poverty, 5–6, 434
  and principle of substitution, 222–223
  real and money parts of, 712–713
  sectors, 52
  of Soviet Union, 936–937
Eddy Match Co., 291
Edsel automobile, 84
Education and development, LDC, 939
Efficiency
  capital, 413–418
  and income distribution, 493
  and perfect competition, 264–268
Effluent charge, 462
Elasticity
  and demand curve, A-12–A-13
  of factor demand, 366–367
  point, A-11–A-15
  and supply curve, A-14
  terminology, 93
Elasticity of demand. See Demand elasticity
Embargo, OPEC, 316–319
Embodied technical change, 921
Employers' association, as potential monopsonist, 389
Employment, 564, 565. See also Full employment; Labor; Labor market; Unemployment; Union(s); Wage(s)
  and discrimination, 405–407
  and minimum wages, 401–404
  opportunities, 436
  and output, 566–567

post-WWII, 860
and protectionism, 520–521
and unemployment in 1970s,
806–807
vs. wages, 400
Employment and Income, 857
Encyclopedia of Social Sciences,
808
Endogenous variables, 26
Ends, and economic systems,
61–62
Energy
debate on price parity, 542–553
as economic problem, 3–4
export taxes, production royalties, and profits taxes,
546–547
international developments, 537
National Energy Program,
553–557
opportunity cost of nonrenewable
resource, 544
policy alternatives, 320–321
prices, domestic vs. international,
537–540
production and consumption,
535–537
two-price system, 535, 540–542
Energy self-sufficiency, 535
Energy substitution, and
productivity, 234
The Engineers and the Price
System (Veblen), 206
England, prices, seven centuries,
715–716
Entry and exit, and long-run
equilibrium in perfect
competition, 257–259
Envelope curve, 226
Equalization payments, 491
Equal net advantage, hypothesis of,
374
Equilibrium
allocative and productive
efficiency of market in,
453–454
firm, when industry is in
long-run equilibrium, A-31
firm and industry, monopoly,
275–276
of household, 156–158,
171–172
of monopolistically competitive
firm, 294

Equilibrium condition, 80, 604
Equilibrium differentials, factor
prices, 377–378
Equilibrium national income,
604–606, 658
and aggregate expenditure, 603
and price level, 782
Equilibrium price, 78–80
agricultural price supports at,
115–116
and demand and supply, 78
short-run, 256–257
Equity capital, 423
Error
normal curve, and law of large
numbers, 24
statistical, control of, 43
Error terms, in economic hypotheses, A-3–A-4
Established programs financing,
492
Europe, wage and price controls
in, 870
European Common Market, 526,
533
joint float, 738
European Economic Community,
526
Evaluation of evidence, 42–43
Eventually diminishing average
productivity, hypothesis of,
217
Ever-normal granary, 115
Evidence, evaluating, 42–43
Evolutionary theories of firm,
356–357
Excess capacity, 217–218
Excess capacity theorem, 294–295
Excess cash reserves, 753
Excess demand, 78
for money, 774–775
and wage and price controls,
858
Excess reserves, bank, 759
Excess supply, 78
Exchange rate, 133–135. See also
Balance of payments;
Money supply
Canadian dollar, 147
central bank management of,
142–147
change in, 135–136, 140–141
defined, 132
determination, 136–138

equilibrium, in competitive
market, 138–140
fixed vs. floating, 147
and inflation, 141–142
management of, 745–746
multilateral, 139
and national pride, 148
and net export function, 654–655
Excise tax, regressivity, 479
Exclusive dealing, as restrictive
trade practice, 334
Execution lag, 683
monetary policy, 788–789
Exogenous variables, 26
Expansion, business cycle, 644
Expansionist monetary policy, 795
Expectation(s)
adaptive vs. rational, 816
and consumption, 630–631
self-realizing, 426–428
Expectational inflation, 814–815
Expenditure(s), 580–582
direct money balance effect on,
572
and fiscal policy, 675–677
value of, 579
Expenditure-changing policies,
840, 842
Expenditure-switching policies,
840, 842
Exploitation doctrine, 518
Export(s), 128. See also Exchange
rates and Canadian dollar
slide, 851
by commodity, 521
determination, 131–132
and GNP, 651
industrialization for, 947–948
and national income, 632
and protectionism, 519–521
Export-Import Bank, 943
Export market, and import, 141
Export multiplier, 652
Export tax, energy, 540, 541–542
vs. royalties, 546–547
External balance
and capital account, 843–844
of trade, 662–663
External costs, of government
attempts to control market
failure, 465–466
Externalities
and Coase Theorem, 464
consequence and correction, 463

Externalities (*Continued*)
  and government activities,
    494–495
  and market inefficiency, 455–458
  and perfect competition, 268
External terms of trade, and
  devaluation, 657
Extraterritoriality, 529

Face value, money, 705
Factor. *See also* Capital; Labor;
  Land; Production factors
  response to change in earnings,
    441–446
Factor demand, 365–369
  derivation, A-37–A-38
  elasticity, 366–367
Factor demand curve, profit-
  maximizing firm, A-37–A-38
Factor earnings
  and market conditions, 438–441
  and regional economic policy,
    443–446
Factor immobility, as market
  impediment, 458
Factor markets, 51
Factor mobility, 374–376
Factor payments, division between
  rents and transfer earnings,
    379–380
Factor payments approach to
  national income, 584–585
Factor prices
  in competitive markets, 376–382
  and cost, 231
  and cost curves, 226
  theory, 364
Factor pricing, Soviet, 944–945
Factor services, and division of
  labor, 47–48
Factor supply, 369–376
Fallacy of composition, 571
Fall in demand, 73
Falling-cost industry, A-35
Family Weekly, 927
Federal Business Development
  Bank, 424
Federal Reserve System (U.S.),
  760, 761
Federation, 392
Fellner, William, 299
Female-male differentials, in labor
  market, 407–409
Ferber, Robert, 179

Fiat money, 708–710
Final products, 580
Finance Department, 17
Financial institutions
  as development barrier, 934–935
  loans from, 424
Financial Post, 700
Financing, of corporation, 423
Fine tuning, 677–678
  and execution lags in monetary
    policy, 789
Firm. *See also* Perfectly competitive
  firm behavior, and market
    structure, 248–251
  control of, 348–351
  cost and profit to, 197–204
  decision making, 50, 208–210
  in declining industry, government
    support for, 262–263
  demand for additional capital,
    418–419
  in economic theory, 195–197
  equilibrium, when industry is in
    long-run equilibrium, A-31
  evolutionary theories, 356–357
  goals, and supply curve shifts, 77
  input decisions, 227–232
  intercorporate control groups,
    349–350
  labor-managed, 354–355
  and manipulation of market,
    344–348
  measurement of opportunity
    cost, 199–203
  nonmaximizing theories, 352–357
  and profits, 357–358
  real choices open to, 208–210
  short-run choices, 210–218
  U-shaped cost curve, A-35–A-36
Firm-created barriers to entry,
  oligopoly, 301–304
Fiscal Arrangements Act (1977),
  491, 492
Fiscal conservatism, 697
Fiscal drag, 682
  and 1964 U.S. tax cuts, 680–681
Fiscal policy, 673–674. *See also*
  Economy; Monetary policy
  in action, 684–698
  and budget balance, 674–675
  built-in stabilizers, 678–682
  and capital account, 843–844
  and cyclical fluctuations,
    890–894

  and exchange rates, 845–846
  Great Depression, 686–687
  and IS curve, A-45
  monetarist and neo-Keynesian
    views on, 893
  and national debt, 694–698
  post-WWII, 688–692
  and private expenditures,
    675–678
  relative effectiveness, A-49–A-51
  stance, 686
  theory, 674–678
  tools, 678–685
  U.S., 680–681
Fisher, Irving, 165n, 429
Five-year plans, Soviet, 944
Fixed capital, 586
Fixed costs, 215
Fixed exchange rates, 143, 729,
  732–739
  and macroeconomic policy,
    844–845
Fixed factors, 209
Fixed stock of capital, 419
Fixed-weight price index, 35
Flat Earth Society, 18
Flanagan, Robert, 870
Flexible exchange rates, 142
  Canadian experience with,
    847–853
  and macroeconomic policy,
    845–853
Floating exchange rates, 142
  de jure vs. *de facto,* 145
  and IMF, 740
  in 1970s, 861–863
Flow of purchases, quantity
  demanded as, 67
Flow variables, 26
Fluctuating exchange rates, 731–732
Fluctuations. *See* Business cycles
Ford, Gerald, 700
Ford Motor Co., 207, 348, 359,
  461, 594
Foreign exchange, 134
Foreign goods, substitution, and
  aggregate demand curve
  shape, 572
Foreign income, and net export
  function, 654, 655
Foreign investment, and R&D
  expenditure, 236–237
Foreign Investment Review Act
  (1973), 530

Foreign ownership, 527–530
  and oil price parity, 547–548
Foreign prices, and net export
  function, 654
Forrester, Jay, 923
Forsey, Eugene, 396
Fortin, Pierre, 806
Fortune, 314
450° line, 599
Fourier, Charles, 354
Fourth world, 948n
Fractionally backed paper money,
  707–708
Freedom of entry and exit, 251
Free exchange rate, 142
Free good, and utility, 162
Free market, and energy policy,
  320
Free-market economy, 51
Free-market prices and profits, and
  resource allocation, 123–124
Free trade, 512
  fallacious arguments, 518
  vs. protectionism, 514–516
Frictional unemployment, 802
Friedman, Milton, 6, 103, 323,
  685, 825, 863, 888, 895, A-39
Fringe benefits, vs. wages, 400–
  401
Full-cost pricing, 353
Full employment. *See also*
  Employment; Labor;
  Unemployment
  and aggregate supply curve,
  568
  and devaluation, 663
  and inflation of 1940s, 856–857
  and national income, 622–623
  1950s goal, 857–859
  and relatively stable prices, 858
  and trade balance, 839–840
  unemployment level at, 899–900
Full-employment GNP, 563
Full-employment income, and
  national income, 823–824
Full-employment surplus, 686
Function(s), 27
  graphing, A-8–A-10
  of three variables, A-10
Functional distribution of income,
  363
Functional forms, A-3
Functional relations, 27, A-2–A-3
Fundamental disequilibria, 735

Funding organizations, as decision
  makers, 51
Future effects of present actions,
  457
Future returns, present value of,
  416–417

Gains from trade, 505, 666
  graphic representation, 510–511
Galbraith, John Kenneth, 6, 344,
  345, 499, 700
Gandhi, Indira, 940
Gap. *See* Deflationary gap;
  Inflationary gap
Garner, James, 384
Gasoline prices, and OPEC,
  315–320
General Agreement on Tariffs and
  Trade (GATT), 524–526
General Motors Corp., 207, 359
General Motors of Canada, 345
General partnership, 193–194
*The General Theory of Employ-
  ment, Interest, and Money*
  (Keynes), 623, 901
Genevra de' Benci (Leonardo),
  175
George, Henry, 381
George V, King, 616
Giffen, Sir Robert, 182
Giffen good, 182–183, A-22,
  A-24
Gillespie, Erwin, 480
Given period price index, 33
Global maximizer, firm as, 352
GNE deflator, 33, 561, 589n
GNP gap, 564, 622. *See also* Gross
  national product (GNP)
Goals of firm, and supply curve
  shifts, 77
Gold. *See also* Exchange rates
  prices, 742
  reserves, and adjustable peg,
  733–734
Gold exchange standard, 732
Gold standard, 707
  in actuality, 730–731
  in theory, 729–730
Gompers, Samuel, 395
Goods
  defined, 7
  Giffen, 182–183, A-22, A-24
  Soviet distribution of, 936
Goods and services

government expenditure on,
  489–490, 581
government purchases of, 587
Goodyear Tire and Rubber Co.,
  475
Gordon, Walter, 529, 530
Government. *See also* Canada;
  Central banks; Fiscal policy;
  Government expenditure;
  Monetary policy; National
  income; Transfer payments
  agricultural policy, 118–121
  agricultural price supports at and
  above equilibrium, 115–117
  central bank as banker to, 761
  and combines laws, 330–334
  control, and development in
  LDCs, 937–939
  current role, 500–501
  and cyclical fluctuations, 642
  as decision maker, 50–51
  demand for services, 498
  economic role, 6
  evaluation of role, 498–501
  expenditures, 487–490
  failure, 466–468
  firm's control of, 347
  oil export tax and import subsidy
  impact on revenue and outlays,
  542
  policies on foreign ownership,
  529–530
  public utility regulation, 334–340
  purchases of goods and services,
  587
  response to market failure,
  460–466, 468–473
  stabilization of farmers'
  revenues by open market
  purchases and sales, 116
  support of firms in declining
  competitive industry, 262–263
  tax revenue by source, 478
Government expenditure. *See also*
  Economy; Government
  as built-in stabilizer, 679
  desired, 602
  and fiscal policy, 679
  on goods and services, 581;
  and cyclical fluctuations, 642
  relative shares, 495
  and resource allocation,
  494–498
  vs. tax rates, 683

Government intervention
  to correct market failure,
    468–471
  New England vs. Atlantic
    Provinces, 472–473
Grants, conditional, 491–492
Graph
  scatter diagram, A-5–A-7
  time-series, A-7
Graphing
  of economic observations,
    A-5–A-8
  functions, A-8–A-10
Gray Report, 530
Grayson, Jackson, 868n
Great Atlantic and Pacific Tea Co.,
  348
Great Britain
  economic system, 59
  wage and price controls in,
    870–871
Great Depression
  economics of, 855–856
  fiscal policy, 686–687
  and fluctuating exchange rates,
    731–732
Greece, development strategy, 943
Green revolution, 945–946
Gresham, Sir Thomas, 706
Gresham's law, 706
Gross business capital formation,
  586–587
Gross investment, 581
Gross national expenditure implicit
  price index. See GNE deflator
Gross national product (GNP), 562,
  563, 583
  Canada vs. U.S., 653
  changes, 633
  in current and constant dollars,
    589
  exports, imports, and, 651
  in Great Depression, 687
  and national debt, 695
  and R&D expenditure, 236
  WWII, 688
Gross private investment, 636
Gross return on capital, 414
Group behavior, vs. individual, 23
Growing stock of capital, 419
Growth
  contemporary view, 919–923
  costs of, 913–916
  as economic problem, 4–5

limits, 923–926
sources, 923
Grubel, H. W., 120
Gulf Oil Corp., 288
Gunderson, Morely, 390

Haircut prices, and control of
  entry, 312–314
Hall, Robert, 353
Hammer, Armand, 175
Hansen, Alvin, 629
Hardcrust, Homer, 625
Harmful, externalities, 456–457
Harrod, Sir Roy, 261
Hawtrey, R. G., 888n
Health care, political economy of,
  496–497
Health services, 437
Helliwell, John, 551n
Hersy, Robert T., Jr., 835
Hicks, Sir John R., 165, A-44
Higher education, subsidy for, 488
Hitch, Charles, 353
Hobbes, Thomas, 46
Hollister, Donald, 323
Homogeneous product, 293
  and oligopolistic behavior,
    297–298
Hospital insurance, 436–437
Hours worked, and total supply of
  labor, 371
Household
  average income, and demand
    curve shifts, 71
  choice, and budget line, 165–168
  consumption, and price index, 34
  demand curve, 158–159; vs.
    market, 153
  as economic decision maker,
    48–50
  equilibrium, 156–158, 171–172
  income, and quantity demanded,
    186–187
  rational decision making, and
    demand theory, 181–182
  Soviet incentives, 937
Housing
  construction, 646–647;
    investment in, 637
  cost of buying on time, 683
  market, special aspects, 103
  shortages, and rent control,
    107–108
  supply, and rent, 106

Hudson's Bay Co., 195
Human capital, 414
Human resources, and economic
  development, 934
Human welfare, omission from
  national income, 591–592
Hume, David, 504
Hunting and gathering society,
  46–47
Hyperinflation, 718
Hypotheses, 82
  proving true or false, 42
  and theory, 25, 27

IBM Corp., 524
Identification, and demand,
  180–181
Ideology, and government
  intervention, 471
Ignorance, nonmaximization due
  to, 352–353
Illegal activities, omission from
  national income, 590–591
Impediments, and inefficiency,
  market, 458–459
Imperfect competition, and
  structure of Canadian
  economy, 290–296
Imperfections, and inefficiency,
  market, 458–459
Imperial Oil Co., 291, 345
Imperial Tobacco Co., 291
Import(s), 128. See also Exchange
  rates
  and aggregate expenditure,
    613–614
  determination, 132–133
  by end use, 522
  and export multiplier, 652
  and GNP, 651
  and protectionism, 519–520
Import cost-push inflation,
  813–814
Imported capital, and development,
  941
Import market, and export, 141
Import subsidy, oil, 540–542
Import substitution industrialization, and development,
  946–947
Import substitution industry, 947
Imputed costs, 201–203
Incentives, structuring, 462
Incentive systems, 61

Income. *See also* Disposable income; Income distribution; National income
  average household, and demand curve shifts, 71
  policies, 882
  and population, by country, 929
  and quantity demanded, 95
Income-consumption curve, 95
Income-consumption line, 172, 173
Income distribution. *See also* Income; Income redistribution
  and consumption, 631
  and demand curve shifts, 72
  and efficiency, 493
  family, 363
  national, 365–382
  personal, and oil price parity, 548
  and poverty, 431–437
  relevance of theory, 437–446
Income effect, 164n
  vs. substitution effect, A-22–A-24
Income-elastic, 94n
Income elasticity of demand, 92, 94, 178–179
Income flow, vs. cash flow, A-27
Income-inelastic, 94n
Income redistribution, 495. *See also* Income; Income distribution
  and growth, 911–913
  intergovernmental transfer payments as, 490–494
  and public expenditures, 490–494
  and tax policy, 483–484
Income statements, A-25–A-29
Income tax
  inflation indexing, 690–691
  progressivity, 479–482
  structural changes, 482–483
Income Tax Act (1972), 479n
Increase in demand, 77
Increasing costs
  and long-run industry supply curve, A-33–A-34
  and returns, 224–225
Increasing returns, 223–224
Incremental cost, 216
Incremental product, 211
Indexing, of money values, 166
Index numbers, 32–33

accuracy and significance, 36
  of physical outputs, 35
  of prices, 33–35
Index of Real Domestic Product in Manufacturing, 35
Indifference curve
  analysis, 165
  derivation from demand curve, A-21–A-24
  and household satisfaction, 171, 172
Indifference map, 170–171
Indirect external costs of government attempts to control market failure, 466
Indirect taxes, 584
Individual(s)
  behavior, vs. group behavior, 23
  consumers' surplus, 164
  federal transfer payments to, 490
  protecting from acts of others, 459
  protecting from themselves, 459–460
Induced components, aggregate expenditure, 604
Induced variable, 26
Industrialization
  for export, and development, 947–948
  import substitution, 946–947
Industrial union, 390
Industry
  foreign ownership, 527–530
  groupings, 290–291
  long-run supply curve, A-32–A-35
  rationalization, MES, and Eastman-Stykolt hypothesis, 302–303
Inefficiency
  and externalities, market, 455–458
  and market imperfections and impediments, 458–459
  monopoly, 276–278
  in resource use, 933–934
Inelastic demand, 90
Inertial inflation, 815–816
Infant industry argument, 516
Inferior goods, 92
Infinite elasticity, and demand curve, 91
Inflation. *See also* Economy
  actual vs. expected, 828–829

and aggregate demand, 812, 876
annual rate, 562
causes, 809–812, 879–880
control, 817, 876, 879–887
current account, PPP exchange rate, and, 838–839
and debasing of coinage, 706
defined, 808
demand-pull, 812
demand-supply, 814–817
as economic problem, 3
and exchange rate, 141–142
expectational, 814–815
experience of, 818–820
and fiscal restraint, 692
foreign, 144–145
and full employment of 1940s, 856–857
full employment without, 857–859
in housing costs, and rent controls, 108
import cost-push, 813–814
inertial, 815–816
and interest rates, 421
monetarist cures, 881–882
and money supply, 791
neo-Keynesian cures, 882–883
in 1970s, 861–864
perceptions of, 810–811
policymaker concern, 808–809
post-Keynesian cures, 884–886
post-WWII, 860
and price level, 561
price-push, 813
and price theory, 82–83
and purchasing power, 11
significance, 715–719
structural rigidity, 814
supply-side, 812–814
target rate, 880–881
and total supply of labor, 372
and unemployment, 820–833
unvalidated demand, 823–824
validated demand, 824–825
Vietnam, and 1968 U.S. tax surcharges, 681
wage cost-push, 813
Inflationary gap, 621–624
  and current account, 838–839
  and fiscal policy, 675–676
  persistent, 785–786
  and price level, 782, 784

Inflation indexing, income taxes, 690–691

Inflation unemployment cycle, 831–833

Inflation-unemployment trade-offs, and demand inflation of 1960s, 859–861

Infrastructure, as development barrier, 934

Innis, Harold, 331, 521

Innovation
incentives, 328–330; and disincentives, 240–242
and invention, 235

Inputs, 196–197

Institute for Policy Analysis, University of Toronto, 619

Institution(s), labor market, 389–393

Institutional climate, and innovation, 242

Intercorporate control groups, 349–350

Interest, 200, 585

Interest income, 584

Interest rate, 200. *See also* Bank(s); Exchange rates; Money
and aggregate demand curve shape, 572
and aggregate expenditure, 776, 777, A-44–A-45
bank administration of, 420
vs. base control, 793
and bond price, 769–770
and business fixed investment, 683
control, 787
and demand for money, 420, 772–773
determination, 418–423
and inventory, 635
many, 422–423
and monetary disequilibrium, 774–776
as monetary policy target variable, 791–796
vs. money supply, 789–791
and mortgage, 638
and national income, macroeconomic equilibrium determination, A-46–A-47

Interest sensitive expenditure, 776n

Interest sensitivities, monetarist and neo-Keynesian views on, 891

Intermediate portion, aggregate supply curve, 574

Intermediate products, 580

Intermediate targets, 786, 787–788

Internal balance of trade, 662–663

Internal costs of government attempts to correct market failure, 465

Internalization, 462

Internal terms of trade, and devaluation, 656–657

International Monetary Fund, 733
and floating exchange rates, 740

International monetary systems
Bretton Woods, 732–739
challenge for 1980s, 745–746
current, 739–745
pre-WWII, 729–732

International Nickel Co., 291, 345

International reserve currency, 745

International Telephone and Telegraph Corp., 351

International trade, 128–129. *See also* Exchange rates
Canadian policy, 521–530
and expansion of consumption possibility set, 129–131
gains from, 505–512
imports and exports determination, 131–133
and protectionism, 512–521
and quantity consumed, 10

Intervention
as energy policy, 321
government, 466–473

Invention, and productivity, 235–240

Inventory, 581
investment in, 635

Inventory cycle, 630, 646

Investment, 581. *See also* Capital; Economic growth
accelerator theory, 640–642
business fixed, 637–640
desired expenditure, 602
and economic system, 59
foreign, and R&D expenditure, 236–237
fund sources, 423–428
in housing, 638

and inventories, 635
and national income, 632–642
in residential construction, 637
short-run and long-run effects, 909

Investment expenditure, 581
and cyclical fluctuation, 890
and price level, 782

Investment goods, 581

Investment income, miscellaneous, 584

Investment opportunities and growth, 918, 919

Invisibles, 665

Irving (K.C.) Limited, 333

IS curve, A-44–A-45
shape, A-49–A-51

Isocost line, 165–166, 229–230

Isoquant(s), 227–230
and principle of substitution, 230–232

Isoquant map, 228–229

Japan
development strategy, 943–944
growth case study, 924

Job security vs. wages, 400

Johnson, George, 408

Johnson, Harry, 237, 517, 862, 871

Johnson, Leland, 337

Joint Economic Committee of the Congress (U.S.), 905

Juno (Rembrandt), 175

Jurisdictional disputes, 391–392

Kahn, David, 314

Kahn, Fred, 877

Kaiser, Henry, 296

Kennedy Round, GATT, 525

Kenya Meat Commission (KMC), 127

Kessel, Reuben, 341

Keyfitz, Nathan, 924

Keynes, John Maynard, 16, 568, 598n, 623, 901

Keynesian model, devaluation, 657

Keynesian portion, aggregate supply curve, 573

Keynesian view, national debt, 697. *See also* Monetarists; Neo-Keynesians

Khalid, King of Saudi Arabia, 18

Khan, Abdul, 245

Killingsworth, Charles, 16

Kinked aggregate demand curve, 783–784
Kinked aggregate supply curve, 621
Kinked demand curve, 305
Knights of Labor, 395, 396
Komoto, Minister, 323
Koppang, Bob, 175
Kosher King Meat Products, 175

Labor, 197, 584. *See also* Employment; Full employment; Labor market; Production factors; Unemployment; Union; Wage(s)
  capital, costs, and, 216
  capital, output, and, 210
  division, and factor services, 47–48
  earnings, and market conditions, 438–441
  foreign, and protectionism, 518–519
  mobility, 375–376
  and productivity, 234–235
  quality, 922
  quantity, 922–923
  quantity of capital per worker, 919
  response to changes in earnings, 442–443
  restricting supply to increase wages, 398–399
  specialization, in market economy, 47
  total supply, 371–372
  variables, 564–566
Laboratory sciences, in testing theories, 37
Labor force, 371, 564–566
Labor-managed firms, 354–355
Labor market. *See also* Labor
  competitive, with union, 386–387
  discrimination in, 404–409
  female-male differentials, 407–409
  institutions, 389–393
  monopoly elements, and earnings, 440–441
  monopsonistic, without union, 387–388
  monopsonistic, with union, 388–389
Labor union. *See* Union
Laffer, Arthur, 481

Laffer curve, 481
Lag, in adjustment of supply, A-17–A-20
Laissez faire, 454
  and development, LDCs, 938–939
Laker, Sir Freddie, 183, 186, 347
Lalonde, Marc, 553
Land, 197, 584. *See also* Production factors
  arable, total supply, 372–373
  earnings, and market conditions, 438
  mobility, 374–375
  response to changes in earnings, 441
  urban, values and taxes, 380–381
Landlords, share of property tax, 485–486
Landon, Alfred, 45
Large numbers, law of, 24
Law(s), 82. *See also* Regulation
  of diminishing returns, 212–214
  of large numbers, 24
LDCs. *See* Development; Economic growth
Learning by doing, 509
Legal tender, 708
Leibenstein, Harvey, 933
Leisure, omission from national income, 591–592
Leitch, Merv, 558
Less-developed countries. *See* Development; Economic growth
Lever Brothers, 290, 295
Lewis, John L., 396
Lewis, W. Arthur, 927
Liabilities, banks, 752–753
Liberal party, 18
Life-cycle hypothesis, A-39–A-43
Life-cycle income, 685
Life style, and growth, 913
Lifetime income, 685
Limited liability, corporation, 194
Limited partnership, 194
Limit price, 301
Linear functions, graphing, A-8–A-9
Liquid assets, bank, 753
Liquidity, 769
Liquidity preference (LP) function, 773
  and national income, A-45–A-46

Literary Digest, 44–45
Living standards
  growth in, 911
  and protectionism, 516
LM curve, A-45–A-46
  shape, A-51
Loans
  bank, 752
  and bank reserve ratio, 755
  day-to-day, 761
  from financial institutions, 424
Local maximizer, firm as, 352
Lockout, 393
Logarithmic scale, A-8
Long run
  cost curves in, 223–225
  decision making in, 209
  and factors, 220–232
Long-run aggregate supply curve, 824
Long-run average cost curve, 223
Long-run competitive equilibrium, A-30–A-36
Long-run costs
  and long-run industry supply curve, A-32–A-35
  vs. short-run, 225–226
Long-run equilibrium, and cost, 259, A-30–A-31
Long-run industry supply curve, A-32–A-35
Long-run supply curve, and housing, 103, 104–105
Long-term disequilibria, and adjustable peg, 735
Lopez-Melton, Nancy, 370
Lorenz curve, 363, 364
  of inequalities among nations and in Canada, 930
Losses, 203
Lower turning point, business cycle, 645–646

McCracken, M. C., 819n
McCulloch, Rachel, 949n, 951
McEachen, Allan, 529n, 539, 692
McFetteridge, Donald, 239
Macintosh, W. A., 13, 331
Mackenzie King, W. L., 331, 332
Maclean's, 524
Macroeconomic performance, 1974–1980, 866
Macroeconomic policy
  and capital account, 841–844

Macroeconomic policy (*Continued*)
and control of inflation in 1980s, 879–887
controversies over stabilization policy, 887.–894
and current account, 836–841
and fixed exchange rates, 844–845
and flexible exchange rates, 845–853
and micro foundations of monetarism and neo-Keynesianism, 894–899
and unemployment level at full employment, 899–900
Macroeconomics, 11–12
equilibrium determination of national income and interest rate, A-46–A-47
of Great Depression, 855–856
issues, 561
vs. microeconomics, 57, 560–561
overview, 55–57
variables, 561–567
Malthus, Thomas, 214, 932, 954
Managed fixed exchange rate, 143, 145
Managed flexible exchange rate, 146–147
Managed float, 739
Manpower and Immigration Department, 436
Manufacturing industries, concentration ratios, 291–292, 293
Marginal cost, 216, 250
and labor market, 387
and price, 325–328
Marginal cost curve, 217
Marginal disutility, 156
Marginal efficiency of capital, 415–416
Marginal efficiency of capital schedule, 415
and growth, 917
Marginal efficiency of investment (MEI) function, 776, 777
Marginal physical product, A-38
Marginal product, 210–211
Marginal product curve, 211
shape, 212–214
Marginal productivity theory of distribution, 367–369
Marginal propensity, 611

Marginal propensity to consume, 597
calculation, 598
and tax rate, 678–679
Marginal propensity to save, 599
Marginal rate of substitution, 169, 228
diminishing, 170
Marginal revenue, 254
defined, 250
monopolist, 273–274
Marginal revenue product, 368
and factor demand, A-37–A-38
Marginal tax rate, 479
and negative income tax, 482
Marginal utility, 154
diminishing, 154–155
vs. total, 159–164
Marginal utility curve, 156
Market(s). *See also* Labor market
allocative efficiency in equilibrium, 453–454
consumers' surplus, 164
coordination, 451–452
and economics, 51–55
and factor earnings, 438–441
failure, 455–460; responding to, 460–466
imperfections and impediments, 458–459
individual, 53–55
manipulation by firm, 344–348
success, 451–455
Market clearing prices, 895
Market demand curve, vs. household, 153
Market economy, 46–48
Marketed production, 52
Market expectations, and interest rates, 420
Market failure
and government intervention, 468–470
and nonmarket goals, 459–460
Marketing, of wheat, 120–121
Market pressures, firm's sensitivity to, 346–347
Market rate of interest, 420–422, 765
Market restriction, 334
Market sector of economy, 52
and cost, 326–328
and firm behavior, 248–251
Market system, 59–60

Market value of nation's output, 579
Markham, Jesse, 329
Markup, 353
Marshall, Alfred, 6, 362
Marx, Karl, 345, 362
Mason, Edward S., 942
Massey-Ferguson, 345
Master card, 751
Mathematical notes, M-1–M-11
Meadows, D. H., 923
Means, Gardiner, 350
Means
and economic systems, 61–62
and government failure, 467
Measurement
and deduction, interaction, 28
of demand, 177–181
of economic relations, 36–43
of monopoly power, 279–280
of opportunity cost, 199–203
Media, and disagreement among economists, 16
Medical insurance, 436–437
Medium of exchange, money as, 703–704
Mellon Bank, 44
Meltz, Noah, 806
Membership, unions, 398
Merchandise trade balance, 666
Metropolitan Museum, 429
Mexico, population policy, 939–940
Microeconomic policy
and government failure, 466–473
and market failure, 455–466
and market success, 451–455
and public expenditure, 487–498
and taxation, 478–487
tools, 460–462
Microeconomics, 10
vs. macroeconomics, 57, 560–561
monetarist model, 895–897
overview, 53–55
Milk withholding, 311–312
Milling, of coins, 705
Minimization, cost, in long run, 221–222
Minimum efficient scale (MES), 300, 302–303
Minimum wages, and employment, 401–404
Minority control, of firm, 349

Miscellaneous adjustments, national income, 584
Miscellaneous investment income, 584
Mixed economies, 52
Mobility
 capital, 375
 labor, 375–376; and changes in earnings, 442–443
 land, 374–375
Modest slack, and aggregate supply curve, 568
Modigliani, Franco, 685, 877, A-39
Molson's Brewery, 348
Monetarism, microeconomic foundations, 894–897
Monetarists
 inflation cures, 881–882
 views on cyclical fluctuations, 888
 views on interest sensitivities, 891
 views on monetary and fiscal policy, 892–893, A-49–A-52
Monetary adjustment mechanism frustration of, 785–786
 and price level, 782–784
Monetary aggregates, controlling, 852–853
Monetary base, 787
Monetary disequilibrium
 defined, 774
 and interest rate, 774–776
 policy-induced, 777–778
Monetary equilibrium, 774, 776
Monetary gradualism, 792–793, 873
 neo-Keynesian alternative to, 874–875
 and wage and price controls, 867
A Monetary History of the United States, 1867–1960 (Friedman and Schwartz), 888
Monetary mechanism, and aggregate demand, A-51–A-52
Monetary policy, 776–777. *See also* Economy; Fiscal policy; Monetarists
 and capital account, 843–844
 control of national income through, 788–789
 and cyclical fluctuations, 890–894
 destabilizing effect, 788–789
 and exchange rates, 845–849
 instruments and objectives of, 786–796

and LM curve, A-46
monetarist and neo-Keynesian views on, 892
and monetary disequilibrium, 777–778
and price level changes, 779–786
relative effectiveness, A-49–A-51
strength, 778–780
targets, 789–791
Money. *See also* Capital; Demand for money; Exchange rates; Interest rate; Monetary policy; Money supply
and aggregate demand curve shape, 572
and bonds, 769
changing concepts of, 712
cost of, 201
creation and destruction of, 753–760
defined, 702–704
deposit, 710–711
and inflation, 715–719
and market economy, 47
metallic, 705–706
and national income, A-44–A-48
need for, 704–705
neutrality of, 713
paper, 706–710
price level changes, 713–715
quantity theory of, 705, 720–725
vs. real output, 910
transactions demand for, 720–721
Money capital, 423
Money flows, 55
Money income
and budget line, 166
vs. real income, 168; after-tax, 690
Money markets
central bank as regulator and supporter of, 762
equilibrium (LM curve), A-45–A-46
Money price, 166
Money rate of interest, 421
Money substitutes, 712
Money supply, 721, 749. *See also* Bank(s); Monetary policy; Money
and balance of payments, 844–845
Canada, 1980, 750

changes in, 723
control of, 761–766
and demand for money, 768–774
determinants, 770
excess, 775–776
vs. interest rates, 789–791
as monetary policy target variable, 791–796
and national income, 778
Money values, vs. real values, 588–589
Monopolist
discriminating, 285
selling at single price, 271–278
Monopolistic competition, 292–296
Monopoly. *See also* Competition; Oligopoly
and combines laws, 330–334
vs. competition, 324–330
defined, 271
innovation under, 328
monopolist selling at single price, 271–278
power, 278–280
price discrimination, 280–287
Monopoly bank, single new deposit, 754–756
Monopsonistic labor market
and minimum wage, 404
with union, 388–389
Monopsony, 386
Moral suasion, 766
Mortgage, and interest rates, 638
Motivation, of firm, 196
Movement along curves, vs. shifts of curves, 72–73, 610–612
Mrs. Weinberg's Kosher Chopped Liver Co., 175
Mueller, Paul, 457
Multibank system
and many deposits, 758–759
and single new deposit, 756–757
Multiple regression analysis, 42
Multiplier
and accelerator, 644–645
balanced budget, 677
Canadian, 619–621
defined, 616–617
export, 652
graphic analysis, 617–618
numerical approach, 620
size, 618–619
Multivariate relation, 68n
Mundell, Robert, 730

Muscovy Co., 195
Myrdal, Gunnar, 942

Nader, Ralph, 339, 344
Namath, Joe, 370
NASA, 219
Nash equilibrium, 297–298
National debt, and fiscal policy, 694–698
National defense, and growth, 913
National Energy Board, 335–336, 537
National Energy Program, 542, 546, 553–557
National Farmers Organization, 311–312
National Health Service, Britain, 126
National income. *See also* Government; Income; Tax(es)
  aggregate demand and aggregate expenditure, 596, 606–608
  and balance of trade, 652–663
  and business cycles, 626–630
  and constant price level, 824
  and consumption, 600–602, 630–632
  control through monetary policy, 788–789
  and demand for money, 771
  desired expenditure, 595–604
  and disposable income, 631–632
  equilibrium, 604–606
  and exports, 362
  factor payments approach, 584–585
  and full-employment income, 823–824
  inflationary and deflationary gaps, 621–624
  and interest rate, macroeconomic equilibrium determination, A-46–A-47
  interpreting measures of, 587–592
  and investments, 632–642
  and liquidity preference, A-45–A-46
  measures, 585
  and money supply, 778, A-44–A-48
  money values vs. real values, 588–589
  and multiplier, 616–621

omissions, 590–592
output-expenditure approach, 579–584
reasons for changes, 610–616
related measures, 585–587
total output vs. per capital output, 589–590
National income accounting, 578–588
National income distribution
  and factor demand, 365–369
  and factor prices in competitive markets, 376–382
  and factor supply, 369–376
Natural barriers to entry, oligopoly, 300–301
Natural gas, Canadianization and nationalization of industry, 554–555
Natural monopoly, 327
  regulation, 334–340
Natural rate of unemployment, 806, 826, 863
Natural resources. *See also* Energy; Oil
  and development, 932–933
  and growth, 923–924
  total supply, 373
Natural scale, A-7
  vs. ratio scale, A-8
NCR Corp., 524
Near money, 711–712
Negative income effect of fall in prices, A-24
Negative income tax, 482–483
Nelson, Richard, 356
Neo-Keynesianism, microeconomic foundations, 897–899
Neo-Keynesians
  alternative to monetary gradualism, 874–875
  inflation cures, 882–883
  and monetary vs. fiscal policy, A-49–A-52
  views on cyclical fluctuations, 888–890
  views on fiscal policy, 893
  views on interest sensitivities, 891
  views on monetary policy, 892
Net exports, 582–584, 587, 652–655
  and aggregate demand, 662–663
  desired, 602

and domestic absorption, 658–661
Net export schedule, 603
Net income, unincorporated businesses, 584
Net investment, 581
Net national product (NNP), 585
Net private benefit, 462
Net profits, 203
Neutrality of money, 713
New Democratic party, 396
New England vs. Atlantic Provinces, government intervention, 472–473
New Industrial State, 345
New International Economic Order (NIEO), and development, 949–951
Newman, Peter C., 345n, 349
Newton, Keith, 806
New York Stock Exchange, 427
New York taxicabs, 447
New York Times, 175, 877, 905, 953
NIEO, 949–951
Nixon, Richard M., 737
Nominal GNP, 562
Nominal income, 563
Nondurable goods, 586
Nonequilibrium price, and quantity exchanged, 99–100
Nonlaboratory sciences, in testing theories, 37–38
Nonlinear functions, graphing, A-10
Nonmarketed economic activities, omission from national income, 591
Nonmarketed production, 52
Nonmarket goals, and market failure, 459–460
Nonmarket sector of economy, 52
Nonmaximizing theories, firm, 352–357
Nonprofit organization, 50n
Nonrenewable resource, opportunity cost, 544
Nontradeables, 656
Nordhaus, William, 835
Normal curve of error, and law of large numbers, 24
Normal goods, 92
Normal profits, 203
Normative aspects, price discrimination, 286

Normative statements, vs. positive, 20–22
Numerical values, demand elasticity, 89–90

Observation and theory, interaction, 28
Occasionally poor, 434
Official account, vs. capital and current accounts, 667–668
Official reserves, 667–668
Oil
  Canadianization and nationalization of industry, 554–555
  export tax, 540, 541–542
  import subsidy, 540–542
  industry reaction to NEP, 556–557
  prices and price parity, 538–553
Oligopolistic behavior, empirically based approaches, 298–300
Oligopoly. See also Competition; Monopoly
  defined, 296
  incentive under, 329–330
  and resource allocation, 306
  theory of, 296–306
Omissions, for national income, 590–592
O'Neill, Thomas P. (Tip), 877
One-year plans, Soviet, 944
Ontario Ministry of Education, 219
Ontario Securities Commission, 335
OPEC. See Organization of Petroleum Exporting Countries (OPEC)
OPEC Fund, 943
Open economy, 129
  national income in, 582–584
Open market operations, central bank, 116, 762–765
Open shop, 392
Opportunity cost, 199. See also Cost
  and choice, 7–8
  and gains from trade, 508–509
  of green revolution, 945–946
  of growth, 915–916
  of holding money, 720
  measurement by firm, 199–203
  of nonrenewable resource, 544
  of war on poverty, 435

Ordinary partnership, 193–194
Organization of Petroleum Exporting Countries (OPEC), 288, 310, 323, 544, 557, 577, 748, 953
  commodity price stabilization agreements, 948
  embargo, 537n
  and international monetary system, 743–745
  and price of gasoline, 315–320
Organization theory, 353, 356
Ottawa Valley Line, 538
Outcome-expenditure approach to national income, 579–584
Output, 196–197
  capital, labor and, 210
  and costs, 216
  and employment, 566–567
  and innovation, 241–242
  least-cost method, 230
  in quantity theory of money, 723–725
  under satisficing, profit maximizing, and sales maximizing, 352
  total vs. per capital, 589–590
  value of, 579
  variables, 561–563
Output per hour of labor, 910
Output per person, 910
Overseas Development Council, 927
Owen, Robert, 354
Ownership, in Soviet Union, 936
Ownership of resources, and economic system, 58–59

Palda, Kristian, 238, 239
Palmer, Arnold, 370
Paper money, 706–710
Paradox of thrift, 615–616, 674
Paradox of value, 152, 159
Pareto, Vilfredo, 165, 265
Pareto-efficiency, 265
Pareto-optimality, 265
Paris, rent control in, 104–105
Parity, oil prices, 538–553
Partnership, 193–194
Patent monopoly, and substitutes, 314–315
Patents, and innovation, 330
Paternalism, 459–460
P/E, 426

Peak, business cycle, 644
Pegged exchange rate, 143
Pensions, old age, 436
Pepsi-Cola Co., 288
PE ratio, 426
Per capital GNP, 589–590
  and population growth, 933
Per capita output, vs. total output, 589–590
Perfect competition. See also Competition
  and efficiency, 264–268
  long-run equilibrium in, 257–264
  short-run equilibrium of firm and industry in, 254–257
  theory, 251–253
Perfectly competitive firm
  demand and revenue curves, 253–254
  short-run equilibrium, 254–257, 258
Perfectly competitive industry
  attempts to monopolize, 309–315
  and technology, 259–261
Permanent-income hypothesis, 685, A-39–A-43
Persistently poor, 434
Personal consumption, 586
Personal costs of growth, 913–915
Personal income, 586–587. See also Disposable income; Income
Personal income taxes, progressivity, 479
Petrodollars, 744
Petroleum and Gas Revenue Tax, 555, 558
Petroleum Compensation Charge, 554, 556
Phelps, Edmund, 825, 863, 895
Phelps-Brown, Professor, 909
Phelps-Friedman theory, 825–829, 863
  implications, 829–833
Phillips, A. W., 822
Phillips curve, 822–823, 859
  trade-off, 863
  unstable, and accelerating inflation, 825–833
Physical outputs, index numbers of, 35
Picket lines, 393
Planning
  and development, LDCs, 938

Planning (*Continued*)
  in Soviet Union, 944–945
Plant, U-shaped cost curves, A-35
Point elasticity, A-11–A-15
Point of diminishing average
  productivity, 210
Point of diminishing marginal
  productivity, 211
Policy, 11, 13–15
Policy conflicts, 13
Policy instruments, 786, 787
Policymaking, 15
Policy variables, 786–787
Political constraints, and
  government failure, 467
Political economy of public health
  care, 496–497
Pollution
  as economic problem, 5
  as harmful externality, 456
  optimal prevention, 468–469
Poor. *See* Poverty
Population
  and demand curve shifts, 72
  and development, 931–932
  and income, by country, 929
  optimal, 922
  and per capita GNP, 933
  and total supply of labor, 371
Population policy
  controversy over, 951
  and development, LDCs,
    939–940
Portfolio investment, 667
Positive statements, vs. normative,
  20–22
Posner, Richard, 339
Post-Keynesian cures for inflation,
  884–886
Post Office, 219, 288
Post-WWII fiscal policy, 688–692
Potential GNP, 563–564
Pound (British), speculation
  against, 736
Poverty
  as economic problem, 5–6
  and income distribution,
    431–437
  and total supply of labor, 372
  vicious circle of, 940–941
  war on, 434–436
Poverty level, 432
PPP exchange rate, 838–839
  and Canadian dollar slide, 850

Prebisch, Raúl, 946
Precautionary motive, 770, 771
Predatory pricing, 301
Predictions, 82
  and theory, 25, 27–29
Preemptive expansion, as
  firm-created barrier to entry,
  301
Preferred stock, 424
Prescriptive rules, 461
Present value
  bond, 769
  of future returns, 416–417
Prestige, 913
Price. *See also* Equilibrium price;
    Factor prices; Inflation; Price
    level
  autarky, 132
  bonds, and interest rate, 769–770
  and budget line, 166
  ceiling, 100, 102, 103
  and demand, 68–69
  determination by demand and
    supply, 78–83
  downward rigidity, 573
  as economic variable, 26
  England, seven centuries,
    715–716
  of factors: and cost curves, 226;
    and supply curve shifts, 76–77
  index numbers of, 33–35
  inflexibility, 305
  and marginal cost, 325–328
  negative income effect of fall in,
    A-24
  and net export function,
    654, 655
  oil, and price parity, 538–553
  other, and demand curve shifts,
    71; and supply curve shifts, 76
  and quantity demanded, 88–92,
    182–183, 186
  and quantity exchanged, 99–100
  and quantity supplied, 95
  quantity theory of money and,
    706, 723–725
  and resource allocation,
    123–124
  on stock market, 425–426
  and Soviet planning, 944–945
  and supply, 74–75
  and taxes on profits, 487
  and TIPs, 884
  of traded goods, 132

Price-consumption line, 173
Price controls
  on gasoline in U.S., 317–318
  theory of, 99–102
Price discrimination
  and dumping, 282–283
  monopoly, 280–287
Price-earnings ratio, 426
Price elasticity of demand. *See*
    Demand elasticity
Price floor, 100, 401
Price index, 33
Price level, 561. *See also* Price
  and aggregate demand, 779–781,
    A-47–A-48
  changes, 713–715; and monetary
    policy, 779–786
  constant, and national income,
    824
  and equilibrium national income,
    782
  and gold flow, 729–730
  and inflation, 808
  and inflationary gap, 782, 784
  and monetary adjustment
    mechanism, 782–784
  in 1930s, 855–856
Price of other commodities, and
  quantity demanded, 187
Price parity, energy, 542–553
Price-push inflation, 813
Price system
  and individual decisions, 55
  as social control mechanism, 53
  statics and dynamics in
    evaluating, A-20
Price taker, 251
Price-taking firm
  revenue curves, 254
  supply curve, 255–256
Price theory, 78
  and attempts to monopolize
    perfectly competitive
    industries, 309–315
  and inflation, 82–83
Pricing
  full-cost, 353
  for natural monopoly, 336
Primary commodities, and NIEO,
  949
Principle of substitution, 222–
  223
  and isoquants, 230–232
Private cost, 456

Private expenditures, and fiscal policy, 675–678
Private sector, of economy, 52
Procter & Gamble, 290, 295
Producer, firm as, 50
Producers' organizations, 310–312
Producers' surplus, and allocative efficiency, 267
Product, homogeneous vs. differentiated, 293
Product differentiation, 293
Production, 210
  defined, 7
  energy, 535–537
  and expansion of consumption opportunities, 129–130
  of goods and services, 9–10
  marketed vs. nonmarketed, 52
  organization of, 193–197; in Soviet Union, 936–937
  value added through stages of, 580
Production costs
  and elasticity of factor demand, 366
  and exchange rates, 141
  and government regulation, 465
Production factors. See also Capital; Labor; Land
  defined, 6
  and firm, 46, 196–197
  in long run, 220–232
  prices, and supply curve shifts, 76–77
  purchased and hired, 199–200
Production possibilities, and choice, 8–9
Production possibility boundary, 8–9, 11
Production royalties, energy, 546–547
Productive capacity, 11
Productive efficiency
  in equilibrium, market, 453–454
  and monopolistic competition, 295
  monopoly, 276–277
  and perfect competition, 265
Productivity, 910
  capital, 413–418
  defined, 232–234
  as economic problem, 4–5
  and government regulation, 465–466

and invention, 235–240
and restraints, 242–244
slowdown, 920–921
sources, 234–235
and very long run, 232–244
Product markets, 51
Product quality, consumer information, and demand, 184–185
Profit, 203–204, 585
  corporation, 584
  and cost to firm, 197–204
  importance of, 357–358
  of monopolist, 275
  and monopoly power, 280
  reinvested, 424–425
  and resource allocation, 123–124, 204
  undistributed, 194
Profit maximization, 50
  and control of firm, 348–352
  monopolized market, 274–275
Profit-maximizing firm, 196
  behavioral rules, 250–251
  factor demand curve, A-37–A-38
Profit taxes
  energy, 546–547
  and prices, 487
Progress and Poverty (George), 318
Progressive Conservatives, 126–127
Progressive tax, 479
Progressivity of taxation, 478–484
Property tax
  payment by landlord vs. tenant, 485–486
  regressivity, 479
Proportionality, 724
Proportional tax, 478
Proprietorship, 193–194
Proscriptive rules, 461
Protectionism, 512–521
Provinces, equalizing per capita incomes and unemployment rates in, 444–445
Proxy, 349
Proxy fight, 349
Public authorities, corruption by firm, 345
Public expenditure, as tool of micro policy, 487–498
Public sector. See Government
Public Service Alliance, 397
Public utility regulation, 334–340

Purchase, on open market, 763–764
Purchase and resale agreements, 761
Purchasing power, and inflation, 11
Purchasing power parity exchange rate, 838–839
Pure rate of interest, 420
Pure return on capital, 414

Quality
  of capital, 919–922
  of labor, 922
  of life, omission from national income, 592
  of product, and demand, 184–185
Quantified joint profit maximization, hypothesis of, 299
Quantity
  of capital per worker, 919
  of labor, 922–923
Quantity actually bought, 67
Quantity actually sold, 74
Quantity consumed, 10
Quantity demanded, 67–68
  and income, 95, 186–187
  and price, 88–92, 182–183, 186
  and price of other commodities, 187
  and taste, 188
Quantity exchanged, 67, 74
  and price, 99–100
Quantity index, 36
Quantity of capital per worker, 919
Quantity produced, 9
  and cost, 325–326
Quantity sold, and revenues, monopolist, 272
Quantity supplied, 74
  and price, 95
Quantity theory of money, 706, 720–725
  and velocity of circulation, 722
Quebec Securities Commission, 335
Quotas, and agricultural marketing boards, 118–120

R. v. Container Materials, Ltd., 333
R. v. Howard Smith Paper Mills, 333
Railway Act (1888), 335

Railway Transport Committee, 291
R&D, 235–239
Random sample, 39
Ratchet effect, and aggregate supply curve, 574–575
Rate base, and natural monopoly regulation, 337
Rate of return on capital, 337, 413–417
Rational expectations, 816, 897
Rationalization
  by formal agreement, 522–523
  industry, and MES, 302–303
  by manufacturer's choice, 524–525
Rationing, 101
Ratio scale, A-7–A-8
  vs. natural scale, A-8
Reagan, Ronald, 340, 877
Reaganomics, 902–903
Real capital, 423
Real flows, 55
Real GNP, 562, 589, 626–629
Real income, 564
  vs. money income, 168; after tax, 690
Real national income, 578
Real national product, 578
Real rate of interest, 421
Real values vs. money values, 588–589
Recession, business cycle, 644
  fixed investment and GNP during, 634
Recovery, business cycle, 644
Redistribution. See Income redistribution
Refusal to supply, as restrictive trade practice, 333–334
Regional Economic Expansion Department, 445, 473
Registered Retirement Savings Plans, 494n
Regression analysis, 40
Regression equation, 40
Regressive tax, 478
Regressivity, of taxes, 479
Regulation
  of combines, 330–334
  myopic, and government failure, 467
  public utility, 334–340
Reid, Frank, 806

Reinvestment of profit, 424–425
Relations among functions and variables, 27
Relative cost of municipal government services, 498
Relative price, 82–83
  and budget line, 166–167
Religious barriers to development, 935
Rent, 584
  and housing supply, 106
  vs. transfer earnings, 380–381
Rental housing, demand for, 107
Rent controls, 102–110
  and housing market, 95–96
  in Paris, 104–105
Report of the Special Senate Committee on Poverty, 437
Required cash reserves, 753
Required reserve, changes in, 765
Required reserve ratio, fixed, 753–754
Research and development (R&D), 235–239
Reserve(s), total, and adjustable peg, 733–734
Reserve currency
  international, 745
  U.S. dollar as, 740–743
Residential construction. See Housing
Resource(s)
  and commodities, 6–7
  common property, and harmful externalities, 456–457
  efficiency in use of, 265, 266
  inefficiency in use of, 933–934
  ownership, and economic system, 58–59
Resource allocation, 9
  and government expenditure, 494–498
  market, 452–454
  and oil price parity, 548–552
  and oligopoly, 306
  and price, 123–124
  and profits, 204
  and scarcity, 48
  and tax structure, 484–485
Resource utilization, 10–11
Restrictive Trade Practices Commission (RPTC), 333–334
Returns, and costs, 223–225
Revaluation of currency, 143

Revenue curve
  monopolist, 272–274
  perfectly competitive firm, 253–254
  price-taking firm, 254
Revenue sharing, 491
Reversibility, need for, 683–684
Reynolds, Milton, 314
Reynolds International Pen Co., 314
Ricardo, David, 362, 372, 378, 504, 506–507
Rigidities, and government failure, 466–467
Ripple effect, minimum wage, 402–403
Rising-cost industry, A-34
Rising supply price, A-34
Risk
  and many interest rates, 422
  and natural monopoly regulation, 337–338
Risk averse, 772
Risk premium, 414
Risk taking, 202–203
Robinson, Joan, 292
Roosevelt, Franklin D., 45, 615–616, 877
Rose, Pete, 370, 384
Rotherhampsted Experimental Station, 212
Rothschild, Emma, 902–903
Royal Commission, 13
Royal Commission on Price Spreads (1935), 291
Royal Commission on the Automobile Industry, 522
Royalties vs. export tax, on energy, 546–547
Ruddick, E., 819n
Rule making, 461–462

Safarian, A. E., 236, 528
St. Lawrence Market, Toronto, 51
Salaries. See Wages
Sales
  maximization, 351–352
  on open market, 764–765
  tied, 334
Sales tax, regressivity, 479
Salmon River, fishing in, 212
Sample, in testing economic theories, 38–39
Sampling error, 213
Samuelson, Paul, 905

Satisfaction, as household goal, 48
Satisficing, 356
  output under, 352
Saving, 597
  and aggregate expenditure, 613, 614
  capital from, 940–941
Saving and consumption schedules, 601
Saving function, 599–600
Say, J. B., 16n
Scarce good, and utility, 162
Scarcity, 7
  and resource allocation, 48
Scatter diagram, 39, A-5–A-7
Schultz, Henry, 177
Schumpeter, Joseph A., 329
Schwartz, Anna, 888
Schwindt, R. W., 120
Science
  economics as developing, 29
  natural vs. social, 23
  in testing theories, 37–38
Scientific theory, nature of, 24–25
Search unemployment, 803–804
Seasonally adjusted series, 629
Secondary reserves, 753
  required ratio, 766
Securities, banks, 752
Securities market, 425–428
Self-realizing expectations, 426–427
Sellers' preferences, allocation by, 101
Semi-durable goods, 586
Services, 7, 586
  curtailment, and government regulation, 338
Shaw, George Bernard, 15, 200
Sherman Antitrust Act (U.S., 1890), 332
Shifts
  in consumption, 630–632
  of curves, vs. movement along, 610–612
  in demand curve, 70–73
  in desired expenditure function, 612–616
  in exports, 632
  in net export function, 653–655
  in supply curve, 75–78
Shop steward, 393
Short run
  cost variations in, 214–218; vs.

long run, 225–226
  decision making in, 208–209
  firm's choices in, 210–218
Short-run aggregate supply curve, 824
Short-run cost curves, 216–217
Short-run equilibrium, perfectly competitive firm and industry, 254–257
Short-run equilibrium price, 256–257
Short-run profitability, perfectly competitive firm, 257
Short-run supply curve
  and housing, 103–104, 105–106
  perfectly competitive firm and industry, 255–257
Significance test, 40
The Silent Spring (Carson), 457
Simon, Herbert, 356
Single price, monopolist selling at, 271–278
Size distribution of income, 363, 381–382
Skills differential, and teenage unemployment, 403–404
Small open economy, 129
  devaluation model, 656
Smith, Adam, 49, 53, 324, 362, 504, 532, 886
Smith, David, 870
Snake, 738
Social barriers to development, 935
Social benefit, 462
Social cost, 456
  of growth, 913–915
Social insurance, 436–437
  as built-in stabilizer, 680–681
Social obligation, as nonmarket goals, 460
Socioeconomic factors, and demand, 179
Solow, Robert, 923
Southern California Edison, 212
Sovereignty, consumer vs. household, 48n
Soviet Union
  economic system, 59, 936–937
  and wheat market, 121
Special drawing rights, 734
Specialization
  in few commodities, and development, 946

gains from, 505–509
  of labor, 47
  surplus, trade, and, 47
Speculation against U.S. dollar, 736–737
Speculative crises, and adjustable peg, 735–736
Speculative motive, 770, 772
Speculative swings, stock market, 426–428
Stabilization and support plans, agriculture, 114–117
Stabilization policy, 673
  controversies over, 887–894
Stabilizer, built-in, 678–682
Stable equilibrium, A-18–A-19
Stafford, Frank, 408
Stagflation, 569, 692
  in 1970s, 864–867
Stalin, Joseph, 936
Standard Oil Co., 332n
Staples theory, 331
Statics
  comparative, A-16–A-17
  and price system, A-20
Statistical analysis, in testing economic relations, 37
Statistics Canada, 35
Stein, Herbert, 887
Stigler, George, 102–103
Stock, 423–424
Stockholders, 423–424
Stock market, 425–428
Stock variables, 26
Stone, Richard, 177
Store of value, money as, 704
Straight-line depreciation, 201
Strike, 393
Strikebreakers, 393
Structural rigidity inflation, 814
Structural unemployment, 802–803
Stykolt, Stephen, 302
Subsidy, for higher education, 488
Subsistence requirements, 432
Substitutes
  and demand curve shifts, 71
  and patent monopoly, 314–315
Substitution
  and elasticity of factor demand, 366–367
  of foreign goods, and shape of aggregate demand curve, 572
  of national income for disposable income in consumption

Substitution (*Continued*)
  function, 601–602
  principle of, 222–223, 230–232
Substitution effect, vs. income
    effect, A-22–A-24
Sun Life Building, .447
Superstars, salaries, 370
Supply. *See also* Demand; Money
    supply; Supply curve
  agriculture, 111–112
  of capital, 373
  change in, 54–55, 78
  of dollars, 138
  of effort, 371
  law of, 80–81
  limitation, as OPEC strategy,
    319–320
  and price, 74–75
  and quantity supplied, 74
  shift and shape of demand
    curve, 87–88
  theory of, 73–74
Supply curve
  for dollars, 138
  and elasticity, A-14
  monopolist, 275
  movements along vs. shifts of,
    78
  and new entrants, 259
  and supply schedule, 75–78
Supply elasticity, 94–96
Supply lag, A-17–A-20
Supply shocks, and stagflation,
    864–867
Supply-side economics, 886–887
Supply-side inflation, 812–814
Surplus, 47
  in balance of trade, 650
Sweden vs. Venezuela, population
    policy and development, 939
Sweezy, Paul, 305

Tacit collusion, 280
Takeover bid, 351
Target variable, interest rate vs.
    money supply, 791–796
Tariff, 512–514
  policy option, 526–527
Taste
  change, and exchange rates, 140
  and demand curve shifts, 72
  and quantity demanded, 188
Tax(es)
  as built-in stabilizer, 678–679

incidence, 485–487
  and income redistribution,
    483–484
  as micro policy tool, 478–487
  on profits, and prices, 487
  progressivity increase,
    481–484
  and resource allocation, 484–
    485
  single, 381
  and urban land values, 380–381
Tax base, 483
Tax-based incomes policies (TIPs),
    883–885
Tax expenditures, 477
Tax rate
  and aggregate expenditure, 614
  and fiscal policy, 675–677
  and government expenditure,
    choice between, 683
  and marginal propensity to
    consume, 678–679
  and total supply of labor,
    371–372
Tax-rental arrangements, 491
Tax-Sharing Act (1957), 491
Technological efficiency, 197
  vs. economic, 198
Technology
  and perfectly competitive in-
    dustry, 259–261
  and supply curve shifts, 77–78
Technostructure, 345
Teenagers, unemployment, and
    skills differential, 403–404
Tenants, share of property tax,
    485–486
Tender offer, 351
Term, 769
Term deposit, 711
Terms of trade, 129, 510–512
Term to maturity, 769
Testing
  of economic relations, 36–37
  of theories, 29, 37–42
Thatcher, Margaret, 905
Theory, scientific, 24–25
  defining, 25–29
  testing, 29, 37–42
The Theory of the Leisure Class
    (Veblen), 183
Third parties, costs, and govern-
    ment regulation, 466
Third-party effects, 456

Third world, 948n
Thrift, paradox of, 615–616, 674
Through the Looking Glass
    (Carroll), 83
Thurow, Lester, 472
Tied sales, 334
Time, and gasoline demand ad-
    justments, 318–319
Time horizons, for firm decision
    making, 208–210
Time lags, 683
Time magazine, 18
Time series, 26, A-6
Time-series graph, A-7
Tobin, James, 772, 811, 816, 835,
    866
Tokyo Round, GATT, 525
Toronto Blue Jays, 384
Total cost, 215
Total cost curve, 217
Total expenditure, and demand
    elasticity, 90–91
Total output, vs. per capita output,
    589–590
Total product, 210
Total product curve, 211
Total revenue, 253–254
  and demand elasticity, 90–91
  monopolist, 273–274
Total supply of capital, 373
Total utility, 154
  vs. marginal, 159–164
Total utility curve, 156
Trade
  and aid to LDCs, 942
  interpersonal, interregional, and
    international, 505
  and protectionism, 516–521
  surplus, specialization, and, 47
  terms of, 129, 510–512
  world interdependence, 743
Tradeables, 656
Trade balance. *See* Balance of
    trade
Trade deficit, 135
Trade policy, Canadian, 521–530
Trades and Labour Congress, 390,
    395, 396
Trade surplus, 135
Trade Union. *See* Union
Trade Unions Act (1872), 410
Transactions balances, 720–721
Transactions costs, and market
    inefficiency, 458–459

Transactions demand for money, 720–721
Transactions motive, 770, 771
Transfer earnings, and economic rent, 378–381
Transfer payments, 581–582, 587
  as built-in stabilizer, 680–682
  and cyclical fluctuations, 642
  government expenditures for, 489–490
  to individuals, 490
  intergovernmental, 490–494
Treasury bill, 675
Treaty of Rome, 526
Trigger prices, 283
Trough, business cycle, 644
Trudeau, Pierre Elliott, 118, 672
Turner, John, 691
Turning points, business cycle, 644–646
Turnover tax, Soviet, 945
Two-price system, 535, 540–542
Tyaack, F. H., 525

Ulman, Lloyd, 870
Unanticipated inflation, 715–717
Uncontrolled experiment, 38
Underdeveloped countries. See Development
Underdevelopment, consequences of, 929–930
Undesirable externalities, avoiding, 464
Undistributed profits, 194, 585
Unemployment, 564–566, 801–802.
  See also Employment; Full employment; Labor; Production factors
  causes, 802–804
  control, 804–805
  and devaluation, 662
  as economic problem, 3
  and employment in 1970s, 806–807
  experience of, 805, 808
  and inflation, 820–833
  level at full employment, 899–900
  measured and nonmeasured, 804
  monthly rate, 629
  and national income, 621–622
  1930s, 855–856
    and per capita income, equilizing, 444–441

policymaker concern, 801–802
post-WWII, 860–861
and protectionism, 520
teenage, and skills differential, 403–404
and total supply of labor, 372
voluntary vs. involuntary, 898–899
Unemployment insurance, 436, 805
  and total supply of labor, 372
Unemployment rate, 564
Unincorporated businesses, net income, 584
Union(s)
  bargaining arrangements, 392–393
  in competitive labor market, 386–387
  evolution, 393–397
  membership, 398
  methods and objectives, 397–401
  and monopsonistic labor market, 387–389
  as potential monopolist, 389–392
Unionism
  international, 396–397
  in public sector, 390–391
Union shop, 392–393
United Automobile Workers, 390, 392, 400
United Farm Workers Union, 393
United Mine Workers, 396, 400
United Nations, Declaration on the Establishment of a New International Economic Order, 949
United States
  concentration ratios in manufacturing, 293
  fiscal policy case studies, 680–681
  GNP, 653
  macroeconomic performance, 1947–1980, 866
  Reaganomics and "McDonalds-ization" of, 900–901
  trigger prices, 283
  wage and price controls in, 871
  and wheat market, 121
United Steelworkers, 392
Unit elasticity, and demand curve, 91
Unit of account, money as, 704
Universal hypothesis, 42
Unreported activities, omission from national income, 591

Unstable equilibrium, A-18–A-19
Unvalidated demand inflation, 823–824
Unvalidated inflation, 817
Upper turning point, business cycle, 644, 645
U-shaped cost curves, plant vs. firm, A-35–A-36
Utility, 153
  and attitude survey, 161
  as household goal, 48
  marginal vs. total, 159–164
  maximizing, 156–159
Utility graph, 155–156
Utility schedule, 155–156
Utilization
  vs. capacity, 910
  and innovation, 240–241

Validated demand inflation, 824–825
Validated inflation, 817
Value
  of asset, 417–418
  and economic system, 60–61
  of expenditure and output, 579
  of infinite stream of payments, 417
  paradox of, 152, 159
  present, 416–417, 769
  of single future payment, 417
Value added, 579, 580
Value and Capital (Hicks), 165
Value system, firm corruption of, 345
Variable(s)
  endogenous and exogenous, 26
  functions of three, A-10
  output, 561–563
  PIH and LCH, A-39–A-41
  relations among, 27, A-2–A-3
  and scientific theory, 25–26
  stock and flow, 26
Variable costs, 215
Variable factors, 209
Variance, 40
Veblen, Thorstein, 183, 206, 345n
Velocity of circulation, and quantity theory of money, 722
Venezuela vs. Sweden, population policy and development, 939
Verdoorn, P. J., 517

Very long run
  decision making in, 209
  progress and productivity in,
    232–244
Vietnam, inflation, and 1968 U.S.
    tax surcharges, 681
Visa card, 751
Visibles, 665
von Hayek, F. A., 888n

Wage(s)
  and discrimination, 405, 406
  downward rigidity, 573
  vs. employment, 400
  vs. fringe benefits, 400–401
  vs. job security, 400
  minimum, and employment,
    401–404
  models of determination,
    386–389
  and other labor income, 584
  and quantity of factor supplied,
    380
  rate, earnings, and drift, 870
  restricting labor supply to in-
    crease, 398–399
  and salaries, 584; of superstars,
    370
  and unions in competitive labor
    market, 386–387

Wage and price controls
  in controlling inflation, 882–883
  and excess demand, 858
  international experience, 870–871
  and monetary gradualism, 867
  U.S. program, 868
Wage cost-push inflation, 813
Walker, Gordon, 127
Wallich, Henry, 884
Walters, Barbara, 370
Wartime demand inflation, 856–857
Wartime Labour Relations
    Regulation (1944), 397
Waverman, Leonard, 552
Wayne, R. E., 698n
Wealth
  and demand for money, 772
  as economic problem, 5–6
The Wealth of Nations (Smith),
    49, 53, 64, 324, 504, 886
Weidenbaum, Murray, 339
Weintraub, Sidney, 884
Welfare
  as built-in stabilizer, 680–681
  provincial systems, 437
  and total supply of labor, 372
Well-being, as household goal, 48
Western Grain Stabilization Plan,
    121
Westinghouse Canada, 524–525

Wheat
  marketing, 120–121
  and perfect competition, 251
  production, 121, 122
Whelan, Eugene, 118, 119
Wholesale Price Index, 33, 561, 714
Wicksell, Knut, 888n
Williams, Ted, marginal vs. lifetime
    batting average, 215
Windfall profits, 106
Winter, Sidney, 356–357
Withdrawal, and bank reserve ratio,
    755
World Bank, 943
World product mandating, 524–525
World War II, fiscal policy, 688
Worldwatch Institute, 877

Xerox Corp., 288, 524
X-inefficiency, 933

Yas's Law, 16
Young, John, 867

Zero elasticity, and demand curve,
    91
Zero expected inflation, short-term
    Phillips curve for, 826–828
Zero-profit equilibrium, 258

:rs

ı)	change in
na)	sum of
a)	elasticity
ı)	profit

ıbreviations

A	Domestic Absorption
AD	Aggregate Demand
AS	Aggregate Supply
AE	Aggregate Expenditure
ATC	Average Total Cost
AVC	Average Variable Cost
C	Consumption
CPI	Consumer Price Index
D	Demand
E	Equilibrium
G	Government Expenditure
GNE	Gross National Expenditure
GNP	Gross National Product
I	Investment Expenditure
I	rate of interest
LP	Liquidity Preference
LR	Long-run
M	Imports *or* Money Supply
M1, M1 B, M2, etc.	Measures of Money Supply
MC	Marginal Cost
MEC	Marginal Efficiency of Capital
MEI	Marginal Efficiency of Investment
MES	Minimum Efficient Scale
MP	Marginal Product
MR	Marginal Revenue
MRP	Marginal Revenue Product
OPEC	Organization of Petroleum Exporting Countries
p	price
P	Price Level
q, Q	Quantity
r	rate of interest, rate of return
S	Supply *or* Saving
SR	Short-run
T	Taxes
TC	Total Cost
TR	Total Revenue
X	Exports
X-M	Net Exports
Y	National Income (generally)
Y_F	Full Employment National Income
Y_d	Disposable Income